San Jose, CA, USA

CHI

May 7 - 12

2016 #chi4good

Association for Computing Machinery

SIGCHI

Proceedings

The 34th Annual CHI Conference on Human Factors in Computing Systems

San Jose Convention Center

https://chi2016.acm.org

Association for
Computing Machinery

Advancing Computing as a Science & Profession

The Association for Computing Machinery
2 Penn Plaza, Suite 701
New York, New York 10121-0701

Notice to Past Authors of ACM-Published Articles
ACM intends to create a complete electronic archive of all articles and/or other material previously published by ACM. If you have written a work that has been previously published by ACM in any journal or conference proceedings prior to 1978, or any SIG Newsletter at any time, and you do NOT want this work to appear in the ACM Digital Library, please inform permissions@acm.org, stating the title of the work, the author(s), and where and when published.

ISBN: 978-1-4503-3362-7 (Digital)

ISBN: 978-1-4503-4627-6 (Print)

Additional copies may be ordered prepaid from:

ACM Order Department
PO Box 30777
New York, NY 10087-0777, USA

Phone: 1-800-342-6626 (USA and Canada)
+1-212-626-0500 (Global)
Fax: +1-212-944-1318
E-mail: acmhelp@acm.org
Hours of Operation: 8:30 am – 4:30 pm ET

Printed in the USA

CHI 2016 is the premier world-wide conference for Human-Computer Interaction (HCI) and this year took place in the heart of Silicon Valley, San Jose, California. The Proceedings and Extended Abstracts represent today's most innovative, novel and creative work in HCI. These Proceedings and Abstracts have added over one-thousand documents in the ACM Digital Library. Across all tracks, CHI received nearly 5000 submissions and accepted over 1000 that can be seen today. These include almost 600 rigorously reviewed papers and notes selected from over 2200 submissions. These Proceedings and Abstracts also document two days of workshops, symposia and meetings involving over 800 participants, a record number for CHI conferences.

2016 #chi4good

The CHI 2016 conference includes two days of focused workshops and four days of technical content, including CHI's prestigious technical program, with 16 parallel sessions of rigorously reviewed research Papers, engaging Panels, Case Studies and Special Interest Groups (SIGs), Conference highlights also include student research, design, and game competitions, and last-minute SIGs for discussing current topics. The popular alt.chi forum enters its eleventh year of provocation within the HCI community. The conference also showcases Interactivity and Interactivity Research Demos, which are hands-on demonstrations of the best in technology and innovation. And we're particularly proud this year to include documents from our new Art Exhibition, held at the *Works/San Jose Gallery* in conjunction with the CHI conference.

We began our conference planning process with three core ideas: "**CHI in Silicon Valley**": emphasizing local engagement in this vibrant community, "**#chiforgood**": HCI in the community, both during the workshop time and at appropriate points during the conference, and a "**More Humane Conference and Planning Process**": lots of transparency, early planning, no surprises, data-driven decisions and taking into account the importance of families, work/life balance, and the like.

From this, the overall theme of the conference emerged, **#chi4good**: addressing issues of social good through the innovation and creativity of the CHI community. To this end we held a Day of Service on the Saturday before the conference with hundreds of CHI attendees working on projects for non-profit and area arts organizations, and we have continued that theme throughout the conference by hosting the Diversity and Inclusion Lunch, brought childcare back to the conference for the first time in many years, and introduced the lunch@chi program to facilitate small group lunches on the first day of the conference. We've introduced CHI's first Diversity & Inclusion Statement, and our keynote speakers, represent the vibrancy, diversity and excitement of the wide field of HCI with particular emphasis on #chi4good. This year's speakers were chosen from among crowd-sourced suggestions from the CHI community and they are: Dayo Olopade, (Journalist and author of *The Bright Continent*); Kimberly Bryant (Founder, Black Girls Code), in conversation with Sarah Guthals, (Co-Founder of ThoughtSTEM); Marissa Meyer (President & CEO of Yahoo), in conversation with Terry Winograd (Professor Emeritus, Stanford University); Vishal Sikka (CEO of Infosys), in conversation with computing pioneer Alan Kay (Viewpoints Research Institute); and Salman Khan (founder, Khan Academy).

With careful consultation from the community, we have enhanced the CHI conference experience from submission and review processes, to more participation possibilities at the conference. Peer-reviewed papers have more space for references and will receive a wider range of better-matched reviews. There are more curated venues and more input into the selection of keynote speakers.

We are deeply indebted to an enormous number of volunteers, without whom CHI 2016 would not be possible, including over 4000 reviewers, 222 senior members of the program committee, nearly 100 members of the CHI 2016 conference organization committee and, of course, the more than 180 student volunteers.

The CHI conference is supported by the efforts of SIGCHI, (the Special Interest Group on Computer-Human Interaction) of the Association for Computing Machinery (ACM) and the ACM, and we are indebted for their ongoing support, organization, and leadership into the future.

Jofish Kaye, Yahoo, CHI 2016 General Conference Co-Chair

Allison Druin, University of Maryland / National Park Service, CHI 2016 General Conference Co-Chair

Cliff Lampe, University of Michigan, CHI 2016 Technical Program Chair

Dan Morris, Microsoft, CHI 2016 Papers Co-Chair

Juan Pablo Hourcade, University of Iowa, CHI 2016 Papers Co-Chair

Loren Terveen, University of Minnesota, President, ACM SIGCHI Executive Committee

Scooter Morris, University of San Francisco, ACM SIGCHI Vice President for Conferences

Table of Contents

VOLUME 1

Table of Contents

Table of Contents

Table of Contents

Table of Contents

Table of Contents

Table of Contents

Table of Contents

Table of Contents

Table of Contents

Table of Contents

Table of Contents

Table of Contents

Table of Contents

Table of Contents

Table of Contents

Table of Contents

Table of Contents

Table of Contents

Table of Contents

Table of Contents

Table of Contents

Table of Contents

Table of Contents

Table of Contents

Table of Contents

Table of Contents

Table of Contents

Table of Contents

Table of Contents

Table of Contents

Table of Contents

Designing for the Other 'Hereafter': When Older Adults Remember about Forgetting

Laura Ramos[1,4]
[1]Faculty of Design, Architecture & Building
University of Technology Sydney
laura.l.ramos@student.uts.edu.au
elise.vandenhoven@uts.edu.au

Elise van den Hoven [1,2,4,5]
[2]Department of Industrial Design
Eindhoven University of Technology
e.v.d.hoven@tue.nl

Laurie Miller[3,4,6]
[3]Institute of Clinical Neurosciences, Royal Prince Alfred Hospital, Sydney
laurie.miller@sydney.edu.au

[4]Australian Research Council Centre of Excellence in Cognition and its Disorders

[5]Duncan of Jordanstone College of Art and Design
University of Dundee

[6]Central Medical School
University of Sydney

ABSTRACT
Designing to support memory for older individuals is a complex challenge in human-computer interaction (HCI) research. Past literature on human memory has mapped processes for recalling past experiences, learning new things, remembering to carry out future intentions and the importance of attention. However, the understanding of how older adults perceive forgetting in daily life remains limited. This paper narrows this gap through a study with older persons (n=18) living independently using self-reporting and semi-structured focus groups to explore what they forget, how they react, and what mechanisms they put in place to recover from and avoid forgetting. Findings include occurrences of prospective and retrospective memory lapses, conflicting negative and neutral perceptions, and techniques to manage forgetting. Participant responses indicate that an awareness of forgetting fosters internal tensions among older adults, thereby creating opportunities for further design research, e.g., to defuse and normalise these reactions.

Author Keywords
Interaction design, Human-computer interaction, Human memory, Everyday remembering, Older persons, Perceptions about forgetting, Diary study

ACM Classification Keywords
H.1.2 User/Machine Systems: Human Factors; H.5.2 User Interfaces: User-centered design; K.4.2 Social Issues.

INTRODUCTION
Facilitator: So, what types of things do you forget?

Participant 1 (P1): Oh, there was one [time] when I went to the room and couldn't remember [why I had gone there]; that's the 'hereafter!' (laughter)

CHI'16, May 07-12, 2016, San Jose, CA, USA
© 2016 ACM. ISBN 978-1-4503-3362-7/16/05...$15.00
DOI: http://dx.doi.org/10.1145/2858036.2858162

We are surrounded by systems and products intended to support our memory – calendars, alarms, and lists, not to mention photos and other objects that jog our memories – as shown in Figure 1 below. Although these solutions may help prevent forgetting, have they taken into consideration how we experience forgetting, how it makes us feel and how we respond to this experience as we age? The ways in which older individuals perceive forgetting could impact how they interact with current and future products and systems relating to memory, but research in this area has been limited to date.

Figure 1. Multiple memory systems at use in the home of P17

The main contribution of our paper lies in surfacing how older persons perceive the experience of forgetting and proposing new ways to consider this experience in design research. We begin with an overview of research on human memory systems and how memory has been approached in the field of human-computer interaction (HCI). We then describe a study on everyday forgetting which involved 18 older persons living independently at two locations in urban and regional Australia, to explore what people forget, how they react to forgetting, and what mechanisms they put in place to manage forgetting. Participants' insightful and sometimes humorous feedback is synthesised in the findings. Implications for interaction design research are presented as inputs for future research.

RELATED WORK

Many definitions of memory and forgetting

To understand how forgetting relates to this paper, we must first define how it relates to human memory. Researchers in psychology have identified multiple – and sometimes overlapping – memory systems [5,8,39,43,44], including systems to process and retain past experiences (*episodic* memories, including autobiographical memories) and facts learned over time (*semantic* memory) [43]. Episodic memory has been linked to *autonoetic consciousness* [44], as memory of one's own history fosters self-belief and a positive sense of self; this is extended in the concept of a 'self-memory system' that accesses and organises past memories into a coherent view of the self [5]. In contrast to memories lived or learned, *procedural* memory covers skills and habits that have become second nature through repeated practice and is part of a range of implicit memory systems which also include other physical and behavioural responses [39]. As episodic, semantic, and procedural memories relate to past experiences, they are referred to collectively as *retrospective* memory. In contrast, *prospective* memory relates to future planning or intentions [8]. Forgetting takes place when the individual is unable to access these memories; the causes of forgetting are equally varied, ranging from errors during memory encoding [1], interference from other memories [33], and lack of attention [4].

The last cause, *attention*, has particular relevance for the study. Momentary breaks in attention lead to memory slips or lapses [28,29]; in an everyday context these are commonly viewed as instances of mind-wandering or absent-mindedness. Absent-mindedness is distinct from forgetting (because what is not noticed cannot be encoded to memory), but this difference may be hard to ascertain in practice [36]. Nonetheless, further research has confirmed a strong relationship between errors in memory and attention [4, 45]. Whilst much has been published on the subject of attention in relation to control systems [see 30], the way in which older individuals perceive lapses in attention and memory has not received as much attention.

Following from previous studies [41,45] everyday forgetting refers to:

- inability to recall things experienced or learned in the past (*episodic* and *semantic memory*),
- failure to do something that had been planned to take place in the future (*prospective memory*), and
- failure to take an intended action due to absent-mindedness or distraction (*attention-based lapse*).

Although forgetting might be commonly viewed as a failing, a more appreciative stance is found in multiple disciplines. There is a long-running thread in psychology that indicates that well-functioning memory enables forgetting and that forgetting supports cognition [37]. More recently, forgetting has been seen as an adaptive, evolutionary response to help the brain process information more effectively [36]. There are also social benefits in forgetting, as individuals can tacitly cast aside memories that decrease their chances of fitting in a group or that do not support the goals of the collective [14]. However, individual and collective forgetting is hampered by the rise of always on and ever present digital media, fueled by falling costs in computing power and storage [22]. Considering implications for HCI, Bannon challenges the view of the human mind as a computer, arguing that human memory is about re-creating experiences, and not about carbon-copy replays; the design of ubiquitous technologies should therefore embrace this notion of memory and also allow for opportunities for "judicious forgetting" [2, p.4].

Memory and ageing

The literature on changes to memory over the human lifespan is voluminous and mixed. Age-related changes to sensory perception (e.g., hearing, sight) and cognition impact how people perceive and interact with the world around them [9]. However, individuals can adapt by using traditional or technological tools (from glasses and hearing aids to multiple digital applications), as well as through a wide range of compensatory mental strategies [21]. A broad survey of literature on attention control and ageing suggests that attention levels decline with age, but that this may be mitigated by greater levels of experience and increased levels of physical activity. [17].

However, one large-scale study of ageing [7], confirms that memory abilities vary substantially depending on the types of memory tasks on which individuals are assessed and how performance in those tasks is measured. Furthermore, a study on stereotype threats [16] finds that negative assumptions about the failing cognitive abilities of older people can compromise their test results, raising the question of whether tactics to promote self-worth and self-efficacy could help individuals rise above negative perceptions and lead to more positive outcomes. The impacts of negative perceptions about forgetting are also explored further in this paper.

Memory, forgetting, and HCI

Due to the negative bias toward forgetting, HCI has focused on preventing or mitigating forgetting. Early examples from the 1990s include proposals for the development of a 'memory prosthesis' and 'augmented memory systems.' [18,32,47]. This has progressed to development of prototypes and full systems for personal use [6,38,46,50], as well as considerable work on design considerations for these types of systems [48], which also propose improving cueing for memory (and possibly forgetting). Forgetting has emerged as an important area for further study as research extends to mechanisms (e.g., cueing) that impact both memory and forgetting [35,46,48,49]. More recent attempts to design for both remembering and forgetting [27,42] reflect Bannon's views [2].

Health and independent living are two major areas where research promises to improve quality of life and reduce cost burdens to the individual and society [26]. However, this will require addressing the extent of diversity among older people, prompting for inclusive and sensitive design principles to deliver tailored, adaptive solutions, and overcoming the practical challenges of effective communication with such broad audiences [13,52]. This awareness is now manifest in the increased use of mixed methods and participatory design for projects ranging from reminder systems for people with disabilities and chronic illness [23] to navigational tools for people with dementia [20]. Furthermore, the case to maintain positive engagement and foster a sense of exploration and fun with older adults during the research process is well articulated in the 'MakeyMakey' case study [34].

RATIONALE FOR STUDY

Solutions to support memory and well-being among older audiences need to be relevant to users' needs; this creates opportunities to unpack perceptions of forgetting in everyday living and to use these as inputs in design. However, there has been comparatively little focus on how older adults perceive forgetting. This study will contribute to the knowledge in this area by exploring how older adults react to forgetting in everyday living and what they do to manage forgetting and support memory. In order to generate insights to inform future designs, this study adopts the Research for Design approach [11] and aims to contribute to answering the wicked problem of designing for memory support systems to help older adults live independently [53].

The key questions that the study will attempt to answer are:

- What happens when individuals realise that they have forgotten something?
- How do individuals realise that forgetting has taken place?
- What actions do individuals take when they realise they have forgotten something?
- How does location and individual context impact how individuals respond to forgetting?
- What tactics do individuals use to avoid forgetting?

METHODOLOGY

Participants

Participants for the study were recruited at two residential villages in Sydney and in Northern New South Wales, Australia as shown in Figure 2 below, providing urban and regional cohorts. The inclusion criteria for the study (older individuals living independently) aligned well with the profile of residents living in those locations (over 55 years of age with minimal need for assistance for activities of daily living). Overall, 18 people provided consent to participate in the study: 14 in both diary study and focus groups, one in the diary study and interview (due to illness), two in face-to-face sessions only (one in a focus group and one in an interview, no diary returned), and one in the diary study only (no focus group or interview).

Figure 2. Regional (top), and urban (bottom) residential village locations

Participant characteristics

Participants completed a brief profile sheet with data on age, education level, gender, marital status, and familiarity with computers. Participants were also asked about prior and current work experiences during interviews (as a number of participants continued working in casual and volunteer roles). Compared to the urban cohort, regional participants were older (median age=79) and better educated; 10 out of 12 had some form of tertiary education. In contrast, only one out of six participants in the urban cohort (median age=68) had tertiary education. Male participants made up one-third (two out of six) of participants in the urban location, compared to one-sixth (two out of 12) in the regional location; this variation may have been due to age differences between cohorts. There was one married couple, and all other participants lived on their own. In terms of familiarity with computers, 15 out of 18 participants reported using computers, mobile phones or tablet devices regularly. There was no cognitive profiling of participants, as this might induce apprehension about participating and influence participants' narratives. In spite of the high proportion of women across the two cohorts, participants had very diverse backgrounds and life experiences and thus provided a reasonable representation of older individuals living independently.

Study methods

As this study focused on forgetting – which is not an easily visible event – self-reporting and focus groups were selected to generate a wider set of data on participants' experiences with forgetting. First, self-reporting in a diary was identified as an indirect observation method to capture forgetting incidents and sensitise individuals about their experiences with forgetting. (Self-reporting through the use of diaries had been used effectively in past research on everyday forgetting, lapses in attention, and reminder systems [29,41,45]). Second, participants were invited to semi-structured focus groups two to three weeks after the diaries were provided to harness insights from self-reporting and generate discussion on their perceptions on forgetting. These methods have been used successfully in prior studies on everyday forgetting among younger persons [45] and older persons [23]. The researchers followed focus-group guidelines specific for design projects involving older participants [9], including:

- keep questions flowing in a cohesive manner and consider different ways to generate responses during the interviews;
- recruit participants with diverse characteristics, but schedule participants with common characteristics into the same groups; and
- keep overall interview length under two hours.

Additional measures were taken to help participants feel at ease throughout the study from recruitment to completion. These included: securing the support of staff at the two residential villages to minimise disruption to established schedules within the community during recruitment and research activities; scheduling briefings and data collection sessions earlier in the day (when energy levels might be higher); taking advantage of comfortable common areas in the residential villages for focus group sessions; sending personal reminders prior to focus group sessions; providing plenty of refreshment and snacks to keep participants comfortable; and starting all briefing sessions with light conversation to defuse any discomfort that participants might have felt in speaking about their experiences with forgetting. These measures helped to create a positive impression and build trust within those communities.

Diary

At an initial briefing session, interested participants were given a pack with materials for the study (two blank diaries, information sheet, consent form, background profile sheet, and a pen to encourage participants to start writing), which are shown in Figure 3 below.

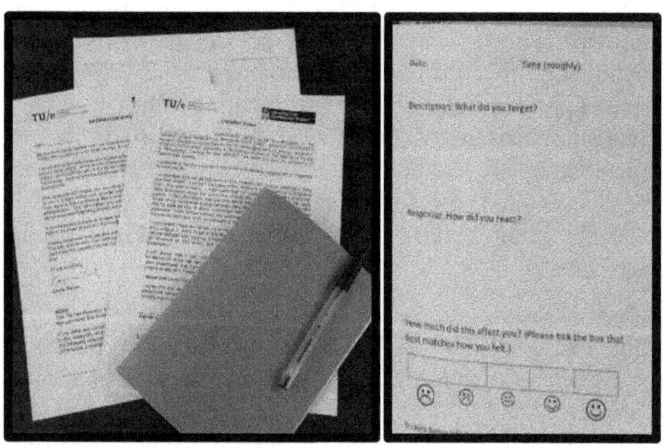

Figure 3. Sample participant pack (L) and blank diary (R)

Participants were asked to self-report in pre-formatted diaries during a period of two weeks. Diaries included a space to note date and time, as well as two pre-printed questions asking participants to describe the incident of forgetting and how it affected them on a five-point Likert scale.

Upon receipt of the consent form for the diary portion of the study, participants were given a short briefing on how to use the diary. Each participant received a reminder note about the diary after the first week, and diaries were collected just prior to the interviews two to three weeks later. Participants briefed on the diaries were invited into focus group sessions to further discuss experiences relating to forgetting.

Focus groups and interviews

Four semi-structured focus groups sessions were held, with six, four, three, and two participants in each session. Two other participants opted for individual interviews due to no-shows at a focus group and illness. Focus groups were selected over individual interviews to normalise forgetting by sharing experiences with peers; during individual interviews, the researcher used stories from other focus groups to this effect. Separate consent was gathered from all participants prior to the sessions.

Interviews lasted about one hour and were facilitated by the same researcher that provided the initial diaries. This aided familiarity and reduced the need for planned warm up activities, as participants were by and large eager to talk about their experiences. Semi-structured discussions were based on questions around experiences with and reactions to forgetting. The same script was used in all sessions, but participants were encouraged to explore different aspects of forgetting as it related to their individual life stories. The sessions were held in the common areas of the residential villages, which provided bright and comfortable spaces for open discussion. (The session with the participant that requested an individual interview due to illness took place at her home.)

Data generated

Diaries from 16 of the 18 participants were returned with some entries; the number of entries ranged from a minimum of two to a maximum of 19, for a total of 129 entries. Each of the 129 entries provided corresponded to an episode of forgetting; 121 included some commentary on how participants responded; and 124 included a rating to the question on how much the incident had affected them. Two participants did not return diaries; one participant responded she did not think she had anything to contribute in the diary, and the other did not have time to complete it (but brought hand-written notes about his experiences to the focus group session).

17 out of the 18 participants joined one of the six interviews conducted. The resulting discussions generated around six hours of audio recordings; all recordings were transcribed for further analysis. Three participants showed the facilitator around their homes to provide additional context following the focus groups and interviews. Photographs were taken before and after the interviews to capture supporting context. All data provided in the diaries and captured in both group and individual interviews was used in the analysis.

Analysis

Diaries and interviews were transcribed and coded using NVivo. Transcripts were analysed using thematic analysis [3]; this data analysis method was seen to be better suited than others (e.g., content analysis) to tease out nuances about forgetting which emerged in the language participants used to describe their experiences and explore their deeper meaning. There were 91 separate codes assigned to the data which were then clustered into three key themes: 1) types of forgetting, 2) perceptions about forgetting, and 3) techniques to recover from and avoid forgetting. A second coder was asked to review the data in the first two themes to assess the validity of the categorisation within these themes. The third theme (techniques) related to participants' actions that could be more easily observed or understood from participants' descriptions than types of forgetting or individual perceptions about forgetting; consequently, the second coder was not asked to review data clustered in the 'techniques' theme.

The reliability of agreement between the two coders was analysed using the Cohen's unweighted kappa statistic, which was seen as an appropriate metric given the nature of the analysis and number of individuals assessing the data [10]. The Cohen's kappa coefficient for data clustered around types of forgetting was 73.9% and 70.6% for data on perceptions on forgetting (both within the 61%-80% band of substantial agreement between coders) [19]. The second coder only had access to typed excerpts of the transcripts, so lacked additional context that might was applied in the initial coding. The variation between results in the types of forgetting was primarily due to differences in categorisation of lapses in prospective memory and attention; the issues in distinguishing between these events has already been noted [4,36]. Nevertheless, there was substantial agreement.

FINDINGS

What types of forgetting emerged during the study?

Participants raised five types of forgetting (prospective, attention-based, episodic, semantic, and procedural) across 154 incidents recorded in diaries and interviews. Every participant reported at least one instance of forgetting. There were 61 prospective memory incidents, 34 episodic memory incidents, 34 semantic memory incidents, 24 attention lapses, and one procedural memory incident. The procedural memory error was reported by a participant (P9) who used a spreadsheet application in her earlier working life but "now can't remember what a spreadsheet is."

Typical examples of *prospective memory lapses* were forgetting the shopping list or an item at the shops (P8, P10, P12, P13, P16), missing times for appointments or meetings (P7, P8, P12, P14, P16), forgetting to make calls (P10, P12, P14), and forgetting to take medication (P2, P13). One participant (P12) noted a prospective memory error and an episodic one in the diary: "[Forgot that] I didn't enter in the last couple of days things I forgot [in this diary]. But then, I can't remember what I forgot!"

Examples of *lapses of attention*, included instances of absent-mindedness and confused intentions, e.g., "picked up my ashtray and took it to the sink believing I was taking my coffee cup and that I could use it to get a cup of coffee" (P16).

Episodic memory lapses related to forgetting things from recent and distant past, as well as losing everyday items (glasses, keys) around the house, such as: "I couldn't find portable phone. Found it in bathroom. I took it with me as I was expecting a call but left it on the sink" (P3). Another participant (P8) expressed her experiences with short-term forgetting as, "I can't remember what I did last week; I remember everything from way back, but [if] you ask me where I was last Tuesday, [...] you've got Buckley's [no chance of remembering]."

Semantic memory lapses related to forgetting words and names of well-known people, things and places. One participant (P6), described his experiences as, "For some reason often I can't remember the name of asparagus." Another participant (P9) wrote in her diary: "Doing cryptic crossword with friends I would read a clue, see a picture of the answer in my mind but couldn't remember the name I needed." Forgetting names was a very common theme and was mentioned by nine participants.

What happens when individuals realise that they have forgotten something?

In the diaries participants were asked to note how each episode of forgetting affected them on a scale with 5 boxes ranging from very negative (rating=1) to very positive (rating=5). Likert-scale ratings were entered in 124 out of 129 total diary entries. There were 57 entries with a neutral rating (3), followed by 45 somewhat negative (rating=2), 9 somewhat positive (rating=4), 6 very negative, and 6 very positive, for an average of 2.7 out of 5 across all entries. The average indicated that forgetting had a neutral (albeit slightly negative) impact on participants. The image in Figure 4 on the following page shows two entries from a diary that were marked as neutral (rating=3).

Separate from the Likert-scale ratings, there were 186 participant comments about forgetting recorded in diaries and interviews, which related to perceptions of forgetting. 150 of these were coded to identify negative, positive, and neutral impacts. The remaining 36 were coded as reflections on forgetting, which are discussed further below.

The most common perception of forgetting was negative and was noted in 88 instances from 16 out of 18 participants. Participants mentioned a range of emotions from annoyance, frustration, embarrassment, anxiety, and guilt. Examples included "I forgot to ring [my granddaughter] and wish her good luck [on the day of the child's concert performance]; she's only five, but you know, that really upset me because, you know I just don't normally do that" (P8), and "I was so very upset [when I couldn't find some clothes I had just bought] but really relieved when I finally found them" (P3). Negative perceptions also included more subtle comments, such as, “It's funny how we don't feel right telling someone ‘listen I've forgotten your name, what is it’” (P3).

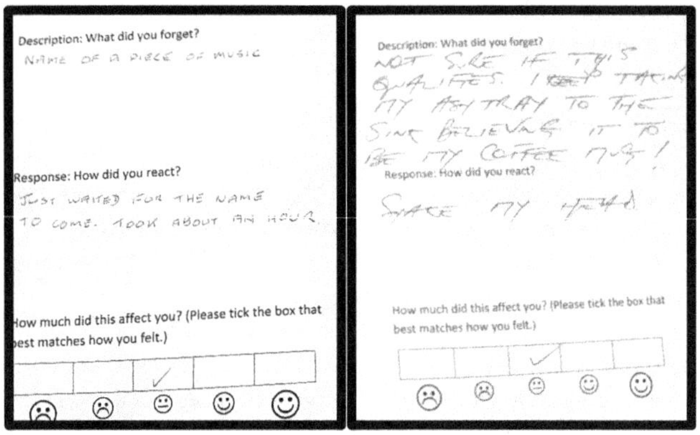

Figure 4. Sample diary entries, both rated as 3 out of 5

The next most common perception corresponded to neutral responses, raised by 15 out of 18 participants, and was noted 46 times in the data. In these instances, participants used language to note that the incident was not a cause for worry or that it was inconsequential, as in, “The things I forgot were essentially trivial” (P16).

Somewhat surprisingly, positive responses were reported in 16 cases of forgetting. An example of this (from a diary entry) was: “I was writing an email to a nurse re my sister's health & told her I didn't want the responsibility of coming for her (my sister). I told her I was 75 years old. Well I'm 76. I forgot I'm a year older. Laughed at myself” (P3).

Even in instances when participants described forgetting in neutral or matter-of-fact terms, they also used negative language to describe how they felt about the incident: “I find that I forget a lot of names of people that I know very well and I just say to them when I see them next ‘I'm sorry, I've lost your name.’ And we go from there, and usually there's no problem about it, but sometimes I feel like a bit of a fool when it's someone who you really know well” (P4).

In addition to positive, negative and neutral perceptions about forgetting, 36 items coded related to reflections on its causes, changes to memory over time, and the need to pay more attention to avoid forgetting. These are covered in further detail later in this paper.

How do individuals realise that forgetting has taken place?

Although this question was raised at all interviews, only four participants described *how* they came to notice that they had forgotten something. In cases of semantic or episodic forgetting, the trigger that made participants realise that forgetting had happened seemed to be the absence of the memory sought (“because it's names, it's very specific” [P6]).

Participants referred to cues which triggered the realisation of something being forgotten, which could have been internal or external. Internal cues related to individual behaviours or habits; for example, one participant described picking up on a lapse in attention as: “[I forgot] that I had taken recycling bag out of cupboard and … I went [back] to the cupboard to [look for] it” (P14). Other participants used mental checking tactics, which would then trigger whether something had been forgotten (often things like keys, wallets and glasses). During instances of prospective memory lapses, external cues ranged from receiving a phone call about a missed appointment (P7 and P16) or seeing a post on social media which reminded them about a future intention which was missed (P14). This realisation could come just as forgetting took place or hours later.

What actions do individuals take when they realise they have forgotten something?

Nine participants referred to techniques they used upon realising that they had forgotten something learned or experienced in the past (semantic and episodic memory). Of the 29 instances of recovery tactics recorded, the most common one was inaction; exercising patience to wait for the forgotten memory to “come back” was mentioned 17 times by six participants. Examples of this approach include: “When we forget something, the challenge half the time is not looking it up like a place name or something; it's letting it come to you,” (P1). The next most commonly used approaches were the use of mnemonics and mental tricks (e.g., going through the alphabet until the letter triggers the word or name forgotten), checking with other people, and using online and offline reference materials (e.g., online search engines, mapping tools, and dictionaries). Responses varied by individual preferences and also by the availability of trusted social networks (i.e., a spouse or friend that could help when memory failed).

In the case of prospective memory and attention-based lapses, the responses were largely reflected in the emotional reactions mentioned above and, where feasible, resulted in a great rush to achieve intended plans with whatever time was available.

What do individuals use to avoid forgetting?

Participants also shared a range of techniques to minimise forgetting and stay across everyday activities and commitments; these were recorded in 72 instances during the study across interviews and photos taken at participants' homes. All 18 participants referred to at least one action taken to manage forgetting.

Paper-based reminders

The most widely used were paper-based tools, mentioned in 42 instances; this category included calendars, diaries, notepads, post-it notes, appointment cards from different specialists and service providers, shopping lists, and lists with unspecified items. One participants found a new use for written reminders to help her cope during a time of life transition: “I've got a diary with dates […] on the cupboard in the kitchen. I've only been doing that since I [moved to this residential village]. My [late] husband was [in a care facility] for 12 months and I found that […] there was so much [to do] moving in here, solicitors, accountants and all sorts of things. I found I had no way of keeping that in my head” (P11).

Special places in everyday spaces and set behaviours

Creating a special place in everyday spaces and keeping to set behaviours, such as habits, routines, and checking, were also commonly used tactics, mentioned in 26 instances during the study. For example, one participant's (P7) method to avoid losing keys relies on using a set place by the door: "I was late one morning and I said to the lady next to me, 'I'm late because I couldn't find the car keys anywhere' and she said 'I've got an answer for that because I used to do that.' She brought me this lovely china dish and she said 'you put that beside the door and you put your keys in it every time you go in or out' So […], I gained a lovely pretty dish beside the door. […] I put the keys in, and it's working." To avoid forgetting things when leaving the house, another participant (P9) said, "I find I put things like the mobile phone or notes that I have to take or something or other, whatever I'm taking with me, all goes on the corner of the dining room table and then I pick up the lot as I go."

Examples of various paper-based tools and special places are shown in Figure 5.

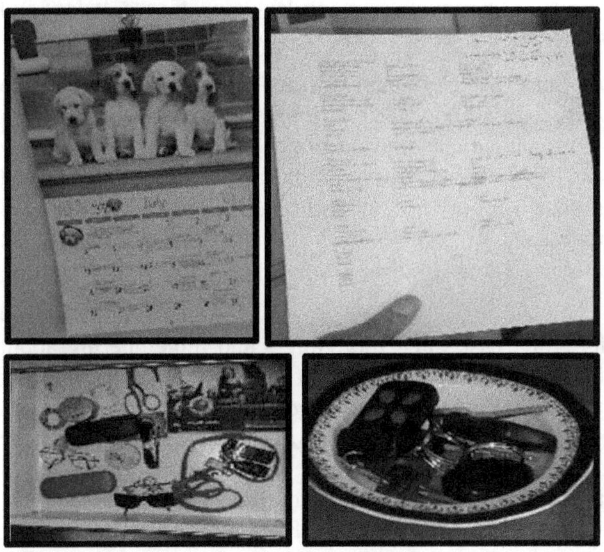

Figure 5. Paper-based tools (wall diary, pre-printed shopping list) and special places (drawer, china bowl for keys)

The use of electronic reminders, such as mobile phone alarms, was only mentioned five times. One participant (P12) mentioned her email archive as one of the places she could check on whether a conversation had taken place.

The techniques mentioned to avoid forgetting are consistent with previous research about the types of reminders used by home-bound older people [23]. Participants' conscientious use of the various tactics used to prevent forgetting is also consistent with findings that older adults are better at managing real-world prospective memory tasks because they are more motivated than younger adults to follow through on these tasks and take more time to plan and manage this [31].

How does location and individual context impact how individuals approach to forgetting?

Participants were asked how the types of techniques they used had changed over time and whether the techniques they used varied within and outside the home. Although there were few direct responses (similar to the earlier question on how individuals realise they have forgotten something), participant observations revealed some possible answers in relation to location and individual context.

Six participants that had moved recently were most aware about organising the space around them, as they were still setting up their homes and establishing regular routines. This included creating special places for reminders and habits based on the layout of their new homes. Changing life circumstances also prompted a similar response. One such example came from a participant with a very busy social life who had recently assumed additional carer responsibilities for an older relative; she managed the anxiety about staying across all this by keeping to do lists at hand. "Even in my bedroom, I have a big A4 writing pad, with a bulldog clip... and I do this [writing notes] in the dark… That's the only [thing] that can help me remember to do things tomorrow... I've been getting pretty good [at writing] in the dark!" (P3).

Outside of the home, the techniques most commonly mentioned were the use of shopping lists and occasional use of small notebooks or paper-diaries and no mention of use of electronic tools outside of the home (perhaps due to low perceived benefits).

Reactions to forgetting outside the home and in the presence of people outside immediate friends and family were consistently negative (with embarrassment and frustration with oneself as common responses).

DISCUSSION

We begin the discussion of our findings with a reflection on the extent and quality of data generated through the study. Study findings point to a number of insights on how forgetting impacts older persons, how these responses could be addressed through design, and how these methods could be extended to generate further knowledge about forgetting.

Participants forgot that they forgot

Compared to previous studies on everyday forgetting [41,45], the volume of diary entries for the current study was relatively low. The 16 diary booklets returned from study participants included a total of 129 entries (one for each incident of forgetfulness). The maximum number of entries provided in one book was 19 and the lowest was two, for an average of eight responses per participant over a period of just over two weeks. By comparison, the number of weekly forgetting incidents was nearly three times higher in another study [45] (even though participants in that study were substantially younger and briefed in far greater detail, which could account for higher response rates). So while it may not be possible to determine how frequently older participants should have been forgetting, there is enough evidence to indicate that participants in the current study under-reported forgetting.

Extreme examples of this lack of acknowledgement of forgetting in the current study came from two participants (one at each of the study locations). One participant (P5) returned two blank diaries at the focus group session, where she reported that, "I didn't write anything because there's no change. I'm the same as I normally am." Another participant (P15) wrote the following diary entries on two separate days: "No problems today. Baked ANZAC biscuits for [local community group]" and "Didn't forget anything. Home all day."

Although identifying the causes for under-reporting of forgetting is outside of the scope of the present study, it is worth exploring potential deliberate and unintentional factors. Individual feedback suggested that some participants were deliberately guarded in their discussions about forgetting. A couple of participants described the research as a 'test,' suggesting they felt that their cognitive capacity was being judged (although this notion was dispelled during the focus groups and interviews). Given that embarrassment was mentioned in relation to forgetting, participants may have sought to attenuate any negative emotions they might have felt about forgetting by refraining from writing in the diary.

However, participants were engaged and responsive during the research session, indicating that under-reporting was more likely unintentional. This could be due to the impact of stereotypes about the behaviour and cognitive abilities of older persons [16], or to age-related declines in cognitive function (even though this is highly variable across older individuals [7]). A further potential factor could be found in the inhibitory control mechanisms of the self-memory system [5] that can reduce the availability of memories that challenge the coherence of the self. This notion is developed further in the next section.

Awareness of forgetting causes internal conflict

All participants acknowledged that forgetting was a normal occurrence among persons of all ages, but that conscious awareness gave way to misgivings about forgetting. It was noted earlier that the prevalence of negative perceptions about forgetting among participants was in sharp contrast with the Likert-scale responses in diaries. This contrast was also evident during focus groups and interviews. Feedback from one participant (P17) encapsulated the dissonance and disparate emotions and reflections about forgetting: "Normally I don't forget; oh, these little things I do, but with names, I'm very good with names. I'm very good with faces. Even my friends are surprised that I can recall everything. ... But little triggers I get annoyed. I don't know, my cup of tea or my glasses; I can't live without my glasses! I mean my reading glasses. I don't wear glasses when I drive. It's annoying, those things, why? Is that part of the ... an ageing human brain?"

In some instances, participants seemed to play down the resulting frustration about forgetting: "I know that my memory isn't as good as it used to be, but I've come to accept it now and I try not to get really irritated by it. I find it funny in some ways, like forgetting the name of asparagus and things like that...but it did used to annoy me because I always had such a good memory" (P6). Another participant mirrored this by responding, "It doesn't annoy me anymore; it's just the time I waste. I get cranky about that" (P7)

This type of feedback was neither isolated nor restricted to any particular type of memory failure (episodic, semantic, prospective, attention-based, or procedural). Around half of participants used language that trivialised forgetting while at the same time expressing annoyance and frustration about having to manage forgetting in their everyday lives. This included labelling an incident as "silly" or "little," as in "it's just little things not so much little things, just small things that waste time and can be very irritating" (P7). It seemed that, as participants became aware of – and, in effect, remembered – the experience of forgetting, this realisation then seemed to provoke varying levels of unease, worry and frustration.

This could be explained by revisiting the relationship between self-knowledge (*autonoetic consciousness*), autobiographical episodic memory [44] and the self-memory system [5]. In other words, if the act of reflecting on past experience supports an individual's sense of self, then an awareness that forgetting has taken place (in effect disallowing access to prior knowledge) could challenge self-belief.

If this is the case, then forgetting - and remembering about forgetting - would cause discomfort regardless of the type of memory that cannot be retrieved or the memory system involved. Acting to trivialise this event would then reduce the impact on the individual's sense of self and defuse internal tensions. A similar motivation would then lead to being "just anxious but not really worried" (P17) about losing something at home.

The contrasting language in these examples is also a window into the experience of forgetting later in life. According to Conway, in the self-memory system memories support beliefs and knowledge about the self, and this requires coherence [5]. Participants seem to be associating perceived faults in their memory to the broader changes they experience as they age (recognising that the ageing process is varied), and they may seek to come to terms with those faults by describing them as "little things" that don't challenge their sense of self. Participants' use of humour (including the comment about the 'hereafter' used at the start of this paper) as a strategy to cope with and normalise these events can also be seen as fostering a coherent view of the self.

No one pretended to trivialise incidents that could have negative implications for personal health, safety, or commitments to others within the person's network. One participant, a diabetic, summarised this as "If I'm not concentrating on taking my blood sugar levels at some points during the day and injecting myself with the right amount of insulin, I could potentially, you know, 'see you later' [So doing these things are] always in the back of the mind. That stuff you don't mess with" (P14). In this instance, the knowledge that one can remember important things could reaffirm the self and boost coherence.

Different types of forgetting need different responses

Overall, the types of forgetting reported were generally consistent with past studies [23,41,45], which identified lapses relating to attention, prospective and retrospective (episodic and semantic) memory. That said, the data points to the need for different responses for the various types of forgetting.

As noted earlier, most of the tactics to recover from forgetting related to episodic and semantic memory lapses, whereas the tactics used to prevent incidents related to prospective memory or attention. For example, reminder systems may be useful to keep an appointment, but they may not be as useful in remembering the name of an acquaintance from many years ago. Similarly, a system to keep keys and glasses from getting lost around the house may not be practical when faced with a tricky crossword puzzle clue outside of the home. In the example of the participant with a specific gap in procedural memory about spreadsheets, none of the systems mentioned above would be of any use; however, it may be that what participant needed most was reassurance about whether this type of forgetting might impact her in the future.

The importance of managing sensitivities in relation to the individual contexts of older persons is well documented in [9,13,23,26,52]. In addition, convenience and ease of use relative to the task at hand seemed to determine participants' choices, consistent with past research [24] that found that if older adults failed to see benefits in a solution they would not engage with it. This has led us to further design considerations to support forgetting.

Design considerations to manage forgetting

The possibility that forgetting is inevitable, unacknowledged, and, when it is acknowledged, a source of mixed emotions and internal tensions creates new opportunities for design research. These are presented as design considerations that can be extended to existing and wholly new design concepts. Although some of these are by no means unique to this study, they are included as they could be relevant for future designs to support memory and forgetting for older users.

Acknowledge and normalise forgetting in the everyday

If forgetting is unavoidable, acknowledging might help some people adapt to it more effectively. This could mean designing solutions that:

- Foster mindfulness and an awareness of everyday actions, rather than avoidance of forgetting; and
- Reassure and acknowledge that forgetting takes place, rather than remind individuals about what they have just forgotten (which is how one participant saw the alarms on his mobile phone);

As an example of the latter point, personal reminder apps could give users the option to mark an item as 'Didn't do it/OK, Forget it!,' which would relegate the item to an archive – or perhaps erase it over time. Whilst this option may not be practical in many instances, it may give some users an alternative way to handle overloaded schedules and manage forgetting in a more positive way.

To expand awareness and acceptance of forgetting, social media could be used to capture, curate and publish stories of (harmless) forgetting to bring the topic out into the open and normalise the experience of forgetting with candour and humour. However, this would require strong moderation to minimise risk of misuse and potential harm to individuals.

Exploit mundane materials

Participants demonstrated great initiative in adapting everyday spaces and objects to remind themselves, e.g., attaching a big clip to a plain paper pad so it could be easier to use in the dark (P3), keeping pre-printed shopping lists on the refrigerator (P7), and putting a canvas bag on a chair as a reminder of things that needed to be packed the following morning (P14). Mundane materials can be put to work on new routines to provide reassurance:

- Give mundane materials around the home new uses and affordances, to display, tag, highlight and connect into digital environments;
- Embed digital interfaces into everyday objects and routines, rather than creating stand-alone applications on electronic devices; and
- Allow for flexible use and re-use of materials.

Past research has involved older adults in the development of reminder systems using smartpens and paper [51] as an extension of everyday reminder tools. The proposed design for the ARENO system [15] uses a digital pen and paper to capture reminders and visualise them on ambient displays. We can envision embedding similar systems in everyday items (e.g., coffee mugs, chairs, doors, or even re-usable shopping bags) to display contextual reminders through visual prompts, as well as sound or haptic feedback.

Enable creative combinations for remembering and forgetting

The techniques that participants used to manage forgetting were often combined (e.g, a particular diary always kept by the phone), with participants creating habits around places and objects in the home to support with ongoing activity. It was interesting to note the low use of electronic tools, even though most participants – even the oldest ones – used computers and mobile phones regularly. This raises a need for creative combinations that:

- Consider digital as just one aspect in a range of interactions (as writing reminders on paper could actually assist in supporting memory formation and retention);

- Give users the option and freedom to opt-in to new uses and to adapt them into existing routines; and
- Consider carefully opportunities for wearable technologies as inputs and with absolute respect for the individual.

The systems noted above apply equally to this set of recommendations. Identifying an opportunity to leverage existing habits, the app proposed in [40] prompts users to nominate routines that could be better suited to timings for medication. This concept could be carried forward to a broader set of tasks, multiple modalities and implementations.

Create discrete and personalised responses

The sheer diversity among participants was consistent with past research [13,23,52] and highlighted the need for:

- Discretion, not only because some material will need to be private, but also because of the emotions and vulnerabilities that can arise from forgetting; and
- Personalisation to cater not only for personal taste and learning preferences, but also to varying physical and cognitive abilities.

A possible extension to an ambient reminder system (e.g., [15]) would allow the user to determine which items remain in a secure location (e.g., paper diary) that only the user can access. In terms of personalisation, future home automation systems may be able to support capture of routines and transfer to reminder systems (see [25] for a recent review of the current state and challenges of home automation.)

These considerations are offered on a preliminary basis, taking into account the perspective that design research should produce knowledge that is "provisional, contingent and aspirational" [12, p. 938], and with a view to contributing to current and future research on interaction design to support memory and forgetting in older adults.

Observations on methods for future research

Overall, the methods applied in this study succeeded in generating valuable data to develop new insights on forgetting. In spite of potential under-reporting of forgetting incidents, the use of diaries in this study helped to sensitise participants to the topic of forgetting, which is not only difficult to observe, but which can also generate avoidance and aversion; the feedback that followed in group sessions and individual interviews benefitted.

There is scope to repeat these methods with a related set of participants to expand the understanding of forgetting, particularly in relation to cues that trigger an awareness of forgetting. Further studies would benefit from additional methods such as home tours or direct observation to deepen the understanding of cues that trigger realisation of forgetting, an area of initial interest for the authors. In addition, recruitment of participants from more diverse backgrounds could provide a broader perspective on perceptions about forgetting.

CONCLUSION

Forgetting is a complex and under-appreciated phenomenon. The core contribution of our paper lies in surfacing internal tensions when older adults perceive forgetting and providing design recommendations to facilitate forgetting and remembering. Through self-reporting, focus groups and interviews, participants (n=18) have revealed that forgetting was most frequently associated with prospective memories (relating to future intentions). The perceptions of forgetting and the tactics used to recover from and prevent forgetting give rise to two insights: First, conflicting negative and neutral perceptions suggest a tension between stated indifference about forgetting and a high proportion of negative emotions about memory failings. Building upon the concept that memory systems support the individual's sense of self [5,43], an awareness of one's own forgetfulness compromises a coherent view of the self and generates discomfort, which individuals may try to resolve by trivialising forgetting to the extent possible. Second, effective solutions to manage forgetting will have to correspond to the types of forgetting experienced, as well as to individual location and context. Resulting considerations for future design research and development include acknowledging, normalising and perhaps even celebrating forgetting to help defuse the internal tensions that may arise from an awareness of the imperfections of memory; exploiting mundane materials which are already embedded in everyday living; enabling creative combinations of different tactics that individuals put in practice to manage forgetting; and creating discrete and personalised solutions. So, although forgetting will continue to be a reality for older persons (and indeed for everyone), systems to support memory can also support forgetting and how it is perceived – perhaps even making an inevitable 'hereafter' moment a bit more liveable.

ACKNOWLEDGMENTS

The authors would like to thank the participants and residential village staff who contributed generously with their time and feedback. This study was approved by the UTS Ethics Committee (#2012000570), and supported by STW VIDI grant number 016.128.303 of The Netherlands Organisation for Scientific Research (NWO) awarded to Elise van den Hoven and by grant number CE110001021 from the ARC Centre of Excellence awarded to Laurie Miller and colleagues from the ARC Centre of Excellence in Cognition and its Disorders.

REFERENCES

1. Alan D. Baddeley. 2004. The psychology of memory. In *The Essential Handbook of Memory Disorders for Clinicians*, Alan D. Baddeley, Michael Kopelman, and Barbara A. Wilson (eds.). John Wiley & Sons, UK, 1-13.
2. Liam J. Bannon. 2006. Forgetting as a feature, not a bug: the duality of memory and implications for ubiquitous computing. *CoDesign* 2, 01: 3-15.

3. Virginia Braun and Victoria Clarke. 2006. Using thematic analysis in psychology. *Qualitative Research in Psychology* 3, 2: 77–101.
4. James Allan Cheyne, Jonathan S. A. Carriere, and Daniel Smilek. 2006. Absent-mindedness: Lapses of conscious awareness and everyday cognitive failures. *Consciousness and cognition*, 15, 3: 578-592.
5. Martin A. Conway, M.A., 2005. Memory and the self. Journal of memory and language, 53(4), pp.594-628.
6. Dan Cosley, Victoria Schwanda Sosik, S. Tejaswi Peesapati, Johnathon Schultz, and Soyoung Lee. 2012. Experiences with designing tools for everyday reminiscing. *Human–Computer Interaction* 27, 1-2: 175-198.
7. Roger A. Dixon, Brent J. Small, Stuart W.S. MacDonald, and John J. McArdle. 2012. Yes, memory declines with aging--but when, how, and why? In *Memory and Aging*, Moshe Naveh-Benjamin and Nabuo Ohta (eds.). Psychology Press, New York, NY, 326-347.
8. Judi Ellis. 1996. Prospective memory or the realization of delayed intentions: A conceptual framework for research. In *Prospective memory: Theory and applications*, Maria A. Brandimonte, Gilles O. Einstein and Mark A. McDaniel (eds.). Lawrence Erlbaum Associates, Mahwah, NJ, 1–22.
9. Arthur D. Fisk, Wendy A. Rogers, Neil Charness, Sara J. Czaja, Joseph Sharit. 2009. *Designing for Older Adults: Principles and Creative Human Factors Approaches.* CRC press.
10. Joseph L. Fleiss. 2004. The measurement of interrater agreement. In *Statistical Methods for Rates and Proportions*, Joseph L. Fleiss, Bruce Levin, and Myunghee Cho Paik (eds.). John Wiley & Sons, Inc., Hoboken, NJ, 598-626.
11. Christopher Frayling. 1993. *Research in art and design.* Royal College of Art, London, UK.
12. William Gaver. 2012. What should we expect from research through design?. In *Proceedings of the SIGCHI Conference on Human Factors in Computing Systems (CHI '12)*. ACM, New York, NY, USA, 937-946. DOI=http://dx.doi.org/10.1145/2207676.2208538
13. Peter Gregor, Alan F. Newell, and Mary Zajicek. 2002. Designing for dynamic diversity: interfaces for older people. In *Proceedings of the fifth international ACM conference on Assistive technologies (Assets '02)*. ACM, New York, NY, USA, 151-156. DOI=http://dx.doi.org/10.1145/638249.638277
14. Celia B. Harris, John Sutton, and Amanda J. Barnier. 2010. Autobiographical forgetting, social forgetting and situated forgetting, In *Forgetting*, Sergio Della Sala (ed.). Psychology Press, 271-284.
15. Adriana Ispas, Sarah Schöni, and Moira C. Norrie. 2012. ARENO: ambient reminder notes. In *Proceedings of the 24th Australian Computer-Human Interaction Conference (OzCHI '12)*, Vivienne Farrell, Graham Farrell, Caslon Chua, Weidong Huang, Raj Vasa, and Clinton Woodward (Eds.). ACM, New York, NY, USA, 253-262. DOI=http://dx.doi.org/10.1145/2414536.2414580
16. Karen A. Kit and Holly A. Tuokko and Catherine A. Mateer. 2008. A review of the stereotype threat literature and its application in a neurological population. *Neuropsychology review* 18, 2: 132-148.
17. Arthur F. Kramer and David J. Madden. 2011. Attention In *The handbook of aging and cognition*, Fergus I.M. Craik and Timothy A. Salthouse (eds.), Psychology Press, New York, 189-249.
18. Mik Lamming, Peter Brown, Kathleen Carter, Margery Eldridge, Mike Flynn, Gifford Louie, Peter Robinson and Abigail Sellen. 1994. The design of a human memory prosthesis. *The Computer Journal* 37, 3: 153-163.
19. J. Richard Landis and Gary G. Koch. 1977. The measurement of observer agreement for categorical data. *Biometrics* 33: 159-74.
20. Stephen Lindsay, Katie Brittain, Daniel Jackson, Cassim Ladha, Karim Ladha, and Patrick Olivier. 2012. Empathy, participatory design and people with dementia. In Proceedings of the SIGCHI Conference on Human Factors in Computing Systems (CHI '12). ACM, New York, NY, USA, 521-530. DOI=http://dx.doi.org/10.1145/2207676.2207749
21. Sophie Martin, Clémence Mazzocco, Pascale Maury, Anne Grosselin, Wim Van der Elst, Roger A. Dixon, Yannick Stephan, and Denis Brouillet. 2015. Compensating for memory losses throughout adulthood: Validation and normalization of the Memory Compensation Questionnaire for non-clinical French populations. *Archives of Gerontology and Geriatrics* 60, 28-38.
22. Viktor Mayer-Schönberger. 2011. *Delete: the virtue of forgetting in the digital age.* Princeton University Press.
23. Marilyn Rose McGee-Lennon, Maria Klara Wolters, and Stephen Brewster. 2011. User-centred multimodal reminders for assistive living. In *Proceedings of the SIGCHI Conference on Human Factors in Computing Systems* (CHI '11). ACM, New York, NY, USA, 2105-2114. DOI=http://dx.doi.org/10.1145/1978942.1979248
24. Anne-Sophie Melenhorst, Wendy A. Rogers and Don G. Bouwhuis. 2006. Older adults' motivated choice for technological innovation: evidence for benefit-driven selectivity. *Psychology and aging* 21, 1: 190-195.
25. Sarah Mennicken, Jo Vermeulen, and Elaine M. Huang. 2014. From today's augmented houses to tomorrow's smart homes: new directions for home automation research. In *Proceedings of the 2014 ACM International Joint Conference on Pervasive and Ubiquitous Computing (UbiComp '14)*. ACM, New York, NY, USA, 105-115. DOI=http://dx.doi.org/10.1145/2632048.2636076
26. Tracy L. Mitzner and Katinka Dijkstra. 2010. E-Health for Older Adults: Assessing and Evaluating User Centered Design with Subjective Methods. In *Human-Centered Design of E-Health Technologies: Concepts, Methods and Applications*, Martina Ziefle and Carsten Röcker (eds.). IGI Global, Pennsylvania, 1-21.

27. Wolfgang Nejdl and Claudia Niederee. 2015. Photos to Remember, Photos to Forget. *IEEE MultiMedia*, 22, 1: 6-11.
28. Donald A. Norman and Tim Shallice. 1986. Attention to action. In *Consciousness and Self-Regulation: Advances in Research and Theory Vol. 4*, Richard J. Davidson, Gary E. Schwartz, David Shapiro (eds.). (pp. 1-18). Springer US.
29. James T. Reason. 1984. Lapses of attention in everyday life. In *Varieties of attention*, Raja Parasuraman and D.R. Davies (eds.). Academic Press, Orlando, FL, 515-549.
30. James T. Reason. 1990. *Human error*. Cambridge University Press, Cambridge.
31. Peter G. Rendell, and Fergus IM Craik. 2000. Virtual week and actual week: Age-related differences in prospective memory. *Applied Cognitive Psychology* 14,7: S43-S62.
32. Bradley J. Rhodes. 1997. The wearable remembrance agent: A system for augmented memory. *Personal Technologies* 1, 4: 218-224.
33. Henry L. Roediger III, Yana Weinstein, and Pooja K. Agarwal. 2010. Forgetting: Preliminary considerations, In *Forgetting*, Sergio Della Sala (ed.). Psychology Press, 1-22.
34. Yvonne Rogers, Jeni Paay, Margot Brereton, Kate L. Vaisutis, Gary Marsden, and Frank Vetere. 2014. Never too old: engaging retired people inventing the future with MaKey MaKey. In *Proceedings of the SIGCHI Conference on Human Factors in Computing Systems* (CHI '14). ACM, New York, NY, USA, 3913-3922. DOI=http://dx.doi.org/10.1145/2556288.2557184
35. Corina Sas and Steve Whittaker. 2013, April. Design for forgetting: disposing of digital possessions after a breakup. In *Proceedings of the SIGCHI Conference on Human Factors in Computing Systems* (CHI '13) 1823-1832.
36. Daniel L. Schacter. 2002. *The Seven Sins of Memory: How the Mind Forgets and Remembers*. Houghton Mifflin Harcourt.
37. Lael J. Schooler and Ralph Hertwig. 2005. How forgetting aids heuristic inference. *Psychological Review* 112, 3: 610.
38. Abigail J. Sellen, Andrew Fogg, Mike Aitken, Steve Hodges, Carsten Rother, and Ken Wood. 2007. Do life-logging technologies support memory for the past?: an experimental study using sensecam. In *Proceedings of the SIGCHI Conference on Human Factors in Computing Systems* (CHI '07). ACM, New York, NY, USA, 81-90. DOI=http://dx.doi.org/10.1145/1240624.1240636
39. Larry R. Squire. 2004. Memory systems of the brain: a brief history and current perspective. *Neurobiology of Learning and Memory* 82, 3: 171-177.
40. Katarzyna Stawarz, Anna L. Cox, and Ann Blandford. 2014. Don't forget your pill!: designing effective medication reminder apps that support users' daily routines. In *Proceedings of the SIGCHI Conference on Human Factors in Computing Systems* (CHI '14). ACM, New York, NY, USA, 2269-2278. DOI=http://dx.doi.org/10.1145/2556288.2557079
41. W. Scott Terry. 1988. Everyday forgetting: Data from a diary study. *Psychological Reports* 62, 1: 299-303.
42. Wenn-Chieh Tsai, Po-Hao Wang, Hung-Chi Lee, Rung-Huei Liang, and Jane Hsu. 2014. The reflexive printer: toward making sense of perceived drawbacks in technology-mediated reminiscence. In *Proceedings of the 2014 conference on Designing interactive systems* (DIS '14). ACM, New York, NY, USA, 995-1004. DOI=http://dx.doi.org/10.1145/2598510.2598589
43. Endel Tulving. 1972. Episodic and semantic memory. In *Organization of Memory*. Academic Press, London and New York, 381-402.
44. Endel Tulving. 1985. Memory and consciousness. *Canadian Psychology/Psychologie canadienne* 26, 1 (Jan 1985), 1-12.
45. Nash Unsworth, Gene A. Brewer, and Gregory J. Spillers. 2012. Variation in cognitive failures: An individual differences investigation of everyday attention and memory failures. *Journal of Memory and Language* 67, 1: 1-16
46. Elise van den Hoven. 2014. A future-proof past: Designing for remembering experiences. *Memory Studies* 7, 3: 370-384.
47. Elise van den Hoven and Berry Eggen. 2008. Informing augmented memory system design through autobiographical memory theory. *Personal and Ubiquitous Computing* 12, 6: 433-443.
48. Elise van den Hoven and Berry Eggen. 2014. The cue is key: Design for real-life remembering. *Zeitschrift für Psychologie* 222, 2: 110.
49. Elise van den Hoven, Corina Sas and Steve Whittaker. 2012. Introduction to this special issue on designing for personal memories: past, present, and future. *Human–Computer Interaction* 27,1-2: 1-12.
50. Sunil Vemuri. 2005. *Personal Long-Term Memory Aids*. Ph.D Dissertation. Massachusetts Institute of Technology, Cambridge, MA.
51. Julie R. Williamson, Marilyn McGee-Lennon, Euan Freeman, and Stephen Brewster. 2013. Designing a smartpen reminder system for older adults. *In CHI '13 Extended Abstracts on Human Factors in Computing Systems* (CHI EA '13). ACM, New York, NY, USA, 73-78. DOI=http://dx.doi.org/10.1145/2468356.2468371
52. Mary Zajicek. 2006. Aspects of HCI research for older people. *Universal Access in the Information Society* 5,3: 279-286.
53. John Zimmerman, Jodi Forlizzi, and Shelley Evenson. 2007. Research through design as a method for interaction design research in HCI. In *Proceedings of the SIGCHI Conference on Human Factors in Computing Systems* (CHI '07). ACM, New York, NY, USA, 493-502. DOI=http://dx.doi.org/10.1145/1240624.1240704

Typing Tutor: Individualized Tutoring in Text Entry for Older Adults Based on Input Stumble Detection

Toshiyuki Hagiya
KDDI R&D Laboratories, Inc.
to-hagiya@kddilabs.jp

Toshiharu Horiuchi
KDDI R&D Laboratories, Inc.
to-horiuchi@kddilabs.jp

Tomonori Yazaki
KDDI R&D Laboratories, Inc.
yazaki@kddilabs.jp

ABSTRACT
Many older adults are interested in smartphones. However most of them encounter difficulties in self-instruction and need support. Text entry, which is essential for various applications, is one of the most difficult operations to master. In this paper, we propose Typing Tutor, an individualized tutoring system for text entry that detects input stumbles and provides instructions. By conducting two user studies, we clarify the common difficulties that novice older adults experience and how skill level is related to input stumbles. Based on these studies, we develop Typing Tutor to support learning how to enter text on a smartphone. A two-week evaluation experiment with novice older adults (65+) showed that Typing Tutor was effective in improving their text entry proficiency, especially in the initial stage of use.

Author Keywords
Text entry; mobile devices; older adults; tutoring system;

ACM Classification Keywords
H.5.2 **Information Interfaces and Presentation**: User Interfaces

INTRODUCTION
Smartphones offer new opportunities to improve the lives of older adults [21]. Although these individuals would like to learn about smartphones [3], those who have never used one may encounter difficulties because of their lack of experience. Some older adults give up using a smartphone and go back to using their old feature phone. Therefore, providing support in the initial stage is very important. To make full use of the functions of a smartphone, it is essential to master text entry on a touch screen. However, text entry is one of the operations that novice older adults find most difficult because considerable background is needed, such as knowing how each key corresponds to a character and how to select a suggestion. In addition, touch interfaces lack both the mechanical stability and tactile feedback of a keyboard, making it harder to accurately select targets [14].

CHI'16, May 07-12, 2016, San Jose, CA, USA
© 2016 ACM. ISBN 978-1-4503-3362-7/16/05...$15.00
DOI: http://dx.doi.org/10.1145/2858036.2858455

Many researchers have tackled the issues associated with making text entry easier using a number of approaches, e.g. changing the layout, adjusting the key target areas, and presenting appropriate suggestions [4, 11, 23]. These aids are effective for users who are accustomed to smartphone operation. However, in addition to the problems mentioned above, smartphone novices, especially older adults, tend to have cognitive problems, such as forgetting and losing how/what to type next [22]. They therefore need patient support during the initial stages of use. According to a study [21], older adults tend to prefer an instruction manual to trial-and-error. An ideal approach is for the system to provide appropriate instructions that can be adapted to the individual user when the user has trouble during the learning process. Accordingly, in this paper, we have designed Typing Tutor, a tutoring system that automatically detects input stumbles and provides instructions that help users resolve the input stumbles independently. We define the word "input stumble" as an occasion when a user makes a mistake or does not know how/what to type next. Because most older adults in developed countries own a mobile, the targeted user group is older adults who have never used a smartphone but have owned a feature phone.

There are five steps in the development of Typing Tutor. First, we verify the acceptability of being given instructions using Wizard-of-Oz (WoZ) [18] and through interviews. Second, we conduct a second user study to clarify the problems the older adults encountered in text entry. Then, we design the structure of Typing Tutor on the basis of the previous user studies. Subsequently, we improve Typing Tutor through two trials. Finally, we evaluate the performance of Typing Tutor in a two-week experiment.

The contributions of this paper are two-fold. The first is to clarify the common difficulties that novice older adults encounter in text entry, and to analyze the relationship between the input stumbles and the user's skill. The second contribution is to develop an individualized tutoring system based on user studies.

RELATED WORK
Interface Design for Older Adults
Many studies have attributed older adults' difficulties in learning how to use technology to a number of user characteristics, such as a decline in perceptual performance and lack of experience in the relevant technology. Fisk *et al.* [7] provided guidelines for older adults. These guidelines emphasize interface changes that respond to age-related changes in perception and cognition: larger displays, fonts, buttons and

accessibility improvements in specific contexts. With respect to the touch interface, Jin *et al.* [15] have investigated optimal target size, spacing and position to derive recommendations and general guidelines for older adults. While these guidelines are very useful, needs can differ among individuals [10]. To respond to older adults' changing needs, researchers have considered adaptive solutions based on user profiles such as user behaviors, knowledge, and skills [6, 25, 28].

Text Entry for Older Adults

Focusing on text entry, many studies proposed methods for transforming detection areas based on language models and users' touch distribution [9, 11, 16, 23, 26, 29]. Rodrigues *et al.* [23] analyzed the influence of the typing behavior of older adults by varying the keyboard layout, including the color and the width of keys. Gunawardana *et al.* [11] proposed methods for varying the detection areas based on typing history using language model. As a different approach, Bi *et al.* [4] optimized an algorithm for presenting suitable suggestions to make correction and completion easier. However, Kurniawan [20] reported that older adults usually dislike text-prediction features. Therefore, Komninos *et al.* [19] proposed a keyboard that makes users aware of any errors through highlighting text in the body of the message and through a color bar at the top of the keyboard. Nicolau and Jorge [22] reported detailed analyses of how older adults learn text entry, and found their most common errors were due to cognitive problems. Therefore, we focus on providing a range of supports for cognitive factors rather than physical factors such as mistyping.

Tutoring System for Older Adults

Effective ways to help older adults have been researched. That most of this extensive research has focused on designing better instructional resources for learning how to use desktop computers. Hichman *et al.* [13] have studied the type of guidance most suitable for older adults. Rogers *et al.* [24] investigated the kinds of resources most useful in the learning process, and found that interactive tutorials were the most effective approach to training older adults. With respect to using smartphones, Leung *et al.* [21] investigated how older adults learned. According to their report, older adults tend to prefer an instruction manual to trial-and-error approaches. Kelleher and Pausch [17] proposed stencil-based tutorials that overlay step-by-step instructions on the screen. Hagiya *et al.* [12] proposed a tutoring system for a typing practice application, and showed its effectivity for older adults.

EXPLORATORY USER STUDY

In previous studies, tutoring systems have been shown to be effective aids to the learning process for older adults. We hypothesize that a tutoring system that operates on free-text input with a smartphone will also be useful for older adults. To support the hypothesis, we first conduct a user study using Wizard-of-Oz (WoZ) [18]. In this study, instructions are provided based on the judgment of a human tutor.

User Study with Wizard-of-Oz

Participants

Five participants took part in this study, two males and three females ranging in age from 65 to 83 years with a mean of age 74.2 (sd = 6.2). They were recruited from a local social institution. They had no previous experience with a smartphone or a tablet, but had owned a feature phone with a 12-key physical keyboard for more than one year and had sent e-mails more than twice a week. They were familiar with this kind of keyboard because the same layout has been used in feature phones for a long time. All of them had used PCs in their jobs. None of them had a tremor disorder, eye problems or other relevant health problems.

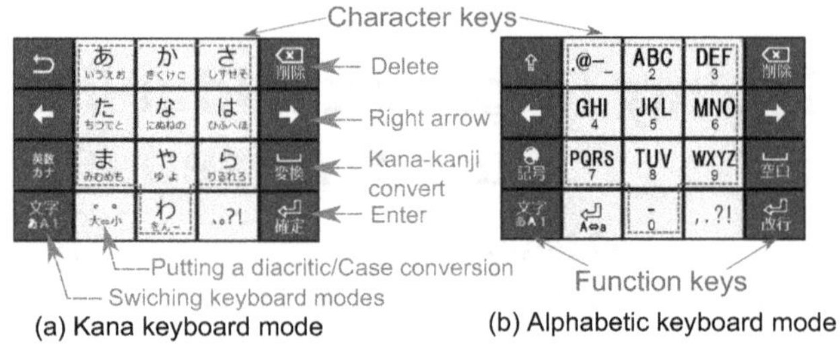

Figure 1. Key layout of 12-key

Figure 2. Screen shot of the instruction with WoZ

Apparatus

A Samsung Galaxy S3 running Android 4.1.2 with a 4.8 inch screen having a resolution of 1280 × 720 pixels (306 ppi) was used in the experiment. The software keyboard of the smartphone had a 12-key multi-tap layout as shown in Figure 1. This layout is common in Japanese smartphones. The smartphone recorded the all touch events in an input log using the standard Android API, plus all linguistic information e.g. typed keys, displayed characters and suggestions. All participant operations were recorded by an overhead video camera and were displayed on a monitor that a human tutor observed.

The human tutor observed the participant's operations via a monitor and operated a PC which was connected to the smartphone using Bluetooth. When the human tutor sent an instruction by selecting from a list of instructions in a PC application, the instruction was provided to the participant by a combination of text instruction and key highlighting overlaid on the key and voice instruction that matched the wording of the text instruction. The list contained eight instructions, such as "how to switch keyboard modes" and "how to enter a symbol", from a reference [12] compiled from research on a tutoring system for typing fixed text. Figure 2 shows one of the instructions. This instruction indicates how to type a punctuation mark.

	A	I	U	E	O
	a (あ)	i (い)	u (う)	e (え)	o (お)
K	ka (か)	ki (き)	ku (く)	ke (け)	ko (こ)
S	sa (さ)	si (し)	su (す)	se (せ)	so (そ)
⋮			⋮		
W	wa (わ)	-	-	-	wo (を)

Table 1. Japanese syllabic alphabet represented by Roman alphabet

Characteristics of 12-key multi-tap for Japanese

First, we describe the characteristics of the keyboard with a 12-key layout. The keyboard has several points in common with QWERTY, such as some function keys (delete, arrow, enter to fix a sentence, switching keyboard, case conversion) and a suggestion list containing autocomplete selections. A character string being edited is not finalized until either a suggestion is selected or a enter key is typed. A point of difference is that the characters are input by the combination of a key and a number being pressed. For example, the letter "c" is input by typing the "a" key three times. Therefore, when typing two consecutive characters allocated to the same key, the first character must be fixed by pressing the right arrow key before typing the second character.

Next, we describe the characteristics of Japanese input. Kana characters, which comprise a Japanese phonetic syllabary, are combinations of a consonant and a vowel as shown in Table 1. In this keyboard, a key corresponds to a consonant, and the number of presses corresponds to a vowel. For some characters, the diacritic key needs to be used after inputting kana. For example, the kana of "gu (ぐ)" is input by pressing a diacritic key after the kana for "ku (く)". Although the suggestion list usually shows the autocomplete list predicted by a typed string, the kanji list is shown after typing the kana-kanji convert key.

Procedure

First, the participants were given explanations and examples of how to operate a smartphone, including touch and swipe operations, by a human tutor. Next, they were briefly instructed on how to use the software keyboard, including the correspondence between each key and a character, and how to correct input text or select suggestions. Then, they typed ten sentences in Japanese using an e-mail application. Participants created the sentences in the form of a response to given sentences, such as "You expect to be ten minutes late for a meeting with a friend. Please create a sentence to let him know." and "Please create a sentence to ask when your son or daughter will arrive home." They operated the smartphone while holding it in their hand or resting it on a desk while sitting on a chair. When the human tutor observing through the monitor judged that the participant needed help with the operation in the instruction list, the human tutor sent the instruction via Bluetooth. They could rest for one minute after writing each sentence. The experimental period was limited to 60 minutes. After the experiment, they filled out a 5-point Likert-scaled questionnaire in which 5 indicated strong agreement, and took part in an interview.

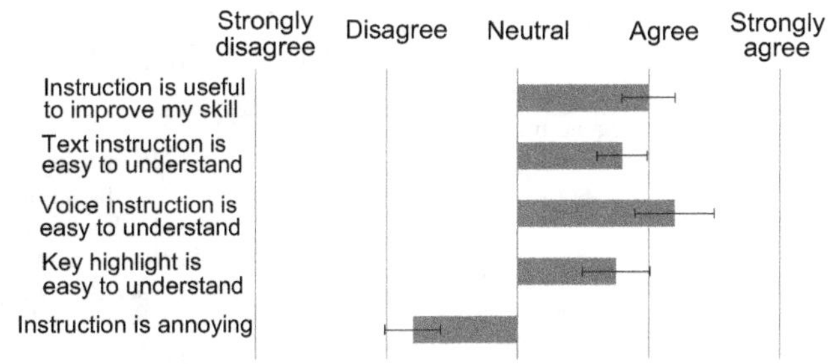

Figure 3. Questionnaire responses regarding WoZ study

Results of WoZ study

Figure 3 shows the results of the subjective questionnaires for the tutoring system using WoZ. There was a positive response to the item *"Instruction is useful to improve my skill."* The instruction methods was also positively rated, particularly voice instruction. These results showed that the tutoring system was generally-supported by the participants. On the other hand, the following negative opinions were expressed:

"I felt irritated when the system gave instructions which I already understood."

"I knew some operations. So I didn't need the instructions for some of the easy operations."

"First, I didn't realize that I could press the overlaid yellow key before the key disappeared. It's confusing to me."

This study showed that older adults found it acceptable to be provided instructions. However, we confirmed that we also needed to consider a user's capability and what they are already accustomed to doing, and we needed to modify the way of expression of the key highlight.

USER STUDY TO CLARIFY HOW NOVICE OLDER ADULTS MAKE INPUT STUMBLES

In the previous section, we verified that older adults found it acceptable to be provided instructions by the WoZ tutoring system. In this section, we describe a second user study to clarify how novice older adults make input stumbles in smartphone text entry, and analyze the relationship between the input stumbles and the user's skill.

Participants

Thirty-five participants took part in this experiment. Five were colleagues who had advanced IT skills, four males and one female, ranging in age from 29 to 48 years with a mean age of 36.6 (sd = 6.6). The other thirty were older adults who were recruited from a local social institution. There were fifteen males and fifteen females, ranging in age from 60 to 83 years with a mean age of 72.1 (sd = 8.2). None of them had any previous experience of using a smartphone but had owned a feature phone for more than one year. Twenty-six of them had often communicated via e-mail, while the others had seldom done so, using the phone only for making phone calls. Twenty-eight had previously entered text with PCs. Ten had used their own PC routinely. None of them had a tremor disorder, eye problems or other relevant health problems.

Input stumble category	Input stumble class
(1) Typing characters allocated to the same key consecutively	(1-1)Typing characters allocated to the same key consecutively
(2) Selecting a suggestion	(2-1) Not selecting despite display the desired word (2-2) Not displaying the desired word due to a long input (2-3) Not displaying the desired word because there are too many suggestions (2-4) Not knowing how to manipulate the suggestion list to find the desired word (2-5) Not knowing how to select a word in the suggestion list in kana-kanji convert mode* (2-6) Not displaying the desired word due to a long input in kana-kanji convert mode* (2-7) Not displaying the desired word because there were too many suggestions* (2-8) Not knowing how to switch the modes*
(3) Enter Key	(3-1) Fixing the sentence (3-2) Linefeed
(4) Delete character	(4-1) Delete the last character (4-2) Delete the character before several characters
(5) Switching keyboard modes	(5-1) Switching the keyboard from kana mode to alphabetic or numeric mode (5-2) Switching the keyboard from alphabetic or numeric mode to kana mode
(6) Moving cursor	(6-1) Moving cursor to previous position (6-2) Moving cursor to the end of sentence (6-3) Moving cursor in order to change target of kana-kanji conversion*
(7) Entering a diacritic	(7-1) Not knowing how to select the diacritic (7-2) Selecting the symbol key by mistake (7-3) Selecting the case conversion by mistake
(8) Case conversion	(8-1) Case conversion of alphabetic character (8-2) Case conversion of kana character*
(9) Entering a symbol	(9-1) Not knowing how to select a period or exclamation mark (9-2) Not knowing how to select a question mark (9-3) Selecting the diacritic key by mistake
(10) Other	(10-1) Touching multiple keys simultaneously (10-2) Failure of key response due to short-duration touch (10-3) Over toggling (10-4) Not knowing how to type emoji (pictorial symbols)

Table 2. The category of the input stumble; the asterisk mark (*) shows the particular input stumble in Japanese.

Procedure and Apparatus

First, the participants were given explanations and examples of how to operate a smartphone in the same way as in the WoZ study. Then they tried to operate the smartphone for one minute. After that, they were briefly instructed on how to use the keyboard by watching a video tutorial on the smartphone. Afterwards, they created ten sentences in Japanese under the same conditions as the WoZ study except for the way of providing instructions. In this study, the human tutor provided instructions directly instead of the WoZ when they judged that participants needed assistance. Although the participants were told to type by themselves if at all possible, they were permitted to ask when they had no idea what to do. After the experiment, they filled out a 5-point Likert-scaled questionnaire and took part in an interview. All colleagues and the fifteen older adult participants used a Samsung Galaxy S3 as in the first study. The other fifteen used a ZenFone5 whose size and weight are similar with Galaxy S3, running Android 4.4 with a 5.0 inch screen having a resolution of 1280 × 720 pixels (294 ppi). The difference of the two conditions was due to a delay in the study. However, we assumed there was little influence on the result because we did not focus on physical factors such as a mistype but on cognitive factors such as input stumble in text entry. The smartphones recorded the input log in the same manner as in the WoZ study.

Annotation

First, three annotators independently extracted the pattern of input stumbles from the logs and the videos of the study, and based on discussion classified the input stumbles into 30 classes. The 30 classes of input stumbles were then grouped into 10 categories based on similarities. Table 2 shows the list of classified input stumbles along with the categories. Next, the three annotators labeled input stumbles and possible stumble opportunities according to the logs of each input. We adopted the labels that were applied by more than two annotators. The concordance rate using Fleiss' kappa [8] showed 0.44. The reason for the low Kappa value was that there were sometimes conflicts in determining when an input stumble started even if annotators labeled the same input stumble as belonging to the same operation. The kappa value of seven input stumbles (4-1), (4-2), (5-1), (6-1), (6-2), (6-3), and (10-4) were under 0.20. The Kappa value without the seven input stumbles was 0.68.

At the same time, the logs for each sentence were also subjectively labeled according to five skill levels. To determine the criteria, the annotators watched a video in which two sentences were being typed and defined the skill level as being from one to five. A sentence of skill level one was typed at a rate of around four characters per minute [2]. On the other hand, that of skill level five was typed at a rate of around twenty characters per minute, which is the same or less than the rate for an average of smartphone users with this kind of keyboard. After watching the video, the annotators placed the sentences in five skill levels subjectively from the standpoints of typing speed, typing errors and the number of input stumbles. We adopted the labels applied by more than two annotators. The concordance rate by Fleiss' kappa was 0.72.

Skill level	1	2	3	4	5
Initial sentence	8	11	9	3	4
Final sentence	7	8	11	6	6
All sentence	56	96	93	43	47

Table 3. The distribution of labeled skill levels for the initial and final sentences of the participants

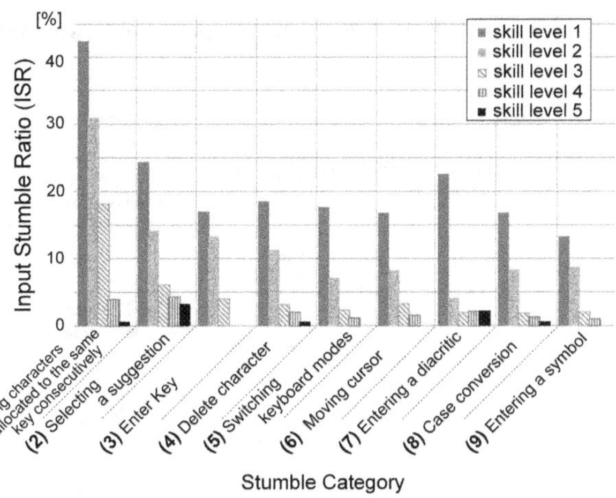

Figure 4. The relationship between the input stumble ratio (ISR) and the input stumble category for each skill level

Results of the second user study

All colleagues and the twenty-eight older adult participants completed the task. The average completion time for colleagues and the older adult participants was 12.4 minutes (sd = 6.0) and 32.4 minutes (sd = 10.9), respectively. The other two participants did not complete the task within 60 minutes. These were the two who had had no previous experience in entering text with their own feature phones.

Table 3 shows the distribution of labeled skill levels for the initial and the final sentences of the participants. Most of the sentences are less than level three, whereas the final sentences of all colleagues are level five. Comparing the skill level of the initial sentences with that for the final sentences, the skill level generally improved.

Figure 4 shows the relationship between the input stumble ratio (ISR) and the input stumble category for each skill level. The ISR was defined as the percentage of the number of input stumbles in the total of possible stumble opportunities for each category. The category "(10) Other" was exclude because it was difficult to define the possible stumble opportunity uniquely. We confirmed that higher-skills had lower ISRs. The category with the highest ISR was "(1) Typing characters allocated to the same key consecutively". This means that when typing two characters allocated to the same key consecutively, the first character must be fixed by pressing the right arrow key before typing the second character. This operation is confusing because no character or string changes when these keys are pressed. Many participants did not seem to realize that they needed to press these keys until the human tutor repeated instructions several times. The category with the second highest ISR was "(2) Selecting a suggestion". The category includes eight classes. These operations need deep knowledge, especially in Japanese because the suggestion list contains the results of auto-complete and kana-kanji conversion. Therefore, this category had the highest ratio among sentences whose skill level was more than four. Many participants found it difficult to judge the timing for selecting the desired suggestion. The "(3) Enter key" error rate was higher than average. The enter key has two functions allocated to it, (3-1) fixing the sentence and (3-2) linefeed. Some participants did not understand the difference so they became confused. On the other hand, there were few errors associated with the other operations because participants only had to check the final character and the next character before typing. Once they had received instructions, most of them were able to carry out these operations.

In the interview after the tasks were completed, some participants said it was not difficult to use the smartphone. However more than half of the participants showed had some concerns and complaints as follows:

"We (older adults) can use a smartphone if we get used to it. But it will be tough to keep using it without any support if we only receive instructions from the tutor on one occasion."

"The tutor's instructions were helpful. But I sometimes couldn't understand why I should do something. If I'm not given the reasons, I will encounter the some problems again."

"I realize that I need to know more about how to use a smartphone. I'd like to acquire this knowledge."

In the interview, we realized two things that need to be incorporated into the instructions provided through the tutoring system: One is that older adults need the instructions for more complex operations to be repeated. The other is that they not only need instructions on how/what to type next but also the reasons and tips on how to perform these operations.

SYSTEM DESIGN OF TYPING TUTOR

In this section, we describe the system design of Typing Tutor based on two previous user studies.

System design

In the first user study, we verified that older adults found it acceptable to be provided instructions, and the instructions have to take user's capabilities into consideration. In the second user study, we confirmed that the tendencies of input stumble were quite different according to the skill level. In the interview, we confirmed that older adults needed instructions to be repeated for more complex operations, and not only needed instructions on how/what to type next but also the reasons and tips of the operations. Therefore, we designed Typing Tutor based on the following rules: The instructions should be provided based on the skill level and whether the user has previously succeeded or not. Typing Tutor should provide not only instructions on how/what to type next but also provide the reasons and tips on how to perform difficult operations.

To realize these rules, we designed Typing Tutor having four functions, as shown in Figure 5: (i) skill estimation, (ii) input stumble detection, (iii) success detection and (iv) instruction control. First, Typing Tutor monitors the input data, such as

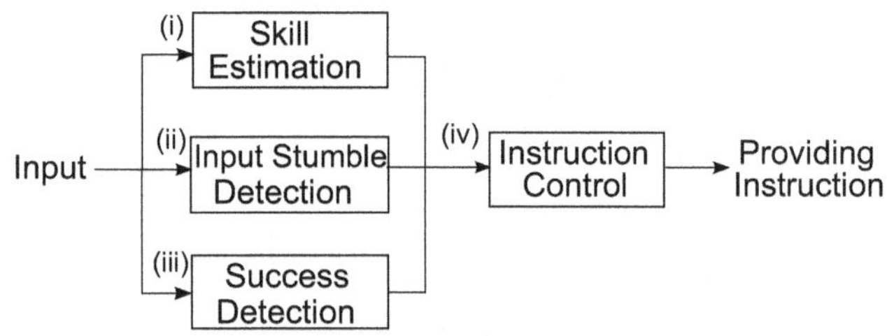

Figure 5. Block diagram of Typing Tutor

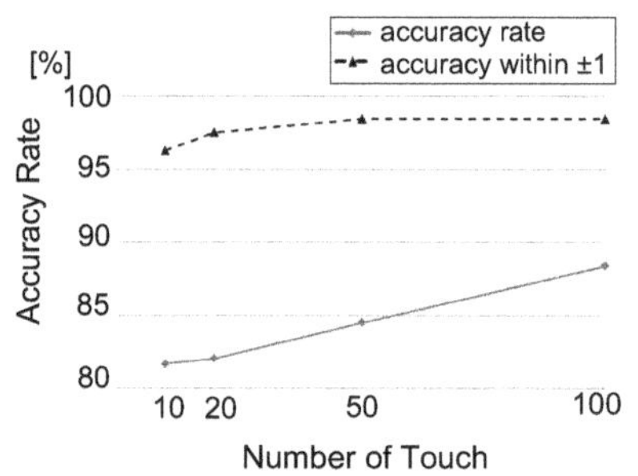

Figure 6. The accuracy of skill classification

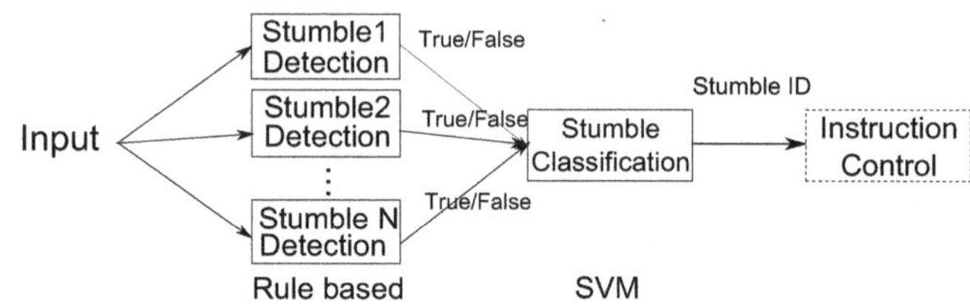

Figure 7. Block diagram of the input stumble detection

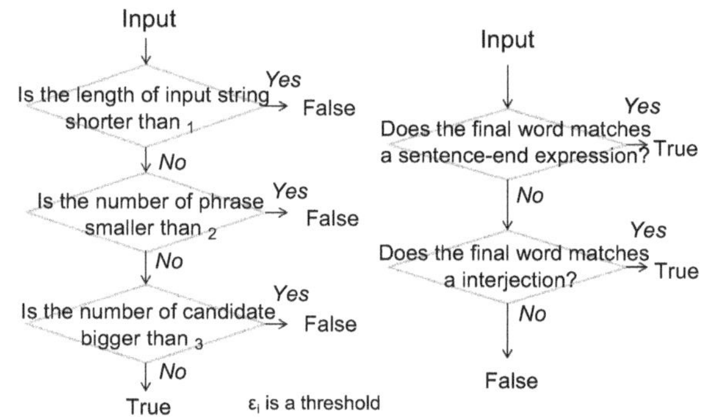

(i) (2-2) Not displaying the desired word due to a long input (ii) (9-1) Not knowing how to select period or exclamation mark

Figure 8. Examples of flowchart for input stumble detection

the keys typed and suggestions. Then, the function of skill estimation classifies the skill level. At the same time, the functions of input stumble detection and success detection work in concert. These functions detect whether the operation was a stumble or successful. Lastly, the function of instruction control determines whether instruction should be provided or not, based on information collected through the other three functions. Specifically, Typing Tutor provides instructions even for easy operations when the skill level is low. In addition, no instructions are provided for operations that the user has already succeeded in doing. This makes it possible to provide only those instructions that are needed by the individual user. We describe the details of each function in this section.

Skill Classification

The skill classification model was constructed based on the data identifying the five skill levels. We trained a linear SVM classifier based on the skill level data. The models are constructed for the number of touches of 10, 20, 50 and 100 from the beginning of typing. The feature amounts for the skill classification are nine dimensions as follows: the average and standard deviation of pressing time, those of the time required to type the same/difference key, the number of input characters, the number of suggestions used, and the number times the delete key was used. The cross validation (CV) for evaluation was conducted 35-fold for each user. As shown by the accuracy rate in Figure 6, we confirmed that the greater the number of touches, the higher the accuracy rate. The accuracy rate of the 10-touch model was 88.7%. Accuracy within ±1 is greater than 95%, even for the 10-touch model.

Input Stumble Detection

Input stumble detection includes two steps: detection and classification, as shown in Figure 7. In the first step, a set of detection functions determines whether an input stumble has occurred or not when the user stops typing for longer than a certain threshold ϵ, defined as $\mu_t + 2\sigma_t$. The variables μ_t and σ_t are the mean and the standard deviation of the touch intervals for the individual user. These functions are rule-based. Two examples of these functions are shown in Figure 8. Figure 8 (i) and (ii) show the algorithm to detect input stumble (2-2) and (9-1), respectively. The others are also implemented heuristically based on data from previous user studies. However, we include detection for only twenty-three stumbles without the seven stumbles for which the kappa value is under 0.2 in the annotation. To detect the input stumbles, 82 features are used, such as the history of the typed key, the displayed character input string, the type of phrase in the input string, the suggestion list, and the current keyboard mode.

In this way, multiple input stumbles can be detected simultaneously. Then in the second step, a function is used that determines what kind of input stumble has occurred. We trained a linear SVM classifier based on the output of each detected input stumble and the labeled data from the second user study. The performance was evaluated for each participant and cross-validated 35-fold with the data that had been labeled as errors offline. The F-value average accuracy rate was 0.72 (recall was 0.58, precision was 0.92).

Success Detection

This function detected successful operations after their completion, unlike input stumble detection. This after-the-fact characteristic made detection easier. However, premature evaluation can lead to errors, so successful operations were registered only if the operation was not canceled before the input of the next two characters.

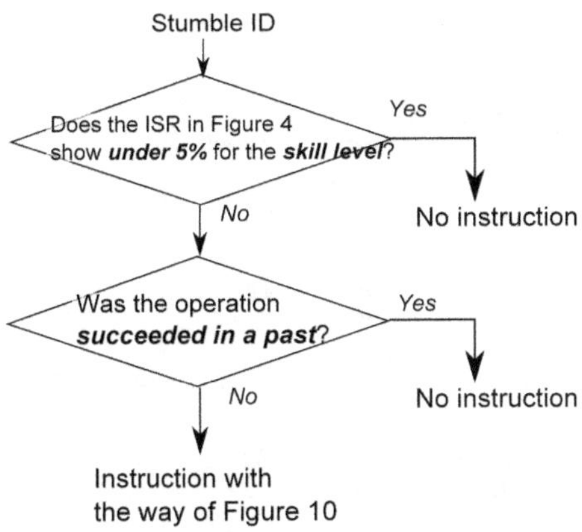

Figure 9. Flowchart for instruction control

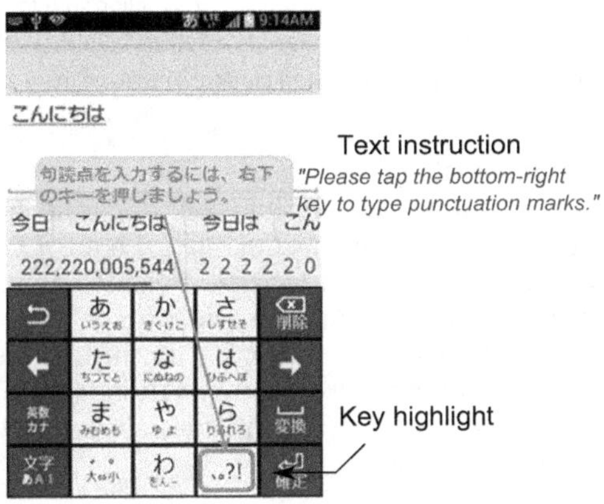

Figure 10. Screenshot showing instruction provision

Instruction Control

This function determines whether instruction on how to correct a detected input stumble is provided or not. The flowchart is shown in Figure 9. Even if an input stumble is detected, no instruction is provided when the relevant ISR in Figure 4 is under 5% for the user's skill level or when the success of the operation without any instruction was detected in the past. Otherwise, instruction is provided. Instruction corresponding to each type of input stumble was given manually, based on the effective advice observed by human tutors in previous studies. Specifically, Typing Tutor provides only operating instructions for categories (4)-(10), but provides both instructions the reasoning behind them and the tips for categories (1) and (3). Both text instruction and voice instruction are provided, plus overlaid key highlighting, the visibility of which was improved as shown in Figure 10.

EXPERIMENT TO IMPROVE TYPING TUTOR

In this section, we describe the preliminary experiment of two trials designed to clarify any problems in Typing Tutor and improve Typing Tutor.

Description of the Two Trials

Participants

In the first trial, six participants, three males and three females between the ages of 65 and 72 years with a mean age of 68.2 (sd = 2.9), took part. The second trial involved the same number males and females between the ages of 66 and 74 years with a mean age of 69.4 (sd = 3.2). They were not participants in the other preliminary experiments, and were recruited from a local social institution. None of them had previous experience with a smartphone, but had owned a feature phone for more than one year. All of them had had previous experience in entering text using a feature phone. Four participants in each trial had used a PC to create documents when employed. Two in the first trial and three in the second trial had routinely used their own PCs. None had a tremor disorder, eye problems or other relevant health problems.

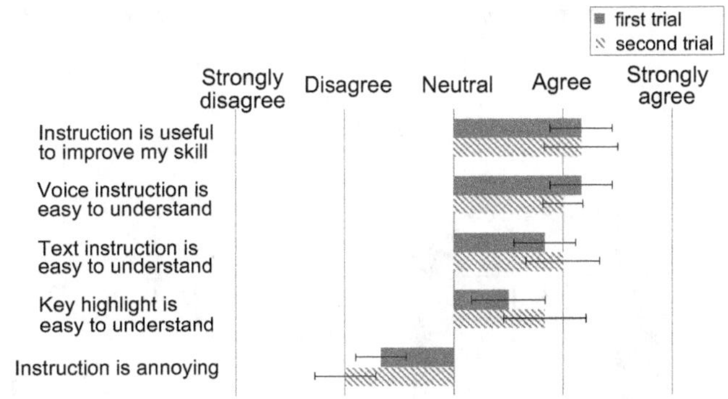

Figure 11. Questionnaire responses regarding the two trials

Procedure and Apparatus

The procedure and apparatus were the same in both trials. The tutorial showing the participants how to use a smartphone and a keyboard was the same as that in the previous experiment. After the tutorial, they typed ten sentences as responses to given sentences, using an e-mail application. Participants in the first trial used Typing Tutor which was designed in previous section. Participants in the second trial used Typing Tutor which was improved after the first trial. All of them made ten sentences in the form of responding to given sentences related to personal conversations, just as in the previous user studies. The experimental period was limited to 60 minutes, with a one-minute rest after each sentence. After the experiment, they filled out a Likert-scale questionnaire and took part in an interview. A ZenFone5 was used in the two trials.

Results of the First Trial

The solid bars in Figure 11 show the results of the subjective questionnaires administered in the first trial. There was a positive response to the item "Instruction is useful to improve my skill." The instruction method was also rated positively, with voice instruction the most favored. These results show that Typing Tutor was well accepted. The interviews yielded some important feedback:

"I am not confident that I can repeat an operation that I did today. I would like to receive instructions again."

"I felt some instructions were annoying because I could understand where to type next, needing only the key highlight."

"The system sometimes did not give instructions. It's helpful if I can confirm what I think I should do, when I'm not confident without that support."

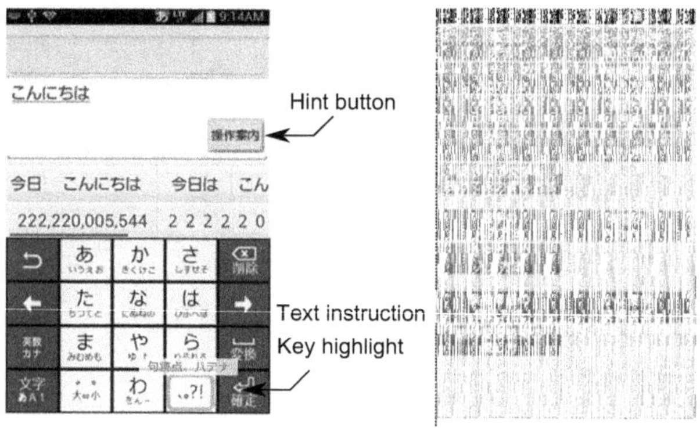

(a) Instruction for easy operation (b) Hint list

Figure 12. Screenshot of instruction after improvement and hint menu

These interviews indicated a need for three improvements: One is to repeat instructions sometimes even though participants have already succeeded in performing an operation. Another is to improve the handling of instructions for easy operations, which can be understood simply from the position and the label. The third is to allow the function to take directions from the learner.

Improvement of Typing Tutor

The three points above, which were deemed to require improvement based on the first trial, were dealt with as follows.

Consideration of forgetting

Typing Tutor in the first trial did not provide further instructions after the participant had succeeded once. To allow the system to forget some successes, we use forgetting curves. This memory retention problem has been examined in many studies [1, 5, 27]. According to the review in [1], the major mathematical models can be classified into three categories: log-linear model, exponential model and hyperbolic model. We used the exponential model in [27] as follows:

$$f = \exp\left(-b_i \sqrt{t}\right) \quad (1)$$

Here f is the retention rate, t is the elapsed days since the last operation, i is the number of times the operation is executed and b_i is the coefficient difference based on i. In the system, the retention rates of each operation are defined, and when the retention rate falls below 50%, the instructions are provided again.

Improvement of instructions for easy operations

Typing Tutor in the first trial provided instructions in a similar way regardless of the degree of difficulty of the operation. Therefore, the operations were divided into two difficulty levels by three annotators. The criterion was whether the operation could be understood simply from an indication of the key position and a word. The input stumbles made when executing the easy operations are the stumble classes (4-1,2), (5-1,2), (7-1,2), (8-1,2) and (9-1,2,3) in Table 2. The instruction for the operations was improved to provide with the key highlight and text above the key highlight, as shown in Figure 12 (a).

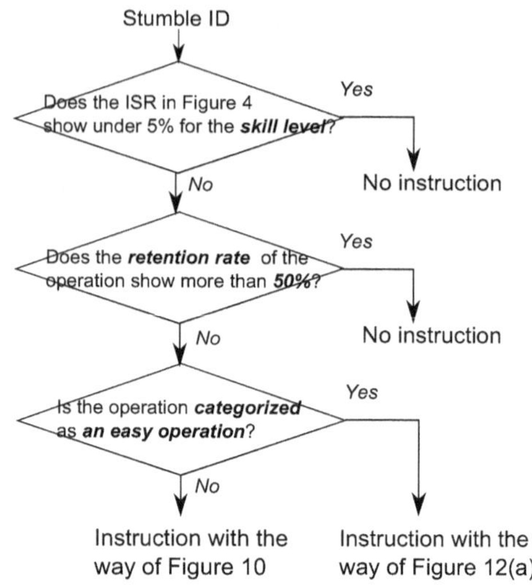

Figure 13. Flowchart for instruction control improved after the first trial

Modification of instruction control

To take the two improvements into consideration, the function of the instruction control was modified. Figure 13 shows the flowchart of the instruction control. Even if a input stumble is detected, the instruction is provided only when the relevant ISR in Figure 4 is not under 5% for the user's skill level and when the retention rate of the operation falls below 50%. Moreover, the way of instruction varies according to the difficulty of the operation.

Implementation of a hint button

In addition to the improvement of instruction control, Typing Tutor was also given a hint button as shown in Figure 12 (a). The hint button is overlaid only when a typing pause exceeds five seconds or a certain threshold ϵ, defined empirically as $\mu_t + 2\sigma_t$. The variables μ_t and σ_t are the mean and the standard deviation of the touch intervals of the user. When the hint button is touched, a list of hints is displayed, as shown in Figure 12 (b). When a hint is selected, instruction is provided as text and voice with key highlight, as shown in Figure 10.

Results of the Second Trial

The hatched bars in Figure 11 show the results of the subjective questionnaires administered in the second trial. Compared to the results of the first trial, there appeared to be an improvement for the items "Key highlight is easy to understand" and "Instruction is annoying," although a Mann-Whitney U test ($\alpha \leq 0.05$) did not show a significant difference due to the small number of participants. Some participants responded negatively to the voice instruction:

"The voice instruction was easy to understand. But I wouldn't like to use it outside because it embarrasses me."

Therefore, Typing Tutor was altered to allow the choice of using voice instruction or not.

TWO-WEEK EVALUATION EXPERIMENT

We developed Typing Tutor, an tutoring system that detects 23 stumbles and provides instructions in two ways according to the difficulty of the operation. Finally, we evaluated the

Skill level		1	2	3	4	5	Average skill level
Group A	First day	0	6	3	1	0	2.5
	Final day	0	1	2	4	3	4.0
Group B	First day	1	4	3	2	0	2.6
	Final day	0	1	4	2	3	3.7

Table 4. The distributions of estimated skill levels on the first day and the final day for each group

performance with a two-week evaluation experiment. In this experiment, the participants would chat for one hour with an operator by using the smartphone's chat application.

Descriptions of the Evaluation Experiment

Participants

Twenty participants, eleven males and nine females between the ages of 65 and 74 years with a mean age of 69.8 (sd = 5.0) who did not participate in other experiments took part in this experiment. They were recruited from a local social institution. Ten of the participants were provided instructions by Typing Tutor (group A). The other ten participants were not provided instructions by Typing Tutor (group B). For these participants of group B, Typing Tutor only obtained the logs in order to estimate the skill level and input stumbles. However, the participants of group B were permitted to ask for advice on how to operate the smartphones through a chat application, but only if necessary. None of them had previous experience with a smartphone, but all had owned a feature phone for more than one year. All of them had entered text using a feature phone before and had often communicated via e-mail. Six participants in group A and seven in group B had routinely used their own PCs. None of them had a tremor disorder, eye problems or other relevant health problems.

Procedure and Apparatus

First, the participants were given explanations and examples of how to operate a smartphone and how to use the software keyboard, just as in previous experiments. After that, they were taught how to use the chat application,"Hangout," which is the default chat application for Android. They kept the smartphone for two weeks (twelve days from Monday to the second Friday) and had a chat with an operator for one hour every day except Saturday and Sunday. The chat topics were not limited and included such subjects as hobbies, their work, and daily events. After two weeks, we held interviews. A ZenFone5 was used in the experiment.

Experimental Results

All participants sent more than six messages each day. The daily averages number of messages and the average length in a message are 7.9 (sd = 1.2) and 45.3 characters (sd = 13.1) for group A and 8.4 (sd = 1.5) and 42.2 characters (sd = 11.0) for group B. We evaluated the performance by four metrics: the skill level, the number of input stumbles, the typing speed and the typing accuracy. Each metric was tested by a Mann-Whitney U-test ($\alpha \leq 0.05$) in each day.

Estimated Skill Level

Table 4 shows the distributions of the estimated skill level on the first day and the final day for each group. On the first day, the skill levels were almost the same. On the final day,

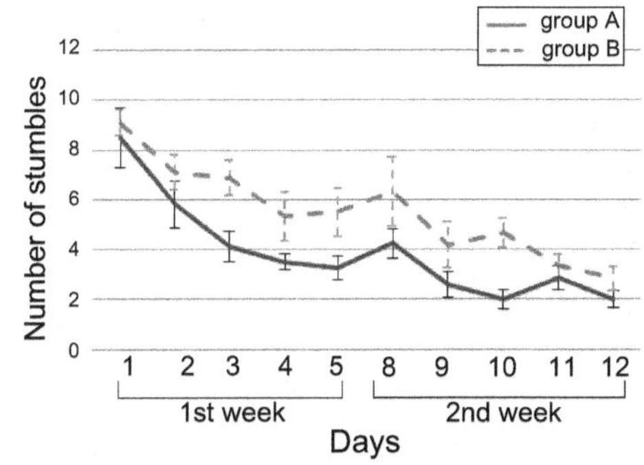

Figure 14. User progress in the number of input stumbles for each group; vertical bars show standard errors

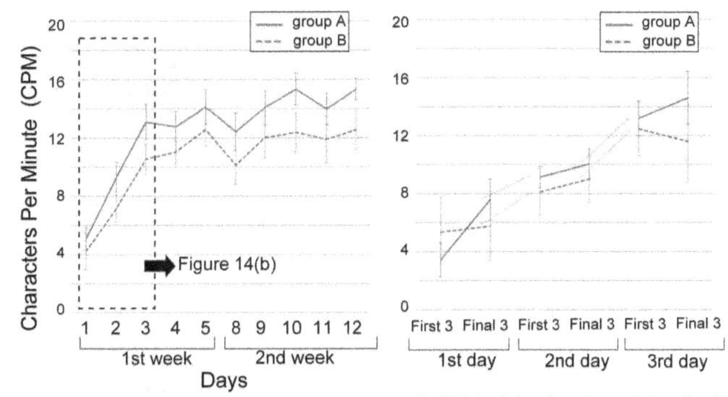

(a) CPM of the average of each day (b) CPM of the first 3 and the final3 sentences of the first three days

Figure 15. User progress in typing speed for each group; vertical bars show standard errors

the skill level of group A was higher than that of group B. However, a Mann-Whitney U-test ($\alpha \leq 0.05$) did not show a significant difference between the two groups.

Number of Input Stumbles

Figure 14 shows the number of input stumbles of both groups. At the beginning of use, the number of input stumbles of both groups was almost the same. After the second days, that of group A was fewer than that of group B. A Mann-Whitney U-test ($\alpha \leq 0.05$) showed a significant difference between the two groups from the third day to the tenth day. The reason why the number of input stumbles on the eighth day became worse than that of the fifth day was that the participants did not use for the previous two days.

Typing Speed

We compared the typing speed in characters per minute (CPM) [2] not including the time used for instructions. Figure 15 (a) shows the CPM of the two groups over two weeks. On the first day, group A was faster than group B. This difference was maintained up until the final day. Figure 15 (b) shows the CPMs of the first three and the final three sentences for the first three days. The CPMs of both groups were almost the same for the first three sentences on the first day. After that, the typing speed of group A increased dramatically. In contrast, that of group B did not increase monotonically. A Mann-Whitney U-test ($\alpha \leq 0.05$) shows a significant difference between the two groups except for the first day and the second day.

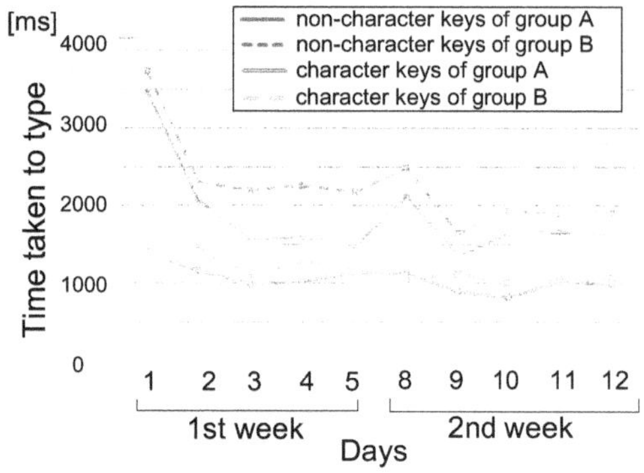

Figure 16. Time taken to type character keys and non character keys for each group

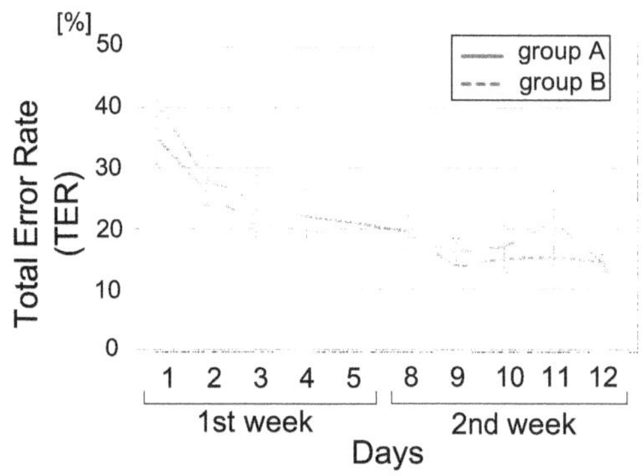

Figure 17. User progress in total error rate for each group; vertical bars show standard errors

Figure 16 shows the time taken by both groups to input character keys and non-character keys. The non-character keys refer to the function keys as shown in Figure 1 and the suggestion list, which require more thinking to select than the non-character keys. The time taken by both groups to input character keys decrease gradually from about 1500 ms to 1000 ms in a similar manner. However, the time taken by group A to input the non-character keys decreased markedly compared with group B, although times on the first day and the final day were almost identical in both groups. A Mann-Whitney U-test ($\alpha \leq 0.05$) showed that a significant difference existed between the two groups from the third day to the eighth day.

Typing Accuracy

We compared the typing accuracy in terms of total error rate (TER) [2]. Although TER is the metrics for typing fixed sentence, sent sentences were used as fixed sentences. The difference between the two groups was negligible as shown in Figure 17. A Mann-Whitney U-test ($\alpha \leq 0.05$) did not show a significant difference between the two groups. The metric is affected by a number of physical factors such as mistyping rather than the cognitive factors. Therefore, this metric is outside the scope of Typing Tutor.

DISCUSSION

The number of input stumbles in group A decreased more rapidly than in group B for the first three days as shown in Figure 14. In a similar way, the CPM of group A increased more rapidly as shown in Figure 15. However, there were no significant differences between the two groups in the first two days. This can be attributed to fact that the participants of both groups were in the process of learning by trial and error during this time. In contrast, significant differences were seen from the third day to the final day. It is considered that the trial-and-error period continued in group B.

Regarding the time taken to type characters, we observed that a difference existed between the time taken to type character keys and non-characters keys, as shown in Figure 16. The time taken to type non-character keys in group A decreased as the number of input stumbles decreased. Typing Tutor focused on support for these operations which have a cognitive dimension. These results show that Typing Tutor is an effective way to improve the skills of participants from a cognitive viewpoint. However, in terms of the time taken to type character keys, the differences between the two groups were negligible. This metric is affected by the ability to construct sentences. These results indicate that the ability construct sentences did not differ between the two groups and Typing Tutor did not affect the performance.

Focusing again on the effectivity of the system to improve the overall proficiency of participants, the average of the estimated skill level of group A on the third day had improved to 3.6, which was the almost same as that of group B on the final day. The CPM in Figure 15 and the number of input stumbles in Figure 14 of group A on the third day were also the same as those of group B on the final day. These results also show the effectivity of Typing Tutor to improve overall proficiency. Furthermore, typing speed is known to be influenced by not only the interval time taken to enter a character but also by the keystroke saving ratio, which is the metric of how the input number is reduced by selecting the auto-complete function in the suggestion list [4]. This ratio on the final day was 13.3% for group A and 9.8% for group B. This means that the participants of group A could input characters effectively using the suggestion list. The result indicates that the instructions provided by Typing Tutor also help participants learn how to use the suggestion list.

There were five participants whose skill level improved by more than two. Their CPM averages improved from 6.21 on the first day to 16.6 on the final day. All of them had previously used their feature phones to e-mail every day. In the interview, they made similar comments:

"At first, I didn't know how to perform the operations at all. But as I came to understand the difference between my feature phone and the smartphone, I gradually became able to operate the smartphone for text entry. I found these kinds of instructions to be useful. "

This comment indicates that Typing Tutor was effective for users who had used their feature phones frequently but had trouble in terms of self-instruction.

Finally, we focus on the participants for whom not much effect was observed. One participant had an estimated skill level of two on the first day and his level remained the same until the final day. His CPM was 3.45 on the first day and 8.28

on the final day, which was the worst result among all participants. During the interview he made the following comment;

"It was difficult for me to operate the smartphone because I pressed the key to the right key of the desired key by mistake."

His TER exceeded 30%, which rate was also the worst rate among all participants. This is caused by physical rather than cognitive factors. Hence, it can be concluded that Typing Tutor was not effective in this case.

Another participant had an estimated skill level of four on the first day and this had advanced to level five on the final day. His CPM was 13.2 on the first day and 17.5 on the final day. During the, he commented;

"Instructions were provided sometimes. But, I didn't need the instructions because I preferred trial and error. "

This comment shows that Typing Tutor is not needed for the users who prefer trial and error and have high IT skills.

LIMITATIONS AND FUTURE WORK

We would like to comment on the generalization to other languages. The skill estimation can be carried out for other languages by training a model based on the data of the targeted language because the feature amounts are not language dependent. In terms of the input stumble detection, it is difficult to apply to other languages directly because the detection algorithm and some input stumbles are specific for Japanese. On the other hand, some input stumbles, especially related to function keys, are common with other language, and some input stumbles related to suggestions are common with the multi-byte-languages such as some Asian languages. However, it is necessary to vary the algorithm of each input stumble according to languages. We will adopt machine learning approach to provide the general framework. In addition, it is essential to research what operation novice older adults tend to have in trouble and how guidance they accept in other languages and countries from the viewpoint of the generalization.

In terms of the detection of input stumbles, the precision was 0.92 in this study. It should be possible to improve precision, but it is difficult to detect input stumbles with perfect accuracy. Therefore, providing instructions in a way that does not interrupt the user's actions is essential.

Finally, we would like to refer to supports for physical factors, e.g. the mistyping problem. Typing Tutor does not focus on this problem, even though this is also a serious problem for older adults [22]. In the field of text entry, many studies have focused on making it easier to type text by adjusting key target areas or presenting suitable suggestions [4, 11, 23]. It should be possible to support both cognitive and physical factors by combining Typing Tutor with these techniques. This is the issue that we will address in a future study.

CONCLUSION

We developed Typing Tutor, a tutoring system for text entry that automatically detects input stumbles and provides individualized instructions for older adults. Through two user studies, we verified the acceptability of the tutoring system for older adults, and clarified the common difficulties that older adults experience and how a user's skill level is related to input stumbles. Based on these studies, we developed Typing Tutor. A two-week evaluation experiment with novice older adults (65+) showed that Typing Tutor was effective for improving to their proficiency in the area of text entry, especially in the initial stage of use compared with instructions through a chat application online. It was particularly beneficial for users who had used their feature phones to e-mail frequently but had trouble in self-instruction.

REFERENCES

1. Michel J. Anzanello and Flavio S. Fogliatto. 2011. Learning curve models and applications: Literature review and research directions. *International Journal of Industrial Ergonomics* 41, 5 (2011), 573–583.
2. Ahmed S. Arif and Wolfgang Stuerzlinger. 2009. Analysis of Text Entry Performance Metrics. In *Proceedings of the International Conference on Science and Technology for Humanity (TIC-STH '09)*. IEEE, 100–105.
3. Beverly Beisge and Marilyn Kraitchman. 2003. Senior Centers: Opportunities For Successful Aging. *Springer Publishing Company* (2003).
4. Xiaojun Bi, Tom Ouyang, and Shumin Zhai. 2014. Both Complete and Correct? Multi-Objective Optimization of Touchscreen Keyboard. In *Proceedings of the SIGCHI Conference on Human Factors in Computing Systems (CHI '14)*. ACM, 2297–2306.
5. Hermann Ebbinghaus. 1885. Memory; A Contribution to Experimental Psychology. *New York by Teachers College* (1885).
6. Rob Edlin-White, Sue Cobb, Mirabelle D'Cruz, Anne Floyde, Sarah Lewthwaite, and Johann Riedel. Accessibility for Older Users through Adaptive Interfaces: Opportunities, Challenges and Achievements. In *Human-Computer Interaction, Part III, HCII2011, LNCS6763*. 483–489.
7. Arthur D. Fisk, Wendy A. Rogers, Neil Charness, Sara J. Czaja, and Joseph Sharit. 2009. Designing for Older Adults: Principles and Creative Human Factors Approaches. (2009).
8. Joseph L. Fleiss. 1971. Measuring nominal scale agreement among many raters. *Psychological Bulletin* 76, 5 (1971), 378–382.
9. Mayank Goel, Alex Jansen, Travis Mandel, Shwetak N. Patel, and Jacob O. Wobbrock. 2013. ContextType: using hand posture information to improve mobile touch screen text entry. In *Proceedings of the SIGCHI Conference on Human Factors in Computing Systems (CHI '13)*. ACM, 2795–2798.
10. Peter Gregor, Alan F. Newell, and Mary Zajicek. 2002. Designing for dynamic diversity: interfaces for older people. In *Proceedings of the Fifth International ACM Conference on Assistive Technologies*. ACM, 151–156.

11. Asela Gunawardana, Tim Paek, and Christopher Meek. 2010. Usability Guided Key-Target Resizing for Soft Keyboards. In *Proceedings of the 15th International Conference on Intelligent User Interfaces (IUI '10)*. ACM, 111–118.

12. Toshiyuki Hagiya, Toshiharu Horiuchi, Tomonori Yazaki, and Tsuneo Kato. 2015. Typing Tutor: Automatic Error Detection and Instruction in Text Entry for Elderly People. In *Proceedings of the 17th International Conference on Human-Computer Interaction with Mobile Devices and Services (MobileHCI '15)*. ACM, 696–703.

13. Jamye M. Hickman, Wendy A. Rogers, and Arthur D. Fisk. 2007. Training older adults to use new technology. *Journals of Gerontology: Series B* 62 (2007).

14. Eve Hoggan, Stephen A. Brewster, and Jody Johnston. 2008. Investigating the effectiveness of tactile feedback for mobile touchscreens. In *Proceedings of the SIGCHI Conference on Human Factors in Computing Systems (CHI '08)*. ACM, 1573–1582.

15. Zhao Xia Jin, Tom Plocher, and Liana Kiff. 2007. Touch screen user interfaces for older adults: button size and spacing. In *Universal Access in HCI, Part I, HCII2007, LNCS4554*. 933–941.

16. Shaun K. Kane, Jacob O. Wobbrock, Mark Harniss, and Kurt L. Johnson. 2008. TrueKeys: identifying and correcting typing errors for people with motor impairments. In *Proceedings of the 13th International Conference on Intelligent User Interfaces (IUI '08)*. ACM, 349–352.

17. Caitlin Kelleher and Randy Pausch. 2005. Stencils-based tutorials: Design and evaluation. In *Proceedings of the SIGCHI Conference on Human Factors in Computing Systems (CHI '05)*. ACM, 541–550.

18. John F. Kelley. CAL - A Natural Language program developed with the OZ Paradigm: Implications for Supercomputing Systems. In *Proceedings of the First International Conference on Supercomputing Systems*. 238–248.

19. Andreas Komninos, Emma Nicol, and Mark D Dunlop. 2015. Designed with Older Adults to Support Better Error Correction in SmartPhone Text Entry: The MaxieKeyboard. In *Proceedings of the 17th International Conference on Human-Computer Interaction with Mobile Devices and Services (MobileHCI '15)*. ACM, 797–802.

20. Sri Kurniawan. 2008. Older people and mobile phones: A multimethod investigation. *International Journal of Human Computer Studies* 66,12 (2008), 889–901.

21. Rock Leung, Charlotte Tang, Shathel Haddad, Joanna Mcgrenere, Peter Graf, and Vilia Ingriany. 2012. How older adults learn to use mobile devices: Survey and field investigations. *ACM Transactions on Accessible Computing* 4, 3 (2012), 11:1–11:33.

22. Hugo Nicolau and Joaquim Jorge. 2012. Elderly text-entry performance on touchscreens. In *Proceedings of the 14th International ACM SIGACCESS Conference on Computers and Accessibility (ACCESS '12)*. ACM, 127–134.

23. Élvio Rodrigues, Micael Carreira, and Daniel Goncalves. 2014. Enhancing typing performance of older adults on tablets. *Universal Access in the Information Society* (2014), 1–26.

24. Wendy A. Rogers, Elizabeth F. Cabrera, Neff Walker, D. Kristen Gilbert, and Arthur D. Fisk. 1996. A survey of automatic teller machine usage across the adult lifespan. *Human Factors* (1996), 38,1; 156–166.

25. David Sloan, Matthew Tylee Atkinson, Colin Machin, and Yunqiu Li. 2010. The Potential of Adaptive Interfaces as an Accessibility Aid for Older Web Users. In *Proceedings of the 2010 International Cross Disciplinary Conference on Web Accessibility 35*. ACM.

26. Keith Vertanen, Haythem Memmi, Justin Emge, Shyam Reyal, and Per Ola Kristensson. VelociTap: Investigating Fast Mobile Text Entry using Sentence-based Decoding of Touchscreen Keyboard Input. In *Proceedings of the SIGCHI Conference on Human Factors in Computing Systems (CHI '15)*.

27. John T. Wixted. 1990. Analyzing the Empirical Course of Forgetting. *Journal of Experimental Psychology: Learning, Memory, and Cognition* 16, 5 (1990), 927–935.

28. Jacob O. Wobbrockand, Shaun K. Kane, Krzysztof Z. Gajos, Susumu Harada, and Jon Froehlich. 2011. Ability-Based Design: Concept, Principles and Examples. *ACM Transactions on Accessible Computing* 3, 3, 9 (2011).

29. Ying Yin, Tom Y. Ouyang, Kurt Partridge, and Shumin Zhai. 2013. Making Touchscreen Keyboards Adaptive to Keys, Hand Postures, and Individuals - A Hierarchical Spatial Backoff Model Approach. In *Proceedings of the SIGCHI Conference on Human Factors in Computing Systems (CHI '13)*. ACM, 2775–2784.

Not For Me: Older Adults Choosing Not to Participate in a Social Isolation Intervention

Jenny Waycott[1] Frank Vetere[1] Sonja Pedell[2] Amee Morgans[3] Elizabeth Ozanne[4] Lars Kulik[1]

[1] Department of Computing and Information Systems, The University of Melbourne, Australia, [jwaycott, f.vetere, lkulik]@unimelb.edu.au
[2] School of Design, Swinburne University of Technology, Australia, spedell@swin.edu.au
[3] RDNS Institute, Melbourne, Australia, amorgans@rdns.com.au
[4] Department of Social Work, The University of Melbourne, Australia, eao@unimelb.edu.au

ABSTRACT
This paper considers what we can learn from the experiences of people who choose not to participate in technology-based social interventions. We conducted ethnographically-informed field studies with socially isolated older adults, who used and evaluated a new iPad application designed to help build new social connections. In this paper we reflect on how the values and assumptions guiding the technological intervention were not always shared by those participating in the evaluation. Drawing on our field notes and interviews with the older adults who chose to discontinue participation, we use personas to illustrate the complexities and tensions involved in individual decisions to *not* participate. This analysis contributes to HCI research calling for a more critical perspective on technological interventions. We provide detailed examples highlighting the complex circumstances of our non-participants' lives, present a framework that outlines the socio-technical context of non-participation, and use our findings to promote reflective practice in HCI research that aims to address complex social issues.

Author Keywords
Non-participation; oldest old; social isolation; reflective practice; ethics.

ACM Classification Keywords
H.5.m. Information interfaces and presentation (e.g., HCI): Miscellaneous

INTRODUCTION
What can we learn from the experiences of people who choose not to use technologies that are designed with their interests in mind? In human-computer interaction research, it is rare to find detailed analyses of the decisions people make to *not* participate in design and evaluation studies. Evaluations tend to focus on the positive impact of the technologies, with decisions to withdraw from the evaluation process typically attributed to a failure in the technology design [17, 19]. In this paper we argue that much can be gained by looking beyond the technology itself, and examining the socio-technical context in which people choose to not participate or discontinue in evaluation studies. This is particularly important when we are designing technologies that aim to support people who might be considered "marginalized" or who typically have limited opportunities to have their voices heard, such as those in the later stages of old age (the "oldest old" [2]).

Technologies designed for (and with) older adults often aim to improve people's lives in some way. Monitoring and assistive devices, for example, can be used to help older adults maintain their independence [22], and there is now a growing interest in the design and use of technologies to improve the social lives of older adults, especially for those considered to be socially isolated ([1, 13], [39]). This brings with it responsibilities for researchers to be sensitive to the diverse needs and experiences of older adults and the possible disruption new social technologies might create for people who are considered vulnerable. When we design technologies to address a social concern such as this, we are effectively intervening in people's lives. As Satchell and Dourish [38] noted, designers and researchers have responsibilities towards the "people in the worlds into which our technologies are introduced [...] responsibilities for taking people – their actions, their statements, and their interpretations – seriously" (p. 15). This means not only "democratizing design" by engaging our intended users in the design process [28, 42], but also listening to, and reflecting on, the experiences of those who choose not to use the designed technologies and who disengage from the evaluation process.

In this paper, we discuss the experiences of older adults who chose to disengage from a project in which they were using and evaluating a specially designed iPad application as part of a social isolation intervention. Our aim is to consider how the experiences of these "non-participants" can help us to better understand our intended users and

CHI'16, May 07-12, 2016, San Jose, CA, USA © 2016 ACM. ISBN 978-1-4503-3362-7/16/05...$15.00
DOI: http://dx.doi.org/10.1145/2858036.2858458

inform our approach to working with older adults. In the following, we position our work by describing the social concern we aimed to address – older adults' experience of social isolation – and discussing related attempts to understand non-use and critique non-participation. We then describe the socio-technical system we developed and the field studies we conducted, which were informed by ethnographic methods and resulted in the creation of detailed field notes describing each participant's experiences. Drawing on the field notes about those who chose to disengage from the project, we present three semi-fictional personas to illustrate the factors that were important in influencing their decisions. These factors were related to personal circumstances (such as health issues and personal preferences), social settings (such as the influence of family members), and the technology context (that is, experience and confidence using technology). Together, these factors form a framework for understanding the socio-technical context of non-participation.

This paper builds on, and contributes to, a growing movement within HCI that promotes critical and reflective practices (e.g., [5, 6, 25, 32, 42]). We argue that taking into account the experiences of non-participants, as well as participants, is crucial when designing and evaluating technologies in sensitive settings. Indeed, the lessons we have gained from understanding the experiences of our non-participants are valuable for informing the future ethical design and evaluation of technology-based social isolation interventions for older adults.

SOCIAL ISOLATION

Although not limited to old age, social isolation is often viewed as a negative experience associated with ageing. As we age, we may outlive family and friends and our mobility may become limited due to deteriorations in physical health. People who are socially isolated are those who have few opportunities to meaningfully engage with others. Older adults are often positioned as being at increased risk of social isolation, and although not all older adults are vulnerable to isolation, social isolation in old age is a significant social concern [44]. It is associated with a range of health problems, such as depression, and can lead to people having limited access to support as they get older ([7], [12], [33], [44]).

Many aged care organizations have devised programs and interventions that aim to address social isolation in old age. These programs often involve face-to-face interactions or require older people to participate in local community activities (e.g., [3], [11], [27], [37]), but interest is beginning to grow in using new technologies to address social isolation (e.g., [13]). Technology-based interventions provide opportunities for older people to communicate with others at a distance or to participate in social activities without having to leave the home, making social groups accessible to those with limited mobility. Recognizing these benefits, researchers have explored the design and use of technologies to enhance older people's social lives – for example, providing opportunities to maintain intergenerational communication [47], to participate in online forums [10], or build connections within the local community [18]. Innovations include a personal reminder and social management system for isolated older adults [13], a design that leverages television as a "ticket-to-talk" to foster social connections [45], and the use of playful technologies to encourage social interaction in a care home setting [8]. These are valuable innovations, and studies have reported a range of benefits, as well as challenges, arising from the use of social technologies by older adults. These studies tend to report on the experience of those who successfully used the technologies being evaluated. The experiences of people who chose not to use the technologies, or to discontinue participating in an evaluation/intervention study, are generally missing from the conversation.

NON-USE AND NON-PARTICIPATION

While it is rare to find research that examines the reasons people choose to not participate in HCI projects, there has been a recent trend in human-computer interaction literature towards studying and understanding "non-use" (e.g., [4], [5], [38]). To date, much of this research has focused on deliberate non-use of social media, such as "leaving" or "refusing" Facebook or "rejecting" the Internet [4], [36], [55]). These studies illustrate that there are various sociocultural forces that both push and pull people towards and away from using apparently ubiquitous technologies and services such as social media. According to this body of work, the distinction between use and non-use can be fluid and is often related to issues beyond the technology itself, such as institutional expectations and cultural rules for established communication practices. In order to understand how people experience and justify their decisions to not use new technologies or applications, then, we need to consider the socio-technical context in which those decisions are made.

Older adults' non-use of new technologies is commonly attributed to limited digital literacy, or experience using technologies and poor accessibility and usability of consumer technologies (see Selwyn [40, 41] for a critique of this argument). Much of the research into technology non-use by older adults has focused on identifying barriers to the adoption and use of new technologies by older adults, such as high costs, concerns about privacy and trust, and attitudes towards social media (e.g., [21], [26], [39]). These studies identify issues that prevent older adults from making use of social technologies before they have familiarized themselves with the available technologies. They provide valuable insight into the reasons older adults might be disenfranchised or excluded from using new technologies. They do not, however, provide detailed analyses of individual experiences of non-use, nor understanding about what happens when older adults make decisions to not use technologies developed with their particular needs in mind.

Technologies designed for older adults often aim to support them (or their carers) in some way, and decisions not to use those technologies need to be understood. In some cases – such as emergency alarms – non-use can lead to serious consequences and impair the support the technologies supposedly provide [22]. There has been some discussion in the sociology and gerontology literature about the need to understand why older people choose not to use e-health systems, which can highlight ethical issues associated with telecare and assistive devices [31, 35]. One recent study, which gained detailed insight into the lives of people using (or not using) assistive devices [22] highlighted the unique needs of older adults, which each individual managed by appropriating technologies according to their own circumstances and preferences; this included, in some cases, choosing not to use particular devices.

While researchers are beginning to recognize that individual responses to assistive technologies need to be taken seriously, technologies designed to address social isolation have rarely received the same scrutiny. Instead, there is an underlying assumption that social technologies are "good" for older adults – that they address an important social concern and empower older people to build and maintain strong interpersonal relationships. However, the research on non-use suggests that we need to adopt a critical stance towards the assumptions that underlie the development of new technologies [5]. We need, as Baumer and Silberman [6] have noted, to critically reflect on whether new technologies are, in fact, an appropriate solution for the particular problems we aim to address.

Alongside growing awareness that HCI researchers need to consider technology non-use, as well as use, recent discussions have critiqued notions of participation in HCI [29, 54, 46]. These discussions tend to focus on user participation in the design process, with limited interrogation of issues surrounding how users participate in the evaluation and use of new technologies. Enabling users to participate in the design of new artifacts and technologies is assumed to be an empowering and democratic process. There may, however, be political issues at play – such as the priorities of researchers and funding bodies – that determine who gets to participate and how [54]. Non-participation, therefore, should be included as part of critical reflection in HCI.

Calls for critical reflection in HCI also tend to focus on design, rather than evaluation and use. For instance, Sengers and colleagues [42] highlighted a number of critical approaches in HCI, all of which are approaches to design, such as participatory design, value-sensitive design, and critical design. They did, however, note that use is an important part of design, and that critical reflection can be valuable for users as well as designers. In addition, they argued that HCI researchers need to "be able to identify when and how a design has failed" (p. 57). One way this can be achieved is by examining non-use and non-participation, thereby broadening our understanding of when and how a technology design or intervention has been successful.

Building on these calls for more reflective practice in HCI, in this paper we go beyond critiques of technology non-use and participation in design (although these are still relevant to our inquiry) to examine non-participation in the context of evaluating and using specially designed technologies. We focus on the experiences of older adults who chose to discontinue participation in a research study in which they were using a new iPad application to trial new forms of communication. The study continued and was successful for the participants who remained in the project, but we believe it is important to interrogate the reasons these non-participants chose to stop using the iPad application. Understanding the decision and its drivers provides us with an opportunity to better understand the lives of the people we are aiming to support – the challenges they encounter on a daily basis and the role technologies can or do play to support them. Just as Greenhalgh and colleagues [22] identified the role individual circumstances play in people's responses to assistive technologies, we identify how individual preferences and the social contexts in which new technologies are introduced play a role in how people respond to and accept social technologies.

EVALUATING A SOCIO-TECHNICAL INTERVENTION

Our research involved designing and implementing a socio-technical intervention: we designed both the technology (an iPad application used to create and share photographs) and the social setting in which it was used (a closed social network comprising a small group of older adults and their care managers). Previous analyses of the data have demonstrated the value of the system for enhancing older adults' creative self-expression and augmenting the psychosocial care provided by aged care workers [48, 53]. Here, we focus on the reasons some participants chose to stop using the iPad and to disengage from the project.

The iPad Application

We developed an iPad application, *Enmesh*, drawing on earlier work that examined the communication needs of older adults [34]. Enmesh ("engagement through media sharing") features an interactive display that shows photographs and messages floating down the screen in a semi-random fashion. Enmesh can be used to both create and view content. Tapping a "speech bubble" icon brings up a dialog box that enables users to take or select a photograph, write a caption, or write a message on its own, without a photograph (see Figure 1). The content is sent to a server, which is used to populate the shared display. The display features photographs and messages created by people who are connected to each other as "friends" on Enmesh. If two or more connected users are viewing the display at the same time, they will see the same configuration of photographs/messages as they move down the screen. Using the touch-screen interface, users can move objects around the display and reduce or enlarge their size; these interactions are visible to other users viewing the display at the same time (see [53] for more information).

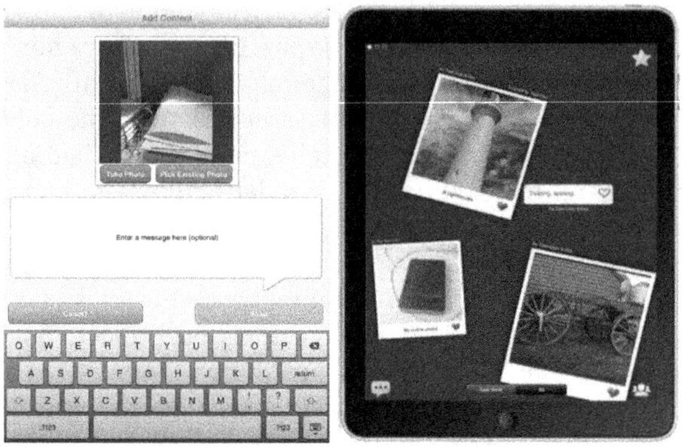

Figure 1. Screen shots showing how to create content on Enmesh (left) and the Enmesh display (right)

Field Studies
The project was conducted in an Australian urban setting, in collaboration with an aged care organization. Participants were clients of the organization who lived independently in their own homes but received home care services. Over the course of the project we conducted three field studies, varying in length from 3 to 12 months. In total, 26 participants agreed to take part in one or more of the field studies. Ten older adults decided to withdraw from the project after using Enmesh for a week or more, leaving 16 participants who remained in the project. Participants were aged in their 70s, 80s, and 90s (mean age 82). All experienced some health or mobility impairments that made them eligible to receive aged care services at home.

Recruitment and Consent
As part of the aged care service, each participant had an assigned "care manager" who visited them each month to oversee care services such as domestic help, healthcare, and personal care. Care managers knew their clients well and were the first point of contact for recruiting suitable participants. Care managers nominated clients who were actively experiencing or were at risk of experiencing social isolation. When nominating suitable clients, care managers spoke to a member of the research team to provide some background information about the client and to describe their social situation. Following this initial pre-selection, researchers contacted the nominated clients directly and met with them to explain the purposes of the study and to introduce them to the technology. The clients then made an independent, informed, and voluntary decision about whether they wanted to be involved in the project and, if they chose to participate, signed a consent form. The project was approved by the university's ethics committee.

Although care managers were often present at this initial meeting, their role was limited to facilitating introductions between the researcher and the clients. They did not play a role in obtaining clients' consent to take part in the project. They did, however, take part as co-participants in the study and used Enmesh to communicate with their clients if clients gave approval to include their care managers in the project. All clients wanted their care managers to be involved. The care manager was someone participants knew and trusted and felt comfortable communicating with; the care managers' involvement therefore provided participants with a "safe" entry point into a new social network. In most cases, care managers co-participated with a single client; in other cases, care managers had two or three clients participating in the project [48].

Creating a Social Network
For the purposes of this study, we created closed social networks, comprising small groups of older adults and care managers who were connected to each other via Enmesh. Participants did not know each other prior to the study. It was therefore crucial that we provided scaffolding to support participants' interactions, as some may have found it difficult to share photographs and messages with strangers. We achieved this by:

1) Involving care managers in the project as co-participants. By using Enmesh alongside their clients and sharing their own photographs and messages, care managers provided crucial support for clients [51]. Their contributions to Enmesh included gentle encouragement, playful messages designed to provoke a response, and photographs and messages that aligned with clients' personal interests [48].
2) Adopting a staged process, so that participants gradually expanded their use of Enmesh. In the first stage, participants were only connected to their care managers until they felt comfortable using Enmesh to create and share photographs and messages. As they gained experience using the application and creating and sharing photographs and messages, participants had the opportunity to meet other participating clients at a face-to-face social event. Following this event, participants were connected to each other through the iPad application and could then see each other's photographs and messages on a shared display.
3) Providing opportunities for participants to meet in person. We held regular social events over morning tea, during which participants and care managers met to talk about how they were using the iPad and to ask questions and provide feedback to the research team. These meetings were important for enabling participants to discover common interests and to share experiences, creating a stronger sense of community within the group. However, not all participants were able or wanted to attend the social events.

Data Collection

During each field study we collected data from a variety of sources, including: 1) In-depth interviews with participants at the beginning and end of the study, as well as informal conversations that emerged during the course of the project; 2) Observations of participants using Enmesh and the iPad both in their own homes and at the social events; 3) Data logs showing how participants had used Enmesh; and 4) Interviews with care managers at the start and end of each field study, along with informal conversations with care managers as the opportunity and need arose. The field studies were not traditional ethnographies, but were informed by ethnographic methods [14]. We spent considerable time getting to know each participant, helping them learn how to use the technology, observing their interactions with each other and with care managers, and learning about their social and family circumstances, which was crucial for enabling us to gain a better understanding of their experiences of social isolation. Because our interactions with participants were not confined to formal interviews and included occasional telephone calls, communication via Enmesh, and other informal conversations, we developed extensive field notes about each participant, which complemented the interview transcripts and other data collected. Our field notes form the basis of the analysis presented in this paper.

Analyzing Reasons for Non-Participation

Ten participants initially gave consent to participate in the project, took part in an interview, and began to use Enmesh, but chose to discontinue participation after a short time (this varied in length from a few days to a few weeks). In three cases, the reasons for non-participation were clearly related to deteriorating health. These participants had been admitted to hospital or started treatment for a specific illness and could no longer commit to the project. Two non-participants chose to withdraw from the project for personal reasons, which they did not disclose to us. In the other five cases we gained a detailed understanding of each person's individual circumstances and the reasons they chose to discontinue participation. Two of these non-participants took part in an exit interview, one provided a detailed explanation of her decision via a lengthy message on Enmesh, and two non-participants explained their decision in a telephone conversation. We gained further insights into the reasons for non-participation through informal conversations with care managers and, on one occasion, a family caregiver, who volunteered additional information about their client/family member's situation. The initial interviews, conducted with each (non)participant, provided further insight into their current circumstances, which helped inform our understanding of their non-participation.

We developed five detailed case studies which were used as the basis for team discussions to interrogate the reasons that some participants chose to disengage from the project. These cases were examined, separately and together, in order to identify features that were common in the five different accounts. However, the core value in the rich data we collected lay in the detailed understanding provided about *individual experiences* of non-participation. While a typical approach to qualitative data analysis would involve identifying common themes across cases, we believed a more fruitful approach was to identify salient factors that led to each individual decision to stop using Enmesh. We did this by reviewing the individual narratives and discussing as a team the salient features of each case. We found that for each case there were highly specific individual circumstances that made it difficult for our non-participants to continue engaging in the project. Sharing these specific details could threaten our non-participants' anonymity and confidentiality. Therefore, we have used the case studies to create three semi-fictional personas, which we describe next.

CHOOSING NOT TO PARTICIPATE

To overcome the challenge of sharing rich data while maintaining confidentiality, we have amalgamated the details about each non-participant to create three semi-fictional personas. Each persona is based on real experiences, but individual experiences have been combined to illustrate three key contextual factors that were important in influencing decisions to not participate: the personal context, social context, and technological context.

Abigail

Abigail is in her early 90s. She lives alone and has limited mobility due to painful arthritis, but is keen to retain her independence for as long as possible. Abigail says she has "always been a loner" and likes a quiet life.

Abigail has never used computers before. Despite this, she makes few mistakes when setting up her profile on Enmesh. In fact, she initially seems delighted with the iPad and enjoys being able to see her care managers' photographs. In the first few days of using Enmesh she takes photographs of the family portraits in her living room, flowers in a vase, and birthday cards she has received. She is pleased to be able to do this but expresses disinterest in being connected to other participants via Enmesh.

The effort Abigail requires for self-care is quite high and this, combined with frequent visits from care workers and the need for regular rest, leaves her with little time or energy for using the iPad. In addition, eye strain causes pain and makes it difficult for Abigail to concentrate. Abigail stops using the iPad after a few weeks and stores it in the "next room" where she can forget about it. She feels guilty about not participating with more enthusiasm and is reluctant to formally withdraw from the project because this means admitting she has found it difficult. Abigail wants to prove to her care manager that she is capable of looking after herself; withdrawing from the project conflicts with the image of independence she is trying to portray.

Martha

Martha is in her 80s and is a full-time carer for her husband Graeme who had a stroke five years ago which left him with impaired mobility and cognitive difficulties. Martha finds caring for her husband extremely difficult and isolating but is reluctant to confide in her family because they are busy and she does not want to trouble them.

Martha wants to learn to use the iPad because she feels left behind by modern society. She would like to be able to understand and use the technologies that her grandchildren and great-grandchildren use. She uses the iPad to take photographs of her great-grandchild's birthday party but is anxious when the child and his brother want to play games on the iPad. She worries about the damage they will do to the iPad and decides to keep it locked in the cupboard so the children will not see it when they next visit.

Martha regularly takes her husband to medical appointments, hydrotherapy classes, and to the local shopping centre. Graeme does not like Martha to be too far away. When they are home and she is in the garden he rings a bell to let her know that he wants something. Martha finds that she has little time or energy left in her day to do anything for herself, let alone to learn something new. Eventually she decides to return the iPad because she feels it is creating an extra burden that she does not have time for at the moment. She believes she has failed in this project and that she has left it too late to learn how to use the technologies that younger people use.

Victor

A widower in his late 80s, Victor has been lonely since losing his wife to illness two years ago. Victor was once a professional photographer and owned a camera shop. He sees himself as knowledgeable and experienced at using new technologies. However, Victor retired thirty years ago and since then has found it difficult to maintain his digital literacy, although he uses email and skype on a desktop computer to keep in touch with his children who all live some distance away. Victor's eye sight is deteriorating and he has started to experience some cognitive difficulties which can make it challenging to learn new things. Because of this, Victor has been unable to continue his hobby as a photographer, an activity he misses greatly.

Victor is keen to learn how to use the iPad. Although he uses a desktop computer, he has never used a tablet device and does not have a mobile (cell) phone, so he feels the need to update his technical skills. He enrolls in a local "iPad for Seniors" course soon after joining the project. However, Victor finds the course to be less than satisfying. Most of the other attendees are recent retirees who are younger than him and have a more up-to-date knowledge of modern technology. Victor is confused by the questions other attendees ask about "apps". He does not fully understand what apps are and what they are used for. He is also confused by the conversation about how to connect the iPad to a wireless internet (his son had set up the internet for him at home). After attending a few classes, Victor realizes he is struggling to keep up and begins to lose enthusiasm for learning to use the iPad.

Victor initially shares photographs of his garden on Enmesh. He is happy to have the opportunity to take photographs and hopes to be able share his skills and knowledge with the rest of the group. However, Victor is frustrated at not being able to take photographs in the same way that he used to (e.g., changing the shutter speed and aperture in response to the light levels); he does not think automatic digital cameras are as good as traditional photography and is concerned about the quality of the images captured on the iPad. In the end, Victor finds taking photographs on the iPad to be a frustrating, rather than enjoyable, experience. Despite being relatively tech-savvy, he struggles to learn how to use the iPad because he is not familiar with Apple products or touch-screens and has to learn new ways of interacting with technology. He worries that deterioration in his cognitive abilities have made it difficult for him to learn new things. In the end, family members advise Victor to stop using the iPad because it is having a negative impact on his self-esteem.

The three personas of Abigail, Martha, and Victor encapsulate the key circumstances that led our non-participants to disengage from the project. Drawing on these examples, we present a framework that illustrates the socio-technical context of non-participation.

SOCIO-TECHNICAL CONTEXT OF NON-PARTICIPATION

We now return to the question posed at the start of this paper: *What can we learn from the experiences of people who choose not to use technologies that are designed with their interests in mind?* From an analysis of the detailed narratives elicited about our five non-participants, we identified a number of individual circumstances that led these older adults to choose to stop using Enmesh and to disengage from the project. We broadly categorized these into three dimensions that together describe the socio-technical context in which participants chose to disengage from the project: 1) the personal context, including individual circumstances such as health and personal preferences, 2) the social context, such as the influence of family members and others, and 3) the technological context, including prior experiences of technology and digital exclusion. Together, these comprise a contextual framework for understanding the circumstances of older adults' non-participation in technology design and evaluation research.

Personal Context

At the time of the study each non-participant was experiencing difficult personal circumstances, such as those described in the profile of Abigail, which prevented their active engagement in the project. Given that we were specifically targeting people in the later stages of old age, it is not surprising that these personal circumstances often included health problems. Abigail, who represents the frailer non-participants, was unable to hold the iPad and suffered eye strain that made it difficult to look at the screen for any length of time.

Difficulty concentrating and learning new things was a common challenge for both our participants and non-participants. Learning to use the iPad sometimes raised feelings of failure and inadequacy, particularly for those like Abigail who had to disengage because of the challenges they faced. In addition to being anxious about frailty, Abigail was disinterested in using Enmesh to communicate with others, challenging the assumptions embedded in the intervention. Like Abigail, some of our non-participants wanted to disengage socially and were content to be disconnected from society. In fact, when we asked if she ever felt disconnected from society, one non-participant replied “yes, but that is a good thing”.

This finding challenges our assumption that designing and introducing a social isolation intervention is the “right” thing to do for all older adults who are socially isolated. Some people experiencing social isolation gained great benefit from this intervention, but it was clearly not right for everybody. This is a reminder that we can’t always predict how people will respond to new technologies, nor what impact the technologies might have. In some cases, our non-participants experienced unexpected strong and negative emotions when taking part in the project. They encountered a range of health problems and personal circumstances that prevented their full participation – problems that were sometimes amplified by the intervention. Notably, other participants who continued in the project encountered similar difficulties. For the very old, daily life is often plagued with health problems and personal challenges. For those who continued in the project these problems were not insurmountable and did not become the barriers to participation that the non-participants faced. Why did difficult personal circumstances prevent some people but not others from fully engaging in the project? To answer this question we broaden our lens to consider the social and technological contexts in which non-participation took place.

Social Context

The social context into which the technology was introduced played a crucial role in driving the decision to disengage from the project. This context included the physical space, family circumstances, and established norms for social activity. Each non-participant did initially choose to use Enmesh but it did not become integrated into their lives. Some non-participants (such as those represented by Abigail and Martha) chose to keep the iPad hidden from view, which limited their opportunities to engage with the iPad. The physical location of technology in people’s homes plays a role in how it is used and how it becomes embedded in people’s daily activities. The decision to keep the iPad locked away or hidden in the spare room could be seen as both contributing to the decision to disengage from the project, and as emerging from that decision.

The domestic environment includes the presence (or absence) of family members. The burden of caring responsibilities made it difficult for some, such as Martha, to fully engage in the project. For others, the absence of family members was keenly felt and may have contributed to the difficulties they experienced learning how to use the iPad (as illustrated by Victor’s reliance on his son to set up the technical infrastructure in his home, leaving him feeling ignorant about what was required). In addition, family members sometimes advised participants to disengage from the project; this may have been because they were concerned about their loved one (as seen in the persona of Victor, whose family members believed the iPad was negatively affecting his self-esteem), or because family members misunderstood the project.

Family could be a source of tension that affected people’s attitudes towards the iPad and the project. Being a full-time carer meant that Martha came to see the project as another burden competing for her time. Meanwhile, the attitude of her great-grandchildren, who saw the iPad as a “toy” left her feeling anxious and worried about protecting the iPad from their intrusion. This concern was echoed by others who remained in the project. Participants noted they had trouble understanding the attitudes that young people had towards new technology because it conflicted with their own upbringing. As children they had been taught to revere expensive technology and equipment; they were told “Don’t touch! You’ll break it”. Understandably the more hands-on and playful approach exhibited by their grandchildren and great-grandchildren provoked some anxiety, although participants were still eager to have a go at using the iPad themselves. In other words, this anxiety was not about participants’ own fear of using the iPad, but their concern about how visiting children might use it. As we saw in the example of Martha, worrying about how children used the iPad could potentially interfere with participants’ own experience of the iPad. This occurred despite our reassurances that the iPad was a robust tool and it was unlikely to be broken. In addition, those who worried about children’s use of the iPad may have missed a valuable opportunity for enriched intergenerational play.

Technological Context

A simplistic response to understanding non-participation in this setting would be to identify limitations relating to old age that prevented participants from successfully using the technology. While these limitations did exist, such as limited eyesight, frailty, and difficulty holding or touching the iPad, participants were initially positive about using the iPad. All were willing to “give it a go,” challenging established understandings of older adults as unwilling to use new technologies. The fact that our application was designed for use on a popular consumer device is important. The iPad can be seen as a status symbol, particularly when contrasted with other technologies designed for older adults, such as monitoring and assisted living devices [22]. Our participants were all eager to learn how to use the iPad, beyond the Enmesh application, because they wanted to gain new skills and to improve their digital literacy so they could feel as though they were a part of the 21st century.

The Enmesh application, with a simple interface and limited functionality, was generally easy for our participants to learn to use, although they did express some uncertainty about the way objects appeared on the display in a semi-random fashion. In addition to learning the basic features of Enmesh, participants needed to learn how to use the onscreen keyboard, the camera, and to understand general features of the iPad, such as the home screen (which was filled with apps), the on/off button (hidden from view), and how the screen orientation could be changed.

The personas we have presented here all had some difficulty learning to use the iPad, which created anxiety and a fear of failure. In Victor's case, family members were concerned about the impact this may have had on his self-esteem. The difficulty he experienced conflicted with his identify as a competent and experienced technology user. Although he had used computers and cameras before, this experience hindered, rather than helped, his ability to learn to use the iPad. This challenges the common view that older adults with limited past experience of using technologies will find it harder to learn to use a new device or application. In contrast, some of the other participants, who continued in the project, had never used computers before but learned to use Enmesh and the iPad quite easily.

For our non-participants, the iPad came to embody their experience of digital exclusion. Disenfranchisement encompasses more than having limited access to new technologies; cultural knowledge is embedded in the technologies that are now a ubiquitous part of our landscape [15] and lacking this cultural knowledge can lead to disenfranchisement. Digital literacy involves more than learning how to *use* technology; it also involves understanding the *language of use* as illustrated by Victor's confusion when attending the "iPad for Seniors" course. This was based on a real experience; one of our non-participants attended a similar course but found it accentuated, rather than ameliorated, a growing sense of digital exclusion. This example suggests that targeted programs for seniors will not solve the problems of digital literacy unless they address the sociocultural knowledge required to actively engage in our sociotechnical world.

LESSONS FOR THE HCI COMMUNITY

Our contextual framework for understanding older adults' non-participation is necessarily broad, as it aims to capture the range of individual circumstances that led our non-participants to disengage from the project. Our aim in developing this framework is not to provide generalizable understandings of non-use and non-participation, but rather to promote consideration of non-participation as a legitimate issue of concern for the HCI community. Here we consider the lessons learned for the HCI community in terms of: a) promoting reflective practice, b) questioning the values embedded in the technologies we design, and c) fostering an awareness of situated ethics. We discuss each of these in turn, focusing on how these practices can inform a sensitive and ethical approach when designing and evaluating technologies with the "oldest old".

Reflective Practice

Five years ago Baumer and Silberman [6] noted that, within the HCI literature, there had been "relatively little reflection about where and when not to apply technology, and arguments that technological interventions might not be appropriate for every situation [were] quite rare" (p. 2271). This appears to still be the case. Although several HCI researchers have called for more reflective practice in HCI (e.g., [32], [42], [52]), detailed reflections about negative experiences with technical interventions remain rare. Baumer and Silberman argued that, sometimes, designing and introducing new technologies might not be the best way to address a particular problem. They cited the example of technology interventions that aimed to promote environmental sustainability where there is clearly a mismatch between the goals of the intervention and the fact that new technologies actually create environmental damage themselves. The answer, Baumer and Silberman argued, is not to stop designing technologies, but to "engage in a critical, reflective dialog about how and why these things are built" (p. 2274). In this paper we have opened up critical dialog about designing and using social technologies with the "oldest old".

Our findings demonstrate the importance of engaging in critical reflective practice. Sengers and colleagues [42] defined critical reflection in HCI as deliberate "reflection on unconscious values embedded in computing and the practices it supports" (p. 49). Reflective practice also means constantly questioning the *value* of the technologies we develop, and our methods of design and evaluation [52]. This means paying attention to the experiences of those who use our interventions, as well as those who do not. By interrogating the reasons that people choose not to use the technologies that are designed with their needs in mind, we can better understand the circumstances of their everyday lives and the social context into which new technologies are introduced. This is particularly important when working in sensitive settings with people who might be considered vulnerable. In these settings, it is crucial to constantly ask: Is taking part in the research a positive experience for the participants or does it cause them anxiety? Is the new technology embraced by participants, or does it cause unwelcome disruption? When the answer to these questions is less positive than we would hope, we need to modify our approach and reflect on the reasons that the experience has been less than positive for our participants.

It is valuable to be reflective when reporting the outcomes of the research, too. Rather than reporting only positive findings, we suggest that researchers working in difficult settings should embrace and acknowledge the challenges involved [52]. As a research community we can benefit from ongoing dialog about how to improve practices. Promisingly, some HCI researchers working with older adults are beginning to embrace this shift towards acknowledging both positive and less than positive experiences with technology (e.g., [2] [20]). At the last CHI conference, Gerling and colleagues [20] highlighted some of the social challenges faced by residents of an aged care facility when they participated in a console games activity. Some participants found it difficult to learn how to play the games and felt uncomfortable doing this in front of other residents. Others were frustrated at having to wait for a turn to play, which created tensions within the group. While the paper also reported positive outcomes, it is useful to reflect on the particular challenges that these participants faced so as to highlight the need for researchers/practitioners to pay careful attention to social structures when implementing similar interventions in the future.

Questioning Values

There is a strong assumption in HCI research that once we have identified common characteristics of specific user groups the process of matching technology design to these characteristics will result in a usable and useful technology [23]. However, the analysis presented in this paper demonstrates that the reality is more complex. Technologies are "not neutral objects but embodiments of our selves and our cultural values" [22, p. 88]. Despite careful user-centered design practices, sometimes the values that technologies embody do not align with the values of the people who come to use them. The term "values" in this sense does not mean how valuable or effective a particular technology is, but refers to "what a person or a group of people consider important in life" ([16], p. 349).

A movement within HCI that can help address these issues is value sensitive design (see [9], [16]). Value sensitive design promotes careful consideration of users' values during the design process, beginning with a conceptual investigation that involves identifying the stakeholders (both direct and indirect), considering how they are or will be affected by the design, noting what values are important, and questioning whether certain values (e.g., moral values) should have more weight than others. This is followed by empirical investigations of the social setting in which the technology is to be used, and technical investigations, which can involve investigating existing technologies or designing systems that aim to support particular values [16]. While this is a useful method for highlighting the importance of values in design, it does have limitations [9] and, like other critical approaches, its focus is on design, rather than evaluation and use.

The challenges discussed in this paper transcend design issues. In some ways, it would not have mattered what the design was, and the tensions around mismatched values did not become apparent until after implementation and use. Our analysis demonstrates that the values embedded in design need to be critiqued by researchers throughout evaluation and use, not only during the design process.

Recognizing mismatched values provides a valuable opportunity to learn more about our intended users. Our design of Enmesh and the broader socio-technical intervention promoted the value of social connectivity. This value and the expectation that older adults would *want* to build new friendships clearly conflicted with some of our participants' personal preferences and their desire to *disengage* from society. By realizing this conflict, we experienced a valuable lesson; it helped us to see more clearly that the lives of the oldest old are complex, and older adults, like many other groups, are heterogeneous and cannot be easily defined by their age alone.

Our technology intervention also, inevitably, communicated that digital literacy and broader societal engagement through the use of new technologies is important. While this value was shared by our participants and non-participants, it created challenges for those who struggled to use the iPad and were unable incorporate it into their lives. We can see this in the tensions that our non-participants experienced: apparent enthusiasm for learning to use the iPad, followed by hesitation and disengagement. The conflict that non-participants felt about using the iPad and Enmesh was not just about the technology but also what it represented: the opportunity (or obligation) to learn to use a new technology, as well as the opportunity (or burden) of communicating with others. For some, it meant coming face-to-face with their deteriorating health and acknowledging a fading ability to learn new things. The iPad came to embody cultural values, including participants' feelings and beliefs about old age. This was quite confronting and presents us with a significant ethical challenge. How do we ensure that those who can benefit from using new technologies are given opportunities and support, while also ensuring that those for whom new technologies cause anxiety are not made to feel burdened by a technological intervention? This is not simply a matter of choosing not to design or not to introduce new technologies. Our research had positive outcomes for the participants who continued to use Enmesh and fully engaged in the project. However, because of the complexities of our participants' lives, we could not predict who among our participants would have a positive experience and who would have a negative experience when using the technology. Therefore, rather than advocating against designing technologies to address social isolation, we believe the appropriate response is for HCI researchers working in sensitive settings to be reflective and to constantly question whether the values embedded in the technology match the values of the people learning to use it.

Situated Ethics

Finally, our analysis of non-participation suggests a need to pay attention to ethical issues, not only when planning and implementing a design or evaluation study, but throughout the project. Recent discussions and presentations at the CHI conference have demonstrated that the ethical issues encountered during "non-traditional" HCI research can be highly complex, emergent, and contingent on the particular contexts in which the research takes place (e.g., [30, 32, 49]). Munteanu et al [32] called these issues "situated ethics"; others have used the term "ethics in practice" [24]. These terms suggest that the ethical challenges researchers face, particularly when working in sensitive settings cannot always be predicted or planned for.

Certainly, in our research it was difficult to fully predict the variety of challenges our participants and non-participants faced. We had to be alert to these challenges and to adapt our methods accordingly. Of course we ensured participants were aware that they could voluntarily withdraw from the project at any time but this was a more complex and sensitive issue than we had expected. As illustrated by the story of our three personas, choosing to not participate could sometimes evoke feelings of failure and inadequacy. If participants did not enjoy using the technology and we (or others) felt their participation was doing more harm than good, this had to be handled very sensitively.

Our experiences highlight a need for flexible practice in response to emergent ethical challenges [52]. Researchers in other disciplines, such as anthropology and sociology, have long acknowledged the need for researchers to respond and adapt to ethical issues as they arise [24]. This is particularly crucial for HCI research conducted in sensitive settings: our research involves not only entering people's lives, but also *intervening* in their lives. Designing technologies that aim to address particular social problems involves "an intervention in a complex situation" ([6], p. 2272). Further, technologies can be "disabling as well as enabling, disempowering as well as empowering" ([22], p. 88). This paper has demonstrated that while social technologies may provide significant benefit for some isolated older adults, they can also be confronting and raise fears of failure for others. There is an ethical obligation for researchers to recognize and respond to these issues. This is difficult; an ethical approach also means not denying people the opportunities and benefits they may gain from taking part in a technology-based intervention. Some of the "oldest old" who took part in our project successfully used Enmesh to build new social connections and to engage in self-expression by sharing creative and personally meaningful captioned photographs [53]. Meanwhile, learning to use the iPad was a positive experience that gave them new skills, a renewed sense of connection to the world, and enhanced confidence. When designing and implementing technologies with this population, then, we need to incorporate flexible methodologies that allow researchers to respond to individual needs. We need to provide considerable time for participants to become familiar with the technology and ensure they feel confident about deciding whether or not they want to use it [50].

CONCLUSION

Why did our non-participants choose to disengage from this social isolation intervention? Our analysis suggests the reasons were highly specific, but together paint a complex picture of the socio-technical context into which new technologies must be integrated. In this paper we have presented a contextual framework that highlights how *personal circumstances* and preferences, *social contexts*, and *technological contexts* inform experiences of non-participation in a socio-technical intervention.

This paper responds to and builds on earlier calls for HCI researchers to engage in considered reflection about the benefits and potential disruption that new technologies can bring. We add to this conversation, by calling for HCI researchers to pay attention to the experiences of those who choose not to participate in design and evaluation studies, as well as those who do, which we believe is especially important when working in sensitive settings. Our experiences highlight the need for researchers to engage in reflective practice, to constantly question the values embedded in the technologies we design and introduce, and to recognize and respond to ethical issues as they arise in the course of the research.

While we acknowledge that the arguments in this paper are based on the experiences of a small group of people, we believe there is great value in undertaking in-depth explorations of individual experiences. The paper's contribution lies in the detailed discussion of the complex circumstances of our non-participants' lives. We argue that design and evaluation in sensitive settings can be improved by taking into account the experiences of non-participants. This perspective has not been fully explored in existing literature, and detailed reflections on the particular challenges faced in these settings remain rare. The examples presented in this paper serve as a valuable reminder of the need to adopt a respectful and sensitive approach when developing and evaluating technologies with the "oldest old". This means respecting the needs, desires, and preferences of the people we design for [38, 50]. In our research, this meant understanding older adults' wishes to disengage from society and honoring their active and considered choice to *not* participate in social isolation interventions.

ACKNOWLEDGEMENTS

This research was supported by Benetas Aged Care Services, the Melbourne Networked Society Institute, and the Australian Research Council (LP120100022). We thank the Benetas clients and care managers who participated in the project and our colleagues John Downs, Hilary Davis, Alan Gruner, and Brendan Lillywhite for their contributions to the project. This research was approved by the University of Melbourne's Human Research Ethics Committee.

REFERENCES

1. Ronald Baecker, Kate Sellen, Sarah Crosskey, Veronique Boscart, Barbara Barbosa Neves. 2014. Technology to Reduce Social Isolation and Loneliness. In *Proceedings of the SIGACCESS Conference on Computers and Accessibility* (ASSETS '14), 27-34.
2. Barbara Barbosa Neves, Rachel L. Franz, Cosmin Munteanu, Ronald Baecker, Mags Ngo. 2015. "My Hand Doesn't Listen to Me!": Adoption and Evaluation of a Communication Technology for the 'Oldest Old'. In *Proceedings of the SIGCHI Conference on Human Factors in Computing Systems* (CHI '15), 1593-1602.
3. Helen Bartlett, Jeni Warburton, C-W. Lui, L. Peach, M. Carroll. 2013. Preventing Social Isolation in Later Life: Findings and Insights from a Pilot Queensland Intervention Study. *Ageing and Society* 33, 7 (2013), 1167-1189.
4. Eric. P. S. Baumer, Phil Adams, Vera D. Khovanskaya, Tony C. Liao, Madeline E. Smith, Victoria S. Sosik, Kaiton Williams. 2013. Limiting, Leaving, and (Re)Lapsing: An Exploration of Facebook Non-Use Practices and Experiences. In *Proceedings SIGCHI Conference on Human Factors in Computing Systems* (CHI '13), 3257-3266.
5. Eric P. S. Baumer, Morgan G. Ames, Jed R. Brubaker, Jenna Burrell, Paul Dourish. 2014. Refusing, Limiting, Departing: Why We Should Study Technology Non-Use. In *Extended Abstracts on Human Factors in Computing Systems (CHI EA '14)*, 65-68.
6. Eric P. S. Baumer and M. Six Silberman. 2011. When the Implication Is Not to Design (Technology). In *Proceedings SIGCHI Conference on Human Factors in Computing Systems* (CHI '11), 2271-2274.
7. D. L. Biordi and N. R. Nicholson. 2013. Social Isolation. In *Chronic Illness: Impact and Intervention*, I. M. Lubkin and P. D. Larsen Eds. Jones & Bartlett Learning (Burlington, MA), 97-132.
8. Mark Blythe, Peter Wright, John Bowers, Andy Boucher, Nadine Jarvis, Phil Reynolds and Bill Gaver. 2010. Age and Experience: Ludic Engagement in a Residential Care Setting. In *Proceedings of DIS 2010*. ACM Press, 161-170.
9. Alan Borning and Michael Muller. 2012. Next Steps for Value Sensitive Design. In *Proceedings of CHI '12*. ACM Press, 1125-1134.
10. Oliver. Burmeister. 2012. What Seniors Value About Online Community. *Community Informatics* 8, 1.
11. Mima Cattan, Martin White, John Bond and Alison Learmouth. 2005. Preventing Social Isolation and Loneliness among Older People: A Systematic Review of Health Promotion Interventions. *Ageing & Society* 25, 01, 41-67. http://dx.doi.org/doi:10.1017/S0144686X04002594
12. E. Y. Cornwell and L. J. Waite. 2009. Social Disconnectedness, Perceived Isolation, and Health among Older Adults. *Journal of Health and Social Behavior* 50, 31 - 48. http://dx.doi.org/10.1177/002214650905000103
13. Sara J. Czaja, Walter R. Boot, Neil Charness, Wendy A. Rogers, Joseph Sharit, Arthur D. Fisk, Chin Chin Lee, Sankaran N. Nair. 2015. The Personalized Reminder Information and Social Management System (Prism) Trial: Rationale, Methods and Baseline Characteristics. *Contemporary Clinical Trials* 40, 35-46.
14. Paul Dourish. 2014. Reading and Interpreting Ethnography. In *Ways of Knowing in HCI*, J.S. Olson and W.A. Kellogg Eds. Springer, 2014.
15. P. Dourish and G. Bell. 2011. *Divining a Digital Future: Mess and Mythology in Ubiquitous Computing*. The MIT Press (Cambridge, MA, London, England).
16. Batya Friedman, Peter H. Kahn Jr, Alan Borning. 2005. Value Sensitive Design and Information Systems. In *Human-Computer Interaction and Management Information Systems: Foundations*, Ping Zhang and Dennis F. Galletta Eds. M.E. Sharpe (Armonk, N.Y; London), 2005, 348-372.
17. Verena Fuchsberger, Martin Murer, Manfred Tscheligi. 2014. Human-Computer Non-Interaction: The Activity of Non-Use. In *Proceedings of the 2014 Companion Publication on Designing Interactive Systems* (DIS '14), 57-60.
18. Chiara Garattini, Joseph Wherton and David Prendergast. 2012. Linking the Lonely: An Exploration of a Communication Technology Designed to Support Social Interaction among Older Adults. *Univ. Acc. in the Inf. Soc.* 11, 2, 211-222. http://dx.doi.org/10.1007/s10209-011-0235-y
19. William Gaver, John Bowers, Tobie Kerridge, Andy Boucher, Nadine Jarvis. 2009. Anatomy of a Failure: How We Knew When Our Design Went Wrong, and What We Learned from It. In *Proceedings SIGCHI Conference on Human Factors in Computing Systems* (CHI '09), 2213-2222.
20. Kathrin M. Gerling, Regan L. Mandryk and Conor Linehan. 2015. Long-Term Use of Motion-Based Video Games in Care Home Settings. In *Proceedings SIGCHI Conference on Human Factors in Computing Systems*, (CHI '15), 1573-1582.
21. Lorna Gibson, Wendy Moncur, Paula Forbes, John Arnott, Christopher Martin and Amritpal S. Bhachu. 2010. Designing Social Networking Sites for Older Adults. In *Proceedings of British Computer Society Specialist Group Conference* (BCS '10). 186-194.
22. Trisha Greenhalgh, Joe Wherton, Paul Sugarhood, Sue Hinder and Rob Procter. 2013. What Matters to Older

People with Assisted Living Needs? A Phenomenological Analysis of the Use and Non-Use of Telehealth and Telecare. *Social Science & Medicine* 93, 86-94. http://dx.doi.org/10.1016/j.socscimed.2013.05.036

23. Peter Gregor, Alan F. Newell, Mary Zajicek. 2002. Designing for Dynamic Diversity - Interfaces for Older People. In *Proceedings of the ACM Conference on Assistive Technologies* (ASSETS '02), 151-156.
24. Marilys Guillemin and Lynn Gillam. 2004. Ethics, Reflexivity, and "Ethically Important Moments" in Research. *Qualitative Inquiry* 10, 2, 261-280.
25. Steve Harrison, Phoebe Sengers, Deborah Tatar. 2011. Making Epistemological Trouble: Third-Paradigm HCI as Successor Science. *Interacting with Computers* 23, 5, 385-392.
26. Vilma Lehtinen, Jaana Näsänen and Risto Sarvas. 2009. "A Little Silly and Empty-Headed" - Older Adults' Understandings of Social Networking Sites. In *Proceedings of British HCI Conf.*, 45-54.
27. Helen Lester, N. Mead, C. C. Graham, L. Gask and S. Reilly. 2012. An Exploration of the Value and Mechanisms of Befriending for Older Adults in England. *Ageing and Society* 32, 307-328 (2012).
28. Ann Light. 2011. Democratising Technology: Making Transformation Using Designing, Performance and Props. In *Proceedings SIGCHI Conference on Human Factors in Computing Systems* (CHI '11), 2239-2242.
29. John McCarthy and Peter Wright. 2015. Taking [a]Part: The Politics and Aesthetics of Participation in Experience-Centered Design. The MIT Press (Cambridge, MA; London, UK).
30. Wendy Moncur. 2013. The Emotional Wellbeing of Researchers: Considerations for Practice. In *Proceedings SIGCHI Conference on Human Factors in Computing Systems* (CHI '13), 1883-1890.
31. M. Mort, C. Roberts and B. Callen. Ageing with Telecare: Care or Coercion in Austerity? *Sociology of Health & Illness* 35, 6 (2013), 799 - 812.
32. Cosmin Munteanu, Heather Molyneaux, Wendy Moncur, Mario Romero, Susan O'Donnell, John Vines. 2015. Situational Ethics: Re-Thinking Approaches to Formal Ethics Requirements for Human-Computer Interaction. In *Proceedings SIGCHI Conference on Human Factors in Computing Systems* (CHI '15), 105-114.
33. Nicholas R. Nicholson. 2012. A Review of Social Isolation: An Important but Underassessed Condition in Older Adults. *Jounral of Primary Prevention* 33, 2-3, 137-152. http://dx.doi.org/10.1007/s10935-012-0271-2
34. Sonja Pedell, Frank Vetere, Lars Kulik, Elizabeth Ozanne and Alan Gruner. 2010. Social Isolation of Older People: The Role of Domestic Technologies. In *Proceedings of OzCHI 2010*. ACM Press, 167-170. http://dx.doi.org/10.1145/1952222.1952255
35. J. Pols and D. Willems. 2010. Innovation and Evaluation: Taming and Unleashing Telecare Technology. *Sociology of Health & Illness* 33, 3, 484 - 498.
36. L. Portwood-Stacer. 2013. Media Refusal and Conspicuous Non-Consumption: The Performative and Political Dimensions of Facebook Abstention. *New Media & Society* 15, 7, 1041 - 1057.
37. E. Raymond, A. Sevigny, A. Tourigny, A. Vezina, R. Verreault and A. C. Guilbert. 2013. On the Track of Evaluated Programmes Targeting the Social Participation of Seniors: A Typology Proposal. *Ageing and Society* 33, 2, 267 - 296.
38. Christine Satchell and Paul Dourish. 2009. Beyond the User: Use and Non-Use in Hci. In *Proceedings of the Australian Computer-Human Special Interest Group Conference* (OzCHI '09), 9-16.
39. Sergio Sayago and Josep Blat. 2011. An Ethnographical Study of the Accessibility Barriers in the Everyday Interactions of Older People with the Web. *Universal Access in the Information Society* 10, 359-371.
40. Neil Selwyn. 2003. Apart from Technology: Understanding People's Non-Use of Information and Communication Technologies in Everyday Life. *Technology in Society* 25, 99-116.
41. Neil Selwyn. 2006. Digital Division or Digital Decision? A Study of Non-Users and Low-Users of Computers. *Poetics* 34, 273 - 292.
42. Phoebe Sengers, Kirsten Boehner, Shay David and Joseph Kaye. 2005. Reflective Design. In *Proceedings of Aarhus '05*. ACM Press, 49-58.
43. T. Sorell and H. Draper. 2014. Robot Carers, Ethics, and Older People. *Ethics and Information Technology* 16, 3 (2014), 183-195.
44. A. Steptoe, A. Shankar, P. Demakakos and J. Wardle. Social Isolation, Loneliness, and All-Cause Mortality in Older Men and Women. *Proceedings of the National Academy of Sciences of the United States of America* 110, 15 (2013), 5797 - 5801.
45. Marcus S. Svensson and Tomas Sokoler. 2008. Ticket-to-Talk-Television: Designing for the Circumstantial Nature of Everyday Social Interaction. In *Proceedings of NordiCHI 2008*. 334-343.
46. John Vines, Rachel Clarke, Peter Wright, John McCarthy and Patrick Olivier. 2013. Configuring Participation: On How We Involve People in Design. In *Proceedings of CHI '13*. ACM Press, 429-438.

47. René Vutborg, Jesper Kjeldskov, Sonja Pedell and Frank Vetere. 2010. Family Storytelling for Grandparents and Grandchildren Living Apart. In *Proceedings of NordiCHI 2010*, 531 - 540.
48. Jenny Waycott, Hilary Davis, Frank Vetere, Amee Morgans, Alan Gruner, Elizabeth Ozanne and Lars Kulik. 2014. Captioned Photographs in Psychosocial Aged Care: Relationship Building and Boundary Work. In *Proceedings of the Sigchi Conference on Human Factors in Computing Systems* (CHI '14), 4167 - 4176.
49. Jenny Waycott, Hilary, Davis, Anja Thieme, Stacy Branham, John Vines and Cosmin Munteanu. Ethical encounters in HCI: Research in sensitive settings. In *Extended Abstracts on Human Factors in Computing Systems (CHI EA '15)*, 2369-2372
50. Jenny Waycott, Amee Morgans, Sonja Pedell, Elizabeth Ozanne, Frank Vetere, Lars Kulik and Hilary Davis. 2015. Ethics in Evaluating a Sociotechnical Intervention with Socially Isolated Older Adults. *Qualitative Health Research* 25, 11, 1518-1528. http://dx.doi.org/10.1177/1049732315570136
51. Jenny Waycott, Sonja Pedell, Frank Vetere, Elizabeth Ozanne, Lars Kulik, Alan Gruner and John Downs. 2012. Actively Engaging Older Adults in the Development and Evaluation of Tablet Technology. In *Proceedings of the Australian Computer-Human Interaction Conference* (OzCHI '12), 643-652.
52. Jenny Waycott, Greg Wadley, Stefan Schutt, Arthur Stabolidis and Reeva Lederman. 2015. The Challenge of Technology Research in 'Sensitive Hci'. In *Proceedings of the Australian Computer-Human Interaction Conference* (OzCHI '15), 240-249.
53. Jenny Waycott, Frank Vetere, Sonja Pedell, Lars Kulik, Elizabeth Ozanne, Alan Gruner and John Downs. 2013. Older Adults as Digital Content Producers. In *Proceedings of SIGCHI Conference on Human Factors in Computing Systems*. ACM Press, 39-48.
54. Peter Wright and John McCarthy. 2015. The Politics and Aesthetics of Participatory HCI. *Interactions*, November-December 2015, 26-31.
55. Sally Wyatt. 2003. Non-Users Also Matter: The Construction of Users and Non-Users of the Internet. In *How Users Matter: The Co-Construction of Users and Technology*, N. Oudshoorn and T. Pinch Eds. The MIT PRess (Cambridge, MA, London, England), 67 - 79.
56. S. Zwijsen, A. R. Niemeijer and C. M. P. M. Hertogh. 2011. Ethics of Using Assistive Technology in the Care of Community-Dwelling Elderly People: An Oveview of the Literature. *Aging & Mental Health* 15, 4, 419 - 427.

The Augmented Climbing Wall: High-Exertion Proximity Interaction on a Wall-Sized Interactive Surface

Raine Kajastila **Leo Holsti** **Perttu Hämäläinen**
Aalto University, Department of Computer Science
firstname.lastname@aalto.fi

ABSTRACT
We present the design and evaluation of the Augmented Climbing Wall (ACW). The system combines computer vision and interactive projected graphics for motivating and instructing indoor wall climbing. We have installed the system in a commercial climbing center, where it has been successfully used by hundreds of climbers, including both children and adults. Our primary contribution is a novel movement-based game system that can inform the design of future games and augmented sports. We evaluate ACW based on three user studies (N=50, N=10, N=10) and further observations and interviews. We highlight three central themes of how digital augmentation can contribute to a sport: increasing diversity of movement and challenges, enabling user-created content in an otherwise risky environment, and enabling procedurally generated content. We further discuss how ACW represents an underexplored class of interactive systems, i.e., proximity interaction on wall-sized interactive surfaces, which presents novel human-computer interaction challenges.

Author Keywords
Human-computer interaction; sports; climbing; movement-based games; exertion interfaces; augmented reality

ACM Classification Keywords
H.5.m. Information interfaces and presentation (e.g., HCI): Miscellaneous.

INTRODUCTION
Utilizing technology to increase excitement and motivation in physical exercise and sport has been increasingly researched in both HCI and sport science [2, 30, 32, 33, 43]. Computer-generated feedback has also been used to enhance movement skill acquisition [23, 26, 37]. However, almost all the studies have been conducted in laboratory setting or as one-off experiments where researchers actively participate in the experiment. Studies in the real world can reveal new aspects of interactive technologies, as participants use the technology on their own terms and without supervision [35].

CHI'16, May 07-12, 2016, San Jose, CA, USA
ACM 978-1-4503-3362-7/16/05.
http://dx.doi.org/10.1145/2858036.2858450.

Figure 1. Our augmented climbing wall in a climbing gym. The climber is playing the Spark game, where the goal is climb from start to end (indicated by stop button) while avoiding the moving electricity lines. The bottom left corner shows the touchscreen used, e.g., to browse game levels. The touchscreen is attached to a cabinet hosting the computer and a Kinect V2 sensor. The projector is mounted on the ceiling.

This paper contributes to the limited knowledge of designing technology and movement-based games[1] outside the laboratory, in real-world sport environments. We have set out to study how climbers interact with technology in a climbing center. This is motivated by the relatively few previous studies on indoor climbing, despite it being a rapidly growing sport [7, 38] and being considered for inclusion in the Olympics [6]. We investigate the following questions that impact the design of interactive systems for sports:

- What are the opportunities and challenges of augmenting a sport with interactive technology?
- How does interactive technology change a sport? More specifically, in what ways can technology affect climbing or watching someone else climb?

Figure 1 shows our Augmented Climbing Wall system installed in a commercial climbing center. ACW combines projected graphics and depth camera body tracking to create interactive games and other training applications. ACW also includes a separate touch screen for more detailed and multiuser interaction, although we do also provide projected buttons on the wall for basic actions such as restarting a game level.

ACW is designed as a research instrument for probing the questions above, and also to solve the problem of providing several interesting climbing challenges and activities in a

[1] By movement-based games we denote games that require active full-body participation [32]

small space. Climbers constantly yearn for new routes to climb (problems to solve), and as shown in Figure 2, fitting multiple routes in a small space easily introduces visual clutter and creates undesired challenges in finding correct holds. Projected graphics allow us to clearly highlight different routes and game levels that reuse the same set of holds. Climbers can quickly browse through the levels, avoiding the sometimes tedious search for routes suitable for one's skills.

Figure 2. Top left: A climbing wall with color-coded routes. Top right: Adding several routes to a small wall may produce a visually cluttered result. Bottom: projected graphics highlight the holds, reducing clutter.

In this paper, we describe the ACW system and three interactive applications (2 games, 1 game level editor). We also present the results from installing ACW for daily use in a climbing gym for four months. Data was gathered in three user studies and by logging game events. We first review related work, then present the system and the design of the applications, and describe the three user studies (N=50, N=10, N=10). Based on the studies and our further observations, we highlight three central opportunities and challenges of augmenting a sport with interactive projected graphics.

RELATED WORK

There has been a substantial amount of research on climbing, mostly concentrating on physiological and biomechanical aspects [9, 29, 41]. The mental side of climbing has also been studied [11], especially the influence of danger and physical risk [25]. There has been less research on using technology, with an exception provided by Climbax [22], which provides climbing statistics by utilizing sensors embedded in a wristband. Similar wrist worn inertial units can also be used for recognizing climbed routes in a climbing gym [21].

In the intersection of climbing and HCI, interactive climbing walls have been developed before our work, but the prior systems have concentrated on attaching sensors and lights to climbing holds [15, 24], or have not utilized full body tracking [40, 45, 46]. Compared to this, our projector and camera setup has many benefits 1) full-body motion tracking for movement analysis and interaction, 2) real-time feedback and interaction with projected graphics, 3) projection on the entire wall instead of just the holds, 4) a configurable system for any climbing wall, and 5) recording the performance for instant replay or later analysis.

Climbing routes (a.k.a. problems) are often "solved" socially with others. The mobile augmented reality application BouldAR by Daibler et al. [8] emphasized the sharing, collaborative training and other social features by providing a way to create, share and define goals and challenges together with friends. Daibler et al. conducted a promising initial study comparing paper and smartphone based route creation, but they underline that collaborative training needs to be explored more in detail. Our work enables collaborative training where climbers can jointly create, edit, grade, comment and share climbing routes by using a touchscreen.

Considering technology and sports on a more general level, there exists a growing body of work on enhancing motor learning and performance using computer-generated augmented feedback (AFB), such as sound effects or visuals that highlight salient aspects of one's performance. When designed properly, AFB can both motivate and guide motor learning [26, 37, 42]. Computer generated feedback can be faster and more accurate than training with a video camera or receiving feedback from an instructor, which allows one to perform more repetitions and evaluations of a skill in a shorter time. Concurrent (i.e., real-time) visual feedback can especially benefit the initial learning of complex skills [37]. However, it should be kept in mind that the learner may develop a dependency on AFB, as explained by the guidance hypothesis [26]. Outside a strict motor skill acquisition focus, we are especially inspired by work such as Jensen et al. [17] and Mueller and Muirhead [31] that derives design knowledge through the study of athletes' experiences of incorporating experimental interactive systems to their practice.

Our key technological components are computer vision and interactive projections, which have a long history in HCI and movement-based games, with examples like the Ping Pong Plus augmented table tennis [16], artificial reality martial arts [12], Kinect trampoline games [14], as well as RoomAlive [18], where multiple computers, cameras and projectors can be calibrated together to transform an ordinary room into a game space.

RELATION TO THE PRELIMINARY ACW STUDY

This paper continues an earlier preliminary study where we developed and evaluated six interactions with eight climbers [19]. For completeness, we briefly review the interactions here:

- **Projected routes**: Projected routes with illuminated circular holds and connecting lines. See Figure 3 left.
- **Route building**: A new route can be defined by climbing. All holds that the climber's hands or feet touch are included in a route.
- **Delayed video feedback**: Falling from the wall triggers a video replay.
- **Hand marks**: A person waiting for their turn uses left and right mouse buttons to define targets for the climber's left and right hands.
- **Route automator**: Endlessly progressing route for endurance training. The system reveals a new random handhold when the previous hold is reached. See Figure 3 middle.
- **Animated Chainsaw**: Climbers avoid animated chainsaws. See Figure 3 right.

Figure 3. Interactions from our earlier, preliminary ACW study [19]. Left: projected routes. Middle: route automator. Right: animated chainsaw.

We build on the preliminary study in three ways: 1) The preliminary study interactions were tested in a light-weight Wizard-of-Oz manner, but our system is technologically complete with computer vision, projector-sensor-calibration, and an additional touchscreen interface for switching and configuring the interactions. 2) We have chosen the three interactions of Figure 3 and developed them further to a level where they work autonomously in a commercial climbing gym. 3) We evaluate the interactions based on three user studies, providing novel data for understanding augmented sports.

INTERACTION DESIGN

This section describes the design of our three applications: the Spark game, Route creation, and the Whack-a-bat game. The applications are illustrated in Figure 1, figures 4-7, as well as the supplemental video.

The high-level interface for selecting and configuring the applications is implemented on the touchscreen shown in Figure 1. In general, our approach is to minimize interface elements such as buttons projected on the climbing wall itself. In principle, everything could be implemented with a projected interface, but using the separate touchscreen yields far more precision, e.g., when editing a route or browsing a large number of user-created routes.

The Spark Game

Evading the chainsaw was the interaction that elicited most excitement in the preliminary work, although some climbers did remark that it is quite far removed from regular climbing. The main change we have made is updating the game theme to avoiding moving electricity lines instead of chainsaws. This allows us to create obstacles of arbitrary shape, and makes visuals less ambiguous; with the chainsaw users were not sure whether they could touch the handle. The resulting Spark game is shown in Figure 1 and Figure 4. The game starts when the user taps the play button, after which the goal is to get to the stop button without touching or overlapping the electric lines. The lines may be static or moving, and some levels also have intermediate waypoints that open up new passages or otherwise change the level.

Although the spark game introduces new aspects to climbing, our goal was to preserve the following familiar and motivating aspects of climbing:

- Each game level has a clear start and end.
- The moves can be planned beforehand and executed while climbing, thus creating both cognitive and motor challenges.
- Each level is predesigned (as opposed to, e.g., randomly created) so that it can be practiced and one can learn from the performances of others.

Route creation and climbing

Our second application combines and further develops the projected routes and route building interactions of the preliminary study. Our touchscreen interface is shown in Figure 6. The screen shows the Kinect RGB view of the climbing wall. Touches are mapped to projected graphics coordinates by using the Kinect 3D coordinate information of each pixel and projector-sensor calibration data. Touching a hold adds or removes a hold mark and an arc between holds. The created routes can be browsed by grade, ratings, times climbed or tried and time of creation. Climbers can also vote for a route grade, input a 1-5 star rating, and add comments.

We first attempted to allow climbers to design routes by climbing, but could not find a 100% reliable way of detecting which holds were used and should be included in a route. In some routes, the climber's whole body may hug the wall closely and cause erroneous selection of holds. It appears that there should be at least some way to edit and refine the route information, which is why we designed and implemented the touchscreen editor. Perfecting the automatic route detection is left as future work. In the end, it turns out to be a fun social activity to edit a route together with a friend, one person using the touchscreen and the other trying out the moves on the wall. This is in line with the positive comments about the sociality of the hand marks interaction of the preliminary study.

The Whack-a-Bat game

Our third application is the Whack-a-bat game (Figure 7), where one attempts to touch a bat sitting on the holds before a timer runs out. When a bat is touched, it flies to a random location on the wall and restarts its timer. The new locations are randomized so that they never overlap the climber's body. As the game progresses, more bats appear, escalating the challenge.

Whack-a-bat extends the idea of the endless route automator of the preliminary study. We chose Whack-a-bat as our third application due to user and climbing gym staff requests about an endless endurance training application. We also wanted to add a simple way of competing with others and monitoring one's own progress in a longer term.

In the first iteration of Whack-a-Bat, the bat simply appeared at each new location, and the users often had difficulty locating it. In the present version, the bat's flight between the holds is animated with ease-in and leaves clear trails. This is inspired by Chang and Ungar [4] who propose using cartoon animation techniques for making it easier for users to track objects and understand what is changing. However, the animation alone is not enough to make it easy to track multiple bats, as the climber is close to the wall and cannot view all of it at a glance. To fix this, the bats also broadcast their locations using visual beacons, i.e., expanding circles that allow one to infer the directions even when looking elsewhere. Previously, Khan et al. [20] have suggested dimming the brightness of other elements to point out the location of a specific object on a large screen, but this is not necessarily compatible with a game's visual design, and only works if one can see the whole screen.

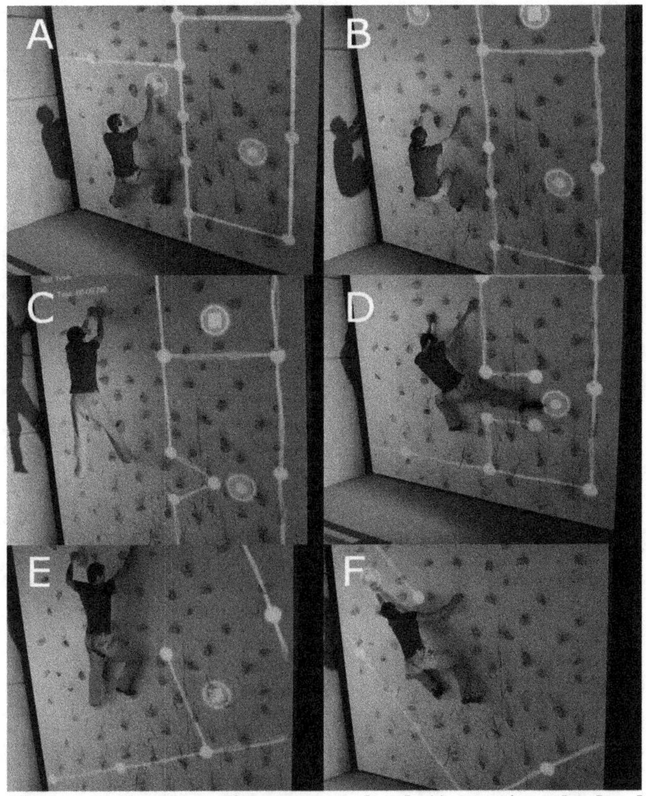

Figure 4. Progress of one game level A) starting the level using the play button, B) Timing a jump to avoid a blinking horizontal electricity line, C) Touching a waypoint opens a door, D) The second waypoint is reached with a challenging move, E) The whole level starts rotating and the climber needs to catch the moving stop button, F) Hitting the stop button ends the level.

CLIMBING WALL SETUP AND TECHNOLOGY

The ACW hardware setup comprises a climbing wall, Windows PC, Kinect V2 depth and color sensor, a projector, and the additional touchscreen. Presently, we have two setups, one at our university, and one at a climbing center. The wall dimensions are approximately 4 x 2.7 and 4.5 x 3.6 meters. While this is not enough for rope climbing walls, such wall height is common in indoor bouldering, which is a rapidly growing segment of climbing [7, 38]. Bouldering denotes climbing without a belay rope on low rocks or walls, with mattresses for safe falling. We use a 50cm thick mattress covered with carpeted polyethylene foam mat, which can be seen in Figure 1. We have further ensured safety by using a slightly overhanging wall. This way, climbers are less likely to scrape themselves against the holds when falling.

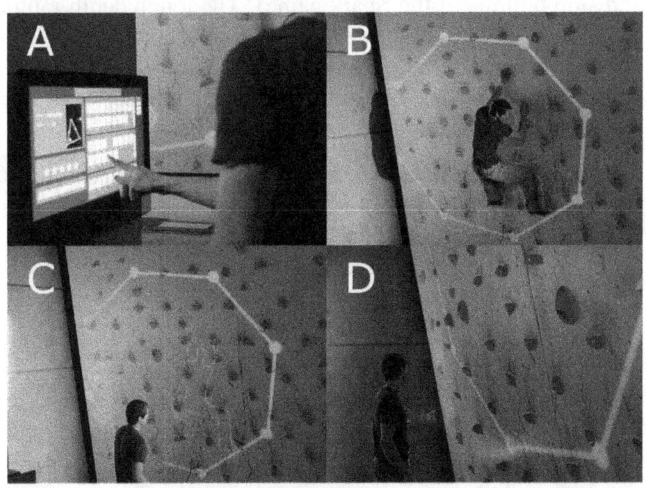

Figure 5. A) A touchscreen can be used to select different game levels and grade the levels (1-5 stars overall rating and a difficulty grade using the French climbing scale). B) The game stops with blue flashes and sound effects when intersecting a line. C) A burn mark silhouette indicates body pose at the time of intersecting the electricity. D) The game level can be restarted using a button on the wall, which is faster than using the separate touchscreen.

Wall size limitations

The climbing wall size is limited by the Kinect's field of view (FoV) and depth measurement noise that increases with distance. A large wall requires placing the sensor far, which makes it difficult to discern details such as fingers from noise. Our sensor is placed at approximately 3.5 meters from the wall. A system designed for adults might work with a sensor further away, but the small hands of children become a problem. Figure 8 shows examples of the depth sensing resolution and noise at various distances. At first, we also tried to implement the system using the older Kinect 1 sensor, which turned out too noisy. In a Kinect 1 depth image at 3.5 meters, one cannot even discern climbing holds from the noise. We have also investigated other depth sensing technologies, but the Kinect V2 appears to provide an unmatched combination of low price, high angular resolution (512x424 pixels with FoV of 70.6x60 degrees, i.e., roughly 7x7 pixels per degree), enough range, and high enough frame rate (30fps) for tracking dynamic movements.

Computer vision

We use custom computer vision software, as the Kinect V2 default skeletal tracking and user detection was found unreliable when not facing the camera and hanging on the wall. This is to be expected as the tracker is heavily based on machine learning training data captured from people's living rooms [36], and the data is unlikely to include the body poses typical to climbing.

When the system is started, we obtain a one second average of the depth map of the static background. At subsequent frames, we perform basic background subtraction, i.e., we segment the pixels to foreground or background by comparing the depth values to the background average. This is straightforward except that one must carefully filter the pixels near foreground object edges, where the depth readings randomly vary between the foreground and background distances. The foreground pixels within 2-8 cm of the wall are labeled as touch points and used for detecting the pressing of projected buttons (e.g., the play and stop buttons of the Spark game). The touch depth range is constrained by both depth noise and occlusions. The upper limit of the range must be quite high to accurately detect touches when the actual point of contact with the surface is occluded by the user's hand or foot.

All foreground points are used for detecting intersections with the electricity lines of the Spark game. Here, the 2D lines are actually considered to signify 3D planes that protrude from the wall, perpendicular to it.

Calibration

Calibrating the system consists of three phases: 1) aligning the projector and sensor so that the wall fits inside their frustums, 2) software keystoning, i.e., the user drags the four corners of a projection rectangle to define the active interaction area on the wall, 3) the software projects a dot pattern and detects the dots by comparing the Kinect's RGB view to a reference image stored before the procedure, and 4) the dots are used to compute the transformation matrices between the game graphics coordinates and the 3D coordinates provided by the sensor. At the climbing center, we ran steps 1 and 2 once, and the software runs steps 3 and 4 every morning when the computer is turned on. We have found this adequate, provided that the Kinect is mounted firmly.

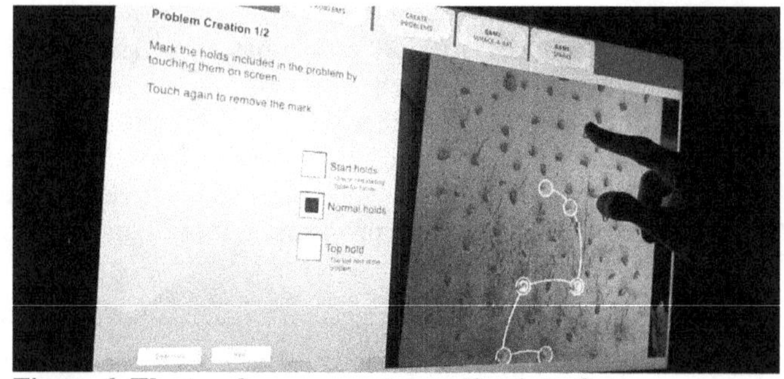

Figure 6. The touchscreen route creation interface.

Figure 7. The Whack-a-bat game. The player scores by touching a bat, after which it flies to another position. The bats emit circular enlarging beacons to help in spatial perception. More bats appear as the game progresses.

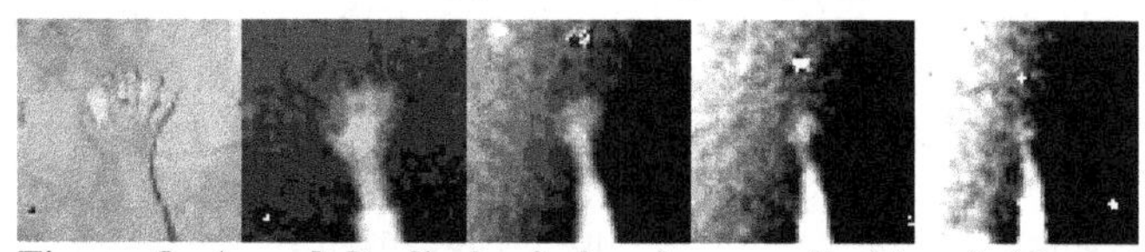

Figure 8. An adult climber's hand on a climbing hold, and corresponding Kinect V2 depth images at distances of 2, 3, 4, and 5 meters.

The game graphics are positioned within a 2D rectangle that is mapped to the projection rectangle. The applications all use 2D graphics which are faster to design and work without low-latency player viewpoint tracking.

USER STUDIES

Our ACW system was first developed at our laboratory and then installed at the Boulderkeskus Isatis climbing center in Helsinki, Finland, May 2015. At the time of submitting this paper, the system had been running for 4 months except for a 4 week break when waiting for a replacement projector. During the time, we conducted one primary user study (N=50) and two supplemental studies (N=10). The primary study 1 investigates the Spark game using questionnaire data, study 2 continues with questionnaire data from all three applications, and study 3 compares two Whack-a-bat interface versions. We also logged game usage data, which we summarize at the end of this section.

Study 1: Spark game questionnaire

In the beginning of our testing period, we only had the Spark game functional, and the other interactions were

Q1: What did you like the least?		Q2: What did you like the most?		Q3: Differences to regular climbing.		Q4: Differences to spectating climbing.		Q5: Suitablility.		Q6: Benefits for climbing practice.	
Category	**N**	**Category**	**N**	**Category**	**N**	**Category**	**N**	**Category**	**N**	**Category**	**N**
Tracking Failure	15	Different / Novelty	18	Climbing Style / Positions	9	Social / Participatory	16	Everyone	23	Endurance	11
User Interface / on Wall	13	Other	16	Tempo	8	Fun	12	Children	14	Other	10
Climbing Routes / Perceiving	12	Fun	12	Climbing Routes / Planning	8	Excitement	9	Other	7	Speed	8
Physical Environment	5	Variety (of routes / training)	12	Concentration / Focus	7	Other	8	Beginners	7	Movement Variety	8
Cheating	5	Motivates Movement Variety	6	Other	7	Nothing	5	Youth	4	None	6
Soundscape	3	Moving Routes	5	Competitiveness	4	Soundscape	3	Groups	3	Concentration / Focus	4
Climbing Routes / Planning	2	Motivates Endurance Training	4	Endurance	3	UI	2			Warm-up	3
Tempo	2	Idea	4	Fun	3					Training small holds	3
Visual Design	2	Fear of Heights	3	Fear of Heights	2					Dynamic moves	3
Difficulty	2	Competitiveness	2	Social	1					Technique	1
Other	2	Excitement	2	Excitement	1						

Table 1. Categories of the questionnaire responses, in order of frequency. Each response can belong to more than one category.

installed in late August. We gathered user feedback from the Spark game using a questionnaire. Printed questionnaires were available at the bouldering gym, and courtesy of the gym management we were able to raffle free climbing passes among respondents who answered all questions. A total of 50 climbers submitted the questionnaire (29 male, 19 female, 2 other. Age median 27, sd 6.9. Climbing experience median 2 years, sd 2.8. Climbing activity median 2.5 times per week, sd 1.2. Maximum climbed grade median 6c, French grade system).

Our questionnaire included eight open-ended questions: Q1) What did you like the least? Q2) What did you like the most? Q3) How does climbing in the game differ from regular climbing? Q4) How does watching someone play differ from watching regular climbing? Q5) Who is this most suitable for? Q6) Would this help your climbing practice? How? Q7) The game had both static and moving levels. Which were better? Why? Q8) Other comments?

Here, we focus on Q1-Q6. Answers to Q7 were inconclusive, and Q8 mainly prompted generic compliments that highlight the overall positive response. To summarize the results of Q1-Q6, two independent coders categorized the responses with a rate of agreement of over 92% for each question. Answers may belong to multiple categories, so typical intercoder reliability statistics such as Cohen's kappa are not usable. The categories and their frequencies are shown in Table 1. The following elaborates on the most relevant findings.

The climber's experience: diversity, fun, forgetting one's fear of heights

Responses to Q2 highlight the versatility, fun, and excitement that the game adds: *"Diverse training", "Fun, new things to do for a climber", "Versatile and different. Moving levels are more fun.", "I noticed I was climbing more in a short time as I had to try again and again :)", "Many routes in a small space. Creates diversity in climbing.", "Easy to change the wall and level of difficulty.", "Forces one to quickly search for alternative routes since the boundaries are moving.", "Fun endurance practice that does not feel like practice. Makes one sweat, panic, and laugh :)"*

Q3 responses further elaborate on the novel challenges of the Spark game regarding endurance, variety of movements, and spatial awareness: *"Movement is different, more sideways movement.", "More different moves",, "Must do more work on the wall (harder to plan the route <before climbing>)", "One chooses the holds oneself and also moves downwards", "Faster pace makes it more addictive", "Must look at other things besides just the holds", "Forces one in strange poses such as head downwards. Forces changes of tempo.", "One must observe sideways and downwards directions as well, can't rest so much", "Spending a longer time on the wall".* Movement variety was also among the most often cited benefits in Q6, in addition to endurance and speed. The appreciation of endurance training is a significant result, as low bouldering walls typically provide more strength than endurance challenges. The "speed" category of Q6 responses also indicate that climbers appreciate being forced to train quick decision making and reactions.

We find it particularly intriguing that three respondents claimed the game made them forget their fear of heights, *"Really great grip practice! I forgot to fear heights and falling", "Excitement provided by the game at one meter above the ground".* We have also observed similar effects in our previous work on trampoline games [14].

Investigating the psychological mechanisms behind this are an interesting topic for future research.

Another specific point mentioned was practicing dynos, i.e., dynamic leaps, *"Dyno practice. Force me to do them in a fun way. Practice timing too."* Here, ACW provides an example of how digital augmentation can actually make training safer and less frightening. Dynos are fun and thrilling, but can also be too scary due to the risk of ripping one's skin painfully when grasping a hold mid-leap. The Spark game has dyno training levels where one only slams the stop button and then falls down. This avoids hand trauma but still allows one to practice the coordinated recruitment of both arms and legs that's needed for efficient high jumps on a wall. Jumping on a wall is substantially different from jumping on the ground, and requires considerable practice.

Interestingly, although digital augmentation might distance the experience from climbing's outdoor roots, one respondent claimed the opposite, *"It's closer to outdoors, because there's no marked route."* Spotting the holds of outdoor routes can be surprisingly hard if one has only practiced indoors with brightly colored holds.

The spectator experience: new forms of interaction with the climber

Answers to Q4 highlight how the new perceptual challenges of observing all directions and dynamically changing levels also change the spectator's role, *"More exciting, one could participate as a spectator by giving instructions related to the moving lines."*, *"More interesting and nice to give guidance and warn the climber about the electricity."*, *"One more often shouts 'HELP!','LOOK OUT!', 'AAAAA' compared to just shouting beta"*. Beta is climbing slang for instructions. In general, spectating the game was also found more fun and exciting. Sound and visual effects also received positive responses.

Technological and perceptual issues

Q1 responses reveal that during our test period, ACW was still a prototype and not a finished product. Especially tracking robustness and/or communicating the limits of the technology were found to require more work. Users criticized the game for *"It was hard to perceive one's body on the wall -> easily hit the electricity"*, *"Electricity borders are imprecise, difficult to estimate whether one's head or limb will hit the electricity"*, and *"Detecting hits based on shadows instead of real body outlines"*. In reality the system is indifferent to the visible shadows of the user, and the comment simply indicates that there was some unpredictable behavior.

There appears to be two main failure cases: 1) tracking glitches due to occlusion and fuzzy object outlines such as hair, which cause random depth readings, and 2) the matching of a 2D shape on the wall surface and one's 3D body being up to interpretation. The first could be fixed by using multiple sensors and developing a custom model-based skeletal tracker to help in ignoring foreground point cloud outliers. The second is a design issue. We first considered detecting the electricity collisions only where one's body touches the wall. This was later discarded in favor of the present game where the electricity lines actually represent 3D planes protruding from the wall. Our rationale was that avoiding the 3D planes presents more interesting spatial puzzles. We believe that this approach is still valid as people clearly learn to play the game after getting "burned" a few times and observing the detected body outline rendered on the wall (Figure 5C). The body outline could also be rendered during play to make it explicit what the game detects, which we have so far avoided to minimize visual clutter and hide tracking and rendering latency.

Target audience: everyone, especially children.

As shown in Table 1, the most common answer to Q5 is that ACW is suitable for everyone (22 mentions). The next most common answers were children, beginners and "other", which comprises characterizations such as *"Everyone, especially people who like games"*, *"Rich people's homes?"*, *"Active climbers."* It should be noted that we deliberately equipped the wall with rather small holds that are more geared at intermediate and advanced than beginner climbers. The inclination of the wall (together with the smaller holds) also makes the wall really hard for beginners. On the other hand, the holds are easier for the small hands of children. During our visits to the climbing gym, we have observed children using ACW for several hours straight, which reflects the fact that adult routes are often too difficult for children and the gym only had little space for dedicated children's routes. It appears that ACW provides a space-effective way of expanding a gym's target audience to children.

A few Q3 responses highlighted negative aspects of how the Spark game changes climbing. *"In normal climbing, the routes are defined and one works on them if one fails. The game does not force one to work on the route and develop one's technique."* In light of this, the game might be more suitable for endurance and strength training or as a warm-up exercise rather than developing perfect climbing technique. Three answers to Q6 also praised the game for providing great warm-up. We conclude that designers should be cautious about how digital augmentation can both expand and limit a sport's target audience.

Study 2: Deploying Whack-a-bat and route creation

We installed the route creation and Whack-a-bat applications 4 weeks before the end of the study. We also made available an updated the Spark game questionnaire with a field that indicates the application(s) that one has tried. According to the 10 filled questionnaires we have received so far, the applications work as intended. Two respondents mention that Whack-a-bat is the best application, and three remark that it is a great form of warm-up. The data is generally in line with the Spark game

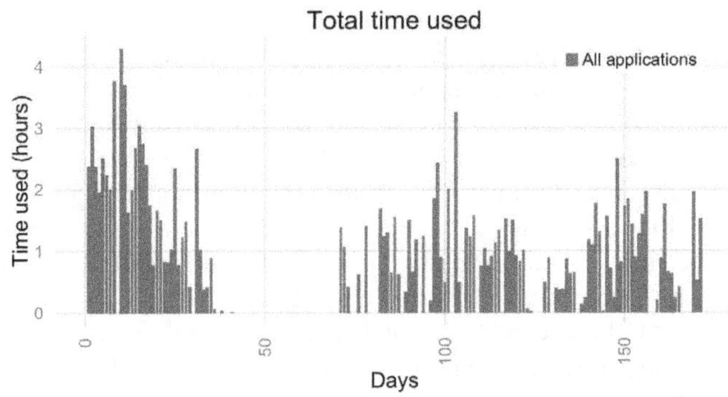

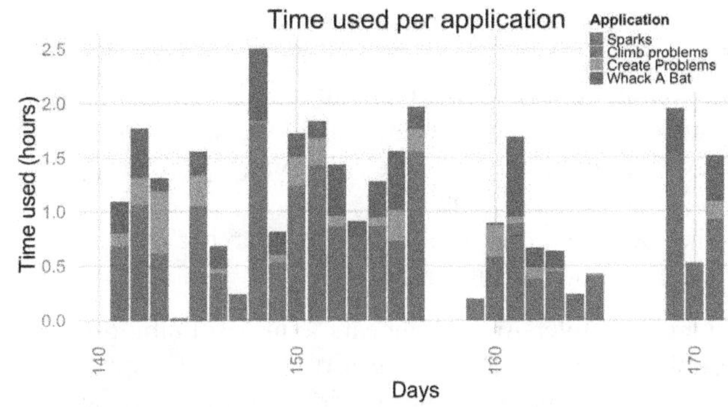

Figure 9. Left: Usage data from 171 days, May-September. Right: Breakdown of the last 30 days when route creation/climbing and Whack-a-bat were installed in addition to the Spark game. In addition to the maintenance break around day 50, there are several days of low or no usage due to the climbing gym being closed or the staff forgetting to turn the system on.

answers. According to our observations from visiting the gym, children in particular seem to like creating new routes, both for themselves and their parents.

Study 3: Improving spatial perception in Whack-a-Bat

Whack-a-bat attempts to improve the player's spatial perception using the circular beacons of Figure 7. Since such beacons are not commonly used and could also introduce undesired visual complexity, we conducted a within-subjects experiment to validate their effectiveness. 10 users were recruited from university students and staff. Each user played the game with and without the beacons in counterbalanced order. The bat transition animations were turned off for both game versions. After experiencing each condition, the users were asked to rate the difficulty of knowing at all times where the bat is on a 7-point Likert-style scale of 1=very easy, 4=not easy or difficult, 7=very difficult. The version with beacons was rated easy (mean=2.7, sd=1.4), and the version without beacons was rated difficult (mean=4.7,sd=1.4). A Wilcoxon signed rank test indicates that the difference is statistically significant ($p=0.0039$). After the test, the participants were also asked how the game versions differed, and how long it took them to realize what the beacons were for. 9 participants had noticed the beacons. All of them stated that they started using the beacon information after 1, 2 or 3 bats, which indicates that the beacons are fairly intuitive.

Game logs

An overview of game usage data is shown in Figure 9. The overall usage time of the system has remained relatively constant after the introduction of the system. The large gap around day 50 is due to projector malfunction and waiting for a replacement projector.

Towards the end, it appears that less new routes have been created and people have been spending more time climbing the already existing routes. We do not have enough data for reliable statistical analysis, but the shift in behavior makes sense as there are now enough routes for most climbers to find something interesting. A total of 53 routes have been created so far.

Further analysis of the data is hindered, because the number of daily climbers greatly varied due to it being summer and most people climbing outside if it was good weather. The duration for which ACW was turned on also varied from 0 to 11 hours each day. The climbing gym staff sometimes forgot to turn the system on at all, which is a result in itself – a system like ACW should not require even a single daily maintenance task for reliable data gathering.

DISCUSSION

To inform the design of future augmented sports, we now articulate the central opportunities and challenges that emerge from our data and experiences.

Opportunity 1: Increasing movement diversity and accessibility

The Spark game data highlights the positive effect of increased diversity of movements and challenges. In previous work, movement-based game players have found creative variation of movement as interesting and enjoyable [32]. Similarly, movement professionals often enjoy a playful exploration of the capabilities of the human body. As dancer and choreographer Steve Paxton puts it, *"I have a hunger to find, and to finish, and to explore, to do essentially what babies do when they begin to move. A hunger to find out more of what movement is or can be."* [1]. This is also in line with studies that have found curiosity as one of the central intrinsic game motivations [27, 28].

Climbing provides highly different movement challenges compared to movement-based games played on a floor, and the Spark game can be considered to further increase diversity in the following ways:

- The targets to reach can be anywhere, whereas in regular climbing the goal is to reach the top of the wall, from where one jumps down on a mattress or is lowered down on a rope. Climbing downwards requires different movements and skills and is often regarded as boring, but a game can make it meaningful and fun.

- In addition to targets to reach, there are also obstacles to avoid, which poses new challenges for spatial perception and movement planning.
- The obstacles and targets can move, which presents new timing challenges, e.g., jumping up or dropping down at the correct time.
- The game requires quick decision making and forces one out of one's comfort zone.

The increased diversity also appears to make climbing more accessible, allowing one to perform more attempts and succeed at least partially on a wider range of difficulty levels. For example, the level in Figure 4 is so hard due to the precise timing and coordination needed that even highly experienced climbers have had to try more than 10 times. Typically, routes of this difficulty are so physically demanding that one simply cannot perform multiple attempts in a short time. Routes above one's own climbing grade also often have so difficult holds that one cannot perform even a single move. As the Spark game is not so focused on grip strength, it is easier to make at least some progress on even the most difficult levels. Note that the importance of grip strength could be easily adjusted by using different holds. The reduced fear of falling and safer practicing of dynos also imply increased accessibility.

Opportunity 2: Enabling user-generated content in sport

The conceptual contribution of the route creation application is that it adds the ability for users to create and share content (routes, game levels) in a sport where one is not typically allowed to modify the environment because of safety reasons. Usually, only the climbing center staff or professional route setters adjust the holds, since an improperly secured hold can cause physical injury, and adding new holds without careful planning may block existing routes.

We believe our safe-to-edit digital content layer could be extended to other sports as well. This can be motivated by the game industry success stories of publishing a level editor together with a game, which can help build a long-lasting following and community around a game, with examples like Little Big Planet, Cities Skylines, and Trials Evolution [44, 47, 48].

Opportunity 3: Enabling procedural content in sport

Whack-a-bat can be considered as a simple example of procedural generation of the augmented digital content layer. Related to this, procedural game level synthesis is an active field of research [13]. In the context of climbing, some progress has been previously made in synthesizing textual route "recipes" such as "R slopey ledge, L match, R medium crimp sidepull..." [34]. In our experience, procedural content in sport is particularly suitable for motivating endurance training, where one can easily run out of handcrafted content.

We find both user-generated and procedural content especially important because they reduce the need for manually adapting content for the physical environment. Presently, we only have two flat walls of nearly equal size, but we have already experienced difficulties in playing the same game levels or climbing the same routes on both walls. Game feel depends on the hold sizes, shapes, and orientations. Further, scaling the visuals has a strong effect on the difficulty of maneuvering between Spark game electricity lines. Adapting content for different 3D wall shapes is even more challenging. Similar problems are likely to be encountered when augmenting other sports with varying physical environments, e.g., skateboarding or parkour.

Challenge 1: Understanding Proximity Interaction on Large Interactive Surfaces

The Spark game data indicates that people sometimes have difficulties of being aware of the extents of their body in space and in relation to the projected graphics. The iterative prototyping and testing of Whack-a-bat have further confirmed that ACW presents an uncommon combination of human-computer interaction challenges:

- Although people around see the whole screen, the person interacting on the wall (at an arm's length) only sees a portion of it at a glance. One's own body also often occludes a portion of the view.
- Due to gravity, the user must stay close to the surface at all times and cannot step back to view the whole.
- Staying on the wall requires heavy exertion and paying attention to holds, which limits the attentional capacity available for other tasks.

We believe that somewhat similar challenges may be encountered in other sports as well, e.g., when designing interactive visuals for a dance floor. More research is needed on interaction techniques that work in such settings. Vision is of course not the only sense that can be utilized, as suggested by Black and Loviscach's research on positional audio for large displays [3].

Challenge 2: Preventing Cheating

The Spark game leaderboards feature several implausible high scores (very low times between pressing the play and stop buttons), which are due to cheating. The most common cheating method we observed was to use two players, one for each button.

The lesson learned is that digital augmentation can introduce cheating even in a sport otherwise strong in self-regulation. Climbers usually avoid cheating despite the ample possibilities. In indoor climbing, the routes are typically color coded, a single wall has holds of multiple colors, and it is up to the climbers to stay honest and only use the correct holds. On the other hand the cheating is not surprising in light of previous gamification studies (e.g., [5, 10]). The Spark game leaderboards add extrinsic goals and motivation to climbing, and it has been found that an extrinsic goal orientation (a desire to engage in learning tasks because of extrinsic goals) is associated with cheating

[39]. It remains as future work to prevent cheating, e.g., by upgrading the computer vision to detect how many persons are on the wall, and focusing on supporting intrinsic instead of extrinsic motivation.

Challenge 3: Robustness and adaptivity to real-life conditions

In our experience, off-the-shelf electronics are vulnerable to the fine magnesium carbonate dust that floats in the air due to climbers applying the substance to their hands. The dust is not necessarily visible but still accumulates on everything, as illustrated in Figure 10. Our first projector drastically degraded in brightness during the first few weeks. In service, it was revealed that the dust had infiltrated the light source container. The lesson learned is that for prolonged use, one cannot avoid investing in hermetically sealed or otherwise dust-proof hardware. Magnesium carbonate is also used in other sports such as gymnastics.

Figure 10. Magnesium carbonate dust quickly accumulates on everything in a climbing center.

Another problem is presented by vibrations caused by people jumping off the walls. Such vibrations are also encountered in other sports such as weight lifting and gymnastics. We mounted our projector on the ceiling, and the resulting long projection distance makes vibrations highly visible – the graphics shake with an amplitude of several centimeters whenever a climber jumps off a nearby wall. Depending on sensor rigging, the vibrations could also interfere with computer vision.

Considering environments beyond our two present setups, we need to expand ACW from small and planar walls to larger and richer 3D shapes. As described earlier, it is a challenge to automatically adapt routes and game levels to different walls, which is however desirable if one aims at a low-cost system that can be installed anywhere without building a new wall. It also remains a technical challenge to accurately track a climber on a large wall with as simple camera setup as possible. The Kinect V2 has a limited range, and affordable long-range depth sensors have limited angular resolution. One solution could be to infer depth and 3D shapes from multiple high-resolution RGB cameras, but it remains unclear how fine precision one can achieve, e.g., for detecting when a climber touches a hold.

CONCLUSIONS AND FUTURE WORK

We have presented Augmented Climbing Wall, a novel sport training and movement-based game system with three prototype applications. The system has been received well, and the Spark game level in Figure 4 was even used as one of the competition problems in the Finnish bouldering cup final competition of 2015. According to our interviews with climbing gym staff members, ACW also makes birthday party and school groups climb for a longer time, and people making bookings have specifically asked whether ACW is available.

Our work highlights three opportunities in digital augmentation of a sport. First, interactive augmented visuals can increase the diversity of movements and challenges, e.g., timing of moves in an otherwise strength-centric sport. Second, a digital malleable content layer can empower users to become content creators with low risk compared to allowing users to actually modify the physical environment. Third, the digital content can also be procedurally generated, which is useful especially for endurance training sessions of non-predetermined duration. Other noteworthy findings include increased spectator-athlete interaction and users forgetting their fear of heights.

We have also highlighted three challenges that provide pointers for future work: 1) facilitating perception and interaction when close to a large display, 2) avoiding and preventing cheating when adding extrinsic motivators such as leaderboards, and 3) improving robustness and adaptivity of technology in real-life sport environments.

Considering generalizability, a climbing gym represents a class of sport environments characterized by 1) challenges defined as routes between two or more points, and 2) the player being bound by gravity in a way that makes it possible to use projected graphics to define the routes and add obstacles. We believe that similar interactions and technology could work in other such environments, e.g., BMX and skate parks. Extending the approach to a larger climbing wall with an automatic belay system should also be possible, but poses more challenges as the computer vision needs to work at a longer distance and tolerate the moving belay ropes. The price of projection technology also grows rapidly with the projection area.

In our future work, we intend to continue exploring the possibilities of user-created and procedural content in sport. It would be intriguing to interview climbers and route creators about their motivations to create routes, what makes a good route, and compare the results to research on game level design. Further, if one can derive a set of design guidelines for good routes or gather enough example data, it should be possible to create a computational creativity system for procedural route synthesis.

ACKNOWLEDGEMENTS

We thank the anonymous reviewers for their comments and feedback. We are also grateful for the support and feedback from Boulderkeskus Isatis climbing center, Helsinki, Finland, as well as all the user study participants and climbers who have used our system.

REFERENCES

1. About reasons to be a mover: 2012. *http://vimeo.com/48276698*.
2. Barnett, A., Cerin, E. and Baranowski, T. 2011. Active video games for youth: a systematic review. *Journal of Physical Activity and Health*. (2011).
3. Black, D. and Loviscach, J. 2010. Locating Sounds Around the Screen. *Proceedings of the 129th Audio Engineering Society Convention* (2010).
4. Chang, B.-W. and Ungar, D. 1993. Animation: From Cartoons to the User Interface. *Proceedings of the 6th Annual ACM Symposium on User Interface Software and Technology* (New York, NY, USA, 1993), 45–55.
5. Cheong, C., Cheong, F. and Filippou, J. 2013. Using Design Science Research to Incorporate Gamification into Learning Activities. *PACIS* (2013), 156.
6. Climbing Gets Second Chance at 2020 Olympics: *http://www.climbing.com/news/climbing-gets-second-chance-at-2020-olympics/*. Accessed: 2015-09-24.
7. Coldwell, W. 2012. Indoor climbing: the rise of bouldering-only centres. *The Guardian, http://www.theguardian.com/lifeandstyle/2012/jun/28/indoor-climbing-bouldering-only-centres*.
8. Daiber, F., Kosmalla, F. and Krüger, A. 2013. BouldAR: using augmented reality to support collaborative boulder training. *CHI '13 Extended Abstracts on Human Factors in Computing Systems* (New York, NY, USA, 2013), 949–954.
9. Fanchini, M., Violette, F., Impellizzeri, F.M. and Maffiuletti, N.A. 2013. Differences in Climbing-Specific Strength Between Boulder and Lead Rock Climbers: *Journal of Strength and Conditioning Research*. 27, 2 (Feb. 2013), 310–314.
10. Glas, R. 2015. Breaking reality: Exploring pervasive cheating in Foursquare. *Playful identities: the ludification of digital media cultures*. V. Frissen, S. Lammes, M. De Lange, J. De Mul, and J. Raessens, eds. Amsterdam University Prress.
11. Green, A.L. and Helton, W.S. 2011. Dual-task performance during a climbing traverse. *Experimental Brain Research*. 215, 3-4 (Oct. 2011), 307–313.
12. Hämäläinen, P., Ilmonen, T., Höysniemi, J., Lindholm, M. and Nykänen, A. 2005. Martial arts in artificial reality. *Proceedings of the SIGCHI conference on Human factors in computing systems* (2005), 781–790.
13. Hendrikx, M., Meijer, S., Van Der Velden, J. and Iosup, A. 2013. Procedural Content Generation for Games: A Survey. *ACM Trans. Multimedia Comput. Commun. Appl.*. 9, 1 (Feb. 2013), 1:1–1:22.
14. Holsti, L., Takala, T., Martikainen, A., Kajastila, R. and Hämäläinen, P. 2013. Body-controlled trampoline training games based on computer vision. *CHI '13 Extended Abstracts on Human Factors in Computing Systems* (New York, NY, USA, 2013), 1143–1148.
15. HRT LED climbing holds: 2013. *http://seanmccoll.com/2013/03/new-hrt-systems/*.
16. Ishii, H., Wisneski, C., Orbanes, J., Chun, B. and Paradiso, J. 1999. PingPongPlus: design of an athletic-tangible interface for computer-supported cooperative play. *Proceedings of the SIGCHI conference on Human Factors in Computing Systems* (New York, NY, USA, 1999), 394–401.
17. Jensen, M.M., Rasmussen, M.K., Mueller, F. "Floyd" and Grønb\a ek, K. 2015. Keepin' It Real: Challenges when Designing Sports-Training Games. *Proceedings of the 33rd Annual ACM Conference on Human Factors in Computing Systems* (New York, NY, USA, 2015), 2003–2012.
18. Jones, B. et al. 2014. RoomAlive: Magical Experiences Enabled by Scalable, Adaptive Projector-camera Units. *Proceedings of the 27th Annual ACM Symposium on User Interface Software and Technology* (New York, NY, USA, 2014), 637–644.
19. Kajastila, R. and Hämäläinen, P. 2014. Augmented Climbing: Interacting With Projected Graphics on a Climbing Wall. *CHI '14 Extended Abstracts on Human Factors in Computing Systems* (2014).
20. Khan, A., Matejka, J., Fitzmaurice, G. and Kurtenbach, G. 2005. Spotlight: Directing Users' Attention on Large Displays. *Proceedings of the SIGCHI Conference on Human Factors in Computing Systems* (New York, NY, USA, 2005), 791–798.
21. Kosmalla, F., Daiber, F. and Krüger, A. 2015. ClimbSense: Automatic Climbing Route Recognition Using Wrist-worn Inertia Measurement Units. *Proceedings of the 33rd Annual ACM Conference on Human Factors in Computing Systems* (New York, NY, USA, 2015), 2033–2042.
22. Ladha, C., Hammerla, N.Y., Olivier, P. and Plötz, T. 2013. ClimbAX: Skill Assessment for Climbing Enthusiasts. *Proceedings of the 2013 ACM International Joint Conference on Pervasive and Ubiquitous Computing* (New York, NY, USA, 2013), 235–244.
23. Liebermann, D.G., Katz, L., Hughes, M.D., Bartlett, R.M., McClements, J. and Franks, I.M. 2002. Advances in the application of information technology to sport performance. *Journal of sports sciences*. 20, 10 (Oct. 2002), 755–769.
24. Liljedahl, M., Lindberg, S. and Berg, J. 2005. Digiwall: an interactive climbing wall. *Proceedings of the 2005 ACM SIGCHI International Conference on Advances in computer entertainment technology* (New York, NY, USA, 2005), 225–228.
25. Llewellyn, D.J. and Sanchez, X. 2008. Individual differences and risk taking in rock climbing.

Psychology of Sport and Exercise. 9, 4 (Jul. 2008), 413–426.

26. Magill, R.A. and Anderson, D.I. 2012. The roles and uses of augmented feedback in motor skill acquisition. *Skill Acquisition in Sport: Research, Theory and Practice*. N. Hodges and A.M. Williams, eds. Routledge.
27. Malone, T.W. 1981. Toward a theory of intrinsically motivating instruction. *Cognitive Science*. 5, 4 (Oct. 1981), 333–369.
28. Malone, T.W. and Lepper, M.R. 1987. Making learning fun: A taxonomy of intrinsic motivations for learning. *Aptitude, learning, and instruction*. 3, (1987), 223–253.
29. Mermier, C.M., Robergs, R.A., McMinn, S.M. and Heyward, V.H. 1997. Energy expenditure and physiological responses during indoor rock climbing. *British Journal of Sports Medicine*. 31, 3 (Sep. 1997), 224–228.
30. Mueller, F., Agamanolis, S. and Picard, R. 2003. Exertion interfaces: sports over a distance for social bonding and fun. *Proceedings of the SIGCHI Conference on Human Factors in Computing Systems* (New York, NY, USA, 2003), 561–568.
31. Mueller, F. "Floyd" and Muirhead, M. 2015. Jogging with a Quadcopter. *Proceedings of the 33rd Annual ACM Conference on Human Factors in Computing Systems* (New York, NY, USA, 2015), 2023–2032.
32. Mueller, F. and Isbister, K. 2014. Movement-based Game Guidelines. *Proceedings of the SIGCHI Conference on Human Factors in Computing Systems* (New York, NY, USA, 2014), 2191–2200.
33. Pasch, M., Bianchi-Berthouze, N., van Dijk, B. and Nijholt, A. 2009. Movement-based sports video games: Investigating motivation and gaming experience. *Entertainment Computing*. 1, 2 (Apr. 2009), 49–61.
34. Phillips, C., Becker, L. and Bradley, E. 2012. Strange Beta: An assistance system for indoor rock climbing route setting. *Chaos: An Interdisciplinary Journal of Nonlinear Science*. 22, 1 (Mar. 2012), 013130.
35. Rogers, Y. 2011. Interaction Design Gone Wild: Striving for Wild Theory. *interactions*. 18, 4 (Jul. 2011), 58–62.
36. Shotton, J., Sharp, T., Kipman, A., Fitzgibbon, A., Finocchio, M., Blake, A., Cook, M. and Moore, R. 2013. Real-time human pose recognition in parts from single depth images. *Commun. ACM*. 56, 1 (Jan. 2013), 116–124.
37. Sigrist, R., Rauter, G., Riener, R. and Wolf, P. 2013. Augmented visual, auditory, haptic, and multimodal feedback in motor learning: A review. *Psychonomic Bulletin & Review*. 20, 1 (Feb. 2013), 21–53.
38. The Next Urban Sports Craze: *http://www.outsideonline.com/1869981/next-urban-sports-craze*.
39. Vansteenkiste, M., Lens, W. and Deci, E.L. 2006. Intrinsic Versus Extrinsic Goal Contents in Self-Determination Theory: Another Look at the Quality of Academic Motivation. *Educational Psychologist*. 41, 1 (Mar. 2006), 19–31.
40. Waterfall climber: *http://exertiongameslab.org/projects/waterfall-climber*.
41. Watts, P.B. 2004. Physiology of difficult rock climbing. *European Journal of Applied Physiology*. 91, 4 (Apr. 2004), 361–372.
42. Wulf, G., Shea, C. and Lewthwaite, R. 2010. Motor skill learning and performance: a review of influential factors. *Medical Education*. 44, 1 (2010), 75–84.
43. Yim, J. and Graham, T.C.N. 2007. Using games to increase exercise motivation. *Proceedings of the 2007 conference on Future Play* (New York, NY, USA, 2007), 166–173.
44. 2015. *Cities: Skylines*. Paradox Interactive.
45. *Interactive Climbing wall: https://www.youtube.com/watch?v=kg2uRGf_04g*.
46. *Level12 - Get the new climbing experience: https://www.youtube.com/watch?v=saKMcnE-BEg*.
47. 2008. *Little Big Planet*. Sony Computer Entertainment.
48. 2012. *Trials Evolution*. Ubisoft.

BitDrones: Towards Using 3D Nanocopter Displays as Interactive Self-Levitating Programmable Matter

Antonio Gomes, Calvin Rubens, Sean Braley and Roel Vertegaal
Human Media Lab, Queen's University,
Kingston, Ontario, K7L 3N6, Canada
{gomes, braley, roel}@cs.queensu.ca, j.rubens@queensu.ca

ABSTRACT

We present BitDrones, a toolbox for building interactive real reality 3D displays that use nano-quadcopters as self-levitating tangible building blocks. Our prototype is a first step towards interactive self-levitating programmable matter, in which the user interface is represented using Catomic structures. We discuss three types of BitDrones: PixelDrones, equipped with an RGB LED and a small OLED display; ShapeDrones, augmented with an acrylic mesh spun over a 3D printed frame in a larger geometric shape; and DisplayDrones, outfitted with a flexible thin-film 720p touchscreen. We present a number of unimanual and bimanual input techniques, including *touch*, *drag*, *throw* and *resize* of individual drones and compound models, as well as user interface elements such as self-levitating cone trees, 3D canvases and alert boxes. We describe application scenarios and depict future directions towards creating high-resolution self-levitating programmable matter.

Author Keywords

Organic User Interfaces; Tangible User Interfaces; Claytronics; Radical Atoms; Real Reality Interfaces; Programmable Matter.

ACM Classification Keywords

H.5.m. Information interfaces and presentation (e.g., HCI): Miscellaneous.

INTRODUCTION

The thought that computer interfaces might someday *physically* embody user interactions with digital data has been around for a long time. In 1965, Sutherland envisioned the "Ultimate Display" as a room in which the computer controlled the existence of matter [42]. According to Toffoli and Margolus [45], such programmable matter would consist of small, parallel, cellular automata nodes capable of geometrically shaping themselves in 3D space to create any kind of material structure. Since then, there has been a significant amount of research conducted towards this goal under various monikers, such as Claytronics [13], Organic User Interfaces [48], and Radical Atoms [18]. All of these seek, at least in part, to utilize programmable matter for user interface purposes to allow for a full two-way synchronization of bits with atoms — something the first generation of Tangible User Interfaces was unable to achieve [17]. While there has been progress towards building hardware modules capable of various forms of self-actuation (known as Claytronic atoms or *Catoms*) [12,38], much of the work on programmable matter has been theoretical in nature. How to create a massively parallel system of Catoms capable of displaying two-way immersive physical user experiences is an enduring research goal. This would promise Augmented Reality (AR) systems physically integrated with real objects, creating Real Reality Interfaces (RRI) that render interactive digital experiences using real matter. The problem we address in this paper is that Catoms need to overcome gravity, typically via structural support by other Catoms, when building larger structures. While there has been some prior work in this area, the movement of individual Catoms in 3 dimensions is generally limited [31]. We propose to address the levitation problem using nano-quadcopters. While there have been explorations of swarms of quadcopters for visualization applications [4,26], there has been little work on interactive, real-time user interface applications of 3D drone displays.

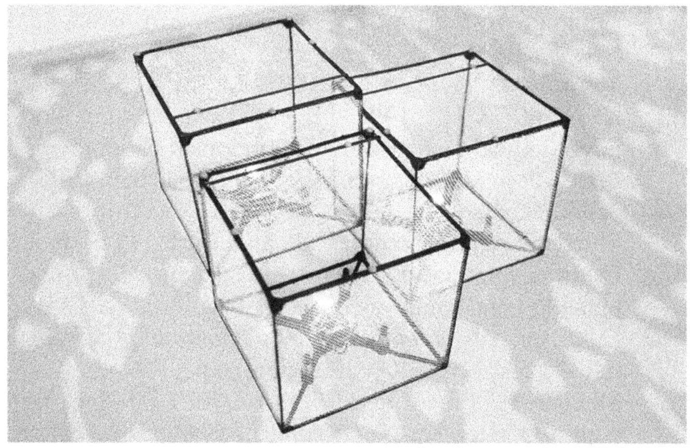

Figure 1. BitDrones hovering in a tight formation.

CHI'16, May 07-12, 2016, San Jose, CA, USA.
© 2016 ACM. ISBN 978-1-4503-3362-7/16/05...$15.00.
DOI: http://dx.doi.org/10.1145/2858036.2858519

Contribution

In this paper, we present BitDrones, an interactive, glasses-free, 3D tangible display that uses nano-quadcopters as self-levitating Catoms that serve as real reality voxels (see Figure 1). Our prototype is a first step towards interactive self-levitating tangible user interfaces with multiple building blocks that are capable of physically representing 3D data on the fly. We discuss three types of BitDrones, each representing Catoms of distinct resolutions: 1) *PixelDrones*, which are equipped with an RGB LED and an OLED display. PixelDrones represent a single illuminated voxel or, optionally, a text label; 2) *ShapeDrones*, which are BitDrones augmented with a lightweight acrylic mesh spun over a 3D printed frame in a larger geometric shape, such as a cube or a sphere. ShapeDrones only have one RGB LED, used to illuminate a lightweight mesh diffuser that covers the 3D frame. ShapeDrones allow users to build higher granularity 3D models without requiring drones to stack on top of each other in mid-flight; 3) *DisplayDrones*, which carry a flexible touchscreen display, molded in an arc, with an Android 5.1 smartphone board. DisplayDrones are able to render high-resolution images, such as contextual menus, pictures and videos. We present both unimanual and bimanual input techniques, including touching, dragging, throwing and resizing of BitDrones and compound models, as well as user interface elements, including flying cone trees, video displays and alert boxes. We conclude with application scenarios in 3D editing, molecular modeling, real reality information visualization and telepresence. While the BitDrones system at present only allows for sparse models of up to 12 Catoms, unlike VR or AR, it promises to fully preserve natural depth and tactile-kinesthetic cues without requiring headsets or simulated haptics.

BACKGROUND

We will first discuss prior work in the areas of Tangible User Interfaces, Augmented and Mixed Reality Interfaces, Actuated Shape Displays, Programmable Matter and Self-Levitating Interfaces, as they relate to the design of our system. Note that we purposefully omitted a discussion of VR interfaces as these systems are designed to be fully immersive, i.e., do not allow the user to interact with the real world. We also discuss ongoing work in the emerging field of Human-Drone Interaction.

Tangible User Interfaces

Tangible User Interfaces (TUIs) leverage our ability to sense and manipulate the material world by providing physical form to digital information, facilitating direct engagement with the physical world. TUIs were introduced by Ishii and Ullmer [17] as an effort to augment the real world by coupling digital information to everyday physical objects and environments. Over the years, tangible interfaces have been extensively explored in electronic music platforms [20], urban planning [34], constructive assembly [35], as well as graspable interfaces [9]. However, TUIs have limited ability to display changes applied to the physical objects by software processes or remote users. To overcome the limitations of tangibles, Radical Atoms [17] described a hypothetical physical material that could be coupled with an underlying digital model, allowing for human interactions with computationally transformable physical materials.

Augmented Reality Interfaces

There is a large body of work aimed at interacting with virtual elements in 3D environments, which we cannot possibly do justice in this review. Robertson et al. [37] designed cone trees as a means of visualizing file hierarchies in a 3D user interface. In cone trees, folders and files are arranged in a circular manner, with each level of the hierarchy containing a horizontal "wheel" of folder or file nodes. Robertson et al. also investigated other forms of navigating 3D Graphical User Interfaces (GUIs), but was limited to a 2D display. By contrast, Augmented Reality systems use partially transparent displays to superimpose graphics onto real objects or environments [15,24]. They can be combined with passive tangible input in the real world, for example, using AR Toolkit markers [16]. HoloLens [15] introduced a semi-transparent head-mounted display that maps the space around the user using a fully integrated depth camera, allowing the system to simultaneously model its environment as well as sense marker-less gestural input. Shader Lamps [36] introduced a method for rendering AR *directly* onto physical objects, thus merging the display with the real world. Researchers have deployed such 3D projection-mapping techniques to create interactive 3D physical objects [1,14] and to simulate textures and material properties of designs [14,19]. 3D projection mapping typically requires expensive capturing of the 3D topography of the projection space. LightSpace [47] showed how cheap arrays of Kinect depth cameras could be combined with multiple projectors to augment any surface in an entire room with rich interactive graphics.

Mixed Reality Interfaces

Mixed Reality [27,28] is a special class of augmented and virtual reality technologies for creating environments wherein real and virtual world objects are presented together in a single display. Milgram and Colquhoun Jr. [28] formulated a global taxonomy to describe how the virtual and real aspects of Mixed Reality environments are combined and experienced, with the ultimate objective of clarifying conceptual boundaries existing among noted research. Benford et al. [5] experimented with projecting a virtual poet into a real theatre as part of a live performance. They suggested that their "early experience of social interaction between physical and synthetic spaces implies the need for a more systematic approach to joining them together". According to them, real-world interactions combine the local with the physical, VR combines the remote with the synthetic, while AR combines the local with the synthetic. They proposed *mixed reality* as a new form of shared space that integrates the local with the remote and the physical with the synthetic. An example mixed reality system, MirageTable [6], allowed users to mix real and virtually projected 3D objects on a curved tabletop. It used a depth camera to map objects and users around the tabletop, then project these back onto a remote table such that remote and local users could interact with one another. This allowed users to virtually share physical objects in a way that was fully spatially congruous. In this paper, we suggest working towards merging the local, remote, physical and synthetic in such a way that they become one and the same, at least when it comes to the sharing of objects.

Actuated Shape Displays

Actuated shape displays provide novel opportunities for experiencing and interacting with digital content in the physical world, by dimensioning the actual displays through actuation. Lumen [33] explored the design of an actuated pixelated relief display. Lumen used light guides actuated through shape memory alloys to display low-resolution images with some *z* dimension. Leithinger and Ishii's Relief system [25] featured an actuated tabletop display that rendered interactive 3D shapes with a wider range of *z* actuation. Their system used a series of motorized pins actuating a fabric display that was top projected with images. More recently, inFORM [11] explored the use of high-resolution dynamic relief to display digital information. inFORM's shape display provided for variable stiffness rendering and real-time user input through direct touch and tangible interaction. Although shape displays can provide a bi-directional interface between bits and matter, including visual, haptic and force feedback experiences, they are limited in the kind of shapes they can render. E.g., the aforementioned explorations cannot render shapes with holes inside their structures.

Programmable Matter

Recently, there has been a significant research effort towards developing a new generation of computer interface capable of displaying physical 3D structures via programmed movement of large quantities of self-assembling nanorobots [38,46]. Goldstein et al. [12] alluded to the creation of physical artifacts using a collection of such Catoms [13], which would eventually be able to mimic an analog object's shape, movement, visual appearance, and tactile qualities. Alonso-Mora et al. [2] presented a display in which each pixel is a mobile robot of controllable color. Their system took images or animations as input and produced a multi-robot display as output. Similarly, Rubenstein et al. proposed a thousand-robot swarm capable of self-assembling into larger, potentially interactive, shapes [39]. Practical attempts at creating claytronic atoms, however, have proven difficult. While the above systems successfully demonstrated programmable self-assembly of complex shapes, thus mitigating some of the limitations associated with shape displays, they are limited to rendering shapes in two dimensions.

Self-Levitating Interfaces

An important problem in the creation of 3D programmable matter is that the structural integrity of the object needs to be preserved while it is changing shape [39]. This can be difficult to achieve with robotic motes as they have to rest on top of one another to overcome gravity. To address this issue, researchers have investigated the use of magnetic [23] and ultrasonic self-levitation [31]. However, these methods pose distinct limitations to the independent motion of multiple Catoms. Karagozler et al. [21] proposed the use of robotic helium balloons, or Giant Helium Catoms. The problem with these structures is that they are inherently difficult to miniaturize.

Drones and User Interaction

While there is a body of work that investigated non-interactive swarms of quadcopters acting together as a scalable production means [10,26], flying displays [30,40,41], augmented sports [29] and feedback mechanisms [42], further research is necessary to ascertain what are the most effective methods to facilitate human-drone interaction [4,8]. Pfeil et al. [32] explored 3D spatial interaction metaphors for interacting with drones. Their approach aimed at generalizing interaction metaphors that could potentially be applied to future user interfaces. This concept was further explored by Cauchard et al. [8], who conducted a Wizard-of-Oz elicitation study to evaluate how users naturally interact with drones. Their results suggested that users interact with drones in a similar way they would interact with a person or a pet. Nitta et al.'s [29] Hoverball demonstrated a flying controllable ball to integrate imaginary dynamics into ball sports. The authors investigated new ball-playing vocabularies, such as hovering, anti-gravity, proximity, or remote manipulation, as a method to extend the way people experience ball-based sports. Researchers have also explored the concept of free-floating midair displays via flying robots equipped with projectors [30,40] and high-resolution displays [41]. In contrast to traditional static displays, free-floating displays have the potential to change their position to appear at any given point in space and approach the user to communicate information. While these explorations facilitated human-drone interaction, they lacked support for multimodal I/O between the drone and the user. Additionally, they were limited to a single drone that primarily acted as a visual information display. Instead, we investigate how users can interact with swarms of nano-quadcopters via direct touch, unimanual and bimanual input techniques and gestural interactions. Our goal is to create the first system that uses multiple drones that act together to create interactive tangible interfaces, and generate real reality 3D displays using nano-quadcopters as self-levitating tangible building blocks.

DESIGN RATIONALE

To inform the design of BitDrones, we considered the following design parameters:

Modularity and Granularity

We designed the system in a modular fashion, like Lego™, allowing users to build structures out of individual, self-levitating building blocks. Structures can have varying granularity, i.e., consisting of a few to a dozen drones, depending on the complexity of the compound object. We compensated for a lack of density in building blocks by

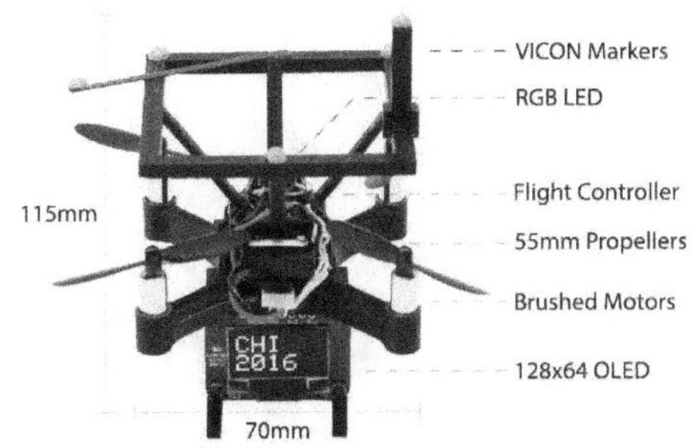

Figure 2.1. PixelDrone with RGB LED and OLED Display.

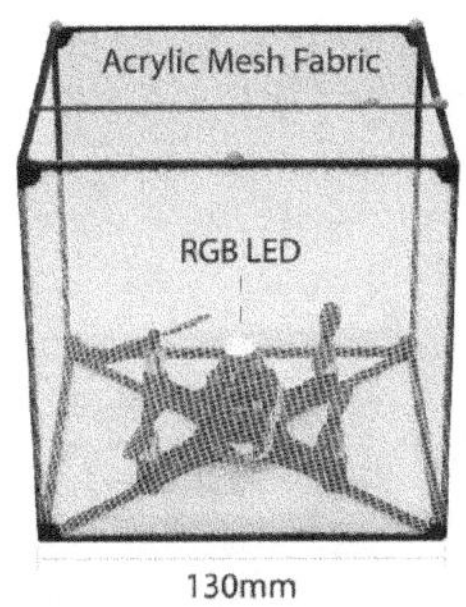

2.2. ShapeDrone with RGB LED and Cube-shaped Diffuser.

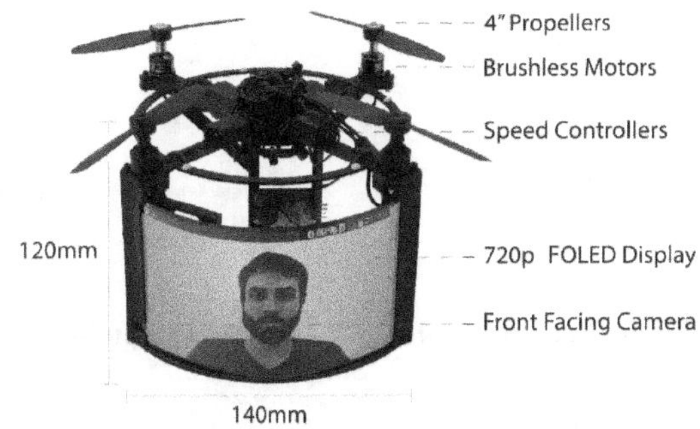

2.3. DisplayDrone with curved 720p FOLED Android display.

allowing the use of higher resolution, sub-voxel imaging via drone-mounted displays.

Drone-Mounted Displays

The original vision for single voxel *Catoms* would require thousands of microscopic drones flying in very close proximity. While this may be feasible in the future, we decided to use sub-voxel imaging techniques to enhance imaging resolution of a sparser drone cloud. We designed 3 types of drones, each with a different sub-voxel imaging resolution, and different form factors: PixelDrones that display a single color voxel; 2) ShapeDrones that display larger shapes and 3) DisplayDrones that carry a high resolution display.

Haptics: Tangible vs. Gestural Interaction

While BitDrones have the ability to follow gestures as well as user's body movements within a tracked space, an important design criterion was for each drone to respond to direct touch. This allows users to directly interact with the real reality interface, without any mapping or prior knowledge of predefined gestural interactions. BitDrones are simply grasped and moved around freespace at will. Groups of BitDrones are manipulated through the use of PixelDrones that serve as handles, allowing for intuitive bimanual 3D translation, rotation and resizing operations. The ability to directly touch and move drones provides haptic experiences not available in VR or AR systems. BitDrones do not require simulation of tactile kinesthetic feedback, as this is naturally provided.

Multiple Form Factors

Due to their sparseness, we designed BitDrones in a multitude of form factors, allowing users to efficiently build larger objects. While BitDrones can carry any type of 3D printed structure, we limited ourselves to constructing basic 3D geometries using very lightweight, wire mesh materials.

Physically Immersive User Interface Elements

The design of our graphical user interface elements was inspired by prior work in the 3D interface space, with the distinction that users *physically* immerse themselves in the interface, without the aid of virtual reality headsets. Borrowing from Robertson et al. [37], e.g., users surround themselves with physical, circular displays showing filenames or content that rotate automatically to stay visible to users at all times.

Physics Engine

We designed the BitDrones system with a built-in physics engine that allows drones to act under the constraint of real-world physics. Single drones, as well as groups of drones, can simulate physical momentum that corresponds to objects moving under friction, to allow greater predictability of their movements.

Other Physical Constraints

Nanodrones are generally limited in payload. The use of specific, lightweight hardware was required to achieve our design goals. For this reason, we used thin-film flexible OLED (FOLED) displays in the design of DisplayDrones. Another physical constraint is the presence of turbulence, mainly caused by the rotors of the drones. This means BitDrones cannot fly directly above or below one another, and need some clearance in order to achieve stable flight. In general, the smaller the drones, the tighter formations they can form.

IMPLEMENTATION

In BitDrones, each nano-quadcopter represents a Catom that can hover anywhere inside a volume of 4m *x* 4m *x* 3m in size. Our system currently supports up to 12 drones in simultaneous flight. BitDrones can hover 15cm from one another and their individual accuracy is 5cm per axis. As an exception, however, when placed against one another, they can fly as a group in tight formations (see Fig. 1). Users can walk around the interaction volume and interact with drones by touching and dragging them. BitDrones can be used for input, output, or for both at the same time. Simple atomic information can be displayed by a few drones, while more complex 3D data displays can be constructed using up to a dozen drones, providing basic elements for a voxel-based 3D modeling system capable of representing sparse 3D graphics in real reality.

Figure 3. Spherical, Cylindrical and Rhombicuboctahedral ShapeDrones.

Hardware

We built three different types of BitDrones, each capable of displaying information at different resolutions: PixelDrones, ShapeDrones and DisplayDrones (Figure 2).

PixelDrone Hardware

Figure 2.1 shows PixelDrone, a nano-quadcopter of our own design. Each PixelDrone is equipped with 4 brushed motors, a Micro MWC flight controller board with an IMU, and an Xbee Wi-Fi radio. PixelDrones run a customized version of MultiWii 2.3.3 as a flight control operating system. An RGB LED provides a colored voxel to the user. PixelDrones are optionally equipped with an Adafruit 128*x*64 OLED display that allows them to display text labels and simple graphics. This display is driven by an ATmega 328p chip which can be programmed wirelessly through the flight controller board. PixelDrones carry a 300mAh battery, providing them with approximately 7 min of flight time. The flight time is reduced to 3 min if an OLED display is included.

ShapeDrone Hardware

ShapeDrones consist of the same hardware as BitDrones without the OLED display. Instead, they carry a lightweight acrylic mesh fabric spun over a 3D printed frame mounted around their propellers (see Figure 2.2). The mesh acts as a diffuser for the RGB LED, allowing the entire shape to be lit up in color to act as a larger pre-shaped voxel. This frame can be printed in any shape. Similar to pre-shaped Lego™ bricks, ShapeDrones allow for the use of larger, more complex shapes that would normally be difficult to produce using a sparsely spaced set of drones. All shapes have holes in the top and bottom for airflow. We printed spherical and cubed shapes, but other shapes are possible (see Figure 3).

DisplayDrone Hardware

Figure 2.3 shows a DisplayDrone, a quadcopter 17.5 cm in size diagonally and capable of lifting heavier loads. DisplayDrone uses the same flight controller and Xbee Wi-Fi radio. MultiWii firmware was modified to drive brushless motor controllers. Each brushless motor is outfitted with a 6A electronic speed controller. DisplayDrones carry a lightweight 1280 *x* 720 LG Display FOLED touchscreen display, with a processor board running Android 5.1 mounted below the propellers. DisplayDrones allow for a high resolution, flying Graphical User Interface (GUI) that can run any Android app. Embedded light sensors measure ambient light and dynamically adjust screen brightness. The display is mounted in a 3D printed frame, curved 90° around the drone, and 15 cm in size diagonally. The Android board runs the Android 5.1 operating system, rendering this drone with full smartphone functionality. A small 2.1MP, 30 fps camera is mounted on the front of the DisplayDrone, to the bottom left of the display, allowing the drone to capture real-time video. Each drone is also outfitted with a small stereo speaker for sound. DisplayDrones carry a 1000 mAh battery, providing them with approximately 7 minutes of flight time.

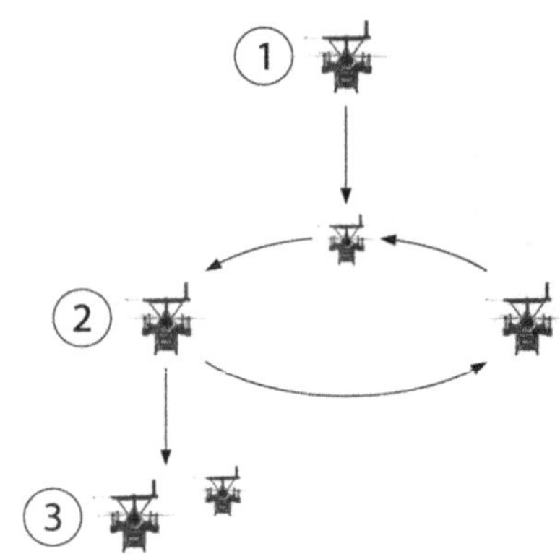

Figure 4.1. Cone tree node; 4.2. Browsing of submenu (rotational wheel); 4.3. Expanded 2nd submenu.

Flight Control

Each BitDrone has a set of reflective markers in a unique configuration, allowing its *x,y,z* position and orientation to be individually tracked by a Vicon MX Motion Capture System running Tracker 3.0 software [49]. A Mac Pro connected to the Vicon system over Ethernet provides location-based flight control information to a second Mac Pro running Windows 8. The BitDrones OS is a C# application running on this computer. It maintains each drone's state in a C# object. Objects representing all user interface elements and application functionality orchestrate the overall BitDrones system's behavior. BitDrones OS also tracks user input to the drones via the Vicon, processing input events as outlined below. For each drone, the BitDrones OS wirelessly sends motor signals to the MultiWii software over Wi-Fi to direct it to a particular location. A set of PID loops controls each drone's movements towards end positions based on user input and interface or application behaviors.

PID Loops

Each drone object in BitDrones OS has its own set of Proportional, Integral and Differential (PID) control loops [44]. These equations model each drone's current location, destination and velocity errors, calculating multipliers that affect the drone's thrust along the *x,y* and *z* axis and about the *z* axis. Each PID loop is tuned to the weight and balance of each individual class of drone. PID loops govern a drone's behavior as it flies to a destination. Once a drone has reached its destination, the MultiWii flight control firmware embedded on the drone controls a hover-in-place. This firmware has its own set of PID loops, one per motor, which controls the stability of the drone. The firmware does not rely on the Vicon system for this purpose, but on the IMU hardware in each drone.

User Input

The Vicon also tracks small reflective markers on the user's hands, allowing for detection of touch and move events by BitDrone OS. By estimating the relative positions between markers on the user's hands and the markers on the drones, the system detects interaction primitives such as touching or dragging of individual drones across the Vicon space. When a user picks up and moves a drone, this allows the BitDrone OS to respond by telling a drone to hover in the new destination. Input primitives can be combined for more complex interactions with 3D compound objects, as outlined below.

INTERACTION TECHNIQUES

Groups of drones were used to construct a number of user interface elements borrowed from 3D user interfaces:

User Interface Elements

3D Conetree Menus, Folders and Files

Figure 4 shows 6 PixelDrones flying in a group that forms a menu structure shaped as a cone tree. Our cone trees begin with a top PixelDrone node representing the root folder (see Figure 4.1). When touched, this expands into a submenu of PixelDrones flying underneath it in a circular arrangement (Figure 4.2). The name of the folder or file is displayed on the corresponding PixelDrone's display. Submenus can be browsed by gentle unimanual horizontal throws of a single drone inside the submenu. This causes the entire submenu wheel to rotate with simulated momentum and friction (Figure 4.2). When a folder in a submenu is touched, a third level of submenus can be displayed (Figure 4.3). Other drones automatically make space for this layer, while drones are automatically recruited to display its contents. When a file node is touched, drones are recruited to show the object inside the file. Currently, file contents are limited to 3D models. Due to the limited number of drones available, files are browsed in place, reusing drones from the cone tree menu to display the file. When a file is open, one BitDrone representing the menu continues to hover above the 3D contents of the file. Users can save the file and return to the menu by touching this drone.

3D Canvas and Handles

When a 3D model file is opened, its 3D boundaries are indicated by 4 PixelDrones, which act as handles to the compound object inside this 3D canvas. When drones are placed inside the boundaries of this 3D canvas, they become part of a compound object, maintaining their relative location within the 3D canvas even when the 3D canvas is moved. Handles also provide a convenient way to resize, move or rotate an entire 3D Canvas using bimanual input techniques.

3D Compound Geometries

Compound objects typically consist of ShapeDrones or PixelDrones acting as sparse voxels representing some physical 3D data structure. The advantage of using a ShapeDrone is that larger, pre-shaped 3D content can be added to the canvas without requiring PixelDrones to render that shape. While this requires a priori knowledge of the rendered shape, it partly addresses the concern that it would require many PixelDrones to create continuous large shapes. Resulting designs are automatically communicated to a Unity 3D engine, from where they can be texture mapped and exported, or 3D printed.

Figure 5. User positioning ShapeDrones within a compound object and releasing them in mid-air.

2D Contextual Flying Menus, Alerts and Video Windows

DisplayDrones are used to represent contextual menus capable of tracking the user, staying within arms length distance as they walk around the Vicon space. Contextual menus can be used to perform menu commands, like copy and paste, on selected drones. DisplayDrones can also be used as a means of alerting the user through a flying notification dialog box, to show images, or to represent remote users via a video window.

Unimanual Input Techniques

We designed a number of unimanual, bimanual and gestural input techniques that implement tangible, direct touch interactions with single drones or compound 3D objects.

Touch

Given the presence of a Vicon system, we sense touch by augmenting the user's hands with small Vicon markers. Touch is triggered when the distance of the user's fingers to a drone is smaller than 0.5 cm. Touch operates similarly to a click in a GUI. E.g., if a drone represents a folder in a menu, touching the drone reveals its content. Touching the drone again closes the content. A touch on a drone in a compound object selects the drone. A touch on two different drones in a compound object selects the entire object. DisplayDrones also sense capacitive touch within their display.

Drag

Drones can be dragged by holding them, then physically moving them to another location within the Vicon space. Upon detecting a drag, drones will hover at their new position. When drones are dragged to within the boundaries of a 3D canvas, they automatically become part of a compound object, maintaining relative position within that object.

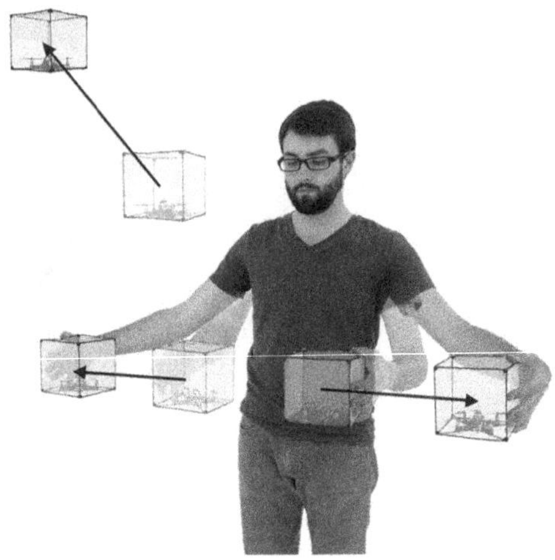

Figure 6. User resizing a compound object using a bimanual pinch gesture, by moving 2 of the total 3 drones.

Throw

Drones can also be moved to out-of-reach destinations by holding them and physically throwing them in the direction of that destination. Upon detecting a throw event, drones will fly in the direction of the throw with simulated momentum and friction that is based on their acceleration when released by the user. The simulated physics allows users to estimate the throw force required to allow a drone to move to the desired destination.

Pick Up/Remove

When not in use, drones are placed on a table in their home location. They can be activated either programmatically when summoned to display content, or by the user picking them up and then releasing them in mid-air (see Figure 5). Upon detecting a pick-up event, drones activate their propellers, hovering in position when released. Conversely, drones can be removed from a model by moving or tossing them towards the home location. Once they arrive within threshold distance of their home location, drones automatically land and spin down.

Bimanual Input Techniques

Drag Group

Holding two drones with separate hands inside a compound object and moving the hands allows users to drag an entire compound object. 3D Canvases can be dragged by moving two of their handles.

Resize Group

Compound objects can be resized by holding two drones inside the compound object, then performing a bimanual pinch gesture (Figure 6). Similarly, 3D Canvases can be resized by holding two handles– one with each hand – and performing a bimanual pinch gesture.

Rotate Group

Compound objects can be rotated by holding two drones inside a compound object and moving the hands in a joint arc, thus performing a bimanual rotation. Other drones in the model automatically adjust their relative position to the orientation of the first two drones. 3D Canvases can be rotated by holding two handles – one with each hand – and performing a bimanual rotation gesture.

While we discussed dragging, resizing and rotation of entire compound objects, our system also supports translation of both compound objects and single elements.

Gestural Input Techniques

Follow the User

Any drone has the capacity to follow the user's movement within the Vicon space. Typically, however, drones stay in their location to provide the user with spatial coherence. DisplayDrones offer a follow-me function that allows them to stay within arm's reach as the user moves around the space. This allows, e.g., contextual menu palettes to hover around the user. Although we could have implemented other gestural input techniques, such as summoning a drone from a distance [7,32], we wanted to emphasize tangibility, and focus on the use of direct touch input in this paper.

Remote Interactions

If two users are working on the same object using the BitDrones system in two different locations, drone actions are automatically synchronized between sites. That is, when a user edits the location of a BitDrone inside a compound object, its movement is automatically replicated in the corresponding remote canvas. This allows users to remotely collaborate on 3D designs with fully synchronized remote Catoms.

APPLICATION SCENARIOS

While the BitDrones OS can be used for a variety of applications, we developed a number of specific scenarios of use that demonstrate the versatility of the system. Since at present, BitDrones OS can only deploy up to 12 drones at a time, most applications were designed with sparse 3D models in mind.

3D Design

Figure 7 shows how the BitDrones OS can be used as a toolbox for 3D real reality modeling applications. In this example, users are building an architectural model out of cubed ShapeDrones. ShapeDrones can be added, removed, and moved around the model freely. PixelDrones form a bounding box that defines a 3D canvas. Users can resize the model within the canvas by holding two ShapeDrones and performing a bimanual pinch gesture. They can rotate the model by holding two ShapeDrones and moving them in an arc. We chose to model the "Cube house project" by Zafari architects [3] as it represents a sparse architecture in which drones need not stack or fly in very close proximity. More traditional architectural models requiring stacking of building blocks are more challenging to represent with the current system. The 3D design application is synchronized with a 3D visualization in Unity 3D, which allows users to render the model with texture maps and shading, as well as 3D print the model after real reality edits are completed (see Figure 8).

Figure 7. 3D editor with architectural model composed out of 3 cubed ShapeDrones.

Figure 8. Unity 3D rendering of resulting "Cube house" model [3].

Molecular Modeling

BitDrones OS allows the exploration of bonds between pairings of atoms in 3D. BitDrones can represent molecular structures in 3D in mid-air using PixelDrones or ShapeDrones, allowing users to interact with these structures in real reality. Spherical ShapeDrones are particularly useful to simulate atoms. Multiple ShapeDrones can be placed in a spatial arrangement that simulates a more complex molecule. To simulate chemical reactions, a user can manipulate individual atoms by dragging drones in or out of a molecular bond. These chemical reactions can be recorded for automated use, for example, to instruct chemistry students about molecular bonds. The drones can also simulate repulsion and attraction forces present in molecular bonding.

Interactive Real Reality InfoVis

The BitDrones system can also be used to represent points in interactive data visualizations. For instance, the position of drones can be determined by a mathematical expression, creating a physical representation of that expression. Manipulating one of the drones modifies some parameters of the expression, such as the curvature of a parabolic function. Other drones adjust their position accordingly, preserving the spatial relations as defined by the mathematical expression. PixelDrones can be used to represent live cloud-based information, such as stock market data or twitter feeds. The location of drones would, in this example, be tied to some parameter of the data. The value of stock or frequency of a retweet can, e.g., be represented by the y coordinate of a PixelDrone.

Figure 9. User inspecting a remote facility using a DisplayDrone with telepresence functionality.

Remote TelePresence

We also developed a remote telepresence application in which users embody themselves via a remote DisplayDrone that displays a Skype videoconference (Figure 9). When reciprocated, this gives users the ability to fly around a model and interact with remote participants at eye level without requiring a robotic structure. The front facing camera on the DisplayDrone shows parallax-free images of the remote user on the local DisplayDrone, and vice versa. Multiple DisplayDrones can be used for multiparty conferences, serving as a self-levitating Hydra system that preserves eye contact and head orientation cues [7].

5D Printing

When polyhedral ShapeDrones are landed on top of one another, they can create complex compound structures that resemble 3D prints. Here, ShapeDrones are connected by magnetic bonds, allowing them to remain in place even when their propellers are spun down. While extremely low-resolution at present, this allows for 5D printing technology with full synchronization between hardware and software editing of prints. We use the term 5D to indicate the real-time bi-directional nature of such edits: Future versions will be capable of real-time 3D animation of parts of the print.

LIMITATIONS

Our current implementation is limited to 12 simultaneously flying BitDrones. One limiting factor is downdraft, which restricts the ability of drones to fly directly over top of each other. A second limiting factor is drift due to turbulence when many drones are flying in a confined space. BitDrones are, however, sufficiently stable to hover within 15 cm from one another. Because of the above limitations, our current design can only be used to represent relatively sparse 3D voxel models.

The lack of pixel density and resolution achievable with our system poses considerable challenges to support tasks that require a lot of detailed information. We considered combining floating voxels with a contextual large graphic display to complement the lack of resolution and density, however, we focused our efforts on developing a proof of principle for a tangible three-dimensional floating interface rather than detailed graphic renderings.

While we claim that BitDrones are immersive without requiring user augmentation, as evidenced by the DisplayDrone touchscreen, our current implementation *does* rely on the use of a Vicon to track user's interactions with ShapeDrones and PixelDrones. Another limitation of our system is that drones produce a clearly audible noise, a considerable challenge for video telepresence.

Finally, the system as presented lacks robustness for a large number of user trials. Specifically, the power requirements to run these trials as well more robust PID loops to correct for air draft and turbulence generated by BitDrones in close proximity are technical challenges that need to be addressed in order to perform a meaning and thorough evaluation of our system.

FUTURE DIRECTIONS

We aim to increase the number of simultaneously flying BitDrones by allowing drones to connect with one another magnetically, and spin down when stacking on top of one another to create vertical structures. Another solution is to use more robust motors to compensate for downdrafts caused by other drones.

That said, we do expect to be able to scale up our architecture to include hundreds of smaller drones. One of the benefits of smaller drones is that they generate significantly less turbulence, allowing them to fly in tighter formations.

To eliminate the need for user augmentation, future BitDrones prototypes will be outfitted with capacitive sensors for all touch and drag operations. Tracking of a remote user's head movements in the video conferencing scenario will be performed using a 3D depth camera, leading to a completely marker-less system that requires no user augmentation to experience immersive 3D tangible interactions.

While we used DisplayDrones to combat the lack of pixel density and resolution, we believe when miniaturized, and with more drones, our system will more fully embody the discussed interaction scenarios.

Currently, the battery life of BitDrones is limited to about 7 minutes. To address this limitation, we propose self-docking drones that use inductive recharge stations when not active. Furthermore, the audible noise produced by BitDrones can be improved by reducing mechanical imbalances associated with off-the-shelf hardware. Although ShapeDrones are currently safe to touch due to their protective mesh, PixelDrones and DisplayDrones have exposed propellers. We will include guards in future designs, thus ensuring user safety. Our next step is to devise and evaluate our interaction language for future self-levitating tangible user interfaces.

CONCLUSIONS

We presented BitDrones, a toolbox for building interactive real reality 3D displays with nano-quadcopters as self-levitating tangible building blocks. Our prototype is a first step towards interactive self-levitating programmable matter, where the user interface is represented using Catomic structures. We discussed 3 types of BitDrones: PixelDrones, with a single color RGB LED and a small OLED display; ShapeDrones, which are BitDrones that carry a pre-molded 3D printed frame in larger geometric shapes; and DisplayDrones, with a curved thin-film 720p FOLED touchscreen and Android functionality. We presented a number of unimanual and bimanual input techniques: touching, dragging, throwing and resizing of individual drones as well as compound models, and self-levitating user interface elements, including cone trees, 3D canvases and alert boxes. Finally, we discussed applications of BitDrones with 3D design, InfoVis and telepresence scenarios that exemplify the potential functionality of this new category of real reality interfaces.

ACKNOWLEDGEMENTS

This work was funded by the generous support of NSERC of Canada and Immersion, Inc. We thank Jordan van der Kroon for his work on the first version of BitDrones OS.

REFERENCES

1. Eric Akaoka, Tim Ginn, and Roel Vertegaal. 2010. DisplayObjects: Prototyping functional physical interfaces on 3D styrofoam, paper or cardboard models. In *Proc. TEI '10*, 49-56.
2. Javier Alonso-Mora, Andreas Breitenmoser, Martin Rufli, Roland Siegwart, and Paul Beardsley. 2012. Image and animation display with multiple mobile robots. *Int. J. Rob. Res.* 31, 6 (May 2012), 753-773.
3. Atelier Zafari, Cube House Project. *http://atelier-zafari.com/cube-house/*
4. Federico Augugliaro, and Raffaello D'Andrea. 2013. Admittance control for physical human-quadrocopter interaction. *Control Conference (ECC)*, IEEE, 1805-1810.
5. Steve Benford, Chris Greenhalgh, Gail Reynard, Chris Brown, and Boriana Koleva. 1998. Understanding and constructing shared spaces with mixed reality boundaries. *ACM Trans. Comput.-Hum. Interact.* 5, 3 (September 1998), 185-223.
6. Hrvoje Benko, Ricardo Jota, and Andrew Wilson. 2012. MirageTable: Freehand interaction on a projected augmented reality tabletop. In *Proc. CHI'12*, 199-208.

7. William Buxton. 1992. Telepresence: Integrating shared task and person spaces. In *Proc. of Graphics Interface'92*, 123-129.

8. Jessica R. Cauchard, Jane, L. E., Kevin Y. Zhai, and James A. Landay. 2015. Drone & me: An exploration into natural human-drone interaction, In *Proc. UbiComp'15*, 361–365.

9. George W. Fitzmaurice, Hiroshi Ishii, and William Buxton. 1995. Bricks: Laying the foundations for graspable user interfaces. In *Proc. CHI'95*, 442-449.

10. Flight Assembled Architecture. *www.gramaziokohler.com/web/e/projekte/209.html*

11. Sean Follmer, Daniel Leithinger, Alex Olwal, Akimitsu Hogge, and Hiroshi Ishii. 2013. inFORM: Dynamic physical affordances and constraints through shape and object actuation. In *Proc. UIST'13*, 417-426.

12. Seth C. Goldstein, and Todd C. Mowry. 2004. Claytronics: A scalable basis for future robots. In *RoboSphere'04*.

13. Seth C. Goldstein, Jason D. Campbell, and Todd C. Mowry. 2005. Programmable matter. *IEEE Computer, 38, 6*, 99-101.

14. David Holman, Roel Vertegaal, Mark Altosaar, Nico Troje, and Derek Johns. 2005. PaperWindows: Interaction techniques for digital paper. In *Proc. CHI '05*, 591-599.

15. HoloLens. 2015. *www.microsoft.com/microsoft-hololens*

16. Eva Hornecker and Thomas Psik. 2005. Using ARToolKit markers to build tangible prototypes and simulate other technologies. In *Proc. INTERACT'05*, 30-42.

17. Hiroshi Ishii, and Brygg Ullmer. 1997. Tangible bits: Beyond pixels. In *Proc. CHI'97*, 234–241.

18. Hiroshi Ishii, Dávid Lakatos, Leonardo Bonanni, and Jean-Baptiste Labrune. 2012. Radical atoms: Beyond tangible bits, toward transformable materials. *Interactions* 19, 1 (January 2012), 38-51.

19. Doug L. James and Dinesh K. Pai. 2002. DyRT: Dynamic response textures for real time deformation simulation with graphics hardware. *ACM Trans. Graph.* 21, 3 (July 2002), 582-585.

20. Sergi Jordà, Günter Geiger, Marcos Alonso, and Martin Kaltenbrunner. 2007. The reacTable: Exploring the synergy between live music performance and tabletop tangible interfaces. In *Proc. TEI '07*, 139-146.

21. Mustafa Karagozler, Brian Kirby, Wei Jie Lee, Eugene Marinelli, Tze Chang Ng. 2006. Ultralight modular robotic building blocks for the rapid deployment of planetary outposts. *RASC-AL Forum*.

22. Brian Kirby, Jason Campbell, Burak Aksak, Padmanabhan Pillai, James Hoburg, Todd C. Mowry and Seth C. Goldstein. 2005. Catoms: Moving robots without moving parts. *AAAI Robotics Exhibition'05*, 1730-1731.

23. Jinha Lee, Rehmi Post, and Hiroshi Ishii. 2011. ZeroN: Mid-air tangible interaction enabled by computer controlled magnetic levitation. In *Proc. UIST'11*, 327-336.

24. Jinha Lee and Cati Boulanger. 2012. Direct, spatial, and dexterous interaction with see-through 3D desktop. In *ACM SIGGRAPH 2012 Posters*, 69.

25. Daniel Leithinger and Hiroshi Ishii. 2010. Relief: A scalable actuated shape display. In *Proc TEI'10*, 221-222.

26. MIT Flyfire. 2014 - *http://senseable.mit.edu/flyfire/*

27. Paul Milgram and Fumio Kishino. 1994. A Taxonomy of Mixed Reality Visual Display. In *IEICE Trans. Information and Systems,* vol. E77-D, no. 12, 1321-1329.

28. Paul Milgram and Herman Colquhoun Jr. 1999. A Taxonomy of Real and Virtual World Display Integration. *Mixed Reality - Merging Real and Virtual Worlds.* Springer Verlag, p. 5-30.

29. Kei Nitta, Keita Higuchi, and Jun Rekimoto. 2014. HoverBall: Augmented sports with a flying ball. In *Proc. AH'14*, Article 13.

30. Hiroki Nozaki. 2014. Flying display: A movable display pairing projector and screen in the air. In *Proc. CHI EA'14*, 909-914.

31. Yoichi Ochiai, Takayuki Hoshi and Jun Rekimoto. 2014. Pixie dust: Graphics generated by levitated and animated objects in computational acoustic-potential field. *ACM Trans. Graph.* 33, 4, 85.

32. Kevin Pfeil, Seng Lee Koh, and Joseph LaViola. 2013. Exploring 3D gesture metaphors for interaction with unmanned aerial vehicles. In *Proc. IUI'13*, 257-266.

33. Ivan Poupyrev, Tatsushi Nashida, Shigeaki Maruyama, Jun Rekimoto, and Yasufumi Yamaji. 2004. Lumen: Interactive visual and shape display for calm computing. In *Proc SIGGRAPH '04*, 17.

34. John Underkoffler and Hiroshi Ishii. 1999. Urp: A luminous-tangible workbench for urban planning and design. In *Proc. CHI '99*, 386–393.

35. Hayes Solos Raffle, Amanda J. Parkes, and Hiroshi Ishii. 2004. Topobo. In *Proc. CHI '04*, 647–654.

36. Ramesh Raskar, Greg Welch, Kok-Lim Low, and Deepak Bandyopadhyay. 2001. Shader Lamps: Animating real objects with image-based illumination. In *Proc. of the 12th Eurographics Workshop on Rendering Techniques*, Springer-Verlag, 89-102.

37. George. G. Robertson, Jock. D. Mackinlay and Stuart K. Card. 1991. Cone trees. *In Proc. CHI '91*, 189–194.

38. Michael Rubenstein, Christian Ahler and Radhika Nagpal. 2012. Kilobot: A low cost scalable robot system for collective behaviors. *ICRA'12*, 3293-98.

39. Michael Rubenstein, Alejandro Cornejo and Radhika Nagpal, R. 2014. Programmable self-assembly in a thousand-robot swarm. *Science 345(6198)*, 795-799.

40. Juergen Scheible, Achim Hoth, Julian Saal and Haifeng Su. 2013. Displaydrone: A flying robot based interactive display. In *Proc. PerDis'13*, 49-54.

41. Stefan Schneegass, Florian Alt, Jürgen Scheible, Albrecht Schmidt, and Haifeng Su. 2014. Midair displays: Exploring the concept of free-floating public displays. In *Proc. CHI EA'14,* 2035-2040.

42. Ivan Sutherland. 1965. The Ultimate Display. In *Proc. IFIP* 65, 2, 506-508.

43. Daniel Szafir, Bilge Mutlu and Terrence Fong. 2015. Communicating directionality in flying robots. In *Proc. HRI'15*, 19-26.

44. Grzegorz Szafranski, and Roman Czyba. 2011. Different approaches of PID control UAV type quadrotor. *IMAV'11*, 70-75.

45. Tomasso Toffoli and Norman Margolus. 1991. Programmable matter: Concepts and realization. *Physica D: Nonlinear Phenomena* 47, 1, 263-272.

46. George Whitesides and Bartosz Grzybowski. 2002. Self-assembly at all scales, *Science, 295(5564)*, 2418-21.

47. Andrew D. Wilson and Hrovje Benko. 2010. Combining multiple depth cameras and projectors for interactions on, above and between surfaces. In *Proc. UIST '10*, 273-282.

48. Roel Vertegaal and Ivan Poupyrev. 2008. Organic user interfaces. *Communications of the ACM* 51, 6, 26-30.

49. Vicon. 2015. *http://www.vicon.com/*

Pmomo: Projection Mapping on Movable 3D Object

Yi Zhou *
Shanghai Jiao Tong University
Shanghai, China

Shuangjiu Xiao †
Shanghai Jiao Tong University
Shanghai, China

Ning Tang
Shanghai Jiao Tong University
Shanghai, China

Zhiyong Wei
Shanghai Jiao Tong University
Shanghai, China

Xu Chen
Shanghai Jiao Tong University
Shanghai, China

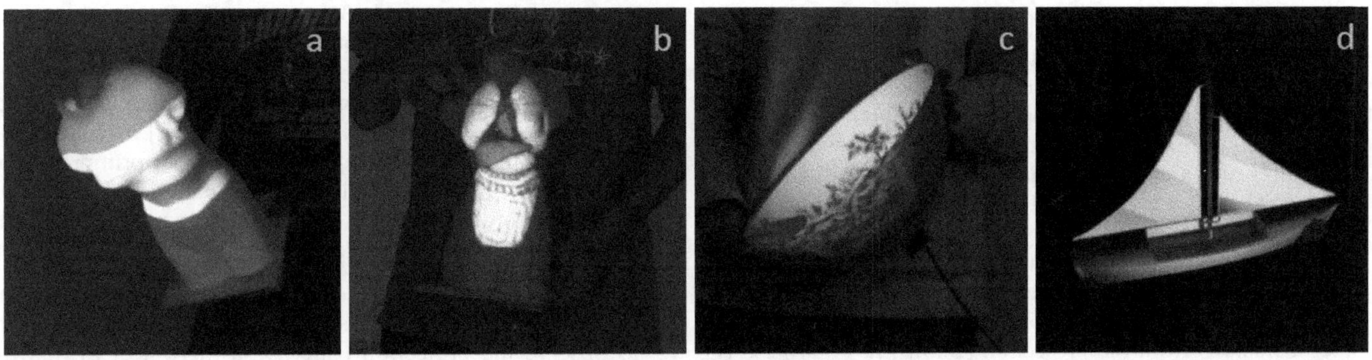

Figure 1. Augmented Reality applications of Pmomo: virtual clothes (a); animated 3D organs with beating heart and breathing lungs inside the bust model (b); virtual porcelain texture on a bowl model (c); virtual canvas on a boat model (d).

ABSTRACT

We introduce Pmomo (acronym of projection mapping on movable object), a dynamic projection mapping system that tracks the 6-DOF position of real-world object, and shades it with virtual 3D contents by projection. The system can precisely lock the projection on the moving object in real-time, even the one with complex geometry. Based on depth camera, we developed a novel and robust tracking method that samples the structure of the object into low-density point cloud, then performs an adaptive searching scheme for the registration procedure. As a fully interactive system, our method can handle both internal and external complex occlusions, and can quickly track back the object even when losing track. In order to further improve the realism of the projected virtual textures, our system innovatively culls occlusions away from projection, which is achieved by a facet-covering method. As a result, the Pmomo system enables the possibility of new interactive Augmented Reality applications that require high-quality dynamic projection effect.

*papagina@sjtu.edu.cn
†xsjiu99@cs.sjtu.edu.cn

CHI 2016, May 7–12, 2016, San Jose, California, USA.

http://dx.doi.org/10.1145/2858036.2858329

Author Keywords

Dynamic Projection Mapping; Tracking; Real-Time; Augmented Reality

ACM Classification Keywords

H.5.2 [Information Interfaces and Presentation]: Graphical user interfaces(GUI), Input devices and strategies.

INTRODUCTION

Projection Mapping, also known as Spatial Augmented Reality (SAR), is a frequently used method to create phantasms in real world. With this method, visual phenomena of real-world objects could be changed or enhanced — colour, texture and even geometry. Static projection mapping is common in multi-media shows, applied on static objects such as sculptures or buildings.

While there have been many researches on Projection Mapping on static sculptures [1][20][30][31], Dynamic Projection Mapping that can keep tracking of a moving target and aligning the projection at interactive level is still a challenge. To achieve high-quality results, the accuracy and the robustness of the system must achieve high requirements as to make light bundles be projected exactly onto the target object in real-time. Also, cumulated errors and delays in tracking can cause visible deviation between the projected texture and the real object, leading to visible artifacts. Last but not least, the users' spontaneous and rapid interactions with the object may lead to occlusions, which makes the tracking and texture projection even more challenging.

There are some works related to dynamic projection mapping. In most of the cases, there is either strong assumption on object's geometry (e.g. quasi-planar), or object's motion (e.g. preset or limited movement). Some works([4][5][11][13][17][18][19][21][32][33][34]) perform adaptive projection on deformable and movable surfaces, e.g. transforming deformable paper into virtual displays; some others perform projection on 3D objects with simple structures [27][23], or on 3D objects with very limited movement range [3].

Our system, in contrast, could handle complex geometries with 6-DOF free motion at the interactive level. In order to achieve a robust real-time alignment between the projection and the object, we developed a novel depth-image based tracking algorithm that can handle rigid objects with arbitrary structures and manage both internal and external occlusions. In addition, we use an AHRS (Altitude Heading Reference System) sensor to improve the real-time alignment performance, also solving the problem that depth-image can't perceive the rotation of symmetrical shapes. As to further improving the realism of projection, our system novelly culls off the occlusions from the projection (Shown in Figure 2). As a result, our system is unique with the combination of these features, and is robust for real interaction. With our system, real-world objects can be projected with realistic virtual exteriors, and transformed into movable 3D displays, bringing the possibility of a variety of interactive AR applications in the field of art, education and entertainment. Figure 1 illustrates some applications of our system.

In summary, we contribute a novel dynamic projection mapping system, Pmomo, that can simultaneously:

1. Align the projection with the object in 6-DOF motion environment in real-time.
2. Support object with complex geometry.
3. Cull occlusions from projection .

We organize our paper as follows: In Section 2, we review background and related techniques in this field. In Section 3, we present the pipeline and algorithm of our system. In Section 4, we report our experiment results and in Section 5 we conclude with future works.

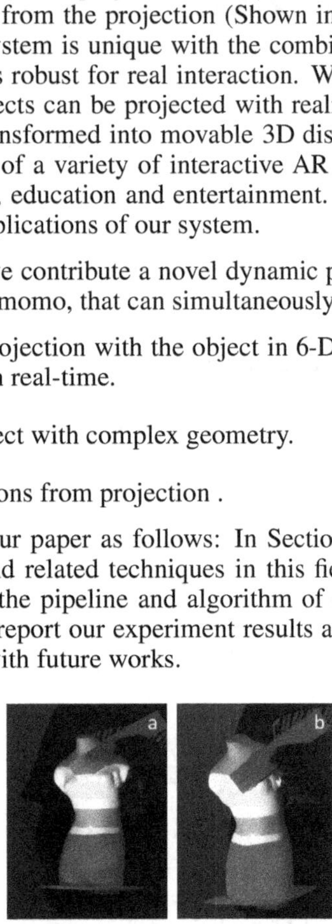

Figure 2. Occlusion culling contrast. (a) shows projection without occlusion culling; (b) shows projection with occlusion culling.

BACKGROUND

Since tracking is the main technical challenge, in this section, we will review the previous work related to dynamic projection systems, with an emphasis on the tracking method.

To achieve projection on dynamic objects, many sorts of tracking sensors have been tested. Bandyopadhyay et. al. [3] suggested to employ the magnetic tracker to obtain the position of the object. But, this type of sensor suffers from a very short working distance and the cost can be impractical. The authors of "Lumipen" [27] used a high-speed vision sensor and a projector with a high-speed optical gaze controller to track objects by keeping the target in the center of the image. This method shows good performance on high-speed balls, e.g. pingpong ball and yo-yo, but it is hard to handle free rotations. Wang et. al. [35] presented an augmented reality surgical navigation system with customized stereo cameras designed to track both the patient and instrument with tracking algorithm based on assumption of the 3-D contour of teeth. In the show of "Face Hacking" [2], optical markers were utilized to track human face and perform projection on the face. However, optical makers can visually interfere with the projection effect, and demand complex setup with multiple infrared cameras setting around the scene.

Some researchers employed the method of explicit tracking by projection features. This kind of method uses the camera to observe the projection patterns on the object to find the correct alignment. Cotting et. al. [8] injected imperceptible codes in a projector. Zheng et. al. [39] aligned the projection and the object by iteratively minimizing the visual distortion. Based on the work of Yang and Welch [37] and the work by Johnson and Fuchs [15], Resch et. al. [28] developed a shader lamp system which used a frame by frame tracking method of comparing discrete features found in the camera and projector image to achieve interactivity close to real-time. A concern of using the projection as an active light sensor is that the object can not be projected with fancy texture or rapidly changing animations since it will interfere with the alignment. Also the occlusion handling can be a problem.

Another kind of tracking method is based on depth camera. The advantage is that the depth camera is not sensitive to light condition, and does not interfere with the projection. Besides, the commodity depth camera like Kinect 2.0 provides a high resolution, a high precision and a wide field of view, making it an accessible and practical technological solution to the issue.

For state of art tracking technology on depth data, KinectFusion [14][26] presented impressive real-time 3D reconstruction capability for static scene. And in recent, DynamicFusion [25] extended the reconstruction to dynamic scene, bringing the possibility of real-time tracking and segmenting 3D objects. But for the scenario of dynamic projection alignment at interactive level, there are still many concerns. For example, it is hard to segment the target object in real interaction when the object is holding by users' hands and is often close to and overlapped with the users' body. Also there are concerns on the accumulated error, the delay for complex computing, and the failures under sharp and continuous motion.

As to registration method for 3D model, ICP(Iterative Closest Point) [6] [29] is a commonly used concept, e.g. KinectFusion employed it to track the motion of the Kinect camera. ICP registers the source and the target by a closest point scheme. It starts with an initial guess of transformation, and in each iteration, it searches for the pairs of closest points on the source and the target and refines the transform vector that minimizes the matching errors. The main worry in using ICP is that the algorithm can easily be trapped in local minima. Thus, it usually depends on the assumptions of simple scene and good initialization when using ICP for real-time tracking. E.g. [12] assumes that the scene for tracking contains only the target, the user's hands and a clear table top so that the target can be easily segmented out of the depth and color images of Kinect. Then it utilizes SIFT (Scale-invariant Feature Transform)[22] with RGB image for getting the rough pose as the initialization for ICP.

A more promising searching approach for registration is CMA-ES (Covariance Matrix Adaptation Evolution Strategy), for it can efficiently provide semi-global optimization. The optimization procedure is initiated with an ancestor, and in each iteration, offspring of the best fitter from the last generation are generated as new samples with Gaussian distribution. It stops when the fitness of the best fitter converges to a threshold, or the number of iterations reaches a threshold. Jordt et. al. [16] provided a tracking method that employs a grid to represent the objects and uses CMA-ES for searching the optimized position of each point in the grid. The number of points determines the dimension of the search space. As a result, this method can support deformable object but can not work for complex structures with large quantity of grid points. The authors of "Flexpad" [33] proposed another method for tracking the deformation of paper for projection alignment. They constructed 16 deformation models of paper and adopted CMA-ES to search the approximate optimum of weighted factors of the deformation.

Occlusion is also a big problem for tracking. Some previous works, e.g. [10] , tackle the occlusion problem by a probabilistic external occlusion map obtained by using the intensity discrepancy. KinectFusion [14] handles occlusion by means of raycasting which is quite expensive. Flexpad [33] detects occlusions created by the user's hands by distinguishing the optical feature of skin on infrared image. And [12] detects hands by building the color model for each user's skin. There are also works using multiple cameras to solve occlusions, e.g., using 16 cameras [9].

In conclusion, the previous tracking methods have the weakness of only handling limited motion range or speed, limited geometry, or limited occlusion, and in some cases, the hardware is too complicated but producing low tracking capability.

METHOD OF PMOMO

The Pmomo system tracks the 6-DOF position of real-world object, and shades it with virtual 3D textures by projection. The work flow of our system is shown in Figure 3.

In preparation phase, a 3D mesh model of the target object needs to be acquired. This can be achieved by either scanning the real object by reconstruction technologies or directly designing and 3D-printing the digital models. Based on the raw 3D mesh model, four models need to be generated for tracking and projection. The first one is a low-density point-cloud model for tracking. The second one is a high-density point-cloud model for occlusion culling. the two point-cloud models are constructed to have even point distribution. The third one is a mesh model that is remeshed from the second one. A point-facet list records the matches of the points in the second model and their adjacent facets on the third one. The fourth model is a textured model designed for projection.

In real-time phase, the first step is to obtain the transform matrix of the target object. This tracking procedure is achieved by registering the low-density point cloud model to the current depth image by a semi-global optimization algorithm. The next step is to generate a layer of facets for occlusion by using the high-density point cloud model and the point-facet list. In the third step, the textured model is covered with the occlusion facets rendered by the background color, and then transformed by the transform matrix obtained from the first step. Finally, the final rendered result is projected onto the real object.

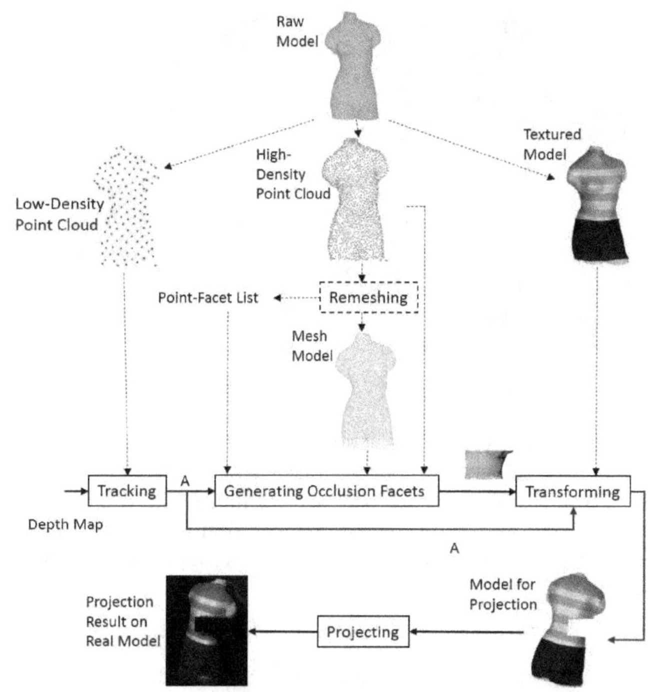

Figure 3. Overall work flow of the Pmomo system. Procedures with solid lines are run in real-time. Procedures with dash lines are done in preparation phase. ***A*** **refers to the transform matrix of the target object.**

Setup and Calibration

To achieve projection mapping, we need to build a virtual scene precisely calibrated to the real scene. Within the virtual scene, there is a 3D model that shares the same pose and position of the real object and a camera that shares the same view port of the real projector. The image rendered from the viewport of the virtual camera determines the projection content.

At each frame of Pmomo, 6-DOF position of the real object is tracked, and its correspondent virtual 3D model is then transformed and updated to that new position. Kinect 2.0 depth camera is used to capture the real-time scene and calculate the translation vector. And AHRS sensor is used to obtain the rotation vector.

The model of the AHRS sensor we use is 3DM-S10A/B from Shanghai Siyue Electronics Co., Ltd, which provides stable orientation angles (±2° for dynamic error and ±0.5° for static error) with high update rate (100fps) and no restriction in 6-DOF range and costs about twice the price of a Kinect 2.0 sensor.

Figure 4 shows the physical setup of Pmomo, consisting of a standard desktop PC (Intel i7 processor, 8 GB RAM, and an NVIDIA GeForce GTX 770 graphics card), an AHRS sensor mounted on the object, a Kinect 2.0 and a projector (Panasonic PT-BX40) placed on a shelf close to each other. The setup creates an interaction volume with best performance of about $1.5 \times 1.0 \times 1.0\ m$.

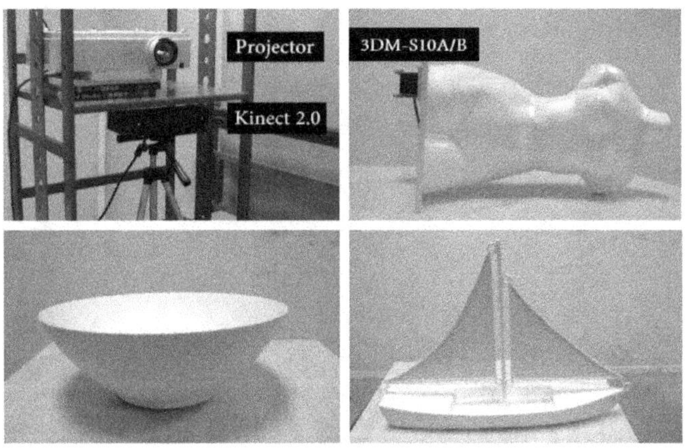

Figure 4. Physical setup and models for testing.

In the calibration work, the AHRS sensor needs to be calibrated to the coordinate of Kinect depth camera. It is mounted on the object in the way that its three axes are aligned to the object's coordinate. Let the rotation of the object in the depth sensor's coordinate be called R^k and the rotation obtained from the sensor be R^s, then,

$$R^k = R^t R^s \quad (1)$$

R^t is the rotation from depth camera's coordinate to the sensor's coordinate. R^t is obtained by the same registration algorithm described in the Tracking Section. As to get the best registration result, the object should be put in the middle of the depth camera's view field without external occlusions.

We use Kinect RGB camera to indirectly calibrate the projector to the infrared camera (the infrared image shares the same view of the depth image). First, we obtain the transform matrix between the RGB camera and the infrared camera by Zhang's method [38]. Then, we calibrate the RGB camera and the projector by [24] and obtain the transform matrix between them. Using the two calibration data, the transform matrix from Kinect infrared camera to the projector can be calculated.

Tracking

In order to achieve robust tracking and texture projection performance for randomly moving rigid object with complex geometry under arbitrary occlusions, we employs the CMA-ES based tracking method with three major modifications:

1. We reduce the complexity of tracking by homogenizing the input geometry to evenly distributed low-density point cloud;
2. We embed an occlusion detection method with self-adaptive threshold in the iterations of CMA-ES;
3. The step size of each iteration is also self-adaptive in order to handle bad tracking conditions.

Our pipeline for object tracking is shown in Figure 5. At each frame n in the running stage, we store a transform matrix A_n and an occlusion list L_n. We use the result from the last frame as the initial guess and search for a transform matrix A_n that best registers the low-density point cloud to the current depth image. Then the occlusion list is updated to indicate which points in the point cloud are occluded in the current frame. The final output of the tracking process is the predicted transform matrix as to compensate the computation and device input delay.

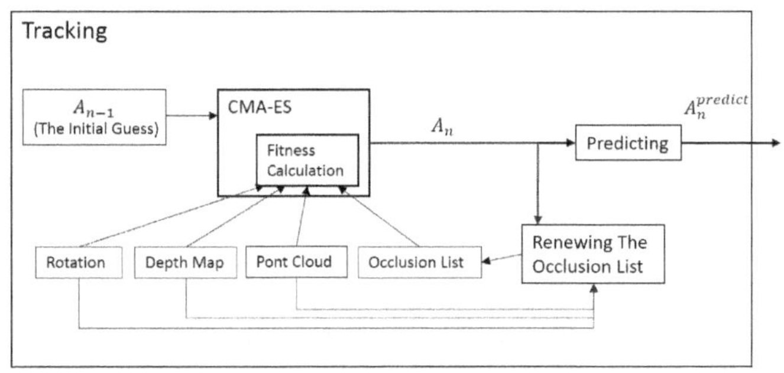

Figure 5. Work flow of Tracking. A_n is the transform matrix of the current depth image frame, $A_n^{predict}$ is the predicted transform matrix, A_{n-1} is the transform matrix of the last depth image frame.

In registration, we use the CMA-ES scheme to obtain the translation vector T_n, while the rotation vector R_n is from the AHRS sensor. First our algorithm initializes with the translation vector T from the last frame, then randomly generates some variants of T using covariance matrix. For each variant of T, the system uses it together with R_n to transform the point cloud $\{p\}$, and then selects the visible points in the transformed point cloud as point set $\{P\}$. Next, the system projects $\{P\}$ to the depth map, getting their 2-D (u, v) position. For each point P_i in $\{P\}$, the system gets its counterpart P'_i by back-projecting the pixel on (u, v) with its depth value on the depth map to the 3-D space. The RMS distance of all the pairs $\{(P'_i, P_i)\}$ is calculated as the fitness error. After that, the system picks up the vector T' that has the lowest fitness error, and updates T by T'. The above steps are iterated until the fitness error reaches a threshold.

We therefore define the following fitness term for each transformation guess.

$$F(A) = \sqrt{\frac{1}{n}\sum_{p_i \in S} ||\phi(\pi(Ap_i)) - Ap_i||^2} \quad (2)$$

where S is a set of sample points, n is the size of S, $P_i = Ap_i$ is the transformed position of p_i in the depth camera's coordinate. $P'_i = \phi(\pi(Ap_i))$ is the counterpart of P_i by depth map. The function $q = \pi(p)$ performs perspective projection of $p \in \mathbb{R}^3 = (x, y, z)^T$ to obtain $q \in \mathbb{R}^2 = (x/z, y/z)^T$ on depth image. The function $p = \phi(q)$ back-projects the q on depth image to world coordination by the depth value.

Transformed sample points invisible to the depth camera are excluded. The visibility of a transformed point P_i is determined by the satisfaction of the following two requirements:

1. If

$$Angle(\vec{n}, \vec{pk}) \leq 90^\circ \quad (3)$$

   where $\vec{n}$ refers to the normal of point P_i, $\vec{pk}$ refers to the vector from point P_i to the center of depth camera, and $Angle(\vec{n}, \vec{pk})$ refers to the angle between $\vec{n}$ and $\vec{pk}$.

2. If p_i is not marked as occluded in the occlusion list.

Self-adaptive Occlusion Detection

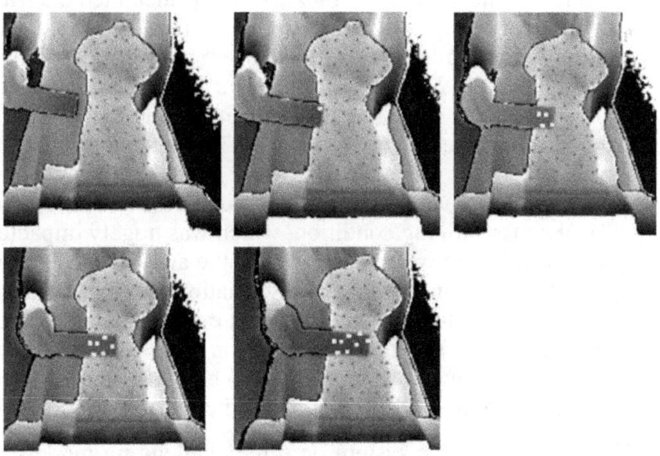

Figure 6. Detection of occluded sample points in real-time. Red points are visible points on the point cloud model, yellow ones are occluded ones at each frame. The background image is a visualized depth map.

For real-time occlusion, we observe that the changes in the set of occluded sample points are very small between two consecutive frames, as shown in Figure 6. Thus, the last frame's occlusion list can be used for the tracking of the current frame, and after obtaining the current A_n, we update the occlusion list for next frame. The occlusion list is updated by checking every transformed sample point with the following two conditions:

1. If the Equation 3 holds.
2. If

$$(depth_{real}(P) - depth_{virtual}(P)) > thr \quad (4)$$

where

$$thr = max(F(A_n), minThr) \quad (5)$$

where $minThr$ is a constant value determined by the precision of tracking. The benefit of the adaptive occlusion threshold is that it can reduce the chance of losing track due to massive misdiagnosis of occlusion points.

Step-size Control

In some cases, the CMA-ES method will fall into incorrect local optimal. For example, when a person holds a object, the algorithm might track onto the person incorrectly instead of the object. To handle this, we use an adaptive step-size for CMA-ES to generate new samples. The step-size σ affects the deviation between the ancestor and the offspring. For each frame, a default value is initially set to σ. In the iterations of CMA-ES, if the Euclidean distance between the fittest translation vector of an iteration and the translation vector from the previous frame exceeds a maximal value, our algorithm will restart the iterations with the step size σ reduced to $k\sigma$. k is the reducing scale, and we empirically set it to be 0.25. With the step-size control scheme, the system also gains the feature that when the tracking suffers from severe errors, the system will hold on around the previous position. This feature, combined with the semi-global searching scheme, provides two advantages for real interaction. First, when the system loses track of the object due to big but instant occlusions (e.g. people walking through the area between the object and Kinect camera), the tracking will hold on to the previous position for a while and when the occlusions are removed, our system can quickly track back the object in seconds. Second, if the system tracks incorrectly to a wrong place, the user can help the system track back the object by moving the object to that place with the indication of the light bundles of projection.

Delay Management

While the AHRS sensor has an insignificant input delay that is negligible, Kinect has a more apparent input delay D_k, with about 90 milliseconds for Kinect 1.0 and about 60 milliseconds for Kinect 2.0. As a result, for the process of real-time depth image registration, the rotation parameter from the AHRS sensor needs to be the one obtained D_k milliseconds before the current frame.

For the real-time projection, we use the latest rotation from the AHRS sensor, and use the predicted translation by a linear model:

$$T_n^{predict} = T_n + f * (D_c + D_k) * (T_n - T_{n-1}) \quad (6)$$

Where D_c is the computation delay, D_k is the Kinect input delay. f is the frame rate, T_n is the estimated translation vector of the nth frame, $T_n^{predict}$ is the predicted one.

Due to the noises in depth image, the tracked position will randomly fluctuate even if the model remains static, and the motion prediction term will amplify the noise. But the fluctuation is not visually evident in fast motion. Thus, Like Wang et. al. [35], we perform Extended Kalman filtering (EKF) to estimate the quasi-static pose to reduce the fluctuation when the model is static or moving slowly.

Model Constructing

In order to achieve best performance, an evenly-distributed point cloud is needed for our system. With unevenly-distributed sample points, if a dense part is occluded, the remaining sample points may not be sufficient for tracking.

The process of generating an evenly-distributed point-cloud $\{p\}$ from a mesh model has two steps. First, we generate Poisson Disk sample points on every facet with a certain density [7]. Second, we initialize $\{p\}$ as an empty point set and traverse all the Poisson-Disk-sampled points on the mesh model. If a point is close to (below a certain threshold) any points in $\{p\}$, we drop it, else add it to $\{p\}$.

Our method also generates a point-facet list while remeshing the point-cloud model for occlusion culling. A point-facet list is a list that tells which facets are adjacent to a certain point. The approach for finding the adjacent facets of point p is to traverse every facet in the remeshed model and choose the facet that contains p as one end point.

Occlusion Culling

In Pmomo, a facet-covering method is used for occlusion culling. The pre-generated high-density point cloud model and its corresponding mesh model are utilized in the method. Using the current transform matrix as input, the high-density point cloud model is aligned to the depth image, and occluded sample points are picked up by the same occlusion detection function in the tracking process. Since we obtained point-facet list for point cloud from mesh, we could easily find facets that are corresponding to the point and add them into the occlusion facets union. Then the occlusion facets are covered on the textured 3D model and are rendered by the background color which is black in the projection scene.

By overlapping black facets on the occluded part of the model, the occluders will be projected in black so that they can be culled from final projection image. The advantage of this method is that for inner occlusion condition, the occlusion facets will be covered on the invisible inner side so that not interfere with the front side.

Computation Complexity

The computation complexity of the tracking process is: $O(NMS)$. N refers to the number of points in the point cloud, M refers to the number of searching iterations, S refers to the number of offspring (translation vector variants) generated in each CMA-ES iteration. Thus, the computation complexity is independent with the size and the shape of the object.

Unlike in the tracking phase where the fitness function is iteratively computed for at most NMS times to find the optimal transform matrix, in the step of generating occlusion facets, the occlusion detection function is calculated only once. Thus, the calculation with high-density point cloud model is affordable. Moreover, the higher the density, the higher precision will the system acquire for occlusion culling.

Initialization

The initial guess of the position of the object is manually set to be around the real position. Then our algorithm will semi-globally search the right position, and within several frames, the system will automatically align to the object. Figure 7 shows the process of the automatic alignment by snapshots extracted from a real-time record.

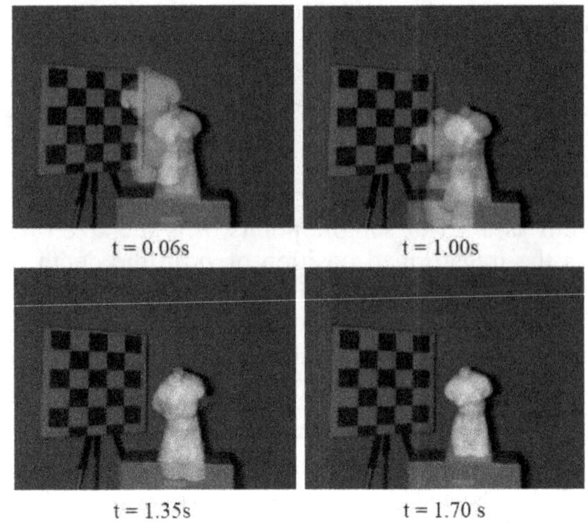

Figure 7. The initialization of tracking. The pictures are snapshots of the virtual scene with the Kinect infrared image rendered as the background.

EVALUATION

For performance estimation in previous works on dynamic projection , The authors of "Flexpad" [33] calculated the RMS depth distance between the paper's surface and the corresponding depth image, showing an average error of 6.47 mm out of over 20,217 frames of data. But it lacked the specification that under what speed of object motion the precision had been measured. The system of [28] presented the evaluation result that its translation error along each x,y,z axis varied from 0.9*mm* to 4.5*mm* for static condition and 2.1*mm* to 31.6*mm* for moving condition, which was hugely impacted by the projection texture according to the authors. Also, they lacked the speed and occlusion information for their test, and the estimation was conducted only on one car model. In our experiment, we estimate the registration error under different speed and occlusion proportion, also estimate the real-time projection alignment error caused by the motion prediction.

We demonstrate our system on three challenging models: a bust, a bowl and a sailing boat. The bust has diverse density of meshes (e.g. denser at navel and sparser on thighs); the bowl has big proportion of internal occlusion (e.g. as shown in the picture c1 in Figure 10, when the inner side is completely occluded by the outer side, the inner occlusion rate reaches 50%); the sailing boat has cut-out and sunken structure, and the area of its frontage changes sharply when it is rotating.

The three models are all 3D-printed, so we have their ground truth 3D models for testing the tracking performance of our system. We also perform test with their comparatively low-quality 3D models reconstructed by KinectFusion with Kinect 2.0 sensor.

In the experiment, ten volunteers are asked to freely move the models in the view field of Kinect camera and occasionally occlude the model by hands or stuff like cards or tapes.

For testing the tracking performance with the ground truth 3D model data, we record around 100,000 frames (30 fps, around 56 minutes in total) of tracking data for the test, with each model at least 18 minutes of testing time. So does the test with 3D model data from KinectFusion.

Tracking Precision

Occlusion Proportion: 0% - 15% Acceleration: 0 - 30 cm/s^2				
Velocity (cm/s)	0 - 10	10 - 20	20 – 30	30-50
Reg-Error (mm) Ground Truth	**5.1**	**6.1**	6.7	7.2
Reg-Error (mm) KinectFusion	**5.7**	**7.5**	8.8	9.3
Occlusion Proportion: 15% - 25% Acceleration: 0 - 30 cm/s^2				
Velocity (cm/s)	0 - 10	10 - 20	20 – 30	30-50
Reg-Error (mm) Ground Truth	9.7	11.2	12.3	18.8
Reg-Error (mm) KinectFusion	10.7	13.2	15.6	29.7
Occlusion Proportion: 0% - 15% Velocity: 0 - 20 cm/s				
Acceleration (cm/s^2)	0 - 20	20 - 40	40 - 60	
Reg-Error (mm) Ground Truth	**5.0**	5.6	9.0	
Pred-Error (mm) Ground Truth	**3.4**	4.0	11.3	
Reg-Error (mm) KinectFusion	**6.3**	6.8	12.3	
Pred-Error (mm) KinectFusion	**4.8**	6.5	15.0	

Figure 8. Average tracking error. Reg-Error refers to the registration error on depth frame; Pred-Error refers to the prediction error.

As to estimate the performance in detail and independently to models, we mix all the testing data and classify them under moving speed, acceleration and occlusion proportion. The tracking precision is estimated by the average RMS Euclidean distance error between the model and the corresponding depth image per frame as defined in equation 2.

The velocity V_n is calculated by

$$V_n = f * \|T_n - T_{n-1}\| \quad (7)$$

T_n is the translation at the frame nth, f is the update rate of the depth image frame.

The acceleration is obtained from the AHRS sensor. We use the function below to subtract the gravitational component from the raw acceleration data.

$$a_n = a_n^s - R_n^s g \quad (8)$$

a_n^s is the raw acceleration vector obtained from AHRS sensor. R_n^s is the raw rotation matrix. g is the acceleration of gravity.

The occlusion proportion includes both the external and internal occlusions. It is calculated by the ratio of sample points satisfying Equation 3 and Equation 4 to sample points satisfying Equation 3.

We set the maximal number of CMA-ES iterations for each frame as 18, number of variants per iteration as 15, with at most 270 times of fitness computation in total. And the sample point clouds we use for tracking have 270 to 280 points. In our test, the overall average time for tracking computation in each frame is 16 milliseconds.

The first two tables in Figure 8 shows the average registration error on depth frame under different categories. It shows that with the ground truth 3D model data, our system has very good real time alignment when the moving speed is under 20 cm/s and the occlusion proportion under 15%. When the velocity exceeds 30 cm/s, and the occlusion proportion exceeds 15%, the average error can exceed 18 mm, but the system is still able to track the object. And for the case of using 3D models reconstructed by KinectFusion, as expected, the tracking error is overall a bit higher, but still feasible.

As to the performance in real-time projection alignment, we demonstrate the prediction error in the third table. It is calculated by the average Euclidean distance between $T_n^{predict}$ (the prediction at the nth frame) and $T_{n+delay}$ (the registration at the future frame after the delay time). According to the result, the prediction error is not evident when the acceleration is not very sharp. But it raises with the increase of acceleration value which conforms to the fact that when the user is sharply changing the motion, e.g. shaking the object, the projection can't be aligned perfectly on the object.

Visual Effect

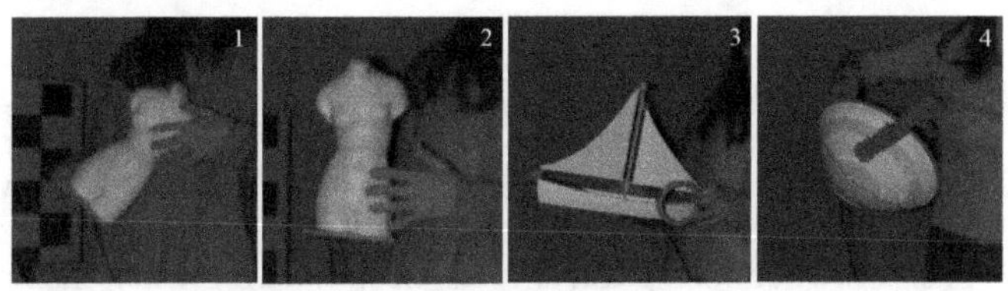

Figure 9. Tracking and occlusion culling performance observed in virtual scene. The pictures are snapshots of real-timely updated virtual scene. Picture 1 and 2 shows occlusion culling of user's fingers. Picture 3 shows occlusion culling of a roll of tape. Picture 4 shows occlusion culling of a piece of paper.

We set a virtual scene to visually monitor the tracking and occlusion culling effect on the screen. As shown in Figure 9, in the scene, we set the virtual camera at the view of the depth camera, render the infrared image as background and update the 3D model's position in real time. The numbers of points in the point-cloud model we use for generating occlusion facets are 3153, 5964, 5800 for the bust, the boat and the bowl respectively. It can be visually perceived that the occlusions are culled in high detail while providing a good real-time tracking. For example, the contour of the user's fingers can be clearly seen in the picture 1 and 2 of Figure 9. The silhouettes are not very smooth yet, but it can be improved by increasing the density of the point-cloud model.

Figure 10 shows the dynamic projection effect in the real scene. The three models in the pictures are originally white, but are shaded with artistic colorful textures. Users are asked to hold the models in hand and freely translate and rotate them. The result shows that the projection can stick on to the real model under arbitrary pose and position. Small visual artifacts of the alignment may occur when the object is in sudden acceleration (e.g. Picture a4 in Figure 10).

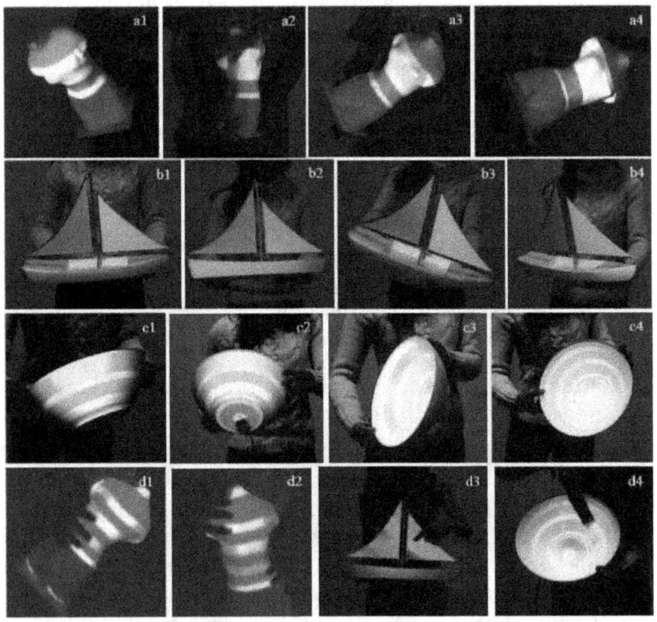

Figure 10. Real projection mapping effect of Pmomo. The white plastic models in the pictures are shaded with colorful textures by projection. All the pictures are video snapshots of projection effect on moving objects.

Failure Handling

The system loses track when the object is occluded with very big proportion or it is moved at extremely high speed. However, since our system will hold on to the previous "right" position when losing track, it can keep tracking when instant big occlusion is passing by (as shown in 11). Also since the system performs semi-global tracking, when the system fails tracking the object and projects the light bundles to an incorrect place, our volunteers can help the system track back the object in no longer than 15 seconds by moving it to the lighted place.

TRACKING WITHOUT AHRS SENSOR

Generally, our tracking algorithm could work without AHRS sensor. However, in such case more iterations would be required in CMA-ES algorithm since estimating both translation and rotation requires larger searching range. For extreme cases (e.g. when the full 6-DOF transformation between frames is very large), the algorithm needs 0.5-1.5 seconds to converge (the converged RMS error is around 10mm). That severely interferes the real-time alignment of our system

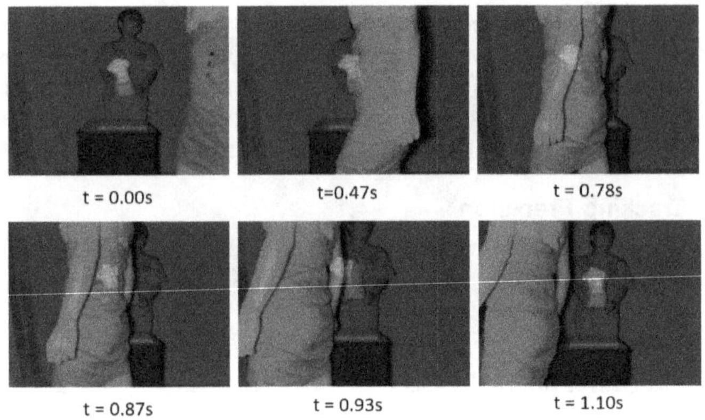

Figure 11. Case of total occlusion. At the first frame the object is tracked. Then someone walks through between the depth camera and the target object, totally occluding the object. At the last frame, the object is tracked again.

and influences its application. By adding an AHRS sensor into the system to provide the rotation data, we can achieve a much better performance at an economical price.

CONCLUSION

As a dynamic projection mapping system, Pmomo system has four notable advantages: real-time alignment for random motion, arbitrary complex geometries, robustness to occlusions and automatical occlusion culling from projection.

To achieve a robust tracking for complex shapes under occlusions, we develop a depth image based tracking algorithm with the novel features of complexity reducing, self-adaptive occlusion handling and self-adaptive step-size control. And, we also develop a facet-covering method to cull occlusions from projection.

The experimental results show that Pmomo system can perform dynamic projection mapping at a very high interactive level. And we believe the technique of Pmomo will lead to a wide range of novel augmented reality applications in art, education and commercials.

Our approach do have some limitations. First, occluders should not be too close to the target object, otherwise it will be unidentifiable on the depth image. Second, large external occlusions might lead to the fail of tracking. When the occlusion proportion exceeds a certain high level, the remaining visible part will not be sufficient for tracking. This limitation can be overcome by employing additional depth cameras with other perspectives. Third, for deformable object, our system can only tolerate small local deformation, as long as such deformation does not impact the overall fitness error of the visible sample points, but can't handle big deformations. Another limitation lies in that the camera and the projector need to be settled close to each other and of similar view direction so as to ensure they can view the same occlusions.

We are planning to develop more advanced features and capability for the system in the future: First, we want to further optimize the system by parallelizing the tracking algorithm on GPU so that the system can perform high-speed 6-DOF tracking only with depth camera. Second, we want to extend our system to support multiple objects simultaneously. Third, we want to enable the possibility of a bigger scene and a wider 360 degree projection by using multiple cameras and projectors or steerable camera-projection systems [36].

ACKNOWLEDGEMENTS

We would like to thank Dong for helping to make the calibration board and all the little gadgets that we used during the research, Wang for helping us settling the equipment, Kan for helping design the 3D models, Xiao and Yue for the revision of the paper, our dear friend Xiong and Shuai for the technical help in coding, Stephane for his emotional support, and all the volunteers, for performing the tests and giving us valuable suggestions.

REFERENCES

1. Daniel G Aliaga, Yu Hong Yeung, Alvin Law, Behzad Sajadi, and Aditi Majumder. 2012. Fast high-resolution appearance editing using superimposed projections. *ACM Transactions on Graphics (TOG)* 31, 2 (2012), 13.
2. Kuwahara Asai, Sakata Lacroix, Koyaku Kobayashi, Yamato Noda, Hiraoka Nakamura, and Doi Nagashio. 2014. "Face Hacking. (2014). `http://www.face-hacking.com`
3. Deepak Bandyopadhyay, Ramesh Raskar, and Henry Fuchs. 2001. Dynamic shader lamps: Painting on movable objects. In *Augmented Reality, 2001. Proceedings. IEEE and ACM International Symposium on*. IEEE, 207–216.
4. Hrvoje Benko, Ricardo Jota, and Andrew Wilson. 2012. MirageTable: freehand interaction on a projected augmented reality tabletop. In *Proceedings of the SIGCHI conference on human factors in computing systems*. ACM, 199–208.
5. Hrvoje Benko, Andrew D Wilson, Federico Zannier, and Hrvoje Benko. 2014. Dyadic projected spatial augmented reality. In *Proceedings of the 27th annual ACM symposium on User interface software and technology*. ACM, 645–655.
6. Paul J Besl and Neil D McKay. 1992. Method for registration of 3-D shapes. In *Robotics-DL tentative*. International Society for Optics and Photonics, 586–606.
7. Robert Bridson. 2007. Fast Poisson disk sampling in arbitrary dimensions. In *ACM SIGGRAPH*, Vol. 2007. ACM, 5.
8. Daniel Cotting, Martin Naef, Markus Gross, and Henry Fuchs. 2004. Embedding imperceptible patterns into projected images for simultaneous acquisition and display. In *Mixed and Augmented Reality, 2004. ISMAR 2004. Third IEEE and ACM International Symposium on*. IEEE, 100–109.
9. Ali O Ercan, Abbas El Gamal, and Leonidas J Guibas. 2013. Object tracking in the presence of occlusions using multiple cameras: A sensor network approach. *ACM Transactions on Sensor Networks (TOSN)* 9, 2 (2013), 16.
10. Vincent Gay-Bellile, Adrien Bartoli, and Patrick Sayd. 2010. Direct estimation of nonrigid registrations with image-based self-occlusion reasoning. *Pattern Analysis and Machine Intelligence, IEEE Transactions on* 32, 1 (2010), 87–104.
11. Chris Harrison, Hrvoje Benko, and Andrew D Wilson. 2011. OmniTouch: wearable multitouch interaction everywhere. In *Proceedings of the 24th annual ACM symposium on User interface software and technology*. ACM, 441–450.
12. Robert Held, Ankit Gupta, Brian Curless, and Maneesh Agrawala. 2012. 3D puppetry: a kinect-based interface for 3D animation.. In *UIST*. Citeseer, 423–434.
13. David Holman, Roel Vertegaal, Mark Altosaar, Nikolaus Troje, and Derek Johns. 2005. Paper windows: interaction techniques for digital paper. In *Proceedings of the SIGCHI conference on Human factors in computing systems*. ACM, 591–599.
14. Shahram Izadi, David Kim, Otmar Hilliges, David Molyneaux, Richard Newcombe, Pushmeet Kohli, Jamie Shotton, Steve Hodges, Dustin Freeman, Andrew Davison, and others. 2011. KinectFusion: real-time 3D reconstruction and interaction using a moving depth camera. In *Proceedings of the 24th annual ACM symposium on User interface software and technology*. ACM, 559–568.
15. Tyler Johnson and Henry Fuchs. 2007. Real-time projector tracking on complex geometry using ordinary imagery. In *Computer Vision and Pattern Recognition, 2007. CVPR'07. IEEE Conference on*. IEEE, 1–8.
16. Andreas Jordt and Reinhard Koch. 2013. Direct model-based tracking of 3d object deformations in depth and color video. *International journal of computer vision* 102, 1-3 (2013), 239–255.
17. Shingo Kagami and Koichi Hashimoto. 2015. Sticky projection mapping: 450-fps tracking projection onto a moving planar surface. In *SIGGRAPH Asia 2015 Emerging Technologies*. ACM, 23.
18. Mohammadreza Khalilbeigi, Roman Lissermann, Wolfgang Kleine, and Jürgen Steimle. 2012. FoldMe: interacting with double-sided foldable displays. In *Proceedings of the Sixth International Conference on Tangible, Embedded and Embodied Interaction*. ACM, 33–40.
19. Mohammadreza Khalilbeigi, Roman Lissermann, Max Mühlhäuser, and Jürgen Steimle. 2011. Xpaaand: interaction techniques for rollable displays. In *Proceedings of the SIGCHI Conference on Human Factors in Computing Systems*. ACM, 2729–2732.
20. Alvin J Law, Daniel G Aliaga, Behzad Sajadi, Aditi Majumder, and Zygmunt Pizlo. 2011. Perceptually based appearance modification for compliant appearance editing. In *Computer Graphics Forum*, Vol. 30. Wiley Online Library, 2288–2300.

21. Johnny C Lee, Scott E Hudson, and Edward Tse. 2008. Foldable interactive displays. In *Proceedings of the 21st annual ACM symposium on User interface software and technology*. ACM, 287–290.

22. David G Lowe. 1999. Object recognition from local scale-invariant features. In *Computer vision, 1999. The proceedings of the seventh IEEE international conference on*, Vol. 2. Ieee, 1150–1157.

23. David Molyneaux, Hans Gellersen, and Joe Finney. 2013. Cooperative augmentation of mobile smart objects with projected displays. *ACM Transactions on Interactive Intelligent Systems (TiiS)* 3, 2 (2013), 7.

24. Daniel Moreno and Gabriel Taubin. 2012. Simple, accurate, and robust projector-camera calibration. In *3D Imaging, Modeling, Processing, Visualization and Transmission (3DIMPVT), 2012 Second International Conference on*. IEEE, 464–471.

25. Richard A Newcombe, Dieter Fox, and Steven M Seitz. 2015. DynamicFusion: Reconstruction and Tracking of Non-rigid Scenes in Real-Time. In *Proceedings of the IEEE Conference on Computer Vision and Pattern Recognition*. 343–352.

26. Richard A Newcombe, Shahram Izadi, Otmar Hilliges, David Molyneaux, David Kim, Andrew J Davison, Pushmeet Kohi, Jamie Shotton, Steve Hodges, and Andrew Fitzgibbon. 2011. KinectFusion: Real-time dense surface mapping and tracking. In *Mixed and augmented reality (ISMAR), 2011 10th IEEE international symposium on*. IEEE, 127–136.

27. Kohei Okumura, Hiromasa Oku, and Masatoshi Ishikawa. 2012. Lumipen: Projection-based mixed reality for dynamic objects. In *Multimedia and Expo (ICME), 2012 IEEE International Conference on*. IEEE, 699–704.

28. Christoph Resch, Peter Keitler, and Gudrun Klinker. 2014. Sticky projections: a new approach to interactive shader lamp tracking. In *Mixed and Augmented Reality (ISMAR), 2014 IEEE International Symposium on*. IEEE, 151–156.

29. Szymon Rusinkiewicz and Marc Levoy. 2001. Efficient variants of the ICP algorithm. In *3-D Digital Imaging and Modeling, 2001. Proceedings. Third International Conference on*. IEEE, 145–152.

30. Behzad Sajadi, Mahdi Abbaspour Tehrani, Mehdi Rahimzadeh, and Aditi Majumder. 2015. High-resolution lighting of 3D reliefs using a network of projectors and cameras. In *3DTV-Conference: The True Vision-Capture, Transmission and Display of 3D Video (3DTV-CON), 2015*. IEEE, 1–4.

31. Christian Siegl, Matteo Colaianni, Lucas Thies, Justus Thies, Michael Zollhöfer, Shahram Izadi, Marc Stamminger, and Frank Bauer. 2015. Real-time pixel luminance optimization for dynamic multi-projection mapping. *ACM Transactions on Graphics (TOG)* 34, 6 (2015), 237.

32. Martin Spindler and Raimund Dachselt. 2009. PaperLens: advanced magic lens interaction above the tabletop. In *Proceedings of the ACM International Conference on Interactive Tabletops and Surfaces*. ACM, 7.

33. Jürgen Steimle, Andreas Jordt, and Pattie Maes. 2013. Flexpad: highly flexible bending interactions for projected handheld displays. In *Proceedings of the SIGCHI Conference on Human Factors in Computing Systems*. ACM, 237–246.

34. Jay Summet and Rahul Sukthankar. 2005. Tracking locations of moving hand-held displays using projected light. In *Pervasive Computing*. Springer, 37–46.

35. Junchen Wang, Hiromichi Suenaga, Keika Hoshi, Liangjing Yang, Etsuko Kobayashi, Ichiro Sakuma, and Hongen Liao. 2014. Augmented reality navigation with automatic marker-free image registration using 3-D image overlay for dental surgery. *Biomedical Engineering, IEEE Transactions on* 61, 4 (2014), 1295–1304.

36. Andrew Wilson, Hrvoje Benko, Shahram Izadi, and Otmar Hilliges. 2012. Steerable augmented reality with the beamatron. In *Proceedings of the 25th annual ACM symposium on User interface software and technology*. ACM, 413–422.

37. Ruigang Yang and Greg Welch. 2001. Automatic and continuous projector display surface calibration using every-day imagery. In *Proc. of 9th International Conf. in Central Europe in Computer Graphics, Visualization, and Computer Vision*. Citeseer.

38. Zhengyou Zhang. 2000. A flexible new technique for camera calibration. *Pattern Analysis and Machine Intelligence, IEEE Transactions on* 22, 11 (2000), 1330–1334.

39. Feng Zheng, Ryan Schubert, and Greg Weich. 2013. A general approach for closed-loop registration in AR. In *Virtual Reality (VR), 2013 IEEE*. IEEE, 47–50.

Combining Shape-Changing Interfaces and Spatial Augmented Reality Enables Extended Object Appearance

David Lindlbauer[1], Jens Emil Grønbæk[2], Morten Birk[2], Kim Halskov[3], Marc Alexa[1], Jörg Müller[2]
[1] TU Berlin, Berlin, Germany
[2] Department of Computer Science, Aarhus University, Aarhus, Denmark
[3] CAVI, Aarhus University, Aarhus, Denmark

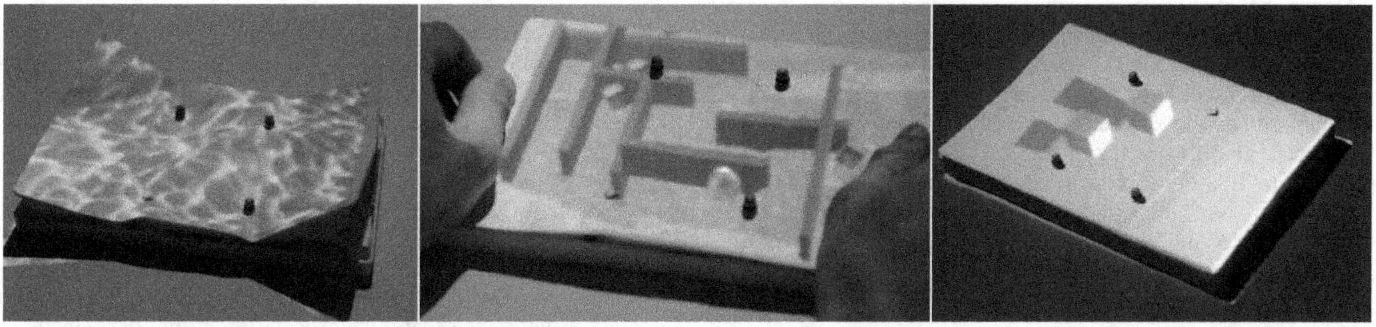

Figure 1. We combine shape-changing interfaces with spatial augmented reality. Shape-changing interfaces physically render coarse shapes and slow movements. Spatial augmented reality is used to display arbitrary textures, objects, and fast motion, directly onto the shape-changing device. This allows us to take advantage of natural depth cues and occlusion. We demonstrate the combination of the two techniques in three applications, i. e. a weather app with waves rendered physically and virtually (*left*) and a game with position of important game elements emphasized through shape change (*center*). We show capabilities of enriching shape-changing interfaces with spatial AR, e. g. the ability to render arbitrary objects and shadows (*right*).

ABSTRACT

We propose combining shape-changing interfaces and spatial augmented reality for extending the space of appearances and interactions of actuated interfaces. While shape-changing interfaces can dynamically alter the *physical appearance* of objects, the integration of spatial augmented reality additionally allows for dynamically changing objects' *optical appearance* with high detail. This way, devices can render currently challenging features such as high frequency texture or fast motion. We frame this combination in the context of computer graphics with analogies to established techniques for increasing the realism of 3D objects such as bump mapping. This extensible framework helps us identify challenges of the two techniques and benefits of their combination. We utilize our prototype shape-changing device enriched with spatial augmented reality through projection mapping to demonstrate the concept. We present a novel mechanical distance-fields algorithm for real-time fitting of mechanically constrained shape-changing devices to arbitrary 3D graphics. Furthermore, we present a technique for increasing effective screen real estate for spatial augmented reality through view-dependent shape change.

CHI'16, May 07–12, 2016, San Jose, CA, USA.

ACM 978-1-4503-3362-7/16/05...$15.00.
DOI: http://dx.doi.org/10.1145/2858036.2858457

ACM Classification Keywords

H.5.m. Information Interfaces and Presentation (e.g. HCI): Miscellaneous

Author Keywords

shape-changing interfaces; spatial augmented reality

INTRODUCTION

Shape-changing interfaces provide benefits with their ability to dynamically alter the physical shape of objects. They allow for dynamic tactile sensation (e. g. [41]), haptic data exploration (e. g. [26]) or in general diverse dynamic affordances (e. g. [23]). However, changing the physical shape of devices to resemble desired target shapes can be challenging. Especially highly detailed shapes and fast motion are hard to achieve for shape-changing interfaces, which oftentimes only feature few actuators (e. g. MorePhone with 4 actuators [18]). Typically, shape-changing devices are limited to their predefined range of possible shapes (i. e. deformations, or *states*), e. g. the faders of 2.5D displays (e. g. [27, 17], or the predefined air-chambers of pneumatic interfaces (e. g. [41]). Additionally, even if fast physical motion is possible, it can be problematic since it could startle users (cf. [26]).

While research on shape-changing interfaces focused mostly on altering objects *physically*, a wide range of prior work aimed at changing the *optical* appearance of objects and environments, for example through spatial augmented reality (*spatial AR*, e. g. [7, 31, 21, 24]) or fish tank VR (e. g. [36]). Spatial AR is defined as augmentation of real surfaces in a physically co-located way, for example through projection or displays. Users need no additional instrumentation such as see-through glasses (cf. [8]). By enriching static physical objects with visual content, users are presented with *the illusion* of different textures, shapes, or motion. These systems benefit from the high resolution of displays and projectors, typically featuring millions of pixels, whereas creating shape-changing devices with even only several hundred individually controllable elements (e. g. the 900 actuators of Relief [17]) is challenging.

However, with spatial AR, only the optical appearance of objects is dynamic, with the physical shape remaining static. Hence, benefits of shape-changing interfaces such as dynamic tactile sensation are not available. Furthermore, the ability of spatial AR to render 3D graphics is limited by the particular display surface. While it is possible to render virtual objects smaller than the surface, it is not possible to render larger objects. Display performance also depends on the viewing position. If users look at a flat display surface from a steep angle, virtual objects cannot be rendered correctly since they would exceed the bounds of the surface and thus are cut off.

In this work, we propose combining shape-changing interfaces, typically mechanically constrained and low-resolution, with spatial AR, which allows for displaying high resolution graphics and arbitrarily fast motion. Our aim is to bridge the gap between desired (real) objects and their physical and virtual representation. We argue that by incorporating perspective-corrected virtual renderings, shape-changing interfaces can come closer to an accurate visual representation of desired arbitrary objects. We use physical shape change for *dynamic tactile sensation and haptic feedback*, and combine it with spatial AR's virtual graphics for *high-frequency texture and the illusion of fast motion*.

Until now, most research has focused on either physical *or* visual change. In the field of shape-changing interfaces, devices showed co-located 2D information (e. g. MorePhone [19]), were augmented with 2.5D height field data (e. g. Relief [27]), or extended with see-through augmented reality (e. g. Sublimate [26]). None of these approaches extends shape-changing interfaces with perspective-corrected 3D visuals in a physically co-located way. We achieved perspective-correction by tracking a user's head, while physical co-location is achieved using projection mapping. In contrast to prior work, we display 3D virtual content directly on the shape-changing device, which allows us to take advantage of natural depth cues and occlusion. Additionally, this allows for leaving users uninstrumented.

Conceptually, we see the connection between shape-changing interfaces and pixel displays analogous to the connection between (coarse) 3D models and high-detail 2D textures in computer graphics. The geometry of a 3D model is created e. g. through polygonal modeling. Subsequently, low complexity is compensated for through sophisticated textures. Therefore, various techniques such as bump mapping, shadow mapping or animated texture mappings are used to increase the realism of virtual objects. We frame our exploration of shape-changing interfaces and spatial AR in this context, which allows us to identify challenges of both techniques and opportunities of their combination.

We demonstrate the concept of combining shape-changing interfaces and spatial AR with a handheld prototype, more specifically a shape-changing tablet enriched with spatial AR through projection mapping. *However, we envision future shape-changing devices to be fully covered with high-resolution displays.* More specifically, we believe that each surface of a device will incorporate controllable pixels, especially with the rise of flexible and printed displays (e. g. [18, 29]). We use projection for *simulating* such future interfaces. We present three applications demonstrating different interaction modalities: a spatial navigation application, an ambient display, and a labyrinth-style game.

In order to map the deformation of a physically constrained shape-changing device to arbitrary 3D graphics of spatial AR, we present a real-time algorithm for matching the two based on what we call *mechanical distance fields* (*MDF*). Our MDF encodes mechanical deformation in a single regular-spaced voxel grid. By matching desired virtual target shapes with MDF, we can determine the necessary deformation to represent any virtual object. This allows us to match the deformation of shape-changing interfaces in real-time to virtual 3D content, even if the device features deformation along 3 dimensions.

Furthermore, we present a technique for enhancing the quality of spatial AR by incorporating a user's perspective, which we call *view-dependent shape-change*. By dynamically altering the display surface, challenges of spatial AR introduced by limited display space can be overcome. This way, we can render virtual 3D objects which would usually be cropped due to the lack of display surface.

Contributions

- An exploration of combining physically changing devices and spatial AR for rendering arbitrary 3D objects and visual effects, framed in the context of computer graphics.
- A technique for extending the design space of shape-changing devices with rendering of complex textures, fast motion, and non-topologically equivalent shape changes.
- A real-time algorithm for matching constrained shape-changing devices to arbitrary 3D models.
- A technique for extending the effective display area for spatial AR based on view-dependent shape change.

RELATED WORK

In the following, we discuss relevant related work from the fields of shape-changing interfaces, spatial AR, and other work which aims at changing the optical appearance of objects.

Shape-changing interfaces

Shape-changing interfaces can change their physical appearance through actuation and serve as input or output devices, or both [23]. They can fulfill a large variety of aims, such as functional (e. g. communication [22], dynamic affordances [17], tactile feedback [41]), hedonic (e. g. aesthetics [41]), conveying emotions (e. g. Thrifty Faucet [38]), or exploration (cf. [23, 33]). To achieve these aims, different strategies are applied, such as different types of shape change or user interaction. 2.5D displays, for example, have been studied as input and output devices for co-located collaboration, telepresence and interaction (e. g. [26, 17]). Their actuated pins allow for user interaction (input) as well as dynamic physical shape and even for actuation of objects placed on top (e. g. inForm [17]). With PneUI [41], the topology of objects is altered with pneumatics for functional aims (e. g. game controller) or hedonic aims (e. g. shape-changing lamp). Alexander et al. demonstrated interactions with a grid of small actuated (tilt) displays [3], whereas we focus on using perspective-corrected 3D graphics.

Rasmussen et al. [33] and Coelho et al. [14] provide taxonomies of shape-changing interfaces and discuss different types of shape change, interaction, and aims. Roudaut et al. [34] quantify the resolution of shape-changing interfaces based on non-rational uniform basis splines (NURBS). As discussed by Rasmussen et al. [33] and Roudaut et al. [34], most research focused on topologically equivalent changes of shape, such as change in volume (e. g. [22]), or texture (e. g. [27, 41]). Other, non-topologically equivalent changes (e. g. dynamically adding holes to a surface) are less explored, arguably because they are hard to achieve with current technology (cf. [34]). Coelho et al. [13] changed the permeability (i. e. create holes in the surface) of a surface for architectural purposes.

Prior work focused mostly on the combination of shape-changing interfaces with 2D graphics, such as caller information or maps on shape-changing mobile phone (e. g. MorePhone[18]). Leithinger et al. enriched their 2.5D displays with virtual graphics through height field data ([27]) and see-through augmented reality ([26]). We extend this line of research by displaying perspective-corrected 3D graphics directly on shape-changing interfaces.

Spatial augmented reality

Spatial augmented reality typically refers to situations when objects are augmented by displaying virtual content onto them (cf. [8]). The virtual content is thereby *registered* to the real objects, which allows for 3D perception while exploiting natural depth cues. No other instrumentation such as see-through displays is needed, since head-tracking is used. We use an interpretation of the term spatial AR, where also displays mounted on a surface can serve as 3D virtual extension of the object (referred to as fish tank VR, e. g. pCubee [36]). With Shader Lamps, Raskar et al. [31] used projection to virtually enhance 3D-scanned objects to alter their appearance dynamically. Techniques for projection mapping (e. g. calibration, compensation for background [20]) are also applied for spatial augmented reality (cf. [8]). These techniques are used for example to support communication (e. g. [15]), urban planning, and media architecture design (e. g. [4]). Furthermore, spatial AR is used for novel interactions (e. g. MirageTable [6]) or increased immersion (e. g. RoomAlive [24]). With Illuminating Clay, Piper et al. [30] augmented a *manually* deformable surface with volume data through projection mapping.

Tangible 3D Tabletop [16, 21] combines tangible tabletop interaction with 3D projection to augment tangible objects with visual content corresponding to its physical shape, position, and orientation on the tabletop. This means that the flat tabletop surface together with the tangible objects becomes a deformable interface.

Among the applications of projection mapping in art we find the works of Valbuena. His installations, for instance Augmented Sculptures [39], are typically composed of very angular and clear-cut geometrical shapes, which, in conjunction with projection mapping, are used to create optical illusions. AntiVJ's installation, Enghien [4], employed projection mapping to create the illusions of the transformation of a building façade. The non-interactive installation first mimics moving light sources to emphasize the 3D effect; then, starts copying and apparently moving the physical, architectural features, such as windows and balconies; finally, it deconstructs these features of the building (cf. [15]).

Bermano et al. [7] augmented an animatronic head with virtual textures. They exploit the dense correspondence between the physical avatar and the virtual shape to increase realism. In our approach, we display *arbitrary* 3D objects and visuals onto shape-changing interfaces.

Appearance control

Besides using projection, researchers changed the optical properties of objects through a variety of other techniques. Alexa and Matusik [2] fabricated objects with different microstructures that yield appearance changes under different viewing angles. Furthermore, a large body of work focused on controlled surface reflectance (e. g. [28]), which allows for objects with dynamic surface properties. All of these works leave the physical shape of objects largely unchanged.

COMBINING SHAPE-CHANGING INTERFACES WITH SPATIAL AUGMENTED REALITY

In this section, we first identify challenges when designing and building shape-changing interfaces taking related work into account. We then address these challenges and frame solutions with analogies to classic techniques of computer graphics.

Challenges of shape-changing interfaces

Looking at work by Roudaut et al. [34] on shape resolution and the taxonomy of shape-changing interfaces by Rasmussen et al. [33], we can identify the main challenges we address in our work:

- *Limited granularity*: The limited number of actuators on many shape-changing interfaces makes rendering more detailed shapes or high frequency textures, such as bumpy surfaces or waves, challenging.
- *Limited speed*: Due to mechanical limitations, actuation speed is limited and high frequency motion is difficult to achieve. Additionally, even if faster motion was possible, it would often not be desirable due to user interaction (e. g. startle users, risk of jamming fingers).
- *Optical appearance relies on physical shape*: Shape-changing interfaces are bound to their physical appearance and environmental influence. Shadows thrown on the device depend largely on (uncontrolled) ambient light. Physical features such as edges of a device depend solely on the current deformation. Current shape-changing interfaces cannot change the ways users perceive them beyond physically possible changes (e. g. perceived levitation or holes).

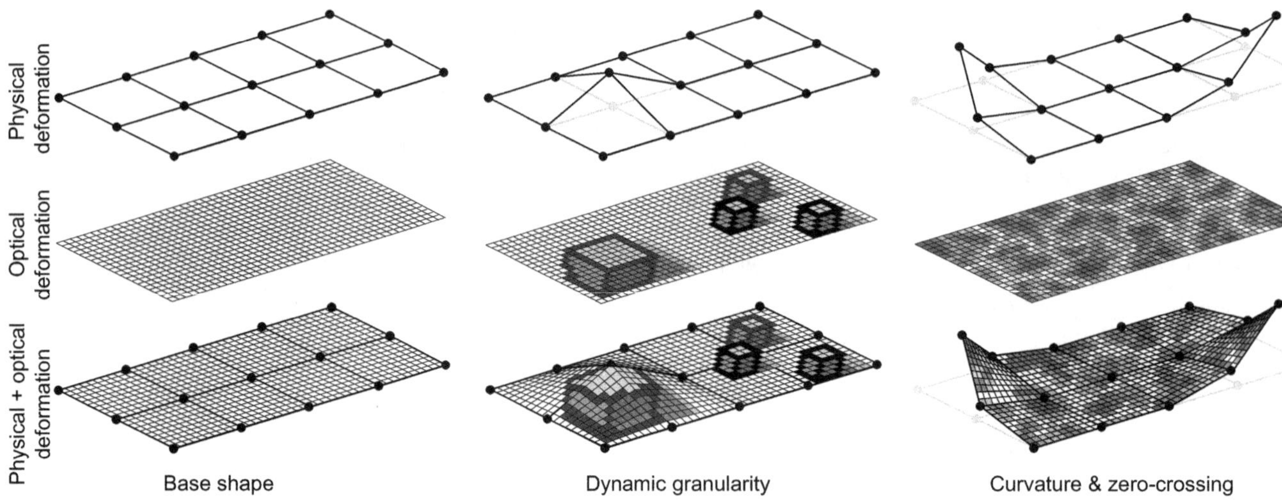

Figure 2. The physical deformation (*top row*) is combined with the optical "deformation" (*center row*), i.e., a shape-changing device with a pixel display (*bottom row*). This allows for higher and changing granularity (*center column*), as well as to render varying curvature and a high number of zero-crossing (*right*). For illustration purposes the display is rather low-resolution (15 × 30 pixels in this case). We envision the optical component to be a high resolution deformable display (e. g. >300 ppi). Figure adapted from [34].

These limitations reduce the expressiveness of shape-changing interfaces and thus their ability to achieve various goals (cf. [33]). Devices with hedonic aims such as conveying emotion (e. g. Thrifty faucet [38]) could benefit for example by not only triggering emotion through bending but also through a highly dynamic surface texture that moves and shows small spikes. Devices with functional aims such as communicating information (e. g. shape-changing mobiles phones [18, 34]) face challenges when trying to express information beyond the capability of their few actuators, e. g. indicating information about upcoming weather (e. g. strength of wind, cloudiness).

Although spatial AR does not allow for tangible change, it can give users the *illusion* of features such as high detail texture or high frequency motion. We argue that the combination with the tangibility of shape-changing interfaces opens more possibilities for researchers and designers. Additionally, we believe spatial AR benefits from the combination with shape-changing interfaces by dynamically altering the display surface.

Connection to computer graphics: 3D models and 2D textures

We frame our proposed techniques in the context of *computer graphics*, more specifically in the context of polygonal 3D models and 2D texturing. We identified three different techniques which we found to be applicable when using spatial AR to address challenges of shape-changing interfaces: *bump maps*, *animated texture maps*, and *shadow maps*. Furthermore, we show how other optical properties of shape-changing devices such as transparency or area (cf. [33]) can be altered, based on the principle of *environment maps*. We applied those principles to our current prototype.

Bump maps: Increasing perceived resolution

Bump mapping is a technique for the depiction of high detail surfaces with only low resolution 3D models, introduced by Blinn in 1978 [9]. The surface normals are changed, e. g. through perturbation, to render effects such as wrinkles or uneven surfaces, highly contributing to the perceived realism of surfaces. The geometry of the object is not modified. This allows for high realism, since the perceived intensity of light is mostly determined by the direction of the surface normal, and less by the position on the surface (cf. [9]).

Like for coarse 3D models, the granularity (i. e. the number of actuators with respect to the device area) of shape-changing devices is rather low (cf. [34]). Increasing the granularity can be challenging, since it means adding actuators and their control mechanisms on a limited area (e. g. within a tablet-sized device), and increased power consumption.

In contrast, traditional displays or video projection feature several million controllable pixels. By adding virtual graphics to shape-changing interfaces, their perceived resolution can be increased. Analogous to using bump maps on 3D geometry, shape-changing interfaces provide the coarse, low resolution geometry. 3D graphics are responsible for *simulating* high resolution spatial and temporal variations (cf. high-detail 2D textures). Like 2.5D shape displays, regular displays can change their perceived granularity through simultaneously changing (i. e. grouping) actuators, ranging from changing only 1 pixel to all pixels simultaneously.

We use shape-changing devices to render the coarse (tactile) shape of a desired target, e. g. a wave-like form mimicking a water surface, or an architectural model. We then use spatial AR for more detailed surface features such as bumps on a map for small hills and valleys, ground textures, or objects for games. Those features are displayed perspective-corrected to appear realistic to the observer. Figure 2 (*center*) illustrates changing a device with multiple control points physically, and multiple boxes added by 3D graphics, as well as the combination of the two.

Granularity also influences other features of shape-resolution, such as curvature, zero-crossings (i. e. ability to produce wave-like shapes), and closure (cf. [34]). As noted by Roudaut et al., curve deformation is challenging to achieve due to different material properties. Shape-changing devices need to be manufactured from, or covered with, flexible material

(e. g. foam or Lycra [12, 27]). Dependent on the amplitude and curvature, only a relatively low number of zero-crossings can be achieved. This problem is even more apparent for devices with only very few actuators, e. g. shape-changing mobile phones. In combination with spatial AR, the number of available perceived zero-crossings, i.e., the frequency of wave-like shapes, can be increased drastically. As illustrated in Figure 2 (*right*), low frequency waves are rendered physically, whereas smaller wave-like structures are simulated.

Animated texture maps: Increasing perceived speed

Animated texture maps are used for presenting predefined animations onto other virtual surfaces, without changing the actual surface geometry. The animations can be of arbitrary speed and size.

Roudaut et al. discuss speed and animation, however mostly in terms of a device's ability to perform actions with varying speed. While the speed of most shape-changing interfaces is fixed (i. e. determined by mechanics, cf. [34]), we argue that in combination with spatial AR, perceived speed of shape-changing devices can be varied as well as increased beyond the physically possible motion of the device. Like with *animated texture maps*, which are used to render motion on static or low resolution surfaces, we render fast virtual motion on the rather slow moving shape-changing interface. Additionally, we render motion of more fine-grained textures (e. g. small waves) and objects (e. g. a rolling marble).

The maximum velocity of a shape-changing interface depends on its implementation. Devices such as 2.5D shape displays with motorized pins rely on the actuation speed of the pins, whereas pneumatic interfaces rely on the pumping and vacuuming speed. Dielectric electro active polymers (DEAP) and shape-memory alloys (SMAs) usually rely on rather high voltage or current, respectively, and oftentimes suffer from low (de-)activation speeds. Higher velocity motion would be possible but poses challenges in terms of manufacturing as well as user interaction. When the velocity is increased above a certain threshold, it is challenging to accurately match a desired target deformation due to the mass of the object and resulting oscillation around the target position. Additionally, high speed deformation poses potential risks to users (e. g. jamming fingers or startling users).

By combining shape-changing interfaces and spatial AR, high velocity movements can be performed virtually. Physical deformation can be performed simultaneously, but with lower velocity, overcoming these potential limitations. In our prototypes, physical actuation is included in our shape-matching algorithm with predefined maximum velocity and a damping factor, allowing for smooth motion which does not distract or startle users.

Shadow maps: Adding virtual depth

Shadow mapping, introduced by Williams in 1978 [40], is a technique for efficiently rendering shadows. A shadow map is generated by rendering the scene from the light source's perspective and storing depth information (z-buffer values). Through comparison of the scene part displayed in each pixel, the position of shadows is determined. This allows for greatly increasing the realism of virtual scenes. Additionally, by moving the virtual light source, different effects such as change in time (e. g. virtual sun clock) and perceived object position (e. g. levitation) can be achieved.

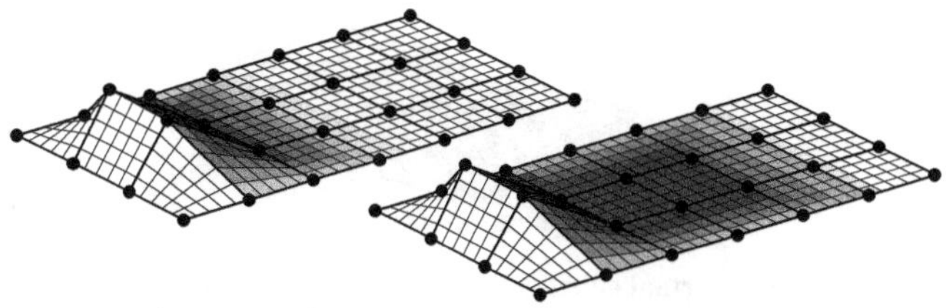

Figure 3. Two different virtual shadows for the same physical shape.

Current shape-changing interfaces are bound to their physical appearance when rendering objects. Occlusion or shadows depend on the current shape of the device and the illumination coming from the environment. Using spatial AR allows for simulating these properties. We change the position of a virtual light source in the "scene" (i. e. the environment where the tracked shape-changing device is in), effectively adding virtual shadows to a physically deformed device (see Figure 3). This allows us to illuminate the device in a way that gives users the impression of different shadows on the device, independently of ambient illumination from the environment. Previously, this was not possible since shape-changing interfaces relied on actual shadows thrown on or through the device. Shadow maps allow designers of shape-changing interfaces to convey different information, e. g. progress of long running processes, or simply time passing, indicated by shadows moving according to the sun (i. e. our virtual light source).

Additionally, *shadow maps* can be used to change optical features of shape-changing interfaces. As illustrated in Figure 4, by emphasizing or blurring physical edges, their appearance can be altered. By emphasizing soft edges with sharp lines, the edges appear more pronounced, and vice versa.

Figure 4. By adding emphasized or blurred virtual edges, perceived shapes such as the sharpness of edges can be altered.

Finally, spatial AR allows for rendering arbitrary objects on shape-changing devices. This makes it possible to render a background texture on the device as well as other objects including their virtual shadow. By exploiting this property, it is possible to create virtual objects on the device that e. g. float above the ground (see Figure 5 and 1), or disappear and reappear on demand. This shadow effect has been used in prior work to make fairies fly in front of a statue as part of culture heritage communication at a historic castle [15].

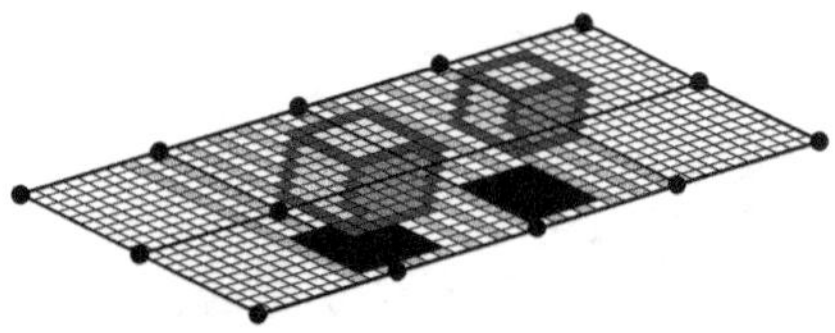

Figure 5. Two virtual cubes are rendered on the shape-changing device. By adding virtual shadows, the illusion of objects hovering over the device can be created.

Extension: Environment maps for optical effects

Besides increasing perceived resolution and speed of shape-changing devices, other optical effects such as transparency can be included in future shape-changing interfaces. By showing the background on top of the device, features such as holes (i. e. partial transparency) can be rendered. This also allows for decreasing the perceived size of a shape-changing device, which is challenging with current technology.

This approach, however, requires knowledge of the environment, such as the surface underneath, beside, or behind the shape-changing device, thus deviates from the other proposed concepts. Therefore, we consider changing these optical properties of shape-changing interfaces as *extensions* of our proposed framework.

In computer graphics, this technique is referred to as environment maps (or reflection maps, [10]). The texture of the environment is captured and stored for later mapping it on a virtual device. This allows for efficient rendering of reflection without having to render the geometry of the environment. Our current implementation uses projection mapping, which allows us to control the appearance of the environment by using it as projection surface (see Figure 6).

Figure 6. By rendering contents on the table, the device blends into the environment and can render apparent holes.

MATCHING PHYSICAL AND VIRTUAL SHAPES

One of our main objectives is to find appropriate physical and optical properties of shape-changing devices to match desired virtual objects. For achieving this goal it is therefore central to match the physical shape of the device to the shape(s) in the virtual environment.

We note that this step was comparatively simple in prior work, as it focused either on 2D information displayed on a shape-changing devices or on height field data displayed on 2.5D shape displays. In our work, however, shapes may cover an arbitrary volume in 3D and they need to be represented by shape change that goes beyond a simple change of height.

Consequently, our goal is to design an algorithm that computes the actuation parameters of the shape changing device so that the virtual model is fit as closely as possible, and in real-time. In the following we develop a model for the problem that makes the idea of a *close-to-optimal fit* precise and facilitates fast computation.

Overview

Our algorithm takes a model of an actuated device (e. g. as a set of 3D models, one per deformation state) as input. The input, representing individual actuators and states, is then encoded into multiple 3D voxel grids. Each voxel holds information on how the device needs to be deformed to cover it. The individual actuators of a device are encoded separately and later combined into a single voxel grid. This representation allows us to store actuation efficiently, and enables real-time matching.

For matching a the shape-changing device to a arbitrary target shape (e. g. given as 3D model), we first decode the target into a voxel grid as well. We then overlay the initially computed voxel grid with the target voxel grid and take the overlapping voxels into account for fitting. Subsequently, we calculate the optimal fit between the initial and the target voxel grid (see below). Figure 7 illustrates the complete algorithm.

Representation

The most important part of the algorithm lies in the representation of the shape changing device. Typically, a shape-changing device is composed of multiple actuators (i. e. degrees of freedom), which, when activated, deform a specific part of the device. The resulting motion need not be linear, which is typical for devices such as shape-changing mobile phones (e. g. [34, 18]). We assume the actuation level of each actuator to be discretized. Then we represent the *state* of the shape-changing device as $\mathbf{s} \in \mathbb{Z}_m^n$, where n is the number of actuators and m is the number of actuation levels per actuator. Note that there is a total of n^m distinct states for the device.

We represent the shape of the device as a discrete grid of voxels above the zero-state $\mathbf{s} = (0, \ldots, 0)$ of the device (i. e. all actuators in state 0). Each voxel is either *covered* or *uncovered* by the device, where covered means the surface has been pushed far enough such that the voxel is below the surface. The status of each grid point is represented by 0 for uncovered and 1 for covered. The shape is a binary vector depending on the state, i. e. $V(\mathbf{s}) \in 0, 1^{x \times y \times z}$, where x, y, z are the dimensions of the voxel grid in space. We note that the discretization need not be rectilinear, however, this is clearly the most convenient choice. We require that the voxel representation can be computed for any state $\mathbf{s}$, i. e. that the shape-changing device is known a priori.

The virtual target shape to be represented by the device is likewise represented in the volumetric grid and denoted $V_T \in 0, 1^{x \times y \times z}$. In a typical scenario the target shape is given as manifold, intersection-free mesh without boundary (sometimes referred to as 'watertight'), which can be scan-converted into the voxel representation. In principle, however, our approach works with every shape representation that can be converted into a voxel grid.

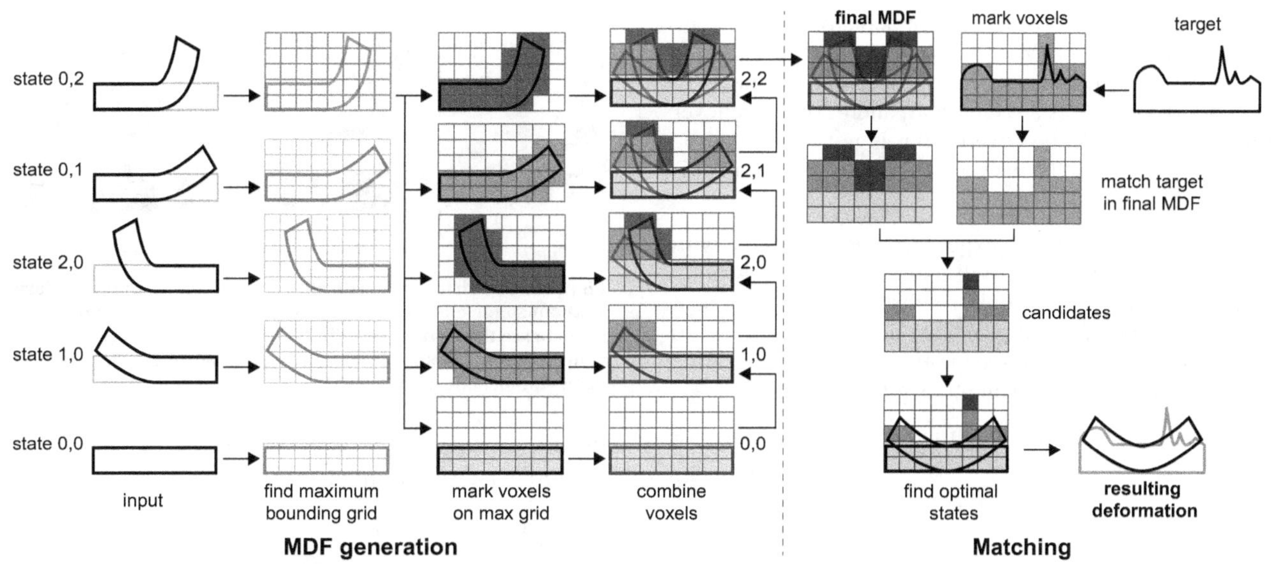

Figure 7. Computation of the initial mechanical distance field (*left*) and matching to a target shape (*right*) in a 2D example. Each state of the device (*left*) is encoded individually, and combined to a single MDF (*center*). The target object is also encoded into a voxel grid and then matched with the initial voxel grid. This gives use candidate voxels (encoding device actuation). We then find the close-to-optimal fit in the MDF, which gives us the resulting deformation for any given target (*bottom right*).

Reduction and simplification

In general it is not feasible to store the grid for each of the n^m possible states, as this would require $xyz \cdot n^m$ bits storage, which is cumbersome for realistic dimensions. In particular, real-time computation would be difficult on this data volume.

Our solution is to *decouple* the individual actuators. This means we will consider the effect of each actuator on the shape changing device *independent* of the state of the remaining actuators. This is justified as only few voxels are actually influenced by more than one actuator. Moreover, we do model the interaction of actuators, albeit probabilistically: we consider the expected value for a voxel depending on the state of an actuator, considering the likelihood of the actuation levels of the other actuators being equal. For example, if a voxel is covered at state j of actuator i for half of the possible states of the other actuators , we consider the value of the voxel to be 0.5. This means we can now store the voxel grid for each actuator i and each actuation level j independently in a real valued vector $\tilde{V}_{i,j} \in [0,1]^{x \times y \times z}$. Note that now the complexity has reduced from using n^m to using nm grids.

We further simplify this representation, making a *monotonicity* assumption: as the actuation levels of the actuators are increased, the enclosed volume never shrinks. This means, if a voxel is covered for actuator i at level j, it will also be covered for any level $j' > j$. We notice that most voxels are affected only by a single actuator. Such voxels will at some actuation level change their value from 0 to 1. Rather than storing all 0's and 1's it suffices to store the actuation level for the change. Furthermore, voxels that depend on more than one actuator usually behave linearly, and we decided to store the values of any voxel for actuator i as a function that is equal 0, then linearly increases to 1, and then stays constant. This means we can store values of each voxel for a given actuator as two actuation levels: the first actuation level at which the value is non-zero, and the first level for which the value is 1. For voxels that are dependent on a single actuator, the two values will be identical. We store this representation as two vectors $V_i^0, V_i^1 \in \mathbb{Z}_m^{x \times y \times z}$. When needed, this information can be used to quickly generate the values $\tilde{V}_{i,j}$.

The representation of the shape for a single actuator has a nice intuitive visualization: the actuation levels V_i^0, V_i^1 symbolize the 'mechanical work' that has to be exerted by the actuator to 'reach' the voxel. Based on this idea, and in analogy to distance fields (cf. [25, 11, 35]) we nickname the representation *mechanical distance field*. The generation of the MDF is visualized in Figure 7 and the result for the set of all actuators combined in our prototype is shown in Figure 8.

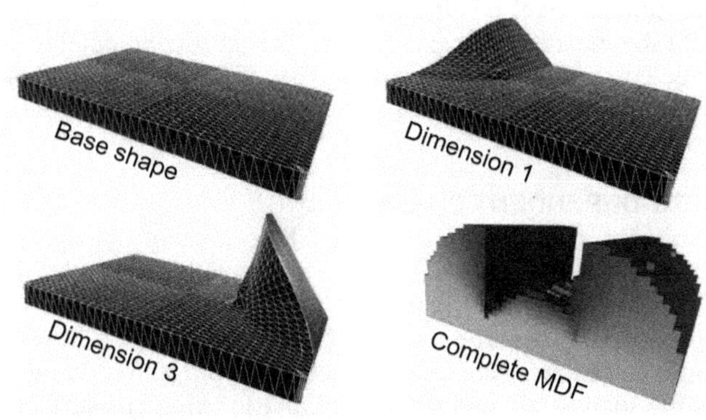

Figure 8. Example of a fully computed MDF (*bottom right*) for a device (base state 0 *top left*). Two of six dimensions of deformation (2 actuated states for dimensions 1 and 3) are illustrated. Darker green indicates larger state.

Real-time matching

Based on the precomputed grids $\tilde{V}_{i,j}$ we use a voting approach to decide on the best state $\mathbf{s}_T$: for each actuator i we check all actuation levels j and try to maximize the fit between the volume represented by the shape changing device and the target shape.

We assess the error of fit for level j for actuator i as the symmetric difference between $|\tilde{V}_{i,j} - V_T|$ (where the absolute value $|\cdot|$ is performed element-wise). Note that this evaluates to zero whenever the values are identical; and to one whenever either the voxel should be covered but is not, or should be uncovered but is. Naturally, we want to choose j such that this value is small.

On the other hand, we cannot expect to cover the shape with a single actuator so the error will usually be large. Among states with large error we would prefer those that represent most of the volume of the target shape, i. e. we would like to maximize the intersection of the target shape and the volume covered by the device. This volume is given by $\tilde{V}_{i,j} \cdot V_T$.

Based on these measures we defined the optimal state for actuator i as

$$s_i = argmin_j \frac{|\tilde{V}_{i,j} - V_T|}{\tilde{V}_{i,j} \cdot V_T}. \quad (1)$$

For numerical reasons we only consider values j for which the common interior volume $\tilde{V}_{i,j} \cdot V_T$ is bounded away from zero. Together these values form the optimal state vector $\mathbf{s}_T$.

Computational considerations

We first determine size of the voxel grid by computing the bounding box of the shape for all states. The smallest side length of the bounding box divided by the resolution r defines the side length of the voxels. In the case of our tablet prototype, as an example, we sample the deformation of each actuator $r = 33$ times, resulting in an initial voxel grid of $x = 83 \times y = 33 \times z = 59$ (~160K total) voxels, which gives us a good balance between resolution of the mechanical deformation and computational effort.

The computation of all best fits can be performed in a single iteration over all voxels, collecting the products and differences for each actuator, and calculating the best fit. For the above mentioned voxel resolution our algorithm runs in real-time, with the most expensive part being the intersection and difference computations. The complexity of the algorithm grows linearly with the number of voxels, actuators, and actuation levels.

VIEW-DEPENDENT SHAPE CHANGE

Typically, the ability of spatial AR to present 3D contents to users is limited by the display surface. If a virtual object extends beyond the bounds of the projection surface, it is cropped. This is true for projection mapping as well as for other techniques such as stereoscopic displays. We make use of the shape-changing devices' ability to extend its surface to avoid cropping without the need to wear glasses. The surface of the device is deformed depending on the angle between the user and the device. In our prototype, this means that an edge is bent upwards to increase the effective projection surface area, as shown in Figure 9.

Figure 10 illustrates the computation of the deformation. The angle α between the user and the device is calculated as the dot product between the viewing direction $\vec{u}$ and the normal of the device $\vec{n}$. We then calculate the deformation simply as $\beta = \theta - \alpha \times \frac{\alpha}{\theta}$, where θ denotes the maximum deformation of

Figure 9. The virtual world displayed on the shape-changing device (*left*). Without shape-change, the display area of the device is not sufficient for users to see the virtual world fully (i. e. walls are cropped, *center*). With view-dependent shape-change, the virtual world can be seen fully (*right*, deformation state *inlay*).

the device (in our case, 90°). We deform the actuators which are furthest away from the user.

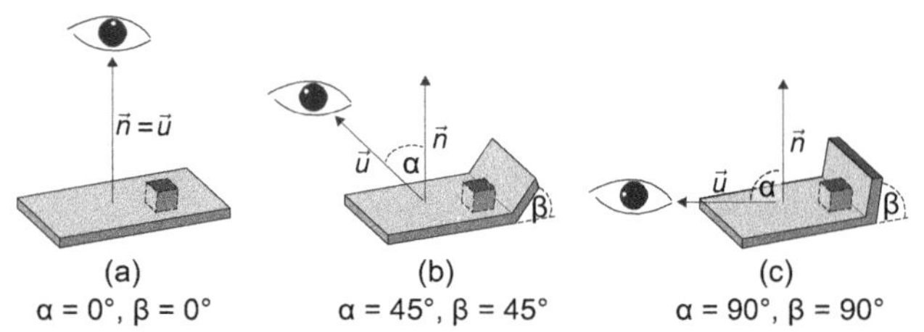

Figure 10. The shape-changing device is deformed to enable the best viewing angle on virtual objects displayed on the device.

IMPLEMENTATION

We built a prototypical shape-changing device enriched with spatial AR through projection mapping to illustrate the concept of combining the two. Software and hardware is released as open-source at `http://www.cg.tu-berlin.de/research/projects/sci-and-ar/`.

Shape-changing tablet

We built a shape-changing tablet (21 cm × 15 cm × 2 cm) from a custom 3D printed housing with 6 servo motors (Flug51 SG90) as actuators. The design of the device was inspired by Rasmussen et al. [32], who were using a smaller, phone-sized and wired version with 4 actuators for their user study. The device is powered by two 2000mAh LiPo batteries. The servo motors are controlled through an Arduino Pro Mini, connected wirelessly via Bluetooth (HC-06 module) to a computer running our custom software. The top of the device is 3D printed from flexible filament (NinjaFlex), which allows for bending according to the servo position. For increased projection quality, the top is additionally covered with a sheet of paper (see Figure 11).

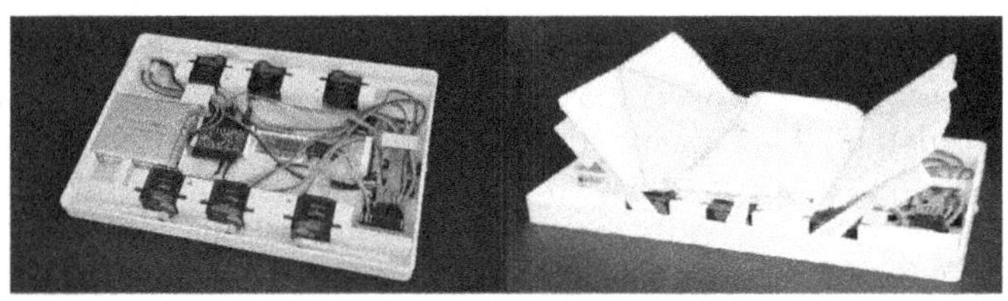

Figure 11. Shape-changing tablet containing 6 servo motors. Each corner can be bent, as well as the center of the tablet.

Projection mapping
3D projection mapping is based on having a 3D model of the physical object(s). This allows us to incorporate the device's geometry into our projection mapping system. We use a rigged 3D model of the tablet within our projection mapping application. By positioning and calibrating the projection system so that the relationship of the projection to the physical object corresponds to the virtual camera's relation to the 3D model, we can project the digital model onto the physical elements of the installation, thereby augmenting the physical object. We track the device as well as the user's head position using an OptiTrack IR tracking system. Projection is done using a single projector positioned ~2 m above the surface.

Software
The control software for our sample applications is written in Unity, with rigged models of our prototypes created in Blender. We use a proprietary software for calibrating our projection mapping system, written in Java. The MDF algorithm is developed in C++ using openFrameworks and CGAL [37]. For voxelization of shapes, we use a simple box-triangle intersection algorithm as described in [1]. The C++ application handles generation and persistence of the MDF. The Unity software handles real-time shape matching.

APPLICATIONS
We demonstrate three different applications showcasing the potential benefits of combining shape-changing interfaces with co-located 3D graphics.

Spatial navigation
Users navigate in a virtual 3D environment, i. e. a 3D map. The shape-changing device deforms according to the geometry, as depicted in Figure 12. Details of buildings and places are rendered onto the device using 3D co-located graphics. Users can rotate the device to explore the map freely. This application uses our view-dependent algorithm. When the user look from an angle, the deformation adapts, making it possible to render features extending the bounds of the projection surface (e. g. by tilting the device 90°).

Figure 12. Users navigate on a 3D map. Tilting of the tablet is compensated for using view-dependent shape-change (*inlay*).

Ambient display
Information of current and upcoming weather and the time are displayed on and with the shape-changing tablet (Figure 13). Virtual shadows of 3D objects convey information about time of the day, following a virtually moving sun. Additionally, a wave simulation is rendered physically through deformation and virtually through spatial AR. The spatial and temporal frequency depends on the strength of wind. The shape-changing tablet deforms according to the wave simulation (i. e. stronger waves result in faster and larger deformation). spatial AR is used for rendering more fine grained details of the simulation. Furthermore, we added virtual fog to convey information of wind strength. The fog seems to float on top of the tablet.

A problem with shape-changing interfaces is that sudden deformations are not always suitable. To solve this, we implemented the concept of *anticipating shape change*. First, only the virtual waves move on top of the device indicating an upcoming shape change. With a short delay, the physical movement starts.

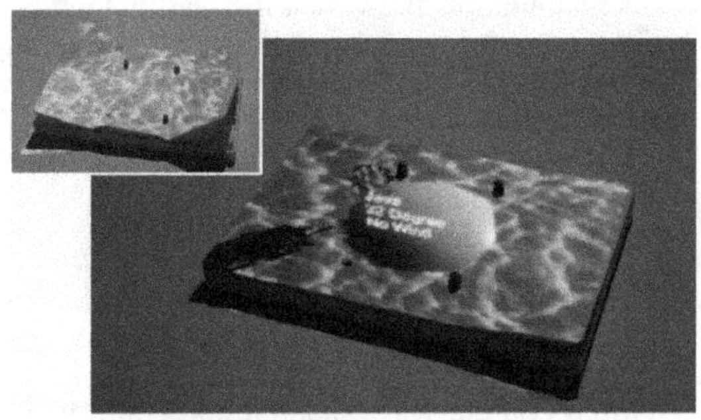

Figure 13. An ambient display conveys information about time and weather. Waves are rendered physically and virtually (*inlay*).

Labyrinth game
We implemented a simple labyrinth game (Figure 14). Users control a (virtual) rolling ball and maneuver it around to pick up colorful objects to complete a level. 3D information of the environment is rendered virtually on the device, including perspective-corrected walls, elevated game objects and high frequency ground textures. The ball also serves as input for our shape-matching algorithm and triggers deformation. Especially for regions covered by player's hands, this seeks to increase the feeling of a physical game object. Additionally, game effects such as stairs are rendered as a combination of shape-changing and virtual graphics.

Figure 14. In the labyrinth game, the position of the ball (*bottom left*) is also rendered physically for greater immersion.

Additional application using dynamic porosity
By using knowledge of the background, we can render holes into the shape. In our current implementation, the background is created by our application, therefore no camera is needed. We implemented this in a simple physical simulation (see Figure 6). The virtual ice first has holes, then breaks apart, thus revealing the underlying surface.

FIRST USER EXPERIENCES

We conducted a small informal user study with 5 participants (24 - 36 years), all students and staff from a local university, for getting first insights into our proposed technique. The study was performed as a think-aloud session. Participants, all unexperienced with both techniques, were first introduced to the applications described earlier. Thereafter, they experimented with the applications themselves.

For the ambient display, participants reacted positively to the combination of the two techniques. Participants immediately understood that physical shape-change corresponds to the virtually rendered waves. One participant noticed: "Oh, now it is clearly getting windy!" after the shape change started on the weather simulation and virtual fog was moving faster. Another participant suggested that the device should spray water, indicating that the device becomes more organic when it is enriched with 3D content. For the labyrinth game, participants felt like the virtual game world was moving whenever the ball was at a position featuring actuation.

This makes us believe that participants considered the device to resemble the objects they saw (i. e. the device *becomes* the water or the game world) and not just serve as a container for the displayed elements. This is different to other work, where virtual content was rendered and controlled through a "container" device, such as pCubee [36]. Therefore, the combination of the two techniques increased the "realism" of the device and, consequently, immersion. Also, the correspondence between the physical and virtual deformation guided users' perception. Designers and researcher can take this into consideration when designing shape-changing interfaces.

DISCUSSION AND FUTURE WORK

The combination of shape-changing interfaces and spatial AR allows for a wide variety of applications and extends the range of perceived appearances of shape-changing interfaces. It enables shape-changing interfaces (with inherently limited spatial resolution) to feature high-resolution 3D content that can overcome physical constraints. Furthermore, shape-changing interfaces only have to render slow and coarse motion, since arbitrarily fast motion can be rendered with spatial AR. Lastly, the combination can be used for rich haptic exploration of 3D visual information, allowing to better convey information.

We also believe by increasing the resolution of shape-changing interfaces, devices can not only serve as a "container" for digital content, they can also come closer to actually representing virtual objects. This would allow them to serve as *avatars* of digital objects, currently only present as on-screen content. By enabling shape-changing interfaces to effectively transition between representations, the space of possible usages can be drastically increased. Incorporating high detail 3D graphics is a step in this direction.

Tangible qualities

Spatial AR allows for changing the optical appearance of a shape-changing device, however these changes are intangible. As soon as users touch the surface which is displaying a high frequency texture, the illusion breaks. Furthermore, only the perceived physical shape of an object can be altered. Other properties such as stretchability, viscosity or strength remain unchanged. They rely completely on the resolution of the shape-changing device. Therefore, it is desirable to increase the range of shape-changing interfaces as well as the resolution of incorporated spatial AR. Including tactile technologies such as TeslaTouch [5] in future devices would help overcome restrictions of combining shape-changing interfaces with pixel displays.

Furthermore, the visual appearance of an object is tightly coupled to its physical shape. While our concept allows for altering an object's perceived appearance, large-scale changes (e. g. doubling its size) are challenging to achieve. Thus, there are limitations in terms of possible optical illusions.

Display quality

Typically, the field-of-view of spatial AR is limited. If users look at a surface from a very steep angle, graphics disappear or are cropped (like with bump maps). We partly overcome this problem with our view-dependent shape-change approach, however, this solves the problem only to a certain extent. Furthermore, spatial AR relies on perspective correction with respect to user perspective. However, we believe that our approach is superior to currently used see-through AR technologies because it features natural depth cues and occlusion.

Our vision is that spatial AR is achieved by OLED-style displays wrapping around shape-changing interfaces, or any other display technology featuring high-resolution flexible displays. Currently, our system only features displaying digital content through projection mapping with a single projector, which gave us the ability to develop and test our concepts. However, we argue that our approach is agnostic to the way the image is generated.

In the future, we plan to extend our prototype with flexible and autostereoscopic displays and an increased number of actuators.

CONCLUSION

The combination of shape-changing interfaces with spatial AR allows for a more accurate and realistic representation of content. The technique features natural depth cues and leaves users uninstrumented, which we believe is important. It allows for displaying high frequency textures, fast motion and other optical effects such as shadows on a low resolution shape-changing device. The shape-changing device complements 3D graphics with tactile sensation and physical deformation. We believe that future shape-changing interfaces should incorporate pixel displays to increase the space of possible interactions and usages.

ACKNOWLEDGEMENTS

We want to thank Alexandra Ion and Christian Lessig for feedback and discussion, and Andreas Fender for support with the projection mapping. This work has been supported by the ERC through grant ERC-2010-StG 259550 ("XSHAPE").

REFERENCES

1. Tomas Akenine-Möller. 2005. Fast 3D Triangle-box Overlap Testing. In *ACM SIGGRAPH 2005 Courses*

(SIGGRAPH '05). ACM, New York, NY, USA, Article 8. DOI:http://dx.doi.org/10.1145/1198555.1198747

2. Marc Alexa and Wojciech Matusik. 2010. Reliefs As Images. *ACM Trans. Graph.* 29, 4 (July 2010), 60:1–60:7. DOI:http://dx.doi.org/10.1145/1778765.1778797

3. Jason Alexander, Andrés Lucero, and Sriram Subramanian. 2012. Tilt Displays: Designing Display Surfaces with Multi-axis Tilting and Actuation. In *Proceedings of the International Conference on Human-computer Interaction with Mobile Devices and Services (MobileHCI '12)*. ACM, New York, NY, USA, 161–170. DOI: http://dx.doi.org/10.1145/2371574.2371600

4. AntiVJ. 2009. Enghien. (2009). Retrieved September 17, 2015 from http://antivj.com/enghien/.

5. Olivier Bau, Ivan Poupyrev, Ali Israr, and Chris Harrison. 2010. TeslaTouch: Electrovibration for Touch Surfaces. In *Proceedings of the Annual ACM Symposium on User Interface Software and Technology (UIST '10)*. ACM, New York, NY, USA, 283–292. DOI: http://dx.doi.org/10.1145/1866029.1866074

6. Hrvoje Benko, Ricardo Jota, and Andrew Wilson. 2012. MirageTable: Freehand Interaction on a Projected Augmented Reality Tabletop. In *Proceedings of the SIGCHI Conference on Human Factors in Computing Systems (CHI '12)*. ACM, New York, NY, USA, 199–208. DOI:http://dx.doi.org/10.1145/2207676.2207704

7. Amit Bermano, Philipp Brüschweiler, Anselm Grundhöfer, Daisuke Iwai, Bernd Bickel, and Markus Gross. 2013. Augmenting Physical Avatars Using Projector-based Illumination. *ACM Trans. Graph.* 32, 6, Article 189 (Nov. 2013), 10 pages. DOI: http://dx.doi.org/10.1145/2508363.2508416

8. Oliver Bimber and Ramesh Raskar. 2005. *Spatial Augmented Reality: Merging Real and Virtual Worlds*. A K Peters.

9. James F. Blinn. 1978. Simulation of Wrinkled Surfaces. In *Proceedings of the Conference on Computer Graphics and Interactive Techniques (SIGGRAPH '78)*. ACM, New York, NY, USA, 286–292. DOI: http://dx.doi.org/10.1145/800248.507101

10. James F. Blinn and Martin E. Newell. 1976. Texture and Reflection in Computer Generated Images. *Commun. ACM* 19, 10 (Oct. 1976), 542–547. DOI: http://dx.doi.org/10.1145/360349.360353

11. Harry Blum. 1967. A Transformation for Extracting New Descriptors of Shape. *Models for the Perception of Speech and Visual Form* (1967).

12. Marcelo Coelho, Hiroshi Ishii, and Pattie Maes. 2008. Surflex: A Programmable Surface for the Design of Tangible Interfaces. In *CHI '08 Extended Abstracts on Human Factors in Computing Systems (CHI EA '08)*. ACM, New York, NY, USA, 3429–3434. DOI: http://dx.doi.org/10.1145/1358628.1358869

13. Marcelo Coelho and Pattie Maes. 2009. Shutters: A Permeable Surface for Environmental Control and Communication. In *Proceedings of the International Conference on Tangible and Embedded Interaction (TEI '09)*. ACM, New York, NY, USA, 13–18. DOI: http://dx.doi.org/10.1145/1517664.1517671

14. Marcelo Coelho and Jamie Zigelbaum. 2011. Shape-changing Interfaces. *Personal Ubiquitous Comput.* 15, 2 (Feb. 2011), 161–173. DOI: http://dx.doi.org/10.1007/s00779-010-0311-y

15. Peter Dalsgaard and Kim Halskov. 2011. 3D Projection on Physical Objects: Design Insights from Five Real Life Cases. In *Proceedings of the SIGCHI Conference on Human Factors in Computing Systems (CHI '11)*. ACM, New York, NY, USA, 1041–1050. DOI: http://dx.doi.org/10.1145/1978942.1979097

16. Peter Dalsgaard and Kim Halskov. 2014. Tangible 3D Tabletops. *interactions* 5, 21 (2014). DOI: http://dx.doi.org/10.1145/2658859

17. Sean Follmer, Daniel Leithinger, Alex Olwal, Akimitsu Hogge, and Hiroshi Ishii. 2013. inFORM: Dynamic Physical Affordances and Constraints Through Shape and Object Actuation. In *Proceedings of the Annual ACM Symposium on User Interface Software and Technology (UIST '13)*. ACM, New York, NY, USA, 417–426. DOI: http://dx.doi.org/10.1145/2501988.2502032

18. Antonio Gomes, Andrea Nesbitt, and Roel Vertegaal. 2013. MorePhone: A Study of Actuated Shape Deformations for Flexible Thin-film Smartphone Notifications. In *Proceedings of the SIGCHI Conference on Human Factors in Computing Systems (CHI '13)*. ACM, New York, NY, USA, 583–592. DOI: http://dx.doi.org/10.1145/2470654.2470737

19. Antonio Gomes and Roel Vertegaal. 2015. PaperFold: Evaluating Shape Changes for Viewport Transformations in Foldable Thin-Film Display Devices. In *Proceedings of the International Conference on Tangible, Embedded, and Embodied Interaction (TEI '15)*. ACM, New York, NY, USA, 153–160. DOI: http://dx.doi.org/10.1145/2677199.2680572

20. Michael D. Grossberg, Harish Peri, Shree K. Nayar, and Peter N. Belhumeur. 2004. Making one object look like another: controlling appearance using a projector-camera system. In *Proceedings of the IEEE Computer Society Conference Computer Vision and Pattern Recognition*. DOI:http://dx.doi.org/10.1109/CVPR.2004.1315067

21. Kim Halskov, Peter Dalsgaard, and Louise Bak Stolze. 2014. Analysing Engaging Experiences with a Tangible 3D Tabletop. In *Proceedings of the Conference on Advances in Computer Entertainment Technology (ACE '14)*. ACM, New York, NY, USA, Article 29, 10 pages. DOI:http://dx.doi.org/10.1145/2663806.2663831

22. Oren Horev. 2006. 'Talking to the Hand' An exploration into shape shifting objects and morphing interfaces. (2006). Master's thesis.

23. Hiroshi Ishii, Dávid Lakatos, Leonardo Bonanni, and Jean-Baptiste Labrune. 2012. Radical Atoms: Beyond Tangible Bits, Toward Transformable Materials. *interactions* 19, 1 (Jan. 2012), 38–51. DOI: http://dx.doi.org/10.1145/2065327.2065337

24. Brett Jones, Rajinder Sodhi, Michael Murdock, Ravish Mehra, Hrvoje Benko, Andrew Wilson, Eyal Ofek, Blair MacIntyre, Nikunj Raghuvanshi, and Lior Shapira. 2014. RoomAlive: Magical Experiences Enabled by Scalable, Adaptive Projector-camera Units. In *Proceedings of the Annual ACM Symposium on User Interface Software and Technology (UIST '14)*. ACM, New York, NY, USA, 637–644. DOI: http://dx.doi.org/10.1145/2642918.2647383

25. Mark W. Jones, J. Andreas Baerentzen, and Milos Sramek. 2006. 3D Distance Fields: A Survey of Techniques and Applications. *IEEE Transactions on Visualization and Computer Graphics* 12, 4 (July 2006), 581–599. DOI: http://dx.doi.org/10.1109/TVCG.2006.56

26. Daniel Leithinger, Sean Follmer, Alex Olwal, Samuel Luescher, Akimitsu Hogge, Jinha Lee, and Hiroshi Ishii. 2013. Sublimate: State-changing Virtual and Physical Rendering to Augment Interaction with Shape Displays. In *Proceedings of the SIGCHI Conference on Human Factors in Computing Systems (CHI '13)*. ACM, New York, NY, USA, 1441–1450. DOI: http://dx.doi.org/10.1145/2470654.2466191

27. Daniel Leithinger, David Lakatos, Anthony DeVincenzi, Matthew Blackshaw, and Hiroshi Ishii. 2011. Direct and Gestural Interaction with Relief: A 2.5D Shape Display. In *Proceedings of the Annual ACM Symposium on User Interface Software and Technology (UIST '11)*. ACM, New York, NY, USA, 541–548. DOI: http://dx.doi.org/10.1145/2047196.2047268

28. Wojciech Matusik, Boris Ajdin, Jinwei Gu, Jason Lawrence, Hendrik P. A. Lensch, Fabio Pellacini, and Szymon Rusinkiewicz. 2009. Printing Spatially-varying Reflectance. *ACM Trans. Graph.* 28, 5, Article 128 (Dec. 2009), 9 pages. DOI: http://dx.doi.org/10.1145/1618452.1618474

29. Simon Olberding, Michael Wessely, and Jürgen Steimle. 2014. PrintScreen: Fabricating Highly Customizable Thin-film Touch-displays. In *Proceedings of the Annual ACM Symposium on User Interface Software and Technology (UIST '14)*. ACM, New York, NY, USA, 281–290. DOI: http://dx.doi.org/10.1145/2642918.2647413

30. Ben Piper, Carlo Ratti, and Hiroshi Ishii. 2002. Illuminating Clay: A 3-D Tangible Interface for Landscape Analysis. In *Proceedings of the SIGCHI Conference on Human Factors in Computing Systems (CHI '02)*. ACM, New York, NY, USA, 355–362. DOI: http://dx.doi.org/10.1145/503376.503439

31. Ramesh Raskar, Greg Welch, Kok-Lim Low, and Deepak Bandyopadhyay. 2001. Shader Lamps: Animating Real Objects With Image-Based Illumination. In *Proceedings of the Eurographics Workshop on Rendering Techniques*. Springer-Verlag, London, UK, UK, 89–102. http://dl.acm.org/citation.cfm?id=647653.732300

32. Majken K. Rasmussen, Timothy Merrit, Miguel Bruns Alonso, and Marianne G. Petersen. 2016. Balancing User and System Control in Shape-Changing Interfaces: a Designerly Exploration. In *Proceedings of the Tenth International Conference on Tangible, Embedded, and Embodied Interaction (TEI '16)*. ACM, New York, NY, USA.

33. Majken K. Rasmussen, Esben W. Pedersen, Marianne G. Petersen, and Kasper Hornbæk. 2012. Shape-changing Interfaces: A Review of the Design Space and Open Research Questions. In *Proceedings of the SIGCHI Conference on Human Factors in Computing Systems (CHI '12)*. ACM, New York, NY, USA, 735–744. DOI: http://dx.doi.org/10.1145/2207676.2207781

34. Anne Roudaut, Abhijit Karnik, Markus Löchtefeld, and Sriram Subramanian. 2013. Morphees: Toward High "Shape Resolution" in Self-actuated Flexible Mobile Devices. In *Proceedings of the SIGCHI Conference on Human Factors in Computing Systems (CHI '13)*. ACM, New York, NY, USA, 593–602. DOI: http://dx.doi.org/10.1145/2470654.2470738

35. Jean Serra. 1983. *Image Analysis and Mathematical Morphology*. Academic Press, Inc.

36. Ian Stavness, Billy Lam, and Sidney Fels. 2010. pCubee: A Perspective-corrected Handheld Cubic Display. In *Proceedings of the SIGCHI Conference on Human Factors in Computing Systems (CHI '10)*. ACM, New York, NY, USA, 1381–1390. DOI: http://dx.doi.org/10.1145/1753326.1753535

37. The CGAL Project. 2015. *CGAL User and Reference Manual* (4.6.3 ed.). CGAL Editorial Board. http://doc.cgal.org/4.6.3/Manual/packages.html

38. Jonas Togler, Fabian Hemmert, and Reto Wettach. 2009. Living Interfaces: The Thrifty Faucet. In *Proceedings of the International Conference on Tangible and Embedded Interaction (TEI '09)*. ACM, New York, NY, USA, 43–44. DOI: http://dx.doi.org/10.1145/1517664.1517680

39. Valbuena, Pablo. 2008. Augmented Sculpture. (2008). Retrieved September 17, 2015 from http://www.pablovalbuena.com/selectedwork/augmented-sculpture-v1/.

40. Lance Williams. 1978. Casting Curved Shadows on Curved Surfaces. *SIGGRAPH Comput. Graph.* 12, 3 (Aug. 1978), 270–274. DOI: http://dx.doi.org/10.1145/965139.807402

41. Lining Yao, Ryuma Niiyama, Jifei Ou, Sean Follmer, Clark Della Silva, and Hiroshi Ishii. 2013. PneUI: Pneumatically Actuated Soft Composite Materials for Shape Changing Interfaces. In *Proceedings of the Annual ACM Symposium on User Interface Software and Technology (UIST '13)*. ACM, New York, NY, USA, 13–22. DOI: http://dx.doi.org/10.1145/2501988.2502037

The Ethics of Unaware Participation in Public Interventions

Annika Waern
Department of Informatics and
Media, Uppsala University
Uppsala, Sweden
annika.waern@im.uu.se

ABSTRACT
Interaction design is increasingly merging with designing our everyday environment. Trialing and evaluating such designs in an ecologically valid way often requires that they be installed in public space without clearly communicating their nature as trials. This leads to *unaware participation* in what, in fact, is an experimental intervention.

This article focuses on the ethical considerations that arise from doing, and studying, interventions in public space, including but not restricted to interactive installations. It argues that under certain circumstances, such as when the known risks are low and the intervention presents sufficient support for avoiding involvement, active participation can be considered *implicit consent.* We revisit some example interventions from literature and press to scrutinize the potential risks and pitfalls associated to unaware participation.

Author Keywords
Research ethics; public intervention; public trial; implicit consent.

ACM Classification Keywords
H.5.m. Information interfaces and presentation (e.g., HCI): Miscellaneous;

INTRODUCTION

In the autumn of 2009, a video called "the piano stairs" went viral. Produced as a commercial, the video showed how a staircase in a subway entrance was visually and aurally augmented to function as the keys of a piano. The video documented how the transformation of the staircase made passers-by start using the staircase instead of the more convenient escalator located right beside it.

We all enjoy the piano stairs. The installation is fun and harmless and has a positive persuasive effect, as using the staircase is a tiny bit healthier. Intuitively, the piano staircase is a harmless intervention. Yet, many ethical boards would have raised issues with its execution: no consent forms were signed, the installation was documented by filming, and it seems like some of this documentation was published without the consent of the participants.

CHI'16, May 07-12, 2016, San Jose, CA, USA
© 2016 ACM. ISBN 978-1-4503-3362-7/16/05…$15.00
DOI: http://dx.doi.org/10.1145/2858036.2858188

At CHI 2015, Williamson and Sundén [44] presented a short article calling for an ethical discussion concerning public installations and covert observation in HCI. They observed that due to the recent 'turn to the wild' it has become increasingly common to install interactive systems in public and semi-public spaces and to study the reactions and interactions from passers-by [12]. In order to capture what Williamson and Sundén call call "users' naturalistic responses to interactive technologies", some form of covert observation is often employed in these studies. Consider again the piano staircase: In order to document the effects of the installation, it was monitored through hidden observers and inconspicuous video filming.

Williamson and Sundén focus on the issue of documentation; scrutinizing what kind of documentation can be gathered from such installations in an ethical manner. This is a well-known issue within social science and ethnography studies and there exist developed principles for observational studies in public space. Williamson and Sundén argue that similar principles can be applied to the public trial of installations.

However, with or without covert observation and data collection, installations in public space are not just observational studies but also *interventions*. They affect the participants and as such face issues not only related to data collection, but to *unaware participation.* In brief, participants that engage with the installations do not completely understand with what they engage.

This article focuses on the ethical considerations that arise from doing, and studying, interventions in public space, including but not restricted to interactive installations. The article does not engage with the question of why these studies are done, but takes as its starting point that they ARE being done. Based in a review of ethical guidelines from various fields of research as well as ethic discussions of art and games, we suggest to structure ethical considerations for public interventions around the idea that under certain circumstances, unaware participation can be considered *implicit consent.* However, this also requires that participants understand and are empowered to manage the *risks* involved with participation. The article focuses on the design of unaware participation in public interventions. It only briefly touches upon issues related to data collection as this was discussed in depth by Williamson and Sundén [44].

ETHICS OF PARTICIPATION - AN OVERVIEW

Ethical guidelines for research revolve around a tight set of concepts. One such concept is the *risk* that a participant faces in getting involved in a study, balanced against its potential usefulness. Another is *informed consent*, the right for the participants to be informed about the purpose, procedure and risk of the study, as well as their right to decline to participate. However, what is considered acceptable levels of risk and the related requirements on informed consent vary greatly between fields.

While ethical guidelines need to be informed by national and international law, they are not entirely defined by it. The discussion below will first summarize such ethical frameworks that have articulated by well-established research associations. These are well in line with legal regulations but will sometimes go beyond them. Next follows a summary of the ethical discussions ongoing in the fields of art and game design. These discussions have not been codified into generally established guidelines and may not even have been vetted against legal concerns.

Medicine and Psychology

Shaped by a history of transgressions, risk assessment and risk avoidance are central concerns to the ethical guidelines in medicine and psychology. While acknowledging that "in medical practice and in medical research, most interventions involve risks and burdens", the World Medical Association declaration on ethical principles for medical research on humans [46] explicitly state that studies must never prioritize knowledge gain over the health of study participants. In a similar vein, the British psychology association states that "where a tension arises between the legitimate needs of research and the avoidance of risk, reasoned judgment should be applied". The same guidelines also stress that psychologists need to be sensitive to any potential impact of their interventions, such as "the possibility of individual distress that may be caused unwittingly".

The APA guidelines [2] do not explicitly require such deliberation, but since they require that participants be informed about reasonably foreseeable factors that may influence their willingness to participate, some such deliberation is still required. The APA guidelines are interesting, as they also deal with the use of deception which has been a common tool in psychology studies. The guidelines state that participants must not be deceived about the nature of studies that are "reasonably expected to cause physical pain or severe emotional distress". showing that such studies are possible. The British guidelines instead highlight the respect of the *autonomy* of participants, advising that studies should ensure that participants can chose their own course of action, including aborting their participation or withdrawing their consent.

Lack of consent is considered ethically problematic in medicine and psychology, but the seriousness of the issue depends on the effects that participation may have on subjects. The most severe restrictions are found in medicine, where the experimental conditions are likely to influence and can have serious consequences for participants. The WMA declaration on ethical principles for medical research on humans [46] disallow it altogether, as consent must be sought from a legal representative of the participant (patient) if the participant herself is unable to give consent. In addition, the WMA guidelines require that such individuals must not be recruited as long as there are alternative participants, that the study must benefit them personally or a group that they represent, and "the research entails only minimal risk and minimal burden". The American psychological association states that psychologists may dispense with informed consent only when "research would not reasonably be assumed to create distress or harm" [1].

Finally, psychology and medical ethics typically take special measures to protect vulnerable populations. The British psychological society [10] stresses that children as well as people who otherwise lack capacity should be "given ample opportunity to understand the nature, purpose and anticipated outcomes of any research participation, so that they may give consent to the extent that their capabilities allow".

To briefly summarize, the ethical guidelines in the fields of psychology and medicine are primarily concerned with managing the risks for harm and discomfort for participants, and for this reason place high demands on informed consent.

Ethics of Sociology and Ethnography

Studies in sociology are less interventionist and typically entail low risk for participants. Hence, the ethical guidelines for sociological studies tend to place less weight on risk management than those of psychology and medicine. The American sociological association explicitly allows sociologists to conduct research in public places without obtaining consent [3]. However, interventionist studies in public places should still acquire consent unless "the research involves no more than minimal risk for research participants, and the research could not practicably be carried out were informed consent to be required" [3].

It must still be acknowledged that even ethnographic studies always entail some level of intervention, and as such risk affecting participants in negative ways. Murphy and Dingwall [35] discuss specifically the risks involved with publication, where participants may be represented in a way that upset them or expose them to less favorable public attention. More direct effects are also non-ignorable, such as the risk to upset, worry or offend participants in ways that can potentially be harmful (such as re-invoking previous traumas [18]). Finally, ethical issues may arise when the ethnographer leaves the field [14], as the ethnographer has developed a double relationship to the observed - as friend as well as observer. A pertinent question concerns what responsibility the observer has towards the observed, once the observations are concluded [42].

As already discussed by Williamson and Sundén, ethnographic studies face ethical issues in closed communities where access is not granted to anybody [25]. This issue has been pertinent in particular in studies of online communities [1,18,26], where the participation in the community means that the observer to some extent also must be active, and in this effectively becomes an intervention. This issue is less pertinent in public settings, but can manifest in semi-public settings.

While risks may be lower for ethnographical studies than in psychology and medicine, establishing informed consent can be complex and difficult. Due to the constant negotiation of the relationship between observer and informants, informed consent cannot be treated as a fixed contract established before observation. Rather, the consensual relation develops over time and can be extended - or retracted - depending on the level of trust that the participants' place in the observer [37]. And even if trust is established, it may not be clear for what consent is negotiated, in particular when it comes to publication and the thick descriptions that ethnographic work typically produces [37]. In the context of ethnography in conjunction with iterative design, Mara et al [27] argue for what they call "agile ethnography", short bursts of vaguely defined observations. The authors argue that ethnographers should "place the concerns of any collaborators front and center". In line with ethnographic action research [41], the participants should be considered active collaborators in the research process and not just objects of study. These requirements are very difficult to combine with unaware participation.

To summarize, ethical guidelines in sociology in general and ethnography in particular are concerned with lower but more insidious risks than those created by medical and psychological studies. The recommendations concerning informed consent are for this reason more varied, so that it under some circumstances can be waivered whereas it under other circumstances must be constantly re-negotiated.

Ethics of participatory art

Participatory art encompasses activities and installations that closely resemble the trialing of interactive technology in public and semi-public settings. Furthermore, it is not uncommon for interaction design scholars to collaborate with artists in creating interesting trials of novel interaction models [4, 5]. Hence, the ethical discussions in art are highly relevant for our investigation.

The ethical concerns put forward in literature on participatory art bring forward very different issues from those that are typical of research ethics from psychology, medicine and sociology. Participatory art has subjected participants to non-negligible risks, to harm, and to humiliation [16] and even though consent is typically acquired, it is not necessarily fully informed and can be coerced. While most artists typically avoid creating physical harm, they are not overly concerned with risks of causing psychological stress or upsetting their audience. The ethical discussions around art are typically politically framed, focusing on the risk of exploiting or humiliating participants. Due to the increasingly international art scene they very often framed from a post-colonial perspective [17].

In a similar manner as Mara et al argues for an action research perspective on ethnography [27], the literature on ethics in participatory art has brought forward a shift of perspective on audiences, from that of passive observers towards being co-creators. A key reference in this context is Borriaud's work on *relational art* [8], in which he analyses a trend in art installations (primarily emerging during the 1990'ies but not without its predecessors) that involve and articulate methods of social exchange. A famous example of what Borriaud classifies as relational art is when artist Rikrit Tiravanija cooked and served Thai food for visitors to the 303 Gallery in New York[1].

Hjort and Sharp [23] discuss the ethics of ethnography in the context of participatory art. They argue that art ethnography is most successful when it moves "beyond a mere aestheticisation" and becomes "an embodied part of creative, social practice". For Hjort and Sharp, a primary concern is to what extent the participatory process itself is considered the outcome, or if it is used as a backdrop for subsequent aesthetic product, e.g. in the form of an exhibition. A key example brought forward by Hjort and Sharp is 'Underground Streams: Shibuya', a local art event where multiple artists were invited to engage in conversation with locals around the theme of the changing urban landscape of Tokyo and more specifically, the burial of the Shibuya River. A range of different works were produced, ranging from city walks to mobile games and community events. The authors stress how the audience in this event was not some anonymous biennal visitor, but local residents and visitors with a relationship to the place. The work was experienced by the same audience as was creating it.

Downey [16] contributes through an interesting discussion of ethically problematic art productions. One of his core

[1] http://www.guggenheim.org/new-york/collections/collection-online/artists/bios/5339

examples is the work by Santiago Sierra, who is known for coercing participants into meaningless and debasing acts for payment. A counterargument is provided by Bishop [7], who uses the very same example in her critique of Borriaud [8]. Bishop argues that there must be room in art for interrelationships that are not collaborative, but that reproduce and maintain tensions from society. The discussion between Downey and Bishop echoes a well-known problem from international law, in balancing the right to privacy and the freedom of (in this case artistic) expression, e.g. as expressed in articles 8 and 10 respectively of the European Convention of Human Rights, (ECHR) [21].

The ethical discussion around participatory art illustrates that interventions can be problematic even if consent is acquired, if the intervention may lead to exploitation. Downey proposes that this has its root in an unbalanced power relation between the artist as a representative of society, and the participant as a subordinate subject of the intervention. This power relation is further emphasized if participants are unaware or only partially aware of the nature of the intervention.

Downey proposes a path towards a solution through a creative reading of Bahktin's work on the ethics of artistic creation:

> "In Bakhtin" ... "we find a blueprint of sorts for contemporary art works that co-opt communities. In his take on the carnivalesque as an integrated form of action that usurps hierarchies, taken in conjunction with his reading of the dialogic as a series of agonistic as opposed to dialectic events, we find the pluralistic underpinnings of collaborative art practices."[16]

Downey appears to propose that participatory art can be ethically as well as aesthetically framed through the transgressive power of implementing a carnivalesque 'world upside down' perspective. One may consider a role reversal also concerning the power relation between the artist or organizer, and the participants of an intervention.

To summarize, the ethical considerations related to participatory art tend to focus on the power relation between artist and participant as a primary, and are less concerned with risk and harm reduction. As consent is part of this power relation, various forms of consent, including coercion, have been explored as art.

The contribution from pervasive games studies

An important observation is that when interventions are done in a public and openly accessible space, it becomes extremely difficult (bordering on the outright impossible) to entirely avoid unaware or only partially informed participation. Even if the intervention is clearly announced, there will always be members of the public that miss this announcement due to lack of attention or inability to access the media of announcement. Children may miss out on a written message, whereas people with low hearing or wearing earphones may miss an audio announcements. Similar issues apply to widely scoped online studies [28]. Even if no data is gathered from unaware participants, they may still be affected by the intervention.

This issue was observed in work on ethics for pervasive games [30, 31, 32]. Montola and Waern [31] exemplify the effect by the mobile game 'Botfighter', a game in which players can play out fictive battles when they are in the vicinity of each other. A bystander may be affected by such a game if, for example, a player bumps into her while running to catch another player.

Work on ethics in pervasive games has thus focused less on creating informed consent, and more on creating ethically acceptable experiences for participants that are not fully aware of what is going on. Montola et al. [31, 32] argue that the awareness of an ongoing game intervention passes through three identifiable stages: the *unaware* state when a passer-by is unaware of the fact that a game is ongoing, the state of *ambiguous awareness* when the person is aware of the fact that something is going on but does not fully grasp its nature, and finally *informed awareness* of the fact that a game is ongoing and at least a partial understanding of the nature of the game. In the context of covert studies in public space, 'full awareness' would correspond the level of understanding that would be required to establish informed consent.

Montola and Waern further argue that an intervention should offer recognizable modes of engagement even when participants are only ambiguously aware of its nature. A very similar argument has been put forward concerning the spectator experience in public space, as one of becoming aware (at varying levels) of a performance frame created by the intervention [5]. To this, Montola and Waern adds the observation that the awareness is not just of the intervention as such, but also of what modes of participation it offers.

The awareness model also resonates with interaction patterns that have been observed in studies of public displays. Brignull and Rogers [9] identified three interaction phases with public displays; *peripheral awareness* when the participants are aware of the display but not giving it attention, *focal awareness* when attention is given to the display and e.g. discussed between participants, and finally *direct interaction.* Michelis & Müller [29] stress that the transitions between these interaction phases constitute major bottlenecks towards active engagement with public displays.

DESIGNING ETHICAL GUIDELINES FOR PUBLIC INTERVENTIONS

As seen from the discussion above, ethics considerations vary between research fields, depending on what is (sometimes tacitly) seen as the major ethical issues for the field. Developing an ethical approach to public interventions must go about in a similar manner, by identifying the major ethical issues and developing guidelines towards addressing them.

Before going into details, we should first make clear who we consider a participant in a public intervention study. In the following, we will consider anyone who is included in the study of the intervention to be a participant, including those who are just captured on record but notice nothing of the intervention themselves. This also implies that the method of data gathering will affect who is considered a participant.

Implicit consent

Williamson and Sundén [44] argue that unaware participation often is desired when trialing installations in public space, for the purposes of ecological validity of the trials. While the 'naturalness' of such studies can be discussed, we have discussed above that informed consent towards participation may be hard or even impossible to achieve in such settings. Hence it makes sense to investigate if there is a way in which public installations can elicit implicit, rather than informed, consent. Could we under any circumstances view the active participation in an intervention as *implicit consent* to participate in a trial? To this purpose, previous work on ethics of pervasive games provides some insight.

The invitation to refuse

A critical consideration brought forward from the work on pervasive game ethics, is that an intervention should offer what they call "an invitation to refuse". This consideration echoes the ethical considerations brought forward by the British psychology association [10], respecting the participants' autonomy. In order to consider the active participation in an intervention as implying implicit consent, it *must* be possible to also ignore the intervention.

Interventions that are disruptive of normality can be very hard to ignore. It is indicative that the right for the state to uphold public safety in international law often is taken to include the right to uphold public order ([39] p. 317).

Montola et al [31, 32] argue that an invitation to refuse should be offered even for players that are only ambiguously aware of the intervention. If players feel the need to engage because they do not fully understand what is going on, this cannot be considered implicit consent: it should be possible to ignore the presence of an intervention without knowing exactly what is refused. This is not entirely straightforward to achieve. An illustrative example is the unfortunate design of a ghost hunt game staged at a university campus [30]. While the gameness of the event was largely hidden for the ordinary campus visitors, these could not avoid being subjected to some of its installations and neither could they leave the area to reject the game intervention. As the installations were uncomfortable or outright scary, the experience became negative to most that were subjected to the game. As noted by Brown et al. [11], unpredictable behavior can be sufficient to induce fear.

For playful installations and games, Montola and Waern [30] further stress the importance of making a game visible only to participants that are prepared to make what they call "a ludic interpretation" of what they see and hear; who are willing or able to assume that what they see is done as unserious or fiction rather than as serious or real. The factors that influence players' willingness to make a ludic interpretation include the connotations of the place of the game: Events taking place in a theme park are more likely to be perceived as playful than events in a hospital. The theme of the game also has an effect: A game about cuddly teddy bears is less likely to be taken seriously than one about ghosts. And finally it matters who is seen playing: playing children are easier to interpret as players, than playing bikers.

The design strategy of offering a ludic interpretation is only possible for playful interventions; other strategies must be developed for other types of interventions. Some possible strategies can still be identified. If the installation fulfills a serious need, the invitation to refuse could be achieved by making involvement *optional*, offering alternative ways to accomplish the same thing. If the intervention is one that calls for attention and engagement, it would be important to ensure that no participant experience a duty to respond.

Professionals

Some participants face particular challenges in ignoring an intervention. Particular care must always be taken with people in their professional capacity, in particular those who have as their job to take things seriously. When approached in their professional capacity, the policeman, the firefighter, the guard, the medical expert etcetera, will have no choice but engage with the intervention. Their engagement cannot be taken as implicit consent, and can in fact lead to numerous issues with ecological validity (as professionals may not engage in the same way as the intended target group), exposing participants to risks and harm, and legal consequences for the organizers. All of these problems surfaced in the case of the ghost hunt game discussed above [30].

Risks

One takeaway from the ethical guidelines from medicine, psychology and sociology, is that the higher is the risk of harm and discomfort is for the participants, the more severe be the requirements on informed consent.

Pervasive risk and risk assessment

When interventions play out in public space, where other activities are going on and other actors are present, the risk for harm or discomfort can be very difficult to assess in advance. Players of a mobile game may for example get distracted and step into traffic; an engaging installation may distract participants in a way that invites pickpockets to take advantage of the situation. A particularly insidious risk is that an intervention may induce a false sense of safety, and by that encourage risky behaviors. An illustrative example is the accident reported in Shelby Logan's run [33 chapter 10], when a player accidentally entered an unprepared mineshaft - only to fall ten meters down and break his back. The participant trusted the game to be safe, missing out on the fact that the instructions explicitly told not to enter any other mineshaft than the one with the right number. The part of the mine that he entered was even closed off and well equipped with danger signs; signals that he most likely semiotically reframed as being part of the game.

Public interventions should - of course - be as safe as possible. For most interventions it makes no sense to deliberately expose participants to neither danger nor discomfort. However, in addition to the difficulties associated to assessing risk, some level of danger and discomfort is sometimes an integral part of an intervention as illustrated by the ethical discussions of participatory art as well in entertainment installations such as e.g. rollercoaster rides [6]. Hence, it is desirable that public interventions keep participants aware of the fact that they are responsible for their own safety, and empower them to manage that risk.

Public interventions *should not pretend to be safe*, even when they are designed to be as safe as possible. Neither is it a good idea to present a comprehensive list of warnings, as it is likely to be incomplete. Interventions are better designed in ways that allow participants to assess and manage their own level of risk, even if this means a higher likelihood of refusing to participate. From this perspective, implicit consent is actually at an advantage over explicit, in that it is less likely to induce an unjustified level of trust in participants. It is much more likely that the participant who signs a consent form to participate in an organized experiment (especially if organized by a known and high-esteemed organization) will trust it to be safe, than that a random passer-by will put the same level of trust in a public intervention staged by an unknown organizer. In some cases, established modes of advertising and framing risk in public settings can be used also for experimental interventions, inspired by how public entertainment communicate their level of uncomfort and risk [6].

There are limits to how far one can take this approach. As with unaware participation in sociological interventionist studies [3], implicit consent requires that known risks are low to negligible. If the organizers know that participants will be exposed to risks, these need to be made fully aware of what they are getting involved with, and explicit consent should be acquired if at all possible. Furthermore, not all participants are capable of assessing their own risk. Children, for example, cannot be considered fully responsible for their own risk assessment. In the light of this, one may question the recommendation from Perry et al. to attempt to engage children, as "children's involvement in interactions appears to warrant more, longer and more engaged interactions than would otherwise be the case" [38]. While this may work to involve groups of adults and children together, it places high requirements on safeguarding unaccompanied children who are drawn to the intervention. Interventions that run a risk of exposing categories of people to risks they are not capable to assess, must find ways to exclude such people from participation.

Risks related to exposition

Public interventions also share some of the risks identified for ethnographic studies. The risk created by publication [35] should be taken into careful consideration. In the era of Internet memes, it can be very difficult for a research team to control how pictures and videos from their data collection will spread, both through the acts of participants themselves [28], as well as once published. The latter concern should influence what data is selected for publication and how it is anonymized. There are also risks associated to retracting installations, similar to those associated with the ethnographer leaving the field [14,42]. Consider for example an intervention targeting a marginalized group: if the intervention is successful, how should the research team handle the negative effects from taking it *out*?

Empowering participants

A potential path towards a solution to the latter type of issues is to empower participants to become active *subjects*, rather than objects, of study [27]. While this may not always be possible, considering it offers an interesting perspective on not just the study of an intervention, but on the design of public interventions as such.

Interventions that benefit the participants

The principle of proportionality has been brought forward as an important consideration in the design of information systems, as a balance between privacy (of information) and usefulness (of system) [24]. While such considerations are important also for public interventions, we must also consider *who* benefits from the intervention. While the world medical association allows for unaware participation by patients who are unable to give consent (when consent is instead given by e.g. a guardian) [46], this form of participation is conditioned in an interesting way: it is considered acceptable only if the experiment is for the benefit of the patient or the specific group that the patient represents. This principle could potentially be considered a guiding principle also for unaware participation in public settings. Intuitively, it is easier to accept an intervention in public space if the sought effect of the intervention is to provide a positive value for participants; such as if it is pleasurable to use, simplifies a necessary task, or contributes to improving the participant's health. By contrast, the covert trial of an intervention that primarily benefits another agent is more difficult to accept. Consider for example the covert trial of a new checkout system in a food store, which adds a cumbersome task to the customer's shopping but saves money for the storeowner.

However, while this can be an important consideration in specific cases, it is of limited value as a general principle. Firstly, as discussed earlier not all interventions need be pleasurable or 'fun' - it is sometimes motivated for art installations to be uncomfortable and provoking. More seriously, as a guiding principle it requires that the designer can determine what is a 'benefit of the participants'. In public settings, any intervention is likely to encounter people that do not share the designers' assessment. The tired and depressed passer-by may not appreciate an engaging and 'fun' game, engaging in healthy exercise may not be fun for the person with back pains. Again, we come back to the invitation to refuse as a crucial requirement, as it empowers participants to reject the intended 'benefit'.

Role reversal

A more multi-faceted form of empowerment could be offered by Dowey's proposal for ethics in participatory art; the offering of role reversals through a carnivalesque "world upside down" view. For example, participants may be offered influence over everyday phenomena that the normally are just subjected to, or installations may present ridiculed commentary to the same. Opening for playful engagement is particularly useful, as it opens for multiple forms of engagement apart from accepting the rules of play or rejecting them altogether; players may for example choose to cheat or create their own rules [40]. However, using a carnivalesque role reversal is a core design choice rather than a consideration for how to stage a study, and is not always a viable option for a trial.

An interesting and useful form of role reversal is to direct it towards the organizers as a way of creating a more even power balance between organizers and participants. Participants can be empowered through ways to referee an intervention, or to affect it directly e.g. by taking it down. A simple version could be to make the results of a study publicly available online and open for comments, ratings and discussions by the people who experienced it.

Co-creation

Finally, we should consider the option of bringing participants into a co-creative role. While this is certainly possible in a public setting as shown for example by "underground streams: Shibuya", it is difficult to combine co-creation with ambiguous awareness and implicit consent. The co-creative art interventions discussed above all require fully informed participation. One reason is that it is only under those circumstances that participants will be able to contribute in a manner that is consistent with the intentions of the organizer. Another is that it can be considered unethical to use the material created within such trials outside the context of the trial, in a similar manner as discussed by Hjort and Sharp [23] for relational aesthetics.

There exist examples of online games that collect data for purposes different than those of the participants (which, we can assume, primarily just want to play a game). For example there exists a range of image-tagging games [22] that are based on this approach. Offering such games online could probably be considered unethical if the players were not informed about its image tagging purpose.

EXAMPLES

This section contextualizes the considerations above through examining three example projects. In order to capture a wide range of issues and risks, these have been retrieved not only from within HCI but also from the adjacent fields of advertisement and art. As the first example, we revisit the 'piano stairs' introduced in the introduction. The second is chosen as a more or less typical public installation project within the HCI community. This installation is in many ways similar to the piano stairs and provides a useful comparison. The third example is a very different, complex and controversial, project taken from the domain of participatory art. It is included as a way to illuminate the complexity of ethical issues involved with unaware participation.

The piano stairs

Let us first go back to explore the ethics of the 'piano stairs' from the introduction in more detail. The piano stairs were not produced as an academic study, but are part of a larger advertisement campaign called 'The Fun Theory'[2]. The core idea is one of gamification [15]: inducing positive behavior change through offering a fun way to do something otherwise uninteresting. Some of the projects involve a public installation, which is documented by a well-produced video illustrating the behavior *before* and *after* the installation is put in place. The videos are published online and the whole project is commissioned by Volkswagen.

The viral video 'The piano stairs' documents one such installation. The location is at a combined staircase and escalator entrance to a subway station in Stockholm. The video tells a story about how almost all passers-by regularly would choose the escalator. Next, the video shows how the design team repaints the stairs to resemble a piano keyboard, and equips it with sensors so that each step would generate the corresponding note when stepped upon. The result (as shown by the video) is that the majority of the passers-by would now choose the stairs. The video also documents some clearly playful engagement with the staircase, especially among children.

Revisiting the ethical considerations from the section above, we can see that the piano stairs fairly clearly affords implicit consent, as the installation offers an invitation to refuse. It is still possible to ride the escalator (which used to be what most passers-by would do). The invitation to refuse could have been strengthened further by using only *half* of the width of stairs for the piano. That way, people who for one or the other reason cannot use the escalator would still be able to use the stairs without activating the piano.

The risks induced by the piano stairs can be considered low to negligible. It is of course possible to imagine accidents that may happen due to the installation; people may for

[2] http://www.thefuntheory.com/

example bump into each other while playing with the stairs. But such risks need to be compared to the risks involved with riding the escalators, which can be very dangerous if somebody falls or get stuck. The overall risk assessment is difficult, but it is not impossible that the overall risk for accidents is lowered by the introduction of the piano stairs. To add, the risks associated to stairs are well understood and we can expect that participants, including children, are able to assess them correctly even when the stairs are painted.

Furthermore, this is an installation that very clearly speaks to our predisposition to accept public interventions if they provide positive effects to the participants. The installation provides an immediate positive effect - fun - and contributes (at least weakly) to a long-term health effect. But it is also here we find the potential ethical issues with the intervention, because this is not its ultimate goal. The ultimate goal is a *viral video*, produced as marketing for the sponsoring company. The video documents a range of behaviors with the stair, including children playing. The publication of the video exposes these participants to known risks associated to viral spread such as getting identified, being exposed to ridicule, and re-appropriation of the video material in less benevolent contexts. (Here, it should be noted that the participants in the videos may very well have consented to its publication - this is not documented on the website.)

Magic Mirrors

Whereas the first example was an advertisement campaign, the second example shows how covert studies in public space have been used within HCI. The study is motivated precisely by the desire to perform a naturalistic study of an interactive installation. Michelis and Möller report on their findings from trialing four interactive "Magic Mirror" displays in a storefront window [29]. Each of these "mirrors" displayed a mirror image of the people and environment in front of it, and applied optical effects to the image that reacted to gestures of their users. In addition to the interactive installations, three projection displays were also installed at the edge of the same building, showing screen shots of interacting users to audiences across the street and down neighboring streets. The purpose of the study was to elicit more knowledge about audience behavior in front of public screen installations; among other things the authors could confirm some previously observed behaviors such as the 'honeypot effect' and develop a model for how engagement develops as a person or a group approaches the installation. The observations were done covertly but not video filmed; instead, researchers stayed close by to take notes. From the publication, it is clear that photographs (and possibly also video) was gathered through the installation camera, and seemingly also captured by observers.

Again, we can see that the installation offers an invitation to refuse; in fact, the authors report that most passers-by ignored the installation altogether. The risk must again be considered low to negligible. In particular, the risk of theft is low as the displays mirror everything in front of them, making it difficult to sneak in on a person engaged in interaction. The researchers have also made an effort to minimize the risk of exposition from publication, by documenting the observations primary through field notes, which ensure participant anonymity. Finally, the reach of academic publications is rather limited at least in comparison with the reach of the viral video in the previous example.

In the light of these precautions, the decision to include public displays at the edge of the house is very difficult to understand. The way these displays expose the participants for public viewing, in a way that makes it unlikely that participants were aware of the exposition, is very difficult to motivate. Furthermore, this part of the installation seems to play a very marginal role in the study and the article reports no findings in relation to it.

Unknown, Woman 2009-349701

The final example does not involve any technological installation but is based on an art intervention. It is included in order to illustrate the complexity of issues surrounding public interventions, and highlights the risks associated to involving people in their professional capacity in particular.

In January 2009, the (at the time) art student Anna Odell staged a public performance where she simulated a psychosis, starting at a bridge in central Stockholm where she pretended to be ready to jump off the bridge. She was taken into custody and released the day after, when she had disclosed for the doctor in charge that she had simulated the psychosis in order to 'expose and document power structures in psychiatric treatment'. The simulated psychosis was part of her exam project at the art school, and based on her previous experiences as an authentic psychiatry patient. The project reached media attention as 'the psychosis bluff', caused public uproar and made medical professionals publish angry debate articles [19]. Consider the following citation, from a debate article authored by a medical authority:

> "Anna Odell wanted, among other things, to show how one becomes a victim within the psychiatric system. But the only victims in this installation are the people passing by, the policemen who answered the distress call, the personnel at the emergency ward, her fellow patients, and the tax payers." [19]

Odell was charged with the crimes of dishonest method, violent resistance and false alarm, and was sentenced to a pay a symbolic fine on the grounds of dishonest method. Her artwork [36] was first exhibited in the exam exhibition at the art school the same year, and has been exhibited at least once after the exam. It includes authentic video documentation from the feigned psychosis at the bridge, and an audio recording of the meeting with a doctor where she disclosed that she was acting.

While the piece raises multiple difficult issues related to unaware participation, the major controversy was caused by the involvement of professionals: the police and the medical ward personnel. Their participation cannot be considered implicit consent, as the simulated psychosis did not give them any option to refuse involvement. This article will not take a stance on whether the political and artistic goals of the project were sufficient to motivate this, but focus on some of the effects of such involvement.

When exposed, the reaction from both the police and the medical ward professionals were strongly negative. They felt duped and unnecessarily bothered. Both the police and the emergency psychiatry are overburdened institutions, manned by stressed personnel. There was a justified reaction against what was seen as a waste of resources. Finally, it is not unlikely that some fear of exposure and ridicule contributed to the strong reactions. Such fear would not have been unjustified: if anybody had been caught on film doing something illegal or strange it could indeed have affected his or her professional career.

At the same time, both the police and the medical ward are powerful and respected institutions, very much in charge of their public perception. This put the *artist* in danger, physically and psychologically as well as in terms of media reception. Right after the events, it was the authorities' perception of the events that dominated media and incited media uproar against the artist and the art school. While Odell had been advised on the ethical issues involved with simulating a psychosis to get into psychiatric care, the art school seems to have underestimated risk for a media storm. It was only when the full artwork was exhibited a couple of months later that the media reporting eventually became more nuanced; recognizing the fact that the artist aimed precisely at exposing the power relationship between patient and institution.

The physical and psychological dangers involved with the artwork primarily affected the artist herself. The artwork is based on a double role reversal: Odell was partially in charge as the psychosis was simulated (and she eventually disclosed this fact), but she also submitted herself completely to the actions of police and medical staff. This, she knew from personal experience, would be uncomfortable and could well be dangerous. During the course of the project she was even warned by psychiatric experts that she might not be released from the ward just because she declared herself sane [12].

To summarize, unaware involvement of people in their professional role can induce a range of risks, both to the participants but also to the organizers. Whether the involvement of police and medical staff was motivated for this particular project will be left for the reader to decide. The final note concern the unaware passers-by who decided to get involved and alert the police. Due to the seeming seriousness of the event, it is difficult to consider their involvement as voluntary, ruling out implicit consent. But with these, there were no double role-reversal. They were not part of the system of psychiatric care and held no power over the artist. There could be no desire from Odell to expose them to risk, discomfort, or public exposure; yet they were exposed to all of those. At best, we can consider their involvement 'collateral art damage'.

DISCUSSION

While the case studies above have been widely scoped to show the variability of ways to approach public interventions, similar concerns can – and will – emerge also within the field. In this section, we will revisit the guidelines developed above in light of cases and similar work within the HCI domain, to highlight risks that seem most pertinent in practice.

Firstly, since it is unlikely that explicit consent can be safely acquired for public interventions, these must either be of a kind that induces 'minimal risk' or else, it must be possible to argue that participation is voluntary. Here, the ability to *offer an invitation to refuse* is a useful way to frame this requirement.

While this is a central concern, it did not emerge as an issue in the HCI examples above, and indeed seldom emerges as a major issue in reported HCI studies. A major reason for this lies in the type of interventions that are trialed, as these often involve a public installation (a screen or a piece of artwork), which participants must voluntarily approach to engage in. Furthermore, many HCI studies are done in semi-public spaces such as art exhibitions or trade fairs, where participants already understand something about the provisional nature of the intervention. However, it is not uncommon that data is gathered also about participants that are not engaging with the installations (see e.g. [29, 38]), effectively treating these as study participants even though they have taken advantage of the 'invitation to refuse'. Furthermore, such installations still may incur risks for involuntary second hand participation through e.g creating a crowd that is difficult to pass.

The risk for involuntary participation is larger when an installation involves aware participants who interact with unaware participants. This is the key element of Odell's work and it is not unusual for pervasive games [5,30,31,32]. Covert observation can in itself lead to such forms of participation, e,g, if participants are shadowed to observe their actions (see e.g. [20).

At the present state, HCI studies seem more troubled by issues related to risk assessment and risk protection. As identified in [28], risks related to data leakage and jigsaw identification can emerge both from the way that data is gathered by the researchers, but also from the actions of participants and spectators who may be taking photos and films and publish this material online. This type of issues plague in particular work on interactive installations, see e.g. [29, 38].

In general, it seems difficult to assess the level of risk involved public installations and even more difficult to install an accurate sense of risk in the participants. This includes both risks related to data leakage, but also more imminent risks related to the physical and social context of the intervention. Muntenau et al [34] have made a call for a more situational approach to ethic planning and approval, with room for adaptation as a study evolves.

CONCLUSION

Unaware participation in public interventions raises very different ethical concerns than classical research ethics. The differences arise primarily from the ways in which the experiment organizer is neither in full control over what is going on in public space, nor who is invited to participate. The concepts brought forward in this article, the idea that consent can be implicit and that participants to some extent must be in charge of their own safety, lie very far from what would be considered ethical in most other forms of empirical work.

Still, as pointed out already by Williamson and Sundén [44], *these studies are already performed*, and they are not always thoroughly considering issues of risk and consent. An example of this is Michelis and Möller's [29] look upon the low number of participants that their mirror installation recruited as a partial failure. Most passers-by would just do that - pass by. If we consider this behavior from a consent perspective, it is an indication that the installation was possible to ignore. The opposite behavior would have been more problematic: if the installation had gathered a crowd, people that were in a hurry would have found it difficult to pass, and by that they would have become unwilling participants.

The issues surrounding unaware participation are complex and not clear-cut, in particular when we take the power relationship between the organizers and the participants into account. The discussion on such topics is very much alive in the context of participatory art, and is worthy of concern also in interaction design. The author would like to conclude by urging HCI researchers to more frequently consider the possibilities of role reversal in order to balance the uneven power relationship between themselves and their study participants, making the latter active *subjects* rather than objects of study. Empowering participants, through allowing them to present judgment on the work or to become co-designers, are strategies worth considering not only for ethical reasons but also because they may produce better results. Eventually, this discussion must challenge not our way of studying public interventions, but also what we choose to design.

ACKNOWLEDGMENTS

The author is in debt to Mareike Glöss and the anonymous reviewers for commenting upon earlier versions of the text and greatly improving the quality of the work.

REFERENCES

1. AOIR. 2012. Ethical decision-making and Internet research 2.0. Recommendations from the aoir ethics working committee. Retrieved July 21st 2015 from http://aoir.org/reports/ethics2.pdf.
2. APA. 2010. Ethical principles of psychologists and code of conduct. Retrieved July 21st 2015 from http://www.apa.org/ethics/code/principles.pdf
3. ASA. 1999. Code of ethics, and policies and procedures. Retrieved July 21st 2015 from http://www.asanet.org/images/asa/docs/pdf/CodeofEthics.pdf
4. Steve Benford, Andy Crabtree, Martin Flintham, Adam Drozd, Rob Anastasi, Mark Paxton, Nick Tandavanitj, Matt Adams and Ju Row-Farr. 2006. Can you see me now? *ACM Transactions on Computer-Human Interaction* (TOCHI), 13,1: 100-133.
5. Steve Benford, Andy Crabtree, Stuart Reeves, Jennifer Sheridan, Alan Dix, Martin Flintham and Adam Drozd. 2006. The frame of the game: blurring the boundary between fiction and reality in mobile experiences. In *Proceedings of the SIGCHI Conference on Human Factors in Computing Systems* (CHI'06), 427-436.
6. Steve Benford, Chris Greenhalgh, Gabriella Giannachi, Brendan Walker, Joel Marshall and Tom Rodden. 2012. Uncomfortable interactions. In *Proceedings of the SIGCHI Conference on Human Factors in Computing Systems* (CHI'12), 2005-2014.
7. Claire Bishop. 2004. Antagonism and relational aesthetics. *October 110*. October Magazine, Ltd. and Massachusetts Institute of Technology, 51–79.
8. Nicolas Bourriaud. 1998. *Relational aesthetics*. Dijon: Les presses du reel.
9. Harry Brignull and Yvonne Rogers. 2003. Enticing people to interact with large public displays in public spaces. *Proceedings of INTERACT Vol. 3*, 17-24.
10. The British psychological society. 2014. Code of human research ethics. 2014. Retrieved July 21st 2015 from http://www.bps.org.uk/system/files/Public%20files/inf180_web.pdf
11. Oliver Brown, Petra Gemeinboeck and Rob Saunders. The machine as autonomous performer. In *Interactive Experience in the Digital Age*. Springer US, 75–90.
12. Andy Crabtree, Alan Chamberlain, Rebecca Grinter, Matt Jones, Tom Rodden and Yvonne Rogers. 2013. Introduction to the Special Issue of "The Turn to The Wild". *ACM Transactions of Computer-Human Interaction (TOCHI)* 20, 3, Article 13.

13. Sofia Curman. 2009. Anna Odell spelade sig själv. (eng. Anna Odell played herself) News clip, Dagens Nyheter. Retrieved September 6th from www.dn.se/kultur-noje/konst-form/anna-odell-spelade-sig-sjalv/

14. Marlene de Laine. 2000. *Fieldwork participation & practice: Ethics & dilemmas in qualitative research*. SAGE Publications Ltd, U.K.

15. Sebastian Deterding, Dan Dixon, Rhilla Khaled and Lennart Nacke. 2011. From game design elements to gamefulness: defining gamification. *Proceedings of the 15th International Academic MindTrek Conference*: Envisioning Future Media Environments, 9-15.

16. Anthony Downey. 2009. An ethics of engagement: Collaborative art practices and the return of the ethnographer. *Third Text* 23, 5: 593-603.

17. Anthony Downey. 2011. Geocentric Conundrums: Aesthetics and Ethics in Contemporary Art; Gemma Lloyd Interviews Anthony Downey. *CAC Interviu* 16-17: 53-60.

18. Catherine Driscoll and Melissa Gregg. 2010. My profile: The ethics of virtual ethnography. *Emotion, Space and Society* 3,1: 15-20.

19. David Eberhard. 2009. Överläkaren David Eberhard: Konstfackseleven borde klippa sig och skaffa sig ett jobb. (eng. The art student should get a haircut and a job) Newsmill. Retrieved September 6th from http://www.dn.se/sthlm/overlakaren-david-eberhard-konstfackseleven-borde-klippa-sig-och-skaffa-sig-ett-jobb/

20. Ernest Edmonds, Bilda Zafer and Lizzie Muller. 2009. Artist, evaluator and curator: three viewpoints on interactive art, evaluation and audience experience. *Digital Creativity* 20, 3: 141-151.

21. European Court of Human Rights. 2002. *European Convention on Human Rights*. Council of Europe, Strasbourg.

22. Dion Hoe-Lian Goh, Rebecca P. Ang, Chei Sian Lee and Alton Y.K. Chua. 2011. Fight or Unite: Investigating Game Genres for Image Tagging. *Journal of the American Society for Information Science and Technology* 62, 7: 1311–1324.

23. Larissa Hjorth and Kristen Sharp. 2014. The art of ethnography: the aesthetics or ethics of participation? *Visual Studies* 29, 2: 128–135.

24. Giovanni Iachello. 2005. Privacy and proportionality: Adapting legal evaluation techniques to inform design in ubiquitous computing. *Proceedings of the SIGCHI Conference on Human Factors in Computing Systems (CHI'05)*, 91-100.

25. John Lofland, David A. Snow, Leon Anderson and Lyn H. Lofland. 2006. *Analyzing social settings*. Belmont, CA: Wadsworth Publishing Company.

26. Heidi A. McKee and James E. Porter. 2009. Playing a good game: Ethical issues in researching MMOGs and virtual worlds. *International Journal of Internet Research Ethics*, 2,1: 5-37.

27. Andrew Flood Mara, Liza Potts and Gerianne Bartocci. 2013. The ethics of agile ethnography. *Proceedings of the 31st ACM international conference on Design of communication*, 101-106.

28. McMillan, Donald, Alistair Morrison and Matthew Chalmers. 2013. Categorised ethical guidelines for large scale mobile HCI. *Proceedings of the SIGCHI Conference on Human Factors in Computing Systems*, 1853-1862.

29. Daniel Michelis and Jörg Müller. 2011. The audience funnel: Observations of gesture based interaction with multiple large displays in a city center. *Intl. Journal of Human–Computer Interaction* 27,6: 562-579.

30. Markus Montola and Annika Waern. 2006. Ethical and practical look at unaware game participation. In Santorineos, Manthos (ed.) *Gaming Realities. A Challenge for Digital Culture.* Mediaterra 2006 Festival, October 6.-8, Athens, 185-193.

31. Markus Montola and Annika Waern. 2006. Participant roles in socially expanded games. In third international workshop on pervasive gaming applications, Pervasive Conference, Dublin, Ireland. Retrieved July 21st from https://annikawaern.files.wordpress.com/2015/07/pg_montola_roles.pdf

32. Markus Montola, Annika Waern, Jussi Kuittinen and Jaakko Stenros. 2006. Ethics of Pervasive Gaming. IPerG Deliverable D5.5. Retrieved July 21st 2015 from http://www.pervasive-gaming.org/Deliverables/D5.5-Ethics.pdf

33. Markus Montola, Jaakko Stenros and Annika Waern. 2009. *Pervasive games: theory and design*. Morgan Kaufmann Publishers Inc.

34. Cosmin Munteanu, Heather Molyneaux, Wendy Moncur, Mario Romero, Susan O'Donnell and John Vines, J. 2015. Situational Ethics: Re-thinking Approaches to Formal Ethics Requirements for Human-Computer Interaction. *In Proceedings of the 33rd Annual ACM Conference on Human Factors in Computing Systems*, 105-114.

35. Elisabeth Murphy and Robert Dingwall. 2007. Informed consent, anticipatory regulation and ethnographic practice. *Social Science & Medicine* 65,11: 2223-2234.

36. Anna Odell. 2009. Unknown, Woman 2009-349701. Exhibition documentation. Retrieved September 6th from http://www.konstfack2009.se/bachelor/bafa/anna-odell/

37. Michael Parker. 2007. Ethnography/ethics. *Social science & medicine* 65,11: 2248-2259.

38. Mark Perry, Steve Beckett, Kenton O'Hara and Sriram Subramanian. 2010. WaveWindow: public, performative gestural interaction. In *ACM International Conference on Interactive Tabletops and Surfaces,* 109-112.

39. Bernadette Rainey, Elizabeth Wicks and Clare Ovey. 2014. *The European convention on human rights*. Oxford University Press.

40. Jaakko Stenros. 2015. Playfulness, play, and games: A constructionist ludology approach. Ph.D. Thesis, Tampere University. Retrieved July 2015 from http://tampub.uta.fi/handle/10024/96986

41. Jo A. Tacchi, Don Slater and Gregory N. Hearn. 2003. Ethnographic action research: A user's handbook. Retrieved July 21st 2015 from http://eprints.qut.edu.au/4399/1/4399.pdf

42. Steven J. Taylor. 1991. Leaving the field: Research, relationships, and responsibilities. *Experiencing fieldwork: An inside view of qualitative research*, 238-247.

43. The Fun Theory. 2009. Piano staircase. Video. Retrieved July 23rd 2015 from http://www.thefuntheory.com/piano-staircase

44. Julie R. Williamson and Daniel Sundén. 2015. Deep Cover HCI: A Case for Covert Research in HCI. In *Proceedings of the 33rd Annual ACM Conference, Extended Abstracts on Human Factors in Computing Systems*, 543-554.

45. Dan Wilson. 2011. Brutally unfair tactics totally OK now: On self-effacing games and unachievements. *Journal of Game Studies* 11,1.

46. World Medical Association. 2015. WMA Declaration of Helsinki - Ethical Principles for Medical Research Involving Human Subjects. Retrieved July 21st 2015 from http://www.wma.net/en/30publications/10policies/b3/index.html.

The Poetics of Socio-Technical Space: Using Craft to Reflect on the Internet of Things

Jessa Lingel
Annenberg School for Communication
University of Pennsylvania
3620 Walnut St.
Philadelphia, PA USA
jlingel@asc.upenn.edu

ABSTRACT

Drawing on semi-structured interviews and cognitive mapping with 14 craftspeople, this paper analyzes the socio-technical arrangements of people and tools in the context of workspaces and productivity. Using actor-network theory and the concept of companionability, both of which emphasize the role of human and non-human actants in the socio-technical fabrics of everyday life, I analyze the relationships between people, productivity and technology through the following themes: embodiment, provenance, insecurity, flow and companionability. The discussion section develops these themes further through comparison with rhetoric surrounding the Internet of Things (IoT). By putting the experiences of craftspeople in conversation with IoT rhetoric, I suggest several policy interventions for understanding connectivity and inter-device operability as material, flexible and respectful of human agency.

Author Keywords

Craft; Internet of Things; workspaces

ACM Classification Keywords

H.1.2. User/Machine systems: Human factors

INTRODUCTION

In the last decade, the IoT has emerged as an increasingly popular paradigm for describing networks of internet-connected devices [1], such as a weight scale that transmits data to a wearable device, a mobile phone and one's social network. Although the term IoT is new, the concept is well established, having overlap with terms like ubiquitous and pervasive computing. In this paper, I start from the premise that the IoT already exists in the arrangements of people and technologies in workspaces, all of which are connected in the service of productivity and work. Rather than looking at internet-based technologies or white collar jobs, I analyze the workplace narratives of craftspeople as a way of thinking more broadly (and more critically) about the IoT. Looking at workspaces of craftspeople offers a vantage point for investigating how spaces are arranged with deliberation and autonomy in the service of creativity and productivity. The narratives surrounding these arrangements and relationships are informative in thinking about how people conceptualize technology, connectivity and space in the context of work, even if the work in that space may look very different from the work referenced in dominant IoT rhetoric.

As a project about technology and the workplace, this research stems from two provocations. First, how do people conceptualize networks of both digital and non-digital technology as arrangements of bodies, tools and space? Discursively, the IoT emphasizes seamless, invisible connectivity. This rhetoric obscures the extent to which the IoT is in fact deeply material, requiring materials and resources that have real consequences for the environment [43] as much as privacy and civil liberties [27]. By looking at how people arrange their workspaces and how they describe their relationships to the tools and technologies used in work life, we gain grounded accounts of networked spaces and practices. In turn, these accounts allow for reflections on rhetorical abstractions surrounding contemporary and emerging paradigms of technology. The second provocation takes up questions relevant to both human computing interaction (HCI) and environmental psychology, namely how workplaces reflect institutional ideologies. For example, Marwick [40] and Saval [49] have documented shifts in office architecture that reflect or encourage particular values, like collaboration or flattened administrative hierarchies. One approach of interrogating a particular design value is to set up a counter-narrative that brings into relief the assumptions underlying dominant narratives, a longstanding approach of science and technology studies (STS) work (e.g. [39]). In this project, I look at the workspaces of craftspeople, drawing on a Latourian [32, 33] framework of actor network theory (ANT) in order to assess paradigms of networks and connectivity, in particular the Internet of Things (IoT), which is increasingly becoming a dominant narrative of

CHI'16, May 07 - 12, 2016, San Jose, CA, USA.

ACM 978-1-4503-3362-7/16/05…$15.00.
DOI: http://dx.doi.org/10.1145/2858036.2858399

relations between humans, computing and work [1, 11, 27, 43].

Within HCI research, the IoT is typically resented as a new way of thinking about how technologies are connected [38], as a design problem to be solved through new techniques of modeling (e.g. [24], [Milojcic et al.]) or frameworks for data management [26]. HCI scholarship on materiality and ubiquitous computing [Jenkins; Wood; 13] have pointed out the tendency to view technological networks as abstract and immaterial. But HCI research is still lacking in terms of how the IoT will be experienced as a set of practical, messy [B&D; 13], everyday experiences [Wood]. At the same time, examples of the IoT are frequently centered on homes of the privileged, with examples stretching at least as far back as the 1969 Honeywell kitchen computer [13, 25], which promised to connect refrigerators, cookbooks and grocery shopping. IoT hype promises convenience and efficiency through invisible connectivity of devices that monitor and communicate on behalf of the consumer, and more specifically, tech-savvy consumers with sophisticated technologies, typically as part of white-collar work or comfortable suburban homes. But this kind of inter-connectedness is already familiar to people who tend not to be depicted in ads or tech review blog posts about near-future technological advancements. As Eubanks [15] has documented, poor people experience the inter-connectedness of the state in monitoring rent, child-care, housing, work and food consumption. One could also apply the IoT to college students, whose daily movements around campus are monitored via ID cards, as are local purchases of food and their participation on online websites [4]. Paraphrasing Bell and Dourish [B&D], the future is already here, it just isn't evenly distributed (p. 141). These differences become meaningful when, as Sadowski and Pasquale [48] have noted, associations between the IoT and everyday and technologies obscure the social justice implications of these same infrastructures and data gathering processes when deployed on a wider scale.

It isn't then a matter of if the IoT will come (indeed, it is already here [B&D]) but what assemblages will be gathered under that name and which will be excluded, and how to understand connections between humans and technologies within these networks. A core project of HCI research is to understand not only how technologies can be designed in concert with everyday goals of both home and the workplace, but also to examine social and cultural implications of the networks that make everyday life possible. This empirically-grounded theory paper contributes to HCI research in two key ways: first, it offers implications for designing workspaces that foster, creativity, productivity and agency. The materiality of handwork and the agency of controlling their workspaces make craftspeople ideal participants for conceptualizing socio-technical environments without abstracting the networks of people, technologies and spaces. Second, I contribute to HCI discourses related to the IoT with grounded accounts of the agency, affect and seams that exist in networks of people, tools and their creations. Taking a cultural studies approach to

Related Work

The relationship between people and their workspaces has been studied in a number of fields, including organizational communication, environmental psychology and HCI. As a means of situating this project in conversation with a broader set of research, I provide a brief overview of environmental psychology studies of the workplace, followed by a discussion of workplaces and craft in HCI literature.

Within environmental psychology, researchers have investigated relationships between people and workplace objects. Bringing things to the office and having routines attached to those items is an important means of managing office tedium as well as stress, and part of how employees designate a degree of personalization [44, 50] and territoriality [8]. Gathering objects and tools as part of one's workplace is not simply about utilitarianism, or even about personalization – it is also tied to an awareness that these artifacts are read by others as indications of personality [12, 23] and relationships to the larger working institution [14]. Personalization of work spaces within office environments is determined primarily by organizational rules and norms, rather than individual preferences (see [59] and [60]). Scheiberg [50] found two key functions of organizing workspaces: "personalizing space appears to provide an unconscious outlet for emotions that otherwise might not have the chance to be expressed" and "to provide specific and concrete stimuli to which the individual will have a predictable emotional response - an emotional response that the individual finds useful for his or her job" (p. 334). Partly, these arrangements emerge in response to and as a means of cultivating routine, in that workers set up their spaces in ways that allow them to respond to changing demands of work. These studies investigate spatial arrangements from a bottom up perspective of how employees curate their personal artifacts, but studies have also examined top-down arrangements of offices, as when employers transition to open floor plans [6, 34, 56]. Within scholarship on workspaces and the tech industry, researchers have noted that open office plans reflect capitalist agendas that privilege productivity and collaboration over privacy or individual subjectivity [40, 49]. Across these studies, the degree of freedom that workers have over their office surroundings has important implications for their sense of individual agency and autonomy, as well as a sense of daily emotional well-being.

Environmental psychologists are largely agnostic to theorizing technology directly, which is where HCI investigations of work environments become relevant. In terms of the specific scope of my interests in craftspeople, within the CHI and CSCW community, scholars have looked to different components of craftwork in order to understand human and computer interaction in terms of materiality [16, 21], professional identity [36] and community [17]. Massimi and Rosner [41] argued that many modern digital artifacts and interactions are contemporary instantiations of traditional objects like mementos, keepsakes and heirlooms. Through interviews with people who create mementos for family and friends to mark significant life events, like weddings, births and moving house, the authors are able to tie online and social media practices to a longer history of documenting everyday life through crafting intimate artifacts (See also, [30]). Goodman and Rosner [22] interrogated the increasingly blurry line between producing objects by hand versus by digital tools, drawing on observations of gardening and knitting. Rosner and Ryokai [47] also used knitting as a means of thinking through the integration of digital versus handmade work in their analysis of knitters who used Spyn, an online app that enabled knitters to record messages with physical locations on knit fabric. In both cases, the authors noted tensions between seeing handmade items as authentic while wanting to embrace and explore the affordances of software programs and computer based tools. Bardzell et al. [3] took a comparative approach, using qualitative interviews with elite craft practitioners in the US and Taiwan, identifying points of commonality (a commitment to integrity) as well as difference (a tendency to value individual expression versus valuing contributions to a community, respectively). Researchers have also investigated the emergence of maker communities, which is associated with a do it yourself (DIY) approach to creating art, artifacts and tools [11, 37, 55].

Many of these projects concentrate on the dialectic between the handmade and the digital (which of course, also tends to rely on the use of one's hands) at the level of individual practices [43, 44] or within particular communities [22, 62]. My project has the most in common with [11] in its attention to how the IoT can be developed in ways that foster creativity and agency, but rather than a manifesto, I've sought to analyze the IoT as a paradigm through analysis of the lived accounts of craftspeople, technology, space and work.

Theoretical Concepts

A key contribution of this project is to develop theories that can account for shifting paradigms of socio-technical connectivity. I draw on two theoretical frameworks for my analysis of the IoT: ANT and companionability.

Given my interests in theorizing networks of people, spaces and technology, ANT offers a particularly useful conceptual framework. When ANT analyzes networks of socio-technical actors, it accounts for human as well as non-human components. In other words, "the project of ANT is simply to extend the list and modify the shapes and figures of those assembled as participants and to design a way to make them act as a durable whole" ([33] p. 72). In terms of applying ANT to grounded accounts of technology and space, I follow Fujimura [18] in being "sociologically (and geographically) interested in understanding why and how some human perspectives win over others in the construction of technologies and truths" (p. 222). Paradigms tend to operate at the level of generalized abstractions; in order to think more concretely about technology in terms of productivity and work, I draw on grounded accounts of people whose workplace arrangements of and relationships to technology offer insight into narratives of connection and interoperability.

Another concept relevant to this study is the idea of companionability. As described by Fox et al. [17] in their research on feminist hacker spaces, companionability refers to "cooperation as a powerful yet silent alliance" between people who shared a workspace. Companionship here means collective practices undertaken in tandem but also in separation, yet with a shared sense of purpose. Drawing together ANT and companionability, my investigation looks at cooperation as a telos of shared workspace, a partnership between human and non-human actors. As such, the following analysis asks, to what extent are agency, affect, seams assigned to people over things/tools? How can the spatial arrangements of production among craftspeople help us analyze and interrogate paradigms of technology, productivity and progress? Taking an ANT approach lends itself to accounting for a broad range of stakeholders (human as well as non-human) and conceptual vantage points (material as well as immaterial).

METHODS

Because I was interested in grounded, holistic accounts of interworkings between people, space and technology, I used qualitative interviews with craftspeople and artists. Restrictions for recruitment centered on gathering a research pool of people who make and sell handmade objects, and who had individual control over their workspaces (as opposed to creating in a makerspace or studio that did not allow artists to reconfigure the space). Within these constraints, participants varied in the extent to which they relied on their craft for income - some, like Jeff and Jennifer, depended on their art for their livelihood. Others, like Dan, had full-time jobs and supplemented their income with their handmade work, whereas Renee and Shannon were retired and made their handcrafted artifacts as a means of staying active and gaining additional income. In terms of the kinds of craft and art that participants produced for work, participants were diverse, including ceramics, woodworking, floral arrangements and soap making. See table 1 for participant details.

I began recruiting through my personal network (n=7), according to the criteria outlined above. I extended this pool by searching on Etsy, a website that allows people to sell their handmade or vintage items. Given Etsy's vast user base, I filtered shops by my location (Philadelphia, PA, USA) in order to be able to interview participants at their workspaces. I also filtered by the high-level category "handmade" and then sent messages to shop owners explaining the project in brief and requesting interviews. In most cases I was able to interview participants at the homes or studios - for a small number, I interviewed them over the phone or via Skype and then visited their workspaces at a later date.

During interviews, I asked participants to describe how they organize their workspace, the tools they use in their work and about their daily routines. I concluded interviews by asking participants to define a series of terms: technology, craft and cheating. Interviews were structured around understanding how people, tools and space converged (or diverged) in the production process. I also asked participants to draw maps of their workspaces, drawing on both cognitive mapping [19] and ethnographic methods [52]. Maps were intended to yield an additional layer of insight into how spaces were arranged in terms of which nodes of participants' sociotechnical networks were included and which dropped out. Interviews were conducted individually, with the exception of Melanie and William, a married couple whose small company produced a range of handmade items from jewelry to handbags to candleholders. I interviewed them together at their studio, although I asked each to draw separate maps of their shared space.

Name	Craft	Recruitment	Age
Anna	Graphic designer	PN	42
Brady	Electronic musical instrument designer	PN	35
Dan	Tile designer	Etsy	31
Eli	Soap maker	Etsy	30
Greg	Woodworker	PN	31
Jennifer	Photographer	Etsy	41
Jeff	Glassblower	Etsy	46
Katrin	Ceramic artist	PN	36
Leah	Ceramic artist	Etsy	32
Melanie	Bookbinder / jewelry designer	Etsy	38
Renee	Florist	PN	61
Shannon	Quilter	Etsy	59
William	Woodworker / leatherworker	PN	28
Heather	Woodworker	PN	28

Table 1: Participant details. The third column refers to recruitment strategy, either through my personal network (PN) or through Etsy (n=7). All participants have been given pseudonyms to provide confidentiality.

Interviews lasted between 45 and 90 minutes and took place throughout the Northeastern US. After verbatim transcription, interviews were coded using NVIVO software. I used a thematic coding approach [7], structured around my primary interests in organization and companionability. High-level themes grew out of this approach, including space, organization, time and tools. At the same time, I used open coding [54] to let additional themes emerge from the data. As a result from this iterative process, I began to develop an outline of tensions surrounding networked workplaces, specifically the ways that tactility and bodies shaped workplace arrangements, the role of flow in productivity and the precarity of maintaining and designing tools and space. The following results section is structured around and expands on these tensions.

RESULTS

Before unpacking the tensions surrounding craft, people and workspaces, I want to clarify a key difference between how participants tended to think of technology and how technology is frequently conceptualized by social science researchers. Particularly in STS, researchers tend to define technology broadly, as in Latour's famous definition that technology is "society made durable" [32]. A small number of participants defined technology in this way, including Heather: "I guess technology is something people develop to help them accomplish a task more easily than if they would just do it themselves." Greg also took an expansive view in defining technology: "This is technology [gestures at pencil]. Technology is just something that gives us tools ... You'll hear a lot of people say, 'We make work driven by technology.' Yeah well, everyone's been making work driven by technology. Everything is technology and everything is hand-made … even if you cut something by hand on a band saw it's still a piece of technology." These comments are very much in line with STS definitions of technology as encompassing a broad range of tools and devices, including long-established and hand-operated artifacts like saws and pencils.

For the majority of participants, however, technology meant internet-based devices or applications like Etsy and Instagram. When I asked Jeff about how he used technology in his work as a glassblower, he responded: "Obviously the computer part of it is huge. I don't currently do a lot of online selling, but I use email, and online searches to locate and communicate with stores and galleries. That's really helpful." Rather than helping in the production of their crafts, technology was associated with ICTs in the specific context of promoting products and connecting to customers. For example, Renee's response to being asked to talk about technology focused narrowly on the flower shop where she worked using social media and email as a means of generating business: "We have a website and we have a Facebook page. We send mass emails. A lot of people send their order in over the computer. That never used to be the case." Similarly, despite the fact that Leah used sophisticated technologies like an electric pottery wheel and kiln in her work with ceramics, she demurred when asked about how technology mattered in her work: "Technology is not my thing. I would love to be able to read up on these things, but even reading, it's just like ... I'd rather leave that to someone else."

I see this divergence as a useful reminder of the disconnect between how theorists think of technology and how it is conceptualized more generally in the context of everyday life. In fact, ANT is in a sense built on the failure to include certain (or all) technologies in accounts of socio-technical networks. This finding reinforces my argument that participant accounts form an important counter-narrative to dominant, narrow characterizations of the IoT solely as censors and cloud-stored datasets rather than a paradigm that encompasses a wide range of design norms and values. With this caveat of diverging definitions in mind - meaning that my analysis of workplace technologies includes tools and devices that most participants would not categorize as such - I can proceed to key themes of socio-technical arrangements in craftspeople's workspaces.

Embodiment and DIY ergonomics

In terms of how participants arranged the tools and technologies in their workspaces, embodiment surfaced as an organizing principle. Participants described fitting spaces to their bodies, or letting their bodies dictate the placement of furniture and tools. For some participants, space and embodiment was structured mostly around convenience, as Jeff described: "[Organization is] based on what shelving I own, and [tools] for the primary thing I'm making, how quickly can I reach the raw materials that I need." Here, individual bodies anchor the spatial structuring of tools and materials, where the placement of objects is literally tied to keeping things at arms' reach. For other participants, bodies and/in workspaces was tied to safety. Katrin was particularly descriptive in terms of how her workspace reflected a need to respect and protect her individual body: "The [height of the] table is really important, where you lean over. Like how I sit. I've had to make a stool especially for the size of my hips. It's just crazy important to take your own body into consideration."

Whereas for Katrin, the arrangement of her workspace and design of her furniture was in direct reflection of her body, for Shannon, a chronic health condition affected the entire process of quilting: "I make the baby quilts because I can't make big quilts anymore, because I can't baste them, because I can't crawl around on the floor. A baby quilt I can baste on the wall, so it makes it much easier." In fact, Shannon first began quilting in response to being diagnosed with chronic obstructive pulmonary disease (COPD), which prevented her from continuing activities she had formerly enjoyed, like hiking. Although quilting took less of a toll on her body, she was still limited in the kinds of quilts she could make, and the setup of her workspace reflected these health issues in that things were arranged in tight proximity rather than spaced out.

For many participants, embodiment was also connected to taking pleasure in the materiality of their craftwork, in contrast to the abstraction and lack of physicality associated with computer-related work. For example, Heather stated: "I'm really drawn to this because I think I just really enjoy the physicality of it. I like being up and moving around ... I like using my coordination. I like using my body." Dan also spoke about taking pleasure in the physical aspects of his work, comparing it to the more abstract process of design: "In design work, you're using your brain, and [then] your hands are doing your brain's work ... You have to wash [tiles]. You have to sand. You have to do this. You have to do that. It's almost like masonry work. [You] get your hands dirty, and it gives you the feeling of 'shit, I'm doing something.'" In keeping with [10], participants valued the physicality of their handmade craft process, as well as the materiality of the actual artifacts, some degree of which was tied to a specific contrast with the abstraction and lack of tactility they associated with computer based work.

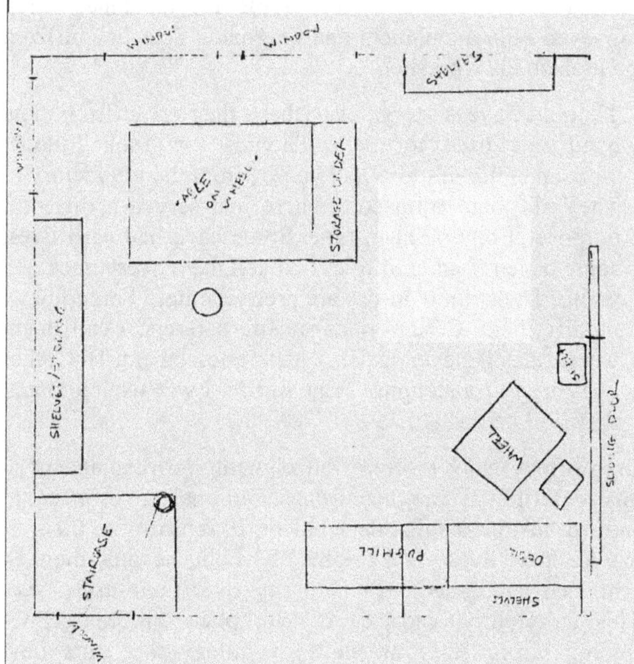

Fig. 1: Katrin's map of her ceramics studio. Interestingly, when asked to draw a map of their workspaces, participants almost never drew themselves. Bodies emerged as highly salient in verbal accounts of how things were organized but absent (for 13 out of 14 participants) in visual representations. Contra ANT, there is an interesting de-privileging of the human here, where non-human actants are elevated to visibility while human actants disappear.

Taken together, these accounts offer a very literal and DIY approach to office ergonomics. As opposed to standing desks or office chairs intended to support healthy posture while working, craftspeople I interviewed described ad hoc assemblages for situating their workspaces in ways that are directly tied to their individual bodies. Rather than conforming to their workspaces, participants described their efforts[1] to make workspaces conform to their individual needs. These efforts enabled smoother, more comfortable workflows in the course of daily productivity, and reflect the extent of autonomy that participants enjoyed in arranging their workspaces.

Provenance

Participants' workspaces become individualized partly in relation to their bodies, in that they customize spaces to meet physical and individualized specifications. Another means of individualizing space emerged from participant accounts of their tools' and materials provenance. Participants took pleasure in describing the histories of different tools and workplace furniture. Anna described inheriting a desk from her father, who worked as a draftsman, while Hannah talked about different bargains she'd found on heavy machinery via Craigslist. The socio-technical narratives of their workspaces thus included narratives of the lives of their tools and machines. Greg conveyed both attachment and pragmatic detachment from the tools in his workshop:

> They all have a story, like where they came from. The band saw used to make Thomas the Tank Engine, wooden children's toys and yo-yos from the toy factory ... They all came from somewhere and served a different purpose at one point in time. Some have had hard lives, some haven't had hard lives … I sell them every once in a while. Their rights in life are pretty limited. Sometimes I modify them. Certain ones are life partners, I call them, where they'll never leave. I just restore them. But other ones are just a stepping stone in life. I will use them and they will go away.

Greg offers many layers of attachment and pragmatism in this description, ranging from emotional investment to shrewd, instrumentalist detachment. In referring to them as having had "lives" and "rights" he both elevates them to sentience and asserts his authority over their usefulness. This storytelling capacity of workplace objects echoes findings from environmental psychology that note how workers arrange workspace artifacts with an awareness that these artifacts will convey meaning to others [12, 23, 50], however, for craftspeople I interviewed, these layers of meaning were attached to machines and tools rather than desktop photos or wall decorations.

Most participants related a preference for buying used equipment, particularly those like Greg, Heather, Melanie and William who needed large machinery for their work. Saving money was an obvious reason for this choice, but there is also a Lefebvre-ian [35] argument that tools and workspaces are imbued more subtly with layers of time and labor, such that participants' expressions of attachment are also reflections of the work that has taken place with their cooperation. Similar to Rosner's [43] design intervention of a platform to embed storytelling into the process of knitting, participants' accounts of their tools revealed a woven layer of origin and provenance in terms of when, where and how they'd located their tools.

Insecurity and making do

A shared experience among participants involved a continual sense of insecurity and instability, sentiments that emerged around three key axes: production, selling and space. Regarding the first category, Katrin talked about the lack of certainty in the production process, even after devoting years to her craft: "There is a lot of anxiety in not knowing. Like, to have a job where you spent a lot of hours working on something and it may or may not turn out, there is no tried and true in this, things crack all the time." Similarly Jeff somewhat ruefully noted that even after many of years of glass blowing, he still had off days of unpredictability in production: "You'd think I'd be a machine by now, right? But on a really good day if everything's going smooth maybe I can make 30 vases, and I'm feeling good, and I drank exactly the right amount of coffee, and it goes really well. On another day, maybe I make two and one breaks. I get frustrated and realize I've been looking at Facebook for an hour." In addition to these anxieties of the reliability of the creative process, participants referenced moments of tools breaking and needing repair. Many craftspeople I interviewed took it upon themselves to learn how to fix or modify the tools they used in their work. Along these lines, Brady noted: "Everything breaks … That was big impetus for only designing my own tools. I use much less stuff that I didn't design or make. Part of the reason is because when it breaks, I know how to fix it, but then, oftentimes, when something breaks then I realize some design flaw and I end up redesigning the tool instead of using the tool." Many participants expressed a sense of satisfaction at being able to repair their own tools, but this expertise in repair also grew out of a need to mitigate financial insecurity.

Participants also talked about the precariousness of not being able to predict a steady flow of orders. Shannon noted the ways that these concerns led to internalized insecurity: "I'm a little slow right now, so I'm a little self-doubting, like, "Nobody likes my stuff!"" Although Melanie and William's business was quite successful, this produced its own form of anxiety. Melanie expressed worry about continuing to make currently popular items rather than developing new ones: "All we're doing is facing the screens. We're not making the stuff we want to make." When I probed about the source of this tension, Melanie set up a contrast between the lure of selling existing products (which she described as taking on a life of its own via the internet) and taking time to allow for creative inspiration: "[The internet] is very absorbing. It creates opportunity for companies like ours to exist in the world. It's very

[1] In a similar vein, I noticed a comparison between craftspeople who brought their pets with them to work (half of participants referenced their dogs and cats in describing their studios) and take-your-pet-to-work initiatives that have become popular among tech start-up companies.

Fig. 2 and 3: Images from Heather's studio. The top image shows a file organizer she had salvaged and then cut to fit the width of a cement divider in her workspace. The lower image shows the various materials that Heather uses to cover chairs, which she suspended from an angled wall. Both images convey the extent to which Heather had improvised space-saving solutions to an oddly-shaped workspace.

beneficial, useful, and necessary. It's also a time-suck and life-suck. It's taken over. I'm trying to push it away to a safe distance that's still effective in the business but not taking my life away."

A third type of insecurity surfaced around the (in)stability of space. Many participants described migrating from one studio space to another, often with improvised home studios in between, typically because of cost and affordability. Heather described the consequences of these transitions as a process of internalizing instability:

> You can't necessarily get too attached to a particular space or environment because sometimes -- in particular with cheap space -- you're just forced to relocate … I always try to keep that in mind when I'm spending a lot of time in here on this space. You can't fall in love with it too much, because you don't own it and you might have to move. The stuff that's yours, that you own, you can take that wherever you want. The way you organize it in the particular space is not permanent.

Heather's studio included a number of very space-specific interventions, making use of an oddly-shaped room and fitting machines and materials into different nooks and corners (see figures 2 and 3). Even for participants who had a fairly established customer base and did not feel it was likely they'd need to move, participants all had recent experiences of having had prior workspaces or ambitions for how to alter their current spaces. The paradox here is on the one hand investing a great deal of energy in customizing workspaces, and on the other hand being prepared to move on to another space on short notice. Insecurity drives a need for improvisation, adaptation and a certain degree of detachment, at odds with the investment of time and effort in customizing their spaces.

Flow

In describing good work days participants almost always described a sense of flow. Among psychologists and researchers who study work, Csikszentmihalyi [10] is often cited as the foundational theorist of flow, which refers to "the state in which people are so involved in an activity that nothing else seems to matter; the experience itself is so enjoyable that people will do it even at great cost, for the sheer sake of doing it" (p.1 – see Liss-Marino [37] for an analysis of flow and craftwork). But beyond a psychological definition, there is an explicitly ANT layer here, in that participants described not just productivity, but a sense of coordination with their surroundings.

About half of participants used the term "flow" specifically, while others described flow more indirectly in terms of fluid productivity, as discussed by Leah: "If I can crank out a lot of stuff, that's a good work day...and finish pieces. If I have unfinished earrings, or something, once I have them all stacked and they're all ready to be fired, that's a really great day." Eli described flow as "A good feeling, there's no rush, just the way you want to do it. You do it and it's easy. It works itself out. You know that you don't have to worry about a late night thing or whether you will have this all done by the time you have to setup shop somewhere." Eli's emphasis on time is characteristic of references to flow, in that it is typically associated with a sense of time lapsing.

For other participants, however, flow was more closely tied to space. Heather offered an illustrative example in her description of a good work day: "Sometimes it just flows, sometimes I have a good flow [during the work day]. Other times I just don't have a good flow, like I can't find things … I spend a lot of time on getting my machinery working properly." Heather's reference to machines and tools as vital to a sense of flow was reiterated by other participants, like Greg: "The second you're trying to do something, and the material or the tool is fighting you. It's the worst thing in the world, like you don't want to do this anymore. When it's right, it's right."

When I asked Greg to elaborate, he explained that in an ideal work environment, "where you can hit a button, and a big saw comes on. You separate a piece of wood, without even thinking about it. Hit another button and flatten it. I'm all about this effortlessness." For participants like Heather and Greg, flow was deeply intertwined with the cooperation of tools, to the extent that they assigned agency to these technologies ("the tool is fighting you"). In this way, tools take on human agency – in ANT terms, they are recognized as actants – in contexts of interrupting or disrupting flow. This sense of autonomy offered the clearest indication of companionability, which I develop more fully in the following section.

Companionability

Initially, I had assumed that participants would describe personal connections to their tools and that companionability would emerge through a kind of anthropomorphizing of workplace technologies. Participants typically had favorite tools that they described with visible fondness, for example, Leah stating "This squeeze bottle is like my heart," and Katrin's comment that "If I can't find my sponge, because my cat has knocked it off somewhere, I'm freaking out. I'm like, 'Where is my tiny little scrubby sponge?'" Although some participants did assign personalities to their tools, for the most part they resisted elevating tools to companions. Instead, companionability emerged in terms of the spatial arrangements of tools, bodies and space as fostering fluid productivity.

Flow was related to assigning agency and affect to tools, which participants tended to characterize as tools wanting or not wanting to work. For example, Heather stated: "The thing about using all these tools is like is it's almost like symphony and it's about how things are working together one after the other. It's kind of a flow, when I think about having made something, I don't necessarily relate one specific tool to that thing I think about all the different tools that I use, one after the other." For Heather, discussing productivity in terms of individual tools was almost nonsensical – they had to operate in concert, as a cooperative network, in order to constitute a production process. With an ANT reading of companionability, participants' workspaces leveraged the support and cooperation of individual tools as well as individual bodies. In turn, the limitations and peculiarities of tools had to be accounted for in order to yield successful pieces.

Greg used similar terms to describe the intimacy in knowing how to respond to the peculiarities of specific tools in order to work with them: "Machines are like an instrument. You have to understand its sensitivities. Right now my joiner's cutting tapers. If I cut on the left-hand side, I won't get a thing called "snipe," which is when it pops off of one table onto the next. At the same time, it's a little high, so it will cut a taper. The tailstock on my lathe is a couple thousandths high right now, so if it's certain kind of work, I know that it will do certain things, but it's going to struggle doing other things." In both cases, connectivity is described as a vital part of enabling tools to cooperate in a productive flow.

Companionability of space itself also come through in expressions of protectiveness over where and with whom one works. Jennifer described a sense of attachment and worry when she rented her studio out to other photographers: "I never hang out in here when I rent the space out. I feel like I'm going to have a heart attack... It's better to just not be here, then come back and see that everything is fine ...There's definitely a level of protectiveness to the space. I'm territorial." Similarly, in talking about the decision to rent her own rather than share studio space, Heather commented: "That's also one benefit of having your own space. A lot of people recommend you do like a collective thing or you're in a wood shop with other people. For me it was like, no. I am so protective of my space. If I clean it up, I want it to be clean when I return to it." These expressions of protectiveness stem from several layers of investment – most obviously financial investment, but also investments of time, effort and individuality. As I noted above, participants often shape spaces around their individual bodies such that their workspaces are shot through with personal preferences and idiosyncrasies.

On some level, it is not surprising that craftspeople would feel protective of their workspace. The degree of freedom agency that craftspeople have over the organization and arrangements of their workspaces meant they had the ability to imbue their surroundings with their individual personalities, which Augustin [2] and Brown [8] have noted are important means of managing everyday frustrations or tensions in the workplace. But in terms of thinking about how companionability emerges in participant narratives of daily working life, the convergence of familiarity with a tools' provenance and determining spatial arrangements produces a sense of concerned attachment, even in the face of financial uncertainty. As such, participants treat their spaces as companions to be cared for, responded to and protected.

DISCUSSION

Beyond gathering ethnographic accounts of how craftspeople arrange their workspaces and relate to their tools and process of production, my aim in this paper has been to interrogate larger paradigms of how people, technology and space are or should be intertwined. In particular, themes that emerged from qualitative interviews about socio-technical relations and production can help analyze core tenets and premises of the IoT as a design paradigm. The IoT has not emerged from a vacuum. Instead it describes a set of relationships that currently exists more informally in the everyday lives of people who are embedded within networks of technology, tools and information. I want to claim craftwork as part of the IoT, in the sense that tools, devices and craftspeople talk to each other in the production of art and artifacts. From this viewpoint, I can redraw and critique the boundaries around what we currently consider belonging to the IoT make suggestions for its further development as sociotechnical infrastructure. In particular, I bring a cultural studies approach to reimagining what the IoT could look like the in the contemporary workplace, concentrating on issues of power, agency and social justice. Although I stated in the introduction that the IoT is already here, I agree with Mosco [43] and Howard [27] that it is still possible to shape the politics of these socio-technical infrastructures. In thinking about policy and design recommendations for the IoT, narratives of craftwork offer two key insights: respecting individual agency and addressing the materiality of IoT infrastructure.

Implications for Workspace Design: Agency at the Office

Although it has become comedy fodder for workplace satire from Dilbert to The Office, how we shape our workspaces offers important insights into the levels of control and autonomy we have as workers. In this context of workplaces, we can think of socio-technical arrangements as a vantage point for understanding agency and power as part of the process of labor and value.

Writing about the working lives of musicians, Stahl [53] has argued that conventional understandings of work are based on a concept of the employment contract which is in itself invalid "because it attempts to do something - and is treated as if it does something - that it cannot do: transform a responsible person into a nonresponsible thing" (p. 219). According to Stahl, working is a process of renting one's labor as well as one's sovereignty. Broadly gathered under Marxist theory, conceptualizing this process of objectification has been one of the major intellectual projects of the 20th century. These questions have long been tied to discussions of technology, from Fordist production lines and Taylorist labor mechanization to big data and workplace analytics [29]. Increasingly, technology and data plays a deciding role not only in terms of how work gets done (e.g. replacing workers with machines) but how work is assigned (e.g. Mechanical Turk and Uber). If Fordism and Taylorism were about drastic changes in how work gets done, current pushes towards connected monitoring and data are about how work is valued. At stake in thinking critically about networks of people, tools and space, is nothing less than understanding changing norms of work and productivity, what counts as labor, what counts as production and how much agency humans retain in the process.

Mobility and interoperability have become such accepted design ethics that it can become difficult to question whether or when these objectives are desirable or valuable. The IoT exemplifies and builds on a sustained push towards mobility and connectedness. In combination with constant, invisible data gathering, the IoT crystallizes a set of socio-technical relationships in which individuals produce data that they do not control and may not even be able to parse. Indeed, individuals are increasingly no longer the most authoritative source of information about themselves [5] and the profoundly uneven exchange of data and agency is one way of characterizing the IoT paradigm. When these exchanges take shape in the workplace, Stahl's [53] arguments about the reduced agency of workers become particularly vital – if work itself requires a contract of highly reduced sovereignty, what does that mean for infrastructural shifts in monitoring, data-gathering, evaluation and compensation? In short, to what extent are shifts in workplace technologies supporting or limiting individual agency?

Craftspeople have a great deal of autonomy in terms of how they work and particularly in how they organize work spaces, which was a key draw in using their experiences to think through the inter-device operations of socio-technical networks. They also have a great deal of autonomy in choosing tools and technologies to use in their work, and are often responsible for repairing or replacing these devices. Using ANT and companionability as theoretical frameworks, this investigation of craft and production has sought to reveal the agency of people as well as things, and has identified different affective dimensions of the networks in which creators, tools, artifacts and space are bound. In particular, participants most frequently assigned human affect and agency to tools in the context of productivity and flow. In terms of what this finding means for IoT as a design ethic, the process of integrating censors and data into work environments should not be undertaken in uncontested acquiescence to constant, invisible connectivity. Rather it should be a process that involves and directly benefits workers [11], respects their need for flexibility, responds to various forms of insecurity, and makes legible rather than obscures paths of data.

Recognizing materiality

As part of accommodating individual agency, policy in IoT design should also acknowledge the materiality at work in its implementation and functionality. What typically drops out of narratives of connectivity and interoperability are the seams [58] between different devices, bodies and spaces. Yet the multiple forms of precarity involved in craftspeople's work exposes the seams and stoppage points within these networks. When participants referenced the deliberate placement of tools and materials in reference to their bodies, they are stitching together a workspace that recognizes rather than obscures seams between sociotechnical actors.

The materiality of craftwork was often a source of pride and pleasure for participants, but it was also a signifier of agency and expertise (see [9, 42, 45]), for example in participants' accounts of repair. As Jackson [28] has argued,

> Repair occupies and constitutes an *aftermath*, growing at the margins, breakpoints, and interstices of complex sociotechnical systems as they creak, flex, and bend their way through time. It fills in the moment of hope and fear in which bridges from old worlds to new worlds are build, and the continuity of order, value, and meaning gets woven, one tenuous thread at a time. And it does all this quietly, humbly, and all the time. (p. 223)

Moments of repair and customization were deeply important for participants' work, partly in pragmatic terms of financial limitations but also as part of creating a work environment that fostered intimacy with their tools and devices, facilitating flow and increasing the simple pleasures of doing work comfortably and well. Because the IoT is structured in ways that we often cannot see and produces data that we cannot access, it threatens to become a structure without repair. Insisting on making repair and rupture a visible part of how IoT networks are designed and experienced would allow for an increased sense of agency and legibility of the different flows of data. It would also ensure more flexibility in how these structures can respond to shifts in user needs and practices. In this sense, resisting descriptions of the IoT as immaterial offers another venue for supporting individual agency within IoT structures.

Attending to the materiality of the IoT is also necessary from a stance of environmental justice. Because it is in the best interest of advertising and marketing firms to gather as much data about consumers as possible [57], there is a contingent advantage to making this process seem invisible, to obscure the processes of information gathering. In fact, the massive creation of data results in massive server farms that require substantial amounts of power [20, 43], with real environmental costs in terms of energy use and waste. Allowing or encouraging abstraction of IoT infrastructure participates in a fiction that these technologies take place invisibly or intangibly, when in fact, these structures have profound and lasting environmental consequences.

DIRECTIONS FOR FUTURE WORK

The approach of analyzing the IoT through investigating space and craft is only one of many for producing a narrative that yields insight into questions of affect and agency as they pertain to socio-technical relationships. By design, participants in this study were craftspeople who make art and artifacts by hand, although digital technologies were fundamental to the design and sale of their products. Future research that compared craftspeople whose use of digital technologies is more fundamental to their work (such as graphic designers or computer-assisted design cartographers) could yield important insights into how findings related to flow, embodiment and companionability may differ for people whose craft is more directly related to computer-based work. An alternative approach to theorizing issues of workspaces and technology in terms of companionability and agency would be to conduct qualitative analysis with people whose workspaces are already deeply connected but perhaps not (yet) recognized as part of the IoT. Examples include university campuses where ID cards are used for purposes as varied as taking a class at the gym, buying food at the dining hall, using library materials and taking exams. Other examples include hospitals, where movements of staff as well as patients are not only monitored but entangled in complex webs of surveillance and response from human as well as non-human agents. By investigating the lived experience of constant data flows and inter-device operability in work environments that are currently only partially (or not at all) claimed within the IoT domain, we can further interrogate the design values and infrastructural politics of this increasingly dominant socio-technical paradigm.

ACKNOWLEDGEMENTS

I am grateful to the participants in this study for their time and hospitality in sharing their work with me. I would also like to thank Megan Finn, Alex Taylor and the anonymous reviewers for their feedback on this paper.

REFERENCES

1. Luigi Atzori, Antonio Iera, and Giacomo Morabito. 2010. The Internet of Things: A survey.*Comput. Netw.* 54, 15 (October 2010), 2787-2805. http://dx.doi.org/10.1016/j.comnet.2010.05.010
2. Sally Augustin. 2004. *The meaning of office things: A study of special objects in office environments.* Ph.D Dissertation. Claremont Graduate University, Claremont, CA.
3. Shaowen Bardzell, Daniela K. Rosner, and Jeffrey Bardzell. 2012. Crafting quality in design: integrity, creativity, and public sensibility. In *Proceedings of the Designing Interactive Systems Conference* (DIS '12). ACM, New York, NY, USA, 11-20. http://doi.acm.org/10.1145/2317956.2317959
4. Christine Borgman. Data, data everywhere — but how to manage and govern? Berkman Center for Internet & Society Luncheon. Harvard University, Cambridge, MA. Jun. 2015. Available at: http://works.bepress.com/borgman/366
5. Jonah Bossewitch and Aram Sinnreich. 2012. The end of forgetting: Strategic agency beyond the panopticon. *New Media & Society*.
6. Aoife Brennan, Jasdeep S. Chugh, and Theresa Kline. 2002. Traditional versus open office design: A longitudinal field study. *Environment and Behavior,* 34, 3: 279-299.
7. Virginia Braun and Victoria Clarke. 2006. Using thematic analysis in psychology. *Qualitative research in psychology,* 3, 2: 77-101.
8. Graham Brown. 2009. Claiming a corner at work: Measuring employee territoriality in their workspaces. *Journal of Environmental Psychology,* 29, 1: 44-52.
9. Matthew Crawford. 2009. The Case for Working with Your Hands or Why Office Work is Bad for Us and Fixing Things Feels Good. Penguin.
10. Mihaly Csikzentmihaly. 1991. *Flow: The psychology of optimal experience.* HarperPerennial.

11. Dries De Roeck, Karin Slegers, Johan Criel, Marc Godon, Laurence Claeys, Katriina Kilpi, and Ann Jacobs. 2012. I would DiYSE for it!: a manifesto for do-it-yourself internet-of-things creation. In *Proceedings of the 7th Nordic Conference on Human-Computer Interaction: Making Sense Through Design* (NordiCHI '12). ACM, New York, NY, USA, 170-179. http://doi.acm.org/10.1145/2399016.2399044
12. Anne S. Devlin, Sarah Donovan, Arianne Novolov, Olivia Nold, Andrea Packard, and Gabrielle Zandan. 2009. "Impressive?" credentials, family photographs, and the perception of therapist qualities. *Journal of Environmental Psychology,* 29, 4: 503-512.
13. Paul Dourish and Genevieve Bell. 2011. *Divining the digital future.* MIT Press.
14. Kimberly Elsbach. 2004. Interpreting workplace identities: The role of office decor. *Journal of Organizational Behavior, 25,* 1: 99-128.
15. Virginia Eubanks. 2011. *Digital dead end: Fighting for social justice in the information age.* MIT Press.
16. Ylva Fernaeus, Martin Jonsson, and Jakob Tholander. 2012. Revisiting the jacquard loom: threads of history and current patterns in HCI. In *Proceedings of the SIGCHI Conference on Human Factors in Computing Systems* (CHI '12). ACM, New York, NY, USA, 1593-1602. http://doi.acm.org/10.1145/2207676.2208280
17. Sarah Fox, Rachel Rose Ulgado, and Daniela Rosner. 2015. Hacking Culture, Not Devices: Access and Recognition in Feminist Hackerspaces. In *Proceedings of the 18th ACM Conference on Computer Supported Cooperative Work & Social Computing* (CSCW '15). ACM, New York, NY, USA, 56-68. http://doi.acm.org/10.1145/2675133.2675223
18. Joan Fujimura. 1991. On methods, ontologies, and representation in the sociology of science: Where do we stand. *Social organization and social process: Essays in honor of Anselm Strauss*. 207-248.
19. Jack Jen Gieseking. 2013. Where We Go From Here The Mental Sketch Mapping Method and Its Analytic Components. *Qualitative Inquiry,* 19, 9: 712-724.
20. James Glanz. 2012. Power, pollution and the Internet. *The New York Times*. Retrieved September 23, 2015 from http://www.nytimes.com/2012/09/23/technology/data-centers-waste-vast-amounts-of-energy-belying-industry-image.html?
21. Connie Golsteijn, Elise Hoven, David Frohlich, and Abigail Sellen. 2014. Hybrid crafting: towards an integrated practice of crafting with physical and digital components. *Personal and ubiquitous computing,* 18, 3: 593-611.
22. Elizabeth Goodman and Daniela Rosner. 2011. From garments to gardens: negotiating material relationships online and 'by hand'. In *Proceedings of the SIGCHI Conference on Human Factors in Computing Systems* (CHI '11). ACM, New York, NY, USA, 2257-2266. http://doi.acm.org/10.1145/1978942.1979273
23. Samuel D. Gosling, Sei Jin Ko, Thomas Mannarelli, and Margaret Morris. 2002. A room with a cue: Personality judgements based on office and bedrooms. *Journal of Personality and Social Psychology, 82,* 3: 379.
24. Sara Hachem, Thiago Teixeira, and Valérie Issarny. 2011. Ontologies for the internet of things. In *Proceedings of the 8th Middleware Doctoral Symposium* (MDS '11). ACM, New York, NY, USA, Article 3 , 6 pages.
25. Daniela Hernandez. 2012. Before the iPad, there was the Honeywell Kitchen Computer. *Wired.* Retrieved September 29, 2015 from http://www.wired.com/2012/11/kitchen-computer/
26. Susmita Horrow and Anjali Sardana. 2012. Identity management framework for cloud based internet of things. In *Proceedings of the First International Conference on Security of Internet of Things* (SecurIT '12). ACM, New York, NY, USA, 200-203.
27. Philip Howard. 2015. *Pax Technica: How the Internet of Things May Set Us Free or Lock Us Up*. Yale University Press.
28. Steven J. Jackson. 2014. Rethinking repair. MIT Press.
29. Jodi Kantor and David Streitfeld. 2015. Inside Amazon: Wrestling big ideas in a bruising workplace. *New York Times*. Retrieved August 15, 2015 from http://www.nytimes.com/2015/08/16/technology/inside-amazon-wrestling-big-ideas-in-a-bruising-workplace.html
30. David S. Kirk and Abigail Sellen. 2010. On human remains: Values and practice in the home archiving of cherished objects. *ACM Trans. Comput.-Hum. Interact.* 17, 3, Article 10 (July 2010), 43 pages. http://doi.acm.org/10.1145/1806923.1806924
31. Rob Kitchin and Martin Dodge. 2011. Code/space. MIT Press.
32. Bruno Latour. 1990. Technology is society made durable. *The Sociological Review* 38, S1: 103-131.
33. Bruno Latour. 2007. Reassembling the social: An introduction to Actor-Network-Theory. Oxford University Press.
34. So Young Lee and Jay L. Brand. 2005. Effects of control over office workspace on perceptions of the work environment and work outcomes. *Journal of Environmental Psychology, 25,* 3: 323-333.
35. Henri Lefebvre. 1991 *The production of space.* Wiley-Blackwell.
36. Jessica Lingel and Tim Regan. 2014. "it's in your spinal cord, it's in your fingertips": practices of tools and craft in building software. In *Proceedings of the 17th ACM conference on Computer supported cooperative work & social computing* (CSCW '14). ACM, New York, NY, USA, 295-304. http://doi.acm.org/10.1145/2531602.2531614

37. Tara J. Liss-Marino. 2014. *Sell (it) yourself: Marketing pleasure in digital DIY*. Ph.D Dissertation. University of Pennsylvania, Philadelphia, PA.
38. Susan S. Lukesh. 2014. The Internet of Things. *ACM Inroads, 5*, 3: 60.
39. Carolyn Marvin. 1997. *When old technologies were new*. Oxford University Press.
40. Alice Marwick. 2013. *Status update*. Yale University Press.
41. Michael Massimi and Daniela Rosner. 2013. Crafting for major life events: implications for technology design and use. In *Proceedings of the 27th International BCS Human Computer Interaction Conference* (BCS-HCI '13), Steve Love, Kate Hone, and Tom McEwan (Eds.). British Computer Society, Swinton, UK, UK, , Article 34 , 6 pages.
42. Malcolm McCullough. 1996. *Abstracting Craft: The Practiced Digital Hand*. MIT Press.
43. Vincent Mosco. 2014. *To the cloud: Big data in a turbulent world*. Paradigm Publishers.
44. Greg Oldham and Yitzhak Fried. 1987. Employee reactions to workspace characteristics. *Journal of Applied Psychology, 72,* 1: 75.
45. Howard Risatti. 2007. *A Theory of Craft: Function and Aesthetic Expression*. University of North Carolina Press.
46. Daniela K. Rosner. 2010. Mediated crafts: digital practices around creative handwork. In *CHI '10 Extended Abstracts on Human Factors in Computing Systems* (CHI EA '10). ACM, New York, NY, USA, 2955-2958. http://doi.acm.org/10.1145/1753846.1753894
47. Daniela K. Rosner and Kimiko Ryokai. 2009. Reflections on craft: probing the creative process of everyday knitters. In *Proceedings of the seventh ACM conference on Creativity and cognition* (C&C '09). ACM, New York, NY, USA, 195-204. http://doi.acm.org/10.1145/1640233.1640264
48. Jathan Sadowski and Frank Pasquale. 2015. The spectrum of control: A social theory of the smart city. *First Monday,* 20, 7.
49. Nikil Saval. 2014. *Cubed: A secret history of the workforce*. Doubleday.
50. Susan Scheiberg. 1990. Emotions on display the personal decoration of work space. *The American Behavioral Scientist, 33,* 3: 330.
51. Richard Sennett. 2008. *The Craftsman*. Yale University Press.
52. James P. Spradley. 1979. *The Ethnographic Interview*. Harcourt, Brace, Jovanovic.
53. Matthew Stahl. 2014. *Unfree Masters: Popular Music and the Politics of Work (Refiguring American Music)*. Duke University Press.
54. Anselm L. Strauss and Juliet M. Corbin. 1990. *Basics of qualitative research*. Sage.
55. Joshua G. Tanenbaum, Amanda M. Williams, Audrey Desjardins, and Karen Tanenbaum. 2013. Democratizing technology: pleasure, utility and expressiveness in DIY and maker practice. In *Proceedings of the SIGCHI Conference on Human Factors in Computing Systems* (CHI '13). ACM, New York, NY, USA, 2603-2612. http://doi.acm.org/10.1145/2470654.2481360
56. Gavin Turner and Jeremy Myerson. 2000. New workspace, new culture. *The Journal for Quality and Participation, 23,* 5: 45.
57. Joseph Turow, Lee McGuigan, and Elena R. Maris. 2015. Making data mining a natural part of life: Physical retailing, customer surveillance and the 21st century social imaginary. *European Journal of Cultural Studies, 18*, 4-5: 464-478.
58. Mark Weiser. 1994. Building invisible interfaces. Keynote talk. In *Proc. ACM UIST.*
59. Meredith Wells, Luke Thelen, and Jennifer Ruark. 2007. Workspace personalization and organizational culture: Does your workspace reflect you or your company? *Environment and Behavior, 39,* 5: 616-634.
60. Meredith Wells and Luke Thelen. 2002. What does your workspace say about you? The influence of personality, status, and workspace on personalization. *Environment and Behavior, 34,* 3: 300-321.
61. Amit Zoran. 2015. Hybrid craft: showcase of physical and digital integration of design and craft skills. In *ACM SIGGRAPH Art Gallery* (SIGGRAPH '15). ACM, New York, NY, USA, 384-398. http://doi.acm.org/10.1145/2810185.2810187

Object-Oriented Publics

Tom Jenkins[1], Christopher A. Le Dantec[1], Carl DiSalvo[1], Thomas Lodato[2] and Mariam Asad[1]

[1]Digital Media Program
School of Literature, Media, and Communication
Georgia Institute of Technology
Atlanta, GA, USA

[2]Center for Urban Innovation
School of Public Policy
Georgia Institute of Technology
Atlanta, GA, USA

tom.jenkins, ledantec, cdisalvo, thomas.lodato, missasad@gatech.edu

ABSTRACT
Social computing—or computing in a social context—has largely concerned itself with understanding social interaction among and between people. This paper asserts that ignoring material components—including computing itself—as social actors is a mistake. Computing has its own agenda and agencies, and including it as a member of the social milieu provides a means of producing design objects that attend to how technology use can extend beyond merely amplifying or augmenting human actions. In this paper, we offer examples of projects that utilize the capacity of *object-oriented publics* to both analyze the conditions and consequences around existing publics and engage with matters of concern inherent to emerging publics. Considering how computing as an actor contributes to the construction of publics provides insight into the design of computational systems that address issues. We end by introducing the idea of the *object ecology* as a way to coordinate design approaches to computational publics.

Author Keywords
Design Research, Computational Agency, Social Computing, Publics, Object Ecology

ACM Classification Keywords
H.5.m. Information interfaces and presentation: Miscellaneous.

INTRODUCTION
Since the turn of the 21st century, publics have gained traction as a productive framing concept for design. The idea of publics as distinctive forms of social organization draw on the work of John Dewey [22], taking as a base assumption that there is not a singular all-inclusive public, but rather a multiplicity of publics. Key to publics, is that they are issue-oriented: a public is directed to the conditions and consequences of a particular condition—or set of inter-related conditions—in order to attend to their consequences [4].

CHI'16, May 07 - 12, 2016, San Jose, CA, USA

ACM 978-1-4503-3362-7/16/05...$15.00
DOI: http://dx.doi.org/10.1145/2858036.2858565

In the 2005 exhibition and accompanying book, *Making Things Public: Atmospheres of Democracy* Bruno Latour reinvigorated the discussion of publics [69]. For Latour, publics are a way to understand how society deals with controversies and dilemmas, and as such, provide a useful bridge to design—issues are not expressed in the abstract, but are encountered through objects. Latour's call for an object-oriented politics, in which issues take place through things, reframed discussions about the politics of artifacts that were occurring at the intersection of design and science and technology studies. Arising from this disciplinary crossroads, there has been a spate of work across design studies [23,52], human-computer interaction and computer-supported cooperative work [2,3,7], participatory design [7,8,27], and science and technology studies [18,56,57] that examine the role of design in articulating issues and constructing publics.

Usually, the central concern when discussing publics is the organization of people. Publics certainly contain people, but that is not all they contain. Publics are, in fact, organizations of humans and nonhumans: animals, plants, atmospheres, buildings, buses, and so on. What is of particular interest to us is the role of computing as a nonhuman actor in publics. The designation "computing," for the purpose of this paper, collapses software, hardware, applications, and networking into a single term; our concern here is to consider broadly the category of computing artifacts and the ways in which they circulate socially and participate in publics.

The critical shift we are proposing is that by extending our understanding of computing beyond that of merely amplifying or augmenting human actions, we gain a new perspective from which to understand and interpret the role and impact of computing in social and cultural terms. We also gain new design opportunities to manifest alternative and speculative visions of future publics.

This maneuver occurs at the intersection of several strains of scholarship within the expansive tent of human-computer interaction. There are clear roots in research through design exemplified by such systems as Drift Table, Plane Tracker, or Prayer Companion [13,30,31]. Each of these examples point toward the ways in which the computational artifacts are in discourse with human actors—rather than simply augmentations of human actors. Furthermore, these projects and other like them and embody a distinct practice of critical design in computing [62]. Likewise, recent turns in computer-supported cooperative work toward sociomaterial design seek to "preserve essential sociomaterial practices in new design interventions" [9], thereby embracing the inseparability of object and social context by recognizing that artifacts participate in, rather than simply inhabit, those social contexts. Even returning to distributed cognition [36,37], we can see the trajectory that externalized cognitive tools are not just repositories of some prefigured human cognition, but are discrete actors with agency engaged discursively with their social context.

COMPUTING AS ACTOR IN PUBLICS

When we say that computing exists as an actor in publics, what we mean is that computing has a character and position of its own, and is an origin of influence and consequence that extends beyond that of either the designer or the user. This is *not* to say that computing does not augment and amplify publics—it does. But computing does something else too: it participates in novel ways in the constitution of publics.

By attending to the ways in which computing acts within publics, we arrive at a more nuanced, descriptive account of its role in society. Our goal is to provide design researchers with an additional perspective on how publics form and can be formed by shifting how we think of social computing where the sociality is not *enacted through* computational tools, but is *composed of* computation.

THE MANY FACES OF HYBRID AGENCY

Notions of agency that extend beyond humans are not new to the humanities, social sciences, or design, but they have gained renewed appreciation and attention in recent years [38,44]. This is broadly part of a nonhuman turn, which draws animals, plants, and other living entities into the endeavor of social and cultural analysis. Even beyond living entities, some social scientists and theorists are looking to understand the role of artifacts themselves and how artifacts and the materials that comprise them might exhibit various kinds of agencies [12,32].

Material Agency

Of the many humanities scholars that might be characterized as part of a "new materialism," Jane Bennett provides an important connection between notions of material agency and political theory [6]. For Bennett, one of the shortcomings of political theory is that it has not attended to the role of objects in the doing and experience of politics. This is not meant as a slight against human agency, but instead an opening of political theory to take into account how all manner of objects should be included in our understanding and analysis of politics.

Material agency provides a way to understand the effects of human and nonhuman collectives as an ecological whole where the effects arise only as a result of the distributed nature of a collective agency—spread among humans, tools, environments, and settings [5]. Much in the way distributed cognition allowed cognition to escape the confines of the skull [36], material agency opens the field of analysis for understanding social effects as the result of hybrid human/nonhuman collectives.

While this perspective on material agency is important to design research, it does not generally engage directly with design itself, neither in regards to the particulars of designed objects, nor in the processes and practices of design. For instance, a particular object might be examined in a general sense as a member of a collective, but the specific qualities of the design itself, in terms of form, construction, and affordances, are overlooked. These approaches also tend to lack a close reading of technology: a given technological system may be called out, as with Bennett's power grid, but the working particulars of the power grid is black-boxed. Some exceptions are found in sub-fields such as software studies or platform studies [59].

Actor-Network Theory

Following on from material agency, Actor-Network Theory (ANT) was developed in the field of Science and Technology Studies through the work of multiple scholars, including (but not limited to) Bruno Latour, John Law, and Michel Callon [47,50]. Despite its name, ANT is less a theory or method than it is a perspective. What was radical about this perspective was that it granted analytic symmetry between human and nonhumans. In addition, where theories of material agency often take nonhumans as black boxes, ANT worked to peer into the particulars of human and nonhuman networks to examine the specific ways technology acted within these networks. One of the central claims of ANT is that to understand a given technology, one must identify and follow the capacities of multiple actors, including but not limited to humans. One implication of this symmetry is that one can speak of the agency of nonhumans, ranging from scallops to doorknobs to speed bumps to algorithms. Rather than considering agency a material quality *per se*, within ANT it is less that any given artifact has agency, but rather that agency is an effect of the configuration of a network in which capacities, responsibilities, and authorities are distributed—delegated—among the variety of human actors and actants (nonhuman actors) that comprise the network [47].

Design research and ANT have crossed before, and continue to cross at many points. These intersections produce exciting exchanges between fields and lead toward new hybrid theories, methods, and perspectives in both design research and science and technology studies. Latour's work in particular has been influential to many designers [7,8,27]; of late, Latour himself has spoken directly about design [46]. There is also an emerging cohort of STS scholars examining the practices and products of design, engaging the field of design research directly. These scholars include Albena Yaneva's research on architecture [73], Noortje Marres' research on material participation and publics [57], Mike Michael's research on speculative design [58], and Alex Wilkie's research on user experience [70].

ANT offers a connection between design and the social sciences that attends to the practices and products of design. Both share a commitment to the "object," or product, as having a capacity for action. Whereas other theories of agency privilege human action—in some cases exclusively—both ANT and design recognize the necessary role of the object in any and every constitution of society. However, while ANT does offer a bridge between the social sciences and design, there are limitations as well. In particular, ANT is useful for analyzing networks that already exist. Unfortunately, it is not a perspective that is well equipped for conceptualizing and generating networks (or products, or services) that do not yet exist. This mismatch for speculating about possible futures limits the utility of ANT for design [52].

Design *Things*

Growing out of ANT, the notion of *things* has begun to take hold within participatory design, particularly around renewed interest in engaging with the political effects and consequences of designed objects and systems [7]. Within design, scholars have advanced the notion of *things*, focusing on the way in which *things* articulate relations between humans and nonhumans [7,8,27]. Even amid the shift from the vernacular thing as a material object, something we would comfortably describe as a product of design, Binder and Ehn point out that the sociomaterial *thing* is also the product of design, and is an attempt to give design a language for imagining and generating networks of effects that include humans and nonhumans [7]. Furthermore, they contend that *things* should explicitly be the aim of design: "the outcome of the design process is a thing that modifies the space where people live: besides and beyond its functions (living for houses, hosting artworks for museums, sitting for chairs, etc.), the designed *thing* aims to change the experience of its users; it is rich in aesthetical and cultural values, opening new ways of thinking and behaving" [7].

This exposition of *thing* and its relation to design grows out of a concern with architectural design but applies broadly to similar kinds of effects and reconfigurations that arise out of actor-networks, whether tied to architectural design, engineering design, or those embodied in interactive technologies. Irrespective of field, the point of departure for analytic and generative engagement is the set of relations within the network of humans and nonhumans and the ways in which those relations exist in a constant state of flux. Here the issues at hand and the attachments to those issues arise from, and give rise to, the *things* themselves. In doing so, *things* are not merely augmenters of human action and agency, but are peers within a complex network of actors from which that agency arises and is enacted.

OBJECT-ORIENTED PUBLICS

Integrating a perspective that attributes agency to the full collective of humans and nonhumans into the notion of publics creates new theoretical opportunities in computing research. At its foundation, this shift in perspective enables a move from thinking about computing as augmentation, a technical appendage to human-centered concerns, and allows us to examine how technical artifacts and systems participate in the constitution and propagation of publics. The theoretical move from computing-as-augmentation to computing-as-actor traces and extends the intellectual and social agendas of contemporary computing research. While previous turns in computing examined the social construction of meaning *around* computing and the ways in which computing created, mediated, and amplified the sites and conditions of that social construction [1,43,66], we are moving into an era where we need to consider the social construction of meaning and action *with* computing.

This new theoretical position opens up both new *analytic* territories as we examine computing artifacts and systems with respect to the ways in which people and computing become conjoined as publics, as well as *generative* territories that take as their departure point the agency of the artifacts being designed. The case studies below help us examine this new landscape of object-oriented publics, highlighting the considerations for an understanding of social computing built around the shared, distributed, and concurrent agency of *things* in the world.

Examples of Object-Oriented Publics

Drawing more specifically on the theoretical perspectives above, we can return to familiar research sites to illustrate the features of publics that arise through the ways in which computing configures human participation and the ways in which computing's agency is made material. These examples constitute a broad category of social action and activity where the present practices require not just embracing the entanglement of social and material elements [9], but where the collective agency and capacity to act necessarily arises out of the shared participation of human and non-human actors.

At first blush, such an analysis may simply ring as a familiar application of ANT to the concept of publics. Where we differ, however, is in attending to the complementary ways in which specific computational capabilities enable new capacities for action and for new publics to convene; and where the particular arrangements of publics enable new computational possibilities to emerge. Our argument here is not just that humans and computing act within a network together, but that we fundamentally encounter social computing as an agentic discourse between people and computation. We contend that *all* computing is social computing, and that such an analysis provides cracks from which to peer into the black box and understand the shared agency in both small-scale, intimate interactions with computing as well as in the large-scale systems that organize and mobilize society.

Cycle Atlanta

Since 2012, we have been involved in a project that has tapped into trends in data-driven governance and crowdsourced models of public participation. Through a smartphone app released in Atlanta, citizens can record their bike rides, uploading route data, ride purpose, and rider demographic data. These data are used by city transportation planners as an empirical basis upon which to make decisions about where and what kind of cycling infrastructure might be necessary to create a robust and diverse urban transportation system.

Beyond the pragmatic, instrumental goal of generating data about where current cyclists were riding, the project provided avenues for public input into the planning process, broadening public input so as to make infrastructure plans both better and better-accepted when implemented. The deployment of the smartphone app channeled two streams of contemporary optimism in how digital technologies can transform urban and public life: the first drew on the vision of smart city projects where sensor networks [60,67], instrumented infrastructure [28,61] and participatory sensing [24,63] are interwoven to improve operational efficiency in city services and planning [61]. The second drew upon moves in digital democracy to decouple public participation in policy development and governance from the physical and temporal constraints of public hearings and other modes of face-to-face interaction between authorities and citizens [34].

The project integrated these two perspectives by linking instrumented data collection with democratic participation: the phones of citizens were enlisted as sensors to generate new streams of data for urban planners and the act of sensing bike routes was a form of advocacy for new infrastructure, one that was decoupled from the public meetings and design charrettes where such advocacy normally took place. However, more than simply augmenting how cyclists participated in an urban planning process, the mere existence of the app enacted a set of political realities with respect to the city. The app enabled the city to position itself as a progressive, data-driven, and technology-embracing place. These realities carried rhetorical weight for elected officials and citizens alike but also introduced the app itself as a material participant in the democratic process.

More than simply amplifying cyclists' public participation in the creation of policy and the design of physical infrastructure, the app acted as a member of a public and had unique relations to different stakeholders involved. Some of these relations came through use, where the communities who used the app provided accounts of geography and mobility that reified existing socio-economic boundaries in an empirical and authoritative way [16]. Others came through non-use where issues of community identity, gentrification, race, and class became viewed through the lens of data-based participation [15]. In some instances, the app participated just by means of existing: in planning meetings, we observed planners and engineers refer to data that might be collected by the app in the future as justification for planning decisions. Here, human participation was inferred—positioned as augmentation to the technology—and the app, as an element of the near-future smart city, enabled new political and policy claims to be made along the contours of who participated with the app and who did not.

Like other infrastructure sensing apps—for example, Street Bump, deployed in Boston to detect pavement quality issues—our app enlisted computing as an active participant in sensing and advocating for public resources. As one of the Street Bump developers explained, these apps create "a new kind of volunteerism," where it was not the citizens themselves, but instead "the devices that are in [citizens'] pocket" who are doing the volunteering [14]. Taking this quip seriously means treating the technology as an actor in a network of concerns and motivations—it is a participant in a social and political exchange, and not simply a medium for such an exchange.

A more familiar analysis of the role of the smartphone app might trace claims that the collection of data amplified the cycling community's ability to have input into the planning process by decoupling it from the limited venues of in-person advocacy. It would also argue that the collected data augmented planners' ability to make rational decisions based on novel sources of ground-truth data. Such an analysis presumes that the agency of collecting data and making use of data rests with human actors, and discounts the role of computing as simply aiding that human agency.

Instead, we would argue that the app and the data both participate as members of a cycling public. Through this participation, issues arise with respect to equity in participation, veracity of representation, and accountability and transparency of civic institutions [15,16]. These issues are all bound up in the human and nonhuman composition of the public, resulting in a *thing*: the computational agent, comprising sensing capabilities and data production that enable an alternate means of contesting urban planning. Around this *thing*, a public emerges where humans and nonhumans engage in negotiating the development of physical infrastructure. This public is both shaped by the participation of the app and the collective agency is materialized through maps, data visualizations, and planning analyses that are built upon the recorded route data produced by the app.

By itself, the app is also only part of the computational agent that participates in this public. The way data are stored, operated on, and analyzed is also part of that computational agency, not just informing the human actors with respect to setting public policy and designing bicycle facilities in a dense urban center, but changing the kinds of questions they ask and the kinds of answers they receive. In short, the app became a new kind of implicated actor in the process, one that in many ways advocated for its own perspective, its own validation and its own self interest. By shifting policy discussion to terms that required the presence of certain kinds of data, data produced by the app, the basis for democratic decision making likewise required the app be a participant, a member of a privileged constituency [16]. Where the basis of digital democracy is "to practice democracy without the limits of time, space and other physical conditions using [computing] as an addition [to], not a replacement for traditional 'analogue' political practices" [34], the facilities that enable that decoupling are not inert. Rather, they are a *thing* that exerts force through material agency.

Issue-oriented Hackathons

Shifting from a context where a new computational agent gave rise to a new public, we now turn to examine a category of publics that give rise to new computational agents: the hackathon. Originally organized within software companies to address labor-intensive development tasks, hackathons have emerged as a widespread activity in recent years. In general, hackathons focus on the development of technical—often digital—prototypes of services and systems. Attendees are presented with tasks (referred to as challenges) and groups form to design and build prototypes that address the topic area of these challenges.

While many of these events are organized around a technical topic, such as smartphones or mapping software, a segment of these events are what we call *issue-oriented hackathons*. These hackathons focus on social topics, such as sustainability, ecological change, civic responsibility, or international relations. Unlike technically-oriented hackathons, issue-oriented hackathons have aspirations of addressing these social issues through technical means.

An example of an issue-oriented hackathon can be found in the Food Data Hack, a one-day hackathon focused on the local food system of Atlanta. The event invited farmers, food advocates, entrepreneurs, service designers, web developers, and community representatives to envision and plan technical prototypes that addressed issues related to land use and food access. While the Food Data Hack emphasized design over development, the event asked participants to consider the role of computational artifacts—smartphones, web servers, and publicly accessible databases—in these issues. Structured around these particular artifacts and this topic, participants used computation and computational systems as a means to express the underlying concerns and dilemmas of land use and food access. For example, one group proposed mapping the available resources in an underserved community. This proposal framed creating, articulating, and storing user-generated data as a means to collectively overcome the lack of infrastructural resources in that community, both providing resources for residents and articulating the community's needs to those outside. As such, digital mapping and the digital map both came to embody the need of the community to be heard as well as legitimizing their concerns materially. If in fact the map had been fully executed, it would have functioned in a manner similar to the cycling app: as a computational thing that gave form to an issue and produced data which could be used as the basis for negotiating actions to be taken on that issue.

Particularly striking about issue-oriented hackathons is the way these events deal with computation as both a means and an end to think through social issues. One might choose to dismiss issue-oriented hackathons because they form around an idealistic—and maybe foolish—premise: that building technological solutions to longstanding social issues is possible over the course of a weekend. Dismissing these events, however, misses a profound insight. These events assume that computing and computation has a role in social issues and are driven by an intuitive alignment of technology as a *thing* and computation as a participant in an object-oriented public constructed to contend with the social issue at hand. Issue-oriented hackathons are based upon an implicit belief that computational artifacts can be designed and deployed as actors to effect change in contexts where human action alone has not succeeded in doing so. As such, issue-oriented hackathons can be viewed as a site to explore computation as a means to articulate both existing as well as new social arrangements.

Issue-oriented hackathons and the Cycle Atlanta project both offer an example of an activity that prefigures the role of computation within these issues, namely, by suggesting computation has a role at all. Furthermore, the role that both suggest points toward participation with collections of computing artifacts: from apps and websites to databases, servers, and libraries of code. This in turn outlines multivalenced, relational orbits among human actors, between human and computational actors, and among computational actors. Some of these valences are better understood, where the social sciences and human-computer interaction have a substantive history mapping bonds like these [25,47,51], but others are less well known—in particular the sociality of computational agents—and require consideration on their own.

Object Oriented Publics as a Design Tool

Object-oriented publics provide a starting point to consider the specific and concrete ways computing material might participate more actively within social computing. More than providing a novel analytic perspective, they enable us to create alternate possibilities for participating in computing, to move beyond computing as a mere augmentation to computing as an agent in its own right. Again, we focus on the notion that all computing is social computing, and that sociality is not just enabled or mediated by computing, but acts *with* computing as a co-participant.

Activist Technology Workshops

We have been working with housing and social justice organizations to understand the sociomaterial work practices that govern different forms of advocacy and activism. Through three years of ethnographic fieldwork and a series of co-design workshops, our investigations have documented the temporal, social, and political constraints in which activism operates; the values of social equality and institutional accountability that guide activists' actions; and the antagonistic tactics deployed to realize their goals [2]. Many of the constraints under which activist organizations operate mirror those of social service non-profits [19,68]; however, while non-profits and non-governmental organizations might try to provide services or influence policy decisions through established channels of influence and power, activists work outside of those channels, relying instead on direct action to bring about social or political change.

To a certain extent, activists' use of computing can be seen as a case study of non-profits pushed to the extreme: resources are more constrained, there is a heavier reliance on volunteers, and moment-to-moment work is contingent and irregular. However, by reframing activist technology use as a kind of information work, their particular use—and often, appropriation—of computing reveals how computing systems and artifacts become crucial co-participants in their political action.

As a result, materiality becomes crucial to activist work, particularly when involving computing. While protests or marches are often seen as spontaneous or unplanned, they are usually quickly organized as a response to an unforeseen development or event. As an example, housing justice activists may need to respond to a resident being evicted without notice. It is in these moments of crisis that computing's materiality is made prominent: the organization needs to respond by marshaling resources through different channels; they need to organize in-person support for the evicted person or family; and they need to personalize the event to build empathy and draw public support to the more general issue of housing justice [2,3].

As part of that information work, an array of computing systems and artifacts become enlisted as participants working under the mandate of the activist organization. For example, social media channels position local action within larger regional or national issues to connect the organization's work to other, related groups and concerns. Social media is also used to broadcast operational information meant to guide and inform local action, as well as to circulate information more widely as evidence of contested social conditions. Likewise, captioned images called "macros" (typically used to propagate humorous internet memes) are created to generate widespread awareness and recruit further support either through in-person action or through visibility online [2]. These computational objects and artifacts are *things* that arise out of the particular circumstances of protest and activism and disperse into the world to marshal support and mediate communication.

Looking beyond the ways in which activists participate with existing computational *things,* we also explored the creation of new computational resources that would advance the political and social aims of the organizations [3]. These workshops revealed a cast of speculative computational actors that could work proactively within the organization—including capabilities for sending messages, monitoring authorities, and sustaining individual and organizational ties. Like the turn to computation in digital democracy, recruiting new computational actors through speculative design created new participants in the activist network.

However, unlike the recruitment of social media platforms in regular operations, the objects that arose out of the design workshops accomplished different goals for the activists. Where the *things* that arose from social media—the Twitter feeds and image macros—worked to create wider shared attachments to the social issue of housing justice, the *things* that resulted from the design workshops served to create a critical reflection on both the conditions of protest and the ways in which those conditions are altered with computing. Like the issue-oriented hackathons described above, the design workshops shifted the frame of who and what could meaningfully participate in acts of peaceful protest by expanding the material of such political acts.

Across these two categories of computational things—the existing social media platforms and visual communication genres, and the speculative creations resulting from a critical making workshop—the individual and organizational work was not simply mediated by these artifacts, but altered and constituted by the collective network of human and computation actors doing the work. Put another way, the work practices of the activist organizations required the participation of an ecology of computing: mobile computing devices, data plans, shared documents, cloud services, and access to social media. It was only through the joint participation of these computing artifacts that the collective agency of the organization was able to activate social networks and constitute an ad hoc public to take action in response to an acute (if otherwise systematically entrenched) event.

Tiny Tinkering Platforms

Our final case study concerns the Internet of Things (IoT) as an assemblage of people, technology companies, concerns around privacy, corporatism, upgradeability, cost, material objects, utopianism, and more [32]. These actors all play a part of the Internet of Things in practice, and understanding what these are and how they operate at a low level is important to understand what kinds of values are being built into the rhetoric driving technical practice—and what might be left out. Participating in the Internet of Things may begin with a person buying a thermostat or smart refrigerator, but it should also include a recognition of how the thermostat and refrigerator are themselves participating, their computational assumptions reflecting choices made in their design and manufacture. Put differently, the IoT is an Internet of *Things*. It is an arrangement of material actants—nonhuman, computational agents—that participate actively in the daily life of the home; however, the modes and rhetoric of participation are usually black-boxed and inaccessible. Algorithmic assumptions about what might be done at a given time, the sensing standards that learn habits from the owner's everyday patterns, the seamless integration into larger systems extending outside of the home, all of these exert forces that are not obvious and often intentionally obfuscated to the end user.

To explore the *things* of the IoT, we designed and constructed a very simple prototyping platform—the "Tiny Tinkering Platform"—to explore building barely-smart materials in the home. These prototypes were aimed at subverting commercial IoT rhetoric [39]. In its place came an IoT that was emergent and contingent rather than centrally controlled; it put an emphasis on material, computational, and human collaboration rather than parameterization of the everyday world for reporting elsewhere. This platform could be used to construct small-scale, human-evaluated systems, as well as to build more complicated, communication-driven devices that still need humans for assessment. In these systems, the output stays *in situ*, and people around them draw conclusions for themselves. In this frame, end user gratification comes not from owning something new and remarkable to show off to the world, but in producing something unremarkable that feels important to an individual or small community. Possible applications might include when to water a particular plant, when hot coffee has reached the correct temperature, when the mail has been delivered, and so on. While these examples are toy problems, to be sure, they served as a useful environment in which to explore a computational ecosystem focused on reducing the complexity of engineering ubiquitous small-scale hardware. In these scenarios, the computational object serves as a rallying point, making possible new arrangements of things.

In prototyping new organizations of sociotechnical material, we have had to take a deep look at how people live and how they interact: what simple, measurable opportunities exist that could become a site for intervention or problem solving? To that end, one unforeseen outcome of developing a platform like this was enforcing a kind of algorithmic lifestyle on prospective users. The platform produced devices that comprised cheap, ubiquitous, computational material assemblages—materializing the experiences that everyday objects have, but only partially translating them into the language of the observer. Rather than emphasizing screen-based interactions with computer-controlled devices, giving directions or setting rules from a cellular phone or personal computer, our Internet of Things instrumented the everyday on its own terms, letting them become partners in ubiquitous meaning-making.

IMPLICATIONS OF PUBLICS BEYOND PEOPLE

In each of the preceding cases, we describe how computing plays an active role in the constitution of a public. This requires that we recognize and appreciate that a) publics are not solely made of people, and b) that to understand the formation and activities of publics, we must take into account the agency and material capacity of computation.

The Political Agencies of Computation

The discourse and debates on the politics of artifacts is long and messy [41,71,72]. As designed and constructed *things*, algorithms, platforms, networks, and other forms of computation are drawn into this discourse. However, there are important material differences between an algorithm or a platform and, say, the freeway bridges of Richard Moses that science studies scholar Langdon Winner famously labeled as racist [71]. The agencies of computational media tend to be more dynamic. Put bluntly, the algorithms and platforms of computational media act with a greater frequency of change than does the concrete of bridges or other aspects of the built environment. However, the legibility of these computational agencies is less than those of other material fixtures. We may see change or effect in computational media, but often the basis of that change is not understandable. For instance, Gillespie has explained how Twitter trending patterns have been incorrectly read as politically biased because of a misunderstanding of how the trending algorithm works [33]. While we may mistake some forms of computational media as political, we may also be unaware of other political algorithms at work—such as those used by the United States National Security Agency to profile and track "suspicious" behavior online. In the former case, the trending algorithm of Twitter may seem to be thwarting the formation of a public, but in fact it is not. In the latter case, the surveillance algorithms may be unseen or even unknown, but nonetheless should be considered as part of the public formed by the U.S. NSA to attend to the perceived issue of terrorism.

Recognizing the political agencies of algorithms, platforms, and data requires that we broaden the space of politics and expand what counts as political engagement and organizing. Most discussions of politics swirl around common civic institutions and mechanisms of government. For example, political engagement tends to mean working with political parties or governmental agencies or civic organizations, such as churches and various clubs. Broadly speaking, most political projects tend to be projects that contribute to the processes of such organizations. This covers a diversity of activities and outcomes, from neighborhood cleanup days that aim to improve and sustain a sense of community through shared pride, to get out the vote campaigns that strive to increase participation in the most basic component of a representative democracy. This work is imperative for the functioning of the state and the well-being of residents. But these ways of framing the space of politics, and of what counts as political engagement, are insufficient to account for the agencies and effects of computation.

Consider, for instance, the data generated of the *Cycle Atlanta* project. These data cohere a public by providing a unifying organization to a range of human actors and their actions. The data collected are thus not only traces of individual actors, but also in the aggregate a bundling of those actors and a binding of them to an issue. The data and algorithmic analysis of those data do even more, though. They become constituents in the public, actors that need to be taken into account on their own terms, and recognized for their potential to effect change independently.

By accounting for the cycling app as an actor we arrive at a position from which we can examine both smart city and digital democracy initiatives. Similar applications exert their agency over the delivery of services, the development and maintenance of infrastructure, and the operations of government. The implicated technologies are not only servicing human goals and desires, but are exerting an influence over representation, governance, and accountability that extends beyond that of human use: the very presence of the app alters what *counts* as representation, governance, and accountability.

A similar example is also found in the *Activist Technologies* work. In that project, an activist public is mobilized through a series of networked hardware and software platforms. These platforms do more than just coordinate action; they also shape the possibilities for action due to a range of medium-specific capacities and affordances. The resulting agency is distinctive and possible only through the enrollment of computation into activist politics.

Considering computation as political actors is not the naïve claim that an algorithm or data exert authority over the person, nor is it an embrace of technological determinism. Rather, it is an acceptance of the capacities of computation into the figuring of a public. This presents two, entwined challenges. One is how to *understand* civics when the platform and the algorithm are considered as actors in the civic endeavor. The other is how to *do* civics when the platform and the algorithm are considered as actors in the civic endeavor.

The Creative Agencies of Computation

The second way we want to interpret the agencies and effects of computation is through the influence they exert on creative endeavors and the formation and support of publics oriented around modes of imaginative production. These agencies are not political agencies, but rather creative agencies. Making, inclusive of so-called maker culture as well as a broader collection of activities and movements is an increasingly important site for design research [40]. The activities of making can be closely aligned to a wealth of scholarship on material agency, particularly with regards to the agencies of materials in craft and arts [44,54,64]. Until recently, less attention was paid towards the material agencies of computation; however, attending to the material qualities of computation provides insight into how inventive publics form to address the issues and opportunities of imaginative making.

Recognizing the creative agencies of computation requires acknowledging how computation shapes the formation of publics around the processes and goals of invention. In his discussion of the agency of materials in the practice of ceramics, Malafouris notes that making pots is an endeavor that involves the negation and collaboration of many factors that extend beyond the potter herself and include the agencies of clay and the various tools of the potter [54]. In a similar way, we can see the activities of invention that come from various forms of computational tinkering as an interplay of agencies beyond the maker. The expressivity of the system is in large part determined by factors other than the human hand. For instance, in *Racing the Beam,* Montfort and Bogost provide a detailed examination of how the computational capacities (and particularly the limitations) of the Atari 2600, together with the capacities and qualities of cathode ray TVs produced the conditions of early gaming that set expectations for the experiences of what "playing a video game" was [59]. The ingenuity of early game designers was not merely in producing creative game mechanics or novel play arcs, but (like the potter) of negotiating between the various agencies of the multiple factors that made video game play possible.

Making, designing, and creating are not always solitary affairs. Communities develop around these practices, and those communities can be considered publics, oriented toward the issues of invention [65]. These publics vary according to the size and scale of their inventive endeavors. The *Tiny Tinkering Platform* is an example of how attending to the agencies of a computational platform can be generative of new publics and experiences of doing computation. The design of the platform—from the level of the microcontroller—was specifically intended to foster a particular orientation towards the issues of making with computation. By purposefully restricting the capacities for expression, the platform was intended to bring into being a public with a distinctive aesthetic approach, one committed to and organized around a kind of material minimalism, quite similar in fact to that of the early Atari.

As a speculative gesture, the *Tiny Tinkering Platform* becomes part of a public concerned with how activities of making are being shaped in relation to dominant discourses of innovation. In a manner similar to *Cycle Atlanta*, the design of the speculative platform intends to both cohere a public through its agencies as well as become an actor in that public, contributing to providing an alternative.

Issue-Oriented Hackathons provide yet another perspective on the creative agencies of computation. It is not simply the human resources that shape the creative output of these events. In these events, the availability of computational resources also shape the possibilities for invention. This is particularly true when regarding data as a material for expressivity. What data is available will exert a strong force upon what kinds of secondary computational expressions get created (for instance visualizations, or maps, or apps). One way to perceive the extent of this agency is through the *absence* of computation resources—in a hackathon where there is no geo-located data, it becomes difficult to imagine, much less produce, a map. Any public that forms at a hackathon, then, is in part determined by the computational resources at that hackathon. The resources themselves become actors in the public by shaping what it can or cannot attend to.

Considering computation as an actor that shapes creativity does not lessen human creativity. It simply extends a line of thinking with regard to how materials shape expression. Moreover, with regard to publics oriented around forms and modes of imaginative making, these agencies extend beyond shaping the expression of the object or system to shaping the community that comes together to explore the inventive opportunities of computation. In these publics, computation is not just the subject of inquiry, it also acts to structure expression both by its capacities when it is present, and by what it thwarts in its absence.

From Networks and Publics to Ecologies

As mentioned earlier, one shortcoming of ANT as it applies to design is that it does not easily support generative design practices. ANT is useful for post-hoc analysis of networks that already exist, but it is not a perspective that is useful for conceptualizing and generating new networks or the products and services that might operate as actants within them. This mismatch for speculating about possible futures limits the utility of ANT for design.

Another frame is needed. One that is *both* analytic and generative, and that offers notions of interconnectedness distributed across multi-faceted agencies.

We propose that one option moving forward is to shift the frame from networks and publics toward a more ecological approach. Ecological thinking requires a broad perspective that foregrounds various connections between objects and systems. By revealing this multiplicity of obligations in an explicit way, and approaching publics as containing computational agency, we expose objects in the world as always having been members of multiple networks, involving themselves in social arrangements in both subtle and dramatic ways. This simultaneous involvement in various networks—information, electronic, legal, cultural, material, and more—means that objects and designed systems cannot and should not be treated as discrete instances. Instead, they must be considered as component members of an assemblage of actants and relations—what we consider an *Object Ecology*.

In HCI, design is being used to propose and articulate possible or even preferable futures [26]. Design assumes the role of speculator, investing rhetoric into objects in order to create artifacts that take a stand, that play an active part in stretching the boundaries of the possible while asserting particular ideological visions. Contemporary HCI design cannot and should not be concerned with a solitary object or interactions with that object alone. Instead, we must take into account how an object becomes contextualized within collectives of people, other objects, values, contexts, social configurations, and so on. We claim that design provides a means to create *things*—in both senses of the word—as giving form to devices, objects, and systems, of course; but also in creating assemblages that let members of an ecology participate and act among the world at large.

Broadly construed, ecological thinking is not new to HCI. Researchers have previously described *product ecologies*, *device ecologies*, and *artifact ecologies*. Each of these carve out different areas of focus, from how the design products come to be used and cared for in a product ecology or milieu [29,55]; to the personal ecosystem of devices that mediate experience and exposure to other personal technological ecosystems [42]; to the way networks of artifacts shape and influence conceptions and potentials for use [10,11]. Each of these ecological perspectives, however, place the focus on the interpretive power of the human user and do not account for any agentic property of the object as such. By considering ecologies instead as containing multiple object oriented publics, each coalescing and offering sites for contestation around various co-imbricated issues, we can do design for publics that take broader social conditions into account.

Running parallel to the developments of different ecological frames within HCI, there has been a recognized need for more deeply engaging material perspectives [21]. As discussed above, scholars like Bogost [12], Latour [45,48,69], Bennett [5,6] and Harman [35,49] have taken a more bidirectional understanding of meaning construction through interaction. In taking the things that surround us as having an active role in shaping and understanding the world, we can move away from the idea HCI design as being primarily interested in creating *products* or *services*—terms that cast things as being primarily transactional—towards something more relational. Here, the scope of an object ecology offers a way to do design beyond an issues interaction with a community. The object ecology provides a theoretical perspective that emphasizes objects, publics, communities, and issues in themselves, for sure, but also the interplay between them.

This may be an alienating move, but one that we feel will pay dividends for design practice. Existing perspectives on materials are beginning to feel inadequate, especially as we consider computation as participating members of publics. This perspective is useful in two ways:

First, the object ecology forces a designer to consider a broader design space—one that might serve to help unpack or take into account complex interactions and interrelations.

From an ecological perspective, the *Tiny Tinkering Platform* provides an opportunity to investigate the interrelation of Internet access, materials, and everyday experience, while emphasizing particular values through design activity. By building a new hardware system that devises different types of connections to materiality, the project critically examines the role of objects in the everyday. It also strives to create a speculative ecosystem of capacities that reduce the complexity in improvising solutions for small-scale, ubiquitous problems.

Regarding *Speculative Activism*, this means that design efforts need to account for mobile computing devices, data plans, shared documents, cloud services, and access to social media not simply as multiple points for interaction, nor even as sites for sociomaterial-design [9], but as an object ecology with its own internal logics. These logics may be governed algorithmically, or materially; they may be legible, or more likely, are rendered opaque or invisible. As a site for productive design and intervention, however, an object ecology spurs speculative claims both about how a public might impact social or political conditions as well as how those new conditions might be maintained through that collection of imbricated agents.

The object ecology also becomes a useful way to consider how designed objects help mobilize a broader ecosystem as members of publics.

In contrast to the more speculative moves an object ecology enables above, projects like the crowdsourced data collection in the *Cycle Atlanta* case illustrate the ways in which the ecology of mobile apps, databases, modeling and analysis make diffuse publics acutely visible. The plural material and human agencies percolating through the cycling public support each other and widen political participation to include computational and human actors. Again, as a site for design and design research, such contexts provide large-scale laboratories for experimenting—speculating—on what a computational civics might look like and what kinds of actants it might regulate.

In the case of *Issue-Oriented Hackathons* the notion of the object ecology is particularly useful because it, at one and the same time, takes into account the material and experiential qualities of the event. In fact, in an object ecology, these are inseperable and they work together to construct the character of the event. The hackathon is itself an ecology of people, code, hopes and aspirations, APIs, pizza, and power cables that comes together with the issue to produce a particular set of relations for a set period of time in a specific configuration of space. An object ecology has us examine those relations and how they are structured to produce (or thwart) a cooperative endeavor, a working together of humans and nonhumans in the context of an issue. Unlike ANT or other perspectives that flatten ontologies, the object ecology appreciates how differences work together to produce different publics. Those different publics are as much as factor of the capabilities of machines as people.

Part of the goal of considering the built environment as an assembly of specific contextual things is to be responsive to the particulars of a particular context or situation. The object ecology takes the everyday built environment as an assemblage of *things*. The role of design in producing new design things from an ecological standpoint is to consider the interrelatedness of these things and to prototype novel, interesting and—more importantly—worthwhile social interactions between and among them.

CONCLUSION

In this paper we have explored how computation, broadly construed, contributes to the constitution of publics. We have also made the argument that computation should be considered an actor in these publics. That is, computation is active in shaping a public: a public is not simply the expression of human desires, fears, and values with regards to an issue, it also includes the capacities of objects and systems that are used to attend to an issue. While there are likely multiple kinds of computational agency, we called out two that were generalized from our cases: political and creative. Certainly, these are not the only agencies and effects of computation on the construction and working of publics.

The notion of an ecology, we propose, is qualitatively different from a network, assemblage, or even the broad claim of material agency. The notion of an ecology suggests a quality to the relations and engagements between the entities—human and nonhuman, living and not living—that compose it. An ecology is not simply interconnected; an ecology exists together. The question for us as designers then, is what do we want the character of that existing together to be? Arguably, the role of design in shaping this ecology should be to construct relations that support a pluralistic approach to *meaningful* and *worthwhile* interactions between these entities, without reducing them to merely the human perspective.

ACKNOWLEDGMENTS

The projects discussed here are the work of multiple collaborations and we would like to thank our partners in the City of Atlanta, the Atlanta Regional Commission, the Atlanta Community Food Bank, and Occupy Our Homes Atlanta.

The research presented here was supported primarily by the Intel Science and Technology Center for Social Computing and in part by NSF grant IIS-1524380.

REFERENCES

1. Philip E. Agre. 1997. Computation and Human Experience (Learning in Doing: Social, Cognitive and Computational Perspectives). Cambridge University Press.
2. Mariam Asad and Christopher A Le Dantec. 2015. Illegitimate Civic Participation: Supporting Community Activists on the Ground. CSCW '15: Proceedings of the 18th ACM Conference on Computer Supported

Cooperative Work & Social Computing, ACM Request Permissions, 1694–1703.

3. Mariam Asad, Sarah Fox, and Christopher A Le Dantec. 2014. Speculative Activist Technologies. iConference 2014 Proceedings: Breaking Down Walls. Culture - Context - Computing, iSchools.
4. Robert Asen. 2003. The Multiple Mr. Dewey: Multiple Publics and Permeable Borders in John Dewey's Theory of the Public Sphere. Argumentation and Advocacy 39, 3: 174–188.
5. Jane Bennett. 2005. The agency of assemblages and the North American blackout. Public Culture 17, 3: 445–465.
6. Jane Bennett. 2010. Vibrant Matter: A Political Ecology of Things. Duke University Press Books.
7. Thomas Binder, Giorgio de De Michelis, Pelle Ehn, Giulio Jacucci, Per Linde, and Ina Wagner. 2011. Design Things. MIT Press.
8. Erling Björgvinsson, Pelle Ehn, and Per-Anders Hillgren. 2010. Participatory design and "democratizing innovation." PDC '10: Proceedings of the 11th Biennial Participatory Design Conference, ACM, 41–50.
9. Pernille Bjørn and Carsten Østerlund. 2014. Sociomaterial-Design. Springer.
10. Eli Blevis, Susanne Bødker, John Flach, et al. 2015. Ecological Perspectives in HCI: Promise, Problems, and Potential. Proceedings of the 33rd Annual ACM Conference Extended Abstracts on Human Factors in Computing Systems, ACM, 2401–2404. http://doi.org/10.1145/2702613.2702634
11. Susanne Bødker and Clemens Nylandsted Klokmose. 2012. Dynamics in Artifact Ecologies. Proceedings of the 7th Nordic Conference on Human-Computer Interaction: Making Sense Through Design, ACM, 448–457. http://doi.org/10.1145/2399016.2399085
12. Ian Bogost. 2012. Alien Phenomenology or, What it's Like to Be a Thing. University of Minnesota Press, Minneapolis.
13. Andrew Boucher and William Gaver. 2006. Developing the Drift Table. interactions 13, 1: 24–27. http://doi.org/10.1145/1109069.1109087
14. M Brown. 2011. "Street Bump" Android app detects and reports potholes (Wired UK). Wired.co.uk.
15. Christopher A Le Dantec, Caroline Appleton, Mariam Asad, Robert Rosenberger, and Kari E Watkins. 2016. Advocating Through Data: Community Visibilities in Crowdsourced Cycling Data. In Bicycle Justice and Urban Tranformation: Biking For All?, Aaron Golub, Melody Hoffmann, Adonia Lugo and Gerardo Sandoval (eds.). Routledge.
16. Christopher A Le Dantec, Mariam Asad, Aditi Misra, and Kari E Watkins. 2015. Planning with Crowdsourced Data: Rhetoric and Representation in Transportation Planning. CSCW '15: Proceedings of the 18th ACM Conference on Computer Supported Cooperative Work & Social Computing, ACM Request Permissions, 1717–1727.
17. Christopher A Le Dantec, Jim E. Christensen, Mark Bailey, et al. 2010. A Tale of Two Publics: Democratizing Design at the Margins. DIS '10: Proceedings of the conference on Designing interactive systems, 11–20.
18. Christopher A Le Dantec and Carl Francis DiSalvo. 2013. Infrastructuring and the Formation of Publics in Participatory Design. Social Studies of Science 43, 2: 241–264.
19. Christopher A Le Dantec and W Keith Edwards. 2010. Across Boundaries of Influence and Accountability: The Multiple Scales of Public Sector Information Systems. CHI '10: Proceeding of the twenty-eighth annual SIGCHI conference on Human factors in computing systems, ACM, 113–122.
20. Christopher A Le Dantec, Robert G. Farrell, Jim E. Christensen, et al. 2011. Publics in practice: ubiquitous computing at a shelter for homeless mothers. CHI '11: Proceedings of the 2011 annual conference extended abstracts on Human factors in computing systems, ACM Request Permissions, 1687–1696.
21. Audrey Desjardins, Ron Wakkary, and William Odom. 2015. Investigating Genres and Perspectives in HCI Research on the Home. Proceedings of the 33rd Annual ACM Conference on Human Factors in Computing Systems, ACM, 3073–3082. http://doi.org/10.1145/2702123.2702540
22. John Dewey. 1954. The public and its problems. Swallow Press, Chicago.
23. Carl Francis DiSalvo. 2009. Design and the Construction of Publics. Design Issues 25, 1: 48–63.
24. Derek Doran, Swapna Gokhale, and Aldo Dagnino. 2013. Human Sensing for Smart Cities. Proceedings of the 2013 IEEE/ACM International Conference on Advances in Social Networks Analysis and Mining, ACM, 1323–1330.
25. Paul Dourish and Genevieve Bell. 2011. Divining a Digital Future: Mess and Mythology in Ubiquitous Computing. The MIT Press, Cambridge, Mass.
26. Anthony Dunne and Fiona Raby. 2014. Speculative Everything: Design, Fiction, and Social Dreaming. MIT Press, Cambridge, Massachusetts ; London.
27. Pelle Ehn. 2008. Participation in design things. Proceedings of the Tenth Anniversary Conference on Participatory Design 2008, Indiana University, 92–101. Retrieved February 12, 2013 from http://dl.acm.org/citation.cfm?id=1795234.1795248
28. Thomas Erickson, Mark Podlaseck, Sambit Sahu, Jing D Dai, Tian Chao, and Milind Naphade. 2012. The Dubuque Water Portal: Evaluation of the Uptake, Use and Impact of Residential Water Consumption Feedback. Proceedings of the SIGCHI Conference on Human Factors in Computing Systems, ACM, 675–684.
29. Jodi Forlizzi. 2008. The Product Ecology: Understanding Social Product Use and Supporting Design Culture. International Journal of Dsign 2, 1. Retrieved March 10, 2015 from

http://www.ijdesign.org/ojs/index.php/IJDesign/article/view/220

30. William Gaver, Andy Boucher, Andy Law, et al. 2008. Threshold Devices: Looking out from the Home. Proceedings of the SIGCHI Conference on Human Factors in Computing Systems, ACM, 1429–1438. http://doi.org/10.1145/1357054.1357278
31. William W. Gaver, Mark Blythe, Andy Boucher, Jarvis Nadine, John Bowers, and Peter Wright. 2010. The Prayer Companion: Openness and Specificity, Materiality and Spirituality. Proceedings of the SIGCHI conference on Human factors in computing systems.
32. Neil Gershenfeld. 1999. When Things Start to Think. Henry Holt and Co., New York.
33. T Gillespie. 2010. The politics of "platforms." new media & society 12, 3: 347–364.
34. Kenneth L Hacker and Jan van Dijk (eds.). 2001. Digital Democracy: Issues of Theory and Practice. Sage Publications, Inc.
35. Graham Harman. 2002. Tool-Being: Heidegger and the Metaphysics of Objects. Open Court.
36. Edwin Hutchins. 1995. Cognition in the Wild. MIT Press.
37. Edwin Hutchins. 2000. Distributed Cognition.
38. Steven J Jackson and Laewoo Kang. 2014. Breakdown, obsolescence and reuse: HCI and the art of repair. CHI '14: Proceedings of the SIGCHI Conference on Human Factors in Computing Systems, ACM Request Permissions, 449–458.
39. Tom Jenkins and Ian Bogost. 2014. Designing for the Internet of Things: Prototyping Material Interactions. CHI '14 Extended Abstracts on Human Factors in Computing Systems, ACM, 731–740. http://doi.org/10.1145/2559206.2578879
40. Tom Jenkins and Ian Bogost. 2015. Escaping the Sandbox: Making and Its Future. Proceedings of the Ninth International Conference on Tangible, Embedded, and Embodied Interaction, ACM, 29–32. http://doi.org/10.1145/2677199.2680558
41. Bernward Joerges. 1999. Do Politics Have Artifacts? Social Studies of Science 29, 3: 411–431.
42. Heekyoung Jung, Erik Stolterman, Will Ryan, Tonya Thompson, and Marty Siegel. 2008. Toward a Framework for Ecologies of Artifacts: How Are Digital Artifacts Interconnected Within a Personal Life? Proceedings of the 5th Nordic Conference on Human-computer Interaction: Building Bridges, ACM, 201–210. http://doi.org/10.1145/1463160.1463182
43. Victor Kaptelinin and Bonnie A. Nardi. 2009. Acting with Technology: Activity Theory and Interaction Design. The MIT Press.
44. Carl Knappett and Lambros Malafouris (eds.). 2007. Material Agency: Towards a non-anthropocentric approach. Springer, New York.
45. Bruno Latour. 1993. We have never been modern. Harvard University Press, Cambridge, Mass.
46. Bruno Latour. 2004. Which Politics for Which Artifacts? Domus.
47. Bruno Latour. 2007. Reassembling the Social: An Introduction to Actor-Network-Theory. Oxford University Press, Oxford.
48. Bruno Latour. 2008. What is the style of Matters of Concern? Vav Gorcum.
49. Bruno Latour, Graham Harman, and Peter Erdélyi. 2011. The prince and the wolf: Latour and Harman at the LSE. ZERO Books, Winchester, UK; Washington.
50. John Law. 1992. Notes on the theory of the actor-network: Ordering, strategy, and heterogeneity. Systems practice 5, 4: 379–393. http://doi.org/10.1007/BF01059830
51. John Law. 2002. Aircraft Stories: Decentering the Object in Technoscience. Duke University Press Books.
52. Kristina Lindström and Åsa Ståhl. 2014. Patchworking publics-in-the-making: design, media and public engagement.
53. Silvia Lindtner, Judy Chen, Gillian R. Hayes, and P Dourish. 2011. Towards a framework of publics: Reencountering media sharing and its user. ACM Transactions on Computer-Human Interaction 18: 5:1–5:23.
54. Dr Lambros Malafouris. 2007. At the Potter's Wheel: An Argument for Material Agency. In Knappett C. & L. Malafouris, (eds) (2008). Material Agency: Towards a non- anthropocentric approach. New York: Springer., Carl Knappett and Lambros Malafouris (eds.). Springer. Retrieved February 13, 2015 from http://cogprints.org/6402/
55. Victor Margolin. 2002. The Politics of the Artificial: Essays on Design and Design Studies. University Of Chicago Press, Chicago.
56. Noortje Marres. 2007. The Issues Deserve More Credit: Pragmatist Contributions to the Study of Public Involvement in Controversy. Social Studies of Science 37, 5: 759–780.
57. Noortje Marres. 2012. Material Participation: Technology, the Environment and Everyday Publics.
58. Mike Michael. 2012. "What are we busy doing?" Engaging the idiot. Science, Technology & Human Values 37, 5: 528–554.
59. Nicolas Montfort and Ian Bogost. 2009. Racing the Beam.
60. Teresa Olivares, Fernando Royo, and Antonio M Ortiz. 2013. An Experimental Testbed for Smart Cities Applications. Proceedings of the 11th ACM International Symposium on Mobility Management and Wireless Access, ACM, 115–118.
61. C Perera, A Zaslavsky, P Christen, and Dimitrios Georgakopoulos. 2014. Sensing as a service model for smart cities supported by Internet of Things. Transactions on Emerging Telecommunications Technologies 25, 1: 81–93.
62. James Pierce, Phoebe Sengers, Tad Hirsch, Tom Jenkins, William Gaver, and Carl DiSalvo. 2015. Expanding and Refining Design and Criticality in HCI. Pro-

ceedings of the 33rd Annual ACM Conference on Human Factors in Computing Systems, ACM, 2083–2092. http://doi.org/10.1145/2702123.2702438

63. Haggai Roitman, Jonathan Mamou, Sameep Mehta, Aharon Satt, and L V Subramaniam. 2012. Harnessing the Crowds for Smart City Sensing. Proceedings of the 1st International Workshop on Multimodal Crowd Sensing, ACM, 17–18.
64. Daniela K Rosner. 2012. Craft, computing & culture. CSCW '12: Proceedings of the ACM 2012 conference on Computer Supported Cooperative Work, 319.
65. Daniela K Rosner, Silvia Lindtner, Ingrid Erickson, Laura Forlano, Steven J Jackson, and Beth Kolko. 2014. Making cultures: building things & building communities. ACM, New York, New York, USA.
66. Lucy Suchman. 2011. Anthropological Relocations and the Limits of Design. Annual Review of Anthropology 40, 1: 1–18. http://doi.org/10.1146/annurev.anthro.041608.105640
67. Athena Vakali, Leonidas Anthopoulos, and Srdjan Krco. 2014. Smart Cities Data Streams Integration: Experimenting with Internet of Things and Social Data Flows. Proceedings of the 4th International Conference on Web Intelligence, Mining and Semantics (WIMS14), ACM, 60:1–60:5.
68. A Voida, Ellie Harmon, and Ban Al-Ani. 2012. Bridging between organizations and the public: volunteer coordinators' uneasy relationship with social computing. CHI '12: Proceedings of the SIGCHI Conference on Human Factors in Computing Systems, 1967–1976.
69. Peter Weibel and Bruno Latour. 2005. Making things public: atmospheres of democracy : [exhibition], ZKM, Center for art and media Karlsruhe, 20.03.-03-10.2005. (Mass.) : MIT press, Cambridge.
70. Alex Wilkie and Mike Michael. 2009. Expectation and Mobilisation: Enacting Future Users. Science, Technology & Human Values 34, 4: 502–522.
71. Langdon Winner. 1980. Do Artifacts Have Politics? Daedalus 109, 1: 121–136.
72. S Woolgar and G Cooper. 1999. Do Artefacts Have Ambivalence: Moses' Bridges, Winner's Bridges and other Urban Legends in S&TS. Social Studies of Science 29, 3: 433–449.
73. Albena Yaneva. 2013. Mapping controversies in architecture. Ashgate Publishing, Ltd.

Repurposing Bits and Pieces of the Digital

Vygandas "Vegas" Šimbelis, Pedro Ferreira, Elsa Vaara[1], Jarmo Laaksolahti[1], Kristina Höök

Mobile Life @ Royal Institute of Technology
10044 Stockholm, Sweden
vygandas, pedropaf, khook@kth.se

[1]Mobile Life @ SICS
16429 Kista, Sweden
elsa, jarmo@sics.se

ABSTRACT
Repurposing refers to a broad set of practices, such as recycling or upcycling, all aiming to make better use of or give new life to physical materials and artefacts. While these practices have an obvious interest regarding sustainability issues, they also bring about unique aesthetics and values that may inspire design beyond sustainability concerns. What if we can harness these qualities in digital materials? We introduce Delete by Haiku, an application that transforms old mobile text messages into haiku poems. We elaborate on how the principles of repurposing – working on a low budget, introducing chance and combining the original values with the new ones – can inform interaction design in evoking some of these aesthetic values. This approach changes our views on what constitutes "digital materials" and the opportunities they offer. We also connect recent debates concerning ownership of data with discussions in the arts on the "Death of the Author."

AUTHOR KEYWORDS
Repurposing; Reuse; Recycling; Upcycling Design; Digital Upcycling; Aesthetics of Deletion; Interaction Design; Interactive Arts

ACM CLASSIFICATION KEYWORDS
H.5.m. Information interfaces and presentation (e.g., HCI): Miscellaneous.

INTRODUCTION
Sustainability has become an increasingly relevant topic of research with concerns regarding overuse of natural resources dominating a large part of the public debate and policy concerns around the world. Reusing our materials is one of the strategies adopted to deal with the mass consumption of goods and elimination of waste. Recycling is one such strategy, but others have emerged in relation to repurposing or upcycling of different artefacts. While these strategies mainly focus on sustainability research, they have also resulted in particular aesthetic expressions, which have become interesting and appealing in themselves, beyond the demands of a strict sustainability perspective.

CHI'16, May 07-12, 2016, San Jose, CA, USA
© 2016 ACM. ISBN 978-1-4503-3362-7/16/05…$15.00
DOI: http://dx.doi.org/10.1145/2858036.2858297

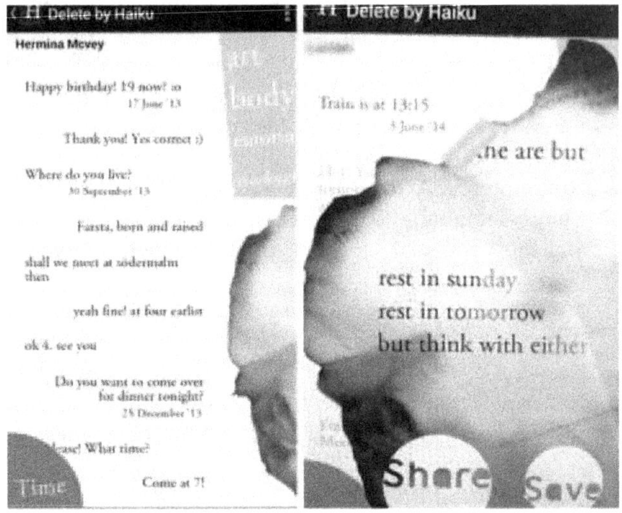

Figure 1. The haiku project: a) SMS thread with themes folder (right). b) The "haiku-bin" with generated haiku.

With growing digital storage capacity space in the cloud, we are accruing an ever-increasing number of digital "things," often rarely revisited, constituting a form of digital waste. While the cost of maintaining those from a sustainability perspective may not yet be a key concern (even if some argue that the cost of storing all this data is an energy cost in itself), from a human perspective the amount of data is reaching an unmanageable level. To live a rich human life in the digital era means engaging in practices, such as, remembering [42], dealing with life and death [5], creating our identity [24,34], managing our social relations, avoiding becoming overwhelmed by all the data we get from life-logging applications [42] and so on. We asked ourselves whether we could borrow the aesthetics of repurposing practices to find novel ways of dealing with our digital possessions. Through designing and building Delete by Haiku, an application that turns old mobile text messages into poems, we show how we can draw from repurposing practices to inspire design for deletion and handling of digital waste – a way of *letting go* – in graceful and aesthetically appealing ways.

This act in turn raises questions regarding the nature of digital waste: what constitutes meaningful pieces we can work with to achieve recycling or upcycling aesthetics? Decomposing an old mobile text message into its "bits and pieces" is only meaningful if we stop at the appropriate level – otherwise users will not recognize their old digital waste in the new.

We start by providing a background from the arts on various repurposing practices, such as upcycling, bricolage, sampling and collage. We then move on to show how those artistic practices and design ideals framed our exploration of what can be done with digital waste. Based on our experiences of designing Delete by Haiku, we discuss different tactics for adopting repurposing aesthetics into interaction design, how those may enable us to see novel affordances of our digital materials, and how the ownership of data debate can be cast in a different light by drawing a parallel to the "Death of the Author" – discussion in the arts.

BACKGROUND

In the physical world, recycling is the practice of deconstructing objects into reusable raw materials; as such, recycling practices are slightly beyond the scope of this paper as it is unclear what it would mean to recycle digital materials (as recycling bits does not make sense from a user experience point of view). *Reuse*, on the other hand, is a practice for using the same object several times without emphasizing exactly how. It is an important practice for extending the lifespan of an object. Repurposing practices form a special case of reuse, as they are concerned with adapting the object for use with a different purpose, thereby also changing the use value of the object.

Upcycling, which plays a key role in our work, is the process through which defunct artefacts are repurposed to obtain a renewed (presumably higher) value. The term upcycling was first coined by a German engineer Reiner Pilz in an article from the Salvo journal in 1994 [36]: "*Recycling? I call it downcycling. They smash bricks, they smash everything. What we need is upcycling, where old products are given more value, not less*" [36]. Instead of deconstructing objects into their raw materials, an upcycling process aims to deconstruct and repurpose, but to keep some properties of the old as well.

The rich aesthetic and conceptual potentials of repurposing have been explored in the arts, and below we review several examples from the arts as a way of explaining what repurposing is and where it comes from. As we are particularly concerned with examining how repurposing can be used to good effect in design using digital materials, we will focus on how creative repurposing practices can be applied to interaction design. We outline and describe a number of generative, creative tactics and values in repurposing practices. Our aim is to introduce repurposing as a sensitizing design practice with potential for opening up new design spaces (rather than attempting to clearly define exactly what repurposing is or is not).

In design and arts, recycling and upcycling have become well-established practices. They are used to cover everything from utilitarian, conceptual concerns to aesthetic ones. For example, McDonough and Braungart use it for utilitarian purposes, focusing on designing for upcycling from the start by, for example, proposing computers built to be disassembled [29]. However, in interaction-design research, the concept has not been explored that widely (with a few notable exceptions [6, 31, 33]). Most reuse and upcycling processes are, therefore, based on materials in which their physical manifestation is central, although examples of reusing digital materials also exist. Prayer Companion [16] is an example of textual upcycling in which sentences from a wide range of global news sites and websites where people write about their experiences and emotions are repurposed to help a group of nuns keep their prayers pertinent.

In the arts, on the other hand, we also see examples of reuse and upcycling more in the form of conceptual practices, without necessarily having a strong connection to actual physical artefacts. From another perspective, we have to mention that our aim in this paper is not to discuss art theory and artistic implications comprehensively, but to find ways for art to be a contributor to interaction design and HCI, and our scope here is from material culture and various practice-driven activities. We even set aside the question of how purpose in itself is related to art, artistic practice and design.

Repurposing Practices in the Arts

The advent of industrialism explains some of the developments of movements such as Modernism as well as establishes practices around the avant-garde [6]. The political values expressed in the avant-garde made a strong impact not only on the art world, but also on broader societal concerns with everyday life in an industrialized era. Conceptualism, introduced by Marcel Duchamp (1887-1968), for example, was a critical inquiry into the status of art at the time. He questioned the institutionalization and audience expectations regarding art. In his endeavour, he drew a strong connection and critique of the notion of the *readymade*. Readymade objects taken from other contexts were brought into the art space, thereby changing their status, value and meaning. An ordinary manufactured artefact could become an artwork, as, for example, when he submitted a urinal to an exhibition – *Fountain* (1917) (see Figure 2) [6]. Through this act, Duchamp showed that the institutional status is inseparable from the values of the artwork. Duchamp's *Fountain* is an example that also clearly shows some of the characteristics of a materialistic repurposing: a flip, rotation, simple change of an existing artefact suddenly turns it into something entirely different. It becomes part of an upcycling process: a commodity turned into an artwork, with a new and higher value.

In the following Modernist tradition in the mid-20th century, artists started to incorporate randomness, chance, indeterminacy [43], ephemerality and destruction in their works. In Postmodernism, the concepts such as originality, appropriation and authorship (that is, who the art can be attribut-

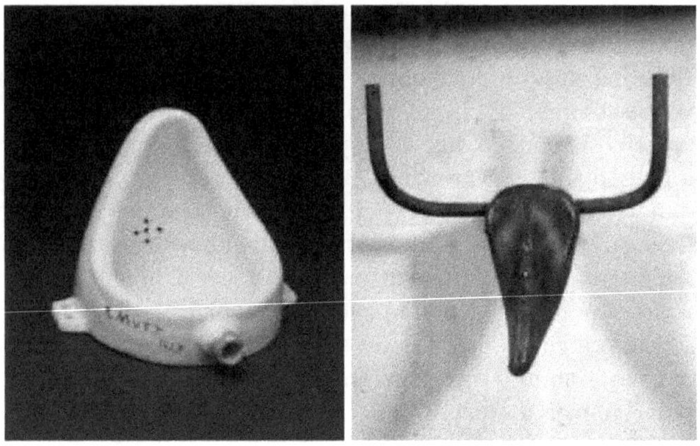

Figure 2. Right: M. Duchamp (1887-1968): Fountain, 1917 [62], **left: P. Picasso (1881-1973): tete de taureau, 1942** [63].

ed to) [20,46] originated and took novel paths to criticizing the established rules and the society at large.

Readymades went further with the use of various objects in neo-avant-garde, Dada and Fluxus, which incorporated those strategies into their art practices. Intentionally humorous situations played a significant part in the works of Fluxus artists, in which George Maciunas (1931-1978) took the lead: "…Dada, an art movement that was often conceptual in nature, as well as subversively humorous" [44]. Jay Belloli discusses the artist Sol Lewitt's (1928-2007) conceptual directions: "…the artist was not there while the piece was being made. Three years later, at the Kunsthalle in Bern, the Silvermans came across a LeWitt exhibition of large wall drawings and other works. It became clear once again that the artist was producing his art by developing directions on how it should be fabricated and leaving its actual construction to others" [44].

The reuse of old artworks by copying or collaging became a permissible practice. Repurposing shares family resemblances with several different concepts and expressions in the arts: *repurposing* of artworks, *compositing*, *cut-and-paste* as artistic techniques, *sampling* in music, *collage*, *reuse* of buildings in architecture, and *cut-up* in literature [20]. Let us explain some of these in more detail.

Repurposing in Remix Culture

Walter Benjamin's work on mechanical reproduction in 1936 [4] discusses the need for a new form of art in the age of mass reproduction – a political way to question the role of originality in an era of mass production. With the possibility of printing and mass reproducing, came replication and possibilities of creating new art through compositions of old (or copied) pieces. An example is the *collage* – an artistic compositing technique that works by putting together various graphic elements (all or parts of existing images) – that arose during the rise of Modernism. Various forms of collage were used in art from manifestations in Cubism, Futurism, and Dadaism [55].

The *assemblage* technique is similar to collage, but it refers to a composition of found objects rather than graphics, in most cases three-dimensional objects protruding from the substrate [55]. Bricolage is a similar technique, using found objects and could take any shape in space. An example of the combination of the bricolage technique, repurposing and upcycling is the insertion of a bicycle seat and handlebar in *Bull's Head* (1942) by Pablo Picasso (see Figure 2). Bricolage is also introduced in interaction design [52] to denote its connection to tinkering and maker culture.

Later, in interactive artworks, collage techniques building on pieces of trash were used, for example, by the artist Danny Rozin in *Trash Mirror* (2001) [38]. Mechanical mirrors, made of various physical trash materials, change and move based on input from video cameras and computers, creating complex mirrors of the viewers standing in front of the art piece. In CollageMachine by Andruid Kerne [25], digital collages are composed by browsing web pages. The machine uses randomness and users' choices when deciding which web links to follow.

Reusing and repurposing are common practices in architecture: for example, a hotel designed in an old ship-to-shore crane or turning a shipping container into a home. It is an adaptive approach for creating new functions from already existing forms, functions and purposes. By applying its *adaptation principles*, such notions of reuse in architecture and in other disciplines could be opposed to one of the most important creative ideals in modern architecture and design – "form follows function" [19]. Instead of making the form follow the function, they make the function adapt to the already existing form – the core feature of repurposing.

Repurposing and Upcycling in DIY

Repurposing and upcycling has a strong role in do-it-yourself (DIY) practices [54] creating something new, with a novel value, from our everyday 'garbage' [7]. We can wear bags designed from used truck tarpaulins [56] or give away souvenirs made from used basket balls [57]. The whole open-source and maker-culture oftentimes centers on reuse, repurposing and upcycling, for example, media art practices as circuit and code bending, and on more visual aspects – pixel and data bending. Another method is repurposing code as a technique used in software industry [41].

As we can see in these examples, there is a focus on low-budget processes and making use of artefacts readily available to us – even garbage. Many of these practices rely on an element of chance in the design process. By placing objects next to one another, turning them, reconfiguring them, ideas arise in and through seeing old objects in a new light. These tactics became of use to us in our design process.

THE CASE OF REPURPOSING

To further explore and open the design space where digital data is seen in the light of being a reusable, upcyclable or repurposable material, we conducted a workshop and subsequently designed an app we named Delete by Haiku.

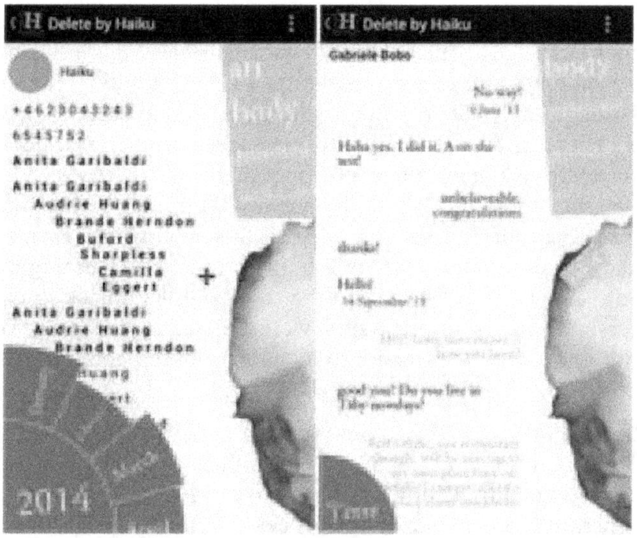

Figure 3. a) Time filter (pink), themes (yellow), and haiku-bin (grey). b) Choosing a theme (right).

To drive the design process forward, we set some rules for ourselves. The first premise was that we would engage with the large amounts of personal data stored in our mobile phones. Text messages in particular become stored in our phones' digital memories, with little to no revisiting (with sometimes dramatic consequences when they are [13]). These messages constitute, in that sense, a form of waste, despite potentially large amounts of effort and emotional value invested at the time of their production. Second, to follow the ideals of repurposing, our aim was to bring new life and a new value to these texts, while at the same time, disposing of them. Third, we wanted to make use of the low-budget, chance-driven, practices.

We will now discuss the Delete by Haiku application and its design process by starting with the idea behind haiku poetry and our motivation to build on this form.

Haiku Poetry

Haiku is a traditional form of Japanese poetry featuring a simple constructive form with a limited number of syllables. In general, haiku poets use a syllabic structure of 5-7-5 for its three verses, resulting in a single strophe. In some cases, this strophe should contain a seasonal indication and also a shift between two parts that creates a feeling of surprise [58]. Contemporary creators of haiku do not always follow the traditional structure strictly and sometimes write without counting syllables or the number of verses. Haiku poetry offers an expressive, very strict and compact form of poetry, building on an artistic tradition and handicraft process that we could pursue [10]. The constrained format of haiku poetry enforces interesting limitations [35], which can also help framing and enhance a playful [9,39,40] and humorous potential [33].

There have been a number of attempts to automate the process of creating haiku poems, for example [59]. Tosa and colleagues [50] discuss the first non-interactive haiku generator Theo from 1959, and in Netzer et al. [32] linguistic passages of building such generators are explained. One contemporary example of a haiku generator is The New York Times Haiku project [60], which simply copies sentences from different articles and creates a haiku through spreading them out on three lines. By building on these research projects and experiments, we want to extend the user experience, control and interaction over the generative process [22,50].

Delete by Haiku

In the Delete by Haiku application, users interactively repurpose selected old text messages on their mobile phone into a haiku poem aided by a haiku-generating algorithm. The interface consists of four main elements: the user's list of contacts, the haiku-bin, the time and the theme filters (see Figure 3a).

Users select messages they want to delete by date and time, by conversation, individually, or any combination of these, and drag them to the haiku-bin. By repeatedly "pinching"[1] the messages in the bin (see Figure 4), the deletion and generation process is moved forward. The generation process is strongly aleatoric, that is, randomness plays an important role. Hence, it is possible to delete identical messages but end up with different poems. However, during the process the syllable structure of haiku poetry influences which words to keep and which to delete in order to create correct haikus. This refers to the repurposing notion of the function being adapted to the already existing form (explained above in the art background) in which the formal count of syllables creates a particular text function, in this case poetry, so the meaning finds its way through the syllable structure. In the process, words that are going to be deleted are greyed-out and eventually fade away. The remaining words in the haiku-bin are animated when "pinched," falling down in a Tetris-like manner and eventually finding their position in the resulting haiku (see in Figure 4). This important step is

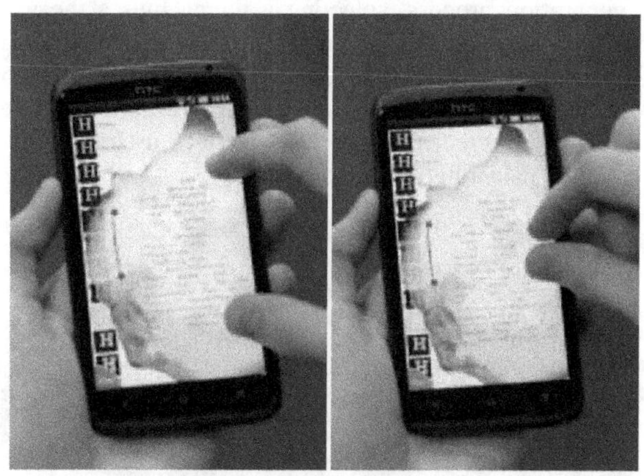

Figure 4. Haiku application, pinching gesture.

[1] By pinching we refer to the multi-touch gesture *pinch to zoom* that most modern mobiles and tablets have [14].

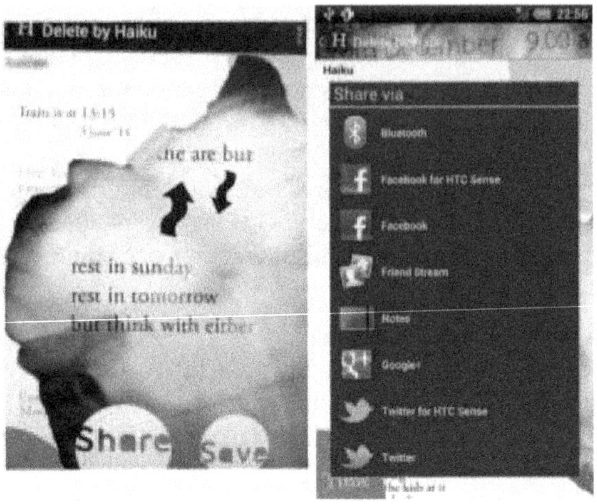

Figure 5. a) Last interaction for a final adjustment by manually moving words (left). b) Sharing window.

animated to slowly expose the work of the algorithm emphasizing the mix of words. Depending on the quantity of text messages that has been selected, users have to repeat the pinching gesture multiple times until nothing but the haiku remains. Since the final poem is dependent on the characteristics of selected messages (expressions, wording, signs, etc.) the initial selection process is fundamental.

A typical haiku poem in the Japanese tradition will refer to nature and convey a certain ambience. While in traditional haiku nature is a standing theme, in our project we wanted to provide users with a broader range of themes to choose from (seen in Figure 3b). Each of the themes directly refers to a library of interrelated words, connected to the haiku-generating algorithm. In the version described here, users could choose to filter the selected messages through one or several of the themes: body, emotion, city and time. Using a theme causes the haiku generation algorithm to favor words from the theme in the generation process. That is, when selecting which words to keep and which ones to delete in the generation process, selecting a theme biases the algorithm to keep words, or synonyms to those, in the resulting haiku. Hence, choosing the emotion theme makes it more likely that the resulting haiku concerns emotions. This feature lets users direct the algorithm towards a certain flavor of haiku by selecting different themes.

Once the haiku is generated, users can choose to keep the poem as it is or interactively change it (see Figure 5a) by rearranging and removing words of the resulting haiku. Through these last rearranging touches by the user, the poem becomes finalized. All text messages used to construct it are thereby transformed into one single haiku. As a final step, users can then share the poem with friends by sending it as a text message or uploading it to social media (such as Facebook) through the app's built-in functions (see Figure 5b). The users can also send the resulting haiku back to the person whose text messages were deleted in the process, and this could be turned into a "poetry"-based communication as both parties start using the app.

Design Process: Repurposing as a Lens for Design

To convey some of the underlying values and directions for upcycling, we will now show how we used repurposing as a generative lens in our design process.

Interviews

As a first investigative step, we joined the Stockholm haiku society and their weekly haiku workshop. During these meetings, we discussed premier haiku rules and alterations; however, we tried to find particularities of those specific meetings of the Stockholm haiku society and focus on what could significantly influence our design process and the project. The iteration process was one of those specific elements we brought into our design process. In these sessions, members anonymously send their haiku poems in advance and get productive discussions and live feedback from other members in the meeting. In those meetings haikus are collectively discussed in detail and eventually get changed in the reflexive process.

Text Repurposing Workshop

To help our understanding of haiku meet repurposing values and practices, we invited eight colleagues to a workshop in which we engaged in a series of playful exercises associated with the creation process of haiku poetry. The participants (see Figure 6b) were all researchers with different backgrounds (arts, design, anthropology, psychology, sociology and computer science). They were all more or less familiar with haiku poetry. The workshop exercises ranged from more generative to associative approaches. A generative approach (see Figure 6c, 7 and 8) involved recy-

Figure 6. The haiku workshop: a) Settings of the workshop (left). b) Participants creating haikus (middle left). c) Haiku Book Hack exercise (middle right). d) Haiku from objects and sounds, an associative haiku approach (right).

cling of already printed texts in various ways, for example, old artefacts were repurposed through using a cut-up technique, by cutting and rearranging headlines, burning away parts of a newspaper and producing haikus from what was left. Restrictions can be engaging [35], and here the restrictive form of the haiku became like solving a puzzle while sticking to a rather restrictive set of rules, and part of the engagement grew out of efforts to outsmart the rule set to create something expressive in spite of it. Later, in the workshop, we applied an associative approach (Figure 6d) in which haikus were created in more interpretative and intuitive ways, through associations to artefacts and without providing the participants with any printed words.

During the workshop, we noticed that the process of creating a haiku was important, perhaps even more interesting than the resulting haiku itself. The tactics we used in the hands-on workshop were purposefully tangible, low-budget and low-fidelity – to make participants focus on the process rather than their poetic abilities. It was low-budget in its choice of materials – newspapers and various old artefacts lying around in our office – and also in its methods – burning, cutting, arranging and rearranging objects and pieces of burnt newspaper. This procedure was in line with original ideas of repurposing in particular from the DIY community.

Implementation of the Workshop Results

The outputs from the workshop provided input to our design: combining mobile phone constraints, the haiku technique, deletion, and repurposing. Some parts of the repurposing methods that we tried with our participants were developed further and implemented in the mobile app. For example, in the Book Hack (see Figure 6c) exercise, participants blended texts from different books, taking random lines from one another and arranging them into a haiku. The Cut and Mix technique (see Figure 7) similarly arranges texts, but instead of books we used headlines and texts from different thematic newspaper pages (sports, culture). The way in which Delete by Haiku works was heavily inspired by these exercises.

The layout and design of the mobile interface was also influenced by the outcomes from the workshop. The interactive haiku-bin, represented by a burnt and crumpled sheet of paper, was inspired by the burnt newspaper, and aimed to symbolize how the bin collects forgotten and fragmented messages. The text and buttons in the interface follow a

Figure 7. The Cut and Mix example of aleatoric method, generative approach in the workshop.

non-symmetrical and non-geometric, natural, colorful and textured, cut-out style expressing aliveness and a messy style that often characterizes the type of defunct and second-hand physical artefacts.

In the development of the haiku generator, we gradually shifted from an initial design, in which we worked with grammar-based rules, to a design combining the theme database with retaining not only the significant words from users' text messages, but whole structures – part of or whole sentences – from the text messages that were being deleted.

User Encounters Shaping the Design

The resulting Delete by Haiku-app was exposed to ten users and haiku-experts through interviews, and was intensively discussed throughout the design process as well as in its final form. There were two focus groups composed of 25 people to discuss the main ideas and so far 64 users have tried it by downloading it. These encounters helped us to iterate on our design and understand some relationships between the concepts we applied and the chosen tactics and directions. These studies, as well as the expert encounters, are not full-fledged studies in themselves but rather orienting and inspirational for the design process.

We learnt from users trying the application that the possibility of tinkering with the haiku material to get a haiku that makes sense and has personal value was crucial (see Figure 9). The feeling of interacting with the poem cannot stop after the pinching gestures, but needs to continue into editing the poem until the user feels satisfied with the result.

Figure 8. The workshop, generative approach: "Newspaper on Fire" aleatoric exercise in progress.

The importance of having some degree of control over the generated result comes not only from the workshop and user encounters, but also from the initial discussion with members of the Stockholm haiku society. Therefore, we added the option for users to rearrange and remove words in the final steps of the haiku creation.

In the example below (see Table 1, left example), a bunch of boring text messages, talking about meeting up for a coffee, are repurposed into an amusing haiku. This haiku captures the main essence of the whole text communication and in the end adds a humorous twist. The final poem became so amusing to this particular user that he decided to post it on his Facebook wall.

coming all order the coffee to departure our mind some coffee	pastry figuring sure but contemporary about midsummer

Table 1. Examples of generated haiku.

In the two examples above (see Table 1) from the end-user perspective, the process can be seen as adding a new, higher value to their mundane everyday messages. They are, using repurposing terminology, *upcycled*.

From one user encounter (Emma), we got feedback about summing up the whole conversation and adding value through creating a haiku, in this case the humorous and playful element works for having a smile:

"Instead of reading the whole conversation I had a day before I could read a small haiku and if that made me smile that would have value for me."

The same user discusses emotional connection to the conversation and also a surprise about a humorous situation:

"I'm an arty emotional person. I think I would like to find the beauty of conversation, that perhaps, it appeals to me that something that very random makes me smile, feel something. I would use it with certain conversations."

Another user (Santiago) emphasizes sentimental and emotional connection to people and conversations, very selective regarding which SMS messages to repurpose:

"Yeah, but you want to get a nice haiku. I made some nice haikus. It was conversation with my friend, very sentimental, some old stuff, then I created a nice haiku. I don't want to use messages with my girlfriend cause those are very personal. And this other friend it was about her stuff, she is a writer as well, so she writes very well and her messages were very long so it was perfect for the haiku. But I don't think I would use it myself."

User (Jonas) focuses on crafting technique in digitally shaping the poem and of that practice relating to getting rid of junk. In this case, the junk is attributed to memorabilia, a process of sort of letting go of your old personal experiences through deleting the core and by creating something substantially new:

"It's like crafting something. It almost feels like you are creating something out of the junk. Also at the same time it's a performance since I aim to share it. You sort of get into the loop of hunting to get the next good haiku. And that helps to get rid of all the junk. It's a way of processing old memorabilia."

Delete by Haiku sometimes has this effect of creating an added value – text messages of little, or forgotten, value to the user are given new life, providing a delightful, humorous surprise, shedding a new light on old, nearly-forgotten, conversations, playing a new role in our communication with others, in some ways similar to but distinct from recent additions to social media platforms, such as building albums and memories from old user data. The messages are perhaps not upcycled in a literal sense, but from the user experience perspective they are.

DIRECTIONS FOR THE DESIGN PROCESS

The practical directions we chose to work with in our project concur with our artistic intentions and fall under the general header of repurposing of digital waste. However, we want to emphasize that the space we are working in is only the initial mapping of a new domain and to suggest interesting directions in this design space. The introduced directions are not really actionable tactics; they are intentionally left open and underspecified as an invitation for the community to join us in engaging with these concepts and populate this novel space within interaction design.

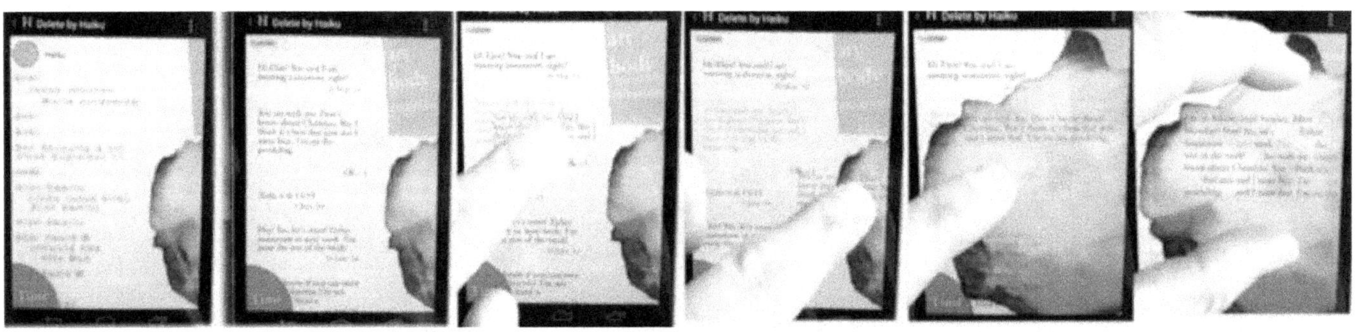

Figure 9. The interaction, from left: the contact list in Delete by Haiku in alphabetic order. A conversation within one contact was chosen. User drags and drops parts of the conversation into the "haiku-bin", which automatically opens up. And finally, user repeatedly pinches the text to compress it into a final haiku poem.

As suggested above, there are various forms of repurposing processes, transformations, constructions and deconstructions that may help designers to render interesting results in their own design cases. By considering one or several of these directions in an early phase of project development, new design spaces can be opened. Throughout our research and design process, we have distinguished between two different types of repurposing: reuse and upcycling. Some practices that help bring out specific repurposing aesthetics, as described earlier, for example, *compose* and *reshape*. In the workshop exercises in which we were rearranging objects, these concepts were guiding us, closely connecting us to our initial aims: to provide a sense of repurposing of the old. Here we will revisit three of the main principles and what we have learned by incorporating them: working on a low budget, introducing chance to design and combining original values with new ones.

At-hand: Working on a Low Budget

In DIY practices, work is usually done on a low budget, using cheap or easily available materials and quick interpretative ideas. There are established activities, such as *freecycling* with dedicated online communities [27,61] that allow for the exchange of old and defunct artefacts. In our Delete by Haiku design case, we chose to work with mobile text messages, which are easily attainable and, for the mobile phone user, free. Others have attempted to repurpose digital content and user interfaces [26].

As we move into the digital realms, there are other methods that require equally low budgets. One such interesting method is *reverse engineering,* in which knowledge is extracted from the artefact (hardware and software), as design features are deduced through deconstructing it [31]. Such a process has a design potential for repurposing and upcycling. Another possible method is *improvised engineering*, that is, solving engineering problems with whatever materials and tools are at hand.

What is perhaps additionally interesting when repurposing old text messages is the underlying political issue. Big Data is often referred to as the "new oil" (Bryan Trogdon) [1] as large corporations make substantial profits from harvesting personal data. Mobile text messages over time, or any other personal and sentimental data, through their abundance on personal users' devices, could be thought of as *Little Big Data*, large in quantity on an individual level, but not really on a "Big Data" scale. That data is of undetermined quality, untouched and not interpreted yet, till it is stored on users' personal devices, and it is not harvested by third parties nor shared with anyone. Most qualities it has are personal, private and mostly valuable on an emotional level, sometimes sentimental, whose importance is its content and information level instead of as data. Although it is not yet converted into data, it contains qualities of data. Oftentimes, those Little Big Data streams, our personal data, are worth so much to corporate entities, and yet so little to us as end-users. Upcycling of those text messages into haiku poems draws our attention to the value of the mundane, putting us in contact with the kinds of data that corporations are already tapping into and using for their own projects. The materials may be cheap and readily available, but its potential value has become enormous. By empowering users to engage with this data, we aim at getting users and the HCI community to explore issues around Big Data – ownership, privacy, and so on – from the bottom up, rather than from a large scale perspective such as Google's or Facebook's handling of it.

Introducing Chance to Design

In repurposing practices, randomness and coincidence are crucial. This is why we purposefully introduced chance into our workshop process as well as into the way the Delete by Haiku algorithm works when selecting words and sentences from the text messages. A creative process within the arts determined by and concerned with processes of chance is called *aleatoricism* [21] (seen in Figure 7).

Dadaism and Fluxus promoting chance procedures [6,44] clearly appear in Duchamp's Erratum Musical (1913) and later in John Cage's music compositions. For example, Music of Changes (1951), textual collages of Fluxus by Maciunas [43,44] and *Silence* by Cage [8] are prominent examples of forms of indeterminacy and aleatoricism in the arts. Matthew Herbert's music production exemplifies how chance can be used in contemporary music. He experiments with whatever artefacts are at-hand and plays live performances, for example, with a can or produces music from body and food signals. Improvisation, interpretation and indeterminacy are important features in those settings where live performance is the end result of the repurposing process. Burning newspapers and using the left-over pieces as we did in our workshop is an example of an aleatoric approach (seen in Figure 8) in which chance is introduced through letting the burning complete the process.

Combining Original Values with the New Ones

In a repurposing process, some of the old properties of the artefact become incorporated and adapted to fit with the new design. However, some of them have to be changed into new properties, qualities and functions in order to add the required new value (in upcycling a higher value is required). There have been some attempts in HCI to facilitate repurposing, as in, for example, repurposing of barcode-technology to facilitate indoor navigation [37] or repurposing a laptop to create a novel musical instrument [23]. As mentioned in the background above, design actions that might be applied in order to bring out this potential are, for instance, simple acts such as flipping, rotating or turning around in order to see an object in a new light. For example, a chair can be turned upside down and fixed onto the wall to become a shelf, adding a substantially new value.

The initial and original properties of an artefact constrain and limit the repurposing process but also help the user to grasp the major constructive parameters of the upcycling and repurposing aesthetics. The properties of a previous design (the shape, materials, functions, damaged parts) of the initial object become the materials for repurposing. Overall, at least some properties or elements of the initial artefact have to be kept evident in the final form of any repurposed artefact – in particular if we aim for upcycling. Through this process repurposing becomes a *critical practice*, calling for new perspectives and new ways of seeing what is there, offering an opportunity to deconstruct the newly designed artefact picking up on materials, values and significant factors there as well as reading the embedded cultural connotations within the material artefact, be it digital or physical.

UPCYCLING AND REPURPOSING AESTHETICS

Similar to other design strategies which have been discussed in HCI, such as: ambiguity [17], defamiliarization [3], or machine aesthetics [49], repurposing is not a one-for-all tool whether for design and art practices, or for information technology and computing. Nonetheless, as we have shown in this paper, it can be one tool in our design repertoires to aid designers in creatively generating designs in a structured manner. In this case, it involves thinking about and building on the materials that have been intentionally created and already have complex and somewhat valuable forms to build on and that are already there for free.

The most important way we see repurposing aesthetics in interaction design is as a lens through which designers develop their design cases in regard to repurposing processes. In this case, however, the upcycling aesthetics mostly refers to the end-user experience, which is shaped by inviting users to take an *active and creative stance*. By inviting participants to take part in shaping the artefact through repurposing, we wanted to create ways of experiencing the project through the upcycling and new value additions. An inherent quality in any upcycling process is the subjective value added by this interpretative process in which new meanings and relationships are created by re-evaluating, recontextualizing or reimagining already existing ones. To the end-user, the creative upcycling process brings forth these aspects in several steps, combining old and new properties of one or several existing pieces of information, contexts, artefacts or users' relationships to them, thereby creating significant and meaningful intersections between the previous and new states. This active, creative process is at the heart of what we mean by upcycling aesthetics.

MATERIALITY OF THE DIGITAL

Research on materiality in HCI is gaining traction and deals with a wide scope of materials, bringing materials into a design process in its early stage [11], working with computational materials for interaction design [53], noticing digital material qualities in design [48], discussing various manifestations of the immaterial through diverse historical and cultural contexts [30], using radio signals as design material and discussing it through an immateriality lens [45], performatively engaging with materials for music production [12], discussing imperfection in relation to interaction design [51], appropriating materiality for meaning and spirituality [16] and lately having a discussion and working with experiential qualities [28] of materials for emphasizing and creating materials experience patterns [18]. Materiality research in interaction design and HCI discusses multiple aspects of materials touching upon physical and digital, meaning and experience and opens relevant design spaces for designers to engage in practical work.

Following on this materiality discussion in interaction design and HCI [15], we see how physical materials are sometimes, but not always, intertwined with the digital materials. We draw our design with both physical and digital, eventually emphasizing the digital aspect and its specificity within recycling-oriented practices, but, in our case, we take account of materiality through a body of text. This specific field of working with text and language, on the one hand, narrows down the complexity of the endeavour, but, on the other hand, makes repurposing even harder as it requires taking semiotics into account.

While the digital world should not be seen as separate from the physical world, the digital materials (or digital waste as in this case) as a basis for our creative efforts are quite different from creativity arising from engaging with physical materials. Some acts are much easier to perform in a digital world, such as moving words, deleting them or treating whole text masses algorithmically. The final sharing process, spreading the resulting poem, can also be accomplished in many ways, reaching many easily in the digital realms, quite different from a physical setting.

We must draw on materiality as a way to understand the components of the digital as well as to contribute to an understanding of digital materiality in itself and bring that to our end-users. It allows users to perceive the power behind what was largely left behind as "waste," how it can be repurposed and given a new life, something which is already happening under the term "Big Data" and which the HCI community as well as users struggle to grasp: "one man's waste, another man's gold".

In the interaction with Delete by Haiku, the end-user is encouraged to engage with the text through a collage technique, selectively moving words in the digital format, setting aside traditional physical writing or digital typing. The algorithm plays a critical role in this process, facilitating and enhancing the making of the poem; the user is, nonetheless, actively involved in the interaction.

The aesthetics and evocative nature of Delete by Haiku relies on a particular stance to what properties we choose to extract from the digital material/waste, that is, from the mobile text messages. We can, of course, choose to regard them as ASCII signs or a bag of letters, but that would not have preserved and then repurposed their value in the eyes of the users. It would have become meaningless. Words, parts of sentences and the structures of the text messages are more relevant to a repurposing process. Using letters would have been a form of recycling – and as such meaningless as any digital process can ultimately be reduced all the way to currents flowing through a circuit, a level at which the recycling metaphor breaks down. What we find especially intriguing here is how the end-users can be empowered through the process of interaction sort of the "upcycling of interactions" view, in which the creation of new values appears. The digital, interactive material affords participants the opportunity to actively engage in the upcycling process – they, in a sense, become authors of the upcycled end-product. The authorship responsibility becomes shared between artist (or designer), system and the user. In that role, upcycling can become a powerful tool in critically and playfully examining the proliferating abundance of digital artefacts, data and applications we all live with, thus creating new relationships and meanings.

THE DEATH OF THE AUTHOR IN THE DIGITAL AGE

The generative and interactive aspects of Delete by Haiku, connects us to Roland Barthes' "The Death of the Author" [2] manifestation and his undermining of traditional literary criticism and the notion of the author's intentions and biographical context in an interpretation of a piece of art. It is a discussion regarding not assigning a single interpretation to the work of art (in this case – a text) as we cannot know the original and precise intentions of the artist. Barthes claims: "The unity of a text is not in its origin, it is in its destination."

This perspective shifts the focus onto the reader instead of the writer. Furthermore, he claims: "The birth of the reader must be ransomed by the death of the Author."

Tying Barthes' theories back to our Delete by Haiku project, paradoxically, we see how the user becomes an author in the production of the generated poem, but also the reader, the receiver of the poem, gets the same credit just by reading it. The mixing and spreading of the authorship to several parties is thus much easier in the digital realm. This fact in turn makes us ask questions about rights and how they can be shared – even for a small and humorous application such as Delete by Haiku: who is the poet behind the resulting poem? Everyone can suddenly be turned into an author, as everyone can change the artwork and in turn share it. Through a limited interaction, a limited creative act, they become authors.

We may also ask ourselves what the role of the haiku-generating algorithm is? What happens when the haiku-generator becomes an active agent, an intelligent supporter, not only a simple matcher of random words or, for example, as in The New York Times Haiku project, in which whole sentences are simply layered down into the three verses? Further, is the algorithm and interface merely a transparent support, so we as users are still in charge of the processes and are able to make decisions on how to use our own data, without any hidden processes underneath?

Another important question is how do we deal with the mechanisms of sharing everything, and who in the end owns digital possessions. Is it the one who collects them and eventually shares an "object" online that has more rights and privileges, or are we all on the same level, all jointly owning it, authoring it? Also on a more political scale – if we see this through the upcycling lens, which values are currently attributed to our Little Big Data (do we want to attribute corporate values to our sentimental data?) and what do we get back from sharing our intimate communications and sentimental data?

CONCLUSIONS

In this paper we started with presenting our main concept in relation to practices in design and the arts. In our discussion of artistic as well as design or DIY practices, we have identified important aesthetic principles that have arisen within traditional repurposing practices: reuse and upcycling. We use our design case, Delete by Haiku, to show how we explored this space, in the digital domain, through repurposing directions dealing with digital waste, and implications for thinking about personal data. Namely, we have suggested that working on a low budget, introducing aleatorism and combining the original values with the new ones are important resources to think about when building these aesthetic expressions within a material digital framework and contributing to the material turn in HCI [15]. While expanding our design space by showing how these aesthetic forms and values can enrich how we think of digital interaction-design was our central focus in this work, it led us to reflect on a wider range of topics: the value, materiality and ownership of our personal data in particular, something which is very timely, thereby tying it to a larger societal debate on what Big Data and Little Big Data really mean.

To live a rich human life means engaging in practices, such as, remembering [42], dealing with life and death [5], creating our identity [24,34], managing our social relations, avoiding becoming overwhelmed by all the data we get from life-logging applications [42] and so on. In many of these settings, design through the lens of repurposing aesthetics and user experience through upcycling aesthetics may open up design spaces previously untapped, helping us to create practices that are manageable on a human scale. Directions for the upcycling and repurposing design processes can provide a means to cope with the masses of information that we generate without losing its sentimental value – a form of *qualified-self* instead of the more famous quantified-self movement.

ACKNOWLEDGEMENT

We would like to thank our workshop participants and user encounters for their input in our project and research. We also thank Indra Motiejunaite for conducting the user study and Fredrik Hagnell – for helping to program the app.

REFERENCES

1. Janna Quitney Anderson and Lee Rainie. 2012. Big Data: Experts say new forms of information analysis will help people be more nimble and adaptive, but worry over humans' capacity to understand and use these new tools well. Washington, DC.
2. Roland Barthes. 1977. The Death of the Author. *Image, music, text.* 145.
3. Genevieve Bell, Mark Blythe, and Phoebe Sengers. 2005. Making by Making Strange: Defamiliarization and the Design of Domestic Technologies. *ACM Transactions on Computer-Human Interaction* 12, 2: 149–173.
4. Walter Benjamin. 2008. *The Work of Art in the Age of Mechanical Reproduction*. Penguin, London, UK.
5. Jed R. Brubaker, Gillian R. Hayes, and Paul Dourish. 2013. Beyond the Grave: Facebook as a Site for the Expansion of Death and Mourning. *The Information Society* 29, 3: 152–163. http://doi.org/10.1080/01972243.2013.777300
6. Peter Bürger. 1984. *Theory of the Avant-garde*. Manchester University Press, Manchester, UK.
7. Otto von Busch. 2008. Fashion-able. Hacktivism and engaged fashion design.
8. John Cage. 2011. *Silence: Lectures and Writings*. Wesleyan University Press.
9. Roger Caillois. 1961. *Man, play, and games*. University of Illinois Press.
10. Erik Stolterman. 2008. The Nature of Design Practice and Implications for Interaction Design Research. *International Journal of Design* 2, 1: 55–65. Retrieved from http://www.ijdesign.org/ojs/index.php/IJDesign/article/view/240
11. Ylva Fernaeus and Petra Sundström. 2012. The material move: how materials matter in interaction design research. *In Proc. DIS'12*, 486–495.
12. Ylva Fernaeus and Anna Vallgårda. 2014. Ajna: negotiating forms in the making of a musical cabinet. *DIS'14*, 915–924.
13. Pedro Ferreira, Pedro Sanches, and Alexandra Weilenmann. 2013. Awareness, Transience and Temporality: Design Opportunities from Rah Island. *In Proc. INTERACT 2*, Springer Berlin Heidelberg, 696–713.
14. M. Frisch, J. Heydekorn, and R. Dachselt. 2009. Investigating multi-touch and pen gestures for diagram editing on interactive surfaces. *In Proc. the ACM International Conference on Interactive Tabletops and Surfaces*, ACM Press.
15. Verena Fuchsberger, Martin Murer, and Manfred Tscheligi. 2013. Materials, materiality, and media. *In Proceedings of the SIGCHI Conference on Human Factors in Computing Systems*, ACM Press.
16. William Gaver, Mark Blythe, Andy Boucher, Nadine Jarvis, John Bowers, and Peter Wright. 2010. The prayer companion: openness and specificity, materiality and spirituality. *In Proc. of the SIGCHI Conference on Human Factors in Computing Systems*, ACM Press, 2055–2064.
17. William W. Gaver, Jacob Beaver, and Steve Benford. 2003. Ambiguity as a resource for design. *In Proc. CHI'03*, ACM Press, 233–240. http://doi.org/10.1145/642651.642653
18. Elisa Giaccardi and Elvin Karana. 2015. Foundations of Materials Experience: An Approach for HCI. *CHI'15*, ACM Press, 2447–2456.
19. Horatio Greenough and Harold Adams Small. 1957. *Form and function: remarks on art, design and architecture*. University of California Press.
20. David J. Gunkel. 2015. *Of Remixology: Ethics and Aesthetics after Remix*. The MIT Press.
21. Stephen A. Hedges. 1978. Dice music in the eighteenth century. *Music & Letters* 59, 2: 180–187.
22. Ingi Helgason. 2012. Beat Haiku: Interactive Poetry Application. *In Proc. NordiCHI'12*, ACM Press, 777–778.
23. Aceituno Jonathan and Ludovic Potier. 2014. The secret life of computers. *CHI'14 Extended Abstracts on Human Factors in Computing Systems*, ACM Press.
24. Oskar Juhlin, Yanqing Zhang, Cristine Sundbom, and Ylva Fernaeus. 2013. Fashionable Shape Switching – Explorations in Outfit-Centric Design. 1353–1362.
25. Andruid Kerne. 1997. CollageMachine: temporality and indeterminacy in media browsing via interface ecology. *In CHI '97 Extended Abstracts on Human Factors in Computing Systems*, ACM Press, 273–274.
26. Nelson Les, Elizabeth F. Churchill, Laurent Denoue, Jonathan Helfman, and Paul Murphy. 2004. Gooey interfaces: an approach for rapidly repurposing digital content. *CHI'04 Extended Abstracts on Human Factors in Computing Systems*, ACM Press.
27. Benny Lin and Elaine M. Huang. 2010. Reuse: promoting repurposing through an online DIY community. *CHI'10 Extended Abstracts on Human Factors in Computing Systems*, ACM Press.
28. Jonas Löwgren. 2006. Pliability as an experiential quality: exploring the aesthetics of interaction design. *Artifact* 1(12): 55–66.
29. William McDonough and Michael Braungart. 2013. *The Upcycle: Beyond Sustainability-designing for Abundance*. Macmillan.
30. Daniel Miller. 2005. *Materiality (Politics, History, and Culture)*. Duke University Press.

31. Martin Murer, Mattias Jacobsson, Siri Skillgate, and Petra Sundström. 2014. Taking things apart: reaching common ground and shared material understanding. *In Proc. CHI'14*, ACM Press, 469–472.

32. Yael Netzer, David Gabay, Yoav Goldberg, and Michael Elhadad. 2009. Gaiku: Generating Haiku with Word Associations Norms. *In Proc. NAACL HLT'09*, Association for Computational Linguistics, 32–39.

33. Anton Nijholt. 2014. Towards humor modelling and facilitation in smart environments. *Advances in Affective and Pleasurable Design*, 260–269.

34. William Odom, John Zimmerman, and Jodi Forlizzi. 2011. Teenagers and T heir Virtual Possessions : Design Opportunities and Issues. 1491–1500.

35. James Pierce and Eric Paulos. 2014. Counterfunctional Things : Exploring Possibilities in Designing Digital Limitations. 1: 375–384.

36. Reiner Pilz. 1994. Thinking about a green future. *Salvo*, 11–14. Retrieved from http://www.salvoweb.com/files/salvonews/sn99v3.pdf

37. Simon Robinson, Jennifer S. Pearson, and Matt Jones. 2014. A billion signposts: Repurposing barcodes for indoor navigation. *Proceedings of the SIGCHI Conference on Human Factors in Computing Systems*, ACM Press.

38. Nicolas Roussel, Helen Evans, and Heiko Hansen. 2004. Proximity as an Interface for Video Communication. *IEEE Computer Society* 11, 3: 12–16.

39. Katie Salen and Eric Zimmerman. 2004. *Rules of Play: Game Design Fundamentals*. MIT Press.

40. Katie Salen and Eric Zimmerman. 2005. *The Game Design Reader: A Rules of Play Anthology*. MIT Press.

41. Joseph Sant. 2015. Code Repurposing as an Assessment Tool. *Proceedings of the 37th International Conference on Software Engineering-Volume 2*, IEEE Press.

42. Abigail J. Sellen and Steve Whittaker. 2010. Beyond Total Capture: A Constructive Critique of Lifelogging. *Communications of the ACM*: 70–77.

43. Gilbert Silverman and Lila Silverman. 1981. *FLUXUS etc.* Cranbrook Academy of Art Museum.

44. Gilbert Silverman and Lila Silverman. 1983. *FLUXUS etc. / Addenda II*. Baxter Art Gallery, California Institute of Technology.

45. Jordi Solsona Belenguer, Marcus Lundén, Jarmo Laaksolahti, and Petra Sundström. 2012. Immaterial materials: designing with radio. *In Proc. of the Sixth International Conference on Tangible, Embedded and Embodied Interaction*, ACM Press.

46. Nikos Stangos. 1981. *Concepts of modern art*. Thames and Hudson.

47. Anne Stevens. Upcycling the Rotary Dial Phone in the Age of the Smartphone.

48. Petra Sundström, Alex Taylor, Katja Grufberg, Niklas Wirström, Jordi Solsona Belenguer, and Marcus Lundén. 2011. Inspirational bits: towards a shared understanding of the digital material. *CHI'11*, 1561–1570.

49. Vygandas Šimbelis, Anders Lundström, Kristina Höök, Jordi Solsona, and Vincent Lewandowski. 2014. Metaphone: Machine Aesthetics Meets Interaction Design. *In Proc. CHI'14*, ACM Press: 1–10.

50. Naoko Tosa, Hideto Obara, and Michihiko Minoh. 2007. Hitch Haiku. *In Proc. DIMEA'07*, ACM Press, 6–7.

51. Vasiliki Tsaknaki and Ylva Fernaeus. 2016. Expanding on Wabi-Sabi as a Design Resource in HCI. *In Proc. CHI'16*, ACM Press.

52. Anna Vallgårda and Ylva Fernaeus. 2015. Interaction Design as a Bricolage Practice. *Proceedings of the Ninth International Conference on Tangible, Embedded, and Embodied Interaction*, ACM Press.

53. Anna Vallgårda. 2013. Giving form to computational things: developing a practice of interaction design. *Pers. and Ubiq. Comput.*, 18(3): 577–592.

54. Ron Wakkary, Audrey Desjardins, Sabrina Hauser, and Leah Maestri. 2013. A Sustainable Design Fiction: Green Practices. *ACM Transactions on Computer-Human Interaction (TOCHI)* 20, 4: 1–33.

55. Eddie Wolfram. 1975. *History of collage*. Macmillan Publishing Company.

56. Freitag. Retrieved from http://freitag.com

57. Baldesigns. Retrieved from http://baldesigns.eu

58. Haiku Society. Retrieved from http://www.haiku-shs.org/haikudef.htm

59. HaikuLeaks. Retrieved from http://haikuleaks.com

60. Times Haiku. Retrieved from http://haiku.nytimes.com

61. Freecycle. Retrieved from https://www.freecycle.org

62. Duchamp, Marcel (1887-1968): Fountain, 1950 (replica of 1917 original). Philadelphia, Philadelphia Museum of Art. Porcelain urinal, 12 x 15 x 18 inches (30.5 x 38.1 x 45.7 cm). Gift (by exchange) of Mrs. Herbert Cameron Morris, 1998 © 2016. Photo The Philadelphia Museum of Art/Art Resource/Scala, Florence.

63. Picasso, Pablo (1881-1973): tete de taureau. Realisee a partir d'une selle et d'un guidon de bicyclette. 1942. Paris, Musee Picasso. Sculpture © 2016. Photo Josse/Scala, Florence.

Five Provocations for Ethical HCI Research

Barry Brown[1], Alexandra Weilenmann[2], Donald McMillan[1], Airi Lampinen[1]

[1]Mobile Life Centre
University of Stockholm, Sweden
[barry, don, airi]@mobilelifecentre.org

[2] Department of Applied IT
University of Gothenburg, Sweden
alexandra.weilenmann@gu.se

ABSTRACT

We present five provocations for ethics, and ethical research, in HCI. We discuss, in turn, informed consent, the researcher–participant power differential, presentation of data in publications, the role of ethical review boards, and, lastly, corporate-facilitated projects. By pointing to unintended consequences of regulation and oversimplifications of unresolvable moral conflicts, we propose these provocations *not* as guidelines or recommendations but as instruments for challenging our views on what it means to do ethical research in HCI. We then suggest an alternative grounded in the sensitivities of those being studied and based on everyday practice and judgement, rather than one driven by bureaucratic, legal, or philosophical concerns. In conclusion, we call for a wider and more practical discussion on ethics within the community, and suggest that we should be more supportive of low-risk ethical experimentation to further the field.

Author Keywords

Ethics; Human Trials; Research Practice

ACM Classification Keywords

H.5.m. Information interfaces and presentation (e.g., HCI): Miscellaneous.

INTRODUCTION

In recent years, there has been increased discussion and debate concerning the role of ethics in HCI research. HCI research projects have generated controversy due to their purported unethicality [22]. While much of these discussions take place in informal venues, recent publications by Benford *et al* [7], and Munteanu *et al* [38], have brought ethical issues into the fore. Questions of how HCI research should be conducted, and the common values that underlie our research community, are receiving renewed scrutiny. In this paper, we similarly engage with the ethical issues in HCI, but our goal is not to summarise or to establish what is ethical and what is not, but rather to question some of the taken for granted foundations of ethics in HCI.

CHI'16, May 07 - 12, 2016, San Jose, CA, USA

ACM 978-1-4503-3362-7/16/05...$15.00
DOI: http://dx.doi.org/10.1145/2858036.2858313

Indeed, we would argue that discussions around ethics frequently suffer from “ethical creep”, where virtuous but impractical positions are advocated, and little attention is paid to how seemingly ethical positions can delay, damage or stop research, with serious implications [48]. In the wake of ethical controversy, the question is asked: "*what is to be done?*", leading to the planning of further ethical scrutiny and regulation, to the submitting of more research to ethical review, and to the enhancement of existing protections and procedures. Yet, these efforts may not lead to any more ethical research and come at considerable cost [42].

Addressing this concern, our paper is not built around exemplary experiences from specific studies but rather an attempt to engender conversation through five *provocations*. These provocations formulate positions that are controversial, and we expect many might disagree with them. A provocation is the discussion and argument for a position that is used to highlight shortcomings in the consensus in order to encourage new, critical thinking [4]. These provocations are *not* guidelines or rules but tools for critical thinking. The aim is to cast new light on decisions that must be made while conducting our research. These five provocations draw on work on ethics from the Internet Research community and the social sciences more broadly. Our goal in writing them is to open, rather than conclude, discussion and to promote a shift away from positions that, while seemingly axiomatic, we believe could result in damage to the whole field. We encourage critical thinking, pushing against the potential chilling effects [2] on academic discourse of overly strong ethical regulation.

Our first provocation argues that informed consent is often unnecessary and can actually mislead by miscommunicating the benefits of participating in research. Second, we argue that research on vulnerable populations should more seriously evaluate who benefits from the research. We turn a sceptical eye onto the important benefits of research to researchers when compared to participants who are left without sustainable benefit after a trial. Third, we question why we preserve anonymity in research, when anonymity may be as much about attempting to imply a generalisability of research findings than a matter of protecting participants. Fourth, we address the *bête noire* of ethical discussions – the institutional review board (IRB). We argue that IRBs can actually damage the ethicality of research, and that we need researcher and institutional responsibility rather than legalistic bureaucracy. Lastly, our fifth provocation goes to the commercial heart of much of HCI research. If research in HCI is based on data that is not generally available, and so cannot be tested or validated, how is this science? We argue that research that is based on privileged commercial access to data should not be published unless access is provided to all researchers.

In the discussion, we ask how we might develop new approaches to research ethics that engage with the interventionist, design-led research that is characteristic of HCI. The five provocations point to unintended consequences of regulation, oversimplifications of unresolvable moral conflicts, a bias in social desirability over what is ethical in effect, and a failure to consider the value of research. Some of the points we make conflict, intentionally, with aspects of current research consensus. We believe this can help advance the debate and chart future work. In conclusion, we call for the community to engage in low-risk experimentation with ethics in HCI.

BACKGROUND

We review briefly prior work on ethics within the HCI and Internet research communities. We will, then, consider in more detail two recent controversies that call into question some of the consensus around ethics and ethical practice.

Ethics in HCI

Much has happened since Wendy Mackay in 1995 outlined ethical guidelines for the then relatively new field of HCI [34]. Focusing specifically on the challenges involved when conducting research involving video, she argued that these guidelines should go beyond legal requirements. While using video in research was relatively new at the time, we have since then seen a range of new tools for conducting research, new domains of study, and a broad sea change in how knowledge is generated and understood in HCI. While SIGCHI members have notionally signed up to the ACM Code of Ethics [1], these 24 general statements are focused on professionals more than researchers.

More recently, Munteanu *et al* [38] draw on their experience in five studies with different populations and interaction structures. From fieldwork with parents of sick children to lab-based studies of interfaces for the blind they highlight the inflexibility of the current ethical review system and suggest mitigating action that can be taken while working within the system. These involve, among others, opening a 'continuous dialog' with members of the review committee and including a number of possible plans for fieldwork in the request sent for approval to allow the researcher to adjust their ethical practice in the field and follow a more 'situational ethics' approach.

In contrast, McMillan *et al* [37] focus specifically on the ethical challenges that have emerged with the possibility of collecting large data sets using mobile apps. The authors suggest a framework where the key dimensions are *identifiability,* and *user expectation*, that is, to what extent the data being collected or logged is on par with users' expectations. When designing applications to be evaluated in a research study, researchers can specifically orient to the amount of relevant data they collect, and whether participants have a reason to expect this particular data to be included. Another relevant point they present, that we will discuss later in relation to issues of anonymity, is that data can easily move beyond control of the study. For instance, users' content might be combined, through mash-ups and generative production, into other products shared beyond the particular study.

Benford *et al* [7] focus in particular on the peculiarities of studying cultural experiences within HCI and the constraints this places on the standard ethical procedure. They note that the notion of informed consent is negotiated with the audience through ticket restraints (age for example), the time, venue, promotional materials, and the artist involved in the performance allow people to use their own judgement without needing full disclosure before hand which may invalidate the performance. They also cover the need to consider the consequences of withdrawal and situations where the artistic integrity and experience can breech traditional ethical concerns such as privacy.

There has also been a series of workshops on ethics at the CHI and CSCW conferences. These have focused on ethics in online social research "in the Facebook era" [11], in large-scale user trials [14], in design research [10], involving co-creation and identity-making, and, most recently, in the study of online socio-technical systems "in a Big Data world" [21]. These workshops illustrate persistent interest in ethical issues as well as continued effort to work on them together as a community, with sensitivity to the shifting social and technological landscape, as well as the multidisciplinary nature of our field.

Ethics in Internet Research

Internet research is a field that shares much with HCI and has, moreover, engaged with ethical issues in depth. In 2002, the ethics committee of the Association of Internet Researchers (AoIR) advocated for "a dialogic, case-based, inductive, and process approach to ethics" in a report on ethical decision-making in internet research [20]. An updated report from 2012 [35] continues to highlight the value of addressing and resolving ethical issues as they come up across the many steps in a research process. Ethical concepts should ground inquiry, instead of being taken as "regulatory hurdles to be jumped through at the beginning stages of research." ([35] p. 4)

The AoIR report acknowledges that there may legitimately be several differing views on norms, values, principles, and practices. Even though there is, at times, broad consensus about whether a particular action was ethical or not, ambiguity and uncertainty are more common. Since different, conflicting judgments are possible, AoIR promotes a deliberative approach to working though ethical issues. This is reflected in that the report provides a set of questions to support ethical decision-making, rather than a set of practices.

Boellstorff *et al* [8] identify *the principle of care* as the most important guideline in conducting ethnographic research – one without which any set of ethics guidelines will be ineffective. In their view, "taking good care" of informants encompasses not only making every effort to avoid doing harm but also working to ensure that informants gain some reward from participation, if possible. This requirement arises from the power asymmetry between researchers and participants, as well as from the common imbalance of benefit between the two parties.

Further debate within the Internet Research community deals with presenting frameworks and supporting discussions around whether, for example, informed consent is necessary or not. When our research data is accessible online, we need to ask if we could use it without the knowledge and consent of the participants. One such framework is presented by Sveningsson [45] to help make the decision about whether or not data could be used for studies. She argues that it is not enough to only consider whether the data was made public or private, it is also necessary to think about the harm that could be done to the participants, and whether the data contained sensitive or non-sensitive material. Various other approaches recognise the need to adapt such guidelines to the unique, practical circumstances of a study at hand. The casuistic approach to ethics, for which the AoIR advocates, can go so far as to argue that "[e]thics should not be treated as *science*, but rather as a practical *art*" ([36] p. 26).

Recent ethical controversies

Facebook has been involved in two recent controversies in social research. In 2008 the "Tastes, Ties, and Time" study used data from Facebook usage to look at social ties amongst collage students [33, 50]. The research group used a corpus of material from university students at a single US university. While the material was collected with the consent of the university and with the acknowledgement of the review board at the university of the researchers, the consent of all those whose data was collected was not obtained. The data was accessed with the collaboration of Facebook, and matched with records provided by the university, to add information about the participants. Even though the researchers took various measures to protect the anonymity of the informants, it did not take long until the university under study was identified. A commentary on the case by Zimmer criticised the research for a misconstrued understanding of the nature of privacy and anonymity on social media [50].

What this situation highlights is also a contextual concern, a need to consider in what context users shared information. In this case there was unauthorised secondary use – when information posted on Facebook for social networking purposes was repurposed for research without authorization from the informants. Or as Zimmer puts it, the research team failed "to recognize that users might maintain strong expectations that information shared on Facebook is meant to stay on Facebook." Finally, and critically for the discussion in this paper, it should be noted that the study set-up was approved by an IRB. According to Zimmer, this shows how review boards despite being experts on ethics do not always have the right expertise to review research protocols for internet research.

A more recent controversy within, and beyond, the HCI community followed the publication of a large-scale experimental study of emotional contagion on Facebook [31]. This study caused controversy over the participation of Facebook users (who had their mood influenced through experimental manipulation of their timeline) without their consent. Jeff Hancock, one of the authors, reflected on the controversy during a keynote talk at CSCW 2015 [26]. Here, he argued that novel, large-scale methods and collaborations between academia and industry raise new ethical questions. He reported the ethical decisions made during the Facebook Emotion study and the reasons why the study attracted such massive attention and criticism. Hancock concluded with thoughts on how the criticisms might act as a gift for the research community, opening opportunities to move the discussion, and practice, forward. The impact of these controversies often takes the form of appeals to broaden the role and scope of institutional review boards [30]. Keegan [ibid.] argues that these appeals are a ill-conceived policy recommendations, emerging from moral panics [48]. Instead of increased oversight, he calls for avoiding "ethics creep" [25] by developing alternative ethical frameworks that reflect enduring moral commitments and apply them to the contemporary circumstances of HCI research.

One workshop at CSCW 2015 set out to document guiding principles for scholars doing research online in a "post-Snowden" world, where "many Internet users are suddenly more aware of who might be watching their digital footprints" ([21] p. 290). This effort is timely and important, since as Zimmer has pointed out, "[c]oncerns over consent, privacy and anonymity do not disappear simply because subjects participate in online social networks; rather, they become even more important." ([50] p. 324). Indeed, if we do not settle these ethical questions ourselves they may be settled for us – by government, the mass media, or the corporations that fund our research. The "chilling effects" of these decisions could inhibit or outlaw research. We are faced with the possibility of researchers being prosecuted, with some suggesting even criminal responsibility [40].

FIVE PROVOCATIONS

Let us move on to our provocations. A provocation is the discussion and argument for a (possibly extreme) position which is used to highlight shortcomings in the consensus, and to encourage rethinking established positions. While the different authors have different positions on each provocation, we believe that each one works to provoke reflection on accepted positions that, although taken for granted, may be wrongheaded or damaging. These provocations are clearly not guidelines, advice or recommendations — they should not be understood or cited as established points but as controversial, conversation enabling, conjectures. As Cavell puts it, "appealing to ordinary language turns to the reader not to convince him without proof but to get him to prove something, test something, against himself" ([13], p76). Through these conjectures we hope to encourage critical thinking in new ways, to present challenges to our ethical reflexes and norms, and to raise discussion on the ways in which we approach our research.

In each of the areas our provocations touch upon, there has been considerable debate about how we should conduct research ethically: How might different ethical models apply to HCI? What might that mean for our research practice? In challenging current shared understandings, our provocations may read as unorthodox. Yet, we hope that considering alternative perspectives can help to sharpen our responses and provide insight into edge cases.

The first provocation takes on informed consent, connecting to questions and debates from medical research about whether informed consent is a realistic and necessary goal. Second, we explore the ethical requirements of working with vulnerable populations and the definition of a 'vulnerable' participant in the eyes of IRBs and researchers. Third, we engage with issues arising from conflicts in the goals and expectations of researchers and participants. Here, in particular, we consider the sharing and co-creation of data in the course of research. Fourth, we challenge the role of IRBs. As has been discussed at length before [42], one issue with IRBs is their overriding concern with bureaucratic and legal functions over their ethical role. We might ask, then, to what extent might these concerns cause IRB boards to harm research (and, as a result, societies) by either delaying or banning inquiry. Lastly, we discuss some of the issues related to the involvement of commercial organisations in HCI and how this can conflict with research practice. This issue is complicated by the availability of large datasets internally to organisations from their related corporate functions, and the problems of privileged access.

Provocation 1: Written informed consent does little to protect participants.

Since Nuremburg [3], the concept of informed consent has become central to medical practice, medical research practice, and, more recently, social science research. It works as a double cure: against researchers misleading or deceiving research participants, but, also, against harm being done to participants without their knowledge. It has, then, both an informational and a duty of care function. It is in medical settings that informed consent has become most broadly institutionalised. Yet it is in medicine where informed consent has also been extensively critiqued. As Katz writes in two articles:

"The phrase "informed consent" evokes [...] magic expectations. Its protagonists often convey that once kissed by the doctrine, frog-patients will become autonomous princes." [28]

"[I]nformed consent in today's world, is largely a charade which misleads patients into thinking that they are making decisions when indeed they are not." [27]

Indeed, studies of consent practices throw light on the ways in which consent is almost always achieved through ritualistic procedures, through the use of professional authority, and where after consent is given patients have little recollection of what they consented to. In 1980, Cassileth *et al* [12] asked patients to recall the contents of consent forms they had completed the day before: *"Only 60 per cent understood the purpose and nature of the procedure, and only 55 per cent correctly listed even one major risk or complication. We found that three factors were related to inadequate recall: education, medical status, and the care with which patients thought they had read their consent forms before signing. Only 40 per cent of the patients had read the form "carefully." Most believed that consent forms were meant to "protect the physician's rights."* [12]

In turn, ethnographic studies [23] in medicine have illustrated how consent is something that is gained from patients, while conducting medical treatment, with doctors passing quickly through the consent procedure, and implicitly making use of their own position of power with respect to patients to obtain the consent they desired. Even in cases where written consent is obtained, this can be achieved in the form of a request by a doctor to "just sign this bit of paperwork", instead of through the careful reflection of patient and practitioner. Looking at this practice in a positive light, we can understand that there are, necessarily, differing levels of expertise between doctor and patient – or researcher and participant – on the topic of the study being conducted. The point of *informing* the participant should not be seen as giving them the same understanding of the study as the researcher has. After all, to what extent can we expect participants to be 'informed' about a research lifeworld to which they might have little or no access (or interest)? How much of participants' time can we demand before the costs of the research outweigh the benefits, or simply that many enough participants drop out to render the research meaningless?

Informing participants enough for them to validly consent is a negotiation, and in this negotiation the level of trust a participant has in the researcher or clinician is a factor in how much information they need to decide whether to participate or withdraw. Having the participants trust that the researcher is not out to intentionally harm them, and that the risks involved are as described, should not be seen as an abuse of power but as fundamental to the trust relationship between participant and researcher. The standard IRB stance that all subjects are 'manipulable victims' [42] infantilizes them. The resulting legalization of the relationship between participant and researcher with a document that casts the researcher as an untrustworthy individual engaged in a dangerous practice and the participant as a victim without agency causes more harm than it prevents. This harm stems from undermining the participants' sense of agency, and, as a result, lessening their sense of altruism, and exposing them to the negative emotional state of feeling that they must be on guard against being somehow *duped* by the researcher who attempts to gain their trust.

In medicine, patients usually describe consent as a way for the doctors to protect themselves legally, rather than as a procedure that protects the patient. [9] There is also the case of research with children, where the parents need to give consent and the children have no legal say in being studied [15]. Another recent HCI example of the asymmetry in power relations is the case of research with animals, where animals cannot give consent to participate in studies and design experiments [47]. We argue that the legalizing of consent obscures the ethical responsibilities in these cases.

We might consider consent in HCI studies to be of a higher quality. Yet, with Mechanical Turk studies and studies that make use of software deployed through app stores, or social media, is this really the case? In these settings, informed consent may be no more than the "click-through" set up around legal agreements which actively force users to lie that they have "read and understood" a long multi-page document in complex legalistic language (cf. [37]).

In many situations, there is no deceit and the possibility of harm to the participants is so slight as to be negligible. In such cases, the act of asking consent in a meaningful way may do more harm to participants (in terms of wasting their time) than the study itself. In interventionist HCI studies of this type, where the deployment of an application, service, or device and the access to it is the compensation for participation, the act of using the system could be interpreted as consent. Indeed, in much of research, participants benefit morally, socially, and personally from participation. Moreover, often research takes place using the passive monitoring of participants (e.g., logging, archival, and public/online observation). The personal benefits, in HCI, are not only of access to novel systems or services, or even the occasional payment for participation. Altruistic acts bring with them a personal benefit, in the form of a positive emotional change [42], and also a social benefit in being seen to be benefiting the wider community. The right to sacrifice oneself for the benefit of others should be respected by researchers.

Our critique of informed consent should not be taken as an argument that it is not an important tool for ethical research, but rather that it should not be considered the 'gold standard' that research must always conform to. Also, gaining informed consent does not absolve the research itself of potential harm. We are arguing that the legal requirements should be separated from the ethical. In other words, not harming or burdening participants is more important than teaching them the intricacies of academic studies, and that given the multifaceted benefits of research, there is a level of harm and effort below which participation can be assumed as the default.

***Provocation 2:* Interventions with vulnerable populations must result in greater benefit for them than for the researchers.**

One longstanding procedure with research is that special procedures need be administered when participants are members of vulnerable populations, such as the young, prisoners, or individuals with mental health issues. Most IRBs' definition of participant implies vulnerability to the influence and power of the researcher. Yet, a member of a vulnerable population is seen to be at a greater risk of this influence. When the power differential, in socio-economic status or political leverage, between the researcher and participant is seen to be unduly strong, or when the risks of revealing membership of a population could harm the participants in some way, the population is seen as vulnerable.

The usual procedure for working with vulnerable populations is thus that special restrictions are placed on the research, extra procedures are implemented, and the research undergoes more extensive review. Certain sorts of research that are possible with non-vulnerable populations, especially those involving forms of deception or social interaction between participants, are often prohibited.

Dealing with these problems can be such a burden on research that researchers are reluctant to take on projects of this nature. For instance, research on patient-centred care is skewed towards excluding the patient, because the process of getting access to the relevant materials is complicated. Another example is research on children, where ethical standards call for informed consent from parents, in a way that makes consent procedures troublesome to the point where such studies are avoided. Even when, for example, children may be keen to be part of a study (and suffer from not being able to participate if their peers do), if their parents withheld consent (or simply do not attend to the request), the children are not allowed to participate.

This is not to say these are not distinctive ethical issues that need to be addressed. Outside HCI, in the development and social policy literature, there has been considerable critique of studies where little benefit comes to the community itself. Some communities are heavily researched, such as poor or migrant populations in cities with strong research communities. This can result in a somewhat jaundiced view on research [16]. We might similarly ask whether some groups such as 'turkers' or 'wikipedians' have been researched out of all magnitude to their number.

Rather than focus on harm we might, instead, ask who benefits: Is it just the researchers? For example, in cases where technology is deployed to vulnerable communities, it is often taken away at the end of the study. The practical realities of research funding make this understandable, yet this is an area where the constraints placed on medical research have not reached HCI – and where they maybe should. With participants in pharmaceutical trials there are considerable post-trial treatment obligations – even if a particular drug does not reach the market [17]. Yet farmers in sub-Saharan Africa are not guaranteed the right to continue using a learning platform or a crop rotation calculator after a research project has dissolved. Instead of focusing on the possibility of participants being pressured into taking part in the study, perhaps the focus should be on reflecting on and engineering lasting benefit to the community being studied. Leaving broken technology, or removing devices at the end of a study can break with the duty of ongoing care that conducting ethical research requires.

The problem of pressure to participate also becomes less worrisome when participants are made to feel that they are actively collaborating in the study of or intervention into their community. While the relationship between participant and researcher is often much closer and more personal than what is expected by IRB rules and regulations [42], formalising this and recognising it as part of ethical practice could put HCI at the forefront of ethical research with vulnerable communities.

***Provocation 3:* Anonymisation should be an option presented alongside co-creation of research with participants, not a default.**

A key premise in how we conduct ethical research is to protect the privacy and integrity of participants. This commitment is often attended to by anonymising data so that participants cannot be identified. There are two assumptions underlying this idea. The first is that it is possible for researchers to effectively anonymise their participants in publication or presentation. The second is that participants want and benefit from anonymity.

There is a relationship between the amount of information in any message and its anonymity [46]. The more information a message entails, be it with a quote, picture, or video, the more there is that can be used for re-identification with the help of other data sources. This means that in order to make a case in a paper or presentation, the researcher has to decide the level of anonymity to afford the participant in balance with the extra information that adds credibility to their claims, and transparency to their justification. Moreover, this means that there is no such thing as an anonymous piece of data from a participant that also supports an argument. Family and friends can still identify an image with a blurred face. A textual snippet as short as a Tweet can be de-anonymised by comparing it statistically against online text posted to IMDB [39]. When we say that we will anonymise our participants, effectively what we mean is that we will not openly point to their identity and that we will not subject them to embarrassment or ridicule them by linking them to compromising data. If we, or the participants, truly wish to hide their act of participation altogether, then effectively no data can be directly shared from a participant.

Anonymity as a default is based on the idea that participants *want* to be anonymous. In the first provocation, we touched on the social benefits of participation. It can be hampered by anonymity. It also goes against some of the driving mechanisms of social media practices, of being seen and recognised for contributions, receiving likes and comments, and reposts in the form of e.g. retweets and regrams. Increasingly, it is being recognised that those who publish material online should be seen as authors or artists who should be referenced and acknowledged. For example, Bruckman argues for *"[t]he need to balance – the right of Internet users to receive credit for their creative and intellectual work, and -- the need to protect vulnerable human subjects in research studies"*. ([11] p. 229).

In one of our own studies of Instagram use [49], it turned out that our study participants did not want anonymity. Rather, they were happy that their social media productions might gain a bigger audience through publication in research outlets. Therefore, we chose not to change the user names when presenting the material. This shows how traditional ideas about privacy and participants' anonymity are no longer valid in certain communities and contexts. However, this is not to say that social media users do not have a strong sense of privacy and what it involves (cf. [9]). In fact, as boyd has argued, it is hard for users to understand the boundaries of the information they share online, since *"[t]he dynamics of mediated social interactions – including invisible audiences, collapsed contexts, and persistent content, complicate things"* ([ibid] p. 61). Publishing the data from our study lead to some discussion with the publisher who first wanted us to exclude all user names in the paper. Later, it was agreed upon that the images included should be considered artwork and we, therefore, needed copyright forms to be signed for each Instagram image being published. In this case, protecting the anonymity of the participants in the study, while seemingly the straightforward thing to do, would have led to going against the morals of the community under study. Similar issues also come up in ethnographic work. In Duneier's book Sidewalk [19], he reports his participants' pleasure in being named in "a book" – their struggles being acknowledged and their lives taken seriously. In another case [5], the decision to change user names to protect the participants' anonymity was considered problematic, as discussed by the authors, since the group under study was marginalised. Disguising the name of an online community for young lesbian women, the authors argue, was in a way unethical because of the political repercussions: the anonymisation of names could be seen as giving into the assumption that homosexuality is something to be ashamed of and could risk further marginalising the group. As the authors put it: "*Overly protective research ethics risks diminishing the cultural capital of those engaging in cultural production through Internet technologies, and inadvertently contributing to their further marginalization.*" ([5] p. 244).

In all research, it is important to recognise the asymmetry between those doing the research and those under study. As HCI researchers, we have an added responsibility because we often deal with system development in some form. This means that we have the power to control and administer the system being used. When publishing material based on studies of systems designed or developed by the researcher, it becomes harder to keep identities hidden. As Bruckman [11] points out, disguising the name of the online community she studied was impossible because she was involved in designing the platform they used. As HCI researchers, we have a different perspective here than social scientists, who are generally not directly involved in system development, but study existing platforms and technologies.

Moreover, often the anonymisation of data is not something that can be done without degrading the amount of information in the dataset [46]. This is an important consideration in terms of the replicability of research, especially given that the re-purposing of datasets by other researchers and in other disciplines is becoming an expected part of the lifecycle of datasets. Indeed, it could be argued that we are ethically bound to use the participation of each participant to the fullest possible benefit for society. We, therefore, ask what the reasonable limits to anonymity are and whether in the future it will be possible to promise participants that their identities are protected.

This becomes particularly challenging, as pointed out by McMillan *et al* [37], when identification techniques are gradually progressing, meaning that what is anonymous at one point in time might not be so in the future. As we saw with the university-based "Tastes, Ties, and Time" Facebook study, even though the researchers in this case thought they had taken "extreme measures" to keep their participants' identities protected, it only took a few days before the different pieces of information were put together and participants' identities revealed [50]. Whenever we promise participants that their data will be 'anonymous', what we are, in fact, promising is a best effort to stop the data being transferred to those with ill intent (already a legal requirement for anyone collecting other people's data in the EU), and a best effort attempt to make tracing an individual piece of data back to a single person a non-trivial task. By using the word 'anonymous', we raise expectations, not only for ourselves as researchers, but also for the participants.

***Provocation 4*: Institutional review boards delay and damage research out of proportion to any harm they prevent. We should replace them.**

Van den Hoonaard's ethnographic work on ethical review boards [48] presents a critical view of how much they understand of the research they are regulating and how much benefit (ethical or otherwise) they bring. Indeed, he goes on to argue that IRBs have resulted in a narrowing of methods, with researchers abandoning covert and action research, IRBs acting to "cut across the grain of social research". Schneider draws on this work, but goes further arguing in "The Censor's Hand" [42] that "imperial IRBs" have led to a widespread mis-regulation of research, with IRBs acting to censor research. According to Schneider, IRBs are propagated by "moral entrepreneurs", drawing on Becker's [6] description of "the crusading reformer who is profoundly disturbed by some evil and who feels that nothing can be right in the world until rules are made to correct it". Schneider goes on to outline ways in which research could be regulated without IRBs, such as drawing more heavily on researchers' own involvement and insights.

It is worth reflecting on the cost of IRBs. Due to the nature of the regulations that guide and bind IRBs, they are charged only to protect the participants from harm – not to weigh the costs in money or time, nor in terms of balancing the potential good the research could cause against the harm it risks doing. Ethical review processes are an extension of organisations and their practices, meaning that some boards will conduct well-balanced reviews, while others will not. At times, review boards will approve unethical research. However, due to their mandate, it is more likely that boards will over-react and reject, or delay, valuable studies.

Dingwall [18] documents the case of a study on hygiene practices in the British National Health Service. This social science study was to understand the practice of reuse of single-use equipment responsible for an estimated seven deaths per year. Yet, Dingwall depicts how this study was delayed and made less effective by the ethical review process he was institutionally forced to undergo. The review board asked for separate approval and review from each hospital. While this might seem like a reasonable request it "potentially generated [the requirement of] 1600 signatures and 9000 pages of documentation" [18]. Moreover, Dingwall argues that through slowing down the research, and the recommendations which helped cut infection rates, the IRB review resulted in a number of deaths. Delaying research can harm studies, slow down research, and delay any positive impacts that might result.

A more pernicious issue concerns the nature of IRB approval. Usually boards use review forms to elicit from researchers the ethical procedures of their research. Yet, much of the ethical work of studies is decided in the field, on a moment-to-moment basis. For qualitative interview work, for example, in discussion with participants the study will be frequently re-described with adjustment to the participants' interaction. Study goals might be simplified or practical outcomes emphasised over academic ones. The nature of research also means that it can change radically post-ethical review. While most ethical procedures request re-review, the real-time nature of research is that it is often responsive to results as they happen. The pre-planned nature of research in HCI is exaggerated beyond credibility by the IRB process, and often research can change radically between design and implementation. This is the case especially where applications or services are being designed and built with the participants' input.

The IRB process comes at a monetary cost as well. Each form must be filled out by a, usually relatively highly paid, researcher, and each of these forms must be reviewed by a number of, usually more highly paid, reviewers. Each delay results in the time of the researchers who could be conducting research to be spent on other things. Moreover, the vast majority of funding for research that is subject to IRBs is funded by public money [42]. Another issue with IRBs is that as a small research field HCI protocols and experiments are reviewed by researchers from other disciplines. Ethical review boards rely heavily on the experience of their participants, their own judgments about ethics and their own knowledge from their own fields of expertise. This can result in nonsensical requirements put onto HCI research.

One way to ameliorate most of the issues this provocation brings up would be to conduct ethical review through peer-review. By placing review in the hands of practitioners on two levels – once during trial planning, and again before publication – the ethical sensitivity to participants that IRBs foster in researchers is kept, but extended through the research with a pre-publication check, allowing them to explain their ethical responsiveness. By publishing these ethical statements and their relationship to the research conducted alongside the results, ethical practice will not only be transparent – it will be something to be discussed and learned from. It would also provide a proof of ethical practice to help protect our field from external regulation and to inform others on our practices. Here, the relatively small size of HCI can be turned to an advantage.

***Provocation 5:* Publication of research performed with, or within, a commercial entity should be blocked until the complete dataset is made available to others – both during review and for future replicability of analysis.**

The last provocation we engage with concerns the interactions between commercial interest and research ethics. This provocation is not only about the replicability of studies performed on corporate data, it also puts attention on HCI research carried out on commercial applications or services where one of the goals is to improve it. By forcing the data to be opened to academics and competitors alike, companies that wish to take advantage of the expertise in the field will have to fund foundational research, the results of which they and others can apply, rather than pushing research into a narrow, blinded, alleyway.

Much HCI research is either funded directly by commercial entities, or is even conducted within those commercial entities. In most cases, there is little conflict or issue – research usually is sufficiently foundational that there is some distance between commercial products and the research. At other times, the research is focused on the invention of new potential products or services, or the identification of user 'needs'. The practical application of computer science is such that its outputs are frequently directed in this direction, and the funding or location of the research is less important.

As others have noted, however, there is at least the potential for problems here [41]. To take an analogous example, research into gambling has long suffered from problems in that funding for the majority of research comes from companies that profit from gambling [43]. To be free to consider whether the products we are designing are harmful in some cases, funding from those who profit from selling them might constitute a conflict of interest. Issues that are damaging to the industry overall, or that question the role of technology itself, may be neglected.

The popular game Candy Crush Saga, for example, is estimated to earn the majority of its money from less than 5% of its users, so called 'whales' [44]. While the publishers may be willing to fund research on the compelling nature of their game for these players, who may spend hundreds of dollars a day on the game, research on the harm caused or the nature of addiction to digital games may find it difficult to get access to the same data. After all, it would be somewhat unreasonable to expect a commercial entity to fund research that would undermine its product. An advantage of the technology field, especially in HCI, is that there is such diversity in organisation and product, that even the largest actors are not monopolistic in the research space. However, while this has not presented itself as a problem so far, it could as the field matures.

As researchers, we present ourselves as being scientifically motivated, when it can be argued that the ultimate purpose of our work in HCI is to make money for the corporations funding the research by informing them in how to build better products. However, there are times when making money might conflict with making a product better. For example, Quicken has conducted considerable user-led research into tax preparation. At first appearances, this would seem to have a noble goal: making financial software easier to use. When the topic was explored at a recent workshop at CHI [29], it was noted that the best tax return may be no tax return, but this is something Quicken has politically lobbied against while funding research on making tax return software easy to use.

To be clear, we are not arguing against corporate funding of research, or even that research with a commercial aim is ethically problematic. Rather, it is that such funding creates blind spots and that it is important to both acknowledge and engage with these issues as topics of research in their own right. As a community, we must face the problem head on and discuss inserting into our everyday research practice the safeguards, checks, and balances that will engender confidence in and respectability of HCI research.

DISCUSSION

Our five provocations put forward problems with current ethical practice within HCI and a series of quite radical and wide-ranging solutions to them. These solutions should not be seen as a manifesto or statement of intent. They are meant as tools to allow us to better discuss the current state of our ethical obligations and practices in light of alternatives that broaden the room for thought. We should emphasise that we are not abating anyone to ignore their current organisational or legal regulation – in nearly all cases research needs to be lawful (see [40] for a rare exception). Yet we are encouraging debate about those regulations and laws.

We are also not arguing for the abolition of IRBs overnight, or against consent and anonymity in all cases, or that corporations could never fund valid research. In some senses the provocations are extremes to counter prevailing wisdoms and to help us consider alternatives. Our provocations work, then, as ways of encouraging new thinking that does not follow the "review and ban" ethical stereotype. The alternative that we argue for here is one that considers ethics more as a situational aspect of our interactions with research participants and communities.

A key notion that underlies our provocations, and ethical discussions and guidelines in HCI and other fields, is the definition of *harm* to participants and beyond. The definition of harm by ethicists and IRB boards is something that goes beyond that defined in law. Here, Schneider [42], notes that in law, at least in the USA, "*because society's 'rough edges' need 'a good deal of filing down,' people are 'expected and required to be hardened to a certain amount of rough language' and 'inconsiderate and unkind' acts*" ([42], quoting from the American Law Institute *Restatement of Torts,* 1965). Yet, the harm envisaged by IRBs across North America and Europe, as well as by professional bodies regulating medical and psychological research, does not take into account the interactions that participants *must* have in everyday life to make them valid participants in the first place. Making someone mildly uncomfortable, slightly irritated, or momentarily inconvenienced, should not constitute a barrier for research. Yet, it does. This is not in itself a provocation as, in our opinion, any call to change the current definition is not a provocative statement.

How the ethics of researchers come into play in the research encounter, and how research ethics and purposes may come into conflict with the concerns and ethics of those who we study is of interest. It is not just that ethical guidelines need to be "applied" but rather that they are artfully manipulated to make research possible while acting ethically towards participants and the wider community [24]. While existing ethical guidelines can provide some information, in this paper, we have explored the gap between rules, regulations and ethical bureaucratic instructions, and the practice of ethical research and judgements in HCI research. We want to open the discussion by bringing out some points that are of particular relevance for HCI.

The distinctive character of ethics in HCI

HCI's ethical challenges are, of course, strongly related to broader ethical discussions in the online social science research communities. As with social science ethics, researchers must grapple with issues such as how to present themselves as researchers, who gets to benefit from research, how is participant anonymity to be handled, and so on. Yet, there are distinctive challenges, even from the growing ethics of HCI research field [7, 14, 37, 47].

First, in HCI we are frequently involved in the creation or design and implementation of particular social environments. HCI researchers are frequently involved in actually building the very environments that they study. This already sets up an interesting position for researchers – they are automatically in a privileged position vis-à-vis the participants. Second, in many cases, the outputs of HCI research are not only constrained to understanding and representing those being researched, but have an orientation towards change in terms of design. Researchers attempt to design systems using and drawing on the studies undertaken. This gives participants a conversely privileged position – they can influence the future shape of the tool they are using. This is not a unique position. For example, in the social sciences, researchers might participate in what they study and policy orientated research can run into similar issues. However, it is a particular challenge for those who might recruit participants with reference to the company that they are researching for, or for what the results could potentially be used for.

Situated, Ordinary Ethics

We suggest a distinctive approach to ethics, one that is grounded not in the bureaucratic or legal concerns but rather in the sensitivities of those being studied and the practice of being ethical. As an contrasting example, in Goffman's view interaction's obligations are more 'etiquette' than 'ethics' proper, and we strain to preserve a semblance of propriety in 'ceremonial' fashion, irrespective of whatever 'substantive' moral sentiments may – or may not – drive them [32]. In the same way we hope to find HCI ethics grounded in everyday practice and judgements, rather than in reflection on philosophical abstracts. Notions such as busyness, getting things done, minimising harm, altruism, and showing respect by understanding that the participants are also striving to behave ethically, need to be adopted to make ethical research become practical and achievable.

To take this approach we suggest three practical measures that could be taken in future work:

1. *Differentiate between ethics as practice versus ethics as law.* As discussed in this paper, and as several of the studies we have referred to have highlighted, it is important to recognize that IRBs do not solve ethical issues, they only transform them. Review boards deal with the legal implications of studies, whereas researchers have to consider a range of different moral and ethical restrictions. Researchers are often doing more than what is asked of them legally, or in fact sometimes promise more than they legally can promise. This does not mean that we should not have review boards, but it means that we need to put emphasis on ethics as practice. One of the practical implications of this could be to focus on learning among peers and providing opportunities for junior researchers to learn from those with more experience, and in doing so keep an open debate on ethical considerations in research practice. As Guillemin and Gillam [24] suggest, ethically important moments in practice should be reflected upon. To keep up this ongoing debate is particularly important in our domain, where we constantly encounter new configurations of users and technology, and where laws, regulations and guidelines are not updated with the same speed.

2. *Support low-risk experiments around ethics.* The idea of experimenting with ethics may seem like a dangerous (even unethical) position. Yet if we take the perspective that ethics is a situated practice then we can argue that we need to discover and explore how different ethical positions might fit different scenarios. There is no set of primary ethics that can be followed in every situation, and in different situations we might need to be inventive to understand how research might be conducted without damaging others. One way of finding out what the particular ethical and moral rules of a particular community are, and how best adapt to them, is simply to start conducting the research and learning from the participants.

3. *Start a conversation on the definition of harm in ethics.* It is almost without question that the broad and sensitive definition of harm used in ethics is, in itself, harmful. Where there are disagreements on the best course of ethical action there will be disagreements on what constitutes harm to a participant. We need to move beyond the current definition which is often taken to mean 'any negative effect; emotional, physical, social, or monetary' and begin to balance harm against not only the good that the research may do in the future but also the good participation can do for the participant and their community.

There is no right to not be offended, but the legal definition of emotional tort may be a step too far. We would not want research to routinely cause the friction and inconvenience that other problematic encounters do in day-to-day life. The political or religious zealot haranguing pedestrians may be something that people must live with, but is not a model for ethical research. However acknowledging the fact that some inconvenience can be caused, and that the benefits can make up for that inconvenience is a step toward a consistent and coherent definition of harm for ethics in HCI.

CONCLUSION

In conclusion, we call for a wider and more practical discussion on ethics within the HCI community. These provocations should be taken *not* as guidelines or recommendations but rather as a starting point for conversations around how, and if, we act ethically in our research. Our goal has been to expand on the assumptions that are embedded within much of the current discussion on ethics in HCI, and in drawing on literature from outwith HCI to show that the taken-for-granted positions may not be as assured as one might think.

In particular, we think that there is an increasingly important role for ethical experimentation to inform our ethical practice. We, as a community, must explore how participants themselves *do ethics* – and in so doing, recognise that ethical practice does not lie solely in the domain of the researcher. As some of the work cited here shows, there is often a divide between participants' views of ethics, and those of researchers, and yet another divide between those and the mandates of institutional review boards. The opportunity presents itself to exploit these gaps in order to find out more – not only about how we strive to behave ethically in our research, but also in how we research the ethics of HCI as a topic in itself.

ACKNOWLEDGMENTS

The research was made possible by LETStudio, University of Gothenburg, and a grant from the Swedish Governmental Agency for Innovation Systems (VINNOVA) to the Mobile Life VINN Excellence Centre. We thank Erin Brady and Pedro Ferreria for a discussion on challenges in ICTD research that led to this paper's second provocation.

REFERENCES

1. 1992. ACM Code of Ethics and Professional Conduct. Retrieved 22/07/2015 from http://www.acm.org/about/code-of-ethics
2. 1969. The Chilling Effect in Constitutional Law. *Columbia Law Review*, 69 (5). 808-842. DOI: 10.2307/1121147
3. George J Annas and Michael A Grodin. 1995. The Nazi doctors and the Nuremberg code. *The Journal of Pharmacy & Law*, 4. 167-245. DOI: 10.1017/S0250569X00020380
4. Jeffrey Bardzell and Shaowen Bardzell. 2015. *Humanistic HCI: Synthesis Lectures on Human-Centered Informatics*. Morgan & Claypool.
5. Elizabeth H Bassett and Kate O'Riordan. 2002. Ethics of Internet research: Contesting the human subjects

research model. *Ethics and Information Technology*, 4 (3). 233-247. DOI: 10.1023/A:1021319125207

6. Howard S Becker. 1995. Moral entrepreneurs: The creation and enforcement of deviant categories. in (Herman, N.J. ed.). *Deviance: A symbolic interactionist approach*, AltaMira Press, 169-178.
7. Steve Benford, Chris Greenhalgh, Bob Anderson, Rachel Jacobs, Mike Golembewski, Marina Jirotka, Bernd Carsten Stahl, Job Timmermans, Gabriella Giannachi and Matt Adams. 2015. The Ethical Implications of HCI's Turn to the Cultural. *ACM Transactions on Computer-Human Interaction (TOCHI)*, 22 (5). 24. DOI: 10.1145/2775107
8. Tom Boellstorff, Bonnie Nardi and Celia Pearce. 2012. *Ethnography and Virtual Worlds: A Handbook of Method.* Princeton University Press.
9. Danah Boyd. 2014. *It's Complicated: The Social Lives of Networked Teens*. Yale University Press.
10. Stacy M Branham, Anja Thieme, Lisa P Nathan, Steve Harrison, Deborah Tatar and Patrick Olivier. 2014. Co-creating & identity-making in CSCW: revisiting ethics in design research. in Proceedings of the companion publication of the 17th ACM conference on Computer supported cooperative work & social computing, ACM, Baltimore, Maryland, USA, 305-308. DOI: 10.1145/2556420.2558859
11. Amy Bruckman, Karrie Karahalios, Robert E Kraut, Erika Shehan Poole, John C Thomas and Sarita Yardi. 2010. Revisiting research ethics in the facebook era: Challenges in emerging CSCW research. in Adjunct Proceedings of the Conference on Computer Supported Cooperative Work ACM, Savannah, GA
12. Barrie R Cassileth, Robert V Zupkis, Katherine Sutton-Smith and Vicki March. 1980. Informed consent -- why are its goals imperfectly realized? *The New England journal of medicine*, 302 (16). 896-900. DOI: 10.1056/NEJM198004173021605
13. Stanley. Cavell. 1969. *Must We Mean What We Say?* Cambridge University Press.
14. Matthew Chalmers, Donald McMillan, Alistair Morrison, Henriette Cramer, Mattias Rost and Wendy Mackay. 2011. Ethics, logs and videotape: ethics in large scale user trials and user generated content. in CHI'11 Extended Abstracts on Human Factors in Computing Systems, ACM, Vancouver, BC, Canada, 2421-2424. DOI: 10.1145/1979742.1979574
15. Pia Christensen and Alan Prout. 2002. Working with ethical symmetry in social research with children. *Childhood*, 9 (4). 477-497. DOI: 10.1177/0907568202009004007
16. Tom Clark. 2008. We're Over-Researched Here!' Exploring Accounts of Research Fatigue within Qualitative Research Engagements. *Sociology*, 42 (5). 953-970. DOI: 10.1177/0038038508094573
17. Sonia Mansoldo Dainesi and Moisés Goldbaum. 2011. Provision of investigational drug after clinical research: review of literature, national and international guidelines. *Revista da Associação Médica Brasileira*, 57 (6). 710-716. DOI: 10.1590/S0104-42302011000600021
18. Robert Dingwall. 2008. The ethical case against ethical regulation in humanities and social science research. *Twenty-First Century Society: Journal of the Academy of Social Sciences*, 3 (1). 1-12. DOI: 10.1080/17450140701749189
19. Mitchell Duneier and Ovie Carter. 1999. *Sidewalk*. Macmillan.
20. Charles Ess. 2002. Ethical decision-making and Internet research: Recommendations from the aoir ethics working committee.
21. Casey Fiesler, Alyson Young, Tamara Peyton, Amy S. Bruckman, Mary Gray, Jeff Hancock and Wayne Lutters. 2015. Ethics for Studying Online Sociotechnical Systems in a Big Data World. in *Proceedings of the 18th ACM Conference Companion on Computer Supported Cooperative Work & Social Computing*, ACM, Vancouver, BC, Canada, 289-292. DOI: 10.1145/2685553.2685558
22. Jennifer Golbeck. 2014. What a Toilet Hoax Can Tell Us About the Future of Surveillance. Retrieved 20/08/2015 from http://www.theatlantic.com/technology/archive/2014/04/what-a-toilet-hoax-can-tell-us-about-the-future-of-surveillance/361408/
23. Michael Goodyear. 2009. Medical research for hire: The political economy of pharmaceutical clinical trials. *JAMA*, 302 (23). 2603-2603. DOI: 10.1001/jama.2009.1779
24. Marilys Guillemin and Lynn Gillam. 2004. Ethics, Reflexivity, and "Ethically Important Moments" in Research. *Qualitative Inquiry*, 10 (2). 261-280. DOI: 10.1177/1077800403262360
25. Kevin D Haggerty. 2004. Ethics Creep: Governing Social Science Research in the Name of Ethics. *Qualitative Sociology*, 27 (4). 391-414. DOI: 10.1023/B:QUAS.0000049239.15922.a3
26. Jeff T Hancock. 2015. The Facebook Study: A Personal Account of Data Science, Ethics and Change. in Proceedings of the 18th ACM Conference on Computer Supported Cooperative Work & Social Computing, ACM, 1-1. DOI: 10.1145/2675133.2697078
27. Jay Katz. 1994. Informed Consent - Must it remain a fairy tale. *Journal of Contemporary Health, Law & Policy*, 10. 69.

28. Jay Katz. 1977. Informed Consent-A Fairy Tale? Law's Vision. *University of Pittsburgh Law Review*, 39(2). 137-174.

29. Jofish Kaye, Janet Vertesi, Jennifer Ferreira, Barry Brown and Mark Perry. 2014. #CHImoney: financial interactions, digital cash, capital exchange and mobile money. in CHI '14 Extended Abstracts on Human Factors in Computing Systems, ACM, Toronto, Ontario, Canada, 111-114. DOI: 10.1145/2559206.2559221

30. Brian Keegan. 2015. Research in the Time of Technopanics. in CSCW 2015 Workshop on Ethics for Studying Online Sociotechnical Systems in a Big Data World,

31. Adam DI Kramer, Jamie E Guillory and Jeffrey T Hancock. 2014. Experimental evidence of massive-scale emotional contagion through social networks. *Proceedings of the National Academy of Sciences*, 111 (24). 8788-8790. DOI: 10.1073/pnas.1320040111

32. Michael Lempert. 2013. No ordinary ethics. *Anthropological Theory*, 13 (4). 370-393. DOI: 10.1177/1463499613505571

33. Kevin Lewis, Jason Kaufman, Marco Gonzalez, Andreas Wimmer and Nicholas Christakis. 2008. Tastes, ties, and time: A new social network dataset using Facebook. com. *Social Networks*, 30 (4). 330-342. DOI: 10.1016/j.socnet.2008.07.002

34. Wendy E Mackay. 1995. Ethics, lies and videotape.... in Proceedings of the SIGCHI Conference on Human Factors in Computing Systems, ACM Press/Addison-Wesley Publishing Co., Denver, Colorado, USA, 138-145. DOI: 10.1145/223904.223922

35. Annette Markham and E Buchanan. 2012. Ethical decision-making and Internet research (version 2.0): Recommendations from the AoIR Ethics Working Committee.

36. Heidi A McKee and James E Porter. 2009. *The ethics of Internet research: A rhetorical, case-based process*. Peter Lang.

37. Donald McMillan, Alistair Morrison and Matthew Chalmers. 2013. Categorised ethical guidelines for large scale mobile HCI. in Proceedings of the SIGCHI Conference on Human Factors in Computing Systems, ACM, Paris, France, 1853-1862. DOI: 10.1145/2470654.2466245

38. Cosmin Munteanu, Heather Molyneaux, Wendy Moncur, Mario Romero, Susan O'Donnell and John Vines. 2015. Situational Ethics: Re-thinking Approaches to Formal Ethics Requirements for Human-Computer Interaction. in Proceedings of the 33rd Annual ACM Conference on Human Factors in Computing Systems, ACM, Seoul, Republic of Korea, 105-114. DOI: 10.1145/2702123.2702481

39. Arvind Narayanan and Vitaly Shmatikov. 2008. Robust De-anonymization of Large Sparse Datasets. in Security and Privacy, 2008. SP 2008. IEEE Symposium on, IEEE, 111-125. DOI: 10.1109/SP.2008.33

40. Geoff Pearson. 2009. The researcher as hooligan: where 'participant' observation means breaking the law. *International Journal of Social Research Methodology*, 12 (3). 243-255. DOI: 10.1080/13645570701804250

41. Lydia Plowman, Yvonne Rogers and Magnus Ramage. 1995. What Are Workplace Studies For? in Proceedings of the Fourth European Conference on Computer-Supported Cooperative Work ECSCW '95, Springer Netherlands, 309-324. DOI: 10.1007/978-94-011-0349-7_20

42. Carl Schneider. 2015. *The Censor's Hand: The Misregulation of Human-Subject Research*. MIT Press.

43. Natasha Dow Schüll. 2012. *Addiction by design: Machine gambling in Las Vegas*. Princeton University Press.

44. Eric Benjamin Seufert. 2013. *Freemium Economics: Leveraging Analytics and User Segmentation to Drive Revenue*. Elsevier.

45. Malin Sveningsson. 2004. Ethics in Internet ethnography. in (Buchanan, E.A. ed.). *Readings in Virtual Research Ethics: Issues and Controversies*, IGI Global, 45-61.

46. Latanya Sweeney. 2002. k-anonymity: A model for protecting privacy. *International Journal of Uncertainty, Fuzziness and Knowledge-Based Systems*, 10 (05). 557-570. DOI: 10.1142/S0218488502001648

47. Heli K Väätäjä and Emilia K Pesonen. 2013. Ethical issues and guidelines when conducting HCI studies with animals. in CHI'13 Extended Abstracts on Human Factors in Computing Systems, ACM, Paris, France, 2159-2168. DOI: 10.1145/2468356.2468736

48. Willy Carl Van den Hoonaard. 2011. *The seduction of ethics: Transforming the social sciences*. University of Toronto Press.

49. Alexandra Weilenmann, Thomas Hillman and Beata Jungselius. 2013. Instagram at the museum: communicating the museum experience through social photo sharing. in Proceedings of the SIGCHI Conference on Human Factors in Computing Systems, ACM, Paris, France, 1843-1852. DOI: 10.1145/2470654.2466243

50. Michael Zimmer. 2010. "But the data is already public": on the ethics of research in Facebook. *Ethics and information technology*, 12 (4). 313-325. DOI: 10.1007/s10676-010-9227-5

Acting with Technology: Rehearsing for Mixed-Media Live Performances

Louise Barkhuus
Stockholm University
Stockholm, Sweden
barkhuus@dsv.su.se

Chiara Rossitto
Stockholm University
Stockholm, Sweden
chiara@dsv.su.se

ABSTRACT

Digital technologies provide theater with new possibilities for combining traditional stage-based performances with interactive artifacts, for streaming remote parallel performances and for other device facilitated audience interaction. Compared to traditional theater, mixed-media performances require a different type of engagement from the actors and rehearsing is challenging, as it can be impossible to rehearse with all the functional technology and interaction. Here, we report experiences from a case study of two mixed-media performances; we studied the rehearsal practices of two actors who were performing in two different plays. We describe how the actors practiced presence during rehearsal in a play where they would be geographically remote, and we describe the challenges of rehearsing with several remote and interactive elements. Our study informs the broader aims of interactive and mixed media performances through addressing critical factors of implementing technology into rehearsal practices.

Author Keywords

Interactive Performance, Ubiquitous Computing, Theater, Rehearsal, Digital Technologies

ACM Classification Keywords

H.5.3 Group and Organization Interfaces: Collaborative computing

INTRODUCTION

Digital technologies are extensively used in the context of artistic experiences, as they provide a multitude of possibilities for interactive performances combining video streaming with live elements, and for elements of audience interaction, both remotely or from the audience rows. Mixed-media performances have a long tradition, both in terms of taking the performances outside the theater through digital and sensor technologies [6, 16] and through using digital material inside theaters [1, 32]. The blurring of theater, dance performances and games has lead to several research projects, particularly within the space of human-computer interaction where interactional practices and sensor technologies have been explored. In 'Desert Rain', for example, artists and researchers embedded a computer system and its use by audience members into a dramatic performance and found that continual monitoring and intervention was essential to the success of the experience [20]. Other studies have used video streaming technologies to augment the audience experience during a live dance performance and found this catered to audience members special interests and deeper understanding of the performance [1].

CHI'16, May 07-12, 2016, San Jose, CA, USA
© 2016 ACM. ISBN 978-1-4503-3362-7/16/05...$15.00
DOI: http://dx.doi.org/10.1145/2858036.2858344

While previous studies have mostly focused on aspects of audience interactions with and within the performance, in this paper we shed light on the mediating role of technology behind the scenes, when the acting and production are being rehearsed. An interesting, and often overlooked, challenge for implementing digital technologies into theater performances is how to rehearse for the actual performances. With technologies often being complex, including live streaming and live production as well as audience interaction, actors are faced with an array of instances and moments that cannot be rehearsed properly before the actual curtain call. This situation resembles what generally happens with traditional theater, where actors in the beginning usually rehearse without props and costumes. Nevertheless, the emerging and often unpredictable practices around the use of digital technologies introduce a number of challenges that for actors become problematic to handle, more than large dresses and breakable china. This paper draws attention to two such challenges, specifically: i) rehearsing without technology, even when the technology itself is a central "actor" of the mixed-media performance, ii) preparing for and managing the audience interaction with the interactive performance.

In this paper we present a case study of two digitally enhanced plays, which we refer to as mixed-media theater. The two plays relate to each other as they were written and directed by the same director, and as they were part of "Women in Science" a trilogy focusing on female scientists. The first play, Lise & Otto, is performed by two actors, located on two different stages, at two different theaters while being connected by real-time streaming. The second play, ADA, makes use of audience interaction through communication technology whereby audience members can send text messages to be displayed on a large screen that is part of the scenography. ADA is a monologue with only one actress on stage. The two plays were commercially produced and played over three days at a national theater, which separates these plays from many earlier CHI studies of mixed-media performance in which the interactive experience has been staged specifically for the research [1, 15, 25].

Using ethnographic methods, we followed rehearsals for both performances from early readings to final dress rehearsals, observing and interviewing the actors, the set designers, the director and the digital producers. Differently from previous studies investigating the *spectators'* experience of using and participating through technology [1, 16], or designing for live performances [18], we shed light on the *actors'* experience of acting with technology. More specifically, we illustrate the challenges arising during rehearsal when the fully working technology only becomes part of the final performance. Our study provides an increased awareness around these practices and challenges, both to understand these better and to make digital performance designers comprehend the difficult tasks actors and directors undertake within this new performance space. Our findings provide insights on how technology is configured (and not merely designed), and certain feelings (i.e. sense of presence) reproduced when technologies are not used with the goal of efficiency, but rather to evoke specific emotions and "felt" experiences.

BACKGROUND

Recent studies have looked at mixed realty and digital performances, particularly in relation to how interactive technologies can support interactive dramatic experiences, but also how exposed technical infrastructure can be studied in relation to interactive experiences. Some researchers have investigated the use of virtual actors for creating novel theatrical elements [30]. An interesting example of virtual performer is Jeremiah [9], an artificial intelligence avatar that is able to interact with a human performer, as the vision and motion tracking system enable him to see what "happens" on the stage. Other investigations include audience participation in a traditional theater/dance setting [16]. Researchers at Nottingham University in collaboration with Blast Theory have staged large mixed reality performances and games [3, 25], some working as large scale participatory events [5, 12]. Most of these interactive dramas require high levels of participation, from riding a bicycle to running around the city, and sometimes a certain level of bravery for the participant (i.e. trusting a stranger).

Although much of this research addresses different issues around the development and implementation of mixed media theater and performances, fewer studies look into the actual rehearsal practices and challenges around that.

Audience Participation

In terms of more subtle and "traditional" audience interaction we find technologies that can assist in parts of the performance. Audience members can for example play a simple digital game on stage with different colored bats [23], or affect a "cheering meter" by clapping and cheering louder [2]. However when considering interactive *drama*, many productions utilize audience participation as part of the narrative, and researchers have looked at different ways whereby the audience can *contribute* to making the narrative into what it is [16]. In the play we studied (i.e. ADA), although audience members can interact through text messages, they are not directly affecting the story as such, which means that the narrative is controlled by the writer and the director. It also provides a simpler entry to experiencing the drama compared to a setup where audience members have to give up all their belongings [12] or go riding on a bicycle [25].

Rehearsal with Augmented or Digital Characters

When considering research in relation to rehearsal for mixed-media performance and theater, most of the productions in this space make use of different electronic partners such as robots and virtual avatars, sometimes in combination with human actors, rather than using technology for enabling human actors to act together remotely such as in Lise & Otto.

When performing "virtual theater", rehearsal can be more flexible and take place at different types of arenas [26]. Early implementations of "remote" acting and rehearsal, for example, include virtual reality technologies connecting remote actors for rehearsal [28]. One important issue is, however, how to obtain "presence", which we also found to be a challenge for the two actors in Lise & Otto. Reeve [27] experimented with acting through virtual reality and found that obtaining a sense of presence by the actors themselves proved very difficult; his work also pointed out that actors found the practical "work" of entering commands to be distracting from the actual rehearsal, something echoing other findings on the production of interactive performances [13, 27]. Another study involving a performance with an interactive technology element is the one by the Robotics Institute at Carnegie Mellon University [33]. The play included a robot as the second actor, and the rehearsal mainly focused on developing gestures for the robot as well as on practicing the operation from the operator independently of the human actor. One challenge found was how to interpret the director's instructions, such as "can you say that more hesitatingly?" into technical outputs. The repeatability of the robot was found to be an advantage; as the robot always replied with the same reaction, it helped the actor practicing [ibid].

The production process is tightly related to the process of rehearsal. Research has looked, for instance, at the work of orchestrating interactive "spectator interfaces", an interactive installation based on movable figurines [13]. This interactive game did not include live performers and rehearsal was therefore limited to technology development and planning. And while rehearsals and production were intertwined, the live production was ultimately about producing a live experience in the moment. Finally, a recent project addresses the challenges of staging interactive costumes in theater productions. The issues arising during preparation was a disjoint between designers and engineers in the theater, leading to complicated collaborations. The researchers also uncovered a lack of continuity of conventional costume design in relation to the interactive costumes [17].

TWO MIXED-MEDIA PLAYS

The two plays analyzed in this paper arc part of a trilogy called "Women in Science", written and directed by Rebecca Forsberg. The trilogy is centered on the lives of three different women who, despite their hardship, have made significant scientific discoveries and contributions. The first play follows the life of Maryam Al-Ijliya, a female Syrian astronomer who lived in the mid-900 AD. It uses location-based technology and is not part of our case study due to it being pre-recorded (a separate study was conducted in relation audience experience [29]). In the sections below we provide a description of the dramas investigated in this paper.

Lise & Otto

The second play in the trilogy is Lise & Otto based on the lives of Lise Meitner and Otto Hahn, the two physicists who worked on radioactivity and nuclear physics eventually contributing to the discovery of nuclear fission in 1938. The two scientists worked closely together from early 1900 through the 30s in Berlin until Lise Meitner had to flee to Sweden in 1938 due to her Jewish heritage. It is commonly acknowledged that while Otto Hahn received the Nobel Prize in 1944, Lise Meitner's involvement and accomplishments were overlooked in this respect. The play takes place in Stockholm, Sweden in 1946 when Otto Hahn travels to receive the Nobel Prize (after being a prisoner of war while receiving the news that he was awarded the Nobel Prize in 1944) and sees his one-time love interest and close research partner for the first time in 8 years. She picks him up at the train station (scene 1), they have a cup of coffee (scene 2) and they go to the ceremony together, taking the elevator up to the ballroom (scene 3) and Otto Hahn gives his acknowledgement speech (final scene).

The play was written for two stages where the two actors perform their roles remotely and simultaneously. This means that while one actor is on one of the stages, the other actor, performing at another theater, is streamed in on a large screen through fast Internet fiber (see figure 1). The audience members have to choose which theater to go to and will consequently see one of the actors in presence, and the other one on the large screen.

Figure 1. Lise and Otto meeting by the train. Here, Lise is on stage, Otto is projected in on the background screen. In the remote theater the setup is reversed.

The writer and director's idea behind this setup is to illustrate the mental and physical distance between the two characters but also to be able to show two different perspectives: his and hers. The technological was thus conceived as a metaphor of the two characters' lives: they had been separated in life and were now separated on stage. This means the technology conveyed a symbolic value and was supposed to evoke certain feelings rather than merely enabling a specific functionality.

Figure 2. Lise on stage, flashback scene in the background.

Twice during the play, the sound through the screen is muted, and each actor gives a monologue, explaining the situation from his/her viewpoint. This means that the audience only hears the viewpoint from 'their' actor. In the production that we studied, Lise was performing on the national scene in the center of the city and Otto was performing on a smaller scene in a suburb. Production cars were set up outside each theater and streamed to one another, but the main production (cut of scenes, music etc.) was managed live from the larger production bus outside the national scene. The play also makes use of pre-recorded video clips for flashbacks by the actors. In these, they are young and in love[1], but on the scene they are masked older (Lise and Otto were 68 and 67 at the time of the Nobel Prize, respectively). At the end, when Otto is giving his

[1]It is well-documented through letters and other sources that the two scientists had a romantic relationship during their early collaborations, but Lise Meitner did not want to get married, possibly because it would have prevented her from continuing her research career as a woman in the early 20th century.

acceptance speech, the cameras on each stage turn to the audience and the audience from each theater is projected onto the screen at the other theater.

ADA

The third play of the trilogy is ADA, recounting the life story of Ada Lovelace, born in 1815 as the daughter of the English poet Lord Byron and Baroness Wentworth. She showed an early interest in mathematics and after meeting Charles Babbage in 1833, they started a life long correspondence about mathematics and logic. When Babbage developed the specifications for the analytical machine, often considered to be the world's first analog computer, Ada Lovelace was a collaborator through her translation work and mathematical input. She died at the early age of 36 from cancer leaving three small children and a legacy of being the inventor of the first general programing language.

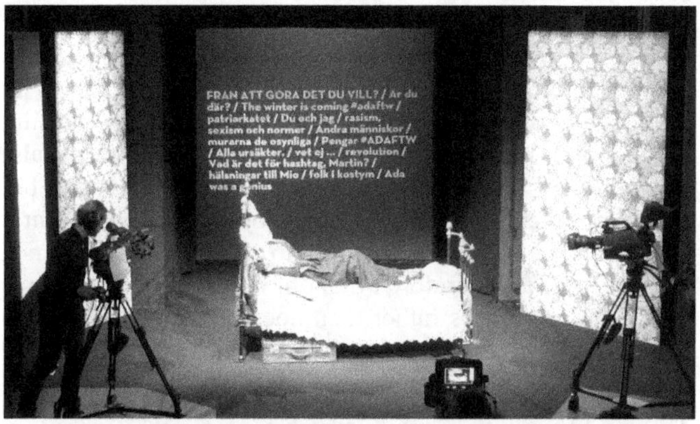

Figure 3. ADA on stage. The text in the background is audience submitted text.

The play is a stage monologue by Ada Lovelace herself; she is the only person on stage as she sits on her deathbed reflecting on her life. The scenography consists of a bed, the wallpaper on the sidewalls and a large digital display in the background (Figure 3). Digital and interactive elements in this play are through audience interaction and live-streaming of the play. Audience members and remote viewers are able to text, tweet or enter in an online form comments and answers to posed questions, which are then published and projected to the background screen. Two cameras are present for recording and live-streaming of the play (Figure 3). In ADA, the choice of the technology, and the design of the interactivity it enables were made considering the audience members – and not the actors – as the main users of the technology. More specifically, the interactive participation was designed around the use of mobile phones and tablets, now common devices in most people's everyday life. During the performance, audience members are encouraged to use their mobile devices to reflect upon their own experiences by answering a number of questions that are presented in the end of each scene. This technological setup was also supported by the underlying assumption that using them during the performance would not hinder the audience's engagement with the dramaturgical narration (which it actually did. See [10]). Similarly to Lise & Otto, the play is live broadcast through the production bus parked outside the theater where the play is performed (see figure 7).

METHOD

To study how actors and producers rehearse for mixed-media performances, we followed rehearsals from the start of collocated rehearsals. That means we did not follow the actors' initial individual rehearsal in which they memorize scripts and practice by themselves or the production planning with the producer team; we started observing when the actors got together (Lise & Otto) or when they started practicing on stage with the digital production in the background (ADA). The rehearsals were planned such that Lise & Otto was rehearsed for one week, then ADA was rehearsed for one week, then Lise & Otto was rehearsed for two days and performed for three days (Thursday, Friday, Saturday) and the week after the same for ADA. That way actors and producers were able to fully focus on one play at a time while performing the plays less than a week apart.

Data Collection

Our case study made use of ethnographic methods, more explicitly observations and informal interviews were carried out over a period of four weeks. Data collection was conducted by the first author who spent the full four weeks with the crew and the actors, immersing herself in the theater setting and talking informally with the actors. Table 1 lists the data collected from each play's set of rehearsals.

The interviews focused mainly on the actors' rehearsal experiences, particularly the challenges related to the use of digital technology in such a setting. The questions focused on the actors' acting practices and their strategies for communicating their role and presence on stage and through the camera. We also inquired into the actor-director relationships and how it was transformed by the inclusion of various digital media in the performance. Interviews were informal conversations, and due to the fluid process of the rehearsal practices and ethnographic nature of the study, there was no prepared interview schedule except for notes that the researcher wrote during rehearsal observation and then inquired into immediately after. Themes for exploration emerged through observations and provided basis for the interviews. Interviews with other people involved in the production focused on their specific task during rehearsal and final production such as the moderator who had to look over each text string submitted by an audience member and decide if it was appropriate to display it on the large screen. A total of 6 interviews (plus short recorded conversations of 3-10 min after each performance) were carried out; they were all recorded and later transcribed. All interviews were conducted in English.

The observations focused on structures and attributes of the rehearsal. More specifically, emphasis was on how the actors and director addressed the interactions between the actors, given that in the final performance they would be acting at a distance (Lise & Otto), the potential interaction with the audience (Lise & Otto and ADA), and how the actors practiced without the media clips in their final format. Observations also focused on how the director coped with technology, media production and live actors. Being actors and used to perform in front of others, they did not report being affected by having one more "audience member" at the rehearsals, rehearsals that are often already semi-public as producers and theater workers walk in and out of the audience area.

	Lise & Otto	ADA
Observations	One week of 3 hours/day, actors together (notes, pictures) Three days of 3 hours/day, actors apart (notes, pictures)	One week of 2 hours/day (notes, pictures) Three days of 3 hours/day stage rehearsal with semi-deployed technologies (notes, pictures)
Interviews	Two 30 min conversations with the two actors about their rehearsal experiences. Short interviews after each performance with the actress playing Lise	Interview with actress about presence (15 min) Interview with actress about her experience with technology (45 min) Interview with set designer (15 min) Interview with moderator of the audience text input
Video	None	Two 15 min clips from dress rehearsal 10 min from technology rehearsal Two 15 min clips from production bus during rehearsal

Table 1. Overview over the data that was collected

Analysis

We analyzed the data as ethnographic data using qualitative methods for comparing and categorizing the themes that we identified. First, we read through all the notes and looked through the transcribed interviews for the two plays in turn. Broad themes were written down in attrition to examples of how these themes were illustrated. The pictures and videos were held up next to the other material for more concrete materialization. Secondly, the themes for each play were compared and we collapsed themes that held up for both plays. The results are therefore presented in terms of themes for both plays, however, one theme was only prevalent for Lise & Otto due to the distinction that there were two actors "on stage" and that they were apart. The data analysis was recursive. We firstly identified themes such as problematic issues around rehearsal and the actors' practices of rehearsing together for being apart; then more detailed categories were determined, separating all the detected problems into sub-categories and splitting the different rehearsal practices into smaller categories.

Participant Observation and Previous Knowledge

When adopting ethnographic methods, an essential element of the fieldwork and analysis is the observer's pre-knowledge and point of view [22]. Subjective analysis is what makes ethnographic methods relevant and powerful, and although an outside perspective is often taken to describe practices in question, it is impossible to take the preliminary experiences out of the ethnographer; in essence the analysis is embedded in the embodied experience of the observer. In our project, an important part of our analysis was the occasional comparison to traditional theater and filmmaking rehearsal due to their relatedness. Yet, the researchers did not actually want to compare directly by observing another movie production or traditional theater production, which would have introduced a bias in terms of topic, type of play and would have required enormous additional time investments. Instead the authors relied on the first author's previous experiences with theater and film production. The first author (and observer of the rehearsals) had not only trained as an actress herself previously, but also part-taken in several international film and theater productions; when comparing to traditional rehearsal practices, we are therefore often drawing on actual previous personal experiences rather than documentation or second-hand experiences.

RESULTS

The weeklong rehearsal period for Lise & Otto took place in a rehearsal room at the national theater where it was later performed (theaters often have large rooms away from the scene for this purpose). The room was empty except for a dozen chairs for visitors and the director, and the props for the scene. When the observations began, the actors knew their lines by heart and the individual scenes were practiced in detail, sometimes several times in a row before going on to run through the full play from the beginning to the end. At this point the mixed media elements such as video clips, music and other effects were included into the rehearsal. The weeklong rehearsal of ADA was very similar, except that they used a bench as the bed (which was a very prominent piece of the scenography in the final production). As the performances came near, a production bus was parked outside the theater, with cables drawn through the windows into the cameras and microphones on stage. The production bus was central as it contained all the technological artifacts needed for the live broadcasting. The inclusion of the live broadcasting meant that the rehearsal also involved three producers who were mixing the plays real-time and controlling the music, in the production bus (see figure 7). Over half the time of these last two days was spent rehearsing non-actor-centric issues such as the timing of the video clips, music and other effects as well as the video production of ADA (which would be streamed online live during the show each evening). The director therefore spent significant time communicating with both the bus bound production crew, the camerawomen and the actors.

We now present our findings, structured according to four themes we discovered during the analysis.

Rehearsing Mixed-Media Performances: The work to make the digital technologies work

Implementing digital performances, as well as performing a play that includes mixed-media, introduce a number of challenges that both the actors and the director have to juggle during rehearsal. During the observations, such challenges emerged as the extra work required to make the technological layer work. While the technology needs to be planned and designed, the actors and director need to consider the actual human-technology interaction of the final performance during rehearsal. In our case, this entailed for instance the challenge inherent in acting at distance (i.e. feeling the presence of the other actor), and in acting while the audience members directly contribute to the scenography. This extra work presents different characteristics that we describe in the following sections, in relation to the director and the actors, respectively.

Directing with technology

One aspect that became noticeable during rehearsal was the sheer amount of work the director had to do, in regards to the technology orchestration, in addition to the directional work of the actors. As the use of interactive media also had to be practiced by the director, its orchestration often resulted in a problem of focus for the director who had to give instructions to the actors as well as juggle the digital elements of the play.

Figure 4: The rehearsal stage of Lise & Otto with screens in the background. One Screen is outside the picture.

For the early rehearsal of Lise & Otto, the director was located in the same rehearsal room with the two actors. Here, she used a computer equipped with a set of external speakers of fairly decent size and quality, in order to be loud enough for the large rehearsal room. The room was also equipped with three large fabric covered (non-digital) screens, exactly as the final stage would be, to indicate the screens where the other actor and flashback video clips would be projected to (not unlike rehearsals for traditional theater where part of the scenography is set up), see figure 4. The director kept all the video clips of flashbacks and the sound files on her computer in a file browser and opened each up when the script called for such clip. As the play alternated elements of live acting and pre-recorded media (both video and audio), it was not possible to merge each clip and music into one large timed file; instead, for the final production, the production crew would have to start each part. This meant that the director had to follow the acting, but also keep focused on the file browser to manage the different files and the audio system. In one episode, for example, the actors started rehearsal from the beginning of the play but to everybody's surprise no sound came out of the speakers. The actor playing Otto, then went out of his role, walked over to plug in the speakers, then back into his role and continued the rehearsal of the scene without comments. Only the director commented on her embarrassment.

While all performance rehearsal in general requires a lot of effort from all people included, this duality of attention on technology and directing lead to occasional problems for the actors. This was particularly true during the last three days of rehearsal, when the production bus managing the production and live streaming of the play was set up. This meant, for instance, that the director moved to the production bus for the majority of her time to check that the cameras were properly angled, not unlike directing for film, or that she was satisfied with the overall scene that would be broadcast to the other theater. As illustrated in the quote below, the two actors referred to the bus as the "control room", the place where the technological layer of the play was ultimately being orchestrated. Although both actors had a positive attitude towards the technology in the play, and they were curious about experimenting with their acting "at distance", they expressed frustration and found it challenging and to a certain extent a bit lonely, particularly in final rehearsals: [Actor playing Otto]: *She [the director] has to sit in the control room [production bus] [...] and that is weird for you because then suddenly you have no director to help you out.* This point was also corroborated by the actress playing Lise, who explained that from an acting point of view, the focus on technology *"takes away the relationship with the director."*

During the final rehearsals, when the actors and production team had access to the actual stage (it is very common that only final rehearsals take place on the actual stage due to lack of access), the rehearsal effort became much more focused on the technology, not unlike a movie production where more than half of the time is usually devoted to setting up cameras and other boundary work. Similarly to the episode recounted above, when the actor playing Otto took the initiative to handle the speaker problem, the temporary absence of the director meant that the actors had to try to solve the problems emerging during rehearsal themselves. For instance, the actor playing Otto explained that towards the end of the rehearsal, when he moved to a stage of a different size (at the remote theater), he realized that elements of the performance were not working in the same way anymore – i.e. the lightening and the dancing parts – due to a different space organization. Thus, while the director was on the production bus, making sure the broadcasting worked, he had to be creative and take the initiative to introduce some changes to make his acting fit to the new settings.

Another characteristic of the directing work was the focus on timing the live acting with the digital media of the performance and with the elements that were broadcast live. Even during early rehearsals, the director was running the full video clips that would be shown in the final production. These video clips showed events the two characters had lived and experienced in the past (flashbacks, see figure 2). When the pre-recorded media were displayed in the final performance, the two actors sat quietly at the stage, still in character. Running the whole clip was therefore a way for the actors to get to practice their "pauses" and the time they would have to wait. In between the clips and the live acting, the director read the action text from the manuscript, such as "Camera on Lise", or "train in the background". The reason for reading the action script was to give the actors an awareness of the images, scenes and angles that were being broadcast live to the theater where the other actor and the other stage where located. This meant that the actors had to combine their focus on live acting and having an audience watching from the pews, with their ability to consider cameras angles and media effects, not unlike directing for movie scenes. We will return to this in a future section.

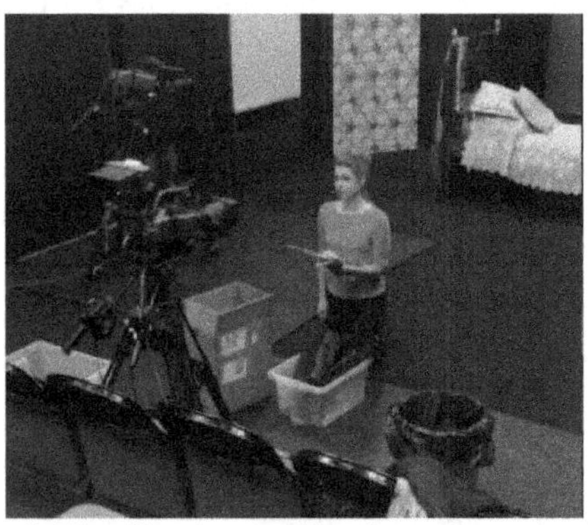

Figure 5: The director reading from the script the day before the premiere, to help the production team adjust sound

During the rehearsal of ADA, that was to include a live film production during the play, the rehearsal work included sound testing, camera angle testing and testing of the Internet broadcasting of the actual production. But to save the actors' time, the director had to be creative in her rehearsal work, which also led to a lot of extra work on her part. The director would, for example, be reading the script on the stage doing the 'work' for the actress and at one point, she sat on her knees for 15 minutes reciting part of the script so the technicians in the production bus could adjust technical aspects such as sound and camera angles, see figure 5.

Acting with technology

In terms of work, the implementation of mixed-media and interactive technologies also introduced more complex issues for the actors during rehearsal, particularly in relation to imagination and choreography. In Lise & Otto, the actors had their own monologue on each stage, which would take place at the same time, and they therefore had to practice them being the same length. Because the actors did not wear earpieces during the final show, they would not know when the other's monologue had finished. If they finished too quickly, they would have to wait quietly before the production team, who could hear both monologues, and then start the next video clip. This challenge was addressed with an old-fashioned timer that the director used to time each monologue.

In general, the actors expressed a need to be more choreographed in their acting, to fit the digital parts of the production. Since neither of them had trained for film, this was fairly new. The actress playing Lise expressed that she felt she needed to be more constrained in her expressions and the actor who played Otto said: *"it's more like choreography, it is more like a dance you do, "okay now it is this part, and now it is this..." It is like choreography... you take step by step."* He added that he felt it was a bit "schizophrenic" to move between camera and audience, a challenge we return to when looking at rehearsing for audience interaction.

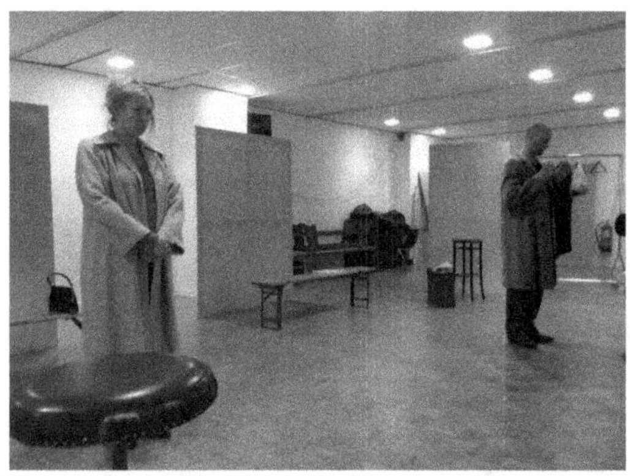

Figure 6: final stage of rehearsal where the actors rehearsed on each side of the stage in order to practice being apart

Maintaining Presence Between Remote Actors

The biggest challenge for the actors of Lise & Otto was the fact that they would be remotely located during the live performance. To our knowledge few, if any, live theater productions have made use of such dual stage setup and this was certainly the first time the actors were to perform in such way. The director wanted to make an allusion to a certain level of closeness between the characters because their previous close friendship (and romantic relationship) and it was therefore important that the actors could project this despite being apart. They therefore started out rehearsing very close to one another, almost touching each other. As rehearsal progressed, they moved further away from each other, and the last few days they were at each side of the room, despite the final production showing them less than a foot apart, see figure 4 and 6.

When inquiring the actors about how they felt on stage after the first show, the actors acknowledged that it was still difficult to convey presence because they are talking to a screen where they cannot see their co-player yet have to make it look like they are talking directly to one another. The actress playing Lise explained: *"...I feel that I take a chance. When I look there [at the spot in front of the screen where Otto is projected], it's like, I don't know. Maybe it's not right, but I rather look there [...]. I hope that if I don't do it right, then the director will tell me."* To help them project a connection between two remote actors, their intense rehearsals had enabled them to sense the presence between them each other. The actress continued explaining how she felt during the play: *"I sense his presence. When we are in the dialogs and we are at the green screen, it's like as if he's there, sort of. [... M]y experience of acting is that you are always there with a distance, so that isn't different. [...] I think that the listening part is even bigger now. You have to concentrate on listening to him so you feel his presence. It sounds religious [laughs]."* The other actor similarly said that he still felt they were on the same stage.

Rehearsing for Audience Interaction

One major challenge in the play ADA was the potential reaction from the audience to the displayed text in the background scenography that was not visible to the actress playing Ada Lovelace. Opposite preparing for a remote co-actor, the actress explained that it was impossible to prepare well for potential text messages on the screen, which in turn made it virtually impossible to react to it. She explained to us, after the first performance, that she had to work hard on ignoring the laughs that occasionally came from the audience, well knowing that they were not necessarily meant for her performance but instead reactions to humorous text on the background of the set. Where most actors are trained in pausing for laughs and applauses, we observed during the live performances that the actress playing Ada was not as capable of doing that (for laughs), due to the occasional disjoint between displayed text and the actual play. As such, the blending of media was not an unproblematic success at the actual performance [10]. The actress explained how she was explicitly not thinking about the questions posed in the background for the audience to answer via text on their mobile phones: *"I don't... I go with my story, what I'm going to tell about Ada and.... because the questions are a bit abstract in my [head] [...] it would only complicate things in the story about Ada if I also thought about the questions and now the audience is answering [...] I can't think about...it wouldn't do good to Ada I think."* She continued using the analogy of thinking about what the other characters in a traditional play would think about, emphasizing that this is not good for the portrayal of a role.

The issue of rehearsing for audience interaction reflects back on the tightly choreographed notion of both plays, that the actors felt the need to have. They lacked the freedom from more traditional theater where small elements of improvisation are not uncommon. Here technology was at a higher priority, a point we will return to in the discussion.

Figure 7: the production bus from the outside and inside

Dealing with Dual Audiences

An observation that we found to be distinctly relevant for mixed-media performances was the difficulty with which the actors had to rehearse (and then act) with two different audiences in mind: the live audience in the theater and the remote audience they knew they would have at the other location, and for ADA, the audience in the cameras watching the streamed live production (see figure 7). When suggesting that the play was both theater and film, the actress said, with respect to Lise & Otto: *"I feel it's weird because it's much thicker anyway [than film] and you have an audience. We both have to [know] everything because [of the] camera but we do have an audience. Now, we decided, or I have decided to think that the audience is [in the camera]. It's film or tv-theater mostly [...] except that they don't see everything [compared to the live audience]."* She continued talking about the live audience as a 'third camera': "*When [we rehearsed,] we talked about the cameras when you look straight. We have a third camera that's in front now that is like the audience camera.*" The actress had similar concerns for ADA, when she had to rehearse with respect to a live audience but still be aware it was a film production as well (see figure 3).

DISCUSSION

In the following discussion we highlight three issues: i) *challenges for rehearsal* ii) *rehearsing presence* and iii) *the overwhelming role of technology*. These points allow us to deepen our understanding of the actors' experience of rehearsing with and for technology, and of their experience in managing audience interactions in the context of mixed-media performances as well as highlighting implications for structuring rehearsal for mixed-media performances.

Rehearsing for mixed-media performances is challenging. The actors in Lise & Otto, for instance, felt that the technology took the director away from the stage, as she had to spend significant time in the "control room" (the production bus) to orchestrate the technology. As we have seen, both for the director and the actors, the technology become yet another "actor" to tune acting with, and that required a mind shift to be able to engage with collocated audience members and at distance ones. To integrate the digital media into the final performance, the rehearsal sessions sometimes focused on practicing how to *ignore* the digital media, such as the text messages audience shared during ADA. Another example is the final scene of Lise & Otto where Otto gives his acceptance speech. This scene blended the actor in (projected into one theater) with a live video streaming of the audience in the *other* theater than the one the audience was sitting in. The rehearsal for this was only able to include numerous empty seats and not the reaction of surprised audience members.

Rehearsing Presence

Mixed-media performances have already experimented with 'beaming' in actors or avatars from afar [9, 26]. However, there is a major difference between human actors being 'beamed' in, and acting with each other through an avatar. Where the avatar actors were not likely to feel much sense of presence, and maybe it was not crucial they would do so, it was pivotal to our actors to be able to feel each other's presence while located on the two different stages. We could observe, for instance, that presence was rehearsed by first practicing next to each other, and then progressively moving away as days went by. As recounted in the interviews, the actress playing Lise described sensing presence during the final performance almost as a supernatural experience, meaning that it had more to do with a way of feeling than with the physical presence of a material body, and it emerged from listening intensively rather than from establishing an eye contact. Interestingly, sensing presence at distance was regarded – and approached by the director – *as an acting skill to be learned and developed through practicing*. Comparing this to remote collaboration in work settings provides and interesting insight. Early studies of video conferencing and remote collaboration comparing this to in-person work, found that "the [collaboration] process [...] changed, however, to require more clarification and more management overhead." [24, p. 152] Similarly, our data show how the actors had to practice a more 'tight' choreography, receive more specific instructions from the director, and had fewer options of ad-hoc adjustments in the final production.

In the plays presented, the sense of presence conveyed by the actors was also intertwined with issues of mixed audiences. With audience members present at the theater and the ones watching the play at distance, the actors were sometimes forced to make a choice rather than rehearse for both simultaneously. The sense of presence that live theater performance is based on, is then adjusted to the mixed-media setting through preparing to give no attention to elements of the setting as well.

The Overwhelming Role of Mixed-Media

The mixed-media technologies enabled the actors to develop a unique way of rehearsing, yet sometimes the technology became very prominent and experienced as constraining. It took the director away from the actors and it disturbed the otherwise stable structure of rehearsal by sometimes requiring extra focus and attention. Although it is easy to suggest that mixed-media rehearsal simply needs more (wo)man-power in terms of assistants and helpers, this would only potentially reduce the number of mishaps and not improve rehearsal practices when they did happen.

As illustrated, the actors had developed their own personal strategies to manage their focus and attention. The actress playing ADA had consciously chosen, for instance, to ignore the dynamic scenography of text in the background, as she felt that a complete immersion in the role was needed to give life to Ada Lovelace. This finding resonates with other studies of mixed-media performances carried out, however, from an audience's perspective. This aspect has been characterized, in fact, as an issue of "understanding unity" [19] between the use of media and representations within performances, and as an issue of fragmented experience between the acting layer of the performance and the technological layer enabling the audience members' participation [10]. Introducing technology brings about changes and sometimes complications. Studies of interactive performances and experiences describe the seamful elements that easily emerge and have to be addressed [4, 8, 11]. However, as illustrated in our findings, as the audience is not there yet, there is not a real possibility to explore and experience the audience's participation during rehearsal. Instead time is spent figuring out how to smooth or ignore the 'seams' of the technology.

Implications For Mixed-Media Performance Rehearsal

Investigations of mixed-media performances have focused on the orchestration of interactive experiences that change through the audience's journey and where audience members can actively contribute to the evolution of the story [14, 20]. The productions we studied did not present elements of audience interactions, which meant that the rehearsal practices were structured, not as much in regards to unpredictable audience members' actions, but instead towards acting on stage with 'invisible' actors – i.e. the producers and the controllers of the digital media broadcast

(Lise & Otto and ADA) and the text messages enabling audience members to participate in the performance (ADA). Essentially, rehearsal did not focus on getting the technology to work but on fine-tuning it and on *learning to act with it* (i.e. how to convey a sense of presence remediated by broadcast media). This meant that the technology became yet another actor to relate to and to practice with. This has important consequences for designers and producers as the focus on technology during rehearsal is not merely to get it to work, but rather to provide an opportunity to rehearse with it, to experience how it feels to act with it, or to learn to perform a new character.

The production of the performances did not include any design iteration and the technology was designed and developed prior to the rehearsal rather than throughout it. For example, the application used for the audience interaction in ADA took much longer to develop than the actual rehearsal. In this play, the absence of the technology during rehearsal was also related to the fact that it was conceived as a tool for the audience; its role and its potential impact was not extensively considered during rehearsal. Another interesting factor was that the creative team did not include digital artists as such; instead all the technologies were envisioned by the director. The team was in fact made up of people with defined and fairly traditional roles: actors, directors, set designer, producers, technicians and the developers of the app (ADA); the latter not present during rehearsal. This point is interesting as it suggests that restructuring rehearsal for mixed-media performances would require more than merely introducing a new production role. We argue instead that this would entail a more holistic reconfiguration of the rehearsing process.

We introduce two points that help us frame implications on how to structure and organize rehearsals of mixed-media performances: One main suggestion in reconfiguring rehearsal is to adopt participatory methods enabling the inclusion of actors in the early stages of technology design. In both our cases, and arguably other studies [9, 30], the design of interactive performances often draws on technological experimentation rather than on the understanding of actors' practices and experience. The issue at stake here is the interplay between the functional aspects of the technology and the creative tension inherent in conveying and evoking a certain feeling through the technology – i.e. presence and closeness. As seen in the analysis (i.e. Otto adjusting his movements to the smaller stage), the actors' professional skills, and their ability to go about emerging problems are highly embodied and situational. This means that it might be difficult to anticipate and recount problems through pre-performance interviews. Another important issue is that the actors' skills evolved with the technology and because of the technology (i.e. learning to feel presence or ignoring the audience text messages). This means that prototyping methods should be complemented with experience-centred methods (i.e. bodystorming or dramaturgical scenarios) enabling to account for contextual factors, bodily, sensorial and emotional aspects emerging when acting with technology [31]. Relatedly, despite the challenges related to the implementation of the technological and digital setup of the performance, it would be misleading to read the related findings merely as problems that could be solved by a better (re)design. The rehearsing for the technology was in fact a way for the actors to develop their acting skills in this new setting. As we pointed out, in Lise & Otto the complete final technological setup was not available during rehearsal, while in ADA it was impossible to predict the form that the audience interaction would take. If we look at our findings through a design lens, a lot of the work the actors and the director engaged, resembled what we would do with a low fidelity prototype, in which the potential interactions with the technology are described in an envisioning scenario. For instance, three large displays in the rehearsing room were used to mark where they would be positioned on the final stage, to rehearse the actors' position on the stage and the exact time they would have to be still in front of the camera (to be broadcast to the other stage), while the actor at distance was talking. Contrary to what one could expect, they were not used to rehearsing presence. Designing for artistic settings requires a shift of focus towards the whole experience, rather than the technical qualities of interactive technologies [21]. When rehearsing for mixed-media performances, this means, for instance, that even low-fidelity prototypes and mockups should be available at the rehearsal stage, allowing the actors and the production team to gain insights on the qualities emerging from the mutual interactions between actors, technologies, and all the other non-human elements present on a stage.

CONCLUSIONS

Rehearsing for mixed-media performances is a subject rarely addressed within HCI, where most interactive performance and experiences have been studied from the audience perspective. We have provided a description of the unique challenges the actors and the director encountered during rehearsals for two mixed-media plays; the challenges included practicing for remote presence, practicing for dual audiences, and managing media and technology control while directing actors in a traditional sense. We pointed out how these challenges lead to a set of implications for structuring rehearsal for mixed media performances. In particular, technology should be viewed as yet another actor for early inclusion of 'prototyping' for the actors and the directors to rehearse with. Finally, our study contributed to a more detailed understanding of structures and practices around rehearsal for mixed-media performances.

ACKNOWLEDGEMENTS

We are grateful to Rebecca Forsberg who facilitated our study of the rehearsals of the plays presented in this paper. We would also like to thank Linda Lönnerfeldt and Andreas Liljeholm who shared their experience with us.

REFERENCES

1. Louise Barkhuus, Arvid Engström, Goranka Zoric 2014. Watching the footwork: Second Screen Interaction at a Dance and Music Performance. *In Proceedings of the SIGCHI Conference on Human Factors in Computing Systems (CHI '14).* ACM, New York, pp. 1305-1314. DOI=10.1145/2556288.2557369
2. Louise Barkhuus and Tobias Jørgensen. 2008. Engaging the crowd: studies of audience-performer interaction. In *CHI '08 Extended Abstracts on Human Factors in Computing Systems* (CHI EA '08). ACM, New York, NY, USA, 2925-2930. DOI=10.1145/1358628.1358785
3. Ben Bedwell, Holger Schnädelbach, Steve Benford, Tom Rodden, and Boriana Koleva. 2009. In support of city exploration. *In Proceedings of the SIGCHI Conference on Human Factors in Computing Systems (CHI '09).* ACM: New York, pp. 1171-1180. DOI=10.1145/1518701.1518879
4. Marek Bell, Matthew Chalmers, Louise Barkhuus, Malcolm Hall, Scott Sherwood, Paul Tennent, Barry Brown, Duncan Rowland, Steve Benford, Mauricio Capra, and Alastair Hampshire. 2006. Interweaving mobile games with everyday life. In *Proceedings of the SIGCHI Conference on Human Factors in Computing Systems* (CHI '06), ACM, New York, NY, USA, 417-426. DOI=10.1145/1124772.1124835
5. Steve Benford, Andy Crabtree, Stuart Reeves, Jennifer Sheridan, Alan Dix, Martin Flintham, and Adam Drozd. 2006. The Frame of the Game: Blurring the Boundary between Fiction and Reality in Mobile Experiences. In *Proceedings of the SIGCHI Conference on Human Factors in Computing Systems* (CHI '06), ACM, New York, NY, USA, 427-436. DOI=10.1145/1124772.1124836
6. Steve Benford, Andy Crabtree, Martin Flintham, Adam Drozd, Rob Anastasi, Mark Paxton, Nick Tandavanitj, Matt Adams, and Ju Row-Farr. 2006. Can you see me now? In *ACM Transaction on. Computer.-Human. Interaction.* 13, 1, pp. 100-133. DOI=10.1145/1143518.1143522
7. Johannes H. Birringer (1999). Contemporary performance/technology. Theatre Journal, 51(4), pp. 361-381. DOI=10.1353/tj.1999.0079
8. Gaetano Borriello, Matthew Chalmers, Anthony LaMarca, and Paddy Nixon. 2005. Delivering real-world ubiquitous location systems. Communications of the ACM 48, 3 (March 2005), 36-41. DOI=10.1145/1047671.1047701
9. Susan Broadhurst 2004. Interaction, Reaction and Performance: The Jeremiah Project. TDR the Drama Review 48(4), December, pp.47-57. http://www.digitalcultures.org/Library/Jeremiah.pdf
10. Teresa Cerratto-Pargman, Chiara Rossitto, Louise Barkhuus L. 2014. Understanding Audience Participation in an Interactive Theater Performance. In *Proceedings of NordiCHI, the Proceedings of the 8th Nordic Conference on Human-Computer Interaction. (NordiCHI '14*). ACM: New York, pp. 608-617. DOI=10.1145/2639189.2641213
11. Matthew Chalmers and Areti Galani. 2004. Seamful interweaving: heterogeneity in the theory and design of interactive systems. In *Proceedings of the 5th conference on Designing interactive systems: processes, practices, methods, and techniques* (DIS '04). ACM, New York, NY, USA, 243-252. DOI=10.1145/1013115.1013149
12. Andy Crabtree, Steve Benford, Tom Rodden, Chris Greenhalgh, Martin Flintham, Rob Anastasi, Adam Drozd, Matt Adams, Ju Row-Farr, Nick Tandavanitj, and Anthony Steed. 2004. Orchestrating a mixed reality game 'on the ground'. In *Proceedings of the SIGCHI Conference on Human Factors in Computing Systems (CHI '04).* ACM, New York, pp. 391-398. DOI=10.1145/985692.985742
13. Andy Crabtree, Steve Benford, S, Mauricio Capra, Martin Flintham, Adam Drozd, Nick Tandavanitj, Matt Adams, and Row Farr, J. 2007. The Cooperative Work of Gaming: Orchestrating a Mobile SMS Game. *Computer. Supported Cooperative. Work* 16, 1-2, 167-DOI=198. 10.1007/s10606-007-9048-1
14. Martin Flintham, Rob Anastasi, Steve Benford, Adam Drozd, James Mathrick, Duncan Rowland, Amanda Oldroyd and Jon Sutton. 2003. Uncle Roy all around you: mixing games and theatre on the city streets. In *DIGRA Conference 2003.*
15. Lesley Fosh, Steve Benford, Stuart Reeves, Boriana Koleva, and Patrick Brundell. 2013. see me, feel me, touch me, hear me: trajectories and interpretation in a sculpture garden. In *Proceedings of the SIGCHI Conference on Human Factors in Computing Systems (CHI '13).* ACM, New York, NY, USA, 149-158. DOI=10.1145/2470654.2470675
16. Gasa Friederichs-Büttner, Benjamin Walther-Franks, Rainer Malaka. 2012. An unfinished drama: designing participation for the theatrical dance performance Parcival XX-XI. *In Proceedings of the Designing Interactive Systems Conference (DIS '12).* ACM New York, pp.770-778. DOI=10.1145/2317956.2318072
17. Michaela Honauer and Eva Hornecker. 2015. Challenges for Creating and Staging Interactive Costumes for the Theatre Stage. In *Proceedings of the 2015 ACM SIGCHI Conference on Creativity and Cognition* (C&C '15). ACM, New York, NY, USA, 13-22. DOI=10.1145/2757226.2757242
18. Jonathan Hook, John McCarthy, Peter Wright, Patrick Oliver P. 2013. Waves: Exploring Idiographic Design

for Live Performance. In *Proceedings of the SIGCHI Conference on Human Factors in Computing Systems* (CHI '13). ACM, New York, pp. 2969-2978. DOI=10.1145/2470654.2481412

19. Carlo Jacucci, Giulio Jacucci, Ina Wagner, and Thomas Psik. 2005. A manifesto for the performative development of ubiquitous media. In Proceedings of the 4th decennial conference on Critical computing: between sense and sensibility (CC '05), ACM, New York, NY, USA, 19-28. DOI=10.1145/1094562.1094566
20. Boriana Koleva, Ian Taylor, Steve Benford, Mike Fraser, Chris Greenhalgh, Holger Schnädelbach, Dirk vom Lehn, Christian Heath, Ju Row-Farr, and Matt Adams. 2001. Orchestrating a mixed reality performance. In *Proceedings of the SIGCHI conference on Human factors in computing systems*, ACM, New York, NY, USA, 38-45. DOI=10.1145/365024.365033
21. Tuck Wah Leong and Peter Wright. 2013. Understanding 'tingle' in opera performances. In *Proceedings of the 25th Australian Computer-Human Interaction Conference: Augmentation, Application, Innovation, Collaboration* (OzCHI '13). ACM, New York, 43-52. DOI=10.1145/2541016.2541026
22. John Lofland, John, John Snow, David Anderson and Lyn H. Lofland. *Analyzing social settings: A guide to qualitative observation and analysis*. 4th edition. Belmont, CA: Wadsworth Publishing Company, 2005.
23. Dan Maynes-Aminzade, Randy Pausch, and Steve Seitz. 2002. Techniques for interactive audience participation. In *Proceedings of the 4th IEEE International Conference on Multimodal Interfaces*, p. 15. IEEE Computer Society.
24. Gary M. Olson and Judith S. Olson. 2000. Distance matters. *Hum.-Comput. Interact.* 15, 2 (September 2000), 139-178. DOI=10.1207/S15327051HCI1523_4
25. Leif Oppermann, Martin Flintham, Stuart Reeves, Steve Benford, Chris Greenhalgh, Joe Marshall, Matt Adams, Ju Row Farr, and Nick Tandavanitj. 2011. Lessons from touring a location-based experience. In *Proceedings of the 9th international conference on Pervasive computing (Pervasive'11).* Springer-Verlag, Berlin, Heidelberg, 232-249. DOI=10.1007/978-3-642-21726-5_15
26. Ian J. Palmer, Nicholas Chilton, Adam Robinson and Carlton Reeve. 2001. The Creation of an Interactive Virtual Theatre: The Mad Hatter's Tea Party. In *Digital Content Creation*, R. Earnshaw and J. Vince (ed.), pp. 184-201. Springer. DOI=10.1007/978-1-4471-0293-9_14
27. Carlton Reeve. 2000. Presence in Virtual Theater. Carlton Reeve 2000. Presence in Virtual Theater. In the journal of Presence: *Teleoperators and Virtual Environments,* MIT Press Cambridge, MA, USA, pp. 209-213. DOI=10.1162/105474600566727
28. Carlton Reeve and Ian Palmer. 1999. Virtual rehearsal over networks. In *Digital Convergence: The Information Revolution*, pp. 101-115. Springer London, 1999.
29. Chiara Rossitto, Louise Barkhuus and Arvid Engström. 2016. Interweaving Place and Story in a Location-Based Audio Drama. To appear in Personal and Ubiquitous Computing. Springer Publishing.
30. Qiong Wu, Pierre Boulanger, Maryia Kazakevich, and Robyn Taylor. 2010. A real-time performance system for virtual theater. In *Proceedings of the 2010 ACM workshop on Surreal media and virtual cloning* (SMVC '10). ACM, New York, NY, USA, 3-8.
31. Peter Wright and John McCarthy. 2010. Experience-centred Design: Designers, users, and communities in dialogue. Morgan & Claypool Publishers.
32. Takuro Yonezawa and Hideyuki Tokuda. 2012. Enhancing communication and dramatic impact of online live performance with cooperative audience control. In *Proceedings of the 2012 ACM Conference on Ubiquitous Computing* (UbiComp '12). ACM, New York, NY, USA, 103-112. DOI=10.1145/2370216.2370234
33. Garth Zeglin, Aaron Walsman, Laura Herlant, Zhaodong Zheng, Yuyang Guo, Michael C. Koval, Kevin Lenzo et al. 2014. HERB's Sure Thing: A rapid drama system for rehearsing and performing live robot theater. In *Advanced Robotics and its Social Impacts (ARSO), 2014 IEEE Workshop on*, pp. 129-136. IEEE, 2014.

What you Sculpt is What you Get: Modeling Physical Interactive Devices with Clay and 3D Printed Widgets

Michael D. Jones
Dept. of Computer Science,
Brigham Young U.
3328 TMCB, Provo, UT 84602
Mike.jones@byu.edu

Kevin Seppi
Dept. of Computer Science
Brigham Young U.
3328 TMCB, Provo, UT 84602
Kevin_seppi@byu.edu

Dan R. Olsen
Dept. of Computer Science
Brigham Young U.
3328 TMCB, Provo, UT 84602
olsen@sparxteq.com

ABSTRACT

We present a method for fabricating prototypes of interactive computing devices from clay sculptures without requiring the designer to be skilled in CAD software. The method creates a "what you *sculpt* is what you get" process that mimics the "what you *see* is what you get" processes used in interface design for 2D screens. Our approach uses clay for modeling the basic shape of the device around 3D printed representations, which we call "blanks", of physical interaction widgets such as buttons, sliders, knobs and other electronics. Each blank includes 4 fiducial markers uniquely arranged on a visible surface. After scanning the sculpture, these fiducial marks allow our software to identify widget types and locations in the scanned model. The software then converts the scan into a printable prototype by positioning mounting surfaces, openings for the controls and a splitting plane for assembly. Because the blanks fit in the sculpted shape, they will reliably fit in the interactive prototype. Creating an interactive prototype requires about 30 minutes of human effort for sculpting, and after scanning, involves a single button click to use the process.

Author Keywords
Physical computing; 3D printing; prototypes

ACM Classification Keywords
D.2.2 Design Tools and Techniques, H.5.2 User Interfaces.

INTRODUCTION

We envision deployable prototypes of physical computing devices similar to that shown in Figure 1. These are single purpose devices that must physically fit into a specific context. The shape of the devices must fit human form and motion. For example, the bicycle mounted music player controller in Figure 1a must be easily accessible by a person on a bicycle. The steering wheel mounted stereo controls in Figure 1b must be carefully placed to lie under the thumb of a hand holding the steering wheel. Similarly, widgets on the camera controller in Figure 1c should be placed to allow operation without looking at the device to locate the controls.

CHI'16, May 07-12, 2016, San Jose, CA, USA
 ISBN 978-1-4503-3362-7/16/05 $15.00
DOI: http://dx.doi.org/10.1145/2858036.2858493

An interactive prototype allows the designer to determine if the shape and interaction will work with human form and motion. It is difficult to make that assessment when looking at a rendering on a computer screen. Finally, it is also important to be able to rapidly iterate the design. The designer needs to be able to go from idea to working prototype quickly so that she can work through many iterations in a short amount of time. Shape alone, is not sufficient. Interactive devices must integrate with the shape and the resulting prototypes must be interactively functional to test usability in context. Finally, it is critical that the functional prototype preserves the shape and widget placements as laid out in the sculpture. Otherwise, widgets may not be correctly placed relative to a user's finger shape, position and movement.

A diverse set of prior approaches to prototyping physical interactive devices share many of these goals. Many of these projects, such as Gadgeteer [15], Phidgets [5] and d.tools [6] and many others, present novel electronics and software systems for building physical interactive devices. We see a need for better methods for integrating the shape of the device with the interactive widgets. The Switcharoo [2], Calder [9], and BOXES [7] projects also describe new methods for creating the device shape but we aim for more fidelity and fluidity in design of the shape than found in these projects.

Savage in Makers' Marks [11] also merges form and function for interactive 3D printed objects using a process based on scanning physical representations of sculpted objects. The maker annotates the object with stickers that represent the approximate positions of input or output elements such as buttons or lights. Sticker positions are recovered after scanning and geometry is added before printing to support assembly using the required components. Stickers provide fluidity but not fidelity in the design process. Stickers do not represent the shape of interactive elements above the surface, do not represent the volume of components beneath the

a b c

Figure 1 Three examples of physical interactive devices.

surface, and may not accurately represent widget locations on curved surfaces. In some cases the captured shape of the housing is extended with a boxy protrusion to make room for components beneath the surface.

Like Makers' Marks, we see value in scanning physical representations of interactive widgets but we envision a process in which the designer works with the actual widget shapes knowing that any sculpted form can be converted into a functional prototype exactly as it was sculpted. Precisely preserving widget placement and device shape is particularly important when designing a device intended to fit comfortably in the hand or to have buttons placed under the fingers when held in a certain way.

Our process begins with sculpting in clay around 3D printed blanks which represent interactive widgets such buttons, sliders and knobs. The blanks are partially embedded in the clay to represent electronics that must fit below the surface and to expose interactive widgets that lie above the surface. Blanks can be easily repositioned in the wet clay. The sculpture is scanned and the scanned mesh is modified to create an identically shaped 3D printable housing with the intended widget placements. After assembling widgets in the housing, the designer has an interactive prototype.

One problem with this process is that there is a significant amount of geometry processing that happens between scanning and printing. The triangular mesh created by the scanner needs to be augmented to support the interactive widgets and prototype assembly. This processing includes adding mounting geometry for the widget parts, cutting holes in the surface for interactive widgets that lie on the surface and making it possible to assemble widgets in the housing. Of these steps, adding mounting geometry is particularly difficult because the geometry must be positioned and oriented precisely to match widget placement in the sculpture.

We present an algorithm that searches through the scanned mesh to find fiducial markers that were 3D printed into the widget blanks. After finding markers, the algorithm searches for groups of markers that match marker placement on the different widget types. Widget type, position and orientation can be recovered from matching groups of markers and then the additional structure can be added in the right places. The process depends on creating several models, included in the model for the blank, derived from a 3D model of the widget and its electronics but this only needs to be done once per widget type. This algorithm allows a designer to convert a scanned mesh into a prototype housing with one button click. The prototypes shown in Figure 1were created using this process. Each prototype required less than 30 minutes of scanning and was correctly processed by our algorithm.

DESIGN PROCESS

Our approach supports a process in which the design is created by physical means. In this section we describe this process and highlight key problems that must be solved to support that process.

The designer sits at a table with clay and 3D printed blanks that represent widgets as shown in Figure 2a. In the photograph, trays of blanks sit to the right of the widgets they represent. There are also 3D printed blanks to represent

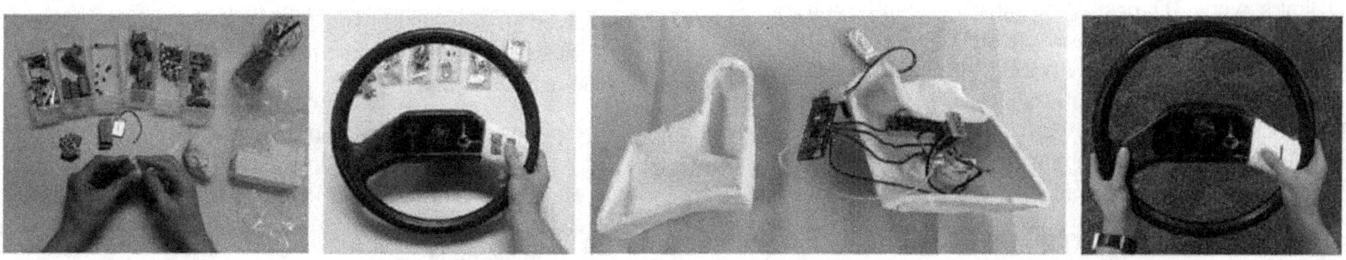

a b c d

Figure 2 Sculpting around printed blanks that represent widgets to make an interactive physical device.

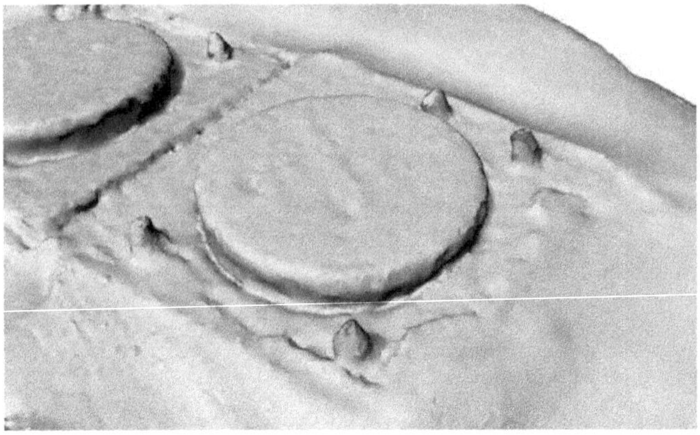

Figure 3 In this scanned model of a sculpted prototype, vertices on fiducial markers are colored red.

batteries, processors and other elements that might be needed in the functional prototype.

The designer molds clay around the blanks while leaving interaction surfaces exposed to create a clay model of the prototype shown in Figure 2b. This clay model includes the interactive widgets embedded in the right places for interaction. In this case, the steering wheel mounted controls are placed comfortably under the thumb when the hand grasps the steering wheel.

Sculpting around blanks is a key part of the process. The resulting prototype will be functional only if the actual widgets can be implemented in their location as specified in the sculpted form. It is not useful to allow the designer to sculpt a housing with a specific placement of widgets only to later discover that that placement is not feasible in the sculpted shape. The printed blanks include volume below the surface to represent the electronics and other parts needed to implement that element above the surface. Later we discuss the use of offset surfaces relative to models of complete widget assemblies as a solution to this problem.

After creating the clay model, the designer scans the sculpture. We used a scanner with resolution of 0.13 mm. The locations of the blanks and the widgets they represent must be recovered from the scanned model and this is done by first finding fiducial markers in the scan. Markers are grouped into predefined arrangements printed into the blank. Blanks were 3D printed using a stereolithography (SLA) process that has a layer thickness of 0.028 mm and a resolution of 600 dpi. Printing blanks at lower resolution using a fusion deposition process (FDM) resulted in misshaped markers that were difficult to find in the scanned model. From these groupings the algorithm recovers widget type, placement and orientation.

The scanned sculpture is processed and printed. The housing and electronics are shown in Figure 2c. Processing the scanned mesh involves adding mount points for electronics and other parts needed to implement a widget, splitting the housing to provide access to the interior, and adding snaps so the housing can be closed after assembly.

The designer can then use the prototype in the intended context as shown in Figure 2d. This allows for evaluation of shape and functionality in ways that are difficult to do when looking at a shape on a computer screen or when using a prototype connected to a workstation by a cable. The designer can repeat the process either by starting over with a new sculpture, modifying the existing sculpture or modifying the scanned model in software.

This design process and the process in Makers' Marks [11] share four key elements. Both involve tangible representation of the device shape, scanning the representation to recover the shape, recovering interactive widgets from the scanned model, and the automatic placement of mounting geometry to support interactive widgets.

The key difference between the Makers' Marks design process and ours is that we represent the physical constraints of widgets to the designer in a natural way using a 3D printed blank. Blanks accurately represent a widgets shape above and below the object surface. Makers' Marks indicate only the widgets position using a stickers as markup on the object surface. In Makers' Marks the design may have to be perturbed to accommodate constraints not represented by stickers.

These two methods offer different design experiences. Stickers are easy to reposition on the surface while moving a 3D printed blank embedded in clay involves moving the clay, repositioning the blank, and replacing the clay. Furthermore 3D printed blanks must be placed inside the object. In order to properly represent the spacing inside of the object we do not allow approaches like the taping together of cardboard tubes as in Makers' Marks' box example [11]. However this approach could be replicated with more effort by cutting holes in the tubes to place the printed blanks inside.

The power of our approach lies in the fact that the designer can manipulate the design without the extra cognitive load of assessing the internals of the design. Thus if the desired parts fit in the design, then it will be possible to assemble the object without further adjustment. Several problems need to be solved to full enable this "what you sculpt is what you get" design process based on clay and 3D printed blanks. These problems are:

- ensuring that widget placements in the sculpture can be implemented as placed,
- finding fiducial markers in the scanned mesh,
- grouping fiducial markers into individual widget placements,
- recovering widget type, position and orientation from widget placement,
- creating the housing by adding mounting points and

- splitting the scanned model for easy assembly and adding snaps to hold it closed after assembly.

In the following sections we describe how we solved these problems and share insights gained along the way.

FINDING FIDUCIAL MARKERS

Our process depends on being able to automatically recover the type, position and orientation of each widget using only a scanned model (mesh) of the design. To do this we need to recover the locations of the fiducial markers that identify each widget type and placement. This involves traversing the vertices in the mesh and labeling vertices that lie on one of these markers. Figure 3 shows markers colored red in a rendering of a scanned model of the sculpture from Figure 2b.

Cones with height 3 mm and a base diameter of 2 mm serve as markers. We chose cones because they have a single point with unique curvature. Cylinders also have unique curvatures, but the unique curvature is found on every point of the rim rather than just one on the tip. We experimented with several cone heights and base diameters before using the 3 mm tall cones with 2 mm bases. Smaller, shorter cones were difficult to locate in scanned meshes. Larger, taller cones poked into the designer's fingers and were more distracting than smaller cones.

We find the tips of cones in the scanned mesh by analyzing the slope at each vertex. The scanned mesh consists of vertices, or points, and edges connected into triangles. At the tip of a cone, the surface slopes downward in every direction. The algorithm computes the slope in the direction of the neighboring vertex. If the slope is downward in every direction, then that vertex must lie on a cone.

We compute the slope to a vertex as shown in Figure 4. To find the slope at A in the direction of vertex B we first compute the vector n which is the normal at A. The vector n is perpendicular to the surface at A and is computed by averaging the normal for the triangles that share A as a vertex. Given n and B we compute a coordinate system at A in which n points in the positive z direction and x is perpendicular to z but parallel to the line that connects A and B. In Figure 4 the x axes from A to each of the other vertices are shown in red. We project the position of B into this coordinate system and then compute dx, the change in x, and dz, the change in z, from A to B. The slope from A to B is dz/dx.

We repeat the process for neighboring vertices B, C, D and E (and for vertices not shown in the illustration). For each neighbor we compute a new coordinate system in which x is parallel to the line from A to the neighbor, and then compute the slope dz/dx in that coordinate system.

After computing the slope in each direction we check that each slope is within the range -0.6 to -1.5. If any slope is outside this range then there is a direction on the surface in which the slope is too flat or too steep for that vertex to lie on the tip of a scanned fiducial marker.

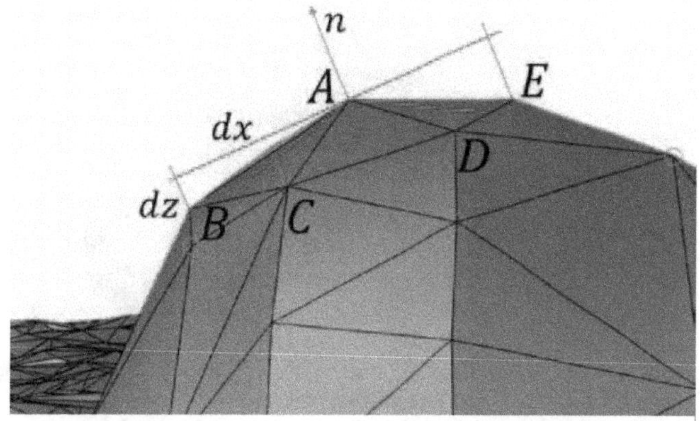

Figure 4 Close up view of mesh vertices on a scanned fiducial marker. We locate vertices on the marker by computing the slope from a vertex to neighboring vertices.

We tried classifying vertices using an estimate of signed mean curvature. The signed mean curvature is the average of the principle curvatures at a vertex. The principle's curvatures are the largest and smallest local curvatures, and the local curvatures are precisely the slopes computed using dz/dx as described above. But signed mean curvature loses too much information and misclassifies more vertices than the threshold method described above. A key feature of a vertex on a bump is that *all* normal curvatures lie within a given range not just that the average of the minimal and maximal normal curvature.

We compute the slope to the neighbors two edges away from a vertex rather than using vertices only one edge away. In Figure 4 this means we use the slope to the vertices circled in blue rather than vertices B, C, D and E. This gives a larger span over which to estimate slope, and makes the algorithm less sensitive to noise. This decision depends on the mesh being at a certain resolution relative to the size of the bumps in a blank. It works well when a vertex on a bump top has at least 2 generations of neighbors that also lie on the bump.

This method for finding vertices on fiducial markers is insensitive to changes in mesh resolution. Reducing the resolution of the mesh matters because processing a mesh with fewer vertices takes less computational time and memory. The mesh resolution reduction algorithm we used preserves a dense collection of vertices on curvy parts of the mesh and leaves a sparse collection of vertices in flat areas. This is because one flat triangle approximates a flat plane just as well as many flat triangles. Because the fiducial markers are curvy, they are left with many vertices which simplifies labeling vertices that lie on them.

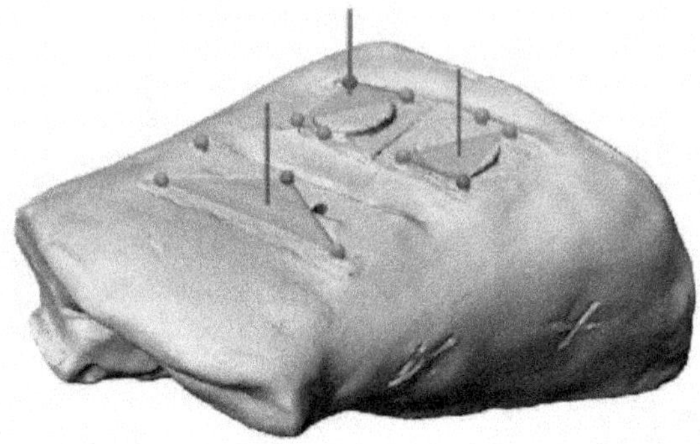

Figure 5 Each colored line connects a marked vertex to 3 other marked vertices with together represent a widget placement. Duplication is due multiple labeled vertices on each marker.

The algorithm often finds several vertices per bump in the scanned mesh. For example in Figure 4 vertices B, C, D and E might also be labeled as lying on bumps. In our approach it is better to identify several vertices on bumps than to miss all of the vertices on a bump. Finding several vertices per bump causes the widget location algorithm to find many widget placements (15 is average) per actual widget blank embedded in the mesh. This happens because each vertex on each bump can be grouped with several vertices on other bumps to create a valid placement. Figure 5 shows vertices labeled on a marker and the connections found on neighboring markers. Each colored line is part of a different widget placement found by the algorithm. We handle these duplicate placements by merging placements that are in close proximity as described in the next section.

Cones used as fiducial markers can be reliably located in the scanned model and this supports recovery of widget type, placement and orientation. Recovering widget placement information is a necessary step in automatically converting a scanned sculpture into an interactive prototype with working widgets.

FINDING WIDGET PLACEMENTS

Finding fiducial markers alone does not identify the type or placement of widgets. What we need to know is which groups of markers represent a widget placement. The algorithm that groups markers into placements should ignore mislabeled vertices that do not actually lie on markers and should find only the valid widget placements.

Figure 6 shows widget positions and orientations recovered from vertices marked on the scanned mesh. Markers are highlighted with colored balls, the plane of the widget is shown with a blue triangle and a vector perpendicular to the plane is shown in purple. Other colors in the image correspond to the vertex order and will be explained in the next section.

The grouping algorithm searches through combinations of labeled vertices to find groups that match the relative positions of markers printed into widgets. The markers on a widget are always arranged into unique asymmetric groups of 4 markers.

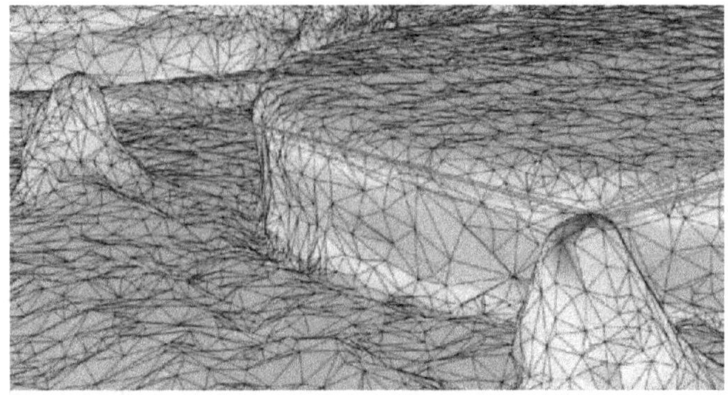

Figure 6 Widget placements recovered by searching for properly spaced clusters of 4 markers and then merging duplicate cluster that lie in close proximity.

Although 3 markers are sufficient to recover position and orientation, we use 4 markers per widget. Using 4 markers rather than 3 eliminates many false positives when finding widget placement. With 3 bumps there are 3 distances to check. With 4 bumps there are 6 distances to check between every pair of bumps. Checking more distances allows the algorithm to exclude more spurious placements.

When checking distances between markers, the algorithm has a tolerance of 0.7 mm. In our tests, we found that about 75% of the distances between vertices on bumps in a widget placement were within 0.5 mm of the expected distance. The other 25% of the distances were between 0.5 and 0.7 mm of the actual distance with larger errors over larger distances.

The algorithm searches through every feasible ordered combination of up to 4 vertices starting with ordered pairs of 2 labeled vertices. We reduce the search space by only searching through labeled vertices that are close enough to the starting vertex. If the greatest distance between two bumps on a widget blank is 31 mm then we only search through labeled vertices within 31.7 mm of a given vertex. The additional 0.7 mm accounts for tolerance in distance matching.

After finding all widget placements the algorithm merges placements in which the center of the placement is closer than 2 mm to the center of another placement. In most cases the actual distance between any two placement centroids is either less than 1 mm or greater than the width of a widget blank on the surface. Merging nearby placements smooths out noise in the widget placements found when several vertices are marked on each marker location.

Finding the widgets in the scanned sculpture is the key step in supporting a design process that includes widgets embedded into clay models. With the bump grouping and

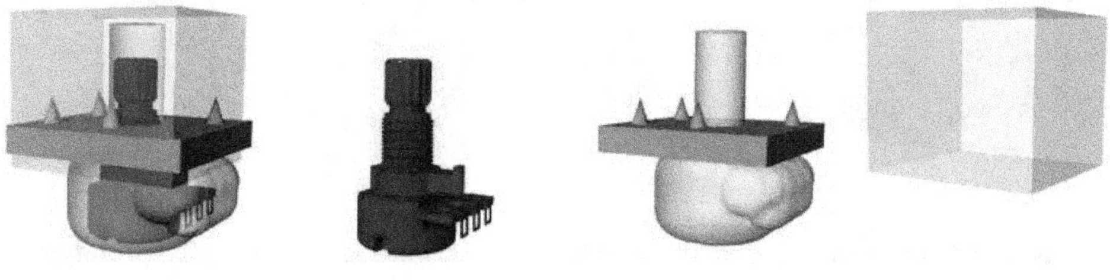

Figure 7 Widget, blank, and slug models for a potentiometer knob.

placement information, we now have what we need to compute widget placement.

RECOVERING WIDGET TYPE AND ORIENTATION

In order to save designer time and effort by automatically placing widget mounts, the algorithm needs to know the type and orientation of the widgets. This information needs to be recovered from the 4 fiducial markers that represent the widget placement.

The widget type is encoded by a unique arrangement of the 4 markers. In this scheme the 4 markers printed into any given widget are positioned at different distances from each other than the 4 markers on any other widget.

After recovering the widget type, the algorithm keeps only the first 3 marker locations rather than all 4. Each marker is numbered and the number is used to compute orientation. We recover vertex numbers from the distances between fiducial markers. The distance between every pair of markers is different for a given widget type. Once the four markers are found, it is simple to match the distances and recover the marker numbers. The plane of the widget placement is defined by markers 1 through 3. In Figure 6 each blue ball gives the location of marker 1 for each widget placement. The yellow line connects marker 1 to 2 and the magenta line connects marker 1 to 3. The plane is shown by the blue triangle. The widgets at the top of the model are both buttons but one is rotated 180 degrees compared to the other. The bottom widget is a slider

The markers used to determine the plane of the placement should be as far apart as possible, should not lie in a single line and should form a right triangle if possible. This gives a larger basis for defining the plane and is less sensitive to noise introduced in scanning.

Given widget placement, orientation and type, the algorithm can now modify the scanned mesh to create a 3D printable housing for the prototype. This will save designer time and effort as the designer does not need to make these modifications by hand.

MODELING WIDGETS

Prototyping with printed widget blanks embedded in clay requires building two models based on the widget geometry. These models ensure that the widget can be implemented in the space allotted and provide fiducial markers for recovery of placements.

Modeling the widgets is not part of the prototype construction process but needs to be done before the process begins. It needs to be done once per widget type and requires CAD skills. Widget models are based on an accurate 3D representation of the widget which includes everything needed to interact with the widget and to implement the widget.

Several additional models are derived from the base widget model. These are shown in Figure 7 with a composite view on the left. The base widget model is shown in blue. The base model is in this figure is a knob implemented using a potentiometer. The mounting bracket is a plate shown in solid orange. This widget attaches to the housing by attaching it to that plate. Other widgets have more complex mounting geometry and this would be included as part of the mounting bracket. The grey box is called the “slug” and used to cut a hole in the housing to accommodate the mounting bracket. The printed blank that represents this widget consists of the mounting bracket and the yellow offset mesh.

The yellow geometry below the plate is a mesh offset by 3 mm from the widget in order to allow space for the widget in the sculpture interior. In this context, offsetting the mesh means moving every vertex in the mesh 3 mm along that vertex’s normal. The offset vertices are remeshed to create a mesh that is 3 mm from the original mesh. Adding this offset to the printed blank allows the designer to sculpt down to the printed widget model while still leaving room for the housing wall to enclose the widget. Without this offset the designer must guess where the widget is inside the opaque modeling clay.

The four fiducial markers need to be added to the visible parts of the orange plate or the visible parts of the blue model above the orange plate. If the 4 markers do not lie on the plane of the orange plate then the widget model must also include the angles between the plane of the first 3 markers and the plane of the orange plate.

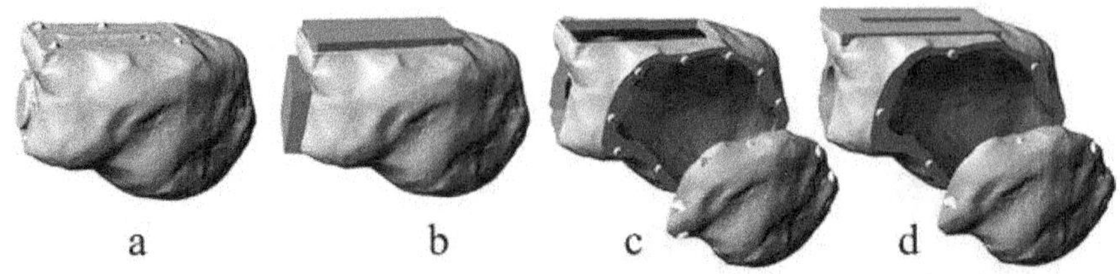

Figure 8 Creating a 3D printable housing from a scanned mesh of sculpted prototype.

We also include 3D printed blanks to represent additional electronic components, such as a processor or a battery, that are completely enclosed in the housing. These blanks are included in the sculpture to make sure that there will be enough space for those parts in the printed prototype without modifying the housing shape. For the devices shown in this paper, we used blanks to represent the volume of an Arduino processor and a battery and embedded those in the sculpture.

We do not locate the blanks that represent embedded electronic components that lie completely within the housing because they are hidden beneath the surface. We also do not add mounting brackets for these elements. Instead, the designer must remember which enclosed electronics belong in the housing and place them by hand.

The blank, slug, bracket and parts should be stored in the same coordinate space in the positions relative to each other. By convention, we stored the widget with the tip of marker 1 on the origin and the tip of marker 2 on the positive x axis. Markers 1, 2, and 3 all lie on the xy plane. The vector created by taking the cross product of the vectors connecting marker 1 with 2 and 1 with 3 points in the positive z direction. This relative placement and alignment is important because it means we know the position and orientation of the parts when they are read into the scanned model space. Any alignment with the model coordinate system will suffice, but it must be unambiguous.

The widget and associated models can now be used in their printed form in sculpting and can be loaded in digital form to prepare the prototype housing for printing and assembly. The investment in modeling time and effort needed to create the widget models pays of in time and effort saved later during prototyping.

CREATING A HOUSING FOR THE PROTOTYPE

Creating a housing involves 4 steps: cutting holes for the interactive elements that support widgets, splitting the housing to allow assembly, adding snaps so the housing can be closed after assembly, and adding mounting brackets and other parts for each widget. These steps are shown in Figure 8, as will be explained in the text below, beginning with the scanned sculpture in Figure 8a and ending with the final printable housing in Figure 8d.

Cutting holes for widgets. Holes need to be cut so that interactive widgets can be exposed on the prototype surface. For each widget placement, the algorithm loads the slug, this is the grey box in Figure 7, which encloses all of the volume needed for interactive elements and for mounting brackets. This slug is shown in brown in Figure 8b. The holes are created by a Boolean subtraction operation which subtracts the slug from the scanned mesh. The holes are visible in Figure 8c (which also shows the housing split into two pieces for assembly).

Splitting the housing. Assembling widgets for the interactive prototype requires access to the interior of the housing. We provide that access by splitting the housing into two pieces. The split must provide a large opening through which electronics can be moved into position. We find a plane for splitting the housing by evaluating 1600 different planes that intersect the housing. Figure 9 shows the feasible planes explored for a mesh with the final selection shown in red. A splitting plane is feasible if it passes through the mesh inner and outer walls and does not intersect a hole cut for widget placement. The optimal splitting plane creates the largest opening in the housing. The area of the opening is the area of the polygon created on the plane when the mesh is intersected with the plane. The plane with the largest area is selected and used to split the housing mesh.

Adding snaps. The housing pieces need to be fastened back together after assembly. The algorithm adds between 6 and 12 post and hole pairs to the matching faces created by splitting the housing. The posts and holes can be seen Figures 8c and 8d. Posts with radius 1.3 mm proved durable in assembly and reassembly of the printed housing. Larger

Figure 9 Finding a plane to split the housing. The red plane was selected from the feasible candidates shown in yellow.

posts would have been more durable but posts and holes need to be small enough to fit on the rim created in the mesh wall.

The hole radius is 0.35 mm larger than the post radius so that the printed post makes a friction fit into the printed hole[1]. The friction fit was tightest when the housing was printed with the plane of the rim parallel to the plane of the print head. Small ridges created in the layer by layer deposition process left small ridges in the post and hole and these ridges fit snugly together with the 0.35 mm tolerance. Other 3D printing process may require different approaches to adding snaps.

Placing brackets. Brackets and other printed pieces needed to implement widgets are added next. These are shown in green in Figure 8d and correspond to the orange bracket in Figure 7. The geometry for brackets and other pieces for each widget placement are loaded, rotated and translated into position. Brackets are joined to either the top or bottom of the split housing using a Boolean union operation. Moving parts that are not attached to the housing are simply left in place to be printed in place.

These modifications to the mesh yield a housing for a functional prototype that is ready for printing and assembly.

EXAMPLES

We have constructed several interactive physical computing prototypes using this process. Prototypes were created by two undergraduate university design students who are part of the research team but who did not write any of the software described above. In each case sculpting required less than 30 minutes of the designer's time, converting the scanned mesh into a printable housing required pressing a button to start the algorithm. The algorithm correctly found widget placement, orientation and type and then prepared the housing for printing and assembly. All sculptures were assembled into functional prototypes. These prototypes are each shown in Figure 1. Four other devices were sculpted by different users and correctly processed by the algorithm to create housings that could be printed and assembled.

Each prototype involves a different hand position relative to the interactive widgets. This means that each prototype shape accommodates different motion of the fingers, hand or arm. Sculpting gives the designer tactile feedback on position and shape needed to support each motion in each context. The camera remote is hand-held. The bike mounted mp3 player control requires moving the arm to access the controls. The steering wheel mounted controller only requires moving the thumb.

Bike mounted mp3 player controls. Using this device involves moving the entire arm while seated on a bicycle.

[1] When printed on a Stratasys Dimension Elite at a layer resolution of 0.25 mm.

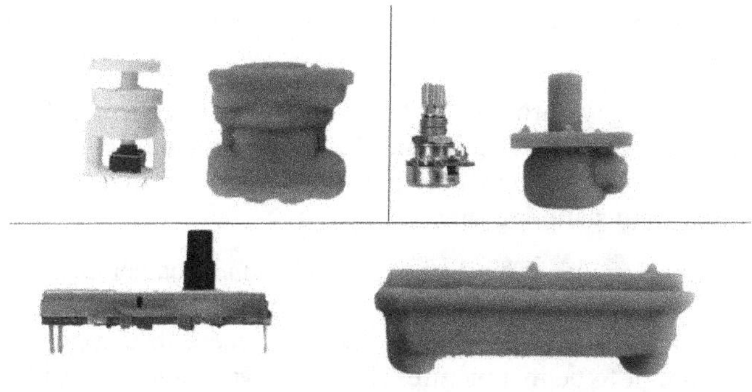

Figure 10 A widget set together with printed blanks used in sculpting. The widgets are a button on the top left, a knob on the top right and a slider on bottom. The button includes a complex mounting bracket printed in white and a moving plunger.

During sculpting the designer sat on a bicycle with the clay wrapped around the bicycle tube that connects the handle bars to the seat (this tube is called the "top tube"). This let the designer check the required arm motion in context. The sculpture wrapped just less than half way around the top tube so that it could be removed for scanning without cutting or moving the clay. The printed controller was attached to the top tube using a thin layer of wet clay. This was sufficient for short test rides (as seen in Figure 1) but double sided foam tape or a stronger adhesive might be needed for longer term testing.

Placing the controller on the top tube is reminiscent of placement of bike gear shifters on the tube connecting the handlebars to the crank arm assembly (this is called the "down tube"). More recent bicycle models put shifters on the handlebars. After testing the interactive prototype on a bicycle ride the designer might decide to place the controls on the handlebars, the down tube, or somewhere else. In either case, designing a new prototype likely involves another 30 minutes of sculpting and pressing a button to create the housing.

Steering wheel mounted mp3 player controls. Unlike the bike mp3 player controller, the steering wheel mounted version does not require moving the entire arm. Placing the controller in the right position on the steering wheel itself allows it to be used with the thumb without changing the hand's grip on steering wheel.

Sculpting the controller shape saved time in two ways in this example. First, the clay and widget models could be pressed into a hole cut in the steering wheel. This gave the prototype housing a shape that would fit in the cut out. Achieving this fit in a CAD tool would require more time. Second, it was easy for the designer to hold the steering wheel with the sculpture in place and test the thumb motion needed to reach the controls.

An interactive prototype of this controller intended to fit a different steering wheel could also be constructed by forming clay on that steering wheel and would likely involve only 30 minutes of sculpting time.

Camera remote. This prototype is a handheld camera remote control. The intended use is to be held in the photographer's hand while they move away from a camera to compose a picture or to be in a picture. The prototype includes a slider under the thumb for controlling zoom and a button under the index finger for taking a picture. It should be usable while looking at the composition or at the camera itself. This means that the interactive widgets should lie under the fingers for easy use without looking at those widgets.

Sculpting around the printed widget models let the designer quickly and accurately place controls under fingers when the device held in the hand. The sculpture required less than 20 minutes to create which was the shortest amount of time across all examples. The final shape was rough but could be refined in either clay or software if testing the functional prototype confirmed that this was a useful application.

A WIDGET SET

Constructing interactive prototypes required a widget set. We need a widget set that keeps the prototype design cycle fast and simple while preserving the feel of interaction with physical objects. This meant using widgets that are simple to assemble, can be printed in any orientation, and which provide good haptic feedback.

After reviewing several widget sets for 3D printed prototypes (see [8, 9, 11] for recent examples) we designed our own widget set based heavily on using existing electronics to convert interaction into electrical signals. Using existing electronics gave up some flexibility in design options but led to simple assembly while providing good haptic feedback. In principle, 3D printable blanks, brackets and slugs as described earlier could be designed and for any of the widgets in [10, 12, 14]. Having a collection of blanks for these widgets on hand would allow the designer to quickly switch between widget types depending on the needs of a project.

The widget set contains a button, a slider, and a knob. Figure 10 shows the widgets together with the printed form used in sculpting. The knob is a potentiometer knob, the slider is a potentiometer slider and the button is a clickable button on a breakout board[2]. The button includes a mounting bracket to hold the breakout board in place, a moving plunger and an enclosure. Choosing a pre-made potentiometer slider limited our designs to straight run sliders with limited lengths. Custom printed sliders would have allowed for curved paths and more flexibility in length. We added additional haptic feedback to the button by placing two ring magnets with polarity mismatched on the button plunger shaft. The magnets are placed in the enclosure after printing. This creates a force that restores the button to its idle position after a button press. We also explored several print-in-place options for providing haptic feedback with the button but the motion varied widely with the print orientation relative to the plane of the 3D printer tray.

All widgets are connected to an Arduino board[3] with Bluetooth. The Arduino board provides power, ground and processes signals from each widget. The Arduino board sends events over Bluetooth to a host for processing.

RELATED WORK

Our work builds on ideas from Switcheroo [1] and Calder [9]. Each of these projects was focus on how to integrate interactive devices with physical shape design. In Switcheroo, passive RF tags could be pinned to a foam surface to place interactive widgets. The Calder project took a similar approach, but involved pinning actual electronic elements to foam. This meant that interactive widgets could be quickly repositioned as the designer explored the feel of the placement of each element. In Calder however, interactive elements protrude from the surface unless the designer creates a cavity in which to embed electronics. This cavity fixes the widget placement and eliminates fluid repositioning. Working with clay, and an oil-based clay in particular, allows the widget to be embedded in the object and to be repositioned as needed. Printing a representation of the widget ensures that elements beneath the surface will fit in the prototype.

Hartmann and Klemmer [6, 8] frame physical design as conversations with the design medium such as clay, paper or foam core, and point to Schoen's reflective practice [13] as a foundation. They were focused on device integration and software and argue that iteration through prototypes is important for designers to understand a problem. Our work shares this foundation but we focus more on integrating the physical shape with the interactive electronics.

The BOXES project merges form and function early in prototyping physical interactive objects [7]. Clever use of cardboard, foil, thumbtacks and masking tape allows a designer to quickly iterate through different shapes and place buttons on those shapes. Our process is a bit less fluid than cutting cardboard, but supports a richer set of shapes and interaction methods beyond buttons. As with some of the other work, the prototype was a mass of tethered wires that was impossible to deploy in a realistic context.

[2] We used a 10k Ohm rotary potentiometer knob (Sparkfun part 09939), small 10k linear taper potentiometer slides (11602), and a mini push button switch (97).

[3] A RedBearLab Blend Micro Arduino board.

Savage et al. in Makers' Marks [11] merge form and functionality in the context of 3D scanning and printing. Approximate widget positions and widget types are recovered by using SIFT and RANSAC to recognize fiducial marks printed on stickers. Our process uses only the sculpted object geometry and does not require recovering the sculpture's surface color and does not use image processing. Makers' Marks supports mechanical elements such as hinges. In principle our process could as well by embedding 3D printed representations of hinges in the clay.

deForm [4] combines the expressiveness of clay with digital interaction using a pair of structured light scanners. While the process is limited to 2.5D deformed surfaces rather than arbitrary 3D shapes, the process may support a fluid environment for creating and modifying interactive physical devices.

In DisplayObjects Akaoka et al. [1] also argue for early merger of prototype form and interaction, but take a different approach based on projecting interfaces onto solid objects. This leads to interesting simulations but is not deployable into usable scenarios.

Many projects have constructed sets of interactive widgets for physical computing and prototypes. They differ primarily in the mechanism used to detect interaction. Interaction has been created using sound [12], pneumatics [14], light [10] and of course electricity [15, 4]. Our focus is different however. Our focus is on supporting the creation of shapes to house the interactive elements, and to do so in such that the shape fits human form and motion. In principle, any widget set could be used with our process given appropriate modeling of each widget. Voodoosketch [3] merges physical widgets with sketched interfaces on interactive surfaces but does not contemplate 3D interactive physical devices.

SUMMARY AND FUTURE WORK

Sculpting keeps physicality in prototype design. We presented a fast and simple method for converting a scan of the sculpture into a printable interactive prototype. The method eliminates CAD skills from the process. The algorithms described were implemented in C# to run in the RhinoCommon API in Rhinoceros 5[4].

This method depends on printing 4 cone shaped fiducial markers into models of widgets embedded into the sculpture. Vertices with negative local slope in every direction are labeled as lying on fiducial markers because cone tips have negative local slope in every direction. We group labeled vertices into widget placements by matching the distance between groups of markers against marker locations on each widget. Widget type and orientation are recovered from the groups of 4 markers. Finally, the scanned mesh is modified based on the widget types, locations and orientations. The printed housing can be combined with electronics to make an interactive prototype.

A key factor in saving designer time and effort is that if widget blanks fit in the sculpture then widget electronics and parts will fit in a housing with the same shape and size. This prevents sculpting a shape and placing widgets that later prove to be infeasible for the given shape.

Future advances in 3D scanning and printing technology will significantly improve this prototyping process. Scanning and printing sculpted prototypes require significant time and effort. Preparing hollowed out scans of sculptures in our example required about 30 minutes of focused effort over the course of an hour by an experienced user[5]. The housings in our examples required 8 to 12 hours each to print. The designer is free to do something else while they wait, but this adds time to the prototype iteration cycle.

There is no guarantee that the splitting plane found by our algorithm will result in an opening that allows electronics to be inserted into the housing. The algorithm worked well in all of our examples—even though designers were not told to consider the feasibility of splitting the housing for assembly. Several methods could be explored to ensure that the split allows assembly. The housing could be split with a curved surface that would allow more possibilities. The function for scoring candidate splits consider the size of the largest object that will through an opening rather than just the area of the opening. In some cases it may be necessary to split the housing into more than 2 pieces.

ACKNOWLEDGEMENTS

This work was supported by National Science Foundation grant IIS-1406578. David Brandt designed the widget set used in this paper.

REFERENCES

1. Akaoka, E., Ginn, T., Vertegaal, R., 2010. DisplayObjects: prototyping functional physical interfaces on 3d styrofoam, paper or cardboard models. In: Proceedings of the fourth international conference on Tangible, embedded, and embodied interaction. ACM, pp. 49–56.
2. Avrahami, D., Hudson, S. E., 2002. Forming interactivity: a tool for rapid prototyping of physical interactive products. In: Proceedings of the 4th conference on Designing interactive systems: processes, practices, methods, and techniques. ACM, pp. 141–146.
3. Block, F., Haller, M., Gellerson, H., Gutwin, C., and Billinghurst, M. 2008. VoodooSketch: Extending

[4] See www.rhino3d.com

[5] Using a NextEngine 3D Scanner HD with ScanStudio HD Pro software and netfabb Professional for repairing and hollowing out the mesh.

interactive surfaces with adaptable interface palettes. In Proceedings of the 2nd International Conference on Tangible and Embedded Interaction (TEI'08). ACM. pp. 55-58.

4. Follmer, S., Johnson, M., Adelson, E., and Ishii, H., 2011. deForm: an interactive malleable surface for capturing 2.5D arbitrary objects, tools and touch. In Proceedings of the 24th annual ACM symposium on User interface software and technology (UIST '11). ACM, New York, NY, USA, pp. 527-536.
5. Greenberg, S., Fitchett, C., 2001. Phidgets: easy development of physical interfaces through physical widgets. In: Proceedings of the 14th annual ACM symposium on User interface software and technology. ACM, pp. 209–218.
6. Hartmann, B., Klemmer, S. R., Bernstein, M., Abdulla, L., Burr, B., Robinson-Mosher, A., Gee, J., 2006. Reflective physical prototyping through integrated design, test, and analysis. In: Proceedings of the 19th annual ACM symposium on User interface software and technology. ACM, pp. 299–308.
7. Hudson, S. E., Mankoff, J., 2006. Rapid construction of functioning physical interfaces from cardboard, thumbtacks, tin foil and masking tape. In: Proceedings of the 19th annual ACM symposium on User interface software and technology. ACM, pp. 289–298.
8. Klemmer, S. Hartmann, B., and Takayama, L. 2006. How bodies matter: five themes for interaction design. In *Proceedings of the 6th conference on Designing Interactive systems* (DIS '06). ACM, New York, NY, USA, 140-149.
9. Lee, J., Avrahami, D., Hudson, S., Forlizzi, J., Dietz, P. and Leigh, D. "The Calder toolkit: wired and wireless components for rapidly prototyping interactive devices" in Processings of the 5th Conference of Designing Interactive Systems: Processes, Practices, Methods and Techniques. 2004. pp. 167-175.
10. Savage, V., Chang, C. and Hartmann, B. "Sauron: Embedded single-camera sensing of printed physical user interfaces" ACM Symposium on User Interface Software and Technology (UIST '13). 2013.
11. Savage, V., Follmer, S., Li, J., and Hargmann, B. 2015. Makers' Marks: Physical markup for designing and fabricating functional objects. In: Proceedings of the 28th Annual Symposium on User Interface Software and Technology (UIST'15). ACM. pp. 103-108.
12. Savage, V., Head, A., Hartmann, B., Goldman, D. B., Mysore, G., Li, W., 2015. Lamello: Passive acoustic sensing for tangible input components. In: Proceedings of the 33rd Annual ACM Conference on Human Factors in Computing Systems. ACM, pp. 1277–1280.
13. Shön, E. 1984. The Reflective Practitioner: How Professionals Think in Action. Basic Books.
14. Vázquez, M., Brockmeyer, E., Desai, R., Harrison, C., Hudson, S. E., 2015. 3d printing pneumatic device controls with variable activation force capabilities. In: Proceedings of the 33rd Annual ACM Conference on Human Factors in Computing Systems. ACM, pp. 1295–1304.
15. Villar, N., Scott, J., Hodges, S., Hammil, K., Miller, C., 2012. .net gadgeteer: a platform for custom devices. In: Pervasive Computing. Springer, pp. 216–233.

On-The-Fly Print: Incremental Printing While Modeling

Huaishu Peng, Rundong Wu, Steve Marschner, François Guimbretière
Computing and Information Science
Cornell University
{hp356, rw489}@cornell.edu, {srm, francois}@cs.cornell.edu

ABSTRACT

Current interactive fabrication tools offer tangible feedback by allowing users to work directly on the physical model, but they are slow because users need to participate in the physical instantiation of their designs. In contrast, CAD software offers powerful tools for 3D modeling but delays access to the physical workpiece until the end of the design process.

In this paper we propose *On-the-Fly Print*: a 3D modeling approach that allows the user to design 3D models digitally while having a low-fidelity physical wireframe model printed in parallel. Our software starts printing features as soon as they are created and updates the physical model as needed. Users can quickly check the design in a real usage context by removing the partial physical print from the printer and replacing it afterwards to continue printing. Digital content modification can be updated with quick physical correction using a retractable cutting blade. We present the detailed description of *On-the-Fly Print* and showcase several examples designed and printed with our system.

Author Keywords
3D printing; fabrication; computational craft; CAD; rapid prototyping; interactive devices.

ACM Classification Keywords
H.5.m. Information interfaces and presentation (e.g., HCI): User Interfaces.

INTRODUCTION

Since the notion of interactive fabrication was introduced by Willis et al. [32], several approaches have been proposed for hands-on digital fabrication. For example, Constructable [17] allows the step-by-step fabrication of functional objects using a laser cutter controlled by a laser pointer; D-Coil [19] enables non-experts to design 3D digital models from scratch using a digitally controlled wax extruder; ReForm [31] merges manual shaping with digital milling and extrusion of synthetic clay. On the one hand, these interactive fabrication systems offer immediate, tangible feedback that can benefit

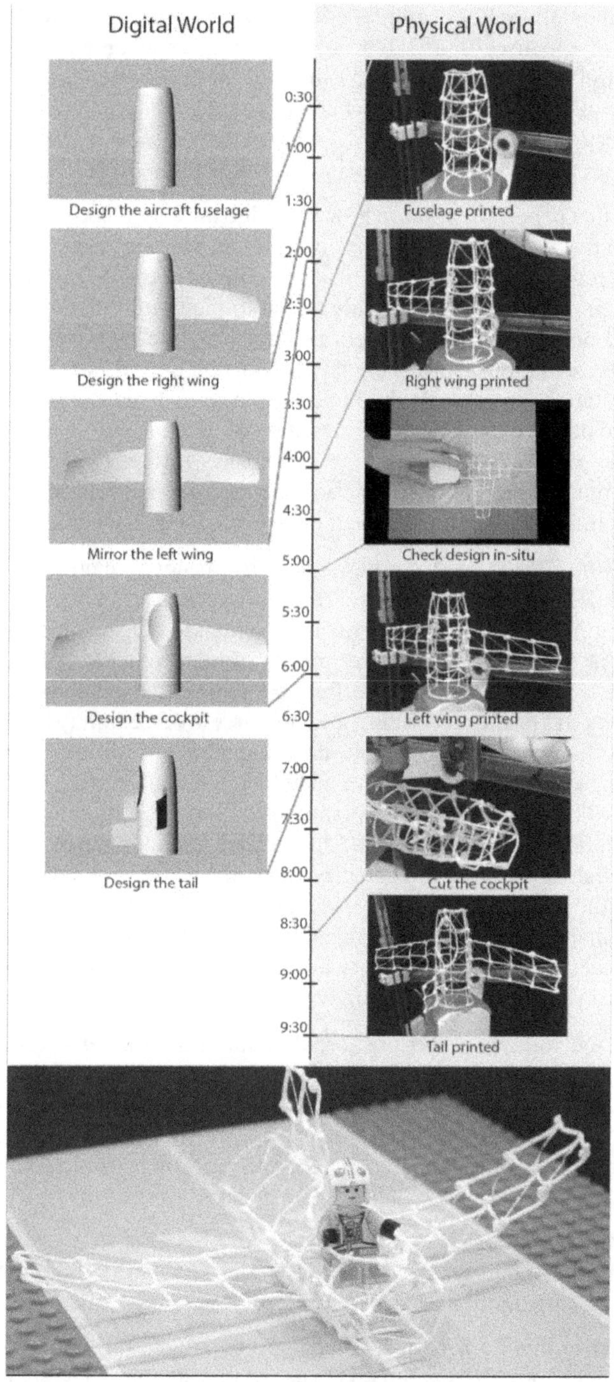

Figure 1: Designing an aircraft model with On-the-Fly Print in 10 minutes.

CHI'16, May 07-12, 2016, San Jose, CA, USA
© 2016 ACM. ISBN 978-1-4503-3362-7/16/05...$15.00
DOI: http://dx.doi.org/10.1145/2858036.2858106

the design process; on the other hand, they are often slow because designers have to instantiate the physical model themselves. Further, CAD users might find them frustrating to use because they lack support for implicit 3D commands (such as construction solid geometry and complex surface creation), which are difficult to implement in interactive fabrication systems.

At the same time, there has been a push to reduce the lead-time between the creation of a 3D model and its actual instantiation. For example, faBrickation [18] and Platener [2] limit the use of a 3D printer to complex geometry, and WirePrint [16] creates a low-fidelity mesh representation of the model. All these approaches serve the traditional "design-fabricate-refine" workflow, which is common in digital fabrication, and focus on printing completed models.

In this paper, we explore how to bridge these two approaches using *On-the-Fly Print*. In our system, printing takes place incrementally, in parallel with the use of the CAD system (Figure 1). As primitives are added to the digital model, our 3D printer instantiates them using a low-fidelity wireframe representation. During the creation of the digital model, the designer can remove the building platform from the printer and observe the model in the context of its future use. She can then return the model to the printer and further modify the digital model as needed while the printer synchronizes modifications to the physical model.

On-the-Fly Print relies on a faster, incremental implementation of the WirePrint [16] system. To speed up the original system up to four times, we extended the reach of the print head and added water mist cooling to quickly solidify the extruded filament. We further modified an off-the-shelf delta 3D printer by adding a two-degree-of-freedom (2DOF) rotation platform to enable incremental prints from a wide range of angles. Finally, we added a retractable cutting blade to allow for subtractive operations and error correction. The printer is controlled by a customized Rhino plug-in [20], which observes the geometry created by the user and can optimize the printing schedule and resolve possible printing collisions to maximize printability. If unsolvable collision is detected, our system can leave parts unprinted, but it will never prevent the user from creating the desired geometry.

In the following sections, we illustrate how the *On-the-Fly Print* could provide CAD designers with tangible feedback during the creation of a digital model (Figure 1). We present a detailed description of our system. We conclude with limitations of our current system and propose possible future directions.

RELATED WORK

Our work builds upon the notions of interactive fabrication, fast fabrication, and hybrid fabrication systems.

Interactive Fabrication

ModelCraft [26] examined the use of pen annotation to create precise 3D digital models with in-situ measurements, but the modifications stayed virtual until the next 3D print cycle. CopyCAD [7] enables a user to remix designs by interacting with and using real world objects. Inspired by traditional craft activities, Willis et al. [32] introduced the concept of interactive fabrication, mixing the hands-on approach of craft with the advantages of digital construction. This concept has been instantiated by several systems. Constructable [17] supports interactive 2D laser cutting for functional objects. Rivers et al. [22] use a digitally controlled 2D router for better cutting precision. FreeD [33, 34] lets users personalize the rendering of a 3D model using a digitally controlled milling tool, and D-Coil [19] uses digitally controlled wax extrusion and cutting to blend digital and physical creation of a model. ReForm [31] combines direct hand shaping, digital extrusion and milling to provide the maximum flexibility to users. Like Constructable, D-Coil and ReForm, our goal is to offer a readily available physical instantiation of the digital model *during* the design process. However, we specifically target CAD users who might not be interested in directly participating in the physical creation their model and prefer that a fast 3D printer create a low-fidelity prototype of the current digital model for them.

Fast Fabrication

The availability of fast prototypes is another approach to a more interactive fabrication process. To this end, several solutions have been proposed by printing with a low-fidelity model. faBrickation [18] replaces most of the building volume with Lego bricks with only the detailed parts being 3D printed. Platener [2] follows a similar path with laser cut sheets being used to create the bulk of the volume, while 3D printed parts are used for complex shapes. One drawback of both approaches is that they require assembly. WirePrint [16], in contrast, saves significant time in 3D printing by printing only a mesh of the shell of the prototype. *On-the-Fly Print* relies on an optimized version of WirePrint for fast and incremental printing. Thus, it provides users with ongoing access to a physical copy of their design while it is being created in the digital realm.

Finally, Carbon3D [30] provides CLIP printing that is 25 to 100 times faster than traditional printing techniques. This hints at a not-too-distant future when there will be reduced trade-offs between speed and quality of rendering. This system is not incremental, however, which might create a large overhead in material and time.

Hybrid and Augmented Fabrication

High DOF CNC machines have been in use in industrial contexts for a long time (e.g., to create complex carbon fiber shapes or in subtractive fabrication). Mataerial [14] introduced a robot arm to create complex 3D shapes, and Song et al. [27] demonstrated a parallel kinematic machine for conformal printing. Gao et al. [8] showed how electronics can be embedded into a 3D print with a rotational cuboidal platform. MultiFab [25] demonstrated vision based approaches for printing on existing objects with multiple materials. To save 3D material and eliminate reprint, Teibrich et al. [29] illustrated a system to patch 3D printed objects using a 3+2 DOF printer. To enhance 3D printed object, Shi et al. [24] introduced a labeling toolkit that can add audio with 3D printed features. Encore [5] allowed the user to augment physical object with printed attachment. Like these systems, *On-the-Fly Print* explores how one could extend the pattern of use of 3D printing in design practice by combining additive and subtractive methods with a 5DOF motion platform. Our system is unique in that it focuses specifically on how to print a low fidelity physical model in parallel with the creation of the digital model.

DESIGN GOAL

Our main design goal with *On-the-Fly Print* is to provide CAD users with a tangible preview of their digital model during the digital design process. To illustrate a typical interaction, we consider the case of a user designing an aircraft model compatible with a Lego airport runway set (Figure 1). After measuring a standard Lego airport size, the user starts the design of the aircraft fuselage in Rhino. The system starts printing the fuselage automatically after the geometry is finalized. As this happens, the designer moves on to specify the right wing using a curved design. She then mirrors the first wing to create the left wing. About 2 minutes later, the first wing is printed and she pauses the printer to remove the model and check if the proportion of the wing matches the Lego runway. Satisfied with the proportion of the design, she puts the model back into the printer and focuses on the design of the cockpit while the printer resumes printing. Her goal is to fit a Lego pilot inside the model. She creates cutting geometry to open a hole in the fuselage, and finally adds a tail. Within 3 minutes of her last addition, she has a finished WirePrint model in her hand (Figure 1), which has already been evaluated in-situ at key design steps. As pointed out by Buxton in the context of interface design [3], this ability to quickly check a design against its intended pattern of use significantly enhances the quality of the final design.

The workflow illustrated above is made possible by the design of a fast incremental WirePrint printer, together with a Rhino plugin that generates the proper printing instructions for each new feature. Our plugin also controls the order in which each feature is executed to limit possible conflicts during the construction process. We now present both aspects in more detail.

Figure 2: Print head design with extended extruder tip and mist cooling sprays.

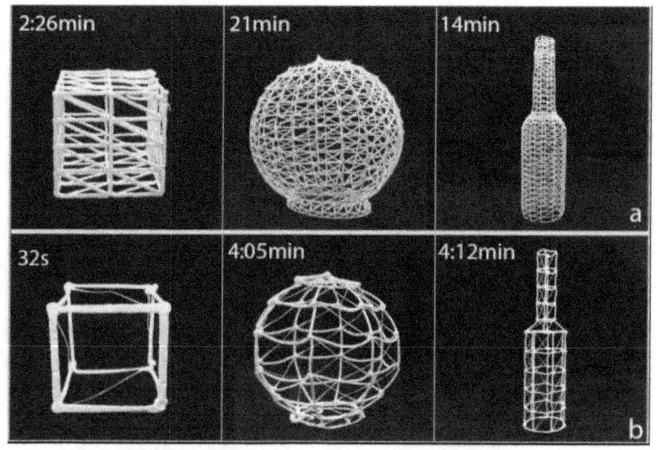

Figure 3: Speed comparison between the original WirePrint (a) and On-the-Fly Print (b).

HARDWARE: FAST AND INCREMENTAL 3D PRINTER

One key prerequisite of *On-the-Fly Print* is the ability to print basic primitives very quickly to catch up with the design of the digital model. In this regard, WirePrint [16] was a natural starting point. We noted that the speed of WirePrint could be increased significantly if one were to reduce the total number of cells to be printed by increasing their size. To do so, we modified the print head with an extended extruder tip to reach deeper into the model without collisions. To maintain the stiffness of the model we also modified the extruder tip to create a thicker (1mm) strand of ABS. One of the drawbacks of creating a thicker filament is longer cooling time. To minimize the need for cooling pauses, we added mist cooling to our system by placing two atomizing nozzles flanking the print head (Figure 2). Together, these modifications allowed us to print a 28 x 28 x 28 mm wireframe cell in 32 seconds as compared to 2:26min reported in the original WirePrint paper (Figure 3). We conducted similar comparisons for two additional models presented in the original WirePrint paper (Figure 3). Our modifications increased speed by a factor of 4.6, 5.1 and 3.3 respectively.

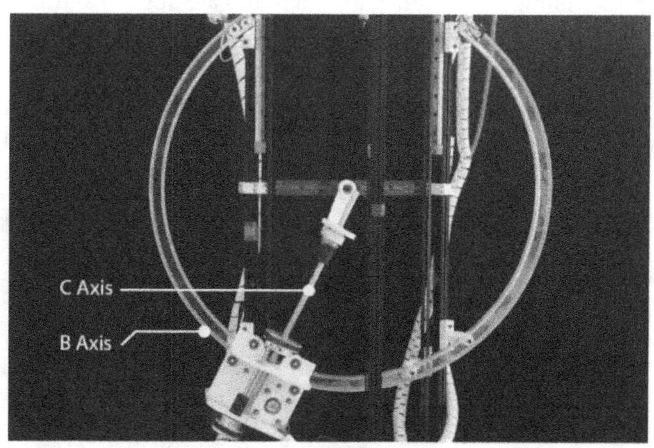

Figure 4: 5DOF add-on design to an off-the-shelf Delta 3D printer.

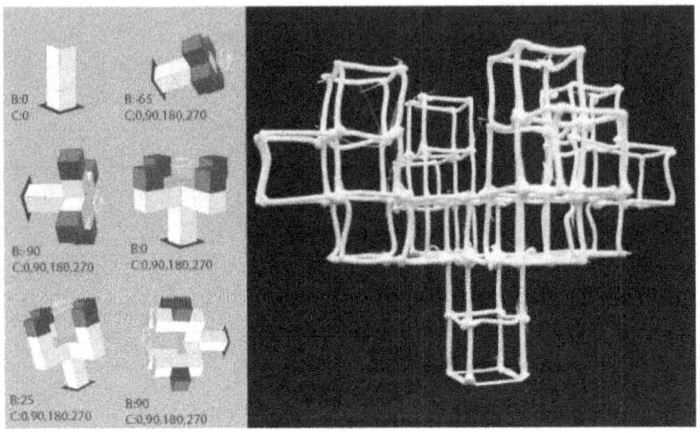

Figure 5: Calibration results. Cubes are printed at the various poses shown at left, yet are properly aligned.

Incremental Printing

Coupling 3D printing and the CAD design process requires the ability to print incrementally to avoid reprinting a model from scratch every time it is modified. Because modifications may affect all parts of the model, not just the easily accessible top, we added two rotational degrees of freedom to an off-the-shelf delta printer, with a B axis (rotating around the Y axis) and a C axis (rotating around the Z axis) (Figure 4). Compared to previous 5 DOF designs [29, 31], our design creates a large open space around the model to ensure easy access for the print head. Further, we used a fully synchronous 6DOF system (5DOF for motion and 1DOF for extrusion) so that instead of printing and cutting in a layer-based manner, we achieve conformal printing and cutting, which offers better physical rendering and quicker cut operations.

Our system is designed with the aim of affordable hardware setup and large open space. Thus, to create robust prints we pay particular attention to the calibration of the rotation platform using a computer vision calibration method [12]. This approach reaches an RMS positioning error of 0.5mm, which is sufficiently small compared to our 1mm diameter nozzle. To demonstrate our calibration results, we show a model with multiple stacked cubes printed from different angles in Figure 5. Notice that all nodes are aligned and well connected. We provide more details in the implementation section.

Cutting Operations

To let the user correct mistakes, adjust geometry and perform subtractive operations, we include a cutting tool in our system.

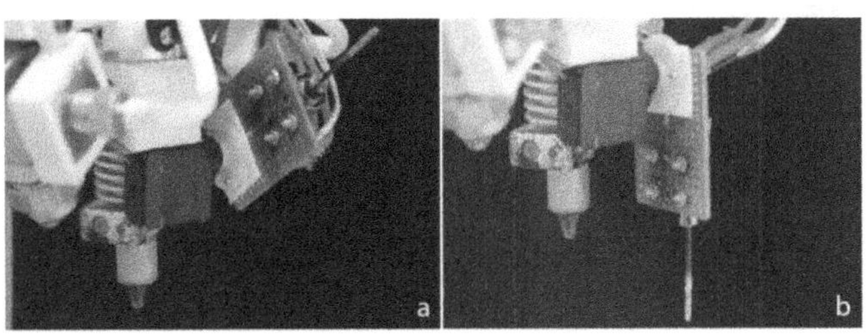

Figure 6: The cutting blade tucks away during the printing process and extends out during cutting.

We first considered using a milling head [29, 31], but this approach is problematic because milling arrangements are heavy and occupy a lot of volume, which could significantly limit the accessibility of the cutting tool. Instead we found that the wireframe shell can be cut using a simple heated blade. Our blade is actuated so it can be tucked away when not in use (Figure 6). When cutting is needed, the blade is moved to the cutting position, which is 15mm lower than the extruder tip to leave as much clearance as possible. This solution is also faster than having to load a new tool.

Moving the Printed Model In and Out of the Printer

As illustrated in the scenario above, to get full advantage of our system, the user should be able to easily remove the model from the printer to compare against real-world constraints and return it later to continue the design. To this end, our system includes a simple removable building platform aligned by a set of magnets.

SOFTWARE

The main goal of the software plugin is to convert the geometry created inside Rhino into a set of printer commands (G-code) suitable for efficient printing. For additive operations, this includes creating a mesh for the shape to be added as well as any connecting structure necessary; for subtractive operations and corrections, this includes converting the input into a cut operation and then creating any repairs necessary. Another important aspect of the plugin is to optimize the print operations to maximize printability without distracting the user. In the following, we first present the basic additive and subtractive approaches, before presenting how they can be modified to take into account print head accessibility.

Additive Geometry

In typical use, the plugin tracks the creation of geometry to decide when a new feature is ready for printing. More specifically, we consider a new feature for printing if it has not been modified for 5s and either lands on the printing platform or is connected with previously printed geometry. For example, in Figure 7, it is only when the sphere is

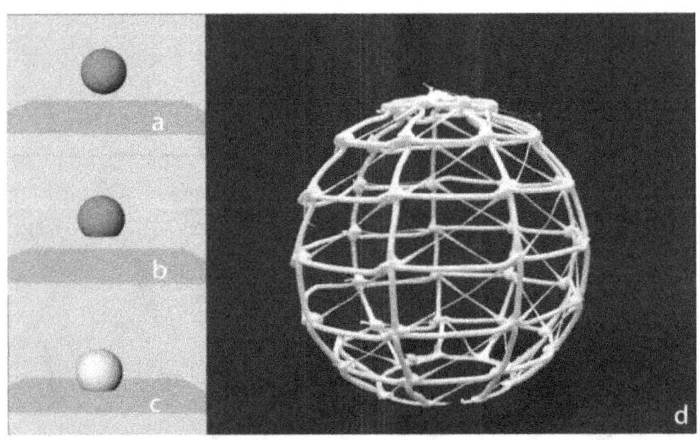

Figure 7: Criteria to commence physical printing. Printing (d) won't start until the digital model intersects with the building plane (a, b, c). Red (a, b) is color coded as unprinted part.

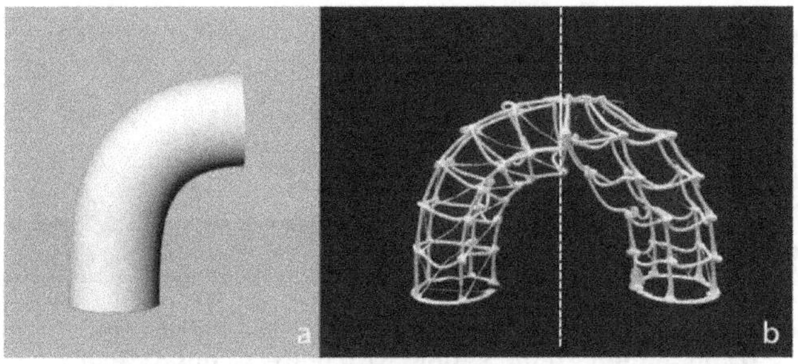

Figure 8: (a): A digital tube model, (b): the model sliced based on UV mapping (left) and traditional parallel slicing (right).

truncated and made to intersect with the building plane that printing starts. Once a new feature is ready to be printed, the plugin uses the UV mapping associated with the feature surface to generate a regular mesh. As shown in Figure 8, using UV coordinates better conveys the structure of the shape when printed in large cells. As UV mapping may lead to non-parallel slicing, our printer rotates the model to extrude upward. The resulting G-code is sent to the printer, which in turn sends an acknowledgement upon completion.

Creating connecting patches

We are using large print cells to speed up the printing process, but this leaves large gaps in the external surface of the object. If new geometry is to be created at the location of a gap, we first need to patch the surface. With speed in mind, we implement this by sub-dividing the patch area and printing the corresponding denser pattern. Because each printed segment rests on an established boundary, this printing is very fast and does not require cooling (Figure 9).

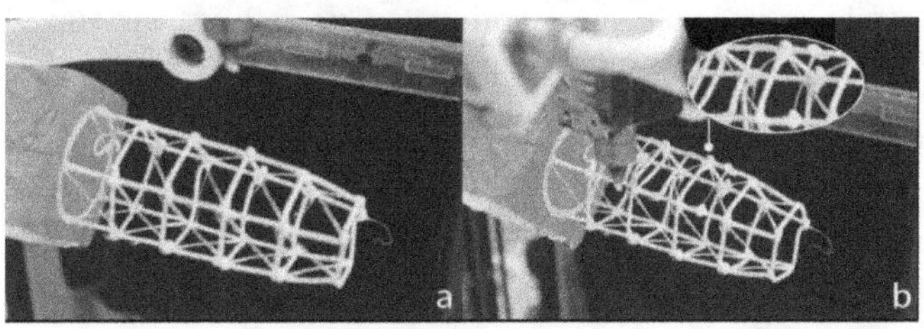

Figure 9: Creating a connecting patch for the wing.

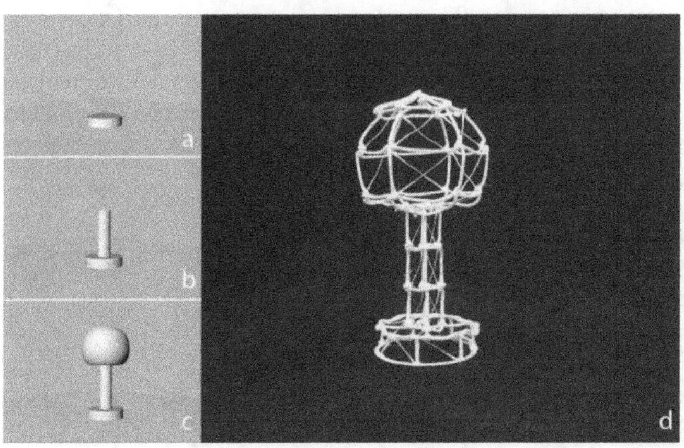

Figure 10: The system accommodates overhang by extending from the contacting curve to the new contour.

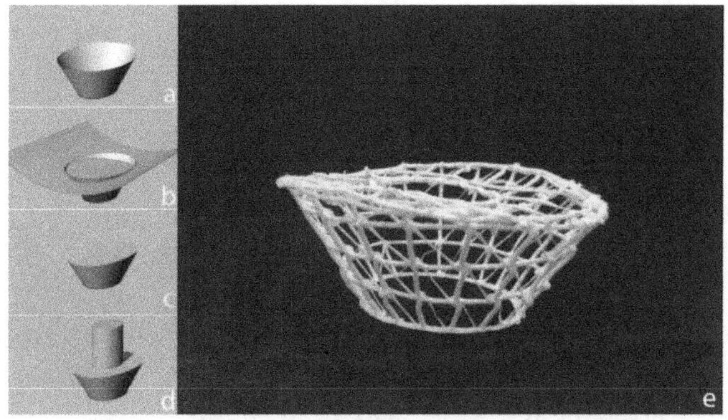

Figure 11: The Bird Nest stadium showing complex cut patching. Green (b, d) is color coded as the cutting geometry.

Another important case to consider is when incremental components create overhangs, such as in the model of the Jucker and Wagenfeld lamp shown in Figure 10. In that case we create a mesh extending from the top surface of the base to the bottom contour of the shade to provide support. A similar approach is used when the design object is bigger than our printing plate. The dinosaur shown in Figure 14a is an example of such a case.

Subtractive Geometry

Our system uses cutting surfaces to carry out cutting operations. Once the user has created the cutting geometry, we compute the intersection curve between the original object and the cutting geometry. This curve is then used to drive the cutting blade. With the help of the rotating platform, the cutting blade is maintained in an orientation normal to the object's surface and the cut is performed with all 5DOF moving synchronously. Once the cut is completed, the print head follows the same contour to "heal" the edge of the cut. This step is necessary because we are using a mesh representation of the model. We then generate the mesh necessary to close any holes as required by the user. In the Bird's Nest stadium example shown in Figure 11, the printer first cuts the tapered geometry (a) and creates a curved patch (b) before creating a new cut in the center (c).

As in the case of additive geometry, when a new cut feature is smaller than the size of the mesh cells, our system can create a supporting patch before performing the cut. We show an example of this feature in Figure 12.

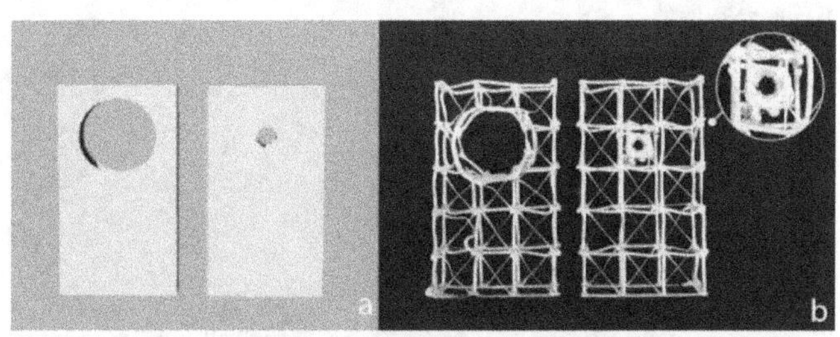

Figure 12: Adding holes to a model. When the hole is much smaller than the cell, we first create a supporting patch.

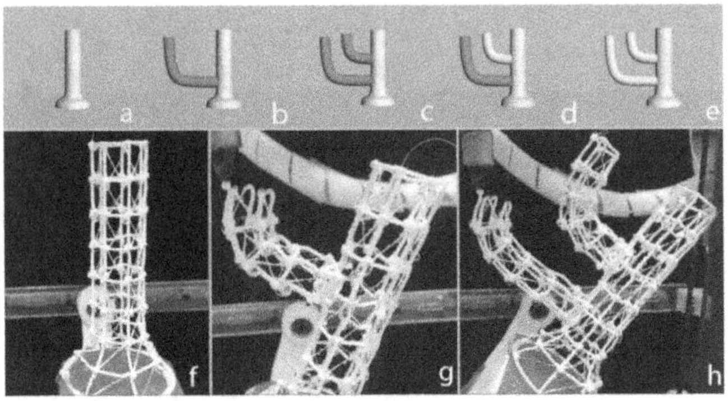

Figure 13: Reordering. The user designs the bottom branch first (b) and the top branch later (c). Noticing that the print of the bottom branch will block the way for printing the top branch, the system reorders the print sequence (g, h).

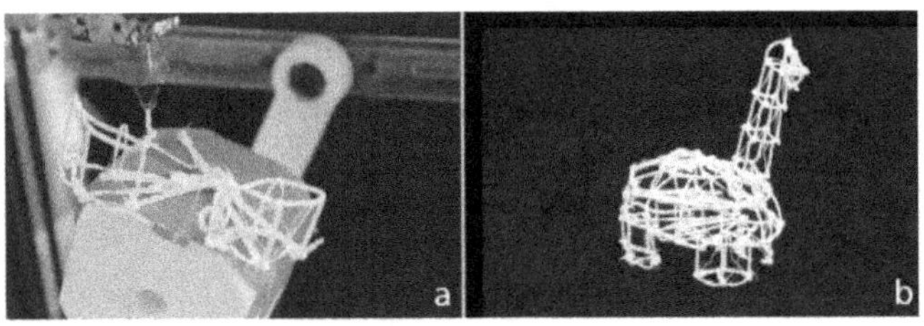

Figure 14: Dinosaur legs are printed at an angle to avoid collision.

Dealing with Collisions

So far, our presentation has ignored the problems caused by collisions. As explained above, our printer was designed from the start to provide maximum tool accessibility, yet it is to be expected that some design sequences will create conflicts between the existing model and the added geometry. We now present how our system uses a staged approach, focusing on early prevention of collisions, to deal with these conflicts.

Out of order printing

Our first step is to explore whether re-ordering the pending primitives will improve printability. This is possible because the printer often lags behind the user's actions. To do so, before printing any new primitive we first observe the queue of pending operations. We compute the possible printing orders and chose the one with the least printing conflicts. For example, in the candelabra shown in Figure 13, the user creates the branches from bottom to top, but we detect that printing the bottom part first will interfere with printing the top branch, so our system prints them from top to bottom instead to limit conflicts. To allow users to easily monitor the progress of the system, features that are delayed in this way can be color coded in red on the screen.

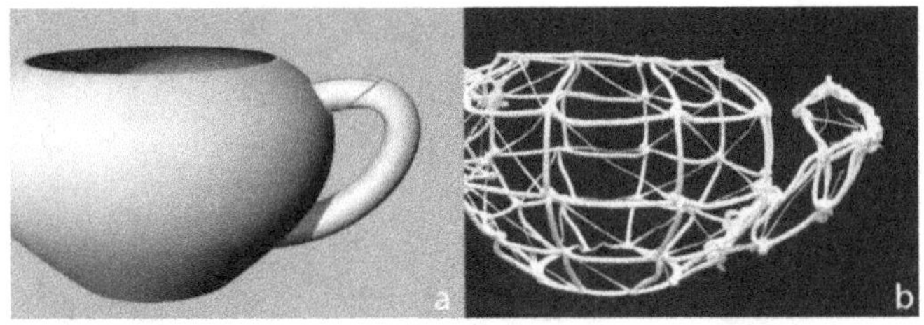

Figure 15: Example of omitted details. Printing the teapot handle would collide with body, so our system omits the part that would cause collisions and prints the rest.

Relaxing printing orientation

Our second approach is to relax the printing orientation using collision detection, similar to [29]. As a default, our system will orient the model so that printing proceeds upward. If this causes a conflict, we will try to repose the object to avoid collision. One example of this approach can be seen in Figure 14, where the system prints the body of the dinosaur sideways to prevent collision between the print head and the previously printed legs. More details about the algorithm are provided in the implementation section.

Omitting geometry

If it is still not possible to print a full feature after sampling different orientations, the system will attempt to print as much of the new feature as possible, leaving the parts that would cause collisions unprinted. This reflects our aim to provide a low-resolution overview of the model as it is designed with minimum distraction to the user's workflow. For example, when creating the handle of the teapot shown in Figure 15, part of the handle is not printed because it is not reachable. Similarly, the system will not attempt to print the walls of the holes shown in Figure 12.

Pause and manual mode

So far, we have described the system working in fully automatic mode. This mode generates a corresponding physical model in parallel to the digital design process. During the design process, the user can also postpone the physical instantiation using a *Pause* command. This allows

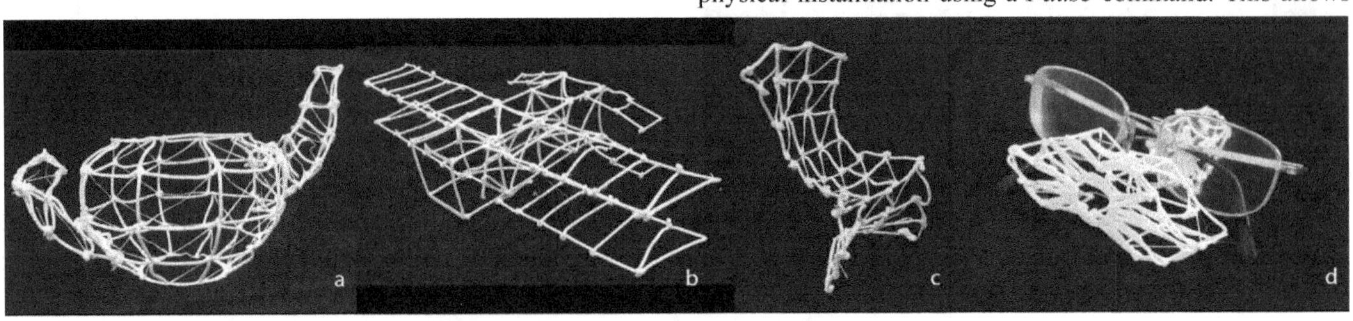

Figure 16: Printing samples. (a): tea pot created printed in 3 steps; (b): Wright brothers' airplane printed in 9 steps; (c): Panton's stacking side chair designed using a loft operation; (d): glasses holder printed in 3 steps.

the user to quickly try several designs in the digital realm without worrying about printability or the physical costs of updates. When printing is resumed, queued primitives may also provide opportunities to our scheduling algorithm to reorder parts for better printability. Finally, if the user would like to have full control of the printing process, our software offers a *Manual* mode. In this mode, the software only prints the primitives that are manually selected by the user.

Further Examples
In Figure 16 we show several examples of models created with our system, including a teapot, a model of the Wright brother's airplane, a chair inspired by Panton's stacking side chair created using a loft operation, and a glasses holder larger than the build platform.

IMPLEMENTATION
Our system has two main components: a custom-built 5DOF printer and a Rhino plugin that processes the geometry and generates the G-code to control the printer. The systems communicate through a job queue, with a notification from the printer to the Rhino plugin to indicate when a job has been completed. Our plug-in was designed to limit user distraction to a minimum. It adds a simple set of controls to the Rhino screen to let the user pause the system, visualize the actual meshing and control the mesh cell size, among other functions. It uses color coding to provide feedback about the state of the print.

Printer Modification
Our Mini Kossel [15] delta printer is driven by a Beagle Bone Black [1] connected to a CRAMPS 2.0 module [6]. It is running LinuxCNC [11] modified to support a 6DOF (5DOF motion and 1DOF extrusion) system.

Extruder
As shown in Figure 2, we modified the standard hot end assembly by adding a 15mm pipe adaptor to extend its reach. The chamber of the extrusion head is kept at 270C to speed up the extrusion of our 1mm filament. We also added two SU11 atomizer nozzles [28], one on each side, to create a mist that rapidly cools the extruded material. In our current prototype, curves in the U direction are printed without cooling to guarantee a firm connection between layers. As a result, the curvature of U might not be preserved as accurately.

Cutter
The cutter (Figure 6) was created by adapting a heating cartridge [9] and a thermistor to fit a cutting blade [13]. The assembly is attached to a small servomotor so that it can be raised when not in use. The cutter's heating cartridge is maintained at 350C so that the cutting tip can easily cut 1mm thick ABS wires.

5 DOF extension
Our prototype uses a circular rail of 260mm radius for the B axis, so as to maximize the accessible print volume. To lower cost, this rail is made of two 6mm-thick acrylic layers glued together to create a butterfly profile. The range of motion is +/– 120°. The C axis can rotate indefinitely. To accommodate the circular rail, we extended the height of the printer by changing the support rails. Our setup is inexpensive and relies only on easily fabricated parts in the spirit of the Mini Kossel design, yet, with the proper calibration, it has enough precision for fast and incremental WirePrint.

Calibration
Our printer was designed for maximum printhead accessibility with affordable hardware setup. As a result, small construction errors adds up during the printing. Our computer vision based calibration system guarantees good accuracy with simple "maker" grade assembly. Two stationary cameras on the side of the machine capture images of a cube placed on the platform for 114 combinations of B and C angles. The OpenCV calibration program [4] recognizes checkerboards attached to five sides of the cube and computes an initial estimate of the intrinsics and extrinsics of the camera-checkerboard system. Given those estimates as input, we used Caliber [12] to recover the exact poses of the platform at the corresponding angles.

With these samples, we can then interpolate the data to predict the pose of the platform given an arbitrary combination of B and C angles. We model the B axis rotation as rigid body motion and fit a circle to the translational part of the pose samples. Then we interpolate the deviation from the best-fit circle to obtain the translation given an arbitrary B angle. We use spherical linear interpolation to obtain the rotational part. The motion of the C axis is well modeled as a rotation, so we only need to solve for the unknown rotation axis using the calibration data.

Key Aspects of Software
Here we present the key features of our Rhino plugin.

UV Mesh and Patch Generation
As a spline-based modelling tool, Rhino offers built-in APIs [21] to generate UV maps. For a given primitive, our plugin first calls the Surface.IsoCurve() function to create a reference V contour. It then samples equally spaced points along this V contour to generate all U contours for printing. The plugin then picks one U contour as the reference to create all V contours for printing.

The connection patches are generated by a similar method. To patch an area, the plugin finds the boundary of the area, sub-samples it to create new V and U lines, and prints accordingly.

Collision Detection and Out of Order Printing
To detect collisions and relax printing orientation, the system positions a built-in extruder model at each of the (U, V) nodes along the primitive mesh and uses the Brep.IsPointInside() function to check for a collision. If a collision is detected at a given node, the system will move the extruder to different orientations until a collision free direction is found (or it decides not to print the edge). Orientations are sampled on a fixed grid over the hemisphere.

A similar method is used to implement out-of-order printing. Given the list of pending primitives, the plugin first

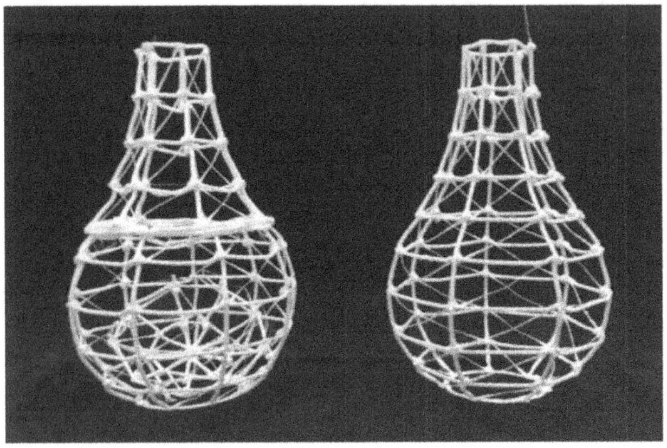

Figure 17: The same vase created in CAD in a multi-step approach (left) versus a single-step approach (right) results different physical appearances. On the left, the top section of the sphere felt into the model during the cutting process.

enumerates all possible printing orders. For each order, it uses collision detection to evaluate the printability (with high printability assigned to the case when the extruder tip doesn't need to be repositioned). The system then picks the highest printability order to print. This computation might take up to a couple of seconds in our non-optimized implementation, but it happens in the background so it has little impact for the user.

DISCUSSION AND FUTURE WORK

The prototype described above illustrates the potential of *On-the-Fly Print* for providing CAD users with a quick tangible feedback on their design. We now consider some aspects of the current prototype that warrant further research efforts.

Printability, Limitation and Future Improvement

A main objective of our system was to limit user involvement during printing. To do so, *On-the-Fly Print* implements a "*best-effort printing*" policy based on limited information about the final shape of the model. We never prevent the user from creating geometry, but we might leave some parts unprinted. Printability or even final results will therefore depend on the steps by which a model is created. As an example, Figure 17 shows the same vase created either in a stepwise modification of a sphere or in a single step via revolution of a profile; each ends up with a different physical rendering.

Similarly, some operations like *Scale* or *Move*, might be costlier than others because they will require the selected features to be reprinted physically. The worst case is a global rescale, which will require restarting from scratch. This costs more time than other operations, but might not be a big issue given the fast printing speed. However, field deployment will be needed to better understand the impact of this and how people approach the design of complex objects with our system.

We should also note that our current printing strategy, which proceeds in a fixed sequence dictated by the UV mapping, makes it difficult to print certain topologies such as a torus (Figure 15). Inner details created after the bulk of the object has been created will also be ignored (or will require a full reprint).

Future Improvement

Currently, our approach stops short of using the cutting tool to selectively remove the part of the model that is in the way of the print head. Instead, new features conflicting with the current model are marked as pending and might never be printed as part of the preview. We envision that making use of the cutting capability would further improve printability. We foresee two general approaches: First, the system could identify which features need to be cut away and returned to the print queue to be reprinted in a different order. Second, the system could identify the minimal flat cut across the model making printing possible and proceed using a standard WirePrint slicing.

Our current implementation does not check for cut-off parts falling into the geometry. For example, in Figure 17 left, the top hemisphere falls into the printed body after the cut operation (but doesn't cause a printing problem). However, several options could solve this as a future improvement. 1) The system could pose the print so that the cut part does not fall inside; 2) The system could pour and shake the cut part out using the rotation platform after cutting (but it might get stuck); 3) The system could pause the print to let the user remove the part if needed.

Finally, our current implementation ignores collisions during cut operations. This has not been a problem in our sample cases, but a complete system would implement this feature using similar approaches as for adding geometry.

Low Resolution Printing

To enable fast preview, we traded speed for accuracy using an extension of the WirePrint method. In the early stages of the design process, the low resolution of the resulting models is not a concern. In fact, low-fidelity models could be a benefit because they clearly communicate to viewers that the design is not finished, but is a sketch to be critiqued [23]. However, low print resolution can become a problem later on when users want to add more details to a design. Like in WirePrint, one solution could be to let users balance the speed/resolution trade-off by giving them the option to incrementally render accurate shells on specific areas of interest. Because our printer is conformal this will not always require a full reprint, as in the case of the original WirePrint implementation. However, it may require a redesign of the cutting mechanism. New printing approaches such as Carbon3D [30] might soon reduce the need for such trade-offs.

High Degree of Freedom Printers

This project and others like the Patching paper [29] are accumulating evidence that adding a rotating platform to the more standard 3D printer might significantly improve the flexibility of these systems when it comes to extending the way they could be used in practice. Both systems demonstrate that the benefits might be worth the extra cost.

Interactive Versus On-the-Fly Print

One of the most interesting aspects of this work is that it makes it possible to empirically study several important questions including: 1) When will users prefer interactive printing over *On-the-Fly Print*? 2) How might both approaches change the way people create digital models? 3) Will either approach bring a more reflective practice to the design of digital models? Traditionally, reflective practice has focused on lower fidelity techniques such as sketching [3], but we believe that the progress in CAD tools and better tangible feedback might change this. We are planning to conduct empirical studies exploring these questions in more detail.

CONCLUSION

In this paper we present *On-the-Fly Print*, a system bridging the gap between hands-on interactive fabrication and purely digital modeling practice. To do so, *On-the-Fly Print* creates low-fidelity physical sketches in parallel with the creation of the corresponding digital model. Throughout the 3D modeling process, the user can hold the physical print in hand to gather tangible feedback and evaluate its fit with external constraints.

As the user creates new features in our CAD software, our system automatically creates a WirePrint representation and sends it to our fast 5DOF printer. Our system can handle both additive and subtractive operations and is designed to minimize the impact of possible interference between the print head and the existing model. We demonstrated how the system can handle a wide variety of shapes and described the limitation of the current implementation as well as ways to limit their impact.

On-the-Fly Print lets CAD users have continuous access to a low-fidelity representation of their design. We believe that this approach has the potential to improve the overall quality of the design process.

ACKNOWLEDGEMENTS

This work was supported in part by NSF Awards IIS-1422106 and IIS-1011919 and by Autodesk Corporation. We thank Corinna Loeckenhoff and Ge Gao for their assistance and the anonymous reviewers for their valuable comments.

REFERENCES

1. Beagle Bone Black. Retrieved Dec 24, 2015 from http://beagleboard.org/BLACK
2. Dustin Beyer, Serafima Gurevich, Stefanie Mueller, Hsiang-Ting Chen, and Patrick Baudisch. 2015. Platener: Low-Fidelity Fabrication of 3D Objects by Substituting 3D Print with Laser-Cut Plates. In *Proceedings of the 33rd Annual ACM Conference on Human Factors in Computing Systems* (CHI '15), 1799-1806. http://dx.doi.org/10.1145/2702123.2702225
3. Bill Buxton. 2010. *Sketching user experiences: getting the design right and the right design: getting the design right and the right design*. Morgan Kaufmann.
4. Camera Calibration with OpenCV. Retrieved Dec 24, 2015 from http://docs.opencv.org/doc/tutorials/calib3d/camera_calibration/camera_calibration.html
5. Xiang 'Anthony' Chen, Stelian Coros, Jennifer Mankoff, and Scott E. Hudson. 2015. Encore: 3D Printed Augmentation of Everyday Objects with Printed-Over, Affixed and Interlocked Attachments. In *Proceedings of the 28th Annual ACM Symposium on User Interface Software & Technology* (UIST '15), 73-82. http://dx.doi.org/10.1145/2807442.2807498
6. CRAMPS 2.0. Retrieved Dec 24, 2015 from http://reprap.org/wiki/CRAMPS
7. Sean Follmer, David Carr, Emily Lovell, and Hiroshi Ishii. 2010. CopyCAD: remixing physical objects with copy and paste from the real world. In *Adjunct proceedings of the 23nd annual ACM symposium on User interface software and technology* (UIST '10), 381-382. http://dx.doi.org/10.1145/1866218.1866230
8. Wei Gao, Yunbo Zhang, Diogo C. Nazzetta, Karthik Ramani, and Raymond J. Cipra. 2015. RevoMaker: Enabling Multi-directional and Functionally-embedded 3D printing using a Rotational Cuboidal Platform. In *Proceedings of the 28th Annual ACM Symposium on User Interface Software & Technology* (UIST '15), 437-446. http://dx.doi.org/10.1145/2807442.2807476
9. Heating Cartridge. Retrieved Dec 24, 2015 from www.makergeeks.com/cecahefor3dp.html
10. Joong Han Lee. Haptic Intelligentsia. Retrieved Dec 24, 2015 from http://studio-homunculus.com
11. LinuxCNC. Retrieved Dec 24, 2015 from http://www.linuxcnc.org
12. Albert Liu, Steve Marschner, Noah Snavely. 2015. Caliber: Camera Localization and Calibration Using Rigidity Constraints. *International Journal of Computer Vision*, pp.1-21. http://dx.doi.org/10.1007/s11263-015-0866-1
13. Master Appliance. Retrieved Dec 24, 2015 from https://www.masterappliance.com/content/35407-tip-assortment-kit-5-tips-1-adaptor
14. Mataerial. Retrieved Dec 24, 2015 from http://www.mataerial.com
15. Mini Kossel. Retrieved Dec 24, 2015 from http://reprap.org/wiki/Kossel
16. Stefanie Mueller, Sangha Im, Serafima Gurevich, Alexander Teibrich, Lisa Pfisterer, François Guimbretière, and Patrick Baudisch. 2014. WirePrint: 3D printed previews for fast prototyping. In *Proceedings of the 27th annual ACM symposium on*

User interface software and technology (UIST '14), 273-280. http://dx.doi.org/10.1145/2642918.2647359

17. Stefanie Mueller, Pedro Lopes, and Patrick Baudisch. 2012. Interactive construction: interactive fabrication of functional mechanical devices. In *Proceedings of the 25th annual ACM symposium on User interface software and technology* (UIST '12), NY, USA, 599-606. http://dx.doi.org/10.1145/2380116.2380191
18. Stefanie Mueller, Tobias Mohr, Kerstin Guenther, Johannes Frohnhofen, and Patrick Baudisch. 2014. faBrickation: fast 3D printing of functional objects by integrating construction kit building blocks. In *Proceedings of the SIGCHI Conference on Human Factors in Computing Systems* (CHI '14), 3827-3834. http://dx.doi.org/10.1145/2556288.2557005
19. Huaishu Peng, Amit Zoran, and François V. Guimbretière. 2015. D-Coil: A Hands-on Approach to Digital 3D Models Design. In *Proceedings of the 33rd Annual ACM Conference on Human Factors in Computing Systems* (CHI '15), 1807-1815. http://dx.doi.org/10.1145/2702123.2702381
20. RhinoCAD. Retrieved Dec 24, 2015 from http://www.rhino3d.com
21. Rhinocommon SDK. Retrived Dec 24, 2015 from http://4.rhino3d.com/5/rhinocommon/
22. Alec Rivers, Ilan E. Moyer, and Frédo Durand. 2012. Position-correcting tools for 2D digital fabrication. *ACM Trans. Graph.* 31, 4, Article 88. http://dx.doi.org/10.1145/2185520.2185584
23. Jutta Schumann, Thomas Strothotte, Stefan Laser, and Andreas Raab. 1996. Assessing the effect of non-photorealistic rendered images in CAD. In *Proceedings of the SIGCHI Conference on Human Factors in Computing Systems* (CHI '96), 35-41. http://dx.doi.org/10.1145/238386.238398
24. Lei Shi, Idan Zelzer, Catherine Feng, and Shiri Azenkot. 2016. Tickers and Talker: An Accessible Labeling Toolkit for 3D Printed Models. In *Proceedings of the 34rd Annual ACM Conference on Human Factors in Computing Systems* (CHI '16). http://dx.doi.org/10.1145/2858036.2858507
25. Pitchaya Sitthi-Amorn, Javier E. Ramos, Yuwang Wangy, Joyce Kwan, Justin Lan, Wenshou Wang, and Wojciech Matusik. 2015. MultiFab: a machine vision assisted platform for multi-material 3D printing. *ACM Trans. Graph.* 34, 4, Article 129. http://dx.doi.org/10.1145/2766962
26. Hyunyoung Song, François Guimbretière, Chang Hu, and Hod Lipson. 2006. ModelCraft: capturing freehand annotations and edits on physical 3D models. *In Proceedings of the 19th annual ACM symposium on User interface software and technology* (UIST '06), 13-22. http://dx.doi.org/10.1145/1166253.1166258
27. Xuan Song, Yayue Pan, Yong Chen. 2015. Development of a Low-Cost Parallel Kinematic Machine for Multidirectional Additive Manufacturing. *Journal of Manufacturing Science and Engineering*, 137(2), 021005. http://dx.doi.org/10.1115/1.4028897
28. Spraying System. Retrieved Dec 24, 2015 from http://www.spray.com/cat70/cat70pdf/ssco_cat70_f.pdf
29. Alexander Teibrich, Stefanie Mueller, François Guimbretière, Robert Kovacs, Stefan Neubert, and Patrick Baudisch. 2015. Patching Physical Objects. In *Proceedings of the 28th Annual ACM Symposium on User Interface Software & Technology* (UIST '15), 83-91. http://dx.doi.org/10.1145/2807442.2807467
30. John R. Tumbleston, David Shirvanyants, Nikita Ermoshkin, Rima Janusziewicz, Ashley R. Johnson, David Kelly, Kai Chen, Robert Pinschmidt, Jason P. Rolland, Alexander Ermoshkin, Edward T. Samulski, Joseph M. DeSimone. 2015. Continuous liquid interface production of 3D objects. *Science*, 347(6228), 1349-1352. http://dx.doi.org/10.1126/science.aaa2397
31. Christian Weichel, John Hardy, Jason Alexander, and Hans Gellersen. 2015. ReForm: Integrating Physical and Digital Design through Bidirectional Fabrication. In *Proceedings of the 28th Annual ACM Symposium on User Interface Software & Technology* (UIST '15), 93-102. http://dx.doi.org/10.1145/2807442.2807451
32. Karl D.D. Willis, Cheng Xu, Kuan-Ju Wu, Golan Levin, and Mark D. Gross. 2010. Interactive fabrication: new interfaces for digital fabrication. In *Proceedings of the fifth international conference on Tangible, embedded, and embodied interaction* (TEI '11), 69-72. http://dx.doi.org/10.1145/1935701.1935716
33. Amit Zoran and Joseph A. Paradiso. 2013. FreeD: a freehand digital sculpting tool. In *Proceedings of the SIGCHI Conference on Human Factors in Computing Systems* (CHI '13), 2613-2616. http://dx.doi.org/10.1145/2470654.2481361
34. Amit Zoran, Roy Shilkrot, and Joseph Paradiso. 2013. Human-computer interaction for hybrid carving. In *Proceedings of the 26th annual ACM symposium on User interface software and technology* (UIST '13), 433-440. http://dx.doi.org/10.1145/2501988.2502023

CardBoardiZer: Creatively Customize, Articulate and Fold 3D Mesh Models

Yunbo Zhang, Wei Gao, Luis Paredes, Karthik Ramani
School of Mechanical Engineering, Purdue University
West Lafayette, IN 47907
{zhan2014, gao51, lparede, ramani}@purdue.edu

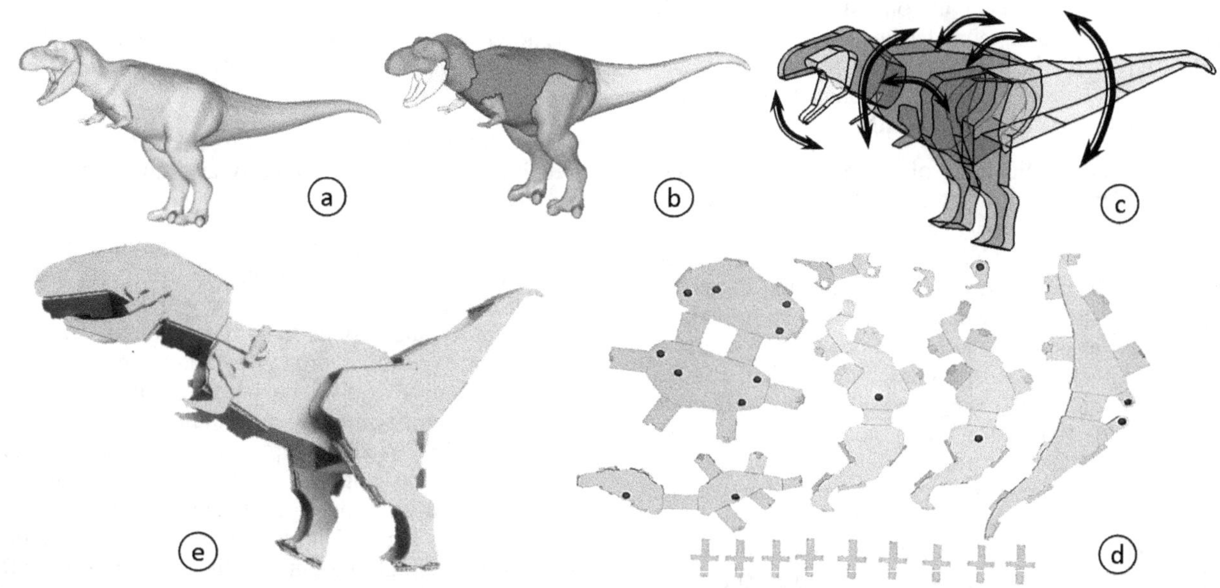

Figure 1. shows the overall building pipeline using CardBoardiZer: Given a 3D mesh T-Rex model as shown in (a), CardBoardiZer allows the user to (b) customize the segmentations at the locations where parts are desired to be articulated, (c) specify the corresponding rotational joint motions, (d) the crease-cut-slot patterns are generated for (e) the user to quickly cut, fold and assemble using cardboard.

ABSTRACT
Computer-aided design of flat patterns allows designers to prototype foldable 3D objects made of heterogeneous sheets of material. We found origami designs are often characterized by pre-synthesized patterns and automated algorithms. Furthermore, augmenting articulated features to a desired model requires time-consuming synthesis of interconnected joints. This paper presents CardBoardiZer, a rapid cardboard based prototyping platform that allows everyday sculptural 3D models to be easily customized, articulated and folded. We develop a building platform to allow the designer to 1) import a desired 3D shape, 2) customize articulated partitions into planar or volumetric foldable patterns, and 3) define rotational movements between partitions. The system unfolds the model into 2D crease-cut-slot patterns ready for die-cutting and folding. In this paper, we developed interactive algorithms and validated the usability of CardBoardiZer using various 3D models. Furthermore, comparisons between CardBoardiZer and methods of Autodesk® 123D™ Make, demonstrated significantly shorter time-to-prototype and ease of fabrication.

CHI'16, May 07-12, 2016, San Jose, CA, USA.

ISBN 978-1-4503-3362-7/16/05 $15.00.
DOI: http://dx.doi.org/10.1145/2858036.2858362

Author Keywords
Foldable design; articulated model; cardboard prototyping.

ACM Classification Keywords
H.5.2. [**Information Interfaces and Presentation**]: User Interface

INTRODUCTION
Current trends in democratization of fabrication make it possible for one to personalize manipulative designs through the choice of geometries, materials, and fabricate them on demand. A variety of rapid, early, but flexible prototyping techniques, such as 3D printing, laser cutting, and home milling

machines, are gaining popularity among the DIY crowds [21]. As a result, common individuals now are able to fabricate artistic and personal objects without being technically trained to use sophisticated computational and production tools.

As an ancient paper craft originating from Japan, origami has been naturally contextualized into many design systems to create foldable 3D structures. The real beauty of folding lies in its elegant simplicity using 2D sheet of material to create complex 3D shapes and forms. During the last 40 years, whys, whats and hows of different origami tessellations and structures have been geometrically and symbolically described by the underlying mathematical rules, such as flat foldability [2] and folding any polygonal shape [11]. With the marriage of computational geometry and origami, systematic design tools have also been developed recently (TreeMaker [24], Origamizer [10], FPME [16], Pepakura Designer [29], Autodesk® 123D™ Make [4], and FoldMecha [33]).

We found the past applications of foldable structures and crafts are limited by the following characteristics: 1) most developments have a typical goal of achieving automation of the design process to construct deterministic shapes and structures. However, in these systems, users are not allowed to participate and customize the desired shape to be folded, determine the parts to be articulated, and decide how the parts are joined. 2) Given any single model with articulated features, it is a daunting task using traditional mechanical design approaches to synthesize and prototype interconnected joints in order to make the model movable. 3) Conventional design and manufacturing tools are highly-procedural and require elaborate training and practice before they can be effectively utilized. Such limitations of these tools impede the integration of designing and making of complex shapes for an independent tinkerer.

Inspired by the development of Do-It-Yourself (DIY) and the maker movement [1], we present a novel customizable prototyping framework, called CardBoardiZer. Using CardBoardiZer, one can repurpose any 3D model that already exists to be foldable and articulable. We aim to democratize the design and fabrication together so that designers who lack specialized knowledge can quickly prototype. It is suitable for novices in the maker movement, K-12 crafting activities, hobbyists and even college level use in prototyping and physical computing classes. The new standards for U.S. STEM education framed by the National Research Council has an explicit focus on engineering and design [41]. Our methodology encourages the design, make, and play through creating, tinkering, using widely available materials, which is essential for engagement [19]. Our approach is targeted towards the DIY community where the versatile prototyping material, cardboard, and a low-cost crafting cutter are used for cutting and then folding is done by hand.

In our work, the overall guiding design philosophy is to allow one to quickly and easily personalize desired designs, through the choice of geometries and articulations, to create foldable cardboard crafts and prototypes. Hence, the barrier to entry into 3D modeling and prototyping is lowered not only by directly repurposing the types of shapes, but indirectly by using cardboard itself as the material. The subsequent folding and assembling using their own hands become a source of pride and satisfaction. In using this guiding principle, the following detailed design elements were adopted for the CardBoardiZer system:

1)The system needs to ensure a rapid cycle of prototyping at early conceptual design stages, including folding and die cutting.

2)The design platform should provide a workflow for different stages of customization, such as shape segmentation and modification, resolution definition, and specification of motion joints.

3)The visual interface should be integrated with the physical behaviors such as foldability, motion constraints and articulation.

4)The physical prototype needs to be easily made out of inexpensive, lightweight and readily available materials that are widely used in the physical prototypes, such as cardboard.

These design elements lead to several geometric and algorithmic challenges to create a human-in-the-loop CardBoardiZer platform. CardBoardiZer is a new genre of cardboard-based rapid prototyping system, that is designed to create new affordances for experimentation and expressiveness of designers. We create a new workflow using the customizable segmentation, shape approximation, articulation specification and unfolding design to allow rapid customization and prototyping. The geometric operations are made accessible for novice designers and use existing 3D sculptural models. Previous works such as Paper Folding 3D [39], generates foldable patterns with a small amount of folds, reducing the effort and time. However the shape approximation of such models is not satisfactory. On the other hand, complex unfolded mesh patterns created by Pepakura Designer, Autodesk® 123D™ Make (*folded panels module*) and Optimized topological surgery [43] approximate the input model well but demand a high effort and time to fold, making these methods accessible only to a few that have the expertise, manual dexterity and patience.

On the other hand, we created affordances for a new intermediate-level foldable crafting form that repurposes and abstracts existing 3D models. This design platform integrates customizable segmentation, contour extraction and approximation, geometric simplification, articulation specification and design of unfolding into a compact design environment to help one easily generate foldable patterns ready for cutting and folding. We retain the ease of foldability of the shape as a key characteristic for the user, but at the same time serve the geometric shape approximation. The alternating curve-and-straight regions (ACSR) form not only retains the curvy shape in curved regions, but also simplifies the folding process for each of the partitions. Only a small amount of straight regions have to be coupled for closing the shape. To automate ACSR, we have developed a new geometric simplification algorithm. By integrating straight portions, this algorithm also provides a basic level of structural integrity. Also by manipulating the ACSR resolution, designers can balance the shape approximation with the total time and folding effort. Several different customization cases that demonstrate the foldability and motion feasibility are discussed later in this paper.

RELATED WORK

Unfolding 3D Meshes

In computer graphics, researchers have studied different geometric processing and rendering techniques to approximate input 3D meshes to 2D patches. Takahashi et al. [43] presented a heuristic approach to unfold 3D triangular meshes without shape distortions. Variation shape approximation [8] applied a mutual and repeated error-driven optimization strategy that provides polygonal plane proxies to best approximate a given 3D shape. Mitani and Hiromasa [32] used a set of triangular strips to approximate an input 3D mesh, while Shatz et al. [37] segmented the mesh into explicitly developable parts that can be cut and glued together. Traditional mesh segmentation [3, 22] and parametrization techniques [38] also provide the implicit mapping between 3D shape and 2D facets. However, all these methods result in a large number of planar segments that are impractical or difficult to join. In addition, physical construction and assembly constraints are rarely considered in these purely digital approximation techniques.

On the commercial side, many computational design tools have been developed for the user to import a 3D textured model and unfold it into flat sheets suitable for printing, such as Pepakura Designer, Autodesk® 123D™ Make (*folded panels module*), Paper Airplane Factory [42], and Paper folding 3D, shown in Fig. 2. In addition, online supportive communities such as Instructables [23] and Robot Living [27] are bringing commercial paper crafting and shipping services directly to customers. In general, all these systems and methods try to focus on the automatic fabrication process from an original mesh model. In our work, we seek a middle ground to empower the DIY community to prototype foldable and articulable shapes.

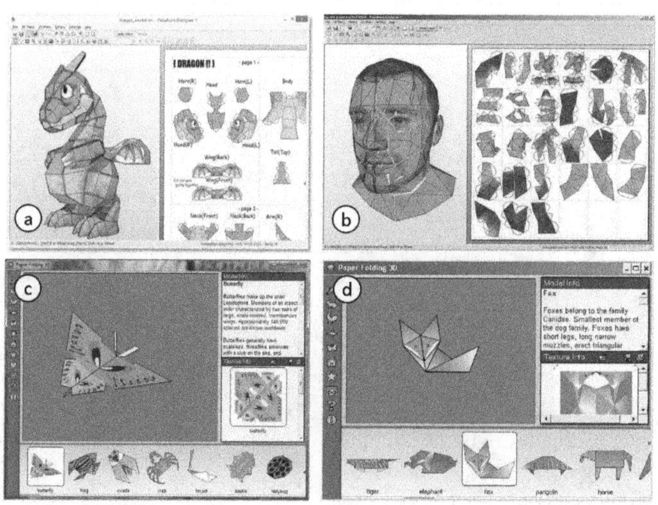

Figure 2. shows (a,b) 3D sculptural models generated using Pepakura Designer; (c,d) animal models generated using Paper folding 3D.

Fabrication-aware Shape Design

3D shape constructions using interlocked planar sections have been widely investigated for the ease of fabrication and assembly [13, 17, 36, 30, 4]. Flatfab [13] enables users to build their own models by sketching and assembling each planar slice one by one, while Crdbrd [17], Schwartzburg et al.'s [36], Slices [30] and Autodesk® 123D™ Make's *interlocked slices module* [4] can automatically convert a 3D model into planar slices. These proposed optimization algorithms derive sets of physical construction constraints to be satisfied in order to guarantee a rigid, stable and collision-free final construct. Nevertheless, the purpose of these methods is to generate a static and decorative object. In all these methods the resultant object has only one body with no joints that have motion and also they cannot house other components due to lack of interior spaces. Lau et al. [25] presented a formal grammar combined with lexical and structural analysis to generate fabricatable parts and connectors from a 3D furniture model. Another study focusses on the constraints and sequences of assemblies by creating geometric puzzles, such as Polyomino [28] and Burr puzzles [47] from a 3D model. Recently, Li et al. [26] developed an algorithm for computing paper architecture using pop-ups.

Some of the trends we notice in the recent work is the introduction of functionality into design and fabrication. Megaro et al. [31] and Coros et al. [9] proposed interactive systems for designing animated mechanical characters by kinematic synthesis based on the output trajectories or configurations specified by users, while FoldMecha [33] focuses on building linkage based toys made of paper. Tubes, ball socket joints and cuboids are embedded into given sculptural 3D models for housing of functionalities and articulation in [35], [5] and [14] and are fabricated by low cost 3D printing processes [15]. In contrast, we enable the creation of inexpensive foldable cardboard patterns for the Maker-DIY community from a wide variety of existing sculptural models.

Cardboard Crafting and Die-cutting

Cardboard, or carton board, is considered as the natural and recyclable material for constructing rapid prototypes and packaging consumer and food commodities [44, 18]. The typical structure consists of two flat panels coupled with a corrugating medium and the fibrous material to provide higher tensile strength and surface stiffness than regular craft papers. The cardboard material not only reduces the weight of the box, but also lends itself to the ease of manufacture, such as die-cutting. As the personal fabrication movement continues to lower the barrier of entry-level manufacturing systems, more and more portable desktop-scale and low-cost craft cutters and 3D printers have gained significant hobbyist, academic, and industry interest. We therefore find that cardboard is the suitable material for constructing 3D models that are found or created by users. In this work, we utilize the paper craft die-cutter to efficiently convert the digital crease patterns into flat cardboard prototypes.

CREATIVE DESIGN FRAMEWORK

CardBoadiZer produces customizable, articulated, and foldable prototypes directly from any digital 3D model. As shown in Fig. 3, our computational design platform workflow unfolds as follows: the designer (1) inputs a desired 3D mesh model, (2) customizes the segmented parts within the model to be articulated, (3) approximates the shape of each partition using a planar contour or an extruded volume, (4) augments the relative articulated movement between partitions, and then (5) develops the crease-cut-slot patterns ready to be die-cut and folded. The user is able to carry their creativity and intent towards the control of the number of articulated partitions, feature details, motion complexity, and the corresponding foldability.

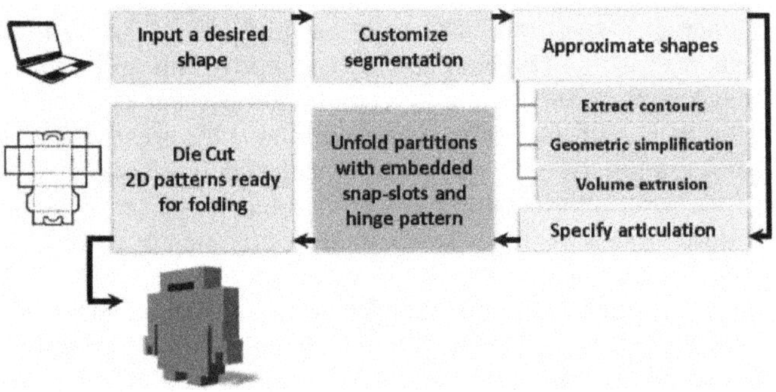

Figure 3. Building process of CardBoardiZer: given a 3D mesh model provided by user, the user customizes the partitions as desired, and enables each partition foldable using planar contour or extruded volumetric representation. The joint motion of articulated partitions are then specified and the system unfolds the crease-cut-slot patterns ready for die-cutting and folding.

Customizable Segmentation

Wong et al. [45] first developed the interactive mesh segmentation approach by specifying points on the cutting boundary and finding the shortest path connecting the points. Later, foreground / background snapping methods such as graph-cut [7], geodesic curvature flow [49], and region growing [46] also provides cutting boundaries to closely follow designers' specification.

In CardBoardiZer, we apply "dot scissor" [50] to capture local concave shape features using concavity-aware harmonic fields, and to select the best cutting boundaries using a voting scheme. The designer first specifies a stroke on the model where the partitioning curves are expected to pass through. A concavity-aware harmonic field is then computed by using the user's specified stroke as constraints. A set of candidate curves are computed upon the harmonic field via extracting iso-value curves. The same voting scheme as [50] is adopted to select the best partitioning curves according to their length and distance to user's stroke. Compared with original "dot scissor" approach, our system with strokes rather than dots representation, affords more of the user intent to be captured by the design process. Besides, the system also allows the users to continue interacting with strokes in the same region without actually partitioning the model. This scheme also increases the flexibility and convenience in using our tool.

Contour Representation

Contours are the basic representation of object shape since it contains explicit and dominant characteristics for determining an object's shape. As seen in Fig. 4, we provide a planar

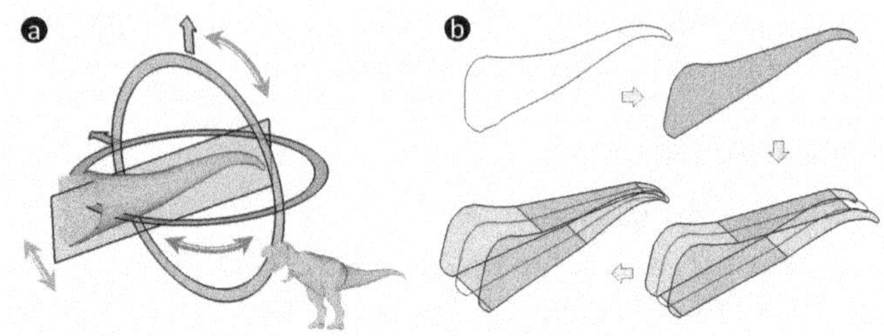

Figure 4. (a) The representative contour of the tail partition can be generated by a widget-based interactive tool, where two circular widgets are used to adjust the normal of a cutting plane. The cutting plane can be translated as well. (b) Once the contour is selected and closed, an extrusion operation is used to generate volumetric models. The tilting operation is for generating a model with non-uniform thickness.

section extraction tool in our platform to cut each partition with a plane and obtain the resultant cross-sectional contour. To generate the initial cutting plane, the system applies the principal component analysis (PCA) so that the plane is created by taking the principal axis with the smallest eigenvalue as the normal and passing through the geometric center. If the initial plane is not satisfactory, a widget-based tool can be used to manipulate the cutting plane until it represents the shape as desired. The tool consists of two circular widgets to rotate the plane and a moving widget to translate the plane. Once the contour is selected, one can either choose to extrude the contour section along the normal vector of the cutting plane to create a prismatic model, or to retain the original planar shape. CardBoardiZer also allows for symmetrically tilting the prism surface with a non-uniform thickness. A sketch completion tool is provided to close the open contour and therefore a generated contour is not necessary to be a closed loop.

Geometric Simplification for Leveraging Foldability and Shape Approximation

When considering unfolding, volumetric models that are extruded from highly curvy contours usually result in massive

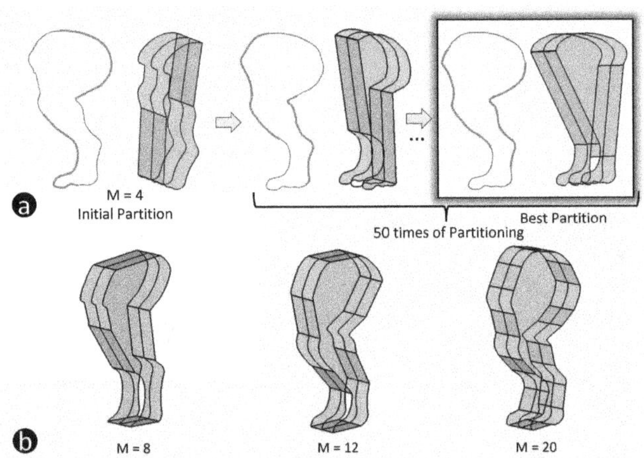

Figure 5. shows (a) when setting M to 4, our simplification generates a region partition with best score according to Eq.1 in the right upper corner. (b) by increasing M to 8, 12, and 20, the simplification results with improved shape approximation are obtained.

number of folding lines and makes the fabrication and assembly impractical. Therefore, it is necessary to geometrically simplify the contours before extrusion. The objectives of our simplification are twofold: 1) generate as little folding edges as possible to alleviate the construction burden, (2) approximate the shape of original curve as much as possible. Existing simplification algorithms such as [20, 40] gives a rough shape approximation and a limited number of retained edges. In these methods, the shape is isotropically coarsened with straight and curvy regions. In this section, we present a geometric simplification algorithm that simultaneously leverages the foldability and shape approximation.

The key idea of the algorithm is to classify the whole contour curve into ACSR, as shown in Fig. 5. Each straight region is approximated by a single line segment and will be extended later with connecting "side walls" to close up the volume, while the curvy regions are left open to preserve the curvy features of the contour. To ensure the folded model to be structurally integral, as a heuristic, we evenly distribute the straight and curved regions along the whole contour length.

To leverage the foldabilty and shape approximation, our simplification algorithm is summarized as follows:

1. **Initial region classification** All the points on each contour are parameterized using an arc length parameterization. Based on this parameterization, by inserting M evenly distributed anchor points, the whole contour can be divided into M regions from R_1 to R_M. The regions are specified into straight and curvy regions alternatively. If R_i is assigned as straight region, R_{i+1} $(i, i+1 \in [1, M])$ will be the curvy regions, and vice versa. This initial classification guarantees the distribution and length of each straight and curvy regions to be the same.

2. **Best classification search** Based on the results of initial region classification, we applied a search algorithm to find out the best region classification that preserves the original shape best. An error evaluation metric is defined as follows:

$$Score = \frac{\sum_{j\in[0,M]} \overline{chordal}(R_j)}{\sum_{k\in[0,M]} \overline{chordal}(R_k)}, \quad (1)$$

   where R_j is a curvy region and R_k is a straight region. $\overline{chordal}(\cdots)$ measures the average chordal length error of each region. The classification search algorithm is designed to find out a classification with max score evaluated by Eq.1. By rotating the contour every small step δ in the parametric domain, we recursively parameterize the same contour and evaluate the score to select the best region classification. Note that, the searching stops when the rotation reaches $\frac{2\pi}{M}$ degrees due to the rotational symmetry of the region classification. The rotation step angle δ is set to $\frac{0.04\pi}{M}$ for balancing the classification quality and speed.

3. **Contour simplification** After a best region classification is selected, we perform the contour simplification by simply linking the starting and ending points of each straight regions. After extruding, the volumetric model will only have Ms set to be under 20, meanwhile the shape of the model is well preserved.

By selecting a different number for M, different levels of detail of the simplified models can be obtained. In this paper, we set M to be the power of 2 up to 16, thereby three levels of details of the simplified models. Besides, a pair of snap-slot patterns are added along each straight region to enclose the volumetric partitions.

Articulation Specification and Motion Hinge Synthesis

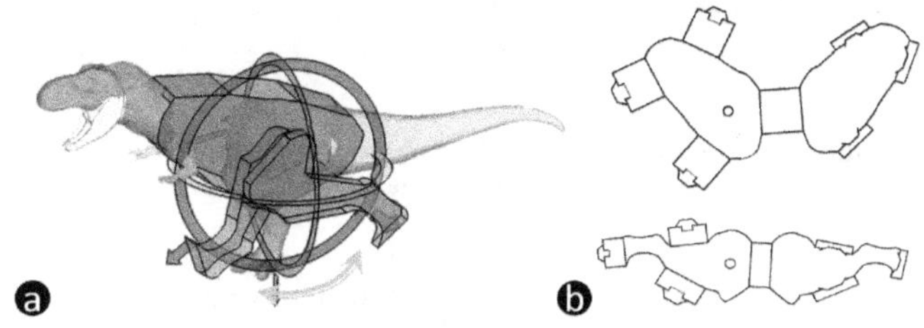

Figure 6. shows (a) a relative rotation specified using our widget based tool by selecting P_b, P_m and rotation axis on widget R. (b) the presynthesized motion hinge patterns are automatically added onto unfolded patterns.

Setting up arbitrary axes or pivots using traditional mechanical approaches is typically tedious and time-consuming. However, it is often the case that the desired manipulation constraint of an object exists in the candidate constraints of another scene object. Our system supports a simple interaction to let users to specify the relative motion between two parts. First, the user interactively specifies a partition P_b that serves as the fixed base, and the moving part P_m that rotates with respect to P_b (see Fig. 6 (a)). The rotation control widget R enables the user to specify which axis they like P_m to rotate about (shown in Fig. 6 (a)). The mating surface S_b on P_b and S_m on P_m can be determined by finding the closest surfaces on two parts. To ensure the relative motion, our system automatically adjusts the orientation of P_m such that two mating surfaces S_b and S_m are coplanar. Currently, our system relies on visual feedback for collision detection during the relative motion between two parts. Once the motion is defined, we assemble each pair of articulated parts P_b and P_m with a synthesized modular and easy-to-assemble motion hinge kit. (see Fig. 6 (b)).

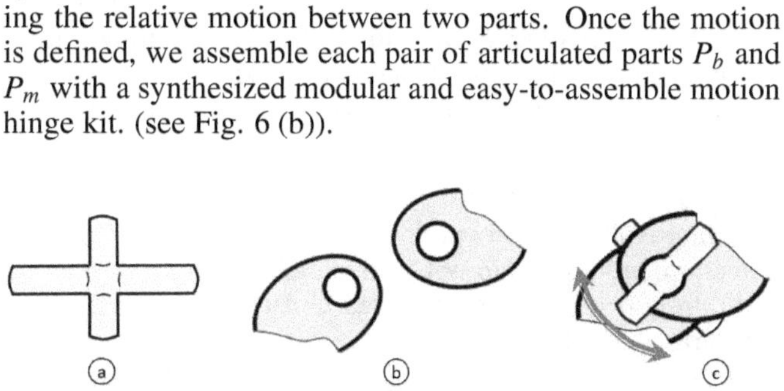

Figure 7. shows a cross-shape stripe (a) for connecting adjacent partitions (b) with revolute joint motion. (c) shows the complete assembly.

Each motion-hinge kit consists of a cross-shape 2D stripe and two circular holes on the patterns of adjacent partitions to be articulated, shown in Fig. 7. In order to generate a revolute motion between two partitions, the user needs to overlap the two patterns together where the holes are aligned to each other, bend the two opposite tips of the stripe towards the

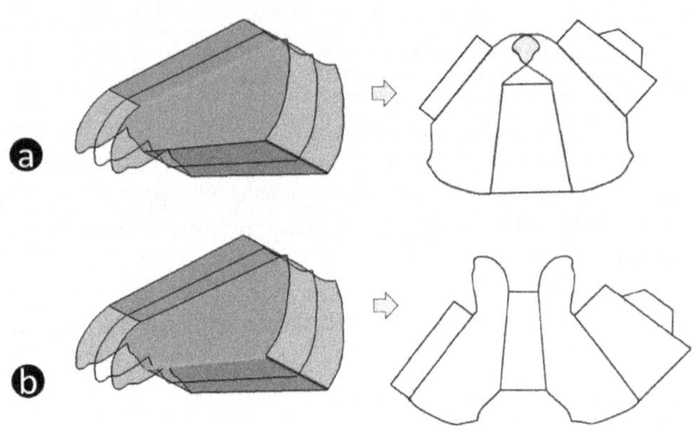

Figure 8. shows by selecting different straight line and curvy regions, overlapping issue occurs in case (a), but not in case (b)

middle, thread them into holes, and then release the tips on the other side.

Design of Unfolding

Our system unfolds each extruded volumetric shape into a 2D pattern with the motion hinges and snap-slot patterns. The design rationale for the unfolded pattern is twofold: 1) to ease the effort of assembly, the 2D pattern for each individual partition needs to be a single connected patch and 2) the pattern requires to be self-overlap-free so that all facets are cuttable. Our unfolding algorithm separates all the ACSR on the contour and leaving one pair of straight regions for connecting facets. During unfolding, the extruded volume can always be flattened ([12]) due to the foldability of polyhedra. Note that, the selection of unseparated straight regions cannot be arbitrary because the self-overlapping of facets might occur (see Fig. 8(a)). We thereby develop a separation algorithm to ensure the a self-overlap-free unfolding result. The algorithm consists of the following two steps:

1. **Edge sorting** All pairs of straight regions are sorted inside a queue Ψ in a descending order of the edge length.
2. **Edge separation & unfolding** One pair of straight region popped up from Ψ is labeled as unseparated while others as separated. Existence of self-overlapping are checked after unfolding.

Step 2 is repeated until Ψ is empty or there exists the unfolding without self-overlapping. In the scenario where self-overlapping areas can not be avoided, the algorithm assigns all straight regions as separated and thus the 2D pattern is separated into two pieces.

PROTOTYPE AND RESULTS

A 1.6 mm-thick single corrugated wall board was used as the substrate material and is shown in Fig. 9 after the 2D pattern is generated and cut. We selected this thickness to facilitate low-cost cutting and folding. We used the 24" Silver Bullet Die cutter Fig. 9(a) along with the 60-degree long blade to cut the crease and motion-hinge pattern. For the overall cutting setup, we use a relatively lower speed (200 mm/s) and higher force (588 grams) for the contour through-cutting, and a higher speed (800 mm/s) and lower force (470 grams) for depth-cutting of folds. Our system requires manual user involvement such as folding and assembling to construct the final prototype (Fig. 9(b)).

Prototypical Results

According to the CardBoardiZer results on a number of humanoid, animal and man-made 3D objects, our creative design framework allows different articulated features of the model to be quickly customized, folded and assembled using cardboard material. Fig. 10 shows our segmentation and prototypical results using 9 demonstrated examples, including 6 sculptural models (T-Rex, Apatosaurus, Michelangelo's David, Stanford bunny, tree frog and tank) and 3 real life objects (desk lamp, clock and plier). In Fig. 11, we show the T-Rex model with 3 different levels of resolutions: M=4, M=8, M=12, respectively. The head and leg are illustrated with the major resolution differences due to many small curvy feature along the contours of this two parts.

Prototyping Time Evaluation

In order to understand the construction efficiency and folding capability using our system, we studied the speed of cutting, folding and assembly using cardboard as a sheet of material. A corrugated cardboard contains 3 sheets of Kraft paper attached together with each other. The internal I-beam structure provides rigidity and strength over the corrugations, while blade cutting and leaving only the bottom substrate layer makes it easy to fold. The 24" Silver Bullet Die cutter enables the through-cuts completed with 0.00625 s/mm for contours, and depth-cuts completed with 0.00125 s/mm. When carefully investigating the folding motion, we observe that typically one first bends the sheet along the pre-cut crease lines and presses on the overlapping side. Our experimental results shows these two motions typically take 1 to 2 seconds. Then the user quickly slides along the crease line within 0.2 ~ 0.4 seconds to complete the folds. Folding each snap into the slot for closing the volumetric partition takes an average of 2 ~ 4 seconds, while assembly the motion hinge takes 8 ~ 9 seconds. Table. 1 shows the time statistics of design, die-cutting, and folding (assembly) of our 11 demonstrated craft prototypes.

Usability Discussion and Comparison

Using CardBoardiZer, the designer is able to customize through the choice of geometries, articulation, joint motions and resolutions, quickly fabricate the patterns using cutters on demand, and complete the model through simple manual

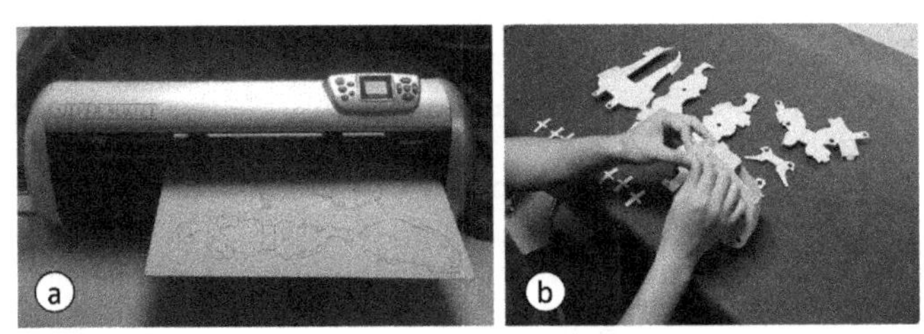

Figure 9. shows (a) 24" Silver Bullet Die cutter, and (b) the 2D T-Rex patterns when folding and assembling

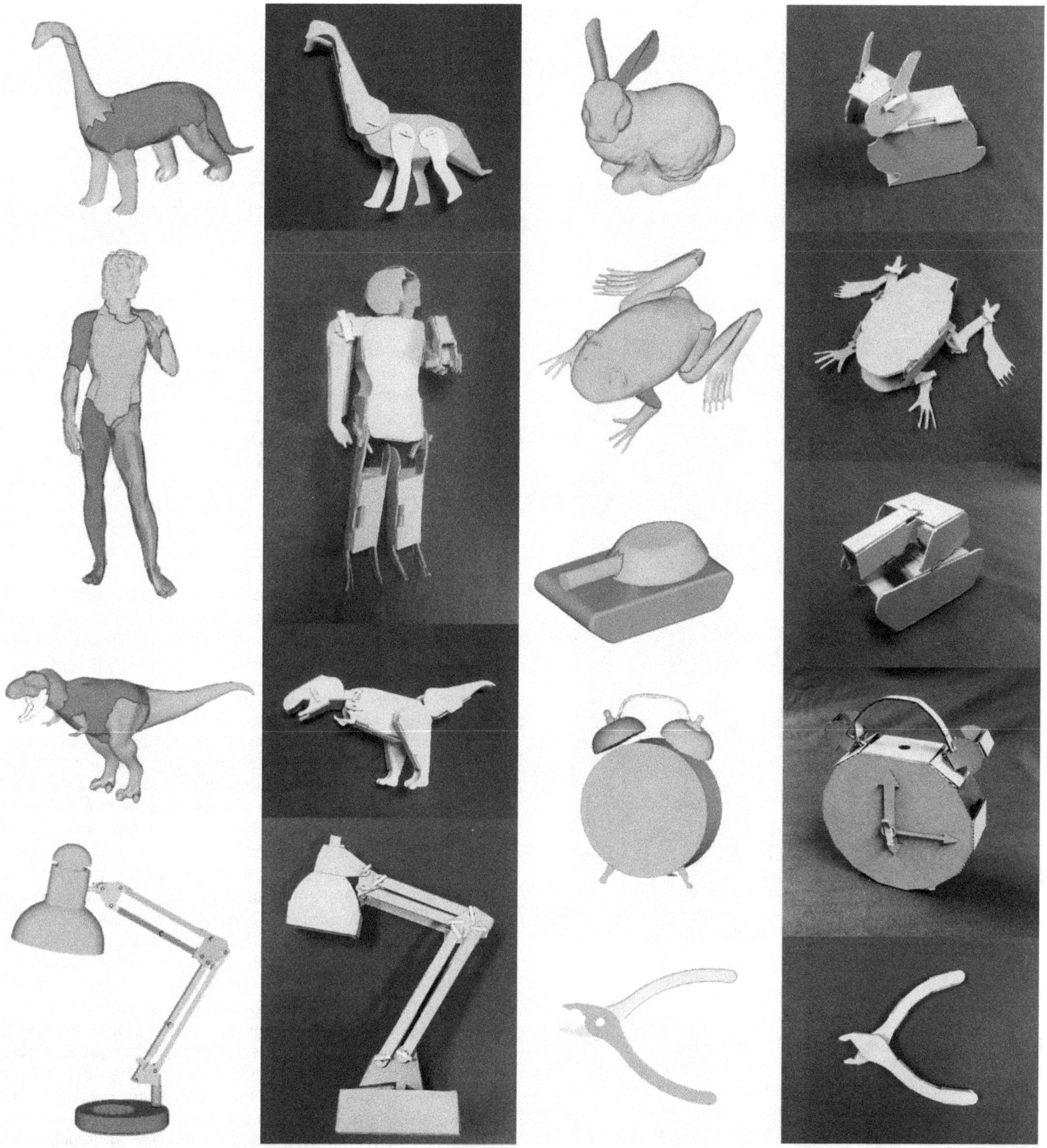

Figure 10. shows prototypical results generated by CardBoardiZer. First column from top down: Apatosaurus, Michelangelo's David, T-Rex and Desk lamp; and second column from top down: Stanford bunny, tree frog, tank, clock and plier.

folding and assembly. It is fast, friendly to use where the users only need to load the digital 3D model, segment the partitions as desired, specify the motions, and finally the system generates the 2D crease-cut-slot patterns ready for cutting, folding and articulation. Compared to traditional manual origami crafting methods, our method allows fast customization of desired shapes and augmented motion features, and fast prototyping by using die-cutting and folding approaches.

Table 1. Design, cutting and folding time statistic for different 3D models using CardBoardiZer

Models		Design Time (mm:ss)	Cutting Time (mm:ss)	Fold & Assembly Time (mm:ss)	Total Time (mm:ss)
T-Rex (47cm x 19cm x 9cm)	M=4	4:25	4:03	5:06	13:34
	M=8	5:38	7:51	7:33	21:02
	M=12	7:03	10:27	12:10	24:37
Apatosaurus (41cm x 44cm x 6cm)		2:19	2:12	1:58	6:29
Tree frog (14cm x 3cm x 18cm)		6:22	5:43	6:09	18:14
Stanford bunny (16cm x 16cm x 7cm)		2:24	1:47	2:01	4:51
Tank (18cm x 8cm x 8cm)		2:01	2:05	1:30	4:36
Michelangelo's David (25cm x 9cm x 4cm)		6:56	6:39	7:13	20:48
Desk lamp (54cm x 35cm x 17cm)		7:23	8:41	10:12	26:16
Clock (19cm x 15cm X 6cm)		1:17	2:20	1:40	5:17
Plier (27cm x 20cm x 3.5cm)		1:02	5:12	2:20	8:34

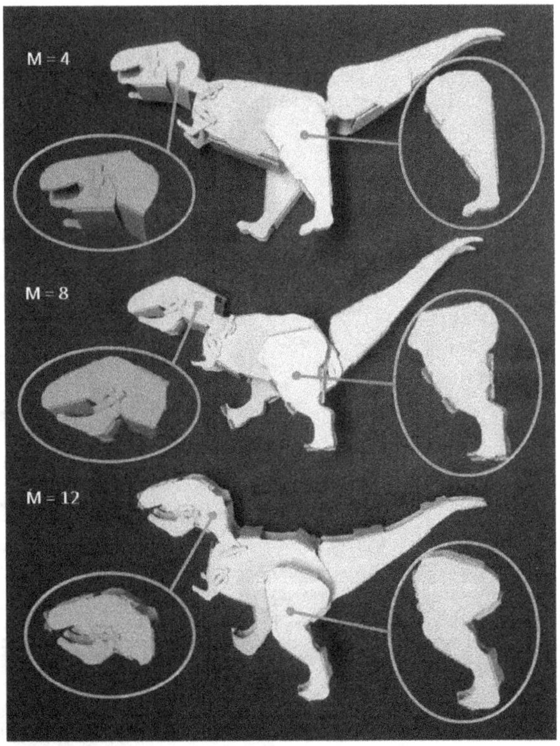

Figure 11. shows the time statistics for cutting and folding the T-Rex model with three different levels of resolutions (top down: M=4, M=8, M=12, respectively).

Our system is applicable for both novice and experienced designers who have basic computer operation skills. The interaction tools of CardBoardiZer are designed for ease of use and enable users to access complex geometric operations. Operations such as segmentation, contour generation and articulation specification, and shape control can be easily performed by simply stroking on model, adjusting a control widget and using a slider bar for different resolutions.

The selection of cardboard as our building material enables accessibility, experimentation and expressiveness by novice users. Cardboard is a low-cost everyday material that users are familiar with and can be easily accessed by novice users. Compared with other materials such as plastics, cardboard can be cut by low cost die-cutters instead of a more expensive laser cutter. The objects generated by CardBoardiZer are tinkerable in many ways: the objects can be easily adjusted and enhanced by users using color pens, scissors, glue and Velcro to paint, cut, make holes and attach other objects or decorative materials (e.g. wheels, levers, textiles, electronics and LED). Tinkering with objects generated by CardBoardiZer and other objects has multiple benefits for both learning and expression [34] as it invites broader participation and deepens the learning outcomes by allowing for a range of new solutions. Cardboard as a material for toys has gained significant attention from the maker community and is also gender neutral [48]. In 2005, cardboard box was inducted by Toy Hall of Fame, Strong National Museum of Play in Rochester and noted to be recognized, respected and remembered while having profoundly changed play or toy design [6].

Autodesk® 123D™ Make provides a variety of rapid prototyping functions for the user to fabricate cardboard-based designs with simplified shapes, including *interlocked slices* and *folded panels*. We herein carefully compare the workflow, ease of interaction, fabrication statistics as well as the final prototypical results using the *interlocked slices* (Fig. 12(a)) and *folded panels* (Fig. 12(b)) of Autodesk® 123D™ Make and our CardBoardiZer (Fig. 12(c)). The T-Rex model was selected for all three methods with identical scales (47cm x 19cm x 9cm) and comparable resolutions. The interlocked planar sections were designed to approximate the shape using successive orthogonal cross-sections. In Autodesk® 123D™ Make, the user is allowed to quickly manipulate the total number and orientation of the planar sections with slots. During the assembly, we found that the Autodesk® 123D™ Make system generates multiple slots along the concave shape regions, which makes it difficult to assemble. Overall, the *interlocked slices* method takes 6 mins to design the pattern, 18 mins to die cut the planar sections, and 38 mins to complete the assembly. Another function in Autodesk® 123D™ Make, *folded panels*, is similar to Pepakura and creates foldable patterns of a model by unfolding its 3D meshes into multiple patches and stripes. It is designed to approximate the shape by generating 2D folding patterns with a high number of folds (198 folds for T-Rex). However, it demands a very high effort and time to fold, assemble, as well as manual dexterity and patience. For example the T-Rex takes, in total 5 mins to design the pattern, 23 mins to die cut the patches, and 3 hours and 32 mins to complete

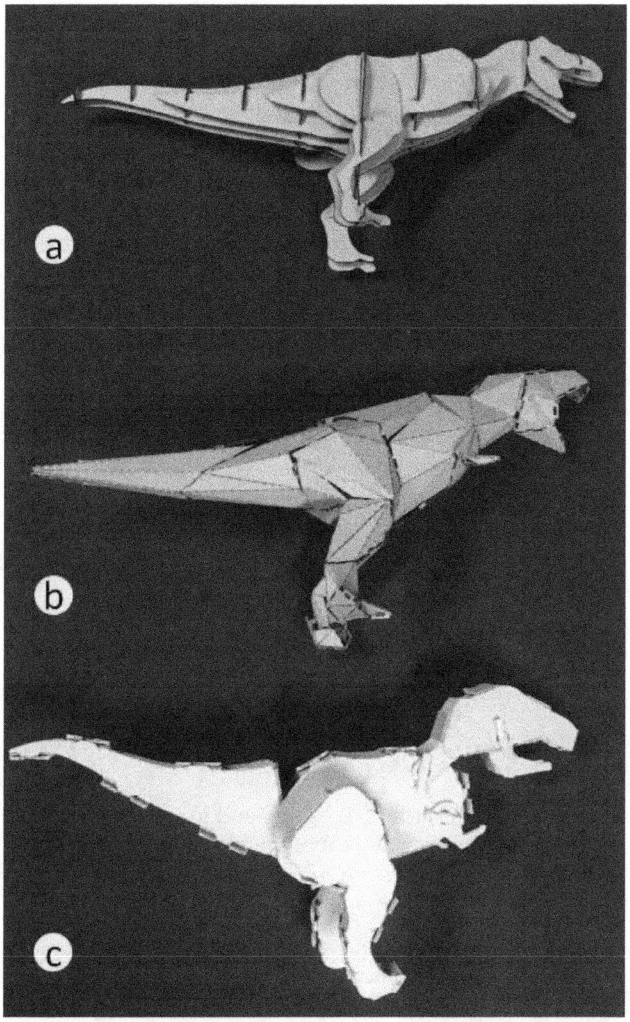

Figure 12. shows 3 fabricated T-Rex models, with identical scale and comparable resolutions, by (a) Autodesk® 123D™ Make *interlocked slices module* taking 6 mins for designing pattern, 18 mins for die cutting and 38 mins for assembly (in total 1 hr), (b) Autodesk® 123D™ Make *folded panels module* taking 5 mins for designing pattern, 23 mins for die cutting and 3 hrs and 32 mins for assembly (in total 4 hrs), and our CardBoardiZer taking 5 mins for designing pattern, 8 mins for die cutting and 7 mins for assembly (in total 20 mins).

the whole assembly. Our method, CardBoardiZer is designed to abstract the 3D shapes and approximate the individual bodies using a simple extruded cross-section. Compared to *folded panels*, CardBoardiZer reduces both the number of folds and time to fold. It also generates articulated features for the model that cannot be achieved using *interlocked slices*. Overall, CardBoardiZer requires 5 mins to design the pattern, 8 mins to die cut, and only 7 mins to fold up the model. The main difference is thus seen in the die cutting, assembly and the folding time. In particular the dexterity and patience to fold or assemble become extraordinarily high that most novices will not attempt crossing this barrier to entry. In addition the users need to keep track of a large number of individual parts and their location and sequence to be assembled.

LIMITATIONS, CONCLUSIONS AND FUTURE WORK

In this paper we present CardBoardiZer, a rapid design and prototyping system that allows a designer to customize, articulate, and fold everyday sculptural models. The computational design platform and prototyping pipeline are explicitly represented to ensure a rapid digital fabrication system. We demonstrate the usability of our system with a number of sculptural models. Currently the system is more suitable for processing shapes with reflectional symmetry, and preferably approximated with extruded features. Models with revolute bodies and massive curvy and protruding features limit our approach towards a good shape approximation. Because CarBoardiZer create shapes via extrusion from contours, models that are spherical-like or those created by revolution operations cannot be approximated well by CardBoardiZer. While repurposing is considered a part of the sharing DIY culture, the transformation from an original 3D model to the paper craft created by CardBoardiZer does raise potential ownership issues.

Several directions are possible for the future work such as understanding the learning that comes from the quick prototyping at early design, algorithmic enhancements to increase functionality, and enabling electromechanical functionalities. We plan to conduct a formal evaluation to further understand how CardBoradiZer helps the novice as well as expert designers to quickly design early prototypes and understand spatial and size constraints, elementary physics such as stability, motion and kinematics through iterative prototyping. CardBoardiZer affords options for further tinkering such as decoration, coloring, crafting and changing the prototype and these aspects will also be studied. Currently, we deal with structural integrity of the objects by heuristically setting the straight and curved regions to be evenly distributed. A more sophisticated strategy for structural stability analysis will further enhance the tool. Also the motion joints are not stable and the individually connected bodies cannot hold relative positions with respect to each other. We would like to address these problems by adding hinges. Another expansion option is towards systematic embedding strategies so that modular electronic components can be preassembled on the flat and encased inside the construction when folded. Integrating different gait patterns for the locomotion of the models would also make an interesting addition. Our CardBoardiZer design platform can serve as an enabler and inspiration for many derivative research works such as cardboard mechanotronics where circuits and sensors can be printed onto the substrate surfaces.

ACKNOWLEDGMENTS

The authors thank all the reviewers for providing valuable insights and suggestions that have helped in substantially improving this paper. This work was partially supported by the NSF IGERT on Sustainable Electronics (DGE 1144842) and by the Donald W. Feddersen Chair Professorship of the School of Mechanical Engineering, Purdue University. Any opinions, findings, and conclusions or recommendations expressed in this material are those of the authors and do not necessarily reflect the views of the sponsors. The authors also would like to acknowledge Youyi Zheng from ShanghaiTech

University for sharing the code of "dot scissor", and Ke Huo and Diogo Nazzetta from C Design Lab, Purdue University for their support.

REFERENCES

1. Chris Anderson. 2010. The new industrial revolution. *Wired magazine18* 2 (2010).
2. Esther M Arkin, Michael A Bender, Erik D Demaine, Martin L Demaine, Joseph SB Mitchell, Saurabh Sethia, and Steven S Skiena. 2004. When can you fold a map? *Computational Geometry* 29, 1 (2004), 23–46.
3. Marco Attene, Sagi Katz, Michela Mortara, Giuseppe Patané, Michela Spagnuolo, and Ayellet Tal. 2006. Mesh segmentation-a comparative study. In *Shape Modeling and Applications, 2006. SMI 2006. IEEE International Conference on*. IEEE, 7–7.
4. Autodesk. 2014. Autodesk 123D Make. (2014). Retrieved September 17, 2015 from `http://www.123dapp.com/make`.
5. Moritz Bächer, Bernd Bickel, Doug L. James, and Hanspeter Pfister. 2012. Fabricating Articulated Characters from Skinned Meshes. *ACM Trans. Graph.* 31, 4, Article 47 (July 2012), 9 pages.
6. James Barron. 2015. New Inductees at Toy Hall of Fame Join the Ball, the Box and the Barbie Doll. *New York Times* (2015), Page A18.
7. Steven Brown, Bryan Morse, and William Barrett. 2009. *Interactive part selection for mesh and point models using hierarchical graph-cut partitioning*. Canadian Information Processing Society.
8. David Cohen-Steiner, Pierre Alliez, and Mathieu Desbrun. 2004. Variational shape approximation. *ACM Transactions on Graphics (TOG)* 23, 3 (2004), 905–914.
9. Stelian Coros, Bernhard Thomaszewski, Gioacchino Noris, Shinjiro Sueda, Moira Forberg, Robert W. Sumner, Wojciech Matusik, and Bernd Bickel. 2013. Computational Design of Mechanical Characters. *ACM Trans. Graph.* 32, 4, Article 83 (July 2013), 12 pages.
10. E Demaine and Tomohiro Tachi. 2010. Origamizer: A practical algorithm for folding any polyhedron. (2010).
11. Erik D Demaine, Martin L Demaine, and Joseph SB Mitchell. 1999. Folding flat silhouettes and wrapping polyhedral packages: New results in computational origami. In *Proceedings of the fifteenth annual symposium on Computational geometry*. ACM, 105–114.
12. M. P. do Carmo. 1976. *Differential Geometry of Curves and Surfaces*. Prentice-Hall, Englewood Cliffs, NJ.
13. Flatfab. 2014. Flatfab. (2014). Retrieved September 17, 2015 from `http://www.flatfab.com`.
14. Wei Gao, Yunbo Zhang, Diogo C. Nazzetta, Karthik Ramani, and Raymond J. Cipra. 2015a. RevoMaker: Enabling Multi-directional and Functionally-embedded 3D Printing Using a Rotational Cuboidal Platform. In *Proceedings of the 28th Annual ACM Symposium on User Interface Software & Technology (UIST '15)*. ACM, New York, NY, USA, 437–446.
15. Wei Gao, Yunbo Zhang, Devarajan Ramanujan, Karthik Ramani, Yong Chen, Christopher B. Williams, Charlie C.L. Wang, Yung C. Shin, Song Zhang, and Pablo D. Zavattieri. 2015b. The status, challenges, and future of additive manufacturing in engineering. *Computer-Aided Design* 69 (2015), 65 – 89.
16. Steven Gray, Nathan Zeichner, Vijay Kumar, and Mark Yim. 2011. A Simulator for Origami-Inspired Self-Reconfigurable Robots. In *Origami 5: Fifth International Meeting of Origami Science, Mathematics, and Education*. CRC Press, 323.
17. Kristian Hildebrand, Bernd Bickel, and Marc Alexa. 2012. crdbrd: Shape fabrication by sliding planar slices. In *Computer Graphics Forum*, Vol. 31. Wiley Online Library, 583–592.
18. Dennis Hine. 1999. *Cartons and cartoning*. Pira International.
19. Margaret Honey and David E Kanter. 2013. *Design, make, play: Growing the next generation of STEM innovators*. Routledge.
20. Pu Huang, Charlie CL Wang, and Yong Chen. 2013. Intersection-free and topologically faithful slicing of implicit solid. *Journal of Computing and Information Science in Engineering* 13, 2 (2013), 021009.
21. Scott E Hudson and Jennifer Mankoff. 2006. Rapid construction of functioning physical interfaces from cardboard, thumbtacks, tin foil and masking tape. In *Proceedings of the 19th annual ACM symposium on User interface software and technology*. ACM, 289–298.
22. Dan Julius, Vladislav Kraevoy, and Alla Sheffer. 2005. D-Charts: Quasi-Developable Mesh Segmentation. In *Computer Graphics Forum*, Vol. 24. Wiley Online Library, 581–590.
23. Squid Labs. 2005. Instructables. (2005). Retrieved September 17, 2015 from `http://www.instructables.com`.
24. Robert J Lang. 1998. Threemaker 4.0: A Program for Origami Design. (1998).
25. Manfred Lau, Akira Ohgawara, Jun Mitani, and Takeo Igarashi. 2011. Converting 3D furniture models to fabricatable parts and connectors. In *ACM Transactions on Graphics (TOG)*, Vol. 30. ACM, 85.
26. Xian-Ying Li, Chao-Hui Shen, Shi-Sheng Huang, Tao Ju, and Shi-Min Hu. 2010. Popup: automatic paper architectures from 3D models. *ACM Transactions on Graphics-TOG* 29, 4 (2010), 111.
27. Robot Living. 2007. Robot Living. (2007). Retrieved September 17, 2015 from `http://www.robotliving.com`.

28. Kui-Yip Lo, Chi-Wing Fu, and Hongwei Li. 2009. 3D polyomino puzzle. *ACM Transactions on Graphics (TOG)* 28, 5 (2009), 157.

29. Tama Software Ltd. 2014. Pepakura Designer. (2014). Retrieved September 17, 2015 from `http://www.tamasoft.co.jp/pepakura-en`.

30. James McCrae, Karan Singh, and Niloy J Mitra. 2011. Slices: a shape-proxy based on planar sections. *ACM Trans. Graph.* 30, 6 (2011), 168.

31. Vittorio Megaro, Bernhard Thomaszewski, Damien Gauge, Eitan Grinspun, Stelian Coros, and Markus Gross. 2014. ChaCra: An Interactive Design System for Rapid Character Crafting. In *Proceedings of the ACM SIGGRAPH/Eurographics Symposium on Computer Animation (SCA '14)*. Eurographics Association, Aire-la-Ville, Switzerland, Switzerland, 123–130.

32. Jun Mitani and Hiromasa Suzuki. 2004. Making papercraft toys from meshes using strip-based approximate unfolding. In *ACM Transactions on Graphics (TOG)*, Vol. 23. ACM, 259–263.

33. Hyunjoo Oh, Mark D. Gross, and Michael Eisenberg. 2015. FoldMecha: Design for Linkage-Based Paper Toys. In *Adjunct Proceedings of the 28th Annual ACM Symposium on User Interface Software & Technology (UIST '15 Adjunct)*. ACM, New York, NY, USA, 91–92.

34. Kylie Peppler. 2013. STEAM-powered computing education: Using e-textiles to integrate the arts and STEM. *Computer* 9 (2013), 38–43.

35. Valkyrie Savage, Ryan Schmidt, Tovi Grossman, George Fitzmaurice, and Björn Hartmann. 2014. A Series of Tubes: Adding Interactivity to 3D Prints Using Internal Pipes. In *Proceedings of the 27th Annual ACM Symposium on User Interface Software and Technology (UIST '14)*. ACM, New York, NY, USA, 3–12.

36. Yuliy Schwartzburg and Mark Pauly. 2013. Fabrication-aware Design with Intersecting Planar Pieces. In *Computer Graphics Forum*, Vol. 32. Wiley Online Library, 317–326.

37. Idan Shatz, Ayellet Tal, and George Leifman. 2006. Paper craft models from meshes. *The Visual Computer* 22, 9-11 (2006), 825–834.

38. Alla Sheffer, Emil Praun, and Kenneth Rose. 2006. Mesh parameterization methods and their applications. *Foundations and Trends® in Computer Graphics and Vision* 2, 2 (2006), 105–171.

39. Softonic. 2015. Paper Folding 3D. (2015). Retrieved September 17, 2015 from `http://origami-windows-8.en.softonic.com/download?ex=SWH-1608.5`.

40. Milan Sonka, Vaclav Hlavac, and Roger Boyle. 2014. *Image processing, analysis, and machine vision.* Cengage Learning.

41. NGSS Lead States. 2013. Next Generation Science Standards: For States, By States. (2013).

42. North Shore-LIJ Health System. 2015. Paper Airplane Factory. (2015). Retrieved September 17, 2015 from `http://www.ihi.org/education/ihiopenschool/resources/Pages/Activities/PaperAirplaneFactory.aspx`.

43. Shigeo Takahashi, Hsiang-Yun Wu, Seow Hui Saw, Chun-Cheng Lin, and Hsu-Chun Yen. 2011. Optimized topological surgery for unfolding 3D meshes. In *Computer Graphics Forum*, Vol. 30. Wiley Online Library, 2077–2086.

44. Diana Twede and Ron Goddard. 1998. *Packaging materials*. Pira International Leatherhead.

45. Kevin Chun-Ho Wong, Tommy Yu-Hang Siu, Pheng-Ann Heng, and Hanqiu Sun. 1998. Interactive volume cutting. In *Graphics Interface*, Vol. 98.

46. Huai-Yu Wu, Chunhong Pan, Jia Pan, Qing Yang, and Songde Ma. 2007. A sketch-based interactive framework for real-time mesh segmentation. In *Computer graphics international.*

47. Shiqing Xin, Chi-Fu Lai, Chi-Wing Fu, Tien-Tsin Wong, Ying He, and Daniel Cohen-Or. 2011. Making burr puzzles from 3D models. *ACM Transactions on Graphics (TOG)* 30, 4 (2011), 97.

48. Sang Ho Yoon, Ansh Verma, Kylie Peppler, and Karthik Ramani. 2015. HandiMate: Exploring a Modular Robotics Kit for Animating Crafted Toys. In *Proceedings of the 14th International Conference on Interaction Design and Children (IDC '15)*. ACM, New York, NY, USA, 11–20.

49. Juyong Zhang, Chunlin Wu, Jianfei Cai, Jianmin Zheng, and Xue-cheng Tai. 2010. Mesh snapping: Robust interactive mesh cutting using fast geodesic curvature flow. In *Computer Graphics Forum*, Vol. 29. Wiley Online Library, 517–526.

50. Youyi Zheng, Chiew-Lan Tai, and Oscar Kin-Chung Au. 2012. Dot scissor: a single-click interface for mesh segmentation. *Visualization and Computer Graphics, IEEE Transactions on* 18, 8 (2012), 1304–1312.

ChronoFab: Fabricating Motion

Rubaiat Habib Kazi, Tovi Grossman, Cory Mogk, Ryan Schmidth, George Fitzmaurice
Autodesk Research
{rubaiat.habib, tovi.grossman, cory.mogk, ryan.schmidth, george.fitzmaurice}@autodesk.com

Figure 1: We bring the stylized motion visualization techniques of 2D pictures into the physical world of 3D printed models. Motion sculptures crafted with our tool from 3D animated objects explicitly visualize objects' motion in static artifacts

ABSTRACT

We present ChronoFab, a 3D modeling tool to craft *motion sculptures*, tangible representations of 3D animated models, visualizing an object's motion with static, transient, ephemeral visuals that are left behind. Our tool casts 3D modeling as a dynamic art-form by employing 3D animation and dynamic simulation for the modeling of *motion sculptures*. Our work is inspired by the rich history of stylized motion depiction techniques in existing 3D motion sculptures and 2D comic art. Based on a survey of such techniques, we present an interface that enables users to rapidly explore and craft a variety of static 3D motion depiction techniques, including *motion lines*, *multiple stroboscopic stamps*, *sweeps* and *particle systems*, using a 3D animated object as input. In a set of professional and non-professional usage sessions, ChronoFab was found to be a superior tool for the authoring of motion sculptures, compared to traditional 3D modeling workflows, reducing task completion times by 79%.

Author Keywords

Motion sculpture; fabrication; animation.

ACM Classification Keywords

H.5.2. Information interfaces and presentation: User Interfaces – Graphical Interface.

CHI 2016, May 07-12, 2016, San Jose, CA, USA
© 2016 ACM. ISBN 978-1-4503-3362-7/16/05…$15.00
DOI: http://dx.doi.org/10.1145/2858036.2858138

INTRODUCTION

"In sculpture, therefore, we are not necessarily looking for pure form, but for pure plastic rhythm, not the construction of an object, but the construction of an object's action."

-Futurist art movement manifestos, 1909 [14]

3D design and digital fabrication is gaining popularity among researchers and makers for rapid prototyping and designing a wide range of artifacts - including toys, jewelry, miniature figurines, mechanical parts and prosthetics. In general, such static, moving [6, 7, 33, 36], or interactive [24, 25, 35] 3D printed artifacts do not reflect movement over time. In contrast, a number of sculptors and artists have explored the notion of physically visualizing motion in static 3D sculptures (Figure 2), often adopting the styles and abstraction techniques used in 2D visual art which depict motion [8]. We refer to such artifacts as *motion sculptures*. Traditionally, sculpting motion sculptures manually- both physically and with digital tools - can be extremely tedious, requiring significant sculpting expertise and familiarity with fabrication constraints. In this paper, we present animation driven dynamic sculpting for *motion sculpture* form finding. By employing time, motion, and dynamic simulation, we explore fundamentally new workflows and ways of thinking for crafting 3D *motion sculptures*.

Psychologists and art historians have categorized the motion depiction techniques in 2D pictures [8, 16] and studied their emotional responses [8], which is a relatively mature form of expression. Compared to their 2D counterparts, motion sculptures are relatively less explored and have received little attention from the research community. To our knowledge, there is no catalog

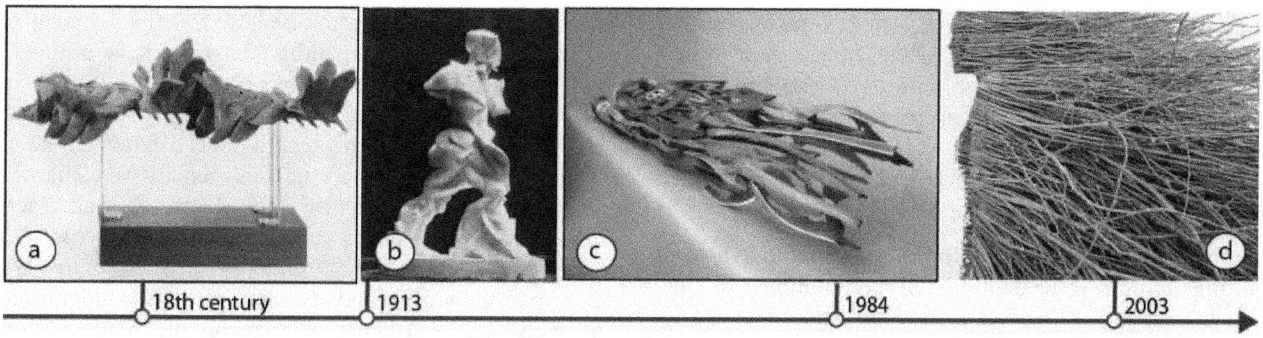

Figure 2. Motion sculpture as an art form has existed for centuries. a) Étienne-Jules Marey's bronze sculpture of a flying gull crafted from his photographic movement studies. b) Umberto Boccioni's sculpture (1913) of "Unique forms of continuity in space" is a notable example of the futurist art movement. Over the years, motion sculptures have become even more vivid and stylized, exploiting creative usage of colors and materials, as in work by Dennis Hoyt (c) and "Stillness in motion" by Olga Ziemska (d).

representing the styles and guidelines for depicting motion for static physical artifacts. We first catalog a list of existing 3D motion sculptures by a wide range of artists and explore the design space of motion depiction techniques. We then explore the materialization of motion into 3D printable geometric objects by employing the temporal dimension for the modeling of such sculptures. We then present ChronoFab, a novel system that allows users to craft motion sculptures, from 3D animated objects, that explicitly visualize objects' motion in static artifacts (Figure 1).The temporal dimension enables the use of motion (3D animation) and dynamic simulation (using Maya's[2] animation engine) as design tools for crafting static 3D forms that are otherwise complicated and tedious. Users can interactively generate and control geometric shapes of four different types of motion effects: *motion lines*, *sweeps*, *multiple stroboscopic stamps* and *particle systems*. The resulting artifacts can then be analyzed for structural strength and stability prior to their fabrication.

We conducted an initial evaluation of our system by having professional and non-professional artists work with both ChronoFab and traditional 3D modeling tools. Our results indicate that ChronoFab simplifies the creation of motion sculptures by intelligently utilizing the motion data to generate the geometries. Overall, task completion times were reduced by 79%, encouraging rapid exploration. We showcase a few resulting artifacts modeled by the authors and the participants which illustrate the expressiveness, ease of usage, and variety of applications of our system.

RELATED WORK

Design and Fabrication

Driven by the increasing availability of 3D printers and laser cutters, HCI and graphic researchers have taken a recent interest in the topic of digital fabrication – including the fabrication of interactive objects, functional mechanical assemblies and data sculptures.

For fabricating interactive objects, researchers have explored a variety of display and sensing techniques, including the use of 3D printed light pipes [35], computer vision to track the movement of interior components [24] and routing pipes through the interior of 3D models [25].

Researchers have also explored the design and fabrication of functional mechanical assemblies that mimic the behavior of an animation. Mechanical toys [36], humanoid motion capture sequences [6] and mechanical characters [7, 33] have all been digitally fabricated. These works optimize the assembly of mechanical components that best approximate the input motion after fabrication. Taking a deformable character and a set of poses as input, the design and fabrication of actuated deformable characters have also been explored [29]. While these works focus on the fabrication of mechanical assembly and actuated objects to reproduce an animation, our work represents motion sculptures, a unique form of art and expression to physically visualize motion within static 3D artifacts.

Helping amateurs for personalized design and fabrication is gaining interest in the computer graphics community. For rapid prototyping, Constructable [18] is a drafting table enabling users to interact by drafting directly on the work piece using a hand-held laser pointer. Other interactive research systems enable non-experts to design plush-toys [17] and personalized chairs [23]. We present an interactive system that enables non-experts to design and explore motion sculptures, using a 3D animated model as input.

Researchers have studied the efficiency of data sculptures [11] for physically visualizing information, and developed tools for fabricating data-driven physical charts [31]. Dragicevic et al. created a curated list of active and passive physical visualizations [9] to motivate and inform the design space of data-driven physical visualization. The vocabulary of the stylized motion effects in our tool is guided by a similar curated list of existing 3D motion sculptures which we contribute.

Motion effects in 2D pictures and 3D rendering

A number of tools and techniques have been developed for generating motion effects in 2D pictures and animation. Among all techniques, photographic blur has received significant attention from the computer graphics community. Sung et al. [30] developed a taxonomy of motion blur approaches and reformulated these approaches in a consistent mathematical framework. Teramoto et al. [32] built a system that enables users to generate a variety of motion effects from a single photograph. Such motion effects have also been used in the context of 2D user interfaces, as an alternative to animated transitions [4].

Researchers in non-photorealistic rendering have explored generating motion effects from 3D animations in the context of real time computer games [10], post-processing operations [12, 15] and programmable shaders [26]. Niehhaus et al. [20] presented a system to generate dynamic glyphs in a 3D scene, guided by scene specifications and user-directed expressions. While these examples serve as inspiration, our work aims to generate motion effects that can be fabricated and viewed from all angles, imposing very different requirements. Furthermore, we provide an interface that enables users to explore a variety of stylized motion effects, without requiring expertise in 3D animation, sculpting or scripting.

BACKGROUND AND DESIGN SPACE

Artists and scientists have crafted a wide range of motion sculptures to visualize motion, for various purposes ranging from aesthetic to analytical (scientific study of motion). To guide our design and explore the variety of motion depiction techniques, we review and categorize motion visualization techniques from our curated list of 3D motion sculptures and installations[1]. We also consulted with motion sculpture artists to gain insight about their existing processes and needs. While prior literature has categorized and discussed a variety of 2D representation styles [8, 16], to our knowledge, no such attempts have been made for 3D motion sculptures.

Motion Depiction Techniques in 3D

Physical 3D sculptures are fundamentally different from graphical 2D content, as the physical objects are tangible and subject to physical forces. However, we have found that many of the motion depiction techniques in 3D sculptures are analogous to the motion depiction techniques commonly used in 2D pictures and cartoons [8, 16]. We have catalogued 79 motion sculptures by 47 distinct artists or entities from art magazines, art history books, film production documentaries, and toy figurines. Taken all together, we identified the following four major types of motion depiction techniques in these artifacts.

Multiple Stroboscopic Stamps

Multiple stroboscopic stamps are commonly used to depict complex motion occurring within a very short period of time. The effect uses a series of discrete, static, slightly different 3D stamps of an object (or parts of an object) taken at different time intervals, overlapped into a single artifact (Figure 3). Depending on how it is utilized, this technique can be effective for portraying the impression of motion without sacrificing clarity or resolution of the moving object. Thus, this technique is used when the object is deforming over time, such as human movements or a flying bird. For scientific purposes, it can facilitate comparison of structure across multiple instances. *Multiple stroboscopic stamps* are commonly used in pictures (Figure 3a), paintings [8] and comics [16]. We identified 22 artifacts by 12 artists using this technique in our catalog.

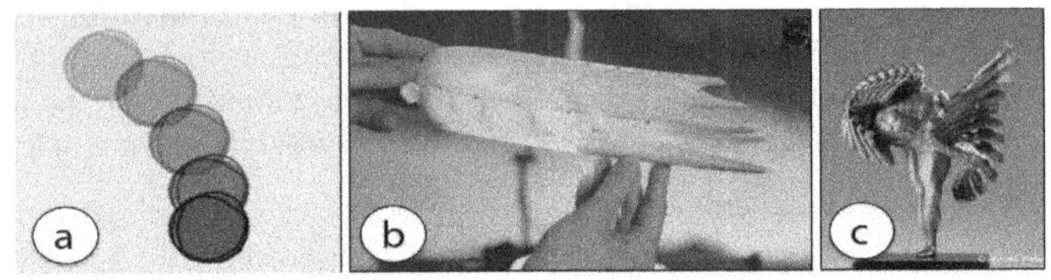

Figure 3: *Multiple stroboscopic stamps* used in (a) photograph (b), 3D printed artifact used in Studio Laika's animated feature film "Paranorman", and (c) Peter Jansen's human motion sculptures.

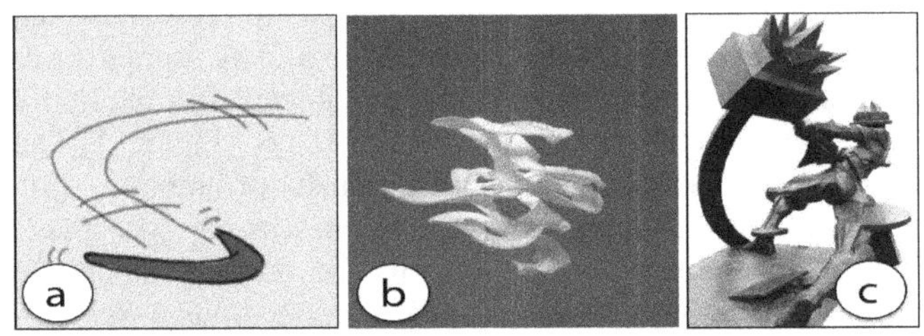

Figure 4: *Sweep* used in (a) comic art, (b) "*Attracted to Light*" by Geoffry Mann, narrating the behavior of a moth flying, and (c) "*Emotions in Motion*" by Michael Sandle

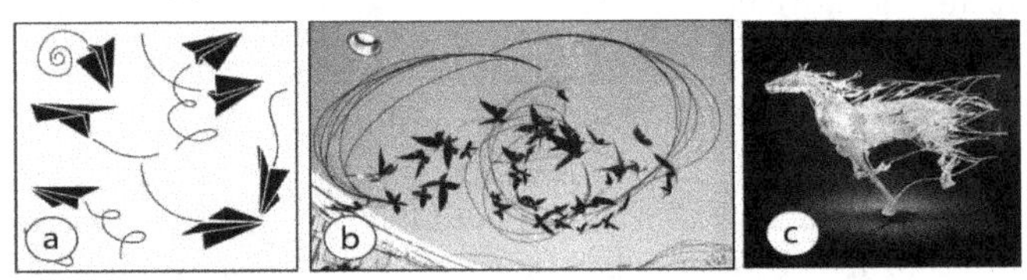

Figure 5: Examples of *motion lines* used in (a) 2D illustration, (b) a wire art ceiling installation by Teressa Leung, and (c) recycled animal art by Sayaka Ganz

Figure 6: Particle systems to depict motion used in (a) comics, (b) "What you see might not be real" by Chen Wenling, and (c) "Nuclear bomb" by Eyal Gever

Sweep

The *sweep* technique generates geometry by sampling numerous instances of a 2D *curve* attached to the surface of an object over a range of time (Figure 4). An analogous effect in 2D pictures is a long exposure photographic blur.

[1] www.autodeskresearch.com/projects/chronofab

Such effects are also common in comics [16] (Figure 4a). We identified *sweep* effects in 19 artifacts by 11 artists.

Motion Lines

Motion lines, also known as speed lines, are generated by sampling numerous instances of a *point* within an object over time to compute the trajectory of that point in space (Figure 5). *Motion lines* are used in cartoons, comics and scientific illustrations to represent the path of a moving object. In motion sculptures, artists sculpt 3D geometry along the trajectory of the *motion line*. We identified this technique in 22 motion sculptures by 15 distinct artists. Similar to comic art, we also identified stylized variations of *motion lines*, such as the use of turbulence (Figure 2d) and tethering (Figure 5c).

Particle Systems

Particle systems, such as smoke and fluid effects, are also used in motion sculptures to depict motion and trajectories (Figure 6). Such effects are also common in comics and illustrations, showing trails of moving objects, such as horses, bikes or rockets (Figure 6a). In the sculpture "*What you see might not be real*" (Figure 6b), geometric shapes of smoke are used to depict the motion of a bull. This technique was used in 8 artifacts by 4 artists in our catalog.

Observations and Discussion

Appropriateness of Techniques

Each of the described techniques has their own advantages and disadvantages [8]. *Motion lines* and *sweeps* are useful for representing abstract motion over a period of time. In contrast, *multiple stroboscopic stamps* and *particle systems* represent a snapshot of a state in time. The actual effectiveness of a technique can depend on the nature of the motion and artist's skill.

Color, Materials and Light

Common materials used to craft motion sculptures include bronze, metal, wires, wood, tree branches and even sand. Among all these motion sculptures, 23 artifacts by 6 distinct artists were multi-colored. We believe the recent advent in multi-material, colored 3D printers offer exciting design possibilities for fabricating these types of motion sculptures.

Uncategorized Techniques

In addition to the four main representation types discussed above, artists and sculptors have also developed a number of ad hoc stylized techniques to portray motion. For example, Umberto Boccioni's "*Unique forms of continuity in space (1913)*" depicts an aerodynamic and fluid form of a human in motion (Figure 2b). Such custom techniques can be very subjective, stylized and irregular which make it hard to formulate procedures for crafting these effects.

Change of parameters over time

We identified examples where artists change the geometric properties (parameters) of the motion geometries over time. For instance, in Figure 6b, the smoke particles spread out more over time. With the *motion lines* and *sweep*, geometries may become tethered (Figure 4c, Figure 5c) and more turbulent (Figure 2d) to represent the passage of time.

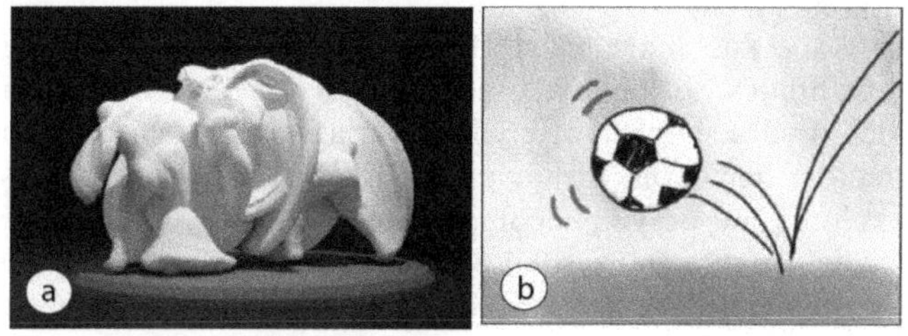

Figure 7: (a) Raphael Perret's "*Bodycloud*" uses multiple techniques together to portray motion (b) *Motion lines* in 2D can be difficult to represent and fabricate in 3D.

Automation in the Authoring Process

The majority of the reviewed motion sculptures were crafted manually. Several motion sculptures were aided by technology during their construction. In project "*BodyCloud*" (Figure 7a) and "*Human motion sculptures*" (Figure 3c), human movements were recorded by motion capture technologies and the final artifacts were generated with digital tools. However, in our correspondences, artists indicated that the process could be tedious and there was a desire for digital tools to enable rapid exploration.

"*To actually do it, took me about a year. Finding the process, getting access to the infrastructure, convincing people and getting the result.*" –Raphael Perret.

Combination of styles

Artists often use a combination of physical representation styles working together to portray motion, similar to comic art [16]. For example, Raphael Perret's "*Bodycloud*" uses a combination of *multiple stroboscopic stamps* and *sweeps* to materialize the motion of human movements (Figure 7a).

Specific Considerations for 3D Fabricated Motion

Even though 2D pictures and 3D sculptures share many techniques for motion depiction, specific considerations must be taken into account when those motion depiction effects are being fabricated in 3D.

Structure Size and Stability

The 2D *motion lines* in Figure 7b are common in cartoons and drawings to provide a jittered appearance, but they may not be feasible in 3D due to their form factor. Unlike their 2D counterparts, 3D printed motion geometries are subject to fabrication constraints, such as minimum thickness and material strength.

Support Structures

Another important consideration is that objects in motion can often be positioned in mid-air. Without support structures, it is challenging to make it stable and balanced. Within our catalog, we identified sixteen examples where the motion geometries themselves also function as support structures (Figure 6b). Such motion geometries that also serve as support structures can assist in both the fabrication process and the balancing and support of the final object.

Summary

Our analysis indicates a rich design space and exciting possibilities to be explored in this art form. We also identified a number of stylized variations of the common motion depiction techniques, which are relatively less explored in previous computational tools. These case studies motivate us to design a tool that facilitates the creation and exploration of 3D motion sculptures.

CHRONOFAB

While many media artists and sculptures have attempted to depict motion in 3D sculptures and installations, there are no specialized interfaces or applications tailored for this purpose. As such, exploring and designing such forms can be tedious and difficult. In this section, we discuss ChronoFab, a new system we have developed, which enables users to model motion sculptures, using a 3D animated object as input. Users interactively author motion geometries by selecting components in the 3D model and adding a range of configurable motion depiction techniques. Once modeled, the resulting artifacts can be exported and prepared for 3D fabrication using existing tools.

Implementation

ChronoFab is implemented with MEL (Maya Embedded Language) scripting using the Maya [2] animation engine. The interface of ChronoFab is developed with QT, a C++ cross platform application and UI framework.

User Interface and Workflow

Our system uses the standard Maya viewport, timeline, selection and navigation tools (Figure 8). The interface has four main panels (Figure 9) for each of the motion depiction techniques – *motion line*, *sweep*, *multiple stroboscopic stamps* and *particle systems*. Within each tab, our interface offers stylized variation of effects for these techniques, with UI widgets for interactive controls.

The system takes an animated model as input. An expert user could use an animated model they designed, while a hobbyist could start with an existing 3D animated model.

The overall workflow to create motion effects is to first select a motion effect type, then specify a time interval, and finally, select a component (vertex, edge or the whole model) of the geometry to apply a desired effect to. The generated effects can be configured using their associated parameters in each tab of the interface. Figure 10 summarizes the overall workflow of the system with the example of a launching rocket.

In this example, the user first selects three vertices of the rocket (Figure 10b), and then generates the associated *motion lines* (Figure 10c). A *Tapered* style variation is then selected. The length of the motion line geometries is determined by the time slider interval, and the user can interactively control the radius and end points of the selected *motion lines*.

To generate a trail of smoke, the user specifies a vertex in the rocket (Figure 10d) and then generates a *particle system* (Figure 10e) which emanates from the selected vertex as it animates through the specified time interval. The user can then interactively control the *particle system* parameters to achieve the desired effect. Once finalized, the user converts the *particle system* into a polygon mesh (Figure 10f) and exports the model for fabrication (Figure 10g). Below we describe each technique in more detail.

Motion Lines

Motion line geometries originate from a point in the object geometry. Users can generate five stylized variations of *motion lines* (Figure 11) - *Cylinder*, *Tapered*, *Turbulent*, *Streak* and *Rugged*. The *Cylinder motion line* generates smooth volumetric curves along the trajectory of the vertex.

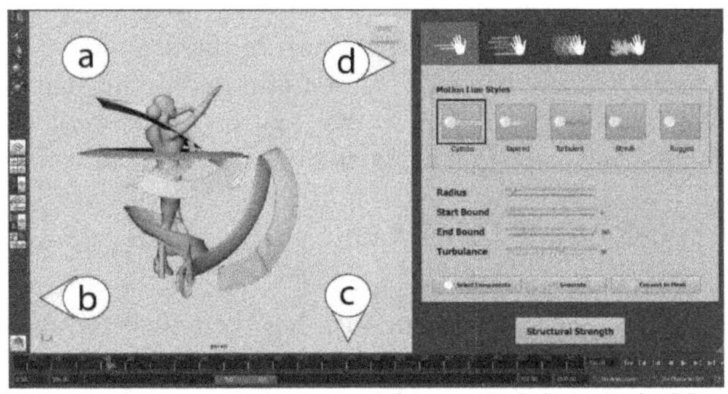

Figure 8: The user interface of ChronoFab is built in Maya (a) Maya viewport (b) Maya selection tool palette (c) Timeline slider (d) ChronoFab user interface.

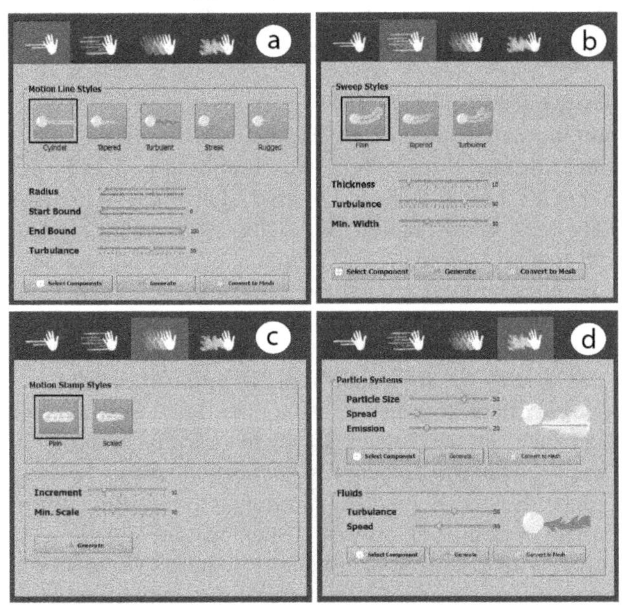

Figure 9. The four ChronoFab effect panels each include parameters for stylizing their own effects (a) *Motion line* (b) *Sweep* (c) *Multiple stroboscopic stamps* (d) *Particle Systems*.

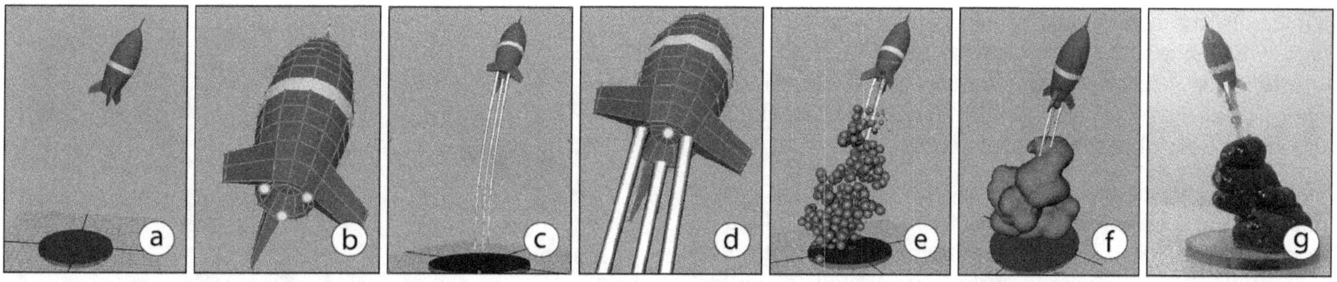

Figure 10: Workflow for crafting motion sculpture using an animated rocket as an input (a) The input animated rocket (b) The user selects multiple vertices (yellow) (b) The system generates *Tapered motion lines* from the selected vertices (d) Preparing to add a smoke trail, the user then selects a vertex (yellow) (e) The system generates a *particle system* emitting from the selected vertex (f) After iterative refinements, the user converts the *particle system* into polygon mesh (g) The 3D printed motion sculpture.

The *Tapered motion line* becomes thinner towards the end while the *Turbulent motion line* adds noise to the path. The *Streak motion line* generates gradually increasing sized motion geometries. The *Rugged motion line* is rough and irregular. To generate *motion line* geometry, the user selects the desired time interval and one or more vertices within the geometry. Pressing the "*Generate*" button creates *motion lines* in the user specified style and time interval.

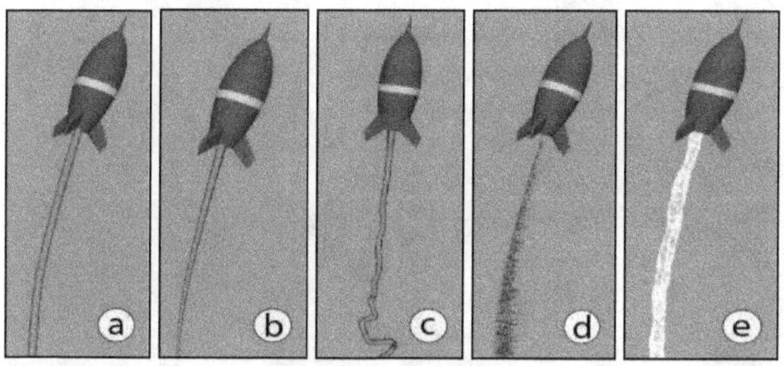

Figure 11: Five stylized variations of *motion line* generated (a) *Cylinder* (b) *Tapered* (c) *Turbulent* (d) *Streak* (e) *Rugged*

Our system computes the trajectory of the selected vertices in 3D space by sampling the target object location at discrete time steps. For *Cylinder*, *Tapered*, *Streak* and *Rugged*, we use existing Maya Paint Effects to generate geometries along the trajectory. For *Turbulent motion line* (Figure 11c), our system attaches a directional Maya Particle system with a point emitter to generate the *motion line*. A turbulence field is attached to the particle system to create the desired irregularities. A *radius* slider controls the thickness of the *motion lines*. The *Start bound* and *End bound* sliders control the starting and end clipping of the *motion line*. A *turbulence strength* slider controls the amount of deformation in the *Turbulent motion line*.

Sweep

Our interface provides three stylized variations of animated *sweeps* (Figure 12) – *Plane*, *Tapered* and *Turbulent*. The *Plane sweep* generates geometry along the trajectory of the 2D animated curve. The *Tapered sweep* becomes thinner towards the end while the *Turbulent sweep* adds geometry deformation over time. To generate a *sweep*, the user selects the time interval and desired *sweep* style. The user then specifies a 2D curve by selecting one or multiple adjacent polygon edges in the geometry surface. Pressing the "*Generate*" button constructs the sweep geometry.

Our system first connects the selected polygon edges to a 2D curve, attached to the surface of the animated object. Next we use Maya's "Animated Sweep" to generate a 2D surface from the animated curve. For a *Tapered sweep*, we linearly scale the animated 2D curve before generating the surface. Our system then extrudes all the polygon faces of the surface to create a volume with thickness for 3D printing. An *initial width scale* slider controls the minimum width of the *Tapered sweep*. The *Turbulent sweep* is implemented by attaching a particle system with a turbulence field to the 2D curve. Upon the generation of the *Turbulent sweep*, users can interactively control the *thickness* and *turbulence* of the geometry.

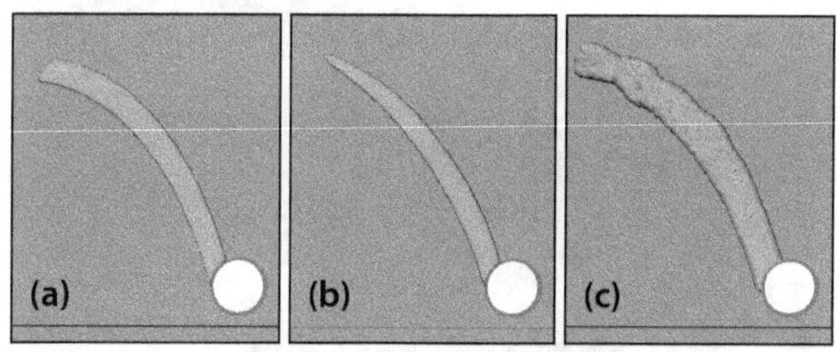

Figure 12: Types of *sweep* (a) *Plane* (b) *Tapered* (c) *Turbulent*

Multiple Stroboscopic Stamps

Users can create stamps of the animated 3D geometry at regular time intervals for a specified time range. There are two variations of this technique – *Plane* and *Scaled*. The *Plane* technique produces stamps without altering the scale of the stamps. The *Scaled* technique linearly scales the stamps over time.

We used Maya's "Animation snapshot" to generate the stamps. The *minimum scale* slider controls the minimum scale of the stamps. An *interval* slider sets the frequency of snapshots. Once generated, users can interactively control the stamp *interval* and *minimum scale* of the stamps.

Particle Systems

Particle systems are used to create smoke and fluid effects along a trajectory of a moving object. The user first switches to the corresponding tab and presses the "*Select component*" button. This switches the system to *vertex selection* mode. After selecting the desired vertex, the user presses "*Generate*" to generate the *particle system* (Figure 10e) along the trail of the selected vertex.

Our system creates and attaches an omni-directional Maya emitter to the selected vertex. A turbulence field is added to the *particle system* to induce irregularities in the motion of our particles. An underlying surface is created to collide with the particles and create a naturalistic smoke effect. Users can interactively control the *particle velocity*, *size* and *emission frequency*. For fluid effects, a fluid emitter is attached to the selected vertex of the object. Users can interactively control the *turbulence strength*. Pressing "*Convert to mesh*" converts the *particle system* into a polygon mesh to be fabricated.

Structural Strength Analysis

Users can often create structurally unsound shape that can easily break after 3D printing. In ChronoFab, users can interactively visualize and analyze the structural strength of the resulting artifacts by pressing the "*Structural Stability*" button. Our system uses Meshmixer [3] python API to visualize the strength of the 3D model through Meshmixer viewport (Figure 13) based on cross-sectional structural analysis that detects critical stress inside the 3D object [34]. In this view, any red coloring indicates structurally weak regions, which the users can then adjust to be thicker.

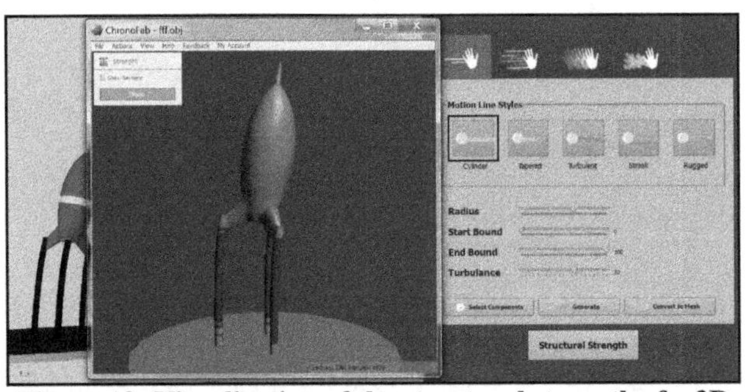

Figure 13: Visualization of the structural strength of a 3D model. Red color indicates structurally weak regions.

Fabrication and Results

Inspired by existing 3D motion sculptures, we used ChronoFab to test our system and fabricate a set of sample objects (Figure 14). We fabricated our models on a variety of 3D printers including the Stratasys Connex 260, Makerbot and ZPrinter 650. Some artifacts were hand-painted (e.g. Figure 10g) and some were printed in full color (Figure 1) and multi-material (Figure 14d).

Figure 14a depicts a creature throwing a tire, with stylized motion techniques inspired by comic books. The trails of the hand and tire are generated using the *sweep* function. In the bouncing ball example (Figure 14c), the motion

Figure 14: 3D printed motion sculptures modeled with ChronoFab. *Sweep* technique applied to visualize a creature throwing a tire (a), a flying plane (b), and the trails of a dance (f). *Tapered motion lines* depict the motion of a bouncing ball (c). *Multiple stroboscopic stamps* technique depicts an action figure fighting (d) and the movement of a snake as a hand bracelet (g). The combination of *Motion lines* and *Multiple Stroboscopic Stamps* portray flying moths around a light (e).

geometries (*Tapered motion lines*) function as support structures for the original object. We used a *Plane sweep* technique for depicting the trail of a flying plane (Figure 14b) and a dancing ballerina (Figure 14f). *Multiple stroboscopic stamps* technique was used to model the fighting action figure (Figure 14d). The abstraction patterns in the stamps were modeled in Meshmixer [3]. 3D animated objects can also be used for product design. The lamp shade in Figure 14e is designed from the flight of an animated moth, using the combination of *Cylinder motion lines* and *Multiple Stroboscopic Stamps*. The moth, its trail and the shell were printed by a multi-material Objet printer using opaque and transparent photopolymers. The jewelry example (hand bracelet) in Figure 14g is designed using the *Multiple Stroboscopic Stamps* technique of a snake moving along the arm. All these examples illustrate the diversified usages of motion sculptures across application domains.

USER STUDY SESSIONS

We conducted a user study to gain insights on how ChronoFab compares to existing 3D modeling tools and workflows for crafting motion sculptures. We invited both professional and amateur users for a comparative user study, and to gain insights about the usability, limitations and creative usage of our system.

Participants

Six participants took part in the user study, aged 25 to 44 years old (average 34). Among them, three participants (*P4, P5, P6*) were expert 3D animators and modelers, having at least 12 years of industry experience. We also invited three amateur users who all had some level of familiarity and experience with 3D modeling and/or sculpting tools, but not as a professional.

Procedure

Our user study sessions for each participant lasted between 50-60 minutes. All the sessions took place in our research lab, consisting of the following two steps.

Overview and Training (20 minutes): In this step, each participant was given a brief overview of the system and was shown some resulting 3D printed motion sculptures made with our system (Figure 14). The instructor walked the participant through seven training tasks. The tasks were designed to familiarize the participant with how to generate and interactively control the motion depiction techniques.

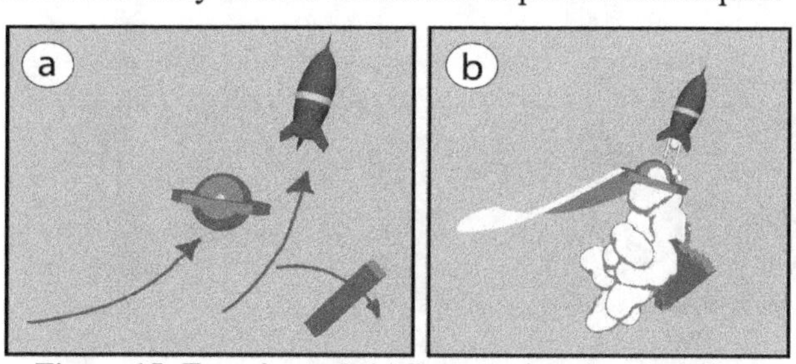

Figure 15: Exercise task (a) Input animation (red lines indicating the motion direction) (b) Target artifact

Exercise Task (30~40 minutes): In this step, participants were asked to reproduce a target motion sculpture (Figure 15) in two separate conditions (*ChronoFab, Traditional*). In the *ChronoFab* condition, the system, as described above, was used. In the *Traditional* condition, participants were allowed to use whichever 3D modeling tool they felt most comfortable with (i.e., Maya, Meshmixer, ZBrush). The target artifact consists of three *motion lines*, a *motion sweep*, a *multiple stroboscopic stamps* effect and a *particle system* effect. Participants were provided with the necessary input files – a Maya animated scene file and all the 3D static models of the individual objects. The condition orders were fully counterbalanced between participants.

Results

All the participants were able to finish the exercise task in both conditions. On average, the task took 4:25 minutes (*SD* 0.6) for *ChronoFab* and 21:10 minutes (*SD* 2.33) for *Traditional* (Figure 17). This effect of condition on completion time was significant ($t_5 = 16.29$, $p<.001$).

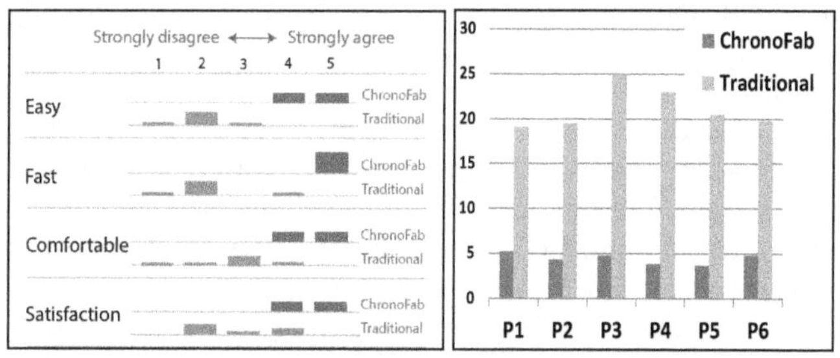

Figure 16: Subjective results from post-study questionnaire (left). Task completion times for each participant (right).

Using *ChronoFab*, participants encountered 2 errors in total, but in both cases recovered independently. *P2* attached a particle system to the flying UFO, instead of the rocket, and later generated the *particle system* from the rocket trajectory. *P5* used *fluids* for the smoke, and later reverted back to a *particle system* for the desired geometry.

For the *Traditional* condition, four participants (*P1, P2, P5, P6*) used Maya and two participants (*P3, P4*) used Meshmixer. Although the animation file was made available for their use, participants mostly used manual sculpting tools (e.g., extrude polygon faces and edges, adding geometric primitives) to generate the geometries.

While our participants (*P1, P2, P5, P6*) had prior experience with Maya, they were often not aware of tools or workflows that could be used to generate geometries using motion data. For example, to create the smoke trail using Maya, two participants (*P1, P6*) repeatedly inserted a number of polygon spheres into the scene. All the participants used sculpting tools to generate the motion lines. This manual use of sculpting tools accounted for longer completion time and lack of precision in the results. Across all participants, there were five instances when participants did utilize the animation – *particle system* (*P2, P5*), *animation sweep* (*P2, P6*), and *multiple stroboscopic stamps* (*P2*). Several participants (*P5*, *P6*) resorted to online help during the task.

In the post-study questionnaire, participants compared the two conditions used to complete the exercise task, based on a set of 1-5 Likert Scale questions (where higher is better). As can be seen in (left), for the given task, participants found ChronoFab to be faster, easier, more comfortable and were more satisfied with the resulting artifacts with ChronoFab compared to traditional tools.

Extended Usage

In addition to the user study, we invited four additional skilled 3D modelers (*P7-P10*) to work with our system to craft motion artifacts of their own. During these usage observations a facilitator assisted the participant when requested. The users authored a range of motion artifacts.

Figure 18a depicts a zoetrope crafted by *P7*, which produces the illusion of motion by using a sequence of 3D models in slightly different poses. The user modeled six different motion sculptures, each of them at a slightly different time interval of an animation. Each of the stamps has *motion lines* added to it. The design took 19 minutes. *P8* modeled a stylized depiction of gaseous emission from a cartoon-like character (Figure 18b). The user started with an existing 3D character and applied the particle system effect to an animated sphere behind the character. The process took 11 minutes. *P9* modeled a procedural geometric shape by first animating a circular disk. He then added *Tapered motion lines* from the vertices in the disc boundary. This artifact took 3 minutes, including the creation and animation of the disc. *P10* crafted an animated rocket artifact with *Tapered motion lines* depicting its trajectory (Figure 18d).

DISCUSSION

In general, the participants responded positively to the simplicity and capabilities of ChronoFab. Participants stated they found our system easy, playful, novel and useful. In the post session questionnaire, the users rated the ease of use as 4.5 out of 5 (*Min.* 4).

Feedback

Participants expressed their high satisfaction to the range of motion effects the system is capable of. Even though our participants never modeled motion sculptures, they expressed their interest in having the tool for a variety of applications, including miniature toy figurines (*P1*, *P2*, *P3*, *P5*, *P6*), jewelry design (*P7*), communicating information (i.e. speed, trajectory, motion in 3D space) in industrial mock-up models (*P5*), procedural geometric modeling (*P8*), public art installations (*P5*), and architectural design (*P2*).

P8: *"If I had the system I would try printing custom jewelry to create intricate and organic looking bracelets or necklaces. Imagine a smoke trail bracelet or necklace generated from a simple animation of a ball going in a circle."*

Users also pointed out a few limitations that could guide future enhancements. Several participants (*P3*, *P4*, *P5*, *P7*) recommended having more sculpting tools in our user interface for greater artistic control and finer details. Users also suggested taking acceleration and velocity into consideration (*P2*, *P8*) when generating motion geometries.

Expressiveness vs. Ease-of-usage

ChronoFab is a special-purpose 3D modeling tool tailored for motion sculptures. As such, it is not directly comparable to general-purpose 3D modeling and animation tools which often have hundreds of controllable parameters Participants (*P3*, *P5*, *P6*, *P8*) commented that the ChronoFab system facilitated rapid exploration by significantly speeding up the process of geometry generation from 3D animated objects and automating the steps. However, it is worth noting that, artists as a user group do not always seek to achieve a task quicker. ChronoFab is more suitable for early stages of design for rapid exploration [28] and form finding. Experienced artists can always use existing sculpting and modeling tools for intricate details and personalization.

P3: *"Although I'll have a lot of control over the shape by sculpting, it will take a lot of time and will be difficult to follow an animation if that's desired. It would be easier just to use your system to make the feature, then add details via sculpting."*

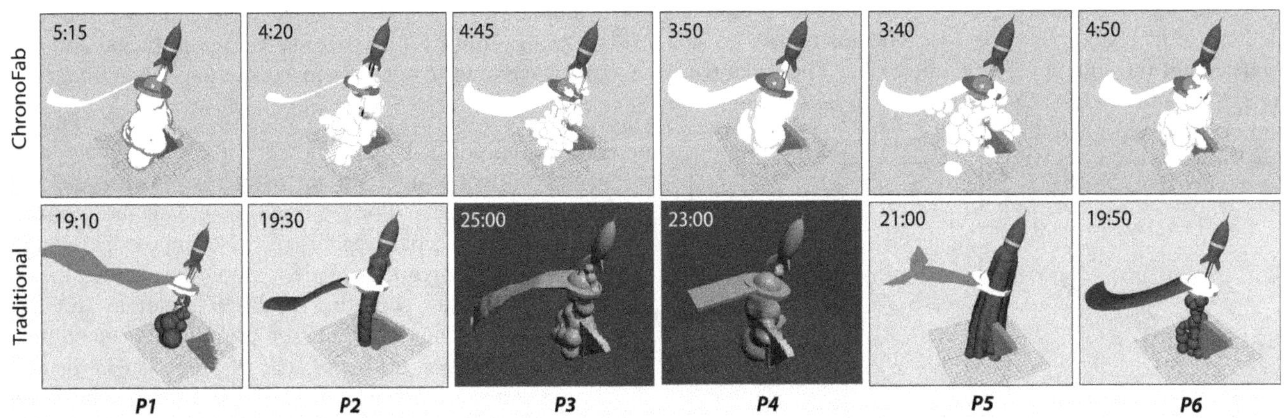

Figure 17: Resulting artifacts in the exercise task using ChoronoFab (top row) and existing tools (using Maya and Meshmixer) by the participants. The number in each panel indicates the time required to complete the task.

Figure 18: Artifacts modeled by external users (a) Zoetrope (b) Gas emission (c) Procedural geometry (d) Rocket

GENERALIZABILITY AND IMPLICATIONS

ChronoFab offers a fundamentally new interactive workflow: Aiding and enhancing 3D modeling techniques by incorporating time, motion, and animation-driven simulations. As we have shown in our work, this is a powerful concept that allows for the efficient and flexible creation of motion sculptures. However, this core concept may extend further with broader implications.

Dynamic sculpting for 3D modeling

One way in which our work may be generalized is the development of 3D sculpting tools that have any awareness of back-end animation data of how a model moves or deforms over time. This would contrast traditional modelling tools which consider only the local geometry and tool parameters. For example, consider having dynamic simulations in a sculpting tool that serve as smart templates or guides for editing manipulation. Or perhaps subtle visualization could reveal local animations that occur at specified areas of a model. We believe there could be a whole class of such "animation-aware" modeling tools and systems, beyond the techniques introduced in our paper.

Novel Approaches to Design Problems and Ideation

Dynamic sculpting can also offer a novel approach to design problems and ideation. While form as a product of dynamic simulation has been explored previously [1], ChronoFab demonstrates the use of motion data as a way of crafting compelling, sophisticated forms quickly and easily. There is a growing corpus of available animation data from motion capture systems, simulation methods, procedural methods, and manually crafted character animations. The integration of such motion data into modeling environments opens up the possibilities for a more dynamic framework in the early stages of design. Static visualizations of motion data, dynamic simulations, and forces over time, can serve as inspiration during the form finding process. For example, as demonstrated in this paper, a flying moth animation may inspire a lamp design (Figure 14e), or a character animation can inspire a jewelry design (Figure 14g).

Generative Design

Another promising avenue for utilizing temporal information in the modeling process is for generative design. In generative design, sophisticated and complex geometries can be represented with small amount of data (e.g., rules, codes, parameters). While the interface components of ChronoFab are inspired from existing motion sculptures, generative designers can write customized rules and codes to generate complex, organic, or repetitive forms using motion data. Together, a number of these tools can be integrated as part of the larger generative design process for new sophisticated designs.

Physical Visualization

By developing tools for crafting physical visualization of motion, our work bridges the gap between 3D animation and physical visualization. Motion is a form of time-varying data. Indexing time in physical artifacts is not just a visual phenomenon, rather it offers new forms of expression for the physical visualization of data [31] that changes over time.

FUTURE WORK

In the future, we intend to explore interfaces that engage motion and time in other forms of 3D modeling. It would also be interesting to investigate the use of static 3D models or video as input for motion sculptures. Currently, our tool only visualizes structurally weak regions of the 3D model. A semi-automatic approach to make the models structurally stable and strong [21] by skewing (e.g., deformation, parameter tweaking) the motion geometries presents an interesting optimization problem. This remains as future work. While previous works analyze the strength of an object as a single material object, balancing the structural integrity of multi-material 3D printed objects also remains an interesting and challenging technical problem.

CONCLUSION

Greg Lynn's seminal book "Animate form" [13] advocates the use of time-based animation techniques for architectural designs that inspired an entire generation of architects to a new way of thinking. Despite the experiments by visionary artists and architects, the use of motion and forces (simulation) as a way of designing static 3D forms is relatively less explored, in particular from an HCI perspective. Guided by our observations, we have designed and developed ChronoFab, a system enabling both amateurs and experts to rapidly explore and craft *motion sculptures* from 3D animated objects using time and dynamic simulation. The user study and resulting artifacts indicate the ease of usage, expressiveness, and creative possibilities of dynamic sculpting for variety of 3D modeling tasks.

REFERENCES

1. Attar, R., Aish, R., Stam, J., Brinsmead, D., Tessier, A., Glueck, M., & Khan, A. (2009). Physics-based generative design. In *CAAD Futures Conference* (pp. 231-244).
2. Autodesk. Maya. tinyurl.com/Adsk-maya.
3. Autodesk. Meshmixer. http://meshmixer.com.
4. Baudisch, P., Tan, D., Collomb, M., Robbins, D., Hinckley, K., Agrawala, M., & Ramos, G. (2006). Phosphor: explaining transitions in the user interface using afterglow effects. *ACM UIST* (pp. 169-178).
5. Braun, M. (1994). Picturing time: the work of Etienne-Jules Marey (1830-1904). *University of Chicago Press.*
6. Ceylan, D., Li, W., Mitra, N. J., Agrawala, M., & Pauly, M. (2013). Designing and fabricating mechanical automata from mocap sequences. *ACM Trans. Graph*, 32(6), 186.
7. Coros, S., Thomaszewski, B., Noris, G., Sueda, S., Forberg, M., Sumner, R. W., et al. (2013). Computational design of mechanical characters. *ACM Trans on Graph (TOG)*, 32(4), 83.
8. Cutting, J. E. (2002). Representing motion in a static image: constraints and parallels in art, science, and popular culture. *PERCEPTION-LONDON*, 31(10), 1165-1194.
9. Dragicevic, P., and Jansen, Y. List of physical visualizations. tinyurl.com/physvis, 2013.
10. Haller, M., Hanl, C., & Diephuis, J. (2004). Non-photorealistic rendering techniques for motion in computer games. *CIE*, 2(4), 11-11.
11. Jansen, Y., Dragicevic, P., & Fekete, J. D. (2013, April). Evaluating the efficiency of physical visualizations. *ACM CHI* (pp. 2593-2602).
12. Lake, A., Marshall, C., Harris, M., & Blackstein, M. (2000, June). Stylized rendering techniques for scalable real-time 3D animation. *ACM NPAR* .13-20.
13. Lynn, G., & Kelly, T. (1999). Animate form.
14. Marinetti, F. T. (1909). The founding and manifesto of Futurism. *Marinetti: Selected writings*, 39-44.
15. Masuch, M., Schlechtweg, S., & Schulz, R. (1999, July). Speedlines: depicting motion in motionless pictures. *ACM SIGGRAPH* (p. 277).
16. McCloud, S. (1993). Understanding comics: The invisible art. *Northampton, Mass.*
17. Mori, Y., & Igarashi, T. (2007, August). Plushie: an interactive design system for plush toys. *ACM Trans. Graph (TOG)* (Vol. 26, No. 3, p. 45).
18. Mueller, S., Lopes, P., & Baudisch, P. (2012, October). Interactive construction: interactive fabrication of functional mechanical devices. *ACM UIST*. 599-606.
19. Muybridge, E. (1957). Animals in motion. *Courier Dover Publications.*
20. Nienhaus, M., & Dollner, J. (2005). Depicting dynamics using principles of visual art and narrations. *Computer Graphics and Applications, IEEE*, 25(3), 40-51.
21. Prévost, R., Whiting, E., Lefebvre, S., & Sorkine-Hornung, O. (2013). Make it stand: balancing shapes for 3d fabrication. ACM *Trans. Graph*, 32(4), 81.
22. Ramachandran, V. S., & Anstis, S. M. (1986). The perception of apparent motion. *Scientific American*, 254(6), 102-109.
23. Saul, G., Lau, M., Mitani, J., & Igarashi, T. (2011, January). SketchChair: an all-in-one chair design system for end users. *TEI* (pp. 73-80). ACM.
24. Savage, V., Chang, C., & Hartmann, B. (2013, October). Sauron: embedded single-camera sensing of printed physical user interfaces. *ACM UIST* (pp. 447-456).
25. Savage, V., Schmidth, R., Grossman, T., Fitzmaurice, G., & Hartmann, B. (2014). A Series of Tubes: Adding Interactivity to 3D Prints Using Internal Pipes. *ACM UIST.*
26. Schmid, J., Sumner, R. W., Bowles, H., & Gross, M. (2010). Programmable motion effects. *ACM SIGGRAPH.* (pp. 1-9).
27. Shah, J. J. (1995). Parametric and feature-based CAD/CAM: concepts, techniques, and applications. *John Wiley & Sons.*
28. Shneiderman, B. (2000). Creating creativity: user interfaces for supporting innovation. *ACM Transactions on Computer-Human Interaction (TOCHI)*,*7*(1), 114-138.
29. Skouras, M., Thomaszewski, B., Coros, S., Bickel, B., & Gross, M. (2013). Computational design of actuated deformable characters. *ACM Trans. Graph*, 32(4), 82
30. Sung, K., Pearce, A., & Wang, C. (2002). Spatial-temporal antialiasing. *Visualization and Computer Graphics, IEEE Transactions* on, 8(2), 144-153.
31. Swaminathan, S., Shi, C., Jansen, Y., Dragicevic, P., Oehlberg, L. A., & Fekete, J. D. (2014, April). Supporting the design and fabrication of physical visualizations. *ACM CHI* (pp. 3845-3854).
32. Teramoto, O., Park, I. K., & Igarashi, T. (2010). Interactive motion photography from a single image. *The Visual Computer*, 26(11), 1339-1348.
33. Thomaszewski, B., Coros, S., Gauge, D., Megaro, V., Grinspun, E., & Gross, M. (2014). Computational design of linkage-based characters. *ACM Trans. Graph* (TOG), 33(4), 64.
34. Umetani, N., & Schmidt, R. (2013). Cross-sectional structural analysis for 3D printing optimization. *SIGGRAPH Asia*, 19-22.
35. Willis, K., Brockmeyer, E., Hudson, S., & Poupyrev, I. (2012, October). Printed optics: 3d printing of embedded optical elements for interactive devices. *ACM UIST* (pp. 589-598).
36. Zhu, L., Xu, W., Snyder, J., Liu, Y., Wang, G., & Guo, B. (2012). Motion-guided mechanical toy modeling. *ACM Trans. Graph.*, 31(6), 127.

Lessons Learned from In-School Use of rTAG: A Robo-Tangible Learning Environment

Victor Girotto[1], Cecil Lozano[1], Kasia Muldner[2], Winslow Burleson[3], Erin Walker[1]

[1]Arizona State University
Tempe, AZ, USA

[2] Carleton University,
Ottawa, Ontario, Canada

[3] New York University,
New York, NY, USA

victor.girotto@asu.edu, cecil.lozano@asu.edu, kasia.muldner@carleton.ca, wb50@nyu.edu, erin.a.walker@asu.edu

ABSTRACT
As technology is increasingly integrated into the classroom, understanding the facilitators and barriers for deployment becomes an important part of the process. While systems that employ traditional WIMP-based interfaces have a well-established body of work describing their integration into classroom environments, more novel technologies generally lack such a foundation to guide their advancement. In this paper we present Robo-Tangible Activities for Geometry (rTAG), a tangible learning environment that utilizes a teachable agent framing, together with a physical robotic agent. We describe its deployment in a school environment, qualitatively analyzing how teachers chose to orchestrate its use, the value they saw in it, and the barriers they faced while organizing the sessions with their students. Based on this analysis, we extract four recommendations that aid in designing and deploying systems that make use of affordances that are similar to those of the rTAG system.

Author Keywords
Classroom integration; social robot; teachable agents; embodied learning.

ACM Classification Keywords
K.3.1. Computer Uses in Education

INTRODUCTION
Technology has become an important element of many classroom environments (e.g., by 2009, 97% of American teachers had computers in their classroom [10]). Students routinely type their assignments on word processors or search for information relevant to their class on the Internet [29]. They can construct knowledge collaboratively in blog posts or discussion forums [6], explore complex concepts within a virtual world [2], and even interact with tutoring systems that analyze problem solving and tailor future exercises [35]. A recent meta-analysis suggests that over the past 40 years, classrooms using digital technologies result in a significant student achievement over classrooms that do not [33]. These benefits are not restricted to students: Educational technology enhances teachers' ability to prepare students for an increasingly collaborative and information-oriented work force [11,36].

To date, the majority of mainstream educational software has been designed for personal computers and related devices. While this kind of software can be beneficial, the WIMP (window, icon, menu, pointing device) paradigm of personal computing does create an artificial separation between the input device, system output, and underlying real-world representation [15]. This paradigm also encourages a style of interaction where students simply sit in front of a computer and interact with a virtual environment on a screen. While tablet and mobile devices have become more popular in recent years, many educational apps still apply a similar style of interaction. Thus, some researchers are beginning to explore the affordances of more embodied and tangible interactions, ranging from collaborative activities surrounding an interactive tabletop [17], to classroom-sized distributed simulations that teach science [22], to interactive robots that teach language learning [32]. Preliminary investigations have highlighted that such technologies can be highly engaging for students and foster learning, but more work is needed to understand the utility of these technologies, particularly in classroom settings.

The Robo-Tangible Activities for Geometry (rTAG) system supports physical, embodied interactions with a robot. The system consists of a Cartesian plane projected onto a white floor mat where a robotic agent, named Quinn, navigates. rTAG facilitates students in mastering the domain through processes related to tangible embodied learning and learning by teaching [24]. Previous work has focused on user studies in laboratory environments [23,24] and there is little in the way of an established body of literature to guide

CHI'16, May 07-12, 2016, San Jose, CA, USA

DOI: http://dx.doi.org/10.1145/2858036.2858454

the translation of rTAG from a laboratory setting to classroom use.

Understanding the barriers that teachers experience in their use of different forms of technology in the classroom is vital for the successful integration of those technologies. Because of the popularity of WIMP-based forms of technology, there is a well-established body of work that examines how to integrate these technologies into classroom practice. For example, a recent review by Bingimlas surveys several barriers to integration at the teacher level (lack of teacher confidence, lack of teacher competence, resistance to change) and at the institutional level (lack of time, lack of training, lack of access to resources, lack of technical support) [4]. Bingimlas' review parallels several related analyses that divide barriers into those constraints imposed on the teachers, and those related to the teacher's attitudes and beliefs [1,3,9].

Recommendations for overcoming these barriers related to traditional WIMP interfaces focus heavily on providing teachers with resources and training. For example, Hew and Brush suggest maintaining a shared vision for technology integration, overcoming scarcity and resources, changing attitudes and beliefs, and providing professional development [13]. It is important to note that professional development should not consist only of instructing teachers on how to use the system, but should also provide a pedagogical background that helps in understanding why the system is effective [3]. To provide this kind of support, it is necessary to understand how teachers perceive the value of the system, what barriers to implementation exist, how they can be overcome, and how teachers can integrate the systems into their current classroom practices.

Since basic technology integration within classrooms has historically suffered from logistics, time, and financial constraints [25], it is reasonable to think that these issues hold, or may even increase when integrating more advanced technologies in the classroom. Teachers may find pedagogical activities using complex technologies too time consuming due to the amount of training required to understand how to use them, or due to the time required to integrate them into classroom activities.

Our overarching research interest is in improving understanding of how to facilitate the integration of non-WIMP educational technologies into classroom practice. As a step towards that, we describe in this paper the design of the rTAG system, with a specific focus on the elements that make it suitable for use in classrooms. We then qualitatively analyze the data collected from the deployment of the rTAG system in a school context using Thomas' General Inductive Approach [34]. This analysis focuses on the teachers' viewpoint, identifying: (1) how they orchestrated the system's usage; (2) The value that they saw in this system; and (3) barriers faced by them in this implementation. From this analysis, we extract design recommendations that can apply to other learning environments that employ nontraditional interactions in a school setting.

RELATED WORK

Integrating Non-WIMP Environments into Classrooms

Kharrufa et al.'s research on the deployment of digital tabletops in a classroom [17] identified five themes, including *control* (how much a teacher felt in control of the classroom), and *awareness* (how aware teachers felt of what students were doing). Their findings show that the deployment had both positive and negative responses from students and teachers. They highlight the importance of supporting teachers through flexibility, or making the system flexible enough to adjust to teachers' plans, and awareness, or making teachers aware of students' progress.

Another similar deployment was made by Hayes et al., who investigated the use of CareLog, a system that aids in the capture and analysis of student behavior information within the context of a special education school [12]. Their five-month study yielded various design principles focusing on empowering teachers to make informed decisions. Poole et al. also discussed the deployment of an ubicomp system that targeted positive health behaviors within a school [29]. Using diverse sources of data, their qualitative analysis also resulted in design recommendations (such as to focus on student-teacher interaction, to be mindful of school boundaries, and to design for group experiences).

As a precursor to the integration of tangible embodied learning environments into classroom practice, Moher [22] describes the integration of "embedded phenomena," which moves technologies off desktop computers into classrooms. These embedded phenomena include simulations of scientific events, such as observations of orbital dynamics and seismic events occurring on a fault line running through the classroom, through media presented on tablets affixed to the walls. Students interact with the simulations over weeks or months, collecting data and making predictions. Although the paper's focus was on describing interactions with the technology, the authors acknowledge that teachers' knowledge of individual students was critical to ensuring that students learn effectively from the simulations. Lui et al. [20] also described the integration of immersive simulations in the classroom, and emphasized the necessity of iterative design and co-design with teachers.

These contributions highlight the importance of teachers in the successful implementation of non-traditional systems in school environments. This paper aims at further expanding knowledge on this form of integration, focusing on the perceptions of the teachers and on the particular affordances of the rTAG system.

Robotic Learning Environments

rTAG is, at its core, a robotic learning environment. The system was inspired by Papert's robotic LOGO system, in which students used LOGO primitives (commands) to control robots [26]. However, rTAG uses embodied interaction and a teachable agent framing in ways that extend beyond the LOGO paradigm. rTAG also leverages principles of robotic learning environments to create more social engagement with the activity, something others are beginning to explore as well. For example, Saerbeck et al. [32] used the iCat robot to investigate how a socially supportive cat influenced the task of language learning. In contrast to a neutral cat, users of the socially supportive version learned more and were more motivated. Leite et al. [19] also relied on the iCat framework, creating a robotic agent that empathized with human chess players. During a game of chess, the robot would generate empathetic messages to the human player, such as "don't be sad, you didn't have better options". Compared to those who had a neutral robot, users who worked with the empathetic version provided higher ratings of degree of companionship with the robot. Kanda et al. [16] conducted a two-month trial in an elementary school with a social robot called Robovie, who could express various social behaviors, such as calling children by name. The focus of this work was to explore the possibility of social human-robot relationships; thus, integration issues were not addressed.

Teachable Agent Environments

The second inspiration for rTAG is teachable agent systems. Teachable agents have emerged from the body of research showing that students benefit from tutoring other students [28]. For instance, when students know they will be tutoring their peers, they are more motivated to attend to educational material. As their partner takes steps and makes errors, they reflect, noticing their own misconceptions; as they give explanations, they elaborate on their knowledge and construct new knowledge [31].

Accordingly, developers have designed educational systems where students teach an agent about the subject they are learning. The most investigated teachable agent system is Betty's Brain, designed to help students learn about causal modeling [5]. Students teach Betty, their agent, by using resources such as text and videos to draw causal networks. Students can ask Betty questions that she will answer based on the network, and at some point, Betty will take a quiz. In Betty's Brain, the teaching mechanism is one of framing--it is the students that create the causal network, and thus, when Betty takes a quiz, it is their work that is being tested. In contrast, other teachable agent platforms such as SimStudent leverage the co-learning potential of teachable agents. After each problem-solving step SimStudent takes, she asks her human tutor if the step is correct, and updates her knowledge with the response. As a result of this learning process, SimStudent makes errors that simulate ones a human student might make, leading human tutors to reflect on their misconceptions [21].

Studies show that students are highly motivated to teach their agents, feel responsible for them, and so try harder and attend more to instructional material [7]. Moreover, peer-to-agent tutors notice their own misconceptions and elaborate on their knowledge as they watch their agents solve problems [5]. Thus, teaching a computer agent is highly beneficial for the student doing the teaching: it can lead to more learning than being taught by a computer agent [18], is nearly as effective as being taught by a human tutor [30], and is more effective than classroom instruction [27]. Recently, Hood, Lemaignan, and Dillenbourg extended a Nao robot so that students could teach it about handwriting [14], further suggesting that the promise of teachable agent interactions can be extended to teachable robot scenarios.

THE rTAG SYSTEM

System Overview

rTAG is designed to teach basic geometry concepts to middle school children [23,24]. It is assembled using components that may already be common in some school settings, including iPod Touches, Wii Remotes, a LEGO® Mindstorms® NXT robot, and a projector.

The system is comprised of three main components. The first is the problem space, which consists of a Cartesian plane projected onto a white floor mat. This plane contains a virtual agent, and can also have zero or more points plotted onto it. The second component is Quinn, a teachable and affective agent that is comprised of a LEGO® Mindstorms® NXT robot and an iPod Touch placed on its top. This iPod Touch displays Quinn's face and outputs its voice, through which it can give affective responses. It also provides the entry point for interacting with Quinn. The last component is the mobile interface, which consists of another iPod Touch, this one held by the student when interacting with the system. Through the mobile interface, the user selects commands for Quinn.

Before using the system, students are told that they need to help Quinn learn how to solve geometry problems—examples of problems are: "*Plot point (3, 1)*" and "*Plot point (-2, 3)*". To solve these problems, students have to issue commands to Quinn, so that it will move to the specified location and plot the point. To give a command to Quinn, students must first touch its face (the iPod Touch screen that is on top of the robot). This triggers a pop-up on the student's mobile interface, from which he or she can select an action for Quinn to perform. Actions include *move n units*, *turn d degrees (counter-clockwise)* and *plot point*. Therefore, a possible solution plan for the problem "*Plot point (3,1)*" could consist of performing the actions *move 3*, *turn 90*, *move 1*, and finally *plot point*. Before each action, the student has to approach Quinn and touch its face in order to trigger the menu on the mobile interface. Since Quinn is always moving, this means that the student will always be moving as well.

After plotting the point, the student can check if the solution is correct or incorrect by tapping on the "Check Answer" button available on the mobile interface, which triggers the system's response with both visual and audio feedback on correctness. Following this feedback, Quinn smiles for positive (correct) outcomes and frowns for negative (incorrect) ones, and then makes a social statement related to the outcome of the problem such as "*We worked hard to solve that problem.*"

Design Principles

The rTAG system combines robotic learning environments and teachable agent learning environments. Quinn is a robotic agent that moves within the physical space. Students also move within the physical space, and thus concepts such as differentiating between axes or translating points may be encoded in movements such as pointing or walking to a point. Further, the rTAG system uses a teachable agent framing where users are told that they are teaching Quinn how to solve the point plotting problems. As described in the related work section, teachable agents have been shown to have a positive impact in learning and engagement, as students attend more to the domain material, reflect on the knowledge required to solve the problem, and feel responsible for the agent's performance.

rTAG was designed to explore the potential for installation in classroom environments. First, it was designed to help address the barrier of insufficient school resources. A fully assembled system costs roughly $2000. While this is too expensive for a typical classroom, it is much more affordable than most embodied learning environments (e.g., US$35,000 for SMALLab [37]), and with optimizations and price drops on components such as the projector, we anticipate that it will be possible to further reduce the cost. Furthermore, the system is built with components that may already exist in a school, such as LEGO® Mindstorms® NXT robots, regular laptops, and portable web browsing devices such as the iPod Touch (Fig. 1 left). In addition, because the system is a physical installation, it allows several students to position themselves around the edges, making observing and engaging with the system more accessible to large classrooms of students.

rTAG also includes design features intended to improve teacher confidence and competence while using the system. It is built from recognizable subcomponents that many teachers are already familiar with: LEGO® Mindstorms®, iPod Touches, and Wii Remotes. As such, its functionality and design aims at being more interpretable than the black box approach of some commercial systems.

We have built both virtual and physical versions of rTAG, which creates a bridge between the familiar WIMP version of the system and the less familiar non-WIMP version of the system. The virtual version, named vTAG, has the same functionality as rTAG, but all the interactions and actions take place through a regular WIMP-based interface. The screen is divided in 3 sections: on the left is the Cartesian plane with a circle representing the robot selected with a mouse click, on the top right is the face of the robot Quinn and on the bottom right is the interface to give commands to Quinn, which looks the same as the iPod interface (Fig. 1 right). It is possible for teachers and students to become comfortable using the WIMP version, called vTAG, before transferring to the non-WIMP version. Collectively, the rTAG and vTAG versions are referred to simply as the TAG system.

Figure 1. rTAG (left) and vTAG (right).

rTAG is designed to leverage teacher objectives in a way that, ideally, engenders positive attitudes and goodwill towards the system. In addition to targeting the geometry domain, it targets cross-curricular skills like collaboration and critical thinking, which are important skills for a successful life, and are being increasingly worked on by schoolteachers due to standards such as the Common Core [8]. It presents an engaging and novel activity that may motivate students to attend more to learning content. We return to implications of these features later.

DEPLOYMENT

We conducted a week long study to evaluate the impact of the TAG system in a school setting, inviting teachers from a California public school district to bring their students to one or more sessions taking place at a room in the district's office in which we had set up several stations of the TAG system. This district is particularly engaged in integrating technology and fostering domain-independent skills. This is clearly visible in their Mission Statement, which highlights the "4 C's": collaboration, communication, critical thinking, creativity, as well as STEAM initiatives. Both the district's superintendent and technology administrator, our contacts within the school, demonstrated great interest in this project, which further shows the district's commitment to adopting technology. In this district, 79% of students qualify for free or reduced price meals.

Twelve teachers, from 4 different schools, scheduled one session each for their classes. Classes had 25-40 students, with 8 classes from 3rd, 3 from 4th and 1 from 5th grade. Five teachers opted to have additional facilitators (parents, administrators, or teacher interns) in their sessions.

Three researchers travelled to the school one day before the study to set up the system, but only two remained to oversee the study. The room was arranged in a semi-circle with a total of 5 stations, as shown in Fig. 2. There was one rTAG station located in the middle of the room, 3 virtual TAG stations (vTAG) and one LEGO® Mindstorms® NXT

2.0 station. We physically separated the vTAG stations to minimize bias from adjacent vTAG stations. The LEGO® station had a robot built similarly to Quinn, but without a face interface. Instead, students used the regular EV3 interface to program it to move. This station, therefore, represented a more common usage of this kind of robot. Each station had a concise system manual and solutions to the problems. Video cameras were arranged around the room to get both a wide angle view of the room and a closer take of the students' interactions with the system, while minimizing interference or distractions as much as possible.

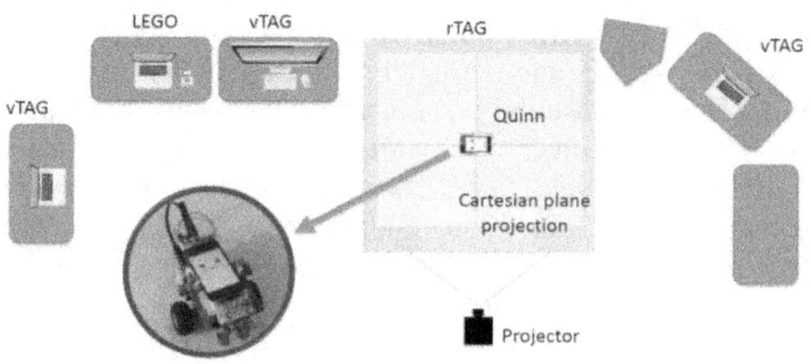

Figure 2. Physical organization of the room.

Consenting teachers were encouraged to be part of all the study activities that took place before, during, and after the immersion session. Before the session, teachers received a summary of the study activities and the description of the system combined with a short video showing how it worked. They were encouraged to send us a new set of problems for their students to match their learning goals (none requested this), send us a lesson plan (1 did) and come to a training session before their scheduled session so they became familiar with the system (less than half did). In the one-hour training session, teachers were debriefed about the goals of the study, the setup and the teaching framing and learned how to give Quinn commands.

The immersion session had a brief introduction from the research team, a training phase followed by an immersion phase, and concluded with a short unstructured debriefing phase. The training phase was intended to be led by the teacher, instructing students on how to perform all TAG actions that they would need to solve problems (e.g., move and turn Quinn, check the answer). Right before the immersion phase, the class was notified that teachers were the ones in charge of the session and experimenters would be available to help only with technical difficulties. The debriefing phase consisted of a few questions from the teacher or experimenter about student impressions of Quinn, the system, and their general experience. After each day, the researchers were responsible for shutting down the system, as well as starting it again on the following day.

After the sessions, the teachers were invited to participate in a 2-hour focus group activity on the final day of the week. Five teachers participated in this activity, in which they reflected on the TAG system (~30 minutes), collaboratively designed a lesson plan (~30 minutes), developed storyboards to show an ideal student interaction with the system (in two groups, ~30 minutes), and shared their designs (~30 minutes).

Finally, two of the five teachers involved in the focus group participated in a follow up semi-structured reflective interview. Both teachers watched the footage of their sessions before the interview.

METHOD

To better understand the affordances and limitations of integrating the TAG system within a school setting, we analyzed teacher's actions and perceptions through three objectives: 1) understand how they orchestrated their sessions, which helps us understand the physical and logistical constraints of the system, 2) understand the value they saw in the system, giving us insight into what worked for them, and 3) understand barriers they faced while using the system, which helps us understand complexities and limitations of the system. By examining how they used the system, why they might want to use it, and what obstacles they faced, we will be able to better understand how to iterate on the design of the system to make it more suitable for classroom use.

Analysis of the interviews, focus groups, and session footage was performed using the General Inductive Approach method outlined by Thomas [34], with the goal of extracting themes from the data. Two members of the research team independently followed this approach, occasionally meeting to converge on the themes that were identified and the quotes that were related to them. The process is as follows: 1) initial reading of the data in order to gain familiarity with it; 2) identifying segments of data (e.g., interview responses, teacher interactions with students) that related to our three objectives (orchestration, value, and barriers); 3) labeling the segments and creating categories; 4) reducing overlap and redundancy between categories; and 5) creating a model that incorporates the most important categories. This procedure followed the *independent parallel coding* strategy outlined by Thomas for checking consistency of qualitative coding [34]. We now describe the themes that arose from this analysis.

RESULTS

Orchestration

Orchestration refers to the activities that the teachers chose to employ in order to facilitate their use of rTAG, including activities both before and during the session. It was analyzed by looking mainly at the session footage, but it was complemented with the data from the interviews and focus groups. The goal was to understand how teachers used the rTAG setup, and if it differed from the more common vTAG setup. We organized orchestration into five subcategories: pre-session instruction, session introduction, student distribution, session management, and rotation of students. Table 1 summarizes the findings for this category.

For the remainder of this paper, we will refer to specific sessions by a code in the form *X-Y*, where *X* is the day of the session and *Y* is the number of the session that happened on that day. Session 3-2, therefore, is the second session on the third day. We will also refer to the two focus groups as FG1 (comprised of T1, T2, and T5), and the second as FG2 (comprised of T3 and T4).

Subcategory	Typical behavior	Atypical behavior
Pre-session instruction	No instruction; teach the domain; teach how to use the system	None
Session introduction	Researcher or teacher handled the system	Teacher chose assigned student to handle the system (1-1, T1)
Student distribution	Teacher distributed students around stations; pre-formed teams	Quinn station not used from the start (1-1, T1); LEGO® station not used at all (1-1, T1)
Session management	Teachers moved around the room; used adult supervisors	None
Student rotation	Within stations: up to the students; between stations: up to the teacher	Between stations: up to the students (1-1, T1; 2-2, T2; 2-4, T2); rTAG managed by supervisor (1-1, T1)

Table 1. Summary of the orchestration strategies and exceptions used throughout the sessions.

Pre-session Instruction

Most teachers did not prepare their students during their regular classes prior to the session, due to time constraints. Some of the teachers who did shared that they showed students the video of the system and Quinn that we sent them, went over the commands to teach Quinn, and described some geometry concepts like positive and negative coordinates, the quadrants, angles, and degrees. While debriefing after the sessions, teachers reflected on how they would prepare their students for the session. Regarding teaching the domain, T5 said: "*See, what I did beforehand, before coming, so they kind of already knew what to do, I taught them the coordinates*". As for showing how the system works, T1 planned on integrating her current practice of demonstrating the system using a projection onto a whiteboard, where she could freely annotate the screen. FG1, of which both T1 and T5 were part of, proposed a lesson plan that followed the same direction, reinforcing the notion of pre-lesson teaching vocabulary and group guidelines. FG2, however, proposed ideas like using YouTube to show how to use the robot and training team captains who could help other students.

Session Introduction

During the introduction phase (explaining how to use the system to the class) in the immersion session itself, six teachers led the session for their students, although three of them couldn't remember some details of the system and required assistance from the researcher. For the remaining six sessions, the researcher was the one performing the training. The main difference between how the teachers vs. researcher introduced the system pertained to time. Teachers spent approximately five minutes showing students how to use the system, while the researcher would spend around fifteen. This finding could relate to the teachers' perceptions that students are able to pick up new technology very fast. T1 says: "*With the technology that we have this school year, I just have found that these kids are really quick. (...) Literally, I did a five-minute demo in front of the class with my computer on the projector of how to make a Google drawing. Five minutes was all they needed, and they were done. They were off. They were running. They were making their Google drawings. It was amazing*". This reflects on the lesson plans and storyboards developed during the focus group session. The only situation similar to an in-session introduction was mentioned by FG2, and it simply stated that teachers should talk about appropriate behavior and good sportsmanship before the session.

As for the content of the instruction, one teacher, who had already taught students the domain before the session, still focused on reviewing the domain content, and not the system usage. But regardless of whether the teacher or researcher introduced the session, the overall strategy was similar: students gathered around a given station (usually a vTAG one), where the teacher or researcher would demonstrate how the system works. One notable exception, however, occurred in session 1-1, where the teacher (T1) chose a "*very tech savvy*" student to man the station while she explained how the system worked.

Student Distribution

After the introduction phase, teachers would distribute the students around the different stations. In six out of the twelve sessions, teachers had already assigned students to teams before the start of the session. In five of the sessions, teachers took some extra time to create the teams and then assigned them to each station. In session 1-1, students could choose which station to go to.

Usually, all stations were used from the beginning of the session. However, on session 1-1, T1 decided to hold off on using the physical system until later, judging that using that setup upfront would have been "*wasted*" time. In this session, rTAG was used only after she gauged that most students had already used the vTAG station. This strategy is reflected in FG1's storyboards, where the rTAG station would be used only after students had already completed a few tasks on pen and paper and using the virtual setup. T1 also didn't make use of the LEGO® station, arguing that it would be "*too much*" for "*that short amount of time*"

Session Management

During the session, teachers usually moved around the room, to ensure each group made progress and that all students had an equal opportunity to try using the system. Five sessions also employed other adult supervisors, such as members of the school staff or some students' parents. Talking about these helpers, T1 says: "*The fact that there was another adult there that they knew and were comfortable with, I think helped, whereas if she weren't there, they probably would have just skirted along the back and probably never even—would have never even attempted.*" Not all helpers were adults: Some students took a leadership role, going around the stations to help other groups. This happened either by initiative of the students, or in some cases, by explicit leadership assignment from the teachers. In fact, teachers in FG2 supplemented this goal in the lesson plans, explicitly assigning some leader students, who would be responsible for coaching their peers. More generally, both groups planned for group interactions. This reinforces the collaboration affordances of this system, which were deemed valuable by the teachers, especially given the new Common Core Standards that are being adopted. T4 stated: "*The good thing, I thought, the Common Core says communication, collaboration. We do some of that, but this was really good.*"

Student Rotation

Rotation of students happened in two levels: within and between the stations. The first relates to how students would control which member of their group would be interacting directly with the station. With the exception of one session (1-2), in which the teacher had a predefined order of which student should be interacting with a station, teachers gave the students freedom to manage this, at most resorting to some organization by the student leaders in each group. Students employed various ad hoc strategies: one group, for instance, used the "rock, papers, scissors" game to decide who would go first. However, many students interacted in very fluid ways, such as sharing the solution generation to a single problem by passing the iPod Touch around, allowing another student to touch Quinn (on the rTAG station), or by passing the mouse around (on the vTAG stations). Rotation between stations was usually controlled by the teachers. They would rotate the groups after a given amount of time which varied among sessions, from 5 to 45 minutes.

The exception happened in sessions 1-1 (T1), 2-2 (T2), and 2-4 (T2), where students were given the freedom to move between stations. While all TAG stations were usually regulated by the students themselves, T1 (session 1-1) decided to have a tighter control over the rTAG station. On session 1-1, a facilitator trusted by the teacher managed the use of rTAG. Students would sit around the setup, while one student, chosen by the facilitator, would use the system. After the student solved a problem, this facilitator would select another student to solve the next problem.

It is interesting to note that even though rTAG is a system with many novel affordances, it was still used much like the vTAG stations were (with the notable exception of session 1-1). Teachers normally did not do anything special with the rTAG station. This warrants further research, but it is possible that some of the principles behind rTAG, such as using recognizable subcomponents, may have helped teachers to perceive it as a more regular system.

Figure 3. Students using rTAG during a session.

Value

Having examined how the sessions were orchestrated by the teachers, we now turn to analyzing the value they saw in the system. The four subcategories we identified are: increase of engagement, physical robot affordances, technology exposure, and domain-general skills.

Engagement

Teachers saw student engagement as one of the positive assets of the system. This was very evident from both the interviews and the footage of the sessions. To illustrate, in the sessions where a teacher or facilitator asked the students who wanted to go next on the rTAG station, students would always promptly raise their hands. Another evidence of engagement was that whenever time was up for a given session, those who had not had the chance to interact with the rTAG station would loudly express their discontent. Teachers perceived this. For example, T1 said: "*They were excited about him [Quinn]. They just thought he was cool*". T2 went deeper: "*That's what I think is really key, is that if they aren't even realizing that they're learning, that they think that they just went on this field trip and had fun, but now they know how to plot points on the positive and negative side. They just think they went and played with a robot, which I think is cool.*" The focus of the excitement, at least in this instance, was on the physical robot.

Robot Affordances

Teachers perceived the physical robot as an important benefit of the system. T1 emphasizes that the novelty of the robot would make this a remarkable experience for students: "*I think this was something that the kids are going to remember because it was separate from the classroom, different from something they were doing on their netbooks. The robot was right there in front of them.*" T1 also mentioned a boost in perseverance due to the robot, especially due to its social attributes: "*I think it would motivate them to persist in a problem and to keep going and to keep trying to get it the way it was supposed to be and get Quinn where he was supposed to go. I do think it makes a difference. I think it's something they can relate to, as opposed to this faceless no name little box with wheels. I think it does make a difference*". In fact, T2 contrasts rTAG with its virtual counterpart: "*the reaction's better with the physical because it's like an actual being. It could be their pet or something. Whereas, on the computer, it's just so second nature.*" It is possible that this heightened engagement may be due to a novelty effect, and would likely decrease over time as they grow accustomed to the system. Teachers may be aware of this. FG1, for example, has proposed gamification additions to the system, which may help to maintain engagement over time.

Technology Exposure

Another common theme among teachers was related to the value of exposing students to technology. Teachers in this school aim to make their students proficient in using digital tools, e.g., most students have their own laptop, and conduct a great amount of the classroom work in them. Teacher T1, for example, integrates Khan Academy into a morning routine: "*the kids are all on Khan Academy. One of our morning activities is the kids' work on Khan Academy. Part of Khan Academy, there is a coding section to it, and I had a group of boys that really wanted to explore it, and so I said sure. I sent about five of them off to a little corner in my classroom, and for several weeks, they explored the coding part of it*". Her goal has been to "*integrate technology into everything that we do as much as possible*". In this context, the teachers saw great value in the rTAG system. To them, this was another opportunity of showing their students some of the affordances made possible by technology, possibly making them more proficient in its use, while also leveraging their curiosity.

Domain-General Skills

Teachers emphasized domain-general skills that can be acquired through the usage of this system, such as critical thinking and problem solving. T1 believes "*that they have to be able to analyze what they're doing and problem solve and decide, what's a more efficient way that I could have done this. I think that's a huge, huge benefit of this program.*" Further evidence is seen through the storyboards, where one group explicitly mentioned the goal of developing the four C's: collaboration, communication, critical thinking, and creativity. The other group planned to attribute the role of leader to some students, giving them the responsibility of coaching other students, which is another valuable domain-general skill. This focus on domain-general skills is possibly due to the increasing requirement for compliance to the Common Core State Standards [8].

For students to collaborate, teachers usually divided them into smaller groups and distributed these groups among the several available stations, allowing students to organize themselves within each station. On vTAG, this led to a few engaged students close to the computers, while others would mostly just sit back and watch, or wander around the room. On the physical setup, however, more students usually tried to participate together with who was currently using the system. Teacher T2 noted: "*I see eight or nine kids jumping in and trying to help, or looking to see if it's time to touch. It's just they're more involved, more willing to maybe offer a solution.*" In many sessions, several students could be seen standing on the foam mat discussing the problem, constantly passing the iPod Touch around and taking turns on who would be interacting with Quinn.

Contrasting the vTAG and rTAG setups, we see that most of the values highlighted by teachers were either present only on the rTAG setup (for example, the values related to the robot affordances), or at least heightened by it (for example, rTAG allowed more room for collaboration. Teachers also perceived it to be more engaging). T1 explicitly contrasted rTAG to "*something they were doing on their netbooks*", that is, their regular computers. Nonetheless, vTAG also proved important, as it was intensively used by most teachers during training, likely due to the larger screen and increased familiarity.

Barriers

Our analysis also identified perceived barriers faced by the rTAG system in a school environment. We identified five subcategories: lack of time for teachers to spend on the system, lack of teacher training, student intimidation, technology limitations, and number of students per station.

Lack of Time

Teachers complained about an overall lack of time to perform activities out of their lesson plans. T2 says: "*Do we have the time? We don't. We don't even have the time to do what we're supposed to be doing.*" This is corroborated by the fact that only one teacher sent the lesson plan which we requested from them. T4 states: "*Well, I don't have time to write a lesson plan, but let me look at what I can do*". This is relevant for rTAG, as it requires a larger setup and training overhead when compared to vTAG, possibly drawing teachers away from using the robotic setup.

Lack of Training

Lack of time could also contribute to another barrier, which is lack of training. In the study we gave teachers two days to come to training before the sessions started, but many of them were not present, which made this problem even more evident. As a result, some teachers could not prepare the students well in both the domain and the system, and were not very well acquainted with it themselves. This resulted in only three out of twelve teachers leading the training completely by themselves, with the remaining nine—including some of those who actually came to training—delegating it partially or completely to the researcher.

Student Intimidation

Teachers also perceived that some students felt intimidated by the rTAG setup, causing them to prefer the vTAG stations. T1 reports: "*I think the ones that stayed on that computer with the larger monitor with my student teacher, those were the ones who were just really afraid and really not quite understanding it.*" This, again, shows the benefit of having vTAG, where students who may be hesitant to try the robotic setup can start to use the system on a more familiar setup. Nonetheless, some were even afraid of the vTAG setup, actively avoiding using it. T1 continues: "*I think there was a little bit of movement of one of those who was afraid and didn't really want to try, was getting close to their turn on one computer, I think they did go to another computer.*" This happened despite the school's adoption of technology on the classroom. She says: "*There were still some that just really were almost afraid of it.*"

Technology Limitations

The limitations of the technology involved in the system could impact the workflow of teachers and students. T2 reported having problems when trying to demonstrate the rTAG system to the students due to the iPod's small screen size, since some could not see the little screen. Whereas the teachers were used to connecting their computers to a projector to demonstrate systems, they were unable to do so with the physical setup of rTAG. In addition, previous experiences led some teachers to worry about the fragility of the setup. T1 recounts an experience with projected smart boards, and the fact that if students moved the projector slightly, there would be significant downtime. T1 says: "*When you have the class's attention, and you're doing something and you're in the middle of a lesson and something happens, then their attention is gone.*"

Number of Students per Station

Teachers also reported limitations related to the quantity of students per station. There were too many students at each station, relegating some of them to the role of passive viewers, while only a few members of the group were actively engaged. T1 suggested that a good number would be five students per station, since it would allow all students to have some time with the system, while allowing more timid students to sit back for a little while to see how the system works. T2 favored a number closer to ten students. T4 suggested only three students, arguing that it would give them more time to perform the tasks.

DESIGN RECOMMENDATIONS

We now turn to four design recommendations based on our analysis of the data. These recommendations target the design and deployment of robo-tangible learning environments such as the rTAG system, so that those who are designing non-WIMP based systems may maximize their value while minimizing the barriers for their adoption.

Target Multiple Learning Objectives

As exposed in the barriers section, one big issue for teachers was lack of time. While even simple activities may already be infeasible, a system like rTAG may suffer from longer setup times when compared to a simple WIMP-based computer application. Additionally, the system's learning curve will probably be steeper for both teachers and students due to novel or uncommon interaction methods and technologies. Therefore, it is important for the system to target multiple learning objectives, including those that are domain-independent. Doing so should help to maximize the value of the system for teachers and the return of their time investment, as it would allow them to combine multiple activities that target one objective into one activity that targets multiple. It would also address the issue that Kharrufa et al. ran into, where teachers reported that students were not used to proper critical thinking and collaborative work [17].

In the case of rTAG, teachers believed that it was a good way of teaching domain concepts, but also saw value in the way that the system could facilitate collaboration, communication, leadership skills, critical thinking, and problem solving. In addition, teachers found the rTAG system to have potential for exposing students to new technologies. rTAG problem sets and related curriculum should be redesigned to more explicitly facilitate these higher-order learning objectives. For example, some of the engineering behind rTAG could be exposed and discussed as a secondary lesson related to student use of rTAG.

Emphasize the Collaborative Affordances of the System

One of the positive aspects mentioned by the teachers was the opportunity for collaboration that rTAG provided. This was also evident on the storyboards and lesson plans developed during the focus group session—all of them included team and collaboration elements. While students normally work on individual computers in the classroom, this setup encouraged them to work in groups. This is seen by contrasting the vTAG and rTAG setups: on the first, students gathered around the computer. Since there was not much room for all of them, a few stayed back and simply watched. On the latter, however, students were able to gather around most of the projected Cartesian plane, sometimes even walking around the physical space while trying to solve the problem together. This result is in agreement with findings from Poole et al., where group experiences seemed to foster participation [29]. This recommendation expands on Poole et al. by emphasizing that systems with tangible and embodied elements should explore their affordances to foster collaboration by design, rather than planning for students to individually use it.

Thus, it follows that rTAG should better leverage the collaborative affordances of the installation so that many students can actively use it at a time. We recommend providing an interface to rTAG that allows multiple students to give the robot commands, potentially by facilitating turn-taking or enabling a voting mechanism.

Optimize Training for the Teachers' Workflows

Since the system employs a novel interaction method, training of both teachers and students becomes an important part of the system's deployment, not only to ensure they correctly use the system, but also to enhance their confidence and reduce apprehension in using the system. To achieve proper means of training, it is important to leverage the familiarity with technology they may already have and to integrate training to their existing workflow. This is analogous, in ways, to findings from Hayes et al., who recommended a minimum disruption of the teacher's classroom organization [12]. For the teachers involved with this current study, they could use a projector hooked up to their computer to perform the training, just as it was their habit. This is only possible due to the capabilities of the TAG system to run in a traditional WIMP interface.

Innovative Use of Commonplace Technology

While the overall interaction with the system may be unusual and requires training, the familiarity with some of the system components may help to bring down this barrier, as well as possibly reducing apprehension of using it. In the case of rTAG, one of the main input methods was through an iPod Touch, which is likely familiar to most students. For example, a student asked: "*Is that an app? I wanna go home and get the app.*" The student had a better understanding of how the system functioned because of his familiarity with its components. The new application of known technology could also motivate students to explore new technology-related possibilities, one of the teachers' desired outcomes. For administration purposes, repurposing technology already owned by a school may reduce costs and facilitate adoption. Something similar was noted by Moher's work on Embedded Phenomena [22], where he chose to use technology already available in the classroom, but for the purposes of scalability rather than familiarity.

DISCUSSION & CONCLUSION

Deploying a non-WIMP based system in a school setting can be a challenging task. While traditional technologies already have barriers to their deployment, a system such as rTAG can increase the complexity of in-school integration. To minimize these barriers, while optimizing the classroom orchestration, and thus maximizing the value in such systems, we proposed four design recommendations for the deployment of non-WIMP (e.g., rTAG) systems in a school setting: 1) target multiple learning objectives, 2) emphasize the collaborative affordances, 3) optimize for training, and 4) innovate the use of known system components.

It is important to note some limitations of the data that we acquired. While we had twelve teachers running sessions, five of them agreed to participate in the focus group session. Of those five, only two participated in an interview session. Therefore, we have much more verbal data from T1 (whose unique behavior was an outlier) and T2 than we have from the other teachers. Furthermore, most teachers could use the system only once for a short session. These factors affect our ability to generalize the results. Nonetheless, the higher-level comments made by these two teachers do not diverge from the goals of the other teachers, as evidenced through the focus group session, such as developing problem solving and collaboration skills. This is compatible with the district's goals, so it may not be so visible in places where there is not so much incentive towards using technology and developing these kinds of skills. Finally, although our recommendations are more focused on the context of the rTAG system and the school we ran our studies in, they have some overlap with the related work on classroom deployment, as discussed in the results, which also contributes to supporting our claims.

As evidenced in the results section, T1 was unique in her approach. While this has implications to generalizability, it can also shed some light into a particular population. T1 is a white, female teacher with 22 years of experience teaching grades 1-3. On a scale from 1 to 10 of technological confidence, she defined herself as an 8+. She employs at least seven different technologies in her teaching, including code.org, Khan Academy, and blogs. This shows that she is extremely confident and engaged in using technology, maybe more so than her peers, which probably motivated her different approach for orchestrating the session.

Throughout the sessions, many of the expected outcomes of the design philosophy behind the rTAG system were clearly observed. Students developed rapport with Quinn, as it was expected from having a physical robotic agent that they could interact with. As expected from the literature available on barriers for the adoption of technology in the classroom, teachers demonstrated some constraints such time, training, and confidence. The design of the TAG system, however, helped to reduce some of those constraints to a certain degree. Future iterations of the system will further develop the system based on the four design recommendations here suggested to maximally facilitate classroom deployments.

ACKNOWLEDGMENTS

The authors would like to thank Elissa Thomas for her help with the data collection, as well as the teachers and administrators of the district. This research was funded by NSF 1249406: EAGER: A Teachable Robot for Mathematics Learning in Middle School Classrooms and by the CAPES Foundation, Ministry of Education of Brazil, Brasília - DF 70040-020, Brazil.

REFERENCES

1. Abdulkareem E. S. Al-Alwani. 2005. *Barriers to integrating information technology in Saudi Arabia science education.*
2. Sasha Barab, Michael Thomas, Tyler Dodge, Robert Carteaux, and Hakan Tuzun. 2005. Making learning fun: Quest Atlantis, a game without guns. Educational Technology Research and Development 53, 1: 86–107.
3. Becta. 2004. A review of the research literature on barriers to the uptake of ICT by teachers: British Educational Communications and Technology Agency (Becta). June.
4. Khalid Abdullah Bingimlas. 2009. Barriers to the successful integration of ICT in teaching and learning environments: A review of the literature. *Eurasia Journal of Mathematics, Science & Technology Education* 5, 3: 235–245.
5. Gautam Biswas, Krittaya Leelawong, Daniel Schwartz, Nancy Vye, and V-TAG. 2005. Learning by teaching: A new agent paradigm for educational software. *Applied Artificial Intelligence* 19, 3-4: 363-392.
6. John Seely Brown and Richard Adler. 2008. Mind on Fire: Open education, the long tail and Learning 2.0. *Educause Review* 43, 1: 16–32.
7. Catherine C. Chase, Doris B. Chin, Marily A. Oppezzo, and Daniel L. Schwartz. 2009. Teachable Agents and the Protégé Effect: Increasing the Effort Towards Learning. *Journal of Science Education and Technology* 18, 4: 334–352.
8. Common Core State Standards Initiative. 2010. Common core state standards for English language arts & literacy in history/social studies, science, and technical subjects. Retrieved Sept. 25, 2015 from http://www.corestandards.org/assets/CCSSI_ELA%20 Standards.pdf
9. Peggy A. Ertmer. 1999. Addressing first-and second-order barriers to change: Strategies for technology integration. *Educational Technology Research and Development* 47, 4: 47-61.
10. Lucinda Gray, Nina Thomas, Laurie Lewis, and Peter Tice. 2010. Teachers' use of educational technology in US public schools, 2009: First look. *National Center for Education Statistics.*
11. Margarete Grimus. 2000. ICT and multimedia in the primary school. *16th conference on educational uses of information and communication technologies*, 21-25.
12. Gillian R. Hayes, Lamar M. Gardere, Gregory D. Abowd, and Khai N. Truong. 2008. CareLog: a selective archiving tool for behavior management in schools. *Proceeding of the twenty-sixth annual CHI conference on Human factors in computing systems - CHI '08*: 685–694.
13. Khe Foon Hew and Thomas Brush. 2007. Integrating technology into K-12 teaching and learning: Current knowledge gaps and recommendations for future research. *Educational Technology Research and Development* 55, 3: 223-252.
14. Deanna Hood, Séverin Lemaignan, and Pierre Dillenbourg. 2015. When Children Teach a Robot to Write: An Autonomous Teachable Humanoid Which Uses Simulated Handwriting. ACM Press, 83–90.
15. Hiroshi Ishii and Brygg Ullmer. 1997. Tangible bits: towards seamless interfaces between people, bits and atoms. *Proceedings of the ACM SIGCHI Conference*, 234-241.
16. Takayuki Kanda and Rumi Sato. 2007. A two-month field trial in an elementary school for long-term human–robot interaction. *Robotics, IEEE Transactions on* 23, 5: 962-971.
17. Ahmed Kharrufa, Madeline Balaam, and Phil Heslop. 2013. Tables in the wild: lessons learned from a large-scale multi-tabletop deployment. *Proceedings of the SIGCHI Conference on Human Factors in Computing Systems*, 1021-1030.
18. Krittaya Leelawong and Gautam Biswas. 2008. Designing learning by teaching agents: The Betty's Brain system. *International journal of artificial intelligence in education* 18, 3: 181–208.
19. Iolanda Leite, Samuel Mascarenhas, André Pereira, Carlos Martinho, Rui Prada, and Ana Paiva. 2010. "Why Can't We Be Friends?" An Empathic Game Companion for Long-Term Interaction. *Intelligent Virtual Agents*: 315–321.
20. Michelle Lui, Alex C. Kuhn, Alisa Acosta, Chris Quintana, and James D. Slotta. 2014. Supporting learners in collecting and exploring data from immersive simulations in collective inquiry. ACM Press, 2103–2112.
21. Noboru Matsuda, William W. Cohen, Jonathan Sewall, Gustavo Lacerda, and Kenneth R. Koedinger. 2007. Predicting students' performance with simstudent: Learning cognitive skills from observation. *FRONTIERS IN ARTIFICIAL INTELLIGENCE AND APPLICATIONS* 158: 467.
22. Tom Moher. 2006. Embedded phenomena: supporting science learning with classroom-sized distributed simulations. *Proceedings of the SIGCHI conference on human factors in computing systems*, 691-700.
23. Kasia Muldner, Victor Girotto, Cecil Lozano, Winslow Burleson, and Erin Walker. 2014. The Impact of a Social Robot's Attributions for Success and Failure in

a Teachable Agent Framework Tangible Activities for Geometry (TAG). *International Conference of the Learning Sciences*.

24. Kasia Muldner, Cecil Lozano, Victor Girotto, Winslow Burleson, and Erin Walker. 2013. Designing a Tangible Learning Environment with a Teachable Agent. *Artificial Intelligence in Education*, 299–308.
25. Shazia Mumtaz. 2000. Factors affecting teachers' use of information and communications technology: a review of the literature. *Journal of Information Techology for Teacher Education* 9, 3: 319–342.
26. Seymour Papert. 1980. *Mindstorms: Computers, children, and powerful ideas*. NY: Basic Books.
27. Lena Pareto, Tobias Arvemo, Ylva Dahl, Magnus Haake, and Agneta Gulz. 2011. A teachable-agent arithmetic game's effects on mathematics understanding, attitude and self-efficacy. *Artificial Intelligence in Education*, 247-255.
28. Rolf Ploetzner, Pierre Dillenbourg, Michael Preier, and David Traum. 1999. Learning by explaining to oneself and to others. *Collaborative learning: Cognitive and computational approaches*, 103-121.
29. Erika Shehan Poole, Andrew D Miller, Yan Xu, Elsa Eiriksdottir, Richard Catrambone, and Elizabeth D Mynatt. 2011. The Place for Ubiquitous Computing in Schools: Lessons Learned from a School-based Intervention for Youth Physical Activity. *Proceedings of the 13th International Conference on Ubiquitous Computing*: 395–404.
30. Frederick Reif and Lisa A. Scott. 1999. Teaching scientific thinking skills: Students and computers coaching each other. *American Journal of Physics* 67, 9: 819-831.
31. Rod D. Roscoe and Michelene T. H. Chi. 2007. Understanding tutor learning: Knowledge-building and knowledge-telling in peer tutors' explanations and questions. *Review of Educational Research* 77, 4: 534-547.
32. Martin Saerbeck, Tom Schut, Cristoph Bartneck, and Maddy D. Janse. 2010. Expressive robots in education: varying the degree of social supportive behavior of a robotic tutor. *Proceedings of the SIGCHI Conference on Human Factors in Computing Systems*, 1613-1622.
33. Rana M. Tamim, Robert M. Bernard, Eugene Borokhovskim Philip C. Abrami, and Richard F. Schmid. 2011. What forty years of research says about the impact of technology on learning a second-order meta-analysis and validation study. *Review of Educational Research* 81, 1: 4–28.
34. David R. Thomas. 2006. A General Inductive Approach for Analyzing Qualitative Evaluation Data. *American Journal of Evaluation* 27, 2: 237–246.
35. Kurt Vanlehn. 2006. The Behavior of Tutoring Systems. *International journal of artificial intelligence in education* 16, 3: 227-265.
36. Angela F. L. Wong, Choon-Lang Quek, Shanti Divaharan, Woon-Chia Liu, Jarina Peer, and Michael D. Williams. 2006. Singapore students' and teachers' perceptions of computer-supported project work classroom learning environments. *Journal of Research on Technology in Education* 38, 4: 449-479.
37. Elizabeth Forward lab enables teachers to use technical tactic dubbed embodied learning. Retrieved Sept. 25, 2015 from http://triblive.com/neighborhoods/2575563-74/students-learning-tactic-elizabeth-forward-game-smallab-eighth-madison-arizona

Human Proxies for Remote University Classroom Attendance

Clarissa Ishak[1], Carman Neustaedter[1], Daniel Hawkins[1], Jason Procyk[1], and Michael Massimi[2]

[1]School of Interactive Arts and Technology
Simon Fraser University, Surrey, BC, Canada
[cishak, carman, drhawkin, jep4]@sfu.ca

[2]Facebook
Menlo Park, CA, USA
mmassimi@fb.com

ABSTRACT

Our research explores the idea of using a human proxy to attend a class on one's behalf where video streaming is used to share the class with the remote student. We explored this idea through an online survey and in-class participation. Survey results show that people favored 'top students' to represent them where gender and race played a much less important role. Students also highly valued a proxy who was also taking the class so they could discuss the course material. In class, students found the setup beneficial and highly valued the pair-wised learning that it afforded. Despite this, proxies found it difficult to concentrate in class and to be a surrogate for someone else at the same time. Together our results highlight the benefits and challenges with human proxies for classroom attendance and raise a series of design sensitivities that should be explored as part of future research.

Author Keywords

Human proxies; telepresence; video streaming; classrooms

ACM Classification Keywords

H5.3. Information interfaces and presentation: Group and Organization Interfaces – CSCW

INTRODUCTION

Rising tuition costs, an increasing slate of school offerings, and options for distance learning have prompted many students to pursue the benefits offered by distance learning [10,17]. Yet such online courses may easily lack the in-person interactions that many people find valuable for learning [17,39]. Given this challenge, we are now seeing a host of new technologies that offer support for telepresence, e.g., online discussion boards with video chat software and remote video presentation setups. There are also technologies that permit one to have a physical embodiment in the remote class such as a telepresence robot.

While telepresence robots offer a compelling scenario, they are still relatively expensive. Instead, we were interested in alternative setups that might include a physical embodiment and still be more affordable for the typical student. In this paper, we explore the idea of using human proxies or surrogates for remote classroom attendance. We were inspired by the use of surrogates in the television show, Arrested Development, where a man on house arrest uses a surrogate to be 'present' at work. In our case, a proxy attends class for a remote student, streams what is happening in the class to him or her via a wearable video streaming technology, and interacts in the class on the student's behalf. The potential benefit is that the student has an actual human presence in the classroom to represent herself. While this technology setup may seem futuristic, in reality it is now possible with present day technology such as relatively inexpensive wearable cameras (each costs about $100-200). Given the cost, students are more likely to have such cameras at their disposal compared to relatively expensive telepresence robots. What is not known is how human proxies may work in practice, what design limitations need to be addressed, and what unintended social consequences might occur when using proxies.

Our paper presents several contributions to the HCI community and, in particular, those exploring telepresence and remote embodiments whom we aim to sensitize to the unique opportunities and challenges brought forward with human proxies. First, we contribute an understanding of human proxy identity through an online survey with 33 university students who described their ideal human proxy. Findings show that students preferred human proxies that were strong students scholastically, favoring problem solvers and organized individuals. This suggests ways in which proxies might be made a reality in the ideal situation.

Second, we contribute an exploration of human proxies in actual classroom settings, which, to our knowledge, has never been done before. Through observations and interviews of student-proxy pairs, we learned that remote students were able to adequately participate in the class and engaged in valued pair-wise learning with a peer. On the other hand, proxies faced a number of challenges relating to camera work, embodiment, autonomy, and interactions.

Third, we articulate design opportunities and challenges for human proxies in classrooms. We describe the social and technical limitations as well as the social questions that still need to be explored. These suggest directions for future research. While we purposely did not explore learning effects in our research because we wanted to first focus on

CHI'16, May 07-12, 2016, San Jose, CA, USA
© 2016 ACM. ISBN 978-1-4503-3362-7/16/05···$15.00
DOI: http://dx.doi.org/10.1145/2858036.2858184

the social situations enabled through the technology, our work brings to light many intriguing questions about how proxies may affect learning processes and outcomes.

RELATED WORK

Video-Based Telepresence in the Workplace

The topic of telepresence has a longstanding research history. Early work on media spaces explored how audio and video feeds could be used to communicate availability information and support casual interactions between distance-separated co-workers [3,12,15,19,50]. The first media spaces connected common areas such as meeting rooms or kitchens and used relatively low-bandwidth to show what was happening at remote locations [3,12,19]. Follow-on work explored media spaces that were designed for office desks [8,14]. In much of this research, privacy was an important consideration [1,4]. Privacy issues typically related to one of solitude, confidentiality, or autonomy [4] and often increased in magnitude when a person was in a mixed context, e.g., telecommuting [37].

Mobile Telepresence

More recently, designs have explored mobile video, such as is the case in our human proxy work. For example, Porta-Person used a laptop-based embodiment that could be transported from one conference room to another through the help of a dedicated human "handler" [51]. Systems have included large, "life-sized" high-fidelity displays to provide virtual presence for the disabled or mobility impaired [31]. LiveSphere [35] provided headgear with six cameras to broadcast an entire scene around a person to remote users. Most similar to our work, Polly [27] provides mobile telepresence through the metaphor of a parrot sitting on a user's shoulder. Here a camera is attached to a stabilized gimbal. Similar to Polly, Misawa and Rekimoto [33] designed ChameleonMask where a human proxy wears a helmet containing a tablet attached to the front. Video of a remote user is streamed to the tablet for local users to see. A pilot study showed that interaction through the proxy worked reasonably well, yet they did not explore social situations to the same extent that we do in our studies.

Studies of mobile video conferencing have explored how wearable or handheld cameras can be used to connect people in settings such as wedding halls [32], restaurants [43], museums [43], malls [21,43], and outdoor parks [21,41,42]. Results showed that the camera holder faces challenges in orienting the camera and providing good views for remote viewers [21,32,42,43]. This can create a sense of social debt to the handler as well as a feeling of helplessness in the remote user who lacks control over remote views [43]. Remote viewers sometimes desire multiple viewing angles [32]. People are also conscious of the public visibility of conversations between remote users and the video handler [43].

Telepresence Robots in the Workplace

Telepresence robots have been designed and studied to allow remote workers to attend meetings with colleagues [49,51]. Despite these efforts, remote users often lack sufficient physical presence at remote locations and can easily begin to feel like second-class citizens causing them to become disengaged from the larger group [26]. The challenge is they are often unable to keep track of conversations and participate in the productive, highly-charged and sometimes chaotic ad-hoc meetings or side conversations that frequently take place [49]. Yet robotic telepresence has been found to provide better attentional information than traditional video conferencing [34].

Research has also shown the importance of wide field-of-view cameras and ranges of audio control from 'whispers' to conversationally-appropriate levels [22,23,25,40]. Video feedback of oneself is also important for self-appropriation [25,30,40,47], while robot height can imply persuasiveness [44]. Lee and Takayama [30] found that telepresence robots can create a sense of social connectedness by supporting casual interactions. The medical community has also been active in testing robotic telepresence systems. Studies have shown high levels of comfort and acceptance for telepresence robots used by doctors [46] though use with elderly patients has had mixed reactions [29].

Distance Learning

Research has also focused on distance learning and telepresence in classrooms or large lectures. Jancke et al. [20] designed TELEP to support presentations in a lecture-style setup. Video of remote audience members was available in a large grid for all to see and discussions took place in a chat room facility. PEBBLES connected children in a hospital to a school classroom [11]. Chen [5] designed a virtual auditorium to support learning that incorporates dialog between instructors and students through an audio link. Subsequent work involved the creation of a gesture-sensitive videoconferencing system where a study of it amongst small groups showed that low fidelity video does not adequately support floor control [6]. Visualizations of classroom participation were able to show 'the pulse' of the audience to instructors [7]. Shi et al. [45] designed a mixed presence classroom that projects views of remote students and supports annotations on projected slides.

To understand the awareness needs for telepresence classroom systems, Birnholtz et al. [2] studied instructors' practices in traditional classroom setups without remote students and suggest that telepresence systems for classrooms should provide both overview and detailed views of remote students. Other researchers have found that how "real" a remote person appears to local students has an impact on social interaction and participation [13,28,48], which are prerequisites for knowledge construction and collaborative learning [16,24].

Overall, we have not seen studies that explore the use of human proxies for remote university classroom attendance. As such, our goal was to build on the related work to understand how people would use a human proxy to support remote classroom attendance, how they would interact with this person, who they would want as their proxy, and what social and technical limitations might exist.

ONLINE SURVEY ON PROXY IDENTITY

Identity is an important attribute when it comes to remote embodiments of oneself [9,36]. In avatar-based environments, it comes with a great number of decisions such as the selection of race, physical appearance, etc. [9,36]. With telepresence robots, it involves deciding how to ensure others recognize who you are [25,30,40]. For these reasons, we decided to first explore what type of person people would select as a human proxy, if given a choice for remote classroom participation. We were interested in learning what types of personality, race, gender, etc. students would want in their proxy, especially compared to their own identity. We created and deployed an online survey focused on these topic areas.

Survey Method

First, our survey described the type of human proxy scenario that students should imagine:

You are a university student and unable to go to class one day. Instead, you send a person to class on your behalf. We call this person a proxy or surrogate. The proxy lets you see and hear a live stream of the class by wearing a technology like Google Glass. You watch on your home computer or laptop. You are also able to participate in the class through your proxy. You can tell this person to ask questions, interact with certain people, etc. - whatever you are comfortable having this person do.

We also included two images to depict the setup. In Figure 1 (left), a blonde haired person is wearing a mobile camera attached to a pair of glasses to stream the classroom activities to the remote student. The remote student is at home in front of a computer and wearing an audio earpiece with microphone to illustrate that the two people can communicate with one another (Figure 1, right). The 'sketch-like' quality of the drawings was purposeful. We wanted survey respondents to comment on the experience rather than any particular hardware or software technology (or potential usability issues with it), which could emerge if they saw a more finalized system.

Figure 1. Drawings illustrating an example technology setup in the classroom (left) and student's home (right).

After reading the scenario and seeing the images, respondents answered our survey. The survey asked basic information about the respondent such as gender, age, race, and languages spoken. These answers were chosen from multiple-choice questions with possible answers. They then rated their technical savvy-ness and scholastic abilities using a 5-point Likert scale. We also asked questions from an abbreviated Myers-Briggs Type Indicator test. Myers-Briggs tests are questionnaires that respondents answer in order to determine their attitude towards behavioral attributes. After being scored, it categorizes people according to combinations of four behavioral dichotomies where a person matches one of the behaviors within each pair. Pairs consist of: introversion (I) vs. extroversion (E); sensing (S) vs. intuition (I); thinking (T) vs. feeling (F); and, judging (J) vs. perception (P). Respondents answered questions about each paired set of terms and are assigned a four-letter personality identifier. For example, "ESTP" represents a person that falls into the dichotomies of extroversion (E), sensing (S), thinking (T), and perception (P) where he or she would have strong personality traits in each area.

Next, our survey asked the same set of questions about the respondent's preferences for a human proxy. Through the same Myers-Briggs Type Indicator Test they selected the ideal behaviors of their proxy. They also chose their preferred gender, race, and languages spoken for the proxy. For example, we asked them, "What gender would you prefer for your proxy? Male, Female, or Doesn't Matter." We followed this up with a question of "Why did you choose this response?" Thus, for each of question, we asked them to explain why they chose a particular attribute. We also gave them options to select if an aspect of identity did not matter to them. Finally, we asked them about their reactions to the idea of using a human proxy to attend class remotely and how they saw this interaction occurring.

Survey Respondents

We received 33 responses to our survey. Respondents were comprised of 28 undergraduate and 5 graduate students who were taking courses within a university program focused on design/media arts. 26 people were 18-24 years old, six were 25-34, and one was 35-44. Only seven respondents were male, which is under representative of the program's roughly 50% split between men and women. Respondents varied heavily in their responses to the Myers-Briggs Indicator Test where between 1 and 4 people fell into each of the 16 possible behavior categories represented by the four letter combinations (e.g., ISTJ, ISFJ); thus, we had a large variety of personality types. All participants rated themselves as moderately to very tech savvy. All lived within a major urban area of North America that is highly multi-cultural. Their university program is equally multi-cultural with students of a variety of races.

Data Collection and Analysis

We used qualitative coding techniques to analyze responses to the open-ended questions in our survey and descriptive statistics to explore responses to closed-ended questions. Our analysis revealed several main themes that we describe next in our results. Here we step through various aspects of identity including personality, gender, race, etc.

RESULTS

Personality

Only four respondents desired to have a proxy that was the same personality type as themselves. Other respondents picked a range of personality types with ESTJ (11 people) being the most popular followed by ISTJ (8) and ESTP (6). Thus, across the three most popular types of personalities, all contained the S and T identity components where S represents mastery of facts, knowledge of resources, and an appreciation of knowledge, and T represents the ability to analyze a situation for its strengths and weaknesses and problem solve. This shows that students would like their proxy to be a careful, analytical thinker. Within the top three personality types there are differences between whether a responded wanted an introvert (11 of 33) or an extrovert (22). This shows that extroversion is desired by a majority of respondents, yet introversion is valued by some.

Gender & Age

When it came to gender, a majority of respondents (22 of 33) felt that the gender of their proxy did not matter because the proxy would be acting on their behalf and gender would have no affect on this behavior. Seven respondents chose the same gender as themselves and four chose the opposite gender. Those who chose the same gender (both men and women) felt they would be able to communicate most easily with someone of the same sex.

A small number of respondents brought up perceived issues with particular genders. For example, three male respondents preferred to have a female proxy because they felt male proxies may be easily distracted by women in the class. Several female respondents brought up perceived interactional challenges with both genders, for example:

"For me personally, it's easier to communicate with male proxy since they talk straight forward and they give opinion straight forward." – P31

A small majority of respondents (17 of 33) favored a proxy that was in the same age range and university year as themselves, while five selected someone in the same age range but a higher university year. Respondents tended to choose people of the same age and university level (or higher) because they wanted have their proxy be someone they could relate to. Four people had no age/university level preference and six people had a mixture of responses. Respondents who were less concerned about age and university level felt that as long as the proxy could be trusted, varying ages/levels were less important.

Class Participation and Scholastic Levels

The majority of respondents (26 of 33) wanted the proxy to be another student in their class. They felt that the proxy would already know what was going on in the class as a result. This would make it easier for them to exchange thoughts with the proxy if they had a question about the course content. Other respondents felt that if there was a cost associated with such a proxy service (an idea brought up by participants, not us), it would be cheaper to have a proxy from within the class since it would be more convenient for this person to act as a proxy in this case. Seven respondents felt that the proxy should definitely not be a student in the class. Instead, they felt that the proxy's sole purpose was to 'be a proxy' and not a student as well.

The majority of respondents (26 of 33) felt that it mattered what kind of grades the proxy received as a student. They felt that grades were an important identifier of the proxy's ability to engage in a class and reflected what type of student they were. Thus, they wanted a proxy who did well in school. On the other hand, seven respondents did not feel that their proxy's grades were important because they felt the proxy was simply a surrogate for them.

Language and Race

All respondents wanted to ensure that their proxy spoke English fluently because all of their classes were taught in English. Respondents also felt it was very important that the proxy know their native language (e.g., Cantonese or Mandarin). This would allow the proxy to translate terms that the student did not understand. Most respondents (24 out of 33) did not have a preference for their proxy's race. What was most important was whether or not the proxy was paying attention in class.

"I would value their intellectual abilities and acuity. Race might play a role in our relationship but I would see this as positive because it would bring an "added value" to the proxy's presence by enriching our "dual" identity." – P9

On the other hand, four respondents felt that communication between themselves and the proxy would be better if they were of the same race. They thought they might share cultural knowledge that would help communication.

Proxy Expectations

When asked what their expectations were for their proxy, a large number of respondents talked about the proxy being able to follow their directions and instructions, be responsible, and pay attention. Smaller numbers talked about wanting the proxy to have good camera control, be able to start conversations on their behalf, be enthusiastic, and not draw too much attention to themselves. They also thought the proxy should periodically interact with the remote person to check if they were understanding the content of the class or repeat content that was missed.

"I would expect them to listen attentatively [sic] to my questions and discussions so they can deliver that to the class. I would expect them to pay attention to important information especially key information about exams. I would expect them to be able to multitask and still pay attention." – P21

SURVEY DISCUSSION

In general, respondents thought of a proxy as more of a friend or partner rather than someone they would explicitly 'control.' There is a chance that when people responded about gender and race that they recorded what they thought was socially acceptable rather than their true opinion. Overall, these findings suggest that if a human proxy service was available or students could ask their friends to fill this role, that there is a broad range of people that would be suitable to be a proxy. Yet if we look at scholastic competencies, we see a different picture. Respondents essentially wanted a human proxy that one might consider to be a 'top student.' The implication is that, given typical student grading (with a small number of high grades), there are likely a small number of individuals that would be considered as ideal human proxies. One may not easily be able to turn to a friend to ask for such a service. Instead, it could be much harder to find an ideal candidate, unless one was willing to compromise.

Our survey is intriguing as it begins to raise questions about what situations might actually arise in a classroom setting with proxies. For example, how will students *actually* interact with their proxy? Will they attempt to 'control' the proxy or will they allow him or her to engage based on their own free will? Many wanted an extrovert who would be good at talking with others, but would extroverted proxies perhaps gain too much autonomy and be too outgoing? Or would control remain with the remote student? We begin to explore such questions next in our study of classrooms.

CLASSROOM USAGE OF HUMAN PROXIES

Our second study explored what would actually happen in a classroom setting with human proxies. We deployed a basic technology setup in two university classes, one graduate and one undergraduate. The goal was to understand how remote students and proxies interact and behave, what works well with the human proxy setup, and what social and technical challenges still need to be overcome. We also wanted to expose any interesting social situations that might arise as a means to sensitive and suggest future direction for research on human proxies.

Participants

We recruited six pairs of students (twelve students in total) from two separate university classes to participate in our study. Recruitment occurred via advertisements in the classes. Table 1 shows information about our participants who are grouped according to each proxy-remote student pair. For example, UG1 (Row 1) was the proxy for UG2 (Row 2) who attended class remotely.

Participants selected their own proxy and could choose anyone they wanted. As it turned out, all chose someone else from the same class. Given this open selection criteria, we also had a mixture of males and females in each role as either the human proxy or the remote student. Participants ranged between 20 and 40 years of age with the majority in their early 20s. Students varied by their personality type in terms of being introverted or extroverted. We did not notice any specific strategies for choosing a partner for the study, aside from choosing someone in the same class. While our previous study showed specific identity and personality attributes as being important for a proxy, when it came to participating in this study, we observed that students quickly asked a friend if he or she would participate with them. This is possibly because it was a study but it could also represent more naturally occurring situations where, in practice, people prefer friends over other identity attributes.

Class	ID	Gender	Role	Personality
Undergrad	UG1	Male	Proxy	Extrovert
Undergrad	UG2	Female	Remote	Introvert
Undergrad	UG3	Female	Proxy	Introvert
Undergrad	UG4	Male	Remote	Extrovert
Undergrad	UG5	Male	Proxy	Introvert
Undergrad	UG6	Female	Remote	Extrovert
Undergrad	UG7	Male	Proxy	Extrovert
Undergrad	UG8	Female	Remote	Introvert
Graduate	G1	Male	Proxy	Introvert
Graduate	G2	Female	Remote	Extrovert
Graduate	G3	Female	Proxy	Extrovert
Graduate	G4	Female	Remote	Introvert

Table 1. Student-proxy pairs in our study.

The first eight participants were students in an undergraduate design course that contained a three-hour class. The first hour was devoted to covering lecture materials using a 'flipped classroom' model, which focused on discussion and questions about course material. The remaining two hours were comprised of design activities and crits. The remaining four participants were students in a graduate course on collaborative technologies. It too contained a single three-hour class. The first hour of this class was seminar-based and involved discussions of papers that students had read before class. The remaining two hours were comprised of design activities, discussions, and informal presentations by students.

Method

Participants pre-selected which class they wanted to do the study in from a selection of six weeks in the term. We purposely had them pick from weeks that included typical class activities, as opposed to weeks containing an exam/quiz or large formal presentation. When the participants' selected day came, the human proxy arrived at class fifteen minutes early and we helped them setup our technology probe. It contained a wearable bag (as a shoulder strap) with a smartphone holder attached to it, as shown in Figure 2. In the holder we placed an iPod Touch (5th generation) with a front facing 1.2 MP camera capable of HD video (720 p) at up to 30 frames per second. A similar wearable setup was previously used in other mobile video communications research [43]. The iPod Touch streamed audio/video to the remote student using Skype. As can be seen in Figure 2, the camera is at chest level. We pilot tested with various locations including the head (a camera attached to a hat) and different chest areas. The selected location was not overly obtrusive and the camera angle changed easily when the proxy moved his body.

Figure 2. A human proxy wearing the technology setup.

At the remote location, students used their own computer. The human proxies used an earbud attached to the iPod Touch in order to talk to the remote student. Participants were told the goal of the human proxy setup was to allow the remote student to see class and participate in it. Beyond this, we allowed participants to choose how they would use the technology and how they would interact as a pair.

In order to speak to others in the class, the remote student had to tell the proxy what to say. We had deliberately not let remote users talk directly through the system (e.g, via the device's speaker) because we felt it may be difficult in a classroom setting without having a broader contextual understanding of what was happening (e.g., frequent interruptions). We thought this understanding would come from the proxy. We also thought that this type of audio might be indicative of situations where students use wearable cameras in a classroom with a proxy on their own accord (given the low cost of cameras and ease of setup) and, perhaps, unbeknownst to the instructor.

During the class, we observed the proxy's interaction with classmates and the instructors and also paid attention to his or her classroom behaviors. After the class, we conducted individual interviews with the human proxy and the remote student to understand their perspectives. We asked them questions about how they interacted using the technology setup, what worked well about it, what did not work well, and what they thought should be done to improve the situation. For example, we asked human proxies, "How did the remote student let you know what s/he wanted you to do?" and "Did this work effectively?" For remote students, we asked similar questions but from their perspective. Interviews lasted between 20 and 45 minutes.

Students in the undergraduate class received a small amount of bonus credit (1%) in the course for participating. Students in the graduate class did not receive any additional credit. Thus, the motivation for a person to be a proxy was at most for course bonus credit, though we expect that students were partly motivated because they saw it as a favor to the remote student. The remote student received the additional benefit of not having to travel to campus.

Data Collection and Analysis

We audio recorded all interviews and kept notes on our classroom observations. We then fully transcribed all interview audio and conducted a series of qualitative data coding activities on the transcriptions, including open, axial, and selective coding. We used our observations to help interpret and guide our coding. The coding drew out main themes related to the benefits of a human proxy, issues around location and privacy, interaction behaviors between the human proxy and the remote student, camera work by the human proxy, and successes and challenges with the remote student's embodiment. In the next section, we step through each of these themes.

THE BENEFITS OF REMOTE PARTICIPATION

Participants generally enjoyed the experience of using a human proxy for classroom attendance. This included both the remote student as well as the student acting as the proxy. Most commented that it was very beneficial for those who might be sick or faced mobility challenges. In fact, two of our participants happened to be sick on the day of their study participation and would have normally not come to class as a result. Other participants talked about the benefits of not having to commute to school, which sometimes took between 45 minutes and an hour via public transportation. One remote student felt human proxies were a good way to overcome shyness in classroom settings.

We asked participants how they felt the experience compared to situations involving Skype and a laptop. Participants overall felt that the proxy experience added benefits beyond just a Skype call alone. The comment most often made was that the proxy added additional mobility beyond a typical video chat call (e.g., via Skype on a laptop). Several proxies commented that they enjoyed having a very close personal connection with another student. In this way, they shared the classroom experience together in a more intimate way than was typical.

G4, Remote Student: "Yeah, I think it was more mobile. Being attached to someone when they broke up into groups, I went with them, and it felt comforting. Like if you're just on a computer, you would feel disconnected. It was nice because I'm friends with <my proxy>, it was nice talking to her one-on-one. It felt really comfortable...more personal than if I was just put up on a big screen on Skype."

Thus, as can be seen, remote attendance had a number of benefits for both proxies and the remote students. But, of course, there were also limitations and challenges that both parties faced and we describe them in the following sections as starting points for design considerations.

LOCATION AND PRIVACY

We had given remote participants the option to connect to class from a location of their choosing and all chose their home bedrooms. This was because it was the most comfortable location for them and they could close the door to avoid hearing sounds from other people that might be around. It also meant 'zero' travel time to get to campus.

UG4, Remote Student: "To be honest, I woke up about half an hour ago at that time, so that's why I was at my home in my room, and that's where my computer and everything is, too. Very comfortable. It's like I was just at home and I just woke up so I don't have to prepare myself or anything."

Some participants considered going to another location, such as a coffee shop, because they thought they may be able to concentrate better there or that it may appear more professional. However, potential background noise prevented this along with the additional effort to leave their home.

We asked remote participants about their privacy and if they were concerned about it, given that they were in their home bedroom. None raised any concerns. They also were generally not concerned about how they looked on camera. Participants described being in their pajamas or having not 'gotten ready' yet for the day. In only one instance did a remote participant talk about changing the view of her camera to not capture herself. When she left her computer area, she would turn her camera to face her cat.

On the classroom side, proxies tended to sit at the front of the classroom in the first available row of seats. They found it easiest for the remote student to hear the instructor from this location after testing out various positions. It also allowed the remote student to easily see a whiteboard on the wall, which sometimes contained writing. At times this location was socially awkward for the proxy because it may not be his or her 'usual' sitting location causing the student to change seating patterns. Students generally tend to sit in the same area each class, though seating is not restricted. They also do not tend to sit at the front of the room. Proxies who did not sit at the front of the room ended up receiving complaints from the remote students about sound quality.

G1, Proxy: "What do I feel about the location? It is awkward because I am the only person in the front row. I have no other choice because if I sit in the back row, due to the limitation of the iPod, <remote student> couldn't see the board, so I have to be in the front."

PROXY-STUDENT INTERACTIONS

The main activity that proxies engaged in was camera work in an effort to properly direct the camera at locations the remote student should be able to see. Because the camera was attached to the proxy's chest, proxies had to orient their bodies towards what was being shown in class or who was talking. Some proxies were very good at this and our observations in class showed that they were often conscious of where the camera was pointed. At times this was awkward because it involved rotating one's chest rather than just their head. Some proxy-student pairs worked collaboratively together to get the best possible view for the remote student. Other remote students did not discuss the camera view because they did not want to 'bother' the proxy, or the view was 'good enough.' Some proxies were less concerned and did not take additional efforts to ensure the view was a good one. Sometimes this led to the remote student seeing awkward or irrelevant views.

Many human proxies said that being a proxy was a challenging task as they had to pay attention to the class itself as well as the desires of the remote student they were representing. Some proxies even felt additional anxiety or worry that they may not be giving the remote student the best possible experience. Because of this, many would go to great efforts to listen to the remote student and ensure the experience was good.

G1, Proxy: "It's hard work. Hard work. Yeah, I need to listen to her first. I need to translate that effectively and clearly and accurately. It's difficult. In that sense, I feel disengaged if there's a very complex idea."

In our setup, remote students had to tell the proxy what to say to others in the classroom. There was no direct audio link for the remote student to speak to the class. This became challenging when complex ideas needed to be communicated. Such interactions often became slow and tedious as the remote student relayed to the proxy what he or she wanted to say.

UG4, Remote Student: "I would actually give her some commands. I would say, "Oh, I've got a question. Can you put your hand up?" kind of thing. Or I would ask her, "Can you ask this for me?" kind of thing."

At times it was difficult for the proxy to hear what the remote student was saying because of other noise in the classroom, such as the instructor speaking or students talking amongst themselves. This meant that interactions between the proxy and the remote student often had to be carefully timed for a point when others were not talking. The proxy faced the additional challenge of sometimes not being able to speak aloud to the remote student to coordinate interactions because of classroom social norms, e.g., not talking aloud when the instructor was speaking.

Some students found workarounds where they would use text chat in Skype or text messaging to talk with the remote student or proxy. This backchannel worked well for proxy-to-student conversations, but it meant that the proxy was limited to mostly sitting down so that they could be at their laptop or in a state where they could easily text message back and forth. During group activities, the remote student could engage in discussion through the proxy, however, it was difficult to do physical activities such as sketching or drawing their ideas.

Sometimes proxies became distracted by classroom happenings and did not hear what the remote student was asking them to do because they were listening to the class or interacting with a local student. Proxies did not always participate on behalf of the remote student exactly as they would have liked. Instead, proxies sometimes filtered interactions with other students. This occurred by either ignoring what the remote student was saying, or by changing its tone or content slightly. Both proxies and students realized that sometimes the proxy could be distracted by other happenings in the classroom and not hear or pay attention to the remote student, this created a sense of plausible deniability as to whether or not the proxy heard an instruction from the remote student. Thus, it could be easily ignored if the proxy did not want to do or say what had been asked.

UG7, Proxy: "I don't want to say exactly what <remote student> said ... Maybe <our partner's> feelings would have been hurt, I don't know."

We also saw other instances where proxies started to develop a deeper sense of autonomy and wanted to interact on their own, rather than as a representative of the remote student. For example, one proxy was a member of a different team (for assignments) than the remote student. When it came time to do activities with team members during the studio lab, tensions emerged between the remote student and the proxy. Each wanted to interact with his or her own team members. The proxy ended up going to be with his team rather than the remote student's and the remote student had to engage with her teammates using an instant messaging channel instead of using the proxy. In this case, the person with the 'stronger' personality (the proxy) ended up getting what he wanted.

EMBODIMENT

Remote students were embodied using a relatively small device. This made it so they were not obtrusively large, yet it also meant that it was difficult for students and the instructor to see the remote student at a distance in the classroom. The remote student's face was much smaller than local student's face and, thus, more difficult to notice. To attract attention to the remote student if they wanted to say something, proxies often performed overt hand gestures. For example, we observed that proxies would sometimes make pointing gestures to the display on their chest when the remote person wanted to say something or when they wanted to be introduced or noticed. This worked some of the time, but could easily not be noticed if the gestures were not large enough.

UG7, Proxy: "I guess I pointed at <remote student> a few times when ...... when people were kind of wondering what I was doing talking to myself or something. Or if I like went up to the teams, I'm like, "Hey say hi to <remote student>," or something. And <remote student> would wave and they would wave."

Several remote students felt that they were not noticed in the classroom because of the small display on the proxy's chest. This was advantageous for those who wanted to remain more discreet. Others wanted to have a larger presence in the classroom setting than the proxy setup afforded. In these cases, many participants talked about having a speaker for their own voice so they could talk aloud, rather than just through the proxy. Here they wanted two options: 1) to be able to talk directly to just the proxy for side conversations and instructions, and 2) to be able to talk aloud to others in the room on an as-needed basis.

G4, Remote Student: "I think, having the ability to speak for myself through maybe a small speaker on the phone than I wouldn't have to be communicating my ideas through someone else's interpretation of what I said. I'd feel more, like I was actually personally contributing to the class."

EXPERIENCING THE CLASS

Remote participants generally felt that they were able to participate effectively in the class through their proxy.

UG4, Remote Student: "I was able to learn effectively because I can hear the lecturer and I can see the lecturer, what he's talking about. I could see the examples. That I find out to be pretty effective.... Aside from the fact that I cannot [directly] interact with other students, otherwise learning direct from the lecturer himself, it's actually just fine. I have no problem with it."

Some participants talked about not wanting to bother the proxy too often with questions. They felt this might compromise *the proxy's* learning. Thus, some were generally concerned about their impact on the other person and his or her ability to pay attention in class.

On the other hand, proxies faced large issues in regards to their own participation and engagement in classroom learning. First, proxies did indeed find it difficult to listen to the remote participant while simultaneously hearing the course instructor. When the remote student was not talking to them, they also had to think about what camera work might be needed to provide a better experience for the remote student.

G3, Proxy: "The idea is interesting, but it was bothering me more than I was benefit from. Being in a classroom and paying attention to someone who is not present. Paying attention to two different locations was more distracting than beneficial. There would be times when she says something and I don't hear it well, or I don't understand, so I have to go back and forth between her and me. I can't follow the content of the class, because I can't tell, let's say to slow down or just to wait for me. So then there were a few critical points where I missed the comment from the class or what someone else said."

DISCUSSION

The goal of our research was to better understand an emerging telepresence opportunity by learning through one type of human proxy setup such that we could sensitize researchers and designers to the types of questions and issues one ought to think about in this design space. Thus, we wanted to use our studies as a means to think critically about the design space. We now discuss our results and detail a series of more speculative thoughts in relation to human proxy design and usage.

Paired Learning

The strongest benefit that we saw in the human proxy experience we studied was the unique learning experience it created. Remote students became engaged in paired learning with their proxy where they would talk with each other, discuss the course content, and help each other out. This was a clear benefit and many remote and proxy students talked about this as their most enjoyable part of the experience. Our survey on identity also reflects this idea where most participants very clearly wanted a proxy who was someone that they could learn *with* and *not through* during their classroom experience. This suggests new opportunities for distance learning as well as how one thinks about remote telepresence and embodiment.

Embodiments such as telepresence robots and laptops place students directly in the class where they represent themselves through the associated computer hardware. This is beneficial for having autonomy over one's actions, yet it means that remote students might feel isolated from others in the class. Thus, while one may imagine that having to interact through a proxy would create many negatives, and it certainly did, it also revealed the potential for opportunities to learn course material in a more intimate fashion with a peer. This type of experience is not normally found in setups that utilize telepresence robots or more traditional video conferencing solutions (e.g., Skype from a laptop). Of course, it also raises questions about how one should think about student learning from an educational perspective. Is such paired learning truly effective? How can student learning be assessed? If, for example, a proxy adds to the discussion in the class and earns some form of participation grade, should the credit go to the proxy or the remote student and how does one truly know where the contribution came from? Such questions already exist for courses that include team-based assignments, yet human proxies raise these issues again in different ways.

Technical Challenges

The human proxy setup we explored certainly created challenges. These included issues with camera work, poor microphone distance, and issues in seeing far away objects. Similar problems have been reported in other contexts [43] and, in particular, with telepresence robots [22,23,25, 40,49]. Design suggestions have included using multiple fixed cameras, direct sharing of meeting slides, and more advanced audio and video setups [22,23,25,40,49]. We advocate that similar solutions may also work for human proxies in classroom settings.

Our proxy setup also created disadvantages for the remote student who did not have autonomous control over their own mobility or speech like they might receive if they were using a telepresence robot instead. This problem has also been articulated in other contexts (e.g., outdoor activities with families [18], proxies at museums and restaurants [43]). We had also thought that remote students might be able to physically interact in class during design activities through their proxy. Such interactions might expose advantages for the use of human proxies as compared to commercial telepresence robots, which currently do not generally have arms. However, the use of proxies for physical activities was not as easy as we had hoped because of the need for detailed instructions between students. Thus, the potential is there but design improvements need to be made for it to be realized.

Social Situations and Questions

Our research also raises intriguing social questions that should be thought about by telepresence designers and researchers, and even potentially instructors of courses where students may use proxies in the future.

First, there are questions around identity and the effects of who one picks to be a proxy. If people do in fact want an ideal proxy who is scholastically strong, and are willing to choose such a person over a friend, there are questions about the effects of a 'stranger' within the classroom setting. It is not clear in these cases if and how the proxy might alter or even potentially disrupt the social dynamics of the classroom and what impact the proxy may have on the relationships between the remote student and her peers. The desire to choose an ideal human proxy could also lead to companies that provide proxy services. Would such proxies be required to 'blend in' with the normal look and interaction style of the class's students, or would the person have to appear and act in a more professional manner (e.g., wearing a suit), akin to business-like expectations that might come along with a paid service? On the other hand, if a student did indeed choose to have a friend be his proxy, what effect might the proxy have on the friendship if the person turned out to not be scholastically strong and this began affecting the remote student's learning?

Second, there are questions around what is socially appropriate in a classroom and if proxies or remote students might disrupt the current classroom social norms. Our participants told us that they wanted a proxy who would understand the normal procedures and behaviors of a post-secondary environment. But who is responsible for ensuring such behaviors are adhered to? Is it the remote student or the proxy? The majority of participants in our classroom study told us that they wanted a mechanism to talk aloud in the classroom without the aid of the proxy. Yet what happens if such interactions are poorly timed because the remote student does not understand the current classroom context and if it is a good time to speak? Is this the fault of the remote student, or should the proxy be held responsible for not informing the student of when and how to talk directly to the class? All of the remote students in our study connected from their bedrooms but some mused about connecting from a more public location like a coffee shop. We might imagine that some would actually do this in practice if proxies were in more widespread use. This raises interesting questions about how the general public might react to seeing and hearing a person engaging with a proxy. For example, would bystanders feel it was socially appropriate for a person to be told what to do by someone who was remote? What social protocols exist around such behaviors and how might they change over time?

Third, our study raised questions about the autonomy of human proxies. From the proxy's perspective, they often found it difficult to perform in the dual role of both a proxy and a student. If they are a student in the class, they may easily decide to focus on their own learning at some stage and begin to neglect the remote student. In our study, some proxies filtered conversations and some ignored certain requests from the remote student. This raises questions around how remote students might be able to deal with such situations. Do social protocols suffice, or should there be 'override' mechanisms designed into the technology that allow remote students to gain back some control over their classroom experience? For example, they may be given the chance to talk directly to those around them rather than through the proxy. Would such control mechanisms then, in turn, unnecessarily infringe on the needs of the proxy?

Fourth, there are questions around scalability. Our study focused on a single proxy, but one could imagine the potential for multiple proxies to be in a single classroom. Multiple proxies could come with the benefit of supporting multiple remote students or they could offer multiple different viewpoints for a single student, if the remote student is able to 'move' between proxies. This also raises further issues about identity and embodiment.

It is highly likely that the use of human proxies in classroom settings is not a complete replacement for attending class. One would not likely want an entire class to consist of proxies, for example, or for students to participate in an entire course through a proxy. Given our experience in trying it out in classroom settings, we feel that it is a system best utilized by a small handful of students, rather than large groups, and in one-off situations such as when someone is sick. However, given the ability for students to easily utilize a proxy (only a smartphone is really needed), one could imagine increased usage of proxies. There is even the potential for surreptitious use of human proxies where instructors do not know proxies are present or that students are 'streaming into class.' This contrasts telepresence robots, which are quite noticeable as compared to human proxy setups. In the latter case, a wearable camera could be easily hidden and not even noticed by instructors. This raises implications around the design of wearable cameras and the feedback mechanisms that might let the class and instructor know they are being streamed. This should be explored in future research.

Limitations

Our explorations of human proxies looked at specific types of classroom setups and did not explore large lecture or theatre-style classes. Further research is needed to understand how our results might generalize or not to these settings. It may be the case that because they do not typically have hands-on design activities, the advantages of a human proxy might diminish. It would also likely be more difficult for a remote student to talk to a proxy via an audio channel because they would feel the need to be quiet during the lecture. We also only explored one type of proxy setup. Future research should explore the use of different embodiment types, including possibly larger device displays. Proxy selection in our classroom study was likely limited in that students were more focused on picking a proxy out of convenience rather than someone who was ideal. Our survey showed that people had an ideal proxy that they would like but in practice they may be less selective. People's usage and selection of proxies may easily change over time as they grow accustomed to the experience and technology. Usage may also change once a period of novelty wears off. Thus, our results should be validated as a part of longer-term research. Lastly, we chose a technology design approach to understand human proxies in classrooms as opposed to an educational approach that might deeply assess the learning potentials or pitfalls of human proxies. This should also be focused on in follow-up research.

CONCLUSION

The use of human proxies to perform tasks for people who are remote is now a possibility given recent advancements in inexpensive mobile video streaming technologies. However, this area of technology usage is relatively unexplored. We chose to study how such technologies might be used for remote classroom attendance, with an emphasis on identity, interactions, embodiment, and privacy. Our results showed that people wanted a specific type of person when it came to proxy use in classroom settings, but this did not focus heavily on attributes such as race or gender. Instead, many idealized traits centered on the proxy's ability to participate in classroom activities such as scholastic abilities, the ability to be outgoing, aptitude, and the language spoken in the classroom. Students also faced challenges with interaction, embodiments, and camera work, which suggest design opportunities for these spaces. Overall, these results show promise for the use of human proxies for remote classroom attendance yet they also have sensitized us and hopefully other researchers and designers to the social and technical challenges that would need to be addressed as a part of future design work.

ACKNOWLEDGMENTS

We thank the Natural Sciences and Engineering Research Council for funding this work. We are thankful to William Odom and Richard Harper for revision suggestions for the paper.

REFERENCES

1. Victoria Bellotti and Abigail Sellen.1993. Design for Privacy in Ubiquitous Computing Environments, Proceedings of the Third European Conference on

Computer-Supported Cooperative Work (ECSCW'93), Kluwer Academic Publishers, Milan, pp. 77-92.

2. Jeremy Birnholtz, Clarissa Mak, Saul Greenberg, and Ron Baecker. 2008. Attention by proxy? issues in audience awareness for webcasts to distributed groups. In Proceedings of the SIGCHI Conference on Human Factors in Computing Systems (CHI '08). ACM, New York, NY, USA, 103-106. DOI=10.1145/1357054.1357071
3. Sara A. Bly, Steve R. Harrison, and Susan Irwin. 1993. Media spaces: bringing people together in a video, audio, and computing environment. Commun. ACM 36, 1 (January 1993), 28-46. DOI=10.1145/151233.151235
4. Michael Boyle, Carman Neustaedter, and Saul Greenberg. 2009. Privacy Factors in Video-based Media Spaces, Media Space: 20+ Years of Mediated Life, Springer.
5. Milton Chen. 2001. Design of a virtual auditorium. In Proceedings of the ninth ACM international conference on Multimedia (MULTIMEDIA '01). ACM, New York, NY, USA, 19-28. DOI=10.1145/500141.500147
6. Milton Chen. 2002. Achieving effective floor control with a low-bandwidth gesture-sensitive videoconferencing system. In Proceedings of the tenth ACM international conference on Multimedia (MULTIMEDIA '02). ACM, New York, NY, USA, 476-483. DOI=10.1145/641007.641109
7. Milton Chen. 2003. Visualizing the pulse of a classroom. In Proceedings of the eleventh ACM international conference on Multimedia (MULTIMEDIA '03). ACM, New York, NY, USA, 555-561. DOI=10.1145/957013.957130
8. Paul Dourish and Sara Bly. 1992. Portholes: supporting awareness in a distributed work group. In Proceedings of the SIGCHI Conference on Human Factors in Computing Systems (CHI '92), Penny Bauersfeld, John Bennett, and Gene Lynch (Eds.). ACM, New York, NY, USA, 541-547. DOI=10.1145/142750.142982
9. Nicolas Ducheneaut, Ming-Hui Wen, Nicholas Yee, and Greg Wadley. 2009. Body and mind: a study of avatar personalization in three virtual worlds. In Proceedings of the SIGCHI Conference on Human Factors in Computing Systems (CHI '09). ACM, New York, NY, USA, 1151-1160. DOI=10.1145/1518701.1518877
10. Ulf-Daniel Ehlers. 2013. Open Learning Cultures: A Guide to Quality, Evaluation, and Assessment for Future Learning. New York: Springer.
11. Deborah Fels, Judith K. Waalen, Shumin Zhai, and Patrice Weiss. Telepresence under exceptional circumstances: Enriching the connection to school for sick children. In Proceedings of Interact, 2001, 617-624.
12. Robert S. Fish, Robert E. Kraut, and Barbara L. Chalfonte. 1990. The VideoWindow system in informal communication. In Proceedings of the 1990 ACM conference on Computer-supported cooperative work (CSCW '90). ACM, New York, NY, USA, 1-11. DOI=10.1145/99332.99335
13. Gina Garramone, Allen C. Harris, and Ronald Anderson. 1986. Uses of political computer bulletin boards. Journal of Broadcasting & Electronic Media, 30, 325–339.
14. Saul Greenberg and Michael Rounding. 2001. The notification collage: posting information to public and personal displays. In Proceedings of the SIGCHI Conference on Human Factors in Computing Systems (CHI '01). ACM, New York, NY, USA, 514-521. DOI=10.1145/365024.365339
15. Steve Harrison. 2009. S. Media Space: 20+ Years of Mediated Life, Springer.
16. Starr Roxanne Hiltz. 1994. The Virtual Classroom: Learning Without Limits Via Computer Networks. Ablex Publishing Corp., Norwood, NJ, USA.
17. H, Hu. 2013. MOOC Migration. Diverse: Issues in Higher Education, 30, 4, 10-11.
18. Kori Inkpen, Brett Taylor, Sasa Junuzovic, John Tang, and Gina Venolia. 2013. Experiences2Go: sharing kids' activities outside the home with remote family members. In Proceedings of the 2013 conference on Computer supported cooperative work (CSCW '13). ACM, New York, NY, USA, 1329-1340. DOI=10.1145/2441776.2441926
19. Gavin Jancke, Gina Danielle Venolia, Jonathan Grudin, J. J. Cadiz, and Anoop Gupta. 2001. Linking public spaces: technical and social issues. In Proceedings of the SIGCHI Conference on Human Factors in Computing Systems (CHI '01). ACM, New York, NY, USA, 530-537. DOI=10.1145/365024.365352
20. Gavin Jancke, Jonathan Grudin, and Anoop Gupta. 2000. Presenting to local and remote audiences: design and use of the TELEP system. In Proceedings of the SIGCHI conference on Human Factors in Computing Systems (CHI '00). ACM, New York, NY, USA, 384-391. DOI=10.1145/332040.332461
21. Brennan Jones, Anna Witcraft, Scott Bateman, Carman Neustaedter, and Anthony Tang. 2015. Mechanics of Camera Work in Mobile Video Collaboration. In Proceedings of the 33rd Annual ACM Conference on Human Factors in Computing Systems (CHI '15). ACM, New York, NY, USA, 957-966. DOI=10.1145/2702123.2702345
22. Norman P. Jouppi. 2002. First steps towards mutually-immersive mobile telepresence. In Proceedings of the

2002 ACM conference on Computer supported cooperative work (CSCW '02). ACM, New York, NY, USA, 354-363. DOI=10.1145/587078.587128

23. Norman P. Jouppi, Subu Iyer, Stan Thomas, and April Slayden. 2004. BiReality: mutually-immersive telepresence. In Proceedings of the 12th annual ACM international conference on Multimedia (MULTIMEDIA '04). ACM, New York, NY, USA, 860-867. DOI=10.1145/1027527.1027725
24. Gregory Kearsley. 1995. The nature and value of interaction in distance learning, ACSDE Research Monograph No. 12, University Park, PA: Pennsylvania State University, American Center for the Study of Distance Education, 83092.
25. Atsunobu Kimura, Masayuki Ihara, Minoru Kobayashi, Yoshitsugu Manabe, and Kunihiro Chihara. 2007. Visual feedback: its effect on teleconferencing. In Proceedings of the 12th international conference on Human-computer interaction: applications and services (HCI'07), Julie A. Jacko (Ed.). Springer-Verlag, Berlin, Heidelberg, 591-600.
26. Eunyee Koh. 2010. Conferencing room for telepresence with remote participants. In Proceedings of the 16th ACM international conference on Supporting group work (GROUP '10). ACM, New York, NY, USA, 309-310. DOI=10.1145/1880071.1880124
27. Sven Kratz, Don Kimber, Weiqing Su, Gwen Gordon, and Don Severns. 2014. Polly: "being there" through the parrot and a guide. In Proceedings of the 16th international conference on Human-computer interaction with mobile devices & services (MobileHCI '14). ACM, New York, NY, USA, 625-630. DOI=10.1145/2628363.2628430
28. Karel Kreijns, Paul Kirschner, Wim Jochems, and Hans van Buuren. 2011. Measuring perceived social presence in distributed learning groups. Education and Information Technologies, 16, 4, 365-381.
29. Anicca Kristoffersson, Silvia Coradeschi, Amy Loutfi, and Kerstin Severinson-Eklundh. 2011. An Exploratory Study of Health Professionals' Attitudes about Robotic Telepresence Technology. *Journal of Technology in Human Services*, 29, 263-283.
30. Min Kyung Lee and Leila Takayama. 2011. "Now, i have a body": uses and social norms for mobile remote presence in the workplace. In Proceedings of the SIGCHI Conference on Human Factors in Computing Systems (CHI '11). ACM, New York, NY, USA, 33-42. DOI=10.1145/1978942.1978950
31. Jason Leigh, Maggie Rawlings, Javier Girado, Greg Dawe, Ray Fang, Alan Verlo, Muhammad-Ali Khan, Alan Cruz, Dana Plepys, Daniel Sandin, and Thomas Defanti. 2000. AccessBot: an Enabling Technology for Telepresence. Proceedings of the 10th Internet Society Conference, INET.
32. Michael Massimi and Carman Neustaedter. 2014. Moving from talking heads to newlyweds: exploring video chat use during major life events. In Proceedings of the 2014 conference on Designing interactive systems (DIS '14). ACM, New York, NY, USA, 43-52. DOI=10.1145/2598510.2598570
33. Kana Misawa and Jun Rekimoto. 2015. ChameleonMask: Embodied Physical and Social Telepresence using Human Surrogates. In Proceedings of the 33rd Annual ACM Conference Extended Abstracts on Human Factors in Computing Systems (CHI EA '15). ACM, New York, NY, USA, 401-411. DOI=10.1145/2702613.2732506
34. Tomoyuki Morita, Kenji Mase, Yasushi Hirano, and Shoji Kajita. 2007. Reciprocal attentive communication in remote meeting with a humanoid robot. In Proceedings of the 9th international conference on Multimodal interfaces (ICMI '07). ACM, New York, NY, USA, 228-235. DOI=10.1145/1322192.1322232
35. Shohei Nagai, Shunichi Kasahara, and Jun Rekimoto. 2015. LiveSphere: Sharing the Surrounding Visual Environment for Immersive Experience in Remote Collaboration. In Proceedings of the Ninth International Conference on Tangible, Embedded, and Embodied Interaction (TEI '15). ACM, New York, NY, USA, 113-116. DOI=10.1145/2677199.2680549
36. Carman Neustaedter and Elena Fedorovskaya. 2009. Presenting identity in a virtual world through avatar appearances. In *Proceedings of Graphics Interface 2009* (GI '09). Canadian Information Processing Society, Toronto, Ont., Canada, Canada, 183-190.
37. Carman Neustaedter and Saul Greenberg. 2003. The Design of a Context-Aware Home Media Space for Balancing Privacy and Awareness, In Proceedings of the Fifth International Conference on Ubiquitous Computing (UbiComp 2003), Springer.
38. Carman Neustaedter, Carolyn Pang, Azadeh Forghani, Erick Oduor, Serena Hillman, Tejinder K. Judge, Michael Massimi, and Saul Greenberg. 2015. Sharing Domestic Life through Long-Term Video Connections. ACM Trans. Comput.-Hum. Interact. 22, 1, Article 3 (February 2015), 29 pages. DOI=10.1145/2696869
39. Scott L. Newstok. 2013. A Plea for "Close Learning." *Liberal Education*. 99, 4, 16-19.
40. Andreas Paepcke, Bianca Soto, Leila Takayama, Frank Koenig, and Blaise Gassend. 2011. Yelling in the hall: using sidetone to address a problem with mobile remote presence systems. In Proceedings of the 24th annual ACM symposium on User interface software and technology (UIST '11). ACM, New York, NY, USA, 107-116. DOI=10.1145/2047196.2047209

41. Jason Procyk, Carman Neustaedter, Carolyn Pang, Anthony Tang, and Tejinder K. Judge. 2014. Shared geocaching over distance with mobile video streaming. In Proceedings of the companion publication of the 17th ACM conference on Computer supported cooperative work & social computing (CSCW Companion '14). ACM, New York, NY, USA, 293-296. DOI=10.1145/2556420.2557635

42. Jason Procyk, Carman Neustaedter, Carolyn Pang, Anthony Tang, and Tejinder K. Judge. 2014. Exploring video streaming in public settings: shared geocaching over distance using mobile video chat. In Proceedings of the SIGCHI Conference on Human Factors in Computing Systems (CHI '14). ACM, New York, NY, USA, 2163-2172. DOI=10.1145/2556288.2557198

43. Irene Rae, Gina Venolia, John C. Tang, and David Molnar. 2015. A Framework for Understanding and Designing Telepresence. In Proceedings of the 18th ACM Conference on Computer Supported Cooperative Work & Social Computing (CSCW '15). ACM, New York, NY, USA, 1552-1566. DOI=10.1145/2675133.2675141

44. Irene Rae, Leila Takayama, and Bilge Mutlu. 2013. The influence of height in robot-mediated communication. In Proceedings of the 8th ACM/IEEE international conference on Human-robot interaction (HRI '13). IEEE Press, Piscataway, NJ, USA, 1-8.

45. Yuanchun Shi, Weikai Xie, Guangyou Xu, Runting Shi, Enyi Chen, Yanhua Mao, and Fang Liu. 2003. The Smart Classroom: Merging Technologies for Seamless Tele-Education. Pervasive Computing IEEE, 2, 2, 47-55.

46. J. Sucher, S. Todd, S. Jones, T. Throckmorton, K. Turner, and F. Moore. 2011. Robotic telepresence: a helpful adjunct that is viewed favorably by critically ill surgical patients. *The American Journal of Surgery*, 202, 6, 843–847.

47. Leila Takayama and Helen Harris. 2013. Presentation of (telepresent) self: on the double-edged effects of mirrors. In *Proceedings of the 8th ACM/IEEE international conference on Human-robot interaction* (HRI '13). IEEE Press, Piscataway, NJ, USA, 381-388.

48. Chih-Hsiung Tu. 2000. On-line learning migration: from social learning theory to social presence theory in a CMC environment. Journal of Network and Computer Applications, 23(1), 27–37.

49. Gina Venolia, John Tang, Ruy Cervantes, Sara Bly, George Robertson, Bongshin Lee, and Kori Inkpen. 2010. Embodied social proxy: mediating interpersonal connection in hub-and-satellite teams. In Proceedings of the SIGCHI Conference on Human Factors in Computing Systems (CHI '10). ACM, New York, NY, USA, 1049-1058. DOI=10.1145/1753326.1753482

50. Steve Whittaker, David Frohlich, and Owen Daly-Jones. 1994. Informal workplace communication: what is it like and how might we support it?. In Conference Companion on Human Factors in Computing Systems (CHI '94), Catherine Plaisant (Ed.). ACM, New York, NY, USA, 208-. DOI=10.1145/259963.260328

51. Nicole Yankelovich, Nigel Simpson, Jonathan Kaplan, and Joe Provino. 2007. Porta-person: telepresence for the connected conference room. In CHI '07 Extended Abstracts on Human Factors in Computing Systems (CHI EA '07). ACM, New York, NY, USA, 2789-2794. DOI=10.1145/1240866.1241080

Ingenium: Engaging Novice Students with Latin Grammar

Sharon Zhou[1] **Ivy J. Livingston**[2] **Mark Schiefsky**[2] **Stuart M. Shieber**[3] **Krzysztof Z. Gajos**[3]

[1]Harvard College
Cambridge, MA USA
sharonz@post.harvard.edu

[2]Harvard Dept. of Classics
Cambridge, MA USA
{livings,mjschief}@fas.harvard.edu

[3]Harvard SEAS
Cambridge, MA USA
{shieber,kgajos}@seas.harvard.edu

ABSTRACT

Reading Latin poses many difficulties for English speakers, because they are accustomed to relying on word order to determine the roles of words in a sentence. In Latin, the grammatical form of a word, and not its position, is responsible for determining the word's function in a sentence. It has proven challenging to develop pedagogical techniques that successfully draw students' attention to the grammar of Latin and that students find engaging enough to use. Building on some of the most promising prior work in Latin instruction—the Michigan Latin approach—and on the insights underlying block-based programming languages used to teach children the basics of computer science, we developed Ingenium. Ingenium uses abstract puzzle blocks to communicate grammatical concepts. Engaging students in grammatical reflection, Ingenium succeeds when students are able to effectively decipher the meaning of Latin sentences. We adapted Ingenium to be used for two standard classroom activities: sentence translations and fill-in-the-blank exercises. We evaluated Ingenium with 67 novice Latin students in universities across the United States. When using Ingenium, participants opted to perform more optional exercises, completed translation exercises with significantly fewer errors related to word order and errors overall, as well as reported higher levels of engagement and attention to grammar than when using a traditional text-based interface.

Author Keywords

Engagement; Grammar; Latin education.

ACM Classification Keywords

H.5.m. Information Interfaces and Presentation (e.g. HCI): Miscellaneous

INTRODUCTION

Reading Latin poses many difficulties for English speakers, because they are accustomed to relying on word order to determine the functional roles of words in a sentence [40, 54]. In Latin, it is the grammatical form of a word that is responsible for determining its function in a sentence, and not its position. For example, *agricolae invenerunt pueros* translates as "the farmers found the boys", while *agricolas invenerunt pueri* is "the boys found the farmers". The two sentences are composed of the same words in the same order, but the different grammatical forms of the words *agricola* (farmer) and *puer* (boy) are responsible for the different meanings.

Despite the necessity of distinguishing between such morphological forms in reading, conventional Latin textbooks [61, 62, 3, 28] tend to accelerate their study, quickly introducing complex sentences with the long-term goal of transitioning students to reading original texts. However, this approach comes at the cost of instilling anxiety in students around grammar and fails to provide students with an adequate grasp of key grammatical concepts to apply to reading [29, 41].

Typically, these textbooks develop knowledge of morphology through repetitive drill exercises. These drills, however, practice words only in isolation [29], which is insufficient preparation for reading complex texts, because word forms are often ambiguous and students must use context to guide their interpretations. Thus, interactions between words in a sentence are extremely important, and pedagogical scholarship has urged development of methods to teach students how to identify the interactions in order to read Latin effectively [52, 20, 12].

In the 1950's, researchers at the University of Michigan designed a relevant pedagogical technique, called the Michigan Latin approach, that addressed the challenge of students' over-reliance on word order and their inadequate attention to grammatical forms and interactions. While studies demonstrated that the Michigan Latin approach was successful in increasing reading comprehension [40], it has not been widely adopted, possibly because it relies on idiosyncratic technical jargon and does not engage students with the material any more than traditional methods [49].

How might we leverage the strengths of the Michigan Latin approach, while minimizing its shortcomings? We found inspiration in block-based programming languages, particularly Scratch [37, 19, 44, 39, 23, 43, 33]. With an interactive and intuitive interface, Scratch is able to effectively engage novices [37]—a feat that the Michigan Latin approach was not able to achieve.

CHI'16, May 07–12, 2016, San Jose, CA, USA.

ACM 978-1-4503-3362-7/16/05...$15.00.
DOI: http://dx.doi.org/10.1145/2858036.2858239

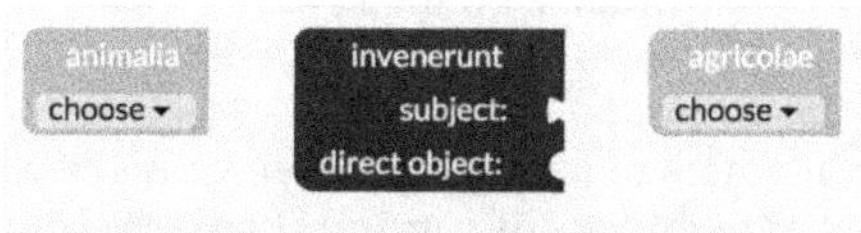

(a) The student encounters the sentence *animalia invenerunt agricolae*, meaning "the farmers found the animals". The sentence is accompanied by Ingenium blocks, horizontally arranged in the same order as the words in the sentence.

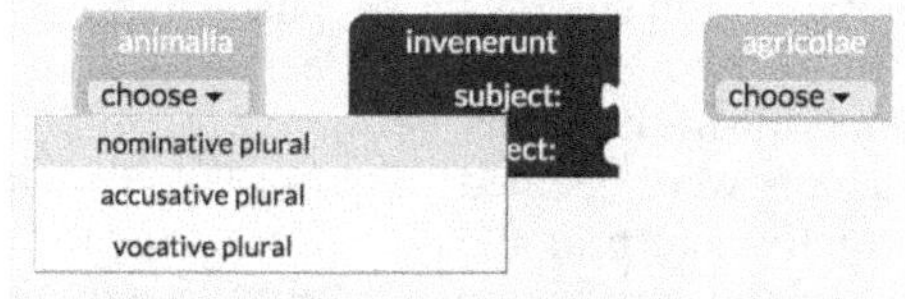

(b) The student inspects possible forms of *animalia* and, guided by word order, assumes that the word should be interpreted as being in the nominative case, which corresponds to the role of the subject.

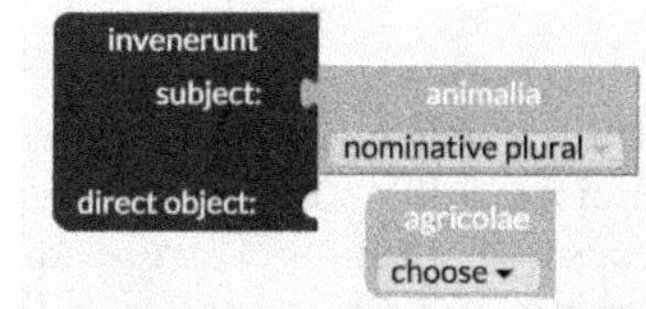

(c) Assigning a grammatical role to *animalia* causes it to change color and to acquire a knob shape corresponding to its case. Because of the grammatical match, the student is able to attach *animalia* to the subject slot of the verb.

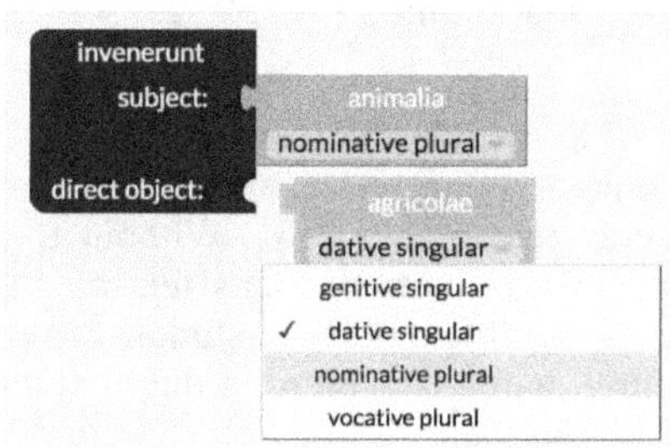

(d) At this point, the verb still needs a direct object. The student realizes, however, that *agricolae* can not be in the accusative case, which corresponds to the role of the direct object.

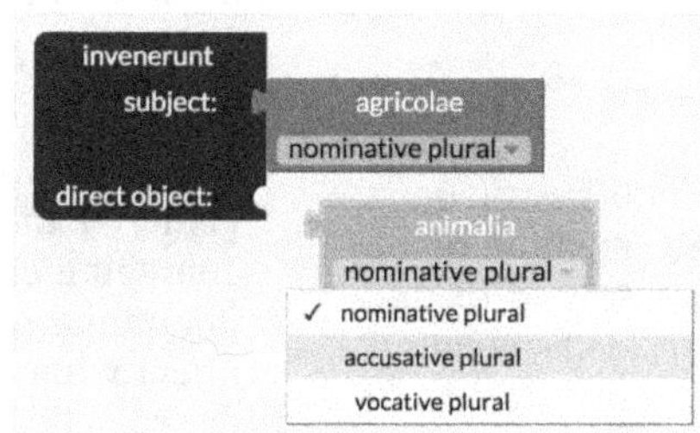

(e) The student backtracks: she removes *animalia* from the subject role and instead assigns nominative case to *agricolae* and places it into the role of the subject. She then assigns the accusative case to *animalia*.

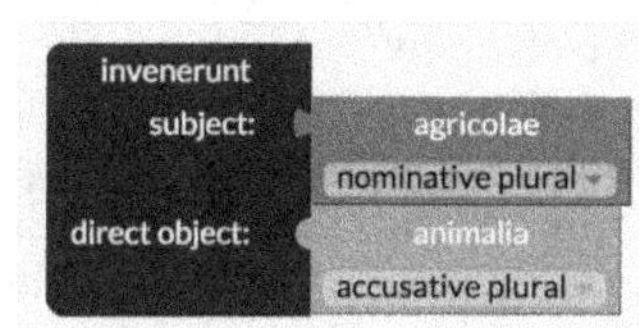

(f) She places *animalia* into the role of the direct object of the verb. The completed puzzle reveals a grammatically valid configuration of the sentence. It is now her responsibility to derive meaning from her understanding of the grammar.

Figure 1: Sample interaction with Ingenium.

Building on the strengths of the Michigan Latin approach and Scratch, we developed Ingenium[1]. Like Scratch, Ingenium uses a visual language, but instead of building new sentences, Ingenium enables learners to visually reconstruct relationships among components of an existing sentence as illustrated in Figure 1. The design of Ingenium addresses the goal of the Michigan Latin approach to focus students' attention on the interactions between words. Ingenium visualizes Latin words as puzzle pieces, whose shapes and colors indicate each word's grammatical functions. As implied by their matching shapes and colors, blocks fit together if their grammatical relationship is sound. However, because the same spelling of a word can often correspond to several possible grammatical forms, students have meaningful choices to make regarding the roles that different words play in a sentence.

Unlike distinct programming concepts whose differences remain consistent in various contexts, forms of Latin words that differ in function can look identical. The correct choice of form depends on the grammatical structure underlying the rest of the sentence, or the context of all words in the sentence. To reflect this, we designed blocks to be mutable so that students could play with each of their forms, and thus each of their roles, in the sentence, so that they may satisfy the constraints of each word in relation to the constraints of all the others.

Importantly, Ingenium is designed so that completing a puzzle does not give away a translation—it only reveals a grammatically permitted configuration of roles for the words in the sentence. Thus, we expect students to reflect more on the grammar, as revealed by the morphology of the words, instead of on the word order.[2] While the constraints of the system allow students to find and verify each word's grammatical role, students are still left with the responsibility of turning these roles into meaning.

We adapted Ingenium to be used for two standard classroom activities: sentence translations and fill-in-the-blank ex-

[1]On the naming of Ingenium, the word *ingenium* in Latin means "innate quality", "invention", and "genius", from which we derive the English words "ingenuity" and "engineer".

[2]We use the term "reflection" here and throughout in its non-technical meaning of "serious thought or consideration". We do so consistently with the attention to grammar as considered by the Michigan Latin approach and as it would be understood by the student participants in the study, who were asked about their reflection, as opposed to in its technical sense that is used by educational psychology theorists.

ercises. We evaluated Ingenium with 67 novice Latin students in universities across the United States. In a within-subjects study, participants performed translation and fill-in-the-blank exercises with and without Ingenium. Students were deemed successful when they were able to correctly interpret the meaning of Latin sentences. Hence, they could not "game the system" by simply completing the puzzles through trial and error, because solving the blocks-based puzzle was only a means toward uncovering the semantics of the sentence. When using Ingenium, participants opted to perform more optional exercises, completed Latin translation exercises with substantially higher accuracy—particularly with fewer errors related to word order—and reported higher levels of engagement and attention to grammar than when using a traditional text-based interface.

RELATED WORK

The Michigan Latin Approach

The University of Michigan created a new set of instructional materials in the 1950's that focused students attention on the grammatical interactions among words necessary to reading a Latin sentence [49, 54, 55, 31, 50]. They trained students to master conceptual techniques instead of repetitive drills, an effective strategy in improving Latin grammar comprehension [35, 27, 18].

The Michigan Latin approach calls its core technique "metaphrasing" [40]. Students apply metaphrasing to reading Latin sentences in order to narrow down the number of possible roles that each word in a sentence can assume. The technique has students analyze and deconstruct each word in a sentence into its possible functions and to consider how each of these functions might predict or affect the functions of other words in the sentence [49, 40]. Students then lay out in English word order the possible configurations of a sentence given their analyses [49]. Through metaphrasing, students are trained to anticipate a constrained set of feasible roles that the remaining words can take. These anticipated predictions, like the blanks in a fill-in-the-blank exercise, form "gaps" in a sentence, and guide students to a grammatically sound interpretation [49, 40].

The approach addresses the common mistake among beginning and more advanced students alike of focusing too little attention on the grammatical construction of a sentence and relying too heavily on word order and isolated dictionary definitions. It teaches students to think consciously about a Latin sentence's grammar before translating, and to use the grammar of the language, not their preconceptions such as word-order dependence, to guide their interpretations [49].

The effectiveness of the Michigan Latin approach lies in breaking down the grammatical construction of a sentence into more manageable parts and establishing a structured and dependable approach to understanding each part [40]. However, the approach fails to capture Latin's flexible ordering of words and thus may not fully remove the influence of word order, a limitation that the creator of the Michigan Latin approach has acknowledged [49]. In fact, second language instructional theory has shown the importance of abstract restructuring and explored how more advanced students, as opposed to novices, newly introduced to a language, restructure parts of a sentence into abstract schemata [42].

Scratch and Other Block-Based Languages

Removing the complexities of a language's syntax and vocabulary, Scratch uses puzzle blocks of varying shapes and colors to represent the concepts, with brief descriptors to help students quickly identify concepts [38]. Instead of memorizing a concept or how it works, students can focus their attention on the concept's application and interaction with other concepts. By using an interactive visual approach both that focuses on the structure behind the concepts and that removes the intimidating concrete syntax of a textual language such as Java [37, 38, 19], Scratch excites, engages, and effectively introduces novices to elementary programming [44, 39, 23, 43, 33, 63, 37].

Another key feature of Scratch is that students cannot make syntactic mistakes in the system, because blocks only fit together if their concepts match [37, 38]. Without the discouraging error-prone environment of many text-based programming languages, Scratch encourages students to experiment with the meaning, while constraining their expression to syntactically-correct programs. Ultimately, Scratch's intuitive environment, the embodiment of the "recognition rather than recall" principle of direct manipulation [26], focus on broad concepts, and prevention of student-made errors make it succeed in engaging novice programmers.

In addition to Scratch, many other block-based languages have been developed for students to learn basic programming, such as Blockly [16], Alice [14], MIT App Inventor [47], Snap! [22], RoboBuilder [60], Storytelling Alice [30], Pencil Code [6], and Droplet [5].

Additional applications of block-based languages have emphasized modeling concepts and substituting code: Polymorphic Blocks that visualize the logic of mathematical proofs and formulas [34], BlockImpress that creates online slideshow presentations with static images, text, charts, graphs, and formulas [56], Pixly that alters images through pixel-level operations [58], Spherly that programs a Sphero robot [58], FabCode that programs 3D models for fabrication such as printing and laser cutting [1], StarLogo TNG that facilitates 3D game design [59], a language that builds SPARQL queries for querying Linked Data [7], and several languages that enable software game design without code, such as Stencyl [36], LEGO Mindstorms [2], Etoys [53], Hopscotch [25], and Pocket Code [10].

We introduce Ingenium as a novel application of a block-based language to natural-language learning and acquisition. Ingenium is also distinctive in that it uses a block-based language to reverse engineer the meaning of an existing artifact, rather than to support learners in constructing new ones.

Ingenium was adapted from the block-based language Blockly [16].

Interactive Language-Learning Technologies

Recent approaches to interactive language learning have focused on relevant vocabulary placement for learning new terminology, such as displaying relevant keywords alongside articles [21], crowdsourcing colloquialisms to native speakers [11], presenting interactive subtitles for learning vocabulary in foreign films [32], and prompting users to practice timely, relevant vocabulary quizzes as they wait for a response from an online chat partner [8]. Gamified language-learning environments, such as Duolingo or Quia word games, have been studied to improve students' motivation [57, 13, 15]. Technology aimed to teach Mandarin Chinese has abstracted out text, using images as definitions [21], or associating spoken words with their pictographic representations [17].

Ingenium, by comparison, moves away from vocabulary recall to emphasize the importance of grammatical structure in informing students of a sentence's meaning. Ingenium associates the text of a word with the abstract visualization of its possible grammatical roles. The interactive, hands-on, and dynamic interface of the blocks, in addition to the positive feedback of snapping together matching blocks, encourages the user to engage with it and gives it a game-like nature.

INGENIUM

We have designed Ingenium with two core objectives in mind: (1) to help students understand the meaning of Latin sentences by focusing their attention on their grammatical structure, and (2) to create an engaging user experience for exploring the complex structure of Latin grammar.

Ingenium allows users to visually contrast possible roles of a Latin word and to explore interactions among different words in a hands-on manner with puzzle blocks representing Latin words. The jigsaw metaphor helps students reason about constraints on each word's role in a sentence, while the mutability of the pieces allows them to realize the range of roles that each word can embody given its spelling. The system prevents syntactically incorrect parsings, giving students the license to experiment without fear of making grammatical mistakes. Additionally, by removing specialized terminology in favor of visual affordances, Ingenium is designed to engage students with Latin grammar.

The act of involving all the blocks focuses students attention on the process of assigning correct grammatical roles to words in a complex Latin sentence. The assignment of grammatical roles aids students in uncovering the correct meaning of the sentence. The success of Ingenium rests in its ability to help students reach a semantic understanding of a sentence by focusing their attention more on the grammar.

Formative Design Research

We designed Ingenium through an iterative process. We started by creating paper prototypes of puzzle blocks from colorful 5 x 8-inch index cards. With them, we experimented with the visualization of the following grammatical concepts:

- Different valid cases of nouns with the same morphology
- Nominative subject and verb agreement
- Accusative case as the direct object
- Adjective and noun agreement
- Prepositional phrases
- Verb transitivity
- Use of linking verbs
- Subordination of relative clauses

We explored two main designs. In one design, shape primarily informed function and color indicated the part of speech. In the other design, the reverse was true: color informed function and shape indicated the part of the speech. In the first design, we explored two sub-designs on the subordination or juxtaposition of an adjective in its relationship with a noun: adjectives could become embedded into a noun or they could attach themselves adjacent to an agreeing noun. All designs enforced a set subject-verb-object word order. Not unlike "gapping" in the Michigan Latin approach, they constructed sentences in a horizontal and linear structure.

We asked instructors at a local Montessori School, who were familiar with pedagogies that use color-coded blocks to represent parts of speech in English, and students at our university with high-school level Latin to play freely with 30 puzzle blocks and the two separate designs.

We observed that shapes more effectively communicated grammatical connections between blocks than colors when there were fewer shapes and clear differentiation among them. As the number of shapes and colors grew, colors performed as more effective indicators. This informed our designs to employ shapes for important indicators that had fewer combinations, such as part of speech and cases, while using color to indicate the many case-number-gender combinations.

Subordinating adjectives was less intuitive initially, yet was preferred once discovered. It allowed participants to group blocks together, and thus to organize them and understand that there were clear separation of roles. We thus observed that different kinds of interactions between parts of speech could effectively convey differences in their relationships.

We found that the grammatical roles of individual words caused more problems than the structural construction of clauses, causing us to focus our subsequent designs on the roles of each word. Since a word's role in a Latin sentence is chiefly determined by its part of speech, we decided to use part of speech to guide the main shape of blocks in order to emphasize grammatically valid connections among words in the design of our system. Ingenium currently illustrates interactions among the following five most common parts of speech, whose interactions are taught earliest in the classroom: nouns, verbs, adjectives, prepositions, and adverbs. (See full interactions in Figure 2.)

Usability Tests

We performed early usability testing of the initial software implementation of the system with five volunteers whose knowledge of Latin ranged from novice to expert.

All parts of speech in both our formative design research and the initial implementation were depicted with colorful blocks. We discovered that applying color to both types of blocks, those that change in color and those that remain the same in color, generated confusion. Communicating the neutrality of the immutable blocks (verbs, prepositions, adverbs) through

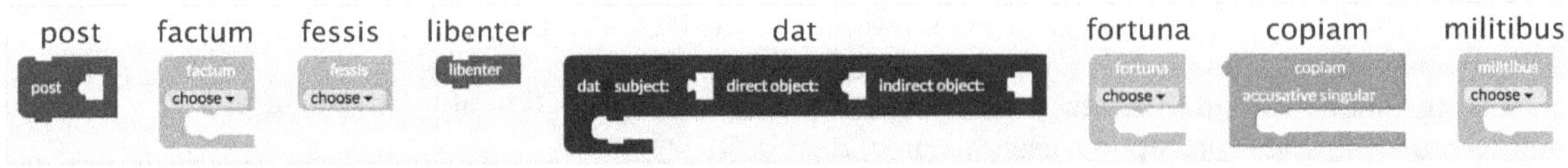

(a) Students are provided these blocks with the Latin sentence that means: "After the deed, fortune willingly gives plenty to the weary soldiers." The verb *dat*, "gives," and preposition *post*, "after," are designed with inline knob cutouts for the nouns that they expect to take. Note that the noun *copiam*, "plenty," is not an ambiguous form, so it has no dropdown menu of alternatives, unlike the other nouns and adjectives that have "choose" written on them.

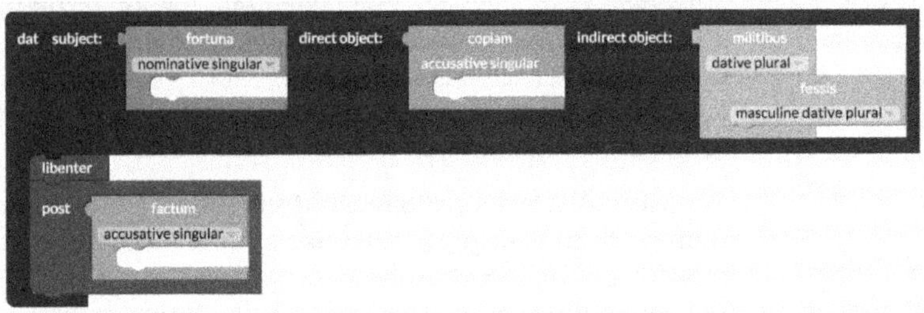

(b) The blocks for the inline design are completely matched. Inside the clamp of the verb *dat*, the adverb *libenter*, "willingly," and the prepositional phrase *post factum*, "after the deed," are nested and stacked. Similarly, inside the clamp of the noun *militibus*, "soldiers," the adjective *fessis*, "weary," is nested.

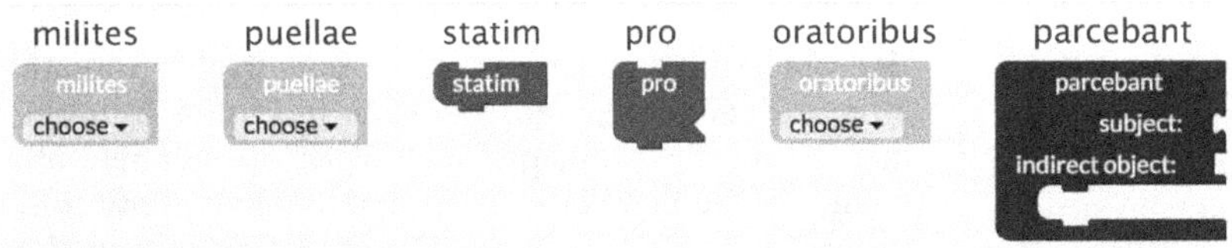

(c) This sentence, meaning "The soldiers immediately spared the girl on behalf of the orators," illustrates the external design of the verb *parcebant* and the preposition *pro*.

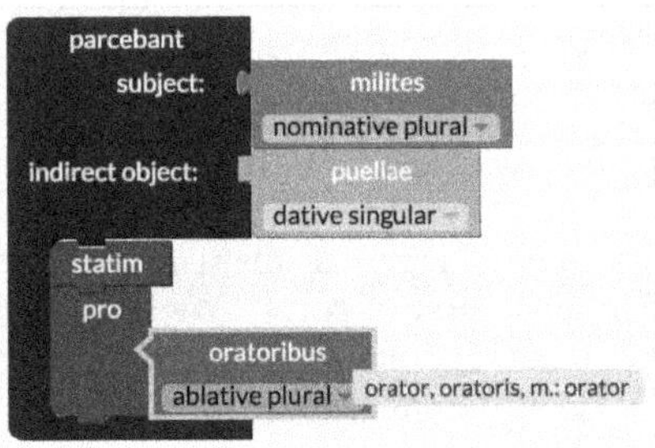

(d) The completed sentence with the external design shows how the verb block expands vertically to accommodate its expected noun blocks. The "clampless" nouns here are to prevent confusing students with unused visual structures, before they have been exposed to the appropriate interactions. Students can also gloss words at any point by right-clicking on a block, such as *oratoribus*, which then shows a text box with the word's dictionary entry, "orator, oratoris, m.: orator," where it was clicked.

Figure 2: Comparison between inline and external designs, and illustration of interactions among all parts of speech.

gray hues (black, charcoal gray, and light gray) reduced this confusion.

One user's embarrassment over forgetting the definition of a word prompted him to stop using the system, while other users were eager to test more blocks. This observation motivated our decision to include dictionary glossing by right-clicking a block, to shift the student's attention to the grammatical, and away from the vocabulary, questions.

Nouns and Verb-Noun Interactions

In Latin, the function of a noun in a sentence is often ambiguous, because a single spelling can correspond to several declined forms—information that a noun carries on its case, number, and gender. Nouns of each case can indicate several different functions, so a single form of a noun can also assume multiple roles. For example, in Figure 2a, *copiam* in the role of direct object could also, as its knob shape suggests, fit inside the preposition *post* to mean "after plenty." Students are responsible for deciding the correct role of the noun by using contextual information about the grammatical constraints of both the noun itself and other words in the sentence.

Verb-noun interactions form the foundation of simple complete sentences. In Ingenium, we make this interaction visually apparent by having verbs and nouns connect like puzzle pieces through matching knob shapes. The noun block has a horizontally projecting knob on its top left corner that, if grammatically appropriate, can fit inside the same shape cut into a verb. (See the nouns *agricolae* and *animalia* fitting the verb *invenerunt* in Figure 1f.) Knob shapes correspond to one of the six declined cases: nominative, genitive, dative, accusative, ablative, or vocative. Through a dropdown menu, students are able to select from all the case-number combinations of the noun that are consistent with its spelling. (See Figures 1b, 1d, and 1e.) Before a selection is made, the block does not have a knob, is a neutral gray color, and has the word "choose" over the dropdown menu, so as not to bias the student's decision. (See *animalia* and *agricolae* in Figure 1a.) Once a combination is chosen and the case-number combination is established, the corresponding knob appears dynamically in the top left hand corner. Students can change the case-number combination of a noun at any time to dynamically change the noun's knob shape and thus its function. (See *animalia* from Figure 1d to 1f.)

Noun-Adjective Interactions

Because a noun's case is the primary factor in determining its possible functions, we wanted to make interactions associated with the noun's case most apparent to the student. The noun's case thus determines the shape of the knob. Along with its case, however, a noun's gender (masculine, feminine, or neuter) and number (singular or plural) indicate which adjectives can modify it, as nouns can only be modified by adjectives of the same case-number-gender combination. A unique color is assigned to each of 36 possible case-number-gender combinations such that agreeing nouns and adjectives have the same color. (See *militibus* and *fessis* in Figure 2b.)

Structurally, the noun-adjective interaction is facilitated by the tooth-shaped concavities above and convexities below on adjective blocks and inside clamp structures beneath the body of noun blocks. (See *fessis* in Figure 2b.) Agreeing adjectives can be stacked unboundedly on top of each other—a grammatically permissible, though semantically improbable, connection—as the enclosing clamp expands to accommodate them.

Verbs, Prepositions & Adverbs: Two Designs

The expectations raised by the verb in a sentence are often the most constraining and thus provide the most helpful information in determining the roles of other words and the overall grammatical structure of the sentence. The knob cutouts in a verb block indicate, implicitly through its shape, the case and, explicitly with text, the roles that the given verb expects. For example, the intransitive verb *parcebant* in Figure 2c has special properties in Latin and expects an object in the dative case, as well as a subject in the usual nominative case. The cutouts in the verb blocks were motivated by the "gapping" concept in the Michigan Latin approach as students form appropriate expectations for blanks, or "gaps," to fill when analyzing the verb's expectations.

We created two designs for the knob cutouts in verbs: *inline* and *external*. The two designs affect the knob cutouts, as shown in *dat* in Figure 2a and *parcebant* in Figure 2c. The inline design has the knob cutouts lie inside the main body of the block in a horizontal and linear layout, like blanks in a fill-in-the-blank exercise. The enclosure of the noun inside of the verb visually suggests that the form of the noun depends on the verb and, in turn, that the verb takes a particular form of the noun. However, the horizontal arrangement of the cutouts in the inline design may inadvertently convey a suggestion of expected word order. In order to minimize any suggestion of word order and to focus students' attention on the roles of words instead, we created the external design with the knob cutouts aligned vertically beneath the body of the block. This design sacrifices clear affordances of the cutouts, but also de-emphasizes the word order. This design was prompted by the shortcomings of fixed horizontal word order in the Michigan Latin approach [49].

Similar to verbs, prepositions take nouns of a certain case as their objects and thus have knob cutouts identical to the ones on verbs. (See *post* in Figure 2a and *pro* in Figure 2c.) However, they only have one functional expectation for their dependent noun, so no textual indication of function is necessary. In order to maintain visual consistency with the inline or external design on verbs, students see the same design on prepositions.

The verb clamp is designed like the noun clamp to enclose arbitrarily many components such as prepositional phrases and adverbs that fit grammatically within the verb phrase. (See *dat* in Figure 2a and *parcebant* in Figure 2b.) To ease students into the use of clamps, the nouns and the verbs are initially "clampless". (See clampless nouns *milites*, *puellae*, and *oratoribus* in Figures 2c and 2d.) Only after the corresponding optional components have been shown and the interaction with them becomes necessary are the clamps necessarily introduced. Furthermore, we have designed the noun and verb clamps to have different teeth shapes, circular and rectangular, in order to visually distinguish the components that can be enclosed by the verb as opposed to the noun. Accordingly, prepositions and adverbs have circular and rectangular teeth, respectively, to correspond in shape with the clamps that enclose them.

Unlike the roles of declined nouns and adjectives, the expectations of a conjugated verb, preposition, and adverb are unambiguous. As changes in color reflect changes in declension, we were informed through usability tests to color the static verb and the preposition and adverb blocks respective shades of neutral black and charcoal gray in order to differentiate them from the mutable noun and adjective blocks. (See static coloring of the verb *dat* in black and the adverb *libenter* and the preposition *post* in charcoal gray in Figures 2a and 2b.)

Interacting With Blocks

When students interact with blocks, grammatical relationships are reinforced with visual highlighting, sound, and automatic snapping of matching pieces. If two blocks do not match, and if the student drops a block near another block with which it shares no connection, the dropped block will be bumped away from the other block to indicate that the connection is not grammatically valid and therefore cannot occur. Students can thus experiment freely without fear of making grammatical errors. Their interactions with Ingenium emphasize how a sentence is grammatically constructed, based on the forms and functions of words and independent of their order.

Ingenium also allows students to see a word's dictionary definition by right-clicking on its block, shifting students' attention to the grammatical problems and away from vocabulary questions. This decision was informed by formative studies in which users were not familiar with all of the words used in the system, making the system less welcoming and engaging.

Classroom Activities

We explored several applications of our system to existing classroom activities.

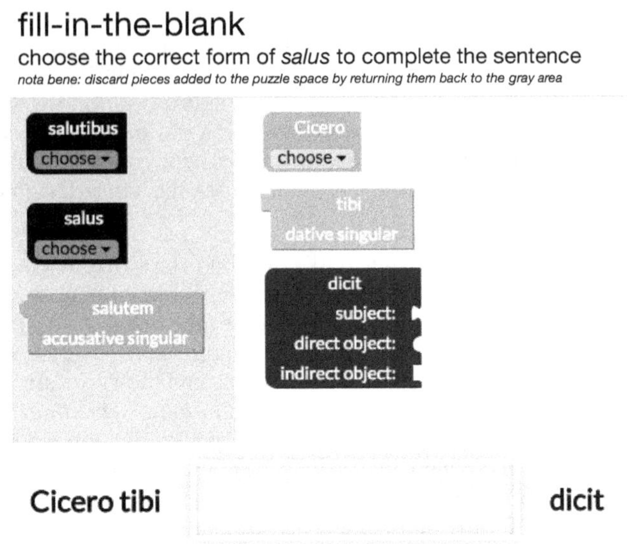

Figure 3: Sample fill-in-the-blank exercise with Ingenium: *Cicero tibi* _______ *dicit.* With the blocks in the gray zone on the left as options, students are free to experiment by dragging them on and off the white canvas to the right. Students can then type the grammatically valid option into the blank.

First, Ingenium applies particularly well to typical Latin-to-English translation exercises. Given a Latin sentence and the given blocks appearing in the same horizontally linear order of the words in the sentence, students can uncover a syntactically correct parsing of the sentence by fitting all the blocks together so that no word is left unattached, or without a grammatical role.

Another common exercise in Latin homework and exam questions is a fill-in-the-blank activity with multiple choice answers, one of which completes the sentence prompted in the question. Inspired by the concept of "gapping" in the Michigan Latin approach, Ingenium is also particularly suitable for this type of task (Figure 3). When given the exercise, the blocks that correspond to the words in the question are present on a main canvas on which students can freely play, and the blocks representing the multiple choice options for the blank appear in a word bank alongside the canvas. From this bank, students can drag the multiple choice blocks onto the canvas to experiment. They can also return the multiple choice blocks back to the word bank.

We also explored a sandbox interface, not deployed for the experiment, in which students can manipulate a wide array of blocks—deleting and adding new ones from a toolbox of various words—to construct grammatically correct Latin text that is meaningful to them.

EXPERIMENT

We conducted an experiment to evaluate Ingenium in comparison to traditional text-only presentation of Latin translation and fill-in-the-blank exercises. We focused in particular on the impact of Ingenium on novice Latin students' engagement, level of attention to grammar, self-efficacy, accuracy in translation, errors related to word order, and overall preference. We define novice to have $\frac{1}{2}$ year to $1\frac{1}{2}$ years of prior college or high school Latin experience.

Hypotheses

The interactive, hands-on, and game-like nature of Ingenium makes it distinct from traditional language comprehension drills and we expected that this change would result in increased *engagement.* Engagement is important in enabling students to improve: the more engaged a student is, the more mindful her practice and the more time she spends on activities, which, in turn, leads to better outcomes [9, 46, 45]. We included both self-reported and trace-based (number of optional exercises completed) measures of engagement. We hypothesize that:

Hypothesis 1: Students will be more engaged with Ingenium than with the traditional text-only versions of the exercises.

In Ingenium, the blocks depict the grammatical constraints and possible grammatical roles of each word. Students are thus compelled to consider the grammatical connections among words, independent of word order, in order to build sentences with the blocks. We therefore expect that:

Hypothesis 2: Students will commit fewer errors related to word order when using Ingenium than using the traditional text-only versions of the exercises.

and

Hypothesis 3: Students will report that they reflected more on the grammar when using Ingenium than when using the traditional text-only versions of the exercises.

Ingenium explicitly encourages learners to focus their attention on the grammar of each sentence. While it makes the grammatical roles of the words particularly prominent, we expect that the overall attention on the grammar will also result in lower incidence of errors, unrelated to word order. For this reason, we expect that:

Hypothesis 4: Students will be able to complete translation exercises with fewer overall errors using Ingenium than using the traditional text-only versions of the exercises.

Ingenium makes examining grammar less intimidating and more intuitive. We therefore expect that:

Hypothesis 5: Students will report a greater positive change in self-efficacy related to Latin grammar and reading comprehension after using Ingenium than after using the traditional text-only versions of the exercises.

Self-efficacy, or task-related confidence, is an effective predictor of motivation [4, 48, 64].

Finally, because Ingenium is more visual, interactive, and hands-on, we expect that:

Hypothesis 6: Students will prefer using Ingenium over the traditional text-only versions of the exercises.

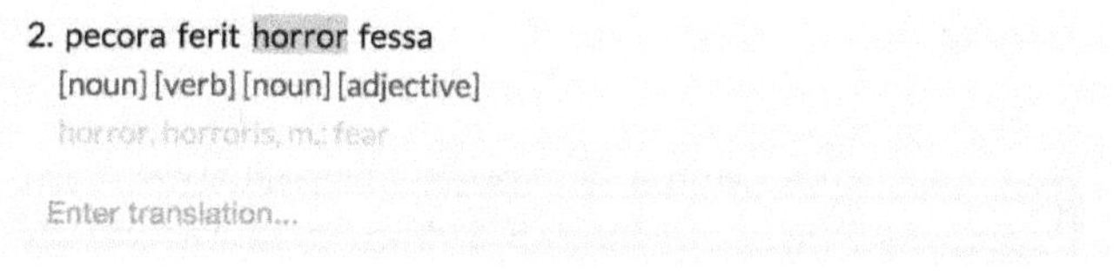

Figure 4: Sample sentence translation in the text-only condition. Parts of speech are indicated in dark gray beneath each word. The user here has right clicked to gloss, or to perform a dictionary lookup, of the highlighted word, *horror*, whose dictionary entry appears in light gray below.

Tasks

We designed two activities that are common in Latin instruction: translation exercises and multiple choice fill-in-the-blank exercises. In the control (text-only) condition, the exercises were presented in textual form (as in Figure 4). In the Ingenium condition, each sentence was additionally accompanied by a set of puzzle pieces. Otherwise, the control and the Ingenium conditions were identical in form and structure. The sentences in the two conditions were isomorphic: for each sentence in one condition there was an equivalent sentence in the other condition that used similar grammatical forms and interactions between words, and used vocabulary words at the same level of difficulty.

Sentences used for translation and fill-in-the-blank exercises were largely quoted or adapted for the novice level from commonly read Latin texts, including Virgil's *Aeneid* and *Georgics*, Cicero's *First Oration Against Catiline* and *Letters to Atticus*, Catullus' *Poem 64*, and Caesar's *Commentaries on the Gallic War*, among others.

In both conditions, students were presented with three rounds of exercises. Each round consisted of a set of four translation exercises and one fill-in-the-blank exercise. The successive experimental rounds increased in the complexity of interactions among words: 1) interactions between nouns and verbs; 2) interactions among nouns, verbs, and adjectives; 3) interactions among nouns, verbs, adjectives, adverbs and prepositions.

In the Ingenium condition, using Ingenium was required for the first two and optional for the last two translations in each round. In all fill-in-the-blank exercises, the use of Ingenium was always completely optional. For both conditions, students could skip the last round (the third set of translations and the third fill-in-the-blank exercise) at any point by pressing a button placed at the top right corner of their screen, which read: "I'm finished using this tool."

Participants

Of the 171 participants who navigated to the study home page, 67 participants completed the entire study. The youngest participants reported to be in the age range of 18–22 and the oldest reported being 51+ years old. Most were college students, who hailed from 42 different colleges and universities across the United States. 4 learners participated in person and 63 remotely. Participants included current and former students of Latin. Their formal study of Latin included representation from over 14 different Latin textbooks.

Participants were compensated $10 for taking part in the study (in-person participants received cash, remote participants Amazon gift certificates).

Procedures

In-person participants were recruited through visits to college Latin classes, and remote participants through email correspondence with Classics departments at over 50 colleges and universities across the United States, email notices to a local college's house lists and other internal lists, and through announcements on social media (Facebook and Twitter).

All the questionnaires and study activities were implemented for web-based use. All participants were asked to begin the study by navigating to the study home page on their computers.

Remote participants were screened through an online questionnaire that asked for their age, and level and years of Latin. Only adults with $^1/_2$ year to $1^1/_2$ years of college or high school Latin were deemed eligible to participate and were given the link to the study.

At the start of the study, in-person participants were told that they should speak out if they found anything confusing, but that the experimenter could not answer their questions or interfere once the study began. All participants were then asked to fill out a questionnaire on their basic demographics and Latin experience. Next, they answered questions related to their self-efficacy, or confidence, with fundamental grammatical concepts in Latin.

Participants were then randomly assigned with a 50% probability to perform either the control or the experimental condition first. They were also randomly assigned with a 50% probability to either the inline or the external design of Ingenium in the experimental condition. Prior to starting each condition, participants were presented with condition-specific instructions. They then proceeded to the three rounds of exercises.

After completing each condition, participants were presented with several questions on a 7-point Likert scale. The questions pertained to self-reported cognitive and emotional engagement, level of attention paid to the grammar, and self-efficacy. The questions were identical in both conditions. After both conditions and post-assessments were completed, participants were asked which tool they preferred: the first or the second.

Adjustments of Data

Due to a programming error, 17 participants were able to complete the study without filling out the demographics questionnaire and the pre-assessment. Because these 17 participants still completed the required sets of exercises, they were only excluded from the self-efficacy analysis, which required pre-assessment data, but were included in the analysis of other measures.

Design and Data Analysis

This was a within-subjects study with one factor (exercise presentation: {text-only, Ingenium}) and the following measures (all subjective measures, except for the overall preference, were collected on a 7-point Likert scale):

- **Trace-based engagement.** In both conditions, as mentioned previously, all the exercises in the third round (4 translations and 1 fill-in-the-blank exercise) were optional. We used the number of optional exercises completed as a trace-based measure of engagement.
- **Self-reported measures of engagement.** After each condition, we asked participants two questions related to their cognitive engagement and two related to their emotional engagement. The answers to all four questions were averaged into a single measure of self-reported engagement prior to analysis.
- **Errors of word order.** For the 9 out of 12 translation exercises per condition that were not given in English word order, the first author flagged the incorrect translations that were caused by over-reliance on English word order. The assessor was blind to the condition in which the answer was generated while grading the accuracy of the answers.
- **Reflection on grammar.** After each condition, we asked participants how much they reflected on the grammar of the sentences during the activity that they just completed.
- **Overall error rate.** For all translation exercises completed by the participants, the first author assessed the accuracy of participants' answers. The assessor was blind to the condition in which the answer was generated while grading the accuracy of the answers.
- **Change in self-efficacy.** We asked participants five self-efficacy questions (related to Latin grammar and text comprehension) at three points during the study: at the beginning of the study and upon the completion of each condition. We computed the change in self-efficacy as the difference between self-efficacy just after and just before each of the two conditions. The answers to the five questions were averaged prior to analysis.
- **Overall preference.** At the end of the study, we asked participants to rank the two tools in the order of overall preference.

We used logistic regression (a generalized linear model with binomial distribution) to analyze trace-based engagement, for which the measures were binary (an optional exercise was either completed or not). We used participant ID as a covariate in those analyses. For all other analyses, we used the Wilcoxon Signed Rank test because normal distribution could not be assumed in our data. We calculated Cohen's *d* for the effect size of errors related to word order and overall error rate.

To guard against Type I errors, we applied the Holm's sequentially-rejective Bonferroni procedure [24, 51] to the analyses. This method introduces fewer Type II errors than the more popular simple Bonferroni correction.

Results

Initial Analyses

We conducted an initial between-subjects analysis to see if the two designs of verb puzzle pieces (the *inline* versus the *external* design illustrated in Figure 2) resulted in different errors rates in translation exercises. Participants made fewer errors when using the external ($M = 43\%$) than the inline ($M = 46\%$) interfaces, but the difference was not statistically significant ($\chi^2_{(959.5,N=1)} = 0.4443, n.s.$). For that reason, in the subsequent analyses we combined results from the two variants of the Ingenium condition.

Main Analyses

The main results are summarized in Table 1.

Participants chose to complete more optional translation and fill-in-the-blank exercises when using Ingenium ($M = 59.1\%$) than when using the text-only interface ($M = 53.4\%$), and this difference was statistically significant ($\chi^2_{(1,N=670)} = 7.55, p = 0.006$). Participants also reported significantly higher levels of self-reported engagement with Ingenium ($M = 5.37$) than with the traditional interface ($M = 3.96$, $S = 643.00$, $p < 0.0001$). Hypothesis 1 is therefore supported.

Participants committed fewer errors related to word order using Ingenium ($M = 7.0\%$) than the text-only interface ($M = 20.0\%$); this effect was large (Cohen's $d = 0.82$) and statistically significant ($S = -386.00$, $p < 0.0001$). Hypothesis 2 was also supported.

Participants reported that they reflected on the grammar more after using Ingenium ($M = 5.54$) than after using the text-only interface ($M = 4.19$), and this difference was statistically significant ($S = 378.00$, $p < 0.0001$). Hypothesis 3 was thus supported.

Participants performed translation exercises with significantly lower overall error rates using Ingenium ($M = 45.1\%$) than using the text-only interface ($M = 57.4\%$); this effect size was moderate (Cohen's $d = 0.49$) and statistically significant ($S = -386.00$, $p < 0.0001$). Hypothesis 4 was supported.

Participants ($N = 50$) reported a positive change in self-efficacy after using Ingenium ($M = 0.196$), while their self-efficacy *decreased* slightly after using the text-only interface ($M = -0.072$). This difference was not statistically significant ($S = 139, n.s.$), however, so Hypothesis 5 was not supported.

Finally, participants preferred Ingenium (*mean rank* = 1.33) over the traditional interface (*mean rank* = 1.67), and this difference was statistically significant ($S = -391$, $p = 0.0042$). Hypothesis 6 was, therefore, supported.

DISCUSSION, FUTURE WORK & CONCLUSION

We developed Ingenium with two goals in mind: (1) to help students focus their attention on the grammar of the Latin sentences in order to aid them with correctly deriving their grammatical, and consequently semantic, compositions, and (2) to do so in a manner that made examining Latin grammar engaging.

Hypothesis		Text-only	Ingenium	Raw p-values	Adjusted p-values	
H1	Trace-based engagement	53.4%	59.1%	0.0060	0.0120	*
	Self-reported engagement	3.96	5.32	< 0.0001	< 0.0006	*
H2	Errors of word order	20.0%	7.0%	< 0.0001	< 0.0007	*
H3	Reflection on grammar	4.19	5.54	< 0.0001	< 0.0005	*
H4	Overall error rate	57.4%	45.1%	0.0010	0.0040	*
H5	Change in self-efficacy	−0.072	0.196	0.0602	0.0602	
H6	Overall preference	1.67	1.33	0.0042	0.0126	*

Table 1: Summary of the results. All subjective measures except the overall preference were reported on a 7-point Likert scale. Overall preference is reported as mean rank; lower indicates greater preference. We used the Holm's sequentially-rejective Bonferroni procedure to account for multiple hypotheses being tested simultaneously. We report both raw and adjusted p-values. Statistically significant results are marked with an asterisk.

In our study, students reported reflecting more on the grammar of the sentences when using Ingenium than when solving the traditional text-only versions of the exercises. This reinforces the main tenets of the Michigan Latin approach of focusing students' attention on grammatical concepts, rather than on word order and vocabulary [40]. This increased attention on the grammar coincided with improved reading comprehension performance: students translated their sentences more accurately when they could use Ingenium. In particular, they made much fewer errors related to word order when using Ingenium (7%) compared to a traditional text-only interface (20%). Other errors, mostly of tense (surrounds/surrounded) and number (animal/animals), were related to individual words in isolation, as opposed to interactions between words, and thus were not targeted by the design of Ingenium. These types of errors still decreased, though to a lesser extent. These findings support the success of the system in enabling students to decipher the meaning of Latin sentences by reflecting more on the grammar.

The results of our study also demonstrate that Ingenium can increase student engagement, both measured as the number of optional exercises they were willing to complete and as their self-reported assessments of emotional engagement and cognitive engagement. Students also indicated a strong preference for doing exercises with Ingenium over the traditional text-only versions. When the use of blocks in the translation exercises was optional, nearly all students still used them at least briefly (97%) and most completed the puzzle (79%).

In the future, we plan to develop ways of visualizing interactions and concepts of greater complexity, such as relative clauses, interrogative questions, clause subordination, etc. We also intend to explore collaborative mechanisms that would allow students to interact with Ingenium together. Because the restructuring of grammar commonly occurs in second language acquisition [42], Ingenium—while particularly fitting for Latin—can also be adapted to a wide variety of other morphologically rich languages, such as those in the Slavic and Finno-Ugric families.

We have already implemented a more open-ended sandbox interface, which was not deployed for the experiment, where students could create spontaneous sentences using novice-level vocabulary from the widely used Cambridge Latin Course, in addition to an interface that enables learners and instructors to input their own words that would generate Ingenium blocks from a lookup in the online Lewis and Short *Latin Dictionary*.[3] We prepare to investigate these more versatile and customizable interfaces of Ingenium with students and instructors.

To conclude, Ingenium addresses a long-standing challenge in Latin instruction: that of helping students make effective use of Latin grammar when comprehending the semantics of complex Latin texts. Unlike prior attempts to address this challenge, Ingenium uses accessible vocabulary of an intuitive visual language instead of idiosyncratic technical jargon. Interactions with Ingenium focus students attention on the process of grammatically unpacking a sentence as a means toward uncovering its meaning. Given its positive impact on students' engagement and performance, and its web-based implementation that allows it to be conveniently accessed online, we hope to develop Ingenium to a point where it becomes an easily adoptable, supplementary instructional tool for Latin students worldwide.

Acknowledgements. This work was supported in part by a Sloan Research Fellowship. We are grateful to Ofra Amir and Jim Waldo for their helpful feedback in the preparation of this paper.

REFERENCES

1. Harshit Agrawal, Rishika Jain, Prabhat Kumar, and Pradeep Yammiyavar. 2014. FabCode: Visual Programming Environment for Digital Fabrication. In *Proceedings of the 2014 Conference on Interaction Design and Children (IDC '14)*. ACM, New York, NY, USA, 353–356. DOI: http://dx.doi.org/10.1145/2593968.2610490

2. Dominik Aufderheide, Werner Krybus, and Ulf Witkowski. 2012. Experiences with LEGO MINDSTORMS as an Embedded and Robotics Plattform within the Undergraduate Curriculum. In *Advances in Autonomous Robotics*, Guido Herrmann, Matthew Studley, Martin Pearson, Andrew Conn, Chris

[3]The Lewis and Short *Latin Dictionary* is a standard and widely used Latin dictionary that is available online through Tufts University's Perseus project at www.perseus.tufts.edu.

Melhuish, Mark Witkowski, Jong-Hwan Kim, and Prahlad Vadakkepat (Eds.). Lecture Notes in Computer Science, Vol. 7429. Springer Berlin Heidelberg, 185–196. DOI: http://dx.doi.org/10.1007/978-3-642-32527-4_17

3. Maurice Balme and James Morwood. 1997. *Oxford latin course. Part II.* Oxford University Press Oxford.

4. Albert Bandura. 1977. Self-efficacy: toward a unifying theory of behavioral change. *Psychological review* 84, 2 (1977), 191.

5. David Bau. 2015. Droplet, a Blocks-based Editor for Text Code. *J. Comput. Sci. Coll.* 30, 6 (June 2015), 138–144. http://dl.acm.org/citation.cfm?id=2753024.2753052

6. David Bau, D. Anthony Bau, Mathew Dawson, and C. Sydney Pickens. 2015. Pencil Code: Block Code for a Text World. In *Proceedings of the 14th International Conference on Interaction Design and Children (IDC '15).* ACM, New York, NY, USA, 445–448. DOI: http://dx.doi.org/10.1145/2771839.2771875

7. Paolo Bottoni and Miguel Ceriani. 2015. Linked Data Queries As Jigsaw Puzzles: A Visual Interface for SPARQL Based on Blockly Library. In *Proceedings of the 11th Biannual Conference on Italian SIGCHI Chapter (CHItaly 2015).* ACM, New York, NY, USA, 86–89. DOI: http://dx.doi.org/10.1145/2808435.2808467

8. Carrie J. Cai, Philip J. Guo, James R. Glass, and Robert C. Miller. 2015. Wait-Learning: Leveraging Wait Time for Second Language Education. In *Proceedings of the 33rd Annual ACM Conference on Human Factors in Computing Systems (CHI '15).* ACM, New York, NY, USA, 3701–3710. DOI: http://dx.doi.org/10.1145/2702123.2702267

9. Robert M Carini, George D Kuh, and Stephen P Klein. 2006. Student engagement and student learning: Testing the linkages*. *Research in higher education* 47, 1 (2006), 1–32.

10. Catrobat. 2015. Pocket Code. https://share.catrob.at/pocketcode. (2015).

11. Yung-Ju Chang, Lezhong Li, Shih-Hsuan Chou, Min-Chih Liu, and Surong Ruan. 2013. Xpress: Crowdsourcing Native Speakers to Learn Colloquial Expressions in a Second Language. In *CHI '13 Extended Abstracts on Human Factors in Computing Systems (CHI EA '13).* ACM, New York, NY, USA, 2555–2560. DOI: http://dx.doi.org/10.1145/2468356.2468829

12. Edith Frances Claflin. 1943. Teaching the Art of Reading Latin. *Classical Journal* (1943), 130–136.

13. Thomas M Connolly, Elizabeth A Boyle, Ewan MacArthur, Thomas Hainey, and James M Boyle. 2012. A systematic literature review of empirical evidence on computer games and serious games. *Computers & Education* 59, 2 (2012), 661–686.

14. Stephen Cooper. 2010. The Design of Alice. *Trans. Comput. Educ.* 10, 4, Article 15 (Nov. 2010), 16 pages. DOI: http://dx.doi.org/10.1145/1868358.1868362

15. S Erhel and E Jamet. 2013. Digital game-based learning: Impact of instructions and feedback on motivation and learning effectiveness. *Computers & Education* 67 (2013), 156–167.

16. Google. 2015. Google Blockly. https://developers.google.com/blockly. (2015).

17. Lindsay Grace, Martha Castaneda, and Jeannie Ducher. 2012. User Testing of a Language Learning Game for Mandarin Chinese. In *CHI '12 Extended Abstracts on Human Factors in Computing Systems (CHI EA '12).* ACM, New York, NY, USA, 865–868. DOI: http://dx.doi.org/10.1145/2212776.2212859

18. John Gruber-Miller, American Philological Association, and others. 2006. *When dead tongues speak: Teaching beginning Greek and Latin.* Oxford University Press.

19. Mark Guzdial. 2008. Education Paving the way for computational thinking. *Commun. ACM* 51, 8 (2008), 25–27.

20. William Gardner Hale. 1887. *The Art of Reading Latin: How to Teach It.* Ginn & Company.

21. Cheng-Hsien Han, Chi-Lan Yang, and Hao-Chuan Wang. 2014. Supporting Second Language Reading with Picture Note-taking. In *CHI '14 Extended Abstracts on Human Factors in Computing Systems (CHI EA '14).* ACM, New York, NY, USA, 2245–2250. DOI: http://dx.doi.org/10.1145/2559206.2581204

22. Brian Harvey, Daniel D. Garcia, Tiffany Barnes, Nathaniel Titterton, Daniel Armendariz, Luke Segars, Eugene Lemon, Sean Morris, and Josh Paley. 2013. SNAP! (Build Your Own Blocks) (Abstract Only). In *Proceeding of the 44th ACM Technical Symposium on Computer Science Education (SIGCSE '13).* ACM, New York, NY, USA, 759–759. DOI: http://dx.doi.org/10.1145/2445196.2445507

23. Brian Harvey and Jens Mönig. 2010. Bringing "No ceiling" to scratch: can one language serve kids and computer scientists. *Proc. Constructionism* (2010).

24. S. Holm. 1979. A simple sequentially rejective multiple test procedure. *Scandinavian Journal of Statistics* 6, 65-70 (1979), 1979.

25. Hopscotch. 2015. Hopscotch. https://www.gethopscotch.com. (2015).

26. E Hutchins, J Hollan, and D Norman. 1985. Direct manipulation interfaces. *Human-Computer Interaction* (1985).

27. Eleanor Huzar. 1957. Structural Linguistics and Latin Teaching. *Classical Journal* (1957), 268–274.

28. Charles Jenney, Rogers V Scudder, and Eric C Baade. 1987. *Jenney's First Year Latin.* Allyn and Bacon.

29. James F Johnson. 1987. Alternative Approaches for the College Elementary Latin Sequence. *Classical Journal* (1987), 246–255.
30. Caitlin Kelleher, Randy Pausch, and Sara Kiesler. 2007. Storytelling Alice Motivates Middle School Girls to Learn Computer Programming. In *Proceedings of the SIGCHI Conference on Human Factors in Computing Systems (CHI '07)*. ACM, New York, NY, USA, 1455–1464. DOI: http://dx.doi.org/10.1145/1240624.1240844
31. Glenn M Knudsvig. 1986. *Latin for Reading: A Beginner's Textbook with Exercises*. University of Michigan Press.
32. Geza Kovacs. 2013. Smart Subtitles for Language Learning. In *CHI '13 Extended Abstracts on Human Factors in Computing Systems (CHI EA '13)*. ACM, New York, NY, USA, 2719–2724. DOI: http://dx.doi.org/10.1145/2468356.2479499
33. Jerry Lee Jr and others. 2009. *Scratch programming for teens*. Cengage Learning.
34. Sorin Lerner, Stephen R. Foster, and William G. Griswold. 2015. Polymorphic Blocks: Formalism-Inspired UI for Structured Connectors. In *Proceedings of the 33rd Annual ACM Conference on Human Factors in Computing Systems (CHI '15)*. ACM, New York, NY, USA, 3063–3072. DOI: http://dx.doi.org/10.1145/2702123.2702302
35. Bob Lister. 2009. Latin in transition. *Arts and Humanities in Higher Education* 8, 2 (2009), 191–200.
36. Jiangjiang Liu, Cheng-Hsien Lin, Joshua Wilson, David Hemmenway, Ethan Hasson, Zebulun Barnett, and Yingbo Xu. 2014. Making Games a "Snap" with Stencyl: A Summer Computing Workshop for K-12 Teachers. In *Proceedings of the 45th ACM Technical Symposium on Computer Science Education (SIGCSE '14)*. ACM, New York, NY, USA, 169–174. DOI: http://dx.doi.org/10.1145/2538862.2538978
37. David J Malan and Henry H Leitner. 2007. Scratch for budding computer scientists. In *ACM SIGCSE Bulletin*, Vol. 39. ACM, 223–227.
38. John Maloney, Mitchel Resnick, Natalie Rusk, Brian Silverman, and Evelyn Eastmond. 2010. The scratch programming language and environment. *ACM Transactions on Computing Education (TOCE)* 10, 4 (2010), 16.
39. John H Maloney, Kylie Peppler, Yasmin Kafai, Mitchel Resnick, and Natalie Rusk. 2008. Programming by choice: urban youth learning programming with scratch. *ACM SIGCSE Bulletin* 40, 1 (2008), 367–371.
40. Donka D Markus and Deborah Pennell Ross. 2004. Reading Proficiency in latin through expectations and visualization. *Classical world* 98, 1 (2004), 79–93.
41. Daniel V McCaffrey. 2006. Reading Latin Efficiently and the Need for Cognitive Strategies. *When Dead Tongues Speak: Teaching Beginning Greek and Latin: Teaching Beginning Greek and Latin* 6 (2006), 113.
42. Barry McLaughlin. 1990. Restructuring. *Applied Linguistics* 11, 2 (1990), 113–128. DOI: http://dx.doi.org/10.1093/applin/11.2.113
43. Mitchel Resnick. 2007. All I really need to know (about creative thinking) I learned (by studying how children learn) in kindergarten. In *Proceedings of the 6th ACM SIGCHI conference on Creativity & cognition*. ACM, 1–6.
44. Mitchel Resnick, John Maloney, Andrés Monroy-Hernández, Natalie Rusk, Evelyn Eastmond, Karen Brennan, Amon Millner, Eric Rosenbaum, Jay Silver, Brian Silverman, and others. 2009. Scratch: programming for all. *Commun. ACM* 52, 11 (2009), 60–67.
45. Timothy Rodgers. 2008. Student engagement in the e-learning process and the impact on their grades. *International Journal of Cyber Society and Education* 1, 2 (2008), 143–156.
46. Timothy Rodgers and Deb Ghosh. 2001. Measuring the determinants of quality in UK higher education: a multinomial logit approach. *Quality Assurance in Education* 9, 3 (2001), 121–126.
47. Krishnendu Roy. 2012. App Inventor for Android: Report from a Summer Camp. In *Proceedings of the 43rd ACM Technical Symposium on Computer Science Education (SIGCSE '12)*. ACM, New York, NY, USA, 283–288. DOI: http://dx.doi.org/10.1145/2157136.2157222
48. Dale H Schunk. 1990. Goal setting and self-efficacy during self-regulated learning. *Educational psychologist* 25, 1 (1990), 71–86.
49. GM SELIGSON. 1983. LATIN AT MICHIGAN 1951-1981. In *Latin Linguistics and Linguistic Theory: Proceedings of the 1st International Colloquium on Latin Linguistics, Amsterdam, April 1981*, Vol. 12. John Benjamins Publishing, 295.
50. Gerda M Seligson. 1964. The Structural Approach, the First Decade. *The Classical World* (1964), 97–100.
51. Juliet P. Shaffer. 1995. Multiple Hypothesis-Testing. *Annual Review of Psychology* 46 (1995), 561–584.
52. Jonah WD Skiles. 1943. The Teaching of the Reading of Latin in the Latin Word-Order. *Classical Journal* (1943), 88–104.
53. Squeakland. 2015. Etoys. http://www.squeakland.org. (2015).
54. Waldo E Sweet. 1957. *Latin: a structural approach*. University of Michigan Press.
55. Waldo E Sweet. 1967. The Continued Development of the Structural Approach. *Didaskalos* 2, 2 (1967), 141–159.

56. V.L. Takacs. 2014. BlockImpress. In *Intelligent Engineering Systems (INES), 2014 18th International Conference on*. 221–226. DOI: http://dx.doi.org/10.1109/INES.2014.6909372

57. Feng Tian, Fei Lv, Jingtao Wang, Hongan Wang, Wencan Luo, Matthew Kam, Vidya Setlur, Guozhong Dai, and John Canny. 2010. Let's Play Chinese Characters: Mobile Learning Approaches via Culturally Inspired Group Games. In *Proceedings of the SIGCHI Conference on Human Factors in Computing Systems (CHI '10)*. ACM, New York, NY, USA, 1603–1612.

58. Jake Trower and Jeff Gray. 2015. Blockly Language Creation and Applications: Visual Programming for Media Computation and Bluetooth Robotics Control. In *Proceedings of the 46th ACM Technical Symposium on Computer Science Education (SIGCSE '15)*. ACM, New York, NY, USA, 5–5. DOI: http://dx.doi.org/10.1145/2676723.2691871

59. Kevin Wang, Corey McCaffrey, Daniel Wendel, and Eric Klopfer. 2006. 3D Game Design with Programming Blocks in StarLogo TNG. In *Proceedings of the 7th International Conference on Learning Sciences (ICLS '06)*. International Society of the Learning Sciences, 1008–1009. http://dl.acm.org/citation.cfm?id=1150034.1150223

60. David Weintrop and Uri Wilensky. 2013. Robobuilder: A Computational Thinking Game (Abstract Only). In *Proceeding of the 44th ACM Technical Symposium on Computer Science Education (SIGCSE '13)*. ACM, New York, NY, USA, 736–736. DOI: http://dx.doi.org/10.1145/2445196.2445430

61. Frederic M Wheelock. 1963. *Latin: An introductory course based on ancient authors*. Number 104. Barnes & Noble Imports.

62. Frederic M Wheelock and Richard A LaFleur. 2005. *Wheelock's Latin*. HarperResource.

63. Ursula Wolz, Henry H Leitner, David J Malan, and John Maloney. 2009. Starting with scratch in CS 1. In *ACM SIGCSE Bulletin*, Vol. 41. ACM, 2–3.

64. Barry J Zimmerman, Albert Bandura, and Manuel Martinez-Pons. 1992. Self-motivation for academic attainment: The role of self-efficacy beliefs and personal goal setting. *American educational research journal* 29, 3 (1992), 663–676.

Social Situational Language Learning through an Online 3D Game

Gabriel Culbertson[1], Shiyu Wang[2], Malte Jung[1], and Erik Andersen[2]
[1]Department of Information Science, [2]Department of Computer Science, Cornell University
{grc74, sw673, mfj28, ela63 }@cornell.edu

ABSTRACT
Learning a second language is challenging. Becoming fluent requires learning contextual information about how language should be used as well as word meanings and grammar. The majority of existing language learning applications provide only thin context around content. In this paper, we present work in *Crystallize*, a language learning game that combines traditional learning approaches with a situated learning paradigm by integrating a spaced-repetition system within a language learning roleplaying game. To facilitate long-term engagement with the game, we added a new quest paradigm, "jobs," that allow a small amount of design effort to generate a large set of highly-scaffolded tasks that grow iteratively. A large-scale evaluation of the language learning game "in the wild" with a diverse set of 186 people revealed that the game was not only engaging players for extended amounts of time but that players learned an average of 8.7 words in an average of 40.5 minutes.

Author Keywords
language learning, video games, situated learning

ACM Classification Keywords
H.5.0. Information Interfaces and Presentation: General

INTRODUCTION
Finding the right balance of abstract learning and situated, communicative approaches has long been a concern for language learners. In an older investigation of "good language learners" teachers found that successful second language learners are willing to experiment in social interactions and make mistakes, but also spend a significant amount of time on abstract practice exercises such as flashcards [36]. Since these findings, the expansion of computer applications has made the abstract learning exercises much more accessible to learners. For example Duolingo [2] enables users to learn by translating isolated sentences and websites such as WaniKani [8] that allow for memorization of individual words.

However, designing a computer application for a situated approach is much more difficult. It requires shifting the focus towards creating social engagements that "provide the proper context for learning to take place" [29]:14. A situated approach also emphasizes the practices involved in becoming skillful. Through his studies of Icelandic fishing practices Gisli Palsson explains the advantages of conceptualizing learning as active engagement with one's environment:

"Becoming skillful means to attend to the task at hand, actively engaged with a social and natural environment. This suggests a notion of enskilment that emphasizes immersion in the practical world, being caught up in the incessant flow of everyday life, and not simply, as many cognitive studies have assumed, the mechanistic internalization and application of a mental script, a stock of knowledge or a 'cultural model', 'what one needs to know in order to behave as a functioning member of one's society"' [32], citing [27], which cited [25].

Specifically in the context of computer applications for learning, Felix [20] argues that taking this perspective is essential to furthering language education in an online environment, but also identified key social, conceptual, political and pedagogical dilemmas that come with adopting a situated approach. It is impossible to fully realize this perspective in an application. However, the question remains, what can we learn from a situated perspective on learning to improve the design of language learning tools?

Some have taken the view that context is primarily visual. For example, *Rosetta Stone* uses images to give learners context without requiring translation. Another game, *Influent*, uses a virtual 3D world to help students learn vocabulary. Yet another tool, Micro-Mandarin [19], pushes the perspective further and uses real-world location for context.

However, we believe a purely visual approach is insufficient in creating a situated learning experience. As we argued above, learning and especially language learning depends on social engagement with others and when we lose the sense of who we are talking to and why we are talking to them, language learning becomes disconnected from reality. We therefore want learners to believe that they are interacting with other real people. To be more precise in our interpretation of situated learning, we describe this as design for social situational language fluency.

Games have a unique potential to provide situate learning experiences. Peterson describes these benefits, citing Gee: "Proponents of game-based learning argue that as games engage players in authentic situated problem solving, they facilitate learning that can be transferred to other domains [21]. Gee claims that as computer games enable language to be put in the context of dialog, they enable language to be situated.

CHI 2016, May 7–12, 2016, San Jose, California, USA.
Copyright © 2016 ACM ISBN 978-1-4503-3362-7/16/05 ...$15.00.
http://dx.doi.org/10.1145/2858036.2858514

This provides an ideal environment for language learning as verbal information is given just in time and is provided in an appropriate context [22]" [33]. Allowing students to engage and shape imagined scenarios can make them more real and engaging.

Furthermore, engagement is a key factor in second language learning. Games have tremendous potential to engage users. Applications such as DuoLingo [40] have made use of game elements to keep users engaged. Games give learners the ability to learn through experimentation rather than through instruction which can improve learning [11].

In order to explore the potential of design for social situational fluency, we created *Crystallize*. An early version of the game is described in [15], and focused mainly on the design and evaluation of joint quests that facilitated collaboration between two players in a highly constrained laboratory setting. This previous work left open the question of whether the ideas behind the game can succeed in the wild and provide a fruitful context for language learning independent of a highly structured laboratory test setting. This work also left open the question of whether we can develop game mechanics that are sufficiently engaging to motivate players who are playing under their own volition.

In this paper, we discuss the challenges and lessons learned from building a socially situated language learning game that can engage players for a long time. The challenges include 1) how to design and maximize the impact of long-term engagement mechanisms, 2) how to represent real-world situations precisely enough that players feel immersed, and 3) how to use game mechanics and player interactions to give the player the feeling of social engagement. We describe the iterative design and development of the game and two user-studies that tested the game in a controlled classroom setting and a final open field-setting on the internet. Through interviews with players, survey responses, direct observation of chat-logs, and analyses of quantitative gameplay data we found that the game engaged learners in socially rich and complex ways for an extended amount of time (40 minutes on average), and with a measurable improvement in language learning. This paper makes three core contributions:

- a language learning game that combines traditional learning approaches with a situated learning paradigm by integrating a spaced-repetition system within a language learning roleplaying game.
- a new quest paradigm to facilitate long-term engagement with the game through, "jobs," that allow a small amount of design effort to generate a large set of highly-scaffolded tasks that grow iteratively.
- a large-scale "in the wild" evaluation with a diverse set of 186 people recruited through Reddit.

RELATED WORK

Language learning tools

Many language learning tools and websites have leveraged context to enhance learning. Some tools make use of content originally designed for native speakers for learning. In order to enable learning while browsing the web in a second language, tools such as Rikaichan [6] allow dictionary look-up of words. Sites such as FluentU [3] make use of publicly available videos with subtitles for learning. Duolingo [2] also has a section where learners can work on translating content for intended for native speakers. These methods allow learners to interact with natural language and have some sense of context, but these methods do not allow for the learner to interact and receive feedback or provide motivation.

Other sites have taken a more social approach to language learning. Italki [4] uses a social network structure to match language learners with native speakers. Another site, LiveMocha [5] encourages users to develop content in their native language for learners of that language to consume. For example, native speakers can create sets of vocabulary combined with audio recordings or provide one-on-one lessons. These methods allow for communicative learning, but the need to coordinate with teachers can make these interactions less accessible. Other work has looked at creating artificial social interactions through a chatterbot [37]. However, the effectiveness of this method needs further study. Furthermore, all of these methods provide only limited motivation frameworks.

Some games have also been developed for language learning to increase engagement for learners. For learning basic skills such as writing, games such as *My Japanese Coach* have been developed. Another game, *Influent* [28] teaches vocabulary in a virtual home and has game modes where the player must rush to find items in the home. These games, while they have some motivational framework, lack real or simulated interpersonal interactions.

Spaced Repetition Systems

Spaced repetition systems (SRS) make use of Ebbinghaus' [18] finding that memory decays over time, but a memory takes longer to decay when it is reviewed at increasingly long intervals. Edge et al. [19] have provided a concise description of the process of learning using an SRS: "Unlike lesson-oriented learning, flashcards operate at the granularity of facts (e.g., word translations) and measure the learners ability to provide the correct response (e.g., a Chinese word) in the presence of a stimulus (e.g., an English word)." SRS are incredibly popular among second language learners. Systems as old as the Pimsleur system [34] and more recently sites such as Duolingo [2] and WaniKani [8] have made use of SRS. Some systems such *Anki* [1] and *SuperMemo* [7] are spaced repetition systems exclusively.

Teachers have examined the use of SRS in classrooms, but found it very difficult to fit SRS in with traditional curricula [12]. Classroom testing prioritizes recall in the short term, which incentivizes cramming strategies. Ebbinghaus' [18] findings have shown these strategies to be inefficient in long term study. Thus SRS is best suited for learners who are self-motivated. We suggest, based on findings that that games can foster intrinsic motivation [16], that a game is an ideal context for SRS learning. Recently, a flash card game called *Picard* combined an SRS with social challenges to create mnemonic devices for remembering language material [39]. We build on this work by addressing the challenges of merging an SRS into a game with a rich quest structure.

Roleplaying and learning

Language is best learned in through experiences. Barsalou [13] argues that people learn language in terms how it relates to real actions and outcomes. Memory of language is connected to memories of the physical surroundings at the site of learning and the outcomes of speaking. In a study by Glenburg et al. [24], it was shown that children manipulating physical figurines while reading or imagining manipulating the figurines led to increased memory and comprehension. Simply imagining scenarios while learning is enough to enhance learning.

Gee [23] drew a connection between these findings and learning in digital games. Games present fictional worlds and simulations. Although there is still a gap between reality and the game scenario, the game enhances the context around the content both by including a virtual world and associating language with an outcome. McGonigal [31] argues that for serious players, there are instances were the lines between game worlds and the real world start to blur.

Some studies have explored the idea of leveraging immersive online games for language learning. In a review of studies of online roleplaying games used to improve language ability [33], Peterson showed that these games have the potential to improve language skills. In one of the studies [35] discussed, intermediate English as a Second Language (ESL) students vastly improved their vocabularies and confidence by playing *Everquest II*. In our previous work on the prototype for *Crystallize*, we found that players with no prior language experience could learn in a collaborative game environment. However, because previous work has been in a lab setting, we lack information about how game design decisions affect experiences in the wild, how engaging these methods are, and what game features are useful to learners.

GAME DESIGN

Overview

Crystallize uses the rich context of a 3D environment with both human and computer controlled characters to create socially situated language learning experiences. Players collect words that they see computer-controlled characters use in the game and complete language puzzles with these collected words to progress in the game. The game also offers players the possibility for social interaction and collaboration with other players in the virtual environment. The game can be downloaded and tried on the game website: `crystallize-online.com/`.

We designed the game to engage learners of Japanese who are tech-savvy and interested in using online tools and games to improve their language skills. We designed the mechanics to have nuance so that learning the game would be engaging in and of itself. However, this complexity makes the game difficult to learn for very young learners. The game is designed to be engaging for anyone old enough to understand the rules. Furthermore, we assume that learners are doing some learning independently, but have difficulty structuring their learning and staying motivated. Thus we provide both a motivational framework and scaffold the learning.

Our first priority is to provide the player with a framework of goals, obstacles and tools to overcome those obstacles. Goals are provided using a questing system. While exploring the world, players can find NPCs (non-player characters or computer controlled characters) who offers tasks for the player to complete. For example, a NPC may ask the player "what is this?" while looking at a bicycle. The player must search the area for other NPCs that can tell the player how to say the word bicycle. All of the quests involve the player responding to prompts using the words that they have collected.

In order to simulate social interaction through conversations using game mechanics, we introduce a system where players construct phrases in order to interact with NPCs. These interactions enable the player to complete quests. First, the player must have the correct words to respond to the prompts provided by the NPCs. In order to better simulate conversational flexibility, there are usually multiple correct responses, and choosing a more complex response will yield a greater reward, but at minimum, the player must be able to construct the simplest response. For example, in Japanese, the subject can be excluded from the sentence resulting in a simple 2-word response to the bicycle prompt: "jitensha desu" (literally is bike). The player may also choose a more complex response for a greater reward: "kore ha jitensha desu" (this is a bike).

In order to encourage reviewing and integrate an SRS into a seamless gameplay experience, we introduced a new game mechanic called *confidence*. When the player sees words that they have not seen before or responds incorrectly to prompts, the player's confidence is reduced. The player begins with some amount of confidence and when the players confidence score falls to zero, the player is ejected from the current conversation and sent to their home where they can review words. Each time an NPC uses a word that the player has not yet collected, the players confidence will drop by 1 point. The player can recover that confidence by collecting the word, but because the players inventory is limited, the player will not be able to complete some conversations before collecting enough words beforehand. Choosing a less desirable response (e.g. if the NPC asks "Can you do this job well?" and the player responds with "Um...") will also cause a reduction in confidence.

To complete quests, the player must (1) collect words and phrases, and (2) review those words and phrases. Collecting words can be accomplished by listening to dialogues of pairs of NPCs, or through the quest conversations. Strategically choosing words that appear more frequently can help the player complete challenges more quickly, but there is no penalty for collecting more words than necessary. Reviewing words and phrases can increase the amount of confidence that the player begins a level with. Therefore, even without having the correct words, players that have spent a long time with the game can complete more difficult quests.

Figure 1. An early prototype of *Crystallize* as used for the laboratory study described in [15]. Because conditions needed to be controlled for the laboratory setting, the game was linear and lacked mechanisms needed for long term motivation and learning.

Iterative development

Crystallize was developed and tested in three stages. First, an early version of the game was designed with a focus on creating a short immersive language learning experience that can be studied in a laboratory setting and is described in [15]. During the second design stage that we report on here we redesigned the game to include mechanics and content to support long term play for an in-class deployment. The goal of the third and final design stage, the outcome of which is the main focus of this paper, we redesigned *Crystallize* to support self-motivated learners on the web and to be conducive to large-scale distributed data collection.

Stage 1 - Crystallize for laboratory deployment

The first prototype of the game was designed for preliminary exploration of the idea for the game in a laboratory based user study. Through the user study we found that participants without any prior Japanese knowledge who played the game for 25 minutes were able to learn, but perceptions of how engaging the game was were highly varied depending on the specific participants interests and background [15]. This initial implementation had several drawbacks. First, the game was highly linear. The game was designed to be played in a lab setting, so we needed participants to follow similar progressions through the game. This meant that players lacked the freedom to explore specific areas of interest in depth. Second, the game lacked mechanisms needed to sustain long-term play. Although players were able to complete challenges in the game, players retained relatively little in the short-term, and we lacked data to make any conclusions about long-term retention. The previous prototype also lacked mechanisms to support long term motivation. The players only goals were to complete the current level and proceed to the next. In the following iterations, we explored methods for addressing these issues.

Stage 2 - Crystallize for classroom deployment

Our main design goal in this iteration was to create mechanics and content to support long term play and engagement. The iteration culminated in a two-week long user study for which we deployed the game in a classroom setting. We recruited 26 high-school aged students from a summer learning program at Cornell University. These students were recruited by email before the learning program began. All of the students came from a single class, but participation was optional and not all students participated. The study was conducted in ten 30 minutes sessions over three weeks. Throughout the study, we conducted interviews with the students, and responded to student comments by adjusting the design. The feedback from this group led to the addition of aesthetic and game-mechanic-related rewards, additional elements of the Japanese language (Hiragana, Katakana and Kanji scripts), and implemented mechanics to reduce repetitiveness.

Figure 3. While exploring the world encountering new words or making language mistakes results in reduced confidence (top). When the player runs out of confidence or chooses to go home, they can review (center) to restore confidence (bottom).

Stage 3 - Crystallize for field deployment

Our primary goals for this iteration were to enrich social interaction in the game and give players more freedom in the game environment. Unlike the classroom study where participants were co-located, the online release of the game required additional features so that players could have a sense of social presence. For this, we expanded on the ideas of the initial prototype. Unlike the initial lab study, we had no control over participants' play schedules and play time. Thus, rather than connecting two players in an interdependent relationship, we designed a more open interaction system where players could come and go as they pleased and have the freedom to interact with players if they desired. This change also required the redesign of the level structure from the earlier prototype. In order for players to have the opportunity to encounter other players, we required a single, central hub for players gameplay rather than a linear progression from one level to the next.

FIELD STUDY

We conducted a field study to evaluate the three design challenges outlined in the introduction. Each challenge has one or more research questions associated with it. The first challenge was about long-term motivation and learning and ad-

Figure 2. In *Crystallize* players explore an open world where they can find and talk to NPCs (1). Players can overhear conversations of groups of NPCs. Speech bubbles show what the NPCs are saying and words that the player has not collected yet are shown as outlined (2). These words can be dragged from the speech bubbles (3) to the player's inventory (9). A map shows the locations of normal NPCs and quest NPCs relative to the player's location (4). Progress on current quests is shown in the quest panel (5). Players can chat with other players using the chat box (6). The players money (7) and confidence (8) are displayed. The player can see how many reviews they have currently available and go home using the home button (10). Other settings can be adjusted and the game can be exited using the control panel (11).

dressed the following research questions: How does the game engage an audience of language learners in the field that do not have the incentives and context that a laboratory study and classroom deployment provide (R1)? Would we be able to measure actual improvements in language learning skills given that we have no control over the makeup of the players in comparison to our laboratory and classroom studies (R2)? The second challenge was about creating immersive as well as situated learning experiences and addressed the following research question: What benefits do learners perceive in a socially situated approach to learning (R3)? The third challenge was about social engagement and addressed the following research question: Would the game give learners the experience of social engagement (R4)?

Reddit Deployment

The game was made publicly available on the web, and advertised using a forum post to the Japanese Learning sub-Reddit (www.reddit.com/r/LearnJapanese). We chose Reddit as a deployment channel because we believed we could reach our desired audience this way. Sub-Reddit communities are focused and active, and the Reddit website provides a simple interface for providing comments and upvotes.

To play Crystallize, players clicked the link in the post that led them to the game website. Upon starting the game, players were informed that the game was part of a research project and consented to have their gameplay data collected. After providing a username and password, participants could create a customized avatar. During the 5 to 10 minute tutorial, users could not see each other or chat with other users. After the tutorial players were free to explore the world and complete quests in an order chosen by the player. At this point, the chat tool was also unlocked and other players in the game world were made visible.

Before beginning the actual game, a prompt appeared asking participants to complete an optional survey. Surveys were completed through a web browser. Participants provided information about perceptions of language learning (e.g. Learning language is easier in a classroom, Language learning causes anxiety) and attitude toward learning Japanese (e.g. I feel excited about learning the Japanese language). All responses used a seven point Likert scale.

Following 15, 30 and 60 minutes of play, participants provided their general impressions of the game (e.g. How much did you like the game?) and rated how well certain words described their experiences (e.g. frustrating, motivating, fun, exciting). The survey then gave participants the opportunity to provide free response feedback. Finally participants were prompted to provide their email if they were willing to participate in a follow-up interview.

The follow-up semi-structured interviews inquired how learners viewed the game relative to other tools they used (e.g. How do other methods you have used compare to the game?), motivation to play the game (e.g. If you were motivated to play, was there something about the game that motivated you?), immersion (e.g. What moment in the game did you feel the most immersed? Least immersed?), how players felt about other players (e.g. How did other players in the game impact your game experience?) and about the mechanisms

Figure 4. Players complete jobs by first initiating a conversation with the "boss NPC" (left), then the player must clean the item specified by the boss (center) and after completing several iterations receives a reward based on performance and progress in the game (right).

Quest or job class	Description
Introduction quest	The player learns basic introductions and how to interact with NPCs in the game
Learning from context	In these quests, the NPC will prompt the player to tell him or her how to identify a thing in the 3D world. For example, the NPC may ask "what is this?" while looking at a tree. The player then goes to other NPCs in the game world and listens to them discussing the thing to learn that word. The player then returns to the original NPC and tells them how to say the word.
Person finding	Player learns to identify people using descriptive characteristics. The prompts are initially very simple. For example: "I lost my friend, he is a boy." The player would then need to search nearby for a male NPC. Later prompts become complex. For example, the quest prompt may become "I lost my friend. He has red hair and is wearing a T-shirt".
Get-to-know-someone	The player learns how to get to know someone in Japanese. Initially, the player will go through an introduction sequence. If the player uses language that is too informal, or does not respond politely to the NPCs prompts, the player will be penalized. After the initial meeting, the player will randomly find the same NPC again in the game world. In following meetings, the NPC may request information from the player ("do you remember my name?", "do you remember where I'm from") or allow the player to ask for new information ("what's your hobby?", "how old are you?").
Take someone somewhere	In this type of quest, the player takes a NPC to a specific location. Initially the NPC prompts the player with a specific location. For example, the NPC may say "I need to go to the restroom, can you take me there?". Later, the NPC will make the request more indirectly. For example, "I'm late to class!". The player completes the quest by navigating to the correct location and telling the NPC that they have arrived.
Chain of information	Players must follow clues provided by NPCs in sequence to solve problems. For example, an NPC my prompt the player with "I can't find my cat... I wonder if Sakura has seen it." The player must then find Sakura and after talking with her she may say "I know where the cat is, but I will only tell you if you help me find out when Kenji's birthday is". The player follows the clues until they reach the final goal. In the example given, this would be finding the cat.
Janitor job	The job is started by completing a kind of interview. By making it difficult to begin the job, we provide a gating mechanism to prevent players from doing the job too early while giving the player the freedom to try if they wish. If the player lacks sufficient confidence they will not be able to complete the interview. Once the interview is passed, the boss NPC will tell the player to clean specific items. For example, the boss may ask the player to "clean the table". After doing the job several times, the items that can be cleaned are expanded.
Cashier job	Similar to the janitor job, the player must first complete an interview before beginning the job. Once the job is started, people will appear who want to buy things. The player must tell the NPC the correct amount of money needed for the items they wish to buy. As the player advances in the job, NPCs will request more complex combinations of items.

Figure 5. Description of activities in the game. After the first quest, players are free to do any of the activities listed here in any order.

for long term learning (e.g. How did you feel about the review system in the game? Did you find it helpful? Annoying?).

Throughout the 15 days during which we collected data, a total of 186 participants created accounts. 69 participants filled out the initial survey and 23 participants filled out the survey in one of the later prompts. Seven participants filled out the survey both at the initial prompt (before starting to play) and at one of the later prompts (15, 30, and 60 minutes into the game). 22 participants provided their email addresses which resulted in 6 participant interviews.

Measures

We collected data through gameplay logs, chat-logs, surveys and interviews to understand (1) players' engagement with the game and (2) learning outcomes. Comparisons between groups were made using independent sample T-tests and correlations were found using Pearon's r.

Measures of engagement: Engagement was measured using the total amount of time that players spent in the game and the number of times the player returned to the game after waiting an hour or more. Many previous "in the wild" experiments with games have used play time to measure engagement [14, 30, 11, 9, 10]. Since players can play many other free games or use other language learning tools if they lose interest in this one, getting players to spend a significant amount of time on a game suggests that the game is engaging.

Measures of progress in the game: After the initial tutorial section of the game, players are free to pursue any content they wish. Thus we measure progress as the number of words and phrases that the player has collected.

Measures of learning: The spaced repetition system used in the game also serves as a continuous test of learning. Each review in the spaced repetition system is a multiple choice quiz where the player must choose the correct English meaning for a Japanese word. We acknowledge that multiple choice questions are not ideal for measuring learning, but the focus of the study was to collect as much information as possible from participants, so we did not wish to drive participants away with mandatory pre and post tests. Thus we use these scores to show evidence that learning occurred rather than an measure of the amount of learning.

For this study, we define learning as the memorization of previously unknown word or phrase meanings. Thus for each word or phrase we first evaluate whether the learner knew the word prior to playing the game. We do this using the first two SRS reviews. Because the review system is multiple choice with 5 choices, there is a 1 in 5 or better chance that the learner can guess the correct answer without knowing the translation. By taking the first two reviews we have a finer value for the probability that the learner knew the word prior to playing the game. All of the following reviews in the spaced repetition system are used to calculate the probability that the learner knew the word after playing the game. Note that this is a conservative measure, because it is possible for the player to see the definition of a word before beginning the review session, so answering incorrectly requires that the player both not know a given word or phrase beforehand and forget the meaning during the first review.

Measures of prior knowledge: A prior knowledge score was calculated by taking the total number of reviews that the player responds to correctly divided by the total number of reviews seen to construct *review accuracy*. We would expect those with less prior knowledge to receive lower scores.

Measures of social engagement: Previous work ([17]) has shown that social engagement is a key motivator in players of online roleplaying games. It can be enough just to see that others are playing the game. Thus we look at players in two groups: those that were online at the same time as another player and those that only played alone. We also take lines of chat to be an indicator of social engagement.

RESULTS AND DISCUSSION

Expert players

We found that many of the players had extensive prior knowledge of Japanese before beginning play. The 58 participants who took the pre-test had an average score of 16.31 (SD=10.67) out of 30 possible on words and phrases available in the game. To better understand the behavior of expert and non-expert behavior, we divided the data in to groups using *review accuracy*. Those with greater than 90% accuracy were considered experts and those with less than 90% accuracy were considered non-experts.

There are 98 experts and 88 non-experts. Number of words learned per hour was higher in non-experts (M = 12.1, SE = 1.6) than in experts (M = 5.8, SE = 0.4, p ¡ 0.001). In survey responses, enjoyment of the game was found to be higher in experts (M = 6, SE = 0.3) than in non-experts (M = 4.6, SE = 0.3, p = 0.010). Playtime was also more than three times as long for expert players (M = 65 minutes, SE = 7.4) than non-expert players (M = 17, SE = 3.0, p ¡ 0.001). Return rate was significantly higher in experts (M = 22%, SE = 2.4%) than in non-experts (M = 6%, SE = 4%, p = 0.002).

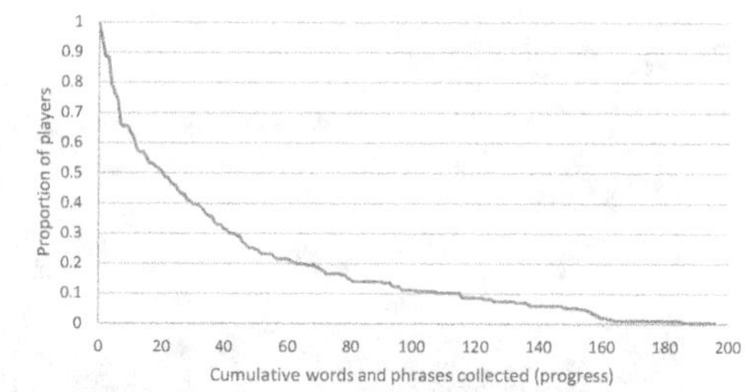

Figure 6. Graph of progress for all 186 players. The x-axis shows numbers of words and phrases collected, and the y-axis shows the percentage of the players who collected at least that many words and phrases. This graph shows that players were motivated to collect many words; the top 20% collected more than 60.

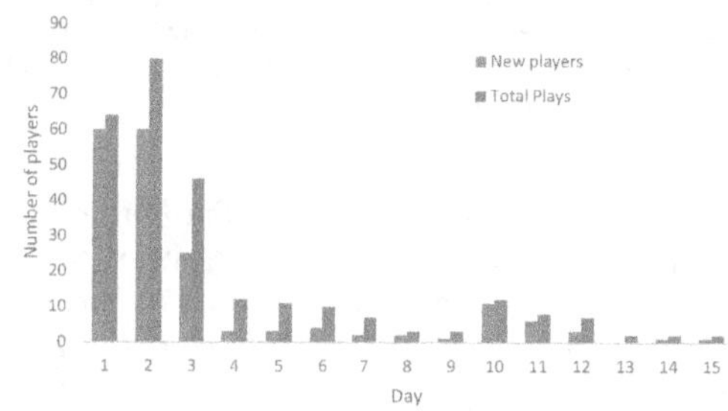

Figure 7. Players over the duration of the study. The majority of the players came in the first two days when the Reddit post was on the front page of the sub-Reddit.

We believe integrating the efficiency-driven SRS with the contextual learning offered by exploring the game environment creates an effective hybrid learning approach. Many learners were already doing this. All but one of the interviewees mentioned that they had used some SRS in the past, the most common being *Anki*.

Evidence that the game is engaging

Addressing R1, we examined various data sources for indicators of engagement. The game was received very positively by the Japanese learning sub-Reddit community. The game thread received an up-vote minus down-vote score of around 115 (for comparison, the posts on the front page of the same sub-Reddit at the time of writing have an average score of 8). There were over 60 comments posted by the sub-Reddit users and half of the people who played the game responded to at least one of the optional surveys. The 186 players spent an average of 40.5 minutes playing the game. Twenty-five (13%) of the players returned to the game after taking a break. We define a break as being logged off for at least 1 hour. For the players that returned at least once, those players returned an average of 2.36 times (SE=0.443). The players that returned at least once played an average of 142 minutes (SE=2.426) while the players that played the game only once played for an average of 24 minutes (SE = 15.925). Charts of play time and progress can be found in Figures 9, 6, and 7.

Many of the comments on Reddit thread were supportive. For example these comments were posted on the Reddit thread:

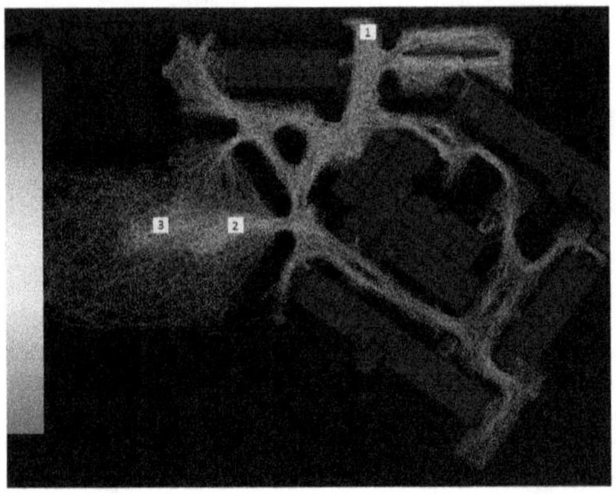

Figure 8. Heat map of player movement. A value closer to red indicates that more time was spent by players in those areas. Players began at (1) and we also see a lot of activity around (2) and (3) which were the popular jobs: janitor and cashier.

This game is really fun; originally, I felt burdened by learning vocabulary (especially in Japanese, when phrases are so long) but this game makes it very exciting to learn new words and phrases! and *I'm actually really enjoying this game, it even covers some vocab that isn't in my textbook!*. These comments were often made despite a long list of issues that the player may have had. Many participants also expressed a long term interest in the project. We also take the high number of participants who responded that they were willing to be contacted for follow-up (22 of the 92 survey-takers) to be indicative of engagement. Some participants asked us to set up a way to communicate updates. For example this was posted on the Reddit thread: *It looks very promising and interesting, but I really miss a changelog on the website. I want to know every bug that was patched and every new feature!*

Of the those who completed the survey after playing the game, 11% said they did not like the game (7-point Likert scale with a score of 3 or less), 18% were neutral (score = 4) and 71% liked the game (score > 4).

We also find evidence for support of the game in the chat log:

maya: I hope this game can become great, though
Breathless: yeah, I hope so
maya: eee
Breathless: it's looking great
Breathless: I hope it doesn't die
...
username: wish their was a korean ver of this
username: would try

Evidence of learning in the game

To gain insight into research questions 2 and 3 that addressed learning, we performed quantitative analyses into the gameplay data. Players collected an average of 29.75 words (SD=33.83) and 7.43 phrases (SD=11.86). For words that player did not know previously, we find a significant difference between review accuracy before (M=0.548, SD=0.142) and after (M=0.873, SD=0.149) the initial set of reviews, $t(184)=-14.68$, $p<0.001$. Learning gains were greater for those who returned (M = 18.3, SE = 2.7) than for those who did not (M = 5.6, SE = 0.7, $p < 0.001$). Using our learning measure, players learned on average 8.7 words and phrases (SD=10). The large difference between words and phrases collected and words and phrases learned is due to three factors: (1) players entered the game with extensive prior knowledge, (2) our learning measure was conservative and (3) we lacked sufficient data to conclude that some of the words had been learned. As we would expect, this is strongly correlated ($r(184)=0.620$, $p < 0.001$) with time spent playing the game. We also measured learning using the pretest and posttest in the survey, but because the surveys were optional and could be taken at any time, only 6 participants completed both the pretest and postest. All of the participants who took both tests had an increase in score, but the difference was not significant, likely due to the small sample size.

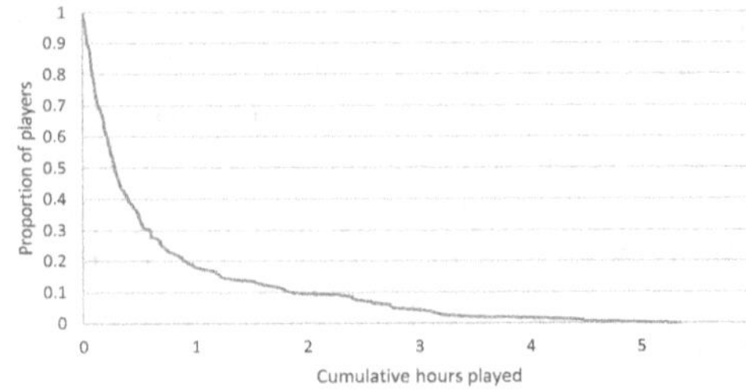

Figure 9. Graph of time played for all 186 players. The x-axis shows lengths of time since starting the game, and the y-axis shows the percentage of the players who played for at least that much time. This graph shows that many players were motivated to continue playing for a long time. 20% of players played for more than one hour.

Evidence that social aspects improved the experience

Our analyses also provided insights into R4 and R5. Although many of the users did not make use of the social features of the game or were always online alone, we believe that designing for social play greatly enhanced the game for some players. Length of play was significantly higher for those learners who entered a line of chat in search of someone to talk to (M = 78.61, SD=62.64) than those who did not (M=32.97, SD=53.27), $t(184)=-4.120$, $p < 0.001$. We looked further looked at players who found another player to chat with, and those that found someone had longer average playtime, but the results were not statistically significant. We speculate that this is because the number of players who found chat partners was small (only 8),

Although none of the interviewees had found chat partners, we do find evidence that the players liked the social of others in the game. *I occasionally ran in to other people, but we didn't talk. It was encouraging to see what other people were doing. ... It would be cool to share the words I learned with other people.* One of the interviewees also speculated on the feature: *it seems like most players in the game have learned some Japanese already so I feel that I can always ask them for help.* We also believe that the shared virtual space enhanced social interactions. Players who saw other players' avatars were far more likely to chat. Furthermore the shared worlds provided grounding for some of the chat: *can't you see the isu here?*. Other chat referred to the in-game jobs: *Gonna try work for the Janitor so I can get some cash.*

Evidence that players prefer roleplaying

We find evidence in the chat logs and survey that players the game reframed activities to have more meaning for players. In the game, rather than simply reading text, the player is "having a conversation" and rather than choosing items from a list, the player is "doing a job". We believe that our players felt that this was qualitatively different from other learning experiences. One interviewee said: *you have quests that make you go talk to people and have a short dialogue with them. I think that's really useful and am glad that the game wasn't just about learning vocabulary like others I've seen in the past. It feels immersing; I really do enjoy it.* Note that although the some of the activities may be similar to to activities in other language learning applications, the language that players use to describe these actions are different. The player says that he was "talking to people", rather than than taking a quiz.

There is also evidence that situating learning using the game world makes learning more meaningful to participants. One of the interviewees described the experience like this: *As a person learning Japanese in a relative vacuum, the illusion of interacting with people who speak the language is valuable, and offering the opportunity to suspend disbelief (that is, I'm not simply filling in the blanks, I'm talking to some dude who has lost some other dude) is useful.* Some participants compared the game to Rosetta Stone. One said: *I tried Rosetta Stone for a while, and I memorized a lot, but I didn't learn anything, you know?* and then *games have a way of showing you something in an interesting way.*

Evidence that simulating situations was motivating

We have evidence that the questing structure of the game encouraged learning. Feedback that we got from participants in the Job prototype study after adding additional reward mechanics was entirely positive. Some participants specifically mentioned that they felt motivated to earn money for new clothes.

In the version of the game released to Reddit, we found instances of players doing jobs in order to earn money in the chat log:

maya: are you playing the janitor thing?
Breathless: to get the new vocab from him (Breathless mistakenly answers the question "*why* are you playing the janitor job")
Breathless: and money to buy clothes
...
username: clothes arent very kawaii desu
Dan: Gonna try work for the Janitor so I can get some cash.

There was also feedback in the Reddit thread and interviews that drew parallels between *Crystallize* and the highly engaging online roleplaying game *World of Warcraft*: *props for the idea, even if the yellow quest markers kind of give me bad flashbacks to being addicted to World of Warcraft. ;)* One interviewee said: *it reminds me of WoW, I like doing quests.*

The rewards that we added only had meaning within the virtual world. The fact that players were motivated to earn these rewards suggests the players were engaged in the imagined world and scenarios.

Evidence for improved social situational learning

By examining the chat logs, we found that there were instances of of players first learning phrases through quests and then using them in conversations with other real players. This finding provides additional insight into R4. For example, Breathless first used the Japanese phrase for "How old are you?" and "what's your hobby?" in quests and then practiced the newly acquired skill in a social context with a real other player :

Breathless: anata ha nan sai desu ka? (how old are you?)
maya: watashi? (me?)
maya: himitsu desu! (it's a secret!)
...
Breathless: anata no kyoumi (your hobby...)
Breathless: ha nan desu ka? (...what is it?)
maya: e wo kaku (painting pictures)

There are around 20 instances of people using the input system in the game (meaning they first collected the words using the game mechanics) to produce Japanese greetings or farewells in social contexts with other real people. One of the interviewees also noted that they used some of the words that they learned in the game in conversations with their real-world friends.

LIMITATIONS

We designed the game to engage learners of Japanese who are tech-savvy and interested in using online tools and games to improve their language skills. This target population is certainly not representative of all language learners, but the Reddit audience reflects this target population very well. Of survey respondents, 48% agreed that learning a second language is best using an application (when compared to classroom or learning abroad) and 41% were neutral between learning through an application and other methods.

Although the return rate of 13% may seem low to readers, it is not unusual in the world of free online video games. In fact, a study of *Hello Worlds!*, a non-educational video game that has been played 1.5 million times, reported a return rate of about 20% [11]. Of course, we would still like to see this improve in future iterations.

Although the system was designed to support long term engagement, in this particular study, we lack sufficient data to answer the question of whether the long-term engagement mechanisms are effective or not. Future work will examine this question in more detail.

CONCLUSIONS AND FUTURE WORK

The problem we set out to address was to build a game that promotes social situational language fluency. We highlighted three major challenges that such a game should address: 1) how to design and maximize the impact of long-term engagement mechanisms, 2) how to represent real-world situations precisely enough that players feel immersed, and 3) how to use game mechanics and player interactions to enable social engagement. To address these challenges, we presented a language learning game that combines traditional learning approaches with a situated learning paradigm by integrating a spaced-repetition system within a language learning roleplaying game. The game features a new quest paradigm to facilitate long-term engagement with the game through "jobs" that allow a small amount of design effort to generate a large set of highly-scaffolded tasks that grow iteratively. Finally, a large-scale evaluation of the language learning game "in the wild" with a diverse set of 186 people revealed that the game was highly engaging for some players. By examining interviews, surveys and chatlogs we found that players were engaged by the roleplaying aspects of the game (R1). Players learned an average of 8.7 new words, despite most players beginning with extensive prior knowledge (R2). Interviews revealed that players felt this method of learning was more useful than more abstract methods because players imagined they were participating in real-world activities (R3). Finally, chatlog analysis and the interviews revealed that only a limited number of players felt socially engaged, but that subset of the players benefited greatly from the presence of the these features (R4). The study also revealed three insights that give promising directions for future work.

Supporting community outside of the game

Releasing the game through Reddit allowed us to engage with the community and troubleshoot issues during the study. It is possible that this engagement with the community encouraged participants to provide more depth in their comments. After helping one Reddit user with an issue, he commended our active participation in the community: *Thank you very much, haven't seen a whole lot of your game yet (but I am sure I will) but you have a damn fine "customer" support so far, lol. ;)* We can also see evidence of our community presence in the chat log:

maya: Did you find this from a reddit thread?
maya: they seem to be working hard to mend problems
...
maya: Maybe report the chat box thing
Breathless: I'll do

The Reddit thread also made it possible to avoid an issue that may have alienated many users. Many of the learners who wanted to try the game already had experience with Japanese and therefore already knew some combination of Hiragana, Katakana and Kanji. Although we allowed Hiragana and Katakana to be unlocked through the game, these learners felt that using the English was too much of step backward. The top comment in thread was *Is it only in romaji? That seems to be a bit of a damper on the "immersion" aspect....* We caught this comment early on and added an option to change the game into Kana initially.

Designing for meta players

When asked about why they came to the game, some interviewees said that they were actually more interested in exploring the ideas and design of the game than using the game for learning. For example, one interviewee when asked about why he played the game said: *I think much of my interest came from curiosity toward how you were going to implement educational ideas.* There was also an interviewee and one poster that mentioned that they had similar ideas for a game and were really excited to see the game being implemented. Many comments we received acknowledged the underlying rationale behind the game mechanics. For example, one interviewee mentioned an annoyance with the limited inventory: *I understand that this is a gating mechanic for language acquisition, but an alternate method needs to be developed to avoid having to pop in and out after every conversation.* This suggests that in designing the game, we can also consider engaging these expert learners by allowing them to contribute to the game design for example through game modifications or mods.

Designing for learning ecosystems

We found that many of the learners did not rely on a single tool or approach for language learning by rather on a complex ecosystem of tools and social engagements such as the sub-Reddit we released our game in. All 6 of the interviewees had tried to learn using more than 5 different approaches (classes, software, Influent, Anki, speaking with native speakers, lang8, pen-pals, to name a few) and some mentioned more than 10 throughout the interview. This finding is in sync with the findings of Townsend et al. [38] who describes the shift in education towards learning from many sources.

Furthermore, interviewees specifically suggested making *Crystallize* more integrated with these larger learning ecosystems. Three separate interviewees recommended that we integrate the game with *Anki*. By integrating the review system in the game with something more portable (such as *Anki*), as one of the interviewees pointed out, it becomes possible to manage the reviews while on vacation using a mobile phone. Another interviewee noted that this would make doing *Anki* reviews much more fun because they would be linked to progress in the game.

The embeddedness of learning tools into an ecosystem also has important implications for how we assess language learning. Learning from many sources means that learners each have qualitatively unique knowledge which means personalization requires more nuance than a simple placement test. For example, one interviewee previously learned Kanji (Chinese characters in the Japanese language) using *Remembering the Kanji* [26] which teaches the meanings of Kanji without teaching pronunciation. There was a similar scenario in the job-driven version of the game: many participants came from China and could understand the meaning of a character without being able to pronounce it.

We believe that this presents an interesting design challenge of designing not just for learning of the language, but also design for integration into larger learning strategies. The many requests for integration with Anki highlight this need. Furthermore one interviewee suggested creating challenges in the game that would require the player to search outside the game in order to solve it.

REFERENCES

1. 2015. Anki. `www.ankisrs.net`. (2015).

2. 2015. Duolingo. `www.duolingo.com`. (2015).
3. 2015. FluentU. `www.fluentu.com/japanese/`. (2015).
4. 2015. italki. `www.italki.com`. (2015).
5. 2015. LiveMocha. `http://livemocha.com/`. (2015).
6. 2015. Rikai Chan. `www.polarcloud.com/getrcx/`. (2015).
7. 2015. Super Memory. `supermemo.com/`. (2015).
8. 2015. WaniKani. `wanikani.com`. (2015).
9. Erik Andersen, Yun-En Liu, Richard Snider, Roy Szeto, Seth Cooper, and Zoran Popović. 2011. On the Harmfulness of Secondary Game Objectives. In *FDG '11: Proceedings of the Sixth International Conference on the Foundations of Digital Games*. ACM, New York, NY, USA.
10. Erik Andersen, Yun-En Liu, Richard Snider, Roy Szeto, and Zoran Popović. Placing a Value on Aesthetics in Online Casual Games. In *CHI 2011*. ACM Press.
11. Erik Andersen, Eleanor O'Rourke, Yun-En Liu, Richard Snider, Jeff Lowdermilk, David Truong, Seth Cooper, and Zoran Popović. The Impact of Tutorials on Games of Varying Complexity. In *CHI 2012*. ACM Press.
12. Richard Bailey and Jesse Davey. 2011. Internet-based Spaced Repetition Learning In and Out of the Classroom: Implementation and Student Perception. *CELE Journal* 20 (2011), 39–50.
13. Lawrence W Barsalou. 1999. Language comprehension: Archival memory or preparation for situated action? (1999).
14. Eric Butler, Erik Andersen, Adam M Smith, Sumit Gulwani, Zoran Popovic, and WA Redmond. 2015. Automatic Game Progression Design through Analysis of Solution Features. In *Proc. of the SIGCHI Conf. on Human Factors in Computing (CHI2015)*.
15. Gabriel Culbertson, Erik Andersen, Walker White, Daniel Zhang, and Malte Jung. Crystallize: An Immersive, Collaborative Game for Second Language Learning. In *CSCW 2016*.
16. Michele D Dickey. 2007. Game design and learning: A conjectural analysis of how massively multiple online role-playing games (MMORPGs) foster intrinsic motivation. *Educational Technology Research and Development* 55, 3 (2007), 253–273.
17. Nicolas Ducheneaut and Robert J Moore. The social side of gaming: a study of interaction patterns in a massively multiplayer online game. In *CSCW 2004*. ACM Press.
18. Hermann Ebbinghaus. 1913. *Memory: A contribution to experimental psychology*. Number 3. Teacher's College, Columbia University, New York City. Originally published in 1885.
19. Darren Edge, Elly Searle, Kevin Chiu, Jing Zhao, and James A Landay. MicroMandarin: mobile language learning in context. In *CHI 2011*. ACM Press.
20. Uschi Felix. 2005. E-learning pedagogy in the third millennium: the need for combining social and cognitive constructivist approaches. *ReCALL* 17, 01 (2005), 85–100.
21. James Paul Gee. 2003. What video games have to teach us about learning and literacy. *Computers in Entertainment (CIE)* 1, 1 (2003), 20–20.
22. James Paul Gee. 2007. Why are video games good for learning. *Unpublished manuscript. Retrieved* 23 (2007).
23. James Paul Gee. 2008. Learning and games. *The ecology of games: Connecting youth, games, and learning* 3 (2008), 21–40.
24. Arthur M Glenberg, Tiana Gutierrez, Joel R Levin, Sandra Japuntich, and Michael P Kaschak. 2004. Activity and Imagined Activity Can Enhance Young Children's Reading Comprehension. *Journal of Educational Psychology* 96, 3 (2004), 424.
25. Ward H. Goodenough. 1957. Oceania and the Problem of Controls in the Study of Cultural and Human Evolution. *The Journal of the Polynesian Society* 66, 2 (1957), pp. 146–155.
26. James W Heisig. 2007. *Remembering the Kanji, Volume 1: A Complete Course on How not to Forget the Meaning and Writing of Japanese Characters*. Vol. 1. University of Hawaii Press.
27. Dorothy Holland and Naomi Quinn. 1987. *Cultural models in language and thought*. Cambridge University Press.
28. Robert Howland, Sachi Urano, and Junichi Hoshino. 2012. SanjigenJiten: computer assisted language learning system within a 3d game environment. In *Advances in Computer Entertainment*. Springer, 262–273.
29. Jean Lave and Etienne Wenger. 1991. *Situated learning: Legitimate peripheral participation*. Cambridge university press.
30. Derek Lomas, Kishan Patel, Jodi L. Forlizzi, and Kenneth R. Koedinger. Optimizing challenge in an educational game using large-scale design experiments. In *CHI 2013*.
31. Jane McGonigal. 2003. A real little game: The performance of belief in pervasive play. *Proceedings of DiGRA 2003* (2003).
32. Gisli Palsson. 1994. Enskilment at sea. *Man* (1994), 901–927.
33. Mark Peterson. 2010. Massively multiplayer online role-playing games as arenas for second language learning. *Computer Assisted Language Learning* 23, 5 (2010), 429–439.
34. Paul Pimsleur. 1967. A memory schedule. *Modern Language Journal* (1967), 73–75.

35. Yolanda A Rankin, McKenzie McNeal, Marcus W Shute, and Bruce Gooch. 2008. User centered game design: evaluating massive multiplayer online role playing games for second language acquisition. In *Proceedings of the 2008 ACM SIGGRAPH symposium on Video games*. ACM, 43–49.

36. Joan Rubin. 1975. What the "good language learner" can teach us. *TESOL quarterly* (1975), 41–51.

37. Guoquan Sha. 2009. AI-based chatterbots and spoken English teaching: a critical analysis. *Computer Assisted Language Learning* 22, 3 (2009), 269–281.

38. T Townsend, P Clarke, and M Ainscow. 1999. Third Millennium Schools: prospects and problems for school effectiveness and school improvement. *T. Townsend, T. Clarke & M. Ainscow, Third Millennium Schools: A world of difference in effectiveness and improvement. Lisse: Swets & Zeitlinger* (1999).

39. Kathleen Tuite, Timothy Pavlik, Sandra B Fan, Tyler Robison, Alexander Jaffe, Yun-En Liu, Erik Andersen, and Steven Tanimoto. 2012. Picard: A creative and social online flashcard learning game. In *Proceedings of the International Conference on the Foundations of Digital Games*. ACM, 231–234.

40. Luis von Ahn. 2013. Duolingo: learn a language for free while helping to translate the web. In *IUI'13*. ACM, 1–2.

Using Gamification to Motivate Students with Dyslexia

Daniel Gooch[1,2], Asimina Vasalou[2], Laura Benton[2], Rilla Khaled[3]

[1]The Open University
Milton Keynes, UK
Daniel.gooch@open.ac.uk

[2]London Knowledge Lab,
Institute of Education,
London, UK
{A.Vasalou, L.Benton}@ioe.ac.uk

[3] Concordia University,
Montreal, Canada
rilla.khaled@concordia.ca

ABSTRACT

The concept of gamification is receiving increasing attention, particularly for its potential to motivate students. However, to date the majority of studies in the context of education have predominantly focused on University students. This paper explores how gamification could potentially benefit a specific student population, children with dyslexia who are transitioning from primary to secondary school. Two teachers from specialist dyslexia teaching centres used classDojo, a gamification platform, during their teaching sessions for one term. We detail how the teachers appropriated the platform in different ways and how the students discussed classDojo in terms of motivation. These findings have subsequently informed a set of provisional implications for gamification distilling opportunities for future pedagogical uses, gamification design for special education and methodological approaches to how gamification is studied.

Author Keywords

Gamification; SEN; Dyslexia; Educational Technology.

ACM Classification Keywords

H.5.m. Information interfaces and presentation (e.g., HCI): Miscellaneous.

K.3.1 Computers and Education: Computer Uses in Education

INTRODUCTION

Developmental dyslexia, or specific reading disability, is a literacy-based learning difficulty. It has been defined as “an unexpected, specific, and persistent failure to acquire efficient reading skills despite conventional instruction, adequate intelligence, and sociocultural opportunity” [13]. While prevalence estimates are susceptible to definitional manipulation [46], and rates differ from country to country, it has been suggested that dyslexia affects around 4%-8% of the UK population [38].

CHI'16, May 07 - 12, 2016, San Jose, CA, USA

ACM 978-1-4503-3362-7/16/05…$15.00
DOI: http://dx.doi.org/10.1145/2858036.2858231

The literacy difficulties associated with dyslexia can result in many children becoming demotivated within school. This is particularly common when students begin the transition to secondary education where literacy forms a substantial part of many lessons and it is assumed that students have acquired the necessary reading skills. To assist with their literacy difficulties, students may be identified as having ‘Special Educational Needs’ (SEN) and consequently receive additional learning support within their schooling. In the UK, this can take the form of one (or more) sessions a week outside of their normal classroom with a SEN teacher or learning support assistant, each of which generally consist of teaching interventions targeting the student’s specific educational needs with the aim of helping them to catch up with their peers. However, often SEN teachers are not specialist dyslexia experts as they have to deal with a wide range of special needs and the student may need more intensive support than the SEN teacher can provide. This can lead many parents to seek additional tuition outside of school from specialist dyslexia teaching centres to help improve literacy skills. Although this can be beneficial it also requires these children to spend additional time undertaking the types of activities that they typically struggle with, an experience that can be demotivating, fuelling their low levels of self-esteem. Indeed, motivation is a substantial issue for most dyslexic students. Research shows that dyslexic students have lower motivation when compared to students without dyslexia in reading as well as other aspects of their learning [48], highlighting the importance of applying motivational teaching strategies for dyslexic students [38].

Looking at education more broadly, the importance of sustaining students’ motivation has been a longstanding concern. One recent mechanism, which has proved to have some success in increasing student motivation, is “gamification”: the use of game elements, such as digital rewards, in non-game contexts [15]. While a variety of studies have explored the use of gamification with University students, showing that the mechanism can increase student motivation [14], the specific needs of primary school students with SEN (such as dyslexia) have not been addressed. Our research stemmed from the belief that a gamification platform could be beneficial for this population, given that students with dyslexia often struggle to be motivated to practice their literacy skills.

In light of the limited previous research in this area, in this paper we take an exploratory approach to understand the implications of the popular gamification platform classDojo[1] on student motivation in the context of specialist teaching sessions for students with dyslexia. Our main contributions are twofold. First, we show how use of the platform impacts on the motivation of the students, deriving a number of provisional best practices for the pedagogically meaningful use of gamification for primary school students with dyslexia. Second, taking a methodological perspective, we show how exploratory approaches to gamification in context enable ecologically valid examinations of its use. We encourage others to utilise similar approaches to develop a deeper understanding of how real, unpredictable, and diverse pedagogical practices can affect the effectiveness and utility of gamification platforms.

BACKGROUND

Gamification as a Motivational Tool

In contrast to "serious games", which are games designed for non-entertainment purposes, gamification entails "the use of game design elements in non-game contexts" [15]. The most commonly employed aspect of gamification is the use of an achievement system, often in the form of badges or rewards [1, 25]. Such systems have analogous "real world" comparisons with famous examples including the medals of the armed forces or the badges awarded within the Scout movement. The root purpose of these awards is based around motivating people to undertake particular tasks and as tokens of recognition for specific achievements. Gamification strives, at its core, to increase motivation.

It is worth considering what it means to be motivated. "To be motivated means to be moved to do something" [41]. Motivation is not a unitary phenomenon for most individuals - different people may have different types and amounts of motivation, which can be shaped by the activity they are undertaking. Someone who is unmotivated to read may be a highly motivated writer.

Additionally, researchers commonly divide motivation into two types based on the source of the motivation: *intrinsic* motivation occurs where no reward is received beyond undertaking a particular activity, while *extrinsic* motivation refers to undertaking an activity in order to receive a desired outcome separate from the activity.

It is not known exactly how gamification affects motivation. Those sceptical of the benefits of gamification have argued that the use of scoring systems as a motivator (which is only one form of gamification) can improve extrinsic motivation while reducing intrinsic motivation (e.g. [27, 35]). Nicholson argues that "the underlying message of these criticisms of gamification is that there are more effective ways than a scoring system to engage users" [35]. These criticisms remain speculative, however, as it does not acknowledge the lack of evidence on whether gamification indeed acts as a tangible reward that decreases intrinsic motivation, or conversely as a form of positive performance feedback which is thought to enhance intrinsic motivation [10, 11, 41]. This will depend on both how the gamification platform is deployed and also what motivates a specific user when they are entering the interaction [45]. Current experimental results are inconclusive with some indicating a positive relationship between gamification and intrinsic motivation [33] and others finding no link [34].

Ryan and Deci's Self-Determination theory [41] breaks down motivation into several different forms based on the perceived locus of causality (i.e. how external the achievement is to the individual). When individuals perceive themselves to be the locus of causality they are intrinsically motivated. As their perception shifts from an internal to an external locus of causality, they become increasingly more extrinsically motivated (moving through the stages of integration, identification, introjection and external regulation). Using this model we would suggest that gamification lies somewhere between introjection (fostering a sense of pride) and identification (where the student recognises the importance of the activity for achieving some goal) [41]. This is educationally relevant as it suggests that the motivation that gamification could provide, even if extrinsic, is about the student improving themselves rather than seeking a reward per-se (what the model terms "external regulation").

Various researchers, most notably Decker [12] and Hamari et al. [25], have argued that while there is the potential for gamification to encourage transient forms of motivation, the effect of gamification is heavily dependent upon the context in which it is being applied [45]. Adults who are trying to get fit through using a gamified exercise program [24] are voluntarily using the program to achieve self-set goals. This is qualitatively different to secondary school students who are compelled by their school to use a gamified platform to learn algebra [42]. Herein lies an unresolved question – does gamification increase motivation even for users compelled to use it? Given the unique nature of the educational context, it is necessary to consider research that has specifically examined the use of gamification in this context.

Gamification in Education

One of the main opportunities for using gamification has been in the field of educational technology. Motivation is an important part of education, strongly influencing the extent to which students use effective learning strategies [36]. Ormrod (2006) identifies six different ways that motivation can affect students including directing behaviour

[1] https://www.classDojo.com

towards particular goals [32], increasing the amount of effort and energy expended in activities related to these goals [37] and leading to increased performance [43]. In terms of reward mechanisms, educators cannot always rely on intrinsic motivation since many learning tasks are not inherently interesting or enjoyable [41]. While extrinsic motivation has often been characterised as being an impoverished form of motivation, we should note that "students can perform extrinsically motivated actions with resentment, resistance, and disinterest or, alternatively, with an attitude of willingness that reflects an inner acceptance of the value or utility of a task… in the latter case, the extrinsic goal is self-endorsed and thus adopted with a sense of volition" [41].

Given the link between learning and motivation, it is unsurprising that gamification has garnered a lot of attention due to its potential to motivate students. However, despite the anecdotal evidence available (e.g. [40]) and examples of popular gamified educational systems (e.g. the Khan Academy) empirical data supporting the educational benefits of gamification in terms of increasing student motivation or linking this motivation to learning outcomes is still in its early stages [1]. While some extant research does examine gamification targeted at primary school student users [4, 16, 19], its focus has not been on motivation. At the same time, empirical work that examines the effect of gamification on motivation (such as [1, 9, 14, 17, 26, 30]) tends to focus on University students, and reports mixed evidence for this user group [45].

For example, Denny (2013) presents one of the most comprehensive empirical studies, analysing 1000 undergraduate students' use of a gamified online learning platform [14]. They established that the students using the gamified version answered more questions and used the system more frequently than those students who used the non-gamified platform. Based on survey data they also argued that the students enjoyed using the badges and indicated a strong preference for their inclusion in the standard interface. Domínguez et al. (2013) demonstrated how a gamified e-learning platform resulted in higher final test scores compared to students who used the non-gamified version [17]. Their survey data indicated high involvement with the tool but with no data from the control group it is difficult to interpret this data. As a third example, Barata et al., (2013) used a gamified version of the e-learning platform Moodle alongside their lecture course for two years, comparing it against the previous three years of the course [1]. While the grade results were somewhat mixed, they examined motivation through lecture attendance, the number of downloaded lecture slides and the number of posts each student made. All three of these measures increased significantly during the gamified years compared to the non-gamified years. This indicates that the gamification may have increased motivation but not performance. As a final example, Sætre (2013) presents a case study of a class of 27 students aged 13-15 using DragonBox, a gamified algebra system, for one month [42]. While focused on comparing scores in pre- and post- study tests, based on a cursory interview he notes that the students reported that the system was "good", while his observations indicated that students did indeed use the software.

RESEARCH AIMS AND APPROACH

While the aforementioned measures in support of gamification are varied, there is some basis for arguing that gamification can increase some students' motivation and learning outcomes. This could be particularly valuable for students with dyslexia who commonly have limited motivation to work on their literacy difficulties [38]. To date, there has been limited research examining the impact of gamification on SEN students. For example, even though scholars such as Ern, [18], have hypothesised that game mechanics could be of use in designing interventions for students with autism, to our knowledge, researchers have not validated these claims empirically. Our work follows on from previous research that highlights how important it is to consider motivation as an intrinsic component to teaching students with dyslexia [38]. We explore how gamification can be used to motivate students with dyslexia who are at a critical transition point in their education, moving up from primary to secondary school.

Previous work on studying gamification and motivation has predominantly relied on quasi-experimental approaches. A number of motivation measures have been used in an attempt to establish the effect of gamification on student motivation with qualitative data primarily used to supplement these quantitative results (e.g. [1, 6, 9, 12, 14, 17, 26, 42]). This approach has yielded mixed results, showing that motivation and learning outcomes increase for some students in some settings. Cautioning against a technology-centred perspective on gamification, Deterding et al. (2011) have shown through illustrative examples of gamified systems that game rewards or badges become meaningful only when users' primary task encourages autonomy, achievement and mastery [15]. The challenge thus remains in separating the effects of gamification from the way in which a gamification platform is used in context. Therefore, the interaction between gamification and the learning environment is of critical importance to those employing gamification in education, and even more so in specialist education where the learning environment is carefully designed and orchestrated. Learning environments tailored to children with SEN are typically constructed to take into account a student's specific educational support needs (such as literacy impairments), cognitive weaknesses (such as organisational and memory weaknesses) and emotional needs (such as low self-esteem), necessitating a highly personalised teaching approach which is distinct from mainstream University tuition [13, 38]. Given the mixed results of previous research, and the extant literature on gamification and SEN, the present paper takes an exploratory approach to understand (i) how gamification can be used by specialist teachers to foster student motivation, and (ii) how students' motivation may be impacted by different pedagogical practices.

METHODOLOGY

Within this research we adopted a case study approach to understanding how gamification could be used in specialist dyslexia teaching sessions. Case study research assumes that the social phenomenon (motivation) and context (situated pedagogical practices) are intertwined; its goal is to illuminate a set of decisions, exploring why they were taken, how they were implemented, and with what result [44]. Aiming at "analytic generalisation" [20, 47], case study research is concerned with elaborating and generalising theories as opposed to generalising to populations, thus requiring in-depth analysis of a small, specific population. Applying an exploratory, inductive case study approach allowed us to explore gamification, focusing on how students were motivated, and why [44, 20] whilst revealing particular pedagogical practices that advance our understanding of the benefits or challenges in applying gamification to a special education setting.

Participants

We recruited three dyslexia specialist teachers, from two different Dyslexia Action (DA) teaching centres in the UK. DA is a national charity whose remit is to provide support to individuals affected by dyslexia and literacy difficulties. Both of these centres follow the same core curriculum. All of the teachers had over 10 years experience in teaching children with dyslexia. Unfortunately, one of these teachers subsequently dropped out of the study as the students she recruited stopped attending her teaching sessions. The remaining two teachers (T:1 and T:2) agreed to use classDojo with seven different students during the summer term (approx. 12 weeks from April 2014 until July 2014). During this time the software was used throughout all 12 of the teaching sessions with each session lasting 1.5 hours. The parents of all seven children also agreed to take part in the study. T:1 recruited two students and T:2 recruited five. All students were taught in pairs with the exception of C:7. Students attended Years 4-7 (equivalent of US grades 3-6). Those students taught in pairs were able to view the performance of their classmate within ClassDojo.

Child	Paired Child	Parent	Age	Student Gender	Teacher
[C:1]	[C:2]	[P:1]	9	Female	[T:1]
[C:2]	[C:1]	[P:2]	9	Female	[T:1]
[C:3]	[C:4]	[P:3]	11	Male	[T:2]
[C:4]	[C:3]	[P:4]	11	Male	[T:2]
[C:5]	[C:6]	[P:5]	8	Female	[T:2]
[C:6]	[C:5]	[P:6]	12	Female	[T:2]
[C:7]	N/A	[P:7]	8	Male	[T:2]

Table 1. Breakdown of the study participants.

Table 1 presents a breakdown of the students taking part in the study. Each of the students had worked with their teacher for at least 1 year with the exception of [C:5] who had attended for 2 months.

Technology

We chose to use classDojo (https://www.classdojo.com) as our gamification platform. A popular platform, classDojo currently has 2.4 million teacher accounts covering 53 million students in 180 countries. classDojo offers customisability, allowing the free-form creation of badges. This enables teachers to create whatever badges they deem necessary for the specific motivational needs of their students. Additionally, the system works on a tablet and only needs two taps to award a badge, allowing it to be easily integrated into teaching sessions.

There are two main components to the classDojo system. The first is the awarding of badges. When a teacher logs into the system (either online or through the tablet app) they first select a teaching session. Once a session is selected, the students within that session are displayed. Each student is represented by a customisable avatar. When an avatar is selected, the teacher can then award a badge from a set list of either positive (green) or negative (red) badges (see Figure 1). The set of badges is fully customizable for each teaching session, allowing the teacher to tailor the awards for the needs of their students. The inclusion of red badges in classDojo is unusual as gamification typically focuses on rewarding achievements rather than recording failures.

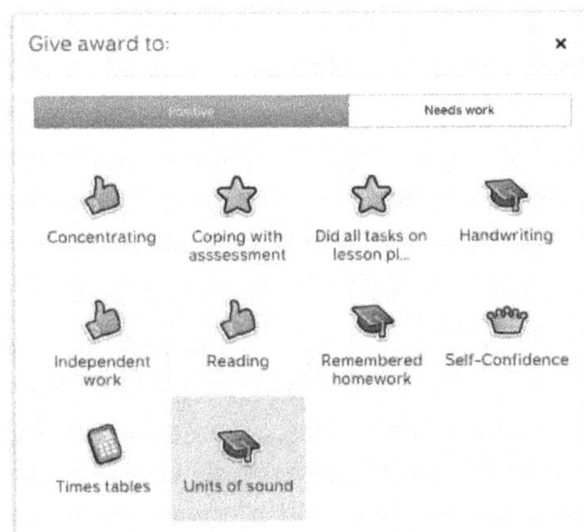

Figure 1. The pop-up showing the positive badges a teacher has customised to award to a given student.

The second element of the classDojo platform is the reporting system, designed to maintain a record of the badges awarded and to keep parents and guardians updated about their child's progress if they sign up to the platform (see Figure 2). A weekly report of a child's badges is automatically emailed to parents every week. This report also contains any comments teachers have written about specific badges.

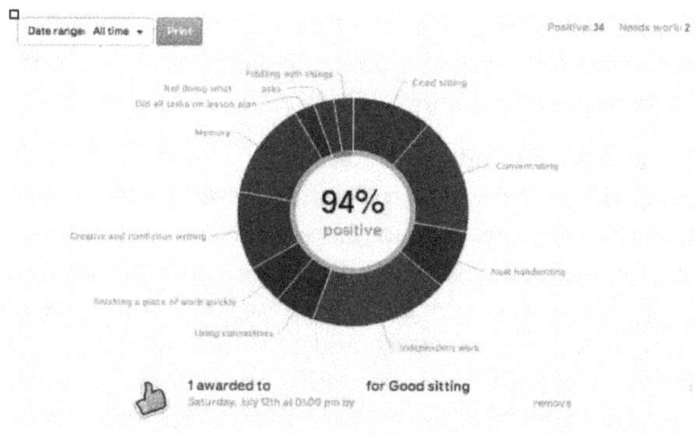

Figure 2. Example student's badges across time (name removed to preserve anonymity).

Having described classDojo, it is important to mention that this technology represents the virtual reward component of gamification and does not address other game elements such as rankings or leaderboards [15]. While virtual rewards are a critical part of gamification and this approach mirrors similar applications of gamification in the education domain [9, 14, 17, 26, 30], it only allows us to understand one facet of "gamification". However, focusing on virtual rewards has particular significance within our case since teachers often motivate students with dyslexia with frequent praise of their achievements [38]. Compared to the traditional equivalent of awarding stickers, classDojo virtual badges offer several benefits. Whereas producing customised stickers is possible, it is time consuming. We postulated that classDojo would enable teachers to instantly and iteratively create badges potentially opening up the space for creative uses of rewards. Moreover, we expected that the points awarded under the badges would offer a historical archive of a child's learning progress. In contrast, stickers can be misplaced or forgotten (e.g. as students change workbooks) as a result limiting the student's ability to view how many stickers have been awarded and what they were rewarded for.

Procedure and Data Collection

Teaching sessions at the specialist centres involve one teacher and one to two students. Focused on improving the students' literacy skills, the sessions are tailored towards each individual student's needs. Although all of the centres follow the same high-level curriculum, each centre and teacher has a high degree of flexibility in how they run their own teaching sessions. While we had a rich understanding of these sessions from previous work, our previous focus had not been on motivational strategies.

To obtain rich data without influencing the behaviour of staff and students during the sessions, we conducted face-to-face interviews both pre- and post- deployment of classDojo. While this limits the data we have collected, it ensures that the teachers were able to use the software within a naturalistic setting, reducing the pressure to use it in 'correct' or 'expected' ways, as can happen when being observed by a researcher.

We performed a pre-study semi-structured interview with each of the teachers, parents and students in order to better understand how the teaching sessions were currently run. It was intended that this baseline data would allow us to contrast the sessions using classDojo with a "typical" session. The teacher interviews lasted on average 39 minutes (SD=2.8) and focussed on how they motivate their students, what achievements they reward and how, and finally what their interest in the platform was. The interviews with parents lasted on average 18 minutes (SD=5.0) and covered how motivated their child was to attend the specialist sessions and whether there were any skills they wanted their child to be rewarded for (such as persistence) that were not currently covered at the teaching centre. The interviews with children lasted on average 11 minutes (SD=5.9) and mainly focused on how they were rewarded within the teaching sessions and how this made them feel. On the request of the parents, some of the interviews with the children were conducted with their parents present.

The post-study interviews took place at the end of the study and focussed on whether the students' motivation had changed after classDojo had been introduced and how well the platform integrated into the sessions. The teacher interviews lasted on average 44 minutes (SD=4.9), the parent interviews lasted on average 14 minutes (SD=3.1) and the child interviews lasted on average 17 minutes (SD=3.9).

In addition to the interview data we kept a daily log of parental and child logins to the system. From the classDojo system itself we were also able to view how many badges were awarded and what badges the teachers created.

Technological Support

Previous work in educational technology research highlights two common methodological considerations we needed to address to support the introduction of a new technology. Firstly, sustained support needs to be provided to both instruct the teachers how to use the technology and to provide assistance when problems are found. Secondly, the technology needs to fit within the teacher's existing classroom practices [8, 31].

In order to provide sustained support to the teachers we remained in contact with them throughout the study period, emailing them fortnightly to ensure they were not experiencing any problems. After some initial issues with the firewalls at the teaching centres, the teachers had no problems with using classDojo. We also made it clear that we would come back into centres to fix any issues they may have been having. With regards to existing classroom practices, during the pre-study interviews we discussed with the teachers how the platform worked and how they might like to integrate it into their teaching sessions. We repeatedly reassured the teachers that they could customise their use of the classDojo platform around their pre-existing teaching practices. Additionally, at the onset of the study, one of the researchers supported each teacher to set up an initial set of badges intended to scaffold the teachers' understanding of the badge creation process.

Analysis

With the participants' consent, the 32 interviews (14 student, 14 parent, 4 teacher) were recorded and transcribed. Taking an interpretive approach, an inductive thematic analysis was conducted, directed by our key focus on gamification, student motivation and teaching practices. Throughout the analysis, we attempted to achieve neutrality with regards to how interviewees' perspectives were represented and interpreted. To achieve this, the first two authors separately coded the interviews and then discussed the uncovered perspectives.

Triangulation was employed during the analysis, comparing data from the interviews against the logs kept by the classDojo platform to help us better understand the phenomenon under consideration. Additionally, when interpreting student motivation, whenever possible we triangulated parent, teacher and student interviews to uncover possible multiple perspectives. Our thematic analysis yielded 13 codes that coalesced into three key themes: *initial motivational strategies and teacher expectations* describes how the teachers motivated their students prior to using classDojo and the expected benefits of using the software; *pedagogy and classDojo* focuses on how the different teachers appropriated the software and how it changed their pedagogy; *inter-individual differences and motivations* captures how different students were affected by the use of classDojo.

FINDINGS AND DISCUSSION

Initial motivational strategies and teacher expectations

Prior to using classDojo, both of the teachers motivated their students with frequent verbal feedback to indicate when progress had been made. As part of this, the teachers frequently praised the students. This was viewed to be particularly important as many of the students did not experience praise or recognition of achievements in school, which was extremely demotivating. As T:1 explained: "*I want them to know that they are doing well, because some of them have got quite fragile self esteem, many of them are used to failure...*"

Although dyslexia is predominantly seen as a literacy impairment, students with dyslexia often have difficulties with meta-cognitive skills, memory, perseverance and organisational ability [11]. Teachers explained that this became an additional impediment to students' progress. Both teachers in the pre-study interviews noted that their assessment framework and strategies do not account for improvements in these broader, non-literacy skills: "*the standardised tests are so insensitive basically, so the student can have made a lot of progress, I must have worked on quite a few spelling patterns and done really, really well and that pattern doesn't come up in the test so it looks like they haven't kind of moved at all...*" [T:2]. This means that even when a student has made progress, it may not be recognised in their test scores.

Both teachers entered the study with a desire to experiment with classDojo, believing that badges may be more tangible than verbal feedback, and as a consequence potentially more motivating for their students. Beyond this tangibility, the badges also reify the notion of progress, which becomes an object for consultation and discussion rather than a comparison process. T:2 pointed out, "*I think it would be nice to have something more concrete rather than just 'look at this page from 6 months ago' and how you've improved...*".

Pedagogy and classDojo

Both teachers had a consistent pattern of use during the study, using the system regularly across the 12 weeks of the study with no decrease of use over time. Despite some shared attitudes and strategies at the onset of the study, the two teachers appropriated and used the gamification platform very differently. T:1 applied an activity-driven pedagogical design basing badges around the activities she typically ran during a given teaching session. She explained that: "*I customised mine to suit the lessons that I had, some of the icons, the badges for the reading packs that they do, spelling packs, the high frequency words, how well they did with dictation sentences*".

	C:1	C:2
Self-Confidence ^	1	2
Reading Speed ^	1	2
Motivation ^	1	1
Fluency ^	1	
Perseverance ^	1	
Dictation*	10	5
Working Independently*	8	6
High Frequency Words*	8	3
Reading Accuracy*	4	5
Spelling Pack*	5	3
Reading Pack*	5	2
Syllable Division*	1	
Total Number of Badges	46	29

Table 2: Badges used by T:1.
^ Indicates positive badges created by the researcher.
*** Indicates positive badges created by T:1 independently.**

Table 2 summarises the badges created and used by T:1 with her students. C2 was awarded less badges overall because she attended one less lesson than C1 and, in general, completed fewer activities than C1. Additionally, T:1 retained complete control over both the decision to award a badge and the interaction with the tablet when awarding a badge: "*I had them there so when I awarded a point I would say 'well that's your reading pack done, well done you did well with that' and then I'd also say you're having a point for your reading pack*".

	C:3	C:4	C:5	C:6	C:7
Memory ^		2			5
Self-Confidence ^	2				
Concentrating*		1		6	6
Independent work*	3	2			7
Finishing a piece of work quickly*		4			2
Coping with frustration*	3	2			
Spelling Pack*	2	3			
Coping with assessment*	2	2		1	
Handwriting*			5		
Did all tasks on lesson plan*			4		1
Working together sensibly*	1	3			
Good sitting*					4
Creative and nonfiction writing*					4
Reading*			2	2	
Units of sound*				3	
Neat handwriting*					3
Remembered homework*				2	
Suffixing rules*		2			
Using connectives*					2
Not insisting on perfection*	2				
Times tables*				1	
Off Task*		1			
Talking out of turn □				1	
Fiddling with things +					1
Not doing what the teacher asks +	1				1
Total Number of Badges	16	22	11	16	36

Table 3. Badges used by T:2.

^ Indicates positive badges created by the researcher.
*** Indicates positive badges created by T:2 independently.**
□Indicates negative badges created by the researcher
+ Indicates negative badges created by T:2 independently.

T:2 took a very different approach, focussing on metacognitive skills and designed badges that reflected unrecognised, underlying skills that were critical to learning. Even though these skills were not formally assessed, T2 was aware that they posed challenges to her students. Thus, when awarding a badge there was an implicit acknowledgment that the student had made an extra effort in a personally challenging area. As she explained, "*I'd say most of the targets I set were either behavioural ones, so things like, good sitting, independent work, not messing around... or reinforcement for the tasks that I knew individual students really hated as a kind of incentive*". T:2 created the badges by iteratively customising them, adding additional ones on-the-fly during her teaching sessions as needed, personalised to the difficulties of her individual students. Table 3 summarises the badges created and used by T:2 with her students. Additionally, T:2 granted her students more autonomy in creating and awarding themselves the badges. Thus, students were encouraged to propose new badges but also to award themselves a badge, or when in a group they gave each other badges.

These contrasting pedagogical uses and strategies had a significant impact on students' perception of the badges. The first cause for this difference in perception were the different levels of **personalisation of the badges**. T:1 customised the badges at the beginning of the study, and following this the badges remained static and applicable to all students on the basis of their activities. One consequence of this activity-based design was that students' progress was comparable across time. As T:1 described, this introduced some tension when a student was away for a week resulting in her receiving less badges overall: "*then sometimes it [classDojo] had both students up there and then one of the students could see the marks for both students and because one was away one week she had much less marks and it looked a bit... and I'm thinking 'oh'.*" This unexpected consequence introduced a comparative element between students that could be damaging to their motivation [7, 38]. While this comparison arose as a result of the teaching context (i.e. two students sharing a single tablet), awarding the same badges to each student creates an equivalence between the badges that enables students to directly compare their achievements.

Conversely, T:2 created personalised badges in a iterative process during the course of the study. As such, badges were not uniformly applicable nor uniformly awarded to students. Across her cohort, students were forthcoming about the sense of accomplishment they felt when being rewarded for something they personally found difficult and challenging. C:6 explained that "*I would get the units of sound one [awarded for using a computer-based literacy program] because T:2 made one up and I liked that one because I hate units of sound.*" Moreover, by using classDojo as a forum for identifying and discussing skills requiring improvement, T:2 promoted some students' meta-cognition and autonomy. During the interview, C:4 described handwriting as a particular challenge explaining his plans to ask his teacher for a corresponding classDojo badge. He went on to attribute this metacognitive awareness to the way classDojo had been used: "*[the badges] have all got a different meaning... [previously] T:2 randomly gave us a sticker when we'd completed a piece of work and we haven't made a link [to skills]. It would just be you've completed a piece of work.*". The explicit link that the classDojo badges build between mastery and particular skills helped students to identify and reflect on the progress they had made during a particular session.

The second cause of the students' different perception of the badges followed from the process taken by T:1 and T:2 to **create and award classDojo badges.** Whereas T:1 based the badges on literacy activities that remained stable over time, T:2 focused on underlying skills to learning, while at the same time inviting students' continuous involvement by allowing them to propose new badges: "*the students start to own it because they will suggest to you why don't we have a badge for this and they will, you know, that's something that they have realised is maybe a strength that they would like to build up and you can do it instantly then and they feel it's more theirs... (T:2)*" The consequence of this was that students appeared to assign personal meaning and significance to the badges. C:3 explained that "*it's like our own little thing and it's lots of different things that they are for, so they've all got a different meaning.*"

Overall, students of both T:1 and T:2 were positive about classDojo and, from the logs, many habitually looked at their badges when at home. Similarly, all students valued the link between progress in learning and the awarding of badges. As C:2 explained, "*I liked seeing how much I'd improved and... being able to check on what I was doing and how many points I was getting...*". Four of the students talked about the pride they experienced when getting a badge: "*they make me feel proud... they make me feel I've done something well*" [C8]. One of the parents, noted how her daughter "*was looking forward every week to seeing the points build up.*" However, whereas T:1's students tended to refer more broadly to progress based on the number of badges they had received, T:2's students' discussions tended to be more directed to specific understanding of skills and a sense of control over these skills.

Thus, we note that even though both teachers followed the behaviourist tradition embodied in the design of classDojo, their pedagogical practices within and around the technology fostered different motivational styles and outcomes. While T:1's use appeared to have highlighted the importance of the number of badges awarded, T:2's use appeared to promote a focus on independence, meta-cognition, and challenge. This in turn encouraged T:2's students to identify specific skills as being important to their learning. Our findings thus highlight how the appropriation of classDojo by the different teachers has a direct impact upon how students interact with, and are motivated by, the gamification platform.

Inter-individual Differences and Motivation

During the post-study interview, T:1 explained that her students were already motivated learners, which one of the parents (P:1) went on to confirm: "*My little one is really improving and her self confidence... she just so looks forward to it [the teaching sessions].*" In part because of this, T:1 pointed out that classDojo made little difference in her lessons: "*I don't think the children took that much notice of it if I'm honest... they probably would have responded as well, if not better, to a star in a book or something like that...*". However it is worth noting that T:1 retained complete control of the system, not allowing the students to explore or use it on their own. In short, T:1 used the classDojo as a traditional reward system and thus her view was unsurprising.

Both teachers agreed that technologies such as classDojo may work best for students who need constant reinforcement. T:1 argued: "*if you've got children that have got problems with attention and things I think you would have to keep them in mode and motivated that way.... I can see it could have a much better application for students who find it hard to stay on task, that's where I see it's strength lying... I don't think its something that you just have and expect it to have the same impact for all of the students that you use it with.*". Within the study, this point was exemplified with one of the children, C:7, who had severe difficulties in attention and motivation. Though C:7 claimed that classDojo had not changed his motivation, both his father and T:2 observed a significant difference. T:2 explained the impact classDojo had had on her student's behaviour within the sessions: "*C:7 in particular was extremely motivated and this was a child who has got concentration and attention problems... and with him you only had to threaten him with a red badge and he'd be back on his seat doing what you wanted, it was amazing...*"

Avoiding negative badges appeared to be a strong motivator for two other students, even though their teacher did not use these badges with them during the course of the study. C:3 in particular mentioned several times that "*I didn't get any red badges like I said so that's made me feel good as well...*" C:4 too seemed to be strongly affected by the mere presence of these badges: "*I think I haven't got any red marks but I'm trying my hardest not to get red marks so it is trying to push you up which is really, really good...*" .

Our findings highlight that students respond differently to the positive and negative badges. In the case of C:7 who lacked motivation, moving him toward extrinsic motivation through the awarding of positive badges was a desirable outcome that translated in his ability to engage with a learning task. Conversely, a subset of students regulated their behaviour to avoid the perceived external sanctions of the negative badges. Given our earlier observations about C:3's and C:4's autonomy and self-endorsement of their learning, we argue that for some students the existence of sanctions may invite undue focus on their avoidance, potentially limiting intrinsic motivation and undermining their independent understanding of their strengths and weaknesses. Thus, introducing negative badges may change the dynamic of gamification platforms, allowing extrinsic and intrinsic motivation to operate in concert with mixed motivational results for students.

IMPLICATIONS FOR GAMIFICATION

Our study has focused on exploring how teachers can appropriate gamification platforms in different ways and whether this appears to affect the motivation of students with dyslexia. This has led to us examining a number of inter-connected issues, which we present below as a set of provisional implications for gamification offered for further exploration in future work.

First we discuss opportunities regarding pedagogical uses for gamification and how these may transfer to other SEN students. Second we focus on the design of the gamification platform to identify some features that appear to mediate teachers' best practices and students' motivation, suggesting design recommendations that follow on from our research. Finally we compare our study methodology and findings to previous research approaches, identifying how these contrasting methodologies impact on our evolving understanding of gamification.

Implications for Pedagogical Practice with Gamification

Our primary research goal was to explore how gamification can be used by teachers to motivate students with dyslexia who are at a critical point in their education due to transitioning from primary to secondary school. Our results indicate that teaching practices with regards to the use of gamification in turn shape the pedagogical and motivational benefits experienced by students. T:1 used the platform primarily to award badges for activities students had completed, awarding the badges in a manner similar to traditional reward systems used in schools (e.g. stars or stickers). We note that this pattern of use has received the most critique by those sceptical about gamification [27, 35]. In comparison, through providing students with a sense of control over the platform, and targeting the badges towards their individual challenges, T:2's practices fostered agency, reflection and meaning making, which are all pedagogically important [36] supporting previous recommendations for using user-generated content and customization as a way to motivate and engage people [35]. In particular, granting students control and agency over the awarding of badges assisted students in identifying their own strengths and weaknesses. We believe that it is these practices that rendered gamification focussed on virtual rewards more meaningful than awarding stickers. Through the highly customised badges students were able to retain a clear connection to a specific achievement (e.g. coping with frustration).

Our findings show that the ways in which gamification platforms are appropriated by teachers are as significant as how they are designed when it comes to fostering educational outcomes. This suggests the importance of facilitating productive uses of gamification and to this end our data suggests three critical pedagogical practices: (1) providing students with badges for overcoming personally meaningful challenges (2) giving students the agency to identify their own weaknesses through a process of negotiation with their teacher, followed by (3) self-reflection and monitoring of their improvements.

Based on our exploration of how gamification can be used by students with dyslexia, we argue that the potential benefits may extend beyond this population to students with other types of SEN, who may face different challenges than those diagnosed with dyslexia. While students in our study experienced linguistic, or meta-cognitive weaknesses, SEN students can face concentration challenges (ADHD), communication and social skills (autism), or intense phobias (anxiety disorders) [3]. Similar to students with dyslexia, these challenges require personalised support. We hope that our work stimulates further research in this area to determine if and how our pedagogical recommendations – where gamification is used to challenge students and give them control over their learning – can transfer to other SEN groups.

Our research identifies a second potential contribution in shaping institutional practices. Often, influenced by top-down pressures, teachers will construct learning tasks on the basis of standard assessment frameworks. As our teachers pointed out, these frameworks can neglect to recognise underlying skills that form an important basis for successful learning. This is, in part, because at a policy level dyslexia is not well understood. Gamification can support a bottom-up approach that leverages teachers' knowledge and practices to overcome the problems caused by institutional and policy shortcomings. This is true of any area of SEN.

When gamification is designed to be customisable and open it can invite teachers to expand beyond the skills assessed through standardised measures, and reward students for otherwise unrecognised achievements. In our study this translated to covering a variety of skills from *concentration* as a necessary condition to engaging with a task to becoming more *self confident* and thus assuring students that they can make mistakes. Therefore, we posit that gamification could support lesson planning by directing teachers away from assessment frameworks in order to integrate pedagogical practices that address a more holistic approach to a SEN student's challenges.

Design Implications for Gamification in Education

Whereas some non-game contexts and tasks where gamification may be employed are more specified (e.g. Foursquare), the context of classDojo is determined by each individual teacher and is highly malleable. Moreover, the difference in practices between the two teachers highlights the contextually-dependent nature of gamification. With this in mind, our results broadly indicate the importance of enabling the enactment of contextual practices and needs through *customisable* educational gamification platforms. The customisation played a key part in convincing teachers that they could adopt classDojo because they felt they could adapt it to their existing practices. Additionally, the customisability of the classDojo badges was a critical feature in motivating students with dyslexia since it allowed one of the teachers in our study to target rewards to a child's individual needs and challenges. The same customisability allowed a teacher to define badge types as both rewards and sanctions. Using badges as sanctions may be particularly effective for students who suffer from a deep lack of motivation [28]. Alongside the importance of teacher agency, our findings also highlighted that *student agency* over the badge creation process can potentially develop students' metacognitive awareness and skills. Gamification designers may thus consider introducing features that enable students to customise badges, e.g. by suggesting new badges to their teachers, or revising existing badges created by their teachers for them. Moreover, the comparative analysis of T:1 and T:2 with regards to their divergent pedagogical practices is illustrative of Deterding's recent argument that the benefits of gamified systems can only be understood by looking at the context of use [15]. We suggest that using technology creatively in education is not straightforward and can be fostered through design supports within the gamification platform, for instance by capturing and providing teachers with access to the effective practices of their peers. Indeed, the pedagogical opportunities captured in this study could be used to design such supports.

Methodological Implications

The majority of previous research has taken a confirmatory approach to examining the effect of gamification on student motivation and learning outcomes, primarily utilising a quantitative research design (e.g. [1, 6, 9, 12, 14, 17, 42]). In contrast, we took an exploratory approach, gathering rich data to show the varied ways in which one particular gamification platform was appropriated. This shifted focus away from the mechanics of the system and its measurable effects on learning or motivation, to the integration of these mechanics in pedagogical practice focusing on how this shapes students' motivation. This allowed us to identify that extrinsic and intrinsic motivation can operate in concert due to the perceived presence of sanctions in the form of negative badges. Future research may examine how this co-existence could impact students' self-determination and volition. In summary, understanding the nuanced interactions between pedagogy, learner and technology can be invaluable in examining the nature of who benefits the most from gamification, why and under what conditions, while suggesting new hypotheses that can be tested in future empirical work.

CONCLUSION

The present research was driven by the important role of motivation in teaching students with dyslexia [38]. Our research goal was to explore how gamification can be used to motivate students with dyslexia who are at a particularly critical transition point in their education due to moving from primary to secondary school. The results of our study show that gamification can foster student motivation, in this instance due to an interaction between a highly customisable design and pedagogically tailored appropriation by teachers.

Our study offers two main contributions. First, we have established a number of provisional opportunities regarding the pedagogical use of gamification. These practices stand to improve how teachers use gamification in the classroom, and thus its resulting impact on students in terms of learning outcomes. We found that teachers' creative customization was critical to the effective use of classDojo. We also found that the way badges were awarded had a significant effect on students' perceptions of them. We argue that encouraging students to customise their badges can lead to reflection of their own abilities and weaknesses. While the practices we identified were limited to students with dyslexia, we have highlighted the ways in which they could be transferable to other SEN students. Our second contribution has been to highlight the value of exploratory approaches to studying gamification, allowing us to carefully examine the pedagogical context and practices required to support student motivation with gamification. We suggest that exploratory research approaches such as our own are invaluable in offering new hypotheses that can be further tested in confirmatory research.

To conclude, this work has highlighted some of the benefits that resulted from the use of a gamification platform with students with dyslexia. We hope that further research will examine more widely the potential uses of gamification to benefit the education of other primary school students both with and without SEN.

ACKNOWLEDGMENTS

This work was funded by the ILearnRW (project no: 318803) FP7 ICT EU project. We thank all of the teachers and children who took part in this research and graciously donated their time. Dominik Lukes and Justine Flower from Dyslexia Action are gratefully acknowledged for encouraging us to continue this work and arranging access to the centers.

REFERENCES

1. Antin, J., & Churchill, E. F., 2011. Badges in social media: A social psychological perspective. In *CHI 2011 Gamification Workshop Proceedings (Vancouver, BC, Canada, 2011)*.
2. Barata, G., Gama, S., Jorge, J., & Gonçalves, D., 2013. Improving Participation and Learning with Gamification. In *Proceedings of Gamification '13*, October 2-4, 2013, Stratford, ON, Canada.
3. Benton, L., Vasalou, A., Khaled, R., Johnson, H., and Gooch, D., 2014. Diversity for design: a framework for involving neurodiverse children in the technology design process. In *Proceedings of the 32nd annual ACM conference on Human factors in computing systems*, pp. 3747-3756. ACM.
4. Boticki, I., Baksa, J., Seow, P. and Looi, C. K., 2015. Usage of a mobile social learning platform with virtual badges in a primary school. *Computers & Education*, *86*, pp. 120-136.

5. Braun, V., & Clarke, V. (2006). Using thematic analysis in psychology. *Qualitative research in psychology*, *3*(2), 77-101.
6. Brewer, R., Anthony, L., Brown, Q., Irwin, G., Nias, J., & Tate, B., 2013. Using gamification to motivate children to complete empirical studies in lab environments. In *Proc. of the 12th International Conference on Interaction Design and Children*, pp. 388-391. ACM.
7. Carroll, J. M., and Iles, J. E., 2006. An assessment of anxiety levels in dyslexic students in higher education. *British journal of educational psychology*, *76*(3), pp. 651-662
8. Cuban, L., Kirkpatrick, H., & Peck, C., 2001. High access and low use of technologies in high school classrooms: Explaining an apparent paradox. *American Educational Research Journal*, 38(4), pp. 813-834.
9. de Freitas, A. A., & de Freitas, M. M., 2013. Classroom Live: a software-assisted gamification tool. *Computer Science Education*, 23(2), 186-206.
10. Deci, E. L. (1971). Effects of externally mediated rewards on intrinsic motivation. *Journal of Personality and Social Psychology*, 18, 105–115.
11. Deci, E. L., Koestner, R., & Ryan, R. M., 2001. Extrinsic rewards and intrinsic motivation in education: Reconsidered once again. *Review of Educational Research*, 71(1), 1-27.
12. Decker, A. and Lawley, E. L., 2013. Life's a game and the game of life: how making a game out of it can change student behavior. In *Proceeding of the 44th ACM technical symposium on Computer science education*, ACM Press, pp. 233-238.
13. Demonet, J., Taylor, M. and Chaix, Y., 2004. Developmental dyslexia. *Lancet*, 363, pp. 1451-1460.
14. Denny, P., 2013. The effect of virtual achievements on student engagement. In *Proceedings of the SIGCHI Conference on Human Factors in Computing Systems (CHI '13)*. ACM, New York, NY, USA, pp. 763-772.
15. Deterding, S., Dixon, D., Khaled, R., & Nacke, L., 2011. From game design elements to gamefulness: defining gamification. In *Proceedings of the 15th International Academic MindTrek Conference*, pp. 9-15. ACM.
16. Dodero, G., Gennari, R., Melonio, A., & Torello, S., 2014. Towards tangible gamified co-design at school: two studies in primary schools. In *Proceedings of the first ACM SIGCHI annual symposium on Computer-human interaction in play*, pp. 77-86. ACM.
17. Domínguez, A., Saenz-de-Navarrete, J., De-Marcos, L., Fernández-Sanz, L., Pagés, C., & Martínez-Herráiz, J. J., 2013. Gamifying learning experiences: Practical implications and outcomes. *Computers & Education*, 63, 380-392.
18. Ern, A., 2014. The use of gamification and serious games within interventions for children with autism spectrum disorder. University of Twente.
19. Filsecker, M. and Hickey, D. T., 2014. A multilevel analysis of the effects of external rewards on elementary students' motivation, engagement and learning in an educational game. *Computers & Education*, *75*, pp. 136-148.
20. Flyvbjerg, B., 2006. Five misunderstandings about case-study research. *Qualitative inquiry*, 12(2), 219-245.
21. Geertz, C., 1994. Thick description: Toward an interpretive theory of culture. *Readings in the philosophy of social science*, pp. 213-231.
22. Gooch, D., Benton, L., Khaled, R., Lukeš, D., & Vasalou, A., 2015. Creating Bridges: The Role of Exploratory Design Research in an Intelligent Tutoring System Project. *Interacting with Computers*, iwv009.
23. Hakulinen, L., Auvinen, T. and Korhonen, A., 2013. Empirical Study on the Effect of Achievement Badges in TRAKLA2 Online Learning Environment, In *Proceedings of Learning and Teaching in Computing and Engineering (LaTiCE) conference*, March 21-24, 2013, Macau, pp. 47-54.
24. Hamari, J. and Koivisto, J., 2013. Social motivations to use gamification: an empirical study of gamifying exercise, In *Proceedings of the European Conference on Information Systems*, Utrecht, The Netherlands.
25. Hamari, J., Koivisto, J. and Sarsa, H., 2014. Does Gamification Work? – A Literature Review of Empirical Studies on Gamification. In *proceedings of the 47th Hawaii International Conference on System Sciences*, Hawaii, USA.
26. Hanus, M. D. and Fox, J., 2015. Assessing the effects of gamification in the classroom: A longitudinal study on intrinsic motivation, social comparison, satisfaction, effort, and academic performance. *Computers & Education*, *80*, pp. 152-161.
27. Hecker, C. 2010. Achievements Considered Harmful? *Game Developers Conference 2010*.
28. Hidi, S., & Harackiewicz, J. M., 2000. Motivating the academically unmotivated: A critical issue for the 21st century. *Review of educational research*, *70*(2), pp. 151-179.
29. Hmelo-Silver, C. E., 2004. Problem-based learning: What and how do students learn?. *Educational psychology review*, *16*(3), pp. 235-266.
30. Landers, R. N., and Landers, A. K., 2015. An Empirical Test of the Theory of Gamified Learning The Effect of Leaderboards on Time-on-Task and Academic Performance. *Simulation & Gaming*, 45(6), pp. 769-785.

31. Livingstone, S. (2012). Critical reflections on the benefits of ICT in education. *Oxford Review of Education*, 38(1), 9-24.
32. Maehr, M. L., & Meyer, H. A., 1997. Understanding motivation and schooling: Where we've been, where we are, and where we need to go. *Educational Psychology Review*, 9(4), 371-409.
33. Mekler, E. D., Brühlmann, F., Opwis, K., & Tuch, A. N., 2013. Disassembling gamification: the effects of points and meaning on user motivation and performance. In *CHI'13 Extended Abstracts on Human Factors in Computing Systems* (pp. 1137-1142). ACM.
34. Mekler, E. D., Brühlmann, F., Opwis, K., & Tuch, A. N., 2013. Do points, levels and leaderboards harm intrinsic motivation?: an empirical analysis of common gamification elements. In *Proceedings of the First International Conference on Gameful Design, Research, and Applications* (pp. 66-73). ACM.
35. Nicholson, S., 2012. A user-centered theoretical framework for meaningful gamification. *Proceedings GLS*, 8.
36. Ormrod, J.E., 2006. Educational Psychology: Developing Learners, fifth edition. Pearson/Merrill Prentice Hall.
37. Pintrich, P. R., Marx, R. W., & Boyle, R. A., 1993. Beyond cold conceptual change: The role of motivational beliefs and classroom contextual factors in the process of conceptual change. *Review of Educational research*, 63(2), 167-199.
38. Rose, J., 2009. Identifying and Teaching Children and Young People with Dyslexia and Literacy Difficulties. Report for the Department of Children, Schools and Families.
39. Rosen, M., 1991. Coming to Terms with the Field: Understanding and Doing Organizational Ethnography. *Journal of Management Studies*, 28(1), pp. 1-24.
40. Ross, M. (2010). Case study: Math teacher uses gamification to help at-risk students succeed. Retrieved from http://www.teachthought.com/trends/a-case-study-in-gamification/
41. Ryan, R. M., & Deci, E. L., 2000. Intrinsic and extrinsic motivations: Classic definitions and new directions. *Contemporary educational psychology*, 25(1), 54-67.
42. Sætre, A. B., 2013. Mathematics on the tablet: Using mobile technology and gamification to support student learning in junior high. MSc Thesis, Universitas Osloensis, 2013.
43. Schiefele, U., Krapp, A. and Winteler, A., Interest as a predictor of academic achievement: A meta-analysis of research. In Renninger, K., Hidi, S. and Krapp, A. (Eds), 1992. The role of interest in learning and development. Hillsdale, NJ: Lawrence Erlbaum Associates.
44. Schramm, W., 1971. Notes on Case Studies of Instructional Media Projects. US Department of Health, Education and Welfare: National Institute of Education
45. Seaborn, K., & Fels, D. I., 2015. Gamification in theory and action: A survey. *International Journal of Human-Computer Studies*, *74*, pp. 14-31.
46. Snowling, M.J., Adams, J.W., Bowyer-Crane, C. and Tobin, V., 2000. Levels of literacy among juvenile offenders: the incidence of specific reading difficulties. *Criminal Behaviour and Mental Health*, 10, pp. 229-241.
47. Yin, R. K., 2014. Case study research: Design and methods. Sage publications.
48. Zisimopoulos, D. and Galanaki, E., 2009. Academic Intrinsic Motivation and Perceived Academic Competence in Greek Elementary Students with and without Learning Disabilities. *Learning Disabilities Research & Practice*, 24(1), pp. 33-43.

Local Standards for Sample Size at CHI

Kelly Caine
Clemson University
McAdams Hall
Clemson, SC 29634
caine@clemson.edu

ABSTRACT

We describe the primary ways researchers can determine the size of a sample of research participants, present the benefits and drawbacks of each of those methods, and focus on improving one method that could be useful to the CHI community: local standards. To determine local standards for sample size within the CHI community, we conducted an analysis of all manuscripts published at CHI2014. We find that sample size for manuscripts published at CHI ranges from 1 – 916,000 and the most common sample size is 12. We also find that sample size differs based on factors such as study setting and type of methodology employed. The outcome of this paper is an overview of the various ways sample size may be determined and an analysis of local standards for sample size within the CHI community. These contributions may be useful to researchers planning studies and reviewers evaluating the validity of results.

Author Keywords

Methodology; research methods; sample size; number of participants; N; evaluation; meta-HCI.

ACM Classification Keywords

H.5.m. Information interfaces and presentation (e.g., HCI): Miscellaneous. H.1.2. Information Systems: User/Machine Systems - *Human Factors*.

General Terms

Human Factors; Design; Measurement.

INTRODUCTION

The CHI community is home to researchers from a wide range of disciplines including computer science, cognitive psychology, design, social science, human factors, artificial intelligence, graphics, visualization and multi-media design. Each of these disciplines has its own research method and manuscript preparation traditions. The CHI community also maintains strong connections with industry practitioners. In industry, methods traditions are often tempered with the need for pragmatism and efficiency.

CHI'16, May 07 - 12, 2016, San Jose, CA, USA

ACM 978-1-4503-3362-7/16/05...$15.00
DOI: http://dx.doi.org/10.1145/2858036.2858498

Methodological rigor and appropriateness are key elements of the peer review process across disciplines. Within the CHI community, the instructions to reviewers about the importance of methodological validity are clear. Reviewers are asked to "assess the validity of the results" presented as a key element of any review. Indeed, the "Ensuring Results are Valid" section of the "Guide to a Successful Archival Submission" states, "reviewers often cite problems with validity as the reason to reject a submission" [1]. Therefore, understanding what constitutes a valid methodology is critical for authors who wish to have their research results accepted and published.

While there are many factors that contribute to the validity of a study such as how well the measures used represent the concepts of interest and how well the sample represents a population, the focus of this paper is on determining the sample size, which is often referred to as *N*.

The goal of the paper is to help readers understand the ways that sample size may be determined, understand the benefits and drawbacks of each method, and to create transparency about local standards for sample size within the CHI community.

Despite its importance to the validity of a study, determining the answer to the question, "how many users do I need?" is often not straightforward for researchers. For example, in an analysis of 55 empirical articles, researchers apologized for the size of their sample in 20%, indicating that even after a peer reviewed publication process, sample size questions remain [3]. There are many methods of determining the appropriate sample size for a given study, each with advantages and disadvantages (see Methods of Determining Sample Size). Reviewers often use sample size as a key determinant in determining validity of results.

Reviewers Incorrectly Use Sample Size to Reject Papers

Given the disciplinary breadth and crossover with industry practice, it is not surprising that there are so many methods for determining the appropriate sample size. It is also not surprising that reviewers often question the validity of the results reported in a manuscript based on the reported sample size, and subsequently recommend rejecting a submission based on a feeling that a "sample size is too small". This rationale, which we refer to as the *sample size fallacy,* has not been empirically studied in the CHI community (though it has been described; see [18]). However, the sample size fallacy is common in other fields, such as the medical field [5; 6]). The criticism by reviewers that a sample size is insufficient has been demonstrated to be a "cover when reviewers cannot pinpoint, or are unwilling to admit, the real reasons why they dislike a proposal" or manuscript [6]. While there are valid reasons to reject a manuscript on sample size grounds, using sample size as a reason to reject a paper when a reviewer is unable to articulate and justify their real reasons is harmful for all parties involved: the authors, the PC members, the community and even the reviewer him or herself.

Why Are We Susceptible to the Sample Size Fallacy?

One reason the sample size fallacy is common is the threshold myth [6]. The threshold myth is that there is a threshold at which a sample size becomes "enough" to be valid. In reality, while the size of a sample is relative to the value of its findings, the relationship is curvilinear rather than square wave shaped (see Figure 1). That is, there is no meaningful cut-off point at which a sample size becomes "too small", inadequate or invalid [6]. Rather, the relationship between the value of a study and the size of the sample incrementally increases with each additional participant up to an asymptote, at which point there are diminishing returns for each additional participant. Therefore, while sample size can be justifiably criticized as inadequate to determine whether there is a reliable effect at a certain level of confidence, there is no point at which a sample size can be justifiably criticized as "too small" without qualification.

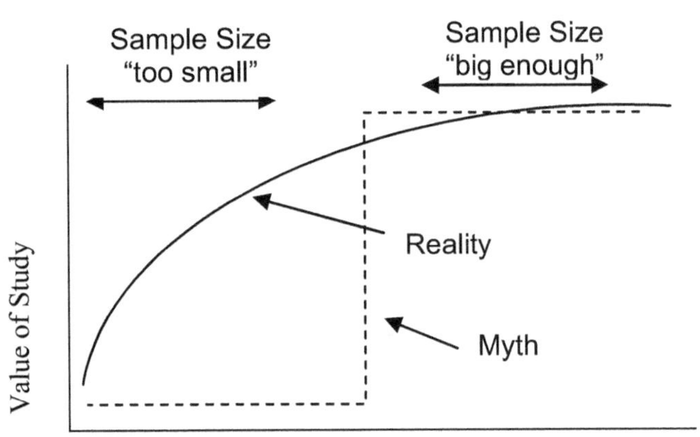

Figure 1. The Sample Size Threshold Myth (adapted from Figure 1, [6])

Despite this, for all studies that involve research participants or "users", researchers must still decide a specific point at which they will cut off or stop testing, observing or interviewing participants. Thus, researchers and reviewers need a way to assess the validity of the size of the sample for a given manuscript or proposal. How is this currently accomplished?

METHODS OF DETERMINING SAMPLE SIZE

There are many methods for determining how many participants are required for a research study including power analysis, saturation, cost or return on investment (ROI) analysis and guidelines, including local standards. We describe these methods below and discuss the limitations and criticisms of each.

Prospective Power Analysis

For quantitative studies, the formal, statistically defensible method to determine how many participants you need for a study where you will draw statistical inferences is a prospective power analysis [15]. A power analysis gives you the probability of rejecting a null hypothesis given the alternative hypothesis is true. Both post-hoc and a priori power analysis consider the type of statistical test you plan to conduct, the significance level or confidence you desire, the size of the effect you expect, the level of "noise" in your data, and the sample size (N). Because these four factors interact with one another, if you know three, you can determine the fourth. This means you can use this type of analysis to determine the sample size you need to be able to confidently and reliably detect an effect as long as you know, or can estimate, the significance level, noise level and effect size [23].

Limitations and criticisms

While power analysis is recognized as a rigorous and defensible method of determining sample size, it is not without limitations or detractors (e.g., [7]). One significant limitation for researchers, who are interested in innovative technology, is that power analysis requires existing quantitative data about the research topic. To conduct a power analysis a researcher must know the significance level, noise level and effect size in order to compute the necessary sample size. For researchers working with new technologies, as is common among the CHI community, this type of preliminary data often does not exist (though one recommendation is to use a general estimate, for example, Cohen's $d = 0.5$, $alpha = 0.05$, and $\beta = 0.85$).

Beyond this, power analysis itself is built upon statistical heuristics. For example, the values for small, medium, and large effect sizes are themselves guidelines produced by an expert, Jacob Cohen [14]. Even the "p-value" was meant by Ronald Fisher, its inventor, to be, "an informal way to judge whether evidence was significant in the old-fashioned sense: worthy of a second look" [26].

Saturation

Data saturation is the point during qualitative data collection at which no new relevant information emerges [16]. Because saturation is not known until it is reached, it is not possible to determine in advance the sample size that will be required before the amount of new information per participant tapers off

Limitations and criticisms

Saturation can be difficult to justify to both stakeholders and reviewers because 1) it cannot be predicted in advance and 2) providing evidence that saturation has been reached is difficult. Furthermore, for the researcher, saturation makes study planning difficult because a researcher does not know in advance when saturation will be reached. This can lead to recruiting too many or too few participants and difficulties coordinating data collection.

Cost and Feasibility Analysis

There are two methods to determine sample size based on resource limitations: cost and feasibility analyses.

Cost or ROI Analysis

When a researcher already knows the limit of funding they have available for research, a cost analysis can help them determine how many participants they can recruit. The simplest, least informed analysis is:

$$\frac{(total\ \$\ available\ to\ pay\ participants)}{(\$\ per\ participant)} = number\ of\ participants$$

Other study variables such as reducing the duration of the study or changing the number of conditions in an experiment, for example, can be manipulated to increase or decrease the number of participants possible.

Feasibility Analysis

Besides monetary costs, there are often other constraints a researcher is aware of as they plan a study. Constraints include: time available to complete a study, participant availability, number of participants that exist (e.g., the population of astronauts is much more limited than the population of laptop users [27]; the availability of surgeons to participate in studies is much less than nurses), number of prototypes, number of researchers available, and space.

With a feasibility analysis, a researcher can use the constraints they know to guide the number of participants they sample. For example, if a researcher only has four prototype devices, a study that takes three hours to complete, and a one-week window within which participants are available, it will not be possible to test hundreds of participants. Instead, the researcher could use these constraints to determine the maximum sample size they can feasibly test given this situation. When a feasibility analysis is used, the typical recommendation is that the researcher should report both the sample size recommended by a power analysis, for example, and the size used for the study, along with an explanation of the constraints that led to the smaller sample size.

Limitations and criticisms

While all study planning involves feasibility analysis even if researchers may not like to admit it, constraints should ideally be only a part of what helps a researcher choose a sample size. Indeed, up to a point, there is only a benefit to each additional participant in a sample size when considered and weighed against the cost and feasibility of conducting the study. Furthermore, despite their ubiquity, cost and feasibility are rarely mentioned in manuscripts reporting research results. This type of analysis is more typical in industry than academia, though some argue it should be more heavily relied upon in scientific funding decisions (e.g., [8; 17]) precisely because it considers the trade-off between cost and return on investment.

Guidelines

There are two types of guidelines for determining sample size: recommendations by experts and local standards.

Recommendations by experts

Experts are people who have worked in a field with particular success and often for a long time. Because of this experience, they are viewed as trusted sources of valuable information about a topic. For example, we conducted a literature search for information about sample size with respect to usability studies and found highly expert recommendations ranging from 4 ± 1 (for think aloud studies [25]) to 10 ± 2 [21] with others recommending a grounded procedure which starts with an estimate, observes the data collected for the estimate and then reevaluates [11]. See [10, pg. 108] for a summary of expert recommendations about sample sizes for various methods.

Limitations and criticisms of recommendations by experts

While expert recommendations are available for some methods (e.g., usability studies), it is difficult to find recommendations for other types of research methods. For example, we found very little in the way of expert sample size recommendations for surveys. Furthermore, relying expertise shares many limitations with local standards.

Local Standards

Local standards are guidelines based on similar or analogous studies that have already been published. Researchers can find out about the local standards in their organization or community by asking colleagues how many participants they have used for studies similar to the one being planned. If a researcher plans to publish his or her work, s/he can determine local norms by reviewing published papers from the venue of interest.

Limitations and criticisms of local standards

First, relying solely on prior work could lead researchers to make an *argumentum ad populum*, fallaciously concluding that simply because many others have used some sample size, it must be appropriate. Rather, researchers must realize that choosing an appropriate sample size depends on a number of factors such as the study approach, effect size and availability of participants. Second, for a researcher to be able to consult local standards, a number of conditions must be met. The researcher must be part of an organization that has other researchers or have a network of colleagues that the researcher feels comfortable querying about sample size practices. While many researchers work in a setting with these amenities, others do not and will thus have difficulty obtaining information about local standards.

The second recommendation for obtaining local standards is to consult recently published papers from the venue where a researcher plans to submit research findings for publication. However, recent summary information about sample size is not available (but see [9] for guidance), so getting this information in any other than an anecdotal way would require a great deal of individual time and effort.

Need for Study
To assist researchers with understanding local standards about sample size in the CHI community, there is a need for a systematic analysis of community-wide practices.

METHODS
We conducted a systematic literature review of all manuscripts published at CHI2014 and manually extracted data from each manuscript. We collected: the contribution type, presence or absence of a user study, sample size, number of studies per manuscript, setting, method, manuscript length, award status, student status and gender breakdown of participants. We used this data to generate summary information about typical sample size at CHI.

Manual Extraction of Category Data
We extracted methods data from each paper/note manually. First, we created a spreadsheet with one row for each manuscript. The spreadsheet contains a column for each of the following fields: title, authors, number of studies reported, method, setting, N, N_male, N_female, Age_data, Age_measure, students (yes, no), funded (yes, no), approach (qualitative, quantitative), other demographics (free text), justification (free text), and notes (free text).

Next, a research assistant used a web browser to view the CHI2014 Proceedings table of contents via the ACM Library. The research assistant then read the title and abstract of an individual manuscript to get an overview of the content. Next, the research assistant opened the pdf of the paper and sought the content required to fill in each field. The following instructions were provided:

1. Glance through the paper to get a sense of what's there; look for the "methods" section, if available.
2. Find the place in the paper that describes the methods of the study. This will vary by paper.
3. Search terms that may help you find the information you need: participants, subjects, male, female, women, men, demographics.
4. Copy and paste the information from the pdf of the paper into the correct column of the spreadsheet. Be sure to include the text you used to determine the method and the number of participants. Use the notes field to explain anything that does not fit neatly into a category.

Research assistants were instructed to use the authors' description/categorization of the work, rather than their own judgment. For example, if an author described their work as "ethnography", we counted that in the "ethnography" category, even if the author described conducting a focus group or interview as part of the ethnography. Similarly, if an author described a study as an "experiment" we counted that in the "experiment" category rather than "mixed-methods" even if data collected included a post-task survey or questionnaire. However, when authors reported their studies using a generic descriptor (e.g., "user study"), we assigned the work to the category that was the closest methodological match to the work they described. For example, if an author called a study a "user study" then went on to describe an experimental set-up with between-subjects tests, we categorized that study as "experiment".

Once the spreadsheet was complete, at least one additional researcher reviewed each entry for accuracy.

Analysis
In consultation with a professional statistician, we considered multiple analysis methods to deal with skewed data and to satisfy the constant variance assumption. We settled on the use of non-parametric tests (e.g., Mann-Whitney U, Kruskal–Wallis), where appropriate. Non-parametric tests were used to compare distributions of sample sizes among levels in categorical variables due to the right-skewness of the distribution of sample size. When the constant variance assumption was not satisfied, we used a natural log transformation of the sample size. A level of 0.05 was used for all tests of significance.

RESULTS
We present the results of our data analysis in the following sections: descriptive statistics, number of studies per manuscript, setting, approach, method, manuscript length, student status and gender breakdown.

Descriptive Statistics
In 2014, there were 465 manuscripts published at CHI [31]. This represents 13% of all manuscripts published CHI between 1994 and 2014 [24]. Of these, 423 included a study with research participants. For simplicity, we will call these *manuscripts with user studies*. The remaining 42 manuscripts were theoretical, methodological, critical, modeling or technical contributions (see Table 1).

Manuscripts	465	100%
User study	423	91%
No user study	42	9%

Table 1. Percent of manuscripts containing user studies.

Number of Studies per Manuscript
Sometimes multiple user studies were reported within one manuscript. These manuscripts came in two styles: "multiple studies" and "mixed-methods". For the purposes of analysis, we considered more than one study with *different* participants reported in a single manuscript "multiple studies" whereas studies using the *same participants* we (and in most cases the authors) labeled "mixed-methods". For example, if a manuscript reported a focus group and an interview with the same participants, we considered this a mixed-methods study. On the other hand, if a manuscript reported an interview and a focus group with different participants for each, we considered this multiple studies. We excluded author-identified pilot studies. A majority of manuscripts reported a single user study (see Table 2).

Number of Studies Reported	Manuscripts	%
Single	289	68
Multiple	134	32
2	*101*	*24*
3	*25*	*6*
4+	*8*	*2*

Table 2: Manuscripts reporting single vs. multiple studies.

Given that some manuscripts reported multiple studies, there were more user studies represented than the total number of manuscripts that reported a user study. There were 606 user studies reported at CHI2014. The mean number of studies reported per manuscript is 1.4. In most of the further analyses we use user study (N = 606), user studies that report sample size (N = 560) or user studies that report a sample size and are not extreme (N = 519; see Outlier Analysis) as the unit of analysis.

Sample Size Reporting

The vast majority of user studies included the number of participants who participated in the user study (see Table 3). However, forty-six studies were published without reporting the size of their sample. Of these, many (39%) were analyses of an existing corpus of data (e.g., blogs, twitter stream). We counted these as user studies since they reported data about users. However, most of these provided the number of data points (e.g., tweets) rather than the number of individual people who may have contributed data. A notable exception is the manuscript that reported the largest N, [19], which reported the number of twitter users, rather than tweets, which was thus counted as reporting an N. The remaining twenty-eight user studies omitted sample size. They were four ethnographies, eleven experiments, two field studies, one focus group, two observations, one participatory design, one usability test and six other user studies that did not fit into one of the defined methods categories (see Section "By Method").

User study	606	100%
Report N	560	92%
Do not report N	46	8%

Table 3. Percent of user studies that provide sample size.

Descriptive Data about Sample Size

For the 560 studies where the number of participants was reported, sample size ranged from 1 – 916,000 (see Table 4 and Figure 2).

Range	Mean	SD	Median	Mode
1 - 916,000	4,119	42,856	18	12

Table 4. Descriptive statistics of sample size at CHI2014.

The most commonly reported sample size was 12. Fifty-seven studies, a full 10% of all user studies, reported a sample size of 12. Twenty percent of studies reported a sample size of ten or less, half of studies reported a sample size of less than 18 and seventy percent of studies reported a sample size of less than 30.

Mean and median sample size differ widely indicating skewed data. A scatter plot that showed a long tail of large sample sizes (see Figure 2) confirmed this skew.

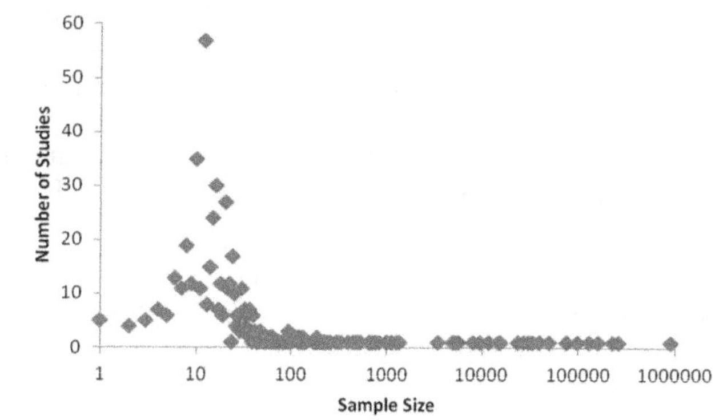

Figure 2. Scatter plot of sample size (log transformed).

Method Frequency

Manuscripts reported a variety of methods for user studies. The type of method employed in a user study was not evenly distributed; some methods (e.g., experiments) were much more frequently represented than others (e.g., diary study). The most common user study method was an experiment (41%) and the second most common was an interview (10%; see Table 5). We combined methods that did not fit within a category into an "other" category. This category included names such as, "first use study", "critical design", "user-elicitation" and "real world deployment".

Type of Method	Frequency	%
Data/corpus/log	30	5%
Diary study	4	1%
Ethnography	13	2%
Experience sampling	3	>1%
Experiment	249	41%
Eyetracking	14	2%
Field Study	32	5%
Focus Group	7	1%
Interview	60	10%
Mixed-method	28	5%
Observation	38	6%
Participatory design	34	6%
Survey/Questionnaire	8	1%
Usability test	21	3%
Other user study	65	11%
Total	606	100%

Table 5: Method Frequency

Outlier Analysis

Because data about sample size were skewed, prior to additional investigation, we conducted an outlier analysis using individual box plots for sample size by setting to identify extreme sample sizes. Based on this analysis we eliminated all cases that were more than three interquartile ranges away from the first or third quartile and the most extreme 5% that were more than 1.5 interquartile ranges away from the first or third quartile. There were 41 studies identified as outliers based on sample size by setting (in person vs. remote). We omitted these outliers from further analysis leaving 519 studies as the final dataset (see Table 6).

For in-person studies we eliminated five experiments, two eyetracking studies, one field study, one focus group, one interview, two mixed methods studies, one usability test and one "other" (14 in total).

For remote studies, we eliminated eight dataset/corpus studies, eleven experiments, one field study, one mixed-methods study, two observations, and one survey/questionnaire (24 total).

User studies that report sample size	560	100%
Included	519	93%
Excluded	41	7%

Table 6. Percent of user studies included in analysis.

Setting (In-person vs. Remote)

Seventy percent of user studies were conducted in-person, while 20% of studies were conducted remotely (e.g., interviews conducted via video chat; experiments via a website). Three percent of studies used a combination of in-person and remote methods, and four percent did not report whether the study was conducted in-person or remotely. There was a significant difference in the sample size for studies conducted in-person vs. those conducted remotely (ln(n) transformed Mann-Whitney $z=10.27$, $p < 0.001$). Studies conducted remotely had a much larger sample size than those conducted in-person (see Table 7). Because sample size varied drastically by setting, we report results for each setting (in-person vs. remote) separately.

Setting	Studies	Mean	SD	Median
In-person[1]	379	18	12	15
Remote[1]	105	197	285	77
Combo	14	15	6	15
Not reported	21	20	11	20
Total	519	54	147	16

[1]Note: ln(n) used in the analysis to compare in-person and remote sample size distributions.

Table 7: Setting (in-person vs. remote)

	In Person			Remote		
	N[1]	Mean	SD	N[1]	Mean	SD
Approach						
Qualitative	163	14	9	41	155	257
Quant.	216	20	12	64	224	300
Method*						
Data/corp	-	-	-	4	549	359
Diary	-	-	-	3	26	10
Exp. Samp.	-	-	-	3	351	562
Ethno.	5	6	4	-	-	-
Other	24	12	10	1	52	-
Usability	58	16	12	3	148	127
Interview	34	16	10	12	15	6
Part Des.	6	20	10	1	23	-
Experiment	182	20	12	31	224	272
-Within	117	17	9	8	252	278
-Between	46	26	16	16	236	325
-Mixed	15	25	13	6	188	87
Observ.	24	18	11	10	97	156
Field	14	19	16	12	89	215
Mixed	15	21	11	6	106	82
FG	5	21	7	-	-	-
ET	12	21	8	-	-	-
Survey	-	-	-	19	371	368
# of Studies						
Single	178	20	12	47	193	268
Multiple	201	16	10	58	200	301
Manuscript*						
Paper	316	18	12	92	208	299
Note	63	19	12	13	119	136
Award*						
Best	18	11	5	3	71	98
HM	62	19	11	16	191	246
None	299	18	12	86	203	297
Funding						
Funded	231	19	12	63	194	285
Not funded	148	17	11	42	201	289
Student*						
Students	81	22	15	10	51	57
Non	145	16	10	70	228	315
Gender	286			65		
Women		7	6		92	131
Men		10	6		117	183

*log(n) used in analyses to satisfy the constant variance assumption

[1] N here refers to the number of user studies; Mean and SD refer to sample size.

Table 8. Descriptive Data by Setting.

Approach: Qualitative vs. Quantitative

A qualitative approach favors data in the form of rich verbal description, while a quantitative approach favors numeric data [28]. Determining whether a study is qualitative vs. quantitative is multifaceted. Qualitative data, such as transcribed interview data, can be counted and analyzed quantitatively; in this case, the data are qualitative but the analysis is quantitative. So what then distinguishes qualitative from quantitative? Is it the type of data collected? The theoretical approach? The analysis method? We chose the following criterion: presence of statistical analysis, in part based on the work of [12]. Those studies that included a statistical analysis we categorized as "quantitative". Those that did not include statistical analysis, we categorized as "qualitative". This definition is clearly imperfect (see the limitations section for a discussion of this), but it provides a useful analog to methods of determining sample size (i.e. a power analysis is applicable only when research involves statistical analysis).

Overall, we found that 44% of studies were qualitative and 56% were quantitative. [12] reported a similar breakdown in HCI studies: 50% of studies he analyzed reported statistical tests.

For both in-person and remote studies, we found a difference in sample size between qualitative and quantitative studies ($z=-5.82$, $p<0.001$ and $z=-2.23$, $p=0.026$ respectively using Mann-Whitney two-sample test). In both cases, qualitative studies had a lower mean sample size than quantitative studies (see Table 8).

By Method

As described above (see section on method frequency), manuscripts reported a variety of methods for user studies. Some methods, for example eye-tracking studies, were all conducted in-person. On the other hand, some interview studies were remote while others were conducted in-person or as a combination of in person and remote. In addition to testing differences across methods, we also specifically tested to determine whether there were differences in sample size across type of experiment (within, between and mixed designs).

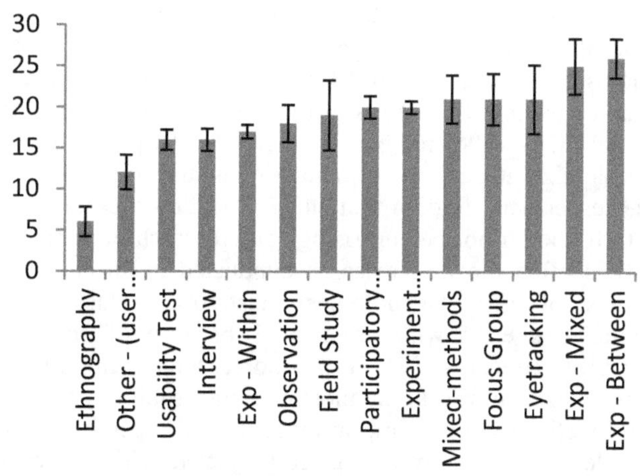

Figure 3. Mean sample size by method (SE) for in-person studies.

In-person

The sample size for in-person studies varied by the type of method (Kruskal-Wallis $X^2=33.67$, $p<0.001$; see Figure 3 and Table 8). Ethnography had the lowest mean sample size (6) while mixed methods and eye-tracking studies had the highest (21; see Table 8).

Experiment Type: For in-person studies, the sample size significantly varied by the type of experiment used (i.e., between-subjects, within-subjects, and mixed design; Kruskal-Wallis $X^2=10.57$, $p=0.005$). The average sample size for within-subjects experiments (17) was smaller than the average for between-subjects (26) or mixed designs (25).

Remote

The sample size for remote studies varied by the type of method used, Kruskal-Wallis $X^2=45.48$, $p<0.001$ (see Figure 4 and Table 8). Interviews had the lowest mean sample size (15) while dataset/corpus had the highest (549).

Experiment Type: For remote studies, sample size was similar across experiment type (between, within vs. mixed studies; Kruskal-Wallis $X^2=0.45$, $p=0.796$).

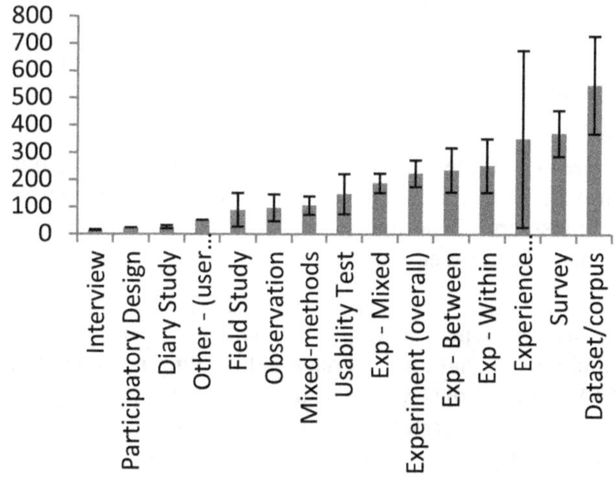

Figure 4. Mean sample size by method (SE) for remote studies.

Paper vs. Note

Manuscripts published at CHI fall into one of two length categories. Papers "must break new ground and provide complete and substantial support for its results and conclusions," whereas notes are "more focused and succinct" and are "likely to have a smaller—yet still significant—scope of contribution" [2]. Papers are at maximum ten pages, whereas notes are at maximum four.

	Single	Multi	Percent Multi-Study
Paper	233	117	33%
Note	58	15	21%

Table 9: Proportion of Manuscripts Reporting Multiple Studies by Type (Paper vs. Note)

Notes are not expected to cover the entire iterative design cycle and may instead focus on providing depth in a specific area. Therefore, we expected a difference in the percent of multiple study manuscripts to single study manuscripts in papers vs. notes. Not surprisingly, more papers than notes reported multiple studies within one manuscript (Fischer exact test: p = 0.037; see Table 9).

Furthermore, because papers must "provide substantial support for its results" while notes are expected to be "more succinct", we expected that papers would report larger Ns.

Contrary to our expectation, there was no significant difference in the sample size of studies reported in papers vs. notes for in-person studies, Mann-Whitney z=0.34, p=0.73, or for remote studies, Mann-Whitney z=-0.43, p=0.67 (see Table 8).

Single and Multiple Studies Have Similar Sample Size

As described in the section on number of studies per manuscript, sometimes multiple user studies were reported within one manuscript (see Table 9).

In-person

For in-person studies, the sample size varied by whether a study was part of a manuscript that reported multiple studies vs. those that reported a single study (z=2.77, p=0.006). Studies part of single study manuscripts reported a higher sample size (20) than those that were part of a multi-study manuscript (16; see Table 8).

Remote

For remote studies, the sample size was similar for studies that were part of a manuscript that reported multiple studies and those that reported a single study, z=0.05, p=0.956 (Mann-Whitney; see Table 8).

Funding

Research presented at CHI is funded in a variety of ways including national and international funding agencies (e.g., NSF) and by industry. We examined the acknowledgments section of manuscripts to determine whether authors noted a funding source. We expected papers that were funded to report larger sample sizes than papers that were not funded.

For both in-person and remote studies, sample size was similar for funded and unfunded studies (Mann-Whitney z=-0.839, p=0.401 and z=-0.278, p=0.781; see Table 8).

Student Participants

Almost three quarters (71%, after removing studies that failed to report an N, outlier analysis, etc.) of the user studies reported whether the participants in the study were college students. Of these, 19% of studies reported college students as the sole participants.

In-person

For in-person studies, the sample size varied by whether participants were students, Mann-Whitney z=2.49, p=0.013 (see Table 8). In-person studies with students reported a higher sample size (22) than those with non-students (16).

Remote

For remote studies, the sample size significantly differed between student and non-student studies, Mann-Whitney z=-2.15, p=0.031 (see Table 8). The average for remote studies without students was higher (228) than the average for remote studies with students (51).

Gender

Almost three quarters of studies (71%; after removing studies that failed to report an N, outliers, etc.) of the user studies reported the gender breakdown of participants.

For both in-person and remote studies, we found a difference in the number of women vs. men that participated in user studies (Wilcoxon Signed Rank S=7851, p < 0.001 and S=327, p=0.012 respectively; see Table 8). In both cases, fewer women than men participated user studies (see Table 8).

DISCUSSION

The goal of this paper is to help readers understand the ways that sample size may be determined, the benefits and drawbacks of each method, and to provide transparency about local standards within the CHI community. An understanding of community practice can complement existing methods of sample size determination.

The Range of Sample Size at CHI is Large

One key takeaway from this analysis is that the range of sample size is extremely large (from N=1 to N=916,000). This is likely due to differences in setting (in person vs. remote), approach (qualitative vs. quantitative) and method choice (e.g., experiment vs. ethnography) that reflect the diversity of the CHI community. No one sample size fits all; researchers and reviewers must take into account a huge number of factors including the research question, method, and availability of participants when determining the appropriateness of sample size for a particular study.

Small N Studies are Publishable

Another key takeaway is that studies with a "small" sample size are publishable. Indeed, seventy percent of those studies published at CHI2014 reported a sample size of less than 30. Twelve was the most common sample size across studies accounting for a full 10% of all studies. The median sample size in 2014 (18) is in line with sample size reports from 1983 – 2006 (ranging from five to 29) [9] indicating sample size at CHI has remained consistent over time. In one respect, the finding that small N studies are published at CHI should not be surprising. The research presented at CHI is often the first research conducted in an area, and studies of new technologies must often start small, "sometimes even with an n of 1 because of cost and feasibility concerns" [7]. Furthermore, studies with a small sample size can reveal the most obvious usability problems [4]. Finally, from a return on investment perspective, small sample sizes "can produce more projected scientific value per dollar spent than larger sample sizes" [7]. On the other hand, especially for quantitative work, it appears that many studies published at CHI are underpowered even to find large effects: a two condition, within-subjects study with 17 participants (the mean for in-person, within-subjects experiments), has a power of 0.49 to find a large effect.

Small N Studies, Especially, Should be Replicated

The median and mode sample size findings, the mean sample size findings for in-person studies, and the finding that many quantitative studies are underpowered, add a new facet to Greenberg and Buxton [18] and Reed and Chi's [13; 29] recommendation that the CHI community embrace replication research. If many studies presented at CHI choose sample sizes because of cost and feasibility concerns, as suggested by [7], it is critical that these studies be replicated for the scientific integrity of our field.

Student Status, Gender and Age of Participants

Despite typically being "weird" (Western, educated, industrialized, rich, and from democratic societies [20]) and unlikely to be representative of even the typical student population [30], college students are often used as a convenience sample because of their proximity to researchers. About half of studies overall and three quarters after removal of outliers, etc., reported whether students were used as participants. Of these, 28% overall and 19% after outlier removal reported using students as the sole participants. For comparison, in 2006, 57% of manuscripts reported student participants [9]. One reason the percentage of studies reporting the use of student participants may be falling is because of the increasing incidence of remote studies; the importance of proximity of students to researchers diminishes for remote studies.

Only around half of overall studies and three quarters after removal of outliers, etc., reported the gender ratio of their sample. This remained roughly unchanged since 2006 [9]. More men than women participated in user studies, though the gap appears to have decreased since 2006 [9]. Notably, similar numbers of women and men participated in remote studies, though there was a statistical difference. Similar to our speculation around student participants, it may be that the increasing availability of remote study facilities can help balance the gender of study participants.

While we did not report it in the results section due to the limited availability and nature of the data and space constraints, it is worth noting that only 58% of manuscripts reported a measure of age of participants. Mean ages were between five and 81. While it is clear that participants ranged in age from children to older adults, it was difficult to ascertain the central tendency of the age of participants.

Summary: Recommendations for Authors

Based on this analysis, we have derived a number of recommendations for authors:

1. Use methods that are appropriate to your approach and analysis strategy to determine sample size. For example, if you plan to perform statistical analyses, use a power analysis; for qualitative work use saturation.
2. *Always* report sample size and the methods used to determine sample size.
3. Include all relevant demographic information (e.g., gender, student status, age) about the sample.
4. Include supplementary information such as power analysis and effect sizes (for quantitative studies, [22]) or the saturation criterion (for qualitative studies, [16]).
5. Note any constraints with respect to sample size. If cost or feasibility concerns played a part in sample size determination, note these [8; 17]. Explain how these limitations affect the interpretation of your findings.

Using Local Standards: Caution Required

Relying on local standards in isolation to assess the validity of a sample size should not be considered "best practice". Using a local standard (from this paper, or any other source), exclusive of other considerations, may lead to a sample size determination that is inappropriate for your research question; an inappropriate sample size could jeopardize the validity of your study. Best practice for choosing a sample size depends on a number of considerations including the disciplinary traditions of your approach, the type of analysis planned, the size of a population, and the cost and feasibility of the study.

Takeaways for Reviewers

Because reviewers and PC members are subject to the sample size fallacy (e.g., [6; 15]), they should, at a minimum, be reminded of this fallacy and asked to consider the method of determining sample size (e.g., saturation, expert recommendation) when assessing the size of a sample reported in a manuscript. If the HCI field is like other fields, then the review process, and the reviews provided to potential authors, would be improved if reviewers focused on unearthing the underlying criticisms of a paper, rather than claiming small sample size as a rejection "cover" [6]. Going beyond the minimum, for quantitative studies, we recommend that the CHI community instruct authors to conduct a power analysis prior to conducting a study, and to note this practice as part of their method section. We also recommend that reviewers insist on the inclusion of a power analysis and rely on this evidence about the adequacy of the sample size.

Another consideration for reviewers is that some reported sample sizes are likely "excessive/too big" which has the potential to lead to the publication of results that are not do not have a practical impact for users, even when statistically significant (i.e., Type I error).

The Evolution of Including User Studies in CHI Papers

In addition to these findings about sample size, a number of other notable findings with respect to general publishing practices at CHI emerged from these data.

First, 91% of manuscripts from 2014 reported a user study of some kind. For comparison, from 1983 to 2006 the portion of manuscripts that included an evaluation ranged from 50% to 97% [9]. This may indicate that reviewers and the PC increasingly expect CHI papers to include a user study. However, perhaps because some portion of the CHI community is not used to including a user study, 28 user studies failed to include the size of the sample. We found it surprising that manuscripts that reported a user study were accepted and published without reporting a sample size, and suggest that any paper published at CHI that includes a user study should report the sample size.

Second, the most commonly reported type of user study is an experiment (41% of all user studies). The second most common is an interview (10%). Following these are many other methods that were less represented at CHI2014. It may be that researchers in the CHI community choose experiments most often because the research questions they are seeking to answer are best addressed through experiments. On the other hand, it could be that reviewers prefer experiments because they perceive them as more rigorous than other methods. While we cannot answer that question with these data, it is one we would be interested in exploring in the future.

Limitations

One major limitation of this study is that we only analyzed data from the proceedings of CHI for a single year, even though we know there is sample size variation across years for studies published at CHI [9]. We chose to analyze data from a single year for three reasons. First, we needed a way to limit our sample size. Previous work has sampled 358 papers [9] and 360 [32]; we used this range as a starting point, though we ended up sampling more manuscripts (465) so that we could cover an entire proceedings. For our purposes, we thought it was preferable to survey an entire proceedings, rather than randomly sampling multiple proceedings, because it provided not only an overview of sample size, but also of the CHI proceedings itself. For example, it allowed us to investigate the frequency of methods (e.g., we were surprised to learn that 41% of studies published at CHI2014 were experiments) and to compare sample size across variables such as method. Finally, for developing local standards, we thought recent data would be the most valuable.

Another limitation, although we feel a defensible, purposeful limitation, is the inclusion of only papers published at CHI. We fully acknowledge that our community is larger than the numbers represented by papers published at CHI. However, as articulated by [24], "considering the relevance of the CHI conference to the field of HCI, an analysis on the CHI articles should enable us to attain a fair overview of the field." Future work should consider papers published in venues that more fully represent the community (e.g., CSCW, UbiComp, TOCHI).

Another limitation of this study is that the data are based on self-report. That is, authors self-report the methods they use and the number of participants they study. It is possible that some of this information is inaccurate or that different communities would call methods by different names. For example, while some in the CHI community would call a study ethnography, some in the anthropology community may not. We addressed this by consistently accepting authors' own description of their methods. However, authors' descriptions were sometimes difficult to resolve within our, admittedly limited and imperfect, categorization scheme. For example, in some cases, authors called their studies "experiments", but no statistical analyses were reported. These cases led to somewhat confusing results such as studies being categorized as qualitative experiments. Furthermore, some authors did not report the size of their sample, gender breakdown, student status, etc. limiting our ability to analyze this data.

Yet another limitation of this work is that the extraction of data from papers was manual, rather than automatic. Humans are fallible and it is possible that we recorded some information incorrectly. We attempted to mitigate this threat by having two or more researchers review each set of data and agree about what was extracted.

Finally, caution is required when using local standards. For example, using solely local standards in quantitative work is considered ineffective by statisticians [14; 15]. Indeed, if the researchers who have published at CHI previously have chosen their sample size based on cost or other constraints analysis and we follow them, our sample size will be similarly constrained; local standards then may not be considered a "best practice", but rather a pragmatic norm.

Future Work

If local standards are considered by the community to be an important method of determining the number of participants for studies published at CHI, it would be beneficial to create a more systematic way of capturing sample size and related data from each paper published. This information could be requested at the time of submission or publication and published via the ACM or SIGCHI website.

CONCLUSION

The size of a sample is critical throughout the research process. At the beginning, when a researcher is choosing the size s/he wants their sample to be, determining how many participants to include is an important, yet sometimes tricky process. At the conclusion of the research process when a reviewer is evaluating the validity of claims made based on data presented, the reviewer must evaluate the sample size presented against conclusions drawn. The goal of this paper is to assist researchers and reviewers in consistently determining and evaluating sample size.

ACKNOWLEDGMENTS

We thank Peter Barnett, Emily Matthews, Keanau Ormson, Subina Saini, Kimberly Shappell, Dane Smith, Natalie Smoot, Justin Stephens, and especially Jenna Derrah for assistance with data collection, Cheng Guo, Byron Lowens Vivian Motti, Richard Pak and especially Bart Knijnenburg for their helpful comments on the manuscript. We also thank Julia Sharp and Bart Knijnenburg for assistance with data analysis. Finally, we thank Kathy Baxter, Catherine Courage, and Audrey Giourard for the inspiration for this study. This work was supported by NSF grants 1513875, 1314342, 1117860, and 1228364.

REFERENCES

1. ACM SIGCHI 2015. Guide to a Successful Paper or Note Submission.
2. ACM SIGCHI 2015. Papers Versus Notes Whats the Difference.
3. Herman Aguinis and Erika Harden. 2009. Sample size rules of thumb: evaluating three common practices. In *Statistical and methodological myths and urban legends: doctrine, verity and fable in the organizational and social sciences.* , Charles Lance and Robert Vandenberg Eds., New York, NY, 267-286.
4. William Albert and Thomas Tullis. 2013. *Measuring the user experience: collecting, analyzing, and presenting usability metrics*. Newnes.
5. Peter Bacchetti. 2002. Peer review of statistics in medical research: the other problem. *BMJ: British Medical Journal 324*, 7348, 1271.
6. Peter Bacchetti. 2010. Current sample size conventions: Flaws, harms, and alternatives. *BMC Medicine 8*, 1, 1-7. http://dx.doi.org/10.1186/1741-7015-8-17.
7. Peter Bacchetti, Steven G. Deeks, and Joseph M. McCune. 2011. Breaking Free of Sample Size Dogma to Perform Innovative Translational Research. *Science Translational Medicine 3*, 87 (2011-06-15 00:00:00), 87ps24-87ps24. http://dx.doi.org/10.1126/scitranslmed.3001628.
8. Peter Bacchetti, Charles E. McCulloch, and Mark R. Segal. 2008. Simple, Defensible Sample Sizes Based on Cost Efficiency. *Biometrics 64*, 2, 577-585. http://dx.doi.org/10.1111/j.1541-0420.2008.01004_1.x.
9. Louise Barkhuus and Jennifer A. Rode. 2007. From Mice to Men - 24 Years of Evaluation in CHI. In *Proceedings of the Proceedings of the SIGCHI Conference on Human Factors in Computing Systems* (San Jose, California, USA2007), ACM, 2180963. http://dx.doi.org/10.1145/1240624.2180963.
10. Kathy Baxter, Catherine Courage, and Kelly Caine. 2015. *Understanding Your Users: A Practical Guide to User Research Methods*. Morgan Kaufmann.
11. Simone Borsci, Robert D. Macredie, Julie Barnett, Jennifer Martin, Jasna Kuljis, and Terry Young. 2013. Reviewing and Extending the Five-User Assumption: A Grounded Procedure for Interaction Evaluation. *ACM Trans. Comput.-Hum. Interact. 20*, 5, 1-23. http://dx.doi.org/10.1145/2506210.
12. Paul Cairns. 2007. HCI... not as it should be: inferential statistics in HCI research. In *Proceedings of the 21st British HCI Group Annual Conference on People and Computers: HCI... but not as we know it-Volume 1* British Computer Society, 195-201.
13. Ed H. Chi. 2011. On the importance of Replication in HCI and Social Computing Research. In *BLOG@CACM.*
14. Jacob Cohen. 1962. The statistical power of abnormal-social psychological research: A review. *The Journal of Abnormal and Social Psychology 65*, 3, 145-153. http://dx.doi.org/http://dx.doi.org.libproxy.clemson.edu/10.1037/h0045186.
15. Paul D Ellis. 2010. *The essential guide to effect sizes: Statistical power, meta-analysis, and the interpretation of research results*. Cambridge University Press.
16. Barney G Glaser and Anselm L Strauss. 2009. *The discovery of grounded theory: Strategies for qualitative research*. Transaction Publishers.
17. Henry A Glick. 2011. Sample Size and Power for Cost-Effectiveness Analysis (Part 2). *Pharmacoeconomics 29*, 4, 287-296.
18. Saul Greenberg and Bill Buxton. 2008. Usability evaluation considered harmful (some of the time). In *Proceedings of the Proceedings of the SIGCHI Conference on Human Factors in Computing Systems* (Florence, Italy2008), ACM, 1357074, 111-120. http://dx.doi.org/10.1145/1357054.1357074.
19. Scott A. Hale. 2014. Global connectivity and multilinguals in the Twitter network. In *Proceedings of the Proceedings of the SIGCHI Conference on Human Factors in Computing Systems* (Toronto, Ontario, Canada2014), ACM, 2557203, 833-842. http://dx.doi.org/10.1145/2556288.2557203.
20. Joseph Henrich, Steven J. Heine, and Ara Norenzayan. 2010. The weirdest people in the world? *Behavioral and Brain Sciences 33*, 2-3, 61-83. http://dx.doi.org/doi:10.1017/S0140525X0999152X.
21. Wonil Hwang and Gavriel Salvendy. 2010. Number of people required for usability evaluation: the 10±2 rule. *Commun. ACM 53*, 5, 130-133. http://dx.doi.org/10.1145/1735223.1735255.
22. Maurits Kaptein and Judy Robertson. 2012. Rethinking statistical analysis methods for CHI. In *Proceedings of the SIGCHI Conference on Human Factors in Computing Systems* ACM, 1105-1114.
23. Helena Chmura Kraemer and Christine Blasey. 2015. *How many subjects?: Statistical power analysis in research*. Sage Publications.
24. Yong Liu, Jorge Goncalves, Denzil Ferreira, Bei Xiao, Simo Hosio, and Vassilis Kostakos. 2014. CHI 1994-2013: mapping two decades of intellectual progress through co-word analysis. In *Proceedings of the Proceedings of the SIGCHI Conference on Human Factors in Computing Systems* (Toronto, Ontario,

Canada2014), ACM, 2556969, 3553-3562. http://dx.doi.org/10.1145/2556288.2556969.

25. Jakob Nielsen. 1994. Estimating the number of subjects needed for a thinking aloud test. *International journal of human-computer studies 41*, 3, 385-397.

26. R Nuzzo. 2014. Statistical errors: P values, the 'gold standard'of statistical validity, are not as reliable as many scientists assume. *Nature 506*, 150, 52.

27. Robert J. Ploutz-Snyder, James Fiedler, and Alan H. Feiveson. 2014. Justifying small-n research in scientifically amazing settings: Challenging the notion that only "big-n" studies are worthwhile. *Journal of Applied Physiology*(2014-01-09 22:33:40). http://dx.doi.org/10.1152/japplphysiol.01335.2013.

28. Jenny Preece, Helen Sharp, and Yvonne Rogers. 2015. *Interaction Design-beyond human-computer interaction*. John Wiley & Sons.

29. Daniel Reed and Ed H. Chi. 2012. Online privacy; replicating research results. *Commun. ACM 55*, 10, 8-9. http://dx.doi.org/10.1145/2347736.2347739.

30. Robert Rosenthal. 1965. The volunteer subject. *Human relations 18*, 4, 389.

31. Albrecht Schmidt and Tovi Grossman. 2014. Proceedings of the SIGCHI Conference on Human Factors in Computing Systems ACM, Toronto, Ontario, Canada, 4206.

32. Wendie Wulff and Dick E Mahling. 1990. An assessment of HCI: issues and implications. *ACM SIGCHI Bulletin 22*, 1, 80-87.

A Comparative Evaluation on Online Learning Approaches using Parallel Coordinate Visualization

Bum Chul Kwon
University of Konstanz
Konstanz, Germany
bumchul.kwon@uni-konstanz.de

Bongshin Lee
Microsoft Research
Redmond, WA, United States
bongshin@microsoft.com

ABSTRACT
As visualizations are increasingly used as a storytelling medium for the general public, it becomes important to help people learn how to understand visualizations. Prior studies indicate that interactive multimedia learning environments can increase the effectiveness of learning [11]. To investigate the efficacy of the multimedia learning environments for data visualization education, we compared four online learning approaches–1) baseline (i.e., no tutorial), 2) static tutorial, 3) video tutorial, and 4) interactive tutorial–through a crowd-sourced user study. We measured participants' learning outcomes in using parallel coordinates with 18 tasks. Results show that participants with the interactive condition achieved higher scores than those with the static and baseline conditions, and reported that they had a more engaging experience than those with the static condition.

ACM Classification Keywords
H.5.m. Information Interfaces and Presentation (e.g. HCI): Miscellaneous

Author Keywords
Interactive tutorial; learning by doing; visualization literacy

INTRODUCTION
We frequently encounter the use of visualizations as a storytelling medium in news media, blog posts, and social media. In addition, people increasingly use visualizations not only for their professions but also for personal matters [5]. In response to this trend, the visualization research community has started to pay attention to non-expert users' cognitive behaviors to understand visualizations [9] and the visualization education for them [16]. For example, the community had workshops on "visualization literacy" [21, 22] and "personal visualization" [20] in recent visualization conferences. These workshops highlighted the need to find effective means for improving the visualization literacy within the larger population that produces and consumes visual data.

CHI'16, May 7–May 12, 2016, San Jose, CA, USA.

ACM 978-1-4503-3362-7/16/05$15.00
DOI: http://dx.doi.org/10.1145/2858036.2858101

Prior education research indicates that multimedia learning environments with the learning-by-doing approaches can increase the effectiveness of learning [11]. For example, a promising approach is multimedia learning in which people learn through verbal and pictorial information. Due to the limited capacity of cognitive processing, learners can only process a limited amount of information over a short period. Researchers stress the importance of learner's "active learning," which refers to learner's cognitive process to construct knowledge by reorganizing inputs from stimuli (e.g., text, image, video) instead of passively viewing materials [17].

Research results are not consistent on which multimedia methods are most effective in encouraging the active processing. While static illustrations can help learners control their learning pace, animated ones can reduce their cognitive efforts in creating mental representation [10]. The "learning-by-doing" approach (a.k.a. experiential learning) allows learners to actively engage in hands-on experience using learning materials [14]. Web-based environments for e-learning allow us to implement interactive activities that follow such approaches, and the effectiveness of multimedia forms may also depend on the education topic. Education of visualization covers from abstract concepts (e.g., how visual elements are mapped from data [18]) to problem-solving skills (e.g., how to read and manipulate visualizations for given tasks [3]). It is yet unclear which media formats yield the best learning outcome for education of data visualization.

To investigate the potential of multimedia learning for teaching novices unfamiliar data visualization, we chose Parallel Coordinates (PC) as a target visualization. PC is an effective way to visualize multidimensional data being used in a wide range of domains including finance and biology. In PC, multiple axes are drawn parallel to one another with data items represented as lines crossing axes (see Figure 1). Due to its unusual representation, it is difficult for novices to learn the meaning of patterns without explicit instruction [12], making it a good candidate to test the effectiveness of the learning-by-doing approach.

The main contribution of this work is to adapt and test the active learning theory (i.e., learning-by-doing) for educating PC. In doing so, we synthesized core concepts and tasks of PC, and translated them into learning-by-doing activities. In addition, through an empirical study using a crowdsourcing platform, we showed that the participants with interactive conditions scored higher in the assessment and felt more confident and engaged than those with the static tutorial.

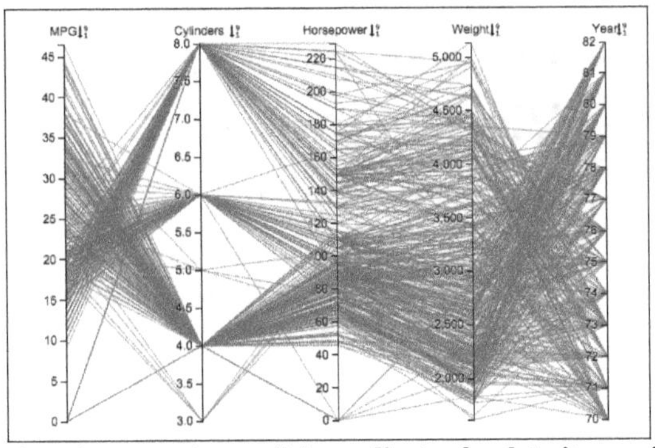

Figure 1. An example parallel coordinates for data items with five attributes (dimensions) used in the study.

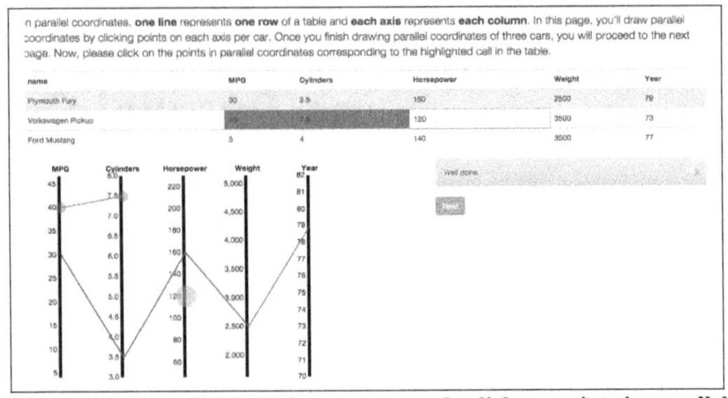

Figure 2. The Build tutorial page: as people click on points in parallel coordinates, lines are drawn connecting them.

DESIGNING INTERACTIVE TUTORIAL

In this section, we describe the design of interactive tutorial. We created three other variations based on the same content, which will be briefly explained in the Evaluation section.

Experiential Learning Model

Experiential learning model defines learning as the process in which knowledge is constructed via concrete experience and reflection on the experience [6]. This principle has been successfully used to design tutorials for education of mathematics (linear equation) [15], design [4], and music [23]. We chose to adopt this model because education of visualization requires conceptual learning as well as practice for problem-solving skills. To achieve learner's concrete experience, we follow the four-stage experiential learning model [7] to build a sequence of interactive tutorial pages each of which is designed to cover one activity type. *Concrete Experience*–in each page, people are asked to complete a mission related to the activity type. *Reflective Observation*–the system interprets learner's mistakes and provides hints at failed attempts. *Abstract Conceptualization*–the system shows the conceptual goal of the activity at a successful completion. *Active Experimentation*–after each activity, the instruction suggests to try repeating the activity to strengthen their learning. As the complexity of tasks increases, the system allows people to proceed to the next page only after they finish the current one.

Developing Tasks

The goal of the tutorial is to help people learn parallel coordinates by leveraging a "learning-by-doing" approach. We compiled a set of tasks for parallel coordinates by reviewing the visualization literature [1, 2, 13, 19]. Adapting the examples for our tutorial purpose, we created and organized 18 visualization tasks into four task categories–"Mapping" between data points and visual elements, "Distribution, Comparison, and Similarities," "Correlation and Cluster," and "Filtering and Multicriteria Evaluation" (see Table 1). We used a simple dataset about cars, having three items and five attributes. In each page, we provided both the table of data items and corresponding parallel coordinates (Figures 2).

Designing Activities

We designed the following two activities to provide concrete experience of parallel coordinates for the four task types.

Mapping Activities

The goal of **Mapping** Activities is to train people in understanding how data items are mapped to visual elements in parallel coordinates. We thus created the following four pages, asking people to read data out of visualizations as well as create visual objects based on data. 1) *Build*: We ask people to draw lines based on a data table by clicking on corresponding points in each axis; as they click on points, lines are drawn connecting them (Figure 2). 2) *Table to Vis*: We ask people to update data values in a table and then watch how the corresponding line changes; they need to change a value at least once for each axis. 3) *Fill in Table*: We ask people to enter correct data values in a table based on given parallel coordinates; they need to fill the five blanks in the table. 4) *Vis to Table*: We ask people to observe how data values in a table change as they manipulate parallel coordinates; as they move the circles for data points on an axis, the data table updates the corresponding values; they need to move lines at least five times. The series of activities strengthen people's understanding of the relation between data and visual elements by engaging in the mapping process in four different ways.

Table 1. Classification of tasks for parallel coordinate visualization.

Task Category	Visualization Tasks
Mapping between data points and visual elements	Choose a row/column in a table that corresponds to a line/axis in parallel coordinates, and vice versa; Count the number of attributes; Find the maximum/minimum value of an attribute.
Distribution, comparison and similarities	Estimate similarities between multiple lines on one/multiple attribute(s); Estimate/compare distributions of one/multiple attributes; Describe the distribution of two lines
Correlation and cluster	Find/describe the correlation between multiple attributes; Find/describe groups of lines with respect to distributions.
Filter and multicriteria evaluation	Describe values of an attribute of lines that satisfy criteria; Choose the best line that satisfies given conditions

Analytics Activities

The goal of **Analytics** Activities is to train people in accomplishing analytics tasks with parallel coordinates. We first taught how to do four different tasks–1) comparison, 2) correlation, 3) distribution, and 4) cluster–with static pages. For each task, we created a page that provides pictures and descriptions on what to look for and how to solve questions. For example, we explain how to estimate correlations between two attributes by looking at line crossings between them.

In following pages, we ask people to interact with parallel coordinates so that they could learn a set of interactions that are useful to achieve analytics tasks. 1) *Sort*: we ask people to sort attributes by clicking on the axis header; they need to arrange all attributes in an ascending order. 2) *Reorder*: we ask people to arrange the axes by dragging them to match the attribute order in a given table of data. 3) *Filter*: we ask people to apply filters by performing a marquee selection on the axis for certain criteria; they need to create filters on at least three different axes. These interaction activities improve people's skills to use visualizations for given analytics tasks.

EVALUATION

Experimental Conditions

Based on the tutorial design described above, we created four experimental conditions: 1) Baseline (i.e., no tutorial), 2) Static, 3) Video, and 4) Interactive. Supplementary materials include tutorial pages used in the study. The Baseline condition provided only a single page description about how data are mapped to visual elements in parallel coordinates. The three other conditions contained, in addition to the description, equivalent tutorial contents using different media types. The Interactive condition provided the interactive tutorial, where participants can draw parallel coordinates, enter values, and perform interactions. It also provided corrective feedback when participants failed to perform actions required to proceed to the next page. The Static condition showed instruction with screenshots taken from the Interactive condition without feedback; the Video condition provided recorded screen activities of a walk-through on the activities in the Interactive mode, so it included the same feedback. Participants could pause or replay the video as many times as they want.

For the Analytic Activities, we provided the description on what patterns to look for and which interactions can be used to solve questions in a static page in all conditions. Then, we provided instructions on how to perform each interactive feature using different media.

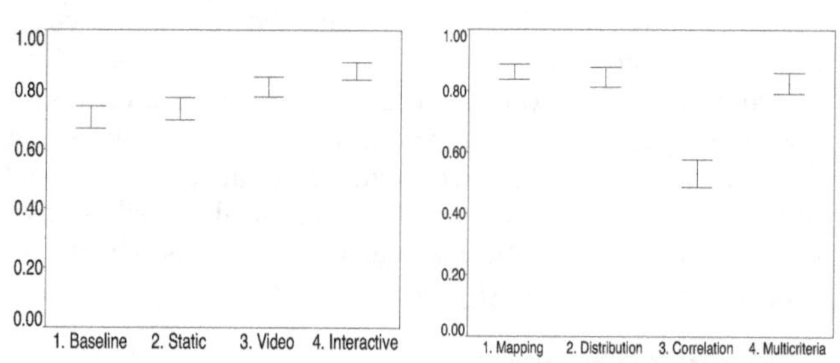

(a) Score by Condition (b) Score by Task Category

Figure 3. The 95% Confidence Interval Plots of Score per Question.

Participants and Methods

We conducted our experiment on Amazon Mechanical Turk with the following recruiting specification, i.e., Compensation: $1.50; Turker requirement: 10,000 # HITs approved, 99 HIT Approval Rate (%). We excluded people who have prior knowledge about parallel coordinates (n = 49). To remove random clickers, we filtered out participants who completed a question under three seconds for more than three times (n = 19). Among the remaining 120 participants (30 participants per condition), 75 were male (62.5%); 78 had some college degrees, 21 had some high school diplomas, and 21 had post-graduate degrees. Each participant was randomly assigned to one of the four experimental conditions. There was no significant differences on self-reported measures between conditions: age, gender, education, and understanding of graph and math. The participants' age ranged from 20 to 61 with an average age of 33.6 years old.

After the tutorial session, we asked participants to answer 18 questions that are related to analytics tasks for parallel coordinates, e.g., "What is the minimum value of Horsepower approximately?" (mapping), "Which attribute has values that are the most proportionally and widely spread?" (distribution), "Which attribute has the highest correlation with MPG?" (correlation), "Which car would you buy if you consider a car with the highest MPG and Horsepower?" (multicriteria). For each question, we provided interactive parallel coordinates (same as tutorial) with a chosen subset of car datasets (100 to 500 data points with the five attributes). We collected task time and accuracy per trial. We also surveyed six questions regarding tutorials (except for the Baseline condition) on the 5-point Likert scale: 1) Engagement, 2) Fun, 3) Interestingness, 4) Easiness of the tutorial; their 5) Confidence and 6) Understanding of parallel coordinates. Lastly, participants provided comments on tutorials.

Results

We analyzed score (i.e., accuracy) and duration (i.e., time in seconds) using an analysis of variance (ANOVA). For score, we found a significant main effect of Condition, $F(3, 2264) = 17.18$, $p < .001$. The Tukey HSD test shows that the mean score was higher in the Interactive condition (M = .86, SD = .11) than both the Static (M = .73, SD = .19) and Baseline (M = .71, SD = .19) conditions, and that the Video condition (M = .80, SD = .16) was higher than the Baseline condition (Figure 3(a)). We also found a significant main effect of Question $F(3, 2264) = 82.39$, $p < .001$. Post hoc analysis shows that the score was lower in Correlation & Cluster than the scores

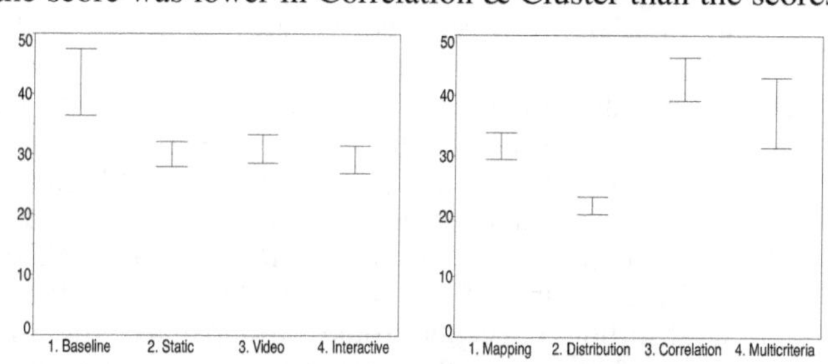

(a) Duration by Condition (b) Duration by Task Category

Figure 4. The 95% Confidence Interval Plots of Duration per Question.

in other task categories (Figure 3(b)). We did not find interaction effects between Condition and Question.

For duration, we found a significant main effect of Condition, $F(3, 2264) = 11.09$, $p < .001$. Post hoc analysis shows that the mean duration of the Baseline condition was significantly higher than the rest (Figure 4(a)). We also found a significant main effect of Question $F(3, 2264) = 24.08$, $p < .001$. Post hoc analysis shows that the mean duration of the Distribution & Comparison category ($M = 21.78$, $SD = 1.83$) was lower than those of Correlation & Cluster ($M = 42.70$, $SD = 1.83$) and Filter and Multicriteria evaluation ($M = 36.70$, $SD = 1.82$), respectively (Figure 4(b)). The mean duration of the Mapping category ($M = 31.65$, $SD = 1.48$) was lower than that of the Correlation & Cluster category.

We analyzed survey responses using a Kruskal-Wallis test, and found a significant association between condition and all survey responses: engagement level of the tutorial ($\chi^2(2, 90) = 12.81$, $p = .002$), the fun level of the tutorial ($\chi^2(2, 90) = 10.93$, $p = .004$), interestingness of the tutorial ($\chi^2(2, 90) = 16.04$, $p < .001$), easiness of the tutorial ($\chi^2(2, 90) = 24.68$, $p < .001$), participants' confidence of parallel coordinates ($\chi^2(2, 90) = 12.92$, $p = .002$), and their perceived understanding of parallel coordinates ($\chi^2(2, 90) = 10.07$, $p = .007$). Pair-wise Wilcoxon test shows that participants with the Video and Interactive tutorials felt more engaged and interested, had more fun, found it easier to follow the tutorial, understood better, and felt more confident with parallel coordinates than those with the Static tutorial.

DISCUSSION AND CONCLUSION

Reflecting upon our results, we discuss implications and future direction from our study.

Potential of Online Learning for Visualizations

Our study showed that crowdsourced non-experts could learn parallel coordinates and perform analytic tasks through 10-minute guided tutorials for learning. As the parallel coordinate is believed to be difficult for the general public to learn and understand, we are pleasantly surprised by the overall accuracy (mean score across all conditions = .77). In particular, participants with Video and Interaction conditions achieved higher scores than those with the Baseline condition, which indicate that this short tutorial can improve students' understanding of parallel coordinates.

In addition, participants generally liked the idea of the online learning tutorials for parallel coordinates regardless of their conditions. They acknowledged that learning parallel coordinates seemed difficult at first, but it turned out to be very easy and fun to follow structured guidance: "*This is how it should be taught in high school and grade school.*" (P54, Interactive); "*I took one look at the beginning and almost backed out but decided to give it a try. I am so glad I did.*" (P16, Video). However, participants of the Static condition reported difficulty in absorbing concepts. Some participants of the Static condition could not grasp the parallel coordinate visualization in the end: "*It was a bit confusing, I had trouble knowing I understood the principles*" (P36, Static).

Interactive Tutorial vs. Video Tutorial

Though we did not find statistical differences between the Interactive and Video conditions in terms of accuracy, participants with the Interactive condition performed better than the Static and Baseline conditions while those with the Video condition performed better than the Baseline condition only. Furthermore, participants feedback generally favored the Interactive condition. Some participants of the Video condition commented that they had to watch multiple times to understand the concept. : "*Some videos I had to watch a few times to grasp the idea*" (P52, Video).

Note that participants of the Interactive condition acknowledged that the tutorials were easy to follow without reporting any difficulty: "*Loved the way it was presented. Coming into this I had no experience in the subject. I found it to be very interesting and easy to follow*" (P17, Interactive). Furthermore, they enjoyed following the tutorial activities: "*I thought the tutorial was fun and interactive. I liked that I got to apply what I learned right away to ensure that I got what it was talking about*" (P77, Interactive).

Learning Core Concepts of Parallel Coordinates

Contrary to our expectation, participants achieved high overall accuracy even with Baseline. This might be because we used a simple and small dataset, which would not overwhelm lay people but would still be useful to teach the core concepts for the PC comprehension. On the other hand, they did poorly on correlation tasks. These results suggest that it is not very difficult to learn how data items are mapped to visual elements in PC, but it is not easy to understand the patterns for correlation and to interact with PC to find the appropriate view to identify those patterns. The real-world datasets would be much larger than the simple datasets we used in our study, and performing an exploratory analysis with real-world data to identify hidden insights would require more advanced skills than understanding the basic concepts of parallel coordinates. Further research is needed to design better activities potentially with more complex datasets, and to study interactive tutorials for advanced tasks such as complex decision-making tasks with large datasets.

Toward Generalizing Guided, Interactive Tutorials

Our results can be generalized to other multidimensional visualizations with unfamiliar layouts such as star coordinates. We also believe that the interactive tutorial approach can be applied to other visualization types (e.g., pixel bar chart, matrix visualization) where one data item can be mapped to graphic elements such as size or color. For example, we could create a guided, interactive tutorial for a matrix-based graph visualization based on existing graph visualization task taxonomies (e.g., [8]). Rows and columns can be coupled with a list of nodes, and each cell can be connected with a list of links. Our study results also encourage the further investigation into a systematic approach to teach visualizations by leveraging the learning-by-doing approach.

ACKNOWLEDGEMENT

We thank Sukwon Lee, Sung-Hee Kim, and Paul Johns for their valuable feedback on the draft.

REFERENCES

1. Robert Amar, James Eagan, and John Stasko. 2005. Low-level components of analytic activity in information visualization. In *IEEE Symposium on Information Visualization*. 111–117.
2. Gennady Andrienko and Natalia Andrienko. 2001. Constructing Parallel Coordinates Plot for Problem Solving. In *In Proceedings of Symposium on Smart Graphics*. 9–14.
3. Jeremy Boy, Ronald A. Rensink, Enrico Bertini, and Jean-Daniel Fekete. 2014. A Principled Way of Assessing Visualization Literacy. *IEEE Transactions on Visualization and Computer Graphics* 20, 12 (2014), 1963–1972.
4. Jonathan Hook, Thomas Hjermitslev, Ole Sejer Iversen, and Patrick Olivier. 2013. The ReflecTable: Bridging the Gap between Theory and Practice in Design Education. In *Human-Computer Interaction INTERACT 2013*, Paula Kotz, Gary Marsden, Gitte Lindgaard, Janet Wesson, and Marco Winckler (Eds.). Number 8118 in Lecture Notes in Computer Science. Springer Berlin Heidelberg, 624–641.
5. Dandan Huang, Melanie Tory, Bon Adriel Aseniero, Lyn Bartram, Scott Bateman, Sheelagh Carpendale, Anthony Tang, and Robert Woodbury. 2015. Personal Visualization and Personal Visual Analytics. *IEEE Transactions on Visualization and Computer Graphics* 21, 3 (2015), 420–433.
6. David A. Kolb. 1984. *Experiential learning: experience as the source of learning and development*. Prentice Hall, Englewood Cliffs, NJ.
7. David A. Kolb, Richard E. Boyatzis, and Charalampos Mainemelis. 2001. Experiential learning theory: Previous research and new directions. Lawrence Erlbaum Associates Publishers, Mahwah, NJ, US, 227–247.
8. Bongshin Lee, Catherine Plaisant, Cynthia Sims Parr, Jean-Daniel Fekete, and Nathalie Henry. 2006. Task taxonomy for graph visualization. In *Proceedings of the 2006 AVI workshop on BEyond time and errors: novel evaluation methods for information visualization*. ACM, 1–5.
9. Sukwon Lee, Sung-Hee Kim, Ya-Hsin Hung, Heidi Lam, Youn-ah Kang, and Ji Soo YI. 2016. How do People Make Sense of Unfamiliar Visualizations?: A Grounded Model of Novice's Information Visualization Sensemaking. *IEEE Transactions on Visualization and Computer Graphics* 22, 1 (Jan. 2016).
10. Richard E. Mayer, Mary Hegarty, Sarah Mayer, and Julie Campbell. 2005. When Static Media Promote Active Learning: Annotated Illustrations Versus Narrated Animations in Multimedia Instruction. *Journal of Experimental Psychology: Applied* 11, 4 (2005), 256–265.
11. Roxana Moreno and Richard Mayer. 2007. Interactive Multimodal Learning Environments. *Educational Psychology Review* 19, 3 (June 2007), 309–326.
12. Tamara Munzner. 2014. *Visualization Analysis and Design*. CRC Press.
13. David Peebles, Devina Ramduny-Ellis, Geoffrey Ellis, and John V. H. Bonner. 2013. The influence of graph schemas on the interpretation of unfamiliar diagrams. In *In Proceedings of the International British Computer Society Human Computer Interaction Conference: The Internet of things*.
14. Maja Pivec. 2007. Editorial: Play and learn: potentials of game-based learning. *British Journal of Educational Technology* (May 2007), 387–393.
15. Leena Razzaq and Neil T. Heffernan. 2008. Towards Designing a User-adaptive Web-based e-Learning System. In *CHI '08 Extended Abstracts on Human Factors in Computing Systems (CHI EA '08)*. ACM, New York, NY, USA, 3525–3530.
16. Holly Rushmeier, Jason Dykes, John Dill, and Peter Yoon. 2007. Revisiting the Need for Formal Education in Visualization. *IEEE Computer Graphics and Applications* 27, 6 (2007), 12–16.
17. Roger C. Schank. 1994. Active Learning Through Multimedia. *IEEE MultiMedia* 1, 1 (March 1994), 69–78.
18. Priti Shah and James Hoeffner. 2002. Review of Graph Comprehension Research: Implications for Instruction. *Educational Psychology Review* 14, 1 (2002), 47–69.
19. Harri Siirtola and Kari-Jouko Rih. 2006. Interacting with parallel coordinates. *Interacting with Computers* 18, 6 (2006), 1278–1309.
20. Personal Visualization Workshop. 2015. Personal Visualization: Exploring Data in Everyday Life, collocated with IEEE VIS 2015. (2015). `http://www.vis4me.com/personalvis15`
21. Towards Visualization Literacy Workshop. 2014a. Visualization Literacy Workshop 2014 collocated with EuroVis 2014. (2014). `http://visualizationliteracy.org/workshop`
22. Visualization Literacy Workshop. 2014b. VisLit 2014 collocated with IEEE VIS 2014. (2014). `http://visualizationliteracy.org/workshop`
23. Anna Xamb, Eva Hornecker, Paul Marshall, Sergi Jord, Chris Dobbyn, and Robin Laney. 2013. Let's Jam the Reactable: Peer Learning During Musical Improvisation with a Tabletop Tangible Interface. *ACM Trans. Comput.-Hum. Interact.* 20, 6 (Dec. 2013), 36:1–36:34.

Lock n' LoL: Group-based Limiting Assistance App to Mitigate Smartphone Distractions in Group Activities

Minsam Ko
KAIST
Daejeon, South Korea
msko@kaist.ac.kr

Seungwoo Choi
KAIST
Daejeon, South Korea
sw.choi@kaist.ac.kr

Koji Yatani
University of Tokyo
Tokyo, Japan
koji@iis-lab.org

Uichin Lee
KAIST
Daejeon, South Korea
uclee@kaist.ac.kr

ABSTRACT

Prior studies have addressed many negative aspects of mobile distractions in group activities. In this paper, we present Lock n' LoL. This is an application designed to help users focus on their group activities by allowing group members to limit their smartphone usage together. In particular, it provides synchronous social awareness of each other's limiting behavior. This synchronous social awareness can arouse feelings of connectedness among group members and can mitigate social vulnerability due to smartphone distraction (e.g., social exclusion) that often results in poor social experiences. After following an iterative prototyping process, we conducted a large-scale user study (n = 976) via real field deployment. The study results revealed how the participants used Lock n' LoL in their diverse contexts and how Lock n' LoL helped them to mitigate smartphone distractions.

ACM Classification Keywords

H.5.m. Information Interfaces and Presentation (e.g. HCI): Miscellaneous

Author Keywords

Smartphone Usage, Smartphone distraction; Group activity

INTRODUCTION

Smartphones have stretched the boundaries of social activities by allowing users to exchange instant messages and easily share daily activities [11, 12]. However, smartphones can sometimes become a distraction in group activities. For example, conversations were found to be disrupted by frequent notifications or habitual checking of online contents. According to our preliminary survey (n=87), 77% of the respondents reported that they experienced distractions caused by smartphones in group contexts. Furthermore, the majority of the participants (90%) agreed that limiting smartphone usage is necessary in order to improve group activities.

Prior studies have demonstrated that limiting smartphone use can improve the quality of group activities. For example, Misra et al. [43] found that people who had conversations without mobile devices reported higher levels of connectedness and empathetic concern than those with mobile devices. In addition, people are more likely to feel social responsibility such as sympathy or engagement in social interaction when smartphones are absent [3]. However, self-regulation of smartphone use is still difficult in many cases due to its various functionality and high accessibility [26]. These difficulties support the need for a device or app to limit smartphone use.

In this paper, we present Lock n' LoL ("locking" smartphones to "laugh out loud" together). This application helps users focus on their group activities by allowing group members to limit their smartphone use together. In particular, it provides synchronous group awareness that all members are currently limiting their smartphones during a group activity. This synchronous limiting feature is motivated by the fact that an individual's smartphone usage can influence others' behaviors. For example, it is likely that the other members are tempted to engage in their phones or they may be also distracted by the other activities [19]. For this reason, Lock n' LoL allows a group of users to temporarily lock their phones in a synchronous manner. For Lock n' LoL design, we followed an iterative prototyping process. Two working prototypes were developed and tested in field trials (n = 20, n = 28).

We studied the in-situ experience with Lock n' LoL and evaluated its effectiveness through a field deployment study that holds a campus-wide Lock n' LoL campaign at a large university in Korea. We uploaded the app to the Google Play store so that anyone could install and use Lock n' LoL for free. During the course of the 25-day study, 976 users installed Lock n' LoL and their limit duration was over 10,000 hours.

In our study, we first discovered that the degree of perceived smartphone distractions was lowered following Lock n' LoL use. Second, we uncovered detailed patterns of group-based use limiting (i.e., how, when, whom, and what) to understand how and why Lock n' LoL either mitigated or failed to mitigate smartphone distractions. Finally, we performed a regression analysis to study how use limiting behavioral characteristics (i.e., activity, social relationship, temporal usage, and location of use) were related to an individual's engagement (e.g., daily use limiting duration and frequency of a user). The results indicated that while the regularity of the limiting events was important for the limit duration, the diversity of the limiting contexts was a stronger predictor of the limit frequency. Users who frequently limited their use tended to reveal their limiting behaviors in diverse situations for diverse purposes rather than frequent trials in limited contexts.

CHI '16, May 07–12, 2016, San Jose, CA, USA

ACM 978-1-4503-3362-7/16/05...$15.00
DOI: http://dx.doi.org/10.1145/2858036.2858568

BACKGROUND AND RELATED WORK

HCI Studies on Technological Distractions

Even though the benefits of multitasking in their overall performance have been reported [9, 21, 38, 46], frequent and unpredictable interruptions can cause people to make mistakes and reduce their efficiencies [8, 29]. Individuals who more frequently switch window screens tend to feel less productive at the end of the day [40]. In addition, the amount of multitasking and interruptions is significantly related to stress [39, 41]. Moreover, multitaskers often enter into a "chain of distraction" with PC use [21] and smartphone use [26, 31].

In the HCI and UbiComp field, researchers studied the practice of technological interruptions in diverse situations [33, 48]. Mehrotra [42] measured the amount of smartphone interruptions based on the phones' content and context (e.g., information about sender and receiver). Leiva et al. [33] demonstrated that interruptions caused either by incoming phone calls or by application switching could be costly. There have been many recent studies that infer opportune moments for interruptions that can lower distraction [6, 42, 53, 56].

These studies provided an excellent foundation for understanding technological interruptions, and for designing tools that help users cope with distractions. Earlier studies on managing technological distractions primarily focused on external stimuli from the technologies (e.g., notifications). However, technological interruptions can also be caused by internal stimuli, also known as self-interruption (or internal interruptions) that Individuals interrupt themselves during ongoing work [1, 10, 22]. According to the prior studies [26, 31], smartphone distractions occur both internally (i.e., habitual usage) and externally (i.e., notifications); the internally cued usage is primarily the result of smartphone functionalities and pervasive accessibility to online content. In addition, we should consider mobile distractions in the group contexts because individuals' usage can influence others' usage [43, 49]. In this study, we considered such smartphone distraction characteristics and developed a group-based limiting assistance to help individuals primarily focus on their group activities.

Negative Effects of Problematic Smartphone Use

The use of mobile devices in interpersonal social interactions has become much more prevalent, as such devices provide valuable functions [13, 44]. However, several studies have reported that smartphone distractions interfere with daily activities [2, 16, 34]. For example, smartphone usage can distract individuals from ongoing tasks such as studying, working, and driving [2, 34]. In addition, Oulasvirta et al. [47] and Bohmer et al. [7] revealed the sources of multitasking: the user's habit of checking updates and frequent content consumption (e.g., checking emails). Furthermore, Lee et al. [31] and Shin and Dey [51] analyzed a smartphone usage log data and identified problematic usages that resulted in negative effects like distractions from daily activities.

It is especially notable that mobile device use sometimes impedes interpersonal experiences by disrupting the introspective processes that accompany in-person social interaction. This disruption prevents one from understanding the psychological states of others and thereby empathizing with them [20]. Turkle [55] revealed that mobile technologies provide multiple spatio-temporalities, which can decrease the quality of face-to-face conversations as people attend to other interests/relationships instead of those individuals who are physically co-located. Gergen [11] noted that online technologies can shift from vertical relationships that require long-term effort and commitment, to horizontal relationships that indicate an expanded network of shallow relationships. Humphreys [19] discussed Goffman's cross talk by mobile phone use in public places. Cross talk is originally referred to as a conversation in which "one member during social interaction momentarily sustains exclusive talk with someone who is not in his/her companions" [14]. This may make other members feel socially vulnerable by triggering feelings of awkwardness and exclusion. Moreover, some studies demonstrated that the mere presence of mobile devices could negatively influence in-person social interaction by interfering with closeness, connection, and the relationship quality in dyadic settings [43, 49].

As such negative effects of mobile distractions have been observed, people's concerns with problematic usage have been increasingly reported [31, 51]. Typical users want to manage their smartphone usage to deal with interferences in their daily lives [32], and Salovaara et al. [50] reported that smartphone users often unavoidably or intentionally limit their use to deal with interruptions. In addition, Shin and Dey [51] found that study participants who had normal usage patterns self-reported that sometimes they used smartphones too much and had concerns about their usage. Thus far, many studies have revealed distractions due to mobile technology use, and their negative effects on daily activities and social relationships. This study extended this research area by examining smartphone distractions in group activities, and acquiring an understanding of their limiting behaviors with our limit assistance tool.

Supports for Self-Regulation of Smartphone Usage

For regular users, managing smartphone distractions is challenging. The participants in Lundquist et al.'s work [37] agreed that they needed to limit some of their smartphone use. In addition, smartphone users have tried several coping strategies for smartphone distractions such as physical separation and setting phones in airplane mode [26]. However, the effectiveness of these strategies tended not to last long, primarily due to users lack of self-regulation [26].

Therefore, HCI studies have been conducted to find computational tools for improving self-regulation of smartphone use. For example, Lee et al. [32] addressed the need for temporary non-use tools in which people actively regulated phone use under various situations. The concept of non-use has been extensively studied with various digital media such as SNS [4] and the Internet [17]. In addition, diverse tools for improving the self-regulation of smartphone usage have been proposed [25, 26, 30, 36]. These tools provide several helpful functions, such as screen and apps locking, usage amounts monitoring, and warnings sent when the usage amounts exceed set limits. Furthermore, some of the apps use social tools to boost social learning and motivation for the smartphone usage self-regulation via comparison [26].

Earlier works primarily focused on presenting an asynchronous awareness of group members' usage behaviors (e.g., presenting members' past limiting behaviors, such as the total amount of time limiting). Asynchronous awareness can be useful for activating competition to motivate usage-limiting behaviors and boost the effects of social learning. However, the group members who shared ongoing activities needed the support of synchronous awareness in order to allow them to manage smartphone distractions together. Our work allows group members to manage usage together, and to have interactions among themselves by synchronously requesting and granting smartphone use. Furthermore, we studied user experiences with our usage-limiting assistance tool in diverse situations, and extracted practical design implications.

PRELIMINARY STUDY ON SMARTPHONE DISTRACTION IN GROUP ACTIVITIES

As a preliminary study, we conducted a survey that consisted of questions answered on a four-point Likert scale regarding how smartphones distract from group activities and what people thought about the necessity of managing smartphone usage in group activities. Following each Likert question, we asked respondents to describe the reasons for their answers in an open-ended question. The survey was posted on online forums and SNSs in Korea. A total of 87 participants responded to the survey (28 females; ages: M = 25.45, SD = 7.75). To supplement the survey, we also interviewed seven participants (two females; age: M = 23.43, SD = 11.87) about their smartphones usage and its effects on their group activities.

Results

77.01% reported that they had experienced smartphone distractions during group activities (M = 2.90, SD = 0.70). Also, 90.8% responded that smartphone usage should be limited to improve group activities (M = 3.23, SD = 0.64). Distractions were specifically found to be triggered by externally cued usages such as push notifications with sound and vibration alarms. However, despite such notification disruptions, the participants simply appeared to forget to set their phones to silent mode for group activities. Some participants argued that there were situations in which they could not set their phones on a silent mode as they are expecting immediate responses. Another type of distraction during group activities resulted from the lack of self-regulation. Other respondents noted that they unconsciously picked up their smartphones, which disrupted ongoing conversations. Here, the problem usually occurred when their usage lasted longer than they had intended. They unconsciously began to check SNSs, and quickly became preoccupied with their phones. As a result, they paid less attention to their group members with whom they were interacting. This result is linked to prior works that found that stimulating content can lead to long usage [31].

In our interview sessions, we discovered that smartphones can also be used to facilitate group activities. Most cases were related to the smartphones' abilities to provide convenient information access. Particularly, the participants acknowledged the need to use smartphones to seek information (e.g., dictionary searches and class sites checks). Some of the participants commented that they sometimes used smartphones to resolve conflicts or find answers for disputes or discussions. In addition, smartphones can enable group members to engage in other online group activities, such as sharing photos and playing mobile games.

Design Implications

Based on our study results, we drew several design implications. First, we found that group activities were often distracted by external usage cues (e.g., notification alarms) and habitual checking patterns (e.g., checking status updates or online contents). Therefore, it appeared to be necessary to design intervention mechanisms to prevent these usage behaviors in order to minimize disruptions to socializing. Second, the study participants also reported the usefulness of smartphones in their group interactions. As smartphones provide diverse functions compared to a traditional cell phones, some aspects of group activities can be extended and facilitated (e.g., taking a photo or posting events onto SNSs). Therefore, slightly different from prior studies regarding cell phone distractions [49, 43], completely limiting smartphones would not be the best solution. Intervention mechanisms for limiting usage should be flexible in order to help users determine when (not) to allow smartphone use during group activities.

DESIGN OF LOCK N' LOL

We present Lock n' LoL, a mobile app that allows users to limit their smartphone usage together and to focus on group activities. The key idea of Lock n' LoL is to foster group awareness that all members are currently limiting their smartphones during group activities. This synchronous limiting feature is inspired by the fact that an individual's usage can influence others' behaviors. For example, it is likely that the other members are tempted to engage in their phones or they may be also distracted by other activities [19].

Iterative Design Process

As part of our iterative prototyping, we performed two pilot studies. After rapidly building the first working prototype, we recruited seven undergraduate students from a large university in November 2014. We instructed them to use the app with their friends during their daily activities for a week. This snowball sampling resulted in seven groups with a total of 20 users (four females; ages: M = 21.2, SD = 1.06). We then interviewed the respondents to understand their overall user experiences with Lock n' LoL. After the interview data was analyzed, we prioritized all of the issues and improved the initial prototype. In February 2015, we conducted the second pilot study for two weeks by recruiting 28 users (12 groups; eight females; ages: M = 22.7, SD = 3.5). Similarly, we performed interviews to gather feedback for improvements.

Lock n' LoL Application Description

Figure 1 shows the final Lock n' LoL design. There are three tabs: 1) "My Info": statistics about a user's limiting behaviors and timeline of the previous limiting behaviors; 2) "Friends": a list of friends who have ever used Lock n' LoL together (also highlights co-location status); 3) "Group Limit Mode": a group's limiting room that displays all the members and their current status (e.g., locked or use). Users can activate a limiting

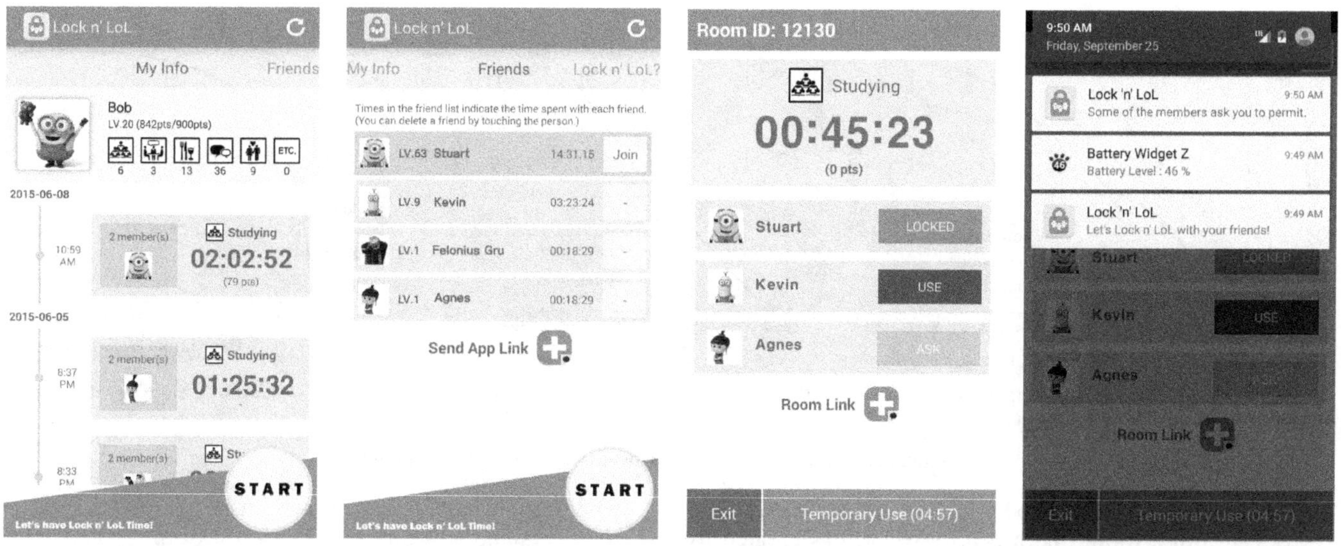

(a) My Info (b) Friends (c) Group Limit mode (d) Co-location reminder

Figure 1. User Interfaces of Lock n' LoL.

mode to lock their smartphones with others by clicking the start button at the bottom of their screens. In the following section, we explain the following three main features of Lock n' LoL: (1) *usage summary and limit behavior timeline*, (2) *group limit mode*, and (3) *co-location reminder*.

Usage Summary and Limit Behavior Timeline

Lock n' LoL records all limiting behaviors and displays them on the front page. We added this feature because people would be encouraged by being able to see their achievements retrospectively. This page allows users to track their previous limiting behaviors. In our early prototype, we had two separate pages that detailed users' statistics and group timelines. For instance, the page for statistics included the current week's total limit time, the weekly average usage time, top friends (ranked by time spent together), and top activities in which the user participated. The group timeline page displayed the user's past activities chronologically. In the second pilot study, we found that the statistics page was rarely used by the participants. Thus, these pages were merged. As a result, a quick statistics summary on a user's limiting behaviors was displayed in the upper part of the front page, and a timeline of the limiting behaviors was displayed in the bottom part.

Group Limit mode

The group limit mode is the most essential aspect of Lock n' LoL. It enables a group of users to lock their smartphones simultaneously. To start the group limit mode, users simply tap the start button. They are then asked to create a new "room" or they can join an existing room. When creating a new room, users also choose the type of group activities (i.e., studying, working, eating, chatting, and dating). After entering a room, users can view the list of group members, members' limiting status, and room information (e.g., the room ID, and the elapsed time in the room). While a user is in a room, notifications are muted to reduce distraction. However, we allow users to answer incoming calls (this call answering feature was added after the first pilot study). To enter a room, our initial design only allowed users to type a room ID. After the second pilot study, a few participants suggested sending an invitation via mobile messaging (i.e., KakaoTalk), which allows them to send invitations to existing group chat rooms.

Lock n' LoL also supports a *temporary unlimit mode*. Our first prototype required users to obtain explicit permission to switch to the temporary unlimit mode in order to prevent its abuse. However, our design iteration found that acquiring explicit permission was too burdensome for short-term usage (less than one minute). We thus revised the system to offer users free access to the unlimit mode for cumulative five minutes after they start the group limit. We determined this five minute duration because it would be sufficient for occasional smartphone use during group activities and was reasonably accepted by users in the second pilot and field tests. When the five-minute allowance is depleted, users have to explicitly obtain unlimit permission from others. This procedure was designed to prevent the temporary unlimit mode from being exploited and thus falling back into *alone together* situations. According to our second pilot study, participants advised that group activities sometimes lasted for a few hours. They requested that we automatically recharge the five-minute allowance at the beginning of each hour. This feature was incorporated in our final prototype.

Co-location Reminder

The co-location reminder notifies users when two friends continue to stay in the same place in order to encourage users to limit their smartphone use with their friends nearby. This function was included based on the pilot study results. Some participants confessed that they often simply forgot to use the Lock n' LoL app during their group activities. Lock n' LoL periodically performs Wi-Fi scans and sends the SSID list and signal strength to the server. The server then calculates the Jaccard similarity between two scan result sets (e.g., the size of the intersection divided by that of the union of the scan result sets). Two smartphones are considered "nearby" when the Jaccard similarity exceeds a threshold value. The server sends push notifications to those devices. In addition, the list

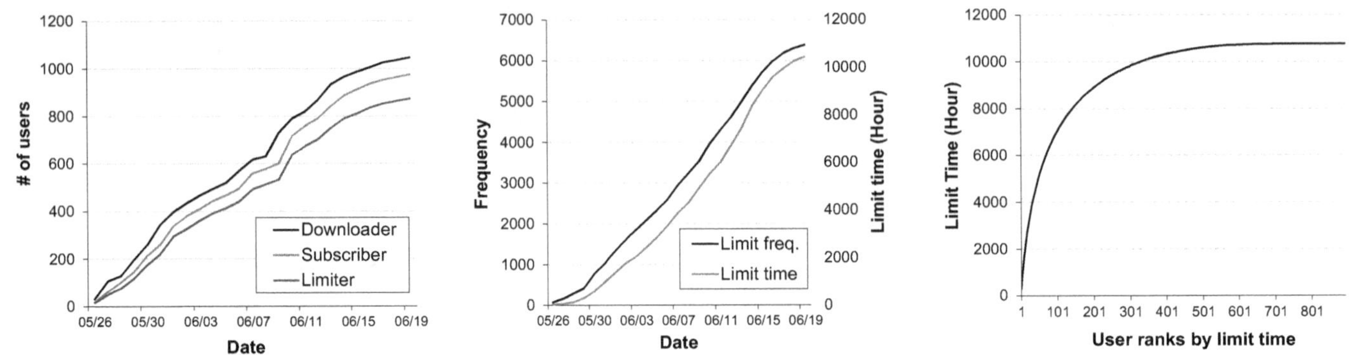

(a) # of downloaders, subscribers, and those who tried use limiting at least once

(b) Limiting time and frequency

(c) Limiting time per user

Figure 2. Statistics of Field Deployment (Cumulative distributions).

of nearby friends is highlighted in yellow in the "Friends" tab. Users can join a room that a nearby friend has created by simply tapping on his or her name.

We wanted to push notifications in a timely manner because users may simply ignore the reminder if they are notified too early prior to meeting with friends. In addition, timely reminders can reduce false-positive cases, as too many alarms can annoy users. Therefore, compared to a previous study [27] that considered co-locations when two devices shared at least one particular Wi-Fi AP, our method has a more rigorous standard based on a threshold of Jaccard similarity in order to detect two devices at distances amenable to in-person social interactions. Based on the results of informal field experiments with four smartphones in twelve places, we determined a threshold of 0.6, which likely guarantees co-location reliably within 20 meters. This is sufficient for our applications, and we used this threshold in the final prototype. After the second pilot study, we set additional rules for reminders. If the group size is large, frequent notification could be generated whenever group churning happens (e.g., whenever a co-worker comes back from a bathroom). To deal with such situations, we limit notification delivery so that only one message per location is pushed in every six hours.

LOCK N' LOL EVALUATION

This section presents our study results from a large-scale field experiment. Our experiment was designed to answer the following three questions:

- Q1. Does Lock n' LoL help mitigate individuals' smartphone distractions?
- Q2. How did people use Lock n' LoL? When and where did they use it? With whom did people use it? What activities did people want to focus on while using it?
- Q3. What aspects of use limiting behaviors are related to its engagement?

First, we studied the effectiveness of Lock n' LoL in mitigating smartphone distractions. This analysis validated whether Lock n' LoL achieved its primary design goal. Second, we aimed to understand users' detailed usage patterns and analyzed usage data by examining various aspects of usage (i.e., how, when, whom, and what). The answers to these questions can allow us to understand how and why Lock n' LoL mitigated or failed to mitigate smartphone distractions. Finally, we performed a regression analysis to study how use limiting behavioral characteristics (i.e., activity, social relationship, temporal usage, and location of use) were related to an individual's engagement (e.g., daily usage duration and frequency).

In-situ Deployment Study Setup

Campaign design

We designed a field deployment study by holding a campus-wide campaign at a large university in Korea. We promoted the slogan "Let's lock our smartphones with Lock n' LoL and laugh out louder with our friends." We chose college students as our target user group because they adopt new technologies relatively well and have dynamic usage contexts, ranging from studying to socializing. We believe that our approach to the field deployment study can help us better capture users' real app usage by minimizing experimental biases. The campaign lasted for 25 days, from May 26 (after the mid-term exams) to July 19, 2015 (the end of the semester). We uploaded the app to the Google Play store so that anyone could install and use Lock n' LoL for free. We prepared a set of campaign advertisements such as online/offline posters. To improve bootstrapping, we offered promotional giveaways. Specifically, the first 300 users who achieved Level 5 in Lock n' LoL (which requires at least 90 minutes of use limiting) were compensated with a gift voucher worth about 5 USD. In addition, those who reached Level 5 received a chance to win a prize (i.e., one digital camera, three Bluetooth speakers, and five gift vouchers worth approximately 50 USD).

Data Collection

To answer our evaluation questions, we collected the following data. First, we asked the participants to complete a pre-survey at the time of registration. This included demographic information (i.e., age, gender, and job) as well as a customized Smartphone Distraction Scale (SDS). We used five questions on daily smartphone distractions, a subscale of the Smartphone Addiction Proneness Scale [24]. We customized the original scale by including daily activities; e.g., *"My daily activity performance (i.e., working, studying, or dating) dropped due to excessive smartphone use."* The higher the SDS score, the more serious was the user's perceived smartphone distraction. Second, we collected Lock n' LoL app usage log data. The data contained a timestamped interaction history; e.g., when an activity was selected or when the group limit mode was enabled. Third, after the campaign we conducted an exit survey to understand the details of their in-situ user experiences. The survey contained several questions about usage context: e.g., the places where they usually executed Lock n' LoL, and the relationships between favorite members who frequently stayed in the group limit mode together. In addition, the SDS questionnaire was administered. Overall, 379 users completed the survey. These participants' demographic and usage characteristics did not significantly differ from those of the entire population. They were aged from 13 to 50 (M = 22.18, SD = 3.70), and 40.3% were females. The survey respondents' average limiting time per day was 89.98 minutes (SD = 130.27). Finally, we solicited short stories about how participants used Lock n' LoL, and 61 users submitted their stories via email.

Deployment Summary

Figure 2(a) illustrates the cumulative distributions of downloaders, subscribers, and those who tried use limiting at least once. The number of users continued to increase over the study period. Overall, a majority of the downloaders registered (93.1%, 976 of 1046 downloads), and most subscribed users tried use limiting with Lock n' LoL (89.6%, 873 out of 976 users). Most of the users were in their early 20s (M = 22.59, SD = 4.76). 37.3% of the users were females. This percentage reflected that fact that the study was held in a technical university in which the proportion of female students was approximately 20% at the time of writing. Most participants were either undergraduate students (52.7%) or graduate students (32.2%). While the study was primarily held at one university, there were also participants from other local universities and secondary schools. A small number of university staff and office staff also participated in the campaign. Overall, 976 users engaged in 10,365 hours of user limiting over the campaign period. Figure 2(b) represents the cumulative distribution of limiting time and frequency over the campaign period. As shown in Figure 2(c), 44.6% of the 976 users showed at least two hours of use limiting, and the mean duration of use limiting per user was noted as 91.4 minutes per day (SD = 123.81).

Distraction Analysis

We evaluated whether Lock n' LoL helped users to manage smartphone distraction. We first analyzed the distraction score differences before and after app use. Next, we analyzed the exit survey and short stories to identify the major usage themes and aspects helpful to mitigating distractions.

Distraction Score Changes

The mean SDS score was initially 3.30 (SD = 0.77). 83.4% of users had SDS scores higher than 2.0, indicating that a majority of participants suffered from smartphone distractions. After the campaign, we found a significant difference in these SDS scores ($p < .000$, Cohen's $d = .993$). The mean SDS score after the campaign was reduced to 2.36 (SD = 0.67), and 50.1% of users had SDS scores greater than 2.0.

Themes of Distraction Reduction

We investigated how Lock n' LoL helped users manage distractions by analyzing the survey data and short story submissions. We determined that the app helped users manage distractions in their primary activities and social interactions.

Distraction in a primary activity: Many of the respondents commented that Lock n' LoL helped to improve their performances in primary activities on which they needed to focus. The most prevalent activity was studying. Some of the users mentioned that their unregulated smartphone usage habits often distracted them while studying or taking classes. One respondent said, *"In a group study, I tended to use my smartphone if other members used their phones. However, after using Lock n' LoL, we all can focus better on our studying together."* (#29) Another respondent (#292) commented on the limit mode's helpfulness (locking apps). He said, *"I think I have a habit of frequently checking my smartphone. I often spent more time than I expected web browsing or messaging. Lock n' LoL's limit mode reminds me that I should focus on my work."* (#137)

There were also examples with other group activities. One office worker said, *"I am somewhat unpleasant whenever a person uses a smartphone during the meeting. Lock n' LoL helps us to concentrate on our meeting without hurting others' feelings."* (#41) In addition, one undergraduate student commented, *"Lock n' LoL use was helpful especially for concentrating on our chorus practice. We usually used smartphones when others in other sections practiced a song. However, we used Lock n' LoL and could focus on how others were doing. This helped us to facilitate our communication and perform better."* (#96)

Distraction in social interactions: The second prevalent responses were related to social interactions. We found that closer rapport [54] between group members was established after Lock n' LoL use. The respondents cited their effective states of mutual attention and positivity in the interviews. They also agreed that they were more aware of and coordinated better with others. One participant even stated, *"I like the time with Lock n' LoL because I could sense my partner's attention, and we had more eye contact."* (#7)

Most participants also agreed that they felt strong *entitativity* (perception as a social unit) [35] when using Lock n' LoL. This is a positive indication of successful collaborative smartphone self-regulation. One participant stated, *"When we use Lock n' LoL together, I often feel that we are doing something together, and this makes me feel at one with others."* (#15) Some participants felt that their main conversation topics evolved from online content to more personal matters. For example, one mentioned, *"We often watched YouTube or read online news articles together when we met, but we could talk about each other's everyday lives when using Lock n' LoL. I think this can improve our relationships."* (#3) In addition, many participants expressed that they listened better to each other during conversations because they were interrupted less. One respondent reported, *"In our conversation, expressions requesting additional information like 'what?' and 'pardon?' decreased because we focused on each other."* (#6)

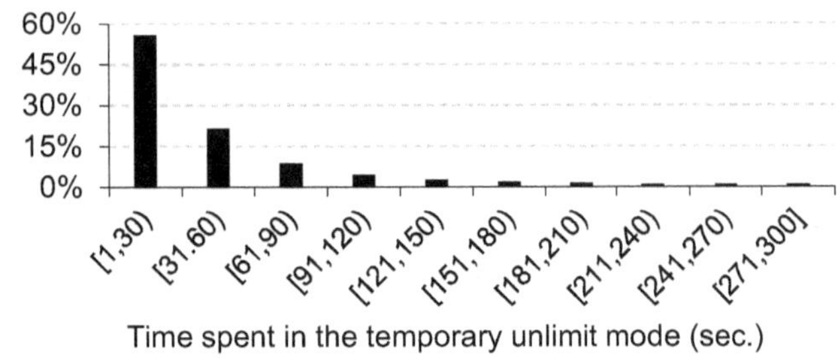

Figure 3. Distribution of time spent in the temporary unlimit mode.

Tool Support for Distraction Reduction

Our next questions focused on how Lock n' LoL helped users to manage distractions. We investigated usage of two key features: group limit mode and temporary unlimit mode

Group Limit mode: Many respondents (57.7%) cited that the group limit mode was the most helpful function. We found that the limit mode screen helped participants become aware of their smartphone usage during group activities. Most participants realized that they habitually checked their smartphones. They initially felt an urge to use the phone during the group limit mode. However, as they kept using Lock n' LoL, they were accustomed to use limiting and perceived an improvement in the quality of their group activities.

Respondents also reported that they could subdue their urge to use their phones during group activities. In particular, peer pressure was a strong factor that encouraged them to limit their usage during group activities. One respondent stated, *"I feel awkward if I use the phone alone because we agreed that we would limit phone use together at first."* (#23) Another respondent commented, *"Whenever I try to use the smartphone, I saw others' status in the group limit mode. Others seemed to be studying hard at the moment, so I decided to continue studying."* (#53) In addition, some of the respondents commented that limiting the smartphone use with others was enjoyable for them. One participant mentioned, *"My girlfriend and I enjoyed locking others' use [when they used the functions of asking/permitting to use]. This is surely a stronger method than verbal instruction like 'you should stop using the phone', but I think that it looks more natural."* (#57)

Temporary unlimit mode: The temporary unlimit mode was also deemed to be useful, with 33.5% of the respondents suggesting it was most helpful mode in Lock n' LoL. We determined that the mode sufficiently addressed the need to answer urgent emails/messages/calls and seek information. In our survey, respondents primarily used the temporary unlimit mode for checking emails (51.6%), responding to SMS and IM (19.1%), and web browsing (15.9%). The remainder of the apps used during the temporary unlimit mode included camera and game apps. Our Lock n' LoL usage log data also indicated that many participants frequently used the temporary unlimit mode. During the campaign period, 976 users had used the temporary unlimit mode 15,069 times. In addition, in 44.3% of the group limiting instances (6,383), the temporary unlimit mode was activated, and the users used it an average 2.36 times per limit instance.

We found that most users perceived five minutes for the temporary unlimit mode as a precious resource. One respondent said, *"I had a feeling that I should not waste the five minutes allowance. Once I finished the app use that I really needed to use, I immediately returned to the group limit mode."* (#120) Most respondents agreed that the five minute duration was appropriate. Our log data also supported this. Figure 3 shows the distribution of time spent in the temporary unlimit mode. In many cases, a session time for the temporary unlimit mode tended to be short, for example, less than one minute (M = 50.2 sec. SD = 63.38). Furthermore, participants made temporary unlimit requests to other members only 3.1% of the time.

Lock n' LoL Usage Context

We explored the details of Lock n' LoL's diverse usage contexts to understand users' limiting practices. We analyzed Lock n' LoL usage contexts as follows: (1) which activities the users wanted to focus on; (2) with whom they stayed in the group limit mode with; (3) when they engaged with the limit mode; and (4) where their limiting behaviors occurred.

Which Activities?

We analyzed the activities in which users reported while limiting their use. Lock n' LoL allows users to select one of the six activities, namely studying, working, eating, chatting, dating, and etc., when they started a group-limit mode. Table 1 shows the distribution of activity selection. "Studying" represented 80% of the selections. The skewness is attributed to the fact that a majority of the users were students. In the exit survey and short stories, we were able to determine that students frequently used the app in classes and group studies.

Next, we studied the activity selection diversity by using an entropy metric. For a given user u, we denote the probability of selecting an activity a as $p_{u,a}$. This probability is calculated by dividing the number of u's selections on an activity a (denoted as $C_{u,a}$) by the sum of $C_{u,a}$ for all activities. The resulting equation is shown as follows:

$$ActivityDiversity_u = \frac{-\sum_{a \in A_u} p_{u,a} \cdot \log_2 p_{u,a}}{\log_2 |A|} \quad (1)$$

Where A_u is a set of activities that user u chose, and $|A|$ represents the number of activity categories (six in our case). Intuitively, higher numbers represent greater randomness; the entropy is maximized when the user uniformly selects all the activities. As a result, most of the users showed the skewed selection of one or two activities (M = 0.19, SD = 0.22). In fact, 69.3% of the users' entropy values were less than 0.3. Interestingly, there were still a significant number of other users who selected diverse activities.

We found that the limit session time varied depending on the activity. Table 1 shows the mean limit session time per activity. A limit session for studying or working tended to be approximately 100 minutes, while a limit time for a chatting or eating activity lasted approximately 40 minutes. Interestingly, the "etc." activity revealed the longest session time. According to our exit survey, users usually selected this category for participating in club activities, watching movies, or exercising.

	Activities					
	Studying	Working	Eating	Chatting	Dating	Etc.
% of selections	80.27%	4.11%	3.51%	3.59%	3.88%	4.62%
Limit minutes per session	99.38	98.57	43.76	37.18	70.54	200.39

Table 1. Activity selection results.

	Night 00:00~05:59	Morning 06:00~11:59	Afternoon 12:00~17:59	Evening 18:00~23.59
Limit duration (hours)	2764.28	1588.81	2652.29	3426.58
Limit frequency	3,620	2,238	4,437	5,533

Table 2. Diurnal usage.

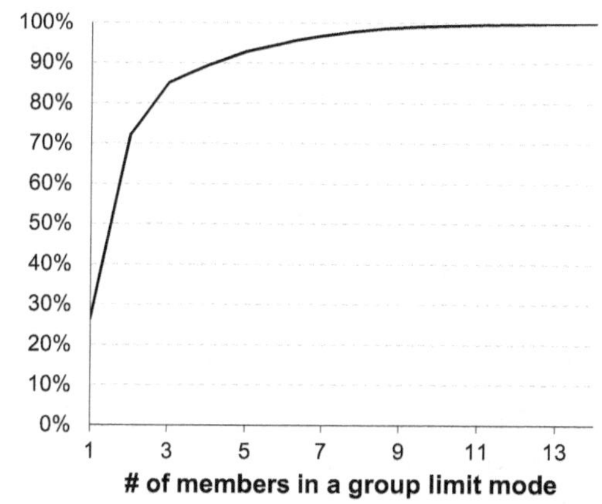

Figure 4. Cumulative distribution of the number of members per group limit mode.

With Whom?

We were curious as to how many members participated in the "group limit" mode. We first calculated the number of members in the group limit mode. Figure 4 shows the cumulative distribution. Here, we only considered the limit trials that lasted more than one minute to exclude any cases of initial trials or user errors. Overall, users preferred to limit usage with other people (alone: 26.26% *vs.* >= two members: 73.63%), which could possibly be due to how we framed the campaign. The most prevalent group size was two or three members. The frequency of group limit mode usage tended to decrease as the number of users increased.

In our exit survey, we asked the participants to identify their relationships with those with whom they frequently activated the group-limit mode through five checkboxes about representative relationships. As the results, notable relationships included friends (53.1%), couples (17.2%), club members (16.6%), co-workers (9.4%) and family members, such as siblings (3.7%). Similar to the activity selection diversity, we calculated the entropy with regard to relationship diversity. The results showed that most of the users tended to focus on one or two relationships ($M = 0.18$, $SD = 0.24$); they were likely friends, couples, and club members.

When and Where?

We analyzed diurnal and weekly usage patterns. Overall, usage amounts during the weekends were longer than those during the weeks (week: $M = 1113.2$ hours, $SD = 125.47$ *vs.* weekend: $M = 1415.52$ hours, $SD = 75.23$). In addition, usage increased during nights and evenings (18:00 – 06:00), as shown in Table 2. These temporal patterns were possibly related to the primary activities during those periods. As illustrated earlier, the primary activities included mostly studying, club activities, and working. These activities generally occurred after the participants' daily routines were completed.

We analyzed the common places for group limiting and the frequency of co-located use limiting. In the exit survey, we asked "Where did you usually limit smartphones with Lock n' LoL?" The most common places were study rooms (e.g., libraries; 42.6%) and classrooms (14.8%). Also listed were places for socializing such as cafes (15%) or restaurants (8%). The diversity of common places for group limiting tended to be skewed into one or two places (but, relatively more diverse compared with the results for activities and relationships). The average entropy value was 0.24 ($SD = 0.24$). Next, we analyzed whether the group-limit mode was activated in co-located or remote situations. Even when members are physically separated, they can still use Lock n' LoL together to focus on the same activity in different places. We analyzed WiFi-fingerprints from the Lock n' LoL usage log data. The group limit attempted was considered a colocation if at least one fingerprint overlapped between two group members. Surprisingly, the majority of group limits were performed remotely, whereas only 23.8% occurred in a co-located setting. While co-location frequency was low, our later statistical analysis indicated that co-location was a critical factor for continued service engagement.

Predictors of Engagement

We performed a regression analysis to study how use limiting behavioral characteristics (i.e., activity, social relationship, temporal usage, and location of use) were related to an individual's engagement (e.g., daily usage duration and frequency of a user). We first considered two independent variables representing limiting engagement: (1) the duration of the group limits per user/day and (2) the frequency of the group limits per user/day. We normalized the duration since the users had heterogeneous start dates. Next, the usage behavioral characteristics reported in the previous section were used as independent variables as follows:

- **Activity:** Activity selection rate (*A_StudyRate*, *A_WorkRate*, *A_EatRate*, *A_ChatRate*, *A_DatingRate*, *A_OtherActivityRate*) and activity diversity (*A_ActivityDiversity*). For the activity selection variables, we divided the number of activity selections by the total number of the limit trials.
- **Relationship:** The average number of members in the group-limit mode (*R_GroupSize*), proportions of relationships (*R_FriendRate*, *R_CoworkerRate*, *R_ClubmemberRate*, *R_FamilyRate*, *R_CoupleRate*); the diversity of relationships (*R_RelationshipDiversity*); and the proportion of co-located members for limits (*R_ColocatedRelationship*).

	Daily Limit Duration		Daily Limit Freq.	
	Beta	Sig.	Beta	Sig.
P_Gender	-	-	-.109	.021
A_StudyRate	.218	.001	.193	.002
A_OtherActivityRate	.156	.004	-	-
A_ActivityDiversity	.216	.000	.265	.000
R_ClubRate	.144	.003	-	-
R_FamilyRate	.125	.008	-	-
R_RelationshipDiversity	-	-	.175	.001
R_ColocatedRelationship	.180	.000	.103	.030
T_MorningRate	.203	.000	.115	.016
L_ClassroomRate	.161	.001	.112	.046
L_LocationDiversity	-	-	.100	.091
R^2	.203 ($p < .000$)		.195 ($p < .000$)	

Table 3. Multiple regression analysis results: Predictors of Engagement (For P_Gender, female and male are coded as zero and one, respectively).

- **Temporal usage:** The proportion of limiting time during weekdays over the entire limiting time (*T_WeekRate*) and diurnal usage proportions (*T_NightRate*, *T_MorningRate*, *T_AfternoonRate*, *T_EveningRate*).
- **Location:** The proportion of the favorite location choices in the survey (*L_StudyroomRate*, *L_ClassroomRate*, *L_CafeRate*, *L_RestaurantRate*, *L_LoungeRate*), and the location selection diversity (*L_LocationDiversity*).

A series of multiple linear regressions were conducted based on the engagement of limiting behaviors with Lock n' LoL (i.e., daily limiting time and frequency). We used the stepwise method for the variable selection. All the regression models were significant, and their R-squared values were comparable to those of earlier studies [23, 52]. We noted that our regressions models were safe from multicollinearity. The Variance Inflation Factor (VIF) for every independent variable was lower than the benchmark 10 [15, 28], which indicated multicollinearity. The highest value was 1.975. Table 3 shows the summary of our regression analysis results.

Several Lock n' LoL usage patterns significantly reflected the duration of limiting time with Lock n' LoL. First, we found that three relational usage variables (i.e., ColocatedRelationship, Family, and ClubMembers) were significantly and positively related to the limit duration. This could indicate that the participation of the members who met regularly and physically contributed to longer limiting behaviors. In addition, relationships such as family and club members were more engaging possibility due to meeting pattern regularities.

The diversity of activity selection was positively related to the duration of limiting time; users' attempts to diversify its usage scenarios positively influenced the duration. Furthermore, we found that those who more frequently limited smartphone use in the morning (06:00 – 11:59) likely revealed a longer period of overall limiting behaviors. The limit attempts in the classroom were the strongest predictors of longer limiting duration. In sum, the duration of the limiting behaviors was considerably related to repeated schedules (e.g., taking classes, club-activities) and regular offline meetings (i.e., colocation, family, and club members), possibly with diverse activities.

The frequency of limiting behaviors was also significantly Lock n' LoL usage patterns. In one regard, some usage variables, such as the use in classrooms, co-location, and morning hours, were positively correlated with the limit frequency as in the duration model. This is probably due to the high correlation between the limit frequency and the limit duration (corr. = .701, $p < .000$). Conversely, unlike with the duration, the frequency was significantly correlated with the gender variable, i.e., females tended to show more frequent limiting behaviors. More importantly, we found that diversity (i.e., activity, relationship, and location) was important for predicting the frequency of limiting behaviors. In sum, the usage patterns related to the limit frequency were similar to those of the limit duration. While the regularity of the limiting events was important to the limit duration, the diversity of the limiting contexts was a stronger limit frequency predictor. Users who frequently limit their use tended to show their limiting behaviors in diverse situations for diverse purposes rather than frequent trials in limited contexts.

DISCUSSION AND CONCLUSION

Dealing with Technology Distractions

We measured the users' active engagement in limiting behaviors with Lock n' LoL during the campaign. Our campaign results indicated that many smartphone users experienced smartphone distractions; however, they were willing to manage these distractions in their diverse situations. This aligns with the results of prior surveys regarding smartphone distractions [26, 32].

In addition to smartphone distractions, several other technological distractions exist in our lives. This phenomenon could become more serious with the advance of these ubiquitous technologies. Therefore, we believe that it will become increasingly important for designers and researchers to address these technological distractions. In particular, it would be interesting if technological distraction studies considered the different characteristics of these diverse devices (i.e., PCs, smartphones, or smartwatches). As the number of devices around users increases, it could be necessary to provide interactive tools for easily managing diverse distractions from multiple sources.

Engaging in Group-Limiting Behaviors

Our regression analysis results showed that several usage patterns were significantly related to engagement in limiting behaviors. In particular, the engagement in limiting behaviors was related to regularity such as repeated schedules (e.g., taking classes, club activities). Therefore, offering a timely reminder about regular events and meetings can be helpful for encouraging limiting behaviors and forming limiting habits. Location-aware techniques can be utilized to detect particular places in which limiting behaviors frequently occur and provide timely recommendations when users enter the location. However, the designers of such reminders would need to be careful that the reminders themselves do not distract users.

We also determined that the relationship factor was considerably important to limiting behaviors. For example, those who had regular offline meetings (i.e., co-location, family, and club members) were likely to show longer periods of limiting behaviors. In addition, we found that some users cited difficulties with enabling the group limit mode due to the strong power-distance (the extent to which the less powerful members expected that power was distributed unequally [18]). For example, an academic teacher obligated his middle school students to install Lock n' LoL, and used it to monitor/control their usage during the class. Even though the teacher's intention was good, these students might not have enjoyed the app. Another case involved a graduate student who wanted to use Lock n' LoL with his seniors or advisors. However, due to hierarchical social cultures in Korea, this kind of usage became mandatory, and they tended to feel too much pressure from seniors or advisors. Further studies should be centered on the design of effective group limiting assistance tools when power distances exist among the group members.

Supporting for Temporary Non-Use Behaviors

Our formative study indicated that many people were concerned about possibly missing important messages/functions when smartphone usage was limited. Furthermore, smartphones are sometimes necessary for group activities. Thus, it is not always effective to entirely limit their use, and it is important to balance enforcement with flexibility. In our case, for flexibility, we proposed the group limit mode that allows a user to decide to start or quit, but used peer-pressure to limit usage. Also, as the prior study suggested [26], we put significant effort into creating a design that allowed users easily decide (not) to use a smartphone based on situations rather than just simply locking the screen. We conducted an iterative design process, resulting in flexible assistance for limits according to user feedback (Ver. 1: allowing for screen checks, receipt of incoming calls, and use with other's permission; Ver. 2: temporary self-use for five minutes per limiting session; Ver. 3: temporary self-use for five minutes per hour). In our exit survey, most of the users were satisfied with this feature while some users reported that they desired a more refined control for the degree of flexibility. For example, one user wanted to be allowed to use particular apps related to productivity (e.g., dictionary/map). It would be interesting to study refined settings for limiting smartphone usage.

Furthermore, balancing enforcement with flexibility would be related with the duration of limiting behaviors. In our case, limiting behaviors occurred mostly for group activities that typically tended not to last a long time (67.8% lasted less than 90 minutes). In prior work about email disruption [21], the participants were asked to mute their email notifications for a week. In this case, their concerns and inconvenience would be relatively more serious thna ours; their study results showed that the participants tended to turn on the notification setting again after the limiting experiment. Therefore, the duration of targeted limiting behaviors should be considered in designing limiting assistance tools.

Regarding this, we extended discussions in conventional non-usage studies [5, 17] that primarily focused on identifying users who decided to stop using the technology and on understanding their motives. We addressed the needs of understanding the "users" who opted to become "non-users" depending on the situation. Earlier technology non-usage smartphone users tended to still remain "users," even though they demonstrated limiting behaviors in particular contexts. Therefore, to better understand the practice of smartphone non-usage, it may be helpful to consider both when users need to use the technology and when they want to limit the usage.

Limitations and Future Work

The generalizability of our work could be limited because it was carried out at a single site in Korea. Hence, additional research in various sociocultural backgrounds is required. However, we believe that Lock n' LoL is not limited to Korea and can work well in other nations. For example, a prior study showed that maintaining smartphone self-regulation is challenging among Korean college students [26], and we note that usage limiting behaviors are also observed in other nations as well (e.g., PhoneStack [45]). There are also other studies performed in different nations, showing that limiting smartphone use can improve the quality of social interaction such as closeness and connection [43, 49].

In addition, our study results should be carefully understood because most of the participants were college students even though we found that Lock n' LoL tends to work well with some other groups such as couples, families, and co-workers. Further studies should certainly be conducted with differently targeted users to confirm whether Lock n' LoL works well in other group settings. For example, we found that Lock n' LoL may need some improvements for particular groups. As we discussed, some user groups, such as teacher-middle school student or boss-worker mentioned their difficulty of enabling the group limit mode due to the power-distance. Also, it would be interesting if group specific study performed such as limiting smartphone usage among couples. For example, we found that either of a couple in our study usually plays a role of initiating the group limit by sending verbal requests via instant messaging. Also, some couples mentioned that the group limit in separated places at midnight makes them relieved because they felt that a partner focuses on one another.

Finally, it would be interesting to analyze how the participants' overall smartphone usage has changed through Lock n' LoL use. For analyzing overall usage, it is required to install logging software to participants' smartphone. In this study, we decided to exclude this to minimize experimental bias due to privacy concerns from usage logging. However, further study with overall usage data can more reveal how the participants limit and use their smarpthones in their daily lives.

ACKNOWLEDGEMENTS

This work was partly supported by Institute for Information & communications Technology Promotion (IITP) grant funded by the Korea government (MSIP) (No.10041313, UX-oriented Mobile SW Platform), Basic Science Research Program through the National Research Foundation of Korea (NRF) funded by the Korea government (MSIP) (No. NRF-2015R1D1A1A01059497), and Microsoft Azure Research Award. The corresponding author of this work is Uichin Lee.

REFERENCES

1. Rachel F. Adler and Raquel Bendunan-Fich. 2013. Self-Interruptions in Discretionary Multitasking. *Computers in Human Behavior* 29, 4 (2013), 1441–1449. DOI:http://dx.doi.org/10.1016/j.chb.2013.01.040
2. Morgan G. Ames. 2013. Managing Mobile Multitasking: The Culture of iPhones on Stanford Campus. In *Proceedings of the 2013 Conference on Computer Supported Cooperative Work (CSCW '13)*. ACM, New York, NY, USA, 1487–1498. DOI: http://dx.doi.org/10.1145/2441776.2441945
3. Omotayo Banjo, Yifeng Hu, and Shyam Sundar. 2006. Cell Phone Usage and Social Interaction with Proximate Others:Ringing in a Theoretical Model. In *ICA*.
4. Eric P.S. Baumer, Phil Adams, Vera D. Khovanskaya, Tony C. Liao, Madeline E. Smith, Victoria Schwanda Sosik, and Kaiton Williams. 2013. Limiting, Leaving, and (Re)Lapsing: An Exploration of Facebook Non-use Practices and Experiences. In *Proceedings of the SIGCHI Conference on Human Factors in Computing Systems (CHI '13)*. ACM, New York, NY, USA, 3257–3266. DOI: http://dx.doi.org/10.1145/2470654.2466446
5. Eric P.S. Baumer, Morgan G. Ames, Jed R. Brubaker, Jenna Burrell, and Paul Dourish. 2014. Refusing, Limiting, Departing: Why We Should Study Technology Non-use. In *CHI '14 Extended Abstracts on Human Factors in Computing Systems (CHI EA '14)*. ACM, New York, NY, USA, 65–68. DOI: http://dx.doi.org/10.1145/2559206.2559224
6. Raquel Benbunan-Fich, Rachel F. Adler, and Tamilla Mavlanova. 2011. Measuring Multitasking Behavior with Activity-based Metrics. *ACM Trans. Comput.-Hum. Interact.* 18, 2, Article 7 (July 2011), 22 pages. DOI: http://dx.doi.org/10.1145/1970378.1970381
7. Matthias Böhmer, Brent Hecht, Johannes Schöning, Antonio Krüger, and Gernot Bauer. 2011. Falling Asleep with Angry Birds, Facebook and Kindle: A Large Scale Study on Mobile Application Usage. In *Proceedings of the 13th International Conference on Human Computer Interaction with Mobile Devices and Services (MobileHCI '11)*. ACM, New York, NY, USA, 47–56. DOI:http://dx.doi.org/10.1145/2037373.2037383
8. Sheldon Cohen. 1980. Aftereffects of Stress on Human Performance and Social Behavior: A Review of Research and Theory. *Psychological Bulletin* 88, 1 (1980), 82–108.
9. Mary Czerwinski, Eric Horvitz, and Susan Wilhite. 2004. A Diary Study of Task Switching and Interruptions. In *Proceedings of the SIGCHI Conference on Human Factors in Computing Systems (CHI '04)*. ACM, New York, NY, USA, 175–182. DOI: http://dx.doi.org/10.1145/985692.985715
10. Laura Dabbish, Gloria Mark, and Víctor M. González. 2011. Why Do I Keep Interrupting Myself?: Environment, Habit and Self-interruption. In *Proceedings of the SIGCHI Conference on Human Factors in Computing Systems (CHI '11)*. ACM, New York, NY, USA, 3127–3130. DOI: http://dx.doi.org/10.1145/1978942.1979405
11. Kenneth J. Gergen. 2002. Perpetual Contact. Cambridge University Press, New York, NY, USA, Chapter The Challenge of Absent Presence, 227–241. http://dl.acm.org/citation.cfm?id=644547.644562
12. Hans Geser. 2004. Towards a Sociology of the Mobile Phone. http://socio.ch/mobile/t_geser1.pdf, *Sociology in Switzerland: Sociology of the Mobile Phone* (2004), 1–47.
13. Hans Geser. 2006. Is the cell phone undermining the social order?: Understanding mobile technology from a sociological perspective. *Knowledge, Technology & Policy* 19, 1 (2006), 8–18.
14. Erving Goffman. 1963. *Behavior in Public Places: Notes on the Social Organization of Gatherings*. Free Press of Glencoe.
15. Joseph F. Hair Jr., William C. Black, Barry J. Badin, and Rolph E. Anderson. 2009. *Multivariate Data Analysis* (7 ed.). Prentice Hall.
16. Ellie Harmon and Melissa Mazmanian. 2013. Stories of the Smartphone in Everyday Discourse: Conflict, Tension & Instability. In *Proceedings of the SIGCHI Conference on Human Factors in Computing Systems (CHI '13)*. ACM, New York, NY, USA, 1051–1060. DOI: http://dx.doi.org/10.1145/2470654.2466134
17. Ellen J. Helsper and Bianca C. Reisdorf. 2013. A Quantitative Examination of Explanations for Reasons for Internet Nonuse. *Cyberpsychology, Behavior, and Social Networking* 16, 2 (2013), 94–99.
18. Geert Hofstede. 1984. The Cultural Relativity of the Quality of Life Concept. *The Academy of Management Review* 9, 3 (1984), 389–398.
19. Lee Humphreys. 2005. Cellphones in Public: Social Interactions in a Wireless Era. *New Media and Society* 7 (2005), 810–833. Issue 6.
20. Mary H. Immordino-Yanga, Andrea McColla, Hanna Damasioa, and Antonio Damasioa. 2009. Neural Correlates of Admiration and Compassion. *National Academy of Sciences of the United States of America* 106 (2009), 1–6. Issue 19.
21. Shamsi T. Iqbal and Eric Horvitz. 2007. Disruption and Recovery of Computing Tasks: Field Study, Analysis, and Directions. In *Proceedings of the SIGCHI Conference on Human Factors in Computing Systems (CHI '07)*. ACM, New York, NY, USA, 677–686. DOI: http://dx.doi.org/10.1145/1240624.1240730
22. Jing Jin and Laura A. Dabbish. 2009. Self-interruption on the Computer: A Typology of Discretionary Task Interleaving. In *Proceedings of the SIGCHI Conference on Human Factors in Computing Systems (CHI '09)*. ACM, New York, NY, USA, 1799–1808. DOI: http://dx.doi.org/10.1145/1518701.1518979

23. Adam N. Joinson. 2008. Looking at, Looking Up or Keeping Up with People?: Motives and Use of Facebook. In *Proceedings of the SIGCHI Conference on Human Factors in Computing Systems (CHI '08)*. ACM, New York, NY, USA, 1027–1036. DOI: http://dx.doi.org/10.1145/1357054.1357213

24. Dongil Kim, Yunhee Lee, Juyoung Lee, JeeEun K. Nam, and Yeoju Chung. 2014. Development of Korean Smartphone Addiction Proneness Scale for Youth. *PLoS ONE* 9, 5 (2014).

25. Minsam Ko, Seungwoo Choi, Subin Yang, Joonwon Lee, and Uichin Lee. 2015a. FamiLync: Facilitating Participatory Parental Mediation of Adolescents' Smartphone Use. In *Proceedings of the 2015 ACM International Joint Conference on Pervasive and Ubiquitous Computing (UbiComp '15)*. ACM, New York, NY, USA, 867–878. DOI: http://dx.doi.org/10.1145/2750858.2804283

26. Minsam Ko, Subin Yang, Joonwon Lee, Christian Heizmann, Jinyoung Jeong, Uichin Lee, Daehee Shin, Koji Yatani, Junehwa Song, and Kyong-Mee Chung. 2015b. NUGU: A Group-based Intervention App for Improving Self-Regulation of Limiting Smartphone Use. In *Proceedings of the 18th ACM Conference on Computer Supported Cooperative Work and Social Computing (CSCW '15)*. ACM, New York, NY, USA, 1235–1245. DOI:http://dx.doi.org/10.1145/2675133.2675244

27. John Krumm and Ken Hinckley. 2004. Proceedings of the Sixth International Conference on Ubiquitous Computing. In *UbiComp '04*.

28. Michael Kutner, Christopher Nachtsheim, John Neter, and William Li. 1989. *Applied Linear Regression Models*. Irwin, Homewood.

29. Kara A. Latorella. 1996. Investigating Interruptions: An Example from the Flightdeck. In *Proceedings of the Human Factors and Ergonomics Society Annual Meeting*, Vol. 40. 249–253.

30. Heyoung Lee, Heejune Ahn, Samwook Choi, and Wanbok Choi. 2014a. The SAMS: Smartphone Addiction Management System and Verification. *Journal of Medical Systems* 38, 1 (2014).

31. Uichin Lee, Joonwon Lee, Minsam Ko, Changhun Lee, Yuhwan Kim, Subin Yang, Koji Yatani, Gahgene Gweon, Kyong-Mee Chung, and Junehwa Song. 2014b. Hooked on Smartphones: An Exploratory Study on Smartphone Overuse Among College Students. In *Proceedings of the SIGCHI Conference on Human Factors in Computing Systems (CHI '14)*. ACM, New York, NY, USA, 2327–2336. DOI: http://dx.doi.org/10.1145/2556288.2557366

32. Uichin Lee, Subin Yang, Minsam Ko, and Joonwon Lee. 2014c. Supporting Temporary Non-Use of Smartphones. In *Refusing, Limitng, Departing: Why We Should Study Technology Non-Use (CHI '14 Workshop)*.

33. Luis Leiva, Matthias Böhmer, Sven Gehring, and Antonio Krüger. 2012. Back to the App: The Costs of Mobile Application Interruptions. In *Proceedings of the 14th International Conference on Human-computer Interaction with Mobile Devices and Services (MobileHCI '12)*. ACM, New York, NY, USA, 291–294. DOI:http://dx.doi.org/10.1145/2371574.2371617

34. Laura E. Levine, Bradley M. Waite, and Laura L. Bowman. 2012. Mobile Media Use, Multitasking and Distractibility. *International Journal of Cyber Behavior, Psychology and Learning* 2, 3 (2012), 15–29.

35. Brian Lickel, David L. Hamilton, Grazyna Wieczorkowska, Amy Lewis, Steven J. Sherman, and A. Neville Uhles. 2000. Varieties of Groups and the Perception of Group Entitativity. *Journal of Personality and Social Psychology* 78, 2 (2000), 223–246.

36. Markus Löchtefeld, Matthias Böhmer, and Lyubomir Ganev. 2013. AppDetox: Helping Users with Mobile App Addiction. In *Proceedings of the 12th International Conference on Mobile and Ubiquitous Multimedia (MUM '13)*. ACM, New York, NY, USA, Article 43, 2 pages. DOI:http://dx.doi.org/10.1145/2541831.2541870

37. Arlene R. Lundquist, Emily J. Lefebvre, and Sara J. Garramone. 2014. Smartphones: Fulfilling the Need for Immediacy in Everyday Life, but at What Cost? . *International Journal of Humanities and Social Science* 4, 2 (2014).

38. Gloria Mark, Victor M. Gonzalez, and Justin Harris. 2005. No Task Left Behind?: Examining the Nature of Fragmented Work. In *Proceedings of the SIGCHI Conference on Human Factors in Computing Systems (CHI '05)*. ACM, New York, NY, USA, 321–330. DOI: http://dx.doi.org/10.1145/1054972.1055017

39. Gloria Mark, Daniela Gudith, and Ulrich Klocke. 2008. The Cost of Interrupted Work: More Speed and Stress. In *Proceedings of the SIGCHI Conference on Human Factors in Computing Systems (CHI '08)*. ACM, New York, NY, USA, 107–110. DOI: http://dx.doi.org/10.1145/1357054.1357072

40. Gloria Mark, Shamsi Iqbal, Mary Czerwinski, and Paul Johns. 2015. Focused, Aroused, but So Distractible: Temporal Perspectives on Multitasking and Communications. In *Proceedings of the 18th ACM Conference on Computer Supported Cooperative Work and Social Computing (CSCW '15)*. ACM, New York, NY, USA, 903–916. DOI: http://dx.doi.org/10.1145/2675133.2675221

41. Gloria Mark, Yiran Wang, and Melissa Niiya. 2014. Stress and Multitasking in Everyday College Life: An Empirical Study of Online Activity. In *Proceedings of the SIGCHI Conference on Human Factors in Computing Systems (CHI '14)*. ACM, New York, NY, USA, 41–50. DOI:http://dx.doi.org/10.1145/2556288.2557361

42. Abhinav Mehrotra, Mirco Musolesi, Robert Hendley, and Veljko Pejovic. 2015. Designing Content-driven Intelligent Notification Mechanisms for Mobile Applications. In *Proceedings of the 2015 ACM International Joint Conference on Pervasive and*

Ubiquitous Computing (UbiComp '15). ACM, New York, NY, USA, 813–824. DOI: http://dx.doi.org/10.1145/2750858.2807544

43. Shalini Misra, Lulu Cheng, Jamie Genevie, and Miao Yuan. 2014. The iPhone Effect: The Quality of In-Person Social Interactions in the Presence of Mobiel Devices. *Environment and Behavior* (2014), 1–24.

44. Shalini Misra and Jamie Genevie. 2013. The Experience of Place: How Digital Technologies are Restructuring Public Places. In *Environmental Design Research Association*.

45. New York Times 2013. Step Away from the Phone. (2013). http://www.nytimes.com/2013/09/22/fashion/step-away-from-the-phone.html?_r=0.

46. Brid O'Conaill and David Frohlich. 1995. Timespace in the Workplace: Dealing with Interruptions. In *Conference Companion on Human Factors in Computing Systems (CHI '95)*. ACM, New York, NY, USA, 262–263. DOI: http://dx.doi.org/10.1145/223355.223665

47. Antti Oulasvirta, Tye Rattenbury, Lingyi Ma, and Eeva Raita. 2012. Habits Make Smartphone Use More Pervasive. *Personal Ubiquitous Comput.* 16, 1 (Jan. 2012), 105–114. DOI: http://dx.doi.org/10.1007/s00779-011-0412-2

48. Antti Oulasvirta, Sakari Tamminen, Virpi Roto, and Jaana Kuorelahti. 2005. Interaction in 4-second Bursts: The Fragmented Nature of Attentional Resources in Mobile HCI. In *Proceedings of the SIGCHI Conference on Human Factors in Computing Systems (CHI '05)*. ACM, New York, NY, USA, 919–928. DOI: http://dx.doi.org/10.1145/1054972.1055101

49. Andrew K. Przybylski and Netta Weinstein. 2013. Can You Connect with Me Now? How the Presence of Mobile Communication Technology Influences Face-to-Face Conversation Quality. *Journal of Social and Personal Relationships* 30 (2013), 237–246.

50. Antti Salovaara, Antti Lindqvist, Tero Hasu, and Jonna Häkkilä. 2011. The Phone Rings but the User Doesn'T Answer: Unavailability in Mobile Communication. In *Proceedings of the 13th International Conference on Human Computer Interaction with Mobile Devices and Services (MobileHCI '11)*. ACM, New York, NY, USA, 503–512. DOI: http://dx.doi.org/10.1145/2037373.2037448

51. Shin, Choonsung and Dey, Anind K. 2013. Automatically Detecting Problematic Use of Smartphones. In *Proceedings of the 2013 ACM International Joint Conference on Pervasive and Ubiquitous Computing (UbiComp '13)*. ACM, New York, NY, USA, 335–344. DOI: http://dx.doi.org/10.1145/2493432.2493443

52. Tasos Spiliotopoulos and Ian Oakley. 2013. Understanding Motivations for Facebook Use: Usage Metrics, Network Structure, and Privacy. In *Proceedings of the SIGCHI Conference on Human Factors in Computing Systems (CHI '13)*. ACM, New York, NY, USA, 3287–3296. DOI: http://dx.doi.org/10.1145/2470654.2466449

53. Hermann Stern, Viktoria Pammer, and Stefanie N. Lindstaedt. 2011. A Preliminary Study on Interruptibility Detection Based on Location and Calendar Information. In *Context-Systems Design, Evaluation and Optimisation*.

54. Linda Tickle-Degnen and Robert Rosenthal. 1990. The Nature of Rapport and Its Nonverbal Correlates. *Psychological Inquiry* 1, 4 (1990), 285–293.

55. Sherry Turkle. 2012. *Alone Together: Why We Expect More from Technology and Less from Each Other*. Basic Books, New York.

56. Liam D. Turner, Stuart M. Allen, and Roger M. Whitaker. 2015. Interruptibility Prediction for Ubiquitous Systems: Conventions and New Directions from a Growing Field. In *Proceedings of the 2015 ACM International Joint Conference on Pervasive and Ubiquitous Computing (UbiComp '15)*. ACM, New York, NY, USA, 801–812. DOI: http://dx.doi.org/10.1145/2750858.2807514

"Silence Your Phones": Smartphone Notifications Increase Inattention and Hyperactivity Symptoms

Kostadin Kushlev
University of Virginia
Charlottesville, USA
kushlevk@gmail.com

Jason Proulx
University of British Columbia
Vancouver, Canada
j.proulx19@gmail.com

Elizabeth W. Dunn
University of British Columbia
Vancouver, Canada
edunn@psych.ubc.ca

ABSTRACT
As smartphones increasingly pervade our daily lives, people are ever more interrupted by alerts and notifications. Using both correlational and experimental methods, we explored whether such interruptions might be causing inattention and hyperactivity—symptoms associated with Attention Deficit Hyperactivity Disorder (ADHD)—even in people not clinically diagnosed with ADHD. We recruited a sample of 221 participants from the general population. For one week, participants were assigned to maximize phone interruptions by keeping notification alerts on and their phones within their reach/sight. During another week, participants were assigned to minimize phone interruptions by keeping alerts off and their phones away. Participants reported higher levels of inattention and hyperactivity when alerts were on than when alerts were off. Higher levels of inattention in turn predicted lower productivity and psychological well-being. These findings highlight some of the costs of ubiquitous connectivity and suggest how people can reduce these costs simply by adjusting existing phone settings.

Author Keywords
Smartphones; interruptions; pervasive computing; multitasking; experimental study; attention management; subjective well-being; psychology

ACM Classification Keywords
H.1.2. [Information Systems]: User/Machine Systems—Human Factors; H.1.2. [Information Systems]: User/Machine Systems—Human Information Processing; H.5.2 [Information Systems]: User Interfaces—Auditory Feedback.

CHI'16, May 07 - 12, 2016, San Jose, CA, USA

ACM 978-1-4503-3362-7/16/05…$15.00
DOI: http://dx.doi.org/10.1145/2858036.2858359

INTRODUCTION
Ken is a married man, a father of four, and the founder and CEO of a digital ad agency. And he is struggling. In his early 40's, Ken noticed a significant decline in his ability to manage tasks, and gaps in his memory and performance. His desk had gotten increasingly cluttered, and when his employees started leaving the company frustrated by his inability to manage it, Ken decided to seek help. He wondered whether he might have an early-onset dementia or a thyroid dysfunction. What he did not expect is that his doctor would diagnose him with Attention Deficit Hyperactivity Disorder (ADHD). Ken wondered whether the recent exacerbation of his symptoms might be due to his increasingly stimulated digital environment.

The real story of Ken [43] is an example of how factors in our contemporary environment might exacerbate ADHD symptoms. Because ADHD is a neurodevelopmental disorder, however, a diagnosis cannot be based only on current symptoms, but also on a lifetime history of such symptoms. Ken's story, therefore does not suggest that digital distractions can cause ADHD. What his story does suggest, however, is that our increasingly pervasive digital technology may be causing inattention and hyperactivity—not only in people already suffering from ADHD, but also in the general population. In a recent survey, for example, one out of every two American smartphone owners reported having been distracted by their phones over the preceding week [31].

When Steve Jobs introduced the first smartphone in 2007, he promised: "This will change everything"; and he was right. Today, we can access the Internet virtually anytime and anywhere. And we do just that. The vast majority of smartphone owners use their phones not only for text messaging and calling, but also to check their email, keep up with their social media feeds, or simply to browse the Internet [31]. Of course, people could access these functions on their stationary computers even before they could carry these powerful computers in their pockets. What smartphones have changed, however, is where and when people access those functions. In a recent poll of smartphone users in the US, for example, almost all (95%) admitted to using their smartphones during their most recent social gathering, including to read incoming messages or emails or simply to check whether they had received any alerts [34]. In other polls, seven out of ten American smartphone owners were found to use their phones while working [31], and one in ten admitted to checking their phone even during sex [17]. According to some estimates people reach for their phones more than one hundred times a day [30] and spend close to two hours a day using their phones [12, 42].

Might the deluge of smartphone alerts and notifications be contributing to an increase in symptoms of ADHD in the general population? According to the Diagnostic and Statistical Manual (DSM-V)—the official guide for diagnosing mental disorders of the American Psychiatric Association—ADHD is characterized by two sets of symptoms: inattention and hyperactivity/impulsivity [4]. Inattention includes symptoms such as having difficulty focusing on one task at a time, being easily distracted, and getting easily bored when trying to focus. Hyperactivity is characterized by symptoms such as fidgeting, having trouble sitting still, and having difficulty doing quiet tasks and activities; in adults, hyperactivity also manifests as a sense of restlessness [22]. Smartphones may contribute to both sets of symptoms in the general population by serving as a readily available source of distraction (causing inattention) and of virtually unlimited array of alternative activities (causing hyperactivity). These effects could be exacerbated by the inflow of new notifications, which can both interrupt ongoing activities and present alternative activities [11; 14]. We propose, therefore, that the interruptions caused by smartphone notifications—from text messages and social media updates to emails and calendar reminders—could cause inattention and hyperactivity even in the general population.

Notifications, Interruptions, and Disruptions

A wealth of basic research and theory documents the toll of frequent task interruptions on attention and cognition. According to the time-based resource sharing model of attention [6], the very act of switching between tasks—even briefly—requires cognitive effort above and beyond the effort required to complete the tasks themselves. Switching attention thus increases cognitive load [6, 28]. And according to load theory of attention [24], the higher the cognitive load, the more susceptible people are to new distractors [36, 26]. To the extent that phone notifications draw users' attention away from other ongoing activities, phones may increase cognitive load. And by making people more prone to distractions, increased cognitive load may in turn make people—even in the general population—suffer from inattention and hyperactivity.

Beyond theory and basic research in cognitive psychology, a large body of work in HCI documents the detrimental effects of digital interruptions, particularly during tasks that require attention [3, 5, 10]. In field experiments, for example, digital interruptions at work (e.g., email alerts) have been associated with feeling more distracted, stressed, and anxious [23, 29]. And experiments in a controlled lab environment have revealed that notifications are disruptive in part because they interrupt people at random times. In one particularly well-designed lab experiment, participants completing common work tasks (e.g., editing text) felt more annoyed and frustrated, experienced greater time pressure, and expended more mental effort when they were interrupted by notifications at random than when uninterrupted [1]. In contrast, people suffered no consequences from being interrupted (i.e., no added frustration, time pressure, and mental effort) when they were interrupted at opportune times in between work tasks. Not all digital interruptions, then, are born equal: When people are interrupted by the random receipt of a new notification, they may be particularly likely to incur attentional and emotional costs.

An emerging body of literature shows that people often attend immediately to notifications received on their phones [8, 32, 37]. This suggests that phone notifications often interrupt other activities at random times, making phones particularly disruptive [1]. Phones' power to interrupt their users is no doubt in part due to their omnipresence throughout our daily activities. Indeed, people attend to new notifications quickly regardless of the alert mode on their phones (e.g., ring vs. vibrate vs. silent) [8, 32]. Still, people are more likely to attend immediately to, for example, new text messages when their phones are in vibrate or ring mode than when they are in silent mode [8]. Above and beyond phones' omnipresence in our lives, then, the rings, dings, and vibrations accompanying new notifications may levy users' attention further by interrupting other tasks at random times. In fact, the very sound of a new alert has been shown to disrupt ongoing tasks. In a recent study, the mere buzz of a new notification was enough to hurt performance on a cognitively demanding task even when people did not attend to the notification (e.g., checked the text message announced by the notification) [41]. Yet, people typically keep their phone alerts on—about 9 in 10 notifications are received in ring and vibrate modes [32]. To the extent that people normally attend immediately to phone notifications and random interruptions tax attention, phone notifications may cause even people not diagnosed with ADHD to suffer from inattention and hyperactivity.

Study Overview

We recruited a sample of university students from the general student population. During an initial study session, we assessed individual differences between participants in inattention and hyperactivity while also measuring how frequently people felt interrupted by their phone notifications. We thus explored correlationally whether feeling interrupted by phone notifications was associated with inattention and hyperactivity. Because ADHD symptoms have been associated with poorer performance at work/school and with relationship and social skills problems [13, 15, 22], we also included exploratory measures of productivity and psychological well-being.

While correlational analyses provide the most naturalistic way to examine the association of phone interruptions with inattention and hyperactivity, such analyses preclude causal conclusions. Accordingly, we ran a two-week within-subjects experiment in which we manipulated how frequently participants felt interrupted by their smartphones. For one week, we assigned participants to maximize phone interruptions by keeping notification alerts on and their phones within their sight and/or reach. During another week, we assigned the same participants to minimize phone interruptions by keeping alerts off and their phones away. By employing this within-subjects design, we were able to examine whether phone interruptions had causal effects on inattention and hyperactivity.

METHOD

Participants

Two-hundred and twenty-one undergraduate students (M_{age} = 19.89; 73.76% female) from the University of British Columbia completed the study in exchange for course credit. Importantly, students were recruited from the university's general participant pool, rather than from a pool of students diagnosed with ADHD. We calculated our sample size based on *a priori* analyses with 80% probability of detecting small effects of d = .20, α = .05, two-tailed[1]. Because we were interested in manipulating how frequently people felt interrupted by their smartphones, we prescreened participants for smartphone ownership; all participants thus had a smartphone[2].

Procedure

Participants attended an introductory session in the lab in groups of up to 10 students. Before assigning them to experimental condition, we assessed our main measures of interest at baseline, including phone interruptions, inattention and hyperactivity, as well as productivity and psychological well-being (see Measures). Participants were then assigned to condition using a randomized counterbalanced within-subjects design. Half the participants were assigned to minimize interruptions for one week and then to maximize interruptions for a second week. For the other half of the participants, the order of these instructions was reversed.

In the *Do-Not-Interrupt* condition, participants configured their smartphones to Do-Not-Disturb settings, disabling auditory (e.g., ring), tactile (i.e., vibration) and visual alerts (i.e., LED flashes). In order to prevent participants from compensating by monitoring incoming notifications on their screens, we additionally asked them to keep their phones out of sight (e.g., in their bags, pockets).

In the *Interrupt* condition, participants configured their phones to enable auditory, tactile, and/or visual alerts. Additionally, participants kept their phones within their sight and/or reach. In situations where their phones may be disruptive to others (e.g., in class), participants in this condition were instructed to use common sense and to switch off audible alerts if necessary. Even in such situations, however, participants were instructed to have their phones at least on vibrate mode.

All participants within a single introductory session were assigned to the same condition. All participants were guided through how to configure their phones in silent, ring, and vibrate settings. Additionally, each participant was given a sheet detailing how to configure his or her phone to the assigned settings; the sheet contained information about the most common smartphones and operating systems (e.g., iPhone, Android).

After the introductory session, participants were sent daily online surveys in the evening on each of the next six days. During the first day of the second week, participants were sent a prompt via email to change their phone settings as shown on their instructions sheets. Then, for each of the following six days, participants again received links to complete daily surveys. In the first five surveys of each week, we assessed how frequently people felt interrupted by their phones during a specified one-hour period of the day. This measure served as our manipulation check (see Measures)[3]. On the seventh and last day of each week, participants received a longer survey asking them to report how they felt over the past week. This survey contained our main variables of interest, including inattention and hyperactivity, productivity, and psychological well-being. At the end of the two weeks, participants returned to the lab to be debriefed in person.

Measures

Smartphone Interruptions

At baseline, we assessed how frequently participants normally felt interrupted by their phones (from 0—*not at all* to 6—*constantly*) when engaging in 14 common daily activities (e.g., attending class, reading for pleasure, commuting, or eating[4]). Interruptions were defined as any time participants' attention shifted from their current

[1] The power analyses were registered on Open Science Framework: http://tinyurl.com/ofx3jjy.

[2] Because we did not want people to get around our manipulation of smartphone interruptions by using other portable devices, we also prescreened people for how much they used tablets. People who reported using a tablet often or all the time in prescreening were not eligible to participate.

[3] These daily questionnaires included other questions beyond the main scope of the present investigation of the effects of phone interruptions on inattention and hyperactivity. The full questionnaire is available here: http://tinyurl.com/nfsux27.

[4] The full version of the baseline survey, including a list of all activities is available here: http://tinyurl.com/nfsux27

activities to their phones because of a notification. We asked people to report interruptions separately for these 14 activities in order to cue people to think about their behavior during specific activities, making their estimates more accurate. We averaged people's responses across all 14 activities to form a single measure of phone interruptions at baseline.

In order to assess the successfulness of the manipulation, we also asked people to report daily how frequently they felt interrupted by their phones (0–*not at all*; 6–*constantly*). We used a self-report measure of interruptions because no available technology can objectively assess how frequently people feel interrupted by their phones. Indeed, people's subjective sense of being interrupted should depend not only on how quickly people attend to notifications but also on what they are currently doing (e.g., trying to pay attention in class versus mindlessly commuting). Still, we used past research to design our self-report measure to be as accurate as possible. Specifically, people have been shown to provide more accurate information about their behavior when asked what they were doing during specific periods of time in the day [e.g., 21]. Accordingly, participants were first prompted to remember what they were doing during a one-hour period of time on each day, and then to report how frequently they felt interrupted by their phones during this period. The specific time period participants were asked about varied by day. To represent the range of activities people engage in during different times of the day, we first selected every other possible one-hour period, starting at 10 am and ending at 7 pm (i.e., 10 am to 11 am, 12 pm to 1 pm, and so forth). We then randomly assigned one of these time periods for each day of the week.

Inattention and Hyperactivity

To measure inattention and hyperactivity (both at baseline and at the end of each week of the study), participants rated the extent to which they experienced 18 symptoms over the past week (1–*never*; 2–*rarely*; 3–*sometimes*; 4–*often*). These 18 items were based on the criteria of the Diagnostic and Statistical Manual – V (DSM-V) for diagnosing ADHD [4, 16]. Nine items assessed inattention (e.g., *How often were you easily distracted by external stimuli, like something in your environment or unrelated thoughts?*); the other nine items assessed hyperactivity (e.g., *How often did you have difficulty waiting your turn, such as while waiting in line?*). We averaged each set of nine items to form our measures of inattention (α = .82) and hyperactivity (α = .79[5]) at baseline and for each of the two experimental weeks.

Productivity

We measured participants' productivity at baseline and at the end of each week of the study with three self-report items used in previous research [23]. We asked participants the extent to which in the previous week they: (1) felt that they got the things done at work or school that were important to them; (2) were satisfied with what they had accomplished at school; and (3) felt a sense of accomplishment from school (α = .88).

Psychological Well-Being

To measure well-being broadly, we assessed several constructs theorized as essential components of psychological well-being. In particular, Ryff [36] has argued for six components of psychological well-being, including a sense of autonomy, environmental mastery, self-acceptance, personal growth, purpose and meaning, and relatedness with others. To reduce the burden on participants from completing measures of all these aspects of psychological well-being, we assessed only four. Specifically, we did not assess people's sense of personal growth and self-acceptance because we deemed it unlikely that these aspects of psychological well-being would be related to inattention and hyperactivity. In contrast, based on past research [13, 15, 22], we theorized that inattention and hyperactivity might have downstream consequences for people's sense of mastery over their environment, autonomy over their actions, relatedness to others, as well as how meaningful they found their daily lives.

To measure participants' environmental mastery, we used the short version of the environmental mastery questionnaire [35], which includes three items (α = .73). To assess mastery during each specific week of the study, we adapted the items so that people reported their sense of mastery over the past week. Participants provided their responses using a scale from 1–*strongly disagree* to 7–*strongly agree.*

Although Ryff [36] has developed scales for all aspects of psychological well-being, Ryff's scales of the other aspects were not adaptable for measuring the constructs over a one-week period (rather than in their life in general). Accordingly, we adapted measures from other commonly used scales to assess the other aspects of psychological well-being. To measure participants' sense of relatedness with others, we adapted 5 items from Social Connectedness Scale [27]. Participants reported, for example, how distant they felt from others and how disconnected they felt from the world around them (both reversed scored). Participants used a scale from, 1–*strongly disagree* to 7–*strongly agree.* This adapted scale demonstrated high reliability (α = .94).

To measure participants' sense of autonomy, we adapted five items from the Perceived Choice Scale [38, 39] (α = .85). For each item, participants were given two statements (A and B) and asked to respond on a scale from 1–*only A feels true* to 5–*only B feels true*. For example, participants were asked to decide between *A—I felt like I always chose the things I did* and *B—I sometimes felt that I was not really choosing the things I did.*

[5] All alphas are reported as averages of the alphas of the three measures of each construct (i.e., baseline, week 1, and week 2)

	Interruptions	Inattention	Hyperactivity	Productivity	Environmental Mastery	Social Connectedness	Perceived Choice	Meaning in Life	Life Satisfaction
Interruptions	–								
Inattention	.31***	–							
Hyperactivity	.30***	.41***	–						
Productivity	−.14*	−.41***	−.09	–					
Environmental Mastery	−.18**	−.52***	−.27***	.34***	–				
Social Connectedness	.01	−.26***	−.27***	0.13*	.29***	–			
Perceived Choice	−.09	−.36***	−.13†	.25***	.35***	.24***	–		
Meaning in Life	−.11†	−.28***	−.11	.36***	.49***	.35***	.38***	–	
Life Satisfaction	−.05	−.41***	−.15*	.42***	.64***	.46***	.39***	.50***	–

Table 1: Table of correlations between baseline measures. *** p < .001; ** p < .01; * p < .05; † = p < .10

To measure participants' meaning in life, we used five items of the Meaning In Life Questionnaire—Presence Subscale [40] (α = .89). Participants reported their agreement with each item on a scale from 1–*strongly disagree* to 7–*strongly agree.*

At baseline, we additionally included a broader measure of life satisfaction in general: *Taking all things together, how satisfied are you with your life these days?* (0–*not at all satisfied*; 6–*very satisfied*) [7].

RESULTS

Are smartphone interruptions associated with inattention and hyperactivity? To explore this question, we first ran a series of correlational analyses using people's self-reports at baseline. We then examined this question causally by comparing whether people reported higher levels of inattention and hyperactivity when they were randomly assigned to maximize (versus minimize) interruptions.

Correlational Analyses at Baseline

As seen in Table 1, people who reported more phone interruptions at baseline also reported higher levels of both inattention (r = .31, p < .001) and hyperactivity (r = .30, p < .001). Consistent with past research, we also found that inattention and hyperactivity were negatively associated with our measures of self-reported productivity and psychological well-being (see Table 1). Notably, inattention was more strongly associated with these outcomes than was hyperactivity. In addition, people who reported feeling interrupted by their phones more frequently felt less productive, experienced a lower sense of environmental mastery, and also reported marginally lower sense of meaning in life.

To explore whether inattention and hyperactivity mediate the relationship between smartphone interruptions and our measures of productivity and psychological well-being, we ran a series of mediational analyses using both bootstrapping with 50,000 replications [18] and Sobel's test of mediation. Inattention mediated the effect of interruptions on productivity, *indirect effect* = −.15, 95% CI [−.23; −.08], *Sobel's Z* = −3.78, p < .001, leaving a nonsignificant direct effect of interruptions on productivity, b = −.02, 95% CI [−.17; .12]. Inattention also mediated the effect of interruptions on environmental mastery, *indirect effect* = −.17, 95% CI [−.26; −.09], *Sobel's Z* = −4.18, p < .001, leaving a nonsignificant direct effect, b = −.02, 95% CI [−.15; .11]. Finally, inattention explained the effect of interruptions on meaning in life, *indirect effect* = −.11, 95% CI [−.19; −.05], *Sobel's Z* = −3.02, p < .01, leaving a nonsignificant direct effect, b = −.04, 95% CI [−.21; .14]. In short, inattention explained the negative associations between phone interruptions and our measures of productivity and psychological well-being.

In contrast to the strong mediating role of inattention, hyperactivity played a less important role in explaining the negative associations of phone interruptions with productivity and psychological well-being. Specifically, hyperactivity did not mediate the association of phone interruptions to productivity, *indirect effect* = −.02, 95% CI [−.07; .03], *Sobel's Z* = .71, p = .48 or meaning in life, *indirect effect* = –.03, 95% CI [–.10; .02], *Sobel's Z* = –1.15, p = .25. And although hyperactivity mediated the effect of interruptions on environmental mastery, *indirect effect* = –.08, 95% CI [–.15; –.03], *Sobel's Z* = –2.79, $p <$ .01, this indirect effect was weaker than the indirect effect of inattention.

The above mediational analyses are correlational; it is, therefore, possible that inattention may make people more susceptible to feeling interrupted by their phones (rather than that phone interruptions cause inattention). If this alternative direction of causality describes the data, phone interruptions should mediate the negative associations of inattention with productivity and psychological well-being. In contrast to this possibility, phone interruptions did not mediate the associations of inattention (b's = –.01 to –.02, p's > .68) with our measures of productivity and psychological well-being. Thus, our correlational analyses at baseline are most consistent with a single causal path: Phone interruptions impair productivity and psychological well-being to the extent that interruptions increase inattention.

Experimental Results

To directly explore whether phone interruptions can cause inattention and hyperactivity[6], we next present the effects of our experimental manipulation.

Manipulation Check

Confirming the success of our manipulation, we found that people felt more frequently interrupted in the *Interrupt* condition (M = 2.64, SD = 1.04) than in the *Do-Not-Interrupt* condition (M = 2.03, SD = .92), $t(210) = 8.06$, $p <$ .001. Interestingly, people felt less interrupted by their phones in the *Do-Not-Interrupt* condition than normal, as assessed at baseline (M = 2.75, SD = 96), $t(210) = 10.20$, p < .001; in contrast, people felt no more interrupted in the *interrupt* condition than at baseline, $t(210) = 1.56$, p = .119.

Main Effects

Did maximizing phone interruptions for a week result in reporting higher levels of inattention and hyperactivity? A paired-samples t-test comparing inattention symptoms between each of the two weeks revealed that participants indeed experienced higher levels of inattention in the *Interrupt* condition (M = 2.38, SD = .58) than in the *Do-Not-Interrupt* condition (M = 2.27, SD = .56), $t(189) = 3.02$, p = .003, d = .44. Mirroring this effect on inattention, people also reported higher levels of hyperactivity in the *Interrupt* condition (M = 2.11, SD = .59) than in the *Do-Not-Interrupt* condition (M = 2.01, SD = .55), $t(189)$ = 3.12, p = .002, d = .45. Notably, both effects were of medium size according to established statistical guidelines in the behavioral sciences [8].

We found no significant main effects of our manipulation on our measures of productivity and psychological well-being, t's < .89, p's > .37. It is, of course, hardly surprising that our minimal manipulation did not produce significant differences in these outcomes within the frame of one week. Still, our correlational findings showed that phone interruptions were negatively associated with productivity and psychological well-being, as well as that these negative associations were explained by inattention. Accordingly, we next examined whether our manipulation of phone interruptions had downstream consequences for productivity and well-being to the extent people suffered greater inattention when maximizing (vs. minimizing) interruptions.

Indirect Effects

To explore the indirect effects of our manipulation on productivity and psychological well-being through inattention, we followed recommendations by Judd and colleagues [20] for conducting mediation analyses with repeated measures. As shown in Eq. (1) below, in each case we predicted the difference scores in the outcome variables (Y) from the sum and difference scores of inattention (X). The regression coefficient of the difference scores of inattention (controlling for its sum scores) is the measure of the indirect effects of the manipulation on productivity and well-being through inattention [20]. As shown in Figure 1, to the extent that people experienced greater inattention in the *Interrupt* (vs. *Do-Not-Interrupt)* condition, they felt less productive and less socially connected, reported less mastery over their environment and lower meaning in life, and perceived less choice over their actions.

$$Y_{\text{diff}} = b_1 X_{\text{sum}} + b_2 X_{\text{diff}} + \varepsilon, \text{ where}$$
$$\text{(a) } Y_{\text{diff}} = Y_{do\text{-}not\text{-}interrupt} - Y_{interrupt}$$
$$\text{(b) } X_{\text{diff}} = X_{do\text{-}not\text{-}interrupt} - X_{interrupt}$$
$$\text{(c) } X_{\text{sum}} = X_{do\text{-}not\text{-}interrupt} + X_{interrupt}$$

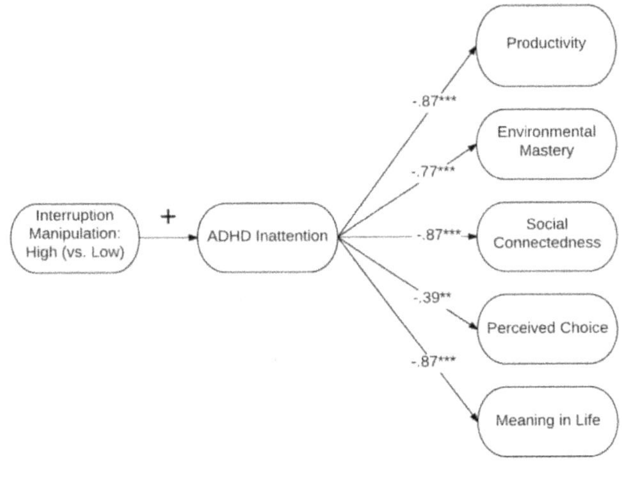

Figure 1. Indirect effects of manipulating smartphone interruptions on psychological well-being via inattention symptoms. Numbers are unstandardized regression coefficients.

[6] Note that degrees of freedom vary slightly between tests due to failure by some participants to complete some measures.

DISCUSSION

We provide the first evidence that interruptions due to phone notifications can cause inattention and hyperactivity in the general population. When people maximized phone interruptions by switching alerts on and keeping their phones within reach, they felt higher levels of inattention and hyperactivity than when they minimized phone interruptions. In line with these experimental findings, correlational analyses at baseline also indicated that people who felt interrupted by their phones more frequently experienced higher levels of inattention and hyperactivity. In both the correlational and experimental analyses, the effects of phone interruptions on inattention had downstream consequences for self-reported productivity and psychological well-being. By triangulating on correlational and experimental methods, therefore, we demonstrated that phone interruptions might cause symptoms of ADHD in the general population. Our findings also suggest, however, that people could mitigate these negative effects by making simple modifications to the notification settings of their phones.

Despite our promising findings, we caution that keeping notifications at bay may not work equally well for everybody trying to reduce phone interruptions. Preliminary qualitative research suggests that for some, disabling alerts may produce anxiety over missing notifications [33]. Such anxiety may drive some to self-interrupt more, resulting in a net increase in interruptions. In one study, for example, information workers disabled their email notifications for one week; while some workers were able to reduce their email checking compared to baseline, others checked their email more to avoid missing important messages [19]. Future research should, therefore, examine what personality characteristics (e.g., neuroticism) and what situational factors (e.g., job type, duration of intervention) determine when and for whom switching off notifications leads to net benefits.

To manipulate phone interruptions in the present research, we asked people to switch alerts on versus off, as well as to keep their phones within sight versus out of sight. Assuming that the old adage—out of sight, out of mind—holds true, our manipulation may have influenced not only external interruptions but also self-interruptions. While past research suggests that the unpredictable timing of external notifications may be especially disruptive to users [1], future research should examine whether self-interruptions contribute to inattention and hyperactivity above and beyond external interruptions. Indeed, even when using silent mode, people normally attend to new phone notifications within 6 minutes [8], suggesting that self-interruptions may account for a large proportion of the interruptions in people's daily activities [cf. 11].

For the purposes of the present research, we used self-report measures to detect differences in how frequently people felt interrupted by their phones. Because people have been shown to underestimate the frequency of their smartphone use [42], the particular values reported by participants should be interpreted with caution. We note, however, that self-report measures were better suited for the purposes of the present investigation than available objective measures. Indeed, past research using objective measures has captured only how quickly people attend to incoming notifications, rather than whether people feel interrupted by these notifications given their current context and activities [8; 32]. Using these objective measures, researchers have shown only small—but statistically significant—differences between how quickly people attend to new notifications in silent versus ring/vibrate modes [8]. By relying on a subjective measure, the present research suggests that even such minor differences in attentiveness to new notifications may make users feel more interrupted by their phones.

By using a subjective measure of phone interruptions, we were able to hone in specifically on how frequently people's attention was drawn to their phone due to a notification. But our measure thus captured only external rather than self-initiated interruptions. In contrast, objective measures in past research have captured both external and self-interruptions (i.e., any time a person attends to a notification [8; 32]). It is possible, therefore, that a subjective measure assessing both external and self-initiated interruptions may have produced a smaller difference between conditions—similar to the available objective measures. Even such a subjective measure, however, would not be conceptually equivalent to the available objective measures. Such measures can accurately assess how frequently users attend to notifications; but they cannot adequately capture how frequently users are interrupted because these measures ignore people's current goals and activities. Attending to a notification may be interruptive when a person is in a meeting or class, but not when she is on the bus or bored at home. The present research thus suggests that subjective measures of interruptions are not simply coarser, less precise versions of the available objective measures; rather, subjective measures can be useful additional tools for studying the psychological effects of our ubiquitous digital devices. We invite future research to use both subjective and objective measures in order to disentangle how the feeling of being interrupted by notifications relates to the objective frequency of attending to notifications.

In order to conduct the first systematic investigation of the effects of phone interruptions, we included a wide range of outcome measures, which included inattention and hyperactivity, but also many other constructs. Given this exploratory approach, it is possible that the significant effects we observed are simply an artifact of the large number of statistical tests we conducted. Importantly, however, we found consistent effects on inattention and hyperactivity both in our correlational analyses at baseline and in our two-week field experiment. This converging evidence of our correlational and experimental analyses make less likely the possibility that our findings are a mere statistical fluke. Still, the present study should be seen as laying the groundwork for further confirmatory research.

Inherent in our within-subjects design lies another limitation of the present study: Participants were aware of the two conditions within our manipulation. To the extent that people might have theories about how their phones affect them, people may have reported how they thought they should feel rather than how they actually felt. But we found the same associations of phone interruptions with inattention and hyperactivity using our baseline measures, which were administered before condition assignment. Viewed in the context of our correlational findings, therefore, our experimental findings are unlikely to be completely explained by participants' lay theories.

We found no direct effects of our manipulation on our measures of productivity and psychological well-being. It is, of course, hardly surprising that keeping notifications at bay for a week did not produce direct effects on, for example, how meaningful people found their lives. Still, to the extent that phone interruptions influenced inattention, they had downstream consequences for productivity and well-being. Future research should explore whether these indirect effects may materialize into direct effects if people minimize phone interruptions over periods of time longer than a week (e.g., one month, an entire semester).

We found that smartphone interruptions were associated with self-reported symptoms of ADHD in a sample drawn from the general population. But our findings do not in any way suggest that smartphone notifications can cause ADHD, which is a neurodevelopmental disorder with complex neurological and early developmental causes [4]. But as with any other disorder, symptoms represent a continuum from the normal to the pathological. Our findings thus simply show that smartphone interruptions may be driving individuals from the general population to feel somewhat more inattentive and hyperactive. The present research can thus be seen only as an initial demonstration of the potential role of smartphones in exacerbating symptoms associated with ADHD.

Just as we do not suggest that phone interruptions can cause ADHD, we by no means claim that reducing phone interruptions can treat ADHD. Indeed, our findings are based on a sample drawn from the general student population, rather than from a population diagnosed with ADHD. What our findings do suggest is that being constantly interrupted by alerts and notifications may be contributing towards an increasingly problematic deficit of attention in our digitally connected society. In an age of incessant digital stimulation, we hope that our findings would spur further research on how people can reclaim control over their attention.

REFERENCES

1. Pitor D. Adamczyk and Brian P. Bailey. 2004. If not now when?: The effects of interruption at different moments within task execution. In *Proceedings of the SIGCHI Conference on Human Factors in Computing Systems* 6, 1: 271–278. http://doi.org/10.1145/985692.985727
2. Lenard A. Adler, L., Thomas Spencer, Stephen V. Faraone, Ronald C. Kessler, Mary J. Howes, Joseph Biederman, and Kristina Secnik. 2006. Validity of pilot adult ADHD Self- Report Scale (ASRS) to rate adult ADHD symptoms. *Annals of Clinical Psychiatry.* 18, 3: 145–148.
3. Rachel F. Adler, and Raquel Benbunan-Fich. 2002. Juggling on a high wire: Multitasking effects on performance. *International Journal of Human-Computer Studies.* 70, 2: 156–168.
4. American Psychiatric Association. 2013. *Diagnostic and Statistical Manual of Mental Disorders* (Fifth ed.). Arlington, VA: American Psychiatric Publishing.
5. Anja Baethge and Thomas Rigotti. 2013. Interruptions to workflow: Their relationship with irritation and satisfaction with performance, and the mediating roles of time pressure and mental demands. *Work & Stress.* 27, 1: 43–63.
6. Pierre Barrouillet, Sophie Bernardin, and Valérie Camos. 2004. Time constraints and resource sharing in adults' working memory spans. *Journal of Experimental Psychology: General.* 133, 1: 83–100.
7. Christian Bjørnskov. 2008. How comparable are the Gallup World Poll life satisfaction data? *Journal of Happiness Studies.* 11, 1: 41–60.
8. Yung-Ju Chang, John C Tang. 2015. Investigating mobile users' ringer mode usage and attentiveness and responsiveness to communication. In *Proceedings of the SIGCHI Conference on Human-Computer Interaction with Mobile Devices and Services* (MobileHCI '15): 6–15. http://dx.doi.org/10.1145/2785830.2785852
9. Jacob Cohen. 1992. A power primer. *Psychological Bulletin.* 112, 1: 155–159.
10. Edward Cutrell, Mary Czerwinski, and Eric Horvitz. 2001. Notification, disruption, and memory: Effects of messaging interruptions on memory and performance. In *Proceedings of the SIGCHI Conference on Human Computer Interaction* (*Interact '01*), 1999: 263–269.
11. Mary Czerwinski, Eric Horvitz, and Susan Wilhite. 2004. A diary study of task switching and interruptions. In *Proceedings of the SIGCHI Conference on Human Factors in Computing Systems* (*CHI '04*) 6, 1: 175–182. http://doi.org/10.1145/985692.985715

12. Tilman Dingler and Martin Pielot. 2015. I'll be there for you: Quantifying attentiveness towards mobile messaging. In *Proceedings of the SIGCHI Conference on Human-Computer Interaction with Mobile Devices and Services*: 1–5. Retrieved December 17th, 2015 from http://pielot.org/pubs/Dingler2015-MobileHCI-Attentiveness.pdf
13. Colleen L. Dobie, W. Brooks Donald, M. Hanson, C. Heim, John Huxsahl, and et al. 2012. Diagnosis and management of attention deficit hyperactivity disorder in primary care for school-age children and adolescents. Institute for Clinical Systems Improvement.
14. Denzil Ferreira, Jorge Gonçalves, Vassilis Kostakos, Louise Barkhuus, and Anind K. Dey. 2014. Contextual experience sampling of mobile application micro-usage. In *Proceedings of SIGCHI Conference on Human-computer interaction with Mobile Devices and Services (MobileHCI'14)*: 91-100. http://doi.org/10.1145/2628363.2628367
15. Julie P. Gentile, Rafay Atiq, and Paulette M. Gillig. 2006. Adult ADHD: Diagnosis, differential diagnosis, and medication management. *Psychiatry* (*Edgmont*). 3, 8: 25–30.
16. James M. Grohol. 2013. Attention Deficit Disorder (ADD/ADHD) Test. Retrieved September 09, 2015 from http://psychcentral.com/cgi-bin/addquiz.cgi#sthash.LxTPdK6V.dpuf
17. Harris Interactive. 2013. Where do you take your phone? Retrieved September 10, 2015 from http://www.zdnet.com/article/phone-sex-using-our-smartphones-from-the-shower-to-the-sack/
18. Andrew Hayes. 2013. *Introduction to Mediation, Moderation, and Conditional Process Analysis: A Regression-Based Approach*. Guilford Press.
19. Shamsi T. Iqbal and Eric Horvitz. 2010. Notifications and awareness: A field study of alert usage and preferences. In *Proceedings of the 2010 ACM Conference on Computer Supported Cooperative Work* (*CSCW '10*): 27–30. http://doi.org/10.1145/1718918.1718926
20. Charles M. Judd, David A. Kenny, and Gary H. McClelland. 2001. Estimating and testing mediation and moderation in within-subject designs. *Psychological Methods*. 6, 2: 115-134.
21. Daniel Kahneman, Alan B. Krueger, David A. Schkade, Norbert Schwarz, and Arthur A. Stone. 2004. A survey method for characterizing daily life experience: The day reconstruction method. *Science*. 306: 1776–1780.
22. Sandra J. J. Kooij, Susanne Bejerot, Andrew Blackwell, and et al. 2010. European consensus statement on diagnosis and treatment of adult ADHD: The European Network Adult ADHD. *BMC Psychiatry*. 10, 1: 67.
23. Kostadin Kushlev and Elizabeth W. Dunn. 2015. Checking email less frequently reduces stress. *Computers in Human Behavior*. 43: 220–228.
24. Nilli Lavie. 2010. Attention, distraction, and cognitive control under load. *Current Directions in Psychological Science*. 19, 3: 143–148.
25. Nilli Lavie, N. and Jan W. De Fockert. 2005. The role of working memory in attentional capture. *Psychonomic Bulletin & Review*. 12, 4: 669–674.
26. Nilli Lavie, Aleksandra Hirst, Jan W. de Fockert, and Essi Viding. 2004. Load theory of selective attention and cognitive control. *Journal of Experimental Psychology: General*. 133, 3: 339–354.
27. Richard M. Lee, Matthew Draper, and Sujin Lee. 2001. Social connectedness, dysfunctional interpersonal behaviors, and psychological distress: Testing a mediator model. *Journal of Counseling Psychology*. 48, 3: 310–318.
28. Baptist Liefooghe, Pierre Barrouillet, André Vandierendonck, and Valérie Camos. 2008. Working memory costs of task switching. *Journal of Experimental Psychology: Learning, Memory, and Cognition*. 34, 3: 478–494.
29. Gloria J. Mark, Stephen Voida, and Armand V. Cardello. 2012. A pace not dictated by electrons: An empirical study of work without email. In *Proceedings of the SIGCHI Conference on Human Factors in Computing Systems* (*CHI '12*): 555–564. http://dx.doi.org/10.1145/2207676.2207754
30. Mary Meeker and Liang Wu. 2013. Internet trends. Retrieved September 10, 2015 from http://www.kpcb.com/blog/2013-internet-trends
31. Pew Research Center. 2015. The Smartphone difference. Retrieved May 22, 2015 from http://www.pewinternet.org/2015/04/01/us-smartphone-use-in-2015/
32. Martin Pielot, Karen Church, and Rodrigo de Oliveira. 2014. An in-situ study of mobile phone notifications. In *Proceedings of the SIGCHI Conference on Human-Computer Interaction with Mobile Devices and Services* (*MobileHCI '14*): 233–242. http://doi.org/10.1145/2628363.2628364
33. Martin Pielot and Luz Rello. 2015. The Do Not Disturb challenge. In *Proceedings of the ACM Conference Extended Abstracts on Human Factors in Computing Systems* (*CHI EA '15*): 1761–1766. http://doi.org/10.1145/2702613.2732704
34. Lee Rainie, and Kathryn Zickuhr. 2015. Americans' views on mobile etiquette. Retrieved on September 10, 2015 from

http://www.pewinternet.org/2015/08/26/americans-views-on-mobile-etiquette/

35. Carol D. Ryff. 1989. Happiness is everything, or is it? Explorations on the meaning of psychological well-being. *Journal of Personality and Social Psychology*. 57: 1069–1081

36. Carol D. Ryff, and Corey Lee M. Keyes. 1995. The structure of psychological well-being revisited. *Journal of Personality and Social Psychology*. 69: 719–727.

37. Alireza Sahami Shirazi, Niels Henze, Tilman Dingler, Martin Pielot, Dominik Weber, and Albrecht Schmidt. 2014. Large-scale assessment of mobile notifications. In *Proceedings of the ACM Conference on Human factors in Computing Systems* (*CHI '14*): 3055–3064. http://doi.org/10.1145/2556288.2557189

38. Kennon M. Sheldon. 1995. Creativity and self-determination in personality. *Creativity Research Journal*. 8: 61-72.

39. Kennon M. Sheldon, Richard Ryan, and Harry T. Reis. 1996. What makes for a good day? Competence and autonomy in the day and in the person. *Personality and Social Psychology Bulletin*. 22: 1270-1279.

40. Michael F. Steger, Patricia Frazier, Shigehiro Oishi, and Matthew Kaler. 2006. The meaning in life questionnaire: Assessing the presence of and search for meaning in life. *Journal of Counseling Psychology*. 53, 1: 80–93. doi:10.1037/0022-0167.53.1.80

41. Cary Stothart, Ainsley Mitchum, and Courtney Yehnert. 2015. The attentional cost of receiving a cell phone notification. *Journal of Experimental Psychology: Human Perception and Performance*. 41, 4: 893–897. doi:10.1037/xhp0000100

42. WNYC. 2015. Bored and Brilliant by the numbers (29 Jan, 2015). Retrieved September 09, 2015 from http://www.wnyc.org/story/bored-and-brilliant-challenge-tracker/

43. WNYC. 2015. Yes, you are distracted. Is it ADHD? (13 May, 2015). Retrieved September 09, 2015 from http://www.wnyc.org/story/you-will-be-distracted-while-you-listen-podcast/

My Phone and Me: Understanding People's Receptivity to Mobile Notifications

Abhinav Mehrotra
University of Birmingham
University College London
United Kingdom
a.mehrotra@cs.bham.ac.uk

Veljko Pejovic
University of Ljubljana
Slovenia
veljko.pejovic@fri.uni-lj.si

Jo Vermeulen
University of Calgary
Canada
University of Birmingham
United Kingdom
jo@jovermeulen.com

Robert Hendley
University of Birmingham
United Kingdom
r.j.hendley@cs.bham.ac.uk

Mirco Musolesi
University College London
United Kingdom
m.musolesi@ucl.ac.uk

ABSTRACT

Notifications are extremely beneficial to users, but they often demand their attention at inappropriate moments. In this paper we present an *in-situ* study of mobile interruptibility focusing on the effect of cognitive and physical factors on the response time and the disruption perceived from a notification. Through a mixed method of automated smartphone logging and experience sampling we collected 10372 *in-the-wild* notifications and 474 questionnaire responses on notification perception from 20 users. We found that the response time and the perceived disruption from a notification can be influenced by its presentation, alert type, sender-recipient relationship as well as the type, completion level and complexity of the task in which the user is engaged. We found that even a notification that contains important or useful content can cause disruption. Finally, we observe the substantial role of the psychological traits of the individuals on the response time and the disruption perceived from a notification.

Author Keywords

Mobile Sensing; Notifications, Interruptibility, Context-aware Computing.

ACM Classification Keywords

H.1.2. Models and Principles: User/Machine Systems; H.5.2. Information Interfaces and Presentation (e.g. HCI): User Interfaces

INTRODUCTION

Smartphones enable a new form of effortless information awareness. Throughout the day, a smartphone user receives a variety of information such as email messages, social network events and birthday reminders. Notifications are at the core of this information awareness, as they use audio, visual and haptic signals to steer the user's attention towards the newly-arrived information.

Notifications are extremely beneficial to the users: however, at the same time, they are a cause of potential disruption, since they often require users' attention at inopportune moments. Indeed, previous studies have found that interruptions at inopportune moments can adversely affect task completion time [11, 12, 25], lead to high task error rate [8] and impact the emotional and affective state of the user [5, 7]. Also, users might get annoyed when they receive notifications presenting information that is not useful or relevant to them in the current context [13]. At the same time, studies have shown that users cannot ignore their smartphones for a long time, because they start feeling stressed and anxious about missing important information until they finally pick up the phone to check for any new notifications [26]. This tension is exacerbated by the fact that individuals deal with hundreds of notifications in a day, some of which are disruptive [23]

Previous studies have investigated the user's *receptivity* to mobile notifications [15, 29, 32]. As defined by Fischer [15], receptivity encompasses a user's reaction to an interruption and their subjective experience of it. For instance, users might quickly respond to a notification when they are idle, but they can still get annoyed because of the content of the notification. Previous studies have shown that the user's receptivity to a notification is determined by: (i) how interesting, entertaining, relevant and actionable its content is for the user [15]; (ii) the type of application that triggers it – communication applications are considered as the most important [32]; (iii) time criticality and social pressure [29]. At the same time, some studies have proposed various mechanisms to infer *opportune moments*, i.e., moments in which a user quickly and/or favorably reacts to a notification [14, 23, 28]. In order to infer interruptibility these studies have used machine learning classifiers provided with different contextual

CHI'16, May 07-12, 2016, San Jose, CA, USA.
©2016 ACM. ISBN 978-1-4503-3362-7/16/05...$15.00.
DOI: http://dx.doi.org/10.1145/2858036.2858566

factors including user's transitions between activities [18], engagement with a mobile device [14], time of day, location and activity [28] as well as notification content [23].

However, none of these studies have deployed the proposed mechanisms in a real world scenario with *in-the-wild* notifications of a regularly used application. The key reason behind this is the fact that the accuracy of these mechanisms is still lower than the user's expectations. In a real world scenario, the users would not accept a system that might defer or stop an important notification. Previous studies have shown that users are willing to tolerate some interruption, in order to not miss any important information [20]. We believe that interruptibility management systems fail to achieve a very high accuracy in predicting the opportune moment because *there is still a lack of understanding concerning the factors influencing the user's receptivity to mobile notifications in different physical and cognitive situations.*

In order to bridge this gap, in this work we conduct an in-situ study to collect objective and subjective data about mobile notifications. We designed and developed *My Phone and Me* (Figure 1), an application that uses a novel experience sampling method (ESM) approach to uncover the factors and motivations impacting the user's reaction and sentiment towards a notification. Through *My Phone and Me*, we collected 10372 notifications, 474 responses for the ESM questionnaires and 11 personality test results from 20 users. Using this data, we investigate users' interaction with mobile notifications in different physical and cognitive contexts. More specifically, the key contributions of this work are the investigation of:

- the impact of a notification's alert modality on the user's ability to perceive a notification alert;
- the impact of the alert modality, sender-recipient relationship, presentation of a notification, the ongoing task type, completion level and task complexity on the response time;
- the impact of the sender-recipient relationship, and the ongoing task's type, completion level and complexity on the perceived disruption;
- the role of the sender-recipient relationship, notification content and the perceived disruption on the user's decision to accept or dismiss a notification;
- the impact of the user's personality on the perceived disruption and response time to a notification.

The findings of our study are wide-ranging, and may have a direct impact on the way future notification management mechanisms are constructed. First, we observe that a sender-recipient relationship, notification priority and an ongoing task's type and complexity influence the response time for the notification, but there is no impact of the ongoing task completion level on the response time. Moreover, our results show that the recipient's relationship with the sender of a notification, the ongoing task's type, completion level and complexity influence the perceived disruption. Our findings imply that the higher the level of disruption perceived by the user the higher the probability of the notification being dismissed. From our results, we also observe that, nevertheless,

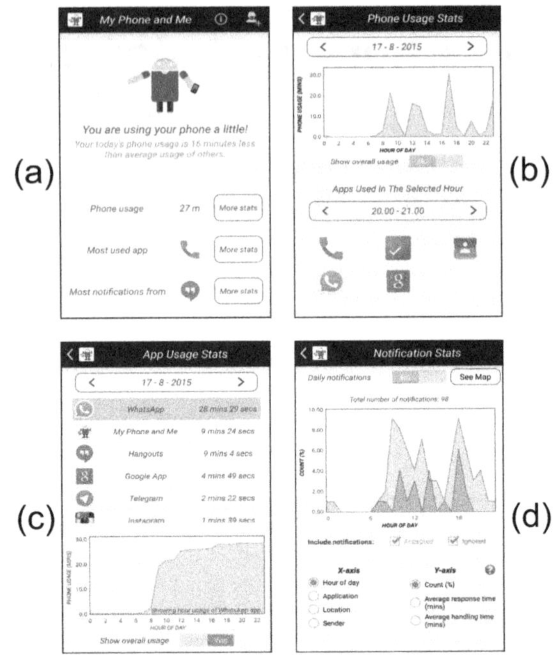

Figure 1. My Phone and Me application: (a) main screen, (b) phone usage statistics, (c) application usage statistics, (d) daily notifications.

users tend to click highly disruptive notifications if they contain valuable information. While users are aware of notifications even when their phone is in silent mode, our analysis shows that the alert modality has a significant impact on the time taken by the users to view the notification. Finally, we observe the substantial role of psychological traits on how a person reacts to a mobile notification, calling for highly personalized interaction between a smartphone and its user.

REASONING ABOUT USERS' RECEPTIVITY TO MOBILE NOTIFICATIONS

An interruption tries to steer a user from an ongoing task to the secondary task signaled by it [8]. As suggested by Clark [10], users can respond to an interruption in four possible ways: (i) handle it immediately; (ii) acknowledge it and agree to handle it later; (iii) decline it (explicitly refusing to handle it); (iv) withdraw it (implicitly refusing to handle it).

A user can respond to mobile notifications in a fairly different way as compared to an in-person interruption. For communication-related interruptions, for example, users might perceive more disruption from an in-person interruption than from a mobile notifications because of the presence of an interrupter in the former case. Mobile notifications enable flexibility in the way an interruption is handled because of the lack of the physical presence of the sender and the asynchronous nature of mobile messaging communication[1]. Thus, the exact moment of handling an interruption can be negotiated and the recipient can decide when and how to attend to a notification.

[1]Certain social norms and expectations from the sender side, however, constrain the flexibility that the receiver has in reacting to a message [30].

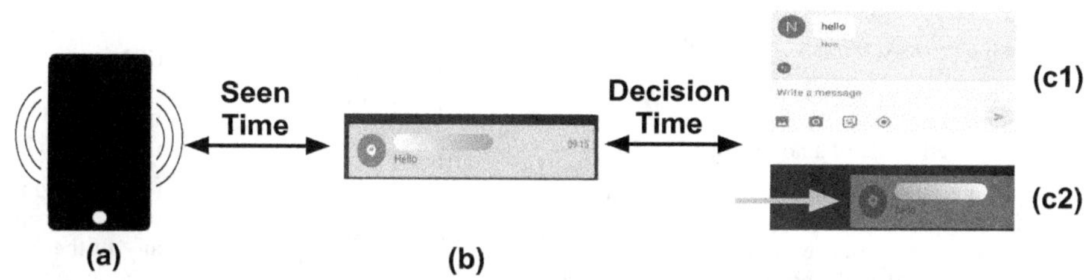

Figure 2. The three time measurements of a notification captured by the My Phone and Me application. The time of notification arrival (*a*), the time when a notification is seen (*b*), and the time when the user accepted (*c*1) or dismissed (*c*2) a notification. The time difference between (*a*) and (*b*) is *seen time* and the time difference between (*b*) and (*c*1 or *c*2) is the *decision time*.

However, this flexibility introduces many other issues. First, notifications can go unnoticed when a user does not register an alert. Second, usually non-persistent notifications may be forgotten about – a user riding a bicycle, might decide to attend to a notification once they arrive at the destination, yet forget to do so. Finally, although designed to signal an interruption but not interrupt themselves, mobile notifications can still induce unnecessary disruption to a user's routine. For instance, the disruption can happen when a user decides to attend to a notification immediately, despite being in the middle of another task, only to find that the notification is about an unrelated promotional offer. Moreover, a disruption may happen even if a notification is not attended to, as the thought of a lingering notification may interfere with the user's current task performance [33].

In this study, we investigate the factors influencing the user's response to a mobile notification, where the response is defined by the time taken to register and react to a notification, and the way in which the notification is handled (i.e., clicked or dismissed). Moreover, we investigate the user's motivation for being self-disruptive by clicking the disruptive notifications.

Our assumption is that the response time for a notification and the disruption perceived by the user are influenced by the different aspects of the notification as well as the user's context. To capture this measure we developed an Android experience sampling method (ESM) application that monitors the actual notifications users receive on their phone, records their reaction to notifications and then queries the users to identify their rating of the disruption caused by the notification. We augment this with questions about the motivation for handling a notification in a particular way. Further, our ESM questionnaires ask the user to provide data on the type, complexity and the completion level of the ongoing task and the user's relationship with the sender. Finally, we collect participants' personality trait measures at the end of the experiment.

First, we investigate the ability of users to adjust their response times to a notification, and see how quickly they can triage different notifications in different situations. As shown in Figure 2, we take three time measurements for each notification: the time of notification arrival (a), the time when the notification is seen (b), and the time when the user accepted (c1) or dismissed (c2) the notification. Note that in order to detect the moment at which a notification is seen, we use the unlock event of the phone and assume that all newly available notifications in the notification bar are seen when the user unlocks the phone. In case a notification arrives when the user is already using the phone (i.e., the phone is unlocked), the seen time of this notification would be computed as zero. We term the time from the notification arrival until the moment the notification was reacted upon as *the response time* for the notification. For our analysis, we break the response time into two intervals:

- Seen time (ST) – time from the notification arrival until the time the notification was seen by the user.
- Decision time (DT) – time from the moment a user saw a notification until the time they acted upon it (by clicking, launching its corresponding app or swiping to dismiss).

We examine the way interruption timing, with respect to the primary task, determines the user's response to the notification. Moreover, we are interested in the way users triage disruptive notifications. Can users quickly discern when notifications are disruptive? We hypothesize that humans might still attend to a notification, even if they know that the primary task is going to be disrupted. For example, in their study of WhatsApp notifications, Pielot et al. [30] show how, due to an inner pressure raised by social expectations, users quickly respond to instant messaging (IM) communication or frequently check their phones, inducing self interruptions just in order to satisfy the social expectations. In our work, we are looking beyond just IM notifications and investigate the way any disruptive message is handled. Through our ESM study we identify the motivation behind reacting to a disruptive notification and the reasoning and the external factors that lead to the exact reaction.

We aim for a comprehensive investigation of interruptibility from a user perspective, thus comparing the effect of different aspects of a notification on its response time and disruptiveness. Finally, we investigate the potential role of individual psychological traits on how users perceive and react to disruptive notifications.

DATA COLLECTION

In order to investigate the nature of disruptive notifications and factors that determine the user's receptivity to mobile notifications in different physical and cognitive situations, we conducted an in-situ field study. More specifically, we developed an Android app called *My Phone and Me* – an Android experience sampling method (ESM) application that collects information about *in-the-wild* notifications, users' interaction

Group	Features
Time	Arrival, seen and the removal time of a notification.
Notification response	Whether the notification was clicked or dismissed.
Notification details	Sender application and the title of a notification.
Alert type	Signals used by a notification to alert the user: sound, vibrate, and flashing LED.
Context data	Physical activity, location, presence of surrounding sound, WiFi connectivity, proximity to the phone, surrounding light intensity. This data is collected on arrival and removal of a notification from the notification bar.

Table 1. Description of features from the My Phone and Me dataset.

with them in natural situations (while they are performing their day-to-day activities), and the physical and cognitive context details.

The My Phone and Me application uses Android's Notification Listener Service [1] to access notifications and Google's Activity Recognition API [3] and ESSensorManager [22] to obtain the context information. Table 1 lists the groups of features captured by the application. The collected context data has not been explored for the analysis presented in this paper. To infer the user's response to a notification, the My Phone and Me application checks whether the application that triggered the notification was launched after the removal time of that notification. We are aware that some notifications are dismissed because they do not require any further action. For this reason, we capture seen time and use the difference between seen time and removal time to understand how long it takes for the user to read and react to a notification.

To collect subjective data from users, the My Phone and Me application triggers four questionnaires in a day. A questionnaire is triggered only when a notification is handled; it contains questions about why the notification was clicked or dismissed by presenting a screenshot of that notification. The application triggers a questionnaire for a randomly selected notification in every four hours time window between 8.00 am and 8.00 pm and the last questionnaire at a random time between 8.00 pm and 10.00 pm. The application did not trigger any questionnaire after 10pm so that the participants do not feel annoyed at responding to the surveys late at night. The application automatically used the local time zones because it relies on the phone's time. Moreover, if the user is busy, the questionnaire can be dismissed by simply swiping it from the notification bar and no questionnaire is shown to the user for the next 30 minutes.

A questionnaire comprises seven multiple-choice and two free-response questions. The list of questions and their options are shown in Table 2. Since we ask the users to enter the free form text for two questions, it could increase time to respond to a questionnaire and may become a source of annoyance. Therefore, the application allows the users to dictate the responses to these questions. These answers are then converted to text using Android's SpeechRecognizer API [2].

Additionally, the My Phone and Me application asks the users to take a personality test based on the 50 item Big-Five Factor Markers from the International Personality Item Pool, de-

Question	Options
Did you notice the alert (e.g., vibration, sound, flashing LED) for this notification when it first arrived?	(i) Yes, and I decided to check my phone immediately. (ii) Yes, but I was already using my phone. (iii) Yes, but I ignored the alert. (iv) No, I didn't notice the alert.
How did you handle the notification when you first saw it?	(i) I decided to immediately click it. (ii) I decided to dismiss it because it didn't require any further action. (iii) I decided to dismiss it because it was not relevant or useful. (iv) I decided to return to it later. (v) Other (descriptive).
Select all factors that made you decide to click/dismiss the notification.	(i) The sender is important. (ii) The content is important. (iii) The content is urgent. (iv) The content is useful. (v) I was waiting for this notification. (vi) The action demanded by the sender does not require a lot of effort. (vii) At this moment, I was free. (viii) Other (descriptive).
What best describes your relationship to the sender?	(i) Partner (ii) Immediate family (children, parents) (iii) Extended family (nieces/nephews, cousins, aunts/uncles) (iv) Friend (v) Acquaintance (vi) Superior at work (vii) Colleague (viii) Subordinate at work (ix) Client (x) Service provider (xi) Sender is not a person (xii) Other relationship (descriptive).
Please describe what the notification was about.	Descriptive response.
Please describe what activity you were involved with when you received the notification.	Descriptive response.
When the notification arrived, I was:	(i) Starting a new task/activity. (ii) In the middle of a task/activity. (iii) Finishing a task/activity. (iv) Not doing anything.
The task/activity I was doing when the notification arrived was complex.	Five-level Likert scale rating between "strongly disagree" and "strongly agree".
I found the notification disruptive.	Five-level Likert scale rating between "strongly disagree" and "strongly agree".

Table 2. Questions and their options from questionnaire triggered by the My Phone and Me app.

veloped by Goldberg [16]. A notification to take this test is triggered once the user has responded to 28 questionnaires. A user can also take the test at any time by clicking on the personality test button present in the application's action bar.

Recruitment of the Participants

The My Phone and Me application was published on the Google Play Store from 12th August 2015. It was installed by 74 participants without any monetary incentive. As shown in Figure 1, My Phone and Me tells the users about their addiction to the phone. It allows users to check statistics on their phone usage and interruptions. The application visualizes a user's phone activities based on different criteria, such as their hourly phone usage (Figure 1 C), hourly usage of individual applications (Figure 1 D) and how much they interact with notifications (Figure 1 B). We believe that displaying this information has a minimal interference with users' actual behavior for interacting with notifications, but provides a valuable functionality in order to make the users keep the application installed on their phones.

In order to ensure privacy compliance, the My Phone and Me application goes through a two-level user agreement to access the user's notifications. Firstly, the user has to give explicit permission as required by the Android operating system. Secondly, the application shows a list of information that is collected and asks for user consent. Moreover, we show the original content of a notification to the user along with the questionnaire in order to avoid any recall bias in the data but we do not collect the notification content for privacy reasons.

DATASET

The data collection was carried out for around two months, during which we collected 19494 notifications, 611 responses for the questionnaire (comprising a set of nine questions listed in Table 2) and 11 personality test results (50 item-based Big-Five Factor Markers by Goldberg [16]) from 74 users who installed the My Phone and Me application. Many users stopped responding to the questionnaires after a few days and some did not respond at all. Therefore, we select a subset of the data for the analysis and include data of users who responded to at least 14 questionnaires. There are 20 users who satisfied this constraint. So, our final dataset comprises of 10372 notifications, 474 questionnaire responses and 11 personality test results. Additionally, during the setup phase we asked participants to enter their age and gender: in our dataset there are 11 male and 9 females aged between 19 and 50 years old. However, we do not ask them to provide any other demographic information.

As we are primarily using the questionnaire responses, we compared the click rate (i.e., percentage of notifications that are clicked out of total notifications) of the overall notifications with the notifications that were linked to questionnaires. The click rate for overall notifications is 62.52%, and for notifications linked with questionnaires is 70.04%. Note that a notification is considered to be clicked either when it is clicked on the notification bar or when its corresponding application is launched directly.

We are aware that our dataset has potential limitations that stem from the inherent nature of an *in-the-wild* study. The dataset remains unbalanced because it is not possible to obtain an equal number of questionnaire responses from all users for each test category. For instance, there is a very small chance that our application triggers a questionnaire for each type of sender from the recipients social circle. Furthermore, in practice, a user might not even receive notifications from each of the sender types during the period of the study. Therefore, we use the data from 20 users who responded to at least 14 questionnaires, i.e., the minimum number of questionnaires that were answered by users in this set. We also make an hypothesis of data independence (i.e., data instances are obtained from different users) which might not hold in reality and can be tested only in a controlled setting.

UNDERSTANDING RESPONSE TIME

In this section we investigate the effect of different factors on the seen and decision time of a notification.

The key findings of this section are:

- Users are aware of the notification alerts even when the phone is in silent mode. However, seen time is fastest when the phone is in vibrate mode and slowest for silent node.
- Notifications are seen fastest when the user is commuting and slowest when idle.
- User's attentiveness increases (reducing the seen time) with the increase in the complexity of an ongoing task.
- The decision time is higher for the notifications from less frequently contacted senders.
- High-priority notifications get quicker response.

The Role of Alert Modality in Perceiving a Notification Alert

A notification can alert the user by means of vibration, sound and/or flashing LED. In order to investigate how users perceive alerts with different alert modalities, we used the responses provided by the users for Q1 (*Did you notice the alert (e.g., vibration, sound, flashing LED) for this notification when it first arrived?*). According to our dataset, when the notifications (with which the questionnaires were linked) were triggered the user's phone was for 25.54% of the times in the silent mode, 21.50% vibrate mode, 41.94% sound mode and 11.03% sound with vibrate.

Users reported that they missed notification alerts for 14.63%, 15.38%, 23.75%, 21.05% of times their phone was in silent, vibrate, sound, and sound with vibrate mode respectively. This provides evidence that when the phone is in silent mode users are still aware of the notification alerts.

What Factors Influence the Seen Time?

We investigate the role of alert modality, sender and the ongoing task type, complexity and completion level, in influencing the seen time of a notification.

The Impact of Alert Modality on Seen Time

In order to perform this analysis, from our dataset of 10372 notifications we use all the notifications of the 20 users who responded to at least 14 questionnaires. However, we ignore the notifications that arrived when the user was already engaged with the phone because we could not calculate the seen time of these notifications. This leaves us with 4929 notifications. A one-way Analysis of Variance (ANOVA) of the seen time was carried out for each alert modality. The results show that the alert modality has an impact on the seen time of notifications, with $F(3, 4925) = 26.41$, $p < 0.001$. A Tukey post-hoc test (by setting the $\alpha = 0.05$) revealed that the seen time is statistically significantly higher for silent notifications (average 7.332 mins). The seen time for the notifications alerting with vibrate only mode is the lowest (average 3 minutes and 21 second). Sound only and sound with vibrate notifications are the second (average 5 minutes and 57 seconds) and third (average 4 minutes and 50 seconds) most quickly seen by users. Quite interestingly, a recent 15-user study by Pielot et al. [29] also found that notifications tend to be seen faster when the phone is in the vibrate mode. Here, we confirm this finding, but also point to the above missed notification percentage in the silent mode (14.63%) and show that setting the phone to silent does not help in escaping interruptions.

The Impact of Ongoing Task Type on Seen Time

To investigate the impact of the ongoing task on the notification's seen time, we require the type of task that the users were involved with when the notification arrived. We classified the information users provided through ESM questionnaires about the ongoing task into the following six categories: work, communication, traveling, maintenance/personal, leisure and idle. The classification was done manually, by two coders who initially disagreed on five entries. Two common labels for these were found after a discussion with three other coders. Note that our app allows users to skip the step of providing the information on the question about their current task by selecting the "Prefer not to say" option. In such cases, we discard the entry from our analysis of the effect of the ongoing task on interruptibility.

A one-way ANOVA of the seen time is carried out for each task type. The results show that the ongoing task type has an impact on the seen time of notifications, with $F(5, 217) = 2.963$, $p = 0.013$. A Tukey post-hoc test (by setting the α as 0.05) reveals that the seen time is the lowest when the notifications arrive while the user is communicating (average 47 seconds) and highest while the user is idle (average 9 minutes and 30 seconds). Other task types do not have a statistically significant effect on the seen time of notifications and have an average seen time of 5 minutes 45 seconds. As shown in a recent study [31] notifications are more welcome when recipients are bored. However, our results show that while the users might be willing to accept more notifications when idle, the time needed to attend to such notifications might be higher compared to the time needed to attend to a notification while a user is busy.

The Impact of Ongoing Task Complexity on Seen Time

To analyze the effect of ongoing task complexity, we first encode the reported task complexity, which was reported as a value on the Likert scale (*Strongly disagree*=1, *Somewhat disagree*=2, *Neutral*=3, *Somewhat agree*=4 and *Strongly agree*=5) to the question "The task/activity I was doing when the notification arrived was complex". The Spearman's rank correlation coefficient is computed to evaluate the relationship between the complexity of an ongoing task and the seen time of a notification. The results show that there is a weak, negative correlation between the two variables, $\rho = -0.183$, $p = 0.005$. Thus, the increase in the seen time of notifications is correlated with the decrease in rating of ongoing task's complexity. We believe that this correlation exists because the users become more alert while performing a complex task and thus, quickly perceive the interruptions. On the other hand, when the users are not performing any complex task, they become less attentive to the interruptions. Finally, we found that factors such as the completion level of the ongoing task and the sender type do not have a statistically significant effect on the seen time of notifications.

What Factors Influence the Decision Time?

We analyze the effect of the type, complexity and completion level of the ongoing task, and the sender type on the time a user takes to decide how to react to a notification. We find that neither of these factors have a statistically significant effect on the decision time of notifications with the exception of the sender.

A one-way repeated measures ANOVA of the decision time was carried out for each sender type. The results show that the sender type has an impact on the seen time of notifications with $F(10, 212) = 2.429$, $p = 0.00936$. A Tukey post-hoc test (by setting the $\alpha = 0.05$) revealed that out of the 11 sender types (shown in Table 2), notifications from partner lead to the fastest decision time (mean DT is 3.315s), followed by immediate family members with an average decision time of 4.891 seconds. On the other hand, notifications from extended family members and service providers have the largest decision time, 11.93 and 8.146 seconds respectively. There was no statistically significant difference in the decision time of the notifications from other senders. These results demonstrate that notifications are quickly handled when they are sent by the close relatives of the user. In other cases users take more time in reading the content before deciding how to handle it. We hypothesize that this behavior stems from the content of notifications from close friends or family members, which might be more predictable, and a part of a daily routine (e.g., "pick kids from school"). *On the other hand, the users have to spend more time on the notifications from less frequently contacted sources, as the content may be less familiar to them.*

The Role of Notification Presentation

In our dataset, 2953 (out of 7795) notifications were received when the user was engaged with the phone. Out of these 2953 notifications, 860 are so-called "low-priority" while 2093 are "high-priority" notifications [4]. Here, a high-priority notification is a foreground notification that gets in the way of the user's ongoing activity and the user cannot perform any action to get it out of the way without clicking or dismissing it (e.g. Viber messages). A low-priority one simply appears on the notification bar without getting in the way of the user's ongoing activity (e.g. Gmail notifications).

We investigate the effect of the notification presentation on the response time (i.e., the sum of seen time and decision time) of a notification. The result of a two sample t-test shows that there is a statistically significant effect of notification priority on the response time, $t(2951) = 17.694$, $p < 0.001$, with high-priority notifications getting quicker response than low-priority notifications. The mean response time for high-priority notifications is 11.94s versus 25.91s for low-priority notifications.

WHY A NOTIFICATION BECOMES DISRUPTIVE

In this section we investigate the effect of different factors on the perceived disruption. Since the perceived disruption was measured with a 5-point Likert scale, we encode the responses as: *Strongly disagree*=1, *Somewhat disagree*=2, *Neutral*=3, *Somewhat agree*=4 and *Strongly agree*=5.

The key findings of this section are:

- Perceived disruption increases with the increase in the complexity of an ongoing task.
- Notifications are perceived as most disruptive if they arrive when the user is in the middle of or finishing a task, and least disruptive if the user is idle or starting a new task.
- Messages from subordinates and system messages (where the sender is not a person) are considered as most disruptive. Whereas, extended family members are considered as the least disruptive.

The Role of Ongoing Task Complexity

We investigate whether the complexity of an ongoing task is associated with the perceived disruption reported by the users. A Kendall's Tau correlation coefficient was computed to assess the relationship between the ongoing task complexity and perceived disruption. We found a strong, positive correlation between the two variables, $R_T = 0.477$, $p < 0.001$. This demonstrates that the users are likely to get more disrupted by a notification that arrives when they are engaged in an intricate task and less disrupted when they are performing a simple task. In our preliminary analysis [27] we have found that when users are engaged in complex tasks they also express more of a negative sentiment towards interruptions.

The Role of Ongoing Task Completion Level

A one-way ANOVA of the reported disruption was carried out for each class of task completion level (starting, in the middle, finishing and not doing anything). The results show that the completion level of an ongoing task has a significant impact on the disruption perceived by the users from the notifications, $F(3, 451) = 19.43$, $p < 0.001$. A Tukey post-hoc test (by setting α as 0.05) reveals that the perceived disruption is the highest when the user is currently involved in a task. The perceived disruption is the lowest when the user is starting a task or idle and there is no statistically significant difference between these groups. These results show that the perceived disruption when the user is highly engaged in a task is very high not only from the desktop notification, as discussed for example in [13, 24], but also from the mobile notifications.

The Role of Sender

We compute a one-way ANOVA of the reported disruption for each type of sender (see Table 2). According to the results, $F(10, 444) = 3.987$, $p < 0.001$, the type of sender has a significant impact on the disruption perceived by the users from the notifications. A Tukey post-hoc test (by setting the α as 0.05) reveals that the perceived disruption is highest when the sender is not a person or is a subordinate at work (no statistically significant difference between these two groups) and the lowest when the sender is an extended family member. Moreover, colleagues and service providers are the second most disruptive sender groups. There is no significant difference between the other groups. Previous studies showed that users express a negative *sentiment* towards the messages not coming from their family and friends [15], and that the more "distant" the sender is, the less likely it is that a notification will be *clicked on* [23]. Results from our study complement this with the finding that the perceived *disruption* varies with the sender of a notification.

The Role of Ongoing Task Type

A one-way ANOVA of the reported disruption is carried out for each type of ongoing task (see Table 2). The results show that the type of task that the user is engaged with on the arrival of a notification has a significant impact on the disruption the user perceives when the notification arrives, $F(5, 380) = 13.03$, $p < 0.001$. A Tukey post-hoc test (by setting $\alpha = 0.05$) revealed that the perceived disruption is the highest when the user is working and the lowest while the user is idle. After work, traveling and then leisure are the tasks where the users perceive the highest level of disruption. When the users are not idle, they perceive least disruption while communicating and doing a personal or maintenance task. Since the communication can involve notifications themselves, e.g. two mobile users exchanging WhatsApp messages, the above result is not surprising. As shown in a recent study [31], users are receptive to information when they are bored. Our results are in line with these findings in showing that perceived disruption is lowest when the user is idle.

UNDERSTANDING THE ACCEPTANCE OF NOTIFICATIONS

In this section we investigate the factors that make the users accept (click) or dismiss a notification.

The key findings of this section are:

- Likelihood of the acceptance of a notification decreases with the increase in the perceived disruption.
- Disruptive notifications are accepted because they contain useful information.

Procedure

Through the questionnaires, we asked the users the reason for clicking/dismissing a notification (see Table 2). If a notification (linked with the questionnaire) is clicked by the user, we ask them to select all factors that made them decide to click the notification, otherwise, we ask them to select the factors that made them decide to dismiss the notification. We provide a predefined list of seven and six options for clicking (see Table 3) and dismissing (see Table 4) the notification. In addition, there is a box for open-ended answers in case users do not find an appropriate answer in the provided list.

In Table 3 and Table 4 we calculate the percentage of times each factor was reported as a reason for clicking and dismissing the notifications. Since, users may select more than one option, the total count percentage in the table adds up to more than 100%. According to these responses, the users mostly accept notifications when they are free, but also the importance of the sender and the usefulness of the content make

Option	Count (%)
Sender is important	31.546
The content is important	27.129
The content is urgent	14.511
The content is useful	31.546
I was waiting for this notification	15.773
The action demanded by the sender does not require a lot of effort	20.189
At this moment, I was free	37.224

Table 3. User response about why they accept (click) notifications.

Option	Count (%)
Sender is not important	19.565
The content is not important	40.580
The content is not urgent	43.478
The content is not useful	38.406
The action demanded by the sender does require a lot of effort	3.623
At this moment, I was busy	19.565

Table 4. User response about why they dismiss notifications.

them accept a notification. On the other hand, users avoid attending to notifications that do not contain important, urgent or useful content. These responses demonstrate that the value of content is used for deciding whether to click or dismiss a notification. Moreover, the users very rarely state that they were busy and thus had to dismiss a notification. This could indicate that the users give precedence to a notification over the primary task, but only if the content is valuable.

Disruptive Notifications are Likely to be Dismissed

We examine the impact of the disruption caused by the notifications on their likelihood of being accepted. In order to quantify this, we encoded the response for perceived disruption with the following values: *Strongly disagree*=1, *Somewhat disagree*=2, *Neutral*=3, *Somewhat agree*=4 and *Strongly agree*=5. In order to detect the acceptance of a notification, we check whether it was clicked by the user. In case it was dismissed, we cross-validate the user's response for the question *How did you handle the notification?* If the user responded that *I decided to dismiss it because it didn't require any further action*, we mark this notification as accepted. Finally, we use 0 to indicate that the notification is dismissed and 1 for an accepted notification.

We fit a logistic regression model to estimate the effect of perceived disruption on the likelihood of the acceptance of notifications. The model was statistically significant $X^2(1) = 48.3$, $p < 0.001$. The results indicate the likelihood of the acceptance of a notification decreases by 0.581 times (95% confidence interval limits for the slope were [0.497, 0.675]) for a unit increase in the perceived disruption (based on the 5-point Likert scale).

However, the coefficient of determination for the fitted model is not high ($R^2 = 0.1434$), which implies that not only the disruption perceived by the user, but also other factors influence the user's decision to accept a notification.

Why are disruptive notifications accepted?

As discussed above, the disruption perceived by the user makes a notification more likely to be dismissed. Our dataset shows that 104 out of 474 notifications (with which the questionnaires were linked) were reported as disruptive. These are the notifications for which the user *somewhat* and *strongly* agreed that they perceived disruption from these notifications.

Option	Count (%)
Sender is important	25.926
The content is important	33.333
The content is urgent	20.370
The content is useful	35.185
I was waiting for this notification	11.111
The action demanded by the sender does not require a lot of effort	16.667
At this moment, I was free	18.519

Table 5. User response about why they accept disruptive notifications.

Variable	Estimated Coefficient	Std. Error	t value	p value
Extroversion	0.017481	0.005694	3.070	0.0278*
Agreeableness	-0.012833	0.005387	-2.382	0.0630
Conscientiousness	0.005942	0.004420	1.344	0.2366
Neuroticism	0.008659	0.004042	2.142	0.0851
Openness	-0.003114	0.005369	-0.580	0.5870

N=11
$R^2 = 0.737$
F(5,5)=2.802(p=0.01413)

Table 6. Results of linear regression with the average disruption as a dependent variable and the personality traits as independent variables.

However, 54% of these disruptive notifications were accepted (clicked) by the users, regardless of the fact that they caused disruption. To investigate the reason for this, we checked users' responses about the factors that made them click these notifications. Table 5 shows the percentage of times each factor was reported by the users for accepting the disruptive notifications. As users were allowed to select more than one option, the sum of the percentages in the table adds up to more than 100. "Content is important" and "Content is useful" are the most dominant reason provided by the users for clicking the disruptive notifications. This tells us that even the notifications containing important or useful content can cause disruption. We suspect that these notifications may contain valuable information, but they were not relevant at the moment of delivery. However, our study remains limited to make such conclusions and provide an understanding about why users perceive disruption from useful notifications.

DOES PERSONALITY MATTER

In this section we investigate the role of personality on the reported disruption, seen time and decision time of notifications. We computed the score for the five personality traits (i.e., the so-called Big Five: Extroversion, Agreeableness, Conscientiousness, Neuroticism and Openness) for each of the 11 users who fully completed the exit questionnaire that includes the 50 questions related to personality traits. For this computation, we used the scoring instructions that come with the personality test [16].

Impact on Reported Disruption

To quantify the relationship between the five personality traits and the disruption perceived by the users from notifications, we fit a linear regression model with the average disruption

Variable	Estimated Coefficient	Std. Error	t value	p value
Extroversion	0.44042	0.14926	2.951	0.0319*
Agreeableness	0.25281	0.14122	1.790	0.1334
Conscientiousness	-0.42050	0.11586	-3.629	0.0151*
Neuroticism	-0.39663	0.10597	-3.743	0.0134*
Openness	-0.05059	0.14074	-0.359	0.7339
N=11 R^2=0.9007 F(5,5)=9.073(p=0.01511)				

Table 7. Results of linear regression with the average seen time as a dependent variable and the personality traits as independent variables.

Variable	Estimated Coefficient	Std. Error	t value	p value
Extroversion	0.45350	0.13446	3.373	0.0198*
Agreeableness	0.29340	0.12722	2.306	0.0692
Conscientiousness	-0.26102	0.10438	-2.501	0.0544
Neuroticism	-0.36975	0.09547	-3.873	0.0117*
Openness	0.08584	0.12679	0.677	0.5284
N=11 R^2=0.9035 F(5,5)=9.366(p=0.01411)				

Table 8. Results of linear regression with the average decision time as a dependent variable and five personality traits as independent variables.

as a dependent variable, and the five personality traits as independent variables. Here, the average disruption is computed as a mean of disruption reported by the user through the questionnaires. All responses were encoded with the following values *Strongly disagree*=1, *Somewhat disagree*=2, *Neutral*=3, *Somewhat agree*=4, and *Strongly agree*=5. Table 6 shows the parameters of the fitted linear regression model. The results show that the extroversion personality trait significantly affects the average perceived disruption and that extroverts are more inclined to be disrupted by a notification. The high value for the coefficient of determination (R^2 = 0.737) shows that the value of average disruption reported by the users is highly influenced by the personality of users, albeit this could be a consequence of our small sample size.

Impact on Notification's Seen Time and Decision Time

We then investigate whether the personality traits influence the seen and decision time. In order to perform these analyses, we compute:

1. the average seen time of notifications for each user: the average time taken by a user to view a notification. It is computed as the mean of the seen time of all notification received by the user.
2. the average decision time of notifications for each user: the average time taken by a user to click/dismiss after viewing a notification. It is computed as the mean of decision time of all notifications received by the user.

We first fit a linear regression model with the average (per user) seen time as a dependent variable, and the five personality traits as independent variables. The parameters of the fitted linear regression model are shown in Table 7. The results demonstrate that the time in which a notification is viewed by the users is significantly influenced by their Extroversion, Conscientiousness and Neuroticism personality traits. We fit another linear regression model with the average decision time as a dependent variable and the five personality traits as independent variables. The parameters of the fitted linear regression model are shown in Table 8, and demonstrate that the decision time for a notification is significantly influenced by the user's Extroversion and Neuroticism personality traits.

The need for individual models of human interruptibility has been identified earlier, both in the desktop office setting [19], as well as with mobile smartphone users [23]. The above results show potential for the interruptibility models to be generalized across groups of users who share the same personality traits.

IMPLICATIONS

Deferring Notifications

Previous studies show that users perceive more disruption from notifications when engaged in intricate tasks and for the first time we confirm this for mobile settings in a quantitative way. Thus, in order to benefit users, the OS should offer more flexibility to them for setting the busy moments so that only time-critical notifications could be triggered. This would potentially allow interruptibility management (IM) systems to learn patterns to predict the user's engagement with complex tasks and prioritize interruptions accordingly.

Improving Notification Presentation

We found that users become more attentive at busy moments, but are likely to perceive most notifications as disruptive and dismiss them. However, disruptive notifications tend to be accepted if they contain useful content. The presentation of notification summaries could be adapted to help users quickly decide whether to click or dismiss notifications, e.g. by highlighting notifications from priority contacts or with priority content that is learnt over time by an IM system.

Building a Personality-Dependent Interruptibility Model

We observed that the perceived disruption, seen and decision time are influenced by the user's personality traits. This demonstrates the potential to take the personality trait into account in interruption models and, for example, generalise interruptibility models across groups of users who share the same personality traits. These findings can be exploited to design more effective machine learning algorithms for intelligent notifications.

RELATED WORK

Multitasking is fundamental in workplaces, where task switching happens every few minutes [17], but also in the private sphere, where an increasing number of personal computing devices mediate the flow of data, be it of entertainment, social or informative nature. Unfortunately, multitasking is seldom seamless, since the limited amount of human attention is sought by a range of competing tasks/themes. The disruptiveness of interruptions was analyzed by Miata and Norman [24], who were among the first to note and explain its variability with the context and particularly their alignment with respect to the primary task a user is working on.

To explain why the interruptions are disruptive, Altmann and Trafton propose the *Memory for Goals model* that explains how users' intention move the necessary mental state of the problem between the foreground and the background of their attention and how such state deteriorates when kept in the background [6]. The importance of the problem state held in the memory corresponds to the complexity of the primary task and, consequently, recovering after a complex task is more demanding than if a routine task is interrupted [9].

In this paper, to the best of our knowledge we are the first to investigate the role of the task complexity on interruptibility in the mobile context. Our results confirm the theory of Altmann and Trafton and we find that interrupting a complex task remains disruptive in the mobile setting. However, the nature of interruptions in our study is fundamentally different from the above work – our users receive notifications signaling interruptions, and are not "forced" into the interruption, per se. This allows us to investigate more subtle phenomena, such as the relationship between the primary task and the time to register a notification. One of our key findings is that *users working on more mentally demanding tasks need less time to notice a notification*. We hypothesize that the "high alert" state in which a user is when working on a complex task [21] also leads to a more agile reaction to a notification.

Multitasking theories are build upon data acquired in highly controlled environments. In reality, however, mobile users engage in unconstrained communication with their friends and family, move about in different surroundings and get notifications from a range of applications. Shirazi et al. [32] show that there is a high variation in the way a notification is handled depending on the application with which it is associated. Personal communication applications, for example, are preferred and attended to faster, than applications associated with utilities and tools. Personal interests, relevance and actionability of the content are additional qualifiers that impact a user's reaction to a notification [15]. In our recent work we uncover that the content and the sender-recipient relationship play a significant role in the decision to accept a notification [23]. In this study, we further refine the role of the sender and find that the messages from extended family members are perceived as the least disruptive. Moreover, the content is one of the main reasons for accepting the notifications even though they interfere with the user's current task.

LIMITATIONS

Most limitations of the work presented in this paper stem from our decision to collect data in the wild, with the minimum amount of intervention from our users. For example, when it comes to the computation of the seen time of a notification, remotely, we can only detect if a user unlocked the phone and assume that all notifications were seen. We cannot detect the precise time when a user starts reading a summary of a message from the notification bar. Moreover, in case a notification arrives when the user is already engaged with the phone, we assume that the user has seen the notification. Further, since our users are not confined to a laboratory, we are limited to self-reported level of disruption from a notification. In reality, the impact on the primary task need not be high even if the perceived disruption level is high. On the other hand, this self perception might be the most important factor that determines the user's long term sentiment towards notifications. When it comes to our ESM sampling, despite being as light as possible (we ask only up to four ESM questionnaires per day from each user), they increase the number of notifications a user sees during the data collection period. The density of notifications negatively impacts the sentiment towards individual notifications [28]. However, we believe that in our case the impact is equally distributed among notifications, and consequently, that the findings about the role of different factors still hold. Finally, while the work is the first to our knowledge to uncover the role of individual psychological traits on mobile interruptibility, it is important to note that we related the traits with the *reported* interruptibility. Therefore, our finding that extrovert people report to be more disturbed by notifications than others, should be interpreted under the fact that general reporting about oneself most likely depends on the person's level of extroversion.

CONCLUSIONS

In this paper we have presented a study of mobile interruptibility, specifically concentrating on the identification of factors that make an interruption disruptive and the impact on the response time to a notification. The contributions of this study are threefold. First, we have confirmed the validity of some past desktop interruptibility studies in a mobile setting. Second, for the first time, we have investigated the role of notification presentation, sender-recipient relationship and personality for modelling interruptibility. Finally, our work confirms findings from recent interruptibility studies.

Through a mixed method of automated smartphone logging and ESM sampling we have obtained a dataset of *in-the-wild* notifications and ESM reports on notification perception from 20 users. We have analysed the data to show that the response time of a notification in the mobile environment is not only influenced by an ongoing task's type, completion level and task complexity, but also by the notification's alert modality, presentation and sender-recipient relationship. Our results have shown that the presentation of a notification and its alert type, as well as the type, completion level and complexity of a task with which the user is engaged, all impact the seen time. Moreover, the relationship with the sender influences the user's decision on accepting a notification or not. The data also reveals how the sentiment (i.e., perceived disruption) towards a notification varies with the type, completion level and complexity of an ongoing task and the recipient's relationship with the sender. Finally, different people exhibit different reactions and we observe a substantial role of the individual psychological traits on how a person reacts to a mobile notification.

ACKNOWLEDGEMENTS

This work was supported through the EPSRC Grants "MACACO: Mobile context-Adaptive CAching for Content-Centric networking" (EP/L018829/2) and "UBhave: ubiquitous and social computing for positive behaviour change" (EP/I032673/1).

REFERENCES

1. *Android's Notification Listener Service.* http://developer.android.com/reference/android/service/notification/NotificationListenerService.html.
2. *Android's SpeechRecognizer API.* http://developer.android.com/reference/android/speech/SpeechRecognizer.html.
3. *Google's Activity Recognition API.* http://developer.android.com/training/location/activity-recognition.htmll.
4. *Heads-up Notifications.* http://developer.android.com/guide/topics/ui/notifiers/notifications.html#Heads-up.
5. Piotr D Adamczyk and Brian P Bailey. 2004. If not now, when?: the effects of interruption at different moments within task execution. In *CHI'04*. ACM, Vienna, Austria, 271—278.
6. Erik M Altmann and J Gregory Trafton. 2002. Memory for goals: An activation-based model. *Cognitive science* 26, 1 (2002), 39–83.
7. Brian P Bailey and Joseph A Konstan. 2006. On the need for attention-aware systems: Measuring effects of interruption on task performance, error rate, and affective state. *Computers in Human Behavior* 22, 4 (2006), 685–708.
8. Brian P Bailey, Joseph A Konstan, and John V Carlis. 2000. Measuring the effects of interruptions on task performance in the user interface. In *SMC'00*, Vol. 2. IEEE, Nashville,Tennessee, USA, 757–762.
9. Jelmer P Borst, Niels A Taatgen, and Hedderik van Rijn. 2010. The problem state: a cognitive bottleneck in multitasking. *Journal of Experimental Psychology: Learning, memory, and cognition* 36, 2 (2010), 363.
10. Herbert H Clark. 1996. *Using language*. Vol. 1996. Cambridge University Press Cambridge.
11. Edward Cutrell, Mary Czerwinski, and Eric Horvitz. 2001. Notification, disruption, and memory: Effects of messaging interruptions on memory and performance. In *Interact'01*. IOS Press, Tokyo, Japan, 263—270.
12. Mary Czerwinski, Edward Cutrell, and Eric Horvitz. 2000a. Instant messaging and interruption: Influence of task type on performance. In *OZCHI'00*. ACM, Sydney, Australia, 361—367.
13. Mary Czerwinski, Edward Cutrell, and Eric Horvitz. 2000b. Instant messaging: Effects of relevance and timing. *People and computers XIV: Proceedings of HCI* 2 (2000), 71–76.
14. Joel E Fischer, Chris Greenhalgh, and Steve Benford. 2011. Investigating episodes of mobile phone activity as indicators of opportune moments to deliver notifications. In *MobileHCI'11*. ACM, Stockholm, Sweden, 181—190.
15. Joel E Fischer, Nick Yee, Victoria Bellotti, Nathan Good, Steve Benford, and Chris Greenhalgh. 2010. Effects of Content and Time of Delivery on Receptivity to Mobile Interruptions. In *MobileHCI'10*. ACM, Lisbon, Portugal, 103—112.
16. Lewis R Goldberg. 1992. The development of markers for the Big-Five factor structure. *Psychological Assessment* 4, 1 (1992), 26.
17. Victor M. Gonzalez and Mark. Gloria. 2004. Constant, Constant, Multi-Tasking Craziness: Managing Multiple Working Spheres. In *CHI'04*. ACM, Vienna, Austria, 113–120.
18. Joyce Ho and Stephen S. Intille. 2005. Using Context-Aware Computing to Reduce the Perceived Burden of Interruptions from Mobile Devices. In *CHI'05*. ACM, Seoul, Korea, 909–918.
19. Eric Horvitz and Johnson Apacible. 2003. Learning and Reasoning about Interruption. In *ICMI'03*. ACM, Vancouver, Canada, 20–27.
20. Shamsi T Iqbal and Eric Horvitz. 2010. Notifications and awareness: a field study of alert usage and preferences. In *CSCW'10*. ACM, Savannah, Georgia, USA, 27–30.
21. Shamsi T Iqbal, Xianjun Sam Zheng, and Brian P Bailey. 2004. Task-evoked pupillary response to mental workload in human-computer interaction. In *CHI'04 Extended Abstracts*. ACM, Vienna, Austria, 1477–1480.
22. Neal Lathia, Kiran K. Rachuri, Cecilia Mascolo, and George Roussos. 2013. Open Source Smartphone Libraries for Computational Social Science. In *MCSS'13*. ACM, Zurich, Switzerland, 911–920.
23. Abhinav Mehrotra, Mirco Musolesi, Robert Hendley, and Veljko Pejovic. 2015. Designing Content-driven Intelligent Notification Mechanisms for Mobile Applications. In *UbiComp'15*. ACM, Osaka, Japan, 813–824.
24. Yoshiro Miyata and Donald A. Norman. 1986. Psychological Issues in Support of Multiple Activities. *User Centered System Design: New Perspectives on Human-Computer Interaction* (1986), 265–284.
25. Christopher A Monk, Deborah A Boehm-Davis, and J Gregory Trafton. 2002. The attentional costs of interrupting task performance at various stages. In *HFES'02*, Vol. 46. SAGE Publications, Baltimore, Maryland, 1824–1828.
26. Antti Oulasvirta, Tye Rattenbury, Lingyi Ma, and Eeva Raita. 2012. Habits make smartphone use more pervasive. *Personal and Ubiquitous Computing* 16, 1 (2012), 105–114.
27. Veljko Pejovic, Abhinav Mehrotra, and Mirco Musolesi. 2015. Investigating The Role of Task Engagement in Mobile Interruptibility. In *MobileHCI'15 Adjunct*. ACM, Copenhagen, Denmark.

28. Veljko Pejovic and Mirco Musolesi. 2014. InterruptMe: designing intelligent prompting mechanisms for pervasive applications. In *UbiComp'14*. ACM, Seattle, WA, USA, 897–908.

29. Martin Pielot, Karen Church, and Rodrigo de Oliveira. 2014a. An in-situ study of mobile phone notifications. In *MobileHCI'14*. ACM, Toronto, ON, Canada, 233–242.

30. Martin Pielot, Rodrigo de Oliveira, Haewoon Kwak, and Nuria Oliver. 2014b. Didn't you see my message?: predicting attentiveness to mobile instant messages. In *CHI'14*. ACM, Toronto, ON, Canada, 3319–3328.

31. Martin Pielot, Tilman Dingler, Jose San Pedro, and Nuria Oliver. 2015. When attention is not scarce-detecting boredom from mobile phone usage. In *UbiComp'15*. ACM, Osaka, Japan, 825–836.

32. Alireza Sahami Shirazi, Niels Henze, Tilman Dingler, Martin Pielot, Dominik Weber, and Albrecht Schmidt. 2014. Large-scale assessment of mobile notifications. In *CHI'14*. ACM, Toronto, ON, Canada, 3055–3064.

33. Cary Stothart, Ainsley Mitchum, and Courtney Yehnert. 2015. The attentional cost of receiving a cell phone notification. *Journal of Experimental Psychology: Human Perception and Performance* 41, 4 (2015), 893.

Voices from the War: Design as a Means of Understanding the Experience of Visiting Heritage

Daniela Petrelli, Nick Dulake, Mark T. Marshall
Sheffield Hallam University
Sheffield, UK
d.petrelli n.dulake m.marshall@shu.ac.uk

Anna Pisetti
Museo Storico Italiano della Guerra
Rovereto, Italy
annapisetti@museodellaguerra.it

Elena Not
FBK
Trento, Italy
not@fbk.eu

ABSTRACT
We use design research to explore ways in which tangible and embodied interaction can be used to create novel experiences of heritage. We identified five design principles and used them to frame the challenge. In collaboration with curators, we co-created an interactive multi-narratives soundscape for the remains of trenches and a fortified camp from World War I. The soundscape is activated by presence and the use of a bespoke device. The design intertwines technology and historical content in context to augment the visitors' experience of the place in an evocative, personal way. The field trial showed that experimenting with different forms is key, as they have an impact on visitors' expectations beyond what they experience directly. It also showed the value in simultaneously designing interaction and content to achieve an effect that goes beyond the contribution of the single components.

Author Keywords
Cultural heritage; tangible interaction; design research.

ACM Classification Keywords
H.5.m : Miscellaneous.

INTRODUCTION
Museums and cultural heritage institutions have always experimented with new technology. For some the Internet of Things is what comes next: paired with wearable technology, it will enable visitors to interact directly with the objects and their surroundings [1]. This is what we explore in the meSch project: we use tangible and embedded interactions, wereables and communication technology to bridge the gap between material and digital collections and explore new ways for the visitors to experience heritage onsite and online [27]. This opens up new ways for design where the shaping of the visitor experience takes into account simultaneously the technical aspects, the interaction and the aim of the museum/heritage in presenting the heritage/collection. In meSch we use a co-design and co-creation approach to combine novel interactions with novel ways to communicate content. Design research and *constructive design research* [18] in particular, is key to explore in depth alternative worlds by means of prototypes and field studies.

CHI'16, May 07 - 12, 2016, San Jose, CA, USA

ACM 978-1-4503-3362-7/16/05…$15.00
DOI: http://dx.doi.org/10.1145/2858036.2858287

This paper describes a case of constructive design research for the remains of the trenches and a fortified camp from World War I in the Italian Alps: in team with curators, designers and technologists created an interactive narrative soundscape and two bespoke interactive devices and observed how visitors interacted with the archaeological site and the devices in the field. The design intertwines technology and historical content in context to augment the visitors' experience of the place in an affective way.

In the next section we use findings from museums studies to define design principles that informed the early stages of idea generation. The concept of 'narratives in place', stories coming directly from the place that they relate to, was developed: the technology disappears to let the immersive experience of the outdoor space emerge while the content, crafted for the place, offers multiple personal stories of war to be interpreted through the visitor's own sensibility. A user-aware multi-point system tracks the visitors' movements and interactions and uses a combination of the visitors' location, their distance from the point of interest, and their preference for a theme to select the appropriate audio. Two different bespoke prototypes were developed, one shaped as a book with a bookmark to select the preferred theme, the other as a belt with a set of cards, one for each theme. We took this tangible and embodied interaction for testing in the wild facing technical (no power or wireless), topical (the war), and contextual (only ruins remain) challenges. We discuss the different phases of the design and development. We conclude the paper by looking at the field-test findings through the lens of the design principles and reflect on the contribution our design approach has for rethinking technology in heritage.

TECHNOLOGY FOR HERITAGE: DESIGN PRINCIPLES
Twenty years have passed since the first studies of technology in museums and some design principles offered in 1992 still hold despite the radical changes in computing [32]. As was the case 20 years ago, not everyone is

attracted by technology and those who are tend to ignore the content: a study of tabletop interaction in a museum showed 50% of visitors did not touch the table, only 17% had more than one-click interaction [16]. One possible explanation is that visitors compete with each other to use the technology and this reduces the availability, but this is not convincing in light of the use of mobile devices, as in such a case every visitor can have one. Usability is often the issue: visitors spend time understanding how the device itself works, whether it is a multimedia PC [32], a PDA [40], or a tabletop [16]. So the principle "make sure instructions are intuitive [...] visitors should be able to learn how to use the interactive in 10 seconds or less" [32] still holds. In HCI different approaches have been used: a facilitator when the interactive is for small children [46], clearly defined steps and instructions [10], automatic triggering that does not require explicit interaction [12, 28]. This last, however, can be confusing if small body movements change the system's behaviour and visitors do not understand how their body controls the system [45]. Therefore what seems a trivial statement, to design straightforward interactions, becomes core for ubiquitous computing as digital technology does not have a form of its own [19, 21], but it takes that of the devices used to interact with it, i.e. the use of a mobile phone automatically shapes the interaction as being for individuals.

Findings from observing tabletop [16] and mobile [40] interactions suggest that technology competes with the heritage or the collection for the visitors' attention. Mobile guides divert the visitor's attention to the screen in their hand, to the point that in some cases they ignore the original [40] or push visitors to choose what to look at on the basis of what is on the screen [36] instead of what is of interest. Tabletops fostered a similar focus on the technology [16]. In 1992 Serrell and Raphling [32] observed that when using computers "visitors are seeking the experience with technology, not content" and this explains the limited use as not everyone is interested in computers. The continuous attempt of museums to adopt the newest technology [1,11] show this is a preferred path to reach new audiences. In a sense technology in museums has its own attracting and holding power [31], terms used in museum studies to define the ability of an object on display to interest visitors [32]. Designers should be aware of this phenomena and design in one of two ways: offer a novel experience with technology that is meaningful in its own rights or make it an understatement with respect to the collection. Successful in complementing the heritage/collection (vs. competing with it) are those interactions that use sound as main medium (e.g. [12, 36, 28]) as this enables the visitors to engage with the heritage visually. Cases of technology as experience often aim to surprise and amuse [13, 46, 25] and are designed as a unique piece within a wider exhibition. However, even when the technology is on its own, authenticity is essential: content must be truthful and the installation sympathetic to the environment [22].

A further issue is the disruption of the social setting of the visit. The vast majority of visitors come in groups [15], but they can only rarely stay in a group because mobile guides [22], games [13], virtual reality [2], augmented reality [5] or soundscapes [12] are often designed for a single user. Social enjoyment and sharing should be a concern for designers [38]. Large screens [41] or tabletops [16] support sharing, while personal devices, particularly if headphones are required, can be designed so that their use is only sparse, leaving time to enjoy the company of others [10] or they can allow visitors to listen in on whatever other members of their group are listening to [36].

Visitors have different needs and even the same person can look at the same exhibit many times, each time in a different way and with different expectations. Factors such as self-identity, companionship, and personal motivations change the way visitors approach and experience the museum [34, 8]. They could come to explore widely or the opposite to go in depth on specific topics; they may aim at the learning of others or seek a personal, contemplative, spiritual experience [8,9]. Despite a clear evidence of such a segmentation of visitors needs [8, 9, 34, 37], the "one size fits all" approach has been dominant meaning that only one type of experience is on offer (except perhaps for organized events). How the visitors react, it depends very much on what the designers propose. Asking visitors to perform actions in public [10] could be a good idea for engagement and some do really enjoy it (see people performing the pose of statues at Gallery One, Cleveland Museum of Art [11]) but to perform in public should be a decision left to the individuals [10]. Design should then consider offering multiple options for visitors to choose from depending on their personality or the mood of the moment [30, 22]. Variety and choice is then another important principle and designers should aim at experiences that are affective too as not everyone visits to be informed, but to be taken through an emotional journey [8, 26, 17].

The increased attention within museum studies to the visitor's experience is shifting methods of meaning-making toward the sensorial and personal [46, 7, 44, 22, 8, 34]. Alternative cases to information delivery include: to inspect an object in a tactile way [6, 39]; to let the aura of the original piece generate emotions [14]; to avoid explicit interpretation and give space to personal connections [44]. When museums lay down traces for multiple interpretations, visitors find personal significance in a number of ways that reflect basic human needs as different as reminiscing, recharging, identity building, and social interaction [34, 8]. Ubiquitous computing and tangible interaction hold much promise in this area. Multisensory and embodied bespoke interactions can be created to enhance the experience of being there or to invite visitor to question what they see or hear.

In summary, we identified five key design principles:

- Technology should be intuitive and straightforward to use and control; if instructions are needed those must be few and clear.
- Beware of the power of technology to engage visitors: exploit it to create a memorable experience as an isolated installation or make sure it does not compete with the exhibition if used throughout.
- Considerations about the social setting should be part of the design from the beginning. If the technology is for individual use then leave space for social interaction.
- Offer multiple experiences and let the visitor choose. Variety is key and information is not necessarily what visitors look for. Consider emotion (vs. cognition) and design for it.
- Explore ways to engage visitors that are physical and active, possibly using multiple senses.

These principles are intentionally open; they help designers to frame the problem and do not aim to guide them toward a specific solution. They are generic to be valid in different contexts, e.g. indoor or outdoor, for a science museum or an archeological site. Indeed each design for museums or heritage should be specific, as we describe in depth in this paper, and the principles should be implemented in different ways in different contexts.

VOICES FROM THE TRENCHES, A DESIGN CASE

A Constructive Design Approach to Design for Heritage

Our research is practice-based, specifically it is an example of *constructive design research* carried out in the field: "Constructive design researchers do not try to analyse the material world …, nor do they see design as in rational problem solving. Rather they imagine new realities and build them to see whether they work. The main criterion for successful work is whether it is imaginative in design terms." [18, pg. 42] Therefore the prototype and its trial with visitors should not be read as a product tested for practical aims, e.g. to assess its usability, but as a means of better understanding how the designers' imagination (embodied in the prototype) "shapes the activities, thoughts and beliefs of those people", the visitors [18, pg. 79].

The design principles discussed above, together with considerations specific to an outdoor context, were our brief at the start of the design process. We aimed at a visitors' experience that intertwines interactivity with content in a way that puts the site and the environment at the centre of the visitors' attention and connects to the visitors at an emotional level. These aims were shared in the team composed of product and interaction designers, computer scientists and curators. The role of curators in the team was well beyond that of a consultative partner: they shared the decisions, designed and created the content in a way that complements and reinforces the emotional effect of sound in place, as described in detail below. Thus while designers and scientists focussed on the devices and the interaction, the curators researched the archives to shape the content.

Two different experience prototypes were produced in the end; although fully functioning and with the intended aesthetics, both prototypes were "rough at the edges" to avoid conveying the idea of a finished product and collect feedback on the design details rather then the overall experience [18, 28]. The prototypes were embodiments of our vision of a different way to experience heritage and served the purpose of revealing, when used in the wild, the effect they had on the visit. Prototypes used in place by potential visitors create the necessary conditions for the experience and the social interaction to emerge [20]. We then use the observations in a naturalistic setting to assess our design choices and, more generally, tangible and embedded interaction in the context of challenging heritage.

Background and Overall Co-Creation Process

The meSch case study that provides the context for the work reported in this paper is set in the remains of the fortifications built across part of the Italian Alps at the outbreak of World War I in what was in 1914 the Austro-Hungarian Empire. The distance between the design team in the UK and the heritage site in Italy meant the iterative design process had to be carried out remotely. To enable designers to perform frequent outdoors assessments of the emerging ideas first and the early prototype after, a local historical cemetery that holds many similarities with the WWI ruins was chosen. Both outdoor settings offer opportunities and pose challenges: they are open with minimal signage; there is no power, network connectivity or technology in place. The Cemetery was used to inform and shape the concept, and to test the technical prototype under development [3]. Some of the observations and reflection of the design team were then fed to the curators at a later stage when the focus was on design for the trenches.

During this early phase the design team periodically met the heritage partners, but the work developed independently. When the concept of the audio narrative in place was presented and discussed at a project meeting, the curators at the Museo proposed to the designers to try it out on site, in the trenches and camp in Italy. This started an intense but remote co-design process: in the UK the initial design concept was revisited and finalised in a form that was considered more suitable for use in the trenches; in Italy the curators designed the visitor experience in terms of which points of interest should be included, which stories should be told and how. Exchanges of the work in progress were frequent enabling the partners to consider and question the choices made, and then tune their effort if needed.

Design Rationale, Concept and Forms

The design process had two phases: (1) the initial conception of the narrative in place resulting in the first prototype for the Cemetery – an interactive book, and (2) its redesign into a form more suitable for trekking, i.e. an interactive belt. Although the form factor is very different, the book and the belt are instances of the same interaction concept. The design and creation of the content for the trenches started in phase (2) when it was decided to port the concept of narratives in place to another site.

Phase 1: Concept design and first prototype

The starting point for the design was the observation that to move attention back to the heritage the story must come directly from the place; we deliberately avoided screens so as to free the visual channel and selected sound as an evocative and potentially group-friendly media. During a small experiment in the Cemetery, we observed that audio played through loudspeakers in place creates a wider *attraction* zone where people become aware of the sound source, and a closer *engagement* zone around the emitting point where one has to get closer and pause to understand what the voice says. The distance from the emitting point captures different degrees of interaction, and different sounds are more suitable when the visitor is at different positions, e.g. voices when far are unintelligible. The scenario we envisaged was that of a small group of visitors walking the grounds of a heritage site, hearing a sound that catches their attention; the group then moves toward the sound source, approaching the narrative point to listen to the story being told in place. The interaction is natural, triggered by the movement of the visitors: stepping into an attraction zone starts the sound; moving closer to the sound source starts the story.

To the experience of narratives in place we added the possibility for the visitors to choose the type of story (or theme) they want to listen to from several available. Besides being an historical site, the Cemetery is also a nature reserve. Four themes were created: facts on nature in the city; the story of the people buried there; weird facts and anecdotes; and the Cemetery volunteers' favourite places [3]. Visitors should be able to change the theme at any point in time so that they can listen to multiple stories simultaneously or follow a single theme consistently from the beginning to the end of the visit. Finally we chose the length of the audio clips to be between 30 and 120 seconds to avoid either overwhelming the visitors with content or, conversely, giving them too little [16, 32].

Figure 1: Narrative in place: book (left) loudspeakers (right).

The concept of *narratives in place* designed and prototyped for the Cemetery consisted of a wooden book with four pages, one for each of the themes; and a set of listening points (loudspeakers concealed in objects sympathetic with the environment) to be placed at points of interest (Fig.1). Visitors walk the heritage holding the book; the selection of the theme of interest is via a magnetic bookmark placed on the corresponding page; the sounds and stories are played at the listening points. The book uses Bluetooth to detect the nearest listening points (via Bluetooth-enabled loudspeaker) and runs a rule-based system to select audio files on the basis of the location (which point of interest), the distance of the visitor from the listening point (such as whether the visitor is within the attraction or the engagement zone), and the current theme selected via the bookmark. The book then sends the audio to play in place [22]. This concept captures the designers' interpretation of the principles as follows:

- *To offer straightforward interaction*: book an bookmarks are well known and should require minimal explanation on the function of the bookmark as selector; walking the ground of the Cemetery is natural and the automatic playback will surprise or amuse;
- *To consider the power of technology*: our purpose was to bring attention back to the heritage so the design conceals the technology and uses audio as the only medium; the strategic placement of the loudspeakers helps focusing attention on the place and engages the visitors by inviting them to get closer;
- *To design with the social dimension in mind*: the audio-based delivery in place is inclusive of whoever is around, whether visitors in the group or passers-by; the book and the selection of the theme via the bookmark mediates the decision of the group on what to listen to;
- *To offer alternatives*: the book holds very different themes, one for each page; selection is via the bookmark; visitors are also free to follow their own path, i.e. they are not required to follow a guide;
- *To engage visitors at many levels*: the visitor is engaged physically by walking and bookmarking, as well as cognitively by listening and interpreting.

The prototype of the book is an interpretation of how the design principles could be implemented into a bespoke device. It is the material expression of an imagined world [18]. Other physical manifestations and the corresponding interactions for the same imagined world would be possible: design is a creative process inspired as well as constrained by the specific situation for which one designs; it is a balancing act between a number of, possibly contrasting, requirements and desired outcomes [21].

Phase 2: Porting 'narratives in place' to the trenches

The proposal from the curators of the Anonym to port the book to the fortified camp and the trenches of WWI gave the designers the opportunity to rethink the concept of narratives in place for another very different context albeit one that shared with the Cemetery the technical, environmental, and topical challenges. While the book was conceived for a gentrified environment the fortified camp is in a rough and at times hostile place. Victorian cemeteries were parks of remembrance where people would stroll on a Sunday afternoon or have a picnic; today users of the Cemetery walk the dog, lie on the grass, bird-watch or read on a bench. The fortified camp is on an uneven terrain that is reached after 20 minutes walk from the car park, has dark caverns, and narrow paths. So despite the same challenges, the two sites inspired very different physical forms for the same concept, each of which better conveys the subtleties of the specific place for which they were designed.

A new brainstorming started and different objects used at the time of WWI were considered such as the recently invented radio or soldier's mess kit. The team converged toward a wearable device easier for trekking on a mountain path where it is useful to have both hands free. Clothes from WWI were inspected and a series of discussions between designers and curators focussed the search within the museum archives towards accessories for the torso. Historical images provided the inspiration for a multi-pocket cartridge box on a belt that is easy for visitors to put on and off, comfortable when walking, and large enough to house the technology. The interactive belt (Fig. 2) contains the same Bluetooth technology as the book, but the theme selection mechanism is implemented using NFC. A set of NFC-enhanced cards is used for the themes: a card inserted in a slot on one of the pockets, selects the matching theme.

Figure 2: The interactive belt (centre) the soldier's equipment that inspired it (left) and the NFC cards – back side (right).

The book and the belt prototypes differ only in their form factor and interaction. Apart from the theme selection mechanisms, all the hardware and software are identical, as is the content used. The form, however, is clearly key to the way people interact. It was then important as part of our constructive design approach to see what effect a different form would have and what are the resulting implications.

Crafting Content for the Place and Its Surround

The work of the designers and scientists on devices and system was complemented by the effort of the curators at the Anonym in defining the context of the interaction (the locations) and the content (the stories) to be used. The interest of the Museo in the book was drawn by the possibility to offer, simultaneously, multiple streams of content relevant to the same setting. In a human tragedy such as war there is no unique perspective or overarching truth, but different personal experiences, such as the commanders planning; the soldiers fighting; the civilians displaced. By providing multiple and contrasting voices curators enable visitors to elaborate their own interpretation of war. This is the role the Museo della Guerra see for themselves today: while it was founded in the 20s to celebrate Italy's role in World War I and was later reshaped to recount the history of events, now the museum's collection offers visitors multiple points of view and different topics that convey the sense of what war meant for the whole of society. By telling the story of the prisoner camps, showing the trophies of aviators or propaganda posters, discussing how the production of armies and uniforms changed industry, or displaying the devastating effect of war on people's life through the drawings and poems of artists, the museum enables visitors to understand and feel for themselves what war was. It drives visitors to engage with the topic at a deeper, personal level. This same approach, used to display the permanent collection within the museum walls, was adopted in designing for the outdoor. The intent was to make visitors walking in the camp and trenches feel the past and aimed at an evocative experience that fuses the physical, sensorial and social dimensions of being there with the history of the place.

The design team briefed the curatorial team on the insights gained during several tests at the Cemetery, specifically: to select stops located far enough apart to avoid signal interferences; to position the speakers above ground level (ideally above the visitors' head) for better listening; to select a variety of themes; to keep the content short (about a minute for narrative); and to select distinct attraction sounds for each theme as a reminder and cue of the theme itself.

Among the several possible the fortified camp used for educational purposes was selected: school groups are guided through an area of about 3.5 hectares (8.5 acres) walking on paths and stopping at specific points of interest. This place is relatively easy to access and requires about 1.5 hours to visit. The camp and trenches are an archaeological site meaning that only ruins remain (Fig. 3): signposts and one information board is all there is for visitors and a leap of imagination is needed to figure out how the place was during the war and what it was like to live there. An holistic and iterative process was used to create the content: the curators took into account physical aspects such as the specificity of the visit (self-directed trail, small groups) and the logistics (easily recognisable stations with comfortable stopping points), but also aspects of content such as which stories could be told at each stop and which themes could develop across the whole site. The striking contrast between today's natural beauty and the hardship of the war was used in the design of the content. The curatorial team searched the museum archives looking for intimate personal stories relevant specifically to the site or the local area. The aim was to create a style of narrative that was personal, at times even intimate, as opposed to more factual, authoritative, detached descriptions typical of an audio guide.

refuge outside (rifugi esterno) refuge inside (rifugi interno) water cistern (cisterna) shooting point (fuciliera) kitchen (cucine) artillery (postaz. artiglieria) trench (trincea) observation point (osservatorio)

Figure 3: The narrative points and the site map. Photos taken during the trial (images of participants used with permission).

This process resulted in the selection of 7 narrative points (Fig. 3) and 4 themes (Table 1) that captured the many voices of the War. The 'Order of the day' is the commander's voice and the most factual theme; 'My dear wife' is the personal experience of war as lived by the soldiers and 'Women in the war' is the little known story of the civilians, again told in the first person; finally 'Poems in the trench' aims for an high emotional impact as in the case of the poem used in the kitchen (Fig.5):

"The smell of war means the smell of rotten leather. That of sweat. The smell of dry excrement. That of fresh blood under the sun, thick, sweet, slightly nauseating. The smell of putrefaction. The smell of anise in the water bottle. The smell of cigarettes "Sport" found in the abandoned Austrian trench, in round packs of brown paper. [...]"

The content is open to personal interpretations. It never says what the place is but contains all the elements to work that out. For example the 'Order of the day' in the trench (Table 1) explains how a trench was constructed so when in place one can see and understand the motivations for a zig-zag path. Effort was put into the delivery form as it explicitly aimed at sparking empathy in the listener, e.g. the 'Order of the day' was read as a military order given by the commander. Explicit references to people and places were introduced, for example a sign outside the artillery commemorates Captain Lewandowski and the 'Order of the day' for the observatory is his own; the villages in the valley visible from the shooting point are mentioned in the theme 'Women in the war'. Two professional actors (male and female) read the final scripts using the intonation proposed by the curators (i.e. a commanding voice for the 'Order of the day'); and appropriate attraction sounds were recorded for each theme.

Although each narrative is independent, their juxtaposition was expected to generate reflection for the complementary and contrasting voices they represented, as shown in Table 1. As the commander states the defensive system, the soldier tells his experience of an assault, the poet the relief of a called back war action and the wife at her angst for missing news. In our "imagined world" [18] visitors in the trench on a beautiful Summer day would listen to the different voices while standing where soldiers stood and, looking out into the valley, would experience strong emotions. We then set out to try our prototypes in the wild with potential visitors and see for ourselves how our "imagined world" works.

Theme (Attraction Sound)	Sources	Content Sample
Order of the day (Trumpet calling soldiers to assembly)	Official documents; laws; bulletins; regulations on the military organisation of the camp.	"The rules for the construction of the defence of fortified camps state that: - the trench must be 2.25 m deep and 80cm wide; - the barbed-wire must be placed 30-40cm before the first line; - between the first and the second line and between the second and a possible third line there must be 100 to 150 m. - the trenches must be connected by communication trenches. Trenches and communication trenches must be built following a zig-zag pattern as to avoid enfilade shooting and to limit the effect of explosions."
My dear wife… (Male choir singing a war song)	Diaries of soldiers; letters sent home.	"Meanwhile above our heads an intense battle was going on. The bullets crossed high above, wailing, with a piercing whistle. Suddenly the command: Auff. Run ahead. In a flash we all climbed up the escarpment of the trench, there we could see the enemy trench 200 steps in front. 200 steps with no cover. A last thought to the family and go. The enemies, when they saw us, threw so much iron at us that, if I think back today, it seems impossible to still be alive. Yet we arrived at the barbed wire, and our job started. The shots whistled in my ears, the machine guns were spewing death, the hand grenades howled, I could not see, I could not hear a thing. For two or three minutes I cut the wire, when I hear a formidable 'HURRAY', and my company arrives charging ahead. In the middle of that hell, with their gunstock they widened the hole already open and they all, as a single man, throw themselves on the enemy, who stands his ground and waits for them. An assault by bayonet. – From the diary of Giovanni Pederzolli, 1915"
Women in the war (Steam train whistle)	Diaries and letters from the family; stories of building work in the camp; stories of refugees moved from the area of war onto camps in Austria.	"Rovereto, 3 October 1914 – Dear sister, it is already two months that Gino left for the war. I remember as if it were yesterday: that morning I accompanied him to Rovereto station. How beautiful he looked in his uniform! He waved to me from the train window, he told me not to cry, that he would be back soon, safe and sound. But I am here alone, with my three small children, and the first news from the front has arrived. Do you remember Luigia? Today she received the news that her dear boy Giacomo is dead. What a pain that poor mother! They say it is terrible on the front line, that men fight in trenches, that they die by the dozens, every day. I am in angst and I pray a lot. I hope I will never get the terrible news. Oh God, what it will become of us?"
Poems in the trench (Fragment of the introduction of the War Requiem by Benjamin Britten)	Edited collections from both Italian and Austro-Hungarian soldier-poets.	"Giulio Barni, The Weather. 1916 If the weather clears up on the 10th we'll act if the weather clears up… And the soldiers scanned the stars and the heavens, their breath weighing the vibrations of the wind. But the 9th saw shining a halo around the moon the moon was veiled by cloudy a veil. Soldiers and commanders whom have been 30 days waiting for the action looked at each other they could have kissed. At dawn on the 10th rain."

Table 1: The four themes, the sound used to attract to the narrative point, the type of sources used and examples of the scripts.

TAKING DESIGN INTO THE WILD: THE FIELD TRIAL

Designers, technologists and curators took active part in the trail in a cooperative evaluation effort. The methodology was naturalistic and qualitative [20], with attention to:

- *Ordinary social setting*: people visit in groups of friends and family, so participants were invited to bring a companion. Familiarity would foster discussions and comments offered to each other in a way one could not expect if the groups were organised by the researchers.
- *Naturalistic research design and methods*: on arrivals participants were shown the device (the book or the belt), were given the map of the place and invited to make their own visit. No preferred order of visit was suggested and the multiple paths on the map (Fig. 3) allowed participants to choose their own route. Some knew the camp and took detours to show their companion interesting points that were not part of our experiment, e.g. the latrines and bath house.
- *Openness*: each group had one prototype, the book or the belt and we looked at how they appropriated it, how they shared the decision on what to listen to or who used it. Of interest were distinct behaviours induced by the two different forms while the embodied experience (to trigger audio by walking) stayed the same.
- *A sufficient time span*: we did not given a time to complete the visit. We also invited them to a post-tour interview, to look at the device they did not use, and to comment on our design and question our research.
- *Special attention to the sequential unfolding of events*: participants were followed at a distance by the researchers who were recording video. The videos enabled us to see how the interaction with the device evolved as well as how the individuals interacted with each other and with their surroundings.

The constructive design approach adopted enabled the members of the team to see how people used the two different forms (product design), how they reacted to the embodied experience of sounds and narratives triggered by movements (interaction design); and how the voices and the content were received (curatorial aim). In the post-visit interview, questions about the type and style of the content were combined with others to further explore the visitor-heritage interaction. The interview, in Italian by native speakers, was audio-recorded and transcribed verbatim. Observation notebooks were used to inform the follow-up interview with specific elements from the visit itself.

Prototypes, Trial Set-up, Data Collection and Analysis

Experience prototypes are a synthesis of our understanding and a tool to probe our design when put in the context of tangible interaction in heritage. Even in their rough form the book and the belt enable us to frame the problem, to create the desired world in which a novel interaction can take place and for us to observe what happens.

Figure 4. Trail setup: the book and bookmark (front) with two sound lanterns and the cards for the interactive belt (back).

Notwithstanding the difference in their form, the two prototypes were made to be as close as possible: the mechanisms of the embodied interaction were identical (walking into an attraction zone and then closer to the engagement zone triggers a sound and then the narrative); they both enable visitors to select a theme at any point in time and even their appearance was as similar as possible (the artistic drawings and historical photos on the cards were on the book pages, Fig.4). The set-up was identical too: 28 stories were uploaded for a total of about 23 mins, plus 4 attraction sounds played when the visitors enter the attraction zone (see video figure). The length of the narratives varied with the shortest poems lasting 30 secs.

The 7 narrative points were distributed across the whole site and were connected by several footpaths (see Fig. 3). The sound lanterns were made of laser-cut plywood for minimal impact on the landscape; they concealed the speakers and were positioned as high as possible to allow a better diffusion of sound and to facilitate listening (Fig. 4).

Participants invited to take part in the study were in the network of the Anonym. Overall 9 people took part in the trial and the following interview; each group spent about 1 hour visiting and 45 min in the interview. The demographic was varied: 3 women and 6 men aged between early 30s and mid 60s. All were local residents; some were also familiar with the place as they come with students or had participated in its restoration, others were not.

Multiple sources of data were collected: the video and the observer notes were complemented by the interaction logs automatically recorded by the devices. The logs captured the full interaction with the bookmark or the cards and enabled us to see if participants followed a single theme for the full visit, or listened to many themes and if there were any patterns. The log recorded the time of arrival at each narrative point and when they left it, so we could compare the length of time spent at the point with the length of time spent listening to the stories. The data analysis was iterative across different sources: backing of findings was sought across the data set, e.g. the observation that visitors listened to more then one story in each position was confirmed by the logs that gave details on how many themes were selected and with which device. In the following discussion we integrate data from observations, interviews and logs.

UNDERSTANDING THROUGH PRACTICE

"[] a prototype is not only a representation of a product of technology ... it consists of both the representation and the social interaction the participants create together" [20]. In this study, the prototype is even more articulated. The experience prototype is a combination of a bespoke device, the embodied interaction, crafted content and sounds, the archaeological site, the landscape and the participants. In this section, we look into how these elements interrelate by unpicking each design principle in turn. It should be noted that the principles intertwine and the same design choice responds to more than one principle.

A straightforward interaction

The book and the belt afforded simple interactions, albeit very different ones: to bookmark the theme of interest, to insert the preferred theme card. As designers we saw pros and cons in both: the book was more aesthetically pleasing and easier to flip through the different themes, but was large (19x23x9cm) although not heavy (about 1kg); the belt left the hands free, but one could easily forget the other themes available when a card was in. We were curious as to the effect each would have.

The book was acknowledged as a beautiful object, but the convenience of the belt was a definite winner: "*two hands are needed to hold the book so I could not take pictures*". Part of the aesthetics of the belt was the cards, which could be taken as a memento as well as an entry point to access content online thus becoming digitally-enhanced souvenirs: "*I'd like to be able to get to the sources used by the museum*"; "*I'd like a bibliography of sort for each card*".

Participants wearing the belt moved around more than those holding the book. The book was kept closed until the point of interest was reached, then it was opened and looked at, the bookmark was used a few times to listen to different narratives before closing it to move away and continue the visit. Sharing of control was clear with the book as partners were taking turns in using it while the belt was worn by the same person throughout the visit. With both prototypes the visitors in a group consulted each other to decide what to listen to next. Early in the visit the members of the groups regularly looked at the book or cards to familiarise themselves with the themes (Fig. 5); as the visit progressed they were just consulting on which theme to listen to next. The logs show that the groups that used the book listened to more themes than those with the belt. This could be due to the book inviting browsing more than the cards. Indeed the modalities of interaction were quite different: the book is always in one's hand, it invites examination while listening; the card selected is folded and put away (in the belt) and there is no browsing while listening. However more interaction with the book could just be a matter of taste (liking some theme less), not of form. The different ways in which participants interacted with the belt and the book highlight the challenge of a design that aims to be holistic and points out competing requirements: the higher number of stories played with the book could be because of the attention being on the book more than the heritage.

Figure 5: A couple negotiating and selecting the theme.

We noted an unexpected behaviour in the use of the bookmark: in a group, while moving from place to place, one member held the bookmark while the other held the book and only when they reached the point they placed the bookmark in the book. This use did not hamper the automatic start of the sounds as the magnetic switch sets the theme until the bookmark is placed on another page. However it made us wonder how what we believed to be a simple metaphor (to bookmark what I am interested in) could be seen rather as a sort of switch: "*at a certain point I thought I did the wrong thing as I moved the bookmark before the sound was over and I was afraid that would interrupt the sound and break the system*".

The most surprising comments where those that explicitly associated the book to a guide book: "*the book feels too much like a tourist guide – don't take me wrong, it is beautiful with its wooden look - it is just wrong in such a place*"; "*the first page should give an introduction, an overview*"; "*at first we were looking at the page expecting the story that is read aloud in the audio to be written on the guide*". The use of a well-known object brought into the interaction more than we expected to the point of reducing, in the view of some, the novelty of the experience.

In summary, the baggage of previous use associated with the book, its form that invites visitors to stand still and look at it, and the possibility to take away a card as souvenir to get more content online suggests that less obvious but still simple designs are worth exploring.

The power of technology on visitors' attention

Our design completely conceals the technology and uses sound in place as a way to focus the attention on the heritage. Sound attracts visitors and leads them to change direction to get closer and listen to the narrative (see video figure) and creates a sense of anticipation. While listening, visitors wandered around, looked at the landscape or at details. All groups listened to more than one story at every stop and the selection of a new theme was seamless, fully integrated with the experience of the place. The effect of sound in place was key in the appreciation and experience of the heritage: "[the attraction sound] *is like the place is welcoming you* ", "[the narrative] *is like someone is imprisoned in the place*", "[in the caverns] *it resounds all around you*". To start the sound by presence and movement with no technology in sight had a magic effect: "*it is amazing!*" Participants easily located and reached the points of interest, but the opinion on whether the sound lanterns should be inconspicuous was split with some visitors liking when the sound played at unexpected times ("*I liked the caverns best because you enter but cannot see - then the music starts, it is of great effect*") and others preferring them to become signposts one can look out for and go to.

Design for the social

Sound in place is social, as the group shares the same experience by listening to the same stories. However we did not expect it to carry a stronger meaning: "*sound in the headphone isolates, it becomes your own thoughts. Sound in place - like here - it is a narrative that comes directly from this place, that past*". The comment highlights the combined effect of the sound, the environment and the content of the narratives. Sharing was part of the way our participants reacted to the content: "*some personal accounts are poignant. We stayed silent as a form of respect.*" A further means of sharing the experience were comments on the content offered to their companions, e.g. a remark on a mother asking her soldier son to send news home "*certain things never change…*". We observed a number of collaborative behaviours triggered by the content, e.g. those who knew the local geography pointed out for their companion the villages and peaks that had been mentioned in the narratives. The interaction logs back our observation as participants stayed in a place, on average, 3 times longer than the playing time, indicating that there was an interaction with the place or their companions beyond the listening of the stories. The value of a shared experience of their local heritage was clear with a participant saying he will come back with his mother to show her this historical site he did not know was at his doorstep.

Offer alternatives

Our design was open in many ways: visitors choose their own path, listen to their preferred stories, draw from the narratives to discuss with their companion and to interpret the place in their own way. The intertwining of the sound in place and the narratives is a link across space and time. The narratives, prepared for this specific place and its locale, link the present time, as experienced by the visitors, to the same place as experienced in the past by others: "*it is a clash between this place where the war was fought and [that] is now so beautiful*". Visitors understand the place by interpreting the narratives for themselves. Some would pick up the reference to a territory they knew well (villages, valleys, lakes and mountains nearby), others to aspects of everyday life such as food, water, or shelter. The curators leave the threads of many lives for the visitors to pick up and to interpret and feel the place individually filtered by their own sensibility.

Many stories were available to visitors simultaneously and visitors did choose. The logs show that all groups took different paths and listened to at least two stories at every stop, but no group listened to all the content all the time. The "Order of the day" was preferred overall and one group never listened to the "Poems". Besides the value of offering choices, we see benefit in proposing something one would not pick of their own accord, an invitation to experience something different: "*I am not one for poems ... but it is different, a poem in here.*"

Engage visitors at many levels

Our design intended to engage visitors in many ways. There is a physical component, the walk around the camp, the embodied interaction of activating sound by presence and the tangible selection of a theme. This is a point of transition toward a cognitive level, as visitors have to take a conscious decision on what to listen next. The content is non-didactic and requires the individuals to make sense of what they are listening to by paying attention to where they are and what they see. While the content triggers personal interpretation, the tone and the topic of the stories provoke emotion. The affective, emotional reaction was evident in the visitors' behaviours, their comments and their silences ("*and now people go on a diet*" commenting on the starvation conditions during war told in the kitchen). The multisensory experience created by combining audio with the sense of the place was very well received ("*this place, that past*"). The seamless integration of technology and content offered to visitors was more than a novel experience; the place itself was brought back to life through the voices of those who lived there.

DISCUSSION AND CONCLUSIONS

We use a constructive design approach to explore tangible and embodied interaction in heritage. Making prototypes that synthesise our understanding and create imagined world is instrumental to the progress of our research and the consolidation or disproval of our understanding. Our study illustrates the potential of this approach in a challenging setting: no power or network; only ruins left to see; and the topic of war - a hard subject to tackle. Guided by the museum literature, we propose five principles: simple interaction; technology to channel attention to the site; be supportive of groups; offer multiple experiences to choose from; challenge visitors to interpret the place in their own terms; engage at many levels including, physical, cognitive and emotional. These principles are broad as to accommodate the diversity of museums and heritage and could help others when starting the design.

Our design process brought us to develop two alternative prototypes for the same concept, one ported from a similar context, one bespoke for the trenches. There was value in implementing two alternative prototypes and exploring the effect of different forms on the experience. We considered the metaphor of the book the ideal means for an easy interaction, but it carried too many expectations and affected the way the experience was received. The belt was not loaded with bias and was therefore best for the exploration of new interactions. This finding invites more design work, more experiments and testing with multiple devices. To do so the technical infrastructure must be flexible at it has to accommodate different forms, possibly partially different technology, to enable exploration of different interactions for the same concept. Much of what we found was unexpected and it could not be revealed in any other way then by trialling, so it is worth investing in designing and making multiple forms. Checking the concept and the prototypes are compliant with the principles is not enough. By observing in the real context how the visitors use the devices, how they behave in situ and what they say we understood in a better way the implications and consequences of our design decisions.

The design approach extended to the creation of content that was not didactic but open to personal interpretation: curators left traces for visitors to pick up; some connected with the surroundings, some with the people who lived there, some with the emotions in the poems. When this happened the experience was deeper, stronger. However, this is not due only to the crafted content designed for personal interpretation or emotional effect. The audio triggered by presence, the selection of the preferred content, the sound and stories coming from the place, all were instrumental to a richer experience. This empathic effect cannot be ascribed to just one component, whether technology or narratives. One empowers the other. An approach that simultaneously considers interaction and content is essential to create a design that exploits the place to a powerful final effect. To embrace this approach museums and heritage institutions have to become more experimental, more design oriented, more willing to have proof of concepts and prototypes to try out before the final commitment to an exhibition is made [35]. Clearly this changes the design process, as curators become creative members of the team in charge of shaping the narratives. It is then not just a matter of rethinking technology for heritage, but to rethink the process and for curators to move from being patrons of technology in heritage to becoming creative with it.

ACKNOWLEDGMENTS

The research described in this paper was conducted as part of the meSch project, Material Encounters with Digital Cultural Heritage. meSch (2013-2017) receives funding from the European Community's Seventh Framework Programme, "ICT for access to cultural resources" (ICT Call 9: FP7-ICT-2011-9) under the Grant Agreement 600851.

REFERENCES

1. Johnson, L., Adams Becker, S., Estrada, V., and Freeman, A. 2015. *NMC Horizon Report: 2015 Museum Edition*. Austin, Texas: The New Media Consortium. Retrieved September 22, 2015 from http://www.nmc.org/publication/nmc-horizon-report-2015-museum-edition/
2. B. Bonis, J. Stamos, S. Vosinakis, I. Andreou, T. Panayiotopoulos. 2009. A platform for virtual museums with personalized content. *Journal of Multimedia Tools and Applications*. 42,2: 139–159.
3. Luigina Ciolfi and Marc McLoughlin. 2012. Of Turf Fires, Fine Linen and Porter Cake: Design for Living History, *ACM Interactions*, XIX.5 September + October, 18-21.
4. Luigina Ciolfi, Daniela Petrelli, Robin Goldberg, Nick Dulake, Matt Willox, Mark T. Marshall and Fabio Caparrelli. 2013. Exploring historical, social and natural heritage: Challenges for tangible interaction design at Sheffield General Cemetery", *Proceedings of Design & Digital Heritage conference* (NODEM 2013), Stockholm December 2013
5. Areti Damala, Pierre Cubaud, Anne Bationo, Pascal Houlier, Isabelle Marchal. 2008. Bridging the Gap between the Digital and the Physical: Design and Evaluation of a Mobile Augmented Reality Guide for the Museum Visit. *Proc. of Digital Interactive Media in Entertertainment and Arts* (DIMEA 2008), 120-127.
6. Betty Davidson, Candace Lee Heald and George Hein, 1991. Increased exhibit accessibility through multisensory interaction. *Curator – The Museum Journal*. 34, 4: 273-290.
7. Sandra Dudley. 2010. Museum materialities: Objects, sense and feeling. In Dudley, S. (ed.) *Museum Materialities: Objects, Engagements, Interpretations*. Routledge, UK, 1-18.
8. John Falk. 2009. *Identity and the museum visitor experience*. Left Coast Press.
9. John Falk. 2011. Contextualizing Falk's Identity-Related Visitor Motivational Model. *Visitors Studies*. 14, 2, 141-157.
10. Lesley Fosh, Steve Benford, Stuart Reeves, Boriana Koleva and Patrick Brundell. 2013. 'See Me, Feel Me, Touch Me, Hear Me': Trajectories and Interpretations in a Sculpture Garden. In *Proceedings of the SIGCHI Conference on Human Factors in Computing Systems* (CHI '13), 149-158.
11. Gallery One, Cleveland Museum of Art. 2013. Video. (7 March 2013.). Retrieved September 22, 2015 from https://www.youtube.com/watch?v=qWJqd6lyJ-E
12. Adrian Hazzard, Steve Benford and Gary Burnett. 2015 Sculpting a mobile music soundtrack. In *Proceedings of the SIGCHI Conference on Human Factors in Computing Systems* (CHI '15), 387-396.
13. Christian Heath, Dirk Vom Lehn and Jonathan Osborne. 2005 Interaction and interactives: collaboration and participation with computer-based exhibits. *Public Understanding of Science*. 14, 1: 91-101.
14. Nuala Hancock. 2010. Virginia Wolf's glasses: material encounters in the literary/artistic house museum. In Dudley, S. (ed.) *Museum Materialities: Objects, Engagements, Interpretations*. Routledge, UK, 114-127.
15. Eilean Hooper-Greenhill. 1994. *Museums and their visitors*. Routledge, UK
16. Eva Hornecker. 2008. "I don't understand it either but it's cool" – Visitor Interactions with a Multi-touch Table in a Museum. *Proc. of IEEE Tabletop*, 121-128.
17. Stephen Kaplan, Lisa V. Bardwell and Deborah B. Slakter. 1993. The Museum as a restorative environment. *Environment and Behaviour*. 26, 6:725-742.
18. Ilpo Koskinen, John Zimmerman, Thomas Binder, Johan Redström and Stephan Wensveen. 2011. *Design Research Through Practice – From the Lab, Field, and Showroom*. Morgan Kaufmann.
19. Mike Kuniavsky. 2010. *Smart Things – Ubiquitous Computing User Experience Design*. Morgan Kaufmann.
20. Esko Kurvinen, Ilpo Koskinen and Katja Battarbee. 2008. Prototyping Social Interaction. *Design Issues*. 23, 3: 46-57.
21. Jonas Löwgren and Erik Stolterman. 2004. *Thoughtful Interaction Design – A Design Perspective on Information Technology*. MIT Press.
22. Mark Leslie. 2011. Applying basic design principles to technology in museums. *Proc. of 2nd Conference on Rethinking Technology in Museums – Emerging Experiences*.
23. Mark T. Marshall, Daniela Petrelli, Nick Dulake, Elena Not, Michele Marchesoni, Elisa Trenti and Anna Pisetti. 2016. Audio-based narratives for the Trenches of World War I : intertwining stories, places and interaction for an evocative experience. *International Journal of Human-Computer Studies, special issue on*

Data Sonification and Sound Design in Interactive Systems, 85, 27-39.

24. David Martin. 2000. Audio Guides. *Museum Practice*, 5, 1: 71-81.
25. David McGookin, Yolanda Vazquez-Alvarez, Stephen Brewster and Joanna Bergstorm-Lehtovirta. 2012 Shaking the Dead: Multimodal Location Based for Un-Stewarded Archaeological Sites. *Proc. of the 7th Nordic Conference on Human-Computer Interaction* (NordiCHI'12).
26. Jan Packer and Nigel Bond. 2010. Museums as Restorative Environments. *Curator – The Museum Journal*. 53, 4: 421-436.
27. Daniela Petrelli, Luigina Ciolfi, Dick van Dijk, Eva Hornecker, Elena Not, Albrecht Schmidt. 2013. Integrating Material and Digital: A New Way for Cultural Heritage. *ACM Interactions*, July + August.
28. Daniela Petrelli, Nick Dulake, Mark Marshall, Robin Goldberg, Matt Willox and Fabio Caparrelli. 2014 Prototyping tangibles: Exploring form and interaction. *Proc. of the Conference on Tangible, Embedded and Embodied Interaction* (TEI'14).
29. Daniela Petrelli and Elena Not. 2005 User-centred design of flexible hypermedia for a museum guide: reflections on the HyperAudio experience. *User Modelling and User Adapted Interaction*, 15: 303-338.
30. Susan Reilly and Daniela Petrelli. 2008. Engaging with Books You Cannot Touch: Interactive Multimedia to Explore Library Treasures. *Co-Design*. 3, 1: 199-210.
31. Cody Sandifer 2003. Technological novelty and open-endedness: Two characteristics of interactive exhibits that contribute to the holding of visitor attention in a science museum. *Journal of Research in Science Teaching*. 40, 2: 121-137.
32. Beverly Serrell. 1997. Paying attention: The duration and allocation of visitors' time in museum exhibitions. *Curator – The Museum Journal*. 40, 2: 109-125.
33. Beverly Serrell and Britt Raphling. 1992 Computers on the Exhibit Floor. *Curator – The Museum Journal*, 35, 3: 181-189.
34. Lois H. Silverman. 1995. Visitors Meaning-Making in Museums for a New Age. *Curator – The Museum Journal*.38, 3: 161-170.
35. Smithsonian Institution. 2002. The Making of Exhibitions: Purpose, Structure, Roles and Process. Report (October 2002.). Retrieved September 22, 2015 http://www.si.edu/Content/opanda/docs/Rpts2002/02.10.MakingExhibitions.Final.pdf
36. Margaret H. Szymanski, Paul M. Aoki, Rebecca E. Grinter, Amy Hurst, James Thornton, and Alison Woodruff. 2007. *Sotto Voce*: Facilitating Social Learning in a Historic House. *Computer Supported Cooperative Work*, 17: 5-34.
37. Bradley L. Taylor. 2010. Reconsidering Digital Surrogates. In Dudley S. (ed.) *Museum Materialities - Objects, Engagements, Interpretations*, Routledge, UK, 175-184.
38. Peter Tolmie, Steve Benford, Chris Greenhalgh, Tom Rodden, Stuart Reeves. 2014. Supporting Group Interaction in Museum Visiting. *Proc. of Computer Supported Cooperative Work* (CSCW '14), 1049-1059.
39. Tessa J. van Schijndel, Rooske K. Franse and Maartje E. J. Raijmakers. 2010. The exploratory behaviour scale: Assessing young visitors' hands-on behaviour in science museums. *Science Education*. 94,5: 794-809.
40. Dirk vom Lehn and Christian Heath. 2003. Displacing the object: mobile technology and interpretive resources. *Proc. of Cultural Institution and Digital Technology*.http://www.archimuse.com/publishing/ichim03/088C.pdf
41. Dirk vom Lehn, Jon Hindmarsh, Paul Luff, Christian Heath. 2007. Engaging Constable: Revealing art with new technology. In *Proceedings of the SIGCHI Conference on Human Factors in Computing Systems* (CHI '07), 1485-1494.
42. Ron Wakkary and Marek Hatala. 2007. Situated play in a tangible interface and adaptive audio museum guide. *Personal and Ubiquitous Computing*, 11: 171-191.
43. Ron Wakkary, Kevin Muise, Karen Tenenbaum, and Marek Hatala. 2007 Situating Approaches to Museum Guides for Families and Groups.
44. Kirsten Wehner and Martha Sear. 2010. Engaging the material world: object knowledge and *Australian Journeys*. In Dudley S. (ed.) *Museum Materialities –* Objects, Engagement, Interpretations, Routledge,143-161.
45. Andreas Zimmermann and Andras Lorenz. 2008 LISTEN: A User-Adaptive Audio-Augmented Museum Guide. *UMUAI - User Modeling and User-Adapted Interaction*, 18: 389-416.
46. Robyn Taylor, John Bowers, Bettina Nissen, Gavin Wood, Peter Wright, Qasim Chaudhry, Lindsey Bruce, Sarah Glynn, Helen Mallinson and Roy Bearpark. 2015. Making Magic: Designing for Open Interactions in Museum Settings. In *Proceedings of the Conference on Creativity and Cognition* (C&C '15). 313-322.

Simplified Audio Production in Asynchronous Voice-Based Discussions

Venkatesh Sivaraman
Bexley High School
Columbus, OH
venkats@mit.edu

Dongwook Yoon
Cornell University
Ithaca, NY
dy252@cornell.edu

Piotr Mitros
edX
Cambridge, MA
pmitros@edx.org

ABSTRACT

Voice communication adds nuance and expressivity to virtual discussions, but its one-shot nature tends to discourage collaborators from utilizing it. Text-based interfaces have made voice editing much easier, especially with recent advancements enabling live, time-aligned speech transcription. We introduce SimpleSpeech, an easy-to-use platform for asynchronous audio communication (AAC) with lightweight tools for deleting and inserting content, adjusting pauses, and correcting transcript errors. Qualitative and quantitative results suggest that novice audio producers, including high school students, experience decreased mental workload when using SimpleSpeech to produce audio messages than without editing. We also found that the linguistic formality of SimpleSpeech is between that of traditional oral and written media. Our findings on formality and workload characteristics of editable speech input help define best practices and use cases for the design and application of such systems.

Author Keywords

Speech editing; transcription-based editing; asynchronous audio communication.

ACM Classification Keywords

H.5.2. User Interface: Voice I/O

INTRODUCTION

Asynchronous audio communication (AAC) is rapidly becoming available to mass audiences through social platforms such as WhatsApp, iMessage, and Facebook. While text is still by far the most prevalent (and often most convenient) mode of communication on the Internet, audio is desirable in many situations because of its ability to convey more expression and nuance than text. For instance, Mayer's work on multimedia learning [?] indicates that audio communication is particularly useful for managing cognitive load where material is primarily conveyed visually (e.g., by pointing), and in situations where an emotional connection between speaker and listener is desirable. AAC therefore holds considerable potential for improving online education, where voice communication has been demonstrated to improve student-student and student-instructor engagement as well as a sense of the instructor's social presence [15, 21, 27]. Our research is primarily motivated by the implications of AAC as a peer-to-peer educational tool, though it is also applicable to other collaborative settings, such as instructor authoring.

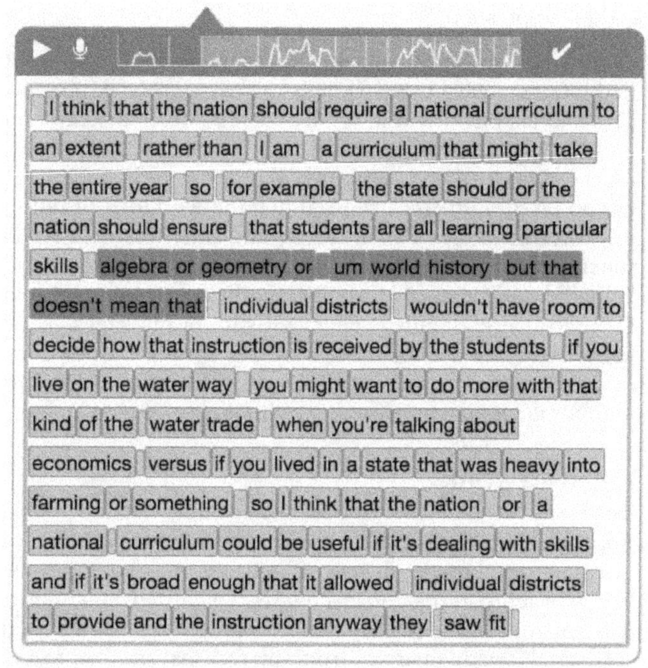

Figure 1. The user interface for SimpleSpeech presents an automatically-generated transcription of a voice comment, which can then be manipulated through normal word-processing operations, such as selection, deletion, and insertion. Word and pause tokens are mapped with audio via time alignment data.

The problem with replacing textual communication with speech, however, is that speakers may face difficulty articulating their ideas vocally. For instance, Marriott and Hiscock's study using Wimba voice boards for discussion forums found that students overwhelmingly preferred text over speech comments, in part because it required them to speak fluently without making errors [20]. Since this problem affects students even in physical classrooms, it could certainly prevent some learners from participating in online oral discussions. AAC platforms in such situations, then, must somehow compensate

CHI'16, May 7-12, 2016, San Jose, California, USA.

ACM ISBN 978-1-4503-3362-7/16/05...$15.00.
DOI string from ACM form confirmation

for the linearity and immutability of audio on the production side.

Our solution is to provide lightweight, easy-to-use editing tools based on automatic speech recognition (ASR)-generated transcripts. Many prior studies have utilized transcription to assist in audio editing [6, 22, 31], but only recently has fast, live editing become possible through advances in ASR technology [7, 23]. We implemented an easy-to-use audio production tool, SimpleSpeech, that allows users to delete and insert segments of the recording in real-time, simplifying quick word-level editing even when transcription errors are present.

Qualitative evidence indicates that SimpleSpeech's simplified interface gave users enough control over the editing process and enabled them to produce more polished audio comments, but that these benefits came at the price of elevated mental workload and formality. Further quantitative investigation on these themes showed that the workload of recording voice messages was in fact significantly less with editing functionality, demonstrating that SimpleSpeech would be a valuable enhancement to online audio communication platforms. Finally, linguistic characteristics of messages created using AAC are also discussed in comparison to other forms of communication, leading to new considerations and insights on optimal applications of this technology.

RELATED WORK

The linear, sequential nature of voice communication not only impedes skimming and navigation capabilities [10], but can also hamper the speech *production* process. Voice production is a temporarily linear process which demands that the speaker thinks and speaks simultaneously [19, 34]. Therefore, cognitive load arises from the fact that one has to keep speaking to prevent undesirable long pauses. In addition, mistakes in recorded speech are harder to revise than textual typos, mainly due to the lack of lightweight voice editing software [19]. Building on the qualitative implications of these previous works, our study presents a quantitative analysis of these burdens when the voice production system includes lightweight editing features.

Because lower-level audio waveform editing is an onerous task, speech manipulation tools have been developed that present audio in semantically meaningful higher-level chunks, such as words and phrases. Acoustic detection of the presence of speech provides binary visual guidance through which users can edit or index the speech recording [1, 14]; on the other hand, a pure acoustic approach has limited recognition granularity. Time-aligned automatic speech recognition (ASR) has now become a popular tool to achieve the word-level structuring of speech [24, 32]. Compared with acoustic structuring, ASR presents semantic information at higher resolution, but has also suffered from high computational load and delay. However, recent technical developments have made ASR faster and more accurate, and we take full benefit of this real-time transcription capability.

Since speech transcription elicits the contents of the recording, researchers have utilized it to assist in visual skimming and navigation. MedSpeak [18] and SCANMail [8] are well recognized as precursors of such systems that use time-alignment data of the transcript for indexing audio. Since transcription errors tend to obstruct visual comprehension, Vemuri et al. suggested a novel visualization of the transcript that adjusts transcription brightness to the word's ASR confidence score [28].

On the production side, there have been several systems that use a time-aligned transcript for editing audio [22, 31, 33] or video [3, 6]. Among them, Whittaker and Rubin's editing system leveraged users' familiarity with text-editing interfaces to adopt audio editing within that paradigm. Since we targeted non-professional users, our interface also took the text-like approach, but emphasizing a *live* production process and going beyond editing previously-transcribed speech.

Just as with listeners, ASR errors can be detrimental for understanding and skimming audio contents during editing [11]. In the MedSpeak interface, Lai et al. provided a separate graphical window for fixing transcription errors [18]. In a speech production system like SimpleSpeech, though, users could easily get lost between the audio editing and transcription correction modes, so we chose to guide the user's attention through these modes via the movement of the editing caret into a quasi-modal interface.

Pauses in speech deliver nuanced meaning such as hesitation or emphasis, so easy and powerful manipulation of pause duration is important. A system called SpeechSkimmer automatically condenses pauses for fast auditory skimming [2]. Other previous systems supported pause editing via a designated button [3] or specialized tags [22]. Rubin et al.'s system used the period key as a shortcut to insert pause tags, but the duration of the gap was preset and required the use of a separate menu. Our approach is based on a traditional text editor, where users adjust lengths of pauses by adding and deleting spaces with the space bar and delete keys. The length of the pause corresponds to the number of spaces.

Perhaps most importantly, studies of the mental and linguistic effects of AAC discourse are limited despite the variety of AAC system designs discussed above. Those studies that exist are focused on the larger category of computer-mediated communication (CMC), which is dominated by textual media such as SMS, email, or Facebook posts. For example, Kiesler, Siegel, and McGuire [16] found more equalized group participation and more uninhibited expression of opinions in synchronous text-based CMC than in face-to-face discussions. Asynchronous CMC, similar to a discussion board, induces more prosocial behavior and, in fact, more informal communication styles over time than face-to-face [30]. On the other hand, formality and politeness in emails has been shown to increase as the social distance, status gap, and importance of a request increase [5]. How these findings about textual media relate to spoken modes of CMC has not been heavily investigated, however.

DESIGNING SIMPLESPEECH

Building on the capabilities developed in these prior studies, SimpleSpeech is a web-based application for recording and editing short voice messages in a discussion setting (see Fig. 1). The design of SimpleSpeech is inspired by the transcription-based speech editing systems developed by Rubin [22], Yoon [33], and Whittaker [31], which also use ASR transcription as a semantic and visual proxy for audio. Conceptual modifications were necessary to suit the "live" editing paradigm, in which the user records and edits spoken comments in a unified workflow.

We followed an iterative procedure to improve the design and interactions of SimpleSpeech. After building an initial prototype of the application, an informal pilot test was conducted with 5 participants. Each user was given a brief introduction to the software and shown how to use the basic features, then given the scenario of creating an audio response to a written claim on an online forum. The prompts used in the tests were adapted from the GRE Pool of Issue Topics. This user feedback helped us improve the capabilities of SimpleSpeech in several ways:

- *Pause manipulation.* An important finding in the pilot study was the importance of being able to introduce and adjust pauses between words, not just to remove them. These gaps in the audio help make natural-sounding cuts between audio clips as well as punctuate claims (e.g., the end of a sentence). The original system only allowed the user to delete pauses, so we added a spacebar action to insert a fragment of silence.

- *Live insertion.* Users often misspoke a word or phrase in the middle of a message. Since re-recording the entire message was a large burden, a partial deletion and re-recording capability was required. Our interface maintains the text-based principle that the cursor position uniformly indicates the focus of editing. Therefore, in SimpleSpeech, clicking the Record button naturally inserts a new stream into the existing audio at the point corresponding to the cursor position.

- *Quasi-modal transcription editing.* In consideration of the recipient, the pilot testers wanted to correct ASR errors. We found that an interface with an audio-editing mode for revising speech and a text-editing mode for correcting mistranscriptions confused users. This led us to design a small, separate quasi-modal editing box (see Fig. 2) that pops up during transcription editing. The movement of the cursor to the modal box clearly indicates that the system is in a separate text-editing mode, accessed by pressing the Return key.

Our text-based approach to speech editing requires a reliable transcription as well as time intervals corresponding to each word. Both of these requirements are fulfilled by the IBM Watson Developer Cloud speech-to-text transcription service, which is reported to have a word error rate of around 10% [25].

QUALITATIVE EVALUATION

The interaction paradigm of SimpleSpeech was tested in a qualitative assessment to determine (1) the practicability of

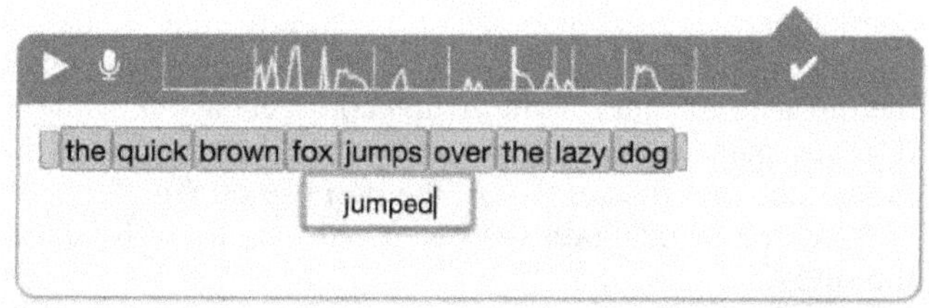

Figure 2. To keep the user interface from becoming cluttered with secondary functionality, the transcription editing feature was implemented as a modal interaction. The pop-up box shown above gives clear visual indication to the user that they are no longer directly editing the audio.

a lightweight text-based audio editor, (2) the effects of minor transcription errors on audio consumption and production, and (3) the implications of being able to edit audio in an asynchronous online discussion.

Participants were introduced to the functionality of the system, then given two untimed tasks. First, to simulate an asynchronous audio discussion, the test users were asked to listen to an audio comment left by the previous tester and create an original audio response. Next, they received a different, textual prompt and created an audio comment which would be consumed by the next user. In both cases the user was asked to edit his or her recording to be polished and clear. The participants were interviewed at the end of the test; these interviews were transcribed with conversational elements filtered out. Themes were extracted from the remaining sentences via open coding, followed by flat coding to sort statements among the themes. Cohen's κ between the two coders was .78, indicating the reliability of the categorized themes.

The sample for the study consisted of 9 test subjects (4 male, 5 female, mean age 22 yrs; henceforth denoted $P_1, P_2, \ldots, P_9$). All participants were native English speakers. Two individuals, P_2 and P_3, were media editors who provided technical feedback and a comparison to professional audio editing. The remainder were interns at edX, an educational technology non-profit, and students at RSI, a summer program for gifted high school students.

Results

The coding process revealed some themes that replicated the findings of Whittaker and Amento [31], as well as some novel results. For instance, the consensus was that a text-based editing paradigm provides sufficient control to render waveform manipulation unnecessary (P_4, P_5, P_6, P_8), as well as being"more accessible, more doable" than pure waveform editing (P_3, P_7). On the consumption side, the transcript was helpful in allowing users to "see all the points [the speaker was] making instead of having to remember them" (P_3, P_4, P_6). Overall the presence of errors was not a heavy distractor from the content of the messages, echoing findings from Whittaker's voicemail study [8], although one user described a greater focus on the audio because of these errors (P_8).

Although users were mostly accustomed to using the transcript for consuming the messages (P_6), they also pointed out that the audio gave them the ability to "feel the emotions coming across, so ... you can still relate to what the persons feeling" (P_1, P_5, P_8). This result indicates that text played the most significant role in *factual* comprehension, while audio was most useful for *tonal* comprehension. Since both modalities seem necessary to the purpose of SimpleSpeech, we decided to maintain the combined paradigm throughout the study.

In addition to these transcript-related results, the qualitative study also yielded the following new themes:

The primary use of lightweight voice editing is to make fine-grained rather than large-scale adjustments. The most commonly-used manipulation during the qualitative study was the removal of disfluencies (P_1, P_2, P_4, P_5, P_7), followed by pause deletion (P_2, P_3, P_5, P_6, P_8). Only P_1 and P_8 edited large chunks of audio by deleting or rerecording, and P_8 reported doing so only to improve the smoothness of a smaller change in a sentence. Perhaps because SimpleSpeech was presented as a tool to be briefly used to "clean up" recordings, participants focused on removing the "embarrassing" and "awkward" sounds (P_1, P_5).

The linearity of audio leads to a pressure to organize one's thoughts during recording. P_4, P_7, and P_9 described a "psychological sort of ... need to get it all out, and the fact that it won't necessarily be as organized there." Another tester, P_5, had "a tendency to get like a blank slate" in which he "couldn't think of anything to say." The elevated mental task load that P_5 describes could be inherent in oral discussion; P_9 noted that "[it] might just be the fact that I was recording," and that "editing would make it nicer." Users likely reported this pressure despite the capability to edit their recordings due to the previous theme of lightweight editing, and also because this pressure arose in the moment of recording rather than throughout the entire message-composition workflow.

Awareness of the recipient and the editability of the audio drive up the quality of contributions. Four users mentioned the formality of their recordings (P_1, P_5, P_7, P_9), which they attributed to "an expectation" to edit, given that "someone else would know that I had that opportunity" (P_8). As P_9 explained her motivation to edit:

> Personally I'm editing to express myself a little more in a polished way when I'm writing.... especially if I know someone else is going to review it and be able to respond, I want to make sure I'm as clear as possible and as concise in a way that doesn't really come across when I'm talking.

Listening to another participant before initiating their own comment may have been a factor in determining the users' performance (P_9), as well as the presence of editing tools: "Since you have the ability to edit things, it feels like you're talking to somebody who's prepared a point or a conversational view" (P_5). The negative viewpoints of a few users on the editing ability were generally expressed in similar terms, so we considered this theme important for the success of AAC.

QUANTITATIVE EVALUATION

Our second, quantitative experiment was conducted in order to validate the three original themes identified in the qualitative evaluation above. In doing so, these measurements collectively assess the efficacy of SimpleSpeech and, indirectly, the usefulness of audio editing tools in general for educational discussions.

Procedure

Two between-subject dimensions were studied: students versus teachers, as well as the formality of initial stimulus recordings (see "Stimuli and Formality Measures" below). In addition, the dimension of no-editing versus editing was studied on a within-subject basis. Participants in the study were given two task parts in random order: recording messages without editing functionality (the **No Editing**, or **NE** task) and using SimpleSpeech (the **Editing**, or **E** task). Each task consisted of "discussion threads," in which users read a prompt statement, listened to another person's opinion on the issue, then produced an original response. Participants responded to two threads for each task, for a total of four messages of about one-minute duration each. (Before starting the E part, participants were given a standardized tutorial to learn how to edit using SimpleSpeech.)

After each task, the NASA Task Load Index (NASA-TLX) questionnaire was used to quantify the pressure or mental task load of producing a voice message [12]. NASA-TLX is a subjective analytical tool that measures task load along six dimensions: Mental Demand, Physical Demand, Temporal Demand, Performance, Effort, and Frustration. Participants in the study completed the TLX ranking and weighting procedure after each task to obtain comparisons between the no-editing and editing situations.

The quantitative study was conducted at a small suburban public high school in the midwestern U.S. with 28 volunteer participants (16 students, ages 16-18, and 12 teachers; 13 male, 15 female). This location was ideal for the study because the sample contained a variety of learning and speaking styles as well as different aptitudes for technology and discussion.

Stimuli and Formality Measures

The criterion used for formality was the F-score, a measure of contextuality introduced by Heylighen and Dewaele in 2002 [13]. The F-score is a purely textual metric based on the frequencies of various parts of speech in a text: nouns, adjectives and prepositions decrease contextuality and increase the F-score since they are independent of the circumstances around the text, while verbs, adverbs, pronouns, and interjections increase contextuality and decrease the F-score.

The initial stimulus recordings for each of the prompt statements were generated by a group of five initial volunteers, who were asked to plan and edit some of the comments and improvise on the others. After splitting the resulting messages by formality, the average F-score was 53.7 for the Group A messages and 49.4 for the Group B messages ($p = .11$ by unpaired t-test), reflecting the likely greater contextuality of the recordings produced on-the-fly. Group A stimuli also tended to use longer words than those for Group B (4.62 versus 4.38 letters, p = .047), to be more concise (113 versus 193 words, p = .0095), and to have higher speaking rates (149 compared to 134 words per minute, p = .076). After obtaining and categorizing these messages, the voices were anonymized by adjusting the pitch randomly.

Since the qualitative study had indicated that prior exposure to other individuals' messages could affect the perceived formality in the discussion, half the participants (Group A) listened to only formal recordings, while the other half (Group B) listened to only informal ones. We hypothesized that the participants in Group A would produce more formal messages due to the stimuli they received.

Results

We analyzed the effects of the live voice editing features by analyzing system logs, speech contents, and the task load survey data. The results fell into the following three categories:

Utilization of SimpleSpeech Features

As in the qualitative study, most participants appreciated and took advantage of the ability to edit their messages. They found the interface intuitive and natural, presumably due to familiarity with text-editing interfaces.

The amount of editing that users engaged in varied widely: on average, about 17.7 edits were made to each comment (*SE* = 2.3, including inserting a new recording, inserting a pause, deleting words, or deleting a pause). Of these changes, the vast majority were subtractive: 6.6 word deletions (*SE* = 1.6) and 6.3 pause deletions (*SE* = 1.1) per message. This was consistent with the previously-observed inclination to remove disfluencies and "awkward" hesitations from the recordings. Both teachers and students exhibited this impetus with no significant difference (12 deletions for students, 16.2 for teachers, p = .36 by unpaired t-test), so correcting misspeeches was fairly universal across participants. Insertions of any kind were less common, at 1.1 per message (*SE* = 0.3), probably because users tended to correct themselves *post hoc* during the initial take and delete the mistakes afterward. Four users went without performing any edits at all on at least one message; three out of these were teachers, and their messages were generally already fluent.

One error that several participants made was to use the Delete key on tokens to fix transcription errors, which resulted in the permanent deletion of that audio token. However, emphasis in the tutorial that the Delete key deleted the audio permanently did help other participants avoid making this mistake. Another misconception we observed in a few participants was a tendency to treat SimpleSpeech as a dictation tool. These users paused for long periods of time during recording sessions and neglected to play back the messages during editing. Furthermore, their inclination after stopping a recording session was to go back and correct transcription errors so that the visual representation made sense.

Effect on Task Load

Since the NASA-TLX scale is subjective, it does introduce variability between participants due to the differences between their perceived skill at the task [12]. For instance, one participant could rate the recording task at a 3 out of 20, while another could rate the very same task at a 15. Therefore, the strongest comparisons of task load were made in the within-subject dimension, which was the ability or inability to edit.

Overall, the students reported significantly *lower* levels of mental task load or pressure during the E task than the NE task (8.70 compared to 10.8, p = .011 by paired t-test). The values for the individual components of the TLX, shown in Table 1, yielded the following contributory dimensions on the TLX questionnaire:

- *Temporal demand*. Students rated the temporal demand at 7.81 for the E task, significantly less than the NE rating of 10.5 (p = .037 by paired t-test). As described by the TLX form, temporal demand refers to "time pressure due to the rate or pace at which the tasks or task elements occurred" [12]. Students verbally described the increase in time demand reported on the TLX in terms of having to think of words quickly, with the knowledge that every second not filled with speech would be an embarrassing silence.
- *Performance*. Students felt more concern about the quality of their messages in the NE task, with a marginally significant difference of 10.0 compared to 8.25 for the E task (p = .083 by paired t-test). Just as the participants in the prior qualitative study had articulated a desire to make their messages better for the sake of their listeners, the students also evidently wanted to improve their recordings in the NE task. The inability to do so resulted in elevated task load due to performance, while for the E task the stress was lower because they were afforded the chance to correct their mistakes.
- *Effort*. Similarly to performance, students reported having to work significantly harder in the NE task to complete it to their desired level (rated 11.6 compared to 9.06 in the E task, p = .014 by paired t-test). This increased effort could correspond to the additional mental activity which had to be expended in order to generate speech fluently and without excessive hesitation.

While the teachers also reported slightly lower average workload levels in the E task, as shown at the right of Table 1, this difference was not significant. In fact, 7 of the 12 participating teachers actually rated the E task as requiring a higher workload than the NE task. This subset of the teachers, 5 of whom were in Group A, reported an average task load greater in the E task than the NE task for *all* dimensions. The reason for this rating, these teachers explained, was that the availability of the editing tools caused them to feel more worried about their performance (likely due to P_8's "expectation to edit"). They were thus made to expend more effort to preserve the existing fluidity of their messages.

Overall, the fact that the differences in perception of workload varied so much among teachers indicates that they were not as heavily affected by the ability to edit as the students,

	Students (N = 16)		Teachers (N = 12)	
Task	E	NE	E	NE
Mental Demand	9.56 (1.0)	11.1 (1.0)	11.4 (1.3)	10.8 (1.4)
Physical Demand	3.69 (0.6)	2.63 (0.5)	4.00 (1.3)	2.83 (0.6)
Temporal Demand	7.81 (1.1)	10.5* (1.0)	7.50 (1.4)	10.0 (1.3)
Performance	8.25 (0.7)	10.0^{+} (0.6)	8.50 (1.4)	9.67 (1.3)
Effort	9.06 (1.1)	11.6* (0.9)	9.83 (1.7)	10.4 (1.4)
Frustration	7.75 (1.1)	8.88 (1.0)	8.42 (1.6)	10.0 (1.7)
Total (weighted)	8.70 (0.7)	10.8* (0.6)	9.47 (1.2)	10.6 (1.3)

Table 1. The unweighted mental work load ratings reported by students and teachers from recording voice messages. *E* and *NE* refer to the tasks in which editing was allowed and disallowed, respectively. Each value ranges from 1 to 20, indicating the subjective level of task load that participants rated for each metric; standard error is given in parentheses. ($^{+}$ – $p < 0.10$, * – $p < 0.05$, paired two-tailed comparison of *E* and *NE*)

who clearly appreciated the security that SimpleSpeech offered.

Speech Formality Between Subject Groups

Contrary to the hypothesis that prior exposure to audio messages would affect the formality or linguistic traits of new messages, the F-scores of the participants' output were unrelated to the group they were in, as shown in Table 2. However, the students' speaking rates in Group A were significantly faster than those in Group B (p = .016 by unpaired t-test). Moreover, students in Group B spoke significantly *slower* than teachers exposed to the same stimulus recordings (p = .0016 by unpaired t-test), but there was no corresponding difference in Group A. This may reflect the auditory component of formality observed by the qualitative test users, if the faster speaking rate was interpreted by students as thought-out or engaging speech.

Interestingly, the same teachers who reported higher task load in the editing task also produced more formal messages than the other teachers (mean F-score 56.6 compared to 53.0, p = .12 by unpaired t-test) and with longer words (4.58 compared to 4.35 letters, p = .0082). In fact, the student participant group also contained members who rated the E task as more demanding than the NE task, though fewer in number (4 out of 16); these students produced much more formal messages than their peers as well (F-score 57.9 compared to 53.5, p = .027 by unpaired t-test). These participants could have had more experience speaking extemporaneously or felt less inclined to speak conversationally, ultimately leading to SimpleSpeech not being as useful to them.

On the whole, the formality of the recordings was not affected by the stimulus message or even whether the participant was a teacher or a student. Considering that the F-score measures contextuality between the speaker and the audience, the principal sources of variation in F-score must have been personal aptitude and preference for the medium and the scenario of an online forum discussion.

FORMALITY COMPARISON

Contextuality in the online voice-based discussion scenario could be highly indicative of AAC's potential applications, and to our knowledge this trait has not been studied extensively. We therefore conducted a comparison between the voice messages composed during this study and several publicly-available corpora. To our knowledge, no corpus exists that was collected in an audio-text situation like SimpleSpeech, so contrasts in formality inevitably arise from the differences in medium.

The SimpleSpeech text, representing AAC, contained 14,569 words from 112 messages. For written documents, we used several sections of the well-known Brown corpus to compile general categories of text: nonfiction, fiction, and technical writing (consisting of government documents, scientific articles, and news) [17]. We obtained chatroom text from the `nps_chat` corpus, face-to-face conversation data from the `webtext` corpus, and telephone data from the `switchboard` corpus, all available as part of the Natural Language Toolkit (NLTK) [4]. Finally, we also analyzed email communication in non-spam messages from the Enron corpus [26], as well as a corpus of Twitter posts [9].

The results of this comparison, shown in Fig. 3, illustrate the middle-ground that AAC takes relative to oral and written media. The least formal and most contextual corpora were those based on oral communication (with the notable exception of web chat messages), while the most formal and least context-dependent were the written texts, including email and Twitter posts. We will note three possible explanations for the formality of each medium based on the ordering of the corpora:

Speaker-audience relationship. Since the F-score is inversely related to contextuality, it is reasonable that the chat and telephone corpora had the lowest F-scores because the participants knew each other and were conversing on a one-to-one basis. On the other hand, the written forms of communication (with the exception of email) were more formal because the audience was defined more loosely and not necessarily acquainted with the speaker. AAC using SimpleSpeech was more closely related to the latter condition (as an online forum discussion), which probably contributed to its greater formality compared to the other spoken corpora.

	Students		Teachers	
Group	*A*	*B*	*A*	*B*
Formality (F-score)	55.8 (1.1)	53.4 (1.3)	54.7 (1.6)	55.5 (1.5)
Word length	4.40 (0.06)	4.44 (0.05)	4.50 (0.06)	4.47 (0.06)
Disfluencies (per 100 words)	1.59 (0.35)	2.38 (0.41)	1.27 (0.27)	1.41 (0.38)
Word count	101 (6.5)	140^{+} (13)	155 (19)	130 (9.4)
Speaking rate (words/min)	130 (5.0)	115* (3.8)	137 (6.8)	138 (4.9)

Table 2. Various metrics describing the formality of the audio messages produced by each participant group. Group A listened to more formal initial stimulus recordings than Group B. There were few significant differences in these criteria between the groups, indicating that formality was dependent on the general context of AAC as well as the speaker's preference, especially for teachers. Standard error is given in parentheses. ($^{+}$ – $p < 0.10$, * – $p < 0.05$, unpaired two-tailed comparison of groups A and B)

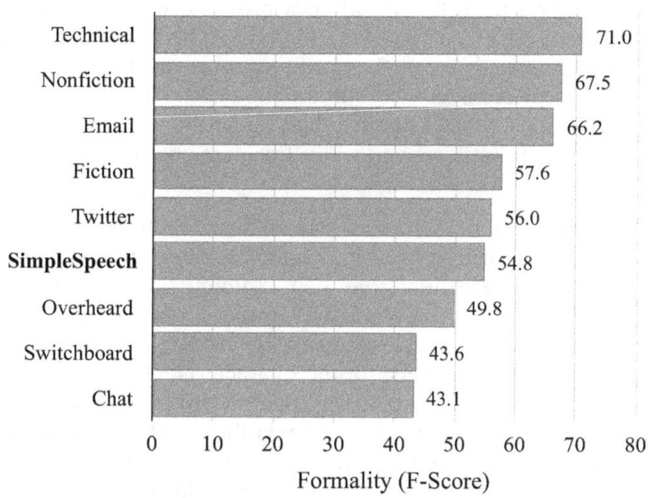

Figure 3. The formality of corpora in different genre and media. The messages produced using SimpleSpeech during the quantitative study are intended to reflect general AAC discussion characteristics, and seem to be more formal than other spoken forms of communication but not as formal as email.

Immediacy of communication. The tendency to speak or write more contextually when the recipient must respond immediately helps explain why the online chat text, though written, was more contextual and less formal than the oral corpora. It also justifies the fact that the email corpus was more formal than all of the other direct communication media. Again, AAC falls toward the more formal end of this spectrum because there is little temporal proximity between the speaker and the audience.

Tendency toward verbosity. Media that pressured the creator to be brief or precise were more formal and less contextual. For instance, writing technical documents requires the preferential use of nouns over pronouns to maximize clarity. Twitter messages are, of course, limited to 140 characters, leading to a greater concentration of meaning that favors less contextual words. For AAC, the ability to edit could potentially influence the contextuality if discussion members were pressured to trim down their recordings. For our study, however, the F-score was not affected by verbosity, because edits were more concentrated on removing disfluencies and misspeeches than on improving concision.

DISCUSSION

In this study two forms of responding to pressure in a communication task were measured: the mental workload involved in completing the task and the degree of formality in the messages created in the task. Using this information, we will evaluate the strengths and weaknesses of SimpleSpeech as a tool for enabling AAC as well as the viability of AAC in educational and collaborative contexts.

Imbalance Between Speaker and Listener

As Grudin notes, it is critical for collaborative software to spread the burden of usage equally on its constituent members. For instance, he cites email as a medium in which "everyone generally shares the benefits and burdens equally" [10]. On the other hand, voice applications create inequality between speaker and listener since the former must expect that the latter will listen thoroughly and carefully to the message, a relatively slow task compared to reading.

However, the premise of SimpleSpeech is that the bias toward the speaker is reversed. ASR transcription can greatly facilitate the listener's task, as has already been demonstrated [8, 29], bringing the workload down and closer to that of reading. Meanwhile, students who record messages could experience a *greater* workload relative to writing because of the linearity of audio, which prevents them from correcting mistakes after the fact and thereby elevates the pressure to do well the first time.

SimpleSpeech was demonstrated to be a useful counterbalance in situations where the speaker's workload is elevated. In the qualitative study, some users noted the pressure "to have organized thoughts" and to "sound composed more" during recording, but that "editing would make it nicer because you can go back and fix the mistakes" (P_2). Furthermore, the level of control was just right for most users: since they focused on deleting the disfluencies and pauses in their speech, the word-tokenized editor for the most part provided exactly the information needed to quickly delete undesirable sounds. For the few users who did want to edit on a larger scale, the audio insertion feature was deemed helpful as well.

In the quantitative evaluation, we found strong evidence to support the use of SimpleSpeech, especially for students. There was a significant decrease in task load on students when given the capability to edit, even in spite of the added time required to listen to the message and perform the editing. On the other hand, teachers did not find SimpleSpeech editing as useful, probably because they already had higher confidence in their recordings as being of acceptable quality. One teacher reasoned that he was "already used to hearing [his] own voice" from lecturing, a medium where statements cannot be retracted as easily as with SimpleSpeech. However, many teachers did use the editing tools, even though their workload levels were not significantly different with or without this opportunity. This would indicate that the editing tools are a valuable option for producers to have, but users should not be obligated to use them.

Implications for Formality in AAC

Our comparative analysis of formality using Heylighen et al.'s F-score [13] is unique in its application to mixed-media discourse. While the corpora against which SimpleSpeech messages were tested were generated through either purely-verbal or purely-written means, users in this study were required to consider both the textual, semantic meaning of the transcript and the auditory, connotative meanings expressed by the voice. As a result, our comparison of contextuality scores inherently lacks the auditory component that may be communicated through slang, dialect, or speaking rate. We do not know of any one single measure that can capture these phenomena across different media. However, our findings are useful for describing the formality of the textual message content, which is arguably the primary purpose of the communication as well as the aspect on which message consumers focused most.

The textual formality of the SimpleSpeech discussions was not significantly affected by the experimental conditions, indicating that for the most part, users are likely to adopt their own style for audio messages suitable for a discussion environment. Nevertheless, it is critical to the success of general-purpose AAC that the formality of discussion be controlled to some extent, so that collaborators feel willing to participate. For students this impetus toward quality is not as problematic, since they felt more relaxed rather than more stressed with editing functionality. If discussion quality were driven up by artificial means, however, such as by grading students on the eloquence of their comments or evaluating employees on the basis of their online interactions, then individuals might gravitate toward socially "safer" modes of communication over which they feel more control (namely, text). Proper acquaintance with audio editing capabilities is essential for AAC's survival under these pressures toward high-quality production.

To provide an example, peer feedback within an online course would be an ideal use of AAC using SimpleSpeech because students could send messages to a well-defined audience, thereby compensating for the additional formality imposed by the spatiotemporal distance between the participants. The editing tools would also drive students to produce better discussion input, increasing productivity and enhancing the learning experience. On the other hand, enabling editing for personal communication, such as WhatsApp voice messages, may reduce the desired informal speaking style of the platform. Since the contextuality demanded by each situation is different, future audio-based collaboration platforms must consider the factors presented here and tailor their functionality accordingly.

CONCLUSIONS

SimpleSpeech's intuitive design alleviates the pressure associated with the linearity of audio because users have the ability to easily fix errors after the fact. Furthermore, we designed SimpleSpeech to clearly distinguish audio and text modalities, from the visual cues provided by the waveform to the quasi-modal interface for correcting transcription errors. Students' use of these editing tools resulted in greater feelings of comfort when producing comments than without SimpleSpeech functionality. The true utility of this software, then, was to (at least partly) un-linearize audio, even making it more text-like.

Because studies of the linguistic and social characteristics of computer-mediated communication have been mostly limited to textual interactions, we also explored the formality and contextuality of AAC. Our finding that it was roughly in between spoken and written media is not discouraging *per se*; however, the relatively formal characteristics of AAC must be taken into account before such a system is implemented in practice. Nevertheless, we feel that the small-scale edits that users engaged in during this study are reassuring for potential applications of AAC. Removing disfluencies and pauses allows users to feel comfortable with their recording while maintaining the spontaneity of thought in a spoken message.

The results of the qualitative study point to new directions for improving SimpleSpeech. For instance, on initial exposure to the application users initially tended to focus preferentially on the text instead of on the voice. Slightly different visual layouts of the application, such as overlaying or juxtaposing the transcription on a more prominent waveform, could help users understand better that the text is a secondary tool. Another possible feature could be automating certain edits, such as removing disfluencies and hesitations, to improve efficiency and edit quality even further. Additionally, the findings in our quantitative study revealed promising trends concerning the benefits of AAC for online discussion, but may need a larger pool of test participants to attain statistical significance.

Our hope in developing SimpleSpeech is that asynchronous audio communication will gain greater usage in education and other collaborative settings. With the combination of ASR transcription for listeners and low-barrier editing tools for speakers, voice-based communication tools can engage students and improve the quality of collaboration on the Web.

ACKNOWLEDGMENTS

We would like to thank all the interns, high school students, and teachers who participated in this study. We owe thanks to the Center for Excellence in Education, whose Research

Science Institute summer program at MIT provided the opportunity to conduct this research. We also thank Nicholas Chen, Abigail Sellen, and François Guimbretière for design inspiration.

REFERENCES

1. Stephen Ades and Daniel C Swinehart. 1986. *Voice annotation and editing in a workstation environment.* XEROX Corporation, Palo Alto Research Center.
2. Barry Arons. 1993. SpeechSkimmer: Interactively Skimming Recorded Speech. In *Proceedings of the 6th Annual ACM Symposium on User Interface Software and Technology (UIST '93)*. ACM, New York, NY, USA, 187–196. DOI: http://dx.doi.org/10.1145/168642.168661
3. Floraine Berthouzoz, Wilmot Li, and Maneesh Agrawala. 2012. Tools for Placing Cuts and Transitions in Interview Video. *ACM Trans. Graph.* 31, 4, Article 67 (July 2012), 8 pages. DOI: http://dx.doi.org/10.1145/2185520.2185563
4. Steven Bird, Ewan Klein, and Edward Loper. 2009. *Natural Language Processing with Python.* O'Reilly Media.
5. Thomas Cho. 2010. Linguistic Features of Electronic Mail in the Workplace: A Comparison with Memoranda. *Language@Internet* 7, 3 (2010).
6. Juan Casares et al. 2002a. Simplifying Video Editing Using Metadata. In *DIS '02 Proceedings*. London, 157–166.
7. Janet M. Baker et al. 2009. Developments and directions in speech recognition and understanding, Part 1. *Signal Processing, IEEE* 26, 3 (2009).
8. Steve Whittaker et al. 2002b. SCANMail: a voicemail interface that makes speech browsable, readable and searchable. *CHI Letters* 4, 1 (2002).
9. Alec Go, Richa Bhayani, and Lei Huang. 2009. *Twitter Sentiment Classification using Distant Supervision.* Technical Report. Stanford.
10. Jonathan Grudin. 1988. Why CSCW applications fail: Problems in the design and evaluation of organizational interfaces. *ACM Conference on Computer-Supported Cooperative Work* (1988).
11. C Halverson, D Horn, C Karat, and John Karat. 1999. The beauty of errors: Patterns of error correction in desktop speech systems. In *Proceedings of INTERACT99*. 133–140.
12. Sandra G. Hart and Lowell E. Staveland. 1988. Development of NASA-TLX (Task Load Index): Results of empirical and theoretical research. In *Human Mental Workload*, P. A. Hancock and N. Meshkati (Eds.). North Holland Press, Amsterdam.
13. Francis Heylighen and Jean-Marc Dewaele. 2002. Variation in the contextuality of language: an empirical measure. *Foundations of Science* 7 (2002), 239–340.
14. Debby Hindus and Chris Schmandt. 1992. Ubiquitous Audio: Capturing Spontaneous Collaboration. In *Proceedings of the 1992 ACM Conference on Computer-supported Cooperative Work (CSCW '92)*. ACM, New York, NY, USA, 210–217. DOI: http://dx.doi.org/10.1145/143457.143481
15. Philip Ice, Reagan Curtis, Perry Phillips, and John Wells. 2007. Using asynchronous audio feedback to enhance teaching presence and students' sense of community. *Journal of Asynchronous Learning Networks* 11, 2 (2007).
16. Sara Kiesler, Jane Siegel, and Timothy W. McGuire. 1984. Social Psychological Aspects of Computer-Mediated Communication. *Amer. Psychologist* 39, 10 (1984), 1123–1134.
17. Henry Kučera and W. Nelson Francis. 1967. *Computational Analysis of Present-Day American English.* Brown University Press, Providence.
18. Jennifer Lai and John Vergo. 1997. MedSpeak: Report Creation with Continuous Speech Recognition. In *Proceedings of the ACM SIGCHI Conference on Human Factors in Computing Systems (CHI '97)*. ACM, New York, NY, USA, 431–438. DOI: http://dx.doi.org/10.1145/258549.258829
19. Philip Marriott. 2002. Voice vs text-based discussion forums: An implementation of Wimba Voice Boards. In *World Conference on E-Learning in Corporate, Government, Healthcare, and Higher Education*, Vol. 2002. 640–646.
20. Philip Marriott and Jane Hiscock. 2002. Voice vs Text-based Discussion Forums: An Implementation of Wimba Voice Boards. In *Proc. E-Learn: World Conference on E-Learning in Corporate, Government, Healthcare, and Higher Education*, M. Driscoll and T. Reeves (Eds.). Chesapeake, VA.
21. Jody Oomen-Early, Mary Bold, Kristin L. Wiginton, Tara L. Gallien, and Nancy Anderson. 2008. Using asynchronous audio communication (AAC) in the online classroom: a comparative study. *Journal of Online Learning and Teaching* 4, 3 (2008).
22. Steve Rubin, Floraine Berthouzoz, Gautham J. Mysore, Wilmot Li, and Maneesh Agrawala. 2013. Content-Based Tools for Editing Audio Stories. In *UIST '13*. 113–122.
23. George Saon, Hong-Kwang J. Kuo, Steven Rennie, and Michael Picheny. 2015. The IBM 2015 English Conversational Telephone Speech Recognition System. *Interspeech* (2015).
24. Christopher Schmandt. 1981. The Intelligent Ear: A Graphical Interface to Digital Audio. In *Proceedings, IEEE International Conference on Cybernetics and Society, IEEE.*

25. Hagen Soltau, George Saon, and Tara N. Sainath. 2014. Joint training of convolutional and non-convolutional neural networks. In *Proceedings of the IEEE Intl. Conference on Acoustic, Speech and Signal Processing*. Florence, 5572–5576.

26. Will Styler. 2011. *The EnronSent Corpus*. Technical Report 01-2011. University of Colorado at Boulder Institute of Cognitive Science, Boulder, CO.

27. Chi-Hsiung Tu and Marina McIsaac. 2002. The Relationship of Social Presence and Interaction in Online Classes. *Amer. Journal of Distance Education* 16, 3 (2002).

28. Sunil Vemuri, Philip DeCamp, Walter Bender, and Chris Schmandt. 2004a. Improving Speech Playback Using Time-compression and Speech Recognition. In *Proceedings of the SIGCHI Conference on Human Factors in Computing Systems (CHI '04)*. ACM, New York, NY, USA, 295–302. DOI: http://dx.doi.org/10.1145/985692.985730

29. Sunil Vemuri, Philip DeCamp, Walter Bender, and Chris Schmandt. 2004b. Improving Speech Playback Using Time-Compression and Speech Recognition. *CHI Letters* 6, 1 (2004).

30. Joseph B. Walther. 1995. Relational Aspects of Computer-Mediated Communication: Experimental Observations over Time. *Organization Science* 6, 2 (1995), 186–203.

31. Steve Whittaker and Brian Amento. 2004. Semantic Speech Editing. *CHI Letters* (2004), 527–534.

32. Lynn Wilcox, Ian Smith, and Marcia Bush. 1992. Wordspotting for Voice Editing and Audio Indexing. In *Proceedings of the SIGCHI Conference on Human Factors in Computing Systems (CHI '92)*. ACM, New York, NY, USA, 655–656. DOI: http://dx.doi.org/10.1145/142750.150715

33. Dongwook Yoon, Nicholas Chen, François Guimbretière, and Abigail Sellen. 2014. RichReview: blending ink, speech, and gesture to support collaborative document review. In *Proceedings of the 27th annual ACM symposium on User interface software and technology*. ACM, 481–490.

34. Dongwook Yoon, Nicholas Chen, Bernie Randles, Amy Cheatle, Corinna E. Loeckenhoff, Steven J. Jackson, Abigail Sellen, and François Guimbretière. 2016. Deployment of a Collaborative Multi-Modal Annotation System for Instructor Feedback and Peer Discussion. In *Proceedings of the 19th ACM Conference on Computer Supported Cooperative Work & Social Computing*. ACM.

Tap the ShapeTones: Exploring the Effects of Crossmodal Congruence in an Audio-Visual Interface

Oussama Metatla
Queen Mary University of London
o.metatla@qmul.ac.uk

Nuno N. Correia
Goldsmiths, University of London
n.correia@gold.ac.uk

Fiore Martin
Queen Mary University of London
f.martin@qmul.ac.uk

Nick Bryan-Kinns
Queen Mary University of London
n.bryan-kinns@qmul.ac.uk

Tony Stockman
Queen Mary University of London
t.stockman@qmul.ac.uk

ABSTRACT

There is growing interest in the application of crossmodal perception to interface design. However, most research has focused on task performance measures and often ignored user experience and engagement. We present an examination of crossmodal congruence in terms of performance and engagement in the context of a memory task of audio, visual, and audio-visual stimuli. Participants in a first study showed improved performance when using a visual congruent mapping that was cancelled by the addition of audio to the baseline conditions, and a subjective preference for the audio-visual stimulus that was not reflected in the objective data. Based on these findings, we designed an audio-visual memory game to examine the effects of crossmodal congruence on user experience and engagement. Results showed higher engagement levels with congruent displays with some reported preference for potential challenge and enjoyment that an incongruent display may support, particularly for increased task complexity.

Author Keywords

Crossmodal congruence, spatial mappings, user engagement, user experience, games, audio-visual display.

ACM Classification Keywords

H.1.2 User/Machine systems: Human Factors; H.5.2 User Interfaces: Auditory (non-speech) feedback, Screen design (e.g., text, graphics, color), Input devices and strategies (e.g., mouse, touchscreen), Evaluation/methodology; K.8.0 General: Games

INTRODUCTION

Multisensory perception is an activity that we do everyday when we combine signals from various sensory channels to make sense of our environment and to act in it. One of the mechanisms that we use to fuse input from multiple sensory channels is referred to as *crossmodal interaction* [35]. A key feature of a crossmodal display is that it relays the same information through two or more senses, for example, when we find it easier to recognise speech when we can see the speaker's lip movements. Research aiming to apply findings from crossmodal perception to interface design has focused on designing support for interaction in complex environments, for example in the design of monitoring systems and warning signals [29, 35], on designing sensory substitution devices for people with sensory disabilities, such as the vOICe system, which uses sonification to convert images into sound [15], and on supporting collaboration between people with different sensory abilities [42, 16]. However, whilst it is increasingly feasible to support crossmodal interaction in a range of general purpose devices, e.g. tablet computers and smartphones provide touch, visual, and speech interaction, little work has considered the implications of crossmodal displays on user experience and engagement. Therefore, we propose that research into the design of effective crossmodal interfaces should consider a wider range of user experiences. In particular, evaluations of crossmodal displays should emphasise elements of both user performance and engagement to provide deeper insights into the application of crossmodal mappings to interactive experiences. This paper contributes to bridging the gap between studies of crossmodal user performance and engagement by examining the effects of crossmodal congruence on performance and engagement in the context of a memory task supported by combinations of audio and visual displays on touch-screen devices. A first study examines the effects of different levels of crossmodal congruence on how audio-visual cues support the mapping of spatial ordering. A second study examines the application of these crossmodal mappings in the design of an audio-visual memory game, focusing on evaluating user experience and engagement with the crossmodal gameplay.

CHI'16, May 07 - 12, 2016, San Jose, CA, USA

ACM 978-1-4503-3362-7/16/05...$15.00
DOI: http://dx.doi.org/10.1145/2858036.2858456

BACKGROUND

Crossmodal interaction underlies the phenomenon by which signals from one sensory modality can affect the processing of information perceived through another modality. One famous example of this phenomenon is the "McGurk" effect [14] where the auditory phoneme "ba" is perceived as "da" when paired with the visual stimuli of lips movements pronouncing "ga". The ideas behind crossmodal interaction stem from advances in cognitive neuroscience, specifically new understandings of brain plasticity and sensory substitution, which refer to the capacity of the brain to replace the functions of a given sense by another sensory modality [1]. Recently, there has been increasing interest in the study of these types of crossmodal interactions between sensory information, and their implications for user interface design. For instance, Ju-Hwan and Spence [12] demonstrated that the presentation of sounds can modulate the number of vibrotactile targets that a person will perceive, particularly when they perform secondary attention-demanding tasks. Shams *et al.* [31] also demonstrated how people's perception of flashing lights can be manipulated by sounds, with people seeing a single flash of light as consisting of two flashes when these are presented simultaneously with multiple auditory beeps. Sensory modalities are therefore far from working as independent modules and findings from these and similar studies challenge the notion that their interaction follows a hierarchy in which vision dominates the sensory experience. Massaro [13] suggests that while all modalities contribute to perceptual experience, it is most influenced by the sensory channel that mediates the least ambiguous information. In the context of this paper, this suggests that different visual and auditory mappings can influence the perception of spatial information and that different combinations may result in more efficient and engaging interactions.

Congruency and crossmodal correspondences

Research examining multi-sensory experience often use the term *congruence* or *crossmodal correspondences* to refer to non-arbitrary associations that exist between different modalities and the consequences that these have on human information processing. For instance, studies found crossmodal correspondences between high-pitched sounds and bright, small objects positioned at higher locations in space, and between low-pitched sounds and darker, bigger rounder objects at lower locations [2, 26]. Other studies found congruent mappings between pitch and vertical location, size and spatial frequency [5]. Spence highlights a further distinction between *semantic* and *synaesthetic congruency* to differentiate between sensory stimuli that vary in terms of their identity and/or meaning, and those that refer to *"correspondences between putatively nonredundant stimulus attributes or dimensions that happen to be shared by many people"* [34]. A number of researchers have demonstrated the benefits of exploiting crossmodal congruency for better user interface design. Hoggan and Brewster [9], for instance, examined the relationships between individual visual button features such as size and height with audio/tactile properties. They showed that perceived quality of touchscreen buttons was correlated to congruence between visual and audio/tactile feedback used to represent them. Fewer researchers have looked at user experience - Huang *et al* developed the MelodicBrush system in which they explored how crossmodal mappings between the shapes of Chinese calligraphy and musical tones can enhance user experience during artistic creation [10], but their system did not ground mapping choices in empirical data.

Attention, memory & motor learning

To explore crossmodal interaction we are interested in how semantically congruent audio and visual stimuli can convey spatial information and guide users' attention when locating items on interactive touch-screen devices as there is extensive evidence supporting the existence of crossmodal links in spatial attention (for reviews, see [33, 36]). In particular, a number of lab-based studies have demonstrated how the presentation of crossmodal as opposed to unimodal cues can significantly facilitate the capture of a person's spatial attention [37]. Stefanucci and Proffitt [38] examined the impact of crossmodal cues on memory tasks involving visual and auditory stimuli with a focus on whether congruency effects between learning and retrieval phases improves retention. Their findings indicated that the presence of sounds provided a strong cue for binding visual display to the information learnt and hence improve retention. Studies have also shown that crossmodal concurrent feedback can enhance motor learning, and positive effects are often explained by a reduction of workload [7]. For example, visual feedback could facilitate learning of spatial aspects of the movement, while auditory feedback could support learning of temporal aspects [32]. Curiously, concurrent crossmodal feedback has been found to enhance performance in the acquisition phase, but the performance gains are lost in retention tests. This finding is explained by the guidance hypothesis which states that permanent feedback during acquisition leads to a dependency on the feedback [30]. The guidance forces learners to ignore their intrinsic feedback which is based on proprioception [32] - our sense of bodily movement and position in space.

SCOPE

The work presented in this paper extends this line of research by examining more complex crossmodal stimuli that support a spatial ordering memory task and by exploring crossmodal congruences from two perspectives: i) task performance, and ii) user engagement. Study 1 builds on previous work on crossmodal perception that demonstrated congruence effects between the auditory feature of pitch and the visual features of size and vertical location [2, 26, 5], as well as the impact of crossmodal feedback on motor learning and the retention of spatial information post-acquisition [7, 30]. The aim is to evaluate users' ability to determine spatial orderings of a sequence of items on the basis of audio, visual, and audio-visual stimuli, in the context of a memory task. Study 2 explores user experience and engagement with a crossmodal memory game building on the results of the first study, and recent work on the evaluation of user engagement in game applications [23, 24, 41]. To do this, we added a number of gamification elements to the apparatus used in the first study that were inspired by current design practices in mobile games. These included the introduction of a game progression logic based on increasing levels of difficulty and scores with corresponding visual and auditory indicators [28]. This is described in more details in later sections of the paper.

STUDY 1: CROSSMODAL MAPPINGS

Apparatus

To examine the impact of crossmodal congruence on mappings of vertical location, motor learning and retention, we designed an interface that consists of a visual and an auditory display component for output and a touch-based component for input. The experimental apparatus was developed as an application that runs on an Apple iPad. It divides the screen horizontally into different sections (top of Figure 1), with each section corresponding to a unique shape and a unique tone (bottom of Figure 1) we refer to as *ShapeTones*.

Visual mappings & congruence levels

We designed three types of visuals to map screen sections; we refer to these as *arbitrary*, *size*, and *spikes* (Figure 1). In the spikes mapping, we used a basic circular shape and increased the amount of spikes attached to it to correspond to a given section; e.g. the shape for section three has three spikes. There is therefore an immediately perceivable relationship between the shapes and the physical layout of the screen, which constitutes a *congruent* mapping. In the size mapping, we used a single shape and we varied its size to correspond to each screen section. The gradual change in size therefore corresponded to the progression of sections, with lower sections corresponding to larger objects [2, 26]. However, compared to the spikes mapping, the exact mapping from a given size to a section has to be inferred. This mapping is therefore *semi-congruent* with the physical layout. In the arbitrary shapes mapping, different shapes are assigned arbitrarily to correspond to each screen section. We designed these shapes so that they bear no obvious relationship to the sections and are therefore *incongruent* with the physical layout of the screen.

Auditory mapping

Tones were mapped vertically to screen sections: lower pitches to lower sections, and higher pitches to higher sections (Figure 1). This mapping is based on crossmodal correspondences between vertical location and pitch [2, 26, 5]. We used musical notes and the sine wave timbre as they are common tones. After trying different scales in terms of tone discernibility with iPad speakers, we chose a mid-range octave: the G4 major scale.

Touch-based input

Users interact with this application by tapping on corresponding sections on the screen to reproduce the spatial order of a sequence of items conveyed to them through ShapeTones.

Experimental design

We manipulated level of congruency as an independent variable in a between-subjects experimental design. Participants were divided into three groups with each group performing the experimental task using one of the three visual mappings; participants used the *spikes mapping* in the *congruent condition*; the *size mapping* in the *semi-congruent condition*; and the *arbitrary mapping* in the *incongruent condition.*

We also manipulated display type in a within-subjects experimental design. Participants in each group performed

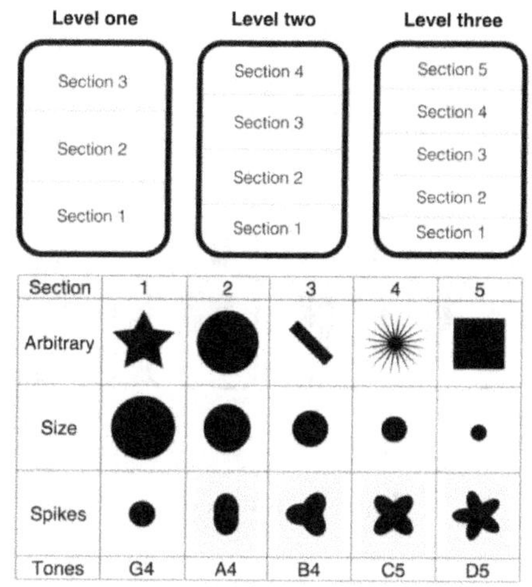

Figure 1. Crossmodal mappings.

the experimental task under three within-subjects conditions; an *audio-visual condition*; *a visual-only condition*; and an *audio-only condition*. The audio-only and visual-only conditions were used as controls to provide baselines to compare crossmodal and unimodal displays, i.e. to examine the effects of the visual and auditory mappings when used independently as a means for judging locations on the touch-screen. A between-subjects design thus ensured that each participant is only exposed to one visual mapping/congruence level, while a within-subjects design ensured that each participant's performance with a given crossmodal congruence level is compared against their own performance on unimodal displays. The combination of between/within-subjects designs also avoids confounding learning effects and fatigue.

Experimental task details

The experimental task was a memory task in which participants were presented with a sequence of three ShapeTones and were asked to reproduce the order of that sequence by tapping the corresponding sections on the touch-screen. This task builds on previous work in the area of point estimation [17] and provides a potential for broader use, e.g. in games. ShapeTones were presented one at a time at the centre of the touch-screen at a speed of 0.3 seconds per item chosen on the basis of previous studies on rapid identification of auditory and graphical stimuli [18, 27]. Depending on the experimental condition, participants were asked to watch and/or listen to a sequence of three shapes and tones and to reproduce the order in which these occurred by tapping on corresponding sections on the touch-screen.

Figure 2 exemplifies the structure of the experimental task. Participants tapped on a "play" button to start the sequence, watched and/or listened to a sequence, then tapped on the touch-screen to reproduce its order. No feedback was presented while tapping the order of the sequence, but the participants' input was played back to them at the end of the tapping (in the form of ShapeTones in the audio-visual condition, shapes only in the visual-only condition, and tones only in the audio-only condition). This was then followed by an in-

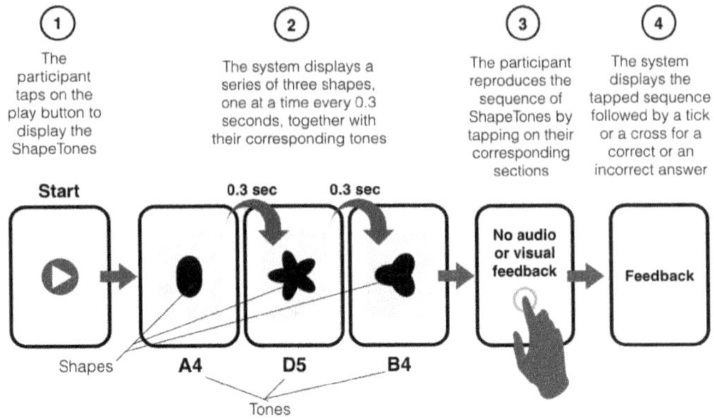

Figure 2. Experimental task

dication of whether their sequence was correct or not (a tick for a correct sequence, and a cross for an incorrect sequence). To avoid ceiling effects in each condition, participants performed sets of experimental tasks using three different complexity levels as shown in Figure 1. We used, three, four and five sections in each level of complexity respectively. The stimuli consisted of three ShapeTones in all complexity levels. Each participant performed 10 trials in each set, totalling 30 trials per condition; thus giving 90 trials per participant and a total of 3240 trials for the whole study.

Experimental setup & procedure

Participants were briefed about the study, signed consent forms and completed an initial questionnaire about demographic details, their musical training (in terms of years of practice), and experience with touch-screen devices. They were then randomly assigned to one of the three groups. Care was taken to ensure different musical abilities were broadly distributed between groups. Before the trials began, participants were trained on the particular display they were going to use. Unlike the tests, training was such that participants could tap around the touch-screen and receive audio, visual or audio-visual feedback that corresponded to the location of where they tapped. They were instructed to take as much time as they needed to memorise the tones and the shapes used for the particular condition they were about to do. Training typically lasted up to 5 minutes. Once familiar with the display, participants performed three trials similar to the actual the testing phase (Figure 2). These were not included in the analysis and were intended to help participants develop their proprioceptive skills. Participants then performed ten trials in each of the three conditions (audio-only, visual-only, and audio-visual) in a given level of complexity before moving on to the next level. They were allowed to familiarise themselves again with the shapes and tones before the start of each new set of trials. We administered short questionnaires and conducted informal interviews at the end of each level to collect feedback. Conditions were counterbalanced. An entire session lasted between 45 minutes and an hour.

Participants

36 participants took part in this study (19 female, 17 male, *mean age* $= 27.9, SD = 4.4$). They were a mixture of university staff (academic and non-academic), undergraduate and postgraduate students and members of the public. Participants received a cash incentive for participating. Seven participants rated their musical experience as expert, eight as intermediate, fourteen as beginner, and six had no musical training. All had experience with using touch-screen devices.

Dependent variables & measurements

The dependent variables were the scores and completion times. Scores were calculated based on the number of correct sequences reproduced by the participants. Completion times were measured as the duration from the time the participants pressed the "play" button to the instant they tapped the third and final point in a given sequence.

Hypotheses

S1H1: Level of congruence will have an effect on participants' performance: in particular, based on existing literature on crossmodal mappings [2, 5, 9, 26, 29], we expected a congruent display using the spikes mapping to lead to better performances than a semi-congruent display using the size mapping and an incongruent display using the shapes mapping. We also expected the semi-congruent display to yield better performances than the incongruent display.

S1H2: Type of display will have an effect on participants' performance: in particular, based on existing literature on the advantages of audio-visual over unimodal displays [4, 38], we expected that the effects of the level of congruence will be more apparent in the audio-visual conditions.

Results

We used single-factor ANOVAs with level of congruence as a factor (three levels: congruent, semi-congruent, and incongruent) to analyse differences in times and scores across groups, and repeated-measures ANOVAs with display type as a factor (three level: audio-visual, audio-only, and visual only) to analyse differences within each group. In both cases, we used Fisher's LSD for post-hoc comparisons of main effects. We used a confidence level of $\alpha = 0.05$ for all tests.

Scores across groups

Level one (three sections)

There was no significant main effect of level of congruence on participants' scores in the audio-visual ($F(2, 34) = 0.104, p = 0.902$) visual-only ($F(2, 34) = 1.578, p = 0.222$) and audio-only conditions ($F(2, 34) = 0.54, p = 0.588$).

Level two (four sections)

There was no significant main effect of level of congruence on participants' scores across groups in the audio-visual condition ($F(2, 34) = 2.834, p = 0.074$). In the visual-only condition, there was a significant main effect of level of congruence on scores ($F(2, 34) = 4.276 p = 0.023, \eta^2 = 0.21$). Post-hoc tests showed that participants in the congruent condition (spikes: *mean* $= 7.16$, *sd* $= 1.99$) scored significantly higher than participants in the semi-congruent condition (size: *mean* $= 5.33$, *sd* $= 1.37$) ($p = 0.015$). Participants in the incongruent condition (random: *mean* $= 7.18$, *sd* $=$

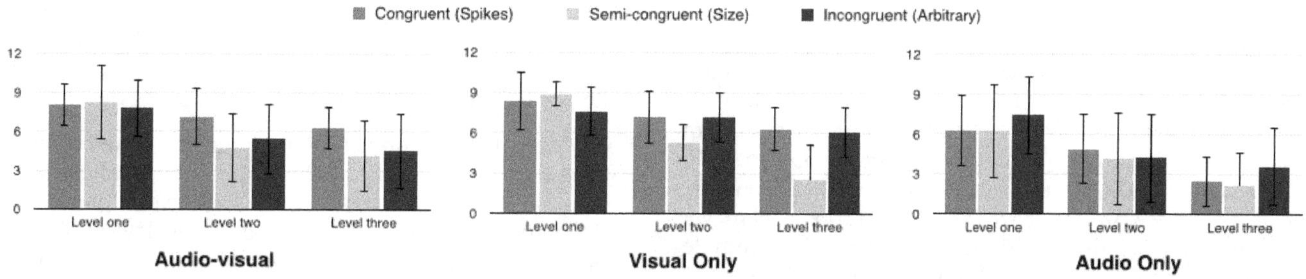

Figure 3. Scores across groups and complexity levels in the audio-visual, visual-only and audio-only conditions

1.88) also scored significantly higher than those in the semi-congruent condition ($p = 0.013$). There was no significant difference between the congruent and the incongruent conditions ($p = 0.984$). There was also no significant main effect of levels of congruence on participants' scores in the audio-only condition ($F(2, 34) = 0.192, p = 0.826$).

Level three (five sections)

There was no significant main effect of level of congruence on participants' scores across groups in the audio-visual condition ($F(2, 34) = 2.565, p = 0.093$). In the visual-only condition, there was a significant main effect of level of congruence on participants' scores across groups ($F(2, 34) = 12.097, p < 0.001, \eta^2 = 0.43$) and post-hoc tests showed that participants in the congruent condition (spike: $m = 6.33, sd = 1.66$) scored significantly higher than participants in the semi-congruent condition (size: $mean = 2.5, sd = 2.67$) ($p < 0.001$), and that participants in the incongruent condition (random: $mean = 6.09, sd = 1.86$) scored significantly higher than participants in the semi-congruent condition ($p = 0.001$). There was no significant difference between participants scores in the congruent and incongruent conditions ($p = 0.746$). There was no significant main effect of level of congruence on participants's scores across group in the audio-only condition ($F(2, 32) = 1.082, p = 0.351$).

Figure 3 summarises these results, which show that: as complexity increased, participants who used the congruent display (spikes mapping) performed significantly better than those who used the semi-congruent and incongruent displays in the visual-only conditions; Participants who used the incongruent display performed significantly better than those who used the semi-congruent display in the visual-only conditions; Augmenting the baseline visual mappings with audio output in the audio-visual conditions seems to have eliminated the observed effects of congruency levels.

Task completion times across groups

Level one (three sections)

There was no significant main effect of level of congruence on task completion times in the audio-visual ($F(2, 34) = 0.456, p = 0.638$), visual-only ($F(2, 34) = 0.679, p = 0.514$), and audio-only conditions ($F(2, 34) = 0.496, p = 0.614$).

Level two (four sections)

There was no significant main effect of level of congruence on task completion times across groups in the audio-visual condition ($F(2, 34) = 0.436p = 0.65$). In the visual-only condition, there was a significant main effect of level of congruence on task completion times across groups ($F(2, 34) = 3.72, p = 0.035, \eta^2 = 0.18$) and post-hoc tests showed that participants in the incongruent condition (random: $mean = 4649.1ms, sd = 971.6ms$) spend significantly longer time to complete the task than those in the semi-congruent condition (size: $mean = 3655.5ms, sd = 1179.2ms$) ($p = 0.04$) and those in the congruent condition (spikes: $mean = 3458.6ms, sd = 1162.8ms$) ($p = 0.015$). There was no significant difference between task completion times in the congruent and semi-congruent conditions ($p = 0.667$). There was also no significant main effect of level of congruence on task completion times across group in the audio-only condition ($F(2, 34) = 0.303, p = 0.74$).

Level three (five sections)

There was no significant main effect of level of congruence on task completion times across groups in any of the audio-visual ($F(2, 34) = 2.977, p = 0.065$), visual-only ($F(2, 34) = 2.792, p = 0.076$) and audio-only conditions ($F(2, 32) = 1.805, p = 0.181$). The above results showed that participants who used the congruent and semi-congruent display were significantly faster than those who used the incongruent display, but this was the case only in the visual-only condition in complexity level two (where the screen was divided into four sections). Again, the introduction of audio output in the audio-visual condition seems to have eliminated these significant effects.

Results within each group

We combined data from all levels of complexity to analyse scores and task completion times within each group.

Congruent group

There was a significant main effect of display type on participants' scores in the congruent group ($F(2, 22) = 13.307, p = 0.001, \eta^2 = 0.547$). Post-hoc tests showed that participants in this group scored significantly higher in the visual-only condition ($mean = 21.41, sd = 4.99$) compared to the audio-only condition ($mean = 13.75, sd = 6.48$) ($p = 0.004$). Their scores in the audio-visual condition ($mean = 21.58, sd = 4.88$) were also significantly higher than in the audio-only condition ($p = 0.002$). Differences between their scores in the audio-visual and visual-only conditions were not statistically significant ($p = 0.861$).

There was also a significant main effect of display type on participants' task completion times ($F(2,22) = 16.584, p = 0.001, \eta^2 = 0.601$). Post-hoc tests showed that participants spent significantly longer times to complete the task in the audio-only condition ($mean = 5574.5, sd = 2100.2$) compared to the visual-only condition ($mean = 3537.5, sd = 1250.9$) ($p = 0.001$), and to the audio-visual condition ($mean = 4325.7, sd = 1898.3$) ($p < 0.001$). There was no statistically significant difference between task completion times in the visual-only and audio-visual conditions ($p = 0.071$). The above results show that participants performance was best when using a visual-only display and that the combination of audio-visual output in a congruent display increased performance times without significantly improving scores.

Semi-congruent group

The effect of display type on participants in the semi-congruent group was not significant for scores ($F(2,22) = 2.216, p = 0.133$) but it was significant for task completion times ($F(2,22) = 3.369, p = 0.043, \eta^2 = 0.249$). For the latter, post-hoc tests showed that participants spent significantly longer times to complete the task in the audio-only condition ($mean = 4579.9, sd = 1608.6$) compared to the visual-only condition ($mean = 3670, sd = 1002.1$) ($p = 0.042$). Difference between the visual-only condition and the audio-visual condition ($mean = 4456.8, sd = 1507.6$) were also statistically significant with participants spending longer time in the audio-visual condition ($p = 0.009$). There was no statistically significant difference in task completion times between the audio-only and the audio-visual conditions ($p = 0.779$). These results show that combining auditory and visual output in a semi-congruent display increased performance times and levelled the scores across the three types of displays.

Incongruent group

There was a significant main effect of display type on participants' scores in the incongruent group ($F(2,22) = 6.212, p = 0.013, \eta^2 = 0.383$). Post-hoc tests showed that participants scored significantly higher in the visual-only condition ($mean = 17.81, sd = 5.61$) compared to the audio-only condition ($mean = 20.9, sd = 4.15$) ($p = 0.011$) and to the audio-visual condition ($mean = 15.36, sd = 8.15$) ($p = 0.024$). The differences in scores between the audio-only and the audio-visual conditions were not statistically significant ($p = 0.18$). There was no significant main effect of display type on task completion times in this group ($F(2,22) = 1.082, p = 0.358$). These results show that combining auditory and visual output in an incongruent display did not have a significant impact on scores and performance times.

Discussion

Our hypothesis that the congruent spikes mapping leads to better performances was only partially confirmed. Participants in the congruent group scored significantly higher than participants in the other groups but only when using a visual-only display. One of the most interesting findings in Study 1, which goes against our initial hypothesis is that the effects of the level of congruence seem to have been cancelled by the introduction of audio to the baseline visual conditions. Differences between participants' performances across groups in the audio-visual conditions were not statistically significant, which suggests participants relied on the audio output to compliment or compensate for the discrepancies in congruence levels used in the size and arbitrary mappings.

We note that a number of participants reported that they sometimes chose to ignore the shapes in the audio-visual conditions. This in turn suggests that those participants relied on the audio output as a primary source for determining spatial orderings of sequences of items, which should mean that they would perform well in the audio-only conditions. The objective data contradicts this analysis, however, showing performances in the audio-only conditions to be overall worse across all complexity levels. The shape mappings used in the audio-visual conditions supported better performances albeit at the expense of more effort.

But our hypothesis that participants would perform significantly better when using audio-visual as opposed to unimodal displays was also not fully supported since participants' scores across the three groups were consistently and often significantly higher in the visual-only conditions. These findings contrast those reported in the literature which often report advantages of crossmodal over unimodal cues in recognition and retention tasks [4, 38]. Interestingly, subjective feedback from the majority of participants did not reflect the analysis obtained from the objective data. For example, many participants across the three groups described how the speed of presentation of the shapes made the task more difficult to complete in the visual-only conditions and that the addition of tones improved this experience. In a recent study, Guastellow et al [8] found that auditory and visual stimuli presented at intervals of about 300ms often produce miss errors in one or the other channel, which could explain the lower scores we obtained in the audio-visual conditions. A possible explanation for these seemingly contradictory accounts is that participants' answers in the interviews and questionnaires reflected perceived as opposed to actual difficulty. The addition of the tones to the crossmodal display may therefore have improved their confidence without necessarily impacting their scores.

Our expectation regarding the semi-congruent mapping was also not confirmed. We expected the semi-congruent size mapping to provide better support for remembering spatial locations than an incongruent arbitrary mapping, but our results showed this the opposite to be the case. The size mapping we used exploits previously reported crossmodal correspondences between vertical location, pitch and object size [2, 26, 5], but the type of task we used in our study could be a possible explanation for why these correspondences did not yield better performance. Whereas crossmodal correspondences have been studied almost exclusively in laboratory settings with simple cues where participants often deal with single or dual items [6, 33], our results show that retention of a sequence of multiple items appears to be more challenging and thus requires more careful design of crossmodal support. Indeed, as complexity increased, participants in the semi-congruent group highlighted that whilst they were able to identify that an extreme location had occurred in a sequence (i.e. small and large shapes), they found it increasingly challenging to accurately reproduce full sequences, particularly those including the middle ranges of the screen (sections two, three and four). So, we suggest that whilst requiring significantly more time to complete, the distinctive visual characteristics of the shapes used in the arbitrary mapping provided a better mapping in this case.

Interestingly, a number of participants from the incongruent group highlighted that whilst they found it challenging to focus on both the shapes and the tones in the audio-visual condition, they also felt that this challenge made the task more enjoyable and engaging. None of the participants in the other groups expressed this opinion when asked about their experiences and preferences. Thus, subjective feedback indicates that, although the incongruent display did not offer complimentary information, the challenge of combining incongruent information across auditory and visual modalities increased enjoyability and engagement with the task.

From the interviews we found that there were two distinct types of responses to the addition of tones to the crossmodal displays. The first was that tones were treated as a dominant output mode, with the shapes ignored or used as a secondary source of spatial information. This was often reported to be the case in the incongruent arbitrary mapping group. The second was that participants preferred to use the shapes as the dominant source of spatial information with tones used as a secondary channel. This was often the case in the congruent and semi-congruent displays. We also observed that participants tended to switch to this "complimentary strategy", where reliance on the secondary modality increased, as the task increased in complexity. These observations are inline with claims that crossmodal perception is most influenced by the sensory channel that mediates the least ambiguous information [13] and that the positive effects of crossmodal concurrent feedback can be explained by a reduction of workload [7]. Our results confirm these findings and highlight that levels of congruency can be a factor in determining complementarity of information display.

STUDY 2: USER ENGAGEMENT

Given the subjective feedback reported in Study 1, we ran a second study focusing on engagement and user experience. This complements the focus on performance-based measures in Study 1, and follows a trend within HCI studies to take experiential issues into account, emphasizing *"the experience of using the technology, rather than the focus on the task that is characteristic of many other approaches HCI"* [11] and aiming to understand *"how the user makes sense of the artefact and his/her interactions with it at emotional, sensual, and intellectual levels"* [43]. This trend has often been ignored in the study of crossmodal displays. In order to facilitate an experience that would be more conducive to engagement and enjoyment, and in response to the reported appeal of 'challenge' identified in Study 1 (particularly with arbitrary shapes), we adapted our test application into a game. With a few exceptions, digital games use the potential of visual display for aesthetic appeal and for elements of game design more than auditory display [20]. Among the exceptions in the field of mobile games are the *Papa Sangre* series

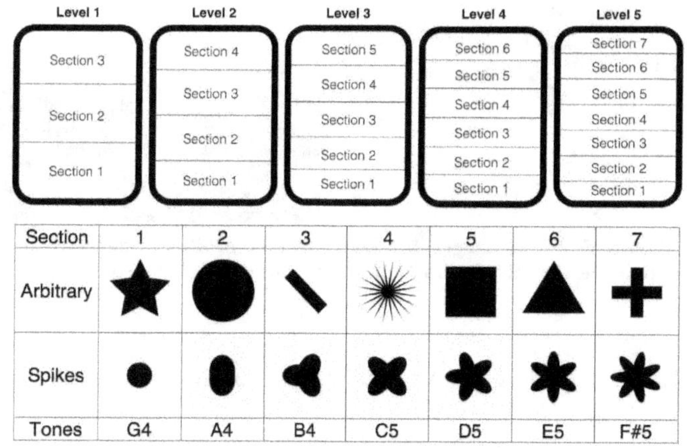

Figure 4. Levels and sections (top), crossmodal mappings (bottom)

[40] and *Dark Echo* [19], which are audio-focused games that cannot be played without sound. Nacke *et al* [20] have reported on the importance of auditory display for gameplay experience across different experiential dimensions (immersion, tension, competence, flow, negative and positive affect, and challenge). We were therefore also interested in examining the role of crossmodal display in gameplay.

Apparatus

We added a number of game design elements based on current design practices in games, particularly mobile games. Levels are a common concept – as the player succeeds in a task, she/he moves to a higher level, often with a higher degree of difficulty. We added a level identity and introduced a progression logic where the environment and challenge remains unchanged unless the player passes the challenge – in which case, the difficulty level will increase. The levels, sub-levels and the progression logic we added were as follows:

1. A player moves to a next sub-level upon successful completion of a trial. A new sequence of ShapeTones is then generated.
2. After ten sub-levels, a new level starts, with an additional ShapeTone – one vertical section is added to the initial three, and so forth, up to seven (Figure 4).
3. A training area is presented to the player at the beginning of each level for testing the new ShapeTones.
4. If the player fails a trial, the sub-level does not progress and the same ShapeTone sequence is played again.

Another common element in games is the score. The usage of scores and visual metaphors such as stars, to indicate degree of success or progress, are common gamification instruments [28]. We added a two-tier score – a star score (1-3 stars, dependent on performance on that level), and a numerical score. The scores and progression feedback we added were:

1. A trial score of one to three stars for passing a sub-level based on speed of playing back the correct sequence (one for slower, three for faster).

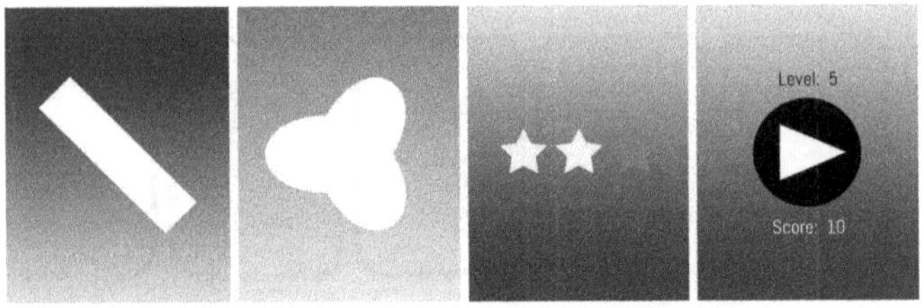

Figure 5. Game images, from left to right: arbitrary shapes version; spikes version; feedback after a trial; followed by global score.

2. Win and lose graphics and sounds for the end of each trial. (Figure 5).
3. The sub-level score accumulates in a global score, presented to the player at the end of each trial (Figure 5).

All other functionalities and application design remained unchanged from Study 1.

Study Design

We aimed to examine user engagement with two versions of the resulting game. We used the spikes and arbitrary shape mappings for each version because these emerged as the most successful visuals mapping in terms of performance in the first study. Several instruments have been developed to measure engagement in games, such as the Game Engagement and Game Experience Questionnaires [21]. Some of these instruments give particular attention to the concept of flow, such as the GameFlow model [39]. However, a range of diverse features contribute to engagement in games [3], we therefore adopted for an instrument that takes into account this diversity, the User Engagement Scale (UES) [24], more specifically the UESz version [41], which unlike other game engagement instruments, has been empirically validated. UES is a self-report measure consisting of a 31-item measured as a 5-point Likert scale that takes into account multiple dimensions of engagement: aesthetic appeal, perceived usability, felt involvement, novelty, focused attention and endurability. [24]. The UES has also been used in comparative studies [22]. Wiebe *et al.* [41] revised the UES for use in games (renamed as UESz) by organising the measures into four subscales: Focused Attention (FAz), Perceived Usability (PUz), Aesthetics (AEz) and Satisfaction (SAz). Later studies on the UES agree with the UESz revised set of subscales [22].

We used a within-subject design and invited participants to play the two versions of the game for 10 minutes each (10 minutes was the minimum duration of gameplay in similar studies deploying the UESz [41]). Before each 10 minute session, participants could play with the game for a short while (typically around 3 minutes), to get acquainted with it. The sequence of versions of the game was randomised and counterbalanced. We then asked participants to fill in UESz questionnaires for each version of the game and logged their scores for later analysis. An additional reason to use UESz as the sole questionnaire was to avoid respondent fatigue, as respondents already had to answer the UESz twice – one for each version of the game. Finally, we conducted a short interview focusing on crossmodal issues, usability and overall satisfaction with the game. We asked questions about the appeal of the tones and shapes, and how well they were connected. We also asked what was more important to play the game: tones, shapes, or both; and if it could be played with only audio or visuals. We also asked participants if they found something frustrating, and if they would play the game again.

Subscale	Arbitrary	Spikes	Significance
FAz	3.4 (0.77)	3.8 (0.85)	W = -2.4, $p = 0.016$
PUz	2.8 (0.81)	3.3 (0.78)	W = -2.764, $p = 0.006$
AEz	3.1 (0.62)	3.6 (0.63)	W = -2.371, $p = 0.018$
SAz	3.8 (0.75)	4.0 (0.84)	W = -1.963, $p = 0.05$

Table 1. *Mean* (*S D*) of UESz subscales for arbitrary shapes and spikes.

Hypothesis

S2H1: The congruent spikes mapping will be more engaging than the incongruent arbitrary shapes mapping.

Participants

Twelve participants took part in this study different from those who took part in the first study (10 male and two female, *mean age* = 36.6, *sd* = 6.7). Participants were a mixture of university staff and students. All participants received a cash incentive for participating. When asked about previous experience in games, on a scale of 1 (not at all experienced) to 5 (very experienced), only one participant declared to be very experienced, with two additional ones answering 4 (*mean* = 2.8). Most of the participants (seven) considered themselves to be very experienced as musicians, with two additional ones answering 4 (*mean* = 3.9). Only one participant considered himself to be very experienced as a visual artist, with three additional ones answering 4 (*mean* = 3.3).

Results

We used a Wilcoxon signed-rank test to analyse data from the UESz questionnaires and Student t-test to compare logged scores. Results from the questionnaire revealed a statistically significant preference for the spikes mapping in all four UESz subscales (Table 1). This preference was higher for Focused Attention (FAz), Perceived Usability (PUz) and Aesthetics (AEz) with differences of 0.4 to 0.5 between means, and less marked with Satisfaction (SAz), with a difference of 0.2 between means. Participants also performed better using the spikes mapping, reaching on average a higher levels (*max level mean* = 39.5, *sd* = 4.6) than with the arbitrary shapes mapping (*max level mean* = 33.1, *sd* = 8.1). This difference was statistically significant ($t = -2.579$, $p = 0.026$).

Based on interview responses, 10 participants preferred the spikes mapping and stated that the relationship between tones and shapes was more effective with spikes. Two participants did not find the two visual mappings to be very different, with one expressing a preference for arbitrary shapes because they were more distinguishable, and another stating that he did not identify any relationship between shapes and tones. One participant who preferred the spikes mapping stated that arbitrary shapes *"are more noticeable, but harder to concentrate [on]"*. Another participant considered that the spikes mapping became more difficult to distinguish in higher levels.

When asked what was more important to play the game, tones or shapes, six of the participants answered that they mostly relied on tones; four stated that they played it mostly as a visual game; one participant mentioned that he alternated between focusing on tones and shapes depending on the visualisation type; and another mentioned that he almost did not notice the visuals. Independently of the main modality, eight of the 12 participants stated that they would use the secondary modality as a backup when the difficulty level was higher. Sample statements, from visual-focused participants: *"when I got lost I relied on sound"*, *"I used sound as a backup"*, *"rely on image then rely on sound as a backup"*, *"sound was used as a check, as a support"*; and from sound-focused participants: *"I would get a visual as something to refer back"*, *"visual element gave me a confirmation"*, *"when you got the first one wrong and do it again, visuals become more important"*. Two of the participants who played the game mostly as a sound game highlighted the importance of visual feedback for seeing the screen and where the fingers were placed. Ten of the participants consider that they could play the game with any single modality (audio or visuals only), with two answering that they would not be able to play without sound.

Regarding usability, participants were asked if anything frustrated them in the game. Nine of the 12 participants mentioned that the strictness of where to tap on the screen to reproduce a given ShapeTones, and the fact that there were no visual aids for this frustrated them. This frustration would increase in higher levels of the game. As one of the participants put it: *"I got the relationship [between the ShapeTones] right but the position wrong – there was a mismatch between my head and the screen"*. Another participant stated that this frustration *"is part of the fun"*. The same frustration was also conveyed when participants were asked to suggest further improvements – six of the participants suggested showing the ShapeTones sections (permanently or only temporarily). We observed that participants used different strategies for solving this issue and achieving a higher precision, by a strict positioning of the hand or by moving the device. Some remarks in the interviews confirm this, e.g. *"I tried to hold it in a different way, shifted and treated it as a piano"*. When asked if they would play the game again, eight of the 12 participants answered affirmatively, with two answering *"maybe"* and two negatively, one of which stating *"I'm not much of a player"* and the other mentioning lack of *"entertainment value"*. Four of the participants mentioned that they would recommend it as a pedagogical game for musical training.

Discussion

The study confirmed our hypothesis S2H1 that the congruent spikes mapping is more engaging than the incongruent arbitrary shapes mapping. The results from the UESz questionnaire point in this direction in all four subscales, although the results from the interviews reveal some slight variations. Mostly, the interviews confirmed the results from the questionnaires, manifesting preference in terms of aesthetics and crossmodal correspondence with spikes and tones. This is illustrated by statements as *"Spikes is more gratifying, easier to play"*. However, one of the participants showed a preference for arbitrary shapes in general, as shapes with a spikes mapping *"were more similar"*. Another participant stated a preference for arbitrary shapes in higher levels of the game (with higher number of ShapeTones) – he argued that in higher sections spikes were harder to disambiguate (it was harder to distinguish shapes with 6 or 7 spikes, for example), while the distinctiveness of arbitrary shapes became more useful. This might point to a problem with recalling the spikes mapping beyond a certain number of spikes. One of the participants who reported preference for the spikes mapping mentioned that the challenge posed by arbitrary shapes could make it more interesting for repeated play. In relation to the perceived importance of audio-visual display in the game, most of the participants (11 of 12) reported relying on both modalities to play the game. Independently of the main modality (audio or visual), most of them (eight) would rely more on the secondary modality as the difficulty increased, as a backup or additional check. This is in line with literature on the importance of audio for user experience in games [20].

Some participants reported frustrations during the study. A common element of frustration was the inability to see the sections, which caused more missed tones as the levels increased. However, one of the participants mentioned that this frustration was *"part of the fun"*. Although the game has a vertical orientation, two of the participants tilted the device, diagonally or horizontally, to better align their hands and fingers with the tablet. When asked about these strategies, one participant mentioned that he was trying to keep a constant hand alignment to the tablet. He observed that accidentally moving the tablet would misalign his hand, leading to a need to *"recalibrate"* his hand. Another participant mentioned that he was trying to align the tablet horizontally as a piano, a musical metaphor which he was familiar with. Two of the participants would hum back in tone a sequence after it was played, and before tapping. When asked why they did this, they replied that it would help memorisation and repetition. It represents a kind of auditory sketching before committing to a sequence. These elements – importance of keeping or removing frustrating elements, spatial strategies outside the frame of the tablet, auditory sketching before playing – could point towards future research directions.

GENERAL DISCUSSION & CONCLUSIONS

In this paper we examined crossmodal congruence in the context of a memory task in which we evaluated users' ability to determine spatial orderings of a sequence of items on the basis of audio, visual and audio-visual stimuli. Two studies were reported which explored task performance and user experience of crossmodal interaction with congruent, incongruent, and semi-congruent displays. In this section we summarise and compare the insights gained from these studies.

Congruent mappings are preferred, but the addition of audio cancelled its advantages: Findings from Study 1 showed that while a congruent spikes mapping led to better results in terms of task performance, its advantages were cancelled out by the addition of audio output. Findings from Study 2, on the other hand, showed that the combination of audio output with a spikes mapping led to more user engagements as measured by UESz. Both studies also revealed problems with the spikes mapping when the complexity of the task increased (levels three, four, and five) and some preferences for the incongruent arbitrary shapes mapping with respect to the challenge and engagement of crossmodal gameplay. Therefore, there could be a threshold at which the clarity and effectiveness of the congruent mapping is saturated. Whilst requiring significantly more time to complete, the distinctive visual characteristics of the shapes used in the arbitrary shapes could provide a better mapping in those cases. Interestingly, the use of the size mapping as a semi-congruent display yielded poor results, even though it was based on crossmodal correspondences between vertical location, pitch and object size [2, 26, 5]. The type of task, in this case recalling the order of a sequence of items, as opposed to identifying a single item, challenged the effectiveness of these particular crossmodal correspondences and therefore calls for more careful design when using this mapping in crossmodal interfaces.

Preference for crossmodal display expressed, but not always confirmed by data: Most of the participants from Study 1 expressed a preference for audio-visual display. In Study 2, the majority of the participants also preferred using both modalities for playing the crossmodal game. However, scores were higher in Study 1 in the visual-only conditions, which contradicted the subjective feedback and observed interaction strategies in both studies. Studies of crossmodal support for spatial attention and motor learning often point out the positive effects of concurrent feedback. However, in general, little work has examined retention tests without audiovisual feedback [32] as we report. The presented studies therefore contribute a systematic evaluation of crossmodal feedback in the context of multimodal information processing. Indeed, our results point toward a subjective preference for crossmodal as opposed to unimodal interaction when task complexity increases. This is evidenced by the diminished effects of levels of congruency observed when auditory output was introduced in the audio-visual displays in Study 1. These findings are inline with accounts of self-management of working memory resources that is associated with multimodal interaction when there is an increase in cognitive demands [25].

Emergence of complimentary strategies using a primary and secondary modality: The above insight is related to a further observation that was also common to the two studies. In both studies, we have seen some users who prefer visuals and others who prefer audio as the primary mode, though both make more use of the secondary mode as task complexity increases. Further research should examine correlations between preferred primary mode and users background and demographics, e.g. musical training or preferred learning style.

Incongruent crossmodal mappings can sometimes be appealing: In both studies, incongruent crossmodal mappings were sometimes associated with positive effects, namely by presenting a challenge and a level of difficulty that rendered the interaction more interesting for some participants. It was *"part of the fun"*. These observations point towards an alternative dimension of crossmodal interfaces when seen from the perspective user experience and engagement, and not merely task performance. Further studies of user engagement through crossmodal interaction should therefore consider addressing this dimension in design.

Contributions, limitations & further research

The presented studies confirmed findings of previous research on the positive performance effect of congruent display for a new task - the memory task. We also found that the addition of auditory display impacts the effects of the levels of congruency and that participants increasingly relied on multiple modalities as task complexity increased. We showed how task and user experience and engagement measures could be used to inform the design of crossmodal interaction which had not been attempted previously. We also demonstrated the deployment of the UESz in a new domain (crossmodal games) where we found it to be an effective measure of engagement.

There are limitations to these findings, however. First, the relatively small number of participants and the specific type of task used in both studies make it unclear how these findings would generalise to other types of interactions. Second, while participants showed superior performances when using the congruent spikes mapping, it is difficult to predict how successful this particular mapping would be for higher levels of complexity, for example when spikes discernibility and hence the ability to count them becomes more challenging as they represent more complex levels (e.g. beyond 10 spikes). Third, while the addition of audio output was perceived as useful, we only used one type of auditory display and did not vary its congruency mappings. It therefore remains unclear how different levels of congruency of the audio output will change the obtained results, for example by using different timbres, or multiple tones that could also be counted to correspond to different levels on the screen. Fourth, we have displayed the ShapeTones such that they are shown in a neutral position on the screen. It would be interesting to examine how displaying ShapeTones in their corresponding sections on the screen would impact participants performances on retention tasks. Finally, in relation to measuring engagement, we have used only one type of questionnaire. Using additional types of measurements could therefore lead to more insights into users engagement with crossmodal displays.

Nonetheless, our findings raise several questions which we would like to explore further. Firstly, further investigation is needed into the relationships between congruity of display, preferred modality, task complexity, and performance. Secondly, explorations of how ‘challenging’ aspects of crossmodal mappings can be used to enhance playful user experiences are needed. Thirdly, exploring how the role of crossmodal elements outside the device, such as proprioceptive mappings, could inform the design of engaging crossmodal interaction. Finally, our long term aim is to explore how crossmodality could be used to inform the design of engaging experiences for people with a variety of sensory capabilities.

ACKNOWLEDGMENTS

This work was supported by EPSRC grant EP/J017205/1 and EU Marie Curie fellowship FP7 REA grant 627922.

REFERENCES

1. P Bach-y Rita. 1988. Brain plasticity. *Rehabilitation Medicine. Mosby* (1988), 113–8.
2. Elisheva Ben-Artzi and Lawrence E Marks. 1995. Visual-auditory interaction in speeded classification: Role of stimulus difference. *Perception & Psychophysics* 57, 8 (1995), 1151–1162.
3. Elizabeth A. Boyle, Thomas M. Connolly, Thomas Hainey, and James M. Boyle. 2012. Engagement in digital entertainment games: A systematic review. *Computers in Human Behavior* 28, 3 (May 2012), 771–780. DOI: http://dx.doi.org/10.1016/j.chb.2011.11.020
4. Alfred O Effenberg. 2005. Movement sonification: Effects on perception and action. *IEEE multimedia* 2 (2005), 53–59.
5. Karla K Evans and Anne Treisman. 2010. Natural cross-modal mappings between visual and auditory features. *Journal of vision* 10, 1 (2010), 6.
6. Thomas Ferris, Robert Penfold, Shameem Hameed, and Nadine Sarter. 2006. The implications of crossmodal links in attention for the design of multimodal interfaces: A driving simulation study. In *Proceedings of the Human Factors and Ergonomics Society Annual Meeting*, Vol. 50. Sage Publications, 406–409.
7. Mark A Guadagnoli and Timothy D Lee. 2004. Challenge point: a framework for conceptualizing the effects of various practice conditions in motor learning. *Journal of motor behavior* 36, 2 (2004), 212–224.
8. Stephen J Guastello, Katherine Reiter, Matthew Malon, and Anton Shircel. 2015. When auditory and visual signal processing conflict: cross-modal interference in extended work periods. *Theoretical Issues in Ergonomics Science* 16, 3 (2015), 232–254.
9. Eve Hoggan, Topi Kaaresoja, Pauli Laitinen, and Stephen Brewster. 2008. Crossmodal congruence: the look, feel and sound of touchscreen widgets. In *Proceedings of the 10th international conference on Multimodal interfaces*. ACM, 157–164.
10. Michael Xuelin Huang, Will WW Tang, Kenneth WK Lo, CK Lau, Grace Ngai, and Stephen Chan. 2012. MelodicBrush: a novel system for cross-modal digital art creation linking calligraphy and music. In *Proceedings of the Designing Interactive Systems Conference*. ACM, 418–427.
11. Joseph 'Jofish' Kaye, Kirsten Boehner, Jarmo Laaksolahti, and Anna Stahl. 2007. Evaluating experience-focused HCI. In *CHI '07 extended abstracts on Human factors in computing systems (CHI EA '07)*. ACM, New York, NY, USA, 2117–2120. DOI: http://dx.doi.org/10.1145/1240866.1240962
12. Ju-Hwan Lee and Charles Spence. 2008. Feeling what you hear: Task-irrelevant sounds modulate tactile perception delivered via a touch screen. *Journal on Multimodal User Interfaces* 2, 3-4 (2008), 145–156.
13. Dominic W Massaro. 1998. Illusions and issues in bimodal speech perception. In *AVSP'98 International Conference on Auditory-Visual Speech Processing*.
14. Harry Mcgurk and John Macdonald. 1976. Hearing lips and seeing voices. *Nature* 264, 5588 (Dec. 1976), 746–748. DOI: http://dx.doi.org/10.1038/264746a0
15. Peter BL Meijer. 1992. An experimental system for auditory image representations. *Biomedical Engineering, IEEE Transactions on* 39, 2 (1992), 112–121.
16. Oussama Metatla, Nick Bryan-Kinns, Tony Stockman, and Fiore Martin. 2012. Supporting cross-modal collaboration in the workplace. In *Proceedings of the 26th Annual BCS Interaction Specialist Group Conference on People and Computers*. British Computer Society, 109–118.
17. Oussama Metatla, Nick Bryan-Kinns, Tony Stockman, and Fiore Martin. 2015. Sonification of reference markers for auditory graphs: Effects on non-visual point estimation tasks. In *PeerJ PrePrints*.
18. Micah M Murray, Sophie Molholm, Christoph M Michel, Dirk J Heslenfeld, Walter Ritter, Daniel C Javitt, Charles E Schroeder, and John J Foxe. 2005. Grabbing your ear: rapid auditory–somatosensory multisensory interactions in low-level sensory cortices are not constrained by stimulus alignment. *Cerebral Cortex* 15, 7 (2005), 963–974.
19. Shaun Musgrave. 2015. 'Dark Echo' Review - Silence Is Golden, And So Is This Game. (Feb. 2015). http://toucharcade.com/2015/02/11/dark-echo-review/
20. Lennart E. Nacke, Mark N. Grimshaw, and Craig A. Lindley. 2010. More than a feeling: Measurement of sonic user experience and psychophysiology in a first-person shooter game. *Interacting with Computers* 22, 5 (Sept. 2010), 336–343. DOI: http://dx.doi.org/10.1016/j.intcom.2010.04.005
21. Kent L. Norman. 2013. GEQ (Game Engagement/Experience Questionnaire): A Review of Two Papers. *Interacting with Computers* 25, 4 (July 2013), 278–283. DOI: http://dx.doi.org/10.1093/iwc/iwt009
22. Heather O'Brien and Paul Cairns. 2015. An empirical evaluation of the User Engagement Scale (UES) in online news environments. *Information Processing & Management* 51, 4 (July 2015), 413–427. DOI: http://dx.doi.org/10.1016/j.ipm.2015.03.003
23. Heather L. O'Brien and Elaine G. Toms. 2008. What is User Engagement? A Conceptual Framework for Defining User Engagement with Technology. *J. Am. Soc. Inf. Sci. Technol.* 59, 6 (April 2008), 938–955. DOI: http://dx.doi.org/10.1002/asi.v59:6

24. Heather L. O'Brien and Elaine G. Toms. 2010. The development and evaluation of a survey to measure user engagement. *Journal of the American Society for Information Science and Technology* 61, 1 (Jan. 2010), 50–69. DOI: http://dx.doi.org/10.1002/asi.21229

25. Sharon Oviatt, Rachel Coulston, and Rebecca Lunsford. 2004. When do we interact multimodally?: cognitive load and multimodal communication patterns. In *Proceedings of the 6th international conference on Multimodal interfaces*. ACM, 129–136.

26. Geoffrey R Patching and Philip T Quinlan. 2002. Garner and congruence effects in the speeded classification of bimodal signals. *Journal of Experimental Psychology: Human Perception and Performance* 28, 4 (2002), 755.

27. Mary C. Potter, Brad Wyble, Carl Erick Hagmann, and Emily S. McCourt. 2013. Detecting meaning in RSVP at 13 ms per picture. *Attention, Perception, & Psychophysics* 76, 2 (Dec. 2013), 270–279. DOI: http://dx.doi.org/10.3758/s13414-013-0605-z

28. Rick Raymer. 2011. Gamification: Using Game Mechanics to Enhance eLearning. *eLearn* 2011, 9 (Sept. 2011). DOI: http://dx.doi.org/10.1145/2025356.2031772

29. Paul Rodway. 2005. The modality shift effect and the effectiveness of warning signals in different modalities. *Acta Psychologica* 120, 2 (2005), 199–226.

30. Richard A Schmidt. 1991. Frequent augmented feedback can degrade learning: Evidence and interpretations. In *Tutorials in motor neuroscience*. Springer, 59–75.

31. Ladan Shams, Yukiyasu Kamitani, and Shinsuke Shimojo. 2000. Illusions: What you see is what you hear. *Nature* 408, 6814 (Dec. 2000), 788–788. DOI: http://dx.doi.org/10.1038/35048669

32. Roland Sigrist, Georg Rauter, Robert Riener, and Peter Wolf. 2013. Augmented visual, auditory, haptic, and multimodal feedback in motor learning: A review. *Psychonomic bulletin & review* 20, 1 (2013), 21–53.

33. Charles Spence. 2010. Crossmodal spatial attention. *Annals of the New York Academy of Sciences* 1191, 1 (2010), 182–200.

34. Charles Spence. 2011. Crossmodal correspondences: A tutorial review. *Attention and Perceptual Psychophysics* (2011). DOI: http://dx.doi.org/DOI10.3758/s13414-010-0073-7

35. Charles Spence and Jon Driver. 1997. Cross-modal links in attention between audition, vision, and touch: Implications for interface design. *International Journal of Cognitive Ergonomics* (1997).

36. Charles Spence and Jon Driver. 2004. *Crossmodal space and crossmodal attention*. Oxford University Press.

37. Charles Spence and Cristy Ho. 2015. Multisensory information processing. In *APA handbook of human systems integration*, D. A. Boehm-Davis, F. T. Durso, and J. D. Lee (Eds.). American Psychological Association, Washington, DC, Ch. 27.

38. JK Stefanucci and DR Proffitt. 2005. Multimodal interfaces improve memory. In *Proceedings of the 11th International Conference on Human-Computer Interaction (HCI'05)*.

39. Penelope Sweetser and Peta Wyeth. 2005. GameFlow: a model for evaluating player enjoyment in games. *Computers in Entertainment (CIE)* 3 (July 2005), 3–3. DOI: http://dx.doi.org/10.1145/1077246.1077253 ACM ID: 1077253.

40. Andrew Webster. 2013. Gaming in darkness: 'Papa Sangre II' is a terrifying world made entirely of sound. (Oct. 2013). http://www.theverge.com/2013/10/31/5048298/papa-sangre-ii-is-a-terrifying-world-made-of-sound

41. Eric N. Wiebe, Allison Lamb, Megan Hardy, and David Sharek. 2014. Measuring engagement in video game-based environments: Investigation of the User Engagement Scale. *Computers in Human Behavior* 32 (March 2014), 123–132. DOI: http://dx.doi.org/10.1016/j.chb.2013.12.001

42. Fredrik Winberg. 2006. Supporting cross-modal collaboration: adding a social dimension to accessibility. In *Haptic and Audio Interaction Design*. Springer, 102–110.

43. Peter Wright, Jayne Wallace, and John McCarthy. 2008. Aesthetics and experience-centered design. *ACM Transactions on Computer-Human Interaction* 15, 4 (Dec. 2008), 18:1–18:21. DOI: http://dx.doi.org/10.1145/1460355.1460360

Maps and Location: Acceptance of Modern Interaction Techniques for Audio Guides

Philipp Wacker **Kerstin Kreutz** **Florian Heller** **Jan Borchers**
RWTH Aachen University
52056 Aachen, Germany
{wacker,kreutz,flo,borchers}@cs.rwth-aachen.de

ABSTRACT
Traditional audio guides in museums and similar spaces typically require the visitor to locate a track number at each exhibit and enter it on a keypad. These guides, however, provide no information on the amount of content available. Current mobile devices provide rich output capabilities, and indoor location tracking technology can simplify the selection of content in modern audio guides. In this paper, we compare the keypad-based interface to a map-based interface with and without automatic localization. Through a field study in a local museum with 84 participants, we found that the usability of all versions is rated high, with the keypad interface coming out ahead. Nevertheless, visitors favored the overview of the map and thumbnails to find the right exhibit, while numbers were considered helpful indicators in the real world. Those who used the self-localizing guide preferred it over manually adjusting the map.

Author Keywords
Audio Guide; Museum; Location Tracking.

ACM Classification Keywords
H.5.2. User Interfaces: Interaction styles

INTRODUCTION
Museums have offered audio and multimedia guides for a long time, and many museums use them [2, 12]. While early versions were based on a predefined audio tour recorded on tape which the user had to follow closely not to lose context, random access players like CD players and later MP3 players allowed visitors to create self-paced tours through the museum [12]. Today, the standard interaction with an audio guide is expected to be entering the number of an exhibit on a keypad (e.g., [11], [15]). While this is certainly a very robust technique, it offers no visibility or information scent [8] about how many exhibits are covered by guide content. The keypad version has a lesser information scent than the map versions

CHI'16, May 07 – 12, 2016, San Jose, CA, USA

ACM 978-1-4503-3362-7/16/05...$15.00
DOI: http://dx.doi.org/10.1145/2858036.2858189

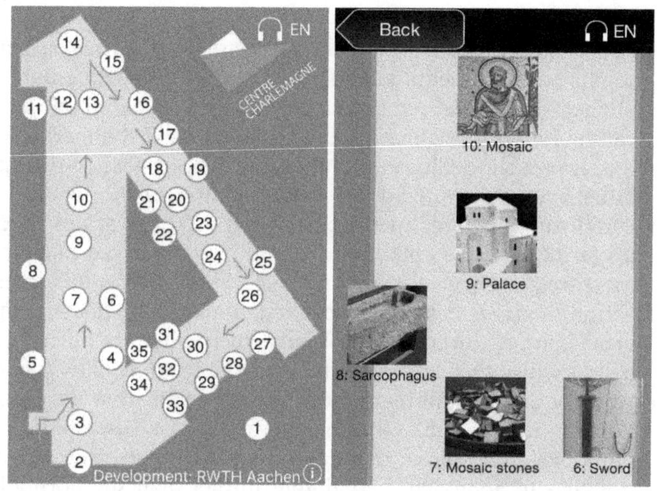

Figure 1. The left shows an overview of all exhibits with according audio content. The right image shows the detailed view which the user interacts with mostly. The area that is shown in this view is determined based on the detected location.

as it does not give a prior hint as to what can be found *behind* a number. It also requires the visitor to find the according number to each exhibit, which can be difficult, especially for large-scale exhibits that require some viewing distance, or that offer no obvious place for signage. Furthermore, exhibitions are modified over time which results in inconsistencies if not the entire numbering is adjusted. The visitor can easily misinterpret a missing number in the sequence as an overlooked exhibit and start a foredoomed search. Also, people are used to rich interaction with smartphones. A regular keypad based audio guide does not fulfill that expectation.

To overcome the problem of having to enter a number, Bederson [5] developed an audio guide in which the according audio track is triggered by an infrared beacon. While the technology to replace the keypad has evolved since then to include QR codes, object recognition, and Bluetooth beacons in the exhibit, it basically offers the same functionality. We evaluated a different approach, which shows a map of the area where the visitor is located, along with the exhibits available in her vicinity (Fig. 1). This has the advantage of providing awareness of the surroundings, along with a visible overview of available information. We deployed such a self-localizing audio guide in a museum and compared its acceptance to a traditional keypad and a manual map-based interface to see whether the prevalent use of a keypad design is due to a superior usability or if other approaches with richer interactions reach the same level. Our results indicate that while the usability of the approaches was rated high, the map versions do not reach the ratings of the keypad version. Nevertheless, visitors favored the overview given by the map and the thumbnails to quickly find the right exhibit while numbers were considered helpful indicators in the real world. Those who used the self-localizing guide preferred it over manual pan and zoom on the map. We therefore suggest a self-localizing map-based approach for visibility, with corresponding numbers on exhibits and thumbnails as a fallback.

RELATED WORK

Ardissono et al. [3] provide a summary of research on personalized multimedia guides. The simplest implementation of a self-paced audio tour guide is the keypad-based one as it can be found in many museums (see [9] for a summary). In this approach, dedicated numbers are placed next to the exhibits and when entered into the guide, trigger the according audio sample. This method has been used in various studies as the baseline condition (e.g., [15]), or referred to as the most frequently used technique (e.g., [11]). While this interaction model is easy to understand, some problems become clear upon a closer look. Usually, the number is placed on a sign with other information about the exhibit. This works well for small exhibits that can be inspected from the same position as the sign. But imagine, e.g., a wall-size painting with its sign beside it; in order to read the number the visitor now has to approach the painting further than she normally would and then move away again to study the painting itself. If no sign is present, there is the additional problem of where to place the number so all visitors find it quickly. An exhibit hanging from the ceiling, e.g., has no obvious place to put a number. The second problem is the visibility of augmented exhibits which arises if only part of the collection has an according audio explanation. A solution would be to hand out a paper leaflet which lists all augmented exhibits, which is of course a suboptimal approach.

To overcome the problem of having to find and enter a number, Bederson [5] combined an MP3 player with an infrared beacon that encodes the number of the exhibit the visitor is standing in front of. While this simplifies the interaction, the problems of visibility and large exhibits remain. For large exhibits, one could place the beacon at the preferred viewing point, but this leaves room for error as different visitors may have different preferences, the center of a room might be a good place to study more than one painting, etc. Wein [15] compared QR-codes and visual recognition of exhibits to numbers. Visitors clearly favored visual recognition, which allows selecting an exhibit from a distance and, if the recognition works well, closely follows the user's intent. However, the study was limited to 2D exhibits. In museums with complex 3D objects the technology might fail much more easily.

None of the above approaches track the visitor's position continuously. This has been done, for example, in PEACH [13], HIPS [6], or ec(h)o [14] for indoor scenarios, and in Cyberguide [1] in outdoor situations. Tracking technologies used in these projects include GPS (only outdoors), WiFi, or beacons (infrared or Bluetooth). Many of these projects notify the user of available content when she is close to an exhibit. Lanir et al. [11] examined the effect of different content presentation styles. In the first condition, content playback was triggered automatically as soon as the visitor got close to an exhibit. In the other two conditions, the system showed an image of nearby exhibits. Exhibits with available audio content were highlighted. After an exhibit was selected, the guide either played one audio piece or offered a choice of multiple audio pieces for the selected exhibit. Visitors disliked the guide triggering playback automatically and preferred the version that offered multiple shorter audio pieces for an exhibit.

Other guide systems offer maps to show the visitor nearby exhibits. Most of these systems are designed for outdoor use, and use GPS to track visitor location. Baus et al. [4] and Kenteris et al. [10] provide overviews of such map-based guides. According to Baus et al., the benefit of maps in mobile guides is the possibility to indicate not only the presence but the location of a point of interest. In a museum scenario this means that exhibits can be displayed on a map at their locations in the museum, rather than in a simple list. Furthermore, they can indicate the current position and surroundings of the user. However, so far no study has compared keypad-based selection of content, manual map-based navigation, and automatic map-based navigation.

EVALUATION

We conducted a between groups field experiment to compare a map-based guide with automatic localization (*tracking*; see the next section for more information), a version with the automatic localization disabled (*map*), and a *keypad*-based implementation as the baseline for currently used audio guides in museums. All ran on iPhones in custom casings. For the *keypad* condition, we attached numbers to all exhibits with audio content. The number was fixed to the information sign if present, or otherwise we placed the number in proximity to the exhibit (e.g., on the glass cover of a display case). We included the map-based version without automatic localization to distinguish between the influences of the map visualization and the location tracking. For this condition, we disabled the tracking code in our location-aware guide software so that the visitor had to manually zoom and pan through the map.

We conducted the study over the course of four days in the Centre Charlemagne in Aachen, Germany with one condition used on each day. One condition was used twice to reach similar group sizes. Normal visitors to the museum were asked whether they would like to participate in the study and were equipped with a free audio guide running that day's software. All materials for the study were available in all four languages of the audio guide (English, German, French, and Dutch) to avoid any language bias. Participants could explore the museum at their own pace. We asked them to fill out a questionnaire when they returned the audio guide. The survey contained questions of Brooke's System Usability Scale [7] as well as questions regarding demographic information (age, nationality, and gender) and the participant's habits regarding museums and audio guides (frequency of visits and frequency of audio guide usage if one is available). We also included a question whether the participant had planned to use the existing audio guide before learning about our study, as our self-locating map-based guide is deployed permanently in the museum. In addition to the survey, we conducted short interviews with visitors who volunteered. The qualitative interview included an open question regarding further comments about problems, ideas for improvement, and general experience. Furthermore, we showed those participants all conditions and asked which system they would prefer, and why.

In addition to this participant-provided information, we logged the number of exhibits each participant selected, to quantify how many exhibits were found and listened to.

We assumed that the keypad-based guide would get the highest usability rating (H1) from visitors, due to its well-known and simple metaphor. However, we expected that visitors would select more exhibits using the map-based methods (H2) because of the increased visibility of available audio content. As for the self-localization, we thought that visitors would prefer the self-localizing map to the manual map (H3) as it reduces the number of necessary interactions and provides awareness of information close-by.

IMPLEMENTATION

Our map interface shows a section of the ground map with thumbnails and names of the exhibits with according audio comments at their respective location (Fig. 1). The thumbnails show the entire exhibit, or a prominent detail. To select an exhibit, the user taps on the according thumbnail on the map. This takes the user either to the audio piece for this exhibit if only one piece of content is associated with it, or to a list of all the content this exhibit has to offer. Along with the audio explanation, the guide presents a timed slideshow of corresponding explanatory images.

Localization Technology

We distributed a grid of 41 Bluetooth beacons in a local museum, and use these for quasi-continuous 2D visitor localization by training an SVM on signal strength fingerprints of predefined regions. While a visitor is moving through the museum, the guide measures the strength of surrounding beacons and feeds this information into the support vector machine (SVM) to assign probabilities for possible regions. Once a region has been characterized with the highest probability for five consecutive times, the device is considered to be located in that area, and the map automatically zooms and pans to display this region. If the user adjusts the visible map region manually, the automatic panning and zooming is disabled until the visitor moves physically into a new region (where it then will center again on this region). This approach does not attempt to display an exact location of the visitor in the museum (e.g., by a blue dot) since such precise tracking would require the use of more complex technology.

RESULTS

A total of 84 visitors (47 female) participated in our study. Of these, 30 were assigned to the *keypad* condition, 29 to the *tracking* condition, and 25 to the *map* condition. All but 8 of the participants reported their age, which ranges from 20 to 77 years with an average of 49 (SD=17). Most of the participants reported to own a smartphone (n=62, 74%).

Of all participants, 61 (73%) go to a museum multiple times a year, 15 (18%) visit a museum less often (one even reported this as his first visit). Only 8 participants (10%) visit a museum multiple times per month, none multiple times per week. Only 6 participants (7%) never take an audio guide, 14 (17%) do so occasionally. Most participants take an audio guide every other time (n=31, 37%), 28 (33%) every time one is available. In case of the current visit, 44 participants (52%) had the intention to use the audio guide even before they learned about our study.

All three implementations received high SUS ratings: *keypad* achieved the highest scores (M=92.4, SD=9.12); both map versions scored slightly lower (*tracking*: M=84.5, SD=9.1; *map*: M=84.7, SD=14.5). An ANOVA on log-transformed SUS scores with user as random factor showed a significant main effect of the input method on the SUS score ($F_{2,76}$ = 4.24, p = .0179). Post-hoc pairwise Tukey HSD tests show that *map* (p = .0314) is rated significantly lower than *keypad* while the remaining differences are not significant. This trend is consistent for every user characteristic we gathered (if the visitor has a smartphone, how often the participant visits a museum, how often she picks an audio guide, and if she planned to take the audio guide on this visit). In all cases, *keypad* received higher or similar usability ratings compared to the other conditions. In conclusion, we can accept H1.

Our assumption that a map enhances the content accessed could not be verified numerically. The average number of accessed descriptions is similar in the *tracking* (M=21.9, SD=8.2), *keypad* (M=19.4, SD=7.9), and *map* (M=20.5, SD=8.5) conditions. However, visitors who always use audio guides access significantly different amounts of content based on the condition ($F_{2,24}$ = 4.53, p = .0213). Post-hoc Tukey HSD test shows that those visitors selected significantly more exhibits in the *tracking* (M=26.7, SD=8.1) condition compared to the *keypad* (M=16.3, SD=6.9) condition (p = .0169). However, as the overall amount of selected exhibits does not change significantly when using a map representation, we reject H2.

Feedback

After filling out the questionnaire, 20 (*tracking*: 8, *map*: 10, *keypad*: 2) participants agreed to stay for our interview regarding possible issues with the audio guide and ideas for improvement. We showed and explained all three implementations side-by-side and asked for their opinions and comments. Participants that had used the *keypad* version mentioned that they liked the ease of use of this input method, but would like to have some form of overview over available exhibits, either as a list or map.

Participants who had used the *map* implementation found it very useful, and mentioned that they liked the thumbnails because they helped find the according exhibits. However, some requested corresponding numbers next to the exhibits (as in the *keypad* condition) to help find the correct match when thumbnails only showed a detail that they could not find immediately. They were also reserved when asked about the automatic localization and assumed it to be confusing.

In contrast to that, people who used the self-localizing guide found this feature to be helpful. One participant mentioned that it felt a little confusing at first but that she quickly understood the principle. Another one liked the localization feature but was concerned that it might be confusing for elderly users.

Overall, none of the participants that used the *map*-based guide, with or without *tracking*, preferred the *keypad*. In conclusion we accept H3 under the condition that visitors need to experience this feature in order to like it.

DISCUSSION

Based on their SUS scores, all three selection methods tested seem suitable for a museum setting. The *keypad*-based selection of audio content appears to be superior in this regard. An influencing factor might be familiarity as many participants mentioned that this method is well known to them and only requires a simple interaction.

We could not verify our assumption that the visualization of exhibits on the map increases their visibility in general as participants selected a similar amount of exhibits during their visits regardless of condition. That visitors who always take an audio-guide if it is available selected significantly more exhibits in the location-based version compared to the *keypad*-version is an interesting finding. If we assume that this visitor group likes to get as much information as possible during their visit, this could mean that the self-localization enabled them to access more of the content in their vicinity. Alternatively—as this group did not select more exhibits in general—they possibly enjoyed a new interaction technique and used it more because of that. However, their usability ratings for the conditions did not show significant differences.

Our qualitative results suggest that visitors like to see visual representations of the exhibits to match the available content to their real-world counterparts, therefore acknowledging the higher information scent of the map visualization. Furthermore, visitors like to have an indicator beside the exhibit that could both show whether an exhibit has a corresponding audio content available and also assist in connecting the digital information to the exhibit. For an optimal solution, the important channel from the exhibit to the visitor should also be included into the map visualization. In addition, the map allows to indicate *difficult* exhibits with no obvious place to attach a number which, so far, would require a workaround.

DESIGN RECOMMENDATIONS

As a result of this experiment, we recommend a combination of the *keypad* and the self-localizing approach. Similar to our implementation, both thumbnails and physical exhibits should be equipped with corresponding numbers (Fig. 2). This still allows to match content and exhibit if the thumbnail fails, e.g., because the thumbnail can only show a small part of the larger exhibit. Furthermore, this assists the visitor in discovering which exhibits have associated audio content without having to check their guide the whole time (to achieve this link, a headphone icon would be sufficient). The

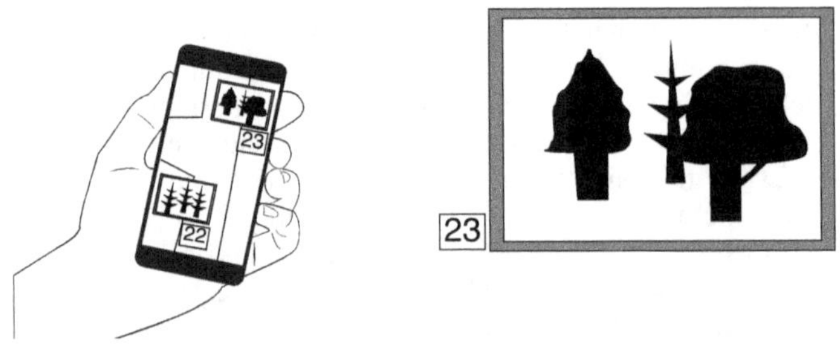

Figure 2. Our design recommendation is to use a self-localizing map-based guide where thumbnails and exhibits are labeled with a corresponding number to provide a channel back to the guide

map and the overview help to discover exhibits that are not directly visible. Modern museums sometimes integrate a notion of exploration into their visits, in which visitors are allowed to pull open drawers or look behind curtains (also noted in [14]), an approach that is certainly engaging but also poses the risk for the visitor to miss something interesting. If all (main) exhibits are represented on a map, the visitor might search a little longer and has a hint what to look for.

The self-localization feature is helpful, but if it is used, it has to work reliably, otherwise this leads to too much confusion. However, with the growing number of people owning a smartphone, automatically localizing the device on a map is a functionality that will be assumed in a modern audio guide. Therefore, we recommend its integration.

CONCLUSION

Many museums offer multimedia guides that allow visitors to explore the museum at their own pace. The traditional approach is to use a number that a visitor has to enter to select an exhibit and get to the associated audio content. This approach does not provide an overview over which exhibits have associated audio content, and some exhibits (e.g., when hanging from the ceiling) may not have obvious locations to place a number. We evaluated a *map*-based approach that visualizes the location of exhibits. As further assistance to the visitor, we also implemented location *tracking* to automatically adjust the map location to the position of the visitor. We tested these three conditions using a field study in a local museum and measured the usability, user preference, and number of selected exhibits. All three conditions received high SUS scores, with the *keypad*-based selection method coming out ahead, likely because of its familiarity. The number of selected exhibits did not differ significantly between conditions. However, visitors mentioned that they liked the visual representation, and none who used a map-based guide preferred the *keypad* version. Furthermore, those who experienced the self-localizing guide found this feature to be helpful. As visitors missed a visual indicator beside the exhibits, we suggest a mixture of the systems: Using a map-based visualization that adjusts to the visitor's location, while providing numbers as visual cues beside each exhibit to link the digital content to it, and also to indicate available content in the real world.

ACKNOWLEDGMENTS

We want to thank the participants of our study for their time and feedback. This work was funded in part by the German B-IT Foundation and the city of Aachen.

REFERENCES

1. Gregory D Abowd, Christopher G Atkeson, Jason Hong, Sue Long, Rob Kooper, and Mike Pinkerton. 1997. Cyberguide: A mobile context-aware tour guide. *Wireless networks* 3, 5 (1997), 421–433.
2. American Association of Museums. 2011. *AAM: 2011 Mobile Technology Survey*. Technical Report. Retrieved September 25, 2015 from http://www.aam-us.org/docs/center-for-the-future-of-museums/aam_mobile_technology_survey.pdf.
3. Liliana Ardissono, Tsvi Kuflik, and Daniela Petrelli. 2012. Personalization in cultural heritage: the road travelled and the one ahead. *User modeling and user-adapted interaction* 22, 1-2 (2012), 73–99.
4. Jörg Baus, Keith Cheverst, and Christian Kray. 2005. A survey of map-based mobile guides. In *Map-based mobile services*. Springer, 193–209.
5. Benjamin B. Bederson. 1995. Audio Augmented Reality: A Prototype Automated Tour Guide. In *Proc. CHI '95 EA*. ACM, New York, NY, USA, 210–211. DOI: http://dx.doi.org/10.1145/223355.223526
6. Giuliano Benelli, Alberto Bianchi, Patrizia Marti, Elena Not, and David Sennati. 1999. HIPS: Hyper-interaction within physical space. In *Proc. ICMCS '99*, Vol. 2. IEEE, 1075–1078.
7. John Brooke. 1996. SUS-A quick and dirty usability scale. *Usability evaluation in industry* 189, 194 (1996), 4–7.
8. Ed H. Chi, Peter Pirolli, Kim Chen, and James Pitkow. 2001. Using Information Scent to Model User Information Needs and Actions and the Web. In *Proc. CHI '01*. ACM, New York, NY, USA, 490–497. DOI: http://dx.doi.org/10.1145/365024.365325
9. Maria Economou and Elpiniki Meintani. 2011. Promising Beginning? Evaluating Museum Mobile Phone Apps. *Rethinking Technology in Museums 2011: Emerging experiences* (2011).
10. Michael Kenteris, Damianos Gavalas, and Daphne Economou. 2011. Electronic mobile guides: a survey. *Personal and ubiquitous computing* 15, 1 (2011), 97–111.
11. Joel Lanir, Tsvi Kuflik, Alan J. Wecker, Oliviero Stock, and Massimo Zancanaro. 2011. Examining proactiveness and choice in a location-aware mobile museum guide. *Interacting with Computers* 23, 5 (Sept. 2011), 513–524. DOI: http://dx.doi.org/10.1016/j.intcom.2011.05.007
12. Nancy Proctor and Chris Tellis. 2003. The State of the Art in Museum Handhelds in 2003. In *Museums and the Web 2003*. Charlotte, NC, USA.
13. Oliviero Stock and Massimo Zancanaro. 2007. *PEACH - Intelligent Interfaces for Museum Visits*. Springer Science & Business Media.
14. Ron Wakkary and Marek Hatala. 2006. Ec(H)O: Situated Play in a Tangible and Audio Museum Guide. In *Proc. DIS '06*. ACM, New York, NY, USA, 281–290. DOI: http://dx.doi.org/10.1145/1142405.1142448
15. Leonard Wein. 2014. Visual Recognition in Museum Guide Apps: Do Visitors Want It?. In *Proc. CHI '14*. ACM, New York, NY, USA, 635–638. DOI: http://dx.doi.org/10.1145/2556288.2557270

Staying the Course: System-Driven Lapse Management for Supporting Behavior Change

Elena Agapie[1,2], **Daniel Avrahami**[1,2], **Jennifer Marlow**[1]

[1]FXPAL
Palo Alto, CA 94304 USA
{daniel, marlow}@fxpal.com

[2]Human Centered Design & Engineering
DUB Group, University of Washington
eagapie@uw.edu

ABSTRACT

The negative effect of lapses during a behavior-change program has been shown to increase the risk of repeated lapses and, ultimately, program abandonment. In this paper, we examine the potential of *system-driven lapse management* – supporting users through lapses as part of a behavior-change tool. We first review lessons from domains such as dieting and addiction research and discuss the design space of lapse management. We then explore the value of one approach to lapse management – the use of "cheat points" – as a way to encourage sustained participation. In an online study, we first examine interpretations of progress that was reached through using cheat points. We then present findings from a deployment of lapse management in a two-week field study with 30 participants. Our results demonstrate the potential of this approach to motivate and change users' behavior. We discuss important open questions for the design of future technology-mediated behavior change programs.

Author Keywords

Lapse management; behavior change; cheat points; tracking; field study.

ACM Classification Keywords

H.5.m. Information interfaces and presentation (e.g., HCI): Miscellaneous

INTRODUCTION

The use of technology for personal behavior change has grown tremendously in the last decade. People use a variety of devices and apps to support their pursuit of diverse goals, from increasing physical activity to changing dietary habits, saving money, or reducing stress/environmental impact. Combined with personal mobile computing, such as smartphones and smartwatches (which themselves contain a wide range of sensors), opportunities for logging and journaling can be easily combined with personal informatics – visualizations of activity and progress.

CHI'16, May 07 - 12, 2016, San Jose, CA, USA.

ACM 978-1-4503-3362-7/16/05...$15.00.
DOI: http://dx.doi.org/10.1145/2858036.2858142

Yet, personal behavior change, with or without technology, is a difficult process that requires motivation, discipline, and perseverance. If a person's goal, for example, is to eliminate an "undesirable behavior" (e.g., taking a long shower), more often than not, that behavior is actually desirable to them in the moment. Conversely, if a person's goal is to pick up a desired behavior (e.g. a daily workout), quite often, that behavior is undesirable to them in the moment (they might rather sleep an extra 40 minutes).

This misalignment between the desirability of the overall behavior change and the desirability (or undesirability) of a behavior in the moment, can lead to lapses. Lapses, in turn, as years of research in behavior change have shown, can lead to other lapses and, ultimately, to quitting the behavior change altogether (in the domain of addiction research, abandoning a behavior change effort and returning to old habits is referred to as "relapse"). When behavior change is supported by use of technology (such as sensing, mobile journaling, etc.), additional risks for lapsing and ultimately quitting exist. For example, as reported in [34], if automatic sensing is used, any failure in tracking for any reason (forgetting the sensor, sensor out of battery, etc.) can make the value of the activity seem wasted. This may also leave data logs incomplete and consequently reduce the effectiveness of the technology. Finally, if a user is afraid or unwilling to track or log a lapse, they may decide to avoid using their tracker (e.g., they don't log a meal where they eat something they shouldn't). As a result, not only do they incur the cost of the lapse itself, but their data become incomplete, which reduces the value of the support the technology offers, and can thus lead to quitting.

The link between lapses (intentional or technology driven) and how technology could be used to manage and overcome lapses is the focus of this work. We investigate whether system-driven lapse management can help users overcome the negative effects of lapsing in behavior change and "stay the course." Specifically, in this work, we explore how accommodating "cheating", operationalized as a lapsing allowance, may ultimately reduce the risk of repeat lapsing and program abandonment. We first review lessons from classic domains of behavior change for addressing lapses (such as smoking). We then examine interpretations of goal-reaching with a lapsing allowance through an online study. Finally, we describe results from a field deployment that explored lapse-management in the context of a specific real-world behavior-change domain – reducing time spent online. Results show that the lapse-management approach we designed was useful for those who lapsed and served as a "safety net" for those who did not. We found that participants were significantly better able to limit their online behavior compared to a control condition, and were marginally significantly less likely to have consecutive lapses.

This work makes the following contributions:

1. A discussion of the design space of system-driven lapse management, reviewing lessons from the domains of dieting, fitness, and addiction research.
2. An investigation of interpretations of a user's progress towards a goal when progress is supported by lapse management.
3. A field deployment and evaluation of a lapse management strategy (cheat points) showing improved goal achievement compared to a control condition.

RELATED WORK

In this section, we first review lessons about the danger of lapses and approaches for dealing with lapses from a range of behavior change domains. We then discuss technologies and tools used for behavior change before discussing the potential design space of tools for lapse management, the focus of this work.

Factors influencing behavior change

People have different reasons for behavior change and different interventional strategies have been implemented to fit these different reasons. For example, behavior change may be goal-based, or motivated by wanting to maintain or increase a behavior (e.g. increase physical activity levels) or to maintain, decrease, or eliminate an undesired state or behavior (e.g. quit smoking, lose weight, etc.) [2, 9]. It may also be influenced by individual characteristics such as intrinsic or extrinsic motivation, [31] or self-efficacy (e.g. how successful a person thinks they will be at changing their behavior [3]. Finally, social factors in the form of other people's influence can either be negative (e.g. smoking) or positive (e.g. providing social support). These factors have been incorporated, in different ways, into the design of technological tools to support behavior change.

Lapses and behavior change

Regardless of an individual's particular goal or the technology they use to help this goal, lapsing during the process of behavior change is a common and sometimes unavoidable experience. Gollwitzer [14] highlights lapsing as the third and final challenge in the behavior change cycle of (1) getting started, (2) staying on track in the face of temptation and (3) facing problems with calling a halt to unsuccessful efforts to reach a goal.

Lapses may occur when an activity requires sustained effort over a long period of time. Many goals require that people keep striving over an extended period, and staying on track becomes difficult when internal or external stimuli interfere with the ongoing efforts [14]. "Tracking fatigue" is a common challenge for people who need to keep a record of their activities or behaviors for purposes such as fitness, sleep, diet, or stress management. Because the burden for these ongoing recording actions is high, many people eventually stop tracking entirely [4]. Personal and situational factors can also cause people to lapse from their ongoing goal pursuit. These include loss of motivation or reduced novelty [34] or external factors such as a change in work schedule, weather, travel, or injury [9].

Prior work on preventing lapses and relapse has focused on changing individuals' cognitions about their actions. For example, building up a behavior change as a habit can make the behavior more resistant to motivation lapses later [13]. Encouraging people to form habits by creating an "if-then" plan (e.g. "If it is sunny out, then I go for a run") can make a person more likely to follow a behavior change plan – they operate on "auto-pilot" [1]. However, habits may take several months to form [28]. In this work, we explore designing system-driven solutions to help with lapses when a break from the behavior change occurs.

Current approaches to lapse management

Previous research work has focused on the role that lapses and relapses play in the cycle of behavior change. Considering the transtheoretical model proposed by Prochaska *et al.* [28], it is acknowledged that people in the maintenance stage of behavior change often exhibit lapses or slips [23]. Thus, relapse prevention methods should make it clear that such mistakes are common and not a sign of personal failure [22]. In other words, a slip "need not be a fall" [9]. As described earlier, one challenge of lapse management is that, on one hand, the negative impact of a lapse should be managed such that it does not lead to quitting. However, when a lapse occurs, its impact should not be ignored or concealed, especially if any direct adverse consequences of the lapse exist (e.g., less money saved, too many calories consumed, etc.). In other words, a lapse should be "forgiven, but not forgotten".

As mentioned previously, external factors such as a change in daily schedule, or vacation can cause people to break a pattern of good behavior. Getting back on track after an initial lapse can be difficult. Gamified online programs such as duolingo [8] or InterviewBit [11] have adopted a "streak freeze" paradigm to help address this issue. In these settings, individuals are encouraged to keep up a "streak" of as many daily visits in a row as they can (in order to practice a language or improve coding skills). In cases where a person does not have time on one particular day to visit the site, they can use virtual tokens to "purchase" a one-day freeze to maintain their streak. Online forum comments suggest that users perceive this as a useful feature.

A similar concept is also employed in the Weight Watchers system, which allots individuals a certain number of "points" to be used on food during a given week. This enables people who have been normally good at eating healthy food but may find themselves in occasional tempting situations (such as going to a restaurant for a social occasion) the ability to use "cheat points" to not go over their weekly limit. The benefits and drawbacks of this concept have been widely discussed on related dieting online forums (the quotes below come from a Weight Watchers community discussion board: [32]). For example, some individuals feel that cheat days allow them to stay on track when unexpected situations arise:

> *Now I do have days when I eat a lot more than normal, like on holidays, pot-lucks or Pie Day at work. I make a broad estimate of points and still list what I ate. Then I get back to precise counting the next meal. It can work if it is infrequent, but I also dislike the word 'cheat day'. It's a planned special occasion.*

An alternate viewpoint is that cheating on one day makes it much easier to break from routine for more days in the future.

> *The realities of life mean that indeed there likely will come a day where you don't track every bite, or where you have to take your best guess. But calling that a "cheat day" encourages you to just throw the whole plan to the wind, and that's an issue.*

> *I understand not everyone has this mindset, but if I have a "cheat meal," it can easily turn into a cheat day, which rolls into a few days, etc. For me it's a huge snowball effect that starts with not tracking one meal and turns into falling entirely off track.*

Technology for behavior change

A variety of technological aids for behavior change have been developed in contexts ranging from smoking cessation [27] to promoting exercise [31] to reducing stress [18]. Michie et al. [25] developed a taxonomy of behavior change techniques (BCT) that are used in behavior change interventions. They come up with a set of 16 categories and 93 subcategories of distinct and precise behavior change techniques. Some of these are based around individual cognitions, others are social in nature. A survey of papers focused around strategies for designing technology to support maintenance of behavior change and decrease lapses reveals different guiding approaches for doing so. Many of these cluster around the following techniques as strategies for behavior change maintenance:

Goals and Planning are mentioned as strategies to support lapse prevention. The most common techniques in this category focus on designing tools that support goal setting, in particular the variety of goals that people might have [19, 30]. Research also suggests that technology should support revision of goals, in particular as behavior-change goals change [9]. Research also proposed that technologies support the creation of action plans that are designed for the context, routines and preferences of the person using them [7, 27]. Goals are effective when they are self-set, realistic, the individual can see his/her progress, and receives positive feedback as progress towards the goal is made [26].

Feedback and Monitoring emphasizes the value of feedback while a user progresses towards their goal, in particular in the case of using tracking technologies: feedback that increases self-efficacy and self-control, feedback on the progress that fits with participant routines [19, 30]. Recommendations for design also include providing feedback on the outcomes of the behavior, which can highlight different benefits a person gains from performing the positive behavior (e.g. money saved by not smoking) [19, 27]. Other recommendations include providing feedback combined with comparison of different outcomes [30], or providing data visualizations to help people return to their behavior after a lapse [9]. The role of visualization can be important. For example, to mitigate motivation loss, amiable visual feedback encourages users to respond to an unfavorable state of the object with the motivation to return it to a favorable state, hence serving as a motivation for immediate task resumption [21].

Repetitions and Substitution of behavior focus on aspects of creating behavioral tasks that are of appropriate difficulty for the stage of behavior change and designing technology appropriate for different levels of task difficulty [27]. Substituting behavior through technology can offer alternatives and flexibility in prompted behaviors [30], and help with technology-driven habit formation [19].

Associations, in particular *Prompts* and *Cues*, refer to recommendations such as reminders, design of messages about behavior change in a personalized and novelty-bringing manner, or choices of recommendations provided by others [7, 16, 27, 30].

Social Support can involves practical tactics and recommendations, such as exchanging devices when goals are no longer being met as well as emotional support by using social features to help a user to connect to friends and online communities [5, 27].

Such a myriad of approaches suggests that any behavior change techniques that are emphasized or employed in a tool should create a match between the behavior, individual goal, and the characteristics of the activity.

SYSTEM-DRIVEN LAPSE MANAGEMENT

In the previous section, we described the potential negative effect of lapsing, and a range of strategies for dealing with lapses. We now turn to discussing potential approaches for incorporating lapse management into a system geared towards behavior change. Specifically, we consider lapse management in which a lapse behavior is tracked, but its negative effect on progress towards a goal is managed. We acknowledge that the range of possibilities for lapse management spans far beyond the list below; exploring the complete design space is beyond the scope of a single paper.

Program (Scenario)	Increase or Reduce	Small or Large	Goal	Available cheat points	Level 1 Goal surpassed	Level 2 Goal met	Level 3 Goal met with cheat points	Level 4 Goal not met	Level 5 Goal severely not met
SNS use	Reduce	Small	10 minutes	2	8	10	12 (-2)	12	14
Water	Increase	Small	8 glasses	1	9	8	7 (+1)	7	6
Calories	Reduce	Large	2,000 cals	200	1,865	1,980	2,160 (-160)	2,140	2,295
Step-count	Increase	Large	10,000 steps	1,000	11,037	10,479	9,156 (+844)	9,289	8,351

Table 1. The four behavior-change program scenarios and 5 levels shown to Study 1 participants.

Manage Before vs. After a Lapse
One important dimension of lapse management is whether lapses are managed after the fact (i.e., they are forgiven), whether a system gives users tools to plan lapses as a resource, or a combination of both. As mentioned earlier, in dieting, for example, people will often have a planned "cheat snack", a "cheat meal", or a "cheat day." Indeed, prior literature described the importance of managing realistic expectations [24]. It is possible that when behavior tracking is difficult but important, a system should allow forgiving a lapse after the fact, thus supporting maintaining a more complete behavior log. One approach for lapse management that we focus on is to provide users a resource (e.g., points) that they can apply towards lapsing.

Granted vs. Earned
Another important dimension is under what circumstances users are given permission (or forgiveness) for lapses. First, one must decide whether the number of lapses possible at any given time, or across a behavior change program is finite or not. We believe that it is important that the number of lapses that can be managed is finite. Otherwise, allowed lapse simply becomes a secondary, potentially unsatisfactory goal. If that number is finite, how and how often is it distributed to the user? One approach is that users "earn" points that allow them to lapse only after exhibiting the desired behavior. A second approach is to grant users points at certain intervals, or even dynamically based on progress towards a goal.

Fixed vs. Personalized
Next, lapse management can be tailored to a user's needs and status within the program. Indeed, flexibility to user current needs is desirable to support behavior change [27, 30]. In our deployed system, lapse management resources are based on a user's individual program (although we did not include any dynamic elements in our system).

Framing and Feedback
Prior research has shown the importance of immediate feedback to support behavior change [27]. Research has also shown that the framing of lapses have direct effects on whether the lapsing behavior is used as a learning opportunity or lead to discouragement and potentially a relapse. For example, the term "cheat meal" or "cheat day" is commonly used in dieting, despite, and perhaps because, of its negative connotations. While high satisfaction with positive outcomes has been shown to lead to better maintenance of behavior [2], it is important that as lapses are managed, they are not ignored. Thus, a lapse-management tool may need to provide a balanced feedback; one that does not encourage lapses, but that does not cause discouragement.

In the work presented in the rest of this paper, we explored the use of "cheat-points" as a mechanism to allow users to manage their own lapses. Cheat points may help people stick to their goal when encountering obstacles, similarly to developing action plans that have been shown to help people achieve goals [15, 17]. Inspired by implementation intentions, people can adopt such strategies to develop plans such as "If I reach my goal today, then I will use cheat points". In our work, cheat points are granted, are personalized to a person's goal, and help them manage (plan) for lapses before they happen. Using cheat-points would occasionally allow a user to recover from a lapse (if they perform a behavior they should not), or allow them to "pad" their progress (if they did not perform enough of a desired behavior to meet their goal). Thus, in order for a system that employs lapse management to be able to permit or forgive a lapse but without actually encouraging lapses, representation of progress should be able to convey a positive and negative message simultaneously. To examine how progress towards a goal while using cheat-points is interpreted, we conducted the study reported next.

STUDY 1: VISUALIZING SUCCESS WITH CHEATING
Providing immediate feedback about progress is commonly used in behavior-change tracking and logging systems (*c.f.*, [26]). Beyond concrete representations of logged or tracked data (the number of steps taken, heart rate, and calories burnt, etc.), many systems also use 'badges' consisting of graphical depictions of items, such as trophies [26], fish [20], a flower [10], a blooming garden [6], etc. These badges afford at-a-glance understanding of one's progress, and offer visual "rewards" to the user (more stars, a prettier garden, etc.). But how should progress towards a goal be represented to help users overcome lapses on one hand, but discourage them from lapsing again?

To test this we conducted an online study in which participants were presented with a 5-day "dashboard" describing a user's progress in a behavior change program (see Figure 1). We created dashboards for four different behavior-change scenarios and with two visualizations (more below). Each dashboard included days in which the goal was met, not met, and a day in which the goal was met

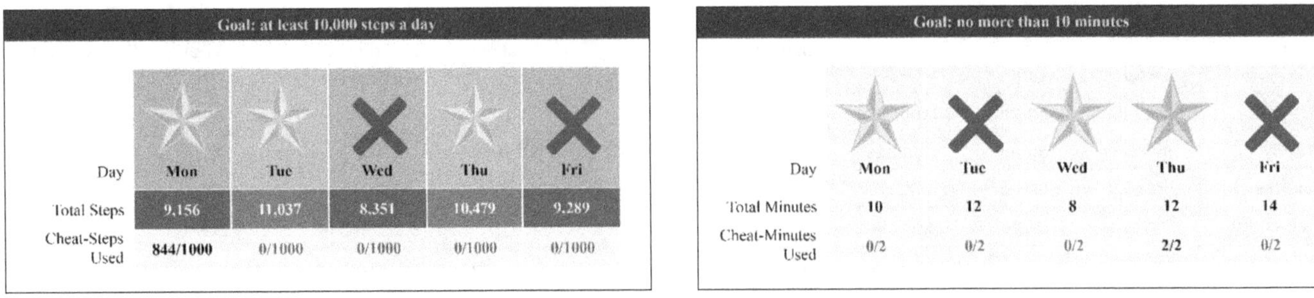

Figure 1. Two example stimuli from the Study 1: Daily step-count (left) and Daily website-visit limit (right). Each dashboard includes a day where a goal was reached using cheat points.

but through the use of cheat points. Participants were asked to rate the user's level of success on each of these five days.

Method

The study was conducted as a between-subject design, with each participant seeing a single 5-day dashboard. We created dashboards depicting progress in 4 behavior-change program scenarios: A daily step-count goal, a daily water-drinking goal, a daily SNS website-visit limit (where a user's goal is to spend no more than a certain number of minutes on a particular website), and a daily calorie limit (Table 1). We chose these four programs as they represent behavior change along two dimensions: Increase vs. Reduce behavior, and Small vs. Large numbers.

Increase vs. Reduce Behavior

One dimension that may influence how progress towards a goal is interpreted is whether the program involves increasing (or starting) a desired behavior such as step-count (an *Increase behavior*), or whether the program involves reducing (or stopping altogether) an undesired behavior such as reducing time spent on an SNS website (a *Reduce behavior*).

Small vs. Large Numbers

The size of numbers in which a program is measured and tracked may affect interpretations of success (and thus, the use of cheat points). For example, reaching 9,000 steps out of a 10,000-step goal may seem different than drinking 9 cups of water out of a 10-cups goal (and thus, the use of cheat-points in those cases may have different impacts).

Visualizations

We tested two visual variations of the dashboard. All the dashboards participants saw included both the daily values tracked (e.g., number of calories consumed per day) as well as a daily badge (either a star or a red *X*). In the first design (Figure 1, left), when a goal is reached (with or without cheat points), a gold star is awarded. Independently, a red or green background is used for each day depending on the daily values tracked. Thus, when a goal is reached using cheat-points, it is represented by a gold star on top of a red background (simultaneously suggesting meeting the goal and failing to meet the goal). In the second design (Figure 1, right), if a goal is reached using cheat points, a bronze star is awarded. No color background is used in this design.

Materials

Table 1 shows the goals and progress levels for each scenario. Goals were based on common values used in practice. Available cheat points were set to ~10% of a goal. We then selected 5 levels of daily progress: Two representing meeting the goal, two representing missing the goal, and one representing meeting the goal using cheat-points. The goals and five levels (Levels 1-5) for each program are shown in Table 1. Importantly, note that in each program, Level 3 (meeting the goal with cheat-points) and Level 4 (missing the goal) contain similar daily values tracked (e.g., 2,160 and 2,140 calories). However, in level 3, a star was awarded due to the use of cheat points. These two levels (3 and 4) will be a focal point for our analysis.

The order of levels in each dashboard was counterbalanced using a 5x5 balanced Latin-square. We thus had a total of 40 dashboards: 4 (programs: Steps, Water, Calories, and Website) x 2 designs x 5 orders.

Participants and Procedure

We recruited US-based participants from Amazon Mechanical Turk. Participants were required to have an approval rate of at least 95%. In the instructions, participants were told that they would see the dashboard of a person and asked to rate their daily success based on a presented goal. Additionally, the instructions included a minimal explanation of the concept of cheat points stating, "The person was given [*two "cheat minutes"*] that they could use whenever they wanted." Each participant was presented one of the 40 dashboards described above and asked to provide a rating of success towards reaching the goal for each day on a 7-point Likert scale ranging from "Completely Unsuccessful" to "Completely Successful". To ensure that participants understood and completed the task correctly we use the sign of the difference in ratings between levels 1, 2, 4 and 5 (see Table 1), since those represent, unambiguously, meeting and missing the daily goal.

A total of 407 participants completed the study, taking a median of 1 minute and 4 seconds to complete the task. Each participant was paid $0.15 for their time. We removed the data of 43 participants (10%) who failed our check. We further excluded the data of 6 participants whose completion time was outside the norm based on a

Mahalanobis outlier analysis (completion time longer than 7 minutes). Our final set contained 1790 ratings provided by 358 participants.

Results

We performed a mixed-model repeated-measures ANOVA, in which the dependent measure was the aligned-ranked ([33]) Likert-scale ratings of success towards the goal. *Level* (1…5, see Table 1) was our main independent measure of interest and was modeled as a fixed effect. We included Program Type (*Increase* vs. *Reduce*), Number Scale (*Small* vs. *Large*), Visualization design and all 2-way interactions as fixed effects. Finally, we included the order of presentation as a control, and Participant ID as a random effect, since each participant provided five ratings (one for each day).

Our results show a main effect of Level on ratings of success ($F[4,1428]=1624.7$, $p<.001$). As can be seen in Figure 2, Levels 1 and 2 were rated as successful (M=6.8 and M=6.5, respectively), while levels 4 and 5 were rated as unsuccessful (M=3.0 and M=2.3, respectively). Level 3 (meeting a goal with cheat points) was rated slightly above the neutral point (M=4.1). A post-hoc Tukey HSD pairwise comparison shows that all levels were rated significantly differently from one another. Importantly for our investigation, Level 3 is considered significantly *more* successful than Levels 4 and 5, but also significantly *less* successful than Levels 1 and 2.

While we found no significant difference between the two design variations, we found significant effects of Program Type and Number Scale. Progress in "Increase" programs was rated as significantly more successful than progress in "Decrease" programs (M=4.7 vs. M=4.3; $F[1,356]=40.0$, $p<.001$). The significant interaction between Level and Program Type ($F[4,1424]=25.0$, $p<.001$) revealed that this difference was most pronounced in the evaluations of failure to meet a goal (Levels 4 and 5). In those two levels, ratings in Increase programs were nearly a whole point higher on the Likert scale. This suggests that participants attributed more value into the effort put into reaching a goal, than the effort needed to avoid a limit – consider the difference between walking 9,900 steps out of a daily goal of 10,000 steps a day, vs. consuming 2,160 calories with a daily goal of 2,000.

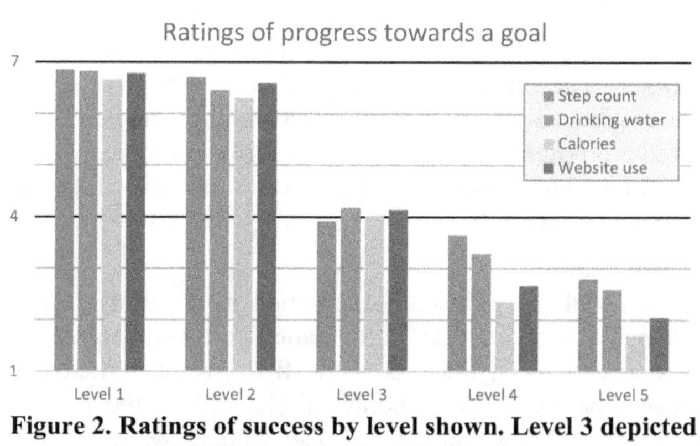

Figure 2. Ratings of success by level shown. Level 3 depicted meeting a goal using cheat points.

Similarly, when represented by large numbers (steps and calories), progress was rated significantly higher than when represented by small numbers (cups of water and minutes on site) ($F[1,356]=7.9$; $p<.01$). The significant interaction between Level and Units Scale ($F[4,1424]=4.6$; $p=.001$) shows that ratings were affected by the number representation in Levels 2, 4, 5, but not in Levels 1 and 3.

To summarize, these results suggest that when interpreting reaching a goal with cheat points, users simultaneously interpret badges as signs of success, but are also sensitive to the actual progress depicted in the dashboard. This result is encouraging; it shows that managed lapses are not seen as failure, but also not seen as simple success. We were now ready to test the effectiveness of the cheat-points lapse-management strategy in a field deployment.

STUDY 2: FIELD DEPLOYMENT OF CHEAT POINTS

To assess the effect of the cheat-points lapse-management approach on behavior and participation, we conducted a two-week field experiment of a real-world behavior-change program. The criteria for selecting a behavior-change program for the study was (a) that behavior is tracked automatically (rather than relies on journaling), (b) that users have measurable daily goals, and (c) that, even in a short duration, participants are likely to exhibit lapsing. We chose a behavior-change program designed for people who wish to reduce the time they spend online on a particular website (e.g., social media, news, or other leisure-based websites). We selected this program in light of recent findings from Sleeper *et al.* [29] that suggest that reducing behavior online is a common goal (44% of Facebook users in their data wanting to spend less time on the social network). We used a two-condition, between-subjects design to compare the online behavior and lapses of participants in a Lapse-Management condition who received *cheat minutes* to participants in a Control condition who did not.

Study Instrument

We designed and implemented a custom browser extension for the Chrome browser. The extension is able to log and visualize time spent on a user-chosen website relative to a selected daily goal. Upon installing the extension, the user first chooses a website they want to reduce their time using (we will refer to this as their *vice website*). The user then selects one of seven possible daily goals (0 to 30 minutes in 5-minute increments). We used 30 minutes as the longest goal based on a pilot survey in which 10 respondents interested in reducing time on certain websites described their current use as ranging from 30 minutes and higher. Finally, the user chooses whether to track their vice website visits all day (24 hours) or only during work hours.

During use, the extension tracks (and logs on our server) attempts to go to the vice website either by entering a URL

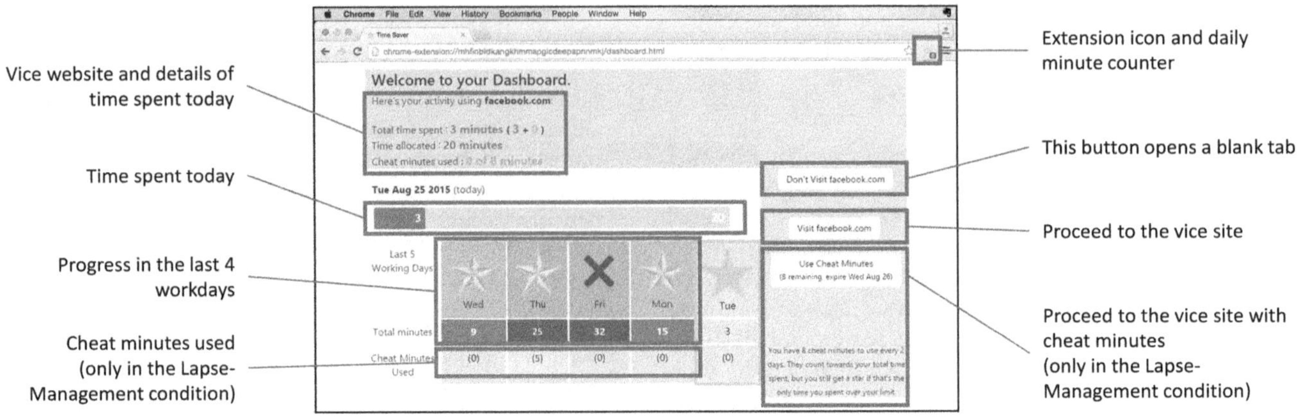

Figure 3. Dashboard of a custom browser extension designed for Study 2 showing progress and progress history. Users see the dashboard when attempting to go to their "vice website" or when they use all the minutes towards their daily goal. From the dashboard users can proceed to their vice website by clicking on right.

or by bringing a browser tab with the site to the foreground. Instead of the vice website, the extension first displays a Dashboard (see Figure 3). The dashboard contains buttons for the user to choose to either proceed to their website or not (selecting this latter option replaces the dashboard with a blank tab). If the user proceeds to their vice site, their time is logged on our servers. If, during their time on the vice site, they reach their daily goal, they are automatically forwarded to the dashboard. As before, they can then choose to return to their vice site or not.

The dashboard also contains information about the current-day's time spent on the site and information about the previous 4 days. Following the first visual design from study 1, the background color for each day conveyed whether the user spent less time than their goal (green) or exceeded their goal (red). A gold star was awarded for days where the goal was achieved, and a red *X* otherwise.

Experimental Conditions

We created two versions of the dashboard, one for each condition, as follows: In the Lapse-Management condition, starting on the second day of the study, participants were granted cheat minutes totaling 20% of a daily limit *every other day*. Cheat minutes expire every two days, whether the participant used them or not (i.e., no "rollover" of cheat minutes). Participants in this condition were instructed how cheat minutes work in both the study instructions and in the dashboard interface itself (*"You have [4] cheat minutes to use every 2 days. They count towards your total time spent, but you still get a star if that's the only time you spent over your limit."*) The decision to have cheat minutes awarded every other day (and expire) was so that they don't simply become a participant's secondary goal. Participants in the Lapse-Management condition were made aware of the concept of cheat minutes. In order to avoid influencing the daily limit goals set, careful language was used that did not guaranteed the availability of cheat minutes at all (specifically, the instructions stated that "It is possible you might not receive cheat minutes at all.").

The dashboard for participants in this condition contained a designated button that had to be clicked in order to use the cheat minutes (see Figure 3, right) as well as information about cheat minutes used and cheat minutes remaining. If a participant stayed under the limit thanks to using cheat minutes, the gold star that they were awarded appeared on top of a red background (as seen in the second day in the dashboard in Figure 3). Participants were redirected to the dashboard if they used up their cheat minutes. Participants in the Control condition did not get cheat minutes. Their dashboard did not contain any mention of cheat-minutes, and included only a single button for proceeding to the website.

Procedure

Participants were recruited through mailing lists and social-network groups at three academic institutions. We targeted participants who were interested in spending less time on certain websites. Participants were asked to fill in a screening questionnaire that asked about the websites they wanted to reduce time on, the amount of time they currently estimate spending on one of these websites, and whether (and how) they have tried to change their behavior with regard to website use in the past.

Based on questionnaire responses, we invited participants who were actively interested or planning to change their behavior (or had been trying to do so already) to install and use our browser extension for one day (we excluded participants who did not use Chrome as their primary browser). Participants were assigned at random to one of the two conditions (recall that no cheat minutes granted on the first day). After using the extension for one day, participants were invited to continue using the extension for the following 9 weekdays (for a 2-workweek study).

Compensation

To ensure that continued participation in the study was not driven by compensation, participants were compensated for the entire study at the end of the first day of participation. Those who chose to withdraw at the end of the first day received a $5 gift card, and those who chose to continue received a $15 gift card. This approach intentionally did not prevent participants from dropping out of the study before the end of the 2 weeks (they were told they could withdraw at any time by uninstalling the browser extension).

Participants

30 individuals participated in the study (16 women, 9 men, 5 did not disclose) and were assigned at random to the Lapse-Management and Control conditions (15 participants per condition). Three additional participants were removed (two who had technical issues with the browser extension one participant who never visited his vice website). Participants were told that the study was set for two weeks but that they could withdraw at any point (by uninstalling the browser extension) or could extend their participation beyond the two weeks. Since our study and dashboard were designed to assist users during the workweek, we only report behavior recorded Monday through Friday.

As described above, before starting, each participant was asked to select a website they wanted to reduce time on and a daily time goal. Of the 30 participants, 23 (77%) chose to reduce time on Facebook, 2 chose reddit.com, and the remaining chose BuzzFeed, hulu.com, Gmail, Pinterest, and a personal livejournal (see Figure 4, left). Two of the participants switched their goal after the first day (from Netflix to BuzzFeed and from YouTube to Facebook).

Participants selected a wide range of daily goals, as seen in Figure 4, right. Twelve of the participants wanted to reduce their time on the site only during workhours (9am-5pm, and in one case 8am-5pm). The remaining wanted to reduce usage throughout the day (3 participants wanted the day to extend past midnight and for them a day in the dashboard started and ended at 4am). We found no statistical difference between the two conditions in the daily limit goals set ($F[1,29]=0.24$; $p=.6$, n.s.).

In their pre-study survey, participants described wanting to reduce time on a site for work-productivity purposes (56%), since it was a waste of time/not worthwhile (46%), or for emotional reasons such as feeling depressed, insecure or less happy (10%). Participants also reported having tried different strategies for quitting or reducing use of a website: six had used extension blockers, three tried deleting an app or bookmark, and six tried using self-control/willpower.

On average, participants in the Lapse-Management condition participated in the study for 9.9 workdays, (Min=2, Max=14, SD=4.1, Median=11). Participants in the Control condition participated for 12.4 workdays, on average (Min=2, Max=24, SD=6.6, Median=13). Two participants (one from each condition) quit the study after two days. Three participants quit after 3 days (2 from the Control condition and 1 from the Lapse-Management condition). Two additional participants quit within 6 days (one from each condition). There was no overall difference between the conditions in days of participation or likelihood of quitting ($F[1,28]=.7$, *n.s*), not surprising for a study of this duration.

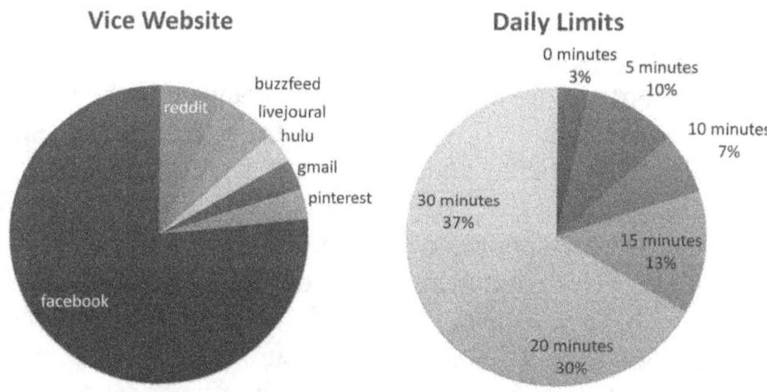

Figure 4. Sites chosen for time reduction and daily goals.

Condition	Average days in study	% of days visiting vice site	Average # of daily visits	% days exceeded time limit
Lapse Management	9.9	84%	9.9	15%
Control	12.4	80%	8.4	23%

Table 2. Average site-use behaviors for Control and Lapse-Management conditions.

RESULTS

On average, participants visited their vice websites 85% of the days they participated in the study (238 days total) spending a grand total of 62 hours on the different vice sites (16 minutes a day, on average) in 2327 visits (9.7 visits per day, on average). To understand the effect of lapsing (exceeding one's daily limit) and the value of lapse management we first examine lapsing occurrences and participants' attitudes towards lapses. We then examine overall differences between the conditions. Finally, we investigate participants' use of cheat minutes and their impressions of the use of cheat minutes in behavior change. We quote participants' responses to the end-of-study survey with LM1-LM15 and C1-C15 for participants in the Lapse-Management and Control conditions, respectively.

Exceeding the Daily Limit (Lapsing)

During the study, 18 of the 30 participants exceeded their time limit at least once: 11 participants in the Control condition lapsed 30 days (out of 128 days), and 7 participants in the Lapse-Management condition lapsed 17 times (out of 110 days). In five of these 17 lapses, using cheat minutes helped participants still receive a star. The remaining participants did not exceed their daily time limit. When asked at the end of the study to describe how they felt about exceeding their daily limit, attitudes varied from neutral (e.g., "*Annoyed me but didn't particularly make me want to do better the next few days.*" <LM11>) to negative (e.g., "*I tried to avoid using Facebook after exceeding the limit.*" <C13>, and "*looking at that big red block was pretty guilt-inducing so I didn't do it again!*" <LM14>). One participant expressed the risk of tracked lapses, "*Going over limit made me care less about going over in future.*" <LM3>.

Time Towards (and Past) a Goal

To identify differences between the Lapse-Management and Control conditions, we examined all days where participants visited their vice site (N=238). We compared the time participants spent on their vice site relative to their daily limit. (In order to avoid giving unfair advantage to the Lapse-Management condition, we count all time spent on the site, regardless of whether cheat minutes were used.) Before analysis, we excluded 3 days from participant <C13> where they spent over 1 hour and 50 minutes on Facebook (with a daily limit of 30 minutes). We conducted a mixed effects model with Time Left at the end of the day (relative to each person's goal) as the dependent measure. Condition (Lapse-Management vs. Control) and Daily Limit were set as fixed effects. ParticipantID was set as a random effect.

The analysis found a significant main effect of Condition, with participants in the Lapse-Management condition having more time left at the end of the day than participants in the Control condition ($F[1,27]=4.21$, $p<.05$). Daily Limit had only a marginally significant effect with more time left at the end of the day with higher goals. To better understand this difference, we repeated the analysis, this time adding to the model a Boolean dummy variable labeled *Lapse,* indicating whether the participant exceeded their daily goal or not, and the two-way interaction Lapse x Condition.

The difference for Condition was again significant indicating that, on average, participants in the Lapse-Management condition had 3:54 minutes *left* on average at the end of a day, while participants in the Control condition had *exceeded* their goal by 4:18 minutes (see Figure 5). This finding is especially interesting given that technically, participants in the Lapse-Management condition were "allowed" to use their vice site more and still receive a star.

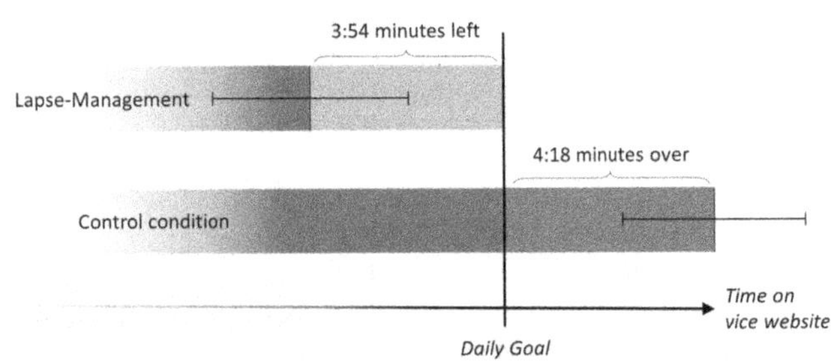

Figure 5. The effect of Condition on how much time is left at the end of the day relative to each user's goal. Includes the time Lapse-Management participants spent on the vice website using cheat minutes.

The interaction was also significant ($F[1,225]=8.1$, $p<.01$) and showed that when going over the limit, participants in the Control condition tended to go over their limit by a significantly greater amount than participants in the Lapse-Management condition (18 minutes *over* vs. 5 minutes *over*, on average). This result suggests that while cheat minutes did not always prevent lapses from occurring, they nevertheless lessened the amount by which people over-shot their stated goals when they did lapse.

Consecutive Lapsing

An important risk of lapsing is the likelihood of them leading to additional lapses (and ultimately a relapse). In order to test whether our lapse management approach helps reduce the likelihood of repeated lapsing, whenever a participant lapsed, we examined the next day they visited their vice site and noted whether they lapsed again, or stayed within their limit. Overall, 38% of lapses were followed by a second lapse. Testing the difference between the two conditions found only a marginally significant difference; 50% of lapses in the Control condition were followed by a second lapse, while only 25% of lapses in the Lapse-Management condition were followed by a lapse ($X^2(1, 44) = 2.73$, $p<.1$).

Using Cheat Minutes

Six of 15 participants in the Lapse-Management condition used cheat minutes. One participant used cheat minutes 5 times, one participant used them twice, and the remaining four used them once, for a total of 11 days. Participants used all their cheat minutes only twice. Recall, that participants in this condition only got cheat minutes every other day.

When asked about their use of cheat minutes, attitudes ranged from feeling guilty to positive. For some, using cheat minutes was seen as something to avoid. As stated by LM14, *"I only really used the cheat minutes once but it was to contact someone for a work-related purpose who I know sits on FB chat all day. Otherwise, I felt guilt using the cheat minutes, which is something I really need!"* Succinctly expressed by LM11: *"It felt like, well, cheating."* For others, however, cheat minutes were seen as useful: *"I think we would feel more guilty if we didn't have them"* <LM5>. Cheat minutes were particularly useful for "special" days: *"The cheat minutes helped me to feel like I'm still minimizing my interaction with the site and staying on the goal while also being realistic about my ability to be distracted and occasional need to use the platform for work"* <LM14>. This is not unlike special cheat snacks or cheat meals in dieting and bodybuilding. However, one participant's response also highlights a potential danger with cheat minutes: *"It felt like a waste not to use what was given to me."* <LM11>

Having, but Not Using Cheat Minutes

We were also interested in understanding participants in the Lapse Management condition who never used their cheat minutes. While two participants stated they did not use cheat minutes because of the need to explicitly "choose" them (i.e., click a different button on the dashboard), others expressed that having the cheat minutes, even without using them was positive. For example, LM13 stated that *"[It was] nice to have them so that if I found a REALLY funny article I wouldn't be cut off in the middle or anything"* and LM15 stated, *"It was good to have the cheat minutes because they provided a safety net for my 20 minute goal."* Finally, for some, not using available cheat minutes was *"sort of like a reward"* <LM1>.

Taken together, these responses indicate that overall cheat minutes were good for those who used them for sporadic (and sometimes unexpected) extra website use needs. At the same time, we also saw that simply having cheat minutes available was seen as a reassuring safety net; their mere availability did not necessarily mean people would use them to go over their limit.

Cheating without Cheat Minutes

Finally, we examined responses from participants in the Control condition who did not have cheat minutes. Using a mobile device to circumvent the extension was described as an available, but undesirable option, *"I didn't cheat much on my phone when I was at my computer working, but if I was away from my computer (say on the bus), I viewed it on the phone more than my 10 minutes allotted."* <C11>

The desire to have the extension represent a goal being met led some participants in the Control condition to increase their use of other means (such as their smartphone) to spend time on their vice site. For example, *"I spent less time on Facebook as I became aware of it. I more carefully used my 20 minute daily allotment. However, I did start accessing Facebook on my phone, which I previous didn't really do, but it wasn't during "real work" time - it was in the bathroom (gross, I know!) or while commuting on public transportation. I still wanted to use Facebook, so I guess I found better times to do it on the mobile device."* <C7>.

These statements illustrate that participants wanted to be compliant with the time limit goals they had set. However, in the absence of any system-driven or "authorized" mechanism to manage lapses, they elected to lapse outside of the tracking environment by circumventing the dashboard and accessing their site of choice via other, non-tracked means such as on their mobile phone. In other words, without "cheat minutes," participants appeared to be more likely to "cheat the system", resulting in a log that does not properly capture their behavior.

Limitations

Our study found both significant quantitative differences as well as qualitative indications for the potential benefits of the cheat-points lapse management approach. However, it is important to remember that the study was relatively short (just over two weeks, on average) and tested one of many possible lapse-management approaches in the context of a single (albeit real-world) behavior-change program. Nevertheless, we believe our findings serve as important and insightful first steps for exploring the general concept of system-driven lapse management. We also note that the first study relies on findings from Mechanical Turk, a participation population that may evaluate reward and success differently.

DISCUSSION

Our work shows the potential value of lapse management for a program that involves reducing an unwanted behavior (time spent on a vice website). Results from the field deployment showed that giving users tools to manage their lapses led to significantly better performance. Despite having cheat minutes to use beyond their goal's limit, participants with lapse management spent significantly less time on their vice site (relative to their goal) compared to a control. It also resulted in positive sentiment toward maintaining realistic progress in the face of changing circumstances.

Other behavior-change programs, however, may differ along a range of dimensions. For example, a program with a goal of picking up a new behavior (e.g., exercising) or one with a goal of abstinence (e.g., eating gluten-free) might require an adapted lapse-management approach. In future work, we plan to investigate system-driven lapse-management in the context of other programs. Additionally, in our two studies, we examined a single instantiation of system-driven lapse management – cheat points. However, as mentioned earlier, the design space of lapse management is broad. Some dimensions include the scheduling, frequency, and quantity of lapses that a system could permit, or the degree of personalization used. For example, a system may choose to increase or decrease the number of lapses permitted dynamically, based on the user's behavior over time.

One dimension of lapse-management that we wish to explore in the future is rewarding users for *not* using their cheat points as a way to ensure that cheat points are only used when necessary. Another important dimension to explore is how lapse-management may interact (or interfere) with behavior change that relies on social support. Would users want to share with others accomplishments and progress that were made with the help of lapse management? Moreover, would they receive the support they need if their network becomes aware of the involvement of lapse management? While our first study provides some initial insights, with participants placed in the role of third-party observers, a more careful investigation is needed.

Still, we believe that successful system-driven lapse management must maintain a delicate balance between supporting unavoidable lapses and encouraging lapses (or at least not sufficiently discouraging them). Our use of the term "cheat minutes" appears to have achieved this goal; participants who used their cheat minutes were thankful to have them, but did not wish to exploit them. Cheat points are similar to other lapse management techniques, by helping people realistically adjust their goals and limits when needed [27]. Further work should examine the set of mechanisms through which cheat points motivate behavior change.

Finally, an interesting observation from the Control condition of Study 2 was the acknowledgement of some participants of increasing use of their mobile device to access the vice site. In the case of Study 2, participants had the ability to go to their vice website on a mobile device, a different computer, or simply a different browser. This challenge is not unique to our study; any tracking system or device can be fooled or circumvented, and journals can have false or incomplete information entered. As mentioned earlier, lapses that are not tracked not only result in the cost of the negative behavior, but also leave an incomplete and potentially meaningless record. Our system demonstrated that allowing users to manage their own lapses can reduce the need to circumvent the system, helping maintain more complete and representative records.

CONCLUSION

In this work, we implemented and deployed a system that helps users manage lapses in a behavior-change program. In a two-week controlled field study, we empirically evaluated the effectiveness of the use of "cheat points" for lapse management. Through quantitative and qualitative data, we describe how lapse management had both positive behavioral and attitudinal effects on participants compared to a control condition. This work gives initial insight into how the design of interventions to support and visualize lapse management can be integrated and used in conjunction with data collected from other devices, interfaces, and systems. Our results suggest the promise of such approaches for supporting and encouraging users in behavior-change programs to "stay the course."

ACKNOWLEDGEMENTS

We thank Tony Dunnigan, Daniel Epstein and Alex Mariakakis for their help and feedback.

REFERENCES

1. Anja Achtziger, Ute C. Bayer, and Peter M. Gollwitzer. 2012. Committing to implementation intentions: Attention and memory effects for selected situational cues. *Motivation and Emotion* 36, 3: 287–300. http://dx.doi.org/10.1007/s11031-011-9261-6
2. Austin S. Baldwin, Alexander J. Rothman, Andrew W. Hertel, Jennifer A. Linde, Robert W. Jeffery, Emily A. Finch, and Harry A. Lando. 2006. Specifying the determinants of the initiation and maintenance of behavior change: an examination of self-efficacy, satisfaction, and smoking cessation. *Health Psychology* 25, 5: 626. http://dx.doi.org/10.1037/0278-6133.25.5.626
3. Albert Bandura. 1977. Self-efficacy: toward a unifying theory of behavioral change. *Psychological review* 84, 2: 191-215. http://dx.doi.org/10.1037/0033-295X.84.2.191
4. Eun Kyoung Choe, Nicole B. Lee, Bongshin Lee, Wanda Pratt, and Julie A. Kientz. 2014. Understanding quantified-selfers' practices in collecting and exploring personal data. *Proceedings of the 32nd annual ACM conference on Human factors in computing systems*, ACM, 1143–1152. http://dx.doi.org/10.1145/2556288.2557372
5. James Clawson, Jessica A. Pater, Andrew D. Miller, Elizabeth D. Mynatt, and Lena Mamykina. 2015. No longer wearing: investigating the abandonment of personal health-tracking technologies on craigslist. *Proceedings of the 2015 ACM International Joint Conference on Pervasive and Ubiquitous Computing*, ACM, 647–658. http://dx.doi.org/10.1145/2750858.2807554
6. Sunny Consolvo, Predrag Klasnja, David W. McDonald, Daniel Avrahami, Jon Froehlich, Louis LeGrand, Ryan Libby, Keith Mosher, and James A. Landay. 2008. "Flowers or a robot army?: encouraging awareness & activity with personal, mobile displays." In *Proceedings of the 10th international conference on Ubiquitous computing*, 54-63. http://dx.doi.org/10.1145/1409635.1409644
7. Felicia Cordeiro, Daniel A. Epstein, Edison Thomaz, Elizabeth Bales, Arvind Jagannathan, Gregory Abowd, and James Fogarty. 2015. Barriers and Negative Nudges: Exploring Challenges in Food Journaling. *Proceedings of the 33rd Annual ACM Conference on Human Factors in Computing Systems*, ACM, 1159–1162. http://dx.doi.org/10.1145/2702123.2702155
8. Duolingo: http://www.duolingo.com
9. Daniel Epstein, Felicia Cordeiro, Elizabeth Bales, James Fogarty, and Sean Munson. 2014. Taming data complexity in lifelogs: exploring visual cuts of personal informatics data. *Proceedings of the 2014 conference on Designing interactive systems*, ACM, 667–676. http://dx.doi.org/10.1145/2598510.2598558
10. Fitbit: http://www.fitbit.com
11. InterviewBit: http://www.interviewbit.com
12. Ira Flatow. "Making Resolutions that Stick." National Public Radio. http://www.npr.org/2012/12/28/168203195/making-resolutions-that-stick (Accessed September 18, 2015).
13. Benjamin Gardner, Kate Sheals, Jane Wardle, and Laura McGowan. 2014. Putting habit into practice, and practice into habit: a process evaluation and exploration of the acceptability of a habit-based dietary behaviour change intervention. *International Journal of Behavioral Nutrition and Physical Activity* 11, 1: 135. http://dx.doi.org/10.1186/s12966-014-0135-7
14. Peter M. Gollwitzer. 2014. Weakness of the will: Is a quick fix possible? *Motivation and Emotion* 38, 3: 305–322. http://dx.doi.org/ 10.1007/s11031-014-9416-3
15. Peter M. Gollwitzer and Bernd Schaal. 1998. Metacognition in action: The importance of implementation intentions. *Personality and Social Psychology Review* 2, 2: 124–136. http://dx.doi.org/10.1207/s15327957pspr0202_5
16. Rúben Gouveia, Evangelos Karapanos, and Marc Hassenzahl. 2015. How do we engage with activity trackers?: a longitudinal study of Habito. *Proceedings of the 2015 ACM International Joint Conference on Pervasive and Ubiquitous Computing*, ACM, 1305–1316. http://dx.doi.org/10.1145/2750858.2804290
17. Richard Koestner, Natasha Lekes, Theodore A. Powers, and Emanuel Chicoine. 2002. Attaining personal goals: self-concordance plus implementation intentions equals

success. *Journal of Personality and Social Psychology* 83, 1: 231-244. http://dx.doi.org/10.1037/0022-3514.83.1.231

18. Artie Konrad, Victoria Bellotti, Nicole Crenshaw, Simon Tucker, Les Nelson, Honglu Du, Peter Pirolli, and Steve Whittaker. 2015. Finding the Adaptive Sweet Spot: Balancing Compliance and Achievement in Automated Stress Reduction. *Proceedings of the 33rd Annual ACM Conference on Human Factors in Computing Systems*, ACM, 3829–3838. http://dx.doi.org/10.1145/2702123.2702512
19. Amanda Lazar, Christian Koehler, Joshua Tanenbaum, and David H. Nguyen. 2015. Why we use and abandon smart devices. *Proceedings of the 2015 ACM International Joint Conference on Pervasive and Ubiquitous Computing*, ACM, 635–646. http://dx.doi.org/10.1145/2750858.2804288
20. James J. Lin, Lena Mamykina, Silvia Lindtner, Gregory Delajoux, and Henry B. Strub. 2006. "Fish'n'Steps: Encouraging physical activity with an interactive computer game." In *UbiComp 2006: Ubiquitous Computing*, 261-278. http://dx.doi.org/10.1007/11853565_16
21. Yikun Liu, Yuan Jia, Wei Pan, and Mark S. Pfaff. 2014. Supporting task resumption using visual feedback. *Proceedings of the 17th ACM conference on Computer supported cooperative work & social computing*, ACM, 767–777. http://dx.doi.org/10.1145/2531602.2531710
22. G. Alan Marlatt. 1996. Taxonomy of high-risk situations for alcohol relapse: evolution and development of a cognitive-behavioral model. *Addiction* 91, Supplement 1 to Issue 12: 37–50. http://dx.doi.org/10.1111/j.1360-0443.1996.tb02326.x
23. G. Alan Marlatt, John S. Baer, and Lori A. Quigley. 1997. 10. Self-efficacy and addictive behavior. *Self-efficacy in changing societies*: 289-315. http://dx.doi.org/10.1007/978-1-4419-6868-5_4
24. G. Alan Marlatt and Dennis Michael Donovan. 2005. *Relapse prevention: Maintenance strategies in the treatment of addictive behaviors*. Guilford Press.
25. Susan Michie, Michelle Richardson, Marie Johnston, Charles Abraham, Jill Francis, Wendy Hardeman, Martin Eccles, James Cane, Caroline E. Wood. 2013. The behavior change technique taxonomy (v1) of 93 hierarchically clustered techniques: building an international consensus for the reporting of behavior change interventions. *Annals of behavioral medicine* 46, 1: 81–95. http://dx.doi.org/10.1007/s12160-013-9486-6
26. Sean A. Munson and Sunny Consolvo. 2012. Exploring goal-setting, rewards, self-monitoring, and sharing to motivate physical activity. *Pervasive Computing Technologies for Healthcare (PervasiveHealth), 2012 6th International Conference on*, IEEE, 25–32. http://dx.doi.org/10.4108/icst.pervasivehealth.2012.248691
27. Jeni Paay, Jesper Kjeldskov, Mikael B. Skov, Nirojan Srikandarajah, and Umachanger Brinthaparan. 2015. Personal Counseling on Smart Phones For Smoking Cessation. *Proceedings of the 33rd Annual ACM Conference Extended Abstracts on Human Factors in Computing Systems*, ACM, 1427–1432. http://dx.doi.org/10.1145/2702613.2732847
28. James O. Prochaska and Wayne F. Velicer. 1997. The transtheoretical model of health behavior change. *American journal of health promotion* 12, 1: 38–48. http://dx.doi.org/10.4278/0890-1171-12.1.38
29. Manya Sleeper, Alessandro Acquisti, Lorrie Faith Cranor, Patrick Gage Kelley, Sean A. Munson, and Norman Sadeh. 2015. I Would Like To..., I Shouldn't..., I Wish I...: Exploring Behavior-Change Goals for Social Networking Sites. *Proceedings of the 18th ACM Conference on Computer Supported Cooperative Work & Social Computing*, ACM, 1058–1069. http://dx.doi.org/10.1145/2675133.2675193
30. Tammy Toscos, Sunny Consolvo, and David W. McDonald. 2011. Barriers to physical activity: A study of self-revelation in an online community. *Journal of medical systems* 35, 5: 1225–1242. http://dx.doi.org/10.1007/s10916-011-9721-2
31. Greg Walsh and Jennifer Golbeck. 2014. Stepcity: a preliminary investigation of a personal informatics-based social game on behavior change. *CHI'14 Extended Abstracts on Human Factors in Computing Systems*, ACM, 2371–2376. http://dx.doi.org/10.1145/2559206.2581326
32. Weight Watchers message board. "Cheat days??" http://www.weightwatchers.com/community/mbd/post.aspx?page_size=25&rownum=15&threadpage_no=1&thread_id=169887989&board_id=1&forum_id=1 (Accessed September 18, 2015).
33. Jacob O. Wobbrock, Leah Findlater, Darren Gergle, and James J. Higgins. 2011. The aligned rank transform for nonparametric factorial analyses using only anova procedures. In *Proceedings of the SIGCHI Conference on Human Factors in Computing Systems*, 143-146. http://dx.doi.org/10.1145/1978942.1978963
34. Rayoung Yang, Eunice Shin, Mark W. Newman, and Mark S. Ackerman. 2015. When fitness trackers don't'fit': end-user difficulties in the assessment of personal tracking device accuracy. *Proceedings of the 2015 ACM International Joint Conference on Pervasive and Ubiquitous Computing*, ACM, 623–634. http://dx.doi.org/10.1145/2750858.2804269

Designing for Future Behaviors: Understanding the Effect of Temporal Distance on Planned Behaviors

Minhyang (Mia) Suh, Gary Hsieh
Human Centered Design & Engineering,
University of Washington,
Seattle, WA, 98195, USA
{miasuh, garyhs}@uw.edu

ABSTRACT
Despite the prevalence of theories and interventions related to behavior change, our knowledge on how intention for a target, or planned behavior, changes over time remains limited. This hinders our ability to consider the temporal aspect in our designs to support behavior change. To understand the effect of temporal distances on planned behaviors, we conducted two studies, building on the Theory of Planned Behavior and Constual Level Theory. We found that attitude about the target is more salient the further away the event, as people focus on the *why* of a behavior. On the other hand, perceived behavior control can influence intention in both near and far future. When the target is in the near future, people generally focus on the feasibility, or the *how* of the behavior. In the far future, people may also consider factors related to behavior control, if they are motivated to do so (i.e., hold a strong attitude towards the action). Findings help advance the Theory of Planned Behavior and offer strategies for designers and event organizers to motivate planned behaviors that are in the near and far future.

Author Keywords
behavior change; Theory of Planned Behavior; temporal distance; time perspective; future behaviors

INTRODUCTION
Persuasive technologies, or "interactive computing systems designed to change people's attitudes or behaviors [18]", continue to be significant area of research in HCI [23]. It could include motivating more physical activity for health [47], improving users' engagement and motivation for games [38], or encouraging users to contribute more to online communities [28,42]. To design effective persuasive technologies, many designs draw upon theories on behavior change to understand what factors influence people's behavior change decisions [16,22,30,39]. One of the most well-known and used is the Theory of Planned Behavior (TPB)[2]. TPB posits that behavior intention is the immediate antecedent to behaviors, and that intention is guided by three components: attitude, subjective norm, and perceived behavioral control [4]. TPB suggests that interventions should target those behavioral, normative, and/or control beliefs to produce positive intentions, and therefore to change behaviors [4]. For examples, in application, behavioral belief has been used to increase physical activity [10], normative belief to reduce HIV sexual risk behaviors [25] and control belief to motivate to quit smoking [6].

CHI'16, May 07-12, 2016, San Jose, CA, USA
 ISBN 978-1-4503-3362-7/16/05...$15.00
DOI: http://dx.doi.org/10.1145/2858036.2858591

However, many of the target behaviors that designers need to encourage are not immediate, but rather in the future. For example, designers build a notification system that encourages users to change food-logging behavior everyday [7], or to start online courses one month after their registeration [44]. But even though someone says they will perform a planned behavior in the future, they will not necessarily do so. People's intentions change with time—we can all recount times when we said we would do something, but decided against it when the time came. Despite the wealth of studies and applications, TPB has not been extended to factor in temporal distances. In fact, meta-analyses of TPB have shown that the predictive power of the theory is significantly reduced when used to model far future behaviors [12,35]. This greatly limitis our ability to support behavior change targets that are in the future.

One obvious explanation for why using TPB to predict future behaviors breaks down is that the temporal distance lowers our ability to accurately judge the future. We may have a fairly good sense of where we are, what we are doing, what we like, who our friends are, and what our environment will be like one hour from now, but we become much more uncertain as we are asked to make those assessments further into the future. As the temporal distance increases, there is a greater chance that unforeseeable events will take place, thus changing our intentions to perform a behavior. This would, unfortunately, imply that the change in intention is random, which would be hard for designers to account for as there are no strategies that they may reliably use.

However, existing research has shown that at least part of the change in intention is systematic. For example, research on the planning fallacy has shown that people generally tend to overcommit to events in the future [8]. Research on temporal discounting also shows how different biases affect our estimation of events or outcomes in different temporal distances, and demonstrates that we tend to overvalue immediate outcomes [19]. More recent research on Construal Level Theory (CLT) [54] integrating both these sets of prior work, states that temporal distance systematically changes people's mental representations of the future, and therefore affects their perceptions of future behaviors. CLT posits that people tend to think about behaviors in the far future more abstractly (using high level construals), while they think about behaviors in the near more concretely (using low level construals) [52].

In a behavior change context, this would mean that when the target behavior is far away, people are more focused on the *why* of an action (high level construals). But as the time approaches, people start focusing more on the *how* of an action (low level construals). The change in salience of these factors suggest that we can and should offer different designs to more effectively nudge behaviors, depending on the temporal distance. But to provide more concrete design guidelines, what is critically missing is a better understanding of how these concepts fit into the common strategies as afforded by TPB. Is attitude about the target more salient in the far future as it is more related to the why? Is perceived behavior control more salient in the near future, as it is more related to the how? How should we change our interventions as the temporal distance changes?

To study the role of temporal distance in planned behaviors, we conducted two studies. In Study 1, we conducted a within-subjects field experiment with 30 participants to examine how intention to attend a free yoga class changes over the period of a month. We found that, supporting prior work [8,12,36,45], people's intention to perform a behavior lowers as the temporal distance decreases. At the same time, advancing prior work, we also found that attitude towards an event is more salient in the far future than in the near future. But contrary to what we had hypothesized, we found that thinking about perceived behavior control is not just limited to when the event is near. In the distal, people may also consider it if they are sufficiently motivated (have a strong attitude towards the target behavior). To replicate our findings, we conducted an additional between-subject study with 423 Amazon Mechanical Turk workers. Results from Study 2 support findings from Study 1.

This work offers multiple contributions. On a theoretical level, it expands our understanding of how temporal distance affects our judgments of attitude and perceived behavior control. It further helps establish links between the Theory of Planned Behavior and Construal Level Theory, and suggests opportunities to use the TPB factors to assess future behaviors. From a practical perspective, the work provides designer and event organizers with insights and strategies to influence near and far future behaviors .

THEORY OF PLANNED BEHAVIOR

Theory of Planned Behavior (TPB) is one of the most predictive persuasion theories [3,5,21], and has been used in various interventions to encourage behavior change [10,26,48,50]. For example, Chatzisarantis & Hagger [10] promoted physical activity participation by providing persuasive messages targeting behavioral beliefs in TPB. Stead et al. [48] changed people's intention to reduce speeding on roads with a 3-year mass media campaign that was explicitely shaped by TPB's main principles.

In terms of technology design, TPB also provides a framework for various persuasive systems. Thieme et al. [50] used TPB to build a BinCam, a social persuasive system that helps users identify barriers in their personal abilities, learn about recycling properties, and improve their planning and sharing of food. BinCam motivated reflection and behavioral change in the food waste and recycling habits of young adults. Kharrazi et al. [26] also developed a computer game to help adolescents cope with the consequences of Type1 Diabetes. They used TPB to understand patients' situations and generate tailored game strategies (e.g., knowledge-based strategies, virtual mentors) and found that those strategies increased patients' rates of compliance and adherence to their treatments [26,27].

TPB proposes that behavior can best be predicted from a person's behavioral intention [3]. Behavioral intention (BI) is an indicator of how hard people are willing to try and how much effort they plan to exert toward performing a behavior [37]. The theory also posits that intention is a function of three variables (Figure 1): Attitude (AT: the degree to which a person has a favorable or unfavorable evaluation or appraisal of the behavior in question), Subjective Norms (SN: the perceived social pressure to perform or not to perform the behavior.), and Perceived Behavioral Control (PBC: the perceived ease or difficulty of performing the behavior)[3]. As a general rule, the more favorable the attitude and subjective norm, and the greater the perceived control, the stronger the person's intention to perform a behavior should be [13]. Therefore, the greater the individual's intention, the more likely he or she will be to perform a behavior [13]. Meta-analytic reviews of the TPB research provide strong support for the predictive power of the TPB variables; these factors explain on

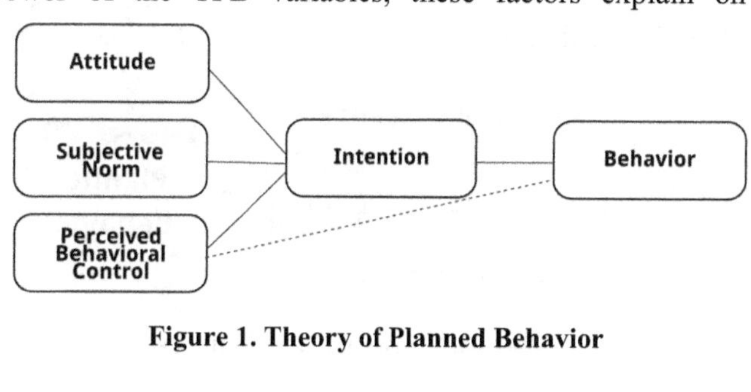

Figure 1. Theory of Planned Behavior

average 40%-50% of the variance in intention, and 19%-38% of the variance in behavior [5,21,49]

Despite the strength of TPB factors in prediciting intentions and behaviors, researchers have raised doubts about the predictive power of the factors as time elapsed between the measurement of intention and the target behavior [49]. In their meta-analysis, Randall & Wolff [41] insisted that the strength of the intention-behavior relationship does not vary according to the time interval between the measurement of intention and behavior (r= -.06, n.s.). Sheeran and Orbell [46], however, argued that the data used by [41] were too sparse to draw this conclusion, and that time interval and behavior type were confounded in their analysis. Instead, they stated that if time interval between the measurement of intention and the target behavior gets larger, the predictive power of intention is attenuated.

While the inconsistent perspective on temporal effect in TPB is problematic for us to use the theory in practice, the general procedure of TPB studies, measuring intention prior to the behavior (1 week, 1 month or 6 months), makes it accerbrated. If intention measured 1 month prior to an event does not actually predict the intention and actual attendance, then is there really a reason to collect that information? The lack of understanding of temporal effect in TPB undermines our ability to utilize the theory to develop strategies and designs to support behaviors. What are the effects of time perspectives on planned behaviors?

TIME PERSPECTIVE & CONSTRUAL LEVEL THEORY

More recent research on Construal Level Theory (CLT) [53] offers an explaination for how factors within TPB may vary as temporal distance to the target behavior changes. CLT states that an individual's temporal distance from a planned behavior is associated with how abstractly he or she will think about the behavior (Figure 2). The mental representation (construal) has different levels (high/low), and the levels of construals affect what information is brought to mind and what is more preferable to the individual [31,51]. Higher-level construal is abstract and more related to the core aspect of a behavior, corresponding to "why" questions. On the other hand, lower-level construal is concrete and more associated with the subordinate aspects of a behavior, corresponding to "how" questions [53]. For example, when planning a behavior (e.g., deciding whether to attend a guest lecture) in the far future, higher-level construal is activated, and thus one tends to focus on the reasons to perform the behavior (e.g., "how interesting the lecture is"). On the other hand, when planning a behavior in the near future, lower-level construal is activated, and one tends to focus on the means to perform the behavior (e.g., "how convenient the time of the lecture is")[31,32,52].

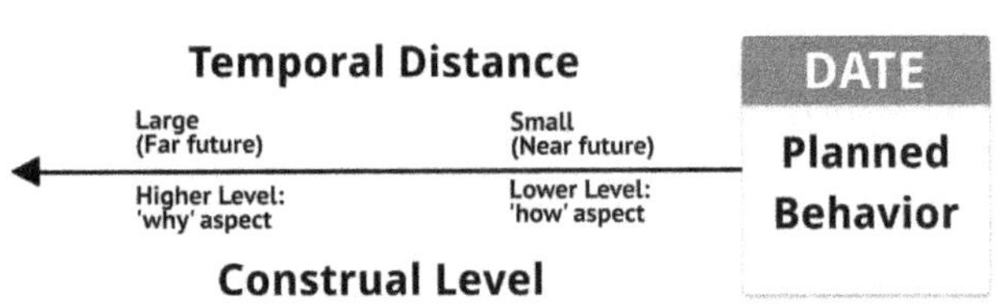

Figure 2. Construal Level Theory

The construal levels, instigated by temporal distances, have been used to explain the actions people prefer as time changes [51]. When thinking about the distant future, people prefer highly desirable behavior as they focus more on the goal of the behavior and less on how to achieve it. On the other hand, when thinking about the near future, people prefer more feasible behaviors even though it might be less desirable because they concern themselves more with the means to reach the goal [32]. Trope & Liberman attribute this tendency to two main reasons [52]. First, people are less likely to have low-level contextual information (e.g., time or places) for behaviors in the further future. Second, people are often not motivated to consider specific, "how" aspects of the situation in which a behavior is to be performed until they get closer in time to that situation. Thus CLT can explain why and how people's intention changes as temporal distance to target behavior decreases. When further away (temporally), desirability (the valence of an action's result) may be driving intention and when closer, feasibility (the ease or difficulty of reaching the result) may be driving intention [53].

Applying CLT into TPB, attitude (AT) may be closely associated with desirability, and perceived behavior control (PBC) with feasibility. Rosenberg [43] has stated that attitude is accociated to important values of the behavior, and is linked to positive versus negative outcomes. Morris considered perceived importance and/or desirability of objects as a cognitive elements of attitude [24]. Furthermore, feasibility is often operationalized and measured as self-efficacy [14,17], which is one of the main components of PBC.

Recent study by Lutchyn & Yzer noted the possible relationship between TPB and CLT [33]. They posit that AT (behavioral) and SN (normative belief) are linked to desirability, and PBC (control belief) is linked to feasibility. They examined how temporal perspectives affect types of salient beliefs. They asked participants to generate thoughts about behaviors (eating fruits and vegetables, condom usage) within various time frames. They found that individuals have more beliefs related to feasibility of the behavior in the near future, but more thoughts related to desirability of the behavior in the distal future [33].

However, the study is limited in several ways. First it does not quite connect the TPB constructs of AT and PBC with the time-dependent beliefs that people generate about the behavior. There is no evidence that AT is considered more in the far future, and PBC in the near future. Further, they were not able to examine what drives intention at different time frames.

Therefore, to build on this idea of connecting TPB with CLT, we conducted two studies to explore how different temporal distances affect peoples' intention to perform behaviors, using TPB factors. First, to replicate results from [33] using TPB concepts, we examine how temporal distance is associated with the amount of a certain type of thoughts. Specifically, we expected people to have more thoughts related to AT (desirability) in the further future, but more thoughts related to PBC (feasibility) in the near future. The hypotheses are:

H1: People will produce more attitude beliefs when considering behaviors in far future than when considering behaviors in the near future.

H2: People will produce more perceived behavior control beliefs when considering behaviors in near future than when considering behaviors in the far future.

Using TPB measures of AT and PBC, we also expect those factors to affect behavior intention differently at different time frames. When making decisions about behavior intention, AT is more salient in the near future, while PBC is more salient in the far future. Our hypotheses are:

H3: AT is a stronger predictor of behavior intention in the far future than in the near future.

H4: PBC is a stronger predictor of behavior intention in the near future than in the far future.

These systematic changes would also help explain why people's general behavioral intention decreases when the date to perform a planned behavior comes. Relating to existing research on the planning fallacy [8], the focus on desirability (while ignoring the various constraints, or the how) in the far future would make people more optimistic [36] and more confident [45] about performing the behavior in the far future. This leads to an over-estimation of intention. But then as the time of enactment closes, the focus on the constraints and costs of participation lowers intention. Thus, we hypothesize:

H5: As temporal distance to a planned behavior decreases, intention to perform the behavior lowers.

STUDY 1

For Study 1, we invited participants to attend a free drop-in yoga class that we had set up for the experiment. Prior to the event, participants were surveyed twice to report their perceptions towards the event, and report on their intentions to attend. The first survey was a month before the yoga class (*far future*), and the second one was a few days before the class (*near future*). We studied how the passage of time affected perceptions of the event.

Participants

Participants were recruited through fliers on public bulletin boards, departmental group mailing lists and the researchers' social networks. Participation was restricted to students at a large University in the Pacific Northwest. This was to ensure that they had access to the university sports complex, where the yoga class was offered. Once participants expressed interest in participating in the study, they received a link to a survey and information about the free drop-in yoga class. They were paid $5 for completing each survey. 45 participants signed up for the study. 38 completed the first survey and out of those, 30 completed the second survey. Responses from the 30 participants who completed both surveys was used for our analysis. 80% of our participants were female (n=24), and participants' mean age was 24.87 (SD=6.85).

Measurements

As a within-subject study, both questionnaires in the far and near future conditions were the same. The survey included three subsets: 1) a open-ended question, "why or why not are you willing to attend the yoga class?" 2) TPB measurements and 3) demographic questions.

TPB measurements included *Behavioral Intention (BI), Attitude, Subjective Norms (SN), and Perceived Behavioral Control (PBC),* all based on [4]. BI was measured with 2 items: 1) I intend to participate in the yoga class; 2) I plan to participate in the yoga class. AT was measured with the following 4 items: For me, participating in the yoga class would be...1) bad-good; 2) useless-useful; 3) unpleasant-pleasant; 4) unenjoyable-enjoyable. SN was measured with 4 items: 1) People who are important to me would approve of my participating in the yoga class; 2) Most people who are close to me would think it is a good idea for me to attend the yoga class; 3) People close to me may think I should participate in the yoga class if they know about it; 4) People I care about would encourage me to attend yoga class. PBC was measured with 4 items: 1) I think I have personal control over participating in the yoga class; 2) It is up to me whether I attend the yoga class or not; 3) If I want, I could easily attend the yoga class; 4) I am confident I could attend the yoga class, if I wanted to. The reliability scale showed our measurments are reliable (Cronbach's α= .95(BI), .93(AT), .92(SN) and .63(PBC); generally if Cronbach's α is larger than .60, the measurement is regarded as internally consistent.)

Analyses & Results

We present our analyses and results. In sum, of our hypotheses, **H1, H2, H5** were supported, not **H3**, nor **H4**.

Thoughts About the Target at Different Time Frames

To test our hypotheses that different temporal distances affect the type of thoughts about the behavior (**H1** and **H2**), we counted the number of thoughts that are related to each TPB construct per person, and examined the difference between the far and near future.

To do so, first, the two researchers separately coded the open-ended responses following the definitions of TPB as coding scheme:

- AT: The degree to which a person has a favorable or unfavorable evaluation or appraisal of the behavior in question (e.g., *"I love yoga for strengthening and stretching my muscles!")*
- PBC: The perceived ease or difficulty ofperforming the behavior (e.g., *"It's free and on campus."*)

Then, they compared what they coded (the agreement rate was 87%), and resolved the discrepancies with a discussion. Once the qualitative coding was finalized, they were converted into quantitative data, using numerical values to statistically test the difference between the far and near future. Each thought was given a numeric value of "+1", and summed up as the total values of each category (AT, PBC). Following [33], each unique thought was considered as one unit. For example, the response "*Yoga is a good way to de-stress. It is challenging yet fun. It's a good form of physical activity.*", was regarded as "3" as the response contains three separate evaluations of performing the behavior: 2 of instrumental attitude (psychological and physical benefit) and 1 of affective attitude (fun). All were related to AT. So this participant had (AT: 3, PBC: 0).

The descriptive statistics show that in total 97 thoughs were generated (the far future: 53, the near future: 44). The average number of thoughts generated per person was 2 (the far future) and 1.53 (the near future). To compare the number of thoughts (AT, PBC) between the far and the near future (**H1**, **H2**), a paired t-test was conducted by comparing the mean number of thoughts per person in two time frames (Table 1). The results show that the mean of thoughts related to AT differs a month before the event (M=1.6, SD=1.00) and a few days before the event (M=.9, SD=1.06) at the .01 level of significance (t(29)=3.00, p<.01). PBC also differs a month before the event (M=.3, SD=.61) and a few days before the event (M=.6, SD=.50) at the .05 level of significance (t(29)=-2.07, p<.05). The results indicate that people have more thoughts related to AT in the far future, compared to the near future; and people have more thoughts related to PBC in the near future, compared to the far future. Both **H1** and **H2** were supported.

Thoughts related to	Far Future	Near Future	Far Future - Near Future (Difference)
Attitude	1.6	.9	.7 **
Perceived Behavioral Control	.3	.6	-.3 *

$*p < .05$, $**p < .01$, $***p < .001$

Table 1. The Number of Thoughts Related to TPB Variables per Person

Salience of TPB Constructs at Different Time Frames

We hypothesized that AT is a stronger predictor of behavior intention in the far future than in the near future (**H3**) while PBC is a stronger predictor of behavior intention in the near future than in the far future (**H4**). To do so we analyzed the prediction of intention at the two time frames separately using logistic regression. Since BI in 7-scales was not normally distributed (u-shaped); we dichotomized it into the lower (BI<4) and the higher (BI>=4) intentions. Independent variables were the TPB constructs (AT, SN, and PBC). Post Hoc, we built another logistic regression model (Model 2), adding the interaction term of AT and PBC into Model 1.

Logistic regression models were statistically significant for both time frames (the far future: $\chi^2(3)$= 13.52, p<.01; the near future: $\chi^2(3)$= 10.90, p<.05). TPB constructs explained 86.7% of intention (Nagelkerke R^2=.57) in the far future, and, they explained 73.3% of intention (Nagelkerke R^2=.42) in the near future (Model 1 in Table 2).

Examining the coefficients of AT and PBC suggests that **H3** was supported (Model 1 in Table 2). AT negatively predicts BI for the planned behavior in the far future (β=-1.37, odd ratio=.26, p=.08); but its statistical significance drops in the near future (β=.24, odd ratio=1.27, p=.66). It indicates that attitude strongly predicts intention to perform the behavior in the further future, but its predictive power gets much weaker in the near future.

On the other hand, **H4** was not supported. For the behavior in the far future, PBC predicts BI 3.01 times more than other constructs (AT, SN) in the far future (β=1.10, odd

	Model 1						**Model 2** (with an interaction term of AT and PBC)					
	Far Future			**Near Future**			**Far Future**			**Near Future**		
	B	*S.E.*	*Exp(B)*	*B*	*S.E.*	*Exp(B)*	*B*	*S.E.*	*Exp(B)*	*B*	*S.E.*	*Exp(B)*
AT	-1.37†	.77	.26	.24	.54	1.27	5.83	4.26	339.02	-3.10	2.25	.05
SN	1.84†	1.00	6.28	.98	.63	2.66	2.35	1.63	10.45	1.33	.82	3.77
PBC	1.10†	.60	3.01	**1.15***	.54	3.17	**11.55**†	6.62	10373.78	-2.52	2.42	.08
AT by PBC							**-1.61**†	.98	.20	.67	.46	1.96
Model χ^2	13.52 (df=3, p<.01)			10.90 (df=3, p<.05)			17.41 (df=4, p<.01)			13.00 (df=4, n.s.)		
Nagelkerke R^2	.57			.42			.70			.46		
Model Accuracy	86.7			73.3			93.3			70.0		

† $p<.1$, $*p < .05$., n.s.=not significant

Table 2. Logistic Regression Analyses on the BI (Attending a yoga class)

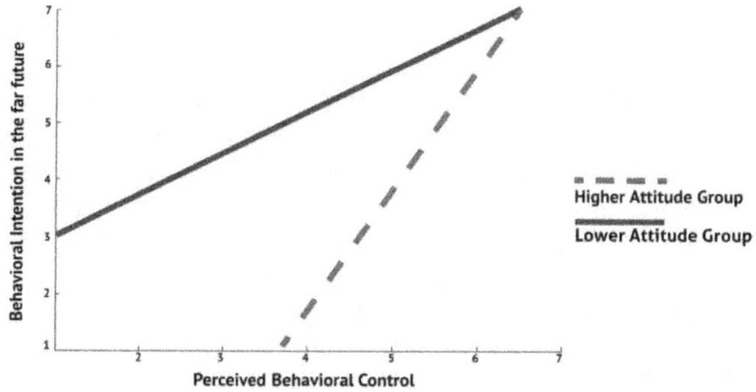

Figure 3. Interaction of AT and PBC in the Far Future

ratio=3.01, p=.07). However, it is not much different from PBC in the near future (β= 1.15, odd ratio=3.17, p<.05), indicating that PBC predicts BI 3.17 times more than other constructs (AT, SN) in the near future.

However, while **H3** seemed to be supported, one concern arose that AT negatively predicts an intention to perform the behavior in the far future, which is contrary to the body of prior work that suggests a positive relation between AT and intention. This led us to further explore the result of the qualitative study to understand what may have caused this. Connecting these ratings with the belief responses, we found that people who hold the most positive attitude towards participating in the yoga class (AT > 6) in the far future actually described more feasibility-related issues to perform the planned behavior. Further, they are also likely to give a low intention rating. For example, one participant (AT= 6.5, BI = 1) wrote: *"I have a meeting 3-5 on Friday. That sounds cool and otherwise I would like to do it though!"*. Another participant (AT = 7, BI = 1) wrote: *"I will be out of town on that date. I would love to attend a free class on a different date."*

Reading these results suggested that there may be a possible interaction between AT and PBC. Those with higher AT are perhaps more likely to factor in PBC in their assessment of BI. Thus, we tested a version of the model with the interaction terms included (Model 2 in Table 2). For the far future, there was a significant interaction effect between PBC and AT in (B=-1.61, odd ratio=.20, p=.10); the Omnibus Tests of Model Coefficients showed that including the interaction term improved the model ($\Delta\chi^2$ =3.9, p<.05). Graphing the relationships between PBC, AT and BI by grouping participants into higher AT (AT>6.00) and lower AT groups confirmed that indeed those with higher AT are more likely to factor in PBC in their judgement of BI (Figure 3). If their rated PBC is low, they are significantly less likely to say they will attend.

On the other hand, for the near future, including the interaction effect did not improve the model fit significantly ($\Delta\chi^2$= 2.11, p=.15).

Change in Intention Over Time

We hypothesized that people tend to have a higher intention to perform the behavior in the far future compared to near future (**H5**). Results of the paired-samples t-test show that the mean of willingness to attend the yoga class differs a month before the event (M=.80, SD=.41) and a few days before the event (M=.60, SD=.49) at the .01 level of significance (t=2.70, df=29, p<.01, 95% CI, for a mean difference .05 to .35, r=.62). We should point out that in the end, only 6 participants actually attended the yoga class (20%). This is a significant drop from 80% to 60% to 20%.

Discussion

In this study, we found that people's focus on their attitudes towards a future behavior decreases as temporal distance to the behavior decreases, while their focus on perceived behavior control increases. This change in salience of TPB factors affects their judgements on intention.

The effects on AT and PBC on behavior, however, is more nuanced than we had hypothesized. We had expected AT to have a stronger influence in the far future and PBC to have a stronger influence in the near future, as people transition from the why (high level construal) to the how (low level construal). However, what we found is that there is an interaction effect. In the near future, PBC is a significant predictor of intention as people focus on the how of behaviors. But in the far future, PBC may not be completely ignored and AT itself may not be the dominant factor. Those who hold higher positive attitudes toward the behavior seemed to also consider PBC in their judgements of intention.

This finding does not necessairily contradict CLT. As discussed earlier, Trope and Lieberman [52] explained that levels of CLT change due to people being less likely to have the motivation to be informed about the situational context of the far future. This also connects to research on dual process models [9,15,40], which suggests that there are

Attitude	Reasons
7	Time conflict.
7	I've never taken an actual yoga class. I'd love to experience it. I've heard great things about yoga.
7	Yoga is good exercise and relaxing.
7	I have work then.
7	I will not be a student on campus this spring.
6.8	I want to begin attending classes at the IMA
6.8	I am always trying to incorporate more yoga into my fitness routine because I find it to be an important and satisfying way to work out I usually just end up going for a run instead.
6.8	Get to experience a different teacher and potentially a different style of yoga

Table 3. Thoughts Generaged by People with the Highest Attitude Towards the Class a Month before the Event (Far Future)

two types of information processing: systematic (central) vs. heuristic (peripheral) process. The former is more detailed and elaborate, which is effortful, whereas the latter uses simple rules and heuristics and less deliberation.

Findings have shown that when a person is motivated to think about an object, he or she tends to process information more systematically and logically, to elaborate on the message, to estimate the missing details, and therefore to eventually predict the future more accurately [9,15,40]. Prior work explored the relationship between CLT and dual-processes [20], but it still remained unclear how they are associated to future behaviors.

Our findings suggest the highly motiaved people may process information systematically, and hence, consider all relevant information more thoroughly. In other words, people who hold stronger AT toward the behavior may be more intrinsically interested in the behavior—and are thus more motivated to consider the planned behavior carefully. While doing so, they consider the various outcomes of the behavior including both desirability and feasibility of the planned behavior. Thus an alternative hypothesis to our **H4** would be:

H6. In the far future, PBC would predict behavior intention more strongly for those who report high AT.

STUDY 2

To further replicate the interaction effect of AT and PBC on the BI, we conducted a second study, a between subject experiment. Using this opportunity, we also expanded on the generalizability of this work by studying three different behavioral contexts instead of one: eating five servings of fruits and vegetables (health), going camping (recreation), and donating to a thrift store (donation).

There are a couple of key differences between Study 1 and Study 2 that we should note. First, unlike Study 1 where participants were invited to and could attend a real yoga event, Study 2 asked about hypothetical future behaviors. This was to enable us to study a wide range of behavior which was harder for us to coordinate (e.g., eating fruits and vegatables). Also, we used a between subjects design to minize problems associated with participant dropout (In Study 1, 8 out of 38 participants dropped out in between two surveys of Study 1). We also tested three different time frames (tomorrow, a week from now, a month from now). Thus there were 9 conditions (3 behaviors x 3 time frames).

Participants

Participants were recruited from Mechanical Turk. They received \$1 for their participation. Workers were restricted to those residing in the US to ensure their basic English proficiency. 457 participants completed the questionnaire, titled "Survey about Intention to Perform an Action." Our manipulation check showed that 34 participants were unable to recall the time frame and behavior they were assigned; they were removed from our analyses. In total, we included the remaining 423 participants (233 male, 189 female, 1 other), who ranged in age from 19 to 68 years (M= 33.89 years, SD=10.9). The breakdown of participants per condition is shown in Table 4.

		Health	Donation	Camping
Far future (n=281)	A month from now	45	52	46
	A week from now	52	42	44
Near future (n=142)	Tomorrow	45	50	47

Table 4. The Number of Participants in each group

Measurements

The questionnaire used was similar to the one used in Study 1, but slightly modified for the different conditions of Study 2 (Appendix). Again, the questions have three subsets: 1) thoughts toward behavior performance in a certain time frame with an open-ended prompt, "Please generate any positive or negative thoughts of performing the given behavior"; 2) TPB questionnaires (BI, AT, SN, and PBC); and 3) demographic questions. All questionnaires were internally consistent (Cronbach's α: BI=.98, AT=.91, SN=.77, and PBC=.83).

Analyses & Results

We present the results of our analyses. Our hypotheses, **H1, H2, H5** and **H6** were supported.

Thoughts About the Target at Different Time Frames

Following the same coding scheme used in Study 1, two researchers coded the responses. Then, they compared the results (the agreement rate was 90%), and resolved the discrepancy with a discussion.

The descriptive statistics show that total 2517 thoughts were generated (far future: 1680, near future: 837). The average number of thoughts generated per person was 5.98 (far future) and 5.89 (near future).

Results of a one-way analysis of variance (Table 5) revealed that the mean of thoughts related to AT differs in the far future (M=4.4, SD=2.30) and in the near future (M=3.8, SD=2.20), and the difference between two time frames is statistically significant ($F(2,422)=3.411$, $p<.05$). PBC also differs in the far future (M=1.2, SD=1.33) and in the near future (M=1.7, SD=1.72), and the difference is statistically significant ($F(2,420)=6.51$, $p<.01$). The result is same as Study 1. Both **H1** and **H2** were supported.

Salience of TPB Constructs at Different Time Frames

Similar logistic regression models used in Study 1 were used here to study the effects of AT, SN and PBC on BI. Interaction between AT and PBC was included to test H6.

Thoughts related to	Far Future	Near Future	Far Future - Near Future (Difference)
Attitude	4.4	3.8	0.56**
Perceived Behavioral Control	1.2	1.7	-0.5***

*$p < .05$, **$p < .01$, ***$p < .001$.

Table 5. The Number of Thoughts Related to TPB Variables Per Person

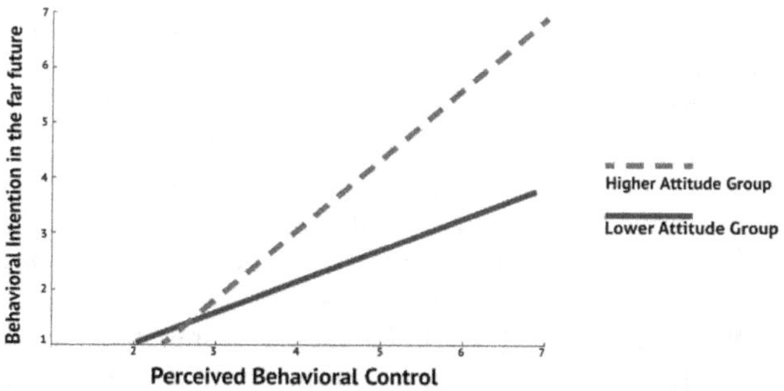

Figure 4. Interaction Effect of AT and PBC

As a control, we included the type of behavior: health, donation or recreation. While we had initially planned to compare the 3 time frames, we found that there was no significant difference between the groups of a week from now and a month from now in terms of intention (Tukey HSD test, mean difference = .054, p=.55). Thus we collapsed those cells together, and focused on the contrast between near future (tomorrow) and far future (a week to a month from now).

To test H6, we built two sets of logistic regression models: Model 1 is with TPB constructs, and Model 2 has an additional interaction term of AT and PBC in Model 1.

Comparing the two sets of models, we found that in the far future, including the interaction term resulted in a better fit (Omnibus Test of Model Coefficients: $\Delta\chi^2$=3.92, p<.05). On the other hand, including the interaction term did not improve the model in the near future (Omnibus Test of Model Coefficients: $\Delta\chi^2$= 1.25, p=.27). These results are similar to what we found in study 1. Thus, we focus our interpretations of finding using the model with the interaction (Model 2) for the far future, while using the model without the interaction (Model 1) for the near future (although they are presented in full in Table 6). In the far future, the factors explain 85.1% of intention to perform a behavior (Model 2: Nagelkerke R^2= .71) ; in the near future, the factors explain 88.7% of intention to perform a behavior (Model 1: Nagelkerke R^2= .62).

Supporting findings from study 1, again we found that PBC is a significant positive predictor in the near future (B=.62, odd ratio=1.86, p<.01) Also that the interaction term was significant in the far future, supporting **H6** (Figure 4 & Model 2 in Table 6). There was a significant interaction effect between PBC and AT in the far future (β=.27, odd ratio=1.31, p<.05), suggesting that PBC moderates the relation between AT and BI when a behavior is planned in the far future.

		Health(%)	Donation(%)	Camping(%)
Far future (n=81)	A month from now	38(84)	16(30)	5(11)
	A week from now	34(65)	9(21)	2(4)
Near future (n= 24)	Tomorrow	27(60)	4(8)	2(4)

Table 7. The Number of Participants in each group who are Willing to Perform Behaviors

We should note that the two interaction graphs are slightly different. For Study 1 (Figure 3), BI is similar for participants at higher PBC and differs at lower PBC, whereas in study 2 (Figure 4), BI is similar for participants at low PBC and differs at high PBC. This suggests that making PBC more salient may have differing effects for those with high attitude—sometimes thinking about the detals may reduce intention, other times improve intention. The specific differences we observed may have been due to the different target activities or participant sample.

Change in Intention Over Time

To test **H5**, we conducted a one-way analysis of variance to compare the difference in intention between time frames, and it was also supported like Study 1.

People report lower intention for behavior when temporal distance is smaller. In the near future, only 33 out of 118 participants (23.2%) intended to perform the behavior. On the other hand, when the behavior is planned in the further future, 104 out of 281 participants (37%) intended to perform the behavior (see details in Table 7). A one-way analysis of variance revealed that the differences are statistically significant (F(1,421) = 8.30, p <.01).

	Model 1						**Model 2** (with an interaction term of AT and PBC)					
	Far future			**Near future**			**Far future**			**Near future**		
	B	*S.E.*	*Exp (B)*	*B*	*S.E.*	*Exp (B)*	*B*	*S.E.*	*Exp (B)*	*B*	*S.E.*	*Exp (B)*
AT	.36*	.17	1.44	.12	.28	1.12	-.92	.70	.40	-.53	.62	.59
SN	1.00***	.22	2.70	.73**	.28	2.07	.89***	.23	2.43	.65*	.29	1.92
PBC	.71***	.18	2.04	.62**	.24	1.86	-.76	.78	.47	-.29	.84	.75
Behavior (Health)	***			***			***			***		
Behavior (Donation)	2.21***	.60	9.12	2.47**	.91	11.81	2.28***	.62	9.75	2.49*	.93	12.04
Behavior (Camping)	.60	.59	1.81	-.60	1.01	.55	.64	.60	1.90	-.52	1.03	.60
AT by PBC							.27*	.14	1.31	.16	.14	1.17
Model χ^2	201.24 (df= 5, p<.001)			75.64 (df= 5, p<.001)			205.16 (df=6, p<.05)			76.89 (df= 6, n.s.)		
Nagelkerke R^2	.70			.62			.71			.63		
Model Accuracy	85.1			88.7			86.1			89.4		

**p* < .05, ***p* < .01, ****p* < .001., n.s.=not significant

Table 6. The Logistic Regression on Intention to Perform a Behavior

DISCUSSION

In this paper, we sought to explore a simple, yet extremely important question: whether and how do the factors that influence behavior intention change as the temporal distance from the planned behavior changes. We found that the salience of different factors that influence intention (i.e., AT, PBC) changes, depending on time. As shown by the belief responses collected in both studies, the salience of the Attitude (AT) towards the behavior decreases as temporal distance decreases (**H1**). At the same time, the focus on the Perceived Behavior Control (PBC) increases as temporal distance increases (**H2**).

But our results are more nuanced than simply AT is dominant in the distal and PBC in the proximal. In both studies, our results indicate an interaction effect between these two factors (**H6**). This interaction effect suggests that in the near future, PBC is a significant predictor of intention, as people focus on the feasibility of the event. But that in the far future, PBC may still be an important predictor of intention, especially for those who hold higher AT towards the planned behavior.

These results offer several contributions to theory. First, they extend the Theory of Planned Behavior (TPB)[2]—one of the most often cited and used behavior change theories—by incorporating the temporal perspective. Many researchers have noted the limitations of TPB when it is used to understand behavior intentions that are not in the proximal [12]. Others have also noted that incorporating time into TPB is a critical and open challenge [11]. Using CLT, we were able to link the different factors that influence intention as proposed by TPB, with the high and low level construals as used in CLT. Specifically, we showed the potential connection between AT component of PBC with high level construals, used to reperesent distal events, and PBC component of TPB with low level contruals, used to represent proximal events. AT is more about the why, or the desirability of an event, while PBC is more about the how, or the feasibility of an event. Incorporating concepts from CLT into TPB, we believe, enables us to better understand how the proposed factors influence future behavioral intention.

In addition, the interaction effect we found also provides important insights about the relationship between TPB, CLT, and dual-process models [9,15,40] that need further exploration. Ajzen posits that AT, SN, and PBC are conceptually separate [2], and lots of prior works have examined the different predictive power of each construct [5,13]. However, others have suggested that some of the factors may interact with each other to influence behavior [13]. Our research suggests that what information people use to base their judgements on is both influenced by time (CLT) and by motivation to process, as suggested by dual-process theories. According to dual theories, when a person is motivated and also has the ability, one uses the central path to process the information, elaborate on the content, estimate the missing details, and eventually predict more accurately. Conversely, when the motivation or ability to think about the information is missing, one uses the peripheral path to process the content heuristically. People's attitude towards a behavior can make them more motivated about the target and use the central route of processing [29]. Thus, in the distal, those who hold strong attitudes may not just consider desirability, but also take the additional step to think about feasibility (PBC). To use an example: imagine if you were asked to participate in an event in the future. You are probably more likely to take out your calendar and check if the event has a conflict (PBC) if you care about the event (high AT). If you do not care about the event (low AT), you will not take the effort to find and process the additional information related to the how. These relationships are important consider. If we do not include this type of interaction effect in our models, it may even be possible to erroneously conclude that AT has a negative influence on behavior, as we had found in Study 1.

While not part of our hypothesis, we do also want to make a note about the subjective norm (SN) component of TPB. Unlike the other factors, subjective norm appears to be a stable predictor of the intentions regardless of temporal distance. This is different from the hypothesis in [33], which argues that SN is closer to desirability and thus should be influenced temporally like AT. We hypothesize, based on our findings, that SN may be both related to desirability and feasibility. Our qualitative analysess provide some supporting evidence. For example, when considering eating five servings of fruits and vegetables tomorrow, one respondent mentioned, *"I could easily be a vegetarian but my husband prefers all meat."* In this case, the normative pressure may be more about PBC (hard to do it). Future research should explore this hypothesis as the influence of SN on intention may also be time-dependent in more subtle ways.

Designing for Temporal Changes of Planned Behavior

From a practical perspective, our results also hold important implications for designing interventions to support behavior change. As highlighted in our findings, people's intention to perform a target behavior decreases as the date to perform the behavior approaches. We found a 15-20% decrease in intention when the target is a few weeks away compared to a few days away. A lot of existing research has talked about nudging and encouraging behavior change, but have ignored the issue of time. The same strategy that works to encourage immediate participation may not be as effective in helping encourage people to make their initial commitments (e.g., RSVP). How might we better design to support behavior change goals at different time frames? Here we outline some strategies.

Goal #1: To Encourage Proximal Participation or Stick to Plans

If one aims to encourage people to participate in a proximal behavior, or stick to their plans in the near-term, our findings suggest that designs need to be salient and support the belief of feasibility of the behavior. This includes reducing the cost of participation (e.g., providing transporation to the event), and also highlighting the ease of doing it (e.g., "you just need to show up!"). To get people to stick to behaviors for something they have already committed to, scheduling systems (e.g., virtual assistant services, calendar systems) or event organizing systems (e.g., RSVP, e-invitation) can also provide tailored notifications, based on temporal distance from planned behaviors. When the planned date gets closer, notifications could offer more information that support the how of performaing the behavior (e.g., showing videos of others performing the tasks, discuss other related performance accomplishments), to help improve users' self-efficacy.

Goal #2: To Get Widespread Attention from People

When marketing a new event, or when promoting campaigns, or when introducing new functions in the system, designers and event organizers may need to gain early and widespread attention from people. Our findings suggest that in these secnearios, one should focus on increasing positive attitudes toward events or activities. One way to encourage people to have positive attitude toward activities is to present the multiple reasons why they should perform the behaviors, focusing on instrumental (e.g., how important or useful the behavior could be) and affective anticipations (e.g., how pleasant or fun the behavior could be) that they may have. For example, if an organizer aims to publicize volunteering events a month in advance, the advertisement should focus on the fun aspects of the event. The high RSVP count and social media shares can then help generate buzz towards an event. Further, research on public commitments has also shown getting people to make those commitments can strengthen behavioral compliance [1].

Due to the potential interaction between AT and PBC, if the target behavior is hard to perform (i.e., low behavior control), the designers or organizers may want to reserve the above strategy to those who are not already vested or motivated to attend (e.g, not on the members' mailing-list or the secondary target market). This might help prevent the set of people who already hold a strong positive attitude towards the target from thinking even more deeply about it and then deciding not to participate right away due to feasibility conccerns, undermining the goal of garnering widespread attention.

Goal #3: To Improve RSVP Accuracy

One of the drawback from the above scenario, is that while that strategy may work to get more people to care and sign up early, there may still be a problem of a high dropout rate due to the decrease in intention over time. There are scenarios where designers and organizers may not care how many people sign up initially, but want a better assessment of how many people will actually attend. Not showing up to an event may disappoint others who would expect him/her to do so (e.g., family), and hamper the best utilization of staff and resources (e.g., over/understaffing)[34].

Based on our findings, what one could do is to motivate people to consider feasibility when making their intention judgements. One strategy to increase processing motivation, as we have discussed, is to encourage positive attitude towards the event. But another way to encourage more detailed considerations, is by providing people the "ability" to participate. For example, when designing the RSVP, designer could include and highlight additional information related to the how of the event, such as actual distance (projected time to travel) to an event, weather forcast, and other costs. The RSVP can also point out potentially conflicting events. Encouraging people to think more and spend more time on the decision, may also enable them to make more accuracte assesssments of the future behaviors.

LIMITATION

Different limitations for the two sets of study results due to the different study designs. In Study 1, as a field study, we focused on one behavior, attending the yoga class. The within-subjects nature of the study also made it hard for us to account for potential confounds that may occur from the dropouts. To address these issues, we replicated the findings in study 2 with additional hypothetical behaviors and using a between-subjects design. However, this came at the tradeoff of reducing the realism of the study. While results from both studies, using these different approaches, supported each other, more research is needed to replicate and build on our findings.

CONCLUSION

In this paper, we studied the role of temporal distance in planned behaviors through two experiments. In Study 1, we conducted a within-subjects field study with 30 participants to examine how intention to attend a free yoga class changes over a month. We found that, supporting prior work, people's intention to perform a behavior lowers as the temporal distance decreases. People also think more about attitude (relating to the why) in the far future than in the near future. But contrary to what we had hypothesized, we found that thinking about perceived behavior control is not just limited to when the event is near. In the distal, people may also consider it if they are sufficiently motivated (strong attitude towards the target). To replicate our findings, we conducted an additional between-subject study with 423 Amazon Mechanical Turk workers. Results from study 2 support the findings from study 1. Findings help extend Theory of Planned Behavior with the temporal dimension, particularly focusing on the interaction effect of each TPB construct. We also conclude with three design strategies for interventions depending on behavior change goals and temporal distance from the target behavior.

ACKNOWLEDGMENTS

We thank Tom Wilson both for his valuable comments and efforts on the qualitative analyses of this work. This work was in part supported by National Science Foundation grant #1348543.

REFERENCES

1. Wokje Abrahamse, Linda Steg, Charles Vlek, and Talib Rothengatter. 2005. A review of intervention studies aimed at household energy conservation. *Journal of Environmental Psychology* 25, 3, 273–291. http://doi.org/10.1016/j.jenvp.2005.08.002
2. Icek Ajzen. 1985. *From intentions to actions: A theory of planned behavior.* Springer.
3. Icek Ajzen. 1991. The theory of planned behavior. *Organizational behavior and Human Decision Processes* 50, 2, 179–211. http://doi.org/10.1016/0749-5978(91)90020-T
4. Icek Ajzen. 2011. The theory of planned behaviour: Reactions and reflections. *Psychology & Health* 26, 9, 1113–1127. http://doi.org/10.1080/08870446.2011.613995
5. Christopher J Armitage and Mark Conner. 2001. Efficacy of the Theory of Planned Behaviour: a meta-analytic review. *The British Journal of Social Psychology* 40, 4, 471–499. http://doi.org/10.1348/014466601164939
6. Sandra K Barta and Richard D Stacy. 2005. The effects of a theory-based training program on nurses' self-efficacy and behavior for smoking cessation counseling. *The Journal of Continuing Education in Nursing* 36, 3, 117.
7. Frank Bentley and Konrad Tollmar. 2013. The power of mobile notifications to increase wellbeing logging behavior. In *Proceedings of the SIGCHI Conference on Human Factors in Computing Systems* (CHI'13), 1095. http://doi.org/10.1145/2470654.2466140
8. Roger Buehler, Dale Griffin, and Michael Ross. 1994. Exploring the "planning fallacy": Why people underestimate their task completion times. *Journal of Personality and Social Psychology* 67, 3, 366–381. http://doi.org/10.1037/0022-3514.67.3.366
9. Shelly Chaiken. 1980. Heuristic versus systematic information processing and the use of source versus message cues in persuasion. *Journal of Personality and Social Psychology* 39, 5, 752. http://dx.doi.org/10.1037/0022-3514.39.5.752
10. Nikos L D Chatzisarantis and Martin S Hagger. 2005. Effects of a brief intervention based on the Theory of Planned Behavior on leisure-time physical activity participation. *Journal of Sports & Exercise Psychology* 27, 470–487.
11. Anna Collins and Barbara Mullan. 2011. An extension of the theory of planned behavior to predict immediate hedonic behaviors and distal benefit behaviors. *Food Quality and Preference* 22, 7, 638–646. http://doi.org/10.1016/j.foodqual.2011.03.011
12. Mark Conner, Paschal Sheeran, Paul Norman, and Christopher J Armitage. 2000. Temporal stability as a moderator of relationships in the Theory of Planned Behaviour. *The British Journal of Social Psychology* 39, 4, 469–493. http://doi.org/http://dx.doi.org/10.1348/014466600164598
13. Mark Conner and Christopher J Armitage. 1998. Extending the Theory of Planned Behavior: A Review and Avenues for Further Research. *Journal of Applied Social Psychology* 28, 15, 1429–1464. http://doi.org/10.1111/j.1559-1816.1998.tb01685.x
14. Dmnsw Dissanayake. 2014. The Impact of Perceived Desirability and Perceived Feasibility on Entrepreneurial Intention among Undergraduate Students in Sri Lanka: An Extended Model. *Kelaniya Journal of Management* 2, 1, 39–57. http://doi.org/10.4038/kjm.v2i1.6543
15. Russell H Fazio and Tamara Towles-Schwen. 1999. The MODE model of attitude-behavior processes. In *Dual Process Theories in Social Psychology,* Shelly Chaiken, Yaacov Trope (eds.), 97–116.
16. Martin Fishbein, Harry C Triandis, Frederick H Kanfer, Marshall Becker, and Susan E Middlestadt. 2001. Factors influencing behavior and behavior change.
17. Jason R. Fitzsimmons and Evan J. Douglas. 2011. Interaction between feasibility and desirability in the formation of entrepreneurial intentions. *Journal of Business Venturing* 26, 4, 431–440. http://doi.org/10.1016/j.jbusvent.2010.01.001
18. B J Fogg. 2002. *Persuasive Technology: Using Computers to Change What We Think and Do (Interactive Technologies).* Morgan Kaufmann Publishers.
19. Shane Frederick, George Loewenstein, and Ted O'donoghue. 2002. Time discounting and time preference: A critical review. *Journal of Economic Literature* 351–401. http://doi.org/10.1257/002205102320161311
20. Kentaro Fujita. 2008. Seeing the forest beyond the trees: A construal□level approach to self□control. *Social and Personality Psychology Compass* 2, 3, 1475–1496. http://doi.org/ 10.1111/j.1751-9004.2008.00118.x
21. Gaston Godin and Gerjo Kok. 1996. The Theory of Planned Behavior: A Review of Its Applications to Health-related Behaviors. *American Journal of Health Promotion* 11, 2, 87–98. http://doi.org/10.4278/0890-1171-11.2.87
22. Harper, F. Maxwell, Sherry Xin Li, Yan Chen, and Joseph A. Konstan. 2007. Social Comparisons to Motivate Contributions to an Online Community. In *Persuasive Technology,* Yvonne de Kort, Wijnand

IJsselsteijn, Cees Midden, Berry Eggen, and B. J. Fogg (eds.). Springer Berlin Heidelberg, 148-159.

23. Eric B Hekler, Predrag Klasnja, Jon E Froehlich, and Matthew P Buman. 2013. Mind the theoretical gap: interpreting, using, and developing behavioral theory in HCI research. In *Proceedings of the SIGCHI Conference on Human Factors in Computing Systems* (CHI'13), 3307–3316. http://doi.org/10.1145/2470654.2466452
24. Morris B Holbrook. 1978. Beyond attitude structure : toward. *Journal of Marketing Research* 15, 4, 545–556. http://doi.org/ 10.2307/3150624
25. John B Jemmott III, Loretta Sweet Jemmott, and Geoffrey T Fong. 1998. Abstinence and safer sex HIV risk-reduction interventions for African American adolescents: a randomized controlled trial. *Jama* 279, 19, 1529–1536. http://doi.org/10.1001/jama.279.19.1529
26. Hadi Kharrazi, Anthony Faiola, and Joseph Defazio. 2009. Healthcare game design: Behavioral modeling of serious gaming design for children with chronic diseases. *Lecture Notes in Computer Science 5613 LNCS, PART* 4, 335–344. http://doi.org/10.1007/978-3-642-02583-9_37
27. Hadi Kharrazi. 2009. Improving healthy behaviors in type 1 diabetic patients by interactive frameworks. *AMIA Annual Symposium*, 322–326.
28. Hyang-Sook Kim and S Shyam Sundar. 2011. Using interface cues in online health community boards to change impressions and encourage user contribution. In *Proceedings of the SIGCHI Conference on Human Factors in Computing Systems* (CHI'11), 599–608. http://doi.org/ 10.1145/1978942.1979028
29. Ziva Kunda. 1990. The case for motivated reasoning. *Psychological Bulletin* 108, 3, 480. http://dx.doi.org/10.1037/0033-2909.108.3.480
30. Yu-Hao Lee and Gary Hsieh. 2013. Does slacktivism hurt activism?: the effects of moral balancing and consistency in online activism. In *Proceedings of the SIGCHI Conference on Human Factors in Computing Systems* (CHI'13), 811–820. http://doi.org/ 10.1145/2470654.2470770
31. Nira Liberman and Jens Förster. 2009. The effect of psychological distance on perceptual level of construal. *Cognitive Science* 33, 7, 1330–1341. http://doi.org/10.1111/j.1551-6709.2009.01061.x
32. Nira Liberman and Yaacov Trope. 1998. The role of feasibility and desirability considerations in near and distant future decisions: A test of temporal construal theory. *Journal of Personality and Social Psychology* 75, 1, 5–18. http://doi.org/10.1037/0022-3514.75.1.5
33. Yuliya Lutchyn and Marco Yzer. 2011. Construal level theory and theory of planned behavior: time frame effects on salient belief generation. *Journal of Health Communication* 16, 6, 595–606. http://doi.org/10.1080/10810730.2011.551991
34. William M Macharia, Gladys Leon, Brian H Rowe, Barbara J Stephenson, and R Brian Haynes. 1992. An overview of interventions to improve compliance with appointment keeping for medical services. *Jama* 267, 13, 1813–1817. http://doi.org/10.1001/jama.1992.03480130129038
35. Rosemary Robin Charlotte McEachan, Mark Conner, Natalie Jayne Taylor, and Rebecca Jane Lawton. 2011. Prospective prediction of health-related behaviours with the Theory of Planned Behaviour: a meta-analysis. *Health Psychology* Review 5, 2, 97–144. http://doi.org/10.1080/17437199.2010.521684
36. Terence R. Mitchell, Leigh Thompson, Erika Peterson, and Randy Cronk. 1997. Temporal Adjustments in the Evaluation of Events: The "Rosy View." *Journal of Experimental Social Psychology* 33, 4, 421–448. http://doi.org/10.1006/jesp.1997.1333
37. Richard Netemeyer, Michelle Van Ryn, and Icek Ajzen. 1991. The theory of planned behavior. *Orgnizational Behavior and Human Decision Processes* 50, 179–211. http://doi.org/10.1016/0749-5978(91)90020-T
38. Eleanor O'Rourke, Kyla Haimovitz, Christy Ballweber, Carol Dweck, and Zoran Popović. 2014. Brain points: A growth mindset incentive structure boosts persistence in an educational game. In *Proceedings of the SIGCHI Conference on Human Factors in Computing Systems*, (CHI'14), 3339–3348. http://doi.org/10.1145/2556288.2557157
39. Dianne Parker, Stephen G Stradling, and Antony S R Manstead. 1996. Modifying Beliefs and Attitudes to Exceeding the Speed Limit: An Intervention Study Based on the Theory of Planned Behavior. *Journal of Applied Social Psychology* 26, 1, 1–19. http://doi.org/ 10.1111/j.1559-1816.1996.tb01835.x
40. Richard E Petty and John T Cacioppo. 1986. The elaboration likelihood model of persuasion. *Springer.*
41. Donna M Randall and James A Wolff. 1994. The time interval in the intention-behaviour relationship: Meta-analysis. *British Journal of Social Psychology* 33, 4, 405–418. http://doi.org/10.1111/j.2044-8309.1994.tb01037.x
42. Al M Rashid, Kimberly Ling, Regina D Tassone, Paul Resnick, Robert Kraut, and John Riedl. 2006. Motivating participation by displaying the value of contribution. In *Proceedings of the SIGCHI conference on Human Factors in Computing Systems* (CHI'06), 955–958. http://doi.org/10.1145/1124772.1124915

43. Milton J Rosenberg. 1956. Cognitive structure and attitudinal affect. *Journal of Abnormal Psychology* 53, 3, 367–372. http://doi.org/10.1037/h0044579

44. Zheng, Saijing, Mary Beth Rosson, Patrick C. Shih, and John M. Carroll. 2015. "Understanding Student Motivation, Behaviors and Perceptions in MOOCs." In *Proceedings of the 18th ACM Conference on Computer Supported Cooperative Work & Social Computing* (CSCW'15), 1882-1895. http://doi.org/10.1145/2675133.2675217

45. Kenneth Savitsky, Victoria Husted Medvec, Ann E Charlton, and Thomas Gilovich. 1998. "What, Me Worry?": Arousal, Misattribution, and the Effect of Temporal Distance on Confidence. *Personality and Social Psychology Bulletin* 24, 5, 529–536. http://doi.org/10.1177/0146167298245008

46. Paschal Sheeran and Shiena Orbell. 1998. Do intentions predict condom use? Meta-analysis and examination of six moderator variables. *The British Journal of Social Psychology* 37, 2, 231–250. http://doi.org/10.1111/j.2044-8309.1998.tb01167.x

47. Aneesha Singh, Annina Klapper, Jinni Jia, et al. 2014. Motivating people with chronic pain to do physical activity: opportunities for technology design. In *Proceedings of the SIGCHI Conference on Human Factors in Computing Systems* (CHI'14), 2803–2812. http://doi.org/10.1145/2556288.2557268

48. Martine Stead, Stephen Tagg, Anne Marie MacKintosh, and Douglas Eadie. 2005. Development and evaluation of a mass media Theory of Planned Behaviour intervention to reduce speeding. *Health Education Research* 20, 1, 36–50. http://doi.org/10.1093/her/cyg093

49. Sutton Stephan. 1998. Predicting and explaining intentions and behavior: How well are we doing? *Journal of Applied Social Psychology* 28, 15, 1317–1338. http://doi.org/10.1111/j.1559-1816.1998.tb01679.x

50. Anja Thieme, Rob Comber, Julia Miebach, et al. 2012. "We've bin watching you": Designing for reflection and social persuasion to promote sustainable lifestyles. In *Proceedings of the 2012 ACM Annual Conference on Human Factors in Computing Systems* (CHI '12), 2337–2346. http://doi.org/10.1145/2208276.2208394

51. Yaacov Trope and N Liberman. 2000. Temporal construal and time-dependent changes in preference. *Journal of Personality and Social Psychology* 79, 6, 876–889. http://doi.org/10.1037/0022-3514.79.6.876

52. Yaacov Trope and Nira Liberman. 2003. Temporal construal. *Psychological Review* 110, 3, 403–421. http://doi.org/10.1037/0033-295X.110.3.403

53. Yaacov Trope and Nira Liberman. 2010. Construal-level theory of psychological distance. *Psychological Review* 117, 2, 440. http://dx.doi.org/10.1037/a0018963

54. Yaacov Trope and Nira Liberman. 2011. Construal level theory. *Handbook of Theories of Social Psychology* 1, 118–134.

ClimbAware - Investigating Perception and Acceptance of Wearables in Rock Climbing

Felix Kosmalla
German Research Center for Artificial Intelligence (DFKI)
Saarbrücken, Germany
felix.kosmalla@dfki.de

Frederik Wiehr
German Research Center for Artificial Intelligence (DFKI)
Saarbrücken, Germany
frederik.wiehr@dfki.de

Florian Daiber
German Research Center for Artificial Intelligence (DFKI)
Saarbrücken, Germany
florian.daiber@dfki.de

Antonio Krüger
German Research Center for Artificial Intelligence (DFKI)
Saarbrücken, Germany
krueger@dfki.de

Markus Löchtefeld
Department of Architecture, Design and Media Technology, Aalborg University
Aalborg, Denmark
mloc@create.aau.dk

ABSTRACT
Wearable sports devices like GPS watches and heart rate monitors are ubiquitous in sports like running or road cycling and enable the users to receive real-time performance feedback. Although rock climbing is a trending sport, there are little to no consumer electronics available to support rock climbing training during exercise. In this paper, we investigated the acceptance and appropriateness of wearables in climbing on different body parts. Based on an online survey with 54 climbers, we designed a wearable device and conducted a perception study with 12 participants in a climbing gym. Using vibro-tactile, audible, and visual cues while climbing an easy route and a hard route, requiring high physical and cognitive load, we found that the most suited notification channel is sound, directly followed by vibro-tactile output. Light has been found to be inappropriate for the use in the sport of climbing.

Author Keywords
Climbing; sports technologies; wearable computing; ambient information; perception; visual alerts; tactile alerts, audible alerts.

ACM Classification Keywords
H.5.m. Information Interfaces and Presentation (e.g. HCI): Miscellaneous

CHI 2016, May 7–12, 2016, San Jose, California, USA.

ACM 978-1-4503-3362-7/16/05...$15.00
DOI: http://dx.doi.org/10.1145/2858036.2858562

Figure 1: The notification device which is worn on the wrist. It is powered by an RFDuino equipped with three RGB LEDs and a vibration motor.

INTRODUCTION
Rock climbing in its original form was only practiced by smaller, more adventurous groups of people who gained expertise in handing the necessary protection equipment such as ropes and bolts while climbing outdoors. In the last several years, a new style of climbing emerged that generally focuses on the athletic aspect and the physical exercise of the climbing activity. The latter is today known as *sport climbing*, differentiating itself from *traditional climbing*. Sport climbing can be performed both indoors and outdoors. Climbing outdoors usually requires the climbers to bring their own ropes, which are clipped into either predrilled bolts or self set protection. Examples for that are nuts, which are a small piece of metal that are stuck in cracks of the rock to hold the climber in case of a fall. In contrast, indoor climbing requires much less material. Artificial climbing walls (see Figure 2) are equipped with colored holds for hands and feet. Although the amount of holds mounted to the wall is large, only a few are part of a specific route and are allowed to be used. Routes can be setup in different difficulties. These can be influenced by the distance, the size, and the orientation of the holds, resulting in body positions which require more grip or body core strength.

The climber may still bring her own rope and do what is called *lead climbing*, i.e. starting with the rope on the ground while clipping into predrilled bolts as she goes up to the top, but the usual and more accessible option is called *top-rope*. In this activity, the climber uses ropes that are already hanging from the top of the wall.

The increased accessibility is one reason why sport climbing, outdoors or indoors, became more and more popular. In the US, there are now 353 climbing and bouldering gyms, including 29 new ones which where built in 2014 [9]. Even though indoor climbing on artificial walls and plastic was initially thought as a form of training for climbing outdoors, many people only engage in this form of climbing because it is easily accessible and does not depend on weather conditions.

High security standards [23] for the walls and the equipment, as well as mandatory introductory courses provide a safe exercise environment for all age groups. Furthermore, climbing is a sport which demands, but also fosters, both physiological and psychological strength. During a climb, the climber uses a large number of muscles in her body while simultaneously concentrating on her next move, grabbing a tiny hold and paying particular attention where to place her feet.

All these factors discussed above outline how different climbing is from other sports such as running or cycling. It represents a more holistic activity that besides muscle force and technique, requires special attention throughout the climb. Green and Helton explored the influence of a memory task on climbing efficiency [5]. They found that climbing efficiency was significantly impaired through the memory task. This hints at the cognitive demands of climbing. If we now consider a climbing training system that aims at giving the climber feedback in-situ as proposed in future work e.g. ClimbAX [13], we need to take into consideration the cognitive capabilities of the climber in mind. If we want to give appropriate feedback to the climber about her performance or how she should adapt her technique during a climb, such a system needs to be well tailored to these capabilities. Finding suited notification channels and positions for devices to deliver the feedback is a crucial point. For example Roumen et al. [22] showed that a simple task like walking has a significant influence on the perceivably of different feedback channels. We expect these effects to be even more prominent for a complex activity such as climbing.

In this work, we investigated whether or not and how a climber can perceive and distinguish notifications, which are sent out from a device worn on her body, even with the high cognitive load described above. Existing interaction concepts that are widely used in other fields, such as sport watches, do not necessarily meet the specific requirements of climbing. We conducted an online survey in which we assessed appropriate body parts on which to place a wearable device and possible notification channels. Based on these results we developed a wrist worn device which was able to notify the user with either vibration or visual cues. In addition to that, we used bone conducting headphones for audible cues and tested all three notification channels in a user study in a local indoor climbing gym using top-rope routes. We propose exemplary use cases for different communication channels based on the findings of the user study.

Figure 2: A climbing route is composed of a number of different holds (often of the same color, or marked with colored tape). Only these holds are allowed to be used.

While parts of the study described below are very specific to rock climbing, we believe that it can inform the design of wearables for activities where high physical and mental demand come together such as white water kayaking or windsurfing.

RELATED WORK

Our work is related to previous studies on (1) wearable devices, (2) the influence of mobility and (3) climbing research in HCI.

Wearable Devices

A variety of different wearable devices have been investigated until now; at this point we will briefly discuss a subset of these that have the potential to be used during climbing. So far most of the related work in this area focused on input techniques and only few investigated the output capabilities in depth. When it comes to interaction with wearables, Profita et al. [21] found the wrist and the forearm to be the most socially acceptable area for such devices. While their study mainly focused on interaction, Harrison et al. [7] investigated reaction time to visual alerts. They found that reaction time performance is not only influenced by the location but also dependent on outside factors such as occlusion. In a climbing scenario, these factors will be even more prevalent compared to every day interaction with wearable devices.

While most of the prior work mainly focused on input on such devices, the limited size makes output as complicated as well. One of the earliest interactive wrist-worn devices has been developed by Hansson and Ljungstrand [6]. Their Reminder Bracelet allowed a connected PDA to notify the user with the assistance of integrated LEDs. Williams et al. presented a wearable ambient display that allowed for semi-public notifications using LEDs as well [24]. Pasquero et al. investigated tactile output on a smartwatch [20]. Besides notifications, they found it to be suitable for obtaining numerical data as well. All of these works have only been tested in well structured lab settings.

The multiple display segments of the Facet system [15] were able to overcome the problems that arise from the small display size of current devices. On the one hand, the multiple viewing angles allowed for different relative head positions while the ability to stretch applications over multiple display segments reduced the effect of the small display size. Nevertheless, the system not only requires a high amount of hardware but also relied on manual adaption which might not be possible during climbing.

Influence of Mobility

When interacting with mobile devices, mobility is an important factor and often neglected in favor of non-mobile lab studies. For example, when walking, users can only keep stable interaction performance at 74% of their preferred walking speed [2]. Furthermore the effect of encumbrance on interaction - carrying an object in one hand and interacting with the other - while for example walking, has a significant influence on task performance for target acquisition on a touchscreen mobile phone [17]. During climbing people are not only carrying an object but also often have no free hands.

Roumen et al. [22] investigated wearable interactive rings regarding the perceivably of different notification channels (light, vibration, sound, poke, and thermal) during five levels of physical activity (laying down, sitting, standing, walking, and running). According to their results, vibration is the most reliable and fastest notification channel, followed by poke and sound independent from level of physical activity. The other two channels, light and thermal, were less noticeable and were affected by the level of physical activity.

Notifications on a wearable add a secondary task to the main task of climbing. This relates to cognitive aspects of how such a secondary task might influence the climbing performance. Green and Helton explored the influence of a memory task on climbing efficiency [5]. They found that climbing efficiency was significantly impaired through the memory task. Helton et al. [10] followed up these results and their findings indicated that climbing is highly cognitively demanding. Based on their results and memory resource theory, they suggested the need for communication equipment that augments the climbers memory. They suggest using visual or tactile modalities but did not investigate their effectiveness. So far, to the best of our knowledge, the effects of climbing on the perception of different output modalities have not been investigated. We are following up on the work of Helton et al. and are investigating these in a real world setting.

Climbing and Human-Computer Interaction

Climbing is a complex activity that is determined by a variety of physiological and anthropometric factors. Mermier et al. [16] found that the variance in climbing performance can be mainly explained by a set of trainable variables and less by specific anthropometric characteristics. While the physiological factors of climbing have gained some research attention, there has also been research on the cognitive factors of climbing [18].

In wearable computing and HCI, climbing received little attention so far. Some related work exists regarding instrumented climbing walls, automated skill assessment, route recognition using a wearable device, and augmented reality [14, 19, 1, 4, 13, 12, 3, 11].

There are various possibilities to track a climber such as body-worn sensors, image processing, or instrumented climbing walls. Liljedahl et al. [14] proposed Digiwall, which consists of holds that can sense the climber's position with built-in capacitive sensors and provide subtle feedback with LEDs. The focus of their work is gaming, competitions, and challenges that can be rather used for playful activities than rigorous training. A very similar instrumentation was done by Ouchi et al. [19] whereas the goal of their work was to model play behavior of children. They used climbing holds that incorporated a LED and a strain gauge. Their work aims to improve the design of age-appropriate and safer playground equipment. Aladdin and Kry [1] proposed an instrumented climbing wall for static pose reconstruction. They used holds equipped with 6-axis force torque sensors that were used to reconstruct the climber's pose during an ascent. An evaluation showed that dynamic motions and higher errors coincided. Fuss and Niegl [4] also used torque sensors in instrumented climbing holds to measure the performance of a climber. Data collected on three climbing events was be segmented into three phases of contact: set-up phase, crank phase, and lock off.

While the previous methods required an instrumented climbing wall, Ladha et al. [13] used wrist worn accelerometer sensors to assess climbing performance. An evaluation of the system during a climbing competition resulted in a positive correlation between the predicted and the actual score of the participants. Kosmalla et al. [12] introduced ClimbSense, a system to record and automatically recognize successfully climbed routes. In their approach, the climber is equipped with wrist-worn Inertia Measurement Units (IMUs). The IMUs were used to collect a set of climbing data and train a classifier that is able to recognize different routes.

Daiber et al. [3] investigated handheld augmented reality for collaborative boulder training. They present a mobile augmented reality application to define, document, and share boulder problems. Kajastila and Hämäläinen [11] also explored augmented reality for climbing walls but they directly augmented the wall with a projector. A preliminary Wizard-of-Oz study with six interaction prototypes and structured interviews showed that users liked the system.

ONLINE SURVEY

To gain a first insight into possible locations of wearables, we conducted an online survey. The participants were asked a set of general questions such as age, sex, climbing experience, and habits, followed by an assessment of body parts concerning appropriateness and perceptibility.

General Questions

54 climbers participated in the survey, of which 11 were female. When asked about their climbing skill, 29 considered themselves beginners, 18 intermediates, and 7 expert climbers. The age of the participants ranged from 18 to 49 with an average age of 27.87 years ($SD = 7.7$). We asked

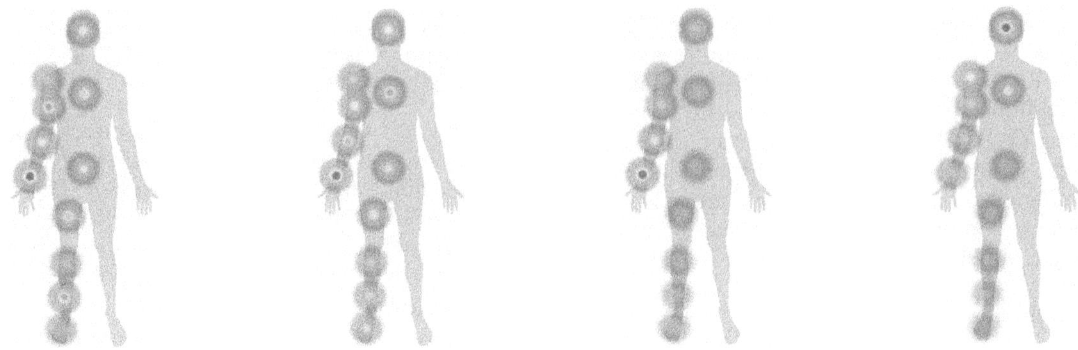

(a) appropriateness (b) vibro-tactile (c) light (d) sound

Figure 3: Cumulated values for the different classifications of body positions. The redder the point, the more appropriate, or perceivable it was considered.

the participants to state whether they would rather boulder (1) or do classic rope climbing (5) on a 5-point likert scale. On average the participants answered 2.7 (SD = 1.05), which means that the participants would rather boulder than climb. For both disciplines the participants had to state whether they train outdoors (1) or indoors (5). On average the participants answered with 1.89 (SD = 1.66) for bouldering and 1.63 (SD = 1.36) for climbing. This shows a tendency for practicing both, climbing and bouldering, outside on a real rock.

Assessment of Body Positions

To get a first insight about possible locations on the body for wearable devices, we investigated eleven body parts for their appropriateness and estimated perceptibility for vibro-tactile, audible, and visual notifications. Appropriateness and perceptibility were questioned by providing the user with an interface, displaying a silhouette of a human with markers placed over the eleven body parts. The participants followed a wizard on the website, leading her from top to bottom.

Appropriateness

In the second part of the questionnaire which assessed the appropriateness, the participants was asked to state how appropriate or inappropriate a device would be when worn during a climbing session. For this, the participants were shown a silhouette of a human body. We selected 11 points on the body to be assessed: head, shoulder, chest, upper arm, lower arm, wrist, waist, upper leg, knee, and ankle (see Figure 3a). Except for the head, chest, and belt area all points where located on the right half of the body for the sake of simplicity.

For each body part, the participant could choose a value from *(1) not appropriate at all* to *(5) fully appropriate.* A generated heatmap of the fixed body parts and their cumulated values for the appropriateness can be seen in Figure 3a. As it can be observed, the wrist, upper arm, and ankle are stated as the most appropriate places on the body. Table 1a gives detailed information about the placements at each body part. For this, we summed up all the answers given by the participants for the given body parts. The feet, lower leg, and shoulder area were perceived as least appropriate.

After the assessment of the appropriateness per point basis, the participants were asked which of the body parts they would consider most suitable for which kind of device and if they could think of concrete examples. The wrist (named 20 times) was clearly in the top position for appropriateness, followed by the upper arm (8), chest (7), ankle (6), head (6) and waist (4). When asked for inappropriate positions, the joints in general (named 8 times), head (7), feet (5), legs (4), hands (4), and shoulders (2) were mentioned as unfavorable position choices.

Some participants also mentioned preconditions for possible body worn devices. The most important requirement for such devices was that it would not hinder the climbing movements and the climbers flexibility at all. Especially the joints and the areas around it were rated as very inappropriate. Another concern of the participants was the risk of injury. The participants feared that devices placed on exposed body parts like knees, elbows or legs, may lead to injuries on the climber herself. A common understanding was that a device worn on the wrist would be the most appropriate, since people are already accustomed to smart watches or bracelets in general. The device should be thin and neither limiting motion nor being uncomfortable.

Followed by the assessment of appropriateness, the participants were asked to estimate the perception quality of the three output channels, vibration, light, and sound. For this, the participants had to state for each channel how perceptible a notification triggered from a device, worn at a specific body position, would be. The participants could answer this question by selecting a point from a five-point scale ranging from *(1) not perceivable at all* to *(5) very perceivable.*

Perception of Tactile Notifications

We asked the participants to state how perceivable a vibro-tactile notification would be when triggered during climbing at the given body positions. Figure 3b shows a visual interpretation of the results. It can be seen that the perceptiveness of vibro-tactile notifications is estimated slightly higher in the upper body half than in the area below the waist. Table 1b summarizes the answers for tactile notifications; While the wrist, chest, and lower leg area were estimated as the most

Position	Score
Wrist	193
Upper Arm	178
Ankle	176
Upper Leg	172
Chest	169
Lower Arm	167
Head	165
Waist	158
Shoulder	138
Lower Leg	136
Foot	129

(a) Appropriateness of body position in descending order.

Position	Score
Wrist	221
Chest	203
Lower arm	199
Head	191
Upper Arm	190
Upper Leg	187
Waist	180
Foot	178
Ankle	170
Shoulder	167
Lower Leg	162

(b) Estimated perception of tactile notifications when induced at different body positions.

Position	Score
Wrist	210
Lower arm	175
Upper Arm	157
Head	151
Chest	138
Shoulder	136
Foot	123
Upper Leg	118
Lower Leg	114
Waist	114
Ankle	106

(c) Estimated visibility of devices placed at various body positions.

Position	Score
Head	225
Shoulder	192
Chest	186
Upper Arm	172
Lower arm2	164
Wrist	158
Waist	126
Upper Leg	111
Lower Leg	108
Ankle	99
Foot	90

(d) Estimated perception of audio notifications when induced at different body positions.

Table 1: Cumulated values for the different classifications of body positions. The redder the point, the more appropriate, or perceivable it was considered.

perceivable areas, the lower leg, shoulder, and ankle were estimated as the least perceivable points to place a tactile notification device.

Perception of Visual Notifications

As for the question of the perception of tactile notifications, we additionally asked the participants how they think visual notifications would be perceived at each of the eleven body parts during climbing.

As it can be seen in Table 1c and Figure 3c, the body areas with the highest estimated perception of visual notifications are all located on the arm (wrist, lower arm, upper arm), while the area with the least estimated perception are the ankle, lower leg, waist, and upper leg.

Perception of Audible Notifications

In contrast to the output channels: vibro-tactile and light, audible notifications are clearly estimated to be the highest around the head area (see Figure 3d). Body parts located further from the head are scored with a low perception of audible notifications. Looking at Table 1d reveals a descending order of body parts, beginning at the head and ending at the foot, confirming the observations made on the heatmap.

Qualitative Feedback to the Output Modalities

As in the *appropriateness* part of the questionnaire, the assessment of the estimated perception of notifications at the different body position was followed by a summarizing question. We asked the participants which body positions would be easier to perceive than others. The wrist, with 19 mentions, leads the list of positions which are thought to be as good places to trigger notifications, followed by the head (9), and arms (8). In contrast, the feet (7), legs (4), and ankles (2) are estimated as places with a low perception.

In general, the participants agreed that the head is the most suitable position for audible notifications, since the distance between the audio source and the ears is the shortest when used, for example, with smart glasses. Additionally, most of the participants stated that both visual and vibro-tactile notifications would be most useful at positions on the arms, especially on the wrist. Concerning the visual feedback, the participant stated that the device has to be in the line of sight, thus, on the arms. *"The arms and hand are closest to the ear and eyes since I am mostly looking upwards when climbing rather than downwards." (P13)* In contrast, all participants agreed that areas on the lower body, with exception for some tactile notifications, are not very suitable for any kind of notification.

Preliminary Design Implications

The feedback of the participants can be generalized as follows: (1) Audio feedback is most suitable around the head, (2) Tactile feedback is most suitable on the arms, (3) Visual feedback should be in the line of sight (4) The wrist is most suitable for a device that combines the two channels light and vibration, and (5) A body worn device should be durable, not obstructive, and not entail any risk of injury.

These results are in accordance with former studies that identified the wrist as the body location at which notifications were perceived the fastest. In particular, this has been shown for the notification with visual cues during other motor activities in which the wrist was located in the immediate field of view [8].

Since one of the main concerns of the participants was the risk of injury, we designed a wristband with a magnetic latch, which opens in case of tangling the device during climbing. Furthermore, we used bone conducting headphones for the audio notifications, since these kind of headphones do not cancel out the climber from her surrounding.

PERCEPTION STUDY

To gain a deeper insight into the findings from the online survey, we conducted a user study in a local climbing gym. Our goal was to test whether climbers would perceive visual, audio, and tactile notifications differently when climbing an easy route, versus climbing a hard route.

Method

Participants

12 climbers (1 female) participated in our user study. Their age ranged from 13 to 60 years, with an average of 34.58 (SD = 11.74) years. For participants under the age of 18 we got written permission from their parents or legal guardians that they were allowed to participate in our experiment. When asked for their climbing skills, seven participants stated to climb *not harder than 5.11*, and five claimed to climb routes rated *5.12 and up*. The difficulties used in the results above are reported in the *Yosemite Decimal System*[1]. As an example, climbing beginners should be able to climb a route graded with 5.4, while professional climbers succeed in routes graded with 5.15. None of the climbers of the perception study participated in the online survey.

Conditions

We tested three different notifications channels that could be perceived by the participants (light, vibration, sound). The first condition consisted of a visual cue, emitted from three RGB LEDs in the colors *red*, *orange*, and *green* for four-seconds. A vibro-tactile cue in form of a one-second long vibration pattern was used as the second condition. The vibrational pattern consisted of either one vibration for one-second, two vibrations within one-second, or three vibrations within one-second. The third cue was an audio signal which also lasted for one-second and consisted of a tone, either played once, twice, or three times. All notifications were manually triggered with the help of a smartphone app, operated by the experimenter.

Tasks

When climbing, the climber undergoes both physical and psychological stress. To investigate the perception in the presence and absence of stress, we selected two different routes. Route *R1* had a difficulty of 5.7 and was equipped with holds which where relatively easy to grab. The second route, *R2*, was picked as the hard route with a difficulty of 5.10c, was slightly slanted and consisted of many holds with a large slope, thus making them hard to grab.

The task for the participants was to climb both routes and to report notifications and their levels as soon as they noticed them (e.g. saying "red" when testing the visual channel).

Design

We designed the experiment so that (1) each order of routes (easy route first, then hard route and vice versa) was climbed by the same number of participants, and (2) each of the six possible orders of notification channels were tested. For two consecutive climbs (easy and hard), only one channel was tested. This resulted in six climbs which each participant had to ascent. To avoid ordering effects, the order of each condition of the tasks was latin square counterbalanced between participants.

Procedure

First, the participant was given an explanation of the experiment and was asked to sign an informed consent to record the data and video capture the study. In the event of participants under 18, we asked their parents or legal guardian for consent. Then we demonstrated the different notification channels and their corresponding levels. Before the first climb, we asked the participant to fill out an initial questionnaire asking for her age and climbing experience. Depending on the current group, the participant started with the easy or hard route and with one of the three notification channels. During the climb, we triggered three notifications in three different levels, where each level was triggered once and in a random order per route. We chose three distinct holds in each route where the participant had to use each of these holds during the ascent. For the hard route, we picked the first hold so that the resulting body position was especially strenuous. We did the same for the easy route, but in this case it was the last hold. As soon as the participant touched the hold, we triggered the specific notification manually and recorded her response by pressing the designated button within the smartphone app.

[1] `http://climber.org/data/decimal.html`

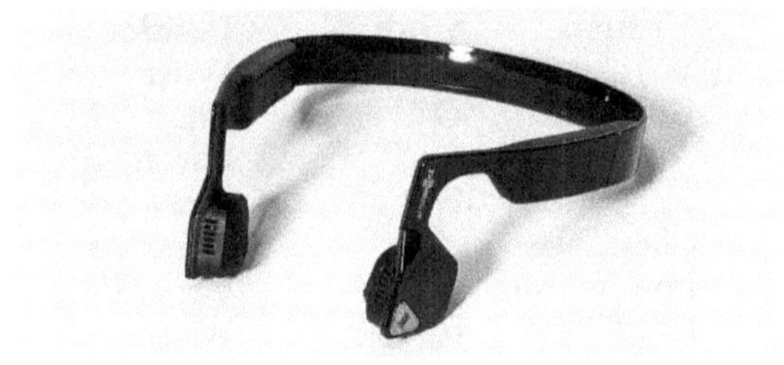

Figure 4: Bone conducting headphones which were used during the study.

After the first climb, the participant directly climbed the second route, which was either the hard route if she started with the easy route or vice versa. When the participant finished the second route, we asked her to fill out a user experience questionnaire, asking how she perceived the notification for this specific channel. This procedure was repeated two more times, testing the two remaining channels while maintaining the order of the routes. A final questionnaire was handed to the participant which assessed the overall experience and how hard she perceived the individual routes. All trials were video recorded.

In summary, the experimental design was: 12 participants × 3 conditions × 6 trials = 216 data points. Overall, the study took roughly 30 minutes and the participants were compensated for their time with 10 Euros.

Apparatus

We conducted the study in a local climbing gym, utilizing two selected top-rope routes. This kind of route ensures the safety of the climber, since the rope runs through a fixed anchor at the top of the route and does not require any additional self-protection except for tying herself in properly. Both routes were approximately 12 meters high.

Based on the guidelines presented above, we designed a wrist worn device which consists of an RFDuino with integrated bluetooth capability and three RGB LEDs, which were able to emit *red*, *orange*, and *green* light. We used LEDs which emitted light that could be perceived in even light conditions.

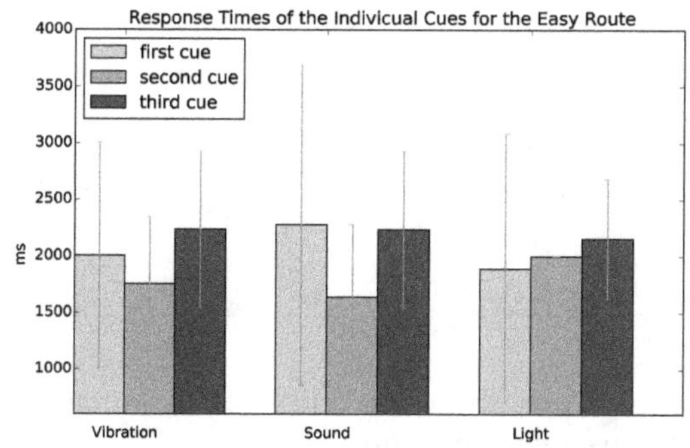

Figure 5: Response times ordered by the time of occurrence and grouped by notification channel for the easy route.

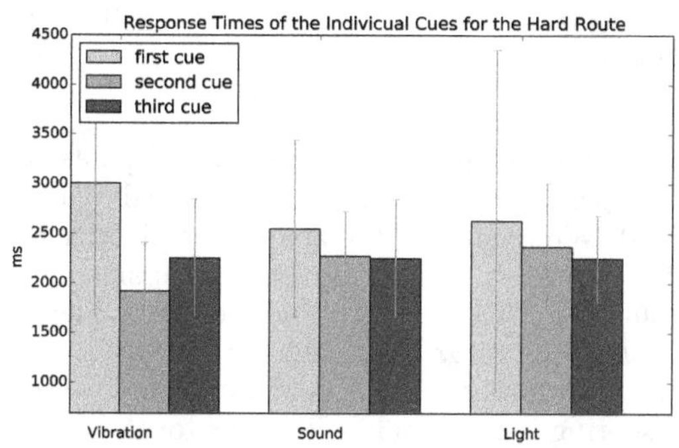

Figure 6: Response times ordered by the time of occurrence and grouped by notification channel for the hard route.

Furthermore, a battery and a vibration motor were included to provide vibro-tactile feedback for the user. An off the shelf 3V vibration motor was used with a vibration amplitude of $0.8G$, which is comparable to smart watches like the Samsung Gear. We used the approach of a custom designed device as opposed to a smart watch because it gives the user a feeling of a more abstract device. A potential bias may occur when using a smartwatch but is therefore counteracted with the use of the device. To meet the need for safety and injury prevention which arose during the online study, we equipped the wrist band with a magnetic latch. The latch is strong enough to hold the device in place, but is sufficiently fragile to open if the wrist band was caught during the climb, preventing serious injury by the wristband in the event of a sudden, unlucky fall.

In addition to this device, we used a pair of AfterShokz BLUEZ 2 bone conducting headphones[2] for audio notifications (see Figure 4). With these headphones, we played back sound chimes with frequencies that ranged from $500Hz$ to $20,000Hz$ We chose these headphones because they do not cancel out the climber from her surrounding, enabling her to hear both the audio notifications and commands from her belayer. The latter is a crucial prerequisite for a safe execution of sports climbing.

[2]http://aftershokz.com/collections/wireless/products/bluez-2

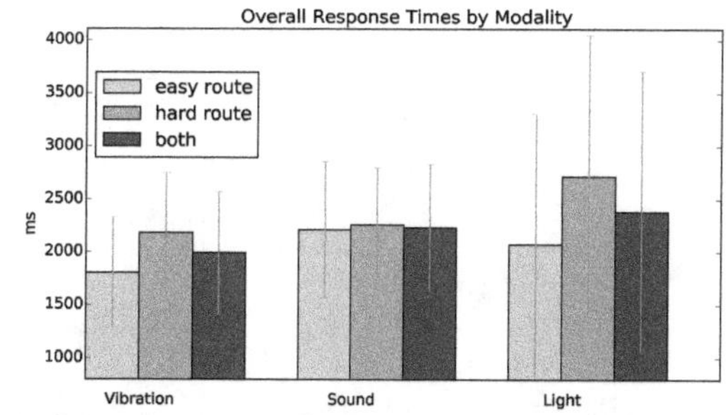

Figure 7: Response times of the participants, ordered by notification channel and climbed route.

To control both notification devices, an Android application was developed to manually trigger notifications to either the wrist-worn device or the headphones. The application was also used to manually record and store response times and the duration of a climb. It furthermore managed the order of routes and notification channels during each individual experiment. When the participant started climbing, a button press started the stopwatch to record the duration of the individual climb. Whenever one of the three designated holds was reached by the climber, a press on the notification button triggered the appropriate notification. As soon as the participant stated the perception of a notification, a stop button was pressed and the response time was saved. The answer given by the participant was transcribed via a dialog within the application.

Results

Response Times

To evaluate the response times, we first averaged the response times for the easy route, the hard route, and then both routes for all channels (see Figure 7). As it can be observed, the *light* channel has a slightly higher mean response time than *vibration* and *sound*. A test of normal distribution followed by a pairwise T-test showed no significant difference of the means between the categories. However, the standard deviation of the *light* (1323.61) channel is notably higher for both *vibration* (575.82) and *sound* (600.37).

We triggered three notifications at three distinct holds for each of the two routes to ensure comparability. Since each hold or position within the route incorporates a different difficulty of the climbing move, we investigated the response times for each position (cue) within a channel and for both routes. As shown in Figure 5 (easy route) and Figure 6 (hard route), the response times differ for each position. In the case of the easy route, the second cue for vibration and sound have a slightly lower response time than the light channel.

Quality of Responses and Missed Notifications

For each notification, the participant had to verbally report the level of the notification by either the number from *one* to *three*, for vibration and sound, or one of the colors *green, yellow,* or *red*, for the visual notifications. Of a total of 216 notifications, 14 notifications were missed and 4 answers where given incorrectly. We could observe that three of the 14 missed notifications were missed in the *vibro-tactile* channel

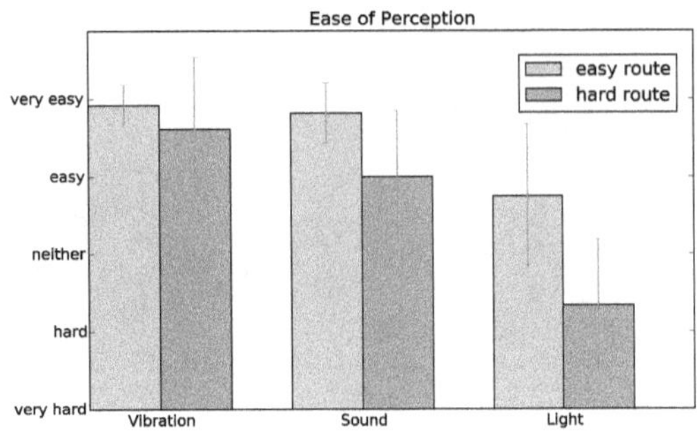

Figure 8: Ease of perception for the three channels, for both, the easy and the hard route.

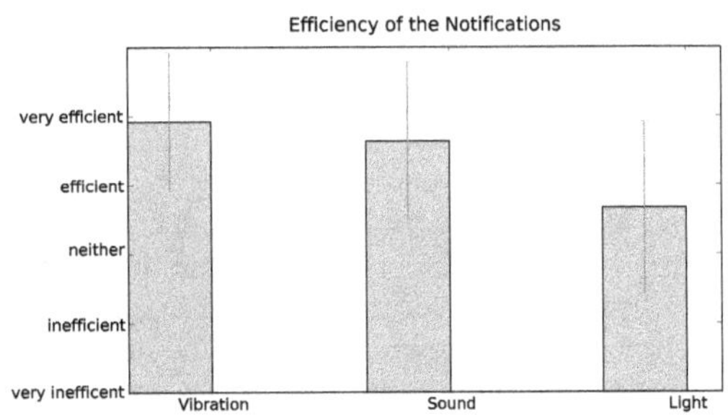

Figure 9: Answers of the questions *How efficient do you think this notification is?*

while the remaining eleven notifications were missed in the *light* condition. Four notifications were missed in the easy route and ten notifications were missed in the hard route. The four notifications that were given incorrectly occurred solely in the hard route while two of them occurred during the visual and two in the vibro-tactile channel. No notifications were either missed or incorrect in the sound condition.

Participant Feedback

After each channel, we asked the participants to fill out a short user experience questionnaire. We wanted to know how the participants felt about the different channels. For this, we asked them how easy they could perceive the notification itself and the different corresponding levels. Furthermore, we asked how comfortable they conceived the notification and how they judged the efficiency of the specific channel. As a final question, the participants were asked how they liked the channel in general.

The participants stated for both, the easy and the hard route, that visual notifications are less easy to perceive than audio notifications and audio notifications are less easily perceived than tactile notifications (see Figure 8).

We asked the participants how efficiently they judged the perceived notification on a five-point scale, ranging from *(1) very inefficient* to *(5) very efficient* (see Figure 9). The light channel was judged as the least efficient with an average of 3.67 (*SD=1.24*), followed by sound with an average of 4.64 (*SD=1.14*). Vibration was rated as most efficient with an average of 4.92 (*SD=0.99*).

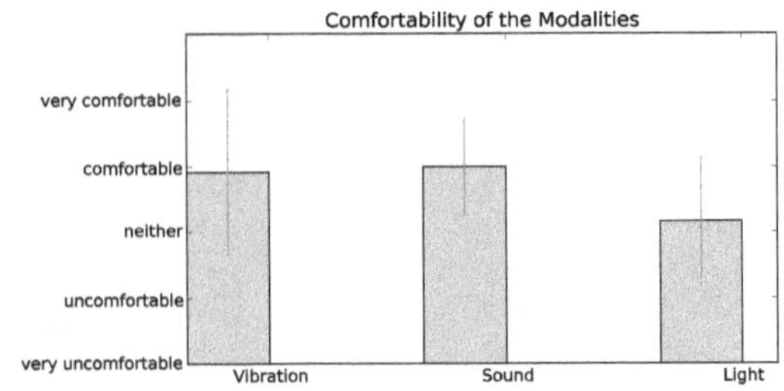

Figure 10: Answers of the questions *How comfortable did you perceive this notification?*

When asking how comfortable the participants perceived the notification on a five-point scale with *(1) very uncomfortable* and *(5) very comfortable*, sound was perceived as the most comfortable (*avg=4.0, (SD=0.73)*), followed by vibration (*avg=3.92 (SD=1.26)*), and light *(avg=3.27 (SD=0.98))*.

In a final questionnaire, we asked the participants how hard or easy they perceived both the hard route and the easy route (see Figure 8). While all the participants perceived the easy route as either *very easy* or *easy*, seven participants perceived the hard route as *hard*, one as *easy* and four participants perceived it as *neither easy nor hard*. As the last task, we asked the participants to order the channels ascending by their priority. When scoring the channels with *three* for the first place, *two* for the second, and *one* for the last place, we could observe the following order: vibration (29), sound (26), light (11).

This feedback is also reflected by the comments the participants gave during and after the study. Most of the participants (10) stated that the visual notification was the most distracting. They stated that this was due to the fact that when climbing during the light channel test, they felt the urge to always keep an eye on their wrist. One participant stated that he even chose his next hand hold so that he could keep the device in sight. Another participant stated that he felt forced to look at the device constantly which hindered him in focusing on the climbing itself. The fact that he missed some of the visual notifications was explained by the features of the selected routes. He reported that due to the slant of the route he needed to keep his feet in sight so that he could place them on small foot holds. This lead to not having the device in sight.

Two participants stated that audible notification were more easily perceived. They claimed that one is more receptive for audible cues than tactile or visual ones.

After the final questionnaire, we asked the participants if they could remember the positions where they received the notifications which were always the same for each route and notification channel. Most of the participants stated that they could not recall all of the positions, but only the ones where they had the most struggle in climbing. Some participants claimed that they did not even notice that there were always three notifications and that these were always triggered at the same positions.

Observed Behavior

In addition to the subjective feedback, we also observed the participants during the experiments and did a video analysis post hoc. When testing the light channel, we noticed that some participants stopped during the climb to check if the wristband lit up during a move. Additionally, there was a large difference in response times for the light channel since some participants responded very quickly, while other participants reacted notably slower (see Figure 7). For all channels, we could observe that most of the participants responded *after* they completed their move to the next hold and very seldomly during a move.

Another observation that surprised us happened during a participant's ascent of the hard route while testing the light channel. We witnessed that he had the wristband in sight during the notifications, but he was so focused that he did not perceive one of the three notifications. After climbing, we asked him if he actually perceived the notification but forgot to report it, but he claimed that he, in fact, did not perceive the visual notification at all.

DISCUSSION

The results of both studies lead to promising results that can inform the future design of climbing technology. After discussing the results, we explore potential application areas to support climbing and address the validity of the perception study.

Evaluation of the Light Condition

Although, in a variety of sports, watches with graphical displays are well established, visual output does not seem to be suited for climbing, as we observed several disadvantages that do not outweigh its advantages. The wristband prototype created simple visual cues, which did not require the participant to read text or interpret graphics. However, the visual output of a plain green, yellow, or red light can be understood as a very simple form of a display. Despite its visual simplicity, the majority of the participants (10 out of 12) stated that they felt the urge to always keep the device in sight, which could explain the similarity in response time to the other notification channels since they were explicitly informed before each climb that they will receive visual cues. The same group of participants also reported a decrease of their climbing performance as they felt distracted by the need to constantly watch their wrist, even in periods when there were no notification.

These observations stay in accordance with objective measures we gathered: light was the slowest channel with an average response time that was 1.2 times higher compared to sound and vibration during the hard climb (see Figure 7). In the easy as well as in the hard climb, the average response times and the standard deviation of the *light* channel are notably higher for both *vibration* and *sound*. Although there was no significant difference, we still think that this is an important finding, which is strongly reinforced by the subjective user feedback. The high standard deviation can be explained by personal strategies of the participants that were revealed by the subjective comments and observations. They either periodically stopped their primary task (climbing) and checked the device or only occasionally glanced at it.

Furthermore, $78,57\%$ (11 out of 14) of complete notification misses occurred during the light condition. It was also subject to the highest standard deviation in terms of response time, which indicates that some climbers reported notifications exceptionally slow, while others responded normally. If we regard the per move analysis in Figure 5 and 6, the light channel can be identified as a clear outlier, while the participants responded similarly to vibration and sound notifications.

Perceptual Differences of Routes

We analyzed the individual moves at which we triggered the notifications in the video footage. Figure 6 shows the average response for each move with the corresponding channels. The hard route was physically demanding right from the start, after which the first notification was directly triggered. The grade of exhaustion and cognitive load also becomes evident in the average response times throughout all modalities. Compared to the other holds where notifications were triggered, the response times of the first hold on the hard route were considerably larger. One explanation for the higher standard deviation in the first as well as in the last move is that some climbers experienced this specific move as easy, for example, due to their reach, and others struggled at this specific part. At the last route, some of the climbers were already exhausted, which accounts for the higher standard deviation but similar response time. This explanation is in line with the video recording of the individual climbs. No climber struggled at the middle part of the route which lead to a small standard deviation and smaller response times compared to the starting move in all channels. The individual moves of the easy route can be explained analogously and also stay in accordance to the observation we made in the video (see Figure 5). It is possible that a low standard deviation and low response time are an indication for a move that was perceived as easy by all climbers and vice versa. When comparing the average response times of the easy and hard route, we noted that the climbers response time was notably slower for the hard route in the vibration and light channel whereas there was only a negligible difference for the sound channel. The error rates and the number of missed notifications in the hard route imply that notifications are more difficult to perceive towards the upper limit of the climber's difficulty spectrum (see Figure 7).

Evaluating the Performance of Vibration and Sound

When looking at the ease of perception in Figure 8, it can be observed that both vibration and sound outperform the light channel. This also applies to the subjectively assessed efficiency and comfortability of the channels. Both channels, vibration and sound, were ranked between very high and high for all three categories (*ease of perception, comfortability*, and *efficiency*). This is also reflected in the evaluation of the final questionnaire where both channels are close to each other on the first (vibration) and second (sound) rank. However, the audio channel outperformed the vibration channel in terms of the average the response time. This is due to the fact that this is the only channel in which only a negligible performance difference could be observed in terms of response time between the hard and the easy route. Moreover, the participants subjectively rated sound as being the most comfortable of all channels (see Figure 10). For climbing outdoors, the pair of wireless bone conducting headphones could also be integrated into a climbing helmet. We did not consider Google Glass as an output methodology as something attached to the forehead could lead to severe injuries in case of a fall. Even though we found the light channel to be less suited when attached to the wrist, it might still be useful when it is located on the top part of a helmet where it could act as a cue in the peripheral view.

The technology we used for audio output, the bone conducting headphones, is well suited for being integrated into a climbing helmet. It also provides eyes-free notifications while climbing, which has shown to be important as it also creates less distraction. For the visual cues, the majority of the participants reported to feel the need to constantly watch and observe the armband, even if there were no incoming notifications.

Limitations

Although the results of the perception study give an insight into climbing indoors, we cannot be sure if the same is valid for climbing outdoors in more extreme environments. Placing self set protection in cracks of rocks adds additional psychological and physiological difficulty, which may result in even more delayed response times as these which were discovered between the easy and the hard route. Furthermore, we would like to emphasize the difficulty of finding and designing routes which are equally hard for a certain group of climbers; every climber perceives the difficulty of the same route different. This is caused by different body height, arms length, body weight, flexibility, etc. For this, having a homogenous group of people with the exact same body characteristics might have resulted in more definitive result of the perception study.

Application Scenarios

Real time on-body notifications in climbing could be used in a variety of situations and systems. We identified two main areas: (1) skill assessment and technique monitoring and (2) climbing assistance. The successful ascent of a route depends on both of these areas. A good climbing technique plays an important role in sports climbing. Examples for that are the efficient use of grip power, the placement of the climber's body's center of mass below the arms, and to keep the elbows unbent whenever possible to save power.

Another important factor is an efficient flow of movements. It is good practice to leave hard parts of a route behind as fast as possible to find a more suitable position to rest the arms. This is only possible if the climber knows which hold to use next such as if a placement of a foot could make her reach a hold which is seemingly far above her or twist herself in a position which optimizes her center of mass.

An experienced climber or trainer can be of great help to assist the climber, but only if both are in immediate hearing distance. A notification system as described and tested above could either facilitate the communication with both parties, or in case of an autonomous climbing assistance system, be used as an output medium.

We think that each channel has its advantages and disadvantages for communicating different information. The results mentioned above suggest that visual notifications are not ideal for time-critical and immediate notifications. In contrast, a gauge that communicates to the climber how much power she has left would be an example of a good use of visual notifications. The climber could glance on the device every now and then to decide whether she should take a break to ensure that her muscles will not harden, so that she can continue to climb later in her climbing session. As opposed to the visual notifications, vibro-tactile or audible notifications could be used in an autonomous system to give the climber an immediate hint to stretch the arms again if the systems detects a lasting contraction of the biceps.

CONCLUSION

In a preliminary online study, we determined the most appropriate body parts for wearables to trigger notifications during climbing. In general, the wrist was found to be most appropriate body part at which we triggered light and vibro-tactile notifications.

The perceptional study revealed that both audible and vibrotactile feedback are suited for ambient notifications during climbing. Overall, sound was rated slightly better than vibration. In accordance with related work, our results indicate that light is inappropriate as a real-time notification channel during climbing (slowest response times, highest error rates, and the most missed notifications).

To conclude, we investigated the acceptance and appropriateness of wearables in climbing with their corresponding body parts. Using these insights, we conducted a perceptional study by triggering vibro-tactile, audible, and visual cues while climbing an easy route and a hard route, requiring high physical and cognitive load. We found that the most suited notification channel is sound, directly followed by vitro-tactile output. Light has been found to be inappropriate for the use in the sport of climbing.

In the future, we plan to cooperate with a competitive climbing team. Training in a professional climbing team is very rigorous. This allows the study of the perception in different states of exhaustion and on a broad variety of difficulties in highly-controlled experimental conditions. Furthermore, varying levels of notifications could be tested or even secondary tasks like solving a math problem. Finally, testing the output modalities in actual applications and not like this study with soley a wizard-of-oz type of setting would reveal the real-world applicability of applications mentioned in the discussion.

ACKNOWLEDGMENTS

This research project is partially funded by the Deutsche Forschungsgemeinschaft (DFG KR3319/8-1) and the Bundesministerium für Bildung und Forschung (16SV7261K).

REFERENCES

1. Rami Aladdin and Paul Kry. 2012. Static Pose Reconstruction with an Instrumented Bouldering Wall. In *Proc. VRST*. 177–184. DOI: http://dx.doi.org/10.1145/2407336.2407369
2. Joanna Bergstrom-Lehtovirta, Antti Oulasvirta, and Stephen Brewster. 2011. The Effects of Walking Speed on Target Acquisition on a Touchscreen Interface. In *Proceedings of the 13th International Conference on Human Computer Interaction with Mobile Devices and Services (MobileHCI '11)*. ACM, New York, NY, USA, 143–146. DOI: http://dx.doi.org/10.1145/2037373.2037396
3. Florian Daiber, Felix Kosmalla, and Antonio Krüger. 2013. BouldAR: Using Augmented Reality to Support Collaborative Boulder Training. In *CHI '13 Extended Abstracts on Human Factors in Computing Systems (CHI EA '13)*. ACM, New York, NY, USA, 949–954. DOI: http://dx.doi.org/10.1145/2468356.2468526
4. Franz Konstantin Fuss and Gnther Niegl. 2006. Instrumented Climbing Holds and Dynamics of Sport Climbing. In *The Engineering of Sport 6*, Eckehard Fozzy Moritz and Steve Haake (Eds.). Springer New York, 57–62. DOI: http://dx.doi.org/10.1007/978-0-387-46050-5_11
5. Alexander L Green and William S Helton. 2011. Dual-task performance during a climbing traverse. *Experimental brain research* 215, 3-4 (2011), 307–313.
6. Rebecca Hansson and Peter Ljungstrand. 2000. The Reminder Bracelet: Subtle Notification Cues for Mobile Devices. In *CHI '00 Extended Abstracts on Human Factors in Computing Systems (CHI EA '00)*. ACM, New York, NY, USA, 323–324. DOI: http://dx.doi.org/10.1145/633292.633488
7. Chris Harrison, Brian Y. Lim, Aubrey Shick, and Scott E. Hudson. 2009a. Where to Locate Wearable Displays?: Reaction Time Performance of Visual Alerts from Tip to Toe. In *Proceedings of the SIGCHI Conference on Human Factors in Computing Systems (CHI '09)*. ACM, New York, NY, USA, 941–944. DOI: http://dx.doi.org/10.1145/1518701.1518845
8. Chris Harrison, Brian Y. Lim, Aubrey Shick, and Scott E. Hudson. 2009b. Where to Locate Wearable Displays?: Reaction Time Performance of Visual Alerts from Tip to Toe. In *Proceedings of the SIGCHI Conference on Human Factors in Computing Systems (CHI '09)*. ACM, New York, NY, USA, 941–944. DOI: http://dx.doi.org/10.1145/1518701.1518845
9. Mike Helt. 2014. 2014 Climbing Gyms & Trends. (2014). http://www.climbingbusinessjournal.com/2014-climbing-gyms-trends/
10. William S. Helton, Alex L. Green, and Neil R. de Joux. 2013. Cognitive Resource Demands During Climbing: Considerations for Communication Technologies. *Proceedings of the Human Factors and Ergonomics Society Annual Meeting* 57, 1 (2013), 1382–1386. DOI: http://dx.doi.org/10.1177/1541931213571306
11. Raine Kajastila and Perttu Hämäläinen. 2014. Augmented Climbing: Interacting with Projected Graphics on a Climbing Wall. In *Proc. CHI EA*. 1279–1284. DOI: http://dx.doi.org/10.1145/2559206.2581139
12. Felix Kosmalla, Florian Daiber, and Antonio Krüger. 2015. ClimbSense: Automatic Climbing Route Recognition Using Wrist-worn Inertia Measurement Units. In *Proceedings of the 33rd Annual ACM Conference on Human Factors in Computing Systems (CHI '15)*. ACM, New York, NY, USA, 2033–2042. DOI: http://dx.doi.org/10.1145/2702123.2702311
13. Cassim Ladha, Nils Y. Hammerla, Patrick Olivier, and Thomas Plötz. 2013. ClimbAX: Skill Assessment for Climbing Enthusiasts. In *Proc. UbiComp*. 235–244. DOI: http://dx.doi.org/10.1145/2493432.2493492
14. Mats Liljedahl, Stefan Lindberg, and Jan Berg. 2005. Digiwall: An Interactive Climbing Wall. In *Proc. ACE*. 225–228. DOI: http://dx.doi.org/10.1145/1178477.1178513
15. Kent Lyons, David Nguyen, Daniel Ashbrook, and Sean White. 2012. Facet: A Multi-segment Wrist Worn System. In *Proceedings of the 25th Annual ACM Symposium on User Interface Software and Technology (UIST '12)*. ACM, New York, NY, USA, 123–130. DOI: http://dx.doi.org/10.1145/2380116.2380134
16. C. M. Mermier, J. M. Janot, D. L. Parker, and J. G. Swan. 2000. Physiological and anthropometric determinants of sport climbing performance. *Br J Sports Med* 34, 5 (Oct 2000), 359–65; discussion 366.
17. Alexander Ng, Stephen A. Brewster, and John H. Williamson. 2014. Investigating the Effects of Encumbrance on One- and Two- Handed Interactions with Mobile Devices. In *Proceedings of the SIGCHI Conference on Human Factors in Computing Systems (CHI '14)*. ACM, New York, NY, USA, 1981–1990. DOI: http://dx.doi.org/10.1145/2556288.2557312
18. Arne Nieuwenhuys, J Rob Pijpers, Raoul R D. Oudejans, and Frank C. Bakker. 2008. The influence of anxiety on visual attention in climbing. *J Sport Exerc Psychol* 30, 2 (Apr 2008), 171–185.
19. Hisakazu Ouchi, Yoshifumi Nishida, Ilwoong Kim, Yoichi Motomura, and Hiroshi Mizoguchi. 2010. Detecting and Modeling Play Behavior Using Sensor-embedded Rock-climbing Equipment. In *Proc. IDC*. 118–127. DOI: http://dx.doi.org/10.1145/1810543.1810557
20. Jerome Pasquero, Scott J. Stobbe, and Noel Stonehouse. 2011. A Haptic Wristwatch for Eyes-free Interactions. In *Proceedings of the SIGCHI Conference on Human Factors in Computing Systems (CHI '11)*. ACM, New York, NY, USA, 3257–3266. DOI: http://dx.doi.org/10.1145/1978942.1979425

21. Halley P Profita, James Clawson, Scott Gilliland, Clint Zeagler, Thad Starner, Jim Budd, and Ellen Yi-Luen Do. 2013. Don't Mind Me Touching My Wrist: A Case Study of Interacting with On-Body Technology in Public. In *Proc. ISWC '13*. ACM, 89–96.

22. Thijs Roumen, Simon T. Perrault, and Shengdong Zhao. 2015. NotiRing: A Comparative Study of Notification Channels for Wearable Interactive Rings. In *Proceedings of the 33rd Annual ACM Conference on Human Factors in Computing Systems (CHI '15)*. ACM, New York, NY, USA, 2497–2500. DOI: http://dx.doi.org/10.1145/2702123.2702350

23. UIAA. 2015. Rock Climbing Safety Standards. (2015). http://www.theuiaa.org/safety-standards.html

24. Amanda Williams, Shelly Farnham, and Scott Counts. 2006. Exploring Wearable Ambient Displays for Social Awareness. In *CHI '06 Extended Abstracts on Human Factors in Computing Systems (CHI EA '06)*. ACM, New York, NY, USA, 1529–1534. DOI: http://dx.doi.org/10.1145/1125451.1125731

Beyond Abandonment to Next Steps: Understanding and Designing for Life after Personal Informatics Tool Use

Daniel A. Epstein[1], Monica Caraway[2], Chuck Johnston[2], An Ping[2], James Fogarty[1], Sean A. Munson[2]
[1]Computer Science & Engineering, [2]Human Centered Design & Engineering
DUB Group, University of Washington
{depstein, jfogarty}@cs.washington.edu, {mcaraway, chuck2, anping, smunson}@uw.edu

ABSTRACT
Recent research examines how and why people abandon self-tracking tools. We extend this work with new insights drawn from people reflecting on their experiences after they stop tracking, examining how designs continue to influence people even after abandonment. We further contrast prior work considering abandonment of health and wellness tracking tools with an exploration of why people abandon financial and location tracking tools, and we connect our findings to models of personal informatics. Surveying 193 people and interviewing 12 people, we identify six reasons why people stop tracking and five perspectives on life after tracking. We discuss these results and opportunities for design to consider life after self-tracking.

Author Keywords
Personal informatics; self-tracking; abandonment.

ACM Classification Keywords
H.5.m. Information interfaces and presentation (e.g., HCI).

INTRODUCTION
Personal informatics is defined as the process of collecting and reflecting on personal information [12], and is now a common practice in the lives of many people [7]. However, people over time come to temporarily lapse or permanently discontinue self-tracking [4,5,6,11]. We study abandonment of self-tracking tools to gain insight into how to design tools that: (1) better align with tracking objectives and practices, and (2) support better abandonment experiences.

This paper extends current understanding of abandonment with insights drawn from people reflecting on their experiences after they stopped self-tracking. As part of this, we examine how designs can continue to influence people even after abandonment. We extend recent work examining self-tracking technology abandonment in health and wellness [4,5,11] by contrasting it with abandonment in other self-tracking domains, specifically finance and location. We frame these findings in models of how people use personal informatics tools [6,12], and we identify and discuss how self-tracking barriers lead to abandonment.

CHI'16, May 07-12, 2016, San Jose, CA, USA
© 2016 ACM. ISBN 978-1-4503-3362-7/16/05···$15.00
http://dx.doi.org/10.1145/2858036.2858045

We survey 193 people who formerly tracked their physical activity, finances, or location, conduct 12 interviews, and distill themes from this qualitative data. We extend prior work by identifying six reasons people stop tracking and five perspectives on life after tracking among the three studied domains. Our results contribute to a growing understanding of self-tracking abandonment, and surface opportunities for design to consider life after tracking.

BACKGROUND AND RELATED WORK
To characterize how people use self-tracking tools, Li et al. introduce a five-stage model of personal informatics, which emphasizes barriers to tracking toward a goal of reflection and presumed action [12]. This model has been modified and expanded, noting people can reflect on data [3] and ultimately change habits [16] in the midst of tracking. Epstein et al. characterize challenges in lived informatics [14], developing a model of tool use in everyday life that surfaces lapsing and stopping as major components [6].

Avoiding or discontinuing the use of technology is common practice. Baumer et al. enumerate motivations for not using Facebook, including concerns for data use and privacy as well as avoiding addiction [2]. In the domains of physical activity and health and wellness more broadly, recent work has explored reasons people stop using self-tracking tools. Schwanda et al. interview people using Wii Fit, finding they begin other exercise activities and abandon the technology, regarding the abandonment as a success [15]. Clawson et al. extend this "happy abandonment," suggesting designs should support people who no longer feel the need to track [4]. Tools sometimes satisfy people's curiosity about their habits, rendering tracking no longer important [6,11]. People find tools frustrating or time-consuming, ultimately not worth the time investment [5,11]. We extend and contrast such findings in the domains of finance and location, building a broader understanding of abandoning tracking.

DATA COLLECTION AND ANALYSIS
We conducted a series of surveys using Amazon Mechanical Turk with people from the United States who had completed at least 1,000 HITs with a 95% acceptance rate. To identify people who had previously tracked, participants completed a 2-minute screener survey ($0.50 compensation). Of 640

completed surveys, we identified 133, 101, and 91 people who had tracked their physical activity, finances, and location (271 unique people). We then conducted two follow-up surveys (screened participants could take either). The first examined self-tracking abandonment practices, requiring about five minutes ($1.00 compensation). The second emphasized life after tracking, requiring about 10 minutes ($2.00 compensation). Of people who tracked physical activity, finances, and location, 64, 61, and 50 people completed the first follow-up survey, and 68, 56, and 42 people completed the second. 193 unique people (aged 18-63, mean 31.6) completed at least one survey, including 109 male, 82 female, and 2 people who declined to report gender. Length of tool use varied substantially, ranging from less than a week to over two years. 49% had used more than one tracking tool (average 1.7 tools used). Additional details and survey materials are in the online appendix.

Based on responses to the first survey, we invited 34 respondents to participate in an interview, targeting people with either particularly representative or unique experiences, yielding 6 interviewees. We supplemented these with 6 interviewees recruited through a convenience sample (university mailing lists and social network posts), for a total of 12 (4 male, 8 female). Interviews lasted about an hour, and interviewees were compensated $20.

Four researchers used open coding to identify themes in responses and transcripts. Two then coded independently, discussing and refining codes to reach high agreement (Cohen's Kappa 0.74 to 1.0 for 11 codes). We quote survey participants with pXX, and interview participants with iXX.

WHY PEOPLE STOP TRACKING

Participants in our study, especially those who had tracked for health and wellness, stopped using their tools for many of the reasons identified in prior research. We also found reasons not previously identified, especially among trackers in other domains. We ground our discussion of why people stop tracking in models of personal informatics [12] and lived informatics [6], and contrast our findings with prior work. These categories do not cover all the reasons people stop tracking (e.g., tools break, people switch phones [14]), but capture the most prominent themes we found in our data.

Cost of *collecting* and *integrating*. The cost of tracking often leads to abandonment, consistent with prior health and wellness results [4,5,11]. People find tracking "*a hassle,*" feel "*lazy,*" or "*lose interest*" and stop tracking (20, 16, and 6 people). The habit of collecting data can often be difficult to maintain in tools that require regular manual entry, such as financial spreadsheets or food journals [5,6]: "*I got behind on keeping up with it and couldn't find the time to start back up*" (p112, 18 others). Others find tracking too tiring "*I got burnt out on [keeping a financial spreadsheet]*" (p14).

Cost of having or sharing the data. 45.2% of respondents who stopped tracking location did so due to concerns for data sharing. This surfaces within Li et al.'s model as part of *integration* between the location data collected and the social context in which it is shared [12]. Although concerns with regard to privacy in location tracking and sharing are well-documented [1,13], we note a connection between sharing concerns and abandonment of location self-tracking. People were concerned about what friends could see "*I don't want people knowing where I am all the time*" (p161, 11 others) as well as companies using information about them "*I don't want a record of my activities being reviewed or sold to try to sell me better ads*" (p61, 6 others). Although these concerns were largely expressed by people tracking location, emerging new domains (e.g., biometric data such as heart rate or blood pressure) may present similar concerns, especially as more personal informatics tools rely on cloud storage or processing.

Discomfort with information revealed. During *reflection*, tracking can highlight perceived shortcomings in behavior or behavior change, and people can find this uncomfortable. p133 "*didn't like being so aware of how little money I had,*" while p178 stopped tracking because she "*had to witness my weight fluctuations every day.*" For p163, entering new expenses was unpleasant: "*I felt guilty every time I tracked an expense that was not a necessity.*" Prior work has found food journals can feel judgmental when people exceed their calorie budgets [5]. We extend this finding, noting that tools in other domains can create feelings of judgment.

Abandoning tracking may be the easiest way to address this discomfort. p23 stopped tracking because she "*felt discouraged with my lack of progress*" and p3 "*didn't feel like I was getting the results that I wanted.*" Tracking emphasized the difficulty of p144's circumstances and made her feel even worse about her situation: "*the decision to stop tracking made me very sad, like it was the final thing in admitting how bad my [financial] situation had become.*" When people do not feel tools help them *act* to change the situation, tracking may only add to their frustration.

Data quality concerns. People often desire greater accuracy than their tools provide [12]: "*the calories burnt seemed so random, and didn't line up with other online sources*" (p123, 19 others), or find data unreliable "*the GPS would lose my location and stop tracking my run*" (p139), leading to imperfect personal data. This problem in *collection* inhibits effective *reflection* and consequently *action*.

Learned enough. People often begin tracking to learn their habits, with a goal of *action* [6,12]. Moreover, Rooksby et al. find people track over short-term periods in support of long-term goals [14]. We also found this practice in our participants. Six people felt no reason to continue tracking after learning what they needed in order to act: "*I was very familiar with the different routes I was taking when I was running, so I eventually just sort of phased out MapMyRun. It wasn't beneficial to me anymore*" (p20). After people develop a skill, the potential benefits of tracking change and it can become unnecessary. p29 "*was able to figure my distance and calories burned without [MapMyRun]*" and p89 "*was able to keep track [of my finances] in my head.*"

People also track to develop and adhere to plans, such as exercise, weight loss, or budgets [6,8,9,10]. Although helpful in developing a plan, some people find that "*once I had that plan, the Fitbit was no longer necessary*" (p171, 5 others). p146 "*felt that I could take charge of keeping my own lifestyle*" and thought tracking was no longer required.

Life circumstances change. As noted in the lived informatics model, lives and routines may change, leading people to intentionally or unintentionally suspend tracking [6]. People regularly change their activities to ones their existing tracking tools do not support, such as p115 who "*gave up running and started to do other types of exercise.*" p127 "*moved to an area that did not have a good walking trail*" and "*had to switch to indoor activity and MapMyRun isn't great for that.*" Other life events may force people to give up the activity they tracked, such as for p17 "*I became pregnant and was not able to exercise anymore because my pregnancy was high risk,*" p181 "*I stopped riding my bike due to a serious injury,*" and 8 others. Other life events often take priority over keeping up with tracking, such as for p133, who used to track finances and then "*got divorced and had other things to focus on.*"

Some people described stopping tracking finances when they did not have any money to track. For i1, "*it came to a point where as soon as I had money it had to immediately go to pay for something that was needed, so there really wasn't anything to keep track of.*" These were often caused by unemployment "*I lost my job and my income dropped*" (p109, 5 others) or career changes "*I went to grad school and thus had no income*" (p82, 5 others). However, stopping tracking can also signal an improving financial situation, such as for p50 "*I was out of debt and making good money*" (2 others).

LIFE AFTER TRACKING

People had varied opinions and feelings about abandoning tracking. Table 1 shows the relationship between reasons for abandonment and perspectives on life after tracking reported by participants in our second survey. Percentages correspond to agreement between the two coders.

No major effect. Interest in tracking often faded without leaving a strong impression, especially for people who felt the cost of tracking was too high to continue. People described this perspective across all three of the tracking domains we surveyed. i7 used MapMyRun, but "*I didn't think about it until your survey, that actually was when I remembered, 'Yeah, I did do that.'*" Some people, such as p55 and 5 others, started to track out of curiosity but were not particularly invested in the activity: "*I felt indifferent about [tracking] because I wasn't that into trying to increase my physical activity.*" Like p55, most who started out of curiosity and later abandoned tracking then feel indifferent about their experience. p110 stopped tracking his location because he "*simply forgot to do so,*" and he had few thoughts about his tracking experiences: "*I don't feel bad. I don't feel much about it. It just kind of happened.*"

	Reason for abandoning tracking					
	Cost of collecting and integrating	Cost of having or sharing the data	Discomfort with the information revealed	Data quality concerns	Learned enough	Life circumstances change
Activity	**45.6%**	**2.9%**	**5.9%**	**5.9%**	**11.8%**	**13.2%**
No effect	22.1%	1.5%	1.5%	2.9%	4.4%	1.5%
Frustration	10.3%	0%	1.5%	1.5%	0%	0%
Guilt	16.2%	0%	1.5%	1.5%	1.5%	5.9%
Freedom	2.9%	0%	1.5%	0%	0%	2.9%
Use skills	1.5%	0%	0%	1.5%	8.8%	1.5%
Location	**42.9%**	**45.2%**	**0%**	**9.5%**	**0%**	**2.4%**
No effect	21.4%	7.1%	0%	4.8%	0%	2.4%
Frustration	0%	0%	0%	0%	0%	0%
Guilt	0%	0%	0%	0%	0%	0%
Freedom	16.7%	33.3%	0%	4.8%	0%	0%
Use skills	0%	0%	0%	0%	0%	0%
Finances	**57.1%**	**1.8%**	**5.4%**	**0%**	**14.3%**	**10.7%**
No effect	25.0%	0%	0%	0%	0%	3.6%
Frustration	5.4%	0%	0%	0%	0%	1.8%
Guilt	8.9%	0%	1.8%	0%	0%	5.4%
Freedom	17.9%	1.8%	3.6%	0%	1.8%	3.6%
Use skills	7.1%	0%	0%	0%	14.3%	0%

Table 1. Participant perspectives on life after tracking grouped by reason for abandonment. The first row shows the cumulative percentage of each reason for why people stop tracking.

Frustration. Tracking tools often do not match people's expectations [4]. After abandonment, some people remain frustrated with their lack of success tracking and attribute that frustration differently. Some felt frustrated with the cost of tracking [11], as witsh p57 who stopped using a Fitbit: "*I feel more frustrated than anything... I want to track my data. I just would rather it be effortless.*" Others felt frustrated that a situation outside their control prevented tracking: "*it was frustrating to know that I needed to make time to do the tracking, but the needs of my family outweighed my own personal goals*" (p23 and 4 others). As tool design evolves and lives change, people may decide to return. Similar to people interviewed by Lazar et al. [11], 16 people planned to return, including p19: "*I'm ok with my decision to stop, but I do think that I will probably do it again in the future.*"

Frustration with the effectiveness of tracking was uncommon among financial and location trackers in our study. This may be because location trackers typically start tracking out of curiosity rather than a desire to change habits [6], while financial trackers often want a *financial touch* (e.g., awareness of current status) [10]. Because they did not initially anticipate action, they may be less frustrated by abandonment.

Guilt. Some people feel guilty for not making tracking a habit, though they found the cost of tracking too high to continue. This was also more common among people who started tracking with the intent of changing physical activity (16.2% of people who tracked activity) or financial habits (8.9% of people who tracked finances). i11 tried to use a spreadsheet to track her finances, stopped, and eventually "*started feeling guilty... I shouldn't have stopped finance tracking.*" She eventually tried to use Mint, but stopped again. She still feels guilty about stopping: "*I really should get back* *to using this or something similar again... I ought to be doing something like this. So yes, guilt.*"

People often blame themselves for not continuing to track, particularly in physical activity. p87 stated, "*I feel like I am wasting my potential by not keeping on top of tracking,*" while p116 felt "*regret because I could have seen my progress or lack thereof over time.*" p188 stopped tracking his activity because "*at the time I thought I could handle it on my own.*" He was sadly unsuccessful: "*I regret it deeply. My workouts have suffered if I do them and most weeks I do not.*" A few felt guilty for abandoning tracking after a change in life circumstances (5.9% and 5.4% of people no longer tracking physical activity or finances): p97 got sick, stopped tracking her activity, and now feels "*ashamed that I haven't restarted, because I was doing so well.*"

Freedom. Self-tracking can be time-consuming, difficult, and "*more of a hassle than a pleasure*" (p65). Some are glad to be done, even if they were not successful. For p52, financial tracking "*felt more and more cumbersome ... it used up a fair bit of my time.*" Ceasing tracking "*felt like a burden was lifted off of me. Although I wanted to continue tracking, I felt this was the right decision... I wanted some of my free time back.*" A few people who stopped after they learned enough felt free from needing to track. After i10 felt she understood her spending, she "*was able to quit.*" p163 avoided the guilt tracking caused and still successfully kept her budget: "*I feel that I am still able to stay within my budget while no longer feeling guilty for any of my purchases that are not necessities.*"

Location trackers most commonly felt free from tracking their data, particularly those who had concerns about having or sharing data (33.3% of people surveyed). p18 felt free from friends knowing, "*I feel like I can move around freely without everyone knowing my every move,*" while p25 appreciated freedom from businesses tracking him: "*I didn't like thinking that outside agencies could see my location tracking and it made me feel very exposed.*" p188 found tracking his location encouraged bad habits: "*I NEEDED to be the mayor of places that were important to me so I spent more time there than I needed to and spent more money... it had turned into a stress rather than something fun.*" Abandoning freed him from the added stress of competition.

Continued use of knowledge or skills. Many people internalize habits developed when tracking and continue to apply their knowledge after abandonment. Financial trackers such as p45 and 11 others learned their spending habits and no longer needed to track: "*I knew that I could spend wisely... my finances are still good, and I haven't had any issues because I've stopped tracking.*" p135 stopped tracking her physical activity because she "*had a very good idea of the amount of steps I was taking without the app... I knew without the app if I was accomplishing my goal.*"

Tracking helps others make structural changes to their lives. p118 "*set a budget that I now carefully follow,*" and felt "*the financial tracking software I used are like training wheels. I used the training wheels to develop balance. It was time for the training wheels to come off.*" p89 changed her habits and felt tracking was no longer important: "*I made changes to my spending and did not need to keep close tabs... I have kept up with my changes and am still doing well.*" p40 started tracking because he "*had a goal of being able to run a 5K without stopping.*" He "*felt tracking did its job*" and stopped, but is "*still running 5K's when I can.*"

People successfully use tracking to change habits, and some feel that continuing to track is unnecessary to sustain the change. 7.1% of respondents no longer tracking their finances reported using knowledge they gained from tracking, despite stopping tracking due to data collection barriers. This suggests *reflection* and *action* can occur long after people abandon data *collection*. Abandonment is thus not always indicative of failure nor the successful end of a process, but could rather be a sign of diminishing returns or a redefinition of goals.

DISCUSSION AND CONCLUSION

Self-tracking is not an effective or beneficial experience for everyone. Many recall their tracking experience with indifference, as just another piece of technology that did not fit in their lives. Others feel frustration that tracking did not support their goals and blame either themselves or the tools. Still others feel guilty for abandoning tracking and wish they had found the will or time to resume. Designers should explore how to appropriately facilitate reengagement and how designs can support a more successful experience in returning. i8 stopped using Mint five years ago, yet "*I still get emails from [Mint] that I ignore... I don't care about them.*" Perhaps tracking tools can promote programs tailored to resuming tracking (e.g., restarting physical activity), rather than nagging notifications pointing out a lack of tracking.

Models of personal informatics in everyday life further include the process of *deciding* to track and *selecting* a tool [6,12]. Our participants had all tried tracking, but we believe many people consider tracking and abandon the idea before ever starting. Future work should study why people abandon tracking before they start, which may inform better design for decisions about whether to track and which tool to use.

We contribute an understanding of life after tracking. Having tracked has no lasting effect for some people, while others continue to apply the lessons they learned about their habits or how to act. For others, tracking was a frustrating experience they wished fit better into their lives. Some felt guilty about stopping, while others felt free from the burdensome or invasive activity of tracking. We surface open opportunities to design for life after tracking, promoting happy abandonment, and designing tools to best support people who want to return to tracking.

ACKNOWLEDGMENTS

We thank Laura Pina for feedback. This research was supported in part by the Intel Science and Technology Center for Pervasive Computing, Nokia Research, AHRQ award 1R21HS023654, and NSF awards OAI-1028195 and SCH-1344613.

REFERENCES

1. Louise Barkhuus and Anind Dey. (2003). Location-Based Services for Mobile Telephony: A Study of Users' Privacy Concerns. *Proceedings of the IFIP TC13 International Conference on Human-Computer Interaction (INTERACT '03)*, 207–212.
2. Eric P.S. Baumer, Phil Adams, Vera D. Khovanskaya, Tony C. Liao, Madeline E. Smith, Victoria Schwanda Sosik, and Kaiton Williams. (2013). Limiting, leaving, and (re) lapsing: an exploration of facebook non-use practices and experiences. *Proceedings of the SIGCHI Conference on Human Factors in Computing Systems (CHI '13)*, 3257–3266. http://doi.org/7wf
3. Eun Kyoung Choe. (2014). *Designing Self-Monitoring Technology to Promote Data Capture and Reflection*. PhD Dissertation. The Information School, University of Washington, Seattle Washington.
4. James Clawson, Jessica A. Pater, Andrew D. Miller, Elizabeth D. Mynatt, and Lena Mamykina. (2015). No Longer Wearing: Investigating the Abandonment of Personal Health-Tracking Technologies on Craigslist. *Proceedings of the ACM International Joint Conference on Pervasive and Ubiquitous Computing (UbiComp '15)*. http://doi.org/10.1145/2750858.2807554
5. Felicia Cordeiro, Daniel A. Epstein, Edison Thomaz, Elizabeth Bales, Arvind K. Jagannathan, Gregory D. Abowd, and James Fogarty. (2015). Barriers and Negative Nudges: Exploring Challenges in Food Journaling. *Proceedings of the SIGCHI Conference on Human Factors in Computing Systems (CHI '15)*, 1159–1162. http://doi.org/bbdt
6. Daniel A. Epstein, An Ping, James Fogarty, and Sean A. Munson. (2015). A Lived Informatics Model of Personal Informatics. *Proceedings of the ACM International Joint Conference on Pervasive and Ubiquitous Computing (UbiComp '15)*, 731–742. http://doi.org/10.1145/2750858.2804250
7. Susannah Fox and Maeve Duggan. (2013). Tracking for Health. *Pew Internet*, 1–32. http://www.pewinternet.org/Reports/2013/Tracking-for-Health.aspx
8. Thomas Fritz, Elaine M. Huang, Gail C. Murphy, and Thomas Zimmermann. (2014). Persuasive Technology in the Real World: A Study of Long-Term Use of Activity Sensing Devices for Fitness. *Proceedings of the SIGCHI Conference on Human Factors in Computing Systems (CHI '14)*, 487–496. http://doi.org/bbdv
9. Matthew Kay, Dan Morris, mc schraefel, and Julie A. Kientz. (2013). There's No Such Thing as Gaining a Pound: Reconsidering the Bathroom Scale User Interface. *Proceedings of the ACM International Joint Conference on Pervasive and Ubiquitous Computing (UbiComp '13)*, 401–410. http://doi.org/bbdw
10. Joseph "Jofish" Kaye, Mary McCuistion, Rebecca Gulotta, and David A. Shamma. (2014). Money talks: Tracking Personal Finances. *Proceedings of the SIGCHI Conference on Human Factors in Computing Systems (CHI '14)*, 521–530. http://doi.org/bbdx
11. Amanda Lazar, Joshua Tanenbaum, Christian Koehler, and David H. Nguyen. (2015). Why We Use and Abandon Smart Devices. *Proceedings of the ACM International Joint Conference on Pervasive and Ubiquitous Computing (UbiComp '15)*, 635–646. http://doi.org/10.1145/2750858.2804288
12. Ian Li, Anind Dey, and Jodi Forlizzi. (2010). A Stage-Based Model of Personal Informatics Systems. *Proceedings of the SIGCHI Conference on Human Factors in Computing Systems (CHI '10)*, 557–566. http://doi.org/bh8zsb
13. Janne Lindqvist, Justin Cranshaw, Jason Wiese, Jason Hong, and John Zimmerman. (2011). I'm the Mayor of My House: Examining Why People Use foursquare-a Social-Driven Location Sharing Application. *Proceedings of the SIGCHI Conference on Human Factors in Computing Systems (CHI '11)*, 2409–2418. http://doi.org/c956b2
14. John Rooksby, Mattias Rost, Alistair Morrison, and Matthew Chalmers. (2014). Personal Tracking as Lived Informatics. *Proceedings of the SIGCHI Conference on Human Factors in Computing Systems (CHI '14)*, 1163–1172. http://doi.org/bbdz
15. Victoria Schwanda, Steven Ibara, Lindsay Reynolds, and Dan Cosley. (2011). Side Effects and "Gateway" Tools: Advocating a Broader look at Evaluating Persuasive Systems. *Proceedings of the SIGCHI Conference on Human Factors in Computing Systems (CHI '11)*, 345–348. http://doi.org/drcwkj
16. Mark Whooley, Bernd Ploderer, and Kathleen Gray. (2014). On the Integration of Self-tracking Data amongst Quantified Self Members. *Proceedings of the International BCS Human Computer Interaction Conference (BCS-HCI '14)*, 151–160. http://doi.org/bbdq

Supporting Comment Moderators in Identifying High Quality Online News Comments

Deokgun Park, Simranjit Sachar, Nicholas Diakopoulos, and Niklas Elmqvist
University of Maryland
College Park, USA
{intuinno, ssachar, nad, elm}@umd.edu

ABSTRACT
Online comments submitted by readers of news articles can provide valuable feedback and critique, personal views and perspectives, and opportunities for discussion. The varying quality of these comments necessitates that publishers remove the low quality ones, but there is also a growing awareness that by identifying and highlighting high quality contributions this can promote the general quality of the community. In this paper we take a user-centered design approach towards developing a system, CommentIQ, which supports comment moderators in interactively identifying high quality comments using a combination of comment analytic scores as well as visualizations and flexible UI components. We evaluated this system with professional comment moderators working at local and national news outlets and provide insights into the utility and appropriateness of features for journalistic tasks, as well as how the system may enable or transform journalistic practices around online comments.

Author Keywords
Computational journalism; online comments; asynchronous collaboration;

ACM Classification Keywords
H.3.3. Information interfaces and presentation

INTRODUCTION
In September 2013, Vladimir Putin published an op-ed article in the New York Times (NYT) [26]. It was an essay critical of the U.S.—some might even say prodding the public. As a result, the comments flooded in: 6,367 of them, in fact. Of those, 4,447 were eventually published along with the piece online, including 85 which were selected as 'NYT Picks', high quality comments with exceptional insights that are highlighted in the commenting interface. What makes this remarkable though is that each of these thousands of comments was read by a human moderator, a trained journalist at the NYT *before* it was published. The New York Times uses a pre-moderation strategy and employs 13 community managers to read such comments, filter out inappropriate ones before publication, and select NYT Picks for highlight [13].

CHI'16, May 07 - 12, 2016, San Jose, CA, USA

ACM 978-1-4503-3362-7/16/05···$15.00
DOI: http://dx.doi.org/10.1145/2858036.2858389

Reader-contributed comments are a double-edged sword: while they increase user engagement, contribute to fostering an online community, and may even provide enriching content to both readers and reporters alike, not all comments are created equally. More specifically, reader comments are sometimes low in quality (in terms of spelling, grammar, or composition), may have a tone not commensurate to the news outlet (e.g., aggressive or obscene), and may be intentionally or unintentionally incorrect or misleading. For this reason, while there is a clear value to including reader comments on online articles, there is also a need for comment moderation to ensure that published comments are representative of the news outlet's policies. Filtering out low-quality comments only addresses half the issue; top news publishers are also interested in selecting high-quality comments that contribute particularly well to the associated article and which set the tone for the site. Crowdsourced approaches have their own limitations: selections don't convey an editorial voice, there is no central oversight to ensure balance, and selections may exhibit undesirable popularity biases.

Managing and moderating online news comments is a particularly challenging task due to the overwhelming volume of content, as well as the nuance and context that moderators sometimes need to understand and consider when dealing with sensitive or political issues. Various strategies for mitigating the scale issue have been tried: leaving comments unmoderated devolves quickly, so post-moderation is often employed to allow the community to flag or report low-quality or otherwise inappropriate comments. The pre-moderation strategy at the New York Times produces a high quality of discourse but is quite resource intensive. As a result they must limit the number of articles where comments are even allowed, as well as the time window for commenting on those limited articles.

This work presents the design and evaluation of a visual analytic tool, CommentIQ, intended to augment comment moderators' capabilities to scale the selection of *high quality* commentary on online news sites. Our design process consisted of iterative requirements gathering from domain experts, prototyping, piloting, and development of analytics and visual representations that enable the selection of comments that are editorially interesting. We evaluated the tool with seven professional community editors and moderators at leading local and national news outlets who used CommentIQ to identify interesting comments on different articles. The evaluation provides insight into how the various analytic dimensions, filters, and visualizations that we built enabled and supported the comment moderation task. Moreover, this evaluation with actual domain experts allows us to reason about current practices and our potential to augment these practices with visual analytics, as well as offer guidelines for the future design and development of computational journalism tools.

Our contributions include (1) the characterization of the comment moderation domain, which includes use cases, user tasks, and other design needs, (2) a web-based moderation tool called CommentIQ that was designed and developed to meet these needs, and (3) the evaluation of the designed tool with domain experts in a way that allows us to reason about current practices and the potential for technological augmentation of those practices. Our results underscore the applicability of visual analytics to enable journalistic activity, and uncover opportunities for future technology development that can enable their practices.

BACKGROUND

This work contributes to a growing body of research in the area of computational journalism, which includes tools that are tailor-designed to suit journalistic tasks and workflows, and which take into account the professional norms and use-cases of journalists. Like previous work in this vein, such as the Overview [4], CityBeat [28], or SRSR prototypes [11], we pursue a design study in this domain. Yet rather than focus on the needs of reporters, we target the CommentIQ system at an underexplored but increasingly important task and user sub-population within this domain: comment moderators. In designing the system we were informed by related work in three areas that we describe next, including *community moderation*, *analytics of comment quality*, and *discourse visualization*.

Community Moderation

Discourse quality and incivility in online comment forums is an issue that has not gone unnoticed in the research literature [6,12,30]. Research has shown that if low-quality commentary goes unchecked it can lead to detrimental and polarized risk perceptions of scientific information [1]. One approach for dealing with discourse quality is that of post-moderation: a user community can flag or report comments that they deem inappropriate and these flags can then be reviewed by professionals [12] to determine whether they should be removed. Users can also rate, tag, and vote on comments which feed into end-user interfaces for sorting and filtering comments [19]. A substantial downside to this approach is that it can take a long time for good comments to be identified, and a reliable ranking depends on having enough votes in the system [20].

Studies have shown that users are more interested in engaging with discussion that is moderated [35]. Evidence is mounting which shows that by signaling norms and expectations for behavior, the overall tenor of discourse can be improved. For instance, lower levels of incivility and a greater use of evidence in comments was found when a reporter engaged directly in a news outlet's comment threads on Facebook [32]. In another study, thoughtfulness cues in comments led to participants posting longer comments, spending more time, and writing more relevant comments [33]. The practice of selecting high quality comments by outlets such as the New York Times fits this strategy of social signaling to set community standards. The CommentIQ system was specifically designed with this approach towards comment moderation in mind, thus we focus not on the removal of low-quality comments (which is still a valid problem in its own right), but on the identification of high-quality contributions that could act as cues for a positive feedback loop with a community.

Analytics of Comment Quality

Various efforts have been undertaken to measure and rank the quality of written texts and comments, including both low quality [31] and high quality written outputs. Natural language processing of text content as well as data analysis of community information (e.g. user history and interactions) have been applied. For instance, Louis and Nenkova [22] predicted the article quality of science journalism based on lower level linguistic features, such as sentence structure. Other work in this domain has considered the measurement of dimensions of text readability [25]. Efforts have tried to automatically predict the quality of online comments, although the reported accuracy of such models makes them difficult to apply practically [3,34]. In addition to textual features such as informativeness and cohesion of text, user features can also be leveraged to rank comments, such as activity level, history of ratings, and degree to which other people respond. In contrast to Hsu et al. [17], however, we do not use community ratings as ground-truth for quality as this can reflect popularity bias. For our ground truth of "quality" we instead utilize a source of professionally curated and selected comments: the NYT "Picks" comments.

Studies in the literature describe journalistic efforts to identify high quality contributions from the public, including how letters to the editor are selected [18], how online comments are selected for print publication [23], and how on-air radio comments are chosen at NPR [27]. Specifically in the domain of online news comments, recent work by Diakopoulos [8,9] has synthesized these journalistic criteria into a set of twelve human-centric criteria including argument quality, criticality, emotionality, entertainment, readability, personal experience, internal coherence, thoughtfulness, brevity, relevance, fairness, and novelty. In this work, we utilize the validated analytic operationalization of several of these criteria to score comments, including readability, personal experience, length, and relevance (i.e., to the article and conversation). We also derive user-based scores of quality by averaging these criteria over user history. We incorporate understanding from other literature in the domain of online reviews which suggests that a measure of user activity level will be usefully correlated to quality [2]. Finally, we train a model on a set of collected comments to arrive at default weights of these various analytic criteria that can orient moderators towards the top comment candidates.

Discourse Visualization

Previous work on comment or discourse visualization has often approached the issue from the end-user's perspective. For instance, the ForumReader tool [7] was designed to help orient and guide readers to areas of interest within large scale online forums, such as Slashdot. Another more recent effort in this area is the ConVisIt system [16], which utilizes flexible user-driven topic modeling to provide an interface that allows for exploration of asynchronous online discussions and an ability to find useful and insightful comments. The Arkose system [24] was designed to help visually distill large online discussions into more succinct summaries. A somewhat related effort is the Opinion Space system, which visualizes comments by projecting sets of elicited scalar opinions relating to controversial statements and led to increased user engagement with comments [14].

Many discourse visualization systems in the literature, including those cited above are not oriented towards sensemaking of comments that can directly enable moderation. In contrast, we designed the CommentIQ system specifically for comment moderators and we present a persona and characterization of the task and use-cases involved which inform our design. More specifically we use analytics to score comments along various dimensions of interest to journalist moderators as discussed above, and we provide interactive visualizations of these scores including map-based and temporal views that align with user needs and requirements in the domain and help orient moderators towards comments that may be high quality.

THE DESIGN PROCESS OF COMMENTIQ

We conducted a multi-phase design study with the purpose of applying both text analytics algorithms and interactive visual interfaces to this domain. The design goal was to develop an interface that would help comment moderators identify high quality comments from online news discourse, and which would allow us to study and evaluate how new tools can augment comment moderation practices.

Our design study process was inspired by the core phase of the nine-stage framework proposed by Sedlmair et al. [29]. More specifically, our work was organized into four distinct stages roughly matching the discover, design, implement, and deploy stages in that framework: (1) Domain Characterization: (discover) characterizing personas, use-cases, and tasks; (2) Design and Analytics: (design) developing design rationale as well as concrete visual, interaction, and algorithm design for analytics; (3) Prototyping and Implementation: (implement) interface prototypes as well as client-side and server-side components; and (4) In-Field Evaluation: (deploy) validation through domain expert feedback. The following sections discuss each of phases 1,2, and 4 in more detail while we elide details on phase 3 as we rely on standard web technologies for implementation.

THE DOMAIN: ONLINE NEWS COMMENTS

In designing the CommentIQ system we adhered to a user-centered design methodology, including undertaking several early semi-structured interviews with domain experts. In particular, we were interested in developing knowledge from our informants that would allow us to (1) build a persona of a comment moderator that would guide our design thinking, and (2) understanding the use-cases and tasks for comment moderation on news sites. Our interviews were informal and targeted individuals who were embedded in newsrooms and had experience moderating online comments in the context of news. We spoke to eight people from news organizations including the Washington Post, National Public Radio (NPR), the New York Times, and the Wall Street Journal. Six of the interviews were conducted face-to-face, two were conducted via phone, and all were uncompensated and lasted roughly one hour. Copious notes were taken during the interviews and these were typed and analyzed afterwards to facilitate our design process. We approached the interviews with several questions in mind, aiming to understand more about comment moderator workflow and goals, editorial criteria for identifying high quality selections, indications of how moderation decisions were made, and challenges, frustrations, and pain points with current tooling.

Persona Development

Personas can be useful design tools that work by capturing and communicating the objectives, motivations, behaviors, and expectations of a group of target users [5]. They are often useful as grounding artifacts to assess how different design options may impact users. In our case, the personas allowed us as designers to crystallize the important facets of moderator work and effectively communicate among the design team and with other stakeholders. Based on our initial interviews, we developed a persona of The Comment Moderator (TCM), an archetype reflecting our understanding of the comment moderators we interviewed.

Perhaps more than any other goal, TCM is motivated by a desire to produce a quality discussion. They want to not only remove off-topic, impolite, or critical and unconstructive comments, but also to identify and highlight original ideas, cogent points, or contributions that rise above the noise. They are interested in discovering local voices and top contributors to give them a spotlight and to create a feedback loop where good behavior is rewarded and readers aspire to have their comment selected. Different outlets employ different terminology for this idea: at the New York Times such selected comments are termed "NYT Picks", at the Washington Post they sometimes badge users as "preferred", and at the Wall Street Journal they refer to them as "featured" comments.

The New York Times is perhaps most sophisticated in their thinking about highlighting perspectives as NYT Picks.[1] The NYT Picks are the most popular comment queue and NYT TCMs try to select those with a broad range of viewpoints. In other words, they strive for diversity in the selections. This might include geographic diversity if that is relevant to the story, or it could involve other types of diversity such as along political perspectives. They want the selections to be representative but they do not necessarily need to be balanced between different viewpoints.

The overall goal of TCM is to set the tone and uphold commenting policies to provide a positive atmosphere for discussion. TCM sees comments not as an appendage but as any other piece of journalistic content, and as such they apply an editorial eye: it's not about finding the "most liked" comment. For instance, they strive for fairness in the editorial standards they apply, and are willing to turn comments off for sensitive topics or stories where they believe civil discussion is unlikely. They seek to build trust and increase engagement with their community.

Use-Cases and Tasks

In our conversations with comment moderators, we learned of several use-cases and analytic tasks that may be accomplished with comments. These include: (1) exclusion of low quality comments, (2) selection, highlighting, or picking high quality comments, and (3) taking other journalistic actions based on comment content.

The first task, that of identifying and filtering out low quality comments is one that dominates the analytic workflow for moderators. To a large extent this is about upholding the community standards and providing a venue for discussion that is free from profanity, hate speech, or personal attacks. In many cases, moderators examine flags that are passed in by community moderators, or in some cases by automated systems (e.g., http://keepcon.com/). Sometimes moderators examine the context of a user to see if they are a habitual violator of community norms and as a result may take additional action such as blocking the user. While this is surely an important analytic task which has received some attention in the research literature [31], we instead focus the current work on the underexplored strategy of selecting high-quality comments.

To select high-quality comments for highlighting on a site, moderators consider many different criteria. At the New York Times, they consider five criteria when choosing NYT Picks: overall quality, such as spelling and grammar, argumentation, and literary value; broad representation and diversity of perspective; conversation between two people making opposing points; unexpected short, funny, or unusual commentary; and relevant personal stories and experiences. Interviews with moderators exposed the importance of flexibility and adaptability in applying these criteria. Different quality criteria apply for different stories and communities: there isn't a one-size-fits-all model for when to apply a given editorial criteria, but rather there are many contingencies. Interviews elucidated openness to employing automation to uncover higher quality comments, with an acceptance of some errors and the understanding that a human moderator is making the final decision.

The final task that moderators might engage in involves some other journalistic action, such as correcting a story based on a comment, or passing a comment on to a reporter for follow-up. Several moderators we interviewed believed that comments were valuable leads for news reporting. People often write fascinating stories about how they are personally impacted by an issue at hand, and this can fuel additional reporting by journalists. For niche communities or blogs, insiders may sometimes comment with valuable knowledge and insight that would otherwise be unavailable. This task is conceptually similar to the previous task insofar as it is about identifying comments of a specific ilk, but instead of choosing comments that should be highlighted it is about using the content of those comments for internal purposes. The essential difference in tasks is thus the final step being one of publication, or one of internal use.

DESIGN AND ANALYTICS

We developed several design goals based on our user-centered requirements gathering, persona development, and user task modeling, particularly the second task relating to selecting high quality comments:

- **DG1. Custom ranked list:** The users can customize the ranking based on their own needs and the contingencies of their context, maintaining user agency in the automation process;
- **DG2. Score by multiple criteria:** Comments are scored by several quality criteria that capture different facets of interest in various discussion contexts;
- **DG3. Overview and filter:** To reflect representative but diverse opinions the system should be able to show the distribution of selected comments;
- **DG4. Learning from user feedback:** The system should learn from the user to accommodate specific recurring scenarios in a newsroom.

In the following subsections we describe the design decisions and rationale that support these goals in the analytics and user interface that we developed for CommentIQ. The process that was informed from our requirements gathering is depicted in Figure 1.

[1] http://www.nytimes.com/times-insider/2014/04/17/a-comments-path-to-publication/?_r=0

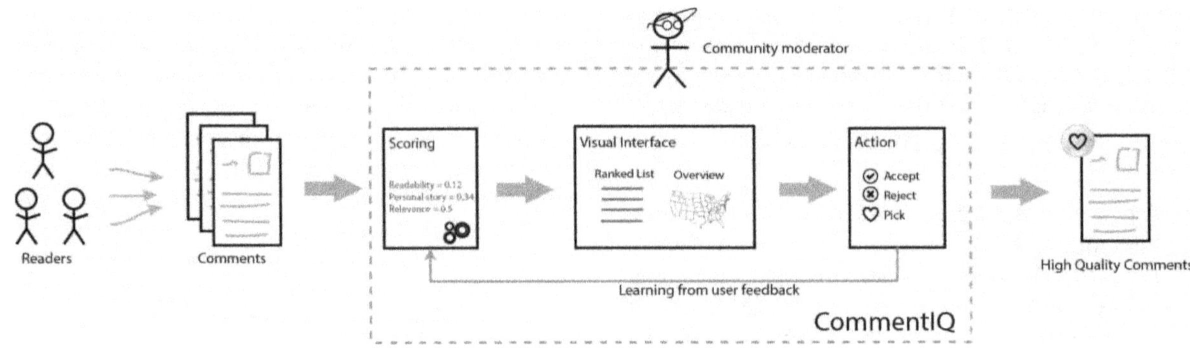

Figure 2. Our design learning suggests the following process for selecting high quality comments: (1) comments submitted by readers are scored using multiple criteria; using these scores, (2) we provide a ranked list of comments as well as the distribution of scores and other meta-data to give an overview and ability to filter; (3) user actions and selection rationale are fed back into the system so that we can learn from users

Analytics

We designed CommentIQ to flexibly support different comment contexts. Thus, instead of using a binary classifier to identify "high quality" comments we employ a customizable weighted ranking of various features (**DG1, DG2**). By allowing the end-user to adjust weights we put the power in their hands to decide when one feature may be more or less salient for their identification of "quality" in that particular context. In addition we provide (1) a smart default weighting for the ranking [10], and (2) several presets to the weighting so that the end-user can quickly switch between contexts.

Selection of Criteria

Instead of computing a large number of textual features and then doing feature selection, we limited our selection of criteria to be legible by humans as motivated by our literature review. Thus we selected criteria that were understandable in this editorial context. This allows us to provide end user customization that is more straightforward (**DG1**). The criteria are based on the content of comments and the history of the user as shown in **Table 1**.

Development of Presets

Tuning of a ranking involves modifying any of 12 weights, one for each criterion. In order to provide a smart starting point for the ranking we trained a classifier to produce a set of default weights. We developed the default weights using a dataset collected via the Times Community API (https://developer.nytimes.com/) which supplies full comment text and metadata such as "NYT Pick" status, and how many recommendation votes it received. The recommendation score was removed during the training of the classifier because a high recommendation score may be a result of a comment being a NYT Pick, rather than the other way around.

Since the final score for the comment is a weighted sum of weights and scores from each criteria, we tested a linear support vector machine (SVM) and a logistic regression. We used 94 'picked' comments and 1574 'not picked' comments. To compensate for the bias in samples, class weight corresponding to the ratio of samples was used. Average precision score using 5-fold cross validation result was 0.13±0.07 with 95 percent confidence interval using linear SVM classifier, and 0.13±0.08 with logistic regression classifier. Average recall for SVM was 0.60±0.39, and 0.60±0.43 for logistic regression. Though these benchmarks are not that impressive, they are adequate to our application since we're interested in providing default settings so that human users can have a useful

Comments Criteria	
Article Relevance	How relevant a comment is with respect to the article, based on word feature vector similarity [8]
Conversational Relevance	How relevant a comment is with respect to preceding comments, based on word feature vector similarity [8]
Length	How long a comment is based on number of words.
Personal Experience	Measures the rate of use of words in Linguistic Inquiry and Word Count (LIWC) categories "I", "We", "Family", and "Friends" [9]
Readability	How readable a comment is according to the SMOG standard index of reading grade level [8,20]
Recommendation	How many recommendation votes a comment has received
User History Criteria	
User Comment Rate	The average number of comments per month a user has written.
User Comment Length	The average comment length score for a user across their entire history.
User Personal Experience	The average personal experience score for a user's comments across their entire history
User Picks	The average rate at which a user's comments are selected as NYT Picks
User Readability	The average readability score for a user's comments across their entire history
User Recommendation	The average recommendation score for a user's comments across their entire history

Table 1. Scoring criteria for comments.

starting point for exploring the rankings and making the final judgment about quality. For both models, weights for the prediction were similar. Readability, article relevance, and user pick history were positively correlated with being an NYT Pick while the conversational relevance and length of comments were negatively correlated with picks. We used the SVM model outputs to create the default ranking.

Other weighting presets were creating using heuristics informed by our interviews with domain experts. We identified the following additional presets that could be useful in different commenting situations:

- **Default:** This preset is for finding generally high-quality comments and was trained using the NYT picks dataset as described above;
- **Personal story:** This sorting favors comments containing personal anecdotes. It is a combination of personal experience and length of comments;
- **Unexpected:** This tries to find short, unexpected comments. This is a combination of short length and high user reputation such as user picks and user recommendation.
- **Best user:** This ranking considers only the user reputation to find a comment written by reliable users.

Interaction and Visual Design

The CommentIQ system is composed of four interface components: article, overview visualization, custom ranking widget, and list of comments. The user can get an overview of comments from the visualization and filter based on making direct selection lassos on the overview visualization (**DG3**). The custom ranking widget provides a way to customize the ranking for one's needs (**DG1**). This section presents the design of these in detail. Figure 2 shows the final interface that was evaluated after soliciting feedback on intermediate designs. The final prototype is online at: http://moderator.comment-iq.com/#/demo

Customizable Ranking View

The goal of the customizable ranking component is to make the custom ranking more intuitive and easy to adjust (**DG1**). The interface is designed for TCMs with various skill levels and goals. At its core is the preset drop-down where the TCM can quickly select weightings for previously identified scenarios, or create a new weighting preset to meet an emerging recognized need. Scoring by different criteria as well as letting the user control the weighting of those scores allows for greater flexibility in the range of contexts where the tool can be employed (**DG2**).

Since our presets cannot cover all of the tasks, we provide a customization so the user can change the weightings of twelve criteria. For example, by giving higher weight to recent posting activity of a commenter, and to user recommendation score, we can surface comments by very active community members with a good reputation.

The different weights are presented with a stacked bar chart, inspired by the multi-attribute ranking visualization by Gratzl et al [15]. It provides a visual signature for each preset as well as feedback to the user about the current weighting distribution.

Overview Visualizations

The goal of the overview visualizations is to show a visual overview of comments according to different scheme, so that moderators can ideally select representative comments along different criteria such as locality, time, or based on quality dimensions (**DG3**). These views can also act as visual filters, where users can select an interesting subset of comments. For example, a user can lasso comments along the west coast on the map view, and only comments from that region will be shown in the comments list. We provide three types of overview explained next.

Map View: This view shows the location of users. We geocoded the location reported by users as free text metadata using the MapQuest Open Geocoding API[2]. This enables the selection of comments from specific geographical regions. Because the location is provided by users as free text, the locations are at various granularities (e.g. state, or city). We applied a force layout algorithm to prevent dots in the same area (e.g. city) from overlapping severely. As a result the map view is suggestive of locations without always being precise.

Commentplot: This view shows scatterplots of criteria scores for all comments. This was intended to provide a quick selection of comments across certain criteria. The axes of the scatterplots were left vague such as "lower" or "higher" because based on design feedback we determined that the relative distribution was more important to show than the absolute score on the overview. These plots show score distributions as well as highlight picked comments to provide feedback to the moderator about where in the score space they have identified quality contributions (**DG3**).

Temporal View: This view shows aggregated scores according to chronological ordering. It can be used for the selection of comments in a specific time window. Also, the change of scores over time such as decreasing article relevance and increasing conversation relevance may be used to make editorial decisions, such as determining when to close the comment functionality on an article.

Brushing and linking between the views is enabled. For example, comment moderators can select the comments from east coast area with long length and high personal story score, and from specific time to find an informative personal anecdote for breaking news for that region.

Learning from User Feedback

Even though comments may be selected by editors for various reasons, the comment data from NYT is annotated simply as a 'Pick' regardless of any of a number of nuanced

[2]http://developer.mapquest.com/web/products/open/geocoding-service

reasons for why it may have been selected. Comments could be selected based on multiple qualifications, such as the presence of personal anecdotes, informative content, or a short and unexpected viewpoint, for example. In some contexts, one feature may have a positive correlation with quality while for others that same feature would have a negative correlation. For example, a comment might be selected either for being short and unexpected, or instead for being long and informative. It may be difficult for a classifier to generalize over the comment length feature.

To address this limitation of the data we have available, we designed CommentIQ to have a feedback loop (**DG4**). When a moderator designates a comment as high quality, they are prompted for information about why it was selected. Along with some predefined options such as "well-written", "informative", "personal experience", "critical", and "humorous" derived from our literature review [9], the moderator can provide free text rationale. When operating at scale the intent is that we could gather selection rationale and correlate the scores and features of those selections to different commenting contexts (e.g. breaking news, different topics or niches). The additional burden of tagging is acceptable because, according to our interviews, only about 1 in 20 comments is selected.

FIELD EVALUATION

We conducted an exploratory evaluation of CommentIQ to gain an understanding of whether and how the tool was helpful to moderators looking to find high quality comments on news articles. We probed users on the tool's utility and asked them to accomplish certain tasks to ensure that they had fully explored system functionality. We piloted the study with a data journalist in order to iterate on the interaction design and UI labeling before we expanded th e study to our target domain users. Based on pilot feedback, we adjusted criteria labels and adjusted the weighting UI to allow for negative weights.

Evaluation Design

We wanted to evaluate whether our approach could be used to enhance current practices as well to know if particular features of CommentIQ were particularly useful or still lacking. We oriented our evaluation according to:

- **Criteria:** Were criteria and the meaning of weights easy to understand? Were they useful in different editorial contexts? Were any criteria missing?
- **Presets:** Was the goal and utility of presets clear to users? Does the algorithm produce results as expected by users? What might be useful presets to add?
- **Rank tuning:** Were users able to create their own custom ranking for their own goals?
- **Overview:** How does the overview and filter approach change the moderation process?

To assess these goals we conducted an in-field evaluation of CommentIQ with domain experts. The following reports our procedure and findings.

Procedure

The study was conducted on a laptop at the place of work of each participant, usually in an area adjacent to the newsroom. After consenting to be in the study, the CommentIQ interface was demonstrated to the participant.

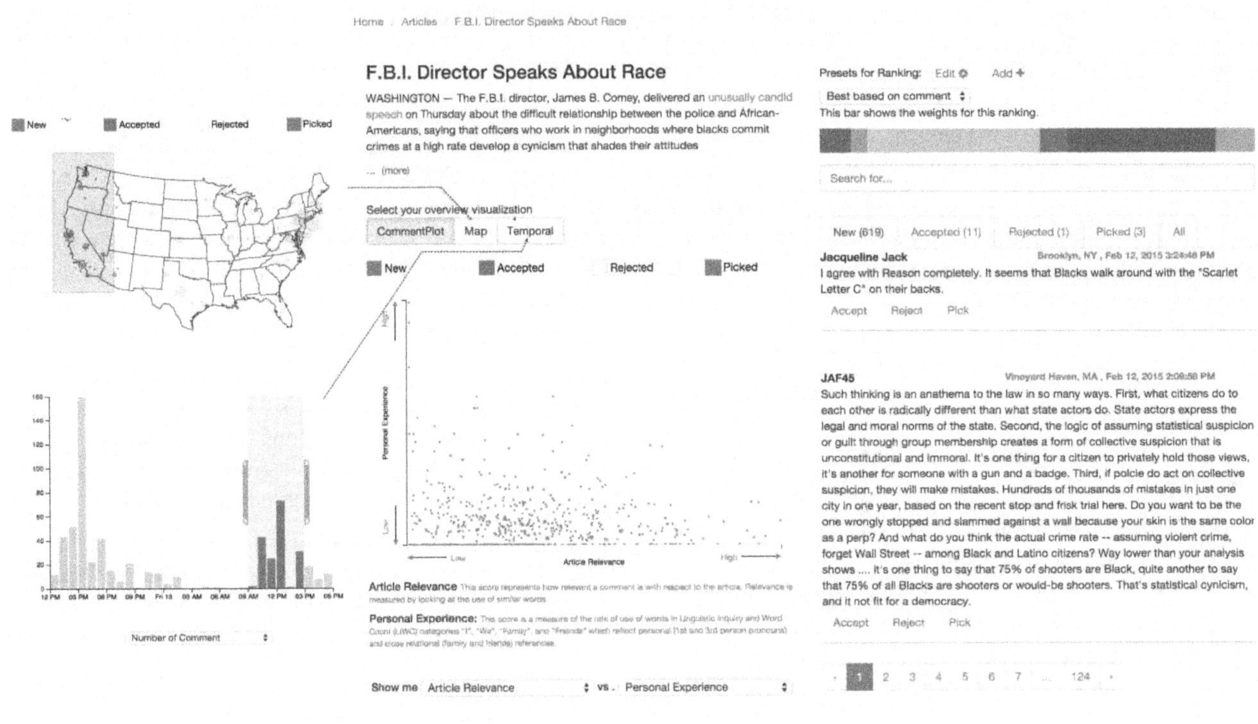

Figure 2. The CommentIQ UI showing toggleable visualizations such as scatterplot, map, and timeline (left) that enable overview and filtering of comments, as well as an adjustable ranking based on various weighted quality criteria (right).

All of the features of the interface were explained, such as how to use and filter on the overview visualizations, how to adjust weights or use the presets on the customized ranking, and the meaning of the various criteria used to score comments. Then the participants were given five minutes for free exploration so they could become acquainted with the system and ask questions if something was not clear. We asked participants to speak aloud as they used the tool. Then we asked users to conduct specific tasks such as using single or multiple criteria to adjust the rankings and weights, as well as using the commentplot and map for selection and filtering. Finally, users were asked to set a goal for target comments that they were interested to find, and then used CommentIQ to pursue finding those comments. After these tasks, we finished the session by asking for the user's general impression and opinion about the advantages and disadvantages of using system. The sessions were audio recorded and transcribed for analysis. Later we summarized important quotes to pull out themes that emerged. Sessions lasted 33 to 75 minutes (M=58).

Content

We made use of three datasets for our evaluation: one for demo purposes, and two for the journalists to interact with. We selected NYT news articles from a range of topics and with varying numbers of comments collected via the NYT Community API. One article, "What Is the Next 'Next Silicon Valley'?" (147 comments), was selected because we thought that it would elicit comments from different geographies that might be interesting for the moderators to consider on the map visualization. Another article, "Who Spewed That Abuse? Anonymous Yik Yak App Isn't Telling" (848 comments), was chosen because we thought that it would elicit comments that included personal stories or perspectives, and it had a much larger and more challenging number of comments. Finally, we chose "F.B.I. Director Speaks About Race" (634 comments) as a demo, since race relations are a hot topic in the U.S. and we thought that comments here might reflect different perspectives that the moderators might want to highlight.

Participants

We evaluated CommentIQ with working professional journalists who have direct responsibilities for comment moderation as part of their duties. Such professionals have knowledge of the real challenges in comment moderation, and the workflows and editorial criteria associated with evaluating online news comments. Combined with the in situ setting in which the study took place, this allows for more ecological validity to reflect on how the tool may be useful in practice. We recruited participants by soliciting industry contacts and asking for referrals. In all, we recruited seven participants (five male, two female) from local (Baltimore Sun) and topical (Wall Street Journal) as well as national (New York Times, Washington Post) outlets. The moderation workflows of the different outlets provided some variability and diversity for the evaluation.

Our participants come from some of the most respected news outlets in the U.S. and are leading-edge practitioners. Their titles and roles include community moderators, community manager, a director of audience engagement development, and a director of digital news projects. Table 1 shows affiliations and related work experience. We will refer to them as 'P1' or 'P2' etc. when citing their comments in the rest of the paper.

Findings

In general participants were positive about the approach and capabilities of CommentIQ. P4 stated that CommentIQ is a great improvement to his existing interface. P3 stated that it is a much more sophisticated and powerful tool than anything she has ever used for comment moderation. The ability to find personal anecdotes quickly and to select comments based on geographic regions received especially positive responses. This reaction was observed from outlets with both pre-moderation and post-moderation processes. Currently, most outlets are just filtering out bad comments, but this is due to resource constraints rather than resistance to selecting and promoting high-quality ones. Participants anticipated that CommentIQ would enable them to find high-quality comments, which is currently not supported by tools that assist in removing low quality comments.

Utility of Analytic Criteria

Participants were able to understand the meaning of the various criteria provided and use multiple criteria to find interesting comments for their goals. Article relevance was used frequently as a comment quality qualification: "I am particularly interested in comments that are on topic," noted P2. And P7 suggested that conversational relevance was also of importance. P1 made an argument that a lower article relevance might also at times be interesting because it is not repeating the article but offering a fresh viewpoint.

The ability to rank comments based on their reflection of personal stories and experiences was met enthusiastically by participants (P1, P3, P4, P5, P6, P7). P3 noted that, "for me personal experience is what makes a productive comments section," underscoring the interest that journalists have in surfacing personal experiences that are

ID	Organization	Field-experience (in years)	Workflow
P1	Washington Post	10	Post-moderation
P2		1	
P3		4	
P4	New York Times	4	Pre-moderation
P5		7	
P6	Wall Street Journal	4	Post-moderation
P7	Baltimore Sun	7	Post-moderation

Table 2. Experience and affiliations of participants.

reported via comments. Initial use of the personal experience score in CommentIQ was hindered because the score counts the frequency of words such as 'I' or 'we', resulting in short one line sentences with 'I' ranked higher. However participants quickly developed various strategies to remedy this, such as selecting comments of a certain length from the CommentPlot (P1, P6) or giving a higher weight to the 'Length' criterion to customize the ranking (P5). For instance, P5 was able to successfully create his own ranking for personal stories. He gave a higher weight to the personal experience criterion, and to the user picks and user recommendation score to select good people. P3 was also able to find good comments for reporters to follow-up on using a combination of the map and a ranking emphasizing conversational relevance and user reputation.

The readability score of comments received mixed reviews. Many participants suggested readability was an important measure, but the result of the current algorithm did not match expectations (P1, P4, P6) as the label did not match their perception of the results they saw. The readability was computed as the SMOG index [21], which is a measure of the grade-level difficulty of the text. However, the score requires further refinement to represent general readability in editorial contexts. As readability features, P1 and P4 suggested the proper use of paragraphs in a comment would make long comments more readable. Sometimes bad comments use meaningless sophisticated language without any hierarchy, resulting in a dense block of text. P6 suggested similar criteria, such as use of 'long ellipsis' or weird punctuation or spacing as features to consider.

Presentation and Visualization

The map view received a lot of positive feedback as a key benefit of the system, with many potential usage scenarios suggested. For example, P1 could find interesting comments from a specific region using the map view. P4 suggested its use to find personal stories via comments from the geographic area where the news is coming from. P6 suggested that the map view could be useful for sport articles, where people are often passionate about their home or school team. Participants compared opinions of Silicon Valley with Florida in the article about Florida being the next Silicon Valley (P1). Also, some users tried to compare conservative states with progressive states, using geography as a proxy for political perspective (P7) and to look for geographic diversity (P5). It was suggested that the granularity of the map might be made flexible to suit different demands: the local outlet wanted a more local map, while national outlets also wanted a global map (P3, P5, P6), with mechanisms to quickly select sub-regions (e.g., a state) using a single click. Geographic information could be improved in the future by using IP geocoding or by extracting location mentions from comments themselves rather than just use metadata.

In the tasks that used CommentPlots, people could select different criteria to get an insight from the scatterplots. Many people used personal experience (P4, P5) and readability (P4) to find interesting comments. P1 successfully used highly relevant but short comments for reporters to quickly find a quote to dress up their story with reactions from users. This shows the adaptability of our approach of leveraging various criteria to accommodate different use contexts.

Elaborate usage scenarios for the temporal view were also suggested. P5 suggested its use for breaking news items, where the ability to find comments from a certain time window can be useful to detect a change of tone or information. Because people do not want to read comments about out-dated news, moderators can put their limited resources on more recent ones. P1 suggested the use of temporal information for getting changing responses of readers as sports events evolve. For example, when there is a new score for an ongoing football game, the sentiment of readers might change accordingly. P6 suggested that the temporal view can be useful when multiple moderators are working together in coordination. P7 articulated that the first wave of comments might contain more personal anecdotes of the event and the last wave of comments will contain more diverse viewpoints about the issues.

The presentation of comments in the ranking view was straightforward but several participants made it clear that threading information should have been reflected there (we lacked this information which was not available from the NYT API at the time of collection). A comment's context within the discussion can be an important element to a moderator's decision as P1, P3, and P4 indicated.

Journalistic Sourcing and Other Use Cases

Several participants emphasized the idea that quality comments were just an entry point for the even more important journalistic goal of identifying potential sources. There was interest in understanding user reputation (P3), repeat commenters and commenting frequency in general (P6, P7), history of negative behaviors like bans, profanity use, or flag history (P3, P6), expertise (P3), and better search access to user comment history. We found that user activity scores, such as average user picks or average user recommendations were frequently combined with comment-based features as a strategy to find reliable people (P5, P6). P7 suggested it would be useful to identify thoughtful users and their expertise and use these to produce future story and article ideas. Our participants thus saw the process of comment moderation not only in terms of the content they were evaluating, but as the potential to identify and engage with potentially new sources. Better user profiling based on past commenting history could thus open up opportunities for new reporting practices.

Some participants expressed that the current tools for comment moderation, which are usually based on chronological or recommendation-based scores, are sub-optimal (P6, P5). Some features of CommentIQ, such as the map-based view and the sorting presets feature may also have value if presented directly to online commenters (P3, P5). P3 stated that, as a community manager, she wants readers to stick around, but the current comment list they use might scare them off. Given the ability to sort comments according to quality might make them stay longer. P5 articulated that he could program some presets for reporters so that reporters could use the intelligent sorts to find interesting content that may inform them. CommentIQ would have utility for longer enterprise stories where there are a surfeit of comments as well as time, resources, and interest in doing follow-up stories (P2).

DISCUSSION AND FUTURE WORK

Our evaluation of CommentIQ along the dimensions of scoring criteria, weighting presets, easy tuning, and overview visualizations showed that the visual analytic system that we designed was productive and useful for comment moderators. Users were able to effectively understand the criteria, compose them into conjunctions of scores that were editorially meaningful, and tune the results to provide access to higher quality comments of editorial interest. The visualizations proved useful for providing an overview of the comment score distribution and helped orient users towards comments according to geography, analytic scores, and temporal characteristics. The evaluation largely validates our design goals **DG1**, **DG2**, and **DG3**. Assessing **DG4** would require a longer-term deployment to study whether the approach can yield enough feedback data to train better models, and is left for future work.

Our evaluation showed that CommentIQ supports a transformational change to the moderation process. One of the more surprising results from our evaluation was the extent to which comment moderators were ready to begin thinking of moderation not as a policing function, but as a first-class editorial position in the newsroom. As P5 explained, CommentIQ positively changed the moderation workflow by *"shifting moderating to a reporting research job."* It changes the role of moderators to editorial knowledge work, because they now think in terms of the qualifications for comments they are looking to publish or use. CommentIQ allows moderators to set up hypotheses and run experiments on presets for the workflows that work well in different contexts and for different types of journalism. Moderators can then publish or share that knowledge with others in the form of custom ranking presets, either internally with other moderators or reporters, or indeed ultimately also with their readers.

By framing comment selection as something that is done to identify interesting content to be published, our users articulated new use cases for comments. Of particular interest is that participants wanted to understand more about the *people* who had written various comments, including aspects such as profession or background knowledge of the commenter. Treating the comments as content, and the commenters as potential journalistic sources, opens new possibilities for leveraging comments in journalistic practices. Future work on deriving user models or profiles based on past commenting behavior and content would allow journalists to tap into comments in new ways.

Through our evaluation we found that journalists (and journalism as a domain) require analytic solutions that place humans in a flexible sensemaking loop with the analytics. Visual analytics is thus a well-suited approach for design in this domain. Journalists do not want editorial decisions automatically made for them per se, but rather seek designs that enable and enhance their own decision-making functions so that they can adapt to new situations and contexts and apply human judgment to editorial decisions.

As an endeavor in value-sensitive design for journalists, CommentIQ necessarily embeds biases and institutional preferences in its representations and analytics. But as a visual analytics system, CommentIQ involves humans in the loop and can thus help offset such algorithmic biases. Moderators can tweak and tune the ranking by re-weighting factors to account for variable contingencies and contexts of work. CommentIQ also visualizes moderation choices within the interface, allowing moderators to get an overview of possible biases in their selections.

While analytic scores were selected to reflect editorial quality, any single score has its limitations. For example, readability was measured using the SMOG index, which likely reflects the educational background of the commenter and could thus be used to privilege certain educated voices. As discussed in the previous work [9] in more detail, each score must be used carefully while critically considering limitations. In a future system it would be interesting to examine the potential for different news organizations to plug in their own scores for measuring different dimensions of quality, thus enabling a wider operationalization of editorial interests than we have currently explored.

Future work in this domain might be oriented towards developing new and better quality scores, including dimensions such as novelty, criticality, and thoughtfulness, [9]. Additional work on natural language processing and analytics needs to develop such metrics to be understandable and useful to moderators. Based on our initial interviews, we identified the desire to maintain diversity and balance in the selected comments. While CommentIQ does provide this to some extent, moderators in our evaluation were looking for minority opinions in terms of sentiment, political thought, or even religious affiliation. CommentIQ can provide limited access to this, such as by proxying political thought to a map view, but the current system lacks the ability to show these dimensions in terms of semantic analysis such as political position. Future work could integrate such advanced analytics.

ACKNOWLEDGEMENTS

We thank our participants for their time and insights. And we thank the John S. and James L. Knight Foundation, which supported this work through a prototype fund grant.

REFERENCES

1. Ashley A. Anderson, Dominique Brossard, Dietram A. Scheufele, Michael A. Xenos, and Peter Ladwig. 2014. The "Nasty Effect:" Online Incivility and Risk Perceptions of Emerging Technologies. *Journal of Computer-Mediated Communication* 19, 3: 373–387. http://doi.org/10.1111/jcc4.12009
2. Saeideh Bakhshi, Partha Kanuparthy, and David A. Shamma. 2015. Understanding Online Reviews: Funny, Cool or Useful? *Proceedings of the 18th ACM Conference on Computer Supported Cooperative Work & Social Computing*, ACM, 1270–1276. http://doi.org/10.1145/2675133.2675275
3. Dirk Brand and Brink Van Der Merwe. 2014. Comment classification for an online news domain. Retrieved January 18, 2015 from https://scholar.sun.ac.za/handle/10019.1/96148
4. M. Brehmer, S. Ingram, J. Stray, and T. Munzner. 2014. Overview: The Design, Adoption, and Analysis of a Visual Document Mining Tool for Investigative Journalists. *IEEE Transactions on Visualization and Computer Graphics* 20, 12: 2271–2280. http://doi.org/10.1109/TVCG.2014.2346431
5. Dan Brown. 2006. *Communicating Design: Developing Web Site Documentation for Design and Planning*. New Riders Publishing, Thousand Oaks, CA, USA.
6. Kevin Coe, Kate Kenski, and Stephen A. Rains. 2014. Online and Uncivil? Patterns and Determinants of Incivility in Newspaper Website Comments. *Journal of Communication* 64, 4: 658–679. http://doi.org/10.1111/jcom.12104
7. Kushal Dave. 2004. Flash Forums and ForumReader: Navigating a New Kind of Large-Scale Online. *Discussion, '' Proceedings of the ACM Conference on Computer Supported Cooperative Work*, 232–241.
8. Nicholas Diakopoulos. 2015. The Editor's Eye: Curation and Comment Relevance on the New York Times. *Proc. Conference on Computer Supported Cooperative Work (CSCW)*.
9. Nicholas Diakopoulos. 2015. Picking the NYT picks: Editorial criteria and automation in the curation of online news comments. *the official research journal of international symposium on online journalism* 5, 1.
10. Nicholas Diakopoulos, Stephen Cass, and Joshua Romero. 2014. Data-Driven Rankings: The Design and Development of the IEEE Top Programming Language News App. *In Proceedings of the Symposium on Computation + Journalism*.
11. Nicholas Diakopoulos, Munmun De Choudhury, and Mor Naaman. 2012. Finding and Assessing Social Media Information Sources in the Context of Journalism. *Proceedings of the SIGCHI Conference on Human Factors in Computing Systems*, ACM, 2451–2460. http://doi.org/10.1145/2207676.2208409
12. Nicholas Diakopoulos and Mor Naaman. 2011. Towards Quality Discourse in Online News Comments. *Proceedings of the ACM 2011 Conference on Computer Supported Cooperative Work*, ACM, 133–142. http://doi.org/10.1145/1958824.1958844
13. Bassey Etim. 2014. A Comment's Path to Publication. *The New York Times*. Retrieved August 8, 2015 from http://www.nytimes.com/times-insider/2014/04/17/a-comments-path-to-publication/
14. Siamak Faridani, Ephrat Bitton, Kimiko Ryokai, and Ken Goldberg. 2010. Opinion Space: A Scalable Tool for Browsing Online Comments. *Proceedings of the SIGCHI Conference on Human Factors in Computing Systems*, ACM, 1175–1184. http://doi.org/10.1145/1753326.1753502
15. Samuel Gratzl, Alexander Lex, Nils Gehlenborg, Hanspeter Pfister, and Marc Streit. 2013. LineUp: Visual Analysis of Multi-Attribute Rankings. *IEEE Transactions on Visualization and Computer Graphics* 19, 12: 2277–2286. http://doi.org/10.1109/TVCG.2013.173
16. Enamul Hoque and Giuseppe Carenini. 2015. ConVisIT: Interactive Topic Modeling for Exploring Asynchronous Online Conversations. *Proceedings of the 20th International Conference on Intelligent User Interfaces*, ACM, 169–180. http://doi.org/10.1145/2678025.2701370
17. Chiao-Fang Hsu, Elham Khabiri, and James Caverlee. 2009. Ranking Comments on the Social Web. *Proceedings of the 2009 International Conference on Computational Science and Engineering - Volume 04*, IEEE Computer Society, 90–97. http://doi.org/10.1109/CSE.2009.109
18. Karin Wahl Jorgensen. 2002. Understanding the Conditions for Public Discourse: four rules for selecting letters to the editor. *Journalism Studies* 3, 1. http://doi.org/10.1080/14616700120107347
19. Cliff A.C. Lampe, Erik Johnston, and Paul Resnick. 2007. Follow the Reader: Filtering Comments on Slashdot. *Proceedings of the SIGCHI Conference on Human Factors in Computing Systems*, ACM, 1253–1262. http://doi.org/10.1145/1240624.1240815
20. Cliff Lampe and Paul Resnick. 2004. Slash(Dot) and Burn: Distributed Moderation in a Large Online Conversation Space. *Proceedings of the SIGCHI Conference on Human Factors in Computing Systems*, ACM, 543–550. http://doi.org/10.1145/985692.985761
21. G. Harry Mc Laughlin. 1969. SMOG Grading-a New Readability Formula. *Journal of Reading* 12, 8: 639–646.
22. Annie Louis and Ani Nenkova. *What Makes Writing Great? First Experiments on Article Quality Prediction in the Science Journalism Domain.*
23. Kathleen McElroy. 2013. Where Old (Gatekeepers) Meets New (Media). *Journalism Practice* 7, 6: 755–771. http://doi.org/10.1080/17512786.2013.774117
24. Kevin K. Nam and Mark S. Ackerman. 2007. Arkose: Reusing Informal Information from Online Discussions. *Proceedings of the 2007 International ACM Conference*

on Supporting Group Work, ACM, 137–146. http://doi.org/10.1145/1316624.1316644

25. Emily Pitler and Ani Nenkova. 2008. Revisiting Readability: A Unified Framework for Predicting Text Quality. *Proceedings of the Conference on Empirical Methods in Natural Language Processing*, Association for Computational Linguistics, 186–195.
26. Vladimir V. Putin. 2013. What Putin Has to Say to Americans About Syria. *The New York Times*. Retrieved August 8, 2015 from http://www.nytimes.com/2013/09/12/opinion/putin-plea-for-caution-from-russia-on-syria.html
27. Bill Reader. 2007. Air Mail: NPR Sees "Community" in Letters From Listeners. *Journal of Broadcasting & Electronic Media* 51, 4: 651–669. http://doi.org/10.1080/08838150701626529
28. Raz Schwartz, Mor Naaman, and Rannie Teodoro. 2015. Editorial Algorithms: Using Social Media to Discover and Report Local News. *Ninth International AAAI Conference on Web and Social Media*.
29. M. Sedlmair, M. Meyer, and T. Munzner. 2012. Design Study Methodology: Reflections from the Trenches and the Stacks. *IEEE Transactions on Visualization and Computer Graphics* 18, 12: 2431–2440. http://doi.org/10.1109/TVCG.2012.213
30. Jane B. Singer. 2010. Quality Control. *Journalism Practice* 4, 2: 127–142. http://doi.org/10.1080/17512780903391979
31. Sara Owsley Sood, Elizabeth F. Churchill, and Judd Antin. 2012. Automatic identification of personal insults on social news sites. *Journal of the American Society for Information Science and Technology* 63, 2: 270–285. http://doi.org/10.1002/asi.21690
32. Natalie Jomini Stroud, Joshua M. Scacco, Ashley Muddiman, and Alexander L. Curry. 2015. Changing Deliberative Norms on News Organizations' Facebook Sites. *Journal of Computer-Mediated Communication* 20, 2: 188–203. http://doi.org/10.1111/jcc4.12104
33. Abhay Sukumaran, Stephanie Vezich, Melanie McHugh, and Clifford Nass. 2011. Normative Influences on Thoughtful Online Participation. *Proceedings of the SIGCHI Conference on Human Factors in Computing Systems*, ACM, 3401–3410. http://doi.org/10.1145/1978942.1979450
34. Nayer Wanas, Motaz El-Saban, Heba Ashour, and Waleed Ammar. 2008. Automatic Scoring of Online Discussion Posts. *Proceedings of the 2Nd ACM Workshop on Information Credibility on the Web*, ACM, 19–26. http://doi.org/10.1145/1458527.1458534
35. Kevin Wise, Brian Hamman, and Kjerstin Thorson. 2006. Moderation, Response Rate, and Message Interactivity: Features of Online Communities and Their Effects on Intent to Participate. *Journal of Computer-Mediated Communication* 12, 1: 24–41. http://doi.org/10.1111/j.1083-6101.2006.00313.x

"Popcorn Tastes Good": Participatory Policymaking and Reddit's "AMAgeddon"

Alissa Centivany
University of Michigan
Ann Arbor, USA
acentiva@umich.edu

Bobby Glushko
University of Toronto
Toronto, Canada
bobby.glushko@utoronto.ca

ABSTRACT

In human-computer interaction research and practice, policy concerns can sometimes fall to the margins, orbiting at the periphery of the traditionally core interests of design and practice. This perspective ignores the important ways that policy is bound up with the technical and behavioral elements of the HCI universe. Policy concerns are triggered as a matter of course in social computing, CSCW, systems engineering, UX, and related contexts because technological design, social practice *and policy* are dynamically entangled and mutually constitutive. Through this research, we demonstrate the value of a stronger emphasis on policy in HCI by exploring a recent controversy on Reddit: "AMAgeddon." Applying Hirschman's exit, voice and loyalty framework, we argue that the sustainability of online communities like Reddit will require successful navigation of the complex and often murky intersections among technical design and human interaction through a distributed participatory policymaking process that promotes user loyalty.

Author Keywords
Information policy; participatory policymaking; value sensitive design; social media; online communities

ACM Classification Keywords
H.5 Information Interfaces and Presentations; K.4.1 Public Policy Issues K.4.3 Organizational Impacts; K.4.m Miscellaneous

INTRODUCTION
Human-computer interaction research and practice traditionally blends interests and aspects of design and human experience. Emergent social computing platforms can constrain and enable new forms of community and practice through design choices. Likewise, human interaction with and amongst emerging computing forms can generate significant changes in the designed or built environments in which they exist. Technical design and human factors thus co-constitute worlds of social computing and these relationships and interactions have long been a chief concern amongst HCI researchers and practitioners.

In this dynamic and emerging environment, policy has sometimes (unfairly) fallen to the wayside. This paper seeks to widen the aperture of CHI's analytic lens to make explicit the implications and significance of policy processes and structures. Policy, along with design and practice, co-constitute emergent sociotechnical forms and systems of interaction. Policy is "deeply intertwined" with design and practice in forceful, subtle, non-linear, interdependent connections [17]. The shared interests of the CHI community can be promoted by incorporating perspectives that foreground the role of policy and policymaking in the emergence, development, and evolution of social computing. (Re)conceptualizing sociotechnical change, innovation, and transformation as a dynamic interplay between design, practice, and policy opens new opportunities for exploring, describing, explaining, and potentially improving the human experience with, and understanding of, emerging technologies.

In this paper, drawing upon a recent controversy involving the popular social media website Reddit, we describe and explain how policies and policymaking processes and structures are deeply and inextricably embedded in the fabric of collaborative online environments. The linkages result from early design choices, the establishment of core values, the behavior of lead users, and emerging community norms, practices, and expectations. In combination, these elements produce an environment suited to distributed participatory policymaking, but how the policymaking process unfolds, and whether or not it is successful, depends on relational factors. We describe and analyze the interplay between technical design, social practice, and policymaking on Reddit through the lens of Hirschman's exit, voice, and loyalty framework, concluding that the success of communities like Reddit depends upon administrators' ability to support participatory policymaking and navigate the policymaking process in ways that promote user loyalty. This research on Reddit's AMAgeddon can provide important clues for CHI researchers and practitioners

CHI'16, May 07 - 12, 2016, San Jose, CA, USA

ACM 978-1-4503-3362-7/16/05…$15.00
DOI: http://dx.doi.org/10.1145/2858036.2858516

working in social computing, online communities, and related fields of human-computer interaction.

HCI AND POLICY RESEARCH IN PERSPECTIVE

With few exceptions, policy has not been a chief concern among the majority of scholars and practitioners working in the field of human-computer interaction. A relatively small but steadfast contingent of the CHI community has sought to raise awareness around the importance of researcher- and practitioner-engagement in technology policymaking. For example, *CHI* has hosted special interest groups and workshops focusing on why and how its members might influence issues of technology policy [19, 2]. The community has organized informal (e.g. the chi-policy@acm.org listserv) and formal mechanisms (e.g. SIGCHI US Public Policy Committee) for discussing and engaging with policy-related aspects of human-computer interaction [28, 20, 27]. In addition, smaller research collaborations have formed to support efforts to generate a workable framework for guiding the interactions between design and practice though greater engagement in public policy processes [13].

This important work, undertaken by a relatively tight-knit cluster of researchers and practitioners, constitutes a disappointingly small proportion of HCI work overall. In addition, the interests described above are notably *public policy* oriented. This sort of high-level, public governance approach is unquestionably important in that it tends to manifest in sweeping changes and broadly applicable rules and regulatory mechanisms. But "policy" for purposes of this research and the interests of CHI should be understood as including the important forms of public law and policymaking processes that regulate the development and use of information technologies but also "a range of rules and procedures set by private firms … that may intersect with formal law and policy in complex ways" [17:4]. The more dispersed, distributed, relatively more modest policies enacted by private companies, non-governmental organizations, and individuals in conjunction with the developments of particular tools, technologies, platforms, applications, and smaller-scale user communities are perhaps equally as important as public policy.

Concerns and issues pertaining to private policies have been discussed and studied in a range of recent human-computer interaction research contexts. For example, policy-authoring mechanisms have been studied, designed, and refined in the context of interface design, usability studies, and information visualization projects [31, 32, 33, 34, 9]. Researchers have studied tradeoffs between security and usability in the context of password policies [16, 25]. Privacy policies have been studied in the context of usability and interface studies and decision-making processes [18, 54, 37]. Researchers have also studied the development and effect of policies in the context of end-user privacy [14], online social science research ethics [4], and emergent collective infrastructures [5]. While the inclusion of policy in this body of work is promising, in the vast majority of instances, policy tends to be a glancing add-on to some other, non-policy-related concern, i.e. policy is rarely confronted head-on, as a first order concern.

That said, there are some areas where policy, and private policies in particular, may been starting to gain momentum as a first-order concern of researchers in the HCI, CSCW, and information science fields. In the context of collaborative information environments such Wikipedia and digg, researchers have explored conflicts arising at the intersection of technical design and social practice, and discussed ways that policy, rules, and norms develop in response conflict [58, 21, 22, 23, 24]. Linkages between early technical design choices, harmful social consequences, and evolving community expectations were explored through a critical feminist lens in the important recent work of Massanari [29]. Researchers in CSCW recently argued that policy is inextricably linked and entangled with design and practice, often preceding and sometimes dominating technical and social factors where emergent technological forms and practices are concerned [17], and that policy is an important source of embedded generativity in sociotechnical systems, functioning as a gatekeeper capable of opening and/or closing spaces of design and practice [7]. In addition, recent research into emerging controversies around values, norms, and behavioral expectations in diverse online communities suggests that participatory policymaking processes may be a necessary condition of such sites' continued success and sustainability [8].

Notwithstanding the aforementioned research, the associations between HCI and information policy seem somewhere mired by ambiguity. Clusters of researchers and practitioners are advancing policy as a priority for public engagement, practice, and research but, for the most part, policy concerns seem disintegrated from the core HCI concerns. This may be a holdover from still dissipating disciplinary strictures, when human-computer interaction research was dominated by computer science and cognitive psychology perspectives, perspectives which coincidentally have tended not to include significant law and policy components in either their teaching or research activities. While it is possible that the under-emphasis on policy reflects a belief that policy is not a relevant, interesting, or integral aspect of HCI work, a more plausible (and less dubious) interpretation may be that it's an unintended consequence of earlier (increasingly outdated) disciplinary divisioning. Many HCI researchers and practitioners simply lack the domain expertise to meaningfully contribute to or engage with complex policy-related issues. This may feed into a contention that policy is best left to "those people over there," (i.e. law, public policy, and governance scholars and practitioners) freeing up members of the HCI community to imagine, build, test, and deploy new technologies and tools unfettered by the policy "what ifs."

Whatever the causes, the sense that policy, "(when it is thought about at all) is imagined to come *after* design and practice, in both time and importance" [17] should be troubling to HCI researchers and practitioners. Human-computer interaction, CSCW, and information science research and practice will have greater reach, depth, and impact if they are able to finds ways to identify and analyze the ways policy interacts with their work. Finding ways to include technology policy, generative policymaking, and studies of participatory policymaking processes more centrally into our research will improve scholarship and foster responsible and ethical practices at the complex intersections of technology and society. Instead of viewing policy as a drag on the fast-paced, dynamic, evolving worlds of human-computer interaction, we must begin recognizing that it is an integral part of it [7].

In the sections that follow, we describe an example of how foregrounding and emphasizing the nexus among policy, design, and practice can have important design and practical implications for social computing research. In particular, we explore the mutually constitutive intersections of design, practice, and policymaking in the context of Reddit and argue that recent, widely publicized controversies involving Reddit administrators, moderators, and users can be traced back to fundamental misunderstandings and/or miscalculations of the nature and role of policy in social media and online communities. We carry forward the arguments made elsewhere that the sustainability and success of social computing sites like Reddit will necessarily depend on the ability of administrators to accommodate and support participatory policymaking processes [8]. In this paper we offer one possible framework, discussed below, for understanding *how and why* the participatory policymaking process emerges in the context of Reddit and demonstrate the value of user loyalty.

EXIT, VOICE & LOYALTY

In his seminal work, economist and political scientist Albert Hirschman developed the exit, voice, and loyalty framework for describing the basic decisions facing consumers of deteriorating goods and services [12]. Before explaining the particulars of his concept, it is important to position Hirschman's perspective on change, broadly construed.

Hirschman's work was grounded in a belief that progress, including technological, economic, political, and social progress, is nonlinear. Cautioning against a tendency to view history through a deterministic lens, Hirschman argued against a view of humanity as steadily climbing up the rungs on the ladder of progress, with each rung representing a new accomplishment or achievement, an improvement in our knowledge, our technology, our social institutions, and so forth. Hirschman stresses that that image of linear accent is not representative of the change process. Humanity undulates, shifting between achievement and lapse, high-performance and slack, opportunity and restriction [12].

The undulating processes of change and progress, he argues, primes human communities to develop a tolerance for deterioration while, somewhat paradoxically, simultaneously developing mechanisms to control against deterioration:

Each society learns to live with a certain amount of dysfunctional or misbehavior; but lest the misbehavior feed on itself and lead to general decay, society must be able to marshal from within itself forces which will make as many of the faltering actors as possible revert to the behavior required for its proper functioning. [12: 1]

Policies and other regulatory mechanisms represent some of the "forces marshaled from within" societies that safeguard against its utter dysfunction and dissolution. Even where a society starts out with relatively few proscriptions and restrictions, Hirschman seems to suggest that social decay is both inevitable and potentially contagious, as are the enhanced policy-based control responses:

[R]ecognition of this unpleasant truth has been impeded by a recurring utopian dream: that economic progress, while increasing the surplus above subsistence, will also bring with it disciplines and sanctions of such severity as to rule out any backsliding that may be due, for example, to faulty political processes.[12: 7]

Moreover, in Hirschman's view, not only is technological progress at risk of the same undulating give and take between progress and deterioration, but the consequences of its flux maybe even direr:

[W]hile technical progress increases society's surplus above subsistence it also introduces a mechanism of the utmost complexity and delicacy, so that certain types of social misbehavior which previously had unfortunate but tolerable consequences would now be so clearly disastrous that they would be more securely barred than before. As a result, society is, and then again it is not, in a surplus situation: it is producing a surplus, but it is not at liberty not *to produce it or to produce less of it than is possible: in effect, social behavior is as simply and as rigidly prescribed and constrained as it is in a no surplus, bare subsistence situation.* [12: 8]

Technical progress never really alleviates the problems of an earlier paradigm or regime; it merely shifts the focus or perspective. In other words, social networks and online communities simultaneously reduce the severity of some social ills (e.g. by improving access to knowledge, communities, and/or companionship) while fueling other forms of "misbehavior," previously dormant, repressed, or alienated but now unleashed and let loose upon the world through newly available information and communication technologies [1]. These will be important considerations to keep in mind as we consider the life-cycle of techno-libertarian ideals on a site like Reddit.

Against this backdrop of inevitable deterioration in products and services, Hirschman tells us that users will be faced with a choice between two alternatives: exit and voice. If exit is chosen, the user simply stops paying for the good or service, perhaps turning instead to a competitor. Exit is essentially an economic principle. Dissatisfied consumers turn to the market to defend their welfare, improve their position, and/or supply them with a better alternative or substitutive product or service. As Hirschman describes, exit is neat, impersonal, and indirect [12].

Voice, in contrast, is volatile and essentially political. When consumers are dissatisfied with a deteriorating product or service, they can choose to voice their dissatisfaction directly, to management or some other authority within the firm, in an effort to induce remedial action and find a fix for the decay. While exit is practical and efficient, voice is messy, graduated, public, articulated, direct and straightforward [12].

While economists tend to favor exit over voice because the former is viewed as a more efficient response to deterioration (what Veblen might call a "trained incapacity" [57]), Hirschman contends that the interests of deteriorating firms and organizations are actually best served by users' exercise of voice. This is particularly the case with users that are particularly invested in and knowledgeable of the product and service because they are uniquely situated to express constructive criticism. But this too poses a problem as:

...those customers who care most about the quality of the product and who therefore are those who would be the most active, reliable, and creative agents of voice are for those very reasons also those who are apparently likely to exit first in the case of deterioration. [12: 47]

In Hirschman's view, the key then is not to safeguard against decay and deterioration (as these are largely inevitable) but to find ways to accommodate and respond to customers' exercise of voice by fostering increased user loyalty. In this context, loyalty includes but signifies more than the feeling of affinity a user has for a product or service. Loyalty influences how much and how long a user will tolerate an imperfect or degraded product or service and it modifies users' decisions between flight (exit) and fight (voice). Loyalty not only makes it more likely that users will choose not to exit when a firm's products or services deteriorate, but it promotes a higher-quality of participation through voice due to these users' investment in, knowledge of, and commitment to the product or service.

Loyalty is therefore the linchpin in Hirschman's exit, voice and loyalty framework. It is the switch that turns lead users (who may otherwise be quick to exit) into lead users committed to sticking it out and wilfully engaging in a potentially messy political process such as participatory policymaking. Loyalty provides pause to those considering instantaneous exit in the face of decay, and quite possibly prevents the quick destruction, dissolution, and collapse many firms and organizations would face at the first (unavoidable) signs of trouble.

With the HCI-policy groundwork and issues set forth, and Hirschman's framework laid out, we now briefly discuss our research methods before turning our attention to Reddit's AMAgeddon.

METHODS

To understand the role of policy in mediating the relationship between technical and social aspects of collaborative online environments, we undertook an in-depth qualitative study of a single specific incident on Reddit, AMAgeddon. We identified and documented the subreddits implicated in the AMAgeddon controversy and manually scraped the data from the relevant time period. The data for this study consisted of publically available comments, conversations, and discussions on and about the effected subreddits.

Using an iterative, inductive process, data was coded for user name, subreddit, user role (e.g. moderator, user, administrator and so forth), exit, voice, and loyalty. User comments were also coded and analyzed for timeliness and popularity. Operating under the assumption that more upvotes a comment received, the clearer it signaled general community sentiment, comments with high scores were interpreted as more representative than lower scored comments. We attempted to triangulate and anchor data wherever possible to foster increased credibility, validity, and trustworthiness. We chose to exclude comments that appeared primarily oriented around or motivated by issues of gender, sexual orientation, and race where they did not also signal exit, voice, and/or loyalty because we determined this data to be of limited relevance to our interest in participatory policymaking processes. In light of Massanari's work, a follow-on study engaging in a critical analysis of these comments may be called for [29]. Stable links to the text of all user comments were also recorded and are provided as needed in the references section of this paper.

In light of the comments of anonymous reviewers, and in the spirit of full disclosure and transparency, we note that the authors of this paper bear no formal affiliation with Reddit. One of the authors is a regular user/participant in the Reddit community but did not play an active role, beyond that of an observer, in the AMAgeddon controversy. The other author is an outsider, engaging with Reddit purely as a research site for the study of distributed participatory policymaking processes in social media environments. The researchers have studied other, similar controversies in Reddit's past including the emergence and suspension of /r/jailbait [8].

By tracing the emergence, evolution, and resolution of a particular controversy, enabling patterns and themes to emerge from the data, we hope to shed light on the entanglements of policy, design, and practice in complex social media environments.

CONTEXTUALIZING REDDIT

Often referred to as "the front page of the Internet," Reddit is a popular social media website and online community that enables users to post, comment on, and vote for (or against) a wide range of user-supplied and/or user-generated content. On any given day, a visit to the site's home page reveals a seemingly random list of posts ranging from a link to an article featuring George Hotz, the hacker credited with first unlocking the iPhone [48], to an "Ask Me Anything" ("AMA") hosted by Ann Wilson from the rock band Heart [38], to a series of photographs depicting spiders eating (surprisingly large) animals [46]. Much of Reddit's success may be owed to the diversity of content on its front page.

In addition, part of Reddit's appeal (which some users characterize as addictive) seems also to stem from its dynamism. Reddit's users (contributing and non-contributing) often find themselves getting lost in the ever-changing life of the site:

I should be applying for jobs but it's so hard when all the people I love are right here :(somebody convince me to get off. [43]

Reddit's content changes moment-to-moment as new posts are created and users' generate responses and comments, and cast their votes. The ever-changing stream of loosely coupled content provides a constant source of stimulation and interest that is sometimes difficult to turn away from.

Reddit's success as a social media platform and online community, and in particular its diversity and dynamism, can be traced to two key value sensitive design choices. First, since its early beginnings when Reddit's co-founders Steve Huffman (/u/spez) and Alexis Ohanian (/u/kn0thing) partnered with Aaron Swartz, techno-libertarian ideals, particularly with respect to freedom of expression, became central to Reddit's core values and identity. As an illustration, when speculating on what the founding fathers of the United States might have thought about Reddit in an interview with *Forbes*, Ohanian replied:

A bastion of free speech on the World Wide Web? I bet they would like it. ... It's the digital form of political pamphlets. [11]

This core value – a bastion of free speech on the World Wide Web — was, in turn, embodied in key design choices. Reddit employs a voting system to whereby users can promote and demote content by clicking an "up" arrow or a "down" arrow. The practical implication of this relatively simple voting mechanism is that content that aligns with the majority's values is promoted while dissenting views tend to be demoted. Even though "down voting" something solely because one disagrees with the viewpoint expressed is a violation of "reddiquette" — shared norms typically expressed and/or ratified by a subreddit's moderator(s) — it is a very common practice.

While numerous popular social media sites employ a voting mechanism (e.g. digg), subreddits are a key feature that distinguishes Reddit from its competitors. Subreddits are niche forums on Reddit, typically created and moderated by users, dedicated to a specific topic. There are currently fifty default subreddits, such as /r/pics, /r/worldnews, and /r/funny, which together funnel the majority of content to Reddit's front page. In addition, there are a multitude of non-default subreddits (over six thousand active ones at last count) that exist in Reddit's extensive digital catacombs.

Within this fairly streamlined collaborative online environment, Redditors let loose to interact and communicate largely as they choose. In other words, the behavior of Redditors are thinly constrained by end-user policies. For example, until some very recent well-publicized controversies [35], all content was welcome so long as it was not illegal (e.g. child porn), was spam (i.e. unsolicited often commercial messages), and did not amount to doxxing (i.e. disclose personally identifiable or confidential information) [30].

An arguably unavoidable consequence of the wide latitude for freedom of expression and thin content policies is that Reddit plays host to a great deal of cultural and intellectual detritus. While particularly offensive or vitriolic content typically never reaches the front page, there are a host of subreddits dedicated to racist, sexist, violent, and particularly disturbing pornographic content. Some of these subreddits (e.g. /r/hitler) are likely trolls, existing only to provoke discord by posting offensive or upsetting material. But others are legitimate, with new content being posted and commented on from an active (though perhaps insular) group of members and users. Several of these offensive subreddits have garnered negative attention both within the Reddit community and in broader public media spheres [6, 10, 36].

Thus, early design choices coupled with established core values, the behavior of lead users primed the way for Reddit to emerge as a social media site and online community strongly oriented around free speech and democratic governance. We see these values reflected in the diverse and dynamic content that flows through Reddit. We also see these values emerge in the ways the community seeks to resolve tensions and controversies through a process of participatory policymaking [8].

Tensions and controversies arise, however, when Reddit's administrators demonstrate reluctance with respect to accommodating and supporting the realities of the participatory world they designed, particularly where policymaking and governance decisions are concerned. The recent controversy surrounding the unexpected and unexplained firing of a beloved Reddit employee illustrates how some of the tensions resolve through a participatory policymaking process that reflects users exit, voice and loyalty.

"AMA"GEDDON: REDDIT GOES DARK

On July 2nd, 2015, many of Reddit's most popular subreddits, including "I Am A" (/r/IAmA), "Ask Me Anything" (/r/ama) and "Ask Reddit" (/r/askreddit) went dark in protest of the termination of Victoria Taylor, /u/chooter.

Taylor was a member of Reddit's administrative team. Her main responsibility was helping high profile users including celebrities, politicians, and other noteworthy figures, handle question and answer sessions in the popular /r/ama ("ask me anything") subreddit. Taylor made strides in upping the quality, depth, breadth, and impact of /r/ama. More generally, she was credited with channelling much-needed goodwill toward Reddit in the wake of several highly-publicized publicized missteps. Needless to say, a large contingent of the Redditors were unhappy about her departure.

Taylor's termination struck a particularly dissonant chord with some members of the Reddit community because it appeared so swift, unexpected, and resolute. She was fired without obvious warning or explanation. Reddit's top administrators, themselves a relatively opaque group aside from the maligned former CEO, Ellen Pao, were viewed as essentially "disappearing" one of the communities own, most-beloved, public, and respected members.

Some disgruntled Redditors began to protest. By changing the access settings on their subreddits to "private," moderators responded to Taylor's termination by essentially "disappearing" some of Reddit's most popular subreddits. To casual visitors of the site, the protest likely went unnoticed; the front page still looked like the front page, albeit an atypically strange and diverse version. To seasoned Redditors, however, the protest was a noticeable and powerful counterpoint to the administrations' move. If it is true that the "most powerful weapon on earth is the human soul on fire" [3] then Reddit's fade into black must have felt like a bomb exploding, sending shockwaves through the administrators and the wider community:

I fully support this decision to shut down /r/IAmA, letting Victoria go is a slap.

To back this up, I am the mod in /r/science that organizes all of the science AMAs, and I am going to have meaningful problems in the /r/science AMAs. Victoria was the only line of communication with the admins. If somebody wants to get analytics for an AMA the answer will be "sorry, I can't help."

Dropping this on all of us in the AMA sphere feels like an enormous slap to those of us who put in massive amounts of time to bring quality content to reddit.

I personally feel like shutting /r/science down as well, that's how much of a bad taste this leaves. [52]

The protest, subsequently dubbed AMAgeddon, represented a breaking point in tensions within the community, particularly amongst administrators, moderators, and users over participation in policymaking and governance. Taylor's termination may have prompted AMAgeddon but the response reflected tensions that had been building for months and even years preceding. Ellen Pao, as CEO of Reddit, was the recipient of much of the initial blame for Taylor's firing. *"Typical Ellen Pao"* was the comment of /u/Oxus007 [53].

The fallout from the protest trickled down through the lower administrative ranks as well, and as it did the darkening spread as well. Other moderators caught on to the protest and they too began to block access. As any web administrator would likely agree, downtime, even when measured in minutes or hours, is a serious problem. The collective darkening of Reddit's most popular subreddits sent many Reddit administrators into crisis-mode. As administrator /u/bluepinkblack commented:

By lunch, I couldn't focus on doing my actual job, as I was overwhelmed trying to keep up with one community after another going private on Reddit. I just couldn't focus on work when the site that we (really do) love so much began imploding in front of our faces. My concerns were all over the place, ranging from "the users hate us" and "the users must understand we're trying," to—selfishly—'No! Don't you shut down r/crappydesign, too!' [40]

/u/bluepinkblack was expressing a complex series of emotional and practical reactions brought on by the AMAgeddon. On the one hand, the protest disrupted functioning of the site and created additional work (and problems) for administrators. On the other hand, the roles of administrators, moderator, and user are not always clearly distinct or separable. Boundary lines within the community are blurred, as are within- and among-group affinities. /u/bluepinkblack can simultaneously react to and engage with AMAgeddon as an administrator, a moderator, *and* a user.

Complicating, and likely spurring, the protest was the reaction of co-founder Ohanian who uttered the now infamous response at the outset of the protest: *"popcorn tastes good"* [47]. Within the Reddit community this phrase has developed a special meaning: Redditors inject this comment when they are voyeuristically observing and enjoying drama, often simultaneously trivial and destructive, between other users. It is a way of expressing detached, smug entertainment, as if munching popcorn in a movie theatre, at the impassioned public displays of others.

When Ohanian said *"popcorn tastes good"* in response to AMAgeddon, it reflected a clear misunderstanding of the significance of the protest and the power dynamics of Reddit. Within minutes of his misstep, Pao was replaced by Ohanian as the primary target of the rising inferno of community outrage on Reddit. His actions even drew the ire of Reddit's former CEO Yishan Wong (/u/yishan) who attempted to simultaneously call out Ohanian and redirected some of the blame that had befallen Pao:

Alexis wasn't some employee reporting to Pao, he was the Executive Chairman of the Board, i.e. Pao's boss. He had different ideas for AMAs, he didn't like Victoria's role, and decided to fire her. Pao wasn't able to do anything about it. In this case it shouldn't have traveled upstream to her, it came from above her.

Then when the hate-train started up against Pao, Alexis should have been out front and center saying very clearly 'Ellen Pao did not make this decision, I did.' Instead, he just sat back and let her take the heat. That's a stunning lack of leadership and an incredibly shitty thing to do.

I actually asked that he be on the board when I joined; I used to respect Alexis Ohanian. After this, not quite so much. [56]

Analyzing AMAgeddon using the exit, voice and loyalty framework can provide some key insights into the intersections of technical design choices, emerging social practices, and policymaking processes on Reddit. The unexplained and seemingly capricious termination of Victoria Taylor represented a serious deterioration in what Reddit's users considered to be its product or service for a number of reasons.

First, the move undermined the core democratic values the community had been built upon and thrived upon for years. The ability to post content and create and moderate largely autonomous subreddits justified, in the minds of moderators and users, their voluntary expenditure of time, energy, and creativity. The sovereign subreddits were one of the key features that differentiated Reddit from other link aggregating sites and the process of Taylor's termination drew the governance structure of Reddit into question.

Relatedly, Taylor's firing triggered a sort of critical self-reflection and questioning within the community around the meaning of Reddit and users' place(s) in it. Redditors had come to believe that Reddit *was* its users both in terms of its content and its organizational infrastructure. Users and, even more so moderators, viewed the opaque, aggressive take-down of one of their friends, who also happened to be a valued administrator, as an affront to their own value and place in the community. One of Reddit's primary moderators and a close collaborator of Taylor responded to her termination by saying:

We all had the rug ripped out from under us and feel betrayed...We have been really blindsided by all of this. As a result, we will need to go through our processes and see what can be done without her. [45]

Objectively, the importance of Redditors like /u/karmanaut cannot be overstated. The moderators of the default subreddits do a tremendous amount of unwaged labor. They clear bad posts, moderate discussions, and ensure that interesting, high quality content is not drowned out in a deluge of spam. Many moderators work essentially full time on their subreddits, and this voluntary participation and contribution is necessary to the functioning of Reddit.

Moderators are, in essence, Reddit's lead users [59]. They are the users who occupy the best position to be able to advise, critique, or direct the political response of Reddit in the face of controversy. Under Hirschman's framework, garnering the loyalty of moderators ought to be the administrators' chief objective. Not only are moderators in the best position to improve Reddit's products and services through the exercise of voice, they are also the users most affected and offended by deterioration of the site such that they are inclined to be the first to exit. "Going dark," was therefore a completely reasonable, perhaps even predictable response of moderators to the seemingly unjustified firing of Taylor.

Relatedly, the AMAgeddon shed light on a growing list of community tensions. It became readily apparent that users viewed Taylor's termination not as a singular, one-off administrative mistake, but rather as a culminating one. A number of content or speech-related collisions had been occurring in the months and years preceding Taylor's termination. For example, several months earlier a conflict had flashed around the administration's decision to ban of a controversial subreddit, /r/fatpeoplehate. While the reasons given for the ban were viewpoint-neutral — the subreddit violated rules against "brigading" or voter collusion – many Redditors believed it was banned *because* it was hate speech (and therefore neither illegal nor prohibited by the site's content policy). In either case, users were quick to point out that other subreddits, whose users engaged in similar conduct, were seemingly arbitrarily granted a stay:

You can't censor one community without running the risk of censoring them all. While boards may be offensive, they are not "wrong" - their discourse is legitimate public dialogue, otherwise the board would have died.

How then, can the "sphere" be determined? The simple answer is that it largely determines itself. If a board has no subscribers, it largely dies in the public eye. No posters - no content - no board. That the board exists as a self-sustaining forum at all indicates that it has a community that considers its topic to be a "sphere of legitimate discourse. [49]

Sensemaking around Taylor's termination thus almost instantaneously merged with a series of other equally inconsistent, awkward, fumbling missteps by Reddit administrators in the recent memory of many Redditors.

One thing was certain. While deep channels of discontent had been brewing amongst Reddit's community for some time, Taylor's termination was a clear breaking point. The central question her firing prompted was not *whether* the community would react, but *how* and *why*. AMAgeddon sent a loud signal of discontent to administrators over the perceived deterioration of Reddit, but it was unclear, perhaps even to those moderating the darkened subreddits, what it all meant. One of the most popular responses, a "top ten" list of Redditors' complaints, seemed to have little to do (at least directly) with Taylor's termination:

The administration has abandoned the concept of reddit as a free speech platform.

Moderators are banning users for activity outside of their subreddit.

Shadowbans are bad and should only be used against commercial spammers.

I no longer trust the Reddit admins to do what they say or say what they mean.

Too much moderator power is concentrated in "cliques" or "cabals" of users.

Subreddits like ShitRedditSays exist as a means of systematically harassing redditors.

Reddit's new harassment definition is too vague, subjective and/or unfairly applied.

Reddit should not cooperate with foreign governments to locally censor content.

Quarantined subreddits should not require a verified email for privacy reasons.

/r/fatpeoplehate and/or related subs should not have been banned and should be restored. [41]

Did the AMAgeddon spurred by Taylor's termination signify that users had simply had enough? Was Reddit "going dark" an act of "exit" such that the subreddits would remain voluntarily and terminally dark? Some Redditors seemed to readily accept this potential reality:

nobody cares reddit blows [54]

Others, however, were less apathetic, encouraging a widespread exodus of users to other, competitor, sites such as digg or the newly emerging "voat," a Reddit clone:

After the banning of many subreddits by Reddit including Coontown and Kiketown, it shows that freedom of speech exists no more in Reddit. Off to Voat! [50]

Another user posted:

I get it. It's Reddit. It's easy. It's comfortable. It's familiar. Fine. Continue to use it. As long as you are here, you are under the thumb of Chairman Pao and you will be stuck in defensive and pointless e-drama and never be allowed to go on the offensive. Your energies will be contained and diminished. [42]

Yet another user, who seemed to be indicating that they would remain on Reddit but diminish their digital footprint (and therefore their potential as a source of revenue for Reddit) said:

I am already doing it by using adblock and not giving reddit any profit. [39]

While the darkening of subreddits and a number of user comments suggest that exit may have been occurring, it is also clear that many users chose to exercise "voice" in response to Taylor's termination. "Going dark" was a way for the Reddit community, and moderators in particular, to communicate their dissatisfaction, exert their political power, and potentially prompt changes in policy and governance processes.

Given this additional context, and the fact that loyalty is the linchpin in the struggle between exit and voice, it becomes excruciatingly apparent how co-founder Ohanian's response of *"popcorn tastes good"* reflected a serious miscalculation and mismanagement of the Reddit communities' expectations and power. The implication that Ohanian positioned himself as a sort of Caesar, gleefully watching the gladiatorial destruction below, was a perspective in need of swift correction. AMAgeddon was, at least in part, directed toward that end. Ohanian had to come to terms with the fact that his extremely popular website would not exist but for the participation, creativity, diligence, and *loyalty* of its users. Ohanian might believe he "owns" the site, but he is not alone at the controls.

Within hours of his *"popcorn tastes good"* comment, Ohanian responded to the growing unrest with a notably different tone:

Your message was received loud and clear. The communication between Reddit and the moderators needs to improve dramatically. We will work closely with you all going forward to ensure events like today don't happen again. At this point, however, the blackout has served its purpose, and now it's time to get Reddit functioning again. I know many of you are still upset. We will continue to work through these issues with you all, but redditors don't deserve to be punished any further over an issue that is ultimately between Reddit and the moderators. [47]

This message signaled an attempt to make amends for his earlier comment, but all was not so easily forgiven. The top comment in response was:

Damn that's condescending.

"redditors don't deserve to be punished any further"

The user's aren't being punished: users will go elsewhere, the internet has many Reddit alternatives just waiting to snap up that traffic. Reddit is not so invaluable, indispensable or irreplaceable that people will be lost without it.

It's the management, executives, and administration of Reddit that is being punished. [44]

Another Redditor observed:

The admins keep dropping the balls on things. I'm concerned that y'all aren't learning from your mistakes. I've been around for nine years and I've never seen anything like these last few months. [51]

A generous interpretation of Ohanian's about-face might be that he was attempting to self-correct his earlier misstep and tap into the loyalty of the user base. He attempted to reach out directly to Redditors who may have felt unjustly harmed by disagreements between moderators and administrators as if to say "but think about the users!" While we might be inclined to dismiss Ohanian's remarks as foolish or misguided, it is difficult to come up with many other sites, or businesses for that matter, of comparable popularity where top administrators, CEOs, co-founders and chairmen of the board engage in public and open dialog about serious and difficult subjects with random users and each other with such fluency and immediacy. This again points to the participatory nature of Reddit, a feature that extends beyond content to the processes of governance and policymaking. It also highlights the fact that exit, voice and loyalty are not uni-directional in a collaborative online environment like Reddit.

AMAgeddon and the subsequent "*popcorn tastes good*" exchange signifies a number of other potentially important observations around questions of loyalty. In particular it suggests that Reddit users' loyalty may be influenced by invisible barriers to exit perhaps not contemplated by Hirschman. Hirschman's framework developed around commercial firms engaged in traditional economic markets. In what ways does a collaborative online environment like Reddit differ from the arrangements envisioned by Hirschman? What kind of buy-in is there for users of Reddit that might impact their decision to exit or not? When they exit are they leaving their community, their friends, and their content? What are the features and characteristics of Reddit that might make exit, voice, and loyalty more or less sticky? Features such as "Reddit gold" and "karma" might coerce user loyalty by granting certain users enhanced privileges which make it exit more untenable. Loyalty can explain why voice is chosen over exit, but it may also explain why a dissatisfied user may choose to do nothing at all (i.e. exhibit apathy) [26]. Reddit's users may remain loyal because they believe in the company or its leaders. They might also remain loyal due to tradition, inertia, sentimental attachment, friendships and other relationships, the lack of availability of reasonable alternatives and substitutes, and/or concern about the potential risk of unforeseen consequences of exiting.

CONCLUSION

This paper argued that CHI research and practice is unnecessarily limited by traditions that ignore or marginalize policy. Our work here was an attempt to pull policy down from its orbit to inform, in a more meaningful and concrete way, understandings of the complex interplay between design and social practice. By demonstrating that policy co-constitutes contemporary social media and online communities, we can generate deeper insights into the ways in which computing technology and human experience interact.

Building on earlier CHI scholarship that stressed the importance of participation in the public policymaking process, this paper argued that participatory policymaking may also be key to the sustained success of many private firms and endeavors. A failure to effectively engage with policy is a choice that will impact not only our understanding of emergent social computing environments but, as demonstrated by the Reddit controversy, may have real and significant detrimental effects on the social media design and practice.

Through the AMAgeddon controversy on the popular site Reddit, we explored the ways in which value sensitive design choices, intended to foster and support core values such as democratic governance and freedom, can have an unintended consequence of generating *de facto* participatory policymaking processes. Despite some of the administrator's beliefs to the contrary, Redditors exercised their political powers of dissent against perceived deterioration of the site and began to establish more explicit expectations around full participation in all facets of the life of Reddit. Users made it clear that they were no longer content with supplying and moderating all of Reddit's content; they also want a voice in the governance and policy determinations impacting the community. Through the exit, voice, loyalty framework, this work also explored the complexity of the notion of user loyalty. While some lead users, typically moderators, were the first to protest Taylor's dismissal, they may also be bound by invisible ties that make swift and complete exit untenable.

Our research shows that whether or not policy is explicitly taken into consideration in the design of online communities, it often emerges through the complex dynamics of human-human and human-computer interaction. User practices can become user expectations which can in turn vest in policies, particularly in highly participatory communities. The AMAgeddon, while sparked by the termination of Taylor, was about much more. It highlights the complex intersections of technical design, emerging social practice, and policy in collaborative online environments. It demonstrates how policies and the policymaking process can play an important role in the evolution and survival of social media sites. In particular, it illustrates how design choices and core communities' values can lead inextricably toward a participatory policymaking process, even where site administrators and owners wish and believe it otherwise.

Reddit and its users differ from the firms and consumers of Hirschman's era. They continuously modify, change, and co-construct the meaning of Reddit for themselves and others. They create the good and service and contribute to its inevitable decay and deterioration. Exit, voice, and loyalty provides a useful framework for describing and understanding this complex co-evolution but this research suggests further refinements may be called for.

Understanding this phenomenon, and developing ways to engage in a more direct and concerted way, can help researchers as we seek to unpack the complicated issues surrounding emerging technology, social practices, and policymaking.

ACKNOWLEDGMENTS

The authors gratefully acknowledge the helpful feedback and comments of the anonymous reviewers.

REFERENCES

1. Paul A. Baran and Robert B. Sutcliffe. *The political economy of growth*. New York: Monthly Review Press, 1957.
2. Benjamin B. Bederson, et al. 2006. Workshop on SIGCHI public policy. *CHI'06 Extended Abstracts on Human Factors in Computing Systems*. ACM Press, New York, NY,1655-1657. DOI: 10.1145/1125451.1125755.
3. Harold Whittle Blakely. 1957. *32d Infantry Division, World War II*. Thirty Second Infantry Division History Commission.
4. Nathan Bos, Karrie Karahalios, Marcela Musgrove-Chávez, Erika Shehan Poole, John Charles Thomas, and Sarita Yardi. 2009. Research ethics in the facebook era: privacy, anonymity, and oversight. In *CHI '09 Extended Abstracts on Human Factors in Computing Systems* (CHI EA '09). ACM, New York, NY. DOI=10.1145/1520340.1520402
5. Brian Butler, Elisabeth Joyce, and Jacqueline Pike. 2008. Don't look now, but we've created a bureaucracy: the nature and roles of policies and rules in wikipedia. *In Proceedings of the SIGCHI Conference on Human Factors in Computing Systems* (CHI '08). ACM, New York, NY, USA, 1101-1110. DOI=10.1145/1357054.1357227.
6. Cbc.ca. (2015). Reddit Bans 'Fat People Hate,' Other Subforums Under New Anti-Harassment Policy. (June 2015). Retrieved September 25th from http://www.cbc.ca/news/trending/reddit-bans-fat-people-hate-other-subforums-under-new-anti-harassment-policy-1.3108425.
7. Alissa Centivany, "Policy as Embedded Generativity: A Case Study of HathiTrust," forthcoming in *Proceedings of Computer-Supported Cooperative Work and Social Computing, 2016* (CSCW '16), San Francisco, CA, Feb. 27-Mar. 2, 2016.
8. Alissa Centivany and Bobby Glushko, "(Shifting) Lines in the Sand: Values, Ethics and Participatory Policymaking in Online Communities," manuscript on file with authors.
9. Kathi Fisler and Shriram Krishnamurthi. "A model of triangulating environments for policy authoring." *Proceedings of the 15th ACM symposium on Access control models and technologies*. ACM, 2010.
10. David Fitzpatrick and Drew Griffin (2012). Man Behind 'Jailbait' Posts Exposed, Loses Job. (October 2012) Retrieved September 24, 2015 from http://www.cnn.com/2012/10/18/us/internet-troll-apology/.
11. Forbes.com,. 'Reddit Co-Founder Alexis Ohanian's Rosy Outlook on the Future of Politics., 2012. Web. 24 Sept. 2015.
12. Albert Hirschman. 1970. "Exit, voice and loyalty." *Cambridge/Mass* (1982).
13. Harry Hochheiser and Jonathan Lazar. "HCI and societal issues: A framework for engagement." *International Journal of Human [#x02013] Computer Interaction* 23.3 (2007): 339-374.
14. Giovanni Iachello and Jason Hong. "End-user privacy in human-computer interaction." *Foundations and Trends in Human-Computer Interaction* 1.1 (2007): 1-137.
15. IAmAMods., 2015. Welcome Back!. Comment. July 3, 2015. Retrieved September 24, 2015 from https://np.reddit.com/r/IAmA/comments/3c0hcz/welcome_back/
16. Philip Inglesant and M. Angela Sasse. "The true cost of unusable password policies: password use in the wild." *Proceedings of the SIGCHI Conference on Human Factors in Computing Systems*. ACM, 2010.
17. Steven J. Jackson, Tarleton Gillespie, and Sandy Payette. "The policy knot: Re-integrating policy, practice and design in CSCW studies of social computing." *Proceedings of the 17th ACM conference on Computer supported cooperative work & social computing*. ACM, 2014.
18. Carlos Jensen and Colin Potts. "Privacy policies as decision-making tools: an evaluation of online privacy notices." *Proceedings of the SIGCHI conference on Human Factors in Computing Systems*. ACM, 2004.
19. Jeff Johnson. "CHI 99 SIG: SIGCHI's role in influencing technology policy." *SIGCHI Bulletin* 31.4 (1999): 43.
20. Maurits Kaptein, Dean Eckles, and Janet Davis. "Envisioning persuasion profiles: challenges for public policy and ethical practice." *interactions* 18.5 (2011): 66-69.
21. Aniket Kittur, E.H. Chi, B.A. Pendleton, B. Suh, and T. Mytkowicz. "Power of the few vs. wisdom of the crowd: Wikipedia and the rise of the bourgeoisie." *World wide web* 1.2 (2007): 19.
22. Aniket Kittur, B. Suh, B.A. Pendleton, and E.H. Chi. "He says, she says: conflict and coordination in Wikipedia." *Proceedings of the SIGCHI conference on Human factors in computing systems*. ACM, 2007.

23. Aniket Kittur, and Robert E. Kraut. "Harnessing the wisdom of crowds in wikipedia: quality through coordination." *Proceedings of the 2008 ACM conference on Computer supported cooperative work.* ACM, 2008.
24. Aniket Kittur, and Robert E. Kraut. "Beyond Wikipedia: coordination and conflict in online production groups." *Proceedings of the 2010 ACM conference on Computer supported cooperative work.* ACM, 2010.
25. Saranga Komanduri, et al. "Of passwords and people: measuring the effect of password-composition policies." *Proceedings of the SIGCHI Conference on Human Factors in Computing Systems.* ACM, 2011.
26. Carl Lagoze, et al. "Should I Stay or Should I Go? Alternative Infrastructures in Scholarly Publishing." *International Journal of Communication* 9 (2015): 20.
27. Jonathan Lazar, Jeff Johnson, and Harry Hochheiser. "Policy at the interface: HCI and public policy." *interactions* 12.6 (2005): 13-14.
28. Wendy E. Mackay. "Ethics, lies and videotape…." *Proceedings of the SIGCHI Conference on Human Factors in Computing Systems.* ACM Press/Addison-Wesley Publishing Co., 1995.
29. Adrienne Massanari. "# Gamergate and The Fappening: How Reddit's algorithm, governance, and culture support toxic technocultures." *New Media & Society* (2015): 1461444815608807.
30. Reddit.com. 2015. Reddit.Com: Content Policy. Retrieved September 24, 2015 from https://www.reddit.com/help/contentpolicy
31. Robert W. Reeder, et al. "Usability challenges in security and privacy policy-authoring interfaces." *Human-Computer Interaction–INTERACT 2007.* Springer Berlin Heidelberg, 2007. 141-155.
32. Robert W. Reeder, et al. "Expandable grids for visualizing and authoring computer security policies." *Proceedings of the SIGCHI Conference on Human Factors in Computing Systems.* ACM, 2008.
33. Robert W. Reeder, et al. "A user study of the expandable grid applied to P3P privacy policy visualization." *Proceedings of the 7th ACM workshop on Privacy in the electronic society.* ACM, 2008.
34. Robert W. Reeder, et al. "More than skin deep: measuring effects of the underlying model on access-control system usability." *Proceedings of the SIGCHI Conference on Human Factors in Computing Systems.* ACM, 2011.
35. Aaron Sarkin. (2014). Is Reddit Broken Beyond Repair? (November 2014) Retrieved September 24, 2015 from http://kernelmag.dailydot.com/issue-sections/staff-editorials/10749/reddit-broken-beyond-repair/.
36. The New York Times. Reddit Removes 5 Groups After Creating Harassment Policy. 2015. Retrieved on September 24, 2015 from http://www.nytimes.com/aponline/2015/06/10/business/ap-us-reddit-subreddit-bans.html?_r=0
37. Eran Toch, Norman M. Sadeh, and Jason Hong. "Generating default privacy policies for online social networks." *CHI'10 Extended Abstracts on Human Factors in Computing Systems.* ACM, 2010.
38. /u/annwilsonmusic. 2015. IamA Ann Wilson, lead singer of "Heart" AMA!. September 24, 2015. Retrieved September 24th, so15 from https://www.reddit.com/r/IAmA/comments/3m559j/iama_ann_wilson_lead_singer_of_heart_ama/
39. /u/BadCompSciMod. 2015. AMA REQUEST: /u/spez . Comment. August 3, 2015. Retrieved September 24, 2015 from https://np.reddit.com/r/circlebroke/comments/3fntzu/ama_request_uspez/ctqdxdu
40. /u/bluepinkblack. 2015. Ask an Admin, Vol 6" On AMAgeddon, Blackout 2015, etc. Comment. September 5, 2015. Retrieved September 24, 2015 from https://www.reddit.com/r/Upvoted/comments/3jn7e9/ask_an_admin_vol_6_on_amageddon_blackout_2015_etc/cuqnfvo
41. /u/GamerGateFan. 2015. Ask an Admin, Vol 6" On AMAgeddon, Blackout 2015, etc. Comment. September 5, 2015. Retrieved September 24, 2015 from https://www.reddit.com/r/Upvoted/comments/3jn7e9/ask_an_admin_vol_6_on_amageddon_blackout_2015_etc/cuqnfvo
42. /u/HistoryOfGamerHatred. June 14, 2015. Retrieved September 24, 2015 from https://np.reddit.com/r/KotakuInAction/comments/39sdy3/do_you_know_why_reddit_banned_you_from/
43. /u/ipissoffthesystem. 2015. I need to get off reddit. Original comment. June 18, 2014. Retrieved September 24, 2015, from https://www.reddit.com/r/teenagers/comments/28h62s/i_need_to_get_off_reddit_other/
44. /u/Isanion. 2015. /r/modclub AMAgeddon discussion thread. Comment. July 2 2015. Retrieved September 24, 2015 from https://www.reddit.com/r/modclub/comments/3bypwq/rmodclub_amageddon_discussion_thread/csqupsf
45. /u/karmanaut. 2015. Why has R/Iama been set to private?. Comment. July 2, 2015. Retrieved September 24, 2015 from https://np.reddit.com/r/OutOfTheLoop/comments/3bw39q/why_has_riama_been_set_to_private/csq204d

46. /u/kentnasty. 2015. The frogs in my neighborhood help to fight against the spider population. Apparently, the spiders are fighting back. September 24, 2015. Retrieved September 24, 2015 from https://www.reddit.com/r/WTF/comments/3m5i2y/the_frogs_in_my_neighborhood_help_to_fight/

47. /u/kn0thing,. 2015. IAmA set to private over mod firing. Comment. July 2, 2015. Retrieved September 24, 2015 from https://np.reddit.com/r/SubredditDrama/comments/3bwgjf/riama_set_to_private_over_mod_firing/csqg24d?context=3

48. /u/mada447. 2015. TIL that George Hotz, then 17 years old, was the first to unlock a first generation iPhone and sold the iPhone for a Nissan 350z and 3 locked iPhones. September 24, 2015. Retrieved September 24, 2015 from https://www.reddit.com/r/todayilearned/comments/3m581q/

49. /u/Mercury. 2015. Content Policy update. AMA Thursday, July 16th, 1pm pst. Comment. July 14, 2015 Retrieved September 24, 2015 from https://www.reddit.com/r/announcements/comments/3dautm/content_policy_update_ama_thursday_july_16th_1pm/ct3pvim

50. /u/MiddlemanOMT. 2015. The Great Migration to Voat begins!. Comment. August 5, 2015. Retrieved September 24, 2015 from https://np.reddit.com/r/Voat/comments/3fx7zc/the_great_migration_to_voat_begins/

51. /u/mrmojorisingi. 2015. Why has R/Iama been set to private?. Comment. July 2, 2015. Retrieved September 24, 2015 from https://np.reddit.com/r/OutOfTheLoop/comments/3bw39q/why_has_riama_been_set_to_private/csq730w?context=1

52. /u/nallen. 2015. Why has R/Iama been set to private. Comment. July 2, 2015. Retrieved September 24, 2015 from https://www.reddit.com/r/OutOfTheLoop/comments/3bw39q/why_has_riama_been_set_to_private/csq3hdm

53. /u/Oxus007. 2015. Admin Chooter, aka "Victoria" has been let go from Reddit, IAMA goes private as a result. Comment. July 2, 2015. Retrieved September 24, 2015, from https://www.reddit.com/r/Drama/comments/3bw66c/admin_chooter_aka_victoria_has_been_let_go_from/.

54. /u/STEAM_0-1-203796. 2015. So long, farewell, auf Wiedersehen, good night!. Comment. July 30, 2015. Retrieved September 24, 2015 from https://www.reddit.com/r/announcements/comments/3f6kqy/so_long_farewell_auf_wiedersehen_good_night/ctlt547

55. /u/whynotanon., 2015. Why has R/Iama been set to private?. Comment. July 2, 2015. Retrieved September 24, 2015 from https://np.reddit.com/r/OutOfTheLoop/comments/3bw39q/why_has_riama_been_set_to_private/csq4tl3

56. /u/yishan. 2015. Kn0thing says he was responsible for the change in AMAs (i.e. he got Victoria fired). Is there any evidence that Ellen Pao caused the alleged firing of Victoria?. Comment. July 12, 2015. Retrieved September 24, 2015 from https://np.reddit.com/r/TheoryOfReddit/comments/3d2hv3/kn0thing_says_he_was_responsible_for_the_change/ct1fsoi?context=3

57. Thorstein Veblen. 1914. The Instinct of Workmanship: And the State of Industrial Arts. Macmillan.

58. Fernanda B. Viégas, Martin Wattenberg, and Kushal Dave. "Studying cooperation and conflict between authors with history flow visualizations."*Proceedings of the SIGCHI conference on Human factors in computing systems*. ACM, 2004.

59. Eric von Hippel. 1986. "Lead Users: A Source of Novel Product Concepts," Management Science 32, no. 7 (July):791-805.

60. Jason Watson, Michael Whitney, and Heather Richter Lipford. "Configuring audience-oriented privacy policies." *Proceedings of the 2nd ACM workshop on Assurable and usable security configuration*. ACM, 2009.

Going Dark: Social Factors in Collective Action Against Platform Operators in the Reddit Blackout

J. Nathan Matias
Microsoft Research
1 Memorial Drive #1
Cambridge, MA 02142
natematias@gmail.com

ABSTRACT
This paper describes how people who lead communities on online platforms join together in mass collective action to influence platform operators. I investigate this by analyzing a protest against the social news platform reddit by moderators of 2,278 subreddit communities in July 2015. These moderators collectively disabled their subreddits, preventing millions of readers from accessing major parts of reddit and convincing the company to negotiate over their demands. This paper offers a descriptive analysis of the protest, combining qualitative content analysis, interviews, and quantitative analysis with the population of 52,735 active subreddits. Through participatory hypotheses testing with moderators, this study reveals social factors including the grievances of moderators, relations with platform operators, relations among moderators, subreddit resources, subreddit isolation, and moderators' relations with their subreddits that can lead to participation in mass collective action against a platform.

ACM Classification Keywords
H.5.3 Information Interfaces and Presentation (e.g., HCI): Group and Organization Interfaces—*Computer-supported cooperative work*

Author Keywords
collective action; sabotage; online platforms; participatory hypothesis testing; reddit; blackout; social factors

INTRODUCTION
The many volunteers who lead online communities exercise tremendous power and influence as they create, maintain, and govern social relations online. For that reason, research has highlighted their role in user activism aimed at online platform operators. In the late 1990s, America Online volunteer community leaders protested their treatment by the company, resulting in a class action lawsuit that was settled in 2011 for $15 million U.S. dollars[39]. Although community leaders have most famously responded to the tensions of unpaid and freely given labor in platform economies[71, 63], forum moderators have also played important roles in collective action by waged crowd workers[65] and political bloggers[68] attempting to change policies on the platforms they use.

What factors lead to collective action against platform operators by these leaders and their communities? In July 2015, moderators of 2,278 "subreddit" community groups on the social news site reddit joined a "blackout," preventing millions of users from accessing major parts of the platform and demanding improved treatment by the company[35]. Within hours, the company promised to meet moderators' demands, and moderators reactivated the communities they had disabled. One week later, reddit CEO Ellen Pao left the company[36].

This paper describes how volunteer community leaders come to participate in collective action to protest and influence platform operators. Through qualitative content analysis, interviews, and quantitative analysis of 52,735 active subreddits, this paper describes the social factors leading to participation in the reddit blackout, testing explanations developed and evaluated together with reddit moderators on both sides of the blackout. This paper finds that participation in the reddit blackout was associated with factors including the grievances of moderators, resources available to subreddits, relations among groups of moderators, the isolation of a subreddit from the rest of the platform, and the internal relationship of moderators to their subreddits.

BACKGROUND AND RELATED WORK
For at least 40 years, online platforms have relied on community leaders to facilitate and support social interactions. In the mid 1970s, the librarians and shopkeepers of Berkeley's Community Memory supported users to contribute, even as a 25 cent per-message fee was introduced to deter unacceptable participation[13]. In the 1980s, the WELL's *conference hosts,* BBS *SysOps*[64], and Usenet *moderators*[14] fostered conversations and maintained order. In the 1990s, tens of thousands of AOL volunteer *community leaders* managed its chatrooms[63]. Moderators remained fundamentally important to on-

line social interactions in the Web 2.0 period, even as platforms attempted to use machine learning[21], voting systems [29, 43, 41], and flagging systems to distribute the work of moderators more widely and disclaim responsibility for governance activity[17]. These roles are played by Wikipedia's *administrators*[1], Facebook's *admins*[23], Slashdot's *moderators*[42], Meetup's *group organizers*[40] and XBOX's *enforcement united*[28]. On platforms like Twitter with no official moderator role, users find the need to invent them[51, 37]. Although this work is often carried out informally[54], formally-defined community leaders are founders, designers, promoters, facilitators recruiters, legislators, responders, and enforcers of online social interactions[15] for millions of people every day.

Moderators and Community on reddit

The popular social news platform reddit hosts conversation threads across more than fifty thousand self-governed discussion groups called "subreddits." Reddit users post and comment on content within these subreddits, voting on contributions to affect their visibility within the subreddit and across a series of public and personalized newsfeeds. Founded in 2006 with the goal of becoming "the front page of the internet," reddit had over 200 million monthly visitors in August 2015, two thirds the number of active users on Twitter in the same period.[1] Practices and interests within these subreddits differ widely, while also sharing common qualities of participatory culture; in an ethnography, Massanari attempts to describe its many dimensions through the metaphors of carnival, performance, play, and community[50]. Subreddit conversations often unfold alongside emerging events; Leavitt and Clark have described participatory news creation on reddit during Hurricane Sandy and other crises[45].

The challenges of reaching diverse audiences and the problems of reddit's combination of newsfeed algorithms with voting mechanisms [49] were present in the earliest versions of the site, motivating the creation of the first subreddit. This group, "NSFW," was created to shift objectionable material away from the site's front page[32]. Over the next two years, the company started dozens of new subreddits, mostly to distinguish conversations happening in different languages. Then in Jan 2008, a year and a half after its acquisition by Condé Nast and 10 months after introducing advertisements[33], the company launched "user-controlled subreddits"[34]. The creators of these subreddits were given special moderator privileges. By June 2008, the final element of reddit governance was in place, per-subreddit machine learning systems for automated filtering of submissions [38]. By July 2015, the platform relied on nearly one hundred fifty thousand moderator roles[2] for over fifty thousand monthly active subreddits.

[1] `https://www.reddit.com/about/` and `https://about.twitter.com/company` accessed Sept 25, 2015.

[2] Since the number of people doing this work is not clear due to the prevalence of throwaway accounts and "alts"[44], this paper uses the term "moderators" to refer to moderator roles.

Subscribing to a subreddit does not always imply an idea of membership in a community. A subreddit's default settings have no barriers to joining, and anyone with a reddit account may post to any subreddit. Furthermore, many users treat subreddits as newsfeeds. Reddit facilitates context collapse[12] at speed and scale, supported by popularity algorithms that tend to draw attention to upvoted content and "drama" alike. The default view for logged-in reddit users is a personalized news feed algorithm that creates "your front page" with "hot" posts from a user's subreddits. In this view, users see only the most prominent posts from their subscriptions. Readers who are not logged in are shown a selection of popular posts from across the site[26].

The reddit Blackout of July 2015

The decisions by moderators to collectively disable over two thousand subreddits occurred in a wider period of crisis for reddit. After a company decision in June to ban several subreddits for harassment[58, 57], some users responded with an influx of posts typical of the banned subreddits. Others manipulated the reddit algorithms to feature protests and insults of then-CEO Ellen Pao, starting a petition calling for her resignation[22].

On July 2, 2015, reddit dismissed an employee who routinely offered essential, ongoing support to moderators who hosted the site's most popular feature: live Ask Me Anything (AMA) question-answer sessions with notable people[35]. Moderators of the /r/IamA subreddit, who heard the news while conducting a live Q&A, describe being caught off guard by this HR decision. They took their subreddit offline mid-conversation to decide how to respond[48]. Moderators of several large, default subreddits agreed to follow suit. They linked the company's lack of a transition plan with reddit's overall lack of communication with moderators and its neglect of moderation software. As more subreddits joined the blackout and the story was featured on international media, a separate group of anti-censorship campaigners who had been protesting reddit's anti-harassment policies redoubled their efforts to remove the CEO and encourage defection to other platforms[35].

After several hours of negotiations with moderators, the company promised to address their concerns, and moderators made their subreddits public again over the next few days. In the following months, the company changed development priorities, established new lines of communications with moderators, and hired its first Chief Technical Officer to address moderator demands[59].

Collective Action Against Platforms

To "black out" and "go dark," moderators modified the configuration of their subreddits to admit participation only from approved submitters. Going dark effectively shut off a subreddit; anyone who was not a moderator or personally approved by one could not access the conversation. Social movement theorists describe such acts as *sabotage*, a common practice where political actors halt the flow of resources, production, transportation, or information to make their demands visible, showcase the importance of their labor, and force powerful institutions to negotiate[7]. Strikes and sit-ins are common examples of this tactic. Notable online acts of political sabotage include a 2013 blackout by Internet platform operators (including reddit and the English language Wikipedia) to protest proposed U.S. intellectual property regulations[9] and the use of distributed denial of service attacks by activists[66].

Before the July blackout, the act of going dark was an isolated incident. In late 2014, a moderator of a popular gaming forum[3] took the subreddit private in an attempt to pressure a game company to release more beta versions of a special feature. Community participants objected strongly, forcing the moderator to restore the subreddit. When one subscriber retaliated by posting private details from the moderator's online dating account, the moderator disabled the subreddit again until reddit employees intervened to resolve the controversy.

Collective Action and Social Movement Theories

The goal of this paper is to describe the factors that led to participation in the reddit blackout. While this paper does not test academic theories of collective action or social movements, it does gesture toward ways that its qualitative and quantitative findings can relate to these theories. A substantial quantitative research tradition has asked what factors come together for a collective action such as a decision or political action to occur or be successful [60, 16]. When explaining a protest or strike, political opportunity theories would focus on the nature of the grievances of movement actors, expecting that those with greater grievances would be more likely to take action [55]. Political opportunity theories would also emphasize network relations among movement actors as important factors in joining a social movement [52]. Resource mobilization theories would focus on group resources as important factors in social movement mobilization, as well as the relative isolation of a group from other participating social movement groups [53].

Online Community Leadership

Although many subreddit participants supported the blackout, the demands made in the blackout were focused entirely on the distinct interests of subreddit moderators, leaders of the site's communities. For this reason, research on the development of distinct interests among online community leaders offers a backdrop for the inductive work of this paper. In studies on a class-action lawsuit by AOL community leaders, Postigo emphasizes poor company relations with community leaders, restrictively-designed moderation software, and coordination among community leaders as three important factors that led volunteers to see themselves as cheated employees rather than freely-contributing volunteers[62, 63]. In a study of 683 wikis drawing from scholarship on union organizations [56, 47], Shaw and Hill test internal characteristics of peer communities that predict the what they term "goal transformation"—the development of interests distinct to a community's leaders. They find goal transformation more likely among older, more complex groups[69].

Approaches and findings from this prior work provide deep influences to the inductive, qualitative work of this paper, while also framing its quantitative methods.

METHODS

To describe factors in collective action against platform operators, this paper carries out mixed methods participatory hypothesis testing, an approach to action research online that combines methods from virtual ethnography and quantitative analysis.

Participatory Hypothesis Testing as Action Research

This study's methods are drawn from the *action research* tradition, which begin in the 1930s with studies by factory workers and university-based researchers in the early years of social psychology. Setting out to produce knowledge with and for workers rather than solely for factory operators, researchers and workers collaborated on studies to answer questions about leadership, cooperation, and management that were led by worker interests[4]. Within HCI, action research has been influential in participatory design[31] and in emancipatory action research, often supporting specific political interests[20][6].

As a study that sets out to describe and explain rather than create, this work of action research brings together virtual ethnography[11] with the emerging practice of "popular data," where researchers and participants create questions and interpretations together[10, 19]. Since participants on reddit commonly create, share, and discuss data about their social behavior[30], reddit is well suited to this approach. Finally, since reddit moderators do not primarily talk about themselves as a well-defined interest group, the researcher has taken a "friendly outsider" stance rather than explicit political objectives[31].

Participatory Data Collection and Hypothesis Building

In practice, the data collection and question formation in this paper have taken three forms:

Firstly, among qualitative methods, the researcher carried out content analysis of 90 published interviews with moderators from before the blackout, over 250 articles outside reddit about the blackout, discussions in over 50 subreddits that declined to join the blackout, public statements by over 200 subreddits that joined the blackout, and over 150 discussions in blacked out subreddits after their communities were restored. The researcher also conducted 90 minute semi-structured interviews with 13 moderators of subreddits of all sizes, including those that joined and declined to join the blackout. These included moderators of communities accessible to anyone and "NSFW" subreddits only accessible to users 18 years

[3]Throughout this study, names, quotations, and subreddit details have been anonymized to protect the identities of participants, many of whom routinely receive threats to their emotional and physical wellbeing.

or older. Moderators of subreddits allegedly associated with hate speech declined to participate.

Secondly, the researcher collected trace data from the reddit API of the population of 52,735 non-corporate subreddits receiving at least one comment in June 2015.[4] Moderator roles were sampled on June 13, July 6, and September 11, 2015, with all roles more recent than the date of the blackout removed from the dataset. The definition of active subreddits was determined from a public archive of all reddit comments from June 2015[8]. A list of subreddits that participated in the blackout was obtained from a public archive created by a reddit user who wrote software to monitor the event[18]. These data sources were combined into a single table with one subreddit per record for analysis.

Finally, the researcher collaborated with reddit users, using a popular data approach to define hypotheses and interpret the results of logistic regression models predicting subreddits' participation in the reddit blackout. Hypotheses were based on reddit users' explanations for blackout participation in comment threads during the blackout, in interviews with moderators, and in a series of three reddit discussions about this research project. In the first discussion, the researcher posted network visualizations of the reddit blackout and recruited moderators for interviews. In the second discussion, the researcher posted a regression model motivated by the questions and comments of moderators. In this second discussion, several participants questioned the validity of the list of blackout-participating subreddits based on their experience of the event. They worked with the researcher to evaluate a higher quality dataset, validating automated and manual supplements to that dataset that had been made by its creator.[5]

In public discussions of statistical results and in private messages, reddit users and interviewees argued the importance of factors that could not be easily measured, convincing the researcher to report key qualitative findings that are not part of the statistical model. These findings are included in the discussion section.

EXPLANATIONS FOR BLACKOUT PARTICIPATION

Rather than testing a central hypothesis motivated by a single academic puzzle[2], this paper tests folk hypotheses about what led moderators to participate in the reddit blackout—explanations offered by reddit users in comments, interviews, and the process of participatory hypothesis testing. For that reason, this section reports common explanations for participation in the reddit blackout by including qualitative findings, connections to relevant scholarly literature, and descriptions of the covariates developed to test each explanation. Although these explanations motivate covariates in a statistical model, each explanation constitutes a qualitative finding in its own right.

Explanations of blackout participation are grouped by categories common to collective action and social movement theories to highlight theory conversations relevant to these findings: *grievances*, *subreddit resources*, *relations among moderators*, *subreddit isolation*, and *goal transformation among moderators*.

Moderator Grievances

Throughout this research, moderators consistently described the workload as a major motivation for joining the blackout and the primary reason they expected others to join. In interviews, moderators of the largest subreddits described spending several hours a day supporting their communities. Even moderators of less prominent subreddits showed the author sophisticated self-built systems for scheduling and coordinating the many hours of work to create content and respond to violations of their community rules. In response to perceived gaps in official moderation tools by reddit, moderator teams use custom bots and custom moderation tools to manage this complex work,[6] creating successor systems that augment reddit's core capabilities through the reddit API[25]. Many interviewees made statements similar to one moderator who claimed that "larger, more active subreddits [were more likely to join the blackout because they] had more of a need."

Even among subreddits that declined to joint the blackout, many moderators described feeling obligated to make a decision one way or an other. This surprised moderators of large subreddits, who described it as an issue for larger groups. Size was a key issue in the hundreds of smaller subreddits that discussed the possibility, with many wondering if they had much in common with larger groups, or whether blacking out their smaller group would make enough of an impact on reddit's advertising revenue to help the protest.

These explanations correspond to grievance models of social movement participation[55], which might expect that larger subreddits with more work and subreddits at greater risk of being banned by the company might have more cause to join the blackout.

H1: More active subreddits with a greater need for moderator tools were more likely to join the blackout.

To test moderators' explanations that subreddits with a greater workload were more likely to join the blackout, this paper includes a predictor for *activity*, represented

[4]10 official subreddits that publish company announcements were removed

[5]In an interview, the creator of the blackout data explained that software monitoring the blackout was deployed several hours after the blackout began, missing several subreddits that were restored early in the protest. When several participants in the participatory hypothesis testing process noted that their blackout participation was not acknowledged in the dataset, the researcher updated the blackout list to include 80 additional subreddits added in subsequent queries by the blackout data creator. These additions were validated from multiple sources. All statistical findings are consistent across both datasets.

[6]`https://www.reddit.com/r/toolbox`

by the total number of comments and posts per subreddit in June 2015. This measure ranged from 0 to 4,190,000 comments with a mean of 1,037.

H2: NSFW subreddits were more likely to join the blackout
In interviews, several moderators reported declining participation to avoid association with hate speech subreddits taken down by the company the prior month[57] or other parts of reddit they preferred not to be associated with. Default moderators denied that their action was associated with hate speech, describing the lengths they went to dissociate from hate speech communities and users that opposed then-CEO Ellen Pao. Nevertheless, moderators of default subreddits had no control over which subreddits chose to join the blackout.

It is possible that "NSFW" subreddits featuring 18+ content, which might have a history of stretching policy boundaries, would be more likely to join the blackout. Another possibility is that NSFW subreddits require more work to maintain high quality content without crossing lines set by reddit and the law. In interviews, one moderator of a moderately-sized NSFW subreddit with roughly 20-30 thousand subscribers reported over 3 million page views per month and 8-10 thousand unique daily visitors, numbers that far outstripped a comparably-sized non-NSFW subreddit that they also moderated. This extra work of moderating NSFW groups would be hidden from the measure of activity in this study, which includes all comments regardless of moderation. Perhaps with more work, NSFW subs were more likely to see the need for better tools and support from reddit.

The NSFW label may be a poor measure of these factors, but many participants emphasized this distinction. For that reason, it is included in the model. In the population, 3741 are labeled NSFW, 7% of active subreddits.

Subreddit Resources

Resource mobilization theories might expect that subreddits with greater capacities might be more likely to take action. Among explanations identified in the qualitative findings, these resources might involve a subreddit's number of moderators, the prominence of the subreddit, or the subreddit's access to employees.

H3: Subreddits with more moderators were more likely to join the blackout
In interviews, several moderators mentioned that a primary difficulty during the blackout involved simply knowing about the blackout and contacting enough moderators to agree on an action. In this situation, subreddits with more moderators had more capacity to take action. In this paper, the *moderator count* includes all moderators of a subreddit who started no later than July 1, 2015. Moderator roles for subreddits accessible to the public were sampled on June 13 and July 6, and moderator roles for NSFW subreddits were sampled on September 11, 2015. The number of moderators ranges from 0 to 908 with a mean of 2.815.

H4: Default subreddits were more likely to join the blackout
In interviews, some moderators pointed out that "most of the conversation about the blackout first took place in the default mod irc channel." Many of these default subreddits, which are added to every new user's subscriptions, receive at least a half million comments per month and have a history of offering extensive original content, including regular live interviews. Many of them were directly supported by the reddit employee whose dismissal prompted the blackout. Moderators of default subreddits also reportedly played a substantial role in negotiations with the company at the height of the protest. In interviews, several moderators described the blackout as an action by and for default subreddits; participation by thousands of smaller subreddits had been a surprise.

To test the hypothesis that *default* subreddits were more likely to participate, this paper uses the set of 49 default subreddits shared across the US, UK, Switzerland, Spain, and Japan at the time of the blackout.[7]

SubsReddit users offered several theories about "admins," their name for company employees. During the blackout, some redditors voiced suspicions that admins who held moderator positions were preventing subreddits from going private. In interviews, moderators tended to voice the opposite opinion. Some argued that subs with more admin contact were joining the blackout to send a message to the company, urging it to pay more attention to the employees who advocated for moderator interests. Moderators of smaller subreddits agreed, with one saying that "we felt 100% independent from admin assistance so it really wasn't our fight." The blackout appears to have succeeded at this goal: in their formal statement after the blackout, reddit announced the creation of a "Moderator Advocate" position for a current employee, promising that this employee's representations would thereafter be given special attention in company decisions[61].

To test the hypothesis that subreddits with more *employees as moderators* would be more likely to join the blackout, this paper uses the Internet Archive record of employee reddit accounts from June 2015 to calculate identify moderators who were among 59 current employees or 34 former employees.[8] This predictor ranges from 0 to 8 with a mean of 0.004. Only 125 subreddits had any current employees as moderators at the time of the blackout.

[7] https://www.reddit.com/r/defaults/comments/2ycn0x/list_of_default_subreddits_march_8_2015/

[8] https://web.archive.org/web/20150621223349/http://www.reddit.com/about/team/

Relations Among Moderators

In any collective action by a class of people advocating for change, it is to be expected that relationships among potential participants would be an important factor. This study does not include data from any private communications or coordination during the blackout and cannot directly estimate the role of moderator relationships in the blackout. Nonetheless, participants suggested predictors that may approximate those relationships. These predictors most closely correspond to discussions in political opportunity theory of the important of social ties to social movement participation[52].

H6: Subreddits whose moderators also moderated other subreddits were more likely to join the blackout

Subreddits are not isolated communities; many moderators have roles in more than one subreddit. For that reason, this paper includes a covariate for *the number of moderator roles in other subreddits* held by moderators of a given subreddit. The predictor ranges from 0 to 2,189 with a mean of 29.22.

Perhaps, for reasons of workload or connectedness to other moderators, subreddits with more overlapping roles with other subreddits might be more likely to join the blackout. The reverse might also be plausible, since self-defined *networks* of subreddits—groups that share common themes and a common governance structure—dissociated themselves from the blackout. These networks include the "ShitRedditSays fempire" of "social justice warriors," the "Imaginary Network" of fictional illustration subreddits, and the "SFW Porn" network that shares beautiful images of landscapes, architecture, and other "safe for work" content[50]. None of these networks joined the blackout, so perhaps subreddits whose moderators participate in other subreddits were less likely to join the blackout.

H7: Subreddits whose moderators also moderated other blackout subreddits were more likely to join the blackout

In studies of risky, costly activism, relationships with other social movement participants and exposure to their choice to participate have been important predictors of participation in activism[52, 3]. If a subreddit shares moderators with another subreddit that joined the blackout, it is plausible to hypothesize that the subreddit is also likely to join the blackout. Furthermore, any single moderator with adequate privileges can take a unilateral action to black out. In many cases, the decision to black out was not a group decision by all moderators. In one instance, a moderator held a vote and joined the blackout with subscriber support before asking other moderators. When the other moderators disagreed and restored the subreddit, this moderator announced voluntary resignation rather than accept punitive consequences.

While a subreddit's *number of shared moderator roles with other subreddits that joined the blackout* cannot produce meaningful estimates of influence or selection[70], these relational predictors offer a general estimate of relational factors among moderators, as well as a control for estimating other factors in the model. The measure ranges from 0 to 180 with a mean of 1.286.

Subreddit Isolation from "The Rest of reddit"

In public statements and private interviews, many moderators distinguish their subreddits from the "rest of reddit." Several moderators described their subreddits as established communities without any special tie to the platform. For these moderators, the blackout controversy and ongoing debates over hate speech had motivated them to test other platforms for migrating their communities. Other moderators who distanced their community from the rest of reddit remained committed to staying on the platform so they could critique and challenge what they described as its dominant culture. Those who moderate self-help subreddits or groups for marginalized people talked about reddit as an important context to offer support and community, even as they distanced themselves from behavior and attitudes elsewhere on the platform. One support subreddit moderator reported that "a lot of the users didn't really identify with the rest of reddit." When subscribers voted against the blackout, the moderator wasn't surprised; it was "a movement we didn't identify with."

Discussion of "the rest of reddit" corresponds with research mobilization theories of social movements, which often expect that more isolated subreddits and constituents will be less likely to join a movement without advertising or incentives [53].

H8: Subreddits that are more isolated from the rest of reddit were less likely to join the blackout

This paper includes a predictor for subreddit isolation. Within the group of all reddit comments made by anyone who commented within a given subreddit in June 2015, this measure is the percentage of those comments made within that subreddit. The measure of isolation ranges from 0 to 1.00 with a higher value representing more isolated subreddits; the mean is 0.08, the median is 0.03.

H9: Subreddits whose moderators participate in "metareddits" were more likely to join the blackout

In interviews, several moderators described learning about the blackout from "meta-reddits" which cover major events on the site, and which mostly stayed active during the blackout. Just like we might expect more isolated subreddits to stay out of the blackout, we might expect moderators who get involved in reddit-wide meta-discussion to join the blackout. Based on a public list of metareddits compiled by reddit users,[9] this predictor includes the total number of metareddit comments made by a subreddit's moderators, divided by the total number of moderators. The measure of metareddit participation per moderator ranges from 0 to 346 with a median of 0 and a mean of 1.28; it is log transformed in the model.

[9] https://www.reddit.com/r/TheoryOfReddit/wiki/meta_subreddits

Moderator's Relations With Their Subreddits

The reddit blackout put strains on moderators' relationships with their communities, whatever decision they made on the blackout. In many subreddits, moderators and subreddit participants already had substantial disagreements. In interviews, many moderators reported that even everyday decisions commonly attract personal insults and threats from reddit users, a problem that became heightened during the blackout. Subscriber support for the blackout was not guaranteed, since moderators were the primary beneficiaries of blackout demands.

When deciding if they should join the protest, moderators differed in how much they included their communities in the decision. Many moderators held votes, asking subscribers to make the final decision. Many others posted threads explaining or defending their top-down decision to join the blackouts. In interviews, many moderators reported receiving large numbers of private messages urging them to join the blackout. In at least one case, a moderator stepped down after joining the blackout, facing a loss of legitimacy with the subreddit.

Ambiguity over who constitues a subreddit member complicated the tension between moderators and subscribers during the blackout, which took many moderators by surprise. Moderators couldn't be sure that the people messaging them were genuine participants in their communities. When votes had occurred, some worried that voting mechanisms had been "brigaded" by outsiders advocating for the blackout. In an interview, one moderator reported posting a vote to appease blackout advocates who the moderator assumed were hate speech campaigners; "it really bought me time to try to get in contact with the other Mods" and coordinate a top-down decision.

Findings on these internal community tensions most closely correspond to "goal transformation" theories on the development of distinct interests by organization leaders[69], informing the following hypotheses:

H10: Older subreddits were more likely to join the blackout

To test expectations that older communities would be more likely to join the blackout, this paper includes an *age* predictor for the number of years since the earliest subreddit, ranging from January 19, 2006 to July 1, 2015.

H11: Subreddits whose moderators participate in moderator-focused subreddits were more likely to join the blackout

In public statements, many of the subreddits that joined the blackout used the language of "solidarity" to describe their choice to join the blackout. Moderator-focused subreddits offer important contexts for that solidarity to develop, as moderators seek technical help, discuss moderator tools, seek advice on difficult decisions, and discuss company policies. Other moderator-focused subreddits function as job boards where moderators can find "internships" and other opportunities to take on a moderator role. Some of these groups only admit moderators of large subreddits. Perhaps moderators who participate in mod-specific subreddits, who have helped and been helped by other mods, would be more likely to join the blackout?

Although several moderator-only subreddits that reportedly played important roles in coordinating the blackout were private, it is still possible to test this hypothesis with public subreddits. Based on content analysis and interviews, this predictor includes the total number of moderator-sub comments made by a subreddit's moderators, divided by the total number of moderators. The measure ranges from 0 to 169.5 with a mean of 0.3.

H12: Subreddits with moderators who participate more in their subreddit were less likely to join the blackout

While the state of relations between leaders and a community or the decision-making processes of each subreddit are not easily quantifiable, redditors did suggest a measure of moderators' relations with their communities. One moderator suggested that "larger groups that didn't join the protest were the more hands-off type."

This paper includes a predictor for *the number of comments made by moderators* within each subreddit. This measure, similar to the measure used by Butler to stratify samples in a study of mailing list leadership[15] is the count of internal comments made by any of a subreddit's moderators in June 2015, including original content, reactions to the posts of others, procedural posts about the workings of the subreddit, and feedback to users whose content had been removed. The measure ranges from 0 to 18,000 with a mean of 21.45 and a median of 0.00.

QUANTITATIVE FINDINGS

The above hypotheses are tested in a logistic regression model with Firth bias reduction[24].[10] Results are shown in Table 1.[11]

Interpretations of the results of this model cannot motivate judgments on the true-ness or false-ness of moderator explanations of the blackout. The predictors in this model are based on important qualitative evidence—very real things that moderators and others on reddit have said when making sense of an event they personally experienced. The regression model offers tests of whether the explanations offered by participants predict the probability of a subreddit to join the blackout, holding constant all the other factors, on average in the population of all active subreddits. In some cases, occurrences unique to a small number of communities may not explain the actions of other subreddits. In other cases, predictors with a p-value greater than 0.05 may still represent accurate observations about the blackout, even though the predictive power of that explanation is not distinguishable from chance. Put simply, the model in Table 1 tests whether participants' explanations of their experience was applicable on average across reddit, accounting for other factors in the model.

[10] Firth bias reduction offers better estimates for issues of linear separation with the *moderator count* predictor. In a sensitivity analysis with non-Firth models, results are robust

[11] Layout formatted with *texreg*[46]

Dependent variable: blackout participation	
(Intercept)	-4.41^{***}
	(0.14)
Moderator Grievances	
H1: ln comments	0.23^{***}
	(0.02)
H2: NSFW sub	0.41^{***}
	(0.10)
Subreddit Resources	
H3: ln moderators	0.58^{***}
	(0.06)
H4: default subreddit	0.36
	(0.34)
H5: ln employee mod roles	−1.19
	(0.79)
Relations Among Moderators	
H6: ln mod roles in other subs	-0.42^{***}
	(0.04)
H7: ln mod roles in blackout subs	2.07^{***}
	(0.10)
ln othersub roles:ln blackout sub roles	-0.24^{***}
	(0.02)
Subreddit Isolation	
H8: ln isolation %	-4.69^{***}
	(0.54)
H9: ln mod participation in metareddts	0.09^{*}
	(0.04)
Moderator's Relations Within Subreddits	
H10: subreddit age in years	0.05^{***}
	(0.01)
H11: ln mod participation in mod-focused subs	0.03
	(0.06)
H12: ln moderator participation in sub	-0.11^{**}
	(0.04)
AIC	11541.59
BIC	11665.82
Log Likelihood	-5756.80
Deviance	11513.59
Num. obs.	52735

$^{***}p < 0.001$, $^{**}p < 0.01$, $^{*}p < 0.05$

Table 1. Logistic regression of social factors predicting subreddit participation in the reddit blackout, July 2015

Estimates are reported with the direction and statistical significance of coefficients at $p < 0.05$, along with relative estimated probabilities for prototypical values, the approach taken when discussing and interpreting the results with participants.

Results for Moderator Grievances

Grievance-focused hypotheses concern moderator workloads and the precarity of subreddits with reddit policies.

H1 result: In a logistic regression model, more active subreddits were more likely to join the blackout, on average across reddit, holding all else constant. With all else at its mean, this relationship can be described for a variety of activity levels. In the 50th percentile, a non-default, non-NSFW subreddit with 6 comments per month had an estimated 1.2% chance of joining the blackout. In the 75th percentile, a subreddit with 46 comments a month had an estimated 1.8% chance of joining the blackout. A subreddit with 1,000 comments a month had an estimated 3.7% chance of joining; one with 100,000 comments per month had an estimated 10.8% chance of blacking out.

H2 result: In a logistic regression model, 18+ "NSFW" subreddits were more likely to join the blackout, on average across reddit, holding all else constant. With all else at its mean, a large, non-default, non-NSFW subreddit with 22,800 comments per month had an estimated 7% chance of joining the blackout, while an NSFW subreddit with the same qualities had a 10% chance of blacking out. At lower levels of activity, a non-NSFW subreddit with 1,000 comments per month had a 3.7% chance of joining the blackout, while an NSFW subreddit of the same size had an estimated 5.5% chance of joining the blackout.

Results for Subreddit Resources

Resource-focused hypotheses expect subreddits with greater resources to be more likely to black out.

H3 result: In a logistic regression model, subreddits with more moderators were more likely to join the blackout,on average across reddit, holding all else constant. Holding all else at its mean, a non-default, non-NSFW subreddit with 1,000 comments per month and 3 moderators (the mean) had an estimated 3.8% chance of joining the blackout. A similar subreddit with 8 moderators had a 6% chance of joining the blackout on average across reddit.

H4 result: In a logistic regression model, default subreddits were no more or less likely to join the blackout, on average across reddit, holding all else constant. Although a single-covariate model shows a large, positive relationship between default status and blackout participation, this predictor is not significant in models that control for the number of moderators and the level of activity. While qualitative findings emphasize the importance of moderators of some default subreddits for organizing the blackout and negoatiating terms with the company, these subreddits were quickly outnumbered by the thousands of others that joined. Consequently, even though visible participation by large, default subreddits may well have influenced others to participate and influenced the company to negotiate, is unsurprising that other predictors offer better explanations of any individual subreddit's blackout participation, on average across reddit.

H5 result: In a logistic regression model, there is no significant relationship between the number of employee moderators and blackout participation, on average across reddit, holding all else constant. Even a single-predictor model finds no statistically significant relationship between the number of employee moderators and blackout participation.

Results for Relations Among Moderators

Participants expected that relations among moderators were important to blackout participation.

H6 & H7 results: In a logistic regression model, the number of roles held by a subreddit's moderators in other groups and other blackout subreddits were significant predictors of blackout participation, relationships that are mediated by each other, on average across reddit, holding all else constant. As stated previously, these predictors are included as controls, so estimates are excluded. Overall, these statistically significant predictors underscore the importance of shared moderation relationships to blackout participation.

Results for Subreddit Isolation from "The rest of reddit"

Isolation-focused hypotheses expect that more isolated subreddits would be less likely to join the blackout.

H8 result: Subreddits that are more isolated from the rest of reddit were less likely to join the blackout, on average across reddit, holding all else constant. Holding all else at its mean, a non-default, non-NSFW subreddit with 1,000 comments per month and an isolation rate of 5% had an estimated 4.2% chance of joining the blackout. A similar, more isolated subreddit with an isolation rate of 50% had an 0.8% chance of joining the blackout.

H9 result: Subreddits whose moderators participate more in "metareddits" were more likely to join the blackout, on average across reddit, holding all else constant. Holding all else at its mean, a non-default, non-NSFW subreddit with 1,000 comments per month and 1 metareddit comment by one of its moderators had an estimated 3.6% chance of joining the blackout, while a similar subreddit whose moderators made 25 comments in metareddits had a 4.5% chance of joining the blackout.

Results for Moderators' Relations With Their Subreddits

H10 result: In a logistic regression model, older subreddits were more likely to join the blackout, on average across reddit, holding all else constant. Holding all else at its mean, a non-default, non-NSFW subreddit with 1,000 comments per month and an age of 0.64 years (the 25th percentile) had an estimated 3.7% chance of joining the blackout, while a similar subreddit 3.8 years old (the 75th percentile) had a 3.9% chance of joining the blackout.

H11 result: In a logistic regression model, subreddits whose moderators comment in moderator-focused subreddits were no more or less likely to join the blackout, on average across reddit, holding all else constant. Although a single-covariate model shows a positive relationship between moderator comments in moderator-focused subreddits and blackout participation, this relationship is not significant in a model that accounts for other factors.

H12 result: In a logistic regression model, subreddits with greater internal participation by moderators were less likely to join the blackout, on average across reddit, holding all else constant. Holding all else at its mean, a non-default, non-NSFW subreddit with 1,000 comments a month and 1 monthly internal comment by moderators (50th percentile) had an estimated 4% chance of joining the blackout, while a similar subreddit with 20 monthly internal comments by moderators had only a 3% chance of joining the blackout.

LIMITATIONS

The chief limitation of the quantitative analysis is the applicability of the covariate measures to the hypotheses, as discussed above. Furthermore, the datasets associated with moderator activity in NSFW subreddits do not include information about moderators who resigned between July 2nd and September 11, 2015. Qualitative content analysis of over one hundred blackout-related discussions within subreddits yielded two cases where moderators resigned after the blackout. While this paper offers connections to relevant theories of collective action and social movements, its inductive methods do not test these theories. Finally, the quantitative findings in this paper generalize only to the population of subreddits during the reddit blackout of July 2015.

DISCUSSION

At a time when many online platforms and communities fundamentally rely on volunteer governance from large numbers of people, the reddit blackout is a powerful voice in favor of supporting those volunteers with meaningful communication and adequate software tools. Moderators do substantial work to create, promote, and maintain social relations online, often at a massive scale. Alongside the meaning they find in that work, many moderators also receive a stream of complaints and threats. Others find pleasure in fostering antagonism and hate, thriving on the drama of controversy and conflict. When these moderators believe that platforms are not supporting them adequately, they can and do organize for change.

What leads such a diverse collection of community leaders to join together in collective action against the platform they share—or to decline participation? On one remarkable moment on reddit in July 2015, more than two thousand community groups forced the company to take notice, negotiate, and change how the company worked. This paper describes how that happened, through qualitative methods and participatory hypothesis testing.

Across reddit, the greatest predictors of blackout participation were related to moderators' grievances: *the work of moderators* and the *precarity of their position with company policies.* Although some subreddits need limited tending, moderators can spend hours each day supporting their communities, creating elaborate systems to coordinate that work with large teams, and developing extended policies across the history of their group. NSFW communities at the edge of company policies were more likely to join the blackout, but it's also possible that moderators of NSFW groups joined because staying within those policies requires more work.

Although default subreddits were no more likely than other subreddits to join the blackout, moderators from those groups started the blackout and conducted important negotiations with the company on behalf of participating subreddits. Reddit employees played a key role in these negotiations, but employee presence as moderators in subreddits was not associated with any significant difference in a subreddit's probability to join the blackout. The blackout was *led by moderators*, who were the central resources in this social movement. Subreddits with more moderators were more likely to join the blackout, controlling for all other factors.

Smaller subreddits also joined the blackout, sometimes using the language of "solidarity" to explain their support. Across subreddits of all sizes, *relations among moderators* were also associated with participation in the blackout. Subreddits who shared moderators tended to stick together in their decision either way, whether or not they participated in formalized networks of subreddits.

Community members also played an important role in action against the platform by pressuring moderators to join the blackout, discussing and voting in decisions, and sometimes even punishing moderators who disagreed. This role was not always explicit. Many moderators describe a sense of their community's connection to the "rest of reddit" as one of the most important factors in their decision. On average across reddit, communities whose participants engaged more with the rest of the platform were more likely to take action against the company, while more isolated subreddits distinct from the rest of the site stayed out of reddit "politics."

Although participants expected that subreddits with moderators who engaged more with their communities were more likely to take action against the platform, the opposite was true on average on reddit. Older communities and those with more detached leaders were more likely to join an action in support of moderator interests.

Implications for Social Movement Mobilization Theories and Collective Action Theories

Insofar as these findings correspond to grievance-based theories of social movement mobilization, they are consistent with expectations that groups with greater grievances are more likely to mobilize[55]. Relations between moderators were also important social factors in the blackout, as expected by political opportunity theories [52]. Yet the nature of grievances among digital volunteerism and online labor are still questions of substantial scholarly discussion[67], at a time when the nature of platforms policies towards users are also still being theorized[27].

Findings on relations among moderators are consistent with expectations from resource mobilization theories. These theories expect that movement organizations with greater resources and less isolation are more likely to take action[53]. This paper finds that subreddits with more moderators and less isolation from the rest of reddit were more likely to join the blackout. However, a deductive test of those theories, which often focus on the comparative resources of opposing parties, might require more covariates for the resources available to a greater variety of actors influencing blackout participation.

Finally, the quantitative findings of this paper do appear to correspond with theories on the development of distinct interests among organization leaders[69]. Older subreddits and those with less engaged moderators were more likely to join the blackout. Research that sets out to test these theories could include further covariates related specifically to subreddit policies and the work of subreddit governance. Special care should be taken to account for overlapping leadership responsibilities across subreddits and wider leadership structures such as "networks" of subreddits[72].

Implications for Social Computing Research

In pursuit of describing social factors in collective action during the reddit backout, this paper demonstrates a method of "participatory hypothesis testing," a way to involve platform users in the development, validation, and interpretation of quantitative models of their behavior. As social computing researchers seek methods for human-centered data science[5], the participatory hypothesis testing methods in this paper illustrate one human-centered approach to studying social behavior in online platforms.

Taking Action Against Platform Operators

Quantitative models tell only part of the blackout story, as participants insistently and repeatedly reminded the author during the process of participatory hypothesis testing. Moderators described tense debates over IRC channels and negotiations in private subreddits as they worked to understand a complex situation rapidly unfolding on reddit and in the press. Participants lamented that it was impossible to include a covariate for voting activity in subreddits that made a democratic decision. Others wished it had been possible to identify subreddits that offer support for people in crisis, news on breaking events, and peer communities among marginalized groups. Many of these support subreddits stayed open rather than cut off their subscribers from needed support.

While the reddit controversies of June and July 2015 included notable employee turnover in the company, including the departure of CEO Ellen Pao, communities were also directly affected by changes the company made. Among subreddits that declined to black out, every moderator interviewed expressed gratitude for the groups that took action, or at least appreciation for changes that the company was forced to introduce.

As the role of online platforms grows in society, mediating our collective intelligence, economic transactions, and social interactions, we can expect that the operators of those platforms will continue to face questions, criticism, and opposition over their management of those societal goods. This paper describes that opposition in action, showing the factors that led community leaders on reddit to join a collective effort to successfully change how the platform and the company works.

ACKNOWLEDGMENTS

This work was undertaken during a summer internship at Microsoft Research. This research would not have been possible without generous contributions from hundreds of reddit users. Tarleton Gillespie, Mary Gray, Molly Sauter, Aaron Shaw, Alex Leavitt, and Katherine Lo offered helpful early feedback on this paper.

REFERENCES

1. 2015. Wikipedia:Administrators. (Sept. 2015). https://en.wikipedia.org/w/index.php?title=Wikipedia:Administrators&oldid=681136693 Page Version ID: 681136693.
2. Andrew Abbott. 2004. Methods of Discovery: Heuristics for the Social Sciences (Contemporary Societies). (2004). http://www.citeulike.org/group/1118/article/150521
3. Lada Adamic and others. 2015. The Diffusion of Support in an Online Social Movement: Evidence from the Adoption of Equal-Sign Profile Pictures. In *Proceedings of the 18th ACM Conference on Computer Supported Cooperative Work & Social Computing*. ACM, 1741–1750. http://dl.acm.org/citation.cfm?id=2675290
4. Clem Adelman. 1993. Kurt Lewin and the origins of action research. *Educational action research* 1, 1 (1993), 7–24. http://www.tandfonline.com/doi/pdf/10.1080/0965079930010102
5. Cecilia Aragon, Joseph Bayer, Andy Echenique, Yun Huang, Clayton Hutto, Jinyoung Kim, Gina Neff, and Wanli Xing. 2015. Human Centered Data Science *(CSCW '16 Workshop)*. ACM. https://cscw2016hcds.wordpress.com/
6. Francois Bar, Melissa Brough, Sasha Costanza-Chock, Carmen Gonzalez, C. J. Wallis, and Amanda Garces. 2009. Mobile voices: A mobile, open source, popular communication platform for first-generation immigrants in Los Angeles. In *Pre-conference workshop at the International Communication Association (ICA) Conference Chicago, Illinois*. http://lirneasia.net/wp-content/uploads/2009/05/final-paper_bar_et_al.pdf
7. Darin Barney. 2013. Pipelines and the politics of sabotage. (Oct. 2013). https://www.youtube.com/watch?v=UjJO5_fjMGU
8. Jason Michael Baumgartner. 2015. I have every publicly available Reddit comment for research. ~ 1.7 billion comments @ 250 GB compressed. Any interest in this? • /r/datasets. (July 2015). https://www.reddit.com/r/datasets/comments/3bxlg7/i_have_every_publicly_available_reddit_comment/
9. Yochai Benkler, Hal Roberts, Robert Faris, Alicia Solow-Niederman, and Bruce Etling. 2013. *Social Mobilization and the Networked Public Sphere: Mapping the SOPA-PIPA Debate*. SSRN Scholarly Paper ID 2295953. Social Science Research Network, Rochester, NY. http://papers.ssrn.com/abstract=2295953
10. Rahul Bhargava. 2013. Towards a Concept of "Popular Data" | MIT Center for Civic Media. (Nov. 2013). https://civic.mit.edu/blog/rahulb/towards-a-concept-of-popular-data
11. Tom Boellstorff, Bonnie Nardi, and Celia Pearce. 2012. *Ethnography and virtual worlds: A handbook of method*. Princeton University Press.
12. danah boyd. 2008. *Taken out of context: American teen sociality in networked publics*. PhD Dissertation. University of California-Berkeley, School of Information.
13. Amy Bruckman. 1998. Finding one's own in cyberspace. *High Wired: On the Design, Use, and Theory of Educational MOOs. Ed. Cynthia Haynes and Jan Rune Holmevik. Ann Arbor, MI: U of Michigan P* (1998), 15–24.
14. Amy Bruckman, Pavel Curtis, Cliff Figallo, and Brenda Laurel. 1994. Approaches to managing deviant behavior in virtual communities. In *CHI Conference Companion*. 183–184. http://www.researchgate.net/profile/Brenda_Laurel/publication/221515969_Approaches_to_managing_deviant_behavior_in_virtual_communities/links/00b495374f7baae77f000000.pdf
15. Brian Butler, Lee Sproull, Sara Kiesler, and Robert Kraut. 2002. Community effort in online groups: Who does the work and why. *Leadership at a distance: Research in technologically supported work* (2002), 171–194.
16. James Samuel Coleman. 1973. *Mathematics of collective action*. Transaction Publishers.
17. Kate Crawford and Tarleton L. Gillespie. 2014. What is a Flag for? Social Media Reporting Tools and the Vocabulary of Complaint. *New Media & Society* (Aug. 2014). http://papers.ssrn.com/abstract=2476464
18. Ethan Dalool. 2015. amageddon - GoldTesting. (July 2015). https://www.reddit.com/r/GoldTesting/wiki/amageddon
19. Catherine D'Ignazio and Rahul Bhargava. 2015. Approaches to Building Big Data Literacy. Bloomberg Data For Good Conference. https://datatherapy.files.wordpress.com/2015/09/big_data_literacy.pdf
20. Jill P. Dimond, Michaelanne Dye, Daphne Larose, and Amy S. Bruckman. 2013. Hollaback!: the role of storytelling online in a social movement organization. In *Proceedings of the 2013 conference on Computer supported cooperative work (CSCW '13)*. ACM, New York, NY, USA, 477–490. DOI: http://dx.doi.org/10.1145/2441776.2441831
21. Karthik Dinakar, Birago Jones, Catherine Havasi, Henry Lieberman, and Rosalind Picard. 2012. Common sense reasoning for detection, prevention, and mitigation of cyberbullying. *ACM Transactions on Interactive Intelligent Systems (TiiS)* 2, 3 (2012), 18. http://dl.acm.org/citation.cfm?id=2362400

22. Jessica Elgot. 2015. Reddit users rebel over banning of fat-shaming subforums. *The Guardian* (June 2015). http://www.theguardian.com/technology/2015/jun/11/reddit-users-rebel-banning-fat-shaming-subforums
23. Facebook. 2015. Group Admin Basics: What is a Group Admin? (2015). https://www.facebook.com/help/418065968237061/
24. David Firth. 1993. Bias reduction of maximum likelihood estimates. *Biometrika* 80, 1 (1993), 27–38. http://biomet.oxfordjournals.org/content/80/1/27.short
25. R. Stuart Geiger. 2014. Successor Systems: The Role of Reflexive Algorithms in Enacting Ideological Critique. *Selected Papers of Internet Research* 4 (2014). http://spir.aoir.org/index.php/spir/article/view/942
26. Eric Gilbert. 2013. Widespread underprovision on reddit. In *Proceedings of the 2013 conference on Computer supported cooperative work*. ACM, 803–808. http://dl.acm.org/citation.cfm?id=2441866
27. Tarleton Gillespie. 2010. The politics of 'platforms'. *New Media & Society* 12, 3 (2010), 347–364. http://nms.sagepub.com/content/12/3/347.short
28. Owen Good. 2013. Does Your Gamertag Have Herpes? Beware Xbox Live Enforcement United. *Kotaku* (Aug. 2013).
29. James Grimmelmann. 2015. *The Virtues of Moderation.* SSRN Scholarly Paper ID 2588493. Social Science Research Network, Rochester, NY. http://papers.ssrn.com/abstract=2588493
30. Alexander Halavais. 2013. Home made big data: Challenges and opportunities for participatory social research. *First Monday* 18, 10 (Oct. 2013). DOI: http://dx.doi.org/10.5210/fm.v18i10.4876
31. Gillian R. Hayes. 2011. The relationship of action research to human-computer interaction. *ACM Transactions on Computer-Human Interaction (TOCHI)* 18, 3 (2011), 15. http://dl.acm.org/citation.cfm?id=1993065
32. Steve Huffman. 2006. what's new on reddit: for those of you with a private office... (Jan. 2006). http://www.redditblog.com/2006/01/for-those-of-you-with-private-office.html
33. Steve Huffman. 2007. what's new on reddit: brace yourself, ads are coming. (March 2007). http://www.redditblog.com/2007/03/brace-yourself-ads-are-coming.html
34. Steve Huffman. 2008. what's new on reddit: new features. (Jan. 2008). http://www.redditblog.com/2008/01/new-features.html
35. Mike Isaac. 2015. Reddit Moderators Shut Down Parts of Site Over Employee's Dismissal. *The New York Times* (July 2015).
36. Mike Isaac and David Streitfeld. 2015. It's Silicon Valley 2, Ellen Pao 0: Fighter of Sexism Is Out at Reddit. *The New York Times* (July 2015). http://www.nytimes.com/2015/07/11/technology/ellen-pao-reddit-chief-executive-resignation.html
37. Nadia Kayyali and Danny O'Brien. 2015. Facing the Challenge of Online Harassment. *Electronic Frontier Foundation* (2015). https://www.eff.org/deeplinks/2015/01/facing-challenge-online-harassment
38. David King. 2008. what's new on reddit: per-reddit automated spam filters. (June 2008). http://www.redditblog.com/2008/06/per-reddit-automated-spam-filters.html
39. Lauren Kirchner. 2011. AOL Settled with Unpaid "Volunteers" for $15 Million. *Columbia Journalism Review* (Feb. 2011). http://www.cjr.org/the_news_frontier/aol_settled_with_unpaid_volunt.php
40. Chih-Hui Lai. 2014. Can Our Group Survive? An Investigation of the Evolution of Mixed-Mode Groups. *J Comput-Mediat Comm* 19, 4 (July 2014), 839–854. DOI: http://dx.doi.org/10.1111/jcc4.12075
41. Cliff Lampe. 2012. The role of reputation systems in managing online communities. *H. Masum, M. Tovey, eds* (2012), 77–88.
42. Cliff Lampe and Paul Resnick. 2004. Slash (dot) and burn: distributed moderation in a large online conversation space. In *Proceedings of the SIGCHI conference on Human factors in computing systems.* ACM, 543–550. http://dl.acm.org/citation.cfm?id=985761
43. Cliff Lampe, Paul Zube, Jusil Lee, Chul Hyun Park, and Erik Johnston. 2014. Crowdsourcing civility: A natural experiment examining the effects of distributed moderation in online forums. *Government Information Quarterly* 31, 2 (2014), 317–326. http://www.sciencedirect.com/science/article/pii/S0740624X14000021
44. Alex Leavitt. 2015. This is a Throwaway Account: Temporary Technical Identities and Perceptions of Anonymity in a Massive Online Community. In *Proceedings of the 18th ACM Conference on Computer Supported Cooperative Work & Social Computing.* ACM, 317–327. http://dl.acm.org/citation.cfm?id=2675175
45. Alex Leavitt and Joshua A. Clark. 2014. Upvoting Hurricane Sandy: Event-based News Production Processes on a Social News Site. In *Proceedings of the 32Nd Annual ACM Conference on Human Factors in Computing Systems (CHI '14).* ACM, New York, NY, USA, 1495–1504. DOI: http://dx.doi.org/10.1145/2556288.2557140

46. Philip Leifeld. 2013. texreg: Conversion of Statistical Model Output in R to LaTeX and HTML Tables. *Journal of Statistical Software* 55, 8 (2013), 1–24. http://www.jstatsoft.org/v55/i08/

47. Seymour Martin Lipset, Martin A. Trow, James Samuel Coleman, and Clark Kerr. 1956. *Union democracy: The internal politics of the International Typographical Union.* Free Press Glencoe. http://library.wur.nl/WebQuery/clc/1627266

48. Brian Lynch and Courtnie Swearingen. 2015. Why We Shut Down Reddit's 'Ask Me Anything' Forum. *The New York Times* (July 2015). http://www.nytimes.com/2015/07/08/opinion/why-we-shut-down-reddits-ask-me-anything-forum.html

49. Adrienne Massanari. 2015a. # Gamergate and The Fappening: How Reddit's algorithm, governance, and culture support toxic technocultures. *New Media & Society* (2015), 1461444815608807. http://nms.sagepub.com/content/early/2015/10/07/1461444815608807.abstract

50. Adrienne L Massanari. 2015b. *Participatory Culture, Community, and Play: Learning from Reddit (Digital Formations): Adrienne L. Massanari: 9781433126789: Amazon.com: Books.* Number 75 in Digital Formations. Peter Lang Publishing Inc.

51. J. Nathan Matias, Amy Johnson, Whitney Erin Boesel, Brian Keegan, Jaclyn Friedman, and Charlie DeTar. 2015. Reporting, Reviewing, and Responding to Harassment on Twitter. *arXiv:1505.03359 [cs]* (May 2015). http://arxiv.org/abs/1505.03359 arXiv: 1505.03359.

52. Doug McAdam. 1986. Recruitment to high-risk activism: The case of freedom summer. *American journal of sociology* (1986), 64–90. http://www.jstor.org/stable/2779717

53. John D. McCarthy and Mayer N. Zald. 1977. Resource mobilization and social movements: A partial theory. *American journal of sociology* (1977), 1212–1241. http://www.jstor.org/stable/2777934

54. Amanda Menking and Ingrid Erickson. 2015. The Heart Work of Wikipedia: Gendered, Emotional Labor in the World's Largest Online Encyclopedia. In *Proceedings of the 33rd Annual ACM Conference on Human Factors in Computing Systems.* ACM, 207–210.

55. David S. Meyer. 2004. Protest and political opportunities. *Annual review of sociology* (2004), 125–145. http://www.jstor.org/stable/29737688

56. Robert Michels. 1915. *Political parties: A sociological study of the oligarchical tendencies of modern democracy.* Hearst's International Library Company. https://books.google.com/books?hl=en&lr=&id=8XX187CLp5cC&oi=fnd&pg=PA1&dq=michels+political+parties&ots=ebokKnRgFJ&sig=pcJkICos-chsYI0nW1k4u3bAKkc

57. Jessica Moreno, Ellen Pao, and Alexis Ohanian. 2015a. Removing harassing subreddits • /r/announcements. (June 2015). https://www.reddit.com/r/announcements/comments/39bpam/removing_harassing_subreddits/

58. Jessica Moreno, Ellen Pao, and Alexis Ohanian. 2015b. what's new on reddit: Promote ideas, protect people. (May 2015). http://www.redditblog.com/2015/05/promote-ideas-protect-people.html

59. Drew Olanoff. 2015. Reddit Names Marty Weiner, Founding Engineer At Pinterest, Its First CTO. *TechCrunch* (Aug. 2015).

60. Mancur Olson. 1965. *The logic of collective action.* Vol. 124. Harvard University Press.

61. Ellen Pao. 2015. We apologize : modnews. (July 2015). https://www.reddit.com/r/modnews/comments/3cbnuu/we_apologize/

62. Hector Postigo. 2003. Emerging sources of labor on the Internet: The case of America Online volunteers. *International review of social History* 48, S11 (2003), 205–223. http://journals.cambridge.org/abstract_S0020859003001329

63. Hector Postigo. 2009. America Online volunteers. *International Journal of Cultural Studies* 12, 5 (Sept. 2009), 451–469. http://ics.sagepub.com.libproxy.mit.edu/content/12/5/451

64. Howard Rheingold. 1993. *The virtual community: Homesteading on the electronic frontier.* MIT press.

65. Niloufar Salehi, Lilly C. Irani, and Michael S. Bernstein. 2015. We Are Dynamo: Overcoming Stalling and Friction in Collective Action for Crowd Workers. In *Proceedings of the 33rd Annual ACM Conference on Human Factors in Computing Systems.* ACM, 1621–1630.

66. Molly Sauter. 2014. *The Coming Swarm: DDOS Actions, Hacktivism, and Civil Disobedience on the Internet.* Bloomsbury Publishing USA.

67. Trebor Scholz. 2012. *Digital labor: The internet as playground and factory.* Routledge.

68. Aaron Shaw. 2012. Centralized and decentralized gatekeeping in an open online collective. *Politics & Society* 40, 3 (2012), 349–388. http://pas.sagepub.com/content/40/3/349.short

69. Aaron Shaw and Benjamin M. Hill. 2014. Laboratories of Oligarchy? How the Iron Law Extends to Peer Production. *J Commun* 64, 2 (April 2014), 215–238. DOI: http://dx.doi.org/10.1111/jcom.12082

70. Christian Steglich, Tom AB Snijders, and Michael Pearson. 2010. Dynamic networks and behavior: Separating selection from influence. *Sociological methodology* 40, 1 (2010), 329–393. http://onlinelibrary.wiley.com/doi/10.1111/j.1467-9531.2010.01225.x/full

71. Tiziana Terranova. 2000. Free labor: Producing culture for the digital economy. *Social text* 18, 2 (2000), 33–58. http://muse.jhu.edu/journals/soc/summary/v018/18.2terranova.html

72. Haiyi Zhu, Robert E. Kraut, and Aniket Kittur. 2014. The impact of membership overlap on the survival of online communities. In *Proceedings of the SIGCHI Conference on Human Factors in Computing Systems*. ACM, 281–290. http://dl.acm.org/citation.cfm?id=2557213

Surviving an "Eternal September" How an Online Community Managed a Surge of Newcomers

Charles Kiene
University of Washington
Seattle, Washington
ckiene@uw.edu

Andrés Monroy-Hernández
Microsoft Research
Redmond, Washington
amh@microsoft.com

Benjamin Mako Hill
University of Washington
Seattle, Washington
makohill@uw.edu

ABSTRACT

We present a qualitative analysis of interviews with participants in the NoSleep community within Reddit where millions of fans and writers of horror fiction congregate. We explore how the community handled a massive, sudden, and sustained increase in new members. Although existing theory and stories like Usenet's infamous "Eternal September" suggest that large influxes of newcomers can hurt online communities, our interviews suggest that NoSleep survived without major incident. We propose that three features of NoSleep allowed it to manage the rapid influx of newcomers gracefully: (1) an active and well-coordinated group of administrators, (2) a shared sense of community which facilitated community moderation, and (3) technological systems that mitigated norm violations. We also point to several important trade-offs and limitations.

ACM Classification Keywords

H.5.3 Information Interfaces and Presentation (e.g., HCI): Group and Organization Interfaces—*Computer-supported cooperative work*

Author Keywords

online communities; newcomers; norms and governance; peer production; qualitative methods

INTRODUCTION

NoSleep[1] is an online community hosted on the social media website Reddit where people share, rate, and comment on original horror stories in an immersive environment. From its inception in May 2010 to May 2014, NoSleep grew organically to more than 240,000 subscribers. On May 7, 2014, Reddit's administrators added NoSleep to a list of communities that every new Reddit user is automatically subscribed to. Less than a month later, NoSleep's subscriber-base had doubled and it has continued to grow at this pace (see Figure 1). Although theory suggests that large influxes of newcomers will challenge, disrupt, and can even destroy online communities, NoSleep appeared to manage this growth without major negative effects. Using a grounded theory-based analysis of interviews of NoSleep members, writers, and moderators, we suggest that NoSleep was able to survive and thrive through this massive influx of newcomers because it had created systems that ensured a high degree of adherence to the community's norms and that minimized the effect of violations. Our findings also point to several important trade-offs and limitations.

[1] https://www.reddit.com/r/nosleep

CHI'16, May 07-12, 2016, San Jose, CA, USA
ACM 978-1-4503-3362-7/16/05.
http://dx.doi.org/10.1145/2858036.2858356

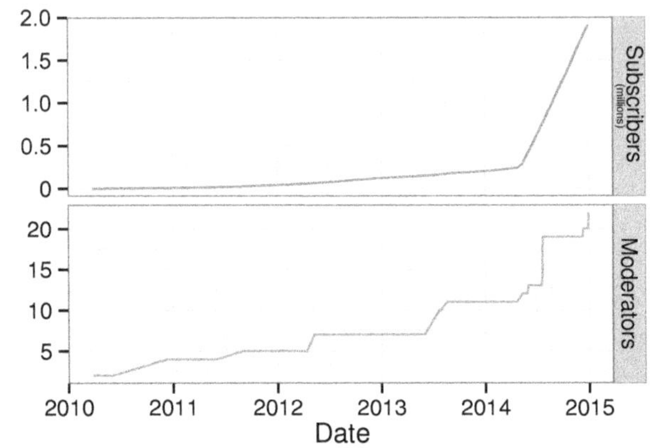

Figure 1. Plots of numbers of subscribers (in millions), and moderators over the life of the community. Data retrieved from snapshots available at archive.org

BACKGROUND

The problem of how to attract newcomers is one of the most important challenges for builders of online communities [13]. A growing body of work considers how leadership, framing, competition, and membership overlap can play an important role in attracting newcomers [17, 21, 13, 22]. However, relatively little research has considered the challenges faced by communities that successfully manage to attract large numbers of new members.

The problems caused by successfully attracting large numbers of newcomers are often invoked in terms of an "Eternal September" [6]. In the 1980s and early 1990s, Usenet participants frequently complained about inexperienced university students joining their communities in September, the beginning of the North American academic year. When America Online connected to Usenet in 1994 and unleashed a large and unremitting stream of new users, Usenet denizens complained of a "September" that never ended and irrevocably damaged their community.

Social computing research suggests that influxes of newcomers can disrupt communities in many ways including increased activity leading to information overload [2, 11] and alienation among established users [10]. Most prominently, research has suggested that newcomers cause disruptions because they do not know and do not follow community norms [13]. As a result, new users can disrupt conversations, contribute low quality content, and annoy existing users. For example, Gorbatai has shown that newcomers tend to make low quality edits to Wikipedia which require fixes by established editors [5].

Because most social computing research treats community growth as a desirable goal, most studies of newcomer activity have focused on how newcomers can be deterred by sanctions leveled at good faith norm violations. For example, studies have shown that Wikipedia editors whose work is undone are less likely to contribute in the future [7, 9, 16]. In response, designers have created welcoming spaces within existing communities [14] and tools to identify and welcome good faith contributors [8].

This work has limited relevance for communities in NoSleep's position in May 2014 whose challenge was widespread norm violation by a surge of newbies. Norm violations included linking to external content in ways that are normative elsewhere in Reddit, marking work as fiction or non-fiction, and misusing the Reddit voting system. Perhaps most importantly, many new users violated a very strong norm of suspended disbelief that requires all commenters to act as if stories are factual. For example, asking if something is true, or even complimenting the author for a "nice story," is not permitted on NoSleep. Violation of this norm by newcomers is disruptive to NoSleep's immersive environment and has historically been treated as a serious threat to the community.

Although the social computing literature points to a deep toll taken by this type of widespread norm violation [13], NoSleep seems to have largely survived its own Eternal September. The NoSleep participants we interviewed suggested that, *"it's gotten bigger but not necessarily worse"* (P1) and that, *"if you went on today, you would see all the comment threads just filled with people going along with it and just enjoying the experience."* (P5). Our analysis asks: How did NoSleep survive, and even thrive, through its Eternal September?

METHODOLOGY

Because large influxes of newcomers are largely unstudied in the social computing literature, the phenomenon is well-suited to qualitative theory-building. Consequently, we adopted a grounded theory interview-based approach [3]. We recruited members of NoSleep in two ways. First, we posted several messages in NoSleep-related forums on Reddit describing the study and requesting that participants contact a member of our research team with information about their individual role and experience in NoSleep. We identified a set of roles (e.g., moderator, writer) and other dimensions (e.g., gender, ex-user) as theoretically important. As is common in grounded theory, we used these dimensions to build a sample that was stratified but did not attempt to be statistically representative [19]. In some cases, we reached out to individuals who we felt would have illuminating perspectives (e.g., a founding member of the

ID	Gender	Role	Joined	Length
1	Female	Lurker	2013	46 min
2	Female	Active	2011	36 min
3	Female	Moderator	2010	41 min
4	Female	Active	2012	42 min
5	Male	Founder / Moderator	2010	52 min
6	Female	Lurker	2010	46 min
7	Male	Ex-Active / Writer	2013	77 min
8	Female	Lurker	2012	41 min
9	Male	Moderator / Writer	2012	62 min
10	Female	Lurker	2013	24 min
11	Female	Active	2013	48 min
12	Male	Moderator	2010	43 min

Table 1. List of study participants with participant ID as used in this paper, gender, primary role(s) in NoSleep, year that they joined the community, and the length of our interview. The term "active" indicates an intense combination of reading, voting, and commenting. "Lurker" indicates reading and voting and was associated with less deep involvement in the community.

community). In total, we interviewed 12 subjects as described in Table 1. All participants were compensated with a $10 Amazon gift card.

Subjects were interviewed over the phone, or via audio/video chat for an average of 47 minutes. Although interviews were semi-structured and open-ended, our protocol was designed to elicit feedback on the large influx of users in May 2014 and is provided in the supplemental materials. All interviews were recorded and transcribed. Following the methodology laid out by Charmaz [3], the first author coded each interview using a series of both inductive codes emergent from the text and deductive codes identified by theory. Transcripts and codes were discussed by all the authors and transcripts were recoded in an iterative fashion. Ultimately, codes were grouped into themes that were elaborated in iteratively created memos.

FINDINGS

Our analysis of coded interviews suggests that NoSleep survived and thrived during its Eternal September because it was equipped with three interconnected systems that ensured a high degree of adherence to NoSleep's norms while minimizing the effect of violations. We present these findings in terms of three propositions and suggest that these attributes could help other online communities survive and thrive in the face of large influxes of newcomers. We also describe ways in which the individuals we interviewed reflected on the trade-offs introduced by these features.

Proposition 1. Consistent Enforcement by Leaders

Participants attributed NoSleep's success in the face of a large influx of new users to the exceptional responsiveness and effectiveness of the community's moderators ("mods") who wield broad authority to remove content and ban users. Figure 1 shows that there were a dozen moderators in May 2014 and that the size of the group has accelerated since then. P1 commented on the quality of moderation saying, *"the NoSleep mods really do a lot as far as keeping everyone not just on track and following rules, but also like keeping everyone interested and active."* NoSleep's moderators were described as a group of community insiders who were committed to, and effective in, keeping the community stable and sustainable.

Moderator work primarily involves rule enforcement and sanctioning. Our subjects commented on the consistency and strictness of NoSleep's moderators and described these qualities as an important component of NoSleep's success in the face of massive growth. Several NoSleep moderators active in other Reddit subcommunities explained that NoSleep had both the strictest and the most consistently enforced rules they had encountered. For example, moderator P3 described how she would enforce community norms at the expense of suppressing friendly conversation: *"If people come on and they say 'that [story] was really great,' that's technically breaking the rules. But, you have to be a real jerk – that's why you're like 'nope you can't – you cannot praise good writing.' "*

Although moderators like P3 mentioned examples of the social and emotional challenges of enforcing NoSleep's norms, they also felt that their work was essential to maintain the stability and immersiveness of the community. Although frequently described as inflexible, subjects also described community leadership as engaged, fair, and legitimate. Echoing the experience of several subjects, P10 described at length how a moderator's interventions helped her learn how to effectively navigate and interact within the community.

In comparison to other communities, the NoSleep moderators were described as extremely organized and engaged. Interviews with moderators revealed a large and sophisticated behind-the-scenes infrastructure including an entire private Reddit community used by moderators to communicate, collaborate, and coordinate with each other to ensure that their actions were responsive and consistent. P3 described the usefulness of this private subreddit: "*We put out drafts of moderator announcements and everybody suggests additions or things that should be changed, so that when we go out and moderate the community – we're really able to show a unified front.*"

Proposition 2. Moderation By Community Members

The community members we interviewed suggested that widespread engagement in norm enforcement by "normal" community members was critically important to handling newcomers. They also suggested that this type of community regulation was only made possible by a strong shared sense of community. For example, there was a striking degree of shared understanding across all participants on what constituted good NoSleep stories. Although subjects could reflect on their individual taste in stories, many respondents echoed P6's claims that excellent NoSleep stories should include "*a strong character voice*" and be "*something that's almost believable.*" Although many newcomers adopt more off-the-cuff styles, nearly every subject interviewed mentioned style and grammar as criteria that they use to judge the quality of stories on NoSleep. Some of this knowledge is made explicit in documentation on the site.

The degree to which this knowledge reflects a shared sense of community was also visible in the way community members described working together to address examples of users violating NoSleep's norms. Described as "burying" material, subjects described collectively rating norm-violating content and comments as low quality (i.e., "downvoting") so that it becomes hidden by Reddit's interface. P1 explained how she approached comments left by newcomers unaware of the suspension of disbelief norm, "*that's when you're like 'All right, if we all downvote this, it will go away. It will be like it never happened.*'" Although P1 did not write content or comments herself, she expressed a feeling of empowerment to act with the community to preserve its norms that was nearly universal among our interviewees.

Although rules are rigid, P8, P9 and P10 each reflected on the way that the community's sense of purpose and shared goals made it possible to identify attempts to game its system, and on the community's ability to "correct themselves" in these cases. Because the number of moderators with explicit authority is limited, this sense of community made collective action among "normal" members possible, scaled effectively, and was able to both minimize damage from, and educate, a sustained influx of newcomers. Because users could work to "bury" norm-violating material, there was much less pressure on moderators to act quickly and in every case of a violated norm.

Proposition 3. Technological Systems Maintaining Norms

Participants suggested that the technological affordances of NoSleep were a third important factor in the community's smooth growth. Several technologies mentioned included basic functionality of the Reddit platform that facilitates community moderation. This included Reddit's voting system giving all members the ability to quickly vote content up or down. As P1 explained, "*in order to be an active member of the community, you just need to hit a button.*" A related tool proved by Reddit facilitates "peer reporting" of problematic content which is presented to moderators who can then hide content and contact users. Moderator P12 explained that, "*if you have individuals committed enough to ... not break immersion, just by clicking a report button on comments that do [break immersion], it brings it into the moderator queue so that we can make them disappear.*"

Building on this system, NoSleep employs a tool called "AutoModerator" that automatically detects rule violations and sanctions violators [15]. Although not visible to many users, several moderators we interviewed explained that the tool, also provided by Reddit, finds and flags problematic content and communicates with moderators in ways that obviates the need for action on many straightforward moderation issues.

Interviewees also credited Reddit's functionality that allows newcomers to edit and improve stories or comments after discovering they have inadvertently broken a rule or deviated from the community's norms and then to resubmit their content. They also pointed to a feature that issues reminders of norms at points of action including an HTML placeholder attribute in the comment box below stories that reminds users of rules before commenting. One moderator described a tool used by the community called "post throttling" which limits users to one story submission every 24 hours. P3 explained that throttling was used to reduce the threat of a newcomer disrupting the community and to provide a limit on the effect of a trend of newbies posting "series" of stories to garner visibility and popularity.

Of course, these technologies rely on social infrastructure to be effective in ways that highlight the interrelated nature of our propositions. Community voting and peer reporting rely on an engaged set of community members with a shared sense of the community as well as an active set of moderators who can effectively remove flagged or downvoted content and sanction repeat violators. Our interviewees suggested that NoSleep effectively combined these three features into a socio-technical system that was able to maintain community standards through a sustained influx of newcomers.

The Cost of Strong Regulation

All three propositions point to systems facilitating strong norm enforcement. Although described as important for managing the influx of new users, these systems were not described as universally positive or costless. For example, a rule requiring stories to be believable was elaborated in the aftermath of the influx of new users to explicitly bar supernatural stories (e.g., stories that involve demons or vampires). Although subjects acknowledged that this pushed newcomers toward creating believable stories, it also annoyed some established users who felt they could navigate the fine line between supernatural content and believability. For example, P3 explained that, "*the rules had been made tighter because of the new subscribers, and that sometimes doesn't allow them as much freedom.*" Similarly, P7 felt that rules were, "*corralling younger users into acting or reading in a particular way...instead of doing what they want.*" Frustrated by this experience, P7 explained that he no longer contributes to the community as frequently.

For others, tough rule enforcement was seen as having a negative effect on commenting and discussion by making the environment feel constrained and contrived. P11 described the difference between her experiences in NoSleep and other Reddit subcommunities, commenting on the rules that forbid any kind of criticism of stories: "*Most subreddits have comment sections that are kind of stream of consciousness—people tend to share their own experiences. On NoSleep, you don't see people really sharing their own experiences; you see people commenting specifically on the story... Again, because of the rules, you don't really see trolling. Kind of nice, kind of not nice ... I think the comment section is kind of – I don't think it's very organic.*" Through a strong system of rules and a complex socio-technical infrastructure to ensure that they are enforced, NoSleep was able to survive and thrive despite the weight of millions of newcomers. However, the cost of NoSleep's survival was described by some interviewees as an uncomfortably strict environment that limited creativity. The systems described as facilitating NoSleep's rapid growth were also portrayed as providing strict limits on what it could grow to become.

DISCUSSION

In one sense, our three propositions seem to be at odds with other social computing research. For example, a body of Wikipedia research has connected stronger systems of norms with inefficient bureaucracies that may cause communities growth to slow or even stop [1, 18, 12]. For example, Halfaker et al. [7] connect increases in social and technical systems for norm-enforcement to lower rates of newcomer retention. In another sense, our propositions should not be unfamiliar to social computing researchers. For example, all three propositions can be found in some form in among Kraut and Resnick's [13] "design claims" and our contribution lies not in the discovery of these features but in our suggestion that they play a critical role in helping groups survive and thrive through what is often traumatic or catastrophic growth. We believe that techniques that minimize the effect of norm violations by newcomers may both help prevent communities from descending into chaos *and* deter newcomers. Techniques that prevent short-term disaster may be inappropriate – and difficult to change – when growth slows.

Of course, our work is limited in many ways. One unavoidable limitation of our inductive grounded theory approach is that findings may reflect the idiosyncrasies and biases of interviewees. For example, we were only able to recruit one user who described themselves as a former NoSleep member. As a result, our findings may reflect "survivor bias" where individuals less negatively affected by an event are the only people available to be interviewed. We gain some confidence in our findings by the fact that our participants did not describe any major exoduses of authors or moderators or major changes in the nature of the community. That said, we only present these findings as propositions for testing in future work.

Our findings offer several important implications for design. The first points toward the importance of emphasizing decentralized moderation. Although previous research has found this to be "underprovisioned" on Reddit as a whole [4], in NoSleep it seems to be sufficient. A second implication is the importance of ensuring enough leadership capacity is available when an influx of newcomers is anticipated. Designers may benefit by focusing on tools to let existing leaders bring others on board and help them clearly communicate norms. Finally, designers should support an ecosystem of accessible and appropriate moderator tools. During a widely reported Reddit uprising, a moderator of a different subcommunity complained that, "the moderation tools we are given are severely lacking" [20].

Our interviews and analysis point to the importance of strong systems of norm enforcement made possible by leadership, community engagement, and technology. Although we propose that NoSleep's socio-technical infrastructure can provide a template for other communities facing similar challenges, we also suggest that they are not without trade-offs. Although not without qualification, NoSleep's example provides a model for how an Eternal September need not mean an inevitable march toward winter.

REFERENCES

1. Brian Butler, Elisabeth Joyce, and Jacqueline Pike. 2008. Don't Look Now, but We've Created a Bureaucracy: The Nature and Roles of Policies and Rules in Wikipedia. In *Proceedings of the SIGCHI Conference on Human Factors in Computing Systems (CHI '08)*. ACM, New

York, NY, USA, 1101–1110. DOI: http://dx.doi.org/10.1145/1357054.1357227

2. Brian S. Butler. 2001. Membership Size, Communication Activity, and Sustainability: A Resource-Based Model of Online Social Structures. *Information Systems Research* 12, 4 (Dec. 2001), 346–362. DOI: http://dx.doi.org/10.1287/isre.12.4.346.9703

3. Kathy Charmaz. 2006. *Constructing Grounded Theory: A Practical Guide through Qualitative Analysis* (1 ed.). Sage Publications Ltd.

4. Eric Gilbert. 2013. Widespread Underprovision on Reddit. In *Proceedings of the 2013 Conference on Computer Supported Cooperative Work (CSCW '13)*. ACM, New York, NY, USA, 803–808. DOI: http://dx.doi.org/10.1145/2441776.2441866

5. Andreea Gorbatai. 2012. Aligning Collective Production with Demand: Evidence from Wikipedia. (2012). http://faculty.chicagobooth.edu/workshops/orgs-markets/past/pdf/gorbatai.pdf

6. Wendy Grossman. 1998. *net.wars*. NYU Press, New York.

7. Aaron Halfaker, R. Stuart Geiger, Jonathan T. Morgan, and John Riedl. 2013. The Rise and Decline of an Open Collaboration System How Wikipedia's Reaction to Popularity Is Causing Its Decline. *American Behavioral Scientist* 57, 5 (May 2013), 664–688. DOI: http://dx.doi.org/10.1177/0002764212469365

8. Aaron Halfaker, R. Stuart Geiger, and Loren G. Terveen. 2014. Snuggle: Designing for Efficient Socialization and Ideological Critique. In *Proceedings of the SIGCHI Conference on Human Factors in Computing Systems (CHI '14)*. ACM, New York, NY, USA, 311–320. DOI: http://dx.doi.org/10.1145/2556288.2557313

9. Aaron Halfaker, Aniket Kittur, and John Riedl. 2011. Don't bite the newbies: how reverts affect the quantity and quality of Wikipedia work. In *Proceedings of the 7th International Symposium on Wikis and Open Collaboration (WikiSym '11)*. ACM, New York, NY, USA, 163–172. DOI: http://dx.doi.org/10.1145/2038558.2038585

10. Robin Jeffries, Sara Kiesler, Jennifer Goetz, and Lee Sproull. 2005. Systers: Contradictions in community. (2005). http://citeseerx.ist.psu.edu/viewdoc/download?doi=10.1.1.111.9648&rep=rep1&type=pdf

11. Quentin Jones, Gilad Ravid, and Sheizaf Rafaeli. 2004. Information Overload and the Message Dynamics of Online Interaction Spaces: A Theoretical Model and Empirical Exploration. *Information Systems Research* 15, 2 (June 2004), 194–210. DOI: http://dx.doi.org/10.1287/isre.1040.0023

12. Nicolas Jullien, Kevin Crowston, and Felipe Ortega. 2015. The Rise and Fall of an Online Project: Is Bureaucracy Killing Efficiency in Open Knowledge Production?. In *Proceedings of the 11th International Symposium on Open Collaboration (OpenSym '15)*. ACM, New York, NY, USA, 13:1–13:10. DOI: http://dx.doi.org/10.1145/2788993.2789844

13. Robert E. Kraut and Paul Resnick. 2012. *Building Successful Online Communities: Evidence-Based Social Design*. The MIT Press.

14. Jonathan T. Morgan, Siko Bouterse, Heather Walls, and Sarah Stierch. 2013. Tea and sympathy: crafting positive new user experiences on wikipedia. In *Proceedings of the 2013 conference on Computer supported cooperative work (CSCW '13)*. ACM, New York, NY, USA, 839–848. DOI:http://dx.doi.org/10.1145/2441776.2441871

15. Kevin Morris. 2012. Reddit moderator bots arrive to protect and serve. (Jan. 2012). http://www.dailydot.com/news/reddit-automoderator-bots/

16. Mikolaj Jan Piskorski and Andreea D. Gorbatai. 2013. *Testing Coleman's Social-Norm Enforcement Mechanism: Evidence from Wikipedia*. SSRN Scholarly Paper ID 1926284. Social Science Research Network, Rochester, NY. http://papers.ssrn.com/abstract=1926284

17. Charles Schweik and Robert English. 2012. *Internet Success: A Study of Open Source Software Commons*. MIT Press, Cambridge, Massachusetts. http://mitpress.mit.edu/catalog/item/default.asp?ttype=2&tid=12792

18. Bongwon Suh, Gregorio Convertino, Ed H. Chi, and Peter Pirolli. 2009. The Singularity is Not Near: Slowing Growth of Wikipedia. In *Proceedings of the 5th International Symposium on Wikis and Open Collaboration (WikiSym '09)*. ACM, New York, NY, USA, 8:1–8:10. DOI: http://dx.doi.org/10.1145/1641309.1641322

19. Jan E. Trost. 1986. Statistically nonrepresentative stratified sampling: A sampling technique for qualitative studies. *Qualitative Sociology* 9, 1 (March 1986), 54–57. DOI:http://dx.doi.org/10.1007/BF00988249

20. Charlie Warzel. 2015. Reddit Moderators Are Fed Up: "I Thought It Couldn't Get Worse" - BuzzFeed News. (July 2015). http://www.buzzfeed.com/charliewarzel/i-thought-it-couldnt-get-worse-reddit-moderators-are-fed-up

21. Haiyi Zhu, Jilin Chen, Tara Matthews, Aditya Pal, Hernan Badenes, and Robert E. Kraut. 2014a. Selecting an Effective Niche: An Ecological View of the Success of Online Communities. In *Proceedings of the SIGCHI Conference on Human Factors in Computing Systems (CHI '14)*. ACM, New York, NY, USA, 301–310. DOI: http://dx.doi.org/10.1145/2556288.2557348

22. Haiyi Zhu, Robert E. Kraut, and Aniket Kittur. 2014b. The Impact of Membership Overlap on the Survival of Online Communities. In *Proceedings of the SIGCHI Conference on Human Factors in Computing Systems (CHI '14)*. ACM, New York, NY, USA, 281–290. DOI: http://dx.doi.org/10.1145/2556288.2557213

"This Post Will Just Get Taken Down": Characterizing Removed Pro-Eating Disorder Social Media Content

Stevie Chancellor
Georgia Tech
Atlanta GA 30332
schancellor3@gatech.edu

Zhiyuan (Jerry) Lin
Georgia Tech
Atlanta GA 30332
zlin48@gatech.edu

Munmun De Choudhury
Georgia Tech
Atlanta GA 30332
munmund@gatech.edu

ABSTRACT
Social media sites like Facebook and Instagram remove content that is against community guidelines or is perceived to be deviant behavior. Users also delete their own content that they feel is not appropriate within personal or community norms. In this paper, we examine characteristics of over 30,000 pro-eating disorder (pro-ED) posts that were at one point public on Instagram but have since been removed. Our work shows that straightforward signals can be found in deleted content that distinguish them from other posts, and that the implications of such classification are immense. We build a classifier that compares public pro-ED posts with this removed content that achieves moderate accuracy of 69%. We also analyze the characteristics in content in each of these post categories and find that removed content reflects more dangerous actions, self-harm tendencies, and vulnerability than posts that remain public. Our work provides early insights into content removal in a sensitive community and addresses the future research implications of the findings.

ACM Classification Keywords
H.5.m. Information Interfaces and Presentation (e.g. HCI): Miscellaneous

Author Keywords
deviant behavior; content removal; social media; eating disorders; health

INTRODUCTION
Social media platforms like Twitter, Instagram, and Facebook are used to discuss a variety of topics, ranging from the mundane to sensitive. Content and user accounts are sometimes moderated to both sustain a healthy community and prevent behavior that violates established rules or social norms [41, 19, 25, 7]. Current moderation practices include platform-enforced policies (e.g., deleting content or banning users) or community-driven assessments (e.g., voting or rating mechanisms, block functionality, reporting infringing content).

The photo-sharing social network Instagram has several moderation approaches for posts that breach their Community Guidelines. Instagram removes sexual photos, illegal behaviors, and spam[1]. It also prohibits self-harm and pro-eating disorder (pro-ED) content — a behavior that promotes eating disorders as legitimate lifestyle choices instead of dangerous psychosocial disorders[2]. Users can also remove their own posts that they feel are not appropriate either for the platform or for the established norms of the community. Whatever the reason, intent, or authority behind removal, users often acknowledge in their posts that, "*this post will just get taken down*". We consider these removed posts as a prime example of deviant behavior [3] because these posts do not conform to the personal or collective norms that the individual, the platform, or the community may have established in tandem.

When individuals experience vulnerability, they tend to reach out to others to "buffer" themselves against negative emotions and actions [16]. To the pro-ED community, social media sites like Instagram provide such an outlet to seek out these kind of "safety valves" to regulate their emotions [1]. Users in this community frequently discuss negative events, like intents to deliberately self-injure [12, 33]; we suspect that the perceived sensitivity expressed in pro-ED posts that removed from the platform is higher than normal – a factor that likely underlies the removal. There is an important opportunity to learn the characteristics of this deviant content for several reasons: learning more about motivations behind post removal, how this removal behavior may carry over to other online communities or technologies, and how other technologies may identify characteristics of deviant behavior on a platform.

Our Contributions and Ethics. This paper examines characteristics of pro-ED posts removed from Instagram. We build a supervised learning approach, a binary logistic regression classifier, to distinguish between the content of public pro-ED posts and removed posts. From here on, we refer to these removed posts as "deviant posts". We build our classifier on a sample of over 30,000 deviant and an equal number of public pro-ED posts. We find that the two classes of posts can be distinguished with satisfactory performance (accuracy of 69% and an area-under-curve measure of 76%). Interpreting the variables with high predictive power, we find that deviant pro-ED posts indeed show heightened vulnerability compared to public posts, and these content markers provide important insights into deviant behavior. We also discuss the implications, future work, and power of this research.

[1] https://help.instagram.com/477434105621119/
[2] http://blog.instagram.com/post/21454597658/instagrams-new-guidelines-against-self-harm

CHI'16, May 07-12, 2016, San Jose, CA, USA
©2016 ACM. ISBN 978-1-4503-3362-7/16/05 $15.00
DOI: http://dx.doi.org/10.1145/2858036.2858248

We recognize that analysis of deleted or removed content is controversial territory in social computing. It has been studied in prior work [37, 4, 14], and we appreciate the authors of [32] for providing insight into the ethics of this research. However, we believe that the important health benefits of our work for those in need justifies the study of removed content in pro-ED communities. In that light, our work extends efforts in the social computing research community where large-scale data analytic approaches have been adopted to extend timely and tailored support to vulnerable communities online [18, 15].

Nonetheless, we took precautions to conduct this study as ethically as possible. The data used in this paper was collected through the official Instagram API when the posts were publicly accessible. There is no research interaction with the users, and the data is only analyzed by the algorithms we develop—i.e., we adopt an "eyes off" quantitative analysis approach (e.g., [11, 30]), since, ethically, users would need to consent to have their deleted content read by researchers. Thus, we did not seek institutional review board approval. To protect the privacy of our participants, we do not disclose any algorithmic output that contains personally identifying information, including usernames or personal tags.

RELATED WORK

Substantial research in HCI and CSCW has examined characteristics of deviant content and deviant behavior, including those associated with content removal or deletion.

Online Deviance. Rafferty et al. [35] qualitatively examined cyberbullying and aggression as forms of deviance (also [27, 44]), and Wang et al. [42] studied the nature of abusive deviant content on Twitter. Other work has examined the dynamics of and motivation behind sharing deviant content [23, 31, 25, 10], the role of online identity choices and accountability in such content [41, 19, 40], and management of design considerations and mechanisms around deviance [9, 38, 39, 5, 2]. Deviant behavior and content sharing has also been studied in specific contexts, such as online gaming [8], online news commentary [6, 14], feminist forums [26], grief expression [34], and peer production communities [43, 36, 28, 2].

Content Deletion on Social Media. Sleeper et al. [37] studied post deletion practices of individuals around regretful experiences on Twitter. Almuhimedi et. al [4] quantitatively examined deleted tweets on Twitter, and Cheng et. al [14] looked at comments removed by moderators that were deemed antisocial and toxic to three online news communities. Close to our work is Chancellor et al. [13] that examined behavior patterns following banning of tags in pro-ED communities; however, this study did not explore the characteristics of deleted and removed pro-ED posts. We build on this larger body of work to offer some of the first quantitative insights into deviant content from a sensitive and controversial online community [22].

DATA AND METHODS

Data Collection

To allow enough removal time for deviant pro-ED posts, our data collection occurred in three phases over ten months. In all phases, we used the tools in the official Instagram API (https://instagram.com/developer/).

skinny	thin	thinspo	bonespo
eatingdisorder	probulimia	anorexia	thighgap
proanorexia	mia	bulimia	promia
thinspiration	secretsociety	ana	proana
anorexianervosa			

Table 1. Example tags used for crawling pro-ED posts in our study.

Phase I: Obtaining Pro-ED Data. In September 2014, we created a large initial sample of *public* posts with pro-ED tags. We consider these posts to be shared by the "pro-ED community" on Instagram; although Instagram does not have defined community structures, users organize around tags to create and share a common identity [24]. To identify pro-ED tags, we first curated a set of nine "seed tags"[3] found to be common tags and structures illustrating pro-ED behaviors and attitudes across different social media platforms [17]. Two researchers then manually inspected posts on each tag to ensure there was sufficient pro-ED content. We crawled these tags for a month, which returned 434K posts and 234K unique tags. We selected 222 tags that had at least a 1% co-occurrence rate with other tags in this dataset.

From this set of 222, we manually filtered tags that did not map to eating disorders for three reasons: (1) Tags that were related to eating disorders but were generic enough to be used in many other contexts, e.g. "beautiful" and "inspiration". (2) Tags related to other mental conditions or disorders, e.g. "depression", "anxious", or "suicidal". Lastly (3) Tags that were tied to the eating disorder recovery community, e.g. "edrecovery". This reduced the filtered co-occurrence tag list from 222 tags to 72 verified to related to eating disorders (see sample tags in Table 1).

In November 2014, we crawled all content across these 72 tags. This returned over 8 million posts between January 2011 and November 2014. We then removed any posts that were cross-posted to any recovery tags as well as any that had three specific tags ("mia", "ana", and "ed") that did not also contain another one of the initial list of 72. Qualitative observation indicated that these three tags used in isolation from pro-ED tags refers to first names (the name "Mia") or references to popular celebrities ("ed" for Ed Sheeran). Our dataset at the end of this phase had 6.5 million posts relating to pro-ED.

Phase II: Gathering Pro-ED Users and Post Timelines. In February 2015, we obtained a random sample of 100K active users from the authors of the 6.5 million posts above. We gathered the public timelines of each of the 100K users. This set contains over 26M posts from 100K users, with posts shared between October 2010 and March 2015.

Phase III: Gathering deviant pro-ED data. In August 2015, we used the Instagram API to check whether the posts from Phase II were still publicly accessible. We randomly sorted our posts and gathered the first 31K posts where the post was no longer available on the platform but the user's account still existed. Note that checking whether the user's account was still active was an important step to prevent confounding resulting from a post being deleted because the user removed their Instagram account altogether — we believe the characteristics of account deletion may be considerably distinct from

[3]Seed tags include: "ed", "eatingdisorder", "ednos", "ana", "anorexia", "anorexic","mia", "bulimia", and "bulimic".

those related to post removal. These 31K posts represent our deviant pro-ED posts for our classification task. To construct an equivalent still-public dataset of pro-ED posts, we gathered the first 31K random public posts, bringing the total number of posts in our dataset to 62K.

Characterization and Prediction Framework

Next, we develop several logistic regression models to learn the characteristics of deviant pro-ED posts as well as to automatically distinguish them from content that remains public. Regularization helps us control for collinearity (since we use the text of posts) and sparsity in our data. In our case, we used the model implementation given in the Python package statsmodels. Our response variable is the binary indicator of whether a post is deviant or still-public. For the predictor variables, we considered four different sets and build a model for each set. These variables capture straightforward linguistic constructs in the post's text. Note that we did not use the visual features of the photo or video included in the post, but it constitutes an important direction toward future work.

TagCt: uses the frequency of tags in a post as predictor variables; we consider all tags which occur 200 or more times, which gives 614 predictor variables.

TagCo: uses the 500 most frequent pairwise tag co-occurrences in posts[4], and the 614 tags with frequencies over 200 (from **TagCt**).

TagCtCo: uses 500 most frequent pairwise unigram co-occurrences in the captions of the posts, the 500 most frequent pairwise tag co-occurrences in posts, and the 614 tags with frequencies over 200 (from **TagCt**).

TagCtCoCap: uses 1,000 most frequent pairwise unigram co-occurrences in the captions of the posts, the 1,000 most frequent pairwise tag co-occurrences in posts, and the 614 tags with frequencies over 200 (from **TagCt**).

RESULTS

Our model used 80% of our data for training purposes and parameter tuning; the remaining 20% were heldout for testing.

On the training data, we first present the goodness of fit of our four models and how they fared against the `Null` model (Table 2). Compared to the `Null` model, all of our models provide considerable explanatory power (statistically significant based on Bonferroni correction) with significant reduction in deviances. Particularly, the `TagCtCoCap` model (that uses tag frequencies, tag co-occurrences and unigram and bigram tokens in post captions) yields the best fit. We find that the difference between the deviance of the `Null` model and the deviance of this model approximately follows a χ^2 distribution, with degrees of freedom equal to the number of additional variables in the latter model: $\chi^2(2613, N = 62K) = 107387 - 54487 = 5.29 \times 10^4, p < 10^{-10}$.

Next we report our results on the 20% heldout dataset. For the sake of brevity, we only report expanded performance metrics on the model with the best performance (the `TagCtCoCap` model) in Table 3. In the confusion matrix, class 1 is deviant posts and class 0 is public posts. We find that the `TagCtCoCap`

[4]Two tags or unigrams co-occur if they are used together in a post.

Model	Deviance	df	χ^2	p-value
`Null`	107387	0		
`TagCt`	61029	613	9.43e+03	$< 10^{-7}$
`TagCo`	58266	1113	6.67e+03	$< 10^{-8}$
`TagCtCo`	57632	1613	6.03e+03	$< 10^{-8}$
`TagCtCoCap`	54487	2613	2.89e+03	$< 10^{-10}$

Table 2. Summary of different model fits. `Null` is the intercept-only model. All comparisons with the `Null model` are statistically significant after Bonferroni correction for multiple testing ($\alpha = \frac{0.05}{4}$).

Actual/Predicted	Class 0	Class 1	Total
Class 0	4433	1913	6346
Class 1	2018	4328	6346
Accuracy	69.85%	68.2%	69.03% (mean)
Precision	.69	.69	.69 (mean)
Recall	.70	.68	.69 (mean)
F-1	.69	.69	.69 (mean)

Table 3. Performance of the `TagCtCoCap` model in distinguishing deviant and public posts.

model gives satisfactory accuracy in classifying both deviant and public pro-ED posts, with a mean precision, recall, and F-1 score of .69 each. The accuracy of the model is 69%, an improvement of 19% over a chance model (50% baseline accuracy due to balanced class sizes). We report the receiver operating characteristic (ROC) curve in Figure 1; the area under curve (AUC) is 76%.

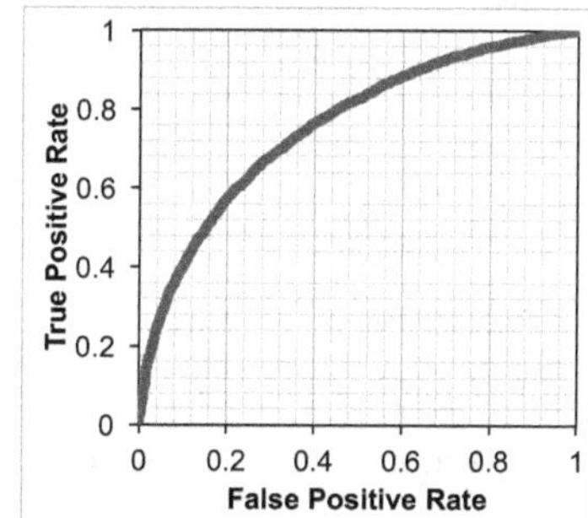

Figure 1. ROC curve for the `tagCtCoCap` model.

We also present 20 of the top 50 positive and negative β values of the `TagCtCoCap` model in Table 4. The positive and negative β values indicate increased likelihood of a post to be deviant or public, respectively. The variables that are most predictive of deviant posts are overwhelmingly associated with attitudes and behaviors that reinforce pro-ED lifestyles as well as self-injurious behaviors. These include "cutting", "bodycheck" (where users invite others to suggest improvements for their body), and the desire to look or be skinny. There are also indicators of high vulnerability and threats to personal safety ("worthless", "suicidal", "razor"). In contrast, predictor variables that increase the likelihood of a post remaining public are closest to those reaching out to the eating disorder recovery community [45]. Public posts also emphasize a larger variety of emotions, cognitions, and confessions ("gourgeous", "angry", "misunderstood").

DISCUSSION AND IMPLICATIONS FOR FUTURE WORK

Our findings show that characteristics in captions and tagging strategies of posts on Instagram can predict whether a post will be considered deviant on the platform and then removed. The beta weights displayed in Table 4 illustrates two important findings from our data. One, deviant posts have a higher chance of being related to self-injury, suicide, and the maintenance of eating disorders, confirming what has been observed in prior work [12]. This implies that, while these communities are allowed to exist on the platform, these particular deviant

Type / Content	β	Type / Content	β
TC/#different	2.22	TP/#edrecovery&#beated	-1.33
TC/#energy	1.95	TC/#eatittobeatit	-1.27
TC/#depressedteen	1.30	TC/#toned	-1.23
TP/#ana & #anorexia	1.10	TC/#nevergoodenough	-1.04
TC/#ptsd	1.08	TC/#angry	-0.97
TP/#anorexia & #anorexianervosa	1.00	TP/#ana & #edsoldiers	-0.92
TP/#cutting & #crying	0.98	TC/#misunderstood	-0.92
TP/#depression & #blade	0.94	CP/today & strong	-0.85
TC/#skinnyplease	0.90	CP/fat & depressed	-0.84
TP/#blade & #suicide	0.87	TC/#gourgeous	-0.80
CP/personal & account	0.86	TP/#anarecovery&#edfamily	-0.78
TP/#ana & #weightloss	0.85	TC/#edarmy	-0.77
TP/#sue&#anorexia	0.82	TP/#prorecovery &#anorexiarecovery	-0.71
TC/#harm	0.80	TC/#nourishnotpunish	-0.71
TP/#anxiety &#depressionquotes	0.80	TC/#eathealthy	-0.71
TC/#anagirl	0.79	TC/#ednosrecovery	-0.70
TC/#selfharmmm	0.79	CP/got & think	-0.70
TC/#bodycheck	0.79	CP/know & friend	-0.69
CP/want & look	0.77	TC/#prorecovery	-0.69

Table 4. Selected 20 out of the top 50 features' positive and negative beta weights in our TagCtCoCap model. There are 3 types of features: TC (tag with at least 200 occurrences), TP (co-occurring tag pair), and CP (co-occurring unigram pair in caption)

posts are either perceived negatively by the authors themselves later or are considered to violate community norms. Second, although further exploration is needed, we find that posts that remain public reach out to the pro-recovery community. This suggests a conscious effort by the community to tacitly endorse these posts, the users' ideas, and promoting a healthier lifestyle despite still being visible on pro-ED tags.

Implications

Because we can identify removed content with straightforward text characteristics, we foresee several exciting research opportunities as a result of this research.

Health and Just-In-Time Interventions. Some platforms have basic intervention systems to bring help to such vulnerable individuals. For example, Facebook's suicide intervention system prompts a user to contact a close friend or assistance hotline if another person reports their post to be suicidal[5]. Beyond these efforts, our predictors show that removed content overwhelmingly shows high vulnerability and threats to personal safety ("worthless", "suicidal", "razor"), making our classifier a good start to identifying moments for just-in-time intervention [29] to users who post this kind of content. Expansion of this approach to contain more cues would boost its accuracy and applicability to real-world systems. Potentials for interventions could include a prompt to direct users to contact a close friend or reach out to a specialist available on a hotline. This would be useful not only for pro-ED posts, but in other cases of mental illness.

Implications for Social Computing Research and HCI. Taking the meaning of intervention more broadly, our deviant post classifier can be used to facilitate better content moderation practices. Social media platforms could build tools leveraging our methodology to assist moderators in identifying deviant posts. Many platforms rely on the report/flag functionality to alert moderators of deviant content. Rather than waiting for reports to manually come in, our classifier could generate a list of posts that are potentially deviant, and then a human well-versed in the community guidelines of the platform can choose an outcome to the post. This way the system brings human judgment to an area where sensitivity and care are needed.

Broadly, through these investigations of deviant pro-ED content, social computing researchers can gain insights into the intent and motivation behind sharing of pro-ED content on a public social platform and the general goals of such sensitive self-disclosure. They can also understand how individuals are repurposing social media platforms in order to connect and bond with others with similar personal challenges relating to mental health, as well as to seek their help and support during moments of heightened physical or emotional vulnerability.

Extending beyond deviant health behavior, HCI researchers could incorporate our approach into analyzing deletion or removal practices behind other forms of user-generated deviant content, ranging from abuse, bullying and hate speech, including how different online communities shape their norms to tackle deviant content.

Limitations and Conclusion

Research has shown that communities like pro-ED can have detrimental effects on the health of the broader community, not just sufferers themselves [21]. Our algorithm could be implemented to help quickly remove deviant posts *before* the post author or the community perceives it to be deviant. However, great care must be taken when implementing any system that filters content. When posts are removed, what are the impacts on the users, their emotional state, and the broader goals of the community? At what point does automated removal shift from improving efficacy to chilling speech, removing important "safety valves" to dangerous behaviors [20], or potentially promote the discussion of more dangerous content [13]?

Future work will need to be delicately crafted to promote positive outcomes, as is the case with health communities. Collaborations between social media researchers, designers, ethicists, and psychologists will be essential in developing what actions are best for particular scenarios and when to deploy these interventions.

Given the constraints imposed by the Instagram API, we are not able to distinguish between post removal initiated by the individual and by the platform. Even though removed content provides a signal that such content is inappropriate and violates norms, some content may be removed due to mundane reasons such as a typo or accidental mis-post. This could potentially introduce noise into our model and analysis. Future work could expand this analysis to understanding deviant content in a deeper way, including how fast posts are removed from the platform as well as interviewing users on the motivation behind these practices.

This paper explored how timely, tailored support could be directed to sensitive online communities like pro-ED when content is removed from the platform. The moral and ethical grounds surrounding content moderation, banning, and removal are important conversations for the social computing community to consider going forward.

[5]http://www.washington.edu/news/2015/02/25/forefront-and-facebook-launch-suicide-prevention-effort/

REFERENCES

1. Jan Paul Acton. 1973. Evaluating public programs to save lives. (1973).
2. B Thomas Adler, Luca De Alfaro, Santiago M Mola-Velasco, Paolo Rosso, and Andrew G West. 2011. Wikipedia vandalism detection: Combining natural language, metadata, and reputation features. In *Computational linguistics and intelligent text processing*. Springer, 277–288.
3. Ronald L Akers. 1977. Deviant behavior: A social learning approach. (1977).
4. Hazim Almuhimedi, Shomir Wilson, Bin Liu, Norman Sadeh, and Alessandro Acquisti. 2013. Tweets are forever: a large-scale quantitative analysis of deleted tweets. In *Proceedings of the 2013 conference on Computer supported cooperative work*. ACM, 897–908.
5. Michael Bernstein, Michael Conover, Benjamin Mako Hill, Andres Monroy-Hernandez, Brian Keegan, Aaron Shaw, Sarita Yardi, R Stuart Geiger, and Amy Bruckman. 2012. Fail whaling: designing from deviance and failures in social computing. In *CHI'12 Extended Abstracts on Human Factors in Computing Systems*. ACM, 1127–1130.
6. Amy Binns. 2012. DON'T FEED THE TROLLS! Managing troublemakers in magazines' online communities. *Journalism Practice* 6, 4 (2012), 547–562.
7. Jonathan Bishop. 2013. *Examining the Concepts, Issues, and Implications of Internet Trolling*. IGI Global.
8. Jeremy Blackburn and Haewoon Kwak. 2014. Stfu noob!: predicting crowdsourced decisions on toxic behavior in online games. In *Proceedings of the 23rd international conference on World wide web*. ACM, 877–888.
9. Amy Bruckman, Pavel Curtis, Cliff Figallo, and Brenda Laurel. 1994. Approaches to managing deviant behavior in virtual communities. In *Conference Companion on Human Factors in Computing Systems*. ACM, 183–184.
10. Erin E Buckels, Paul D Trapnell, and Delroy L Paulhus. 2014. Trolls just want to have fun. *Personality and individual Differences* 67 (2014), 97–102.
11. Moira Burke, Cameron Marlow, and Thomas Lento. 2010. Social network activity and social well-being. In *Proceedings of the SIGCHI conference on human factors in computing systems*. ACM, 1909–1912.
12. Stevie Chancellor, Zhiyuan (Jerry) Lin, Erica Goodman, Stephanie Zerwas, and Munmun De Choudhury. Quantifying and Predicting Mental Illness Severity in Online Pro-Eating Disorder Communities. In *Proceedings of the 19th ACM Conference on Computer Supported Cooperative Work & Social Computing (CSCW)*.
13. Stevie Chancellor, Jessica Pater, Trustin Clear, Eric Gilbert, and Munmun De Choudhury. 2016. #thyghgapp: Instagram Content Moderation and Lexical Variation in Pro-Eating Disorder Communities. In *Proceedings of the 2016 Conference on Computer Supported Cooperative Work & Social Computing(CSCW)*. ACM. in press.
14. Justin Cheng, Cristian Danescu-Niculescu-Mizil, and Jure Leskovec. 2015. Antisocial Behavior in Online Discussion Communities. In *International Conference on Weblogs and Social Media (ICWSM)*. AAAI.
15. Glen Coppersmith, Craig Harman, and Mark Dredze. 2014. Measuring post traumatic stress disorder in Twitter. In *Proc. ICWSM*.
16. James C Coyne and Geraldine Downey. 1991. Social factors and psychopathology: Stress, social support, and coping processes. *Annual review of psychology* 42, 1 (1991), 401–425.
17. Munmun De Choudhury. 2015. Anorexia on Tumblr: A Characterization Study. In *Proc. Digital Health*.
18. Munmun De Choudhury, Scott Counts, and Eric Horvitz. 2013. Predicting postpartum changes in emotion and behavior via social media. In *Proceedings of the 2013 ACM annual conference on Human factors in computing systems*. ACM, 3267–3276.
19. Judith S Donath and others. 1999. Identity and deception in the virtual community. *Communities in cyberspace* 1996 (1999), 29–59.
20. T Emmens and A Phippen. 2010. Evaluating Online Safety Programs. *Harvard Berkman Center for Internet and Society.[23 July 2011]* (2010).
21. Christopher G Fairburn and Paul J Harrison. 2003. Eating disorders. *The Lancet* 361, 9355 (2003), 407–416.
22. David Giles. 2006. Constructing identities in cyberspace: The case of eating disorders. *British journal of social psychology* 45, 3 (2006), 463–477.
23. Lynne Hall and Carlisle E George. 1999. Law and Punishment in Virtual Communities. *Proceedings of Cybersociety* (1999).
24. Kyungsik Han, Jin Yea Jang, and Dongwon Lee. 2015. Exploring tag-based like networks. In *Proceedings of the 33rd Annual ACM Conference Extended Abstracts on Human Factors in Computing Systems*. ACM, 1941–1946.
25. Claire Hardaker. 2010. Trolling in asynchronous computer-mediated communication: from user discussions to theoretical concepts. *Journal of Politeness Research* 6, 2 (2010), 215–242.
26. Susan Herring, Kirk Job-Sluder, Rebecca Scheckler, and Sasha Barab. 2002. Searching for safety online: Managing" trolling" in a feminist forum. *The Information Society* 18, 5 (2002), 371–384.
27. Sameer Hinduja and Justin W Patchin. 2014. *Bullying beyond the schoolyard: Preventing and responding to cyberbullying*. Corwin Press.
28. Sara Javanmardi, David W McDonald, and Cristina V Lopes. 2011. Vandalism detection in Wikipedia: a high-performing, feature-rich model and its reduction through Lasso. In *Proceedings of the 7th International Symposium on Wikis and Open Collaboration*. ACM, 82–90.

29. Predrag Klasnja and Wanda Pratt. 2012. Healthcare in the pocket: mapping the space of mobile-phone health interventions. *Journal of biomedical informatics* 45, 1 (2012), 184–198.

30. Cliff Lampe, Rebecca Gray, Andrew T Fiore, and Nicole Ellison. 2014. Help is on the way: Patterns of responses to resource requests on Facebook. In *Proceedings of the 17th ACM conference on Computer supported cooperative work & social computing*. ACM, 3–15.

31. Danielle Lawson. 2008. Negotiating social and moral order in internet relay chat. (2008).

32. Jim Maddock, Robert Mason, and Kate Starbird. 2015. Using Historical Twitter Data for Research: Ethical Challenges of Tweet Deletions. In *CSCW 2015 Workshop on Ethics for Studying Sociotechnical Systems in a Big Data World*. ACM.

33. Jessica A Pater, Oliver L Haimston, Nazanin Andalibi, and Elizabeth D Mynatt. 2016. "Hunger Hurts but Starving Works:" Characterizing the Presentation of Eating Disorders Online. In *Proceedings of the 19th ACM conference on Computer Supported Cooperative Work & Social Computing (CSCW)*. ACM. in press.

34. Whitney Phillips. 2011. LOLing at tragedy: Facebook trolls, memorial pages and resistance to grief online. *First Monday* 16, 12 (2011).

35. Rebecca Rafferty and Thomas Vander Ven. 2014. âĂIJI Hate Everything About YouâĂİ: A Qualitative Examination of Cyberbullying and On-Line Aggression in a College Sample. *Deviant behavior* 35, 5 (2014), 364–377.

36. Pnina Shachaf and Noriko Hara. 2010. Beyond vandalism: Wikipedia trolls. *Journal of Information Science* 36, 3 (2010), 357–370.

37. Manya Sleeper, Justin Cranshaw, Patrick Gage Kelley, Blase Ur, Alessandro Acquisti, Lorrie Faith Cranor, and Norman Sadeh. 2013. I read my Twitter the next morning and was astonished: A conversational perspective on Twitter regrets. In *Proceedings of the SIGCHI Conference on Human Factors in Computing Systems*. ACM, 3277–3286.

38. Janet Sternberg. 2000. Virtual misbehavior: breaking rules of conduct in online environments. In *Proceedings of the Media Ecology Association*, Vol. 1. 53–60.

39. Janet Sternberg. 2012. *Misbehavior in cyber places: The regulation of online conduct in virtual communities on the Internet*. Rowman & Littlefield.

40. John Suler. 2004. The online disinhibition effect. *Cyberpsychology & behavior* 7, 3 (2004), 321–326.

41. John R Suler and Wende L Phillips. 1998. The bad boys of cyberspace: Deviant behavior in a multimedia chat community. *CyberPsychology & Behavior* 1, 3 (1998), 275–294.

42. Wenbo Wang, Lu Chen, Krishnaprasad Thirunarayan, and Amit P Sheth. 2014. Cursing in english on twitter. In *Proceedings of the 17th ACM conference on Computer supported cooperative work & social computing*. ACM, 415–425.

43. William Yang Wang and Kathleen R McKeown. 2010. Got you!: automatic vandalism detection in Wikipedia with web-based shallow syntactic-semantic modeling. In *Proceedings of the 23rd International Conference on Computational Linguistics*. Association for Computational Linguistics, 1146–1154.

44. Jun-Ming Xu, Benjamin Burchfiel, Xiaojin Zhu, and Amy Bellmore. 2013. An Examination of Regret in Bullying Tweets.. In *HLT-NAACL*. 697–702.

45. Elad Yom-Tov, Luis Fernandez-Luque, Ingmar Weber, and Steven P Crain. 2012. Pro-anorexia and pro-recovery photo sharing: A tale of two warring tribes. *Journal of medical Internet research* 14, 6 (2012).

Accountable Artefacts: The Case of the Carolan Guitar

Steve Benford, Adrian Hazzard, Alan Chamberlain, Kevin Glover,
Chris Greenhalgh, Liming Xu, Michaela Hoare, Dimitrios Darzentas
Mixed Reality Laboratory, The University of Nottingham, Nottingham, UK
{firstname.lastname}@nottingham.ac.uk

ABSTRACT
We explore how physical artefacts can be connected to digital records of where they have been, who they have encountered and what has happened to them, and how this can enhance their meaning and utility. We describe how a travelling technology probe in the form of an augmented acoustic guitar engaged users in a design conversation as it visited homes, studios, gigs, workshops and lessons, and how this revealed the diversity and utility of its digital record. We describe how this record was captured and flexibly mapped to the physical guitar and proxy artefacts. We contribute a conceptual framework for *accountable artefacts* that articulates how multiple and complex mappings between physical artefacts and their digital records may be created, appropriated, shared and interrogated to deliver accounts of provenance and use as well as methodological reflections on technology probes.

Author Keywords
Internet of Things; Digital Record; Physical Artefact; Guitar; Music; Technology Probe; Provenance; Archiving; Augmented Reality; Tangible and Embedded Interaction.

ACM Classification Keywords
H.5.m. Information interfaces and presentation (e.g., HCI): Miscellaneous.

INTRODUCTION
We are entering a world in which everyday things become networked to create the Internet of Things [1]. Embedding sensing and communications into things promises to make them smart [34] and social [2], enabling new applications in logistics, healthcare and smart environments [24]. These networked things will generate digital records that reflect where they have been, who they have met and what happened to them. They may therefore serve as memory objects, helping us construct our identities and self-histories [50], or as narrative objects, enabling us to tell stories [43]. Their records will enhance their economic and social value [7], support provenance [44] and extend their utility [18].

CHI'16, May 07-12, 2016, San Jose, CA, USA
 ISBN 978-1-4503-3362-7/16/05...$15.00
DOI: http://dx.doi.org/10.1145/2858036.2858306

HCI has begun to explore the opportunities and challenges of connecting everyday things to their digital records. The Tales of Things and Electronic Memory (TOTeM) project [7,48] deployed technology probes based on RFID, QR and Web technologies to reveal how scanning an object might replay its past associations, locations and the memories of its owners, and proposed novel applications such as enhancing the value of second hand goods through stories of prior use [17], an idea also explored in the Significant Objects project where narratives enhanced the value of goods on eBay [26]. An ethnographic study of the lives of war-gaming miniatures revealed the complex ways in which players captured and used digital records, often carefully documenting their making, recording their use in gameplay and telling stories afterwards [18].

Inspired by this previous research, we were motivated to further explore the nature and utility of the digital records of everyday things. Our distinctive focus has been on the rich nature and diverse uses of the digital records that are generated and shared as things *pass from person to person.* Like TOTeM, we have employed a technology probe [33], creating a unique augmented thing that could tour to diverse people and settings as part of an unfolding design conversation. In our case, this took the form of an acoustic guitar that was decorated with interactive inlaid patterns so that it could be scanned using a mobile device so as to access its history.

We offer three contributions from this work. First, we present the design and experience of our guitar as an example of the rich ways in which long-lived everyday things may be mapped to their digital records. Second, we draw on this example to derive the strong concept [30] of *accountable artefacts* – things that can be interrogated to deliver diverse accounts of their histories – so as to guide future study and design. Third, we draw out methodological implications of augmenting an everyday but valuable artefact with digital functionality as a technology probe.

A TOURING TECHNOLOGY PROBE
Our overarching approach has been one of Research Through Design [55] in which research findings emerge from processes of designing interactive systems and may be documented in an annotated portfolio [28]. Research Through Design has emerged as a broad umbrella under which one can find various specific methods ranging from cultural probes that capture inspirational materials in the early stages of design [29], to participatory approaches that engage users as design partners [49], to critical design

where provocative products challenge norms and foreground values and ethics [8,21]. We have adopted the method of technology probes. A technology probe is an "instrument [quite literally a musical instrument in our case] that is deployed to find out about the unknown – returning with useful or interesting data" [33]. A probe embodies a specific design idea, embedding inspiration *within* design rather than providing inspiration *for* design [23]. Hutchinson *et al* propose that technology probes balance three goals: the design goal of inspiring reflection on new technologies; the social scientific goal of understanding needs and desires; and the engineering goal of field-testing [33]. They maintain that a good probe is simple yet flexible, open-ended, adaptable, co-adaptive [38] (i.e., users can adapt it too) and gathers data.

The Carolan guitar

We have chosen to augment an acoustic guitar as a probe object. Acoustic guitars are played and owned by millions of people worldwide, are readily portable (rather than being installed in one setting) and can have long lifetimes, potentially spanning decades, during which they accrue rich stories, from personal memories of learning and performing to the widely reported histories of 'celebrity' instruments. Our probing proceeded in two phases. First, we engaged a luthier (a traditional instrument maker) to hand-make an acoustic guitar. Our aim was to create an unusual, valuable and functional instrument that people would naturally wish to host and play. We augmented our guitar by inlaying interactive decorative patterns into its woods that could be scanned using a mobile device in order to access its digital record. We chose an augmented reality technique called D-Touch in which computer-readable visual codes are embedded into the topology of images [13]. Previous research has applied this technique to handmade craft artefacts and suggested that it affords creative flexibility to visual designers [39]. It therefore appeared to be a good fit with our goal of hand-crafting an acoustic guitar. We gave our guitar a distinct identity and backstory in order to establish its uniqueness, naming it 'Carolan' in tribute to the legendary 18th century Irish harpist who was himself a nomadic performer and storyteller. We hired a graphic designer to create a series of interactive Celtic knot work designs that were then inlaid by our luthier (Figure 1). Finally, we implemented a mobile app to scan the patterns and trigger interactions, releasing this through Google Play and iTunes and updating it with new functionality in response to emerging ideas as the probing unfolded.

The second phase was to release Carolan into the wild, building up its digital record as it travelled. Our aim was to engage a diverse set of stakeholders in an inspirational design conversation, jointly exploring the nature and potential value of the guitar's digital record through a deliberately broad series of encounters in diverse settings. We followed a snowballing approach to recruitment, initially drawing on our own contacts with local players, venues and shops but then quickly reaching out through their contacts to engage people further afield, ultimately internationally. We progressed from early engagements where we accompanied Carolan on its travels so as to field-test the probe and seed its initial record to loaning the instrument for weeks at a time. Participants were encouraged to use the guitar as they wished. We then rapidly responded to their design ideas by reconfiguring our app. Participants and researchers jointly documented Carolan's history throughout its travels, capturing a corpus of photos, recordings, notes and interviews and drawing on these to create a series of blogposts (on carolanguitar.com).

SIX ENCOUNTERS WITH CAROLAN

Over a period of a year, Carolan travelled to 6 homes, was played at 3 gigs and 2 recording sessions, visited 8 clubs or jam sessions, hosted an 'open mic' event, resided in a shop and undertook an international road-trip. During this time 30 players contributed to its record, 8 being professional and 8 female. This produced over 100 video recordings, 5 studio audio recordings, and hundreds of photos that contributed to 50 blogposts. Participants responded enthusiastically to Carolan, although were mixed in their attitudes to its interactivity, ranging from those who immediately embraced the possibilities to those who were keen to experience the guitar itself but claimed little interest in digital technologies. In what follows, we distil this complex history into a series of six encounters that illustrate the nature and uses of its digital record in different settings.

In the luthier's workshop

We begin with the birth of our guitar in the luthier's workshop over a period of six months. We captured extensive documentation of this process including design sketches, photographs of the luthier at work, time-lapse videos of the front and back being laser etched and an official photoshoot. These were written up as a series of 23 blogposts constituting the initial digital record of the instrument from first concept through to a video of the luthier performing its first ever song {1-23}[1].

The build process involved specifying body size, shape and tonewoods {4, 8}; designing Celtic patterns {5}; and deciding which surfaces of the guitar to decorate {9}. We aimed to provide a flexible platform for exploring the creative possibilities of scanning the guitar and so choose to extensively decorate the instrument so as to provide multiple points of connection to its record, each with a distinct visibility and access. We eventually decorated six surfaces with distinct visual codes (Figure 1) the *headstock, front, back, top soundhole*, a small 'nook' in the *cutaway* underneath, and a *fretboard* marker at the 12th fret. The latter requires the strings to be removed before scanning.

Construction involved traditional processes of hand-crafting {21}, with some use of a laser cutter to prepare surfaces for inlay {14, 17}. The intricate inlay on the front led to the

[1] References in braces refer to posts on www.carolanguitar.com (verified January 2016) that provide additional documentation.

innovation of a removable soundhole on the top (being held in place by small magnets) to enable access to the inside {19}. We were inspired to create three further digital resources at this stage, configuring our app to attach them to different surfaces. A certificate with official details of the model, maker, birthdate and materials was attached to the headstock, conventionally home to the maker's logo. A user-guide explaining how to control the pickup inside the guitar was connected to the removable soundhole. A technical specification with details of internal structure (bracings and truss rod), electronics (pickup specification) and maintenance history was attached to the 12th fret.

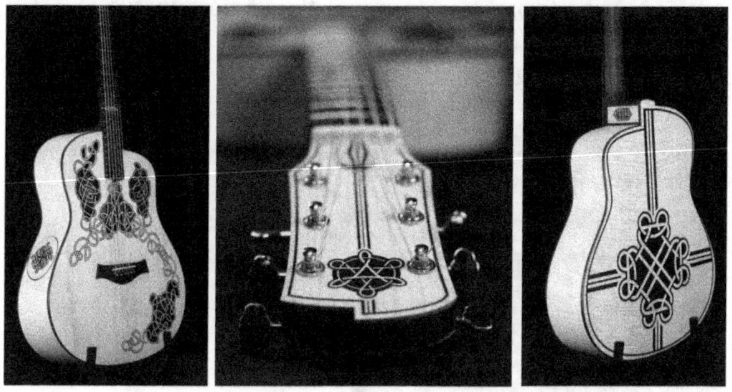

Figure 1. Patterns applied to the front, top soundhole and fretboard (left), headstock (middle), back and cutaway (right)

At home

Carolan was hosted in 6 homes for a week at a time (revisiting one for a second week). Owning a handmade guitar, if only temporarily, was an extraordinary experience for amateur players, one that was greatly enhanced by viewing recordings of it being played by the professionals who had helped us seed the initial record (e.g. {27, 31, 35, 39, 48}). In turn, players were keen to record themselves, using the camera we provided to capture videos {45} (one player recorded over twenty). These were typically of a sketchy nature, capturing pieces they were learning or composing. Naturally, they were cautious about sharing these publicly, so the resulting collections, while extensive, assumed the character of personal archives of 'works in progress' to support their own reflection. Carolan visited regular clubs and jam sessions, where it was played by various attendees {25, 40}. Players also discovered the guitar's distinctive quirks (e.g., the gypsy-jazz style fret marker at the 10th fret rather than the more conventional 9th) leading us to extend the user-guide with 'playing tips'.

These experiences inspired us explore the idea of personalized mappings between Carolan and its digital record and we began to adapt the guitar's behaviour to each player it visited. We typically left the headstock, top soundhole and fretboard mappings unchanged, but reconfigured the front, back and cutaway patterns to map to personalized content such as curated playlists of existing recordings they might appreciate, links to their own websites and social media, and a personal archive of their own experience with Carolan. Some of these resources such as websites felt more suited to being attached to the public front of the instrument while others such as the private archive felt more suited to the hidden cutaway. Visits to regular clubs and sessions also inspired us to consider how these personalized mappings might dynamically adapt to location and time, for example recommending songs and tunes known to be popular at a given session.

Players evidently wished to keep in contact with Carolan once it had moved on, both to follow its future progress and to retain access to their own materials. We therefore created a series of interactive mementoes that could act as proxies for the guitar itself. These took the form of familiar guitar accessories that were decorated with Carolan's interactive patterns, including sets of plectrums, button badges and stickers (widely used to personalise instrument cases) {44}. We envisaged that these might also be distributed to friends who encountered Carolan, especially if they featured in its record. One player decorated his own guitar with a sticker, while a second, who felt a particularly strong affinity with Carolan, requested that we permanently painted our patterns onto an old acoustic guitar that he owned.

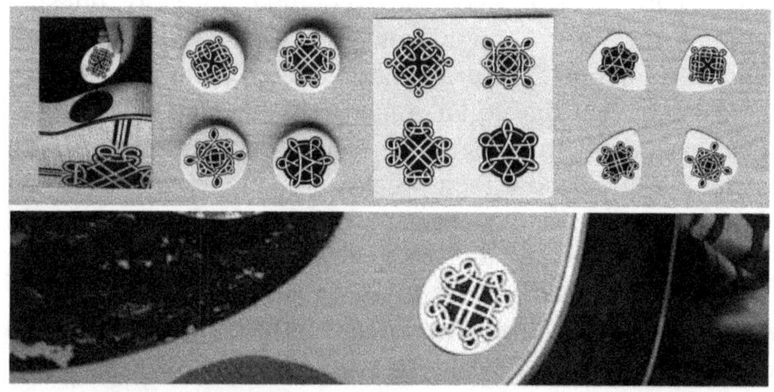

Figure 2. Early designs for interactive accessories

Writing and recording

Carolan joined a professional band at the early stages of composing a new album {43}. They used the guitar to record a sketch of a new song, contributing the original lyrics and chord sheet to its record. A second musician employed their week-long engagement with Carolan to compose a new instrumental, capturing multiple versions of the piece as it evolved. These players raised the idea of an instrument that passes among chains of musicians gathering songs for a new album. Inspired by this idea, we prototyped some interactive album artwork that could be inserted into a CD cover and that used Carolan's patterns to link to bonus materials such as early sketches of compositions.

We undertook two recording sessions with Carolan, the first using budget equipment in a home studio {38} and the second with a professional engineer using high-grade equipment in a recital hall {41}. These produced six polished audio recordings along with photo and video documentation. They also delivered extensive technical know-how about choices and placements of microphones, equalization and effects settings to best capture Carolan's distinctive voice that were added to the growing user guide.

Performing

Live performance is perhaps the most exciting and yet demanding of situations in which a musician plays their instrument. Carolan took part in public performances that contributed further data to its record. In one early case, a touring professional musician took the guitar onstage, played a piece on it and described its concept and history to the audience at some length {35}. This inspired us to consider how scanning and retrieving songs and stories from the digital record might be interleaved with live performance. We therefore staged an Open Mic session in which we invited six musicians to perform with Carolan while we in turn scanned it to conjure up and project videos during the breaks between performers {52}. In order to further engage the audience with scanning, we manufactured a set of decorated coasters that were left on tables around the venue. Scanning these revealed the programme for the show with links to performers' websites.

Learning

Several of those who hosted Carolan noted how it might support learning. A retailer who accommodated Carolan in their shop {29, 33}(and who recounted stories of unusual guitars they had bought and sold) stressed how their business involved selling tuition along with instruments, suggesting that the guitar might deliver video lessons and enable students to upload their responses. One player spoke at length about how their weekly lessons drew heavily on Internet videos and proposed that Carolan's codes could "point to the future" as well as the past, meaning that they might recommend videos to "take you to the next level". They speculated that the guitar might be enhanced with sensors to recognize what you were playing {50}.

We were therefore inspired to explore how Carolan might deliver tuition. Our discussions turned to how teachers often accompany their pupils during lessons. Not only might Carolan recommend new pieces to learn, but it might also play a second complementary part along with them. Inspired by Carolan's Celtic theme, we created some traditional Irish music lessons {51}. For each tune to be learned, we recruited musicians to record the melody as if playing in a traditional session. We then recorded a separate guitar accompaniment. We configured Carolan with three modes of scanning. Scanning the front triggered it to play a melody part, inviting the player to play along on the guitar (we chose the front with the idea that the player might mount a tablet on a music stand and sit facing it ready to play). Scanning the back played Carolan's accompaniment so that the player could study it in isolation or play along on another instrument. Finally, scanning the cutaway yielded the sheet music, chord charts and other notes. We envisaged that the same approach might enhance live performance with players dueting with themselves, especially if the scanning were integrated with live performance systems.

On the road

It is part and parcel of a guitar's life to be on the road, whether being carried in a gig bag to a local session or packed in a flight case and shipped between countries during touring. We equipped Carolan with two sensors to help document its travels: an Affectiva Q Sensor logged accelerometer and temperature data for thirty hours at a time, while a small Autographer camera automatically captured hundreds of photos, along with GPS coordinates, triggered by movement and light levels. Armed with these sensors and inspired by the popular narrative device of the roadtrip, we grasped the opportunity of exhibiting Carolan at a conference to document its first journey overseas, capturing encounters with new people and places including airline staff and passengers who readily recounted their own guitar stories {46, 47}. Mounting the camera inside Carolan delivered an unusual guitar-eye view of the world {49}, with the movement triggered camera often capturing images of people as they played and scanned the instrument (Fig. 3, left). We used these and other images to annotate movement and temperature data, creating a 'life-logging' visualisation of Carolan's end-to-end journey (Fig. 3, right).

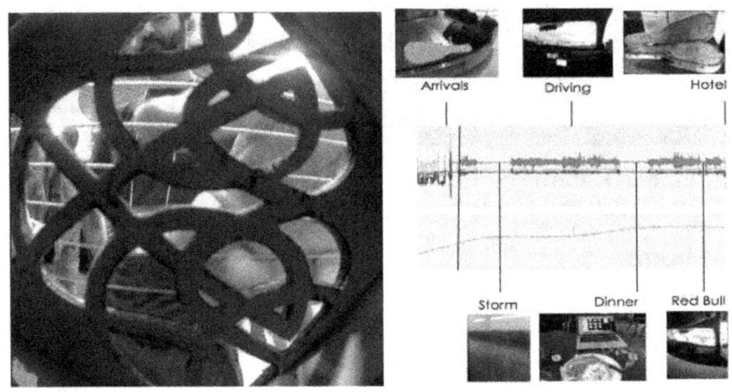

Figure 3: Capturing and visualizing Carolan's road trip

Sensor data offered insights into the stresses and strains experienced by a travelling instrument. The music press abounds with stories of damaged instruments along with travelling advice (e.g., the conundrum of whether to try to carry your instrument as hand-baggage or to check it into hold). Even when not travelling, concerns about how best to store an instrument have stimulated a market for custom humidity sensors and dehumidifiers. Carolan's sensors revealed moments of stress such as the temperature inside the case exceeding 40 degrees Celsius when it was left in the trunk of a car (fortunately without the guitar inside) as well as various jolts when being moved. This reminded us that the digital record might help address familiar Internet of Things concerns of security, safety and logistics.

Finally, our experience highlighted significant challenges for the automatic capture of images and sensor data. Automated cameras raise privacy concerns, especially when hidden inside an everyday object that enters private places such as hotel rooms and homes or sensitive ones such as airports. Airline regulations insist that devices powered by lithium-ion batteries are powered down when in the hold. Consequently, it was vital that Carolan's travelling companion retained control over when sensors were placed in the instrument and when they were collecting data.

MAPPING CAROLANS'S DIGITAL RECORD

We now draw on these six encounters to illustrate the nature and uses of Carolan's digital record. We reflect on the broad composition of the record, the uses to which it was put by different people, how it became flexibly connected to the instrument, how its reach was extended through proxy artefacts, and how it was captured.

Composition, users and uses of Carolan's record

Our experiences reveal how Carolan's broad digital record comprises five primary types of information:

- *Historical provenance* including certification of its maker, when and where it was made, sustainable sourcing of materials, maintenance log, and a documented history of ownership (including loans).
- *Personal and public archives* of performances, recordings, and compositions, documented as video, audio, lyric sheets and chord charts.
- *Historical and fictional stories* inspired by Carolan, including stories of other found, owned, lost, damaged and regained instruments that people recounted.
- *Documentation to support ongoing use* including an extended user guide (with playing and recording tips contributed by players), personal set-lists, playlists to be called up during live shows and materials for lessons.
- *Data pertaining to long-term wellbeing* including measurements of movements and environmental conditions during transportation and storage that might encourage good practice or account for any damage.

We have also seen how diverse stakeholders might share and contribute to this record. These include: makers and legal owners (ourselves); temporary owners (players); their friends and collaborators (at clubs and sessions); various technicians (from luthiers to recording engineers); teachers and learners; and audiences who encounter the instrument at performances. We have envisaged multiple ways in which the digital record might add value to how these stakeholders experience Carolan. Owners may enjoy a richer emotional attachment through the stories it can tell. Learners might summon up recordings to accompany them during practice or be recommended new exercises based on how they play. Makers can follow where their instruments go. Technicians can inspect the guitar to get detailed usage and maintenance information. In short, the digital record of an acoustic guitar is a complex beast spanning multiple forms of documentation, users and potential uses.

Connecting Carolan and its record

Our approach of decorating Carolan with six distinct interactive patterns led to an exploration of how it might best be connected to its digital record. A relatively complex artefact such as a guitar offers multiple surfaces as potential points of interaction that vary in their cultural meanings (the headstock is traditionally reserved for the maker's logo, the top sound-hole provides access to internal controls, the front might be thought of as the public voice) and availability to different audiences (the large back can be read from several meters away, the front and headstock require approaching close-up, the top sound-hole and nook require holding the instrument and turning it over, while scanning the fretboard requires the strings to be removed).

Carolan's encounters quickly revealed the need for multiple, dynamic, personalized and contextualized connections between these six surfaces and its digital record. We configured personalized mappings for individual players, adapting Carolan's playlist to their own interests and linking to their repertories. We configured event-based mappings for performances such as the Open Mic and task-based mappings for activities such as learning. As a result, we established some rules of thumb as to appropriate uses of Carolan's surfaces. Three retained more or less consistent 'canonical' uses throughout:

- The headstock remained linked to the instrument's official provenance (the maker's certificate and officially curated history on the public blog).
- The top sound-hole remained linked to the user-guide, though this might be personalized to particular users and tasks such as learning, performing or recording.
- The fretboard inlay under the strings remained linked to the technical specification and maintenance history.

The three remaining surfaces were employed more fluidly, though again with some general tendencies:

- The front was often adopted as the 'public voice' of the instrument, connecting to playlists of recordings.
- As a small intimate code, the nook tended to be associated with personal, hidden or bonus materials.
- The back has been treated as a somewhat general surface, being variously mapped to players' profiles, concert programmes and other supporting information.

A further question concerns who should make and control these connections? So far, we (as developers and owners) have made them for other people, but it seems likely that players would wish to control at least some aspects of mappings for themselves, for example setting up the guitar for a particular performance, lesson or recording session. We also note the possibility for players to specify the location and temporal characteristics of mappings so that they become applied or recommended at particular events.

Our final reflection on this topic concerns how scanning these connections might be more gracefully integrated with the situated use of the guitar. 'Looping' technologies already enable guitarists to play along with themselves live on stage, but demand flexible, reliable and discrete control (typically via foot pedals). How might we make Carolan's scanning more usable in a live setting?

Keeping in touch with Carolan

A striking and unanticipated practice that emerged during Carolan's travels was the fabrication of various physical mementoes that served as proxies for the guitar's actual presence. These were decorated with Carolan's knotwork designs so that they could also be scanned to conjure up material from the digital record. Examples included plectrums, stickers, button badges, coasters, album inserts, and the more extreme case of permanently painting patterns onto another guitar. Such mementoes meet multiple needs:

- They enable people to maintain an emotional connection with the instrument once it has moved on. Players were keen to keep in touch with Carolan and one luthier reported a strong emotional attachment to his guitars, expressing a desire to follow their progress.
- They add value to albums and other musical products, for example drawing on Carolan's patterns and record to create interactive album artwork. This reflects previous accounts of how amateur musicians associate digital downloads with handcrafted physical artefacts so as to add value through personalization [32].
- Merchandise such as button badges enable fans to publicly display their affiliation while also promoting the instrument, its players and associated events.
- They extend the physical presence of the object, allowing it to be scanned at a distance, both spatially (an audience can scan coasters on tables if the guitar is not in view or is too far away) and temporally (when the instrument has left the venue).

Our choice of employing interactive decorative patterns is especially pertinent here as these are both publically visible and can be readily applied to many new artefacts. This said, other approaches such as embedded electronics might be used to the same effect.

Capturing Carolan's record

Our final reflection concerns how the digital record was captured. We experimented with various approaches from the use of off-the-shelf technologies such as video cameras to capture performances and both professional and amateur audio equipment to capture recording sessions, to less conventional technologies such as automated photography from inside the guitar and the use of movement and environmental sensors. This said, our approach throughout was largely manual. Participants were provided with a toolbox (actually a small suitcase) of devices and could choose how to best deploy them in a given situation. They/we then collated and curated the resulting material, uploading it to familiar and robust services such as Soundcloud and YouTube and writing a series of blogposts.

While this manual approach allowed us to easily engage participants in exploring the diverse nature of the digital record, various people commented on the potential for greater automation. The luthier who borrowed Carolan noted the difficulties of documenting the build process, raising concerns about the additional time required to capture and edit videos as well the risks of revealing to customers some of the 'messier' aspects of handcrafting, the rough and unfinished state of the instrument at some points and making mistakes. Similar concerns about balancing ease of capture with editorial control will apply to composing, performing and recording. Our engagement with music tuition also raised calls for greater automation, with participants suggesting that the guitar might analyse their playing and recommend new lessons. Finally, our deployments of sensors during roadtrips highlights the potential for Carolan to self-document its movements and stresses and strains for logistical purposes.

ACCOUNTABLE ARTEFACTS

So far, our discussion has been grounded in the specific example of the Carolan guitar. We now seek to generalise our findings beyond this unique case to consider potential implications for a far wider range of everyday things. This involves developing a general conceptual framework for reasoning about the complex connections that may exist between physical artefacts and their digital records. Our overarching concept is that of an ***accountable artefact*** – a 'thing' that becomes connected to an evolving digital record over its lifetime and that can be interrogated to reveal diverse accounts of its history and use. We anticipate a wide variety of such accounts, from those concerned with conventional IoT issues such as logistics, to practical guidance over usage and maintenance, to formally tracing provenance, to telling personal 'tales' of ownership [7].

We intend our framework to provide sensitising concepts [4] to guide future studies, attuning researchers to the kinds of digital records that artefacts might generate and their potential uses, while also providing a language for describing findings and relating them to the wider literature. We also intend our framework to help generate future designs. In the terms of Höök and Löwgren, our notion of an accountable artefact is therefore intended to be a *strong concept*, a form of intermediate design knowledge that carries a core design idea; bridges specific instances and generalized theory; addresses interactivity; speaks of use over time; and generates designs [30]. We now expand our overarching concept of an accountable artefact into a series of more specific concepts that express different aspects of how a 'thing' may be structured and connected to its digital record so as to deliver various kinds of account.

Physical artefacts and digital records

Our first group of concepts focuses on the structure of accountable artefacts. First there is an identifiable ***physical artefact***. Thus, our focus here is on material artefacts. Moreover, we are interested in artefacts that are readily identifiable as things, whose essential qualities, properties or characteristics give them an identifiable *haecceity*, i.e., sense of 'thisness' [25], making them worthy of a name and the responsibilities of ownership. We are especially interested in long-lived artefacts that may move between contexts and owners. We also note that such artefacts may have complex physical manifestations comprising multiple parts, including various components, accessories and even proxies that project their presence across space and time.

This physical artefact then becomes connected to a ***digital record*** that grows over its lifetime to potentially encompass an extensive history of its making, maintenance, ownership, use and travels. Just as people generate digital footprints as they use computers, browse the Internet and carry or wear sensors [47], so this digital record may include logs of digital interactions alongside location, environmental and other contextual data. However, it may also include user-generated documentation arising from making, maintenance and use, including social media generated by those who encounter it. This broad digital record may be captured though a combination of automated and manual means, though given the goal of creating narrative 'tales' and the privacy concerns that may arise when the artefact enters new and possibly unforeseen contexts, we anticipate a high degree of human involvement in its capture and curation.

Mappings

Having laid some groundwork, we now turn to the essence of accountable artefacts, the notion of ***mappings*** between the physical artefact and its digital record that configure it to deliver different accounts. We stress two key aspects of mappings. First, as we saw with the Carolan guitar, *multiple mappings* may be created over the artefact's lifetime as it is owned by different people, travels to various places and is used in diverse ways. Thus, it is the choice of mapping that yields a particular account when the artefact is interrogated (e.g., is scanned). Second, each individual mapping comprises a *bundle of links*, each connecting a facet of the artefact to a facet of its digital record (Figure 4). Thinking in terms of bundles of links is important because it allows a given mapping to support complex uses or address different stakeholders who may be present in a given context. Thus, Carolan can be given a distinct mapping for each performance, home visit, music lesson or writing session with its six links variously targeting players, audiences, owners, and technicians who may be present in each.

We can draw on Bieber *et al*'s survey of hypermedia to help clarify some key properties of individual links [6]. Like augmented reality systems in general, our links tend to be *transclusive* [41], bringing digital information to the physical artefact, rather than navigating the user away from the artefact to some new thing. As in Carolan's case, they may often be *unidirectional*, linking from the physical artefact to its digital record but not vice versa. This said, we note some intriguing possibilities for linking the other way: perhaps following a link from the digital record could summon the physical artefact or even trigger the fabrication of a new physical proxy? Support for multiple mappings suggests that bundles of links will be maintained in external *linkbases* rather than being *embedded* [31]. Finally, link *anchors* may be physically manifested on the artefact. In such cases, the form of a physical artefact both affords and constrains possibilities for interaction while also conveying semantic and cultural meaning [40]. In particular, designers need to account for the visibility and accessibility of different surfaces at varying degrees of intimacy. Some are visible at a distance, others only when standing nearby, others when holding the artefact, and yet others when opening it up or removing parts of it. They also need to reflect on their cultural associations, for example the front of the artefact being its public face. The need for a principled mapping of surfaces to anchors is readily apparent when following the augmented reality approach of visibly decorating the artefact with interactive patterns. However, the same issues are likely to apply no matter what technologies are employed, for example when embedding electronic tags into an artefact.

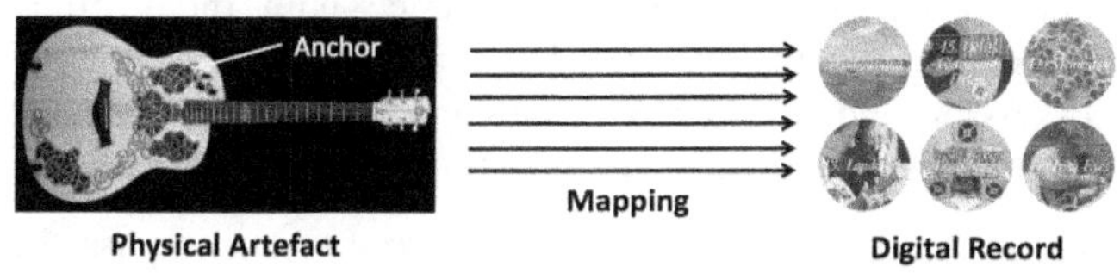

Figure 4. Physical artefacts, digital records, mapping and links

Appropriation

Our second group of concepts addresses how accountable artefacts evolve through various processes of appropriation. The idea that users appropriate technologies, adapting them to their specific needs and contexts, has been discussed widely in HCI. Dourish notes how people adopt and adapt technologies during the course of practice [20] in order to bridge Ackerman's social-technical gap [3]. Carroll *et al* propose a model in which processes of appropriation, non-appropriation and disappropriation move technologies between being designed, in-use and rejected [12]. Rather than seeing appropriation as a sign of technological failure, Dix celebrates it as supporting situatedness, dynamics and ownership, and offers guidelines to design for appropriation including: provide visibility, aim to support rather then control, encourage sharing and learning from appropriation, and enable plugability and control [15].

Following Dix, we propose that it is important to design accountable artefacts for appropriation so that they can be adapted for diverse owners, uses and contexts over their lifetimes. We therefore introduce two further concepts to deal with different kinds of appropriation. ***Digital appropriation*** involves changing an existing mapping so that some of its links reconnect to alternative facets of the digital record (e.g. configuring the front of Carolan to point at new playlists for various performances, lessons and home visits). In contrast, ***physical appropriation*** involves creating proxy physical artefacts (e.g., Carolan's plectrums, badges, stickers, CD inserts and so forth) that then connect back to the digital record. Both these forms of appropriation require support for Dix's notions of interpretation, visibility, sharing and plugability. For digital appropriation, it should be easy to add new content to the digital record (e.g., through social media), inspect an existing mapping to see its current links, and then alter these to point at this new content. For physical appropriation, it should be possible to reapply existing anchors to new artefacts, for example acquiring Carolan's existing patterns and applying them to new things. In turn, all of this requires being able to share mappings among a community of users, including support for recursive appropriation in which derived mappings are themselves appropriated to create yet more mappings.

From owners to custodians

Our final group of concepts addresses the question of ownership. There is a growing literature in HCI around notions ownership, especially with regard to the curation of digital possessions and personal identity, for example digital photos in the home [14], social media profiles [54], teenagers' virtual possessions [42] and the Web as a personal archive [36]. Our experience with the Carolan guitar suggests that we need to extend these notions of possession and curation with new concepts that reflect the complex lives of long-lived and valuable artefacts.

We introduce the concept of ***custodians*** to encompass the diverse stakeholders that might take responsibility for an accountable artefact, including its digital record. These may include its original makers, a succession of legal owners, but also those who assume temporary custodianship (e.g., borrowing the artefact).

Then there are the custodians of the mappings themselves – those who have at some point configured the artefact to yield a particular account when interrogated. Each new mapping should have an identifiable custodian, responsible for maintaining its links over time. Inspired by the approach of trajectories through experiences [10] and subsequent proposals that this thinking should be applied to designing the trajectories of everyday things [18], we propose that the custodian of a mapping might dynamically update it to design ***encounters*** with the artefact, configuring it to deliver distinct information before, during and after meeting an individual or entering a context. For example, Carolan was configured to deliver different information before, during and after its Open Mic performance.

The custodians of mappings can influence appropriation through two final concepts. First, they can specify the ***mutability*** of each of link, meaning whether this link can be pointed at new content when the mapping is appropriated or whether it remains fixed. Thus, the original maker of Carolan might set up a mapping where the headstock is immutably linked to their maker's certificate but where other surfaces can be freely remapped. A subsequent legal owner may further appropriate this in a new mapping that ensures that the back always points to their personal information in case of loss or theft, while leaving the remaining surfaces free to be appropriated by players, venues and other more temporary custodians.

Our final concept, ***acknowledgement***, is intended to ensure that the custodian of a mapping derives benefit from its appropriation. First, they may be credited for their contribution through something akin to a Creative Commons license. Second, a mapping may be inspected to reveal the chain of 'upstream' mappings from which it was derived, back to an original source mapping. Finally, they might harvest usage data from appropriated mappings, collecting information about where the artefact has gone and who has interacted with it. For example, the original maker of the artefact might be notified of subsequent transitions of legal ownership as part of a product registration scheme, while the current legal owner might keep in touch with the artefact when loaned to others. This notion of harvesting data from derived mappings reflects the findings of a study of amateur musicians that revealed how they were often happy to distribute their material freely in return for feedback and connections to fans, but often struggled to capture this feedback [32].

Figure 5 summarises the processes of recursive physical and/or digital appropriation supported by the further concepts of mutability and acknowledgement.

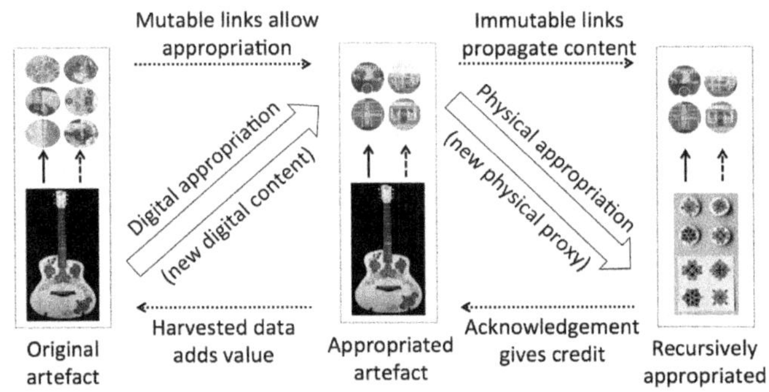

Figure 5. Physical and digital appropriation

These concepts of mutability and acknowledgement raise one final question. Where do mappings actually live in practice and what authority controls how they are appropriated? Schemes such as ours imply controls on digital copying that can be notoriously difficult to enforce in practice, especially in an age in which digital (and increasingly physical) copying is widely practiced as part of a 'remix' culture [35]. We therefore identify one final form of custodianship to be considered when designing accountable artefacts – responsibility for storing and enforcing mappings. This might be achieved in various ways, from reliance on legal authorities to register contracts of ownership and responsibility (think of houses and cars), to added-value commercial services provided by makers and retailers, to people voluntarily signing-up to fair and appropriate use under Creative Commons. We also note the possibility of physically embedding an initial mapping and digital record into the physical artefact itself at the point of creation as an immutable baseline that always travels with the artefact and from which other more flexible mappings can be appropriated.

PUTTING OUR CONCEPTS TO WORK

In line with Höök and Löwgren's proposal for *strong concepts* [30], we now explore how our notion of accountable artefacts might help generate new designs. Many everyday things meet our broad criteria for being accountable artefacts (identifiable, valuable, long-lived, passing among multiple custodians, generating rich digital records), from collectible antiques and artworks to cars and houses. Our concepts suggest various ways in which these might be enhanced through richer connections to their digital records.

Provenance. The first concerns authenticating the provenance of products, meaning their chronology of origination, ownership, alteration and use. Although originating in the world of historical art and antiquities, the notion of provenance has since spread to many fields, and through e-Science has been applied to the attribution of data in databases and trust on the Web [37]. The Open Provenance Model and standard [52] embeds concepts of usage, generation, derivation and association into provenance-graphs [53]. HCI research has explored how scientists understand such graphs [19], the provenance of design [44] and whether the public can engage with provenance concepts [5]. Our concepts support provenance in two ways. First, mappings connect artefacts to their digital records, making it easier to access provenance documentation. Second, our concept of appropriation with mutability and acknowledgement addresses the provenance notion of derivation and enables people to establish provenance graphs as an assertion made about provenance in a given mapping (e.g., claim to ownership) can be tracked back through a chain of mappings to a source.

Storytelling. Our concepts allow people to associate their artefacts with rich stories, from recollections that transform them into memory objects [50] to creative fictions [43]. Our concepts draw attention to the storytelling potential inherent in travelling artefacts in which 'road-trip' narratives provide the muse for new compositions or inspire chain-narratives as they pass among people and places (e.g., [22]). We also note how the performativity of an artefact may be enhanced by recalling recordings during live use. The open and flexible sharing and appropriation of mappings among custodians is key to these kinds of creative storytelling.

Servicing. Our concepts support the management and servicing of complex artefacts such as cars and houses where multiple custodians (e.g., the maker, owner, local garage and insurer for a car) will negotiate access to digital records. Our notions of multiple mappings with ownership and mutability offer a framework for reasoning about how such records are shared, retained or passed on by various parties as the artefact is used and changes ownership.

Collecting. There is a trend in the guitar industry for releasing collectable, limited-edition, celebrity-endorsed instruments that command high prices. This inspires a final idea to create limited-edition collections of artefacts that gain in value by sharing elements of a common history. Each artefact in the collection would come with an initial mapping to a shared history. Its custodian would be free to appropriate some links for their own purposes, while others would immutably connect to maker's documentation as well as regular updates from the original celebrity artefact. Local custodians would be able to share their own updates to create a wider social network of connected things.

Archiving. The cultural sector and especially museums and galleries have a longstanding interest in preservation and archiving. Recent writing in Science and Technology Studies has stressed the increasingly social, emergent and reflexive nature of contemporary archives that are becoming open to interpretation by diverse audiences [51]. These writings also stress the performative nature of archives, meaning the ways in which they are brought to life and iteratively developed through various social performative practices. Our framework might provide archivists with concepts for exploring how archives can be further opened up to more iterative, emergent, appropriated and performed mappings between preserved artefacts and their records.

A reference implementation

We we are aware of the notorious difficulty of translating HCI concepts into practice [45]. We have therefore produced a reference implementation of our framework in the form of an app called Artcodes that enables people to create, share and appropriate mappings between physical artefacts and their digital records and that is freely available on both iTunes and Google Play. Artcodes empowers users to create their own recognizable patterns (following the D-Touch approach) that they can then apply to their own artefacts so as to link them to web resources. The app includes an editor for creating mappings with multiple links. This supports digital appropriation through the editing of existing mappings and physical appropriation by reapplying existing decorative patterns to new artefacts. Implementations of mutability and acknowledgement allow custodians to manage how mappings are appropriated.

METHODOLOGICAL REFLECTIONS

We finish with some methodological reflections on our particular interpretation of technology probes. Perhaps the most striking aspect of this has been to create a travelling probe whose functionality has been improvised and extended as it has toured among different participants and contexts. Our choice of a handmade guitar was significant here. An acoustic guitar is *portable*, being easily transported to different users and settings and installed with minimal fuss. It balances *niche interest*, appealing to knowledgeable and enthusiastic users who are keen to host it and able to venture design suggestions, with being *democratic* in the sense that many people can play it to some extent and many more understand and may appreciate it. Our handmade guitar is *valuable* (costing us several thousand dollars to build), which piques curiosity and motivates people to host it and show it to their friends. It is however, actually rather *durable*, allowing us to engage users over the course of a year and potentially being available for years to come. Finally, our choice of decorating an acoustic guitar is *provocative*, not in a critical design sense [16], but because such extensive and visible application of digital technology to a traditional instrument raises eyebrows among players and makers.

While the guitar itself was stable, its associated digital record and mappings were far more fluid, rapidly evolving in response to its travels. We adopted an improvisational approach to generating the digital record and connecting it to instrument. First, we provided users with a kit of off-the-shelf accessories (tablets and cameras) to support documentation {34}. Thus, the physical manifestation of our probe (guitar and accessories) comprised robust and familiar technologies, facilitating flexibly improvisation by users with minimal intervention from us. Second, we evolved our app to dynamically edit and publish new mappings as described above, allowing us to extend interactions with the guitar remotely and on-the-fly. This separation between a stable and robust physical probe kit and remotely improvised digital interactions enabled us to respond rapidly to users' ideas as our probe travelled.

Finally, we reflect on the nature of users' engagements with Carolan. Over the course of our probing we transitioned from shepherded encounters, intended to seed an initial record with interesting materials, to more 'wild' encounters in which Carolan spent longer periods living in diverse settings. Players' evident knowledge of guitars and skill at playing them tended to place them on an equal footing with researchers in the design conversation, while seeing public documentation of previous engagements in the record enabled them to respond to and build on others' ideas. We suggest that, as a result, our probe was good at inspiring new ideas. Conversely, these engagements were less ethnographic or evaluative in nature, neither capturing rich materials about situated everyday use nor critically and objectively testing emerging designs. We would broadly characterize the nature of our engagement with users as being an iterative 'design conversation' in which a chain of users and designers positively engaged with the concept of a digital record, proposing many new ideas.

Looking back at Hutchinson *et al*'s three initial goals for technology probes [33], we suggest that our approach emphasises the design goal of inspiring reflection over the social scientific goal of understanding real-world use. Their third-goal was to field-test new technologies, with the suggestion that probes are not prototypes. Here, we argue for a more nuanced interpretation in which an adaptable travelling probe offers rich possibilities to transition from early prototyping to field-testing over its lifetime. What began with a prototype guitar ended up with the public release of a functional and tested app. Perhaps Carolan might even be further adapted to become a more ethnographic or evaluative probe in future years?

CONCLUSIONS AND FUTURE WORK

By deploying the Carolan guitar as a travelling technology probe we have revealed the complex relationships between things and their digital records, leading us to propose the strong concept of accountable artefacts:

- An ***accountable artefact*** comprises a ***physical artefact*** and ***digital record*** that grows over its lifetime.
- These become connected via multiple ***mappings***, each providing a specific account of the artefact for particular people in a given context. Each mapping comprises multiple *links* that connect a facet of the physical artefact to a facet of its digital record.
- Mappings can be created through recursive processes of ***digital appropriation*** that involves relinking an existing physical artefact to new aspects of its digital record and ***physical appropriation*** that involves making new physical proxies that project the presence of the artefact across space and time.
- Mappings are associated with identified ***custodians*** who can control the ***mutability*** of their links so as to preserve some aspects of the original mapping. In turn, appropriate mappings, ***acknowledge*** their source, sharing credit and possibly helping harvest usage data.

We have proposed various ways in which these concepts might prove useful in designing future interactive products including enhancing provenance, enabling creative collaborations and producing limited-edition collectibles.

We finish by noting two key caveats that suggest directions for further research. First, we recognize that Carolan is an unusual thing and moreover, is one with a relatively high financial value. It is an open question as to how our findings and framework will generalise to other kinds of artefact, including more mundane ones with a lesser financial value (or whose value lies in other areas such as personal meaning or utility) as well as more socially or culturally provocative ones. Second, as noted earlier, engagement with Carolan tended to be largely creative and constructive, centred around a series of 'forward looking' design conversations. Other kinds of artefacts, mundane or provocative, might reveal more of the problems and challenges associated with our approach. Thus, we are careful to position Carolan as an early probe into this space that sits somewhere between the mundane and provocative and that has served to inspire new ideas. We hope that this will stimulate further work to explore associations between a richer diversity of things and their digital records.

ACKNOWLEDGMENTS

We are grateful to Nick Perez for his expert luthiery, Liz Jeal for her beautiful graphic design and to all those who hosted, played or commented on Carolan. This research was supported through the following EPSRC projects: Fusing Semantic and Audio Technologies for Intelligent Music Production and Consumption (EP/L019981/1); Living with Digital Ubiquity (EP/M000877/1); and EPSRC Centre for Doctoral Training in My Life in Data (EP/L015463/1).

Data access statement: the ethics approval obtained for this project allows for the publication of selected and participant-approved research data on the project website carolanguitar.com. Other personal data must be withheld for ethical reasons.

REFERENCES

1. Luigi Atzori, Antonio Iera, and Giacomo Morabito. 2010. The Internet of Things: A survey. Computer Networks 54, 15: 2787–2805. http://doi.org/10.1016/j.comnet.2010.05.010
2. Luigi Atzori, Antonio Iera, and Giacomo Morabito. 2014. From "smart objects" to "social objects": The next evolutionary step of the internet of Luigi Atzori, Antonio Iera, and Giacomo Morabito. 2010. The Internet of Things: A survey. Computer Networks 54, 15: 2787–2805. http://doi.org/10.1016/j.comnet.2010.05.010
3. Mark S. Ackerman. 2000. The intellectual challenge of CSCW: the gap between social requirements and technical feasibility. *Hum.-Comput. Interact.* 15, 2 (September 2000), 179-203. DOI=10.1207/S15327051HCI1523_5 http://dx.doi.org/10.1207/S15327051HCI1523_5
4. Glenn Bowen, (2006) Grounded Theory and Sensitizing Concepts, *International Journal of Qualitative Methods*, 5 (3), September 2006
5. Khaled Bachour, Richard Wetzel, Martin Flintham, Trung Dong Huynh, Tom Rodden, and Luc Moreau. 2015. Provenance for the People: An HCI Perspective on the W3C PROV Standard through an Online Game. In Proceedings of the 33rd Annual ACM Conference on Human Factors in Computing Systems (CHI '15). ACM, New York, NY, USA, 2437-2446. DOI=10.1145/2702123.2702455 http://doi.acm.org/10.1145/2702123.2702455
6. Michael Bieber, Fabio Vitali, Helen Ashman, V. Balasubramanian, And Harri Oinas-Kukkonen. 1997. Fourth generation hypermedia. *Int. J. Hum.-Comput. Stud.* 47, 1 (July 1997), 31-65. DOI=10.1006/ijhc.1997.0130 http://dx.doi.org/10.1006/ijhc.1997.0130
7. Ralph Barthel, Kerstin Leder Mackley, Andrew Hudson-Smith, Angelina Karpovich, Martin de Jode, and Chris Speed. 2013. An internet of old things as an augmented memory system. Personal and Ubiquitous Computing 17, 2: 321–333. http://doi.org/10.1007/s00779-011-0496-8
8. Jeffrey Bardzell and Shaowen Bardzell. 2013. What is "critical" about critical design?. In *Proceedings of the SIGCHI Conference on Human Factors in Computing Systems* (CHI '13). ACM, New York, NY, USA, 3297-3306. DOI=10.1145/2470654.2466451 http://doi.acm.org/10.1145/2470654.2466451
9. Steve Benford, Adrian Hazzard, Alan Chamberlain, Liming Xu, Augmenting a Guitar with its Digital Footprint, Proceedings of NIME 2015, Proceedings of the International Conference on New Interfaces for Musical Expression, Baton Rouge, LA, USA, May 31-June 3, 2015 https://nime2015.lsu.edu/proceedings/264/0264-paper.pdf
10. Steve Benford and Gabriella Giannachi, *Performing Mixed Reality*, MIT Press, 2011
11. Steve Benford, Peter Tolmie, Ahmed Ahmed, Andy Crabtree, Tom Rodden, 2012. Supporting traditional music-making: designing for situated discretion. In *Proceedings of the ACM 2012 conference on Computer Supported Cooperative Work* (CSCW '12). ACM, New York, NY, USA, 127-136.
12. Jennie Carroll, Steve Howard, Frank Vetere, Jane Peck, Jane, John Murphy, Identity, Power And Fragmentation in Cyberspace: Technology Appropriation by Young People (2001). *ACIS 2001 Proceedings.* Paper 6. http://aisel.aisnet.org/acis2001/6
13. Enrico Costanza and Jeffrey Huang. 2009. Designable visual markers. In *Proceedings of the SIGCHI Conference on Human Factors in Computing Systems* (CHI '09). ACM, New York, NY, USA, 1879-1888. DOI=10.1145/1518701.1518990 http://doi.acm.org/10.1145/1518701.1518990
14. Abigail Durrant, Alex S. Taylor, David Frohlich, Abigail Sellen, and David Uzzell. 2009. Photo displays and intergenerational relationships in the family home. In *Proceedings of the 23rd British HCI Group Annual Conference on People and Computers: Celebrating People and Technology* (BCS-HCI '09). British Computer Society, Swinton, UK, UK, 10-19.
15. Alan Dix. 2007. Designing for appropriation. In *Proceedings of the 21st British HCI Group Annual Conference on People and Computers: HCI...but not as we know it - Volume 2* (BCS-HCI '07), Vol. 2. British Computer Society, Swinton, UK, UK, 27-30
16. Anthony Dunne, Hertzian Tales: Electronic Products, Aesthetic Experience, and Critical Design Paperback – 17 Oct 2008
17. Martin De Jode, Ralph Barthel, Andrew Hudson-Smith, Tales of Things: The Story So Far. Proc. NOMe-IoT, ACM (2011), 19–20.
18. Dimitrios Paris Darzentas, Michael A. Brown, Martin Flintham, and Steve Benford. 2015. The Data Driven Lives of Wargaming Miniatures. In Proceedings of the 33rd Annual ACM Conference on Human Factors in Computing Systems (CHI '15). ACM, New York, NY, USA, 2427-2436
19. Nicholas Del Rio and Paulo Pinheiro Da Silva. 2007. Probe-it!: visualization support for provenance. In Proceedings of the 3rd international conference on Advances in visual computing - Volume Part II (ISVC'07), Vol. Part II. Springer-Verlag, Berlin, Heidelberg, 732-741.

20. Paul Dourish, Where the Action Is, MIT Press, 2004
21. Anthony Dunne, Hertzian Tales: Electronic Products, Aesthetic Experience, and Critical Design, The MIT Press, 2006
22. Raphael Eidenbenz, Li Yu, and Roger Wattenhofer. 2013. Reading Up on Bookcrossing. The International Journal of the Book 10, 2: 11–26.
23. Dan Fitton, Keith Cheverst, Mark Rouncefield, Alan Dix, Andy Crabtree, Probing Technology With technology Probes, Equator Workshop on Record and Replay Technologies, February 12-13 2004, London: EPSRC http://citeseerx.ist.psu.edu/viewdoc/download?doi=10.1.1.209.664&rep=rep1&type=pdf
24. Daniel Giusto, Antonio Iera, Giacomo Morabito, Luigi Atzori (Eds.), The Internet of Things, 1661 Springer, 2010. ISBN: 978-1-4419-1673-0.
25. Etienne Gilson, The Philosophy of the Middle Ages, 1955, London: Sheed and Ward
26. Joshua Glenn and Rob Walker. 2012. Significant Objects. FANTAGRAPHICS, Seattle, WA.
27. Bill Gaver, Cultural commentators: Non-native interpretations as resources for polyphonic assessment, International Journal of Human-Computer Studies, Volume 65, Issue 4, April 2007, Pages 292–305
28. Bill Gaver, What Should we Expect from Research Through Design, In Proceedings of the SIGCHI Conference on Human Factors in Computing Systems *(CHI'12),* May 5–10, 2012, Austin, Texas, USA.
29. Bill Gaver, Tony Dunne, and Elena Pacenti. 1999. Design: Cultural probes. *interactions* 6, 1 (January 1999), 21-29. DOI=10.1145/291224.291235 http://doi.acm.org/10.1145/291224.291235
30. Kristina Höök and Jonas Löwgren. 2012. Strong concepts: Intermediate-level knowledge in interaction design research. ACM Trans. Comput.-Hum. Interact. 19, 3, Article 23 (October 2012), 18 pages. DOI=10.1145/2362364.2362371 http://doi.acm.org/10.1145/2362364.2362371
31. Wendy Hall, Hugh Davies, Gerard Hutchings, Rethinking Hypermedia: The Microscosm Approach, Klumer Academic Publishers, 1996
32. Michaela Hoare, Steve Benford, Rachel Jones, and Natasa Milic-Frayling. 2014. Coming in from the margins: amateur musicians in the online age. In *Proceedings of the SIGCHI Conference on Human Factors in Computing Systems* (CHI '14). ACM, New York, NY, USA, 1295-1304. DOI=10.1145/2556288.2557298 http://doi.acm.org/10.1145/2556288.2557298.
33. Hilary Hutchinson, Wendy Mackay, Bo Westerlund, Benjamin B. Bederson, Allison Druin, Catherine Plaisant, Michel Beaudouin-Lafon, Stéphane Conversy, Helen Evans, Heiko Hansen, Nicolas Roussel, and Björn Eiderbäck. 2003. Technology probes: inspiring design for and with families. In *Proceedings of the SIGCHI Conference on Human Factors in Computing Systems* (CHI '03). ACM, New York, NY, USA, 17-24. DOI=10.1145/642611.642616 http://doi.acm.org/10.1145/642611.642616
34. Gerd Kortuem, F. Kawsar, Dan Fitton, V. Sundramoorthy, Smart objects as building blocks for the Internet of things. IEEE Internet Computing 14, 1 (2010), 44–5.
35. Lawrence Lessig, Remix: making art and commerce thrive in the hybrid economy, 2008, Penguin Pres
36. Siân E. Lindley, Catherine C. Marshall, Richard Banks, Abigail Sellen, and Tim Regan. 2013. Rethinking the web as a personal archive. In *Proceedings of the 22nd international conference on World Wide Web* (WWW '13). International World Wide Web Conferences Steering Committee, Republic and Canton of Geneva, Switzerland, 749-760.
37. Luc Moreau, The Foundations for Provenance on the Web, Foundations and Trends in Web Science, v.2 n.2–3, p.99-241, February 2010 doi>10.1561/1800000010
38. Wendy Mackay, (1990). Users and Customizable Software: A Co-Adaptive Phenomenon. Ph.D. Thesis. Massachusetts Institute of Technology.
39. Rupert Meese, Shakir Ali, Emily-Clare Thorne, Steve D. Benford, Anthony Quinn, Richard Mortier, Boriana N. Koleva, Tony Pridmore, and Sharon L. Baurley. 2013. From codes to patterns: designing interactive decoration for tableware. In *Proceedings of the SIGCHI Conference on Human Factors in Computing Systems* (CHI '13). ACM, New York, NY, USA, 931-940. DOI=10.1145/2470654.2466119 http://doi.acm.org/10.1145/2470654.2466119
40. Don Norman, The Design of Everyday Things: Revised and Expanded Edition, MIT Press, 2013
41. Ted Nelson. (1995). The heart of connection: hypermedia unified by transclusion. Communications of the ACM, 38(8), 31—33.
42. William Odom, John Zimmerman, and Jodi Forlizzi. 2011. Teenagers and their virtual possessions: design opportunities and issues. In *Proceedings of the SIGCHI Conference on Human Factors in Computing Systems* (CHI '11). ACM, New York, NY, USA, 1491-1500. DOI=10.1145/1978942.1979161 http://doi.acm.org/10.1145/1978942.1979161
43. Daniela Petrelli, Steve Whittaker, and Jens Brockmeier. 2008. AutoTopography: what can physical mementos tell us about digital memories?. In *Proceedings of the SIGCHI Conference on Human Factors in Computing*

Systems (CHI '08). ACM, New York, NY, USA, 53-62. DOI=10.1145/1357054.1357065 http://doi.acm.org/10.1145/1357054.1357065.

44. Daniela K. Rosner. 2011. Tracing Provenance. interactions 18, 5: 32–37. http://doi.org/10.1145/2008176.2008186
45. Yvonne Rogers, (2012) *HCI Theory: Classical, Modern and Contemporary,* Morgan & Claypool.
46. Yvonne Rogers, Interaction design gone wild: Striving for wild theory. Interactions 18(4), 58–62.
47. Abigail Sellen, Yvonne Rogers, Richard Harper, and Tom Rodden. 2009. Reflecting human values in the digital age. *Commun. ACM* 52, 3 (March 2009), 58-66. DOI=10.1145/1467247.1467265 http://doi.acm.org/10.1145/1467247.1467265
48. Chris Speed and Simone O'Callaghan. 2011. The Hidden Histories of Objects; Provenance, Storytelling and Tagging Technologies. International Symposium for Electronic Art. Retrieved July 14, 2014 from http://www.research.ed.ac.uk/portal/en/publications/the-hidden-histories-of-objects-provenance-storytelling-and-tagging-technologies(e1755569-1ad6-4078-a0e1-84c08ccd1c51).html
49. Douglas Schuler, Aki Namioka, (1993). Participatory Design: Principles and Practice. New Jersey: Lawrence Erlbaum.
50. Elise van den Hoven and Berry Eggen B (2008) Informing augmented memory system design through autobiographical memory theory. Personal and Ubiquitous Computing, 12(6), 433-443.
51. Claire Waterton, Experimenting with the Archive: STS-ers as Analysts and Co-constructors of Databases and Other Archival Forms, Science, Technology & Human Values, 35 (5), 645-676, 2010, SAGE
52. World Wide Web Consortium, PROV-Overview: An Overview of the PROV Family of Documents, W3C Working Group Note, Moreau, L. and Groth, P., eds, 30th April 2013. http://hdl.handle.net/10421/7487
53. World Wide Web Consortium, W3C Provenance Working Group. PROV Graph Layout Conventions. 2012. Accessed 2014-09--22. http://www.w3.org/2011/prov/wiki/Diagrams
54. Xuan Zhao, Niloufar Salehi, Sasha Naranjit, Sara Alwaalan, Stephen Voida, and Dan Cosley. 2013. The many faces of facebook: experiencing social media as performance, exhibition, and personal archive. In *Proceedings of the SIGCHI Conference on Human Factors in Computing Systems* (CHI '13). ACM, New York, NY, USA, 1-10. DOI=10.1145/2470654.2470656 http://doi.acm.org/10.1145/2470654.2470656
55. Zimmerman, J., Forlizzi, J., Evenson. S. (2007) Research through design as a method for interaction design research in HCI. In Proceedings of the SIGCHI Conference on Human Factors in Computing Systems (CHI '07). ACM, New York, NY, USA, 493-502

Things We Own Together: Sharing Possessions at Home

Jane Gruning
School of Information
The University of Texas at Austin
1616 Guadalupe St., Suite 5.202
Austin, TX, 78701, USA
jane.gru@gmail.com

Siân Lindley
Microsoft Research
21 Station Road
Cambridge, CB1 2FB, UK
sianl@microsoft.com

ABSTRACT
Sharing is an important facet of human relationships, yet there is a lack of research on how people share ownership of possessions. This paper reports on a study that investigates shared ownership of physical and digital possessions through interviews with couples and families in 13 households. We offer a more nuanced definition of shared ownership and show that certain practices, which are central to sharing physical objects, are not supported in the sharing of digital content. We suggest potential approaches to address this, focusing in particular on how the sharing of possessions plays a role in the building of relationships and is done against a backdrop of trust.

Author Keywords
Ownership; sharing; home; virtual possessions.

ACM Classification Keywords
H.5.m. Information interfaces and presentation (e.g., HCI): Miscellaneous.

INTRODUCTION
Sharing ownership of objects is a powerful way that people establish and maintain relationships with one another. As Belk states, "Sharing tends to be a communal act that links us to other people. It is not the only way in which we may connect with others, but it is a potentially powerful one that creates feelings of solidarity and bonding" [2, p. 717]. However, while sharing practices involving physical objects are well established in daily life, the ways in which sharing functions when it comes to digital content are neither well understood nor well supported. Indeed, research has demonstrated that ownership *per se* of digital things is more fraught and uncertain than that of physical objects, especially when that content is in the Cloud [16,19,21]. Further, when digital content is stored in shared repositories it tends to be seen as 'mine' or as 'yours', but rarely as 'ours' [22].

CHI'16, May 07 - 12, 2016, San Jose, CA, USA

ACM 978-1-4503-3362-7/16/05...$15.00
DOI: http://dx.doi.org/10.1145/2858036.2858154

There is, then, a recognized need to better support shared ownership of digital content. However, research on the topic has often focused on the workplace [e.g. 4] and educational settings [e.g. 22], with the aim of enabling finding or re-finding of content in shared repositories, and preventing a build-up of clutter. Little attention has been paid to how systems could be designed to enable sharing and joint ownership practices around digital objects, with an eye to how these help define and strengthen relationships between people.

In the study reported in this paper, we explore how shared ownership is handled in the home, with the broader aim of considering how we might design to support shared ownership of digital possessions. Our contribution is threefold. Firstly, we clarify definitions of shared ownership, which, we will argue, varies by degrees. Recognizing distinctions across the ownership spectrum has implications for how we might design to support shared ownership.

Secondly, we offer insights into how shared ownership of digital content is accomplished in the current landscape of services and devices. We detail various approaches to sharing adopted by our interviewees, including the appropriation of single user accounts and the establishment of workarounds for service agreements.

Thirdly, we demonstrate some of the ways in which shared ownership is bound up with relationships. People become accountable to one another through their use of shared objects, and so shared ownership plays a role in how parents socialize their children and how couples exhibit trust in one another. These findings highlight how shared ownership at home is distinct from previously studied settings, and is worth focusing on in its own right. In the next section, we outline what is known about shared ownership at home.

RELATED WORK
To date, little research has focused specifically on shared ownership. As Belk observed, "Despite its pervasiveness, the ubiquitous consumer behavior of sharing remains not only theoretical terra incognita, but a nearly invisible and unmentioned topic in the consumer behavior literature" [2,

p.716]. Relevant research has primarily been undertaken in the field of consumer studies, and has focused on topics such as the sharing of resources, space, and knowledge in addition to the sharing of objects. [2,3,12]. Outside of consumer studies, research focused on domestic spaces has uncovered insights on sharing practices [13,23]. These areas of research have produced nascent definitions of shared ownership, insights into how it is managed in practice, and an initial understanding of what sharing implies for those doing the sharing. We review this literature, alongside relevant work done in HCI, here.

Beginning with definitions of sharing, Furby (a consumer studies scholar) made a distinction between 'collective possession' and 'sole ownership.' She found that collective possession was tied to the right to use an object, whereas sole ownership was tied to the right to control use of it, including use by others [12]. Belk and Llamas further distinguished between 'sharing' and 'joint use.' They identified sharing as "possession or ownership [that] is joint. The shared object is effectively ours rather than mine or yours…" [3, p.627]. This is contrasted with joint use, or "borrowing something or feeling that it is free for another person to use" [3, p.635]. Belk and Llamas argue that joint ownership is more likely to occur within the family than outside of it, where they say that joint use is more common.

This emphasis on family runs through the literature on sharing. Belk noted that "sharing within the Western family is centered primarily within the home" [2, p.724], and Furby argued that "Even within American society, most individuals experience many cases of collective ownership, particularly within the family setting" [12, p.165]. The focus on the home and family is bound up with three further themes. Firstly, sharing implies responsibilities to others in the home. Belk found that these "may include taking care not to damage shared possessions, not overusing these things to the detriment of others, and cleaning up so that others will find these resources in a similar state of readiness for their own use. Such responsibilities underscore a difference between shared possession and sole ownership" [2, p.717].

Secondly, research on domestic spaces has found that sharing is key in the construction of shared identities. The home is an important space in which couples and families construct their shared identity through common preferences and aesthetics, as well as through compromise [23]. The latter is especially relevant in the context of shared spaces within the home: Gorman-Murray's participants "emphasized the importance of juxtaposing personal objects together at home… as a way of symbolically bringing two lives together, generating a shared identity which is a combination of two individuals" [13, p.160].

Thirdly, and related to the point made above, the home offers a particular backdrop for how sharing is accomplished. In two HCI studies of communication in the home, researchers noted that spatial locations of objects conveyed information to household members [9,11]. Elliot et al. noted that "Each location within the home has an owner…" [11, p.261], although spaces could belong to everyone in the house or to some subset of residents, as well as to an individual. Rouncefield and Tolmie's study similarly found that locations of books communicated expectations regarding the appropriate use of those objects [24]. They highlight the importance of communal space, contrasting what is signified by a personal pile of books in a private space with books kept in a 'general store' (typically on bookcases), these being "…places where people put books that are *not* being currently read and these are understood to be available for reading" [24, p.147].

Notably, Rouncefield and Tolmie observe that in contrast to physical books, in the case of e-books "The book is not located within the broader topology of the home" [24, p.143]. Meanings that are associated with physical spaces in the home support the sharing of physical belongings. However, these meanings do not necessarily extend to digital content, such as when content that might otherwise be placed in a general store is located on a personal, portable electronic device. That said, in other cases, digital content is accessed via situated devices, such as family computers and games consoles, which are often located in communal areas of the home.

While work in HCI has looked at the sharing of accounts for family PCs [7,10], it hasn't focused in detail on what this implies for possession of the content stored on them. Additionally, and as already noted, HCI research on shared repositories has largely focused on collaborative work rather than home settings. This research has highlighted various challenges when it comes to sharing digital content, including that it is often understood as individually rather than jointly owned [22], that it is rarely organized or decluttered [22], that it is difficult to find content in group repositories organized by others [4], and that use of the same Cloud service across collaborations can result in content being problematically aggregated across faceted identities [25]. Research has indicated a continued preference for managing collaborative work through email, for reasons including reliability, notification, simplicity, and a sense of control [4].

These findings resonate with Bannon and Bødker's [1] earlier analysis of the construction, use and maintenance of common information spaces. They argue that these spaces are boundary objects, packaged and turned into immutables to allow for sharing across contexts and communities of practice, and over time. Work is needed to place items in common, so that they are understandable to others. Recent examples of what this work might entail are provided by Massey et al. [17], whose participants collaboratively organized content (e.g. by generating 'ContentMaps' using wikis or GoogleDocs to link directly to collaboration materials), and by Birnholtz and Ibara [5], who describe how collaborators consider the effects of their edits on their co-authors, producing social messages as well as functional edits that have implications for group maintenance.

These practices for sharing digital objects clearly differ from those described by Rouncefield and Tolmie in relation to books. There are multiple reasons as to why this might be, and it is likely that all have a role to play: office vs. home, work vs. leisure, and physical vs. digital are all important distinctions that influence how sharing is done. While we cannot address all of these possibilities, in the study we present here we seek to learn more about how the sharing of digital content is managed at home, and whether and how it differs from the sharing of physical things. We articulate our research questions in the following section.

RESEARCH AIMS

We focused on three research questions in this study. First, we aimed to consider whether existing definitions of shared ownership are sufficient to capture behaviors around and attitudes towards a varied range of possessions, including electronic devices and digital content. Second, we aimed to understand how shared ownership in relation to these things is accomplished; how is shared ownership *done*, for physical and digital possessions at home? Thirdly, we aimed to explore how shared ownership is bound up with relationships. As indicated above, sharing implies responsibilities to others and plays a role in the construction of shared identities. We were interested in understanding how shared ownership of both physical and digital belongings was intrinsic to relationships.

Together, these aims comprise a broader goal. In understanding shared ownership practices and how they are bound up with human relationships, we sought to gain insights into how to design to support the sharing of digital possessions, and how to encourage people to make use of additional affordances provided by the digital environment.

METHODS

The home is a location where sharing happens readily [2,12], so although focusing our research there excluded examination of sharing practices more broadly (such as between friends), we felt that this tradeoff was worthwhile. Accordingly, our methods consisted of interviews in which we asked participants to discuss objects that were shared within the home (where they were kept and how they were used), with the aim of unpacking how their shared status was indicated, what rights and responsibilities they (and others) had in relation to those objects, and how they felt about them. We prompted participants to discuss physical goods, electronic devices, and digital content, while avoiding introducing distinctions between these in the structure of the interview.

Interviews lasted for 1-1½ hours, were conducted in participants' homes, and culminated in short home tours. In cases where participants shared devices with other members of the household, we also asked for tours of the devices to investigate the ways that participants organized shared content. Interviews were audio-recorded and photos were taken, with consent, during the home tours.

We recruited participants through advertisements and mailing lists. Participants received a £30 gift voucher to thank them for their participation. We interviewed 18 people in 13 households (referred to as H1-H13 below), which had 39 members in total, in the United Kingdom. Participant names have been changed for anonymity. Interviews were arranged with a primary participant, and other household members participated if they were interested and available (5 of 13 interviews included multiple participants). Participants' ages ranged from 15-52. Seven of the thirteen households were comprised of couples without children and the remaining six were families, with children ranging in age from 1-22. Participants worked at a variety of occupations, including dressmaker, software engineer, puppet-maker, biologist, archaeologist, graphic designer, homemaker, and student.

Data Analysis

The first author analyzed transcribed interviews using open and axial coding [8]. Emergent themes were consolidated in a master list of themes and sub-themes with relevant quotes related to each one. The second author analyzed four of the transcripts, discussing each with the first author until agreement with regards to themes and sub-themes was reached. Themes included joint ownership, primary ownership, shared accounts, sharing experiences, locations of objects, and lending out, among others.

FINDINGS

We begin by drawing nuanced definitions of shared ownership from our data, describing how objects come to be shared, how people know that objects are shared, and what can be done with shared objects. Following this, we discuss specifics of sharing devices and digital objects. Finally, we draw out what it means to share objects, in terms of building relationships and a sense of home.

Defining Shared Ownership

Our data indicates a distinction between two kinds of shared ownership: *joint ownership*, where something is considered to be jointly (and equally) owned by a number of people, and *primary ownership*, where an object is considered to be primarily owned by an individual who allows others to use it. Note that primary ownership is distinct from borrowing (and from Belk and Llamas's 'joint use', which combines primary ownership and borrowing). We define borrowing as access to or use of an object belonging to someone else for a limited time, whereas primary ownership is a more open arrangement, in which others have an expectation of being able to use an object freely so long as this doesn't impinge on the primary owner's use.

The distinction between joint and primary ownership has implications for the ways in which things are perceived and used. For instance, one participant described how she treated her partner's books, which we would define as primarily owned by him, differently to her own:

Girlfriend: *But if I was going to read something I wouldn't think twice about reading one of Tommy's books.*

Interviewer: *Yeah.*

Girlfriend: *I probably wouldn't like write in one or something, you know... I would take pencil to mine, but I wouldn't necessarily, I wouldn't probably do that.*

Interviewer: *To his, yeah.*

Girlfriend: *But I wouldn't have a problem with like, you know, taking it with me somewhere or anything like that.*

Interviewer: *Yeah, yeah. What about lending it out?*

Girlfriend: *Yeah, I probably wouldn't lend it out.* (H12, 25, girlfriend in couple)

The boyfriend's books were kept in their apartment and while the participant felt she could read them without constraint, she was uncomfortable performing other kinds of actions that would normally be associated with ownership.

This contrasts with joint ownership, an example of which comes from a participant with three siblings who bought computer games together with his brother:

We had quite a few discs and things for like Sonic Heroes and stuff that we used to play back in the day ...me and my older brother saved up together to buy several of them, and so we shared those, we generally had priority over them as well, so sometimes share them with our siblings, sometimes didn't. (H5, 18, son in family with four children).

In this case, the games belonged equally to both brothers and either was free to make decisions about whether their other siblings could play them.

We also draw a distinction between types of ownership that are not shared: *sole ownership by design* and *sole ownership by default.* The former refers to objects that people view specifically as their own. These might be borrowed by others with permission, but they are not viewed as shared. For instance, in the four-sibling household mentioned above, one brother had a collection of comics that were kept in a drawer under his bed. Other siblings were expected to ask permission any time they wanted to read one of these, as they were understood as belonging to him. Sole ownership by default refers instead to objects that could fall into the categories of shared or primary ownership, except that others simply refuse to use or accept ownership of them. These are possessions that would normally be considered shared, but that in some specific cases, were not.

For example, in a house where music was generally shared, the mother told us how the stack of CDs in the kitchen were considered her own: "*So like all the old stuff I've got here which nobody else would touch with a bargepole. These are definitely mine*" (H7, 44, wife and mother of two teens). A similar sentiment, described from the opposite perspective, was voiced by a woman living with her boyfriend; she generally considered all of the artwork in the home to be jointly owned by them, except for one particular piece that she disliked. This she defined as belonging to her partner alone.

The spectrum of ownership that we introduce here is broader than that presented in prior work, which has not distinguished between joint and primary ownership inside the home, and which has not identified instances of sole ownership by default. In the following sections, we unpack what it is about an object that makes it jointly or primarily owned, what implications this has for responsibility and accountability, and how it is bound up with relationships and home-making.

Determining and Indicating Ownership

Our analysis highlights two factors that indicate ownership: an object's origin and its location.

Origin and Acquisition

One means of determining an object's ownership is its origin. Purchasing, gifting, and association with shared experiences were all cited by participants when describing who owned an object. Objects that had been purchased jointly were typically interpreted as jointly owned, as seen in the computer games example above. In contrast, objects purchased by an individual were seen as being primarily owned by that person, even if others could use them freely. Similarly, gifts to couples or families were associated with joint ownership while gifts to individuals indicated primary or sole ownership:

Son: *I think we have got a pretty big collection of movies. Generally I think most of them people will watch just on their own choice, but there's certain ones that sometimes people get a bit tetchy about if people don't ask first.*

Mum: *Well it's if they were gifted to you isn't it?*

Son: *Yeah, really...*

Mum: *Because then there's an ownership.*

Son: *If we receive them as a gift.* (H5)

Alternatively, jointly owned objects were those that were created together or acquired as part of some shared experience:

Yeah, well when we moved in we had to like get all the furniture and we didn't really see a table that we liked for the price we could afford. So me being an engineer just said 'Oh, let's just make one' and then, yeah, we just had, my parents had these planks of wood and then we just like worked out, looked on the Internet, found a design, worked it out... I would say that's something that we share, like probably did the same amount of making. (H12, 25, girlfriend in couple).

More mundane examples of joint ownership included photographs from events and vacations that had been experienced together, even when these were taken by individuals (in some cases with a camera that was seen as solely owned). One couple considered travel guides used in vacations that they took together as jointly owned for this reason as well (see Figure 1). Additionally, where objects were representative of the family or couple, they could be seen as belonging to everyone within the relationship. For example, a baby book in H11 that was carefully created by the mother was nevertheless considered to be owned by the father as well. She noted that *"...he makes all the right sounds with regards to showing an interest... But he wouldn't put any legwork in."* Even so, she felt that the album belonged to both of them because *"Jamie is just as important to me as he is to Ray"* (H11, 40, wife and mother of a young child).

Figure 1: Jointly owned travel guides from vacations a couple took together (H4).

In some cases, origin seemed to be the only factor that could be used to identify primary ownership. Some primarily owned belongings were kept in 'general stores' [24] and could be used by anyone in the household, within reasonable constraints (as with the girlfriend's reluctance to write in her boyfriend's books). Although we did not introduce the topic, some participants noted that the only instance in which primary ownership might be re-expressed was in the circumstance of breaking up:

Girlfriend: *So there has been a joining of stuff. So you would probably be like 'Oh yeah, that's Allie's Eddie Izzard DVD' whereas I'd probably now, we'd just be like 'Those are our DVDs.'*

Boyfriend: *Yeah.*

Girlfriend: *Unless you left me crying in a ditch for some other harlot then I'd be like 'That is totally my DVD.'* (H4, 28 & 30, couple)

Here we see that the DVD collection is assumed to be shared, but the knowledge of where things originally came from persists.

Physical Place

A second, and no less important, factor in determining ownership is where an object is stored. As noted in previous research [24], the placing of books can signify their status for purposes of sharing. We also saw that shared books were kept on bookshelves in communal areas such as living rooms, front halls, and staircase landings, whereas solely owned books were kept in bedrooms, and as noted above, sometimes under beds when bedrooms were shared. Essentially it held that if someone did not want other people to use an object they owned, they kept it out of the communal areas of the house. As noted, this does not necessarily mean that things in communal areas are always shared (people other than the primary owners have to want to use them, otherwise they are solely owned by default), but storing an object in a communal area is typically a sign that it is open for use by others in the household. Indeed, in one case a mother moved a series of horse books she had loved as a teen into the general store of books, in an (unsuccessful) attempt to encourage her teenage daughter to read them (H7).

Our study also supports the idea that the lack of physical presence of digital possessions has ramifications for how shared ownership is signified and enacted, as noted in previous research [24]. This differs according to whether digital possessions are stored on shared or personal devices, and whether they take the form of shared content or shared streaming accounts. Next, we address each of these in turn.

Sharing Digital Possessions

Shared digital possessions included music, photos, movies, games, and e-books. The ways in which these were shared was not consistent across households, and did not necessarily entail these objects being placed in communal areas – either digital or physical. Here we describe how participants shared digital objects through different types of repositories, both online and on devices, and how sometimes objects were considered shared even when only one person had direct access to them. We will now describe these practices, which both complement and contrast with those we found with physical possessions.

Shared Repositories

Participants used various kinds of shared repositories to store shared digital objects, some of which were housed on shared devices (such as family PCs) and some of which were accessed via shared accounts. Family PCs were bought to be shared, unlike many other shared devices such as tablets or older laptops, which often became shared over time. Family PCs also differed from other shared devices in that they housed both shared and personal files. This mix of content necessitates maintenance and organizational work; like shared communal spaces of a home, household members' use of the family PC could affect others who also used the device.

Shared content on family PCs, such as photos and music, was typically considered as jointly (rather than primarily) owned, and was made up of contributions from multiple family members. Photos were often stored in shared folders, and music was typically associated with, and sometimes bought via, a single iTunes account:

Strangely the children seem to like our music, so eventually, Danny's been doing it over a few years, all our CDs he has put them all on the computer... And everybody's music is all shared, so anybody can have anything. So for example if you buy an album on iTunes it goes on there, then anybody else in our family can have it... (H7, 44, wife & mother of two teens).

Households that did not share devices adopted other mechanisms for building shared repositories. None of the couples without children in this study had the equivalent of a family PC, but they did use Cloud services such as OneDrive and Dropbox to store shared objects such as photos. One couple (H8) had appropriated Facebook as a shared repository for photos, because it was seen as free, having plentiful storage, easy to use, and accessible to far away friends and family:

Husband: *So in the end I think Facebook is an acceptable compromise.*

Wife: *Yeah, because everybody gets to see them after we've been there so it's kind of actual, it's easy, it's accessible, people don't have to spend a lot of time, you know, you don't have to spend a lot of time sending those photos. It's very, yeah, it's nice.* (H8, 31 & 31, husband and wife)

In other instances, accounts were used to build online shared repositories, such as in one couple's use of Amazon Kindle:

Wife: *Yeah, I think when we first wondered about whether or not to get a Kindle in the first place sharing was a question, it was like 'Well, I would get a Kindle but not if I can't lend you a book that I've just read.' ...Because that would be silly. So I think it was only, we wanted to know that there was a way of doing it and if you can have more than one device on your account then that's fine.* (H13, 34, wife & mother of two young children)

In this example, personal devices mediated access to the shared store, and this was also the case for shared iTunes accounts and shared Cloud folders. So while these repositories could work in much the same way as a family bookshelf or CD rack in a living room, an important difference is that one person's use of an object does not necessarily mean that another cannot use it at the same time.

Personal Devices & Accounts

Another way in which shared digital possessions differed from their physical counterparts was that they were sometimes stored in places that only one person had direct access to.

Interviewer: *...speaking of photos do you guys have like shared photos anywhere? Are there...?*

Boyfriend: [to girlfriend] *They're all on your camera aren't they?*

Girlfriend: *Yeah, well I've taken them off... yeah, you wouldn't know where they were would you? So trusting. All over the Internet, doctored and, no, I just dumped them in my OneDrive because I keep, kept a backup...* (H4, 28 & 30, couple)

Although they agreed that these photos were jointly owned, they were stored on a device (and Cloud service) that was only used by one partner in the couple. Here, there is a sense of there being no need to create a copy of photos taken by another person; one person takes responsibility for the shared possessions, which are located on a solely-owned account.

Sharing Streaming Services

In addition to building repositories of shared content, some households shared accounts that enabled digital content streaming, which might be accessed via shared or personal devices.

Shared devices

Shared laptops and tablets were frequently used as a way to access streamed movies or music. These devices were often left logged into accounts that were shared amongst household members, therefore allowing everyone who had access to the device to use the accounts. For instance, in one home the two small children could log in to watch TV on the shared family laptop:

You know, so I think the only time when they might watch something on their own would be if Liam wakes up early in the morning and we don't want him to wake us up, "Go away and, yes, you can, yes, you can watch TV." (H13, mother of two young children).

This kind of arrangement has similarities to the storage of content on shared devices, with two key differences: there is no real perception of ownership when it comes to streamed content, and no expectation of long-term, persistent access to that content.

Personal Devices

Personal devices were also used to access shared accounts. For example, one couple both used the boyfriend's Premium Spotify account. This initially led to trouble because Spotify does not allow multiple users to access one account simultaneously:

Boyfriend: *So we've had like battles in the past when we've been in different locations...*

Girlfriend: *And you, as soon as you hit play the other person gets kicked off. And you, it's happened a couple of times, like 'Right, I'm going to win this' and eventually found that peace could be found by one of us being on offline mode.* (H4, 28 & 30, couple)

This example highlights some of the constraints associated with sharing digital content, and workarounds participants used to circumvent them. In the next section, we look at some of these constraints more closely, asking what responsibilities they entail but also what opportunities they offer.

What does Sharing Mean?

Prior work has indicated that possession is bound up with being accountable for something and being able to act upon it in certain ways, including getting rid of it [19]. When possessions are shared, actions may need to be negotiated with others, and accountability is not only to the object itself but also to other people, as mediated by the object. In this section, we focus on what sharing *means* in the context of family and home.

Accountability

Rules and norms for sharing were not standard across households. In some households it would be acceptable to lend out shared books, whereas in others this would be frowned upon. Despite these kinds of variations in sharing practices, the status of an object as shared always implies constraints on any one person's use of the object because they can be called to account for it by others. Sharing objects necessitates that they are treated well, so that they can continue to be used by all members of the household. Our data highlighted a few ways this took shape with shared devices and digital possessions, including keeping them organized and comprehensible to others, and avoiding impeding others' use of them.

Organization was often led by a manager of a shared space, who would prompt others to deal with the content they had stored there, including deleting it; participants made clear that limited digital storage was a major factor in 'cleaning' shared devices. In one household, the father had configured the shared PC to have multiple backup drives, and he also managed others' use of that PC: *"Dad manages to make sure there's nothing, it doesn't get too full and we're only allowed to put certain things on certain drives"* (H7, 15, son). In both digital and physical spaces, the standard rule was to check with all sharers of a collection of objects before getting rid of any of them:

...I did check with the children first of all about any DVDs that they don't watch anymore, I said 'Can we, tell me which ones we can get rid of and I'll just sell them.' So I did that, yeah, of course I'd double check it with them first. (H9, 40, mother of two teens).

Parents also enforced rules on children's use of shared devices that taught the children to consider the effects their actions could have on other people who relied on the device. For example, a mother and son discussed how the son was careful to avoid infecting the family computer with viruses, which was especially important because the mother ran her own business and kept work files on the family PC:

Son: *Normally if it's like a dodgy kind of file or something like that I'll sort it out on my laptop, send it to myself on the computer, because it's like our pride and joy with all the work.*

Mum: *...We've taught the children all about viruses and things and we never take any risks with that because it has all my work on there.* (H7, 15 & 44, son and mother)

In these examples, people who used the shared devices were accountable to one another: they had to act in such a way that the devices did not run out of storage or become infected with viruses. In the same way that the couple who shared a Spotify account took measures to avoid impeding one another's access, use of shared devices was undertaken with others in mind.

Additionally, building repositories of shared content also required that sharers made the repositories meaningful for all users, as the girlfriend in H12 describes:

Like if you open up a Dropbox folder and someone's just got their own structure it's like quite hard to understand that. Like the way I organise my documents is completely different to the way Tommy organises them.

While this was negated to an extent with accounts such as iTunes and Kindle, and services such as Spotify where default organizations exist, shared folders allow the opportunity but also necessitate the effort to create structures that all parties can understand.

Figure 2: The shared family PC in H7.

Trust

Taking account of the needs of others within the household means that sharing not only entails general consideration but also builds trust between sharers. As one teenager said about sharing:

I think it's good because it shows that you have a level of trust with your own family, at least that's always nice to know you can trust each other. (H5, 18, son in family with four children).

We saw that parents used sharing as a way to teach children about responsibility, fairness, and generosity. For instance, two families with shared PCs made a practice of applying all iTunes gift cards to a shared account. Purchases were not constrained, although family members would check with one another before making a purchase, and perhaps make some kind of repayment if the desired item wasn't wanted by others:

If Andy really wants something that maybe nobody else wants and I'll say 'Well hold on, that's £5, that's quite a lot' and then he'll say 'Well I'll give you my money' or he'll mow the lawns or something, say 'I'll mow the lawn and I'll clean the car for it' so we do that kind of thing as well. (H7, 44, mother of two teen children).

This arrangement both relies on and reinforces trust between those who share the account.

Trust played an important role in other sharing arrangements for digital objects as well. For instance, when asked about differences between sharing digital and physical objects, one mother argued that there weren't real differences because *"I guess if you live in the same house it doesn't make any difference because you have just as much access to them because [the other person is] there"* (H11, 40, wife and mother of a young child). This recalls the couple in which the boyfriend did not know where their jointly owned photos were stored, but trusted his girlfriend to keep them. Because digital objects are not necessarily accessible even when present in a house (due to password protection and social norms about accessing other people's devices and personal accounts), their accessibility for non-primary owners often relies on the primary owner in a way that is not necessary for physical objects. Such arrangements demonstrate trust in the other person and in the strength of the relationship.

Building Relationships and Shared Identities

Sharing also provides a mechanism for members of the same household to share their knowledge about which objects others might enjoy. It was central to sharing practices that people knew each other's tastes and preferences, and so knew which objects other people might want to use, often making recommendations to each other. Indeed, recommendations were one way in which objects became shared. These objects represented shared experiences and cultural references for family members, and their accumulation was bound up with shared identity and home making. One example of this is a family who collected Studio Ghibli movies and enjoyed watching them together:

We've got a massive collection of Studio Ghibli because every birthday or whatever someone gets someone else a Studio Ghibli film, which is always really great because we love Studio Ghibli. (H5, 18, son in family with four children).

Notably, this works differently when digital objects are accessed primarily through streaming services. In those cases, the objects being used were not part of a collection built by a family over time because they were accessed through a service and not owned by family members. One effect that this has is that the work of maintenance and curation is done by the service rather than by the family.

Figure 3: Physical objects "are more about building a home" (H12).

Another difference between physical and digital possessions was that physical objects are part of people's shared experience of living in a home. They are a persistently visible and accessible resource, the use and availability of which is connected to membership in the household. As one participant put it, while digital objects were *"more of a store of your own personal stuff,"* physical objects *"are more about like building a home"* (H12; see **Figure 3**). For couples especially, shared objects (frequently those jointly owned by the couple) could be seen as a representation of the couple's relationship. These were often put on display in the home, as in the case of a set of favorite photos a couple took together of places they had lived (H4). Digital objects, being essentially invisible to any potential sharers who are not primary owners, do not seem to share the same capability of home-building.

DISCUSSION

The analysis presented above allows us to make three contributions in this paper. First, we offer more nuanced definitions of shared ownership and sole ownership, drawing distinctions between joint ownership and primary ownership, and between sole ownership by design and sole ownership by default. Second, we offer insights into how shared ownership is managed in practice, and third, we highlight what this means for those doing the sharing. In this Discussion, we draw out the relevance of our findings for HCI.

We emphasize here that, as indicated by our data, only the extremes of the ownership spectrum are fully supported when it comes to shared digital possessions, and that the ways in which shared ownership is accomplished are different for digital in comparison to physical possessions. This raises various implications for design, which, while made tentatively, are offered to illustrate how we might facilitate the sharing of digital possessions and further support the ways in which this is bound up with human relationships.

Supporting the Ownership Spectrum through Action

Our data suggest that different types of shared ownership are not supported equally when it comes to digital possessions. While sole ownership can be maintained and even extended (for example, owners can provide copies of objects to others), and joint ownership can emerge (e.g. through the use of shared repositories), primary ownership was not supported. We saw no evidence for digital communal spaces where primary owners retained their ownership of a digital possession but shared access to it with others.

If richer support for the ownership spectrum is needed, one way of designing for this might be to support more breadth when it comes to how people are able to act upon their digital possessions. Prior work has highlighted the need for a richer grammar of action in relation to digital possessions [15] and has indicated how *giving* rather than *copying* digital content enables different opportunities for design [18]. Here, we suggest that different types of ownership could imply different sets of actions, including loaning out content that is solely owned, making freely available content that is primarily owned (perhaps with select constraints, such as making it read-only), and opening up access to jointly owned possessions, in the context of a system that might nevertheless draw a distinction between different users (and, for example, apply metadata accordingly).

Support for such actions could underpin some of the ways in which accountability is made manifest when sharing physical possessions. Our data show that constraints that are integral to the trust and consideration bound up with sharing physical belongings are weakened when it comes to digital possessions: if a person creates a copy of a digital possession in order to share it with someone else, or if sharing is mediated by personal devices such as iPods or Kindles that sync with shared accounts (essentially copying items from them), then if one person changes or destroys their version of an object, it does not affect others. Thus, our data show that issues of accountability and trust were restricted to the use of shared devices and shared accounts, rather than shared repositories of digital possessions (such as Kindle or iTunes).

One approach to incorporating the need for trust into actions such as lending out content, or making it available to others at home, would be to mimic the ways in which this is currently accomplished with physical belongings. With material possessions, the artifact in question is effectively given up on trust until it is returned, a situation that contrasts starkly with the system-reinforced and time-limited (14 days) action of loaning that is currently enabled by Kindle. Indeed, reintroducing some of the vulnerabilities bound up with ownership could ironically reinforce feelings of ownership; as Odom et al. [19] note, an important part of feeling in possession of something is being able to give it away.

However, people may feel that an expected digital affordance is being removed if limits are placed on their ability to create multiple copies of the things that they own. An alternative way forwards would be to consider how to replicate some of the desirable outcomes of the constraints that are associated with physical sharing, such as their role in relationship building, by looking to other ways of necessitating trust or building knowledge of shared tastes and interests. So while a digital equivalent to loaning or otherwise accessing a primarily-owned object might avoid imposing limitations on its owner, it could have other ramifications. As an example, links could be maintained between copies of a digital possession that are created when an item is shared. These could, at an abstract level, highlight when the object is being used and so underpin awareness and connectivity, or alternatively, they could influence its metadata, resulting in a plural history of use. As an example, an eBook that has been shared in this way might become imbued with metadata (or a digital patina [14,20]), that highlights when and where it has been read, and by whom, or it might be inscribed with comments created by multiple people. These possibilities raise implications for awareness and trust, just as loaning out a physical object would.

Furthermore, there is scope for these possibilities to differ across the ownership spectrum. Plural histories might be more pertinent for joint ownership, whilst loaning out solely owned content could entail the prevention of the borrower's actions from affecting permanent metadata.

Supporting the Ownership Spectrum through Representation

These suggestions shift our argument from considering ways to support ownership through design for actions, such as giving and loaning, to design for representations, such as of histories of use. We can stretch this further by considering how accumulations of digital possessions might be meaningfully represented and made visible in the home.

As noted, we saw plenty of examples of digital possessions that were considered jointly owned in our data. However, these were rarely presented as meaningful representations of families or couples, nor were they easily distinguished from content that others were not interested in (that which might be considered solely owned by default). Jointly owned repositories were often established through the appropriation of single-user accounts simply because they worked with a particular service and device (such as the creation of shared iTunes accounts on shared computers), and these accounts, which contained everybody's content, did little to elevate or make visible collections that were meaningful to everyone in the home. Likewise, shared streaming services did not separate a history or preferences that was representative of common interests from those targeted at individuals.

Current efforts to support 'family accounts' (e.g. in iTunes) allow certain rights to parents, but they do not facilitate the building of collections that are of interest to the family as a whole. Were this to be supported, these collections might be made visible (such as via screensavers), thus reinforcing family identity. Furthermore, use of jointly owned content could contribute to a family history that, for instance, makes visible preferences and consumption habits over time – the type of information that is often shared when it comes to jointly owned physical objects through knowledge of who is using them. While this has implications for privacy, work on tracking the locations of family members has highlighted how what might be interpreted as an invasive technology can instead underpin feelings of reassurance and connection [6]. Thus, designing transparency into a family collection could reinforce its status as belonging to all of its members, whilst facilitating knowledge sharing and capitalizing on trust.

Sharing at Home and the Role of Trust

The notion of trust runs through this discussion: sharing at home is sometimes wholly dependent on it. Our data shows how content on personal devices (such as photo collections) was in some cases considered jointly owned, even if others did not know where it was or how to access it. Whilst this is partly indicative of the difficulty of building shared repositories (what data we do have on the use of these resonates with findings from CSCW [1,22] – making shared folders comprehensible to others does not seem easier in home settings), it also emphasizes that people may see no need to create additional copies of content that is under the care of their loved ones. Indeed, their not doing so is an indicator of their confidence in their loved ones. In addition to the need for better design for shared repositories, this highlights a separate set of design opportunities that may be unique to the home, and which speaks to the need to allow significant others easier access to jointly owned, but privately held, stores. We might ask what the technological equivalent would be to saying to a family member, 'The photo album is in the bottom drawer,' when that photo album is a digital version that resides on a password-protected Cloud service. Ways of supporting this could perhaps draw on NFC (Near Field Communication) or Bluetooth technologies to open up temporary access to co-owners, without the need to email a link or dictate a password to them. The resulting expansion of access would signify the connection between the owners of the photos, whilst also acknowledging that sometimes joint ownership is most simply mediated through a human relationship, rather than the building of a shared file store.

CONCLUSION

This paper supports previous assertions that sharing helps people "establish and maintain relationships with one another" [2] and further, shows how that happens in practice across a spectrum of types of shared ownership. In addition, it provides insights into how sharing digital possessions is done at home, filling a gap between prior examinations of sharing physical objects at home and digital repositories at work. Sharing at home is different. It builds, and is done against, a backdrop of trust; it is integral to relationships and it plays a role in home-making. Consequently, it demands something different to the requirements of digital repositories in the workplace. Designing for this entails recognizing more nuanced differences in the ownership spectrum, and supporting their enactment and representation.

ACKNOWLEDGMENTS

We are grateful to our participants for their time, generosity, and openness.

REFERENCES

1. Liam Bannon and Susanne Bødker. 1997. Constructing Common Information Spaces. In *Proceedings of the 5th European Conference on Computer Supported Cooperative Work* (ECSCW '97), 81–96.
2. Russell Belk. 2010. Sharing. *Journal of Consumer Research* 36, 5: 715–734. http://doi.org/10.1086/612649
3. Russell Belk and Rosa Llamas. The Nature and Effects of Sharing in Consumer Behavior. In *Transformative Consumer Research for Personal and Collective Well-Being*, David Mick, Simone Pettigrew, Cornelia Pechmann and Julie Ozanne (eds.). 625–646.
4. Ofer Bergman, Steve Whittaker, and Noa Falk. 2014. Shared files: The retrieval perspective. *Journal of the Association for Information Science and Technology* 65, 10: 1949–1963. http://doi.org/10.1002/asi.23147
5. Jeremy Birnholtz and Steven Ibara. 2012. Tracking Changes in Collaborative Writing: Edits, Visibility and Group Maintenance. In *Proceedings of the 2012 Conference on Computer Supported Cooperative Work* (CSCW '12), 809–818. http://doi.org/10.1145/2145204.2145325
6. Barry Brown, Alex S. Taylor, Shahram Izadi, Abigail Sellen, Joseph Jofish' Kaye, and Rachel Eardley. 2007. Locating Family Values: A Field Trial of the Whereabouts Clock. In *Proceedings of the 9th international conference on Ubiquitous Computing* (UbiComp '07), 354–371.
7. A. J. Bernheim Brush and Kori M. Inkpen. 2007. Yours, Mine and Ours? Sharing and Use of Technology in Domestic Environments. In *Proceedings of the 9th international conference on Ubiquitous Computing* (UbiComp '07), 109–126.

8. Juliet Corbin and Anselm Strauss. 2008. *Basics of Qualitative Research*. SAGE Publications, Los Angeles, CA.
9. Andy Crabtree and Tom Rodden. 2004. Domestic Routines and Design for the Home. In *Proceedings of the 2004 Conference on Computer Supported Cooperative Work (CSCW '04)* 13, 2: 191–220. http://doi.org/10.1023/B:COSU.0000045712.26840.a4
10. Serge Egelman, A.J. Bernheim Brush, and Kori M. Inkpen. 2008. Family Accounts: A New Paradigm for User Accounts Within the Home Environment. In *Proceedings of the 2008 Conference on Computer Supported Cooperative Work* (CSCW '08), 669–678. http://doi.org/10.1145/1460563.1460666
11. Kathryn Elliot, Carman Neustaedter, and Saul Greenberg. 2005. Time, Ownership and Awareness: The Value of Contextual Locations in the Home. In *Proceedings of the 7th international conference on Ubiquitous Computing* (UbiComp '05), 251–268.
12. Lita Furby. 1980. Collective Possession and Ownership: A Study of its Judged Feasibility and Desirability. *Social Behavior and Personality: an international journal* 8, 2: 165–183. http://doi.org/10.2224/sbp.1980.8.2.165
13. Andrew Gorman-Murray. 2006. Gay and Lesbian Couples at Home: Identity Work in Domestic Space. *Home Cultures* 3, 2: 145–167. http://doi.org/10.2752/174063106778053200
14. Rebecca Gulotta, William Odom, Jodi Forlizzi, and Haakon Faste. 2013. Digital Artifacts As Legacy: Exploring the Lifespan and Value of Digital Data. *Proceedings of the SIGCHI Conference on Human Factors in Computing Systems*, ACM, 1813–1822. http://doi.org/10.1145/2470654.2466240
15. Richard Harper, Siân Lindley, Eno Thereska, et al. 2013. What is a File? In *Proceedings of the 2013 Conference on Computer Supported Cooperative Work*, (CSCW '13), 1125–1136. http://doi.org/10.1145/2441776.2441903
16. Cathy Marshall and John C. Tang. 2012. That Syncing Feeling: Early User Experiences with the Cloud. In *Proceedings of the Designing Interactive Systems Conference* (DIS '12), 544–553. http://doi.org/10.1145/2317956.2318038
17. Charlotte Massey, Thomas Lennig, and Steve Whittaker. 2014. Cloudy Forecast: An Exploration of the Factors Underlying Shared Repository Use. In *Proceedings of the SIGCHI Conference on Human Factors in Computing Systems* (CHI '14), 2461–2470. http://doi.org/10.1145/2556288.2557042
18. Helena M. Mentis, Siân E. Lindley, Stuart Taylor, Paul Dunphy, Tim Regan, and Richard Harper. 2012. Taking As an Act of Sharing. In *Proceedings of the 2012 Conference on Computer Supported Cooperative Work* (CSCW '12), 1091–1100. http://doi.org/10.1145/2145204.2145366
19. William Odom, Abi Sellen, Richard Harper, and Eno Thereska. 2012. Lost in Translation: Understanding the Possession of Digital Things in the Cloud. In *Proceedings of the SIGCHI Conference on Human Factors in Computing Systems* (CHI '12), 781–790.
20. William Odom, John Zimmerman, and Jodi Forlizzi. 2011. Teenagers and Their Virtual Possessions: Design Opportunities and Issues. In *Proceedings of the SIGCHI Conference on Human Factors in Computing Systems* (CHI '11), 1491–1500. http://doi.org/10.1145/1978942.1979161
21. William Odom, John Zimmerman, Jodi Forlizzi, et al. 2013. Fragmentation and Transition: Understanding Perceptions of Virtual Possessions Among Young Adults in Spain, South Korea and the United States. In *Proceedings of the SIGCHI Conference on Human Factors in Computing Systems* (CHI '13), 1833–1842. http://doi.org/10.1145/2470654.2466242
22. Emilee Rader. 2009. Yours, Mine and (Not) Ours: Social Influences on Group Information Repositories. In *Proceedings of the SIGCHI Conference on Human Factors in Computing Systems* (CHI '09) , 2095–2098. http://doi.org/10.1145/1518701.1519019
23. Suzanne Reimer and Deborah Leslie. 2004. Identity, Consumption, and the Home. *Home Cultures* 1, 2: 187–210. http://doi.org/10.2752/174063104778053536
24. Mark Rouncefield and Peter Tolmie. 2011. Digital Words: Reading and the 21st Century Home. In *The Connected Home: The Future of Domestic Life*, Richard Harper (ed.). Springer London, 133–162. Retrieved September 24, 2015 from http://link.springer.com.ezproxy.lib.utexas.edu/chapter/10.1007/978-0-85729-476-0_8
25. Amy Voida, Judith S. Olson, and Gary M. Olson. 2013. Turbulence in the Clouds: Challenges of Cloud-based Information Work. In *Proceedings of the SIGCHI Conference on Human Factors in Computing Systems* (CHI '13), 2273–2282. http://doi.org/10.1145/2470654.2481313

Mailing Archived Emails As Postcards: Probing the Value of Virtual Collections

David B. Gerritsen[1]*, Jennifer K. Olsen[1]*, Dan Tasse[1]*, Tatiana A. Vlahovic[1]*
Rebecca Gulotta[1], William Odom[2], Jason Wiese[3], John Zimmerman[1]
[1] Human-Computer Interaction Institute, Carnegie Mellon University,
{dgerrits, jkolsen, dtasse, tvlahovi, rgulotta, johnz}@cs.cmu.edu
[2] School of Interactive Arts + Technology, Simon Fraser University, wodom@sfu.ca
[3]FXPAL, jwiese@acm.org
* Contributed equally to this paper

ABSTRACT
People accumulate huge assortments of virtual possessions, but it is not yet clear how systems and system designers can help people make meaning from these large archives. Early research in HCI has suggested that people generally appear to value their virtual things less than their material things, but theory on material possessions does not entirely explain this difference. To investigate if changes to the form and behavior of virtual things may surface valued elements of a virtual archive, we designed a technology probe that selected snippets from old emails and mailed them as physical postcards to participating households. The probe uncovered features of emails that trigger meaningful reflection, and how contextual information can help people engage in reminiscence. Our study revealed insights about how materializing virtual possessions influences factors shaping how people draw on, understand, and value those possessions. We conclude with implication and strategies for aimed at supporting people in having more meaningful interactions and experiences with their virtual possessions.

Author Keywords
Virtual Possessions; Technology Probes; Self-Reflection; Design; Revisitation.

ACM Classification Keywords
H.5.m. Information interfaces and presentation (e.g., HCI): Miscellaneous.

INTRODUCTION
We live in a world in which people are accumulating large, heterogeneous archives of virtual possessions. The ongoing transition of traditionally physical artifacts (e.g., books, photographs, movies, etc.) into digital forms has produced a range of benefits, such as lower costs, more flexible access, and a smaller physical footprint. People are also acquiring growing collections of things that never had a material form, such as digital communication archives (e.g., email and SMS), video game avatars, and metadata from social networking sites (e.g., photos tags, Facebook likes, comments, etc.). Given this shift, researchers have begun to examine how the forms and affordances of virtual materials shape how people perceive their value and meaning.

Virtual possessions open up a wide range of opportunities to support meaningful experiences—from reflecting on previous life experiences to connecting with loved ones across space and time. Despite these benefits, a nascent and growing body of research has shown that people often view their digital collections as less valuable than collections of material things [e.g., 38, 45, 55]. Current theory on how people perceive and construct value with their material things fails to describe why the same value often does not accrue to the same extent for virtual things. Additionally, research from archival studies and HCI suggests a number of challenges that arise from trying to make sense of large collections of virtual things [17, 28, 54]. There are still a number of open questions regarding how people construct value with virtual possessions [3], leaving designers with little guidance to create new opportunities for people to create value and meaning with their virtual things.

Recent research speculates that changes to the form or behavior of virtual things might increase people's perceptions of value or attachment to them [37]. Yet, it is unclear (i) how designers can support meaningful engagement with archived artifacts, (ii) how interaction with those artifacts influences perceptions of the archive as a whole, and (iii) how designers can support meaningful engagement with those artifacts. To investigate this further, we designed and deployed a technology probe [18] that altered the form and presentation of potentially valuable messages within people's email archives by sending them as physical postcards. We deployed this system in eight households, sending one postcard every seven to ten days over the course of three months, and interviewed the recipients to understand the properties of messages that did and did not encourage self-reflection—a behavior

CHI'16, May 07 - 12, 2016, San Jose, CA, USA

ACM 978-1-4503-3362-7/16/05···$15.00
DOI: http://dx.doi.org/10.1145/2858036.2858541

associated with value creation [37, 40]—and to consider the meaningfulness of the items they received through the mail.

Building on existing research on designing for reminiscence [8, 14], the field study revealed that people were most likely to experience meaningful reflection on the past when the postcards represented cues from some substantial life event, a memorable social relationship, or a transformative experience. In line with prior work from archival studies and information science, the study also revealed challenges associated with making meaning from content that has been removed from its original context, a problem that results from the mutable nature of virtual content. The paper makes two main contributions. First, it provides an example of the design, implementation, and field deployment of a technology probe that alters the form and behavior of a virtual archive. Second, it offers new insights about how designers can build systems that help people to perceive the value of their virtual possessions archives as well as design strategies that ought to be avoided.

RELATED WORK

Related work spans three areas: theories of material possessions; research on virtual possessions archives; and research on designing for digitally mediated experiences of self-reflection and reminiscence.

Theories of Material Possession Attachment

Psychologists have long considered possessions to be an integral part of people's self-concept [19]. Goffman spoke of possessions as props in self-presentation [12] and Csikszenthmihalyi and Rochberg-Halton [10] noted how people invest psychic energy in the things they use, both with meaning-making activities and with self-reflection on who they were or wish to be. Belk's work in consumer behavior research [2, 3] describes how people extend their sense of self through their use of objects. People come to understand the value of a thing as they use it socially, and also as they reflect on and re-evaluate it in relation to their self. Research building on Belk's idea of self-extension has emphasized the importance of social roles and life story [1]. People grow attached to the things that connect them to the important social roles they enact, as well as to the things that play a role in the events and activities that make up their *life story*—the many stories that tell of who they were, who they are, and who they desire to be [1, 26].

Dispossession also plays a critical role, though it has been researched somewhat less [32, 44]. As people acquire new things, they often get rid of other things to make space [26, 42, 44]. The practice of dispossessing things is ongoing, but it is most easily viewed at life transitions. For example, when a person has a child, they may accumulate many new objects, such as a crib and a stroller. These all intrude into their domestic space, forcing them to reassess the value of their other possessions, to curate their collections, and to dispossess the things that are no longer reflective of who they are. Dispossession has value as a way of constructing and communicating one's identity [25], as a way of establishing an enduring life narrative [42], and as a way of highlighting significant values and relationships [42].

Research on Virtual Possessions and Archives

Research in archival studies and information science provides a foundational understanding of how people engage with large archives of virtual things. Though much of this work is focused on the practices of archivists and of people interacting with data that they did not generate, there is a limited corpus of research that has investigated how people engage with personal archives, including archives of their own information and media. With regards to our work, this research highlights that metadata and other contextual information may provide valuable insights about the significance of the information they describe or accompany [17, 22, 29]. Work in these areas also describes tensions regarding people's perceptions of the value of their virtual archives. For example, although people take steps that maintain and add to their archives [53], they are often unsure of the future value of these archives or the information they hold [20, 28].

HCI researchers have begun to investigate collections of virtual possessions. Early work examined specific types of possessions, such as music [6, 51], photos [6, 23, 42], videos [24], money [52] and, later, social media [46, 58, 59]. More recently, researchers have begun to investigate virtual possessions as a class of artifacts [36, 38].

One recurring finding has been that virtual possessions are often considered less valuable than material possessions. When investigating this issue, prior work has speculated about the nuances of virtual possessions that limit their ability to become valued objects and has suggested how we might draw from aspects of both physical and digital objects to support this type of value creation [13, 42]. Work by Brown and Sellen theorizes that the inability to display digital music collections might erode their value [6], a finding that could extend to other types of virtual possessions. Similarly, other work in this area suggests that e-cards may seem less valuable than traditional greeting cards because people perceive e-cards as a low effort alternative to physical cards [37]. This finding points to the ways in which the context of a virtual object impacts the way it is perceived.

Delving deeper into the ways people use their virtual possessions, other research has observed people engaging in behaviors similar to value construction with material things [3]. This applies to virtual possessions that do and do not have a material form. Studies on teens demonstrated that valued virtual possessions are those that support self-presentation and self-reflection [37]. Other work investigating practices of young adults showed that they valued assortments of virtual possessions that represented their life stories, and that they desired to organize and access their collections in terms of relationships, events, activities, and life stages [36]. This is in line with larger narratives around how people collect and curate physical objects as a way of constructing their identity and cultivating personal values [26].

Nonetheless, there are clear differences between the qualities of a virtual possession and material things—differences that change how these objects are perceived and used. In a synthesis of fieldwork people's uses and perceptions of virtual possessions, Odom et al. noted three paradoxical properties of virtual possessions that increase their functional value while eroding their ability to accrue deeper meaning: spacelessness, placelessness, and formlessness [38]. Because of differences like these, it is unclear how digital things can be integrated into existing practices and rituals in a way that is meaningful [41]. This process is complicated, in part, by the means through which people store and manage their virtual possessions [27]. The scale of the archives that people generate also can make it more difficult to manage those records [57].

Our work advances research on virtual possessions by examining how changes to form and behavior impact perceptions of virtual possessions. Specifically, we investigate how materializing elements within virtual archive might diminish its placeless, spaceless, and formless qualities, and provide a way for people to draw on these artifacts as resources in everyday life.

Reflection and Reminiscence

Our work investigates self-reflection and reminiscence through use of email archives. These archives present the opportunity for operating as a rich resource for reflection due to their size, message length, and temporal depth; several researchers have created systems that visualize email archives in support of reminiscence. Across systems, these visualizations often represent online social behavior and overviews of relationships [34, 47, 49, 50]. Different systems offer more or less depth in terms of archive navigation [14, 40, 50], but for the most part users found each of these systems useful for reflecting on their own patterns of behavior and reminders of past life events, and show that users find value in using these tools to engage in self-reflection.

In addition to an analysis of individual systems, our work draws from research that directly articulates how we might design systems that enable people to reflect and reminisce using virtual materials [8, 35, 56]. In particular, this work suggests that experiences of reflection can be supported through three related strategies: (i) materializing one's virtual possessions, (i) providing lightweight methods for people to select and organize meaningful records, and (iii) integrating one's records into everyday life. To better understand the process of reflection on one's virtual information, we also examined a number of existing systems and practices—such as TimeHop [48], Facebook's Year in Review, and the use of hashtags on Twitter, Instagram, and Facebook for 'throwback Thursday' posts, in which people resurface content from their past. The popularity of these systems and practices suggests that people have the desire to reflect on and share information from their virtual archives. However, none of the research work examining reflective practices online engages with questions about how this reflection and examination impacts people's perception of value for the whole of their virtual communications or archives.

Our goal is to bring these threads together to examine how people's perceptions of value with physical and virtual possessions differ. Theories of material possession attachment do not fully explain the difference, but provide a starting point. We aim to build on this foundation, while incorporating insights from prior research on virtual possessions. In advancing these ideas, we explore how materializing key elements in an email archive might shape their capacity to function as resources for reminiscence and reflection. We also seek to better understand how people construct value with their virtual things in the service of opening new opportunities for designing more meaningful interactions with virtual archives in the future.

TECHNOLOGY PROBE DESIGN

The overarching goal of our work is to investigate how changes to the form and behavior of virtual possessions shape people's perception of their value in the context of self-reflection, identity formation, and construction of one's physical environment. The concept for the probe we design was influenced by prior research that simulated a similar idea using the user enactments design research method [37]. This prior work suggested there might be value in providing people with materialized versions of their virtual possessions, but did not use participants' actual archives.

We extended this work by adopting a technology probes approach [18] that involved creating a concrete, functional system, and subsequently deploying and studying people's everyday experiences and interactions with it over time. This method is particularly beneficial in situations where there is little knowledge to guide designers in what they should make or how people might interact with a new thing. Importantly, technology probes do not aim to 'solve' a particular problem. Rather, they aim to explore the benefits (e.g., what participants enjoy), the unexpected uses, and the unintended consequences and tensions produced from people's real, lived-with experiences. In this way, it is a generative approach for researchers to develop an under-investigated area in order to identify both opportunities and areas of concern.

We chose to focus on archives of email messages because they hold long histories of social exchanges and have been shown to be valuable resources for self-reflection [40]. We initially considered SMS or social media archives, but we chose to use email instead for three reasons. First, email has no length limit, which offers the potential to support more in-depth communication than text messages, Tweets, or status updates. Second, it presents one of the oldest and most persistent virtual archives people have. Email has existed since the early 1970's [4], long before any social networking service. Notably, Gmail, the world's largest email service [33] has encouraged archiving instead of deletion since its launch in 2004 [27]; many of its hundreds of millions of account holders have uncurated archives spanning several years. Research on email archives also demonstrates the high frequency with which people choose to hold on emails they've received [54]. Third, email is a private, directed communication medium as opposed to a broadcast medium like social media [7], making it potentially more apt to contain intimate or personal information that could be a trigger for self-reflection.

We chose to materialize email communication as postcards. As a cultural artifact, postcards are a familiar, slower communication medium, often used for personal messages such as holiday wishes and vacation updates [21]. Unlike letters, postcards are often displayed informally in the home and signify some information about the relationship between the sender and recipient. In addition, postcards are often used to share information about a particular memory or experience. As such, the form and function of a postcard aligned with the kind of engagement we hoped to foster with participants. By materializing electronic messages in the physical world as postcards, we were interested in whether participants would feel more inclined to re-examine the potential significance of each message against the backdrop of their everyday lives and to consider the value of their archives as a whole.

Message Selection

In designing the probe, we were interested in giving participants the chance to engage with their virtual archives through a discrete interaction. We tried to select emails that could reasonably be expected to trigger self-reflection as an indication of meaning making and value attachment, should such messages actually exist. Email contains rich structure: long messages within conversations or threads. However, due to space limitations, we could not tell an entire story on a single card. Instead, we printed a portion of an email (a "snippet") on each postcard with the intention of sparking a memory and triggering reflection under the assumption that people would remember the context from which the snippet was drawn.

To select snippets, we wrote software to extract potentially meaningful segments from a person's archive based on several heuristics. We induced these heuristics from our

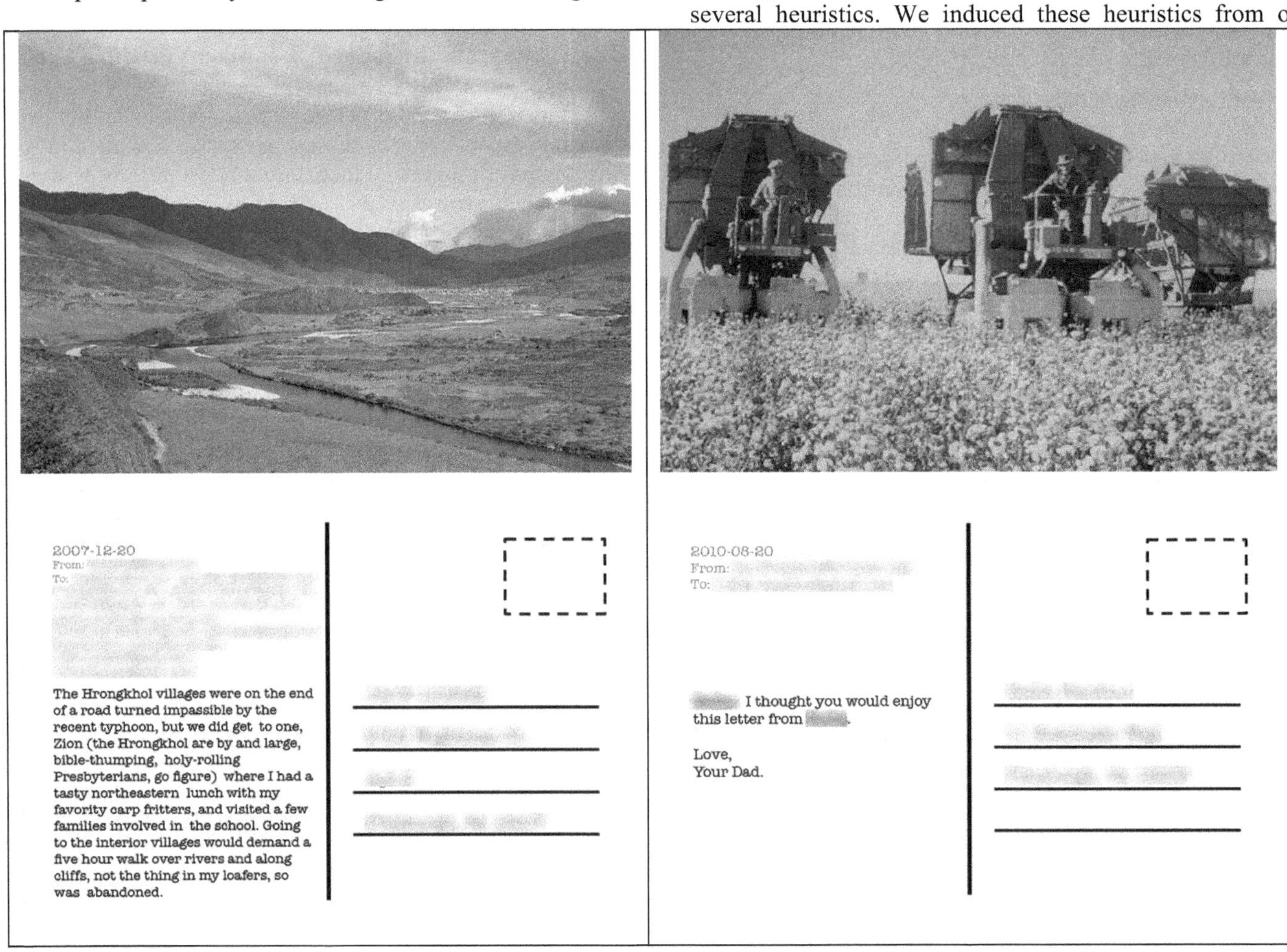

Figure 1: Examples of postcards we sent. A postcard that triggered self-reflection (left) and a postcard that was mundane and lacked context (right)

own email archives and from prior work that suggested cues for identifying meaningful messages and threads. Based on our analysis, we created the following rules to help select messages:

- High-frequency words that appear mainly in messages from a single person. For example, if a participant often discusses theology with one friend, but rarely with others, then conversations about theology with that one friend might be meaningful. We employed the TF-IDF statistic [15, 50] to determine which words were statistically improbable for each sender.
- Keywords and key emoticons, such as lol, love, I feel, xoxo, haha, :), :-). Research on the MUSE system suggests that these emotional cues may help identify significant or meaningful content [15].
- All-caps words with four or more letters, which may signal excitement within an email message. (We excluded shorter words to avoid acronyms.)

To determine which emails to mine, our software generated a list of each participant's most frequent correspondents. We then asked them to specify people from whom they did not want to receive messages (this process is described in more detail in the study design section). The software then applied the heuristics we developed to select specific sentences from the emails both to and from these topmost correspondents. After identifying a plausible sentence, the software then expanded each snippet by adding surrounding sentences from the same message until the snippet was between 400 and 500 characters—a comfortable number for a postcard. Messages less than 400 characters long were included in full. Each snippet was printed on the left of the postcard. The "To" and "From" email addresses and the date the email was originally sent were above the snippet. The participant's home address was printed on the right, as in a standard postcard (see Figure 1).

It is important to note that our approach to identify potentially interesting or meaningful messages, though based on prior work, is one of many possible approaches to this problem. Similarly, the decision to shorten long messages was made due to space considerations, but other approaches (such as summarizing content or only using messages that can be represented in full) may have elicited other reactions from participants. However, the snippets generated by the probe did yield reflections from the participants that inform our understanding of how we might increase the value associated with virtual possessions.

Image Selection

Materializing virtual artifacts introduces unintentional side effects in which some users could potentially find meaning. This was evident for us in selecting images for the front of the postcards. We were not specifically investigating the value people attach to images, and we wanted to avoid, when possible, using pictures that could significantly change the meaning people attributed to the original text. We used Google Image Search to randomize image generation for each snippet. To do so, we used the entire snippet as our input, with parameters set to large, wide-format images, with moderate safe search. If we found no results from this, we removed the last three words and searched again, taking the first image that we found. We rejected images that were only text or that were potentially upsetting (e.g., a picture taken just before the April 2013 Boston Marathon bombing). Our goal was to generate photo selections that would support, but not overtly influence, the process of reflecting on the message.

FIELD STUDY PROCEDURE AND PARTICIPANTS

Participants

Participants were recruited through Facebook, and then through word of mouth. In total, there were 8 participants (4 male, 4 female) in this study. They ranged in age between 25 and 32 years old (mean 28) and all lived in the same medium-sized city in the United States. All participants had been using their email account for at least 3 years. Despite the limited age range, the participants had a wide range of technological proficiency. The number of messages each participant had in their archive ranged from a low of approximately 800 to a high of approximately 80,000. The amount of personal correspondence each participant regularly receives varied, but each participant had some experience sending and receiving letters and postcards.

Study Design

We conducted the study over a three-month period. We sent a postcard to each participant at a random interval between 7 to 10 days so that they received each new postcard on a different day of the week across the duration of the study. This was meant to reflect the pleasantly unpredictable nature of receiving traditional postcards. We also conducted three in-home interviews with each participant that lasted from 30 minutes to 2 hours apiece. Interviews were semi-structured and each of the three served a different purpose.

The first interview was used to learn more about participants, explain the study, and collect the information to use for the probes. We asked participants about their living situation, occupation, their communication patterns, how they interact with their archived emails, and their relationships with sentimental objects (e.g., postcards or other mementos), as well as where such items are kept. We also described our data protection policy and downloaded their entire email archive. Participants knew before the interview that we would be requesting access to the archive.

After downloading the emails, our software output the email addresses with which the participant had exchanged the most messages. For each correspondent we collected information characterizing the relationship, and then asked the participant for permission to send postcards containing information from this person. We wanted to give participants control to avoid receiving messages from relationships they would rather not revisit (one participant removed a correspondent for this reason). Participants sometimes chose to exclude certain email addresses as inappropriate, such as mailing lists or business associates. Most participants also had a set of emails in which they had emailed themselves information, and these were also excluded. For each participant, we settled on a selected set of 8 to 12 email addresses that corresponded to friends, family, and other personally relevant contacts.

After selecting correspondents, we generated the postcards, as described in the previous section. We then manually checked each postcard to ensure that it did not contain sensitive information, exceedingly emotionally fraught conversations, or simply automatic or business communication. If it did, we replaced it with a different snippet and image. We rejected 24% of the snippets at this stage, the vast majority of which fell into the later category of business and promotional communications, such as advertisements. It is possible that some rejected snippets could have triggered the participant to reflect on some aspect of their life. However, regarding sensitive and emotionally fraught messages, we made the decision to exclude those to protect the rights of participants and reduce the emotional risks of being involved in the study. This decision reflects findings from recent work that highlights the potential impact of systems exposing people to difficult or negative content over time [11, 16, 39].

The remaining two interviews were conducted after the participants had used the system for one month, and again then two months later (totaling three months of system use). During each interview we discussed participants' experiences receiving the postcards, what they did with them, and any further reflections on their communication or archives. We recorded the audio from each interview and took pictures to document how people display their meaningful objects and where the postcards were stored after they were received.

Data Analysis

To analyze results, we reviewed field notes taken during and immediately following an interview and employed affinity diagramming to reveal and structure salient themes. This was an ongoing and iterative process involving clustering and coding themes emerging in the data over time [31]. Throughout this process, we reviewed the recordings to resolve ambiguity in our notes, to locate particular quotes or ideas, and to better understand the data we'd collected.

FINDINGS

Our data analysis revealed a number of significant findings and themes. The first theme describes insights about value construction for virtual possessions—insights that come from the intrinsic features of messages and whether they did or did not trigger meaningful reflections. The second articulates challenges associated with deriving meaning from large virtual collections and allows us to reflect on how these challenges might be addressed through the design of the systems that capture and archive this information. The third theme explores how the technology probe and its materialized form of virtual messages caused behavioral tensions for the participants. Finally, the fourth describes participants' higher-level reflections about their virtual collections.

Value Construction Through Reflection

Not all of the 8-11 postcards sent to each participant were successful in triggering some form of reflection. Though an email account is only one of the many ways that people generate and accumulate content, it is still a large archive of content, much of which may not be all that meaningful. In this section, we describe the types of reflection that our postcards generated (or failed to generate) and we use that information to frame a discussion about how designers and developers might help people engage in value creation with heterogeneous virtual collections.

Our interviews revealed that people were primarily interested in engaging in two distinct but related types of reflection. The first type of reflection relates to events and time periods in one's life. This type of reflection often involved revisiting significant periods of one's life and thinking about how one's life had changed since that time. The second type of reflection was centered around relationships. As one would expect, different participants displayed different levels of enthusiasm for reflection in general, but within their level each engaged in narrative exposition about important people or life events. Though one type of reflection usually dominated each narrative, it was often the case that both types would be present in a single narrative. For example, it was rare for someone to reflect about a life event without it having been triggered by a memory of a specific person. In the following sections, we describe participant's experiences reflecting on the information shared on the postcard and describe how the findings could be used to inform the design of systems that help people engage with their virtual collections.

Reflection on Events and Place

When describing a memorable postcard, participants would often begin with "This was when…", framing their story around a specific event or time period in their life. This notion of 'events' was frequently tied to place; it is clear that events that reference changes of place, such as traveling, leaving a workplace, or moving to a new city, are often transformative experiences that offer a rich resource for reflection. As systems capture more information that connects to these transformational experiences in people's lives, we can begin to think about how those systems can use the data they've captured to provide more meaningful opportunities for reflection.

For P3, who described herself as someone who loved to reminisce, the two most memorable postcards triggered her to reflect on events and periods of time from her past. The first was from an old interaction with a former employer.

The message itself was mostly mundane *("It would most likely be part time or internship type work, but I'll see what I can do!")*, but P3 joyfully described how the message brought back fond memories of a time of her life and a job she had enjoyed. The second snippet was from a message that she had sent while on a trip. She was fond of this postcard because it reminded her of something she would write in a journal—that is, it brought her back to that time and allowed her to reflect on that experience.

Events were also accessible anchors for participants who described themselves as not being particularly interested in saving or holding on to things. For example, P4, who thought of keeping old cards and accomplishments as a form of "hoarding," told us that her email was mostly recipes from her mom, which she kept because of their utility, and conversations that reminded her of when she studied abroad in China. Many of P4's postcards had messages from this time that she had spent abroad. In each interview she told us that the postcards were not meaningful and that she intended to throw them out, but she continued to tell us these stories of when she was abroad and the people that were in her life at that time. Her interest in sharing these stories illustrates that the postcards—and the contents of her virtual archives—were capable of calling up important times from her life that helped construct her evolving life story.

Reflection About a Person

For several of the participants, an event referenced by a snippet was less important than the person that it reminded them of. For example, P5 described receiving a postcard that reminded him of a fondness he had held for a former high school teacher. The snippet from the card read, "*The Hrongkhol villages were on the end of a road turned impassible by the recent typhoon, but we did get to one, Zion (the Hrongkhol are by and large, bible-thumping, holy-rolling Presbyterians, go figure) where I had a tasty northeastern lunch with my favority* [sic] *carp fritters…*" P5 explained that this snippet had come from an email sent as a greeting when the teacher was on a trip to India. P5 did not go on that trip, and the details of it were not particularly important to P5, but the card functioned as a reminder of a teacher that had played an important role in his life. P7 also enjoyed a card that reminded him of a friend with whom he is no longer in touch. The postcard snippet repeated a disclosure from that friend: "*Completely clean for 6mos ish*" which reminded P7 of a transformative time for his friend, and prompted him to reflect on their relationship.

Other participants shared stories about how cards triggered reflection on important family members, friends, and even acquaintances that had left an impact on their lives. P8 spoke of a sequence of postcards that serendipitously happened to come from the same conversational thread. It started with a snippet from her grandmother: "*Have you any ideas? I last had the key ring when I drove into the driveway yesterday about noon after getting groceries and mail, so they must be here…*" The thread continued with another postcard two weeks later: "*Gma- Last I knew, the keys were on top of the pine box for wood. I looked through my purse and my pants pockets, and I couldn't find them, so I don't think I still have them. I'm sorry, I hope you find them*" [P8]. P8 shared that she was able to recognize what she described as the quintessential nature of her grandmother from these two decontextualized snippets. Although people reflected on important life stages and humorous stories throughout each of the follow-up interviews, many of the initial triggers that people mentioned were the relationships connected to messages captured by the postcards.

Clearly, revisiting relationships was an important part of how the participants engaged in reflection and reminiscence with the probes. Many existing systems focus almost exclusively on highlighting content that they think will be relevant to the user. This is no doubt a reasonable goal. However, these insights illustrate how systems that can incorporate a broader understanding of what makes something relevant or valuable to a user may be able to surface content—like that of an old relationship or about a person that has passed away—in a way that illustrates the potential richness captured in their virtual archives.

Context and Interpretation

While a subset of postcards successfully triggered reflection or amusement, many left participants feeling bemused or disinterested because they could not place the message in context. When designing the probe, our expectation had been that people would recognize messages selected from their own archive as well as the email addresses of their most frequent correspondents. However, it turned out that many people did not recognize the addresses without their accompanying names and that the short snippets sometimes did not contain enough information to provide the context of a larger thread of messages. This is in line with prior work [17, 22], and prompts questions regarding how designers can make use of aspects of both physical and digital artifacts to support reflection and meaning-making with virtual possessions and archives.

P2 shared that reading the cards felt like looking "through a keyhole." It was difficult to make sense of what was being viewed, and in response, he suggested that a collage of messages might be a more beneficial design strategy. P3 likewise lamented a lack of context. P7 complained that in many cases he could not extract the meaning of a snippet without going back to the source email, but that the motivation from the curiosity did not outweigh the effort to find the snippet in the archive. This lack of context stands in contrast to traditional postcards, which provide contextual clues. P2, P3, P5, and P6 discussed how the image, location, event, postmarks, handwriting, and signature all add context that helps them make sense of or form an attachment to a traditional postcard, most of which was missing from or unrelated to the technology probe.

Several participants mentioned their inability to connect the randomly selected image on each card to the selected snippet. P1, P2, P5, and P6 tended to like the postcards when they could draw a connection between the picture and the text. However, for most cards, the two seemed disjointed. For example, P6 expressed a desire for the photos to come from her archive: "I don't know what the pictures are, like how those are being generated. It might be, I know I have a lot of emails that included pictures... It'd be neat if they were actual pictures that are relevant to the text." P5 thought the postcards should include photos from his photo archive, such as those saved on a local drive or on cloud services such as Flickr. P7 shared that he felt rather uncomfortable when one of the randomly selected images appeared to be someone he knew, but in fact was not. As we had anticipated, the Google Image Search images did not directly support the meaning of the accompanying text, but disconnected images may have influenced perceptions at times when they seemed to disrupt reflection on the message itself.

Though providing longer snippets or more relevant images might have mitigated some of the difficulty of making sense of decontextualized information, we believe these issues also reflects a larger set of difficulties resulting from the scale of people's virtual collections. Future systems may benefit from drawing more deeply from an analysis of the contextual information that is available about the data people generate. For example, a system might make decisions about how to present information to people based on how often it has been revisited and the people to whom it is connected. Furthermore, this points to the difficulty associated with finding appropriate physical representations for virtual content. Despite similarities between the form and function of the probe and the format and meaning of participant's emails, there were clearly ways in which the probe did not adequately capture what makes either of those meaningful or valued.

Form and Curation

One way to examine the value people placed on these materialized elements of their virtual archive was to understand how they engaged with, and made use of, the postcards. In their original form as email messages, none of the snippets were particularly important to its owner. Each of the emails represented a single message within a large, unwieldy collection of virtual information. As has been noted by previous work, it is immensely difficult to manage and derive real value from one's email archive given the scale and breadth of that archive [57].

In contrast to the activities that a person might undertake with their email archive on a daily basis, our probe reframed how a person engages with the contents of that archive. That is, the probe provided participants with an opportunity to reflect on a single, disconnected piece of their larger archive. When the snippet arrived as a material postcard, the fact that it was in their hand forced them to evaluate the message from a new perspective and to determine its next location in the world. Most participants felt uncertain about where to place a postcard after it arrived.

Although the probe took the form of a postcard, its origins and content lead people to rethink its place in their home. Participants described the place they regularly put most postcards, but in some cases did not feel as though the probe belonged in that place. For example, P6 would normally place the postcards she (infrequently) received from friends or family members on the refrigerator in the kitchen. Our postcards appeared different enough from the traditional medium that she described leaving them piled up with the other collecting mail as it migrated through the house. This pattern of postcards moving between designated spots for untreated mail repeated for several participants. P8 reported that she normally puts postcards on the refrigerator, but only one of our postcards made it to this landmark. She ended up scattering most of them across various places within her home, even using one as a bookmark because it was handy. She compared the postcards we mailed her to a photo booth image that she carries in her wallet because it has "...no other place that it belongs."

P3 regularly displays postcards by tacking them to a wall in her bedroom. The images on the cards we sent complicated this practice, however, because the pictures did not resonate with her like normal postcard photos do. She described being more connected to the text, and so she mounted them with the message facing out. P5 absentmindedly left our first postcard in the bathroom. He proceeded to place each subsequent postcard there as well, building a collection in this unexpected place. He shared that he did this because he did not know where else to put them.

A few discarded the postcards. At the end of the third interview, we observed P4 disposing of all of the cards. She had kept them only to discuss in the interviews. P7, on the other hand, kept the cards because they were reminders of having participated "in a cool study." Others, such as P1 and P2, simply discarded them over the course of the study. P1 explained that these postcards had no instrumental value, such as "save the date" cards that would normally go on the refrigerator.

Although participants viewed some of the postcards more like unfamiliar intrusions rather than treasured artifacts, this did not diminish the findings, but rather helped us to classify which messages were more or less meaningful. In this way participants' evaluations helped us determine the categories of important messages as described above.

After the Postcards

Considering the Archive

At the end of the study, a few participants spoke to us about how being a part of the study had lead them to consider changing their email archiving practices. P6 mentioned becoming "...aware of how I see [my email archive] as sort of a burden." She talked about possibly creating a new email account and making a fresh start with building a more manageable archive. This exposes that some parts of the archive are indeed meaningful, even if all of the messages that are "worth keeping" may not be. Nevertheless, none of the participants claimed they viewed their email archive as more valuable at the end of the three months. This is not unexpected, as material possession attachment research shows changes in perception of value happen over many years and through repeated use [2].

To get a sense of the conscious value people placed on their extant archive, we asked participants if they would look through their email if the entire record was printed out in book form. Only P4 would, and she had the smallest email archive. However, if we printed out only a small subset of their personal messages, all except P1 reported that they would look at it. Similarly, P3 even considered printing out a few selected emails to save in a memory box.

We also saw that our participants were quite unaware of the contents of their email archives. On reflection, P5 noted that his archived contained things he had forgotten since high school. P7 was surprised by how much of his archive was of little value. In the beginning of the study, P4 was sure that the majority of her email archive was saved recipes and messages from when she was traveling. By the end of the study, she decided those two categories of messages must have taken up only a third of her archive, and that nearly half of it must have been nothing more than bills, receipts, bank statements, and saved contact information. In addition, many were surprised by the list of frequent correspondents, especially by how many of those correspondents were mailing lists or otherwise not humans. Although the probe may not have changed how our participants considered the value of their email archives, these findings indicate that it would be worthwhile to explore how materializing aspects of one's virtual archives may change how people interact with those materials.

Privacy Concerns

Although not a formal area of research for the current study, we anticipated participants would have concerns with the privacy of their emails, particularly since we planned to select snippets without their input and send them as a postcard that could be read by many before reaching their hand. We assured them that we would check each postcard before sending it, to avoid sending out credit card numbers or other sensitive information. We were surprised that we encountered no resistance save one participant who expressed mild discomfort in the first interview. This might be a selection effect; people who are more concerned about privacy might not have signed up to participate. However, it might indicate that participants either do not know what is in their archives or do not feel their archives hold things of private value that need to be protected.

DISCUSSION

Interaction designers bring together elements, resources, and interactions meant to trigger personally meaningful experiences, and sometimes they do this by mining a user's collection of virtual possessions. Prior research indicates that people can see their virtual possessions as being less valuable than their material possessions. The spaceless, placeless, and formless aspects of these immaterial things provide new utility while paradoxically undermining lasting value [38]. By not being present in the physical world, virtual artifacts provide fewer opportunities to encounter, curate, and reflect on the meaning of the individual items or the entire collection [20]. We examined how manifesting an archived email snippet as a postcard might enable people to re-experience their virtual collections. This physical artifact invited people to engage with their virtual archives in a new way and allowed users to talk about their virtual possessions in a more critical light.

Our findings also indicate that people have strong positive regard for materialized possessions when those artifacts have specific features: they carry a context, they remind people of cherished moments or relationships, or they remind people of transformative experiences in their life. Requiring people to curate these materialized emails provided a new way for participants to view and assess the relative value captured in their personal virtual archive. Moving forward, creating meaningful virtual objects may rely on designs that leverage contextual data in order to create a coherent connection to people's personal histories.

Struggle to Trigger Meaningful Reflection

The probe succeeded in engaging participants to discuss the meaningfulness of their email archive, however participants did not feel that the postcards shifted their sense of value for this archive. Given our goal to investigate how changes in form and behavior of virtual possessions can increase perceptions of value, in this section we reflect on this design issue and how our experience with the probes has shaped our understanding of how to engage with this issue.

The postcards we sent to participants often lacked enough context of any previous relationship, event, activity, or life stage to trigger meaningful reflection. This is in line with research from the archival sciences [17, 29], but here it suggests avenues for future research. For example, this evokes questions regarding how system designers can discover critical aspects of context within an archive and how designs can more effectively communicate this to users. Similarly, it highlights the need for systems designers to be judicious about where context should and should not be included. It allows us to reflect on the ways in which people are unresponsive when prompted to reflect. Additionally, when considered in contrast to prior work in this area [35], this work emphasizes the importance of the form of the physical representation of some virtual possession. In this study, information was materialized as postcards. For the most part, participants did not treasure these postcards and did not integrate them into areas of their home where valued objects were kept or displayed. Despite the analogy one could make between an email and a letter or postcard, it is clear that this functional similarity did not serve the goal of fostering value creation. Given that, future research could investigate how best to adapt physical artifacts to represent and foster attachment to particular types of digital information.

Regarding directions for future research, this work articulates a number of considerations regarding the design of the physical object and the information selected or contained within the resulting artifact. The materialized items must have clear connections to time, place, relationship, event, or life stage. In addition, researchers need to acknowledge the originating media from which the data is extracted. Features of the materialized artifact should be individually considered as either direct representations of the individual's life, or else signposts that orient the individual toward the type of experience the material represents. For example, postcard senders select specific images for people and often connect the image to the meaning of the message they share. Our probe could have avoided disorienting participants by better selecting images that support the intention of the sent email message.

Features of Common, Meaningful Virtual Possessions

At the beginning of the study, several participants expressed the belief that their email archive held little value. Some participants, such as P6, were overwhelmed to discover the amount of messages in their archive, many of which she did not find valuable. She was ready to abandon the archive in order to start fresh with a new email account to better curate her meaningful emails. This arguably drastic response indicates that the email archive could be seen as valuable if its meaningful messages were more salient. In our results, we found that it is not as easy as just pulling archived messages from important people to the forefront. People want to see messages that remind them of an important relationship, a memorable life stage, or a transformative event. However, these features are not sufficient for providing value to the user. In failing to provide enough context, our probe demonstrated that users must be able to reconstruct the story which surrounds individual elements of the archive.

Email, like many virtual archives, can swell in size in nearly undetectable or unnoticeable ways. Often only those items that have utility on the day they arrive stand out as valuable. All messages, no matter what their expected future value is, are stored in the same place. Future research might attempt to draw from these findings to support the saliency of uniquely personal messages as they arrive, i.e., those that carry the potential for future value. As these more significant messages accumulate, and eventually reappear as tools for reflection, the challenge would then be to provide sufficient context. This process may involve finding the meaningful aspects of a person's virtual archive, or even creating new content that carries the same types of features. To add value to a virtual collection, it may be necessary to better facilitate the personal processes through which people attach meaning to their possessions.

Providing Value Through Curating Virtual Collections

Dispossession is a critical process for value construction with material things. People must continually reevaluate an item's worth when they acquire new material things. However, the spaceless quality of virtual things makes it easy to never engage in dispossession and, thus, to never reevaluate an item's worth. We suspect that this repeated reengagement and reevaluation of things may be a critical activity in constructing value for things, and the fact that this so rarely happens with virtual possessions may be a major factor reducing their ability to accrue value.

In addition to the spaceless quality of virtual possessions not catalyzing reevaluation, curation, and dispossession, the interaction design of most digital communication systems tends to guide people away from these kinds of activities. In other words, that these systems often direct people to advance to the next new message reinforces passive archiving of mundane content. Our postcards interrupted this practice by placing a proxy of an email into a participant's hand, forcing them to decide, even temporarily, where to place this thing. These interrelated aspects of large quantities of mundane content and lack of reevaluation may individually or even collectively contribute to people's current beliefs that their virtual possessions are less valuable. There is a clear opportunity to investigate designing interactive systems that actively subvert this process by reversing those capabilities and requiring users to take a more active role in the organization of their virtual collections.

CONCLUSION

In this study, we designed, implemented, and deployed a technology probe to better understand what people value in virtual archives. In the process of rendering email snippets as postcards and mailing them to people, we discovered that people most often like to reflect on important people, events, and humor. However, virtual possessions can easily be experienced out of context, which obscures their value. Findings also revealed how people fail to continually reengage with and reevaluate their virtual things, which can lead to meaningful messages being "lost." Based on these findings, we proposed that encouraging archive curation and the compilation of virtual possessions of different types into unique new assemblies could open up new value construction activities. In this way, designers could take advantage of virtual possessions' spacelessness, placelessness, and formlessness, while still enabling meaningful, unique, and self-determined experiences as people's life stories evolve and virtual archives evolve, over time and into the future.

ACKNOWLEDGEMENTS
We thank the participants who took part in this project. We also thank our colleagues at the HCII for their feedback.

REFERENCES

1. Aaron D. Ahuvia. 2005. Beyond the extended self: Loved objects and consumers' identity narratives. *Journal of Consumer Research* 32, 1: 171 – 184.
2. Russell Belk. 1998. *Possessions and Self.* John Wiley & Sons, Ltd.
3. Russell W. Belk. 2013. Extended self in a digital world. *Journal of Consumer Research* 40, 3: 477 – 500.
4. Abhay Bhushan, Ken Pogran, Ray Tomlinson, and Jim White. 1973. RFC #561: Standardizing Network Mail Headers. Retrieved from https://tools.ietf.org/html/rfc733
5. Kirsten Boehner, Janet Vertesi, Phoebe Sengers, and Paul Dourish. 2007. How HCI interprets the probes. In *Proceedings of the SIGCHI Conference on Human Factors in Computing Systems* (CHI '07). ACM, New York, NY, USA, 1077 – 1086.
6. Barry Brown and Abigail Sellen. 2006. Sharing and listening to music. In *Consuming music together: social and collaborative aspects of music.* K. O'Hara and B. Brown (eds.), Springer Netherlands, 37 – 56.
7. Moira Burke, Robert Kraut, and Cameron Marlow. 2011. Social capital on Facebook: differentiating uses and users. In *Proceedings of the SIGCHI Conference on Human Factors in Computing Systems* (CHI '11). ACM, New York, NY, USA, 571 – 580.
8. Dan Cosley, Victoria Schwanda Sosik, Jonathan Schultz, S. Tejaswi Peesapati, and Soyoung Lee. 2012. Experiences with designing tools for everyday reminiscing. *Journal of Human-Computer Interaction,* 27, 1-2: 175 – 198.
9. Andy Crabtree, Tom Rodden, Terry Hemmings, and Steve Benford. 2003. Finding a place for UbiComp in the home. In *Proceedings of the 5th International Conference on Ubiquitous Computing,* 208 – 226.
10. Mihaly Csikszenthmihalyi and Eugene Rochberg-Halton. 1981. *The Meaning of Things: Domestic Symbols and the Self.* Cambridge University Press.
11. Doménique van Gennip, Elise van den Hoven, and Panos Markopoulos. 2015. Things that make us reminisce: Everyday memory cues as opportunities for interaction design. In *Proceedings of the 33rd Annual ACM Conference on Human Factors in Computing Systems.* ACM, New York, NY, USA, 3443 – 3452.
12. Erving Goffman. 1959. *The presentation of self in everyday life.* Anchor Books.
13. Connie Golsteijn, Elise van den Hoven, David Frohlich, and Abigail Sellen. 2012. Towards a more cherishable digital object. In *Proceedings of the 2012 Conference on Designing Interactive Systems* (DIS '12). ACM, New York, NY, USA, 655– 664.
14. Lars Hallnäs and Johan Redström. 2001. Slow technology – Designing for reflection. In *Proceedings of the 2001 ACM International Conference on Personal and Ubiquitous Computing.* ACM, New York, NY, USA, 201 – 212.
15. Sudheendra Hangal, Monica S. Lam, and Jeffrey Heer. 2011. MUSE: Reviving memories using email archives. In *Proceedings of the 24th annual ACM symposium on User Interface Software and Technology* (UIST '11). ACM, New York, NY, USA, 75 – 84.
16. Daniel Hawkins, Carman Neustaedter, and Jason Procyk. 2015. Postulater: the design and evaluation of a time-delayed media sharing system. In *Proceedings of the 41st Graphics Interface Conference.* Canadian Information Processing Society, Toronto, Ont., Canada, Canada, 249 – 256.
17. Catherine Hobbs. 2001. The character of personal archives: Reflections on the value of records of individuals. Archivaria 52: 126 – 135.
18. Hilary Hutchinson, Wendy Mackay, Bo Westerlund, Benjamin B. Bederson, Allison Druin, Catherine Plaisant, Michel Beaudouin-Lafon, Stéphane Conversy, Helen Evans, Heiko Hansen, Nicolas Roussel, and Björn Eiderbäck. 2003. Technology probes: inspiring design for and with families. In *Proceedings of the SIGCHI Conference on Human Factors in Computing Systems* (CHI '03). ACM, New York, NY, USA, 17 – 24.
19. William James. 1890. *The Principles of Psychology.* Henry Holt, New York.
20. William Jones. 2007. Personal information management. In *Annual Review of Information Science and Technology* 41, 1, 453 – 504.
21. Chris Kennedy. 2005. 'Just perfect!': The pragmatics of evaluation in holiday postcards. In *Discource, communication, and tourism.* A. Jaworski and A. Pritchard (eds.), Channel View Publications, 223 – 246.
22. Liadh Kelly, Yi Chen, Marguerite Fuller, and Gareth J.F. Jones. 2008. A study of remembered context for information access from personal digital archives. In *Proceedings of the Second International Symposium on Information Interaction in Context,* 44 – 50.
23. David Kirk, Abigail Sellen, Carsten Rother, and Ken Wood. 2006. Understanding photowork. In *Proceedings of the ACM Conference on Human Factors in Computing Systems,* Rebecca Grinter, Thomas Rodden, Paul Aoki, Ed Cutrell, Robin Jeffries, and Gary Olson (eds.). ACM, New York, NY, USA, 761 – 770.
24. David Kirk, Abigail Sellen, Richard Harper, and Ken Wood. 2007. Understanding videowork. In *Proceedings of the SIGCHI Conference on Human Factors in Computing Systems* (CHI '07). ACM, New York, NY, USA, 61 – 70.
25. Robert E. Kleine and Susan Schultz Kleine. 2000. Consumption and self-schema changes throughout the

identity project life cycle. *Advances in Consumer Research,* 27, 279 – 285.

26. Susan Schultz Kleine and Stacey Menzel Baker. 2004. An integrative review of material possession attachment. *Academy of Marketing Science Review* 1, 1: 1 – 39.
27. Siân E. Lindley, Catherine C. Marshall, Richard Banks, Abigail Sellen, and Tim Regan. 2013. Rethinking the web as a personal archive. In *Proceedings of the 22nd International Conference on World Wide Web,* 749 – 760.
28. Catherine C. Marshall. 2007. How people manage personal information over a lifetime. *Personal Information Management,* 57 – 75.
29. Catherine C. Marshall and Frank M. Shipman. 2014. An argument for archiving Facebook as a heterogeneous personal store. In *Proceedings of the 14th ACM/IEEE-CS Joint Conference on Digital Libraries,* 11 – 20.
30. Kathryn McGarr. 9 Reasons to Archive. 2008. Retrieved from: http://gmailblog.blogspot.com/2008/04/9-reasons-to-archive.html
31. Matthew B. Miles, A. Michael Huberman, and Johnny Saldaña. 2013. *Qualitative data analysis: A methods sourcebook.* SAGE Publications, Incorporated.
32. Daniel Miller and Fiona Parrott. 2009. Loss and material culture. *Journal of the Royal Anthropological Institute* 15, 3: 502 – 519.
33. Rani Molla. Gmail finally beats Hotmail, according to third-party data. 2012. Retrieved from: http://gigaom.com/2012/10/31/gmail-finally-beats-hotmail-according-to-third-party-data-chart/
34. Tiffany Ng, Ou Jie Zhao, and Dan Cosley. 2011. pieTime: Visualizing Communication Patterns. In *Proceedings of Privacy, Security, Risk and Trust*, 720 – 723.
35. William Odom, Abigail J. Sellen, Richard Banks, David S. Kirk, Tim Regan, Mark Selby, Jodi L. Forlizzi, and John Zimmerman. 2014. Designing for slowness, anticipation and re-visitation: a long term field study of the photobox. In *Proceedings of the 32nd annual ACM Conference on Human Factors in Computing Systems* (CHI '14). ACM, New York, NY, USA, 1961 – 1970.
36. William Odom, John Zimmerman, and Jodi Forlizzi. 2011. Teenagers and their virtual possessions: Design opportunities and issues. In *Proceedings of the SIGCHI Conference on Human Factors in Computing Systems* (CHI '11). ACM, New York, NY, USA, 1491 – 1500.
37. William Odom, John Zimmerman, Jodi Forlizzi, Hajin Choi, Stephanie Meier, and Angela Park. 2012. Investigating the presence, form and behavior of virtual possessions in the context of a teen bedroom. In *Proceedings of the SIGCHI Conference on Human Factors in Computing Systems* (CHI '12). ACM, New York, NY, USA, 327 – 336.
38. William Odom, John Zimmerman, and Jodi Forlizzi. 2014. Placelessness, spacelessness, and formlessness: Experiential qualities of virtual possessions. In *Proceedings of the 2014 Conference on Designing Interactive Systems* (DIS '14). ACM, New York, NY, USA, 985 – 994.
39. William Odom. 2015. Understanding long-term interactions with a slow technology: An investigation of experiences with FutureMe. In *Proceedings of the 33rd Annual ACM Conference on Human Factors in Computing Systems* (CHI '15). ACM, New York, NY, USA, 575-584.
40. S. Tejaswi Peesapati, Victoria Schwanda, Johnathon Schultz, Matt Lepage, So-yae Jeong, and Dan Cosley. 2010. Pensieve: Supporting everyday reminiscence. In *Proceedings of the SIGCHI Conference on Human Factors in Computing Systems* (CHI '10). ACM, New York, NY, USA, 2027 – 2036.
41. Daniela Petrelli, Simon Bowen, Nick Dulake, and Ann Light. 2012. Digital Christmas: An exploration of festive technology. In *Proceedings of Designing Interactive System Conference* (DIS '12). ACM, New York, NY, USA, 348 – 357.
42. Daniela Petrelli and Steve Whittaker. 2010. Family memories in the home: Contrasting physical and digital mementos. *Personal and Ubiquitous Computing* 14, 2: 153 – 169.
43. Linda L. Price, Eric J. Arnould, and Carolyn Folkman Curasi. 2000. Older consumers' disposition of special possessions. *Journal of Consumer Research* 27, 179 – 201.
44. Catherine A. Roster. 2001. Letting go: The process and meaning of dispossession in the lives of consumers. *Advances in Consumer Research* 28, 425 – 430.
45. Abigail J. Sellen, Andrew Fogg, Mike Aitken, Steve Hodges, Carsten Rother, and Ken Wood. 2007. Do life-logging technologies support memory for the past?: an experimental study using sensecam. In *Proceedings of the SIGCHI Conference on Human Factors in Computing Systems* (CHI '07). ACM, New York, NY, USA, 81 – 90.
46. Victoria Schwanda Sosik, Xuan Zhao, and Dan Cosley. 2012. See friendship, sort of: how conversation and digital traces might support reflection on friendships. In *Proceedings of the ACM 2012 Conference on Computer Support Cooperative Work* (CSCW '12). ACM, New York, NY, USA, 1145 – 1154.
47. Daniel Smilkov, Deepak Jagdish, and César Hidalgo. Immersion: a people-centric view of your email life. 2013. Retrieved from: https://immersion.media.mit.edu/
48. Timehop Application. Retrieved from: http://timehop.com/
49. Fernanda B. Viégas, danah boyd, David H. Nguyen, Jeffrey Potter, and Judith Donath. 2004. Digital artifacts for remembering and storytelling: posthistory and social

network fragments. In *Proceedings of the Hawaii International Conference on System Sciences,* 1 – 10.

50. Fernanda B. Viégas, Scott Golder, and Judith Donath. 2006. Visualizing email content: portraying relationships from conversational histories. In *Proceedings of the SIGCHI Conference on Human Factors in Computing Systems* (CHI '06). ACM, New York, NY, USA, 979 – 988.

51. Amy Voida, Rebecca E. Grinter, Nicolas Ducheneaut, W. Keith Edwards, and Mark W. Newman. 2005. Listening in: practices surrounding iTunes music sharing. In *Proceedings of the SIGCHI Conference on Human Factors in Computing Systems* (CHI '05). ACM, New York, NY, USA, 191 – 200.

52. Yang Wang and Scott D. Mainwaring. 2008. Human-currency interaction: learning from virtual currency use in China. In *Proceedings of the SIGCHI Conference on Human Factors in Computing Systems* (CHI '08). ACM, New York, NY, USA, 81 – 90.

53. Peter Williams, Jeremy Leighton, and John Ian Rowland. 2009. The personal curation of digital objects. In *Aslib Proceedings* 61, 4: 340 – 363.

54. Steve Whittaker. 2011. Personal information management: From information consumption to curation. *Annual Review of Information Science and Technology* 45, 1.

55. Steve Whittaker, Ofer Bergman, and Paul Clough. 2010. Easy on that trigger dad: a study of long term family photo retrieval. In *Proceedings of the 2010 ACM International Conference on Personal and Ubiquitous Computing.* ACM, New York, NY, USA, 31 – 43.

56. Steve Whittaker, Vaiva Kalnikaite, Daniella Petrelli, Abigail Sellen, Nicolas Villar, Ofer Bergman, Paul Clough, and Jens Brockmeier. 2012. Socio-technical lifelogging: Deriving design principles for a future proof digital past. *Journal of Human-Computer Interaction* 27, 1 – 2: 37 – 62.

57. Steve Whittaker, and Candace Sidener. 1996. Email overload: Exploring personal information management of email. In *Proceedings of the SIGCHI Conference on Human Factors in Computing Systems* (CHI '96). ACM, New York, NY, USA, 276 – 283.

58. Xuan Zhao, Niloufar Salehi, Sasha Naranjit, Sara Alwaalan, Stephen Voida, and Dan Cosley. 2013. The many faces of Facebook: Experiencing social media as performance, exhibition, and personal archive. In *Proceedings of the SIGCHI Conference on Human Factors in Computing Systems* (CHI '13). ACM, New York, NY, USA, 1 – 10.

59. Xuan Zhao and Siân Lindley 2014. Curation through use: Understanding the personal value of social media. In *Proceedings of the 32nd annual Conference on Human Factors in Computing Systems* (CHI '14). ACM, New York, NY, USA, 2431 – 2440.

Finding Email in a Multi-Account, Multi-Device World

Marta E. Cecchinato
UCL Interaction Centre
University College London
WC1E 6BT, London, UK
m.cecchinato@cs.ucl.ac.uk

Abigail Sellen, Milad Shokouhi, Gavin Smyth
Microsoft Research Cambridge
CB1 2FB, Cambridge, UK
{asellen,milads,gavin.smyth}@microsoft.com

ABSTRACT
Email is far from dead; in fact the volume of messages exchanged daily, the number of accounts per user, and the number of devices on which email is accessed have been constantly growing. Most previous studies on email have focused on management and retrieval behaviour within a single account and on a single device. In this paper, we examine how people retrieve email in today's ecosystem through an in-depth qualitative diary study with 16 participants. We found that personal and work accounts are managed differently, resulting in diverse retrieval strategies: while work accounts are more structured and thus email is retrieved through folders, personal accounts have fewer folders and users rely primarily on the built-in search option. Moreover, retrieval occurs primarily on laptops and PCs compared to smartphones. We explore the reasons, and uncover barriers and workarounds related to managing multiple accounts and devices. Finally, we consider new design possibilities for email clients to better support how email is used today.

ACM Classification Keywords
H.5.m. Information Interfaces and Presentation (e.g. HCI): Miscellaneous

Author Keywords
Email; multi-device; cross-device interaction; information retrieval; searching; archiving

INTRODUCTION
Despite the ongoing debate in popular media on whether email is dead[1], forecasters predict that the number of messages exchanged per year will grow at an average rate of 3% over the next four years for both business and consumer purposes [19], suggesting that, for the foreseeable future, email is here to stay. This is all the more interesting in the face of the growing popularity of other social media and instant messaging platforms [19], that not only are popular among the younger population[2], but are also starting to be used in the working environment[1]. Alongside its staying power, however, are some of email's equally persistent, attendant problems.

"Email overload", for example, has long been recognised as a universal problem [39] and there is now a substantial body of work dedicated to understanding how people manage and file their email in order to deal with the incoming deluge and growing archives. Over the years, there have been several taxonomies of managing habits (e.g. [4, 17, 26]), distinguishing for example between people who frequently, sporadically or never file their email. Regardless of the managing strategy used, there is a trend toward users receiving and retaining more messages [21], reinforcing email's role as an important digital archive. Given this archiving role, understanding how people manage and retrieve email is more important than ever. Previous work has found that how messages are managed is inextricably linked to how users expect to be able to find any given message or set of messages in future [38].

However, the majority of previous studies have overlooked two key factors which have become even more important in recent years: continued growth in the number of accounts per user [19], and the growing number of devices that people use to access their email [30]. Email management across multiple accounts such as work and personal has been largely ignored with only a few exceptions [7, 11, 18]. Email use across devices has only been touched upon as an example of multi-device usage (e.g. [14, 29]), rather than being thoroughly investigated.

We argue that it is now increasingly important to understand user's current email retrieval and management practices across devices and accounts. It may be that the more complex modern ecosystems create new challenges in managing or finding email; it is also possible that having access to multiple devices and accounts have made email management and retrieval easier for some users. Exploring this in depth may point to opportunities for improving email tools. Indeed most have changed very little in the past couple of decades, suggesting they have not kept pace with fundamental changes in the way email is now used.

To this end, we present an in-depth qualitative study with 16 diverse participants who took part in a week-long diary study. We examine their general email habits, their management habits, and how they look for information in their email. Specifically, we investigate how their practices differ across accounts and devices. The results also illustrate issues

[1]Forbes 2015, http://onforb.es/1gQ8fXE
[2]Forbes 2014, http://onforb.es/1s5pT1K

CHI'16, May 07 - 12, 2016, San Jose, CA, USA

ACM 978-1-4503-3362-7/16/05...$15.00
DOI: http://dx.doi.org/10.1145/2858036.2858473

participants encountered during retrieval and workarounds to make finding easier. Consequently, our research confirms and extends previous work in a number of ways and makes the following contributions:

- It further unpacks the differences between work email and personal accounts, with the former relying more on structure and preparatory mechanisms, and the latter relying more on opportunistic retrieval.
- It proves the importance of considering multiple devices when investigating email behaviour. We find how email retrieval occurs primarily on laptops and desktop PCs, and how mobile search is infrequent and often problematic.
- It helps identify current issues with email retrieval and users' workarounds, both in terms of having to manage multiple accounts and deal with device constraints.
- It considers how the design of today's email clients could be improved to better support how email is used in a multi-account, multi-device ecosystem, and points to trends toward more flexible, integrated tools.

LITERATURE REVIEW

Most previous research in this area has focused on email as a communication channel at work [37]. Email has also been characterized as a habitat [15] for information management, and as a means of time and task management [26]. As a result, several taxonomies have been created to reflect users' email management strategies, distinguishing between *frequent filers, spring cleaners, no filers* [39] and *few folder filers* [17], *cleaners and keepers* [20], to name but a few. While each of these papers highlights slightly different management strategies, all studied only work-related email.

Email Retrieval

Managing, filing and archiving work email has been the subject of deeper research than the other side of the coin: retrieving messages in email. Early work, such as Mackay [26], and Whittaker and Sidner [39], distinguished between "preparatory behaviours", where users take time to file and label email in anticipation of retrieving the information, and "opportunistic access", where users rely on sorting, scrolling or searching at the time of need, delaying the burden. However, it was not until later that Whittaker *et al.*'s work [38] more explicitly showed the relationship between management and retrieval strategies. They compared the benefits of preparatory retrieval using folders and tags with opportunistic search and threading, and showed how these relate to email management strategies. Their findings suggest opportunistic behaviour is better and that preparatory strategies are inefficient and do not necessarily improve successful retrieval. They proposed that filing strategies are a reaction to the large number of messages received and a way to better visualise tasks.

Retrieving email is an intricate research area not only studied in HCI, but also in the information retrieval literature. Of relevance, studies focussed on prototypes called Phlat [13] and *Stuff I've Seen* [16]. The latter study was aimed at exploring how information is found and re-found on computers, including in email [16]. The system facilitates information re-use, by offering a unified indexing from one's own emails, web history, calendars, and files. The authors found that time frame and people's names are powerful contextual cues used when retrieving personal information, as later reinforced also by Cutrell *et al.* [12].

Personal vs. Work Email Accounts

While, on average, people have more than one account to reflect the various facets of one's life [11], most academic research has concentrated on work email to the exclusion of personal email. Smith *et al.* [34] were the first to point towards a tension between work and personal email, finding in 2003 that 54% of their participants had two separate accounts, particularly as a way to keep spam out of work email. Ten years later, Capra *et al.* [7], found that this separation was growing, with 84% of their survey respondents having separate accounts as a way of managing boundaries between work and personal life. However, it is only more recently that research has shown how work and personal accounts are managed differently. Grevet *et al.* [18] replicated and extended two seminal studies [17, 39] updating our understanding of email management strategies and adding a comparison between work and personal accounts among Gmail-only users. They found that personal inboxes are usually considerably larger in terms of archive size, inbox size and number of unread messages when compared to work inboxes. While these findings are important, more work is needed to unpack personal vs. work use of email in multi-account settings and extending this to other email clients.

Multi-Device Use and Email Access

Understanding user interactions across multiple devices has emerged as an active area of research in recent years. Takkinen and Shahmeheri [35] were the first to investigate email use on multiple devices exploring how often email is accessed on different computers, and using different email clients as a function of communication context (social, work, educational, etc.) and role. More generally, one's choice of device depends not only on the nature of the task, but also on the context of use (physical space, social environment, etc.) [23, 25], and the access and initialisation time vs. actual usage time [27]. Santosa *et al.* [31] discussed how email is frequently used to transfer information to others and across devices, especially for quick access, re-access and *hot* documents [32].

Despite these prior studies, there is relatively little known about cross-device retrieval of email. Montanez *et al.* [28] investigated multi-device search behaviour in a search log dataset. While they found that there are learnable patterns of device transitions – such as how different devices are used to search different content, and how the choice of device is dependent on the time of the day – their focus is only on browser search and does not mention email use. Carrascal and Church [8] used qualitative and quantitative methods to investigate how mobile search interacts with other mobile apps. They found that "browsers, email, SMS, social networking, shopping & retail and entertainment related apps are used more intensively when people engage with mobile search, both in terms of app launches and duration of app usage" [*ibid, p.2745*].

Research Questions

In summary, an examination of related work highlights the need to understand how email retrieval differs between work and personal accounts, especially with respect to multi-device use. Specifically, our work aims to answer the following two research questions:

- What kinds of content do users look for and what strategies do they employ in work vs. personal email accounts for managing and finding email?
- Do users' email retrieval strategies differ across devices? How does this influence users' choice of activity or choice of devices?

METHOD

In order to get in *situ* data and maintain high ecological validity, we opted for a mixed methods approach which included a weeklong diary study, with pre- and post-interviews. The study took place in July 2015. Prior studies on email retrieval have relied on observations [14], interviews [29], diary studies [23], and data logging [24]. Our methodology was refined through a series of pilot tests using a diary method which adheres to Carter & Mankoff's [9] guidelines, asking participants to record instances of retrieval as they occurred, adding more details later if needed and following up with interviews. We defined 'retrieval' for users as a range of behaviours in support of finding information, messages or attachments including: entering keywords in the search bar; accessing one or more folders; glancing or scrolling in folders or inbox; and sorting email based on metadata (date/sender/etc.). Therefore some activities would be more like goal-directed search in pursuit of a particular piece of information (e.g. when using the search bar), whereas other activities such as scrolling or glancing through collections of messages might involve behaviour which would be more like scanning or browsing.

Participants

Sixteen people completed the study (9 women, 7 men), aged between 22 and 52 (Median: 28). All lived in the south-eastern area of U.K. Occupations included: a physiotherapist, two nurses, two PhD students, two research assistants, three post-doctoral researchers, a high school teacher, a teaching associate, a barista, a software engineer, a graphic designer, and a marketing coordinator. We screened participants based on occupation, striving to include as many different ones as possible given the initial 35 people who signed up, to ensure a wider spectrum of experiences with email and expertise in computer literacy. Participants were recruited through flyers, social media ads, and word-of-mouth. All participants received an Amazon gift voucher.

Procedure

Initial Survey

Participants began with a survey covering: general demographics, their email accounts, the total number of folders in both main work and main personal accounts, and their preferred filing strategy for both their main work and main personal accounts (following the classification in [39] of frequent filers, spring cleaners and no filers), the type of devices they owned (including who bought it and where they often used it), and how they accessed their email accounts on each device.

Pre-diary interview

Participants were asked to bring along devices they used to access email to prompt contextual explanations about their general email habits, including management and retrieval strategies. We asked participants to distinguish between personal and work devices, and accounts when answering questions, collecting pictures of their physical desktops at home and work, and screenshots of their folder structures. The first interview also included observation of retrieval tasks which we assigned in order to create an initial understanding of their practices before the diary study. We asked participants to retrieve messages or information within (e.g. attachments, login details, pictures) from people or services they frequently, rarely, or no longer received emails from. In order to ensure ecological validity, these tasks were based on elements mentioned by themselves during the interview. For example, P12 mentioned going on holiday to Berlin, so we asked him to look for the flight confirmation, as he would normally do. Notes were taken for each step and participants were free to choose which device to use to complete the task.

Diary

Starting the day after the first interview, participants were then asked to diarise for a week their *retrieval activities* related to email, ranging from goal-directed search to more general browsing or scanning. We specifically asked them to include, as they occurred, any instances that somehow involved email: whether they were looking for a particular message, or an attachment, or a piece of information within a message, or even if they were just looking through their email in a more serendipitous way. To help them understand what we were interested in, we included examples on each page of the diary. They could choose between a digital (n=12) or paper (n=4) diary, to accommodate their everyday routine. For each entry participants had to specify their location, which device they used and which account they searched. A link to the digital diary was sent out once during the evening of the first interview; reminders to complete the diary were sent daily.

Post-diary interview

The follow-up interviews were scheduled within a week from the end of the diary, based on participants' availability. The purpose of this interview was to walk the researcher through each diary entry, in order to provide more details and more contextual explanations, building on the in-depth data collection. Both semi-structured interviews took place either in participants' homes, offices, or in our lab. The first interview lasted on average 53 minutes, while the follow-up lasted on average 46 minutes.

Activity logging

To ensure greater external validity and compensate for under-reporting issues in qualitative studies, we asked participants' permission to collect logged data on their usage of email across devices, using RescueTime[3]. To make sure participants were comfortable sharing their data, we made this optional, but only six installed it on compatible devices. As a result, logs were only used as an aide-memoir during follow-up interviews, and to validate self-reported data when possible. Before each of the six follow-up interviews, diary entries were compared with logged data to ensure accuracy of self-reported data and we found that no searching activities were missing from the diaries. As previously discussed [3], logs are difficult to collect for different devices due to technical issues (e.g. operating system compatibility) and privacy concerns.

Analysis

To build a holistic understanding of participants' searching practices across devices and accounts, we compiled interview transcripts, diary entries, notes, photographs, and logged data for the 16 participants, and analysed the data thematically [6]. Open and axial coding was used to define themes, which were then discussed amongst all authors. We looked at differences between work and personal accounts, both in terms of types of email retrieved and strategies used. We then focused the analysis on devices used, and how the type of email, context and affordances defined users' choices. For each stage, we also identified issues and workarounds created by participants, as suggested by [22].

FINDINGS

Together with the interviews, a total of 239 diary entries was recorded, averaging 15 entries per participant over the course of seven days. In addition, during the first interview, participants completed a total of 42 finding tasks, averaging almost three each. From the initial survey, participants listed having on average three email accounts each (Min: 2, Max: 9, Median: 3). On average people had four devices each (Min: 2, Max: 7, Median: 4), including smartphones, tablets, laptops and desktop PCs, and all participants had devices from a mix of platforms (i.e. Windows, Apple, Android, Linux). Two participants also had a smartwatch: P1 had a Pebble, and P11 had an Apple Watch.

Participants used different email clients, based on device and type of account, i.e. email clients used to access personal and/or work accounts on laptops and PCs were not necessarily the same used on mobile devices. For example, P11 accessed his work and personal accounts on a laptop and PC through webmail (Roundcube and Gmail, respectively), while on his smartphone and tablet he accessed his accounts through the Mailbox app[4]. A list of email clients used across multiple devices and participants is as follows: Work accounts were accessed primarily through Outlook (n =15), followed by Roundcube (n=8), Inbox by Gmail (n=4), Gmail (n=2), Mutt (n=2), Mailbox app (n=1), Android email app (n=1), Windows Phone email app (n=1), and finally through K9 app (n=1). Personal accounts, instead, were accessed primarily through Gmail (n=14), followed by Mail app (n=8), Outlook (n=7), Yahoo (n=3), Inbox by Gmail (n=2), Libero (n=2), Mailbox app (n=2), Mutt (n=2), and finally the K9 app (n=1).

[3] `https://www.rescuetime.com`

[4] `http://www.mailboxapp.com`

We found that reported instances of email retrieval varied by type of account and device used, and also as a function of physical location and activity. Instances were somewhat more frequent for work accounts (55%) than personal accounts (45%), loosely overlapping with the location in which these finding activities were conducted: 53% at work, followed by home (40%) and other locations (7%). In terms of devices used, 85% of finding instances were completed on a laptop (54%) or desktop PC (31%), followed by the phone (15%) and a tablet in just one case, because their "*iPhone was on charge, iPad* [was the] *nearest quickest thing*" (P6, diary).

Due to the small sample size and the perhaps low number of self- reported retrieval instances, we need to be cautious in generalising from these numbers, however, the diaries and interviews do give us deeper insights into people's strategies and motivations when looking for email. In the following sections we start by distinguishing between management practices based on different accounts, and then move to *what* users looked for in work and personal accounts, discussing the *why* and the *how*, followed by issues and workarounds. We later discuss how email retrieval differs across devices, based on strategy used, issues encountered and workarounds created when retrieving information across multiple devices.

Email Management in Work vs. Personal Accounts

All participants had at least one main work-related and one main personal account as a way to maintain separate life roles, and 11 of them had at least one additional account. Only one participant, P10 (who had four email addresses), used her main Gmail account for both personal and work reasons, despite having other work-related accounts. Reasons for having additional accounts confirm those found in Cecchinato *et al.* [11] (e.g. having legacy accounts, separating one's many life roles, or filtering out junk email), and, if used at all, they were rarely checked or accessed for retrieving email.

The way in which accounts were organised and managed differed between work and personal ones, with work email giving rise to more structured filing. From the initial survey, most participants (n=10) reported having the same overall filing strategy between personal and work accounts: six were frequent filers (P1, P3, P5, P6, P12, P14); two were spring cleaners (P7, P13); and two were no filers (P10, P11). However the remaining six participants (P2, P4, P8, P9, P15, P16) had different strategies for different accounts. Of these, five filed email more frequently in their work account compared to their personal one, while the remaining participant (P4) was more organised in her personal account: this participant, a nurse, reported that she received very few work-related emails relevant to her. Participants tended to have more folders in their work account, suggesting they try to be more organised or used work email more as an archive. P2 described this well: "*Somehow I had accepted that I didn't really care that my Gmail* [personal] *inbox was huge. But* [· · ·] *I might star things* [· · ·]. [In] *my small inbox at work* [Outlook] *I labelled* [categorised] *it and archived it*".

These findings are reflected in the average number of folders or labels that participants had in their work and personal accounts (Table 1). Here we treat both folders and labels as equivalent

	Main work account	*Main personal account*
# Folders/labels + subfolders	32 (87.51)	8.81 (10.10)
# Folders/labels with 3 or fewer items	1.1 (2.73)	0.71 (1.73)
# Folders/labels not used for at least 6 months	18 (66.97)	4 (6.23)

Table 1. Average number of folders/labels (with standard deviation), excluding P10 who did not distinguish between work and personal accounts.

for the purpose of this analysis. Not all email clients offer the same features: for example, Gmail does not have folders *per se*, but its labels can be assigned to the same email, unlike Outlook where an email can only belong to one folder, but can have multiple categories. However, other research also claims that folders and labels are comparable, as their ultimate purpose is to "file messages away from the inbox" ([18], p.797). With regard to the use of different email clients, it is of course possible that other aspects of their design can impact on both management and retrieval strategies which might confound our comparisons of work versus personal email. However, we did not find obvious evidence of this in our sample.

Notably, in our sample, the three healthcare workers (P4, P6, P7) did not have any folders in their work account, but organised their personal email with folders to store important files, such as insurance documents, login details (P7) or emails related to their owned properties (P6). Despite having folders for "*important documents*" and university-related emails, P4 admitted not having accessed those folders in over a year. This suggests that occupation may play a role in email strategies, as seen in [11], and points towards the idea that for workers who do not rely heavily on email, folders in personal accounts are valuable for long term archiving. However, the findings may not be generalisable to other professions.

What People Looked for in Work vs. Personal Accounts

From the interviews and diaries, we found that what users looked for differed between work and personal accounts, confirming recent findings [18]. Highlighting how the content differs is relevant for understanding the ways in which they looked for it, given the range and diversity of reasons people need to find things in their accounts.

In personal accounts, participants mainly reported retrieving details and documents such as: order confirmations; travel related information (e.g. booking references); money related email (e.g. bank details, and bills); and to-do lists or reminders. In addition, participants sometimes searched their personal account to go through past correspondence in a more reminiscent or nostalgic way: "*A friend of mine (high school) sent me a link to a video on YouTube* [$\cdots$] *I was just nostalgic and went to that email again and watched the goal.*" (P14, diary). In work accounts, instead, participants retrieved information which was more central to, and entwined with, ongoing work tasks. Finally, some types of information were reported being looked for in both work and personal accounts: meeting details such as location or time; attachments; links; login details; and pictures. The most frequent reasons for searching either type of account were "double checking" and forwarding information.

In summary, retrieval in work accounts seemed to be more motivated by needing to refer to email in the course of *information gathering* for larger tasks, as described in [33]. While this can be the case in personal accounts too, retrieval in the latter among our sample tended to involve more directed search for email that contained quick facts (similar to the *finding* category in [33]).

How People Retrieved Work vs. Personal Email

Participants were generally good at finding email within one or two attempts, with a 97.5% success rate from the diary entries and 81% in the 42 tasks performed during the first interview. When unsuccessful, they still managed to obtain the information needed by other means. For example, they either remembered it was stored somewhere else ("*I found the file in my Dropbox*" – P11, diary), or asked to have the information sent to them ("*So I gave up I said hello to her on WhatsApp*[5] *and Facebook*[6]" – P15, diary), suggesting that people usually find what they are looking for.

Overall, diary entries showed that participants had preferred retrieval strategies depending on the account: for personal accounts the most common methods were using the search bar and glancing or scrolling the inbox, while for work accounts the most common ones were clicking on a folder and using keyword search within it (*folder+search*), using the *search bar*, or simply opening a folder and scrolling through its contents (*folder+scroll*) (Figure 1). This confirms the heavier reliance, in work email, on the use of structured filing to support retrieval and shows a hybrid combination between preparatory (*folder*) and opportunistic (*search bar/scroll*) strategies. It is important to note that strategies depicted in Figure 1 were often used in combination, when the first attempt was not successful, but with no recurring pattern.

Further analysis of the diary entries together with the interview transcripts allowed us to abstract the strategies reported in the diaries and shown in Figure 1. As a result, participants can be described as falling into three different categories:

1. Those whose retrieval strategies referred to only one of their accounts because, despite having multiple accounts, they used only one (P4, P10, P13): "*Gmail.com* [$\cdots$] *was my personal one but I actually use it for work as well*" – P10, who despite having other two accounts for part-time jobs, prefers keeping everything in the same inbox.
2. Those who used similar strategies when retrieving information from both their work and personal accounts (P1, P5, P6, P7, P11, P12, P14, P16): "[I] *primarily use the search bar. It's usually order one operation, it's not order N.*" – P1,

[5] `https://www.whatsapp.com`

[6] `https://www.facebook.com`

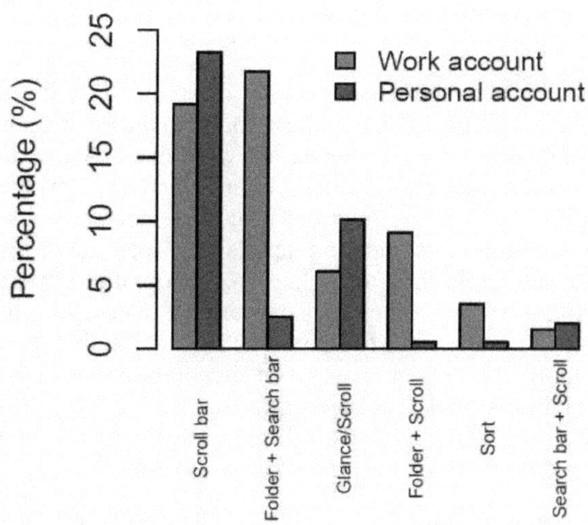

Figure 1. Combined retrieval strategies used for work and personal accounts, as reported in diary entries.

suggesting that he preferred the quickest route for retrieval, with the least number of attempts.

3. Those who used different retrieval strategies for work and personal accounts (P2, P3, P8, P9, P15). While in their personal account they tended to rely on the search bar or scrolling through their inbox, in work accounts they relied more heavily on accessing a folder and then using the search function within it. This is nicely illustrated with comments from P3. Talking about her work account, she said: "[I create folders] *to try and group emails that have a common theme together.* [· · ·] *It's just easier to reference* [and] *find them if they are altogether somewhere.*" By contrast, when P3 talked about her personal account, she reported usually just scrolling or using the search bar: "*What I tend to do is, if it's really important I don't touch it. But if it is just general crap I would just tend to move it to* [archive]."

With regard to the effect of different email clients on patterns of retrieval and management, we could discern no clear relationship between email clients and type of account. While this does not exclude it as a possibility, it is fair to say that differences between work and personal accounts were more salient than any that might be due to particular features of the email client used.

Cross-Account Issues and Workarounds

In general, despite the overall success reported in diaries of participants finding email, they nonetheless complained about how hard and frustrating it can be, especially considering their many accounts. As a result of this frustration, workarounds were used to guard against these difficulties, including moving away from email altogether.

Making messages conspicuous

Some participants ensured that the information they needed would be at the top of their inbox, either by using built-in features, such as Save for Later in the Mailbox app "*so that it pops up when I need it, which* [is] *incredibly useful because then it's just at the top of my inbox, it's like 'a-ah!'*" (P11, first interview), or repurposing existing features, such as: "*I mark important conversations as unread and leave them there in my unread upper-portion of the screen. This way I don't really have to search for them by using the engine*" (P15, diary).

Email to self

Other issues related to retrieving email from oneself. We know from previous literature that self-emails are often used as reminders and to-do lists [2] and as such, they might have a short lifespan until they serve their purpose. However, we found that having to retrieve self-emails can cause issues: "*This one it's annoying because* [· · ·] *it includes me. If I am looking for an email that I sent myself, it also includes an email where I have replied to someone,*" (P8, first interview). It also created redundant information, "*if I send myself a message then I get two copies in the inbox and* [in the sent folder]. *It's a really silly little thing but it's sort of like kind of irritating*" (P11, first interview).

As a result of this, P11 started using Pushbullet[7] to send himself things, "*I can just push this to myself wherever I want it to be and it's kind of, it's more like a dedicated app for it and it feels less messy than sending myself an email, because emails have a lot of sort of metadata and information on it*". Pushbullet allows users to share web content such as links with oneself and friends. Other workarounds for searching for self-emails included changing "*my name for myself on my Gmail account to me. And then I just type 'me', it returns 'me'.*" (P15, first interview), and creating a folder just for self-emails (P13). In this case, P15 used self-email for short-lived reminders and to-do lists, whereas P13 sent himself emails with long-lived information, e.g. bank details.

Account and channel boundaries

Another set of issues emerged as a direct result of having multiple email accounts for different purposes. We found that participants experienced difficulties in finding email sometimes because the boundaries between accounts were not well-defined. This affected their filing strategies but also their retrieval behaviour, as this quote exemplifies: "*I think the problem arises from the fact that it's personal and work email and sometimes there's tons of overlap* [· · ·] *so like my sister might send me this, really interesting thing to do with academic things* [· · ·] *and she might have put like, I don't know, some personal information in there as well about a holiday· · · I'd be really confused about where to put that and so like, that's why I didn't use the filing system*" (P10, first interview).

By contrast, P12 found these concerns were no longer relevant when using Slack[8], an instant messaging tool advertised for work purposes that allows users to communicate with team members through public channels, private groups and direct messages. As a result, it made it easier for him to retrieve older messages: "*Before* [my colleague and I] *set* [Slack] *up, it was really horrid,* [· · ·] *it would all be like, 'Oh, I sent you an email three months ago' or 'I sent you a text' or, like, 'I've got this like WhatsApp chat thing'. But it is all in there and it's*

[7] `https://www.pushbullet.com`

[8] `https://slack.com`

all curated heavily and there's no, like, subject changing", in fact, he explains how this is beneficial to maintaining separate work and personal roles, "*you're not posting something about going for drinks in the thread about the job we're working on*" (P12, first interview).

More generally, we found our younger participants (n=8, age¡30) were moving away from email for personal communications, in favour of other dedicated channels, as has been suggested in popular media[9]. P12 explained this very well, distinguishing the use of email from instant messaging tools and social networks: "*I'm not really sure where email sits at the moment* [· · ·] *not that long ago it was the only option for communicating with people via computers. Now I've got one machine in my hand that can do, like, 50 different types of email sending* [· · ·] *I don't use* [email] *the same way I might use, say, Facebook chat or like texting or like Snapchat.*" (P12, first interview).

He went on to explain how other people may not be aware of personal preferences, blurring the boundaries not only between work and personal, but also between communication channels, making it more difficult to manage and retrieve information: "*People message me on my Facebook to give me a job so I* [· · ·] *maybe screenshot and email* [it to myself], *or if someone's emailing me on the wrong account* [· · ·] *rather than asking them to email me on the proper account* [· · ·], *I would kind of do it for them.* [· · ·] *I mean it's putting it where I would end up looking for it*" (P12, first interview).

We also found a movement away from email when it came to sharing pictures, choosing different communications channels instead, such as WhatsApp. Participants sent and received photos via email only in two cases: when the sender was not a user of social media or instant messaging services (e.g. sharing with other family members); or when wanting to maintain a certain image quality. "*Me and my friend, we are constantly* [sharing] *pictures or screenshots via WhatsApp. Also Snapchat... But yes, never really on email for social reasons*" – (P6, first interview).

In summary, we see a shifting landscape where email is finding a new role and niche amongst other channels. The evidence suggests that the difficulty of managing email across account boundaries, along with issues in trying to find information across them, may be contributing factors.

Email Retrieval Across Devices

Moving on from cross-account issues, we now turn to issues linked to the use of different devices for accessing email. Here we found that 85% of email retrieval tasks reported in the diaries occurred on laptops and PCs, with only 15% on mobile devices. More than this, the device used depended on the type of email being sought for or the location of use. Laptops and PCs were used primarily at work and for retrieving work-related content (e.g. correspondence, tasks, instructions), together with important information from personal accounts (e.g. bills, bank details, passport). This is perhaps not surprising given that many work-related tasks, including email, require larger screens and keyboards, for example when creating documents.

Although 15 participants accessed at least one of their email accounts on their phone, the majority of them did not search on their mobile devices either because it was not an easy process or they "*never had cause to*" (P1). Phones were used primarily for searching quick reference information, such as: booking confirmation numbers, meeting details (e.g. location or time), emails to self containing to-do lists (e.g. shopping list). They were also used where other devices were not handy, such as in bed or at a restaurant. Of those who did search on their phone, some had different strategies from their laptops or desktop PCs, as P3 describes: "*it's weird, if I am typing it out on the phone I don't think to do* [advance search options] *but if I was using my Gmail on a laptop I probably would*".

Other types of mobile devices (tablets and smartwatches) were not used to search email. Eight participants owned a tablet, and two of them never used it to access email. Tablet use for email was limited and echoes previous findings [18] that suggest tablets are more for information-consumption, such as "*for reading eBooks*" (P1). While both smartwatch users received email notifications on their wrist, they did not use them for searching. As P1 explains, "*the wrist is not the place to search emails*".

The relatively little amount of retrieval activity on smartphones despite high engagement with such devices is somewhat surprising. Our interviews revealed that frustration and user unfamiliarity with search features may explain this discrepancy to some extent: "*For me it's easier on Outlook* [on laptop] *but that's probably because I know how to use it better really, because you don't really spend time figuring out how to search for things on your phone*" (P16, first interview). Similarly, P6 explains: "*I have never really noticed it on my phone and it's my phone that I always check my emails on*". Interestingly, we found that not knowing about the search button was not related to technology expertise.

In addition, participants complained about the phone being "less effective" at finding what they were looking for, due to limited storage capabilities or connectivity problems: "*I find that on mobile searching is not as good because it's, particularly when you're out and on a 3G connection, it's struggling to find* [· · ·] *the search heuristic isn't fast enough* [· · ·] *I sometimes end up with emails that are like from ages ago because it's something that's cached* [· · ·] *not really relevant to what I'm looking for, just because it's not got enough storage*" (P11, first interview).

Cross-Device Issues and Workarounds

Our findings show how searching email, especially on different devices, can cause frustration: "*I've never had particularly good results with searching for emails.*" (P12, first interview). To avoid this, participants relied on a series of workarounds, especially when anticipating having to retrieve email on the phone and sometimes as a result of the email client.

External copies

Some of these workarounds were closely linked to general personal information management practices, such as copying

[9]Forbes 2014, `http://onforb.es/1s5pT1K`

information onto scraps of paper or into a separate application. For example, P1 used Google Keep[10], a note-taking app, to keep track of any trip related information: "*It's like keeping a single post-it note for it* [···] *so its ephemeral. I mean I don't search in the same way* [···] *I don't keep an archive of all the post-it notes that are on the fridge, because once that's reached its purpose it's often in the recycle bin*" (P1, follow-up interview).

Sending

Other workarounds included sending oneself an email, a strategy also used across accounts, so to avoid having to search or scroll the inbox when they have already anticipated needing to retrieve an email, as P9 explains: "*So say I'm going to* [a shop] *to pick up an order* [···] *it's been a few days since I got the email saying the number of the order, then I will forward that email to myself again so that it will be at the top when I get to the shop and I can tell them the number.*"

Application switch

Of note, three people did not use their usual email application when they had to search for an email, especially for old ones, as they were not easily accessible from their preferred application. For example, "*generally* [I use my phone] *if I'm out and about, but I will normally go on the web browser and go on Hotmail itself, rather than the app because··· on* [the Mail app], *it only has my most recent ones*" (P7, first interview). Mail app has been criticised for its poor searching capabilities[11] and indeed two of the five Mail app users switched applications when they needed to retrieve a message: P4 switched to the Outlook app on her phone; P7 switched to the webmail on her phone. Other Mail app users did not feel the need to switch application (but some did use other workarounds). This suggests that, as much as email clients do impact user engagement, there are clearly other factors involved.

Pictures and screenshots

To overcome some of the annoyance with having to search, but particularly the limitations of mobile devices not always having signal, or enough memory to store email, some participants took screenshots of their emails that they could then search for in their photo collection. P7 reported in the diary taking a screenshot of her train confirmation a couple of days before leaving for Paris. She then explained that on her the way back, looking for that screenshot was more difficult, "*because I had taken quite a lot of photos on holiday, I did have quite a bit of scrolling to have to do for that one*" (P7, follow-up interview). These ephemeral scraps of information were not always deleted from the phone gallery once they served their purpose, adding to the phone's storage problem. This builds on previous work on how scraps of information are needed for rapid capturing [36].

Interestingly, pictures or screenshots were also used to share the content of email with others via different channels, as a means to curate communications: "*I will occasionally* [···], *screenshot an email and send it to him* [via WhatsApp] *so he can deal with it and he doesn't have to be in a thread*" (P12, first interview). It is worth mentioning that screenshots and pictures of email were taken by all participants who were in their 20s (n=8) but none of the older participants relied on this workaround.

[10] `http://www.google.com/keep`

[11] MacWorld, `http://bit.ly/1TI9BWv`

DISCUSSION

To the best of our knowledge, this study is the first to provide insights into how people retrieve information across work and personal email accounts, and across devices. By using a mixed method approach, we confirm and extend previous findings, along with presenting several novel insights.

Work versus Personal Email

We found that work email continues to provide a central archive for work-related tasks, as a key part of knowledge work and in support of structuring tasks, creating documents, and controlling the workflow of tasks. This confirms that email archives continue to be an important hub for working life. Personal email archives, by contrast, are more likely to be searched in order to access important details (e.g. booking references) and documents (e.g. passport). As a result, it is not surprising that work email accounts are searched more often than personal ones because they are in service of these work-related tasks. Moreover, given that our evidence from younger participants suggests that they are moving away from email as a personal communication channel (preferring other channels instead), we might surmise that in time personal email may well evolve primarily into an archive for what could be called "domestic paperwork".

We also consider retrieval and management practices in light of participants' email clients, extending previous work [18]. We find that participants using the same clients had different experiences and the choice of email client alone does not explain issues encountered and workarounds created: personal preference and type of account also play a significant role. Further work should expand on this by including a larger sample.

We find some points of contrast with earlier work related to how people retrieve email in the context of their management practices. For example, whereas previous work [18] found similar management habits for work and personal accounts, we found that work accounts were usually more structured, with more folders than personal accounts. This partially confirms what Whittaker *et al.* [38] concluded, that folders are created as a way of managing the increasing number of messages, at least in work accounts. In personal accounts, instead, the small number of folders confirms how users may not want to put effort into organising information [5]. However, we did also see how some participants relied on additional accounts to filter out unwanted messages from their main accounts.

These differences in management strategies were also reflected in different retrieval strategies between work and personal accounts. Table 1 and Figure 1 provide a good summary that highlights the trade-off between preparatory and opportunistic mechanisms [38]: we found that folders in work accounts were used for later retrieval, as opposed to in personal accounts where opportunistic retrieval was more common due to the lack of a filing system. While the overall most common retrieval strategy was using the search bar, work accounts were primarily searched starting with a folder, and then searching or scrolling within it, thus combining preparatory (*folder*) and opportunistic (*search, scroll*) mechanisms. This means that the two strategies are not mutually exclusive, as was suggested by [38] but rather represent a kind of hybrid approach.

Management Through Multiple Channels

Another set of findings take us outside of the conventional email ecosystem to look for other ways in which email was managed. For example, there is a trend toward new kinds of dedicated work-related tools that are becoming popular, such as Slack[8] and Asana[12], among others, which incorporate email-like functionality. Slack is an instant messaging (IM) tool advertised for work purposes that allows users to communicate and share files with team members through public channels, private groups and direct messages. Asana, too, offers team collaboration functionalities that allows users to communicate, share, and monitor progress on individual projects, with the purpose of moving away from email. In addition, both tools offer the possibility to integrate a wide range of other applications, such as Dropbox[13] and Evernote[14], supporting users' flexibility and preferences by creating a tailored tool. In essence, what we are seeing here might be described as a trend towards greater curation of content for particular purposes, which also serves as a way of managing it for later retrieval, which tools such as Slack, Asana and others afford.

Another way of viewing this is that using other channels to transfer information, communicate, share pictures, and store data, is a way for users to step away from having to rely on email retrieval, which they find frustrating and not always efficient. Our younger participants in particular were more aware of other communication channels and articulated more frustration with the current limitations of email systems. By contrast, people who were heavier users of email appeared more willing to put up with the limitations perhaps because they had not been exposed to alternatives.

We might surmise, however, that using ever more channels also exacerbates both managing and retrieving information sent between people. Indeed we saw this as a result of trying to deal with multiple email accounts where participants often struggled to remember from which account an email was sent or where it was received, a problem that was most prevalent when the cross-over happened between work and personal accounts. This highlights the fact that the boundaries between accounts are not always well defined, both in terms of how a user thinks of them and how others perceive them. This was despite the fact that, by having multiple accounts, clearly reflecting different life roles (personal, professional, social, etc.), at least some participants were striving to draw those boundaries to make management and retrieval easier.

To the best of our knowledge no work has looked at the use of these new kinds of tools, particularly comparing them with email. Nor has it examined the added benefits or difficulties that might ensue by using more and different channels to take over from email. While our findings point to why these new tools are becoming popular, more research is needed to explore these issues in depth and to examine their consequences.

Management Through Workarounds

We have seen that both filing strategies as well as the use of multiple channels or accounts have important implications for how email is retrieved. However, taking a cross-device view also highlights other strategies that users take in order to anticipate the need for later retrieval. We saw this particularly in the case of mobile devices, where our participants avoided the need to search for email as much as possible. In part, this was because of storage and connectivity issues; in part, this was due to a perception that search tools on mobile devices are ineffective and difficult to use. As a consequence, our participants used a variety of workaround strategies. For example they took screenshots of booking references, or transferred information through dedicated apps for easier and quicker access to information when needed. Indeed, such workarounds which made certain email messages more conspicuous and easily accessed could also be seen within accounts, such as the practice of highlighting email in the inbox. This seems symptomatic of the difficulty of quickly finding the information one is after. We also found that other mobile devices, like tablets and smartwatches, were not used for searching email. Such findings, although more anecdotal than anything, are interesting as new research is considering how smartwatches are being used [10].

CONSIDERATIONS FOR DESIGN

Whilst our findings are not representative of the whole population, they do provide useful insights on current retrieval practices in today's email ecosystem which is increasingly one based on multiple accounts and multiple devices. While aspects of these behaviours will continue to change with technology, we believe that the themes and insights from our data provide useful pointers on how email clients could be re-designed, or email functionality could fit within the larger scope of new applications and services. Some suggestions are as follows:

- *Better email integration for work.* Our findings suggest that work and personal email both serve important archiving functions, but in different ways. Work email archives are tied more closely with knowledge work tasks and hence communication functions could be better integrated into authoring and workflow tools. More than this, however, the findings suggest that email as an archive is equally important, but when it comes to work-related email, the fractionation of multiple accounts and devices creates additional silos that complicate management and finding. We propose that design should aim to counteract this trend and find more opportunities to tie together email archives with work resources, as well as binding across accounts and devices.

- *Learning from other communication tools.* As popular IM tools take over not only in personal, but also for work communications, email clients could, and perhaps should,

[12] https://asana.com

[13] https://www.dropbox.com

[14] https://evernote.com

learn from such tools. For example, Microsoft recently announced Send[15], a mobile app that allows sending quick messages masked as work emails (similar to Gmail Hangout conversations[16]). However, these systems are still unlinked to email content and cannot be easily searched. They also add to the problem of managing different communication channels. Tools such as Slack, instead, nudge users to curate content in a more easily retrievable way, but the move toward quick, more synchronous communication may change the nature of work in other ways. More work is needed to explore the benefits and drawbacks of IM in the workplace.

- *Designing for short-lived and long-lived content.* Changing our focus from work email, personal email teaches us that email could be imbued with more features which allow paperwork, forms, and facts to be accessed and filed, either for quick access or long term storage. With regard to quick access, strategies that make email content quickly accessible, but then obsolete once used, suggest that it might be useful to look for ways to automatically classify them as such. Self-email largely falls into the category of being utility based, but only useful in the short term. We need to think about mechanisms for making such information conspicuous but temporary. Likewise, some emailed documents such as warranties, instructions, and visas are more likely to be needed long term but can be kept in "cold storage". There is no need for visibility, rather the emphasis is on safe-keeping and back-up. This points to more diverse options for storing and archiving information sent by email.
- *Optimising smartphone search.* Finally, it is clear from our findings that search on mobile devices needs to be improved. While storage and connectivity may be less of an issue in the future, we urge designers to learn from the workarounds we presented. For example, searching on mobiles could be enhanced by allowing users to pin emails from any device in a separate application or to the lock screen, thus providing a new feature to quickly refer to *ephemeral scraps of information*[1]. By moving outside of the inbox, this would also avoid messages on the top being hidden by new incoming emails, and bypass connectivity or storage issues.

CONCLUSIONS

In this paper we present findings from an in-depth qualitative field study which takes a new look at how email management and retrieval occurs in today's multi-account, multi-device world. The findings point to how users' attempts to manage their email through a proliferation of accounts comes with its own problems: different accounts are used for different purposes, the boundaries between accounts can be blurred, and the mechanisms and strategies for managing and retrieving are account-dependent. Likewise, it is clearly important that we have access to and engage with email through a variety of devices, yet when it comes down to it, finding email on handheld devices such as phones is still seen as difficult. Some of this is doubtless due to the need to intertwine work email with the tools of work which mainly reside on the laptop and PC, though we have also pointed to other limitations in the way mobile devices are designed. In all of this, we suggest that one way forward is to think about new features for email tools based on these findings. In the longer term, however, we may well see email evolve not as a stand-alone application, but as a tightly integrated set of communication and archiving functions within more flexible applications and services.

[15] `http://bit.ly/1CSOAGT`

[16] `https://hangouts.google.com`

REFERENCES

1. Deborah Barreau and Bonnie A Nardi. 1995. Finding and reminding: file organization from the desktop. *SIGCHI Bulletin* 27, 3 (1995), 39–43.
2. Victoria Bellotti, Nicolas Ducheneaut, Mark Howard, and Ian Smith. 2003. Taking email to task: the design and evaluation of a task management centered email tool. In *Proc. Conf. on Human Factors in Computing Systems*. ACM, 345–352.
3. Ofer Bergman, Maskit Tene-Rubinstein, and Jonathan Shalom. 2013. The use of attention resources in navigation versus search. *Personal and ubiquitous computing* 17, 3 (2013), 583–590.
4. Richard Boardman and M Angela Sasse. 2004. Stuff goes into the computer and doesn't come out: a cross-tool study of personal information management. In *Proc. Conf. on Human Factors in Computing Systems*. ACM, 583–590.
5. Olha Bondarenko and Ruud Janssen. 2005. Documents at hand: Learning from paper to improve digital technologies. In *Proc. of the Conf. on Human Factors in Computing Systems*. ACM, 121–130.
6. Virginia Braun and Victoria Clarke. 2006. Using thematic analysis in psychology. *Qualitative research in psychology* 3, 2 (2006), 77–101.
7. Robert Capra, Julia Khanova, and Sarah Ramdeen. 2013. Work and personal e-mail use by university employees: PIM practices across domain boundaries. *Journal of the American Society for Information Science and Technology* 64, 5 (2013), 1029–1044.
8. Juan Pablo Carrascal and Karen Church. 2015. An in-situ study of mobile app & mobile search interactions. In *Proc. Conf. on Human Factors in Computing Systems*, Vol. 15. 2739–2748.
9. Scott Carter and Jennifer Mankoff. 2005. When participants do the capturing: the role of media in diary studies. In *Proc. Conf. on Human Factors in Computing Systems*. ACM, 899–908.
10. Marta E Cecchinato, Anna L Cox, and Jon Bird. 2015a. Smartwatches: the Good, the Bad and the Ugly?. In *Extended Abstracts on Human Factors in Computing Systems*. ACM, 2133–2138.
11. Marta E Cecchinato, Anna L Cox, and Jon Bird. 2015b. Working 9-5? Professional Differences in Email and Boundary Management Practices. In *Proc. Conf. on Human Factors in Computing Systems*. ACM, 3989–3998.

12. Edward Cutrell, Susan T Dumais, and Jaime Teevan. 2006a. Searching to eliminate personal information management. *Commun. ACM* 49, 1 (2006), 58–64.
13. Edward Cutrell, Daniel Robbins, Susan Dumais, and Raman Sarin. 2006b. Fast, flexible filtering with phlat. In *Proc. Conf. on Human Factors in Computing Systems*. ACM, 261–270.
14. David Dearman and Jeffery S Pierce. 2008. It's on my other computer!: computing with multiple devices. In *Proc. Conf. on Human Factors in Computing Systems*. ACM, 767–776.
15. Nicolas Ducheneaut and Victoria Bellotti. 2001. E-mail as habitat: an exploration of embedded personal information management. *Interactions* 8, 5 (2001), 30–38.
16. Susan Dumais, Edward Cutrell, Jonathan J Cadiz, Gavin Jancke, Raman Sarin, and Daniel C Robbins. 2003. Stuff I've seen: a system for personal information retrieval and re-use. In *Proc. SIGIR Conf. on Research and development in informaion retrieval*. ACM, 72–79.
17. Danyel Fisher, AJ Brush, Eric Gleave, and Marc A Smith. 2006. Revisiting Whittaker & Sidner's email overload ten years later. In *Proc. 2006 20th Anniversary Conf. on Computer Supported Cooperative Work*. ACM, 309–312.
18. Catherine Grevet, David Choi, Debra Kumar, and Eric Gilbert. 2014. Overload is overloaded: email in the age of Gmail. In *Proc. Conf. on Human Factors in Computing Systems*. ACM, 793–802.
19. Radicati Group. 2015. Email Statistics Report , 2015-2019. (2015).
20. Jacek Gwizdka. 2002. Reinventing the inbox: supporting the management of pending tasks in email. In *Extended Abstracts on Human Factors in Computing Systems*. ACM, 550–551.
21. Benjamin V Hanrahan, Manuel A Pérez-Quiñones, and David Martin. 2014. Attending to Email. *Interacting with Computers* (2014).
22. Daniel Harrison, Paul Marshall, Nadia Bianchi-Berthouze, and Jon Bird. 2015. Activity tracking: barriers, workarounds and customisation. In *Proc. Joint Conf. on Pervasive and Ubiquitous Computing*. ACM, 617–621.
23. Tero Jokela, Jarno Ojala, and Thomas Olsson. 2015. A Diary Study on Combining Multiple Information Devices in Everyday Activities and Tasks. In *Proc. Conf. on Human Factors in Computing Systems*. ACM, 3903–3912.
24. Amy K Karlson, Brian R Meyers, Andy Jacobs, Paul Johns, and Shaun K Kane. 2009. Working overtime: Patterns of smartphone and PC usage in the day of an information worker. In *Pervasive computing*. Springer, 398–405.
25. Fahim Kawsar and AJ Brush. 2013. Home computing unplugged: why, where and when people use different connected devices at home. In *Proc. Joint Conf. on Pervasive and Ubiquitous Computing*. ACM, 627–636.
26. Wendy E Mackay. 1988. Diversity in the use of electronic mail: A preliminary inquiry. *ACM Transactions on Information Systems* 6, 4 (1988), 380–397.
27. Tara Matthews, Jeffrey Pierce, and John Tang. 2009. No smart phone is an island: The impact of places, situations, and other devices on smart phone use. *IBM RJ10452* (2009).
28. George D Montañez, Ryen W White, and Xiao Huang. 2014. Cross-device search. In *Proc. Conf. on Information and Knowledge Management*. ACM, 1669–1678.
29. Antti Oulasvirta and Lauri Sumari. 2007. Mobile kits and laptop trays: managing multiple devices in mobile information work. In *Proc. Conf. on Human factors in Computing Systems*. ACM, 1127–1136.
30. Pew Research. 2014. Device Ownership. (2014).
31. Stephanie Santosa and Daniel Wigdor. 2013. A field study of multi-device workflows in distributed workspaces. In *Proc. Joint Conf. on Pervasive and ubiquitous computing*. ACM, 63–72.
32. Abigail Sellen and Richard Harper. 2002. *The myth of the paperless office*. MIT press.
33. Abigail J Sellen, Rachel Murphy, and Kate L Shaw. 2002. How knowledge workers use the web. In *Proc. Conf. on Human Factors in Computing Systems*. ACM, 227–234.
34. Hilary Smith, Yvonne Rogers, and Mia Underwood. 2003. Managing personal and work email in the same box: overcoming the tensions through new metaphors. *Proc. HOIT Conf.* (2003).
35. Juha Takkinen and Nahid Shahmehri. 1998. Delegation of tasks and dissemination of information in organizations: Restructuring internet e-mail for doing things. *Proc. American Information Society* (1998), 166.
36. Max G Van Kleek, Michael Bernstein, Katrina Panovich, Gregory G Vargas, David R Karger, and mc schraefel. 2009. Note to self: examining personal information keeping in a lightweight note-taking tool. In *Proc. Conf. on Human Factors in Computing Systems*. ACM, 1477–1480.
37. Steve Whittaker, Victoria Bellotti, and Jacek Gwizdka. 2006. Email in personal information management. *Commun. ACM* 49, 1 (2006), 68–73.
38. Steve Whittaker, Tara Matthews, Julian Cerruti, Hernan Badenes, and John Tang. 2011. Am I wasting my time organizing email?: a study of email refinding. In *Proc. Conf. on Human Factors in Computing Systems*. ACM, 3449–3458.
39. Steve Whittaker and Candace Sidner. 1996. Email overload: exploring personal information management of email. In *Proc. Conf. on Human factors in Computing Systems*. ACM, 276–283.

Novel Optical Configurations for Virtual Reality: Evaluating User Preference and Performance with Focus-tunable and Monovision Near-eye Displays

Robert Konrad
Stanford University

Emily A. Cooper
Dartmouth College

Gordon Wetzstein
Stanford University

ABSTRACT

Emerging virtual reality (VR) displays must overcome the prevalent issue of visual discomfort to provide high-quality and immersive user experiences. In particular, the mismatch between vergence and accommodation cues inherent to most stereoscopic displays has been a long standing challenge. In this paper, we evaluate several adaptive display modes afforded by focus-tunable optics or actuated displays that have the promise to mitigate visual discomfort caused by the vergence-accommodation conflict, and improve performance in VR environments. We also explore monovision as an unconventional mode that allows each eye of an observer to accommodate to a different distance. While this technique is common practice in ophthalmology, we are the first to report its effectiveness for VR applications with a custom built set up. We demonstrate that monovision and other focus-tunable display modes can provide better user experiences and improve user performance in terms of reaction times and accuracy, particularly for nearby simulated distances in VR.

Author Keywords

virtual reality; focus cues; user comfort; user performance

INTRODUCTION AND MOTIVATION

Virtual and augmented reality (VR/AR) technologies have the potential to profoundly impact our society in the near future. With a wide range of applications in education, simulation and training, collaborative work, teleconferencing, scientific visualization, remote-controlled vehicles, telesurgery, basic vision research, entertainment, and phobia treatment, VR and AR provide a platform for immersive user experiences and unprecedented interaction techniques unmatched by other consumer electronics devices.

Recent advances in immersive near-eye display technologies promise consumer products to be within reach. Along with further reducing latency, increasing display resolution, and providing compelling and interactive multi-modal experiences, the support for visually comfortable experiences may be one of the most important characteristics to determine the success of VR/AR technology. Current-generation

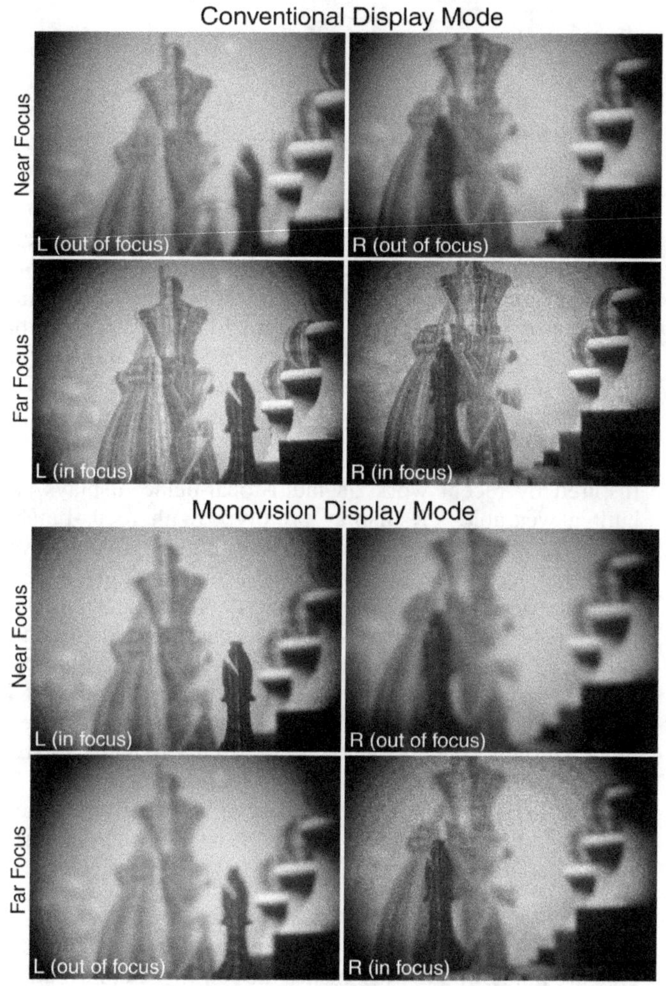

Figure 1. Focus-tunable near-eye display with different rendering modes. In the top panels, we illustrate via photographs how the images seen by each eye in a typical near-eye display are only focused properly when the eyes are focused at a relatively far distance (lower row). When the eyes focus near, to match objects simulated to be near, both eyes' images are blurry (upper row). Monovision is an alternative display mode where the lenses of the two eyes have different focal lengths, allowing for each eye to accommodate at a different distance. The bottom panels illustrate this mode. When the camera is focused relatively far, the left eye's image is out of focus and the right eye's image is sharp (lower row). When the camera is focused near, the relationship reverses. We asked whether this display mode could improve visual comfort and performance.

near-eye displays can simulate many of the depth cues typically available to the visual system, including both monocular and binocular cues (disparity and vergence). Unfortunately, focus cues (accommodation and retinal blur) are usually not

CHI 2016, May 7–12, 2016, San Jose, California, USA.

ACM ISBN 978-1-4503-3362-7/16/05 ...$15.00.
http://dx.doi.org/10.1145/2858036.2858140

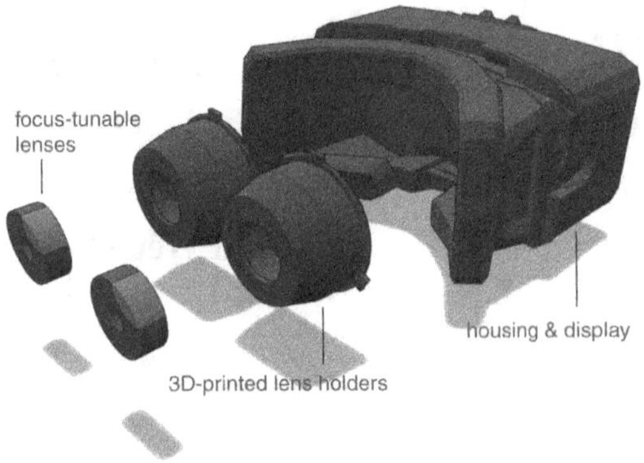

Figure 2. Focus-tunable near-eye display prototype configuration.

supported, resulting in conflicting visual stimulation known as the vergence-accommodation conflict (Fig. 1, top panels) (see [21] for review). This conflict can cause visual discomfort and fatigue, and compromised visual clarity [37]. Using benchtop *multi-focal-plane displays*, it has been shown that correct or nearly correct focus cues that reduce this conflict can also improve stereoscopic correspondence matching [16], 3D shape perception [42], and discrimination of larger depth intervals [14].

Inspired by recent work on multi-focal-plane displays, we built a wearable VR display prototype with focus-tunable optics (programmable liquid lenses) and perceptually-driven rendering algorithms that allows the accommodative state of the observer's eyes to be adjusted adaptively and independently (see Figs. 1, 2). This system can be used to generate correct or nearly-correct focus cues via time-multiplexed or adaptive focus image presentation, or via *monovision*. In monovision, an optical augmentation that is currently a treatment option for patients who lose the ability to focus, the two eyes observe the world through two lenses with different focal lengths. For some wearable display applications, monovision may be an effective tool to counteract the vergence-accommodation conflict.

Contributions to Human-Computer Interaction

While the ideas of gaze-contingent retinal focus and monovision are not new, our work makes the following contributions that advance the field towards integrating these improvements into standard VR applications:

- We quantify the perceptual benefits of multiple different focus-tunable display modes.
- We demonstrate and evaluate monovision for mitigating the vergence-accommodation conflict in VR displays.
- We directly compare monovision and focus-tunable modes w.r.t. user preference and performance.
- We examine factors that are relevant to typical HCI applications, such as reaction time and perceptual accuracy.

Our user studies advance our understanding of human factors in VR and suggest that monovision is a viable and low-cost path to mitigate the vergence-accommodation conflict. A system capable of producing both monovision and adaptive focus can be implemented with focus-tunable optics, as done in our studies, or with actuated displays. Such flexible systems can provide a valuable tool for HCI and graphics research. However, low-cost monovision setups can also be implemented using static lenses with different focal lenths or using two staggered screens.

However, it is also important to note that the current prototype has several limitations, most importantly a limited FOV and a lack of gaze tracking. In the current study, we employed a somewhat constrained setting with the field of view afforded by our prototype, and we encouraged users to fixate on one target at a time. Furthermore, the potential long-term effects of the monovision configuration on comfort in individuals with normal vision are unknown. Nevertheless, the insights we gained will directly benefit future HMDs as technology advances to overcome these limitations.

RELATED WORK

Focus-supporting Near-eye Displays

Sutherland's vision of electronic head mounted displays [40] has become practical and affordable with recent developments in the consumer electronics industry. However, providing accurate focus cues remains a major challenge for these types of displays. Possible options include *volumetric displays* that mechanically [10, 20] scan a projection surface to create a 3D display volume within which an observer can accommodate. Unfortunately, the form factor of these devices is not suitable for wearable displays. *Multi-focal-plane displays* approximate such a volume using a few virtual display planes that are generated by beam splitters [7, 1] or focus-tunable optics [34, 41, 17, 24, 27, 36, 25, 32]. Two possible ways to create focus cues with focus-tunable optics have been described: temporal multiplexing and gaze-contingent display. For temporal multiplexing, the focus is periodically swept through the volume and synchronized with the display update. However, display refresh rates beyond those offered by current-generation microdisplays are usually required and flicker may be perceived. Gaze-contingency can be achieved using eye tracking (e.g. [35]) by either estimating the vergence angle of the eyes or by analyzing the depth buffer of the displayed images at the gaze-tracked location. An example *gaze-contingent focus display* was implemented by Sugihara and Miyasato [39]: two monitors are physically moved towards or away from the observer based on their gaze direction. Although Peli [33] outlines prior work that proposes the idea of gaze-contingent focus, we are not aware of anyone having reported a practical gaze-contingent, focus-tunable display prototype yet, although this would be an obvious next step.

Monovision

Monovision refers to a common treatment for presbyopia, a condition that often occurs with age in which people lose the ability to focus their eyes on nearby objects. Currently, there is no treatment available for presbyopia that restores the eyes' ability to adaptively focus. As such, the goal of treatments such as surgery, bifocals, and monovision is to augment the presbyopic patient's optics in the way that restores the range of distances over which they can experience clear vision [13, 11]. To accomplish this goal, the monovision treatment method involves focusing one eye at a fixed near distance, and the other eye at a fixed far distance. This is accomplished via contact lenses, spectacles, or surgery. Ideally, this correction allows the patient to experience clear vision over a range of distances via whichever eye is closest to the correct focus (see [9] for a review). However, the differing focal distances of the two eyes means that one eye is necessarily out of focus at any given distance, so patients with monovision can experience overall decreases in acuity and stereoscopic depth perception (likely because the two eyes' images are dissimilar) [2, 13]. Nonetheless, patient satisfaction after monovision correction tends to be quite high [9]. Thus, it seems possible that a technique similar to monovision might be able to ameliorate some of the perceptual and visual-comfort consequences of the vergence-accommodation conflict in near-eye displays, by essentially minimizing the conflict in one eye at a time. Indeed, the idea of exotic optical configurations for near-eye displays, including monovision and bifocal lenses, was first described by Marran and Schor [30]. The idea for using monovision for this application has continued to be of interest [33] and benchtop implementations were proposed [26]. An evaluation of these ideas had not been reported when we conducted our work; however, we recently because aware of a concurrent study [19]. Our display prototype enabled us to assess the effectiveness of a monovision optics configuration, along with a variety of other focus-tunable display modes.

Retinal Blur Rendering

In addition to the prior work investigating the perceptual improvements associated with benchtop multi-focal-plane displays (which include both accommodative and retinal blur cues) summarized in the introduction, other researchers have investigated the perceptual effects of *gaze-contingent retinal blur* rendering on its own. Because gaze-contingent retinal blur rendering only requires a gaze-tracker and fast/realistic blur rendering techniques—no specialized optics are needed—it is useful to know if this type of display mode on its own offers improvements over standard displays. Several previous studies have examined the effect of this rendering technique on visual experience and performance with benchtop displays [5, 15, 28, 31, 8]. In these studies, gaze-tracking and estimated or ground-truth depth maps were used to adaptively update the depth of field of an image depending on the distance of the object that the participants were fixating. Several studies reported improvements in subjective viewing experience [15, 31], however, the results for performance improvements on a variety of visual tasks were more mixed [5, 31]. One study showed that combining this technique with stereo display significantly decreased the time needed for participants to achieve binocular fusion under some conditions [28]. Given the mixture of results, it seemed worthwhile to assess an implementation of retinal blur rendering in the current near-eye display system.

Light Field Displays

Recently, microlens-based near-eye light field displays have been shown to support focus cues [23], albeit at low spatial resolution. Building on emerging compressive light field display technology [22, 43, 29], Huang et al. [18] recently demonstrated the first high-resolution near-eye light field display for VR applications. Whereas Huang's work achieves focus cues at moderate spatial resolution without temporal multiplexing, eye tracking, or focus-tunable optics, the required light field factorizations place a high demand on computation. Furthermore, reduced light throughput and diffraction blur of stacked liquid crystal displays are problematic for see-through AR display modes. The focus-tunable display modes evaluated in this paper are complimentary to recent developments in near-eye light field displays. By exploring focus-tunable stereoscopic displays, we hope to provide new insights and quantify the advantages of focus-tunable displays for both AR and VR applications. Finally, we anticipate the proposed techniques to enhance visual comfort also in light field displays, for example by optimizing the perceived depth of field in possible future implementations of focus-tunable near-eye light field displays via monovision.

Field of view	$26°(H) \times 26°(V)$
Resolution	488×488 px
Accommodation range	10.5–∞ cm
Latency	11.5 ms rendering 15 ms focus adjustment

Table 1. Overview of focus-tunable HMD characteristics.

Figure 3. Photograph of HMD prototype and focus-tunable lens.

FOCUS-TUNABLE NEAR-EYE DISPLAY SYSTEM

Hardware

Building on commodity electronics and optics components, we built a focus-tunable display based on the Oculus Rift DK2. The original lenses are replaced by two independently controllable Optotune EL-10-30-VIS-LD focus-tunable liquid lenses, driven by an Optotune Lens Driver 4 (see Fig. 3). Each of these plano-convex lenses has a diameter of 10 mm and they are tunable to a focal length range of 52–140 mm (19.23–7.14 D) throughout the visible spectrum. The lenses are mounted at a distance of 6 cm from the display panel. In our system this corresponds to an accommodation range of 10.5–∞ cm. The response time is approximately 15 ms at room temperature. The update of the lens focal state and display were synchronized. The focus tunable lenses are connected to a host computer (Dell XPS 8700 workstation, Intel 378 i7 CPU, 8 GB RAM, NVIDIA GTX 690 GPU) via USB and all rendering software is written in C++ and OpenGL.

The main limitation of the prototype are the small apertures of the focus-tunable lenses, which severely restrict the observed field of view and also crop most of the screen. When the lenses are set to a focal length of 8.5 cm the field of view is approximately 26°, which corresponds to a 488 × 488 px viewing area. The field of view changes by 1° within the focal length range. Note that the field of view limitation is specific to of our dynamically-switchable prototype; large fields of view with any of the discussed display modes on their own can be easily achieved with fixed-focus lenses.

Software

All hardware, including the display, the internal measurement unit (IMU), and the focus-tunable lenses are controlled from a C++ program. The render engine is embedded in that code; we use OpenGL with a physically plausible approximation of retinal blur / depth of field effect implemented in a fragment shader. We implemented an approximation of retinal blur via adaptive depth of field (DOF) rendering.

To perform the rendering, we used image space with the aid of a depth map. As explained in [4], there are several criteria that image space methods would ideally satisfy to simulate DOF blur: choice of point spread function (PSF), lack of intensity leakage, lack of depth discontinuity artifacts, proper simulation of partial occlusions, and high performance. However, no post-processing is able to achieve all of these simultaneously. In the experiments run, only a portion of the above were necessary. Depth discontinuity artifacts never occurred in the foveal region because the in-focus target was never occluded, and although our algorithm could handle such artifacts, they were not prevalent. Therefore, we focused on implementing two criteria well: lack of intensity leakage (a blurred background never blurs on top of an in-focus foreground) and high performance (critical for VR applications).

We followed the method in [44] which uses accurate circles of confusion to simulate DOF effects by adjusting weights of a non-linear filter. In our prototype system, we render two 960 × 1080 px scenes to one framebuffer for each eye and then apply the retinal blur to the whole framebuffer. The process of rendering the scenes and applying the blur takes 11.5 ms (86.9 FPS) on average across the three scenes that we tested. On average the retinal blur takes 7.67 ms to render. Note that focus adjustment in the lens can be triggered prior to applying the depth of field shader, which minimizes overall latency.

EVALUATION

We conducted three user studies to assess the effects of the focus-tunable display system and adaptive DOF rendering on VR applications. The goal of these studies was (1) to determine if users have a *preference* for engaging with VR environments using different display modes, and (2) to determine whether user *performance* on tasks within VR environments is affected by different display modes. The research protocol was approved by the Institutional Review Board at Stanford University and all participants gave informed consent.

Participants: Twelve users participated in all three studies. Participants were recruited from the university population (age range 18-28, 3 females). All participants reported having normal or corrected-to-normal vision, and passed a standard Randot stereo vision test. Two volunteers were excluded from participating because they did not pass the stereo vision test.

Display modes: For each study, we compared 5 modes:

- *Normal* mode: equivalent to standard usage of the Oculus, the focus-tunable lenses were disabled (but present) and VR environments were rendered with infinite DOF
- *Adaptive DOF* mode: the focus-tunable lenses were disabled, but VR environments were rendered with adaptive DOF that placed the main point-of-interest in the scene at the center of the DOF
- *Adaptive Focus* mode: the focus-tunable lenses were engaged and focused adaptively to the distance of the main point-of-interest, and VR environments were rendered with infinite DOF
- *Adaptive Focus + DOF* mode: the focus-tunable lenses were engaged and focused adaptively to the distance of the main point-of-interest, and adaptive DOF was used to also put this point at the center of the DOF
- *Monovision* mode: the focus-tunable lenses were fixed at two different focal distances for the two eyes, 2 diopters for the left eye and infinity for the right eye, and adaptive DOF rendering was enabled

Throughout the descriptions of these user studies, we will refer to the simulated distances of objects in the VR environment in terms of diopters (D), which are measured in inverse meters, as well as in meters (m). Also, note that our prototype does not include eye-tracking. Thus, in each user study, the participants were instructed as to where to look in the scene via the presentation of specific targets.

User Preferences Study

Methods: In this study, we asked users to visually explore a VR environment and rank the overall quality of their experience for different display modes. Users were fitted with the display system, and then allowed to switch freely through the five display modes for a single VR environment; the screen was not blanked when switching between display modes. The environment consisted of a static scene with a single target floating dynamically within the scene (Figure 4, left panel). For the four adaptive conditions (*Adaptive DOF*, *Adaptive Focus*, *Adaptive Focus + DOF*, and *Monovision*), this target was treated as the main point-of-interest for which the DOF and/or focus were set. The simulated distance of the target ranged from 3.33 to 0.25 D (0.3 to 4 m). For the non-adaptive, fixed focus reference mode, the in-focus accommodative distance was 1.3 m (0.77 D)[1]. For all display modes using a rendered depth of field, we assume a pupil diameter of 4 mm. The users were asked to rank the modes from 1-5 in terms of their general viewing experience, with 1 being the best score. As the users set their rankings, a number on the floating target was updated to indicate the ranking of the current mode. The initial display mode and the order through which they were switched was randomized for each session, and users were encouraged to view each mode at least once before starting to rank them. They were also encouraged to focus on the floating rectangle during the task, although this instruction was not strictly enforced. They repeated their ranking three times for three different VR environments.

[1]Similar to DK2; see Oculus Best Practices Guide

Figure 4. Example screenshots from the user studies. For the user preference study (left), we ask users to fixate on a target moving periodically in depth within a static scene. The target shows a number with the user's ranking of the current display mode, while the character is randomly associated with the display mode. For the visual clarity (center) and depth judgment (right) tasks, we display small targets that are magnified in the insets.

Results: On average, the users ranked the normal mode the lowest, and they preferred the display modes with adaptive focus. Figure 5 shows the results for each condition. The bar heights indicate the mean ranking (and standard error) across subjects. Individual circles show the mean rankings for each individual user. The rankings for the Adaptive Focus and Adaptive Focus + DOF conditions were highest (2.2 and 2.4, respectively). Individual user data reveal that these two modes were often selected as either the first or second choice. Normal mode and Adaptive DOF alone had the lowest rankings (3.9 and 3.5, respectively). The Monovision mode fell in the middle (3.2).

To test for statistical significance, we performed a Friedman test and follow up multiple comparison tests (using the Tukey-Kramer method) on the mean ranking, after averaging the repeated trials for each subject. These tests determined if display mode had a significant effect on user mean rankings, and which specific display modes resulted in significant improvements above Normal mode, respectively [38]. The Friedman test indicated a significant effect of display mode ($p < 0.01$). A followup multiple comparison test with a significance threshold of $p < 0.05$ showed that the rankings for Adaptive Focus and Adaptive Focus + DOF were significantly better than Normal mode, but the other display modes were not.

These results suggest that manipulating focal distances adaptively can improve subjective viewing experience. While the two other display modes (Adaptive DOF and Monovision) did not significantly improve user rankings, the results indicate that they also did not degrade viewing experience. Thus, if either of these display modes confers a performance advantage, they might be able to do so without any cost to subjective experience.

After each user completed this experiment, we also conducted an informal debriefing interview. Users consistently commented that their rankings were affected by the "blurring of the background" and not being able to fuse the floating square at close distances. Also, many commented that the lenses tended to get warm.

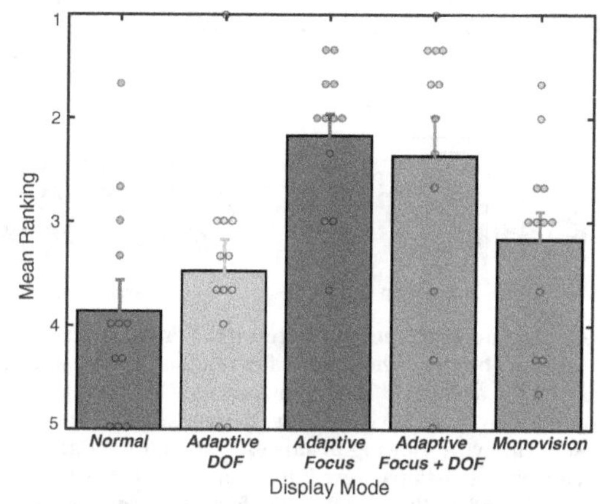

Figure 5. User preference study results. Bar heights indicate the mean ranking for each display mode across all users. A ranking of one is for the best experience, and five the worst. Note that one is at the top of the ordinate axis and five is at the bottom. Error bars are the between-subjects standard error of the mean. Circles indicate the mean ranking for each individual user across three repetitions.

User Performance Studies

Methods: In this study, we asked if user performance on two different tasks in a VR environment was affected by the different display modes. In the *Visual Clarity* task, users identified the orientation of a small letter "E" placed on a target within a VR scene. In the *Depth Judgment* task, users made a relative depth judgment between two targets within the scene. The procedure and stimulus for each task were almost identical. At the start of each trial, the user was instructed to fixate an initial target, a textured gray square, presented in the center of the visual field. This target could appear at one of three simulated viewing distances: 0.4, 1, and 2 D (2.5, 1, and 0.5 m). Once they were fixating, the user initiated the trial with a key press. After a random delay (uniformly distributed between 0 and 1 seconds), the first target disappeared and a second target appeared at one of five simulated depths relative to the viewing distance. In diopters, these relative distances were the same for each viewing distance: -0.5, -0.2, 0, 0.2, and 0.5 D. That is, sometimes the second target appeared in the same distance plane as the first, sometimes it was closer to the user, and sometimes it was farther away. Obviously, the relative depth in meters depended on the viewing distance of the first target. For the farthest viewing distance (0.4 D), the relative distance of -0.5 D was excluded because this was an impossible object distance. The second target appeared randomly within a circle indicated by the intersection of a 2° cone and that distance plane. In both experiments, all of the

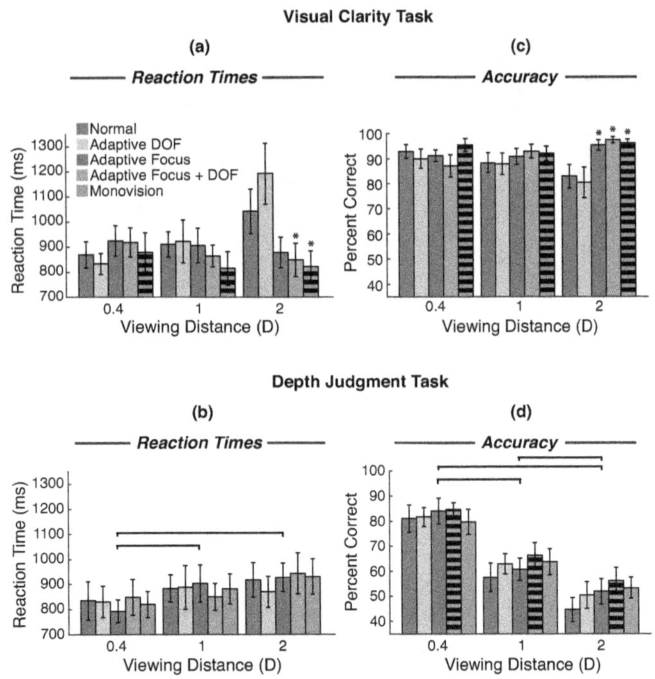

Figure 6. User performance study results. For each performance task, panels (a) and (b) show the results for reaction times, and (c) and (d) show results for accuracy. Each bar indicates the results for one of the display modes, averaged across users (see legend). Bars are grouped and plotted separately by viewing distance. Note that the data for each user from each viewing distance were initially averaged over the different target depths. To reflect the ANOVA, the farthest target depth for viewing distances of 1 and 2 D are excluded, so that the same set of four target depths are included in each group. For data from all individual targets (see Fig. 7). Error bars indicate standard errors across subjects.

targets subtended the same visual angle regardless of the simulated distance.

In the *Visual Clarity* task, the second target had a small letter "E" (6 pixels in height, or 22.59 arcminutes), which was facing upwards, downwards, leftwards, or rightwards (Figure 4, middle panel). Users responded with a key press to indicate the letter's orientation. In the *Depth Judgment* task, the second target instead simply had a number "2" on it, and the users responded whether this target was closer, farther, or at the same distance as the first target (Figure 4, right panel). In both tasks, the users were instructed to make their response as quickly as possible. The two tasks were run in two separate sessions. Within each task, each combination of viewing distance and relative distance was repeated five times for each user, and the order of presentation was randomized. We recorded the reaction times (time between when the second target appeared and when the user logged their response) and accuracy (whether or not they responded correctly).

Analysis: To examine differences in reaction time, for each user we calculated the median reaction time over all repetitions of a given trial type (display mode × viewing distance × target relative depth). We used the median in order to reduce the impact of outlier trials with very long reaction times. To examine differences in accuracy, we calculated the percentage of trials in which each subject responded correctly for each trial type. For each of the user performance studies, a 5 × 3 repeated measures analysis of variance (ANOVA) was performed to test for statistically significant main effects and interactions of two fixed factors (Display Mode and Viewing Distance). Display Mode had five levels (Normal, Adaptive DOF, Adaptive Focus, Adaptive Focus + DOF, and Monovision) and Viewing Distance had three levels (0.4D, 1D, and 2D). To avoid having a large number of factors, we did not examine the effect of each individual target depth with the ANOVA. Thus, this analysis was performed on data collapsed across target depths for each viewing distance, with the farthest target depth (-0.5D) excluded from analysis because it was not present at all viewing distances. We also calculated generalized eta squared (GES) measures of effect size [3]. Follow-up t-tests were performed using all data points to examine the statistically significant effects from the ANOVA, and p-values were corrected for multiple comparisons using the Holm method. These t-tests were further limited to three different planned comparisons which were focused on examining effects of viewing distance, and differences between Normal mode and the other display modes: (1) comparing reaction time/accuracy for each viewing distance, (2) comparing each augmented display mode to Normal mode, (3) comparing each augmented display mode to Normal mode for each viewing distance separately.

Results

The analyses suggest that adaptive focus and monovision display modes can result in better user performance under a number of conditions. The results for both performance studies are summarized in Figure 6 and Figure 7. Figure 6 shows the average reaction time and accuracy across users for each combination of display mode and viewing distance. The results for the Normal display mode are shown in blue. Display modes that were significantly different from normal (main effects), are indicated by striped bars, interactions between display mode and viewing distance are indicated by asterisks above the bars that were significantly different from the normal mode, and main effects of viewing distance are indicated by horizontal lines. Figure 7 shows the same data, separated out for each individual target location, and thus reveals under which conditions some of the largest differences between display modes appear. For simplicity, in Figure 7 we show the mean reaction times and accuracy data for each mode relative to the Normal mode. This way of plotting makes it clear whether the added features (DOF, focus-tunable lenses, monovision) increased or decreased reaction times. Points that lie near zero indicate that reaction times and accuracy were similar to those in Normal mode. Points above zero (white portion) indicate faster reaction times and better accuracy, points below zero (gray portion) indicate slower reaction times and worse accuracy. For both reaction times and accuracy, differences were calculated by taking the difference between the Normal mode data and the other display modes, such that differences are represented as changes in reaction time in ms, and changes in percent correct in percentage points, rather than ratios. Each column shows the results for all target depths for a single simulated viewing distance.

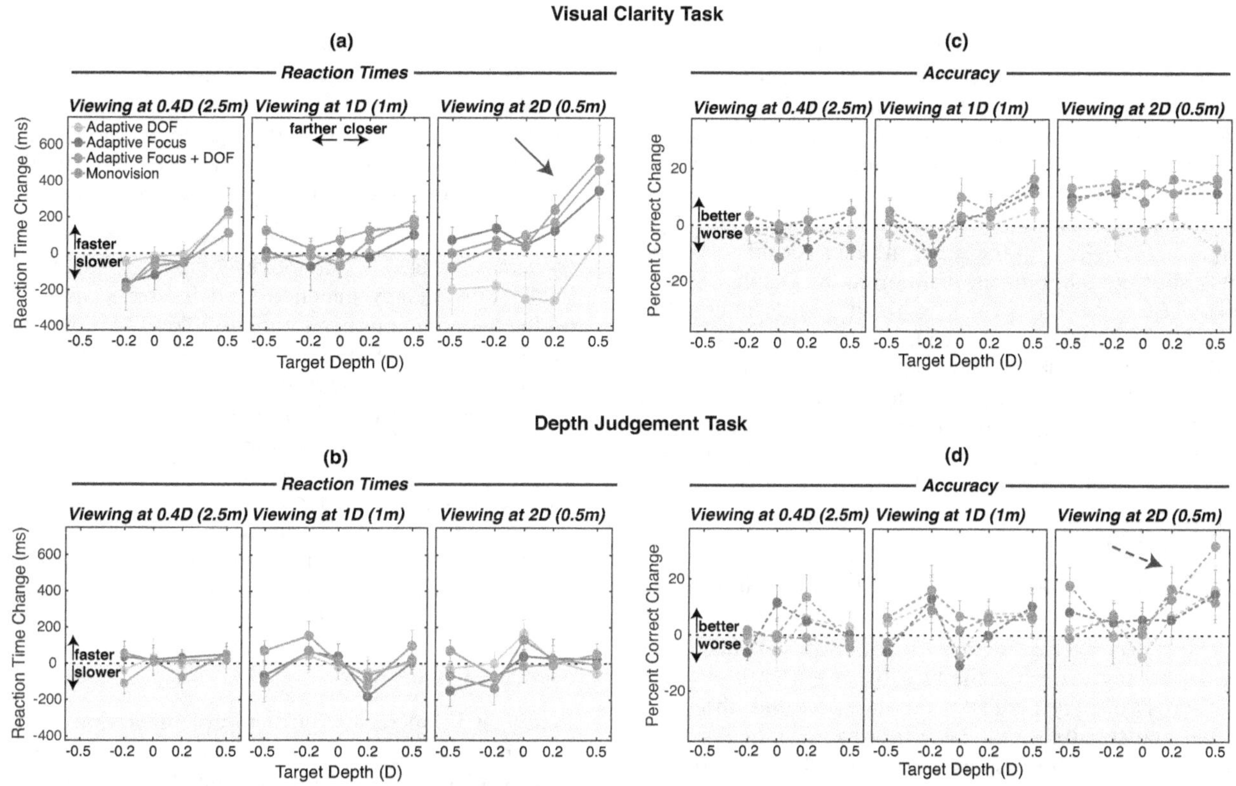

Figure 7. User performance study results for all targets. Panels (a) and (b) show the results for reaction times, and (c) and (d) show results for accuracy. Each colored line shows the results for a different display mode (see legend). Results for Normal mode are not shown, because the results for each of the other modes were normalized by taking the difference from the reaction time or percent correct for Normal mode. These differences were calculated for each user, and the mean and standard errors of these differences across users are shown as circles and vertical bars.

Visual Clarity/Reaction Times: Across all trial types, the average reaction time in the Visual Clarity task was 913 ms. Particularly for the nearest viewing distance (2 D, 0.5 m), several display modes resulted in faster reaction times than the Normal mode. The ANOVA showed a significant main effect of Display Mode, F(4,44) = 3.8, $p < 0.01$, and a significant interaction between Display Mode and Viewing Distance, F(8,88) = 6.4, $p < 0.001$. The sizes of these effects (GES) were 0.04 and 0.09, respectively. These and most other effects in these data were in the range of small to medium [3]. Follow up t-tests showed that the reaction times for the Monovision mode across all viewing distances were significantly faster than for Normal mode ($p < 0.05$), and that at the nearest viewing distance (2 D), the reaction times for Monovision and Adaptive Focus + DOF were also significantly faster ($ps < 0.05$) (See Figure 6(a)). Figure 7(a) shows that the display modes with Adaptive Focus and Monovision resulted in faster reaction times than the Normal mode particularly when the simulated distances were relatively close to the user (2 D/0.5 m or less; blue arrow in right panel). This advantage was largely due to the fact that reaction times in the Normal mode slowed down at these distances, whereas reaction times in the adaptive focus conditions remained relatively stable. In Normal display mode, the virtual screen is optically placed at 0.77D, therefore simulating a viewing distance at 2 D results in the strongest vergence-accommodation conflict (targets appearing from 1.5 D to 2.5 D). The larger conflict may lead to longer image fusion/response times, hence the increased baseline reaction times. At the 2 D viewing distance, the Adaptive DOF mode actually tended to result in slower reaction times than Normal mode (yellow line), however, this slow down did not reach statistical significance.

Depth Judgment/Reaction Times: Unlike the Visual Clarity task, reaction times in the Depth Judgment task did not vary substantially as a function of display mode. Across all trial types, the average reaction time was 884 ms. The ANOVA showed a significant main effect of Viewing Distance, F(2,22) = 7.3, $p < 0.01$, $GES = 0.03$, but no effect of Display Mode and no interaction. Follow up t-tests showed that pair-wise comparisons between the farthest and two closer viewing distances were significant ($ps < 0.01$), indicating that reaction times tended to slow down for closer targets, but that there was no significant effect on reaction times of the different Display Modes (See Figure 6(b) and Figure 7(b)).

Visual Clarity/Accuracy: The reaction time data suggest that the adaptive focus display modes offer an advantage in terms of being able to react quickly to nearby stimuli within a VR environment. However, if this increase in speed was also associated with a decrease in performance accuracy, it might be undesirable. Thus, we also asked whether users' response accuracy was affected by the different display modes. Across all trial types in the Visual Clarity task, average accuracy was 91% (chance performance would be 25%). This is not surprising, because all users reported having normal vision, and the "E" was large enough that it was clearly visible if the eyes were properly fixated and focused. Thus, incorrect trials likely result from users choosing to respond before the target was clearly focused, in order to comply with the instruction to respond as quickly as possible. Interestingly, user accuracy did not decrease for the display modes with faster reaction times, but actually increased slightly (See Figure 6(c) and Figure 7(c)). As with the reaction times for this task, the ANOVA showed a significant main effect of Display Mode, F(4,44) = 3.6, $p < 0.05$, $GES = 0.07$, and an interaction between Display Mode and Viewing Distance, F(8,88) = 4.9, $p < 0.001$, $GES = 0.08$. Follow up t-tests showed that the accuracy results followed a similar pattern to the reaction times results: Monovision had better accuracy across all distances ($p < 0.01$), and at the nearest viewing distance (2D), the accuracy for Monovision, Adaptive Focus + DOF, and (in addition) Adaptive Focus display modes were also significantly more accurate ($ps < 0.01$).

Depth Judgment/Accuracy: In the Depth Judgment task, the overall performance was worse than the Visual Clarity task (67% correct on average across all trial types, chance was 33%). Surprisingly, despite the fact that reaction times were similar across display modes in this task, we did observe a small but statistically significant improvement in accuracy with one adaptive focus display mode (See Figure 6(d)). The ANOVA showed a significant and large main effect of Viewing Distance, F(2,22) = 44.7, $p < 0.001$, $GES = 0.39$ and a main effect of Display Mode, F(4,44) = 2.7, $p < 0.05$, $GES = 0.02$. Follow up t-tests showed that all pair-wise comparisons between viewing distances were significant, indicating worse accuracy for closer targets ($ps < 0.001$). There was also a significant improvement in accuracy relative to Normal mode for the Adaptive Focus + DOF mode ($p < 0.01$). An examination of the individual target data (Figure 7(d)) reveals a similar pattern to that observed in the Visual Clarity Task reaction times: the most improvement in performance with the adaptive focus and monovision modes occurs when the simulated distances are relatively near to the observer (purple arrow).

DISCUSSION

In summary, we introduce and evaluate monovision for mitigating the vergence-accommodation conflict in VR displays, we quantify the perceptual benefits of newly available focus-tunable display modes, and we directly compare monovision and focus-tunable modes w.r.t. user preference and performance. Our user studies reveal that monovision and adaptive focus can offer higher-quality VR experiences and better user performance than conventional display modes, particularly for objects and tasks performed at nearby depths. Gaze-contingent depth of field rendering on its own, as proposed in previous work, may not offer the same benefits as monovision or gaze-contingent focus.

Interpretation of User Study Results

The results of our user studies support the idea that focus adaptability and monovision can improve user experience and performance with stereoscopic near-eye displays. We can conclude that particularly in cases where it is desirable to simulate object distances that are relatively close to the user (less than 0.5 m), focus adaptable technology provides desirable benefits. This makes sense, because without adaptable lenses, the fixed focal distance of the display we used for testing is 1.3 m. Thus, without the adaptable lenses, simulated near distances produce a large vergence-accommodation conflict.

Somewhat surprisingly, the improvements of the adaptive refocusing conditions (Adaptive Focus and Adaptive Focus + DOF) were nearly matched, and in some cases surpassed, by the Monovision display mode. This is an intriguing finding, because while implementing eye-tracking to guide adaptive focusing in near-eye displays with focus tunable optics poses substantial technical challenges, monovision can easily and inexpensively be implemented by simply placing two fixed lenses of different powers. What we do not know is whether any potential long-term discomfort associated with decoupling the accommodative distances of the two eyes in monovision would be any greater than the discomfort that is already associated with the vergence-accommodation conflict in near-eye displays. In the current work, the user studies were relatively short in duration, so this will be an interesting avenue for future work.

Lastly, it is unclear why our implementation of the Adaptive DOF display mode alone reduced reaction times, in the context of prior work showing that retinal blur cues can aid binocular fusion [28]. Although neither of our tasks explicitly tested binocular fusion, it would be reasonable to assume that if time to fusion was substantially faster, the users might have responded faster in the Visual Clarity and/or Depth Judgment task. One possibility is that we used computer generated scenes, which are likely less cluttered and detailed than the natural images used the prior study.

Alternative Hardware Implementations

The insights drawn from our experiments can serve as guidelines for the design of future near-eye displays. If the user's gaze direction can be either measured (i.e. using gaze tracking) or otherwise predicted, gaze-contingent focus is the most natural viewing condition and should be used if possible. The primary benefit of monovision, as an alternative to gaze-contingent focus, is its simplicity. It can be implemented using focus-tunable lenses, as demonstrated in our prototype, using actuated screens in the HMD, or using conventional, fixed-focal length lenses. The latter option can be readily implemented with any existing HMD - simply mount two different lenses in the HMD and adjust the stereo rendering. We chose focus-tunable lenses for our prototype, because it allows us to quickly switch between different rendering modes to quantify and compare them with user studies.

Additional Limitations

Focus-tunable lenses require a fair amount of power and, unfortunately, much of this power is dissipated as heat. The lenses tend to heat up particularly when pushed to low focal lengths. According to the manufacturer, when the lenses heat up the fluid inside of the lenses expands in volume. Therefore the focal length of the lenses decreases by as much as 0.67 D per 10°C temperature increase. We accounted for this by calibrating the interaction between current, focal length, and temperature of the lenses. On average, there was a 0.08 D error over the range of focal lengths used, with the highest error being 0.17 D. However, we know that the accommodation system of the human visual system is not perfect. People can naturally have fairly large accommodative lags during natural viewing situations (i.e. they do not accommodate enough to a near stimulus) [12] and the accommodative state of the eye can fluctuate by several 10ths of a diopter [6]. Thus, it is currently unclear how precisely the focus tunable lenses need to be calibrated in order to provide perceptual benefits.

Future Work

In the near future, we would like to run more user studies that evaluate these new display modes for VR applications. Our current study included a typical user sample size (see [28, 31, 15]), however, it would be advantageous in the future to increase the sample size, the variety of tasks, and the duration of time during which the prototype is worn. Furthermore, for the monovision display made, the choice of focal length could be varied to determine the best accommodative state for VR. With a setting of 2 D, we follow typical settings reported in the clinical literature [2, 9], but other settings are certainly possible. Testing monovision for see-through augmented reality applications would be interesting, because in that setting the real world provides natural focus cues that are optically overlaid with the virtual image and may make monovision display modes even more comfortable and interesting. In the long run, the effectiveness of monovision should be tested as a function that varies over the entire visual field, such that unconventional fixed optics (e.g., bi-focal and multi-focal lenses) can be optimized for spatially-varying, wide field of view monovision display modes in VR and AR.

CONCLUSION

Emerging near-eye displays have the potential to profoundly impact our society by providing a fundamentally new tool for education, collaborative work, scientific visualization, remote-controlled vehicles, training and simulation, and surgical training. Providing visually comfortable experiences with these displays, however, is a long standing challenge. With this work, we provide possible ways to decrease visual discomfort using focus tunable display modes and monovision. We have evaluated monovision and demonstrated that it can help users to detect targets more accurately and in less time than what is possible with conventional stereoscopic HMDs, without sacrificing comfortable viewing experiences. We believe our technology to be a crucial advance towards more immersive and comfortable VR experiences.

Acknowledgements

We thank Tom Malzbender, Bennett Wilburn, and Marty Banks for fruitful discussions and Intel, Meta, Huawei, and Google for generous support.

REFERENCES

1. K. Akeley, S.J Watt, A.R Girshick, and M.S Banks. 2004. A Stereo Display Prototype with Multiple Focal Distances. *ACM Trans. Graph.* 23, 3 (2004), 804–813.
2. A. Back. 1995. Factors Influencing Success and Failure in Monovision. *Int. Contact Lens Clinic* 22, 7 (1995), 165–72.
3. R. Bakeman. 2005. Recommended effect size statistics for repeated measures designs. *Behavior research methods* 37, 3 (2005), 379–384.
4. B. A. Barsky and T. J. Kosloff. 2008. Algorithms for Rendering Depth of Field Effects in Computer Graphics. In *Proc. Int. Conf. on Computers*. 999–1010.
5. J. P. Brooker and P.M. Sharkey. 2001. Operator performance evaluation of controlled depth of field in a stereographically displayed virtual environment. *Proc. SPIE* 4297 (2001), 408–417.
6. WN Charman and G. Heron. 1988. Fluctuations in accommodation: a review. *Ophthalmic & physiological optics* 8, 2 (1988), 153–164.
7. E. Dolgoff. 1997. Real-Depth imaging: a new 3D imaging technology with inexpensive direct-view (no glasses) video and other applications. *Proc. SPIE 3012* (1997), 282–288.
8. A. T. Duchowski, D. H. House, J. Gestring, R. I. Wang, K. Krejtz, I. Krejtz, R. Mantiuk, and B. Bazyluk. 2014. Reducing Visual Discomfort of 3D Stereoscopic Displays with Gaze-contingent Depth-of-field. In *ACM Symposium on Applied Perception*. 39–46.
9. B. J. Evans. 2007. Monovision: a review. *Ophthalmic and Physiological Optics* 27, 5 (2007), 417–439.
10. G.E. Favalora. 2005. Volumetric 3D Displays and Application Infrastructure. *IEEE Computer* 38, 8 (2005), 37–44.
11. R. Gil-Cazorla, S. Shah, and S. A. Naroo. 2015. A review of the surgical options for the correction of presbyopia. *British Journal of Ophthalmology* (2015).
12. E. Harb, F. Thorn, and D. Troilo. 2006. Characteristics of accommodative behavior during sustained reading in emmetropes and myopes. *Vision Research* 46, 16 (2006), 2581–92.
13. M. G. Harris, J. E. Sheedy, and C. M. Gan. 1992. Vision and Task Performance with Monovision and Diffractive Bifocal Contact Lenses. *Optometry and Vision Science* 69, 8 (1992), 609–14.
14. R. T. Held, E. A. Cooper, and M. S. Banks. 2012. Blur and Disparity Are Complementary Cues to Depth. *Current Biology* 22, 5 (2012), 426 – 431.
15. S. Hillaire, A. Lecuyer, R. Cozot, and G. Casiez. 2008. Using an Eye-Tracking System to Improve Camera Motions and Depth-of-Field Blur Effects in Virtual Environments. In *Proc. IEEE VR*. 47–50.
16. D. M. Hoffman and M. S. Banks. 2010. Focus information is used to interpret binocular images. *Journal of Vision* 10, 5 (2010), 13.

17. X. Hu and H. Hua. 2014. Design and Assessment of a Depth-Fused Multi-Focal-Plane Display Prototype. *Journal of Display Technology* 10, 4 (2014), 308–316.

18. F.C. Huang, K. Chen, and G. Wetzstein. 2015. The Light Field Stereoscope: Immersive Computer Graphics via Factored Near-Eye Light Field Display with Focus Cues. *ACM Trans. Graph. (SIGGRAPH)* 34, 4 (2015).

19. P. V. Johnson, J. A. Q. Parnell, J. Kim, C. D. Saunter, G. D. Love, and M. S. Banks. 2015. Dynamic lens and monovision 3D displays to improve viewer comfort. *ArXiv e-prints 1512.09163* (2015).

20. A. Jones, I. McDowall, H. Yamada, M. Bolas, and P. Debevec. 2007. Rendering for an interactive 360° light field display. *ACM Trans. Graph. (SIGGRAPH)* 26, 3 (2007).

21. M. Lambooij, M. Fortuin, I. Heynderickx, and W. IJsselsteijn. 2009. Visual Discomfort and Visual Fatigue of Stereoscopic Displays: A Review. *Journal of Imaging Science and Technology* 53, 3 (2009).

22. D. Lanman, M. Hirsch, Y. Kim, and R. Raskar. 2010. Content-Adaptive Parallax Barriers: Optimizing Dual-Layer 3D Displays using Low-Rank Light Field Factorization. *ACM Trans. Graph. (SIGGRAPH Asia)* 29, 6 (2010), 163:1–163:10.

23. D. Lanman and D. Luebke. 2013. Near-eye Light Field Displays. *ACM Trans. Graph. (SIGGRAPH Asia)* 32, 6 (2013), 220:1–220:10.

24. S. Liu, D. Cheng, and H. Hua. 2008. An optical see-through head mounted display with addressable focal planes. In *Proc. ISMAR*. 33–42.

25. P. Llull, N. Bedard, W. Wu, I. Tosic, K. Berkner, and N. Balram. 2015. Design and optimization of a near-eye multifocal display system for augmented reality. In *OSA Imaging and Applied Optics*.

26. G.D. Love and M.S. Banks. 2014. Stereoscopic Image Generation with Asymmetric Level of Sharpness, Patent Application WO2014199127A1. (2014).

27. G. D. Love, D. M. Hoffman, P. J. Hands, J. Gao, A. K. Kirby, and M. S. Banks. 2009. High-speed switchable lens enables the development of a volumetric stereoscopic display. *Optics Express* 17, 18 (2009), 15716–25.

28. G. Maiello, M. Chessa, F. Solari, and P. J. Bex. 2014. Simulated disparity and peripheral blur interact during binocular fusion. *Journal of Vision* 14, 8 (2014).

29. A. Maimone, G. Wetzstein, M. Hirsch, D. Lanman, R. Raskar, and H. Fuchs. 2013. Focus 3D: Compressive Accommodation Display. *ACM Trans. Graphics* 32, 5 (2013), 153:1–153:13.

30. L. Marran and C. Schor. 1997. Multiaccommodative stimuli in VR systems: problems and solutions. *Human Factors* 39, 3 (1997), 382–388.

31. M. Mauderer, S. Conte, M. A. Nacenta, and D. Vishwanath. 2014. Depth Perception with Gaze-contingent Depth of Field. *ACM SIGCHI* (2014).

32. R. Narain, R. Albert, A. Bulbul, G. J. Ward, M. S. Banks, and J. F. O'Brien. 2015. Optimal Presentation of Imagery with Focus Cues on Multi-Plane Displays. *ACM Trans. Graph. (SIGGRAPH)* 34, 4 (2015).

33. E. Peli. 1999. Optometric and perceptual issues with head-mounted displays. In *Visual Instrumentation: Optical Design & Engineering Principles*. McGraw-Hill.

34. J. Rolland, M. Krueger, and A. Goon. 2000. Multifocal planes head-mounted displays. *Applied Optics* 39, 19 (2000), 3209–3215.

35. J. Rolland and L. Vaissie. 2002. Head mounted display with eyetracking capability. U.S. Patent 6,433,760B1. (2002).

36. B. Schowengerdt and E. Seibel. 2006. True 3-D scanned voxel displays using single or multiple light sources. *J. SID* 14, 2 (2006), 135–143.

37. T. Shibata, J. Kim, D.M. Hoffman, and M.S. Banks. 2011. The zone of comfort: Predicting visual discomfort with stereo displays. *Journal of Vision* 11, 8 (2011), 11.

38. S. Siegel. 1956. *Nonparametric statistics for the behavioral sciences*. McGraw-Hill.

39. T. Sugihara and T. Miyasato. 1998. 32.4: A Lightweight 3-D HMD with Accommodative Compensation. *SID Digest* 29, 1 (1998), 927–930.

40. I. E. Sutherland. 1968. A Head-mounted Three Dimensional Display. In *Proc. Fall Joint Computer Conference*. 757–764.

41. M. Waldkirch, P. Lukowicz, and G. Tröster. 2004. Multiple imaging technique for extending depth of focus in retinal displays. *Optics Express* 12, 25 (2004).

42. S. J. Watt, K. Akeley, M. O. Ernst, and M. S. Banks. 2005. Focus cues affect perceived depth. *Journal of Vision* 5, 7 (2005), 834–862.

43. G. Wetzstein, D. Lanman, M. Hirsch, and R. Raskar. 2012. Tensor Displays: Compressive Light Field Synthesis using Multilayer Displays with Directional Backlighting. *ACM Trans. Graph. (SIGGRAPH)* 31, 4 (2012), 1–11.

44. T. Zhou, J. X. Chen, and M. Pullen. 2007. Accurate Depth of Field Simulation in Real Time. *Computer Graphics Forum* 26, 1 (2007), 15–23.

Augmenting the Field-of-View of Head-Mounted Displays with Sparse Peripheral Displays

Robert Xiao[1,2] **Hrvoje Benko**[1]

[1] Microsoft Research
One Microsoft Way, Redmond, WA 98052
benko@microsoft.com

[2] Carnegie Mellon University, HCI Institute
5000 Forbes Avenue, Pittsburgh, PA 15213
brx@cs.cmu.edu

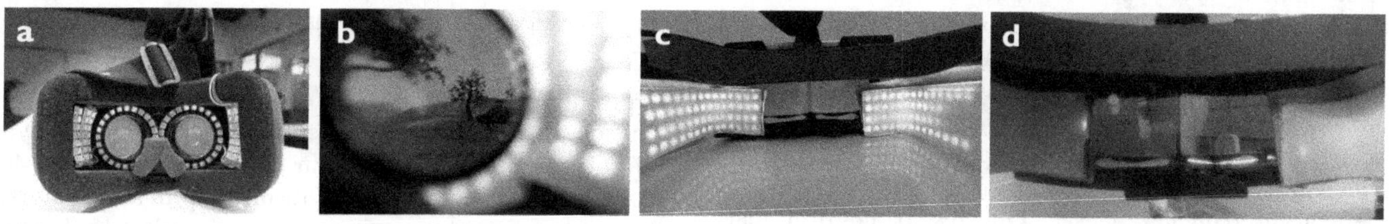

Figure 1. Our sparse peripheral display prototypes: (a) Virtual reality prototype SparseLightVR, with a 170° field of view, showing LED arrangement. (b) SparseLightVR imaged from the inside showing a forest scene. (c) Augmented reality prototype SparseLightAR, with a field of view exceeding 190°. (d) SparseLightAR showing a scene with butterflies and beach balls.

ABSTRACT
In this paper, we explore the concept of a *sparse peripheral display,* which augments the field-of-view of a head-mounted display with a lightweight, low-resolution, inexpensively produced array of LEDs surrounding the central high-resolution display. We show that sparse peripheral displays expand the available field-of-view up to 190° horizontal, nearly filling the human field-of-view. We prototyped two proof-of-concept implementations of sparse peripheral displays: a virtual reality headset, dubbed *SparseLightVR*, and an augmented reality headset, called *SparseLightAR*. Using SparseLightVR, we conducted a user study to evaluate the utility of our implementation, and a second user study to assess different visualization schemes in the periphery and their effect on simulator sickness. Our findings show that sparse peripheral displays are useful in conveying peripheral information and improving situational awareness, are generally preferred, and can help reduce motion sickness in nausea-susceptible people.

Author Keywords
Augmented reality; virtual reality; wide field-of-view; sparse peripheral display; peripheral vision

ACM 978-1-4503-3362-7/16/05···$15.00
DOI: http://dx.doi.org/10.1145/2858036.2858212

ACM Classification Keywords
H.5.1. Information interfaces and presentation (e.g. HCI): Multimedia information systems: Artificial, augmented, and virtual realities.

INTRODUCTION
Head-mounted Augmented and Virtual Reality (AR and VR) devices are increasingly popular due to a recent resurgence in interest, driven by technological improvements such as better displays, processing power and mobility. Such mixed-reality systems offer the promise of immersing a person in a virtual environment or digitally augmenting a person's vision, enabling diverse applications in areas including gaming, information visualization, medical assistants, and more immersive communication.

However, one common limitation of such devices is their limited field-of-view (FOV). The human visual system has a binocular FOV exceeding 180° horizontally, yet current head-mounted virtual reality devices, such as the Oculus Rift, are limited to around 90° horizontally (Figure 3). Augmented reality devices such as Lumus DK-40 glasses and the upcoming Microsoft Hololens are even narrower, at around 40° horizontal (Figure 6). Notably, this means that the users of such displays either see pitch black (in VR) or an absence of virtual content (in AR) in their peripheral vision. This restricted FOV limits the immersive potential of mixed-reality systems, reduces the situational awareness of the person, and leaves the vast information-processing capabilities of the human visual system underutilized.

We propose the concept of *sparse peripheral displays*, which fill the periphery of a head-mounted display using a low-resolution, high-contrast array of diffused, colored LED lights, rendering of which is tightly coupled to the content presented on the device (Figure 1). Because sparse peripheral displays can be lightweight and inexpensive to construct, they can easily be retrofitted to existing head-mounted displays, enhancing existing devices. To demonstrate our concept's applicability to a range of form factors, we implemented two proof-of-concept implementations: a virtual reality display, called *SparseLightVR*, and an augmented reality display, called *SparseLightAR*.

We evaluated the effectiveness of our concept using our SparseLightVR prototype in a pair of user studies. In addition to confirming the benefits of increased situational awareness, our experiments showed that participants preferred SparseLightVR, reporting less effects from simulator sickness or nausea compared to the plain VR display. In particular, our participants found our novel *peripheral countervection* visualization to be particularly beneficial in reducing nausea. Our results confirm that sparse peripheral displays can be used to expand the field-of-view in mixed-reality environments while also countering the common nauseating effects of enlarged field-of-view [8, 16].

In summary, this paper makes the following three contributions:

- The concept of *sparse peripheral displays* and two proof-of-concept implementations: a virtual reality display (*SparseLightVR*) and an augmented reality display (*SparseLightAR*), along with a detailed description of their hardware and software designs.
- A *peripheral countervection* visualization, designed to reduce the effects of simulator sickness by presenting motion stimulation on the retina that counters any additional motions not generated by the user's head movement itself (e.g., motion derived from controller input).
- A 17-person evaluation of SparseLightVR testing its ability to provide additional context to mixed-reality interactions, and a follow up study examining the effects of various rendering strategies on simulator sickness.

BACKGROUND AND RELATED WORK

In contrast to foveal vision, which senses detail, color, and textures [27], peripheral vision is much lower resolution and attuned to sensing contrast [1] and motion [20]. Thus, displays targeting the periphery have different requirements than displays for the fovea, leading us to design our sparse peripheral displays to to complement the high-resolution foveal display.

FOV and Simulator Sickness

Simulator sickness is a type of motion sickness induced by visual information that conflicts with vestibular and proprioceptive sensory cues [23]. The principal source of simulator sickness is induced perception of self-motion, or *vection*, caused by motion cues in the visual field that are not corroborated by vestibular sensory data [14]. In turn, vection is primarily derived from peripheral visual cues [5, 6], with the central visual field playing only a small role.

Consequently, research has confirmed that wide FOV displays can often induce simulator sickness more easily than narrow FOV displays [8, 16]. However, because wide FOV displays also result in higher presence and immersion [16], system designers face a difficult decision when choosing an appropriate FOV. In addition, technical difficulties in producing commercial devices with wide FOV (e.g., complicated optics, increased weight etc.) often limit the available FOV, limiting the depth of virtual experiences available to users.

Explorations of Wide FOV

Outside of AR/VR, many systems have explored displaying information or visualizations in the visual periphery. Most commonly, these peripheral displays provide additional context to a foveal display, an arrangement referred to as a *focus plus context* display [3]. Such displays often feature low-resolution context displays paired with a high-resolution focus display, similar in concept to the present sparse peripheral displays.

Other systems have explored using the periphery to present information and notifications [15], enhance user experiences through immersive peripheral projections [10], or expand the effective size of a display through low-resolution ambient light [26]. Recently, FoveAR [4] combined optically see-through glasses with wide FOV background projection as another example of such focus + periphery hybrid displays.

In the HMD space, Jones et al. [11] found that strategically placed static, bright areas in the peripheral visual field resulted in more accurate distance perception by HMD users, suggesting that even static illumination in the periphery can improve HMD experiences. In contrast, Knapp and Loomis found that reducing the FOV did not directly cause distance underestimation [13]. Watson et. al. [28] found that degradation of peripheral resolution did not significantly affect user performance on a complex visual search task.

Wide FOV HMDs

A few recent AR research prototypes [2, 18, 19] demonstrate higher FOVs (up to 92° horizontal, compared with 40° for commercial devices) albeit with significantly reduced image quality across the entire display. For example, Pinlight Displays [19] use a special light field display consisting of an LCD backed with an array of point light sources. These displays require significant computational power to render a full light field. Furthermore, the ultimate resolution of the display is diffraction-limited.

In VR, a number of systems have attempted to widen the field of view with complex optical configurations. For example, StarVR [9] (210° horizontal) and Wearality Sky [29] (150° diagonal) both use complex Fresnel lenses which

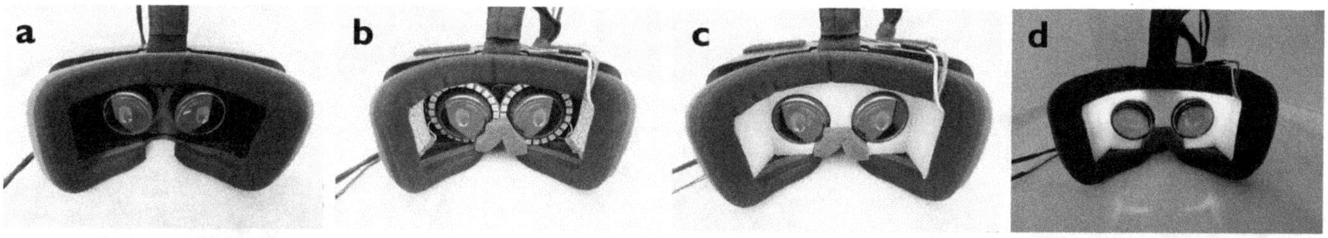

Figure 2. SparseLightVR device. (a) Unmodified Oculus Rift DK2 device. (b) Rift with LED arrays installed. (c) Rift after Delrin diffuser installed. (d) SparseLightVR in operation. Note that the LEDs above the nose are disabled to avoid crosstalk, since those can be seen by both eyes.

are challenging to manufacture and design, and introduce optical distortions which are hard to mitigate. Nagahara et al. [21] (180° horizontal) use a novel optical arrangement (catadioptrical optics), significantly increasing the weight of their device (3.75 kg headset).

Other approaches are possible. For instance, Yang and Kim [30] compress the virtual environment to provide higher virtual FOV. Similarly, Orlosky et. al. [24] warp the display using fisheye lenses. Although these warping approaches result in higher virtual FOV, they trade off physical accuracy to do so.

Most related to our approach are systems that explicitly place low-resolution displays in the periphery. Nojima et al. [22] demonstrate a prototype peripheral display consisting of four 16x32 LED arrays worn on the user's head. These display a moving random dot pattern as the user operates a normal computer monitor, increasing the user's sense of self-motion. Baek et al. [2] place a pair of low-resolution LCDs on the either side of an HMD, but do not evaluate their prototype or describe its implementation in detail.

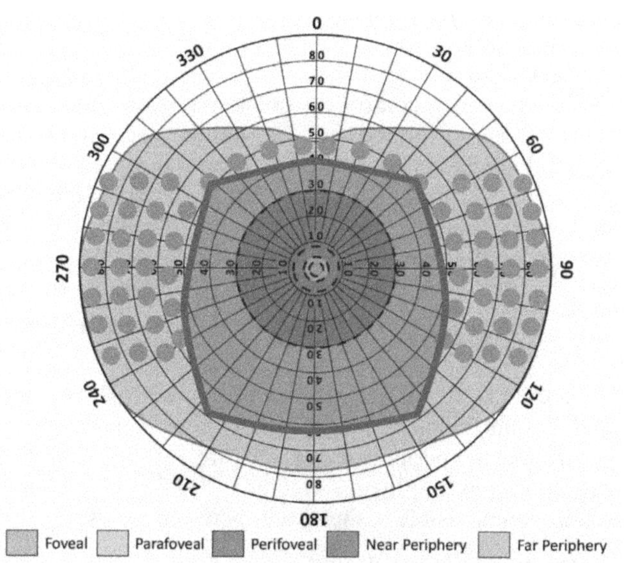

Figure 3. LED placements in SparseLightVR relative to the visual FOV of human vision. Purple box: Oculus Rift DK2 binocular FOV. Purple circles: SparseLightVR LEDs. Figure adapted from Jones, et al. [11].

IMPLEMENTATION DETAILS

Both our VR and AR prototype displays share some of the same core components. The displays consist of a number of individually-addressable RGB LEDs (WS2812S 5050), connected in series to an Arduino microprocessor. These LEDs provide 24-bit color (8 bits per channel), and are all controlled from a single Arduino pin using a cascading serial protocol. Due to the high brightness of these LEDs coupled with their proximity to the eyes, we covered the LEDs with laser-cut diffuser material to absorb some of the light and smooth out the LED hotspots (Figures 2c, 5d).

To further reduce the brightness of these LEDs (which are designed for outdoor lighting applications), we undervolted the LEDs, driving them at 3.0 V instead of the recommended 5.0 V. We also performed a quick manual calibration of the LEDs to the central display, adjusting our software's per-channel scale values so that the LEDs match both the brightness and color gamut of the display.

The rendering device continuously streams color data to the Arduino over a serial connection running at 500 kilobits per second. The rendering device is responsible for computing the color value output by each LED.

SparseLightVR

Our VR prototype, called SparseLightVR, is built on a commercial Oculus Rift DK2 head-mounted virtual reality device (Figure 2a). This device has a central high-resolution display of 960x1080 per eye, updating at 75 Hz. The binocular high-resolution field-of-view is approximately

Figure 4. Close-up image from the inside of SparseLightVR. The sparse peripheral display shows the sky (top), ground (bottom), and a nearby off-screen red helicopter (left).

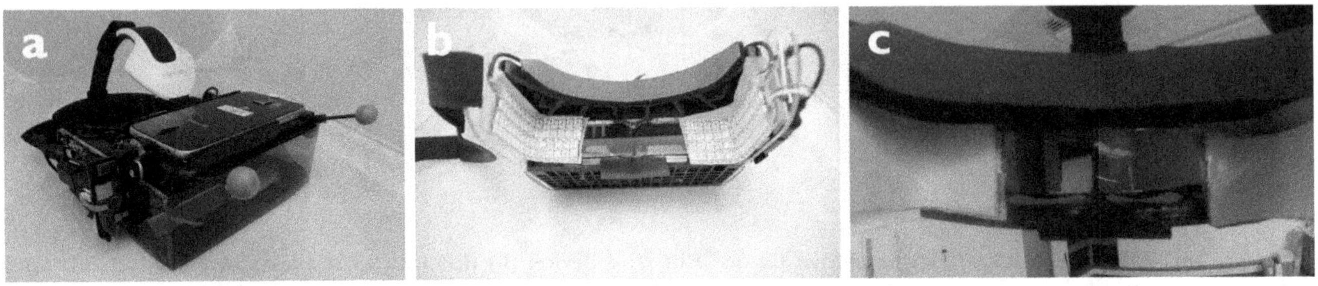

Figure 5. SparseLightAR construction. (a) Our custom AR head-worn display prototype. A Samsung Galaxy S6 is mounted on top, connected to the external IMU and the SparseLightAR controller (left assembly). (b) SparseLightAR LED arrays installed. (c) SparseLightAR with paper diffusers added, in operation showing a scene with flying butterflies (blue).

84° horizontal. The SparseLightVR peripheral display consists of 70 LEDs broken up into four groups, arranged as shown in Figures 3b and 4. Two groups of LEDs are placed in the far periphery inside the left and right edges of the display, and the other two groups are configured as rings in the near periphery surrounding the Oculus' two eye displays. Laser-cut pieces of Delrin plastic cover the LEDs to diffuse the light (Figure 2c). The total sparse FOV is approximately 170° horizontal (Figure 3). The sparse peripheral display is driven at 100 Hz using an Arduino Duemilanove microprocessor, slightly faster than the Oculus' native display refresh rate of 75 Hz.

SparseLightVR is driven by a desktop computer running Windows 8.1, a Core i7-3770 CPU and an NVIDIA Quadro K5000 graphics card. Applications were developed in Unity 5 using the Oculus VR 0.6 SDK.

SparseLightAR

Our AR prototype, called SparseLightAR, is built on a

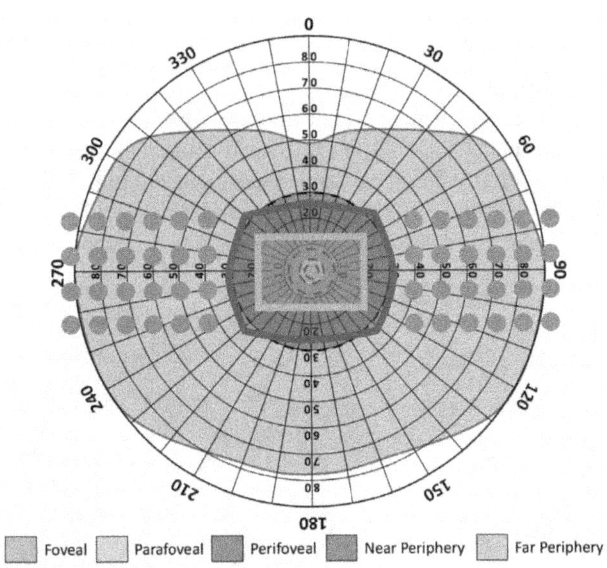

Figure 6. LED placements in SparseLightAR relative to the visual FOV. Gray box: Lumus AR [17] FOV for comparison. Purple box: Our custom AR display's binocular FOV. Purple circles: SparseLightAR LEDs. Figure adapted from Jones, et al. [11].

custom-built head-mounted see-through augmented reality device. This AR device is a modification of the commercial Samsung Galaxy Gear VR device. It consists of a smartphone (Samsung Galaxy S6) mounted flat across the top, connected to an external inertial measurement unit (Figure 5a). Collimating lenses opposite the display split the display output into two halves, one per eye, with each image individually projected at infinity. A half-silvered mirror mounted at a 45° angle between the display and lenses redirects the collimated images onto the eyes. The effect is that the display's contents are overlaid onto the environment, creating a see-through augmented reality experience. The Samsung S6 display provides a resolution of 1280x1440 per eye at a refresh rate of 60 fps. The horizontal FOV of our AR display is 62°, comparable with similar wide FOV AR systems [7].

The SparseLightAR peripheral display for this prototype consists of 112 LEDs (Figure 5b) updated 75 times per second and arranged as two 4x14 rectangular matrices, one along each edge of our unit. In total, the field of view exceeds 190° horizontally (Figure 6). A DFRobot Beetle microcontroller drives the sparse peripheral display and is connected to the smartphone via USB On-The-Go. All rendering, microcontroller communication and motion tracking is performed on the phone itself without an external computer, and all LEDs are powered from the phone's USB port. SparseLightAR applications are written in Unity 5 using Unity's Android SDK and a modified version of the Samsung Gear VR SDK. As the Gear VR SDK is itself based on the Oculus VR SDK, most of our Unity code is common to both SparseLightVR and SparseLightAR.

As the LED arrays are opaque, we chose to leave the top and bottom areas of the field of view clear to preserve environmental peripheral cues (Figure 5c). We later discuss future designs employing smaller LEDs that could keep the environment visible in the spaces between LEDs.

Scene and LED Rendering

We used the Unity 5 game engine to implement the 3D virtual scenes and scenarios for our sparse peripheral displays. We implemented a reusable rendering component, which we called a *light probe*, responsible for updating a

Figure 7. Light probes used to render SparseLightVR. In the center, light probes for both eyes overlap.

single LED. The designer can place many such light probes in the scene, matching the arrangement of the LEDs of the sparse peripheral display they are representing (Figure 7). This configuration is easily attached to the user's view and is updated as the user moves around the scene.

For each eye, a virtual camera renders the scene into a color buffer (Figure 8a). The color buffer is partitioned using a Voronoi diagram (Figure 8b), assigning each pixel in the buffer to the nearest light probe. The output color from each probe is the average color (using the CIELAB colorspace) of all pixels assigned to it. In this way, we guarantee that every object in the field of view contributes to at least one light probe, allowing even small details to be seen.

Our rendering implementation and light probe configurations are packaged into a prefabricated Unity object, enabling existing projects to be augmented simply by dropping this object in the scene. Furthermore, these light probes can be added to the Oculus VR SDK's prefabricated headset object, allowing applications using the SDK to automatically support our sparse peripheral displays.

The actual color values sent to the LEDs are adjusted to match the colorspace of the central display (converting

Figure 8. LED rendering using light probes. (a) Original rendered color buffer. (b) Colors averaged using a Voronoi diagram with a distance cutoff. Each solid region corresponds to a single light probe.

Figure 9. Countervection rendering. (a) Sphere with motion bars in Unity. (b) Countervection rendering as it appears in SparseLightVR.

from the standardized sRGB colorspace to linear RGB), and then multiplied by predetermined per-channel scale factors, which correct for color gamut mismatches and brightness discrepancies. We took special care to match the gamut and brightness of our sparse peripheral display to the central display, as that makes the experience seamless and comfortable for longer use.

Peripheral Visualizations

As has been shown in several focus + periphery hybrid displays (e.g., Focus+Context [3], IllumiRoom [10]), designers have many options when creating content to be displayed in the periphery. They can choose to purely extend the FOV as faithfully as possible, or use the periphery for highlighting of a particular feature or style. We developed a number of proof of concept visualization schemes to explore how to effectively use the sparse peripheral displays in head-mounted displays.

In particular, we implemented the following three visualizations: *full environment*, *objects only*, and a novel rendering mode called *countervection visualization*.

Full Environment

This is the most naïve visualization, in which the periphery extends the FOV of the main display as faithfully as possible. All objects and scenery are rendered into the sparse display.

Objects of Interest Only

As an alternative to rendering the full environment, the designers can choose to render only select objects in the periphery. This can be helpful to draw the person's attention to a particular object in their periphery that is currently not visible on the main foveal display.

Countervection Visualization

We contribute a novel visualization particularly suited to peripheral displays, which attempts to counteract motions not generated by physical head movement. We designed this visualization to reduce the negative effects of vection-induced simulator sickness caused by motion cues in the visual field [14].

Our countervection visualization consists of a series of vertical bars, placed in a spherical arrangement around the person's avatar and only visible in the sparse peripheral

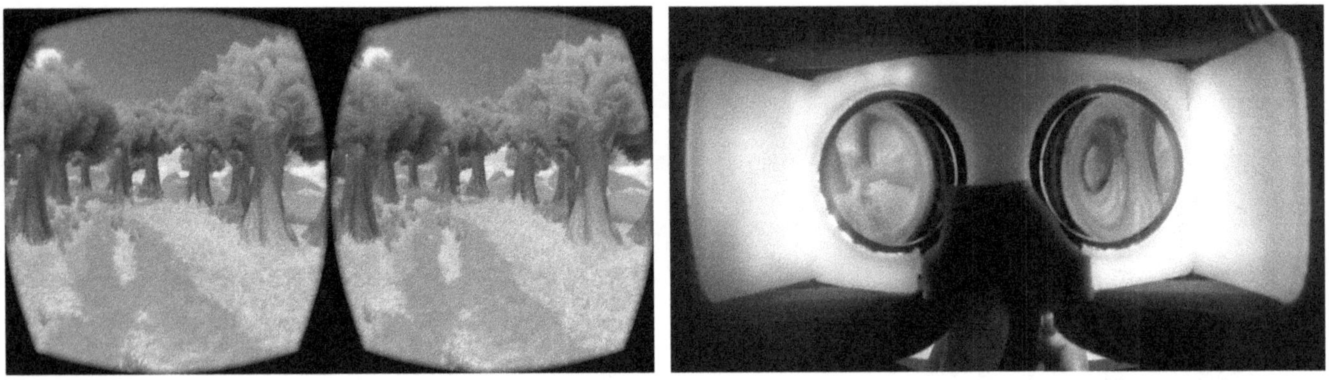

Figure 10. The forest scene used to introduce users to SparseLightVR. Left: the virtual scene as rendered for the Oculus Rift DK2. Right: scene as it appears inside the unit with SparseLightVR enabled.

display (Figure 9). The sphere does not respond to physical head motions. However, when the user's avatar moves or rotates (e.g., due to user input), the bars are shifted (via texture manipulation) so that they move *in the same direction as the motion*, i.e., opposite to what normally would occur. We call these contrary motions *countervection cues*, as they oppose the motion cues of the central display and thus reduce the feeling of vection (self-motion). For example, if the user walks forward, the bars will also move forward. The bars are configured to move slightly slower than the actual motion, as we found that a 1:1 mapping produced an overwhelming motion effect in the opposite direction during pilot testing.

The countervection visualization is designed to partially cancel the vection experienced in the peripheral regions of the VR display. As such, we aimed to balance the strength of the effect (in terms of brightness) and the speed of the motion with the VR periphery.

Additionally, we implemented a dynamic switching strategy in which the full environment is rendered while the user is not moving or when the movement comes only from their physical movement of their head, but countervection cues fade in when the user begins to move via external input (*e.g.*, joystick input). This means that we fade in the contervection cues only when the person is experiencing visual-vestibular mismatch. This allows the user to attain the benefit of a wider field of view (better immersion, more information) while also benefiting from the reduced vection (and thus reduced visual-vestibular conflict) of the countervection visualization. Our second study specifically examines the effects of countervection visualization and full environment visualizations on simulator sickness.

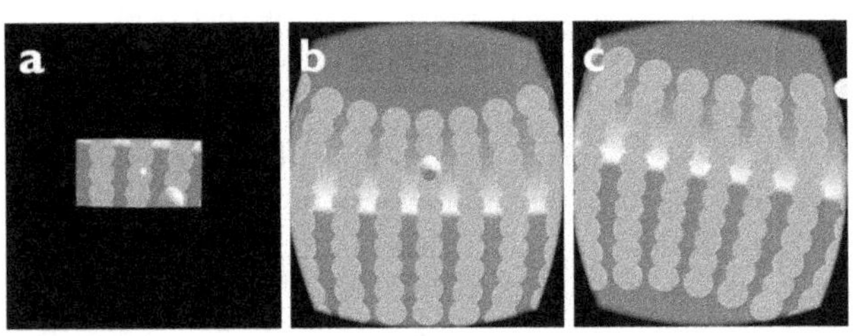

Figure 11. Search task. The user uses a cursor in the middle of the screen to select a white target from a grid of circles. (a) Narrow FOV condition. (b) Regular FOV condition. (c) SparseLightVR condition: the white dot (top-right) is rendered to SparseLightVR as an activated LED.

USER EVALUATIONS

We conducted two evaluations with 17 participants (6 female, mean age 28). Participants completed the two studies in a single session lasting 60 minutes: a *search* task where participants moved their head to locate an object, and a *simulator sickness* evaluation in which participants were asked to evaluate their subjective nausea over a range of rendering conditions.

Participants were given the option to stop the experiment at any time. Each participant was compensated $10 for participating, regardless of how much they completed. All 17 participants completed the search task, while 14 participants completed the sickness evaluation.

Procedure

Participants were first asked about their experiences with virtual reality. Only one person mentioned using virtual

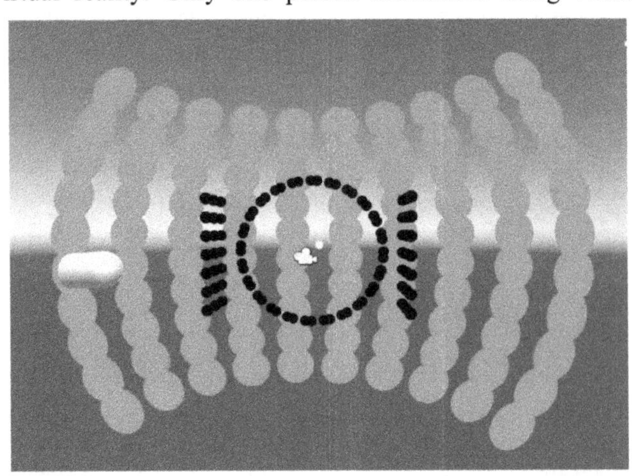

Figure 12. Virtual scene of the first study search task. Target shown at left. The LEDs are configured to only show the target.

reality devices regularly; the remainder had either used them on a small number of occasions just as a trial, or had never used them. The experimenter then had the participant wear the SparseLightVR device and had them move around a simulated forest environment (Figure 10) using a gamepad controller, without the sparse peripheral display enabled. After a minute of familiarizing the participant with the device and the virtual reality experience, the experimenter switched on the sparse peripheral display, which rendered an expanded view of the forest. The participant was asked to describe their reaction and first impressions of the system. After this initial induction phase, the participant began the first study.

Study 1 – Search Task

The goal of the first study was to examine the effect of field of view on performance in an object search task. Three fields of view were tested, as shown in Figure 11: a simulated "augmented reality" field of view measuring 25 degrees vertical and 50 degrees horizontal (slightly larger than the field of view of the Lumus AR glasses), a full "virtual reality" field of view employing the Oculus Rift's full foveal resolution (84 degrees horizontal); and a wide "peripheral" field of view which used the Oculus Rift's full foveal field-of-view alongside SparseLightVR for a total of 170 degrees horizontal. In this task, SparseLightVR was configured to render in "object-of-interest only" visualization mode. For consistency, we term these tasks, Narrow, Regular, and SparseLightVR, respectively.

Participants were presented with a virtual 10x10 grid of circles, arranged in a hemispherical arc 1 meter from the participant and occupying a field of view of 160 degrees horizontal and 80 degrees vertical (shown in Figure 12). Upon beginning the task, a white target would appear in a random hole. The participant was to move their head until a cursor in the center of their gaze aligned with the target, and click a button on the gamepad to select it. This constituted a single trial. The target would then disappear and reappear at a different grid point. The participant performed three blocks of 75 trials each, with each block having a different field of view condition. Condition (block) order was randomized per participant to control for order effects, and the first 25 trials for each block were discarded to reduce learning effects.

Following this first study, participants were asked to give their impressions of the system, and then took a short break before the next study.

Study 2 – Simulator Sickness

Wide FOV displays are commonly cited in the literature as increasing the sickness and nausea experienced by users of virtual reality devices [8, 16]. Consequently, we sought to evaluate whether sparse peripheral displays suffered from the same limitation and whether our countervection cues helped people reduce the effects of simulator sickness. We compared three conditions: full Oculus Rift FOV without the sparse periphery, extended FOV using the full environment visualization in the sparse periphery to render an extension of the scene, and countervection extended FOV in which the sparse periphery displayed countervection cues while the user was in motion.

Our second study proceeded in two parts. In the first part, participants acquainted themselves with our rendering conditions through a simple *chase task*, following a glowing orb as it moved around a forest clearing (Figure 13). The orb moved along a predetermined path, stopping at 20 waypoints (Figure 14). At each waypoint, the orb stopped to orbit a nearby tree and waited for the participant to approach it; once they moved close enough, the orb moved to the next waypoint. Participants controlled their movement in the game environment using a gamepad and their head movements. The participants repeated this task under each of our three rendering conditions, with the orb moving along the same path each time.

Of the 17 participants in this experiment, three participants did not complete this chase task; all three tried the task once or twice and felt too sick to continue to a another repetition.

Following each task repetition, participants filled out the Simulator Sickness Questionnaire [12] and were given a five-minute rest to alleviate any lingering nausea.

Figure 13. Chase task. Participants follow the red orb to each waypoint. The orb leaves a long translucent trail for users to follow.

Figure 14. Orb path for the chase task. The orb's path consists of a mix of sharp and shallow turns, so that participants try out different turning radii.

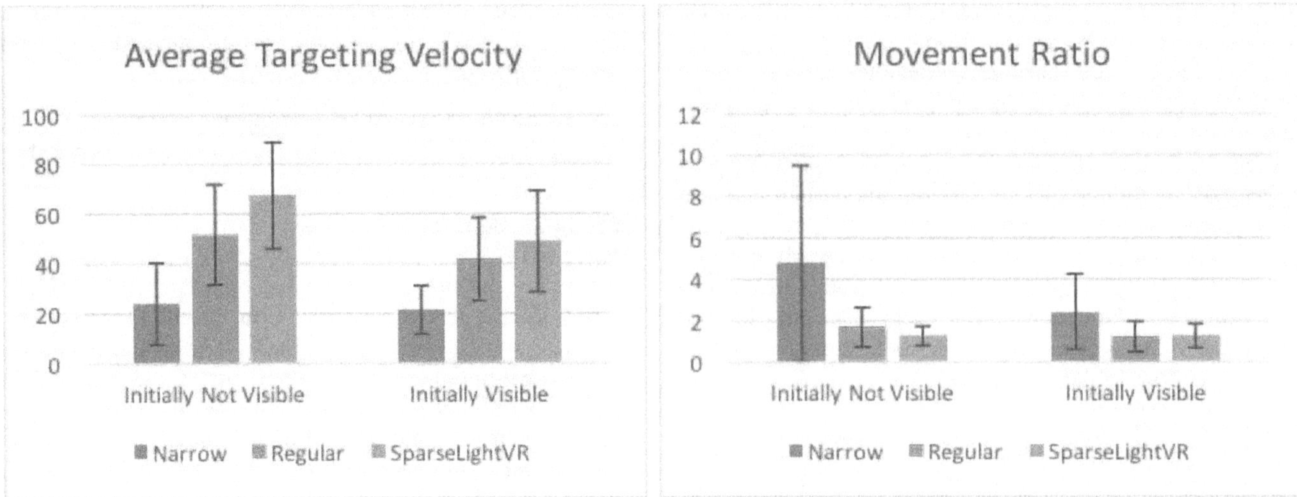

Figure 15. Results of the search task in Study 1.

Following the chase task, participants were asked if they were willing to continue with a final, possibly difficult task in which they were *involuntarily* moved around a space (i.e., moved on "rails"). In this task, participants were able to switch between the three conditions from study 2 using buttons on the gamepad, and try different conditions out as they moved through the space. Participants were asked specifically to rank the conditions in order of *comfort* based on which conditions they felt minimized their nausea. Participants were given as long as they wanted to make this determination, and were asked to stay until they had fully determined their ranking.

Participants who declined the involuntary "rails" task were asked to complete it with voluntary movement instead, i.e., where they both moved themselves around and changed the rendering mode using the gamepad. Of the 14 participants who completed the chase task, three participants chose this option.

In the involuntary movement-on-rails task, participants moved along a looping path which repeated until they stopped the experiment. Along both straightaways, the participant's avatar accelerated gradually to the midpoint then decelerated to a stop. At the end of each straightaway, the avatar jumped about 1.2m into the air to provide some vertical motion, then proceeded to execute the turn and the next straightaway.

RESULTS

Although we did not explicitly ask participants to rate our system overall, many participants reacted positively to the system, noting that they "liked this much more" (P2), "[SparseLightVR] felt the most natural" (P12), or that tasks were "a lot easier with [SparseLightVR]" (P4). Two participants (P3, P12) found the LEDs to be too bright, while others found it hard to see cues (P8), suggesting that the brightness of SparseLightVR could be made customizable per-person to improve the experience.

Study 1 – Search Task

Completion time of a trial in this task depended strongly on two factors: whether the next target was visible in the field-of-view at the start of the trial (i.e., whether the participant had to actively move his head to find the next target), and the angular distance to the next target. We also recorded the total angular distance traveled – due to the Oculus Rift's orientation smoothing, this total distance incorporates very little noise.

We discarded trials in which participants missed the target on their first click attempt (162 trials in all), and trials in which the target appeared in the same location as the previous trial (21 trials in all). Of the remaining 2367 trials, 988 had initially-visible targets.

To measure task performance, we use two measurements: the *average targeting velocity* measure – the ratio between the angular distance to the next target and the completion time – and the *movement ratio* – the ratio between the total angular distance travelled and the angular distance to the next target. The former measures in effect how quickly the person targets the object, and the latter measurement measures how efficiently they locate the target.

Results are summarized in Figure 15. All significant differences were determined through repeated measures Tukey HSD at a $p<0.05$ significance level.

For trials with initially visible targets, all three conditions were significantly different for average targeting velocity (SparseLightVR 49.2°/s, Regular 41.4°/s, Narrow 21.2°/s), and Narrow was significantly different from the other conditions for movement ratio (Narrow 2.35, Regular 1.29, SparseLightVR 1.28).

For trials without initially visible targets, all three conditions were significantly different for average targeting velocity (SparseLightVR 70.7°/s, Regular 53.1°/s, Narrow 24.2°/s), and AR was again significantly different from the other conditions for movement ratio (Narrow 4.79, Regular 1.70, SparseLightVR 1.28).

The poor performance of the Narrow condition (very low average targeting velocity and very high movement ratio) can be explained due to the very small field of view of the "augmented reality" condition: when the object was not immediately visible in the view, participants had to execute a time-consuming grid sweep to locate it, and each motion only revealed a small amount of the grid. By comparison, with SparseLightVR, the grid was revealed rapidly as the participant moved their head.

In the post-study survey, participants were asked to choose the condition that was most helpful, most comfortable, and most preferable. Participants uniformly chose SparseLightVR as being the most helpful, with several noting that the expanded field of view helped find the target faster ("amazing how much those little [peripheral] cues help" (P12)). 15 participants chose SparseLightVR as being the most comfortable, with two participants choosing the Regular experience instead due to the brightness of the LEDs. Finally, all participants indicated they would prefer SparseLightVR in a VR experience (e.g. "I hate the black rim" (P1), "this would be useful in [a first person shooter]" (P2)).

Study 2 – Simulator Sickness

Although we attempted to use the Simulator Sickness Questionnaire [12] to gauge participant nausea after each chase task repetition, we found that the SSQ results were extremely subject to order effects. In some participants, their sickness scores consistently rose through the experiment, indicating mounting nausea (despite being given breaks to get up, walk around, drink water, etc.). In other participants, their sickness scores consistently dropped through the experiment due to increased familiarity with the scene. Three participants noted almost no nausea across all three conditions. Consequently, we did could not use the collected SSQ scores to establish the effect on nausea. However, the participants also had a chance to directly compare the three conditions and come up with a ranking when specifically asked to rank them in terms of how nauseating the experience was.

10 of our participants felt comfortable enough after the chase task to do the high-intensity movement-on-rails task, while the remaining 3 participants moved themselves through the scene. Remarkably, all participant rankings fall into only 3 particular orderings: 9 of the 14 participants ranked countervection first (followed by wide, then no-periphery); 2 participants ranked wide field of view first, followed by countervection in second place; and three participants ranked the no-periphery condition first, followed by wide field of view, followed by countervection.

Thus, in total, 11 of the 14 participants preferred the countervection rendering to the no-periphery condition.

Several participants expressed a clear difference between countervection and wide FOV rendering (e.g., P8 felt "immediate relief" when switching to countervection rendering, P10 noted it was less jarring during rotations, while P15 noted that "[countervection] stabilized me during turns"). However, a few participants also found the countervection rendering to be distracting, noting that the ordinary wide field of view "looks better" (P15) or simply expressing a general preference for the ordinary rendering.

These results indicate that participants strongly preferred SparseLightVR in motion-heavy tasks, and the high ranking of the countervection rendering condition suggests that appropriate peripheral cues can help mitigate user sickness.

DISCUSSION AND LIMITATIONS

Although the SSQ questionnaire results were inconclusive, the direct comparison ranking in our study showed that the SparseLightVR display was preferred over no periphery for being less sickness-inducing, even without the stabilizing effects of the countervection cues. As this conflicts with prior research results on wide FOV mixed-reality systems (e.g. [16]), we believe this merits further investigation.

We note that the low resolution of the display may contribute to decreased nausea. Duh, et al. [8] found that high-resolution content in the foveal area tended to make users lose their balance more often than low-resolution content. This finding that may extend to the peripheral display, and should certainly be explored in future work.

Sparse peripheral displays do suffer from a number of limitations compared with other means of expanding the field of view. Because they are low resolution, it is inherently difficult to display small objects or fine detail. We partially mitigate this in our implementation using Voronoi rendering to ensure that all objects contribute to the nearest LED, but ultimately system designers will have to carefully design environments and objects to produce optimal sparse periphery renderings. This could involve, for example, rendering only targets or relevant objectives (as we did in the search task), or rendering simplified low-detail geometry to make relevant objects stand out more.

Because the sparse peripheral display requires a separate virtual camera for each eye, in addition to the two eye cameras already required for the VR/AR headset, rendering sparse peripheral display content can cause a significant performance impact. Furthermore, because the sparse peripheral displays cover a large field of view, the graphics pipeline must render many more objects, incurring performance penalties. In our implementations, we use very low resolution render textures for the sparse periphery (128x128 or lower) and disable most shader effects which are imperceptible in the low-resolution sparse periphery. However, the additional rendering load is still significant, limiting the complexity of scenes we can render. The problem is especially acute in SparseLightAR, with its smartphone GPU. Designers will have to carefully consider what is rendered to the sparse periphery to minimize rendering cost, and learn optimization techniques specific to the sparse periphery.

While sparse periphery displays can usefully expand the field of view for a user who is attending to the central high-resolution display, the displays are much less useful if the user looks directly at them. Thus, users will have to avoid glancing around too much, which can be limiting and artificial. With a reasonably wide-FOV central display (such as the Oculus Rift display), users may not have to look directly at the periphery as often, partially mitigating this issue.

Although super-wide FOV displays are not yet practically available, some designs on the market (such as the Weareality Sky [29]) are moving in that direction. Should wide FOV displays become widespread, we argue that sparse peripheral displays may still be useful. As our results, and past work (e.g., [8]) suggest, lower resolution peripheral displays can help to reduce motion sickness. Thus, even wide FOV displays could have a resolution toggle to display lower resolution imagery to motion-susceptible individuals, emulating a sparse peripheral display in software.

While we did not explicitly evaluate our AR prototype, we believe that our results for improved situational awareness in VR (study 1) should apply to AR systems as well. Our "narrow" condition simulated the same field of view as a typical AR system, and we showed that SparseLight produced a significant improvement over a narrow field of view.

Finally, our current implementations use fairly large LEDs (5x5 mm). However, extremely tiny SMD LEDs are available (as small as 0.65x0.35 mm), making it possible to make the LED itself nearly imperceptible when placed near the eye. This in turn would make it possible to develop a see-through AR display where the environment is fully visible, with a sparse peripheral display of miniature LEDs in similar arrangement as SparseLightAR. In this way, the full benefits of see-through AR could be realized in conjunction with a wide FOV sparse peripheral display.

FUTURE WORK

The literature contains many examples of uses for wide field of view displays, as covered in the related work section. Exploring which of these uses are practically feasible with sparse peripheral displays would produce further insights into the capabilities of this concept. For instance, exploring the various peripheral rendering modes used by IllumiRoom [10] would dramatically increase the richness of peripheral rendering options available to designers. Another promising area of research would be to integrate peripheral flicker [25] notifications, like those developed by Kooi et al. [15], into a sparse peripheral display, providing unobtrusive but immediately visible notifications.

Because our countervection visualization helped mitigate user sensations of motion sickness, we suggest further research should be done on its applications to various VR devices and approaches. For instance, studying the countervection visualization in a high-resolution wide-FOV display would determine whether its properties depend on the resolution used.

Repeating our Study 2, but with longer trial exposure and significantly longer time delay between trials, might reveal statistically significant differences in the simulator sickness questionnaire data, which would be a welcome validation of our direct comparison results.

Further investigations on the relationship between peripheral resolution, field-of-view and simulator sickness in general would also be very valuable to the research community. In particular, we believe that our sparse peripheral display concept could offer a practical solution to the simulator sickness problem, but further investigations are needed to potentially allow a substantial number of motion-sickness-sensitive users to enjoy VR experiences previously unavailable to them.

CONCLUSIONS

In this paper, we presented the concept of the sparse peripheral display, which adds a matrix of colored LEDs to the periphery of an existing high-resolution head-mounted display. We contribute two prototype implementations, SparseLightVR and SparseLightAR, which demonstrate the feasibility of retrofitting such lightweight, inexpensive display enhancements on top of existing VR/AR hardware. We also evaluated our SparseLightVR implementation in two studies that found that people have increased situational awareness, preference for the experience, and presence in the 3D scene when using our prototype. Lastly, we found that our novel countervection visualization holds promise in reducing the effects of simulator sickness experienced by VR users. We believe that sparse peripheral displays offer an inexpensive, light and highly customizable way to significantly improve existing AR and VR head-mounted displays. We are particularly encouraged by our results demonstrating that they can also help make mixed-reality experiences more comfortable and less nauseating.

ACKNOWLEDGEMENTS

We thank Jaron Lanier, Victor A. Mateevitsi, Patrick Therien, Josh Hudman, Javier Porras Lurashi, Wayne Chang and all the members of the Microsoft Research COMRADRE and Hardware Labs for developing the custom AR display and helping us adapt it for the SparsePeriphery project.

REFERENCES

1. Randall William Adams. 1971. Peripheral vision and visual attention. *Retrospective Theses and Dissertations*. Paper 4933.
2. Jin-uk Baek, Jaehoon Jung, and Gerard J. Kim. 2005. Head mounted display with peripheral vision. In

Proceedings of the 2005 international conference on Augmented tele-existence (ICAT '05). ACM, New York, NY, USA, 282-282. http://doi.acm.org/10.1145/1152399.1152472

3. Patrick Baudisch, Nathaniel Good, and Paul Stewart. 2001. Focus plus context screens: combining display technology with visualization techniques. In *Proceedings of the 14th annual ACM symposium on User interface software and technology* (UIST '01). ACM, New York, NY, USA, 31-40. http://doi.acm.org/10.1145/502348.502354
4. Hrvoje Benko, Eyal Ofek, Feng Zheng, and Andrew D. Wilson. 2015. FoveAR: Combining an Optically See-Through Near-Eye Display with Projector-Based Spatial Augmented Reality. In Proceedings of the 28th Annual ACM Symposium on User Interface Software & Technology (UIST '15). ACM, New York, NY, USA, 129-135. http://dx.doi.org/10.1145/2807442.2807493
5. A. Berthoz, B. Pavard, and L.R. Young. 1975. Perception of linear horizontal self-motion induced by peripheral vision (linearvection) basic characteristics and visual-vestibular interactions. *Experimental Brain Research*, 23(5): 471-89.
6. Th. Brandt, J. Dichgans, and E. Koenig. 1973. Differential effects of central versus peripheral vision on egocentric and exocentric motion perception. *Experimental Brain Research*, 16(5): 476-491.
7. Dewen Cheng, Yongtian Wang, Hong Hua, and Jose Sasian. 2011. Design of a wide-angle, lightweight head-mounted display using free-form optics tiling. *Optics Letters,* 36(11):2098-2100.
8. Henry Been-Lirn Duh, James J. W. Lin, Robert V. Kenyon, Donald E. Parker, and Thomas A. Furness. 2002. Effects of Characteristics of Image Quality in an Immersive Environment. *Presence: Teleoperators and Virtual Environments*, 11(3): 324-332
9. InfinitEye. StarVR Tech Specs. http://www.starvr.com/#techspecs. Retrieved September 23, 2015.
10. Brett R. Jones, Hrvoje Benko, Eyal Ofek, and Andrew D. Wilson. 2013. IllumiRoom: peripheral projected illusions for interactive experiences. In *Proceedings of the SIGCHI Conference on Human Factors in Computing Systems* (CHI '13). ACM, New York, NY, USA, 869-878. http://doi.acm.org/10.1145/2470654.2466112
11. J. Adam Jones, J. Edward Swan II, Mark Bolas. 2013. Peripheral Stimulation and its Effect on Perceived Spatial Scale in Virtual Environments. *IEEE Transactions on Visualization & Computer Graphics*, 19(4): 701-710. http://doi.ieeecomputersociety.org/10.1109/TVCG.2013.37
12. Robert S. Kennedy, Norman E. Lane, Kevin S. Berbaum, and Michael G. Lilienthal. 1993. Simulator Sickness Questionnaire: An enhanced method for quantifying simulator sickness. *International Journal of Aviation Psychology*, 3(3): 203-220. DOI: 10.1207/s15327108ijap0303_3
13. Joshua M. Knapp and Jack M. Loomis. 2004. Limited field of view of head-mounted displays is not the cause of distance underestimation in virtual environments. *Presence: Teleoper. Virtual Environ.* 13, 5 (October 2004), 572-577. DOI: http://dx.doi.org/10.1162/1054746042545238
14. Eugenia M. Kolasinski. 1995. Simulator sickness in virtual environments. Technical Report 1027 (ARTI-TR-1027). Alexandria, VA: Army Research Institute for the Behavioral and Social Sciences.
15. Frank L. Kooi and Marcel Mosch. 2006. Peripheral Motion Displays: Tapping the Potential of the Visual Periphery. Proceedings of the Human Factors and Ergonomics Society Annual Meeting, 50(16): 1604-1608. DOI: 10.1177/154193120605001619
16. James Jeng-Weei Lin, Henry B.L. Duh, Donald E. Parker, Habib Abi-Rached, and Thomas A. Furness. Effects of field of view on presence, enjoyment, memory, and simulator sickness in a virtual environment. In *Proceedings of IEEE Virtual Reality 2002* (IEEE VR '02), 164-171. http://dx.doi.org/10.1109/VR.2002.996519
17. Lumus, Ltd. Lumus OE-32. http://www.lumus-optical.com/index.php?option=com_content&task=view&id=9&Itemid=15. Retrieved September 23, 2015.
18. Andrew Maimone and Henry Fuchs. Computational Augmented Reality Eyeglasses. In *Proceedings of the 2013 IEEE International Symposium on Mixed and Augmented Reality* (ISMAR '13), 29-38. http://dx.doi.org/10.1109/ISMAR.2013.6671761
19. Andrew Maimone, Douglas Lanman, Kishore Rathinavel, Kurtis Keller, David Luebke, and Henry Fuchs. 2014. Pinlight displays: wide field of view augmented reality eyeglasses using defocused point light sources. *ACM Trans. Graph.* 33, 4, Article 89 (July 2014), 11 pages. http://doi.acm.org/10.1145/2601097.2601141
20. Suzanne P. McKee and Ken Nakayama. 1984. The detection of motion in the peripheral visual field. *Vision Research,* 24(1): 24-32. http://dx.doi.org/10.1016/0042-6989(84)90140-8
21. Hajime Nagahara, Yasushi Yagi, and Masahiko Yachida. 2003. Super wide viewer using catadioptrical optics. In *Proceedings of the ACM symposium on Virtual reality software and technology* (VRST '03). ACM, New York, NY, USA, 169-175. DOI=10.1145/1008653.1008683 http://doi.acm.org/10.1145/1008653.1008683

22. Takuya Nojima, Yoshihiko Saiga, Yu Okano, Yuki Hashimoto, and Hiroyuki Kajimoto. The Peripheral Display for Augmented Reality of Self-motion. In *Proceedings of the 17th International Conference on Artificial Reality and Telexistence 2007* 308-309. http://dx.doi.org/10.1109/ICAT.2007.44
23. Oculus VR. Best Practices Guide. Published December 5, 2014. Retrieved September 23, 2015. https://developer.oculus.com/documentation/intro-vr/latest/concepts/book-bp/
24. Jason Orlosky, Qifan Wu, Kiyoshi Kiyokawa, Haruo Takemura, and Christian Nitschke. 2014. Fisheye vision: peripheral spatial compression for improved field of view in head mounted displays. In *Proceedings of the 2nd ACM symposium on Spatial user interaction* (SUI '14). ACM, New York, NY, USA, 54-61. http://doi.acm.org/10.1145/2659766.2659771
25. Małgorzata Perz. 2010. Flicker perception in the periphery. MSc. Thesis, Technische Universiteit Eindhoven.
26. Phillips Television. Ambilight. http://ambilight.philips.com. Retrieved September 23, 2015.
27. D. Purves, G.J. Augustine, D. Fitzpatrick, et al., editors. Neuroscience. 2nd edition. Sunderland (MA): Sinauer Associates; 2001. Chapter 11: Anatomical Distribution of Rods and Cones.
28. Benjamin Watson, Neff Walker, Larry F. Hodges, and Aileen Worden. 1997. Managing level of detail through peripheral degradation: effects on search performance with a head-mounted display. *ACM Trans. Comput.-Hum. Interact.* 4, 4 (December 1997), 323-346. http://doi.acm.org/10.1145/267135.267137
29. Wearality Corporation. Wearality Sky. http://www.wearality.com/wearalitysky/. Retrieved September 23, 2015.
30. Ungyeon Yang and Gerard Jounghyun Kim. 2010. Increasing the geometric field of view in head mounted displays through proprioceptive task and multimodal feedback for effective close range interaction. *Behav. Inf. Technol.* 29, 2 (March 2010), 175-186. http://dx.doi.org/10.1080/01449290903160459

SnapToReality: Aligning Augmented Reality to the Real World

Benjamin Nuernberger[1,2] **Eyal Ofek**[1] **Hrvoje Benko**[1] **Andrew D. Wilson**[1]

[1]Microsoft Research
Redmond, WA, USA
{eyalofek, benko, awilson}@microsoft.com

[2]University of California, Santa Barbara
Santa Barbara, CA, USA
bnuernberger@cs.ucsb.edu

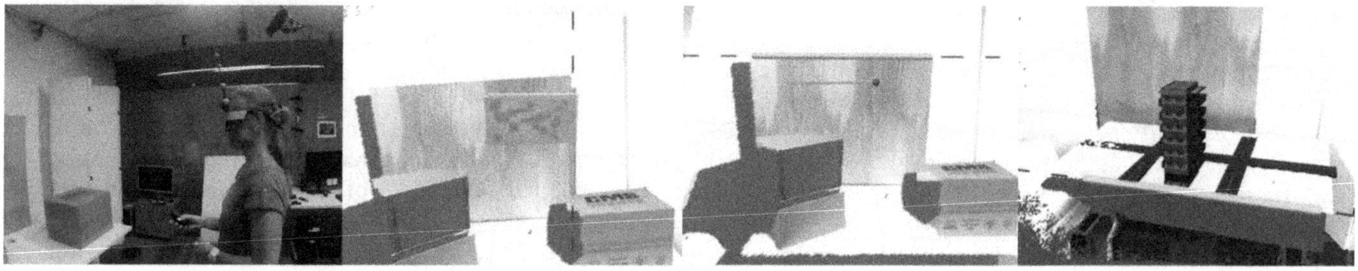

(a) (b) (c) (d)

Figure 1: *SnapToReality* allows users to easily position, orient, and scale AR virtual content with respect to real world constraints. Our prototype (a) extracts real world planar surfaces and edges as constraints so that users can easily align virtual content to the real world via snapping (b, c). *SnapToReality* techniques enable the seamless integration of AR content into the real world (d).

ABSTRACT

Augmented Reality (AR) applications may require the precise alignment of virtual objects to the real world. We propose automatic alignment of virtual objects to physical constraints calculated from the real world in real time ("snapping to reality"). We demonstrate *SnapToReality* alignment techniques that allow users to position, rotate, and scale virtual content to dynamic, real world scenes. Our proof-of-concept prototype extracts 3D edge and planar surface constraints. We furthermore discuss the unique design challenges of snapping in AR, including the user's limited field of view, noise in constraint extraction, issues with changing the view in AR, visualizing constraints, and more. We also report the results of a user study evaluating *SnapToReality*, confirming that aligning objects to the real world is significantly faster when assisted by snapping to dynamically extracted constraints. Perhaps more importantly, we also found that snapping in AR enables a fresh and expressive form of AR content creation.

Author Keywords

Interaction techniques; snapping; augmented reality; 3D user interaction; user studies.

CHI'16, May 07 - 12, 2016, San Jose, CA, USA

ACM 978-1-4503-3362-7/16/05...$15.00
DOI: http://dx.doi.org/10.1145/2858036.2858250

ACM Classification Keywords

H.5.1. Information interfaces and presentation (e.g., HCI): Multimedia Information Systems—Artificial, augmented, and virtual realities.

INTRODUCTION

In the real world, the positioning of objects is often guided by physical constraints (e.g., stacking objects on the table, or aligning a chair against the wall) or design constraints (e.g., aligning collinear objects, or resizing objects to have the same dimensions).

Performing similar actions in Augmented Reality (AR) may be difficult as virtual objects do not necessarily follow the rules of physics. Meanwhile, positioning virtual content in space around a user is an important task in many AR applications, such as industrial design, home redecoration, games, etc. While it is possible to position objects without regard to the real world surrounding the user, many AR experiences require a precise alignment between virtual objects and the real environment (e.g., Figure 2).

In traditional desktop computing, many sophisticated techniques are available to achieve precise alignment, such as dynamic guides and snapping behaviors [4]. Snapping is a common technique that helps users precisely align content with respect to certain constraints. A typical approach is to automatically align an object with a constraint whenever the user moves the object near to that constraint. For example, Microsoft PowerPoint uses "Smart Guides" to snap content so that it is parallel to other content, directly touching other content, etc. Snapping is also readily used in many 3D modeling programs, such as SketchUp and AutoCAD, making typically difficult 3D positioning tasks easier.

We introduce *SnapToReality*, the concept of snapping *virtual* content to *physical* constraints calculated from the real world in real time. In addition to supporting traditional alignment tasks in AR, SnapToReality enables new forms of interaction due to the world's dynamic nature: A door may be opened, a chair may be moved, and objects may be added or taken away, creating new opportunities for alignment. Furthermore, users may stack objects to generate a new snapping constraint, or even use physical tools (e.g., a measuring tape) to guide the formation of virtual objects.

Snapping to physical constraints is inherently more difficult than snapping to virtual constraints because the physical constraints are not known *a priori* and therefore must be extracted on-the-fly. If such constraints are extracted perfectly, the snapping procedure may be considered identical to snapping to virtual constraints. However, due to sensor noise, complexity of the environment, and AR hardware limitations, it is easily possible to extract the wrong constraints, causing an overall negative impact on performance. To our knowledge, our prototype is the first to demonstrate the extraction of 3D physical constraints to enhance the performance of 3D snapping in AR.

Our main contributions are as follows:

- A proof-of-concept prototype that implements two SnapToReality alignment techniques—snapping to real world edges and planar surfaces in real-time—enabling new expressive forms of interaction by utilizing dynamic real world scene content. Special care is taken to visualize the constraints in the real environment and outside the field of view.
- A detailed analysis of the important design considerations for SnapToReality alignment techniques, including the user's limited field of view, noise in constraint extraction, issues with changing the view in AR, issues concerning dynamic scenes, and visualization of physical constraints.
- A user evaluation demonstrating (a) that positioning and rotating AR objects to be aligned with a real world target is faster with snapping than without snapping; and (b) that snapping enables expressive forms of interaction for creating AR content aligned to the dynamic real world.

RELATED WORK

Snapping to Virtual Constraints

Snapping virtual content to virtual constraints has been investigated in many ways. Eric Bier's work on snap-dragging [3,4] was one of the first. In its 3D version, snap-dragging enables the precise placement of a 3D cursor (the "snap-dragging skitter"), which snaps to points, curves, and surfaces whenever it is close to existing geometry. Snapping between objects using simple affine transformations was also available, thus making precise, relative 3D modeling easier. The AR content creation mode in our prototype draws inspiration from the snap-dragging skitter.

Over the years, snapping has been improved in various ways [1,10,13,17,27]. Today, snapping is also used in many popular desktop and web applications, such as Microsoft PowerPoint, Google Slides, SketchUp, AutoCAD, etc. However, most if not all of these applications apply snapping to virtual constraints only. Snapping to real physical and dynamically changing constraints makes SnapToReality stand apart from previous works.

Snapping to Real Constraints

Important early works on extracting real-world constraints from 2D images for snapping were Gleicher's image-snapping [16] and Mortensen & Barrett's intelligent scissors [23]. More recently, Lee et al. [20,21] applied the idea of image-snapping to helping users annotate objects in 2D images in augmented reality. Nóbrega and Correia [26] also applied the idea of augmenting 2D images by extracting vanishing points and coarse depth from pairs of images. In SnapToReality, we take the idea of extracting real world constraints a step further, going from 2D to 3D.

To the best of our knowledge, no previous work exists on extracting 3D physical constraints in real-time specifically for snapping in augmented reality. With our prototype, we focused on snapping to real 3D edges and planar surfaces. Edge detection has traditionally been approached by using variants of the Hough Transform [8,9,18], or other 3D methods if such data is available [7,15]. Planar surface detection has also used variants of the Hough Transform [5,8,18,28] and we follow this approach.

Constraint Optimization Approaches

An alternative to snapping is constraint optimization [2,14,22,30,31]. Here, rather than allowing a user to manipulate an object to snap to a set of constraints, objects and constraints are jointly optimized to automatically achieve an optimal configuration of the objects with respect to the constraints. FLARE [14] is a recent example of such a system, in which a rule-based framework is used to lay out AR content with respect to real world planar surfaces. One shortcoming of constraint optimization approaches is that opportunities for user input are limited as the system attempts to achieve optimal configurations automatically. Perhaps the ideal system would first suggest automatic placement of objects via constraint optimization and then allow users to precisely manipulate individual objects thereafter. SnapToReality focuses on this latter part.

SNAP-TO-REALITY CONCEPT

SnapToReality allows snapping virtual objects to physical ones using constraints extracted in real-time. This can be used to position, rotate, and scale AR virtual objects to align with the physical world. Such snapping may be as simple as mimicking physical behaviors of real objects not penetrating each other, or as sophisticated as snapping to lie at evenly spaced distances, or to fit harmoniously with the environment color palette.

Motivating Scenarios

We envision alignments to real-world constraints as one of the core interactive requirements of most AR scenarios that deal with 3D modeling or 3D positioning of virtual content. Imagine the AR task of setting up virtual toys in a child's room. The user builds a train bridge from the bed, stretching virtual columns from the floor up to the height of the bed, and then installs tracks on the bed and a bridge that stretches along the wall. Or maybe a person would like to redecorate her room in AR, hanging virtual pictures on the wall, parallel to the existing artwork, walls, and the floor. Lastly, imagine being able to position a variety of 3D virtual content at different available spaces in the room (e.g., above the fireplace, on top of the kitchen cabinet, at the corner of the tabletop) as envisioned in Figure 2. These are just a few of the interaction scenarios made possible by SnapToReality.

Figure 2: An artistic vision of an AR desktop scenario as depicted by Microsoft's HoloLens[1]. Notice the precise positioning of AR apps in various locations in the kitchen—the "Recipes" app is centered over the cabinet doors; the sports game app over the fireplace; etc.

EXTRACTING PHYSICAL CONSTRAINTS

The core capability of our proof-of-concept SnapToReality alignment techniques is the real-time extraction of real world constraints—specifically linear edges and planar surfaces in the environment. These features are common in man-made scenes and often come from semantically important structures such as floors, supporting horizontal surfaces, walls that separates spaces, and more.

While there are potentially many other geometric and non-geometric constraints that can be deduced from the environment, we believe that linear edges and surfaces represent a good starting point in our exploration of SnapToReality techniques. The principles of our work may be extended to other types of constraints, which we leave as future work (cf. Semantic Snapping). We now describe the details of our extraction algorithms.

Extracting 3D Linear Edges

Typical man-made environments contain many linear features. Some of those edges distinguish objects from other objects behind them, others represent a change in an object's surface normal, and some come from a visible change of the object's color. We would like to recover a representation of such features in the scene so that virtual objects may be aligned to them.

We use a Microsoft Kinect 2.0 camera to capture the scene continuously in several modalities. First the depth channel is used to detect depth edges. The noisy depth data is temporally smoothed using an exponential filter:

$$filteredDepth_t = \alpha \times depth_t + (1 - \alpha) \times filteredDepth_{t-1}$$

where $\alpha = 0.3$ (found by trial and error) is a midpoint between good noise reduction (low α) and reaction to dynamic scenes (high α). Surface normals are computed at each point in the depth image [19] and are used to detect surface normal edges. Finally, the color channel is used to detect color edges. We now describe the pipeline, shown in Figure 3, for the edge extraction in each of these modalities.

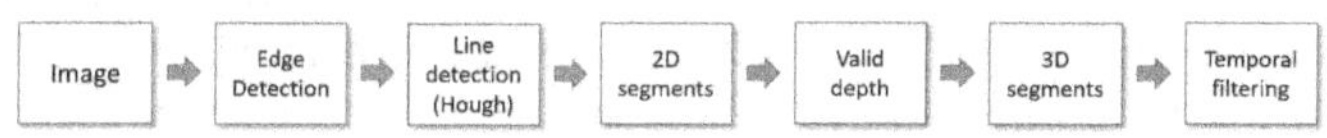

Figure 3: Edge extraction pipeline.

The most dominant lines are extracted from each depth, normals component, or color image by running the Hough Transform [9] on edge points detected by Canny edge detection [6]. A variant of RANSAC [11] is used to extract inlier edge points along each Hough line and to generate a more accurate line equation. Finally each 2D line is divided into segments having a density of edge points greater than some threshold (each line must have at least 35px in our implementation). Special care is given to depth edges, whose location may need to be shifted slightly to lie on the nearby occluding object that originated the edge.

2D line segments, extracted from all modalities, are back projected to 3D space if there are enough valid depth values along their length. RANSAC is used to fit 3D linear segments through the 3D edge points.

Special care is given to ensure the consistency of the recovered constraints over successive frames. We reduce temporal noise in positioning, orientation, and extent, by using a Kalman filter. Extracted segments are associated with existing edges based on proximity and similarity of their orientation. In addition, we require edges to have been seen in at least five frames prior to allowing the edge to be used for snapping; this minimizes the chance of the user relying on false positives from the edge extraction. Once detected, constraints will be maintained and updated unless they are not seen for one second, at which point they are removed; this helps overcome short periods of occlusion of constraints that may occur as a result of the user's motion or the scene object moving. Our edge extraction algorithm runs around 15 Hz in our prototype implementation. See Figure 4 and the supplementary video for typical results.

[1] https://www.microsoft.com/microsoft-hololens/en-us

Figure 4: An example of Kalman filtered edges; please see the supplemental video for more examples.

Extracting Planar Surfaces

Planar surfaces are detected in a fashion similar to that of recent plane and scene analysis methods [28]. Depth image normals vote for a plane equation parameterized by its azimuth, elevation, and distance from the origin. A Hough transform on 3D depth points is used to detect major plane equations in the scene.

Next, a greedy strategy is used to associate scene points with those planes. Unassigned 3D points that lie in the vicinity of each candidate plane (up to ~10 cm), with compatible normal directions, are associated with the plane (~10° angle, and may increase to 20° as depth noise grows for farther away planes; see Figure 5). This surface extraction algorithm runs around 4 Hz on our prototype implementation.

Figure 5: Plane extraction stages: IR image (top left), depth image (top right), shaded mesh indicating surface normals (bottom left), and recovered major planes (bottom right).

SNAP-TO-REALITY TECHNIQUES

We now discuss how the extracted constraints are used in precise alignment and snapping. In our prototype, a virtual object snaps to real edges and planar surfaces that are found to be compatible with the object's own edges and planes. The object's own edges and planes are referred to as "internal constraints" since they originate from the virtual object, while the physical constraints are external to the

Algorithm 1

```
SnapToRealConstraint:
  BestRealConstraint ← null
  MinCost ← ∞
  for each Internal {Edge, Planar Surface}
Constraint I:
    for each Real {Edge, Planar Surface}
Constraint R:
      if IsCompatible(I, R):
        cost ← Cost(I, R)
        if cost < MinCost:
          BestRealConstraint ← R
          MinCost ← cost
        endif
      endif
    endfor
  endfor
  return BestRealConstraint

D ← {edge, plane} distance threshold
A ← {edge, normal} angle threshold
IsCompatible(I, R):
  if distance(centroid of I, R) > D
    return false
  if angle_between(I, R) > A
    return false
  return true

Cost(I, R):
  c ← α × distance(centroid of I, R)
  c ← c + β × distance(centroid of I, centroid
of R)
  if R was previously BestRealConstraint
    c ← γ × c
  endif
  return c
```

object. Our approach is designed to support the interactive selection of compatible physical constraints. For example, an AR designer may decide that a virtual toy soldier's internal constraints should simply be its bounding box, thus allowing snapping to physical planes and edges.

We now describe the two SnapToReality alignment techniques implemented in our prototype—*edge snapping* and *planar surface snapping*.

Edge & Planar Surface Snapping

Our edge and plane snapping algorithm is summarized in Algorithm 1 and described as follows. For each internal edge (plane) constraint, we search through all physical edge (plane) constraints for *compatible* edges (planes).

An edge (plane) is compatible if the distance between the internal edge midpoint (plane centroid) and its projection onto the physical edge (plane) is less than some threshold (e.g., 20 cm), and the internal and physical edges are approximately parallel (e.g., within 20° for edges and 60° for planes). We keep the physical edge (plane) with the lowest cost, where the cost is a linear combination of (a) the distance between the internal edge midpoint (plane centroid) and its projection onto the physical edge (plane) and (b) the distance between the internal edge midpoint (plane centroid) and the physical edge midpoint (plane centroid); in our experiments, $\alpha = 1, \beta = 1$. The second component of this linear combination (b) aids in favoring edges (planes) that are nearby. For temporal consistency, previously selected edges and planes are favored ($\gamma = 0.1$). If a compatible physical edge (plane) is found, we rotate and translate the AR virtual content so that its corresponding internal edge (plane) is parallel to and overlapping the physical edge (plane).

Visualization of Compatible Physical Constraints

To minimize user distraction, compatible edges and planes are visualized only when snapping to them. Compatible edges are visualized via a green cylinder and a dotted red cylinder edge extending outward from the edge (see Figure 6, left). Compatible planar surfaces are visualized via a fading circular region on the surface's centroid and a red line connecting the snapping virtual content to the surface's centroid (see Figure 6). This red line visualization is important for small field of view AR displays, as the user may otherwise not know what the virtual content is snapping to (cf. User's Limited Field of View).

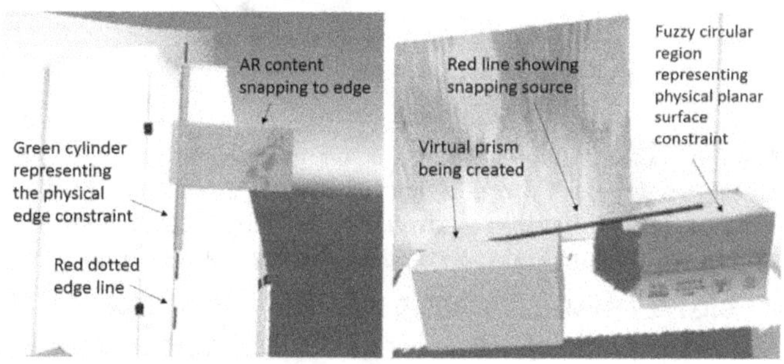

Figure 6: Visualizations for compatible physical edges (left) and planar surfaces (right).

PROTOTYPE SNAP-TO-REALITY IMPLEMENTATION

In our AR system, the user wears an optical see-through head-mounted near-eye display (Lumus DK-32[2] 1280x720) calibrated with a method similar to the single point active alignment method [29]. Figure 7 shows the view through the Lumus display. Our glasses are equipped with 6 retro-reflective spheres that are tracked using a ceiling-mounted motion capture system, Natural Point's OptiTrack Flex 3 system[3] (12 cameras). Our glasses are also augmented with a 9 degrees-of-freedom inertial measurement unit (SparkFun's Razor SEN-10736[4]) which provides a smoother estimate of the unit's orientation. The orientation data from the IMU (~160Hz) is integrated with the orientation and position data from the OptiTrack system (~100Hz) for a relatively smooth, low latency operation. We render at 60Hz, matching the refresh rate of the glasses. Figure 8 shows the hardware components.

We used a Microsoft Kinect 2.0 sensor to obtain RGB+Depth images in real-time for extracting the real world 3D edges and planar surfaces. Virtual content was created using the Unity 5 game engine and was shown to the user via the Lumus glasses. In our current prototype configuration, the Kinect camera is mounted above the user to observe the physical scene (see Figure 8).

Figure 7: View through Lumus display (left); note that the virtual content does not appear as bright to the human eye. Screenshot of Unity player view (right). The red dot indicates the user's gaze direction.

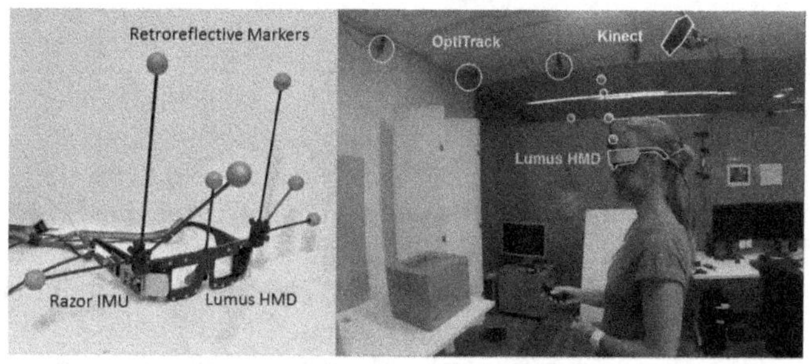

Figure 8: Hardware used in our prototype.

User input was obtained through a Kensington Wireless Presenter remote controller. All processing was done on a single PC with an Intel Xeon E5-1620 processor with 16 GB of RAM and an NVIDIA GeForce GTX 980 GPU.

To correctly render the occlusion of virtual objects by real objects, the depth image acquired by Kinect camera is rendered as a black (invisible in the glasses) mesh. AR virtual objects are rendered offset by about 5cm towards the head-worn glasses to help overcome any noise in the depth image and system calibration.

Demo Applications

To showcase our SnapToReality alignment techniques, we developed two prototype AR scenarios—*content placement* and *content creation*. In each, the user interacts with a virtual object in the following way: A ray is cast from the center of the tracked glasses, and its point of intersection with the scene geometry is regarded as the object or cursor position. The user can then interact with objects that intersect the ray using the buttons on the remote controller.

We considered other interaction methods such as using a ray cast from the handheld remote. After preliminary usability evaluations we settled on head gaze-based interaction, which was simpler to implement as display and interaction share the same location. We leave finding the

[2] http://www.lumus-optical.com/

[3] http://www.optitrack.com/products/flex-3/

[4] https://www.sparkfun.com/products/10736

most ergonomic interaction method for snapping in AR as future work.

AR Content Placement

A virtual AR app window is positioned in space and is highlighted whenever the user gazes at it (see Figure 7). The user can "pick up" the highlighted window by pressing a button on the remote controller. The window can then be positioned, oriented, and scaled by the user's head gaze direction, until the user drops the object by pressing the same button again. While picked up, the AR app window is positioned at the intersection point of the user's head direction and the geometry, and oriented towards the user's head gaze. To scale an app window, the user drops the window in place, and then gazes at a corner of the window. Pressing a button toggles scaling mode, resizing from that corner while the opposite corner is fixed. Scale snapping works by finding the lowest cost compatible external constraint for each internal constraint used in scaling (using Algorithm 1).

AR Content Creation

This demo application is inspired by SketchUp's line, rectangle, and push/pull drawing tools[5]. As the user gazes at a planar surface, the detected surface is visualized by a fuzzy circle and a surface normal (see Figure 9, top left). Pressing the remote's right button begins drawing a 3D edge on the plane starting at the intersection point of the user's gaze direction and the plane. The edge's end point is controlled by the user's gaze direction (see Figure 9, top right) and can snap to nearby physical edges. Furthermore, the edge can snap to be made parallel or perpendicular to nearby edges. Pressing the right button a second time fixes the edge's end point and begins extending a rectangular area away from the fixed edge. Again, the user's current gaze direction determines the size of the rectangular plane, and a third right button press fixes the plane (see Figure 9, bottom left). Now a 3D box can be extruded upwards away from the plane. The height of the 3D box is determined by finding the closest intersection between the user's head direction and the ray in direction of the 3D box extrusion starting from the 3D box's center. This height can snap to compatible planar surfaces and also to nearby edge endpoints (see Figure 6, right). A final right button press finishes the box creation process (see Figure 9, bottom right). In each step of the process, the left button of the remote performs an 'undo' operation. Figure 9 illustrates this entire process.

Users can optionally scale a face of a completed box by directing their gaze toward the face and pressing the right button. In a similar fashion, the height of the 3D prism with respect to that face is determined by the closest intersection between the user's gaze direction and the ray in direction of the extrusion, starting from the 3D box's center.

[5] http://www.sketchup.com/learn

Prototype Limitations

One limitation of our prototype is that the Kinect camera is statically mounted above the user. However, we envision similar interactions would be possible using a depth camera worn by the user or mounted on the glasses.

Another limitation is that the accuracy of the Kinect depth map is limited, contributing a significant source of noise. More sophisticated surface reconstruction methods such as Kinect Fusion [25] or DynamicFusion [24] might help.

Figure 9: Flow of AR content creation. Top left: The user's head direction defines a cursor on a physical surface. Top right: Clicking a button starts drawing a line on the surface. Bottom left: Clicking again extrudes the drawn line to a rectangle. Bottom right: Extruding the rectangle to a 3D box.

DESIGN CONSIDERATIONS FOR SNAP-TO-REALITY

In this section, we discuss practical design considerations, limitations, and insights gained while developing SnapToReality techniques. Because these observations are not limited to our current prototype, we hope that this discussion will help developers and researchers extend and apply the SnapToReality concept. We note that in addition to what we discuss here, traditional snapping design issues (not specific to SnapToReality) are also important when designing any snapping system (e.g., snapping hierarchies, the amount of constraints to show to the user, etc.).

The main considerations and challenges in enabling SnapToReality systems are: limited field of view, noise in constraint extraction, changing the view in AR, issues concerning dynamic scenes, and visualization of physical constraints. We now discuss each in detail.

Limited Field of View

User's Limited Field of View

Today's AR glasses typically have a very limited field of view (e.g., the Lumus glasses have about a 40° diagonal FOV). Thus, many constraints that an object may snap to are outside the user's field of view. In addition, even if AR glasses had an unlimited field of view, a particular constraint could still be behind the user, out of sight. There are at least two ways to address this problem.

First, the system can visualize available constraints that are outside the field of view. This is the approach taken in our prototype. When virtual content begins to snap to a compatible constraint, we visualize those constraints in case they are out of sight: for edges, by extending them with red dotted edges; for planes, by drawing a red edge from the virtual content to the plane's centroid (see Figure 6).

Another possible way to overcome this problem is to let the user actively preselect a constraint by bringing it into the field of view and then returning the view to manipulate the virtual content. For example, the user may gaze directly at a constraint and then press a button to select it. A positive consequence of this approach is that the user's current field of view can aid in the physical constraints extraction process. For example, the system may simply follow the user's gaze to limit its extraction there.

Camera's Limited Field of View

The camera's limited field of view also means that extracting many physical constraints is challenging. If the user wants to snap virtual content to many different constraints, the camera must first be able to see all those constraints. Thus, unless snapping is limited to the camera's field of view, a global analysis of the scene is required.

Noise in Constraint Extraction

In contrast to typical virtual scenes, the complexity of real world geometry, texture, and sensor noise may lead to a very dense and noisy set of potential constraints. As with any snapping technique, high density of constraints will negatively affect the utility and usability of snapping.

Active selection of constraints by the user is again one way to overcome this problem. By putting the user "in the loop" of the constraint extraction process, the effects of sensor noise can be diminished. The user can either select the constraint directly or explicitly discard it.

We can also substantially minimize the effects of sensor noise by limiting the types of compatible constraints we extract. This can be achieved by adjusting the virtual content's snapping abilities (called "internal constraints" in our prototype). For example, a cube has 6 planar surfaces; each of the cube's planar surfaces may only snap to physical planar surfaces, not corners or edges. Therefore, under this assumption, we can limit the types of physical constraints to extract to those that are compatible with the virtual content. Used by our prototype, this approach mitigates problems with sensor noise.

Changing the View in AR

In AR, users see virtual objects interacting with real objects as if they were life size. Users may move themselves closer to the real and virtual objects to inspect them more closely, or move to encourage the extraction of a physical constraint. However, users are limited by the physics of the real world in how they may change their view. This limits the ability to see more detail, perform more precise manipulation, zoom out to see an overview, or look behind objects that are occluded. In addition, physically moving around the environment may introduce user fatigue. Future SnapToReality systems need to account for these considerations, including snapping at far distances and helping the user know about available snapping constraints outside the field of view (cf. User's Limited Field of View).

Interacting with Dynamic Constraints

When constraints are obtained in real-time from the dynamic physical world, new types of snapping interaction are possible. Physical constraints can be altered on the fly to enable virtual content to be translated, rotated, or scaled more appropriately. For example, virtual content can be scaled to different physical extents by simply moving physical objects in the scene. The possibilities of actively manipulating reality to alter virtual content in precise ways via snapping could be explored further.

One interesting question that arises with dynamic constraints is how to deal with a constraint that is currently being used, but then suddenly disappears in the real world during the interaction (e.g., a real object moves away). In our prototype, we chose to simply keep the constraint alive until the end of the interaction. However, the constraint does not move with the real object as it moves away. Such capability may be desired and we leave it as future work.

Visualizing Physical Constraints in AR

Choosing how to visualize extracted physical constraints is another important matter of design. Should the system visualize all available constraints, none, or only those currently being snapping to by virtual content?

In some simple cases it may be obvious which physical object a virtual object is snapping to without rendering the available constraints. In others, it may be necessary to render all available constraints. Visualizations are particularly important when snapping to physical constraints whose source is far away or outside the user's field of view (e.g., snapping virtual content to be aligned with the top of a table that is behind the user). In this case, clear guides should let the user be aware of the source. This is especially important when using today's available AR displays which have a narrow field of view. Figure 6 shows how our prototype visualizes edge constraints and planar surface constraints, drawing inspiration from common snapping applications using dotted linear edges to represent linear constraints.

USER EVALUATIONS

We conducted three preliminary evaluations of various aspects of our prototype.

Evaluation of Constraint Extraction Algorithms

To evaluate our constraint extraction algorithms, we recorded eleven scenes showing a large range of physical environments. We asked four participants (all male, 24 to 33 years old, avg. 28 years old) to indicate up to ten edges and ten surfaces they would envision aligning AR content to for each of the scenes. Participants indicated this by drawing on the color image of each scene.

We compared the edges and planar surfaces drawn by users to those extracted from our algorithm by aggregating the responses of the four participants and visually comparing them to the extracted constraints (see Figure 10 and the supplementary video). Our algorithm was able to detect 51.95% of user drawn edges (min. 30.43%, max 77.78% across all scenes) and 60% of user drawn planar surfaces (min. 41.67%, max 81.82% across all scenes). We note that for each scene, we did not modify any of the edge or plane detection algorithm parameters. Had we done so for each scene, we believe the percentage of detected user drawn constraints would only increase.

Figure 10: Living room scene overlaid with user drawn edges (top left) and planar surfaces (bottom left) compared to the edges and planar surfaces detected by our algorithm (top right and bottom right, respectively).

Evaluation of SnapToReality Techniques

We invited 8 different participants (all male, 23 to 49 years old, avg. 30 years old) to evaluate our SnapToReality techniques. Participants received $10 for their participation and each session lasted approximately one hour. The physical scene used for interaction included a table, several boxes, a wooden board, a white panel folding screen, and a wall in the background (see Figure 11).

Participants filled out pre-study and post-study questionnaires and separately evaluated both AR Content Placement and AR Content Creation demos. They were given a few minutes to familiarize themselves with the interface for each demo.

Evaluation of AR Content Placement

To evaluate the potential benefits of snapping, we asked the participants to place and size a box representing a mock AR application window at various locations around the room. After verbally confirming that the person understood the interface, they were given a set of five training trials. Next, each participant completed twenty trials, each composed of a positioning and orienting stage followed by a resizing stage. The position, orientation, and size for each trial were chosen beforehand to align with various physical objects, and the order of the trials was chosen randomly. Ten trials were completed with snapping and ten trials without snapping. The order of snapping and no-snapping conditions was counterbalanced over the eight participants. Interaction in the no-snapping condition was identical to that of the snapping condition except that snapping was disabled (physical constraints were extracted but not used).

Figure 11: View from the Kinect camera for the user evaluation of SnapToReality techniques.

In the positioning and orienting stage, participants were shown an AR app window placed randomly near a target window, which at first was invisible. They then picked up the window by gazing at it and pressing the top button on the wireless remote. At this point, a timer began and the target window location was now shown as a white transparent box. Participants were asked to place the AR app window at the target location as quickly as possible, and end the trial by pressing the top button again. If the window was placed too far away from the target (distance between the center points of the windows greater than 10 cm) or not close enough in orientation (angle between the surface normals of the windows greater than 10°), text appeared notifying the user that the window is not close enough to the target. Participants then had to pick up the window and try again. Once the window was positioned and oriented closely enough to the target, the timer stopped and the user saw the text, "Correct!"

Next, during the resizing stage, a target transparent box appeared, showing the desired dimensions of the window and a second timer began. Participants then had to scale the window to match the target (measured in terms of both position and scale, within 10 cm). To make this second stage similar between snapping and no-snapping conditions, we adjusted the starting position and orientation of the window to be the same for all trials.

In all trials, a one minute timeout was used and treated as outliers in the data, removed before analysis. With snapping enabled, participants took an average of 4.45s (median 2.74s, std. dev. 5.34) to position and orient AR app windows correctly. With snapping disabled, participants took an average of 11.36s (median 9.89s, std. dev. 6.75). A paired t-test indicated a statistical significance (p-value << 0.001). For scaling, participants took an average of 8.18s (median 7.89s, std. dev. 3.97) with snapping and 8.71s (7.43s, std. dev. 5.12) without snapping. A paired t-test did not indicate any statistical significance.

In the post-study questionnaire, participants were asked to compare their experience with and without snapping. Here we list some of their feedback:

"With snapping, I trusted the system to take me there and it allowed me to be a bit careless and [speed] things up. I would just go to the nearest corner and trust the system to pick the best spot up for me."

"Snapping objects [...] was a more subtle interaction. Small head movements were enough to get the job done. Whereas without snaps I had to use my whole body to get the object where I wanted."

Evaluation of AR Content Creation

In the second part of the study, we sought to assess qualitatively how well participants can create simple virtual objects in AR. After explaining the interface, we allowed participants to play with this mode freely as long they wished. For this task, snapping was always enabled.

Participants created various structures of 3D geometry using the simple prism creation tool. Figure 12 shows an example of such a structure created by a participant. Participants were made aware of the ability to place virtual content aligned to dynamic elements in the scene, such as boxes that had been moved into place, and a measuring tape used to extrude prisms to certain heights. Please see the supplemental video for more examples.

Figure 12: Example of virtual content created by a participant using AR Content Creation. Here, physical walls (planar surfaces) were used as constraints to create "virtual shelves."

In the post-study questionnaire, participants were asked to describe their approach of creating 3D boxes with snapping. Here we list some of their feedback:

"I started by positioning the cursor near the edge of another object, like the table or box, and then moved to another edge to set the area. Then setting the volume was fairly easy once the other two were in place."

"I started by choosing the 'right plane'. I moved until I saw the angle of the plane I wanted. Then I drew one face on that plane, not caring too much about the snapping. Finally, I adjusted the height, mostly trying to match the height of the surrounding objects using snapping. I resized it sometimes to match different heights."

Additional Questionnaire Results

In the post-study questionnaire, participants were asked to rate several statements using a Likert scale. The statements were as follows: "With{out} snapping, I can easily {place, orient, resize} objects {where, how} I want," "While interacting with snapping {enabled, disabled}, I felt fatigued," and "Snapping in augmented reality is useful." Responses are shown in Figure 13. The Wilcoxon signed-rank test found that for the placing, orienting, and feeling fatigued statements, participants rated snapping significantly better than without snapping at a 0.05 level of significance. As with the timing results, no statistical significance was found comparing resizing with and without snapping. Finally, all participants agreed or strongly agreed that snapping in AR is useful.

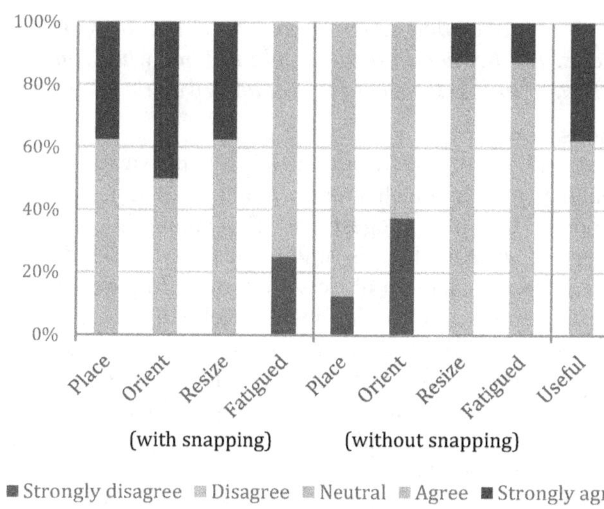

Figure 13: Chart visualizing post-study questionnaire responses (best viewed in color).

We also asked participants several open-ended questions. Some representative quotes with their corresponding questions are as follows:

Q: When did you find snapping most helpful? Least helpful?
"Snapping was most helpful when moving something quickly across the scene to a general target area. Movements requiring more finesse or accuracy on behalf of

the user are more frustrating when snaps suddenly make drastic shift."

"When snapping worked it was very helpful because I didn't have to move very much to achieve success..."

(Referring to the Likert scale statements): Please briefly describe why you chose the ratings in the previous question.
"Placing objects is quite easy even without snapping. Certainly snapping helped a bit, just did not affect the overall experience too much. Orienting and scaling things, on the other hand, when done imprecisely, can often be quite obvious and seem bizarre, so snapping helps a lot more in these cases. [...] snapping reduces the time needed, hence less fatigue."

"Overall snapping is a useful feature. However, just as with other design programs like Photoshop, it can become obtrusive in certain situations. Easily being able to toggle between snapping and non-snapping behavior would be ideal. In this specific study, it seemed like when the tracking found the surfaces correctly and the world locking was working that snapping was fairly helpful. When either of those two breakdown, snapping becomes more of a hassle."

Q: What snapping features would you like to have for augmented reality?
"It would be great if I could put my hand or finger in the field of view and point where I want the object to snap to, or where I want the edge to scale to. Manual pointing/direction would be nice. I envision it as sort of a physical mouse pointer for the virtual objects."

"Snap to planes and edges of various virtual and physical objects. It'd be nice to also be able to filter what you snap to (kind of like AutoCAD's [...]) at any given time."

Discussion
In general, we observed that participants physically walked around the room much more without snapping than with snapping. This may suggest that 3D snapping is even more important in AR than in traditional 2D or 3D desktop environments where all objects are virtual. In purely virtual environments, "magical" navigation techniques (e.g., flying and teleporting) enable quick and easy viewpoint positioning for easier interaction with virtual content. In AR, however, users are limited to physical navigation and thus are not always able to quickly and easily assume different viewpoints.

The lack of a statistically significant difference in scaling times in our evaluation of AR Content Placement is most likely due to the fact that only two degrees of freedom were being manipulated, and that we did not allow snapping to position content arbitrarily within the snapping threshold (by deactivating snapping or by automatic methods [1,10]). Adding such features and also comparing scaling in three dimensions may change results for future experiments.

In addition to comments that may apply to any snapping system, participants' open-ended responses also verified certain unique points about snapping in AR. For example, one participant noted needing to move their whole body to achieve object positioning when not using snapping; while with snapping, he only needed small head movements (see comment in Evaluation of AR Content Placement).

FUTURE WORK
Selecting Constraints via Other Modalities
We imagine many other ways in which users can actively select constraints. For example, users should be able to physically touch a constraint to select it. Natural language processing along with computer vision scene understanding is also an interesting avenue for future work (e.g., "place the app parallel to and to the right of the door").

Using Snapping for Physical Objects
An interesting idea that has previously been proposed by Forster and Tozzi [12] but still remains an open area of research is the use of snapping in AR to align *physical* objects to *physical* constraints. An application for this might be interior design.

Semantic Snapping
Usually when we refer to snapping, we imply a geometric relationship of snapping. This may include geometric proximity in translation or rotation; objects being perpendicular or parallel to one another; aligning to dominant directions/axes (e.g., gravity); aligning to mid-points; etc. However, using *semantic* relationships is another possible way to achieve snapping. For example, an AR app related to cooking may favor snapping to relevant physical areas of a kitchen (cf. Figure 2). This, however, would require a detailed semantic understanding of the physical scene. In our SnapToReality prototype, we chose to focus on simple geometric relationships.

CONCLUSION
SnapToReality alignment techniques allow users to position, rotate, and scale virtual content to dynamic, real world scenes. Our prototype system extracts physical linear edges and planar surfaces in real-time and allows users to manipulate and create AR content precisely aligned to the real world. We contribute a set of design considerations and insights for future designers of AR snapping systems. In particular, we note the issues of a small field of view in AR, sensor noise in the constraint extraction process, changing the view in AR being limited to physical movements (thus making SnapToReality an important interaction paradigm to quickly achieve precise positioning), interacting with dynamic constraints, and considerations on how to visualize physical constraints. Finally, our user evaluations show that aligning virtual content to physical constraints in our prototype system is significantly faster with snapping than without snapping. Snapping in AR was also shown to enable novel forms of AR content creation interaction.

ACKNOWLEDGMENTS
We thank Michael Waechter and the anonymous reviewers for their helpful feedback.

REFERENCES

1. Patrick Baudisch, Edward Cutrell, Ken Hinckley, and Adam Eversole. 2005. Snap-and-go: helping users align objects without the modality of traditional snapping. In *Proceedings of the SIGCHI Conference on Human Factors in Computing Systems* (CHI '05), 301-310. http://doi.org/10.1145/1054972.1055014

2. Blaine Bell, Steven Feiner, and Tobias Höllerer. 2001. View management for virtual and augmented reality. In *Proceedings of the 14th Annual ACM Symposium on User Interface Software and Technology* (UIST '01), 101-110. http://doi.org/10.1145/502348.502363

3. Eric A. Bier and Maureen C. Stone. 1986. Snap-dragging. In *Proceedings of the 13th Annual Conference on Computer Graphics and Interactive Techniques* (SIGGRAPH '86), 233-240. http://dx.doi.org/10.1145/15922.15912

4. Eric A. Bier. 1990. Snap-dragging in three dimensions. In *Proceedings of the 1990 Symposium on Interactive 3D Graphics* (I3D '90), 193-204. http://doi.org/10.1145/91385.91446

5. Dorit Borrmann, Jan Elseberg, Kai Lingemann, and Andreas Nüchter. 2011. The 3D Hough Transform for plane detection in point clouds: A review and a new accumulator design. *3D Research*. 2, 2, Article 32 (June 2011): 1-13. http://dx.doi.org/10.1007/3DRes.02(2011)3

6. John Canny. 1986. A Computational Approach to Edge Detection. *IEEE Transactions on Pattern Analysis and Machine Intelligence* (PAMI). 8, 6 (Nov. 1986): 679-698. http://doi.org/10.1109/TPAMI.1986.4767851

7. Changhyun Choi, Alexander J. B. Trevor, and Henrik I. Christensen. 2013. RGB-D Edge Detection and Edge-based Registration. In *Proceedings of the IEEE/RSJ International Conference on Intelligent Robots and Systems* (IROS '13), 1568-1575. http://doi.org/10.1109/IROS.2013.6696558

8. Richard O. Duda and Peter E. Hart. 1972. Use of the Hough transformation to detect lines and curves in pictures. *Communications of the ACM*. 15, 1 (Jan. 1972): 11-15. http://doi.org/10.1145/361237.361242

9. Leandro A. F. Fernandes and Manuel M. Oliveira. 2008. Real-time line detection through an improved Hough transform voting scheme. *Pattern Recognition*. 41, 1 (Jan. 2008): 299-314. http://dx.doi.org/10.1016/j.patcog.2007.04.003

10. Jennifer Fernquist, Garth Shoemaker, and Kellogg S. Booth. 2011. "Oh Snap" – Helping Users Align Digital Objects on Touch Interfaces. In *Proceedings of the 13th IFIP TC 13 International Conference on Human-Computer Interaction* (INTERACT 2011), 338-355. http://dx.doi.org/10.1007/978-3-642-23765-2_24

11. Martin A. Fischler and Robert C. Bolles. 1981. Random sample consensus: a paradigm for model fitting with applications to image analysis and automated cartography. *Communications of the ACM*. 24, 6 (June 1981): 381-395. http://doi.org/10.1145/358669.358692

12. Carlos H. Q. Forster and Clésio L. Tozzi. 2001. An architecture based on constraints for augmented shared workspaces. In *Proceedings of the 14th Brazilian Symposium on Computer Graphics and Image Processing* (SIBGRAPI '01), 328-335. http://doi.org/10.1109/SIBGRAPI.2001.963073

13. Mathias Frisch, Ricardo Langner, and Raimund Dachselt. 2011. Neat: a set of flexible tools and gestures for layout tasks on interactive displays. In *Proceedings of the ACM International Conference on Interactive Tabletops and Surfaces* (ITS '11), 1-10. http://doi.org/10.1145/2076354.2076356

14. Ran Gal, Lior Shapira, Eyal Ofek, and Pushmeet Kohli. 2014. FLARE: Fast layout for augmented reality applications. In *Proceedings of the 13th IEEE International Symposium on Mixed and Augmented Reality* (ISMAR '14), 207-212. http://doi.org/10.1109/ISMAR.2014.6948429

15. Natasha Gelfand and Leonidas J. Guibas. 2004. Shape segmentation using local slippage analysis. In *Proceedings of the 2004 Eurographics/ACM SIGGRAPH Symposium on Geometry Processing* (SGP '04), 214-223. http://doi.org/10.1145/1057432.1057461

16. Michael Gleicher. 1995. Image snapping. In *Proceedings of the 22nd Annual Conference on Computer Graphics and Interactive Techniques* (SIGGRAPH '95), 183-190. http://doi.org/10.1145/218380.218441

17. Seongkook Heo, Yong-Ki Lee, Jiho Yeom, and Geehyuk Lee. 2012. Design of a shape dependent snapping algorithm. In *CHI '12 Extended Abstracts on Human Factors in Computing Systems* (CHI EA '12), 2207-2212. http://doi.org/10.1145/2212776.2223777

18. Paul V. C. Hough. 1962. Method and means for recognizing complex patterns. (Dec. 1962). *US Patent 3069654 A,* Filed Mar. 25, 1960, Issued Dec. 18, 1962.

19. Klaas Klasing, Daniel Althoff, Dirk Wollherr, and Martin Buss. 2009. Comparison of surface normal estimation methods for range sensing applications. In *Proceedings of the 26th IEEE International Conference on Robotics and Automation* (ICRA '09), 3206-3211. http://doi.org/10.1109/ROBOT.2009.5152493

20. Gun A. Lee, Ungyeon Yang, Yongwan Kim, Dongsik Jo, and Ki-Hong Kim. Snap-to-feature interface for annotation in mobile augmented reality. In *Augmented*

Reality Super Models Workshop at the 9th IEEE International Symposium on Mixed and Augmented Reality (ISMAR '10), Retrieved September 14, 2015 from http://www.icg.tugraz.at/Members/arth/arsupermodels/04_lee.pdf

21. Gun A. Lee and Mark Billinghurst. 2012. Assistive techniques for precise touch interaction in handheld augmented reality environments. In *Proceedings of the 11th ACM SIGGRAPH International Conference on Virtual-Reality Continuum and its Applications in Industry* (VRCAI '12), 279-285. http://doi.org/10.1145/2407516.2407582

22. Paul Merrell, Eric Schkufza, Zeyang Li, Maneesh Agrawala, and Vladlen Koltun. 2011. Interactive furniture layout using interior design guidelines. *ACM Transactions on Graphics* (TOG). 30, 4, Article 87 (July 2011): 1-10. http://dx.doi.org/10.1145/2010324.1964982

23. Eric N. Mortensen and William A. Barrett. 1998. Interactive segmentation with intelligent scissors. *Graphical Models and Image Processing*. 60, 5 (Sept. 1998): 349-384. http://dx.doi.org/10.1006/gmip.1998.0480

24. Richard A. Newcombe, Dieter Fox, and Steven M. Seitz. 2015. DynamicFusion: Reconstruction and tracking of non-rigid scenes in real-time. In *Proceedings of the 28th IEEE Conference on Computer Vision and Pattern Recognition* (CVPR '15), 343-352. http://dx.doi.org/10.1109/CVPR.2015.7298631

25. Richard A. Newcombe, Shahram Izadi, Otmar Hilliges, David Molyneaux, David Kim, Andrew J. Davison, Pushmeet Kohli, Jamie Shotton, Steve Hodges, and Andrew Fitzgibbon. 2011. KinectFusion: Real-time dense surface mapping and tracking. In *Proceedings of the 10th IEEE International Symposium on Mixed and Augmented Reality* (ISMAR '11), 127-136. http://doi.org/10.1109/ISMAR.2011.6092378

26. Rui Nóbrega and Nuno Correia. 2012. Magnetic augmented reality. In *Proceedings of the International Working Conference on Advanced Visual Interfaces* (AVI '12), 332-335. http://doi.org/10.1145/2254556.2254620

27. Ji-Young Oh, Wolfgang Stuerzlinger, and John Danahy. 2006. SESAME: towards better 3D conceptual design systems. In *Proceedings of the 6th Conference on Designing Interactive Systems* (DIS '06), 80-89. http://doi.org/10.1145/1142405.1142419

28. Nathan Silberman, Lior Shapira, Ran Gal, and Pushmeet Kohli. 2014. A contour completion model for augmenting surface reconstructions. In *Proceedings of the 14th European Conference on Computer Vision* (ECCV '14), 488-503. http://dx.doi.org/10.1007/978-3-319-10578-9_32

29. Mihran Tuceryan and Nassir Navab. 2000. Single point active alignment method (SPAAM) for optical see-through HMD calibration for AR. In *Proceedings of the IEEE and ACM International Symposium on Augmented Reality* (ISAR '00), 149-158. http://doi.org/10.1109/ISAR.2000.880938

30. Ken Xu, James Stewart, and Eugene Fiume. 2002. Constraint-based Automatic Placement for Scene Composition. In *Proceedings of the Graphics Interface Conference* (GI '02), 25-34. Retrieved September 14, 2015 from http://graphicsinterface.org/wp-content/uploads/gi2002-4.pdf

31. Pengfei Xu, Hongbo Fu, Chiew-Lan Tai, and Takeo Igarashi. 2015. GACA: Group-Aware Command-based Arrangement of Graphic Elements. In *Proceedings of the 33rd Annual ACM Conference on Human Factors in Computing Systems* (CHI '15), 2787-2795. http://doi.org/10.1145/2702123.2702198

Virtual Objects as Spatial Cues in Collaborative Mixed Reality Environments: How They Shape Communication Behavior and User Task Load

Jens Müller, Roman Rädle, Harald Reiterer
Human-Computer Interaction Group, University of Konstanz
{Jens.Mueller,Roman.Raedle,Harald.Reiterer}@uni-konstanz.de

ABSTRACT
In collaborative activities, collaborators can use physical objects in their shared environment as spatial cues to guide each other's attention. Collaborative mixed reality environments (MREs) include both physical and virtual objects. To study how virtual objects influence collaboration and whether they are used as spatial cues, we conducted a controlled lab experiment with 16 dyads. Results of our study show that collaborators favored the virtual objects as spatial cues over the physical environment and the physical objects: Collaborators used significantly less deictic gestures in favor of more disambiguous verbal references and a decreased subjective workload when virtual objects were present. This suggests adding additional virtual objects as spatial cues to MREs to improve user experience during collaborative mixed reality tasks.

Author Keywords
Mixed reality; collaboration; virtual spatial cues.

ACM Classification Keywords
H.5.2. Information interfaces and presentation (e.g., HCI): User Interfaces.

INTRODUCTION
Mixed reality (MR), as introduced by Milgram and Kishino [11], describes the blending of physical and virtual objects on a single display. Virtual objects are rendered on top of a video see-through display which creates the illusion as if they were situated in the same physical space (see Figure 1). Users can benefit from such MR applications when viewing and manipulating virtual objects becomes a familiar physical interaction. MR has been proven not only to be beneficial for single user applications such as education, manufacturing, and architecture [2], but has also been proposed as a tool for computer supported

CHI'16, May 07-12, 2016, San Jose, CA, USA
© 2016 ACM. ISBN 978-1-4503-3362-7/16/05…$15.00
DOI: http://dx.doi.org/10.1145/2858036.2858043

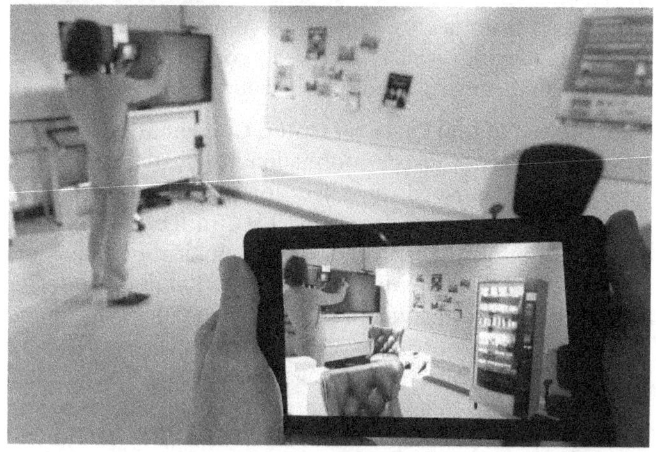

Figure 1. Dyads solving an object identification task in a mixed reality environment with additive virtual objects (e.g., armchairs and a vending machine) that serve as spatial cues.

collaborative work. Billinghurst [3], for instance, refers to two inherent qualities of MREs that are crucial to collaboration: First, MREs provide seamless transitions between the shared workspace (the task area in which collaborators are situated) and the speakers' interpersonal space (the communication space which allows for social interactions). Second, MR can enhance reality and may thereby "satisfy the needs of communication." [3] Closely related to the question of how to enhance reality in MR is the aspect of artificiality, which can be described as "the extent to which a space is either synthetic or is based on the physical world". [1]

For collaboration, shared visual information such as spatial cues are known to play a crucial role to coordinate collaborators' actions (see [5–7,13]). Given that virtual objects are highly customizable in their appearance and their behavior (e.g., they do not represent physical obstacles), it raises the question whether spatial cues can be synthesized in MREs. In this note we investigate how additive virtual objects shape communication behavior and user task load in co-located MREs.

RELATED WORK
Our work is based on two strains of research: *influence of visual cues on individual cognition* and *influence of visual cues on group coordination*. For each strain, we introduce related work and summarize with the formulation of a hypothesis.

Influence of Visual Cues on Individual Cognition

The importance of visual information for cognition during navigation tasks has been well established both in physical and in virtual environments. Montello [12] discusses the visual and structural properties of physical environments and how they determine the ease of navigation therein. Based on research on landmark design in physical environments, Vinson [14] provides a set of design guidelines to support navigation in virtual environments (VRs). A reoccurring aspect refers to the "distinctiveness" of landmarks, e.g., that "a landmark must be easy to distinguish from nearby objects and other landmarks," and that "Landmarks must carry a common element to distinguish them, as a group, from data objects." [14]

Influence of Visual Cues on Group Coordination

The importance of visual information in a shared workspace has been established in terms of the coordination of collaborative activities (e.g. [5–7,13]). In the field of MR, Kiyokawa et al. [8] investigated communication behaviors in co-located collaborative Augmented Reality interfaces. In a target identification task they found that "the more difficult it was to use non-verbal communication cues, the more people resorted to speech cues to compensate." [8] Chastine et al. [4] investigated referencing behaviors in a collaborative modelling task in an MRE. They found that groups make heavy use of deictic speech, and that with increasing concreteness of the model, some groups created their own vocabulary to identify elements of the workspace.

These findings show that 1) spatial cues play a crucial role for individual cognition during navigation tasks, 2) that they represent an important coordination mechanism in collaborative tasks, and 3) that they can be synthesized in VRs. Based on these findings, we hypothesize that spatial cues can also be synthesized in MREs and that their presence positively influences collaboration.

EXPERIMENT

To investigate how additive virtual objects influence collaboration in co-located MREs, we conducted a controlled lab experiment. The study used a counterbalanced within-subjects design with the provision of additive virtual objects being the independent variable ("additive" in the sense of "additional to the actual data objects the participants had to work with," henceforth referred to as "objects" and "no objects"). The dependent variables were user task load (NASA TLX), communication behavior (video analysis), user experiences (semi-structured interview) and spatial memory" (reconstruction task).

Participants

We recruited 32 participants (8 female, 24 male) between 16-39 years of age (*M* 26.06, *SD* 5.63), forming 16 dyads. 19 participants were university students, 9 employed persons, and 4 secondary schools students. 4 participants reported prior experiences with MR technologies. 16 participants indicated regular tablet usage.

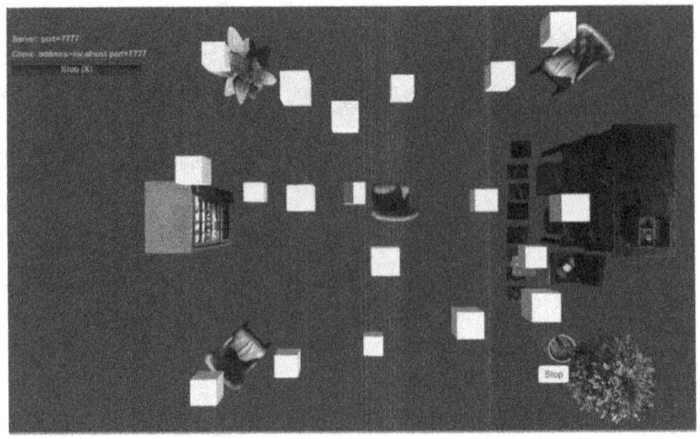

Figure 2. Bird's eye view of the virtual MR space in the condition with additive objects (including the memory cubes).

Apparatus and Study Environment

In our lab we allocated physical space of 4×4×2m, where participants could move freely. As MR displays we used Project Tango Tablets (370g, 1920x1200 pixels on a 7.02″ display (323 ppi) [15]). Due to the tablets' capability of area learning no additional tracking hardware was required to locate their position and orientation in space (6DOF). This guaranteed a high external validity since they can also be used outside of research lab facilities. We developed an MRE with Unity [16]. As potential physical cues we placed a waste paper basket, a clothes hook, a chair, a double ladder, several wall papers, and a floor lamp at the border of the interaction space. As virtual objects we used three armchairs, a bookshelf, two house plants and a vending machine (see Figure 2).

Study Task

For the design of our study task we referred to spatial planning tasks (such as architecture [3]). Such tasks require the collaborators to identify particular objects in the workspace (henceforth *object identification task*). There are also situations, when collaborators need to position a virtual object at a specific position in the workspace (henceforth *object positioning task).*

Object identification task

To create a dynamic situation in which collaborators have to exchange spatial information, we let collaborators play a modified (3D) version of the memory card game. In our version there were 10 pairs of white memory cubes as data objects (25cm edge length) which were randomly distributed in the MRE (see Figure 2). Each pair was texturized with the same symbol from the Wingdings font. Cubes were initially in the "covered" state. A cube could be "uncovered" by touching it. Unlike the original version of the game, dyads had to find matches collaboratively. Due to the collaborative nature of our version, collaborators benefited from each other's spatial knowledge, whereby communication was stimulated. In line with the original memory game, non-matching pairs of uncovered cubes had to be covered to continue with the next move. Accordingly, matches were removed from the MRE.

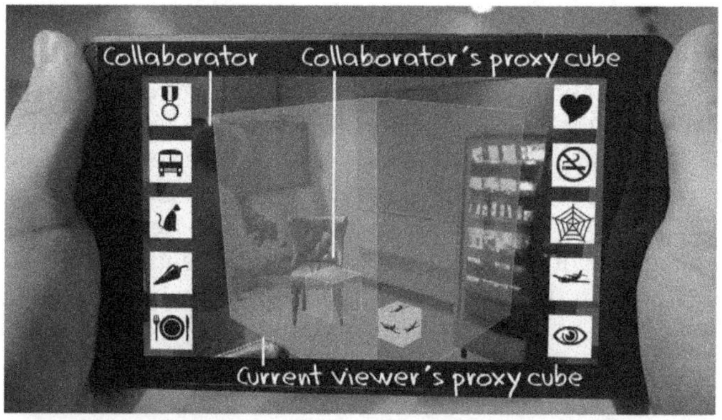

Figure 3. A semi-translucent proxy cube (displayed in front of each tablet) provides a dynamic positioning hint.

Object positioning task

The object identification task was followed by an object positioning task. In this task, dyads had to collaboratively position the memory cubes within the MRE according to their positions in the preceding objects identification task. The 10 symbols were displayed as buttons on each tablet (see Figure 3). A virtual semi-translucent proxy cube was displayed 0.5m in front of each tablet, which allowed participants to estimate the position where a memory cube would appear in the MRE when the corresponding button was pressed. To enable collaborative fine-tuning of positions, participants could see each other's proxy cube on their display. Deposited cubes could be repositioned.

Procedure

Participants were welcomed and introduced to the study. Afterwards, they were asked to fill out a demographic questionnaire. Then participants were introduced to the object identification task and were provided with a training phase (no additive virtual objects were provided, and a test set of symbols and coordinates was used for the memory cubes) to familiarize themselves with the devices and the task. Then, the objects identification task started in their assigned first study condition (≈ 10 mins). Afterwards, the NASA TLX questionnaire was provided to the participants. Then, participants started with the object positioning task in the same condition (≈ 15 mins). Afterwards, participants were provided with the NASA TLX questionnaire. This procedure was repeated in the respective other condition. After completion of the tasks in the second study condition a concluding, semi-structured interview on participants' experiences was conducted. Each session took about 60 minutes. Participants were compensated for their time.

RESULTS

The reporting of study results is structured into the two study tasks. Non-parametric tests were used when the assumption of normal distribution was violated. Results are marked with the subscript $_{NO}$ for the condition when no additive virtual objects were provided, and $_{O}$ when additive virtual objects were provided.

Object identification task

For analysis of *communication behavior,* video material from half of the sessions was analyzed for participants' spatial expressions. A cluster analysis yielded a set of 8 categories (see Figure 4): *deictic speech* (spatial indications, which "cannot be fully understood by speech alone" as explained by Kiyokawa et al. [8], e.g., "here," "over there,"), *participant* (e.g., "in front of me"), *region* (e.g., "in the center of the room"), *physical object* (e.g., "at the chair"), *other virtual cube* ("left of the uncovered cube"), and the *virtual object* ("near the shelf"). For non-verbal spatial expressions we identified *hand gestures* as the most prevalent ones. *"Non-assigned"* summarizes spatial expressions that occurred extremely seldom (e.g., pointing on the tablet, head-, and feet gestures) and those that could not be assigned to one of the other categories. Finally, all videos were coded using these categories as a coding scheme. A Wilcoxon signed rank test revealed that deictic speech, virtual cubes, and hand gestures were used significantly less frequently when objects were provided (deictic speech: M_{NO} = 18.1, SD_{NO} = 8.5, M_O = 10.3, SD_O = 4.5, p = .010; virtual cube: M_{NO} = 4.1, SD_{NO} = 3.0, M_O = 2.2, SD_O = 1.4, p = .025; hand gesture: M_{NO} = 3.8, SD_{NO} = 3.6, M_O = 1.9, SD_O = 2.5, p = .039) (see Figure 4).

User task load was analyzed with the Wilcoxon signed rank test. The test revealed a significantly lower cognitive task load when virtual objects were provided (M_{NO} = 33.2, SD_{NO} = 15.4, M_O = 27.0, SD_O = 12.4, p = .009). Analysis of mean values in the TLX subscales yielded a significantly lower temporal demand and a lower value in the performance subscale when objects were provided (temporal: M_{NO} = 30.5, SD_{NO} = 21.2, M_O = 20.31, SD_O = 13.6, p = .009; performance: M_{NO} = 38.0, SD_{NO} = 21.4, M_O = 30.9, SD_O = 21.9, p = .049).

Object positioning task

For *communication behavior*, the Wilcoxon signed rank test revealed that deictic speech was used significantly less frequently when objects were provided (M_{NO} = 19.7, SD_{NO} = 4.8, M_O = 14.9, SD_O = 6.3, p = .036) (see Figure 4).

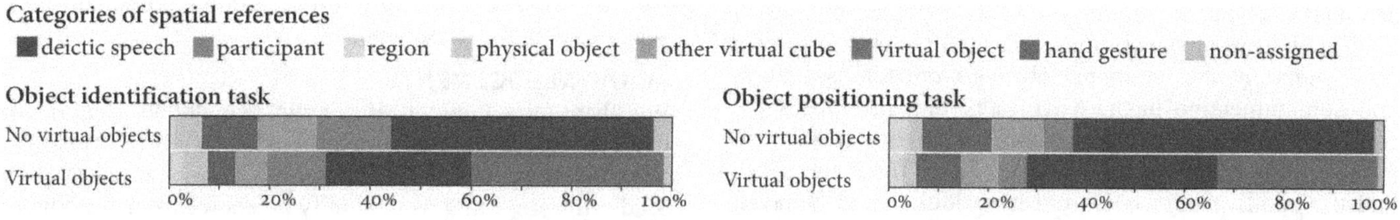

Figure 4. Categories of spatial references (top) and the mean proportions of occurrences in each study task and each condition.

For *user task load*, a pairwise comparison in the NASA TLX neither revealed a significant difference in the overall user task load nor in any subscale.

Recall precision was defined as the minimum error of the distance of positioned cube pairs compared to their former position in the object identification task. A Friedman test revealed that the minimum error was significantly lower when additive virtual objects were provided ($\chi^2(2) = 4.9$, $\tilde{x}_{NO} = 1.59$, $\tilde{x}_O = 1.41$, $M_{NO} = 3.02$, $SD_{NO} = 1.32$, $M_O = 2.62$, $SD_O = 1.17$, $p = .032$).

Further results from the concluding interview

When asked how well target objects could be identified, from 0 (very poorly) to 10 (very well), the condition with additive objects reached a significantly higher rating ($t(31) = 9.031$, $M_{NO} = 5.34$, $SD_{NO} = 1.84$, $M_O = 7.91$, $SD_O = 1.15$, $p = .000$). 10 participants reported to have perceived the physical environment to a very limited degree and other 10 reported to have not consciously perceived it at all. When additive objects were provided, they were accepted as part of the 3D interaction space, e.g., *"the room looks strange, now that all these objects are missing,"* or *"this cube was where the snack machine stood earlier."* (No additive objects were provided at the time the statement was made).

DISCUSSION, IMPLICATIONS, AND LIMITATIONS

Results from communication behavior clearly indicate the positive effect of the additive virtual objects: they were used extensively as shared spatial cues to identify target cubes and the use of the less specific deictic expressions decreased significantly along with the hand gestures which often occurred together. In line with the lower task load in the object identification task and participants' statements, the additive objects supported the participants in expressing spatial references. The object positioning task yielded a similar communication behavior, but no significant differences in the task load. This can be explained by participants' statements that positioning without the additive objects often was a mere matter of guessing, what indicates that participants put only little mental effort in recalling their positions. This aspect, however, shows that results in workload must not be explicitly attributed to communication behavior but also include individual spatial memory which might have been profited from the presence of additive objects.

Nearly all participants reported that they did not regard the physical environment in general. By some, this was explained as being because the data objects were obviously artificial and that the additive objects appeared similar in contrast to the physical environment. This clearly shows how important the additional objects were for navigation and communication in the MRE. Yet, this also raises the following question: Would the physical environment have gained more attention if the virtual objects (both the cubes and the additive objects) would have looked and behaved more like physical objects (e.g., realistic rendering, no hovering in space, etc.)? In addition, as perception within an MREs presumably depends on the proportions between the physical environments and the virtual content, communication behavior may depend on the proportions we used and the physical features of our lab. Similarly, this applies to our choice of virtual objects: other objects might have produced other results. Furthermore, and as stated by Kiyokawa et al. [8], the type of display technology is crucial in MR. The tablets required participants to focus on a rather narrow field of view. Thus, collaborators' attention was set on a small portion of the environment. Our findings may therefore not be fully generalizable as they might be specific to task design and the design of our MRE. Possible influencing factors (e.g. proportion of virtual and physical content, type and degree of abstraction of present objects, and display technology) and are subject of further research.

In the analysis of communication behavior we identified several categories of spatial expression that participants made use of. These categories only partially overlap with those identified by Chastine et al. [4]. Hence, we do not claim the classification as complete but rather task specific. Furthermore, our classification did not take the complexity of natural language into account. This should be further investigated from a linguistic point of view. Logan [10] and Levinson [9], for example, provide a deeper understanding of cognition and space in language that focuses on the rather complex relationship between 1) the observer, 2) the addressee, 3) the target object (here: a target cube), 4) the referenced object, and 5) several types of frames of reference. One interesting aspect refers to the concept that objects provide their own intrinsic coordinate systems that differ in their expressiveness (e.g., a chair has its clear front side, a bottle without a label does not). Thus, expressiveness of an object's intrinsic coordinate system may further help to disambiguate spatial expressions in MREs and should therefore be studied.

CONCLUSION

This note contributes to a better understanding of the effects of spatial cues in collaborative MREs. Results from our study, consisting of an object identification task and an object positioning task, provide three major insights: 1) The physical environment plays only a minor role in the collaborators' perception and their communication behavior, whereas 2) the virtual objects are extensively used as spatial cues by collaborators, and 3) their presence positively influences collaborators' communication behavior, decreases user task load, and improves user experience. This suggest adding virtual objects to MREs to reduce user task load and improve groups' communication behavior and user experience.

ACKNOWLEDGEMENTS

We thank the German Research Foundation (DFG) for financial support within project C01 of SFB/Transregio 161. We also thank VIS Games, Jason Wong, and Vertex Studio for providing us the Unity assets we used as additive virtual objects.

REFERENCES

1. Steve Benford, Chris Greenhalgh, Gail Reynard, Chris Brown, and Boriana Koleva. 1998. Understanding and Constructing Shared Spaces with Mixed-Reality Boundaries. *ACM Transactions on Computer-Human Interaction* 5, 3: 185–223. http://doi.org/10.1145/292834.292836
2. Mark Billinghurst, Adrian Clark, and Gun Lee. 2015. A Survey of Augmented Reality. *Foundations and Trends® in Human–Computer Interaction* 8, 2: 73–272. http://doi.org/10.1561/1100000049
3. Mark Billinghurst and Hirokazu Kato. 1999. Collaborative Mixed Reality. *Proc. of ISMR '99*, Springer, 261–284.
4. Jeffrey W. Chastine, Kristine Nagel, Ying Zhu, and Luca Yearsovich. 2007. Understanding the design space of referencing in collaborative augmented reality environments. *Proc.of CGI '07*, 207–214. http://doi.org/10.1145/1268517.1268552
5. Susan R. Fussell, Robert E. Kraut, and Jane Siegel. 2000. Coordination of Communication : Effects of Shared Visual Context on Collaborative Work. *Proc. of CSCW '00*, 21–30. http://doi.org/10.1145/358916.358947
6. William W. Gaver. 1992. The Affordances of Media Spaces for Collaboration. *Proc. of CSCW '92*, 17–24. http://doi.org/10.1145/143457.371596
7. Darren Gergle, Robert E. Kraut, and Susan R. Fussell. 2013. Using Visual Information for Grounding and Awareness in Collaborative Tasks. *Human-Computer Interaction* 28, August 2014: 1–39. http://doi.org/10.1080/07370024.2012.678246
8. Kiyoshi Kiyokawa, Mark Billinghurst, Sohan Hayes, Arnab Gupta, Yuki Sannohe, and Hirokazu Kato. 2002. Communication Behaviors of Co-Located Users in Collaborative AR Interfaces. *Proc. of ISMAR '02*: 135–144. http://doi.org/10.1109/ISMAR.2002.1115083
9. Stpehen C. Levinson. 2003. *Space in language and cognition: Exploration in cognitive diversity*. Cambridge University Press. http://doi.org/10.1017/CBO9780511613609
10. Gordon D. Logan. 1995. Linguistic and Conceptual Control of Visual Spatial Attention. *Cognitive Psychology 28*: 103–174. http://doi.org/10.1006/cogp.1995.1004
11. Paul Milgram and Fumio Kishino. 1994. Taxonomy of mixed reality visual displays. *IEICE Transactions on Information and Systems*, 1321–1329. http://doi.org/10.1.1.102.4646
12. Daniel R. Montello. 2005. Navigation. In *The Cambridge handbook of visuospatial thinking*, Pritt Shah and Akira Miyake (eds.). 257–294. http://doi.org/10.2277/0521001730
13. Kjeld Schmidt and Carla Simone. 1996. Coordination mechanisms: Towards a conceptual foundation of CSCW systems design. *Computer Supported Cooperative Work (CSCW)* 5, 2-3: 155–200. http://doi.org/10.1007/BF00133655
14. Norman G. Vinson. 1999. Design Guidelines for Landmarks to Support Navigation in Virtual Environments. *Proc. of CHI '99*, 278–285. http://doi.org/10.1145/302979.303062
15. 2015. Project Tango Tablet Development Kit User Guide. Retrieved January 3, 2016 from https://developers.google.com/project-tango/hardware/tablet#technical_specifications
16. 2015. Unity – Gaming Engine. Retrieved January 3, 2016 from https://unity3d.com/

VR-STEP: Walking-in-Place using Inertial Sensing for Hands Free Navigation in Mobile VR Environments

Sam Tregillus
tregillus@cse.unr.edu

Eelke Folmer
efolmer@cse.unr.edu

Human+ Lab - Computer Science - University of Nevada

ABSTRACT

Low-cost smartphone adapters can bring virtual reality to the masses, but input is typically limited to using head tracking, which makes it difficult to perform complex tasks like navigation. Walking-in-place (WIP) offers a natural and immersive form of virtual locomotion that can reduce simulation sickness. WIP, however, is difficult to implement in mobile contexts as it typically relies on bulky controllers or an external camera. We present VR-STEP; a WIP implementation that uses real-time pedometry to implement virtual locomotion. VR-STEP requires no additional instrumentation outside of a smartphone's inertial sensors. A user study with 18 users compares VR-STEP with a commonly used auto-walk navigation method and finds no significant difference in performance or reliability, though VR-STEP was found to be more immersive and intuitive.

Author Keywords

Virtual reality; pedometry; walking-in-place; virtual locomotion; head-mounted display; motion-sickness; games;

ACM Classification Keywords

I.3.7 Graphics: 3D Graphics and Realism–Virtual Reality;

INTRODUCTION

Virtual reality (VR) has reached potential for mainstream adoption due to the introduction of low-cost smartphone adapters, such as Google Cardboard, that can transform any smartphone into a head-mounted VR display. Navigation is an essential 3D interaction task [7], but a challenge with head-mounted displays is that their input options are limited [10]. Because the smartphone is inside the adapter, touchscreen input is not possible. A controller cannot be used with Google Cardboard adapters because its users are required to hold the adapter with both hands. Doing so limits head rotation speed to the torso, which may minimize simulation sickness [1]. Due to these constraints, input typically relies on head-tracking using the smartphone's inertial sensors. Several VR apps feature an auto-walk button that is rendered at the user's feet. Users toggle the auto-walk by looking down at the button briefly, which then starts moving the user in the direction of their gaze. Besides being limited to a fixed locomotion speed, this method requires users to interrupt their focus on the virtual environment to look down at the button, which may be detrimental to immersion and undesirable in gaming contexts.

CHI'16, May 07-12, 2016, San Jose, CA, USA.
©2016 ACM. ISBN 978-1-4503-3362-7/16/05 $15.00
DOI: http://dx.doi.org/10.1145/2858036.2858084

Walking-in-place (WIP) allows users to perform handsfree virtual locomotion using step-like movements while remaining stationary [26]. WIP resembles walking and offers a natural, immersive form of input [25]. When compared to using a controller, WIP allows for better spatial orientation [15] while approximating the performance of real walking [23].

Simulation sickness is a major concern to the mass adoption of VR [19] and is caused by –among other factors– a sensory mismatch between visual and vestibular stimuli [29]. Because WIP generates proprioceptive feedback, users are less likely to experience simulation sickness than when using a conventional controller [13]. Unfortunately, current WIP implementations aren't feasible in mobile contexts, as they rely either on external cameras [24], which may require calibration, or expensive, bulky treadmill controllers [33].

This paper addresses a need for a low-cost virtual locomotion technique [33] by presenting VR-STEP: a novel WIP implementation that requires no instrumentation beyond the sensors already present in smartphones. VR-STEP is immersive, has low latency, and is easy to learn. We show a quantitative and qualitative comparison of our system with another handsfree navigation technique that is found in several VR apps. We provide a detailed description of our virtual locomotion implementation. Our results highlight the importance of smooth, natural movement and low starting/stopping latency in VR locomotion.

BACKGROUND

Exploring natural, immersive types of input for virtual locomotion is an active field of research (see [26] for an survey). Using a joystick for navigation is a simple and common approach. Gaze based navigation with joystick control of locomotion speed was found to be superior to navigation using a joystick alone [23]. Real walking, where the user actually moves in real space, is the most natural and effective method for virtual locomotion [23, 30]. Real walking can be implemented using an optical tracking system [31, 30], but this approach doesn't scale very well since the tracked space and the virtual space need to be the same size. Omnidirectional treadmills [9] circumvent physical space limitations, but these are often expensive and bulky, which restricts their use in mobile contexts.

Walking-in-place [24] has many advantages over other methods for virtual locomotion. WIP can be used to control locomotion speed just as effectively as using a joystick [11], but WIP has also been found to be much more immersive [25]. Maintaining spatial knowledge of the virtual world is difficult in VR environments [21], but WIP was found to allow for better spatial orientation than when using a joystick [15]. WIP has also been found to be almost as efficient as real walking [23] but is not subject to space constraints and is therefore more cost effective to implement.

A challenge with implementing WIP is starting and stopping latency [26], i.e., how quickly a step is detected and translated into virtual motion, or how long it takes the virtual avatar to stop after the user stops taking any steps. High stopping and starting latency makes precise navigation challenging [11]. Latency can be a result of the step detection algorithm implementation, noise reduction, or damping based on which part of the body is being tracked. In general, step detection is most accurate when tracking motions closest to the feet [12]. The first WIP [24] implementation used an optical motion tracking system to track head movements to infer steps. However, due to "false steps" being detected, they did not start actual motion until 4 consecutive steps had been taken, which resulted in a large delay between walking and actually moving. Other implementations used optical tracking of knee or shin motions [26, 32], and had a latency of a "half-step", or about 400ms at a normal walking pace. Another method by Feasel [11] used a magnetic tracking system for detecting heel motions, with a starting latency of 138ms and stopping latency of 96ms.

The optical & magnetic tracking systems used in the above studies are typically expensive [11, 33], and their weight and size makes them difficult to employ in mobile contexts. Low-cost implementations have also been explored. To enable desktop VR, a basic webcam has been used to detect head oscillations, which are then interpreted for virtual locomotion [27]. A user study found this approach to be faster and more immersive than keyboard input when seated. A commercially-available pressure-sensitive game controller (Wii Balance Board) was explored for step detection [33]. A study found no significant difference in latency when compared with joystick and real walking input, but limitations included difficulty controlling small motions and a risk of users falling off the balance board. Other notable WIP implementations include using a Kinect [34] and a CAVE system [14, 22] but these implementations aren't feasible in mobile contexts.

IMPLEMENTATION OF VR-STEP

Inertial measurement units (IMU) have become ubiquitous in smartphones and typically consist of a 3-axis accelerometer and 3-axis gyroscope. Various studies have investigated the accuracy of pedometry for different smartphone/sensor placements on the body [8, 16] and found that steps can be detected most accurately for a sensor worn closest to the feet[12]. Rather than using an external sensor, VR-STEP uses the smartphone's accelerometer for step detection. Since the smartphone sits in the head-mounted adapter, latency is a major concern for effective virtual locomotion [11]. A challenge with our approach is that a smartphone worn on the head may dampen the acceleration signal (due to the larger distance from the feet), causing problems for accurate step detection. In prior work [5], we evaluated the accuracy with which pedometry can be achieved on a head mounted display (Google Glass), which had not been investigated before. We found no significant difference in accuracy on the head when compared with a smartphone worn on in the pocket or held in the hand. This supports the feasibility of our approach, since with mobile VR, users basically wear a phone on their head.

Though various step detection algorithms exist [8], we use a real-time algorithm proposed by Zhao [35]. This algorithm has little computational overhead and ensures the smartphone can maintain a high frame rate, which is important for VR simulations [17]. This algorithm averages every 5 samples to smooth the acceleration signal, which minimizes noise while still yielding a near real-time response of between 100-200ms. A step is detected if the accelerometer values pass a dynamic threshold level with a large enough negative slope. The dynamic threshold changes every 50 samples from the accelerometer to account for different step intensities. The slope acts as a sensitivity setting, which we can tune to make sure that small steps that the user uses to turn left and right are not translated into forward movement.

Once steps are detected, they need to be translated into virtual locomotion, in the direction of the user's gaze. A limitation of existing WIP implementations is that most provide few details on how virtual locomotion is implemented [11]. For our implementation, we wanted users to feel like they have precise control over their velocity, to be able to move reasonable distances quickly, but also be able to make small changes in position if needed. Because users walk in place, there is no way to detect the length of their stride to determine how far users might want to move. A discrete approach where every detected step is translated into moving a fixed distance forward leads to jarring and unnatural movement [11]. A high stopping latency can make users experience a frustrating sensation of gliding [11].

We query the accelerometer and gyroscope values to determine acceleration along the gravity axis, which we feed into the Zhao's algorithm described above. A sensitivity value, S, can be used to tweak how sensitive the algorithm is. When a step is detected, an event is fired, which the step handler listens for. The step handler measures the time between steps, (t_{step}) to determine the virtual velocity (v). A large t_{step} indicates that the user is walking slowly, so we set v to a low value. A small t_{step} value indicates faster steps, so we set v to a higher value. We establish bounds on $t_{step} \in [I_{min}, I_{max}]$, and a maximum and minimum velocity, $[V_{min}, V_{max}]$. If $t_{step} > I_{max}$, it means that a step has not been detected in some time (the user has been standing still before they took this step), so we set v to V_{min}. $t_{step} < I_{min}$ is not possible, as it is filtered out by the step detector, but if $t_{step} < I_{min}$, velocity is set to V_{max}. If $t_{step} \in [I_{min}, I_{max}]$, we linearly interpolate v between $[V_{min}, V_{max}]$ according to:

$$v = \frac{t_{step} - I_{min}}{I_{max} - I_{min}} * (V_{max} - V_{min}) + V_{min} \quad (1)$$

By modifying their WIP speed, users have precise control over their virtual speed. We also adjust the velocity of the avatar between steps by applying friction. This slows down the user between steps, giving a natural feeling of walking, and it reduces stopping latency, since the user begins slowing down immediately after taking their last step. If the user continues walking, the velocity is maintained.

EVALUATION

A number of studies have already compared WIP with joystick based virtual locomotion [23, 11, 25, 15, 33]. We also felt that comparisons to other WIP methods that involve extensive instrumentation weren't as useful, as users of mobile VR would not typically have access to such instrumentation. Because VR-STEP is hands free and requires no instrumentation, it is more meaningful to compare its performance with another hands free navigation method, "look down to move" (LDTM), which is used in several VR apps, such as the popular Oculus "Tuscany" demo [4]. Users toggle a button at their feet by briefly looking down at it, then back up. When activated the user will move with a fixed horizontal velocity in the direction of their gaze. Similar to other WIP evaluations [23, 11, 25, 15, 33, 6], we compare VR-STEP to LDTM by having users perform a number of navigation tasks.

Instrumentation

For our smartphone mount, we used a Zeiss VR One. The VR One features Zeiss precision lenses with a 100 degree field of view. The VR One features a strap and weighs 590 grams. We used an Android Nexus 5 smartphone with a Qualcomm Snapdragon 800 CPU (2.3 GHz quad-core) and an Adreno 330 GPU which can render 3D simulations with a high frame rate. The Nexus 5 features a InvenSense MPU-6515 six-axis (gyro + accelerometer) with a 50Hz sample rate. The user study was implemented using the Google Cardboard for Unity SDK and the Unity 5 engine.

Because LDTM uses a fixed velocity (V_{LDTM}), a precise quantitative comparison with VR-STEP is challenging, as VR-STEP allows variable locomotion speeds. Even if we limit V_{max} to be the same as V_{LDTM}, the average speed for VR-STEP will be smaller than LDTM unless the participant consistently runs at the highest speed. To allow for a fair comparison, we modified VR-STEP such that when $t_{step} < I_{max}$, we set v to V_{LDTM}. If no step has been taken for I_{max} seconds, we immediately set v to 0. This means that velocity is the same for both methods at all times when moving, but it does make stopping latency for VR-STEP equal to I_{max}, which causes a minor gliding issue, where after not taking any steps, you continue to move forward for I_{max} seconds. For the user study, we set I_{max} = .7s, and V_{LDTM} to 6 m/s.

Participants

We recruited 18 participants (9 female, average age 28.83, SD=7.93) to participate in our user study. None of the subjects self-reported any non-correctable impairments in perception or limitations in mobility. Individuals who had previously experienced simulator sickness were excluded from participation as they were at a high risk of not completing the study. User studies were approved by an IRB. On average users had 4.97 years experience (SD=8.05) navigating 3D environments and 11 subjects had prior experience using a VR headset, such as the Oculus Rift.

Figure 1. A view of the navigation task in the virtual environment. The blue area is the target zone, and the white rectangle is an obstacle.

Procedure

A criticism of existing WIP studies is that they have mostly included navigation tasks that use a straight trajectory [28], which isn't very realistic for many VR applications. Our study had participants perform two different navigation tasks: an unobstructed navigation task with a straight trajectory, and an obstructed one requiring them to circumnavigate an obstacle. We designed our navigation task to be similar to one described by Bowman [6]. Our virtual environment consists of a flat plane featuring a checkerboard pattern. Participants must find a target zone (a blue transparent column), navigate to it, and remain inside the area for 2 seconds before the next target zone becomes visible. This column changes color when participants enter it, and auditory feedback indicates success. The locations of the target zone were initially determined at random, with each new location a minimum distance of 10 meters away from the prior location. Obstructed navigation tasks feature a rectangular box (Size: 1x3 meters) halfway to the target zone. To decouple the visual search task from the navigation task, we started measuring time and distance traveled as soon as participants started moving. Each participant tests both navigation methods, but which method they use first is randomly assigned (half of the participants used VR-STEP first, then LDTM). Participants performed 20 navigation tasks for each navigation method with 10 tasks containing an obstacle. The specific locations of the target zones and the obstacle ordering was the same for all users and both methods. Before the data collection, participants were fitted with the VR One headset and we ensured the HMD was firmly attached to their head using the straps. Some participants with eyeglasses took them off but others kept them on. A built-in tutorial explained how each navigation method worked and let participants practice three navigation tasks. After the trials, basic demographic and qualitative feedback was collected using a questionnaire. The entire session, including training and questionnaires, took about 10 minutes.

Results

Table 1 lists the results for all users. For our analysis, we used a two-way repeated measures ANOVA where we evaluate efficiency of each navigation method using time and distance

Method-trajectory	Time (s)	SD	Distance (m)	SD
LDTM-straight	59.12	25.0	225.31	127.1
VR-STEP-straight	61.88	8.7	198.18	13.3
LDTM-curved	65.31	19.2	243.25	65.4
VR-STEP-curved	77.45	23.3	224.87	32.3

Table 1. Total time and distance traveled averaged per user.

traveled. There was no statistically significant two-way interaction between navigation type and trajectory for navigation time ($F_{1,17}$ = 1.680, p = .212), or distance ($F_{1,17}$ = .107, p = .784). Pairwise comparisons using a Bonferroni correction found a statistical significant difference between navigation methods for time for a curved trajectory (p = .012) but not for distance or straight trajectories.

Qualitative results. After the trial, we let participants rank each navigation method based on a number of criteria which included: efficiency, reliability, learnability, immersion and overall preference. If participants had no preference, they could also select both as a 3rd option. The summarized results are shown in Figure 2. A Chi square test found the rankings for learnability (p = .0023) and immersion (p = .0045) to be statistically significantly different. Non-directed interviews with open-ended questions were used to collect general experiences and identify areas for improvement. For LDTM, ten participants stated that having to look down to activate the button was awkward or strenuous for their neck. Six participants suggested using a larger button or placing the button at eye level. For VR-STEP, eight participants said they found it difficult to stop precisely in the target zone due to gliding. Two participants wanted control over their velocity as they felt their avatar was moving too fast. Three participants wanted better step detection.

DISCUSSION

Overall, we demonstrated the feasibility of VR-STEP as a low-cost virtual locomotion technique for mobile VR. Participants found VR-STEP more immersive and easy to learn than LDTM. Though LDTM was perceived to be more reliable and efficient, quantitative results only showed LDTM to be faster for curved trajectories. An analysis of paths revealed that some participants overshot the target zone, requiring them to turn around. Overshooting would occur with LDTM as well, but not as frequently as with VR-STEP. If users failed to stop, the switchback they took back to the target zone significantly increased both time and distance, leading to much larger standard deviation values for these metrics.

Ironically, the main user complaints about VR-STEP, high stopping latency (gliding) and no control over speed, are issues that are absent when variable locomotion speed is used. Though we wanted to be able to compare quantitative values, such as navigation speed, between the two methods, the changes we made to equate velocities ended up hurting user perception of efficiency and reliability. However, these results do highlight how stopping latency impacts user perception. Overshooting is very frustrating to the user, and enabling them to stop intuitively where they would like to is very important. LDTM can have large stopping latency, as users must stop looking at the world to look down at a button.

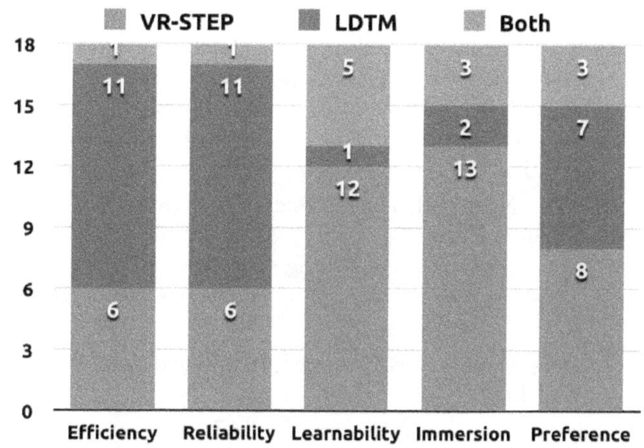

Figure 2. Ranking of navigation methods based on usability criteria.

Some participants found a way around this by looking forward and down while navigating, but if your goal is to create an immersive world, this is obviously not what you want your users to be doing. The trade off we made to allow for a fair comparison did clearly demonstrate participant's qualitative preferences for VR-STEP.

For VR-STEP, we selected a step detection algorithm [35] with a low computational overhead to assure a high frame rate. Some participants initially expressed that our step detection wasn't sensitive enough, but when we instructed them to "jog in place" so their head bounced, they were able to use VR-STEP quite efficiently. If a user is already moving, it may be challenging –based on visual feedback alone– to know whether the system has detected a step. When we added audio feedback, e.g., the sound of a footstep, users were able to better anticipate how the system works and modify their stepping input accordingly.

LIMITATIONS & FUTURE WORK

VR-STEP requires users to stand and provide continuous stepping input. This may not be desirable when using mobile VR for longer periods of time. However, popular VR headset manufacturers recommend that users take regular breaks from using VR [3], so standing may not be a major issue. VR-step moves the user in the direction of their gaze, but this is rather limited compared to how humans navigate in real life. For future work, we will explore the use of head tilt to indicate a direction for navigation which may allow users to walk other directions. For step detection feedback, we will explore haptic feedback, since audio feedback may be obfuscated in gaming contexts. Besides detecting steps for walking, other feet related actions may be detected using acceleration. We were able to implement jumps in VR-STEP using a threshold for vertical acceleration. A promising application area of VR-STEP is exercise games [18]. Jogging-in-place has already been found to get users into moderate-to-vigorous levels of exercise [20]. In addition, bringing the immersion of VR to exergames could engage players for longer, which may stimulate larger health benefits. This may address some of the current criticisms of exergames that they don't provide sufficient health benefits [2].

REFERENCES

1. Works with Google Cardboard Guidelines and Best Practices, http://static.googleusercontent.com/media/www.google.com/en//get/cardboard/downloads/wwgc_best_practices.pdf. (September 2015).
2. 2012. New York Times, 'Exergames' Don't Make Children Fitter, http://parenting.blogs.nytimes.com/2012/06/25/exergames-dont-make-children-more-fit/. (June 2012).
3. 2014. Oculus Best Practices: Health and Safety Warnings, https://developer.oculus.com/documentation/intro-vr/latest/concepts/bp_app_health/. (January 2014).
4. 2015. Tuscany Demo, http://play.google.com/store/apps/details?id=com.FabulousPixel.TuscanyDive. (August 2015).
5. Ilias Apostolopoulos, Daniel S. Coming, and Eelke Folmer. 2015. Accuracy of Pedometry on a Head-mounted Display. In *Proceedings of the 33rd Annual ACM Conference on Human Factors in Computing Systems (CHI '15)*. ACM, New York, NY, USA, 2153–2156. DOI: http://dx.doi.org/10.1145/2702123.2702143
6. Doug Bowman, David Koller, Larry F Hodges, and others. 1997. Travel in immersive virtual environments: An evaluation of viewpoint motion control techniques. In *Virtual Reality Annual International Symposium, 1997., IEEE 1997*. IEEE, 45–52.
7. Doug A Bowman, Ernst Kruijff, Joseph J LaViola Jr, and Ivan Poupyrev. 2004. *3D user interfaces: theory and practice*. Addison-Wesley.
8. Agata Brajdic and Robert Harle. 2013. Walk Detection and Step Counting on Unconstrained Smartphones. In *Proceedings of the 2013 ACM International Joint Conference on Pervasive and Ubiquitous Computing (UbiComp '13)*. ACM, New York, NY, USA, 225–234. DOI: http://dx.doi.org/10.1145/2493432.2493449
9. Rudolph P Darken, William R Cockayne, and David Carmein. 1997. The omni-directional treadmill: a locomotion device for virtual worlds. In *Proceedings of the 10th annual ACM symposium on User interface software and technology*. ACM, 213–221.
10. David Dobbelstein, Philipp Hock, and Enrico Rukzio. 2015. Belt: An Unobtrusive Touch Input Device for Head-worn Displays. In *Proceedings of the 33rd Annual ACM Conference on Human Factors in Computing Systems*. ACM, 2135–2138.
11. Jeff Feasel, Mary C. Whitton, and Jeremy D. Wendt. 2008. LLCM-WIP: Low-Latency, Continuous-Motion Walking-in-Place. In *Proceedings of the 2008 IEEE Symposium on 3D User Interfaces (3DUI '08)*. IEEE Computer Society, Washington, DC, USA, 97–104. DOI: http://dx.doi.org/10.1109/3DUI.2008.4476598
12. Randal C Foster, Lorraine M Lanningham-Foster, Chinmay Manohar, and et al. 2005. Precision and accuracy of an ankle-worn accelerometer-based pedometer in step counting and energy expenditure. *Prev Med* 41, 3-4 (2005), 778–83. DOI: http://dx.doi.org/10.1016/j.ypmed.2005.07.006
13. Beverly K Jaeger and Ronald R Mourant. 2001. Comparison of simulator sickness using static and dynamic walking simulators. In *Proceedings of the Human Factors and Ergonomics Society Annual Meeting*, Vol. 45. SAGE Publications, 1896–1900.
14. Ji-Sun Kim, Denis Gračanin, and Francis Quek. 2012. Sensor-fusion walking-in-place interaction technique using mobile devices. In *Virtual Reality Short Papers and Posters (VRW), 2012 IEEE*. IEEE, 39–42.
15. William B Lathrop and Mary K Kaiser. 2002. Perceived orientation in physical and virtual environments: changes in perceived orientation as a function of idiothetic information available. *Presence* 11, 1 (2002), 19–32.
16. Catherine G Ling and Sheila O Smith. 2010. Alternative placements for women wearing pedometers. *J Am Acad Nurse Pract* 22, 5 (May 2010), 264–9. DOI: http://dx.doi.org/10.1111/j.1745-7599.2010.00502.x
17. Michael Meehan, Sharif Razzaque, Mary C Whitton, and Frederick P Brooks Jr. 2003. Effect of latency on presence in stressful virtual environments. In *Virtual Reality, 2003. Proceedings. IEEE*. IEEE, 141–148.
18. Florian 'Floyd' Mueller, Martin R. Gibbs, and Frank Vetere. 2008. Taxonomy of exertion games. In *OZCHI '08: Proceedings of the 20th Australasian Conference on Computer-Human Interaction*. ACM, New York, NY, USA, 263–266. DOI: http://dx.doi.org/10.1145/1517744.1517772
19. Noah Nelson. 2015. NPR - All Tech Considered - Virtual Reality's Next Hurdle: Overcoming 'Sim Sickness' http://www.npr.org/sections/alltechconsidered/2014/08/05/338015854/virtual-realitys-next-hurdle-overcoming-sim-sickness. (August 2015).
20. Nicolaos Papazoglou, Panayotis Loussidis, Andreas Giannoulopoulos, and et al. 1991. Comparison of respiratory response of jogging in place and Bruce treadmill exercise test. *Clinical cardiology* 14, 11 (1991), 913–916.
21. Patrick Péruch, Loïc Belingard, and Catherine Thinus-Blanc. 2000. Transfer of spatial knowledge from virtual to real environments. In *Spatial Cognition II*. Springer, 253–264.
22. Sharif Razzaque, David Swapp, Mel Slater, and et al. 2002. Redirected walking in place. In *ACM International Conference Proceeding Series*, Vol. 23. 123–130.

23. Bernhard E. Riecke, Bobby Bodenheimer, Timothy P. McNamara, andet al. 2010. Do We Need to Walk for Effective Virtual Reality Navigation? Physical Rotations Alone May Suffice. In *Proceedings of the 7th International Conference on Spatial Cognition (SC'10)*. Springer-Verlag, Berlin, Heidelberg, 234–247. http://dl.acm.org/citation.cfm?id=1887093.1887121

24. Mel Slater, Martin Usoh, and Anthony Steed. 1994. Steps and ladders in virtual reality. In *Proceedings of the ACM Conference on Virtual Reality Software and Technology*. World Scientific, 45–54.

25. Mel Slater, Martin Usoh, and Anthony Steed. 1995. Taking steps: the influence of a walking technique on presence in virtual reality. *ACM Transactions on Computer-Human Interaction (TOCHI)* 2, 3 (1995), 201–219.

26. James Templeman, Patricia S. Denbrook, and Linda E. Sibert. 1999. Virtual Locomotion: Walking in Place through Virtual Environments. *Presence* 8, 6 (Dec 1999), 598–617. DOI: http://dx.doi.org/10.1162/105474699566512

27. Léo Terziman, Maud Marchal, Mathieu Emily, and et al. 2010. Shake-your-head: Revisiting walking-in-place for desktop virtual reality. In *Proceedings of the 17th ACM Symposium on Virtual Reality Software and Technology*. ACM, 27–34.

28. Léo Terziman, Maud Marchal, Franck Multon, and Anatole Lécuyer. 2011. Comparing virtual trajectories made in slalom using walking-in-place and joystick techniques. In *EuroVR/EGVE Joint Virtual Reality Conference*. Eurographics.

29. Michel Treisman. 1977. Motion sickness: an evolutionary hypothesis. *Science* 197, 4302 (1977), 493–495.

30. Martin Usoh, Kevin Arthur, Mary C Whitton, andet al. 1999 Walking > walking-in-place > flying, in virtual environments. In *Proceedings of the 26th annual conference on Computer graphics and interactive techniques*. ACM Press/Addison-Wesley Publishing Co., 359–364.

31. Mark Ward, Ronald Azuma, Robert Bennett, and et al. 1992. A demonstrated optical tracker with scalable work area for head-mounted display systems. In *Proceedings of the 1992 symposium on Interactive 3D graphics*. ACM, 43–52.

32. Jeremy D Wendt, Mary C Whitton, and Frederick P Brooks Jr. 2010. Gud wip: Gait-understanding-driven walking-in-place. In *Virtual Reality Conference (VR), 2010 IEEE*. IEEE, 51–58.

33. Betsy Williams, Stephen Bailey, Gayathri Narasimham, andet al. 2011. Evaluation of Walking in Place on a Wii Balance Board to Explore a Virtual Environment. *ACM Trans. Appl. Percept.* 8, 3, Article 19 (Aug. 2011), 14 pages. DOI: http://dx.doi.org/10.1145/2010325.2010329

34. Preston Tunnell Wilson, Kevin Nguyen, Alyssa Harris, and Betsy Williams. 2014. Walking in place using the Microsoft Kinect to explore a large VE. In *Proceedings of the 13th ACM SIGGRAPH International Conference on Virtual-Reality Continuum and its Applications in Industry*. ACM, 27–33.

35. Neil Zhao. 2010. Full-featured pedometer design realized with 3-Axis digital accelerometer. *Analog Dialogue* 44, 06 (2010).

"Will I always be not social?": Re-Conceptualizing Sociality in the Context of a Minecraft Community for Autism

Kathryn E. Ringland[1], Christine T. Wolf[1], Heather Faucett[1], Lynn Dombrowski[2], Gillian R. Hayes[1]

[1]Department of Informatics
University of California, Irvine
{kringlan, wolfct, hfaucett, hayesg}@uci.edu

[2]School of Informatics and Computing
Indiana University, IUPUI
lsdombro@iupui.edu

ABSTRACT
Traditional face-to-face social interactions can be challenging for individuals with autism, leading some to perceive and categorize them as less social than their typically-developing peers. Individuals with autism may even see themselves as less social relative to their peers. Online communities can provide an alternative venue for social expression, enabling different types of communication beyond face-to-face, oral interaction. Using ethnographic methods, we studied the communication ecology that has emerged around a Minecraft server for children with autism and their allies. Our analysis shows how members of this community search for, practice, and define sociality through a variety of communication channels. These findings suggest an expansion in how sociality has traditionally been conceptualized for individuals with autism.

Author Keywords
Autism; Communication; Social Interaction; Virtual Worlds; Minecraft; Social Media.

ACM Classification Keywords
K.4.2 Social Issues: Assistive technologies for persons with disabilities.

INTRODUCTION
Positive social interaction can contribute to increased feelings of wellbeing. For people with autism[1], however, social interactions can be challenging, particularly in person and on the telephone [35,71]. Challenges include difficulty initiating social encounters, using and interpreting non-verbal cues (*e.g.,* gestures, eye contact), displaying emotional reciprocity, and a tendency to focus exclusively on one interest intently [1,49,59]. Such challenges in social interactions can be isolating, often leading to decreases in feelings of social connectedness or belonging [3,32,59,67] and increases in feelings of loneliness, depression, and anxiety [3,36,45,67]. Adolescents who feel cared for and as though they are part of a social group tend to report higher levels of emotional wellbeing and are less likely to abuse substances or engage in dangerous behavior [13,55,56,61]. Likewise, low levels of social connection, support, and competence tend to predict depression and low self-esteem [69].

Despite their challenges in social interactions and popular misconceptions about their sociability, individuals with autism typically express a desire to create social connections with others [45,48,52]. Some assistive technologies address difficulties surrounding social interaction by supporting discrete kinds of communication (*e.g.,* verbal speech). This focus on a single avenue for communication, however, may be inadequate in addressing the myriad ways in which people with autism can be expressive and social that extend beyond a singular medium. Alternatively, online communities, including social networking sites [7,24,25], can create multiple avenues for communication for those who struggle with face-to-face interactions, such as those with autism [52].

Despite the potential advantages online communication has for people with autism, these interactions also bring their own challenges. It can be difficult to know who is trustworthy in a space where multiple identities, some fraudulent, are easily created [7]. Cyberbullying can be harder to avoid than in-person bullying with increasing mobile and home connectivity [21,58,64]. Finally, as the norms of online communities rapidly change, and there are limited ways to explicitly indicate those changes, it can be particularly difficult to detect and emulate those changing norms [7,58].

CHI'16, May 07-12, 2016, San Jose, CA, USA
© 2016 ACM. ISBN 978-1-4503-3362-7/16/05···$15.00
DOI: http://dx.doi.org/10.1145/2858036.2858038

[1] The term *autism* will be used throughout this paper to denote Autism Spectrum Disorder as well as Asperger's Syndrome as previously defined before the DSM-V changes [1].

In this paper, we present the results of an ethnographic study of an online community surrounding a Minecraft server dedicated to children with autism and their allies. By studying the communication ecology surrounding this community—including social networking sites, online videos, a community website, and the Minecraft server itself—we describe how people with autism and their allies search for community and how they practice and define sociality (*i.e.,* the state of being social).

RELATED WORK

In this section, we first describe prior research focused on sociality among people with autism. We then examine technological supports developed to help individuals with autism communicate and interact socially with others.

Autism and Sociality

There has been much debate surrounding the sociality of individuals with autism. Autism is often accompanied by difficulty making eye contact, interpreting certain nonverbal cues, and, in some cases, performing coherent verbal utterances [1]. These challenges can often be interpreted as an inability or lack of desire for social interaction. However, autism is complex, nuanced, and occurs on a spectrum. Accordingly, researchers have begun exploring how sociality might be different, not less, for those with autism.

Müller *et al.*, for instance, found during interviews that individuals with autism do, in fact, desire social interaction with other people [45]. These social interactions are often complicated by sensory overload and other experiences associated with autism. These personal challenges are only partially at the heart of difficulties that individuals with autism experience when socializing [48]; sociality also depends on circumstance and context. For instance, face-to-face conversations may be much more difficult for a child with autism than an interaction that takes place side-by-side, without the need for eye contact or facial cues. Thus, enabling flexibility in the nature, context, and form of interactions may ease some of the challenges faced by these individuals.

The range of therapies available for those with autism is as wide and varied as the symptoms of autism itself [60]. In aiding the sociality of individuals with autism, therapies often support the social skills and social needs of individuals with autism but tend to support a particular view of sociality [48]. For instance, one such view may be that to be social, an individual must communicate in face-to-face conversations using body language, inflections in vocal tones, and eye contact. This social behavior is a large focus of therapies and technologies to support these therapies [48].

More recent work, notably in Anthropology and Psychology, has begun exploring other social behaviors and interactions that might be of use to individuals with autism. Social supports—such as structured social activities, creative outlets, and mediating objects—can facilitate alternative social interactions [45]. These social supports often lend themselves to being technologically mediated. Communication mediated by technology may reduce sensory overload and improve one's overall ability to socialize to the preferred level [48,52].

Social Play

Social play is how children practice and develop their social skills. Children engage in a range of playful practice roles and test the boundaries of social rules during social play sessions [16]. These skills are vital not only for children to grow into competent, functioning adults, but also to discover who they are and what kind of adults they want to become [16,41].

Difficulties in social play arise for children with autism because they often have challenges in the development of social skills and communication [1,33,34]. Thus, children with autism can be caught in a cycle of being unable to engage in social interactions which leads to impoverished social play which, in turn, leads to further deficits in social skills as the children age [33]. Children with autism have a tendency to become fixated on one toy, object, or theme, which can lead to alienating their peers with demands for more rigid and less attractive types of play [70]. Libby *et al.* found that while children with autism did not have difficulty with most forms of play (*e.g.,* sensorimotor play), they did exhibit less symbolic (*i.e.,* pretend) play than other children [38]. Looking more broadly, children with disabilities are found to engage in play, but the forms that play takes may not be "typical" [17,54]. For example, a child may be in a wheelchair and unable to play traditional outdoor running games (*e.g.,* tag), but can play in other ways, such as a game that uses only the upper body or modifies the game to fit their specific needs. Children with autism fall into this category of both wanting and being able to play, but are not able to engage in play in ways other children may consider typical.

Recognizing these difficulties, work has been conducted in the area of teaching children with autism how to engage in social play. These include peer-play training with models [31], using Integrated Play Groups [70], and adult-child interventions [2]. Strain and Schwartz demonstrate that social play cannot be taught with a discrete skillset because it is a highly contextual experience [62]. This has led to a need to mediate the play experience, either naturally occurring play or artificially produced play experiences, rather than teach children how to play. However, some therapies still teach specific social skills (*e.g.,* eye contact, joint attention), which may then be reflected on and practiced during social play [2]. Therapists can create structured play environments where a child with autism may have directed play, getting cues and positive feedback when exhibiting appropriate play behavior. Therapists have also found that narrative construction and storytelling are both useful in helping teach social skills, such as reciprocation and emotion recognition, necessary to engage in social play [10,15,37,40]. These techniques are useful because they are already found in play and, when used in therapy, they can help children with autism gain social skills and enhance their play experience [15].

Technology to Support Social Interaction for Autism

Assistive technologies can support communication and act as social supports for people with autism [11,42]. Assistive technologies focused on socialization have taken many forms including, but not limited to, tabletops (*e.g.,* SIDES [53]), tablets (*e.g.,* [6,26,27]), and social media (*e.g.,* [23–25]), each with their own advantages and disadvantages, as we detail here.

Tabletops provide a large common focal point and all users can be collocated comfortably [53]. While tabletop applications have promise for creating a supportive environment for socializing, they have not been seen as feasible for general distribution, due to their high price point, large size, and lack of portability. Tablets provide many of the same advantages without the these large barriers and thus have been used for social support, creating a focal point for joint attention, and encouraging sharing and creativity [6,26,27].

Social media, which can be accessed from tablets or any other platform, can be also be a means of social support for people with autism or a way to deliver social skills based therapies. For example, SocialMirror was designed to connect people with autism to their social network and get support as they transition into adulthood [23–25]. On the other hand, Burke *et al.* have found that it may be difficult for users with autism to maintain online relationships [7]. As social media and its users continue to change, individuals with autism may find that computer-mediated interactions are effective for socializing regardless of these challenges [52]. In this work, we explore what these challenges and opportunities look like in the context of an online community using a virtual world and its surrounding technological artifacts to support people with autism, their allies, and broader social community.

METHODS

The data presented in this paper are from an on-going, immersive digital study of the community that has grown around a Minecraft server known as Autcraft[2]. The Autcraft community was created for children with autism and their allies. This community originated with the customized Minecraft virtual world initially, but a variety of channels are now used in tandem including YouTube, Twitch[3], Twitter, Facebook, and a community maintained website (including an administrator's blog, community forums, member profiles, and an in-browser web messenger). These are all included in this work. Data were collected through interviews, participant-observations, field notes, directed and non-directed forum discussions, chat logs, and the retrieval of digital artifacts.

Setting

The Autcraft community populates social media, live video streaming, and a Minecraft virtual world. We describe each of these in turn in this section as part of the overall site.

Minecraft. Minecraft is an open-ended virtual world with no particular goals or play requirements [12,43,63]. Players can build and create new objects by manipulating blocks in the game. Minecraft virtual worlds are each unique, procedurally-generated environments [12,20]. Players can use Single Player Mode (in which case a unique world will be created just for them), or Multiplayer Mode, in which a unique, shared world is created and hosted on a server other players may join.

The multiplayer virtual world in our study, Autcraft, is a semi-private server on Minecraft created for children with autism and their families. As such, anyone wishing to join must first complete an application to be added to the white list. This application includes a declaration of having autism or being a friend or family member of someone with autism who plays on the server. Only those who have been added to the white list can access the server. Autcraft currently has more than 5,000 white-listed members with a daily average of approximately 50 players in-world at peak hours of the day. Because the Autcraft server requires all chat activities to be in English, most players are located in English-speaking countries. This server has strict rules for behavior that are enforced both by software modifications and a group of volunteer administrators and "helpers."

Video. Autcraft community members use two main outlets for creating and publishing video content: Twitch and YouTube. Twitch is a live-streaming video platform used for streaming video game content while the user is playing [19]. Members use this platform to stream live videos of their activities within the Autcraft virtual world. Other Twitch users can search for the Autcraft keyword or find users by username to watch the desired community related content. Live stream videos are meant to be watched in the moment, but are occasionally recorded. Videos recorded and published on YouTube are generally edited before publishing, including title screens denoting the player's username and video title. YouTube videos are shared with other Autcraft members through the community's website.

Social Networking Sites. Autcraft administrators maintain a Twitter account and a Facebook group page, which are used to disseminate community news, post inspirational blogs by members of the community, and keep in touch with community members. Community discussions happen across these sites and are member-driven.

[2] http://Autcraft.com

[3] http://www.twitch.tv/

Autcraft Community Website. Autcraft administrators maintain a website that includes a main page with news and blog posts, a status page for the virtual world, forums, member profile pages, and an in-browser web messenger. The website allows members to "friend" each other through profile pages and displays "top forum posters" on the front page for those who have posted the most in the forums.

Data Collection

Our work employs methods established by other studies of virtual world communities [4,5,28,46,51]. The first author has four years experience playing Minecraft recreationally approximately 15 hours per month. As Autcraft is a semi-private server, we gained access to Autcraft via permission of the server's creator for the purposes of this study. From here, the first author created an account with an avatar labeled as a researcher. The researcher's presence and purpose was made clear to the community through both the Autcraft web-based forum as well as in the in-game chat. Additionally, community members were able to ask the researcher questions about the study through the forums or by visiting the researcher at an in-world home office created by the researcher during participant observations. Parents were informed of the lead researcher's presence via a parent message board and the Facebook page of the community. Parents and children were encouraged to voice their concerns and ask questions about the research through all communication platforms utilized by the community. The lead researcher also maintains a public website where members of the community are directed to see updates from the study, including any publications. The lead researcher collected approximately 60 hours of immersive in-game observations, including participating in activities on the server, recording chat-based dialogue, and field-notes on everyday practices and events as they occurred in the virtual world. The lead researcher also participated in community activities outside the virtual world, including observing discussions in the forums and on the social networking sites. In addition, focus groups were created informally on the forums through forum posts prompts, wherein the lead researcher asked open-ended questions of the community. Additionally, the first author collected a variety of digital artifacts from the various platforms used by the community. These data were collected over a period of sixteen months and include approximately 5000 forum threads and 150 blog posts created by players, parents, and administrators.

Data Analysis

Using an iterative, inductive approach, emergent phenomena were identified, named, and categorized following techniques similar to those employed in grounded theory [8]. We used an inductive method of analysis to understand how participants defined and enacted sociality through practice, rather than testing theoretical definitions found in the literature because we were explicitly interested in understanding how the community views and experiences sociality. Using open coding, the research team met weekly to discuss recurring themes in the data. As dominant codes emerged, they were incorporated into the categories presented in this paper. Through these preliminary codes, types of practices and meanings emerged, particularly patterns of common behaviors and situations around community, definitions of sociality, and practices of sociality. Additionally, through directed coding around the theme of social behaviors, we identified the dimensions and degrees of variation around these behaviors (*e.g.*, the various ways in which Autcraft community members define and practice sociality). We used affinity diagramming and axial coding to understand the relationship between, across, and within these codes.

RESULTS

Our analysis demonstrates how members of the Autcraft community search for, practice, and define sociality. These results indicate more broadly how people may increasingly find new ways to express themselves and create a sense of community as emergent forms of media change the nature of our social landscape.

Searching For and Finding Community

In this section, we describe how people with autism and their allies search out and find social interactions through Autcraft. Specifically, we examine how members of the Autcraft community articulate their entry into, and continued involvement with, this community. These results highlight how online communities can serve as sites of sociality and how the people who are a part of them seek out social interactions through the varied platforms available to them.

Early adolescence (*i.e.*, typically ages 9 to 13) is known to be a time of discovering one's own identity marked by shifting priorities from family to peer relations and a strong desire to conform to and be accepted by one's peers [72]. By middle adolescence (*i.e.*, typically ages 14 to 16), individual relationships become more important but "fitting in" remains a key value. There are no clear data on the average age of Minecraft players, but our extensive time spent in game and on forums would indicate that early adolescence and adolescence are sizable age groups for players on Minecraft and even more so for members of the Autcraft community. Thus, it is not particularly surprising that the awareness of, and a strong concern about, feelings of difference are salient aspects for Autcraft members. Being "different" can result in feelings of isolation, realized isolation, or even bullying. In this context, game play and the associated online communities can be a place of escape for those who are socially isolated or bullied in other areas of their lives. For example, one member describes being unhappy with the behavior of his school peers and notes that the forums are a place to vent these frustrations:

Everything I do just makes me more and more unhappy and stressed.....it's not like [me] to feel depressed but I just feel so depressed and down and stupid and just bad about myself. People are saying mean things to me. I......don't want to post this but I need to get out of my system... (forums, P27, age 12, m)[4]

Using the forums, members of Autcraft are able to express their emotions, something they may not be comfortable doing elsewhere or be able to in "conventional" ways. These slower-paced, text-based interactions allow members to decide what and how to share—thus reducing the stress of improvised interactions and the need for interpreting nonverbal cues found in face-to-face interactions (*e.g.*, gestures, eye contact).

Despite enjoying the benefits of this outlet, Autcraft players must still navigate other places in their lives, where, in many cases, they feel bullied and isolated. As one member posted:

"Still hard in the rest of the day - can't spend all day on Autcraft - Seriously!!" (forums, Q9, P23, age ?, m).

Similarly, one member posted about her difficulties with bullying at school:

...so today i was thinking about how much i have been bullied and how many friends ditched me. so i need some advice on how to make friends plz help thx guys (forums, P10, age ?, f)

Here, we see her ability to cope with bullying at school, in part, related to her ability to leverage her online social network. Still, she is actively seeking out in-person friendships and asks her online friends for help.

Autcraft was created with the intent of being a Minecraft server free of bullying and as such attracts a large number of players with autism seeking a "safe" space [58]. Sometimes this support comes in the form of the implicit reassurance that there are other "people like me" in the world. For example, one poster in the forums asked how to deal with life when it becomes "overwhelming" due to sensory impairments that make many physical sensations uncomfortable for her:

When I'm getting to the point that I'm freaking out over something ... everything feels really overwhelming (like if I had to be out in a loud place with loads of people for a while it all builds up) and when it is being I guess let out everything feels horrible. Like I get to the point where I want to cut my hair off because the feeling of it on me gets too much. I'm not sure if anyone else gets like that or if it is just me being weird but it feels really horrible ... (forums, P21, age 14, f)

In this forum post, the writer wonders if her feelings are "weird" or if "anyone else gets like that." Although she is describing a *physical* discomfort, she is seeking *emotional* and *social* comfort from her network of peers, and she is not denied. Another poster quickly responded:

Yeah.. I'm so glad someone feels the same way - It's hard to find the words to explain it, especially with peers. Good to make friends on here. (forums, P23, age ?, m)

Not only were other posters supportive, they dispense advice related to these physical world problems such as *"crying it out"* or going to the school's *"learning support room"* and discussing these problems with a supportive teacher *(forums, P2, age 13, m)*.

Thus, a dedicated social network of supportive people with relatable personal experiences can help members of the online community overcome challenges, both on and offline, and normalize the experiences of those with autism. This in and of itself is not particularly surprising. We know from the literature that online communities can support people with chronic health conditions [9,14,39], those who are members of minority groups [57], and typically developing adolescents [66]. What is unique here is the particular role that a game coupled with other, more common, forms of online community have on a population particularly known to struggle with finding social support [63]. Autcraft—including the game, forums, Facebook page, and community-related videos—helps community members to not feel "alone:"

I guess that's what Autcraft is for, meeting people who go through the same thing as you, so you don't feel alone? xD (forums, P28, age ?, m)

Autcraft members' descriptions of "hanging out" with their friends mirrors those of other youth online [30]. They spend time with their online friends by interacting through forums, instant messenger, and "hanging out" in the Autcraft virtual world. Although not typically physically collocated, members consider these relationships to be meaningful friendships. Autcraft, by its very nature of blending social interaction with strict rules of behavior and appealing game mechanics, comes together to form a space of cohesion, not difference, and of support, not scorn. This type of community allows people to redefine their views on sociality and of community more broadly as we examine in the next section.

Defining Sociality and Community

Although Autcraft community members often seek out social relationships through Autcraft as an augment to in-person relationships, some do not wish to seek out these in-person friendships. Those who prefer the bulk of their sociality to occur online struggle with what it means to be "social." For example, one teen described himself on the forums as "not social" while, in the same post, describing many online, and offline, social interactions:

So, I dont ever social lize. The only way i am social is online. I never hang out with my family or do anything. The only time i come out of my room is if we watch a family

[4] Each quote includes: (source of quote, participant number, age of participant, and identified gender if available in member profile).

movie, i play baseball we go for a car ride or i go to work. Other than that i am in my room 24/7 on PC, YouTube texting etc. Anyone else like this? Will i always be not social :(I really want to be social but its hard D: (forums, P22, age 13, m)

This participant questions his own sociality by comparing his social behavior to more normative views of sociality. While he describes thinking that he should be communicating more face-to-face, he finds his online communications satisfying in their own right. For individuals with autism, face-to-face interactions can prove difficult and take a great deal of energy. Therefore, these users may find that online interactions are less "costly" and derive from them the same satisfaction as face-to-face interactions.

Some interview participants, on the other hand, directly defined their online activities in Autcraft as social. For example, one called it out as particularly social, noting that it was a way to find people with common interests, an issue to which we return in the following section:

Even being on [Autcraft] is social. Those are good ways of talking to people. ... I asked [my dad] and he said try to find people with similar interests. (forums, P5, age ?, ?)

Of course, online interactions are not always positive, and, in other online environments, negative interactions can erupt around labels and definitions. For example, one Autcraft player described responses to the word "Autistic" as part of his username when playing Minecraft on another server:

*"people would swear call me names break my builds etc...becuz i am defrent... i didnt relize people would be mean about [the username]... and i liked the name... theres other people on here [Autcraft] with *autism* or *Autistic* in there names...Yeah... thats another reason i am happy to have [autism]" (interview, P22, age 13, m)*

For P22, having autism was something he wanted to disclose to others until that label led to negative responses from other Minecraft players. Recognizing this commonality with other Autcraft players then led him to play exclusively on the Autcraft server rather than other places in Minecraft. He was able, in this way, to define not only what being social meant for him but also who his community might be.

Members of Autcraft find that they can lean on one another for social support. In turn, they learn the valuable lesson of social reciprocity by providing aid and comfort for other members when they are troubled. For example, one member described being *"so into talking"* that he would forget to actually play the game, going on to express:

"i like to help people with there problems... Like if someone is sad about bullies i help cheer them up" (interview, P22, age 13, m)

For many members, being helpful and supportive is one of the most important parts of their sociality. The community has found this important enough to write into their rules, and has actively encouraged helpful behavior by giving the most helpful members advanced ranks and other rewards.

More broadly, Autcraft community members frequently articulate their membership as being part of the Autcraft "family." In much the same way players of MMOs might feel a strong bond with their guild members, members of the Autcraft community bond with each other and feel connected to one another [47,68]. Particularly for adolescents, who are actively exploring their identities and places in the world, this "family" membership allows them a sense of connection and affiliation with others beyond their biological family.

Being a part of the Autcraft "family" means being a member of the group, having a support network to lean on, feeling included, and participating in activities and events together. A participating parent details:

Well, I love being a member of the [Autcraft] community and love spending time with my 'family' here. ...finally just felt like I found a place that I fit in. A place I was accepted for being shy ... and just being "different" than others. ... Most of my life I've never felt like I fit in anywhere and never could make friends my age. Here--it doesn't matter where I live, my age, how shy and/or anti-social i can be at times, that I have anxiety over really weird things, or that I can talk too much--I'm accepted. And for that, I want to go to these events and just either hang out and have fun with other people, or help make an event happen. (directed forum, P25, age 45, f)

As we see in the above quote, "family" as it relates to the Autcraft community, incorporates the idea of being accepted for who you are, including faults and quirks. Across our analysis, we saw this acceptance as a cornerstone to making being "different" more tolerable and reducing the social isolation and loneliness that frequently surrounds difference. Definitions—whether of sociality, community, or even family—are shaped both by conceptualizations and ways of thinking, but also through practice. Thus, in the next section, we examine the ways people in the Autcraft community practice sociality.

Practicing Sociality

In this section, we consider practices of social connection at both the community and interpersonal level. For the Autcraft community, these social connections are formed and maintained through a variety of media technologies, allowing members to use communicative practices best suited for them, both as individuals and as a group.

Community: Setting the Stage for Sociality

The guidelines of the Autcraft community explicitly encourage people to *"Be Kind, Be Respectful, Be Responsible" (community rules, from website).* Reminders of these rules are automatically sent to the personal chat window of Autcraft players. However, no rules would matter if the community were not engaged in these supportive behaviors. Additionally, the emergent ecology of other non-Minecraft platforms around Autcraft makes rule enforcement difficult, if not impossible. What makes the Autcraft community noteworthy is that the culture and norms of the community ensure positive behaviors cross these platforms and are adapted to the features of the particular communications media being used.

Administrators foster the sense of "family" that is core to this community's definition of sociality by creating community events, including parties, special battles during which members collaboratively fight monsters, and even local in-person events. For example, when the community celebrated its second anniversary, there were dragon fights, a dance party in-world, live-streaming of the weekend's events through Twitch, YouTube, and giveaways:

"Well, the day is coming to a close... Autcraft's 2nd birthday.

I have been up for a very long time but we did 4 epic community dragon fights, shared tons of great memories and had lots of fun partying in the ballroom on the server." (Facebook post, P29, age 39, m)

Community members hold these events in places that are marked with in-world monuments that honor the events. Given the importance of these events, administrators have worked to expand their reach beyond Minecraft players to curious parents or others who are interested. For example, an administrator who helped run a major community event posted a recap on Facebook and used Twitch to live stream the event:

I've heard from parents that told me that they were able to see their children interacting with others in the videos. They loved to see their kids having fun! Another parent told me that her son saw himself in one of the videos and he couldn't stop talking about what a great day it was. (Facebook post, P29, age 39, m)

Even members who may not be able to participate fully, such as parents who have other obligations, are still able to connect:

This year for autism awareness day I had to work, but was able to listen to [Autcraft]'s stream off and on and participate in chat once in awhile. (directed forum, P25, age 45, f)

Members are able to watch these videos and read posts about the event in order to relive the experience. One member told the story of when *"famous youtubers"* (*i.e.*, Minecraft players who produce YouTube videos and have a substantial following) came to visit the virtual world:

On April 2nd, 2015 (Autism Awareness day) We had a bunch of famous youtubers come and visit, including some of my favorites that I never thought I would be able to see. It was one of the best days ever for me! (directed forum, P30, age 16, m)

The poster included links to the YouTube videos created by an administrator who recorded the event, showing again the ways community members and administrators are creating, capturing, and assembling content in new and ever evolving ways. Various modes of creating and capturing community events give members a variety of options for participating in the events and fostering their own sense of belonging.

...I am still feeling really great [about the event] because even though they were just words on the screen, I could see the happiness in so many people today. They had the time of their lives. And so, I did too." (Facebook post, P29, age 39, m)

To P29, the happiness felt by other members of the community was still impactful and meaningful to him, even though "they were just words on the screen." Being able to navigate between video, audio, and text-based communication enhances the community's ability to express shared joy.

When asked why they would participate in community events, such as the dragon fight, members recalled stories of working together to complete a goal. These events create a sense of shared pride that directly connects to an overall sense of belonging.

It's cool to be slaying a huge dragon with other people, because then you can all be proud when it dies! (directed forum, P25, age 13, f)

Another member described that everyone had a common goal in slaying the dragon. When the dragon died it left behind loot for the players, including a dragonhead, which is used for various recipes and decorating.

Trying to get a head was what everyone was doing, and that was part of the fun! I ended up getting one, and so did a lot of others because of how many dragons there were. (directed forum, P26 , age 13, f)

The poster also included a screen shot as part of his story about the dragon fight, to give readers a sense of what the in-game experience was like. When the event "lagged" or

Image 1. Fire arrows frozen in the air due to lag during dragon fight.

froze on screen because too many people were online at once, all the arrows were frozen in the sky (See Image 1). Again we see here the merging of varying media types all in an effort to help others experience this highly social interaction. Although reading forum posts and viewing screenshots may not seem traditionally "social," the participants in these events are actively redefining belonging, community, and sociality.

The inherent nature of how tasks are accomplished within the virtual world forces members to seek out connections in their network. To create new objects within the game, players must go to their network of other players to get the information, or "recipes" they need [44] from Reddit, YouTube, forums, or direct communication.

The Autcraft community engenders a sense of "family" in its members employing the different platforms at its disposal. As members each have their own unique communication needs and desired levels of participation with the group, there are a variety of available platforms for them to use. Events held within the Autcraft virtual world are also available across the Autcraft community's many platforms, allowing members to participate at their own desired level and ability (*e.g.,* direct participation, in-world observation, or through the website or live-streaming). Indeed, having these multiple options not only enables members to feel like part of the "family" as they occur, but also facilitate the remembrance of events after they have passed, enabling a sort of retelling of the "family stories."

Interpersonal Relationships Across Platforms

For adolescents, the Internet can be an important social space for developing and maintain one-on-one friendships. Contrary to early findings regarding online socialization, more recent research indicates that Internet use has positive social consequences [65]. Autcraft provides powerful common ground for players, a key foundation to many friendships. Not only do those who join the community share a common interest in Minecraft, they also all have claimed to be either an ally of, or someone with, autism. This is a requirement the community regulates carefully. These two components of the community help lay the groundwork for friendship because they represent part of a person's shared interest. Of course, this foundation is not enough to foster long-term friendships, and indeed not every player on Autcraft likes every other player nor considers them friends. However, the shared space of the Autcraft server facilitates making new acquaintances with some assurance that you have some commonality. In-game chatting, text-based communication out of game, gift giving, and shared activities work together to enable players to strengthen the bonds of friendship, a phenomenon we unpack in this section.

In-game chat, which is by far the dominant mode of communication for Autcraft players, includes everyone who is currently online in the virtual world regardless of their location within said virtual world. Much of the discussion occurs within this main chat, making this space a powerful venue for establishing new friendships:

I wasn't feeling well at that time and needed someone to talk to. [Another player] listened to everything I said and made me feel better that's when we became friends. Since that day we talked a lot we joked around and had a lot of [fun]. after some time we ended up talking every day, when I was sad she would cheer me up, she would make me laugh through my tears and eventually I learned to trust her. I don't trust many people (except for some people on [Autcraft]) so that was really special for me. And I think that's why I'm able to call her a friend. We still talk everyday and we have so much fun. We have so many inside jokes and she is always there for me. (directed forum, P31, age 15, f)

When one is feeling emotionally fragile and in need of friendship, online communications can fill that void. However, this quote also brings to mind issues with trust online. Burke *et al.* found that individuals with autism had difficulty knowing who to trust and when to disclose information in online communications [7]. Autcraft administrators enforce server rules to ensure that no abuse occurs; this protection, however is only a first step in building trust—P31, for instance, say that she only trusts "some people" on Autcraft. Trust can be essential in developing deeper friendships.

Members also reported installing applications on their mobile devices to continue chatting with those in-world, without accessing Minecraft. This technology enables continued connection without Minecraft game features, demonstrating how Minecraft has been appropriated as a platform for social media beyond game play.

In addition to text communication, virtual possessions and gifts are also a way members demonstrate friendship. One member described how he made one of his friends when they first joined the community:

...another new person joined. She was fun and I felt like I could be myself with her. At the end of the first day we met, she gave me a lead[5] named 'Friendship Bracelet' that I still have today and we are still really good friends. (directed forum, P30, age 16, m)

In this instance, an in-world object bestowed as a gift signified the importance of the relationship. Sharing objects created by users and sharing virtual space (*e.g.,* jointly owned houses, villages, common play areas) contribute to relationships in much the same way as equivalent physical objects and space might contribute to out of game sociality.

[5] In-world object that is a rope for leading horses or cows, used here as a bracelet because jewelry does not otherwise exist in the world as of this writing.

Building objects was originally, and still is, the main attraction of Minecraft for most players. While building can be done by an individual, having a partner or team enables the creation of more complex architecture. Formation of building teams can also be a way to make friends:

while building that village I met this friend name [player name] and to this day he is still my friend (directed forum, P32, age ?, m)

To form these teams, a member usually asks others if they would like to help build the project. In some cases, the project is advertised on the forums or in-world to see who would like to join in (See Image 2). While administrators and parents sometimes organize these teams to help build large-scale projects, by and large, the younger members organize the teams. This is significant because in other social situations, it is challenging for individuals with autism to take on leadership positions [45]. Müller *et al.* found that while small groups were a desirable format for social interaction for individuals with autism, a facilitator was needed to sustain the group. It seems in the context of the Autcraft community, the technology facilitates younger members practicing leadership roles.

Usually, one member has a project idea that they would like to see realized. They then organize the rest of the team to fulfill the project goal, as in the following:

i sometimes ask others to help me... Usally i would show them a picture on how to build it and we pick either get the items or start the build... i usally let them start becuase i am not the best builder ;p (interview, P22, age 13, m)

P22 explained his process for leading his team in a build project. He would send images of project ideas found through Google Images or Minecraft videos on YouTube to his project team through the Autcraft website's messenger. The team would then coordinate the actual building in-world through the chat functionality.

While chatting and working in groups both require one-on-one communication and interaction, other activities can be done in parallel, reducing the stress of interacting. These parallel activities are favored by members who are younger, are less skilled at communicating via text, or just want a less intense social interaction. As found in Müller *et al.*, having the options for one-on-one interaction *and* parallel activities is preferable for individuals with autism [45]. Parallel interactions give individuals a shared focus, allowing them to still form friendships and foster social connectedness, as we see in the following vignette:

A member asks in chat if anyone wants to mine with them. Another player volunteers. Together they go to the mining world within the virtual world armed with pickaxes. There is very little talking, the first player takes the lead in choosing a dig site. Together they work in parallel digging down into the earth, looking for minerals to take home to use as building materials. When they hit lava, the first player says he has to get off for now because dinner is ready and asks the second player if they will be on again tomorrow. The second player says yes. The first player logs off. (adapted from field notes)

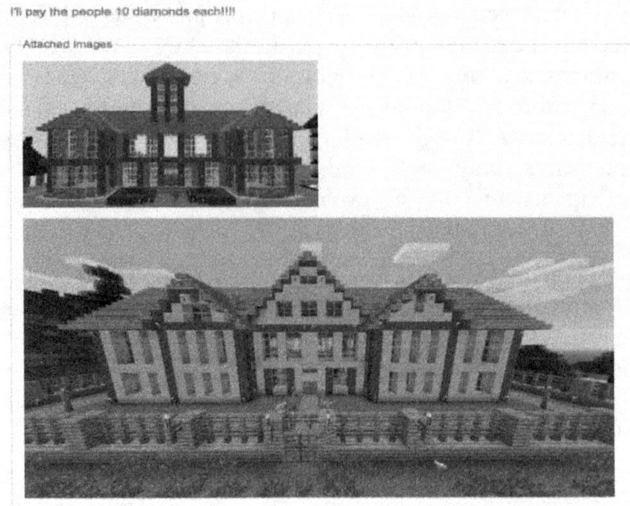

Image 2. Advertisement for a team to build the picture project.

By using various platforms, members of the Autcraft community are able to form deeper friendships with one another, if so desired. Being able to foster these relationships across the myriad platforms creates cohesion in the community. Two members may meet through an advertisement on the forums for builders, build a project together, and then go on to create YouTube videos together of the experience. This facilitates the expansion of how members can socialize with one another, giving them opportunity to explore their own sociality, expand how they would like to be able to socialize, and deepen their connection with other members of the Autcraft community.

DISCUSSION

Over the past two years, members of the Autcraft community have been organically incorporating many different communication channels to support the social interactions of community members. These practices have created a communication ecology, enabling sociality by providing flexible means of social expression. For this community, key aspects of sociality include searching for and finding community, defining sociality and community, and practicing sociality. Through these practices, this community creates and shapes social norms and relations that flourish throughout multiple platforms. By examining this network of communication channels, we are able to tease apart a variety of social behaviors that Autcraft community members are engaged in, witnessing how even taking screenshots and videos of game play or building oneself a fort can be seen as a social community-building practice. Rather than a focus exclusively on face-to-face, oral interactions, Autcraft is a community built by members who interact through a variety of computer-mediated channels, such as chats, forum message boards, videos, Minecraft avatars, and creations in-world. There are many ways to be social and Autcraft's communication ecology gives members technological options to express that diversity.

The social practices of Autcraft community members demonstrate that individuals with autism are as social as anyone else and that the social interactions of those with autism can be as complex and intimate as those without. Exploring these social practices—with all their richness and diversity—extends our understanding of what forms of technology we might consider to be "assistive." Although neither the game Minecraft itself, nor any of the online platforms in Autcraft's communication ecology are explicitly designed as assistive technologies, their flexibility allows for them to take on assistive qualities when brought together in practice. This flexibility allows for nuance, multiplicity, spontaneity, and personal preference, all touchstones of communicative, social skills.

There is a tension found in this form of communication as well. Using computers to mediate communication will not work for every child, in every situation. The children on this server must also learn how social engagement works in other parts of their world, such as school and home. As we saw in this work, they sometimes rely on the relationships formed online as the only place they perceive themselves to be socializing, which may constrain offline social behavior. At the same time, emergent evidence indicates that contrary to what we may believe instinctively, these online activities can actually improve and enhance offline behaviors. We leave this interesting area of research open for future inquiry.

Part of the challenge, particularly as new media continue to emerge, is expanding definitions of sociality that help to weave on- and offline behavior and resonate with the people engaging in them. At one time, talking on the phone was considered an asocial activity compared with face-to-face encounters. As popular opinion changes and more evidence is amassed in the research, we must be prepared as a scholarly community to understand—if not accept—these community-based definitions of terms we may think we already know. Similarly, methods and modes of communication may differ across these contexts, though the resulting feelings of connection and affiliation endure. Relying solely on any individual form of communication may make it more difficult for people to connect with people in alternate environments. For children with autism, for whom structure and predictability can be such a comfort, the challenges are even greater. While learning to communicate solely online may understandably inhibit children in connecting with others in environments that require face-to-face communication in adulthood, being able to socialize in an online environment that feels safe and supportive may encourage children to socialize offline. Similarly, pre-established online relationships can pave the way to in-person connections, such as is seen regularly with services like online dating. In particular, for this population, the online environment may, in fact, be the first place these children have ever experienced social support and friendship. Having success in this environment then lays the basic foundation for practicing and honing a wide variety of social skills to be used in a wide variety of environments, a good first (not final) step towards enhanced social experiences.

The communication ecology we see emerging around Autcraft mirrors broadening practices of online communities whose communications can sometimes span multiple platforms. As people communicate, they bring together many devices and platforms, extending beyond any one singular website, app, or game. For example, members of virtual world games frequently continue their in-world interactions on websites and forums [4,50,63]. Our exploration of Autcraft adds to this work by showing how flexible, multimodal communications not only "keep the game going" but also can have profound effects for self-expression and feelings of social belonging.

CONCLUSION AND FUTURE WORK

In this work, our results have demonstrated both how a community can organically create its own communication ecology through multimodal, multisensory technological options and how that ecology represents the diversity of sociality amongst the community's members (both those with autism and their allies). Our results show how individuals with autism search for community and define and practice sociality.

While this work looks explicitly at the Autcraft community, the sociality revealed here could also be explored in other online communities (*e.g.,* those dedicated to other hobbies or interests). Further work could reveal more about how this sociality exhibits itself in the physical world (*i.e.,* at school, home, or work) and also what kind of therapeutic impact this kind of community has on its individuals.

ACKNOWLEDGEMENTS

We thank the members of Autcraft for the warm welcome to their community. We would like to thank members of LUCI for their feedback on this paper. We would also like to thank Robert and Barbara Kleist for their support. This work is covered by human subjects protocol #2014-1079 at the University of California, Irvine.

REFERENCES

1. American Psychiatric Association. 2013. *Diagnostic and Statistical Manual of Mental Disorders*.
2. Michael Arthur, Sandra Bochner, and Nancy Butterfield. 1999. Enhancing Peer Interactions Within the Context of Play. *International Journal of Disability, Development and Education* 46, 3: 367–381. http://doi.org/10.1080/103491299100551
3. Nirit Bauminger, Cory Shulman, and Galit Agam. 2003. Peer interaction and loneliness in high-

functioning children with autism. *Journal of autism and developmental disorders* 33, 5: 489–507.

4. Tom Boellstorff. 2010. *Coming of Age in Second Life: An Anthropologist Explores the Virtually Human*. Princeton University Press.
5. Tom Boellstorff, Bonnie Nardi, Celia Pearce, and T.L. Taylor. 2012. *Ethnography and Virtual Worlds: A Handbook of Method*. Princeton University Press.
6. Louanne E. Boyd, Kathryn E. Ringland, Oliver L. Haimson, Helen Fernandez, Maria Bistarkey, and Gillian R. Hayes. 2015. Evaluating a Collaborative iPad Game's Impact on Social Relationships for Children with Autism Spectrum Disorder. *ACM Transactions on Accessible Computing* 7, 1: 1–18. http://doi.org/10.1145/2751564
7. Moira Burke, Robert Kraut, and Diane Williams. 2010. Social use of computer-mediated communication by adults on the autism spectrum. *Proceedings of the 2010 ACM conference on Computer supported cooperative work*, 425–434. Retrieved January 12, 2014 from http://dl.acm.org/citation.cfm?id=1718991
8. Kathry Charmaz. 2006. *Constructing Grounded Theory: A Practical Guide to Qualitative Analysis*. Sage Publications Ltd.
9. Neil S. Coulson, Heather Buchanan, and Aimee Aubeeluck. 2007. Social support in cyberspace: A content analysis of communication within a Huntington's disease online support group. *Patient Education and Counseling* 68, 2: 173–178. http://doi.org/10.1016/j.pec.2007.06.002
10. Joshua J. Diehl, Loisa Bennetto, and Edna Carter Young. 2006. Story Recall and Narrative Coherence of High-Functioning Children with Autism Spectrum Disorders. *Journal of Abnormal Child Psychology* 34, 1: 83–98. http://doi.org/10.1007/s10802-005-9003-x
11. Florence D. DiGennaro Reed, Sarah R. Hyman, and Jason M. Hirst. 2011. Applications of technology to teach social skills to children with autism. *Research in Autism Spectrum Disorders* 5, 3: 1003–1010. http://doi.org/10.1016/j.rasd.2011.01.022
12. Sean C. Duncan. 2011. Minecraft, beyond construction and survival. *Well Played: a journal on video games, value and meaning* 1, 1: 1–22.
13. Jacquelynne S. Eccles, Diane Early, Kari Fraser, Elaine Belansky, and Karen McCarthy. 1997. The Relation of Connection, Regulation, and Support for Autonomy to Adolescents' Functioning. *Journal of Adolescent Research* 12, 2: 263–286.
14. Marilyn Evans, Lorie Donelle, and Laurie Hume-Loveland. 2012. Social support and online postpartum depression discussion groups: A content analysis. *Patient Education and Counseling* 87, 3: 405–410. http://doi.org/10.1016/j.pec.2011.09.011
15. Eynat Gal, Dina Goren-Bar, E. Gazit, et al. 2005. Enhancing social communication through story-telling among high-functioning children with autism. In *Intelligent Technologies for Interactive Entertainment*. Springer, 320–323. Retrieved January 29, 2015 from http://link.springer.com/chapter/10.1007/11590323_43
16. Catherine Garvey. 1990. *Play*. Harvard University Press, Cambridge, MA.
17. Dan Goodley and Katherine Runswick-Cole. 2010. Emancipating play: dis/abled children, development and deconstruction. *Disability & Society* 25, 4: 499–512. http://doi.org/10.1080/09687591003755914
18. Roy Richard Grinker. 2007. *Unstrange minds: remapping the world of autism*. Basic Books, New York.
19. William A. Hamilton, Oliver Garretson, and Andruid Kerne. 2014. Streaming on twitch: fostering participatory communities of play within live mixed media. ACM Press, 1315–1324. http://doi.org/10.1145/2556288.2557048
20. Ken Hartsook, Alexander Zook, Sauvik Das, and Mark Owen Riedl. 2011. Toward supporting stories with procedurally generated game worlds. *Computational Intelligence and Games (CIG), 2011 IEEE Conference on*, IEEE, 297–304. Retrieved August 10, 2015 from http://ieeexplore.ieee.org/xpls/abs_all.jsp?arnumber=6032020
21. Sameer Hinduja and Justin W. Patchin. 2008. Cyberbullying: An Exploratory Analysis of Factors Related to Offending and Victimization. *Deviant Behavior* 29, 2: 129–156. http://doi.org/10.1080/01639620701457816
22. H. Honda and Y. Shimizu. 2002. Early Intervention System for Preschool Children with Autism in the Community: The Discovery Approach in Yokohama, Japan. *Autism* 6, 3: 239–257. http://doi.org/10.1177/1362361302006003003
23. Hwajung Hong, Eric Gilbert, Gregory D. Abowd, and Rosa I. Arriaga. 2015. In-group Questions and Out-group Answers: Crowdsourcing Daily Living Advice for Individuals with Autism. Retrieved February 18, 2015 from http://comp.social.gatech.edu/papers/chi15.autismQA.hong.pdf
24. Hwajung Hong, Jennifer G. Kim, Gregory D. Abowd, and Rosa I. Arriaga. 2012. Designing a social network to support the independence of young adults with autism. *Proceedings of the ACM 2012 conference on Computer Supported Cooperative Work*, ACM, 627–636. Retrieved April 28, 2014 from http://dl.acm.org/citation.cfm?id=2145300
25. Hwajung Hong, Jennifer G. Kim, Gregory D. Abowd, and Rosa I. Arriaga. 2012. SocialMirror: motivating

young adults with autism to practice life skills in a social world. *Proceedings of the ACM 2012 conference on Computer Supported Cooperative Work Companion*, ACM, 41–42. Retrieved May 2, 2015 from http://dl.acm.org/citation.cfm?id=2141533

26. Juan Pablo Hourcade, Natasha E. Bullock-Rest, and Thomas E. Hansen. 2011. Multitouch tablet applications and activities to enhance the social skills of children with autism spectrum disorders. *Personal and Ubiquitous Computing* 16, 2: 157–168. http://doi.org/10.1007/s00779-011-0383-3
27. Juan Pablo Hourcade, Stacy R. Williams, Ellen A. Miller, Kelsey E. Huebner, and Lucas J. Liang. 2013. Evaluation of tablet apps to encourage social interaction in children with autism spectrum disorders. *Proceedings of the 2013 ACM annual conference on Human factors in computing systems*, ACM, 3197–3206. Retrieved March 9, 2014 from http://dl.acm.org/citation.cfm?id=2466438
28. Lilly C. Irani, Gillian R. Hayes, and Paul Dourish. 2008. Situated practices of looking: visual practice in an online world. *Proceedings of the 2008 ACM conference on Computer supported cooperative work*, ACM, 187–196. Retrieved January 31, 2014 from http://dl.acm.org/citation.cfm?id=1460592
29. Ellen Isaacs, Margaret Szymanski, Yutaka Yamauchi, James Glasnapp, and Kyohei Iwamoto. 2012. Integrating local and remote worlds through channel blending. *Proceedings of the ACM 2012 conference on Computer Supported Cooperative Work*, ACM, 617–626. Retrieved August 10, 2015 from http://dl.acm.org/citation.cfm?id=2145299
30. Mizuko Itō, Sonja Baumer, Matteo Bittanti, et al. 2010. *Hanging Out, Messing Around, and Geeking Out: Kids Living and Learning with New Media*. MIT Press, Cambridge, MA.
31. Erik Jahr, Sigmund Eldevik, and Svein Eikeseth. 2000. Teaching children with autism to initiate and sustain cooperative play. *Research in Developmental Disabilities* 21, 2: 151–169.
32. Lisa E. Jobe and Susan Williams White. 2007. Loneliness, social relationships, and a broader autism phenotype in college students. *Personality and Individual Differences* 42, 8: 1479–1489. http://doi.org/10.1016/j.paid.2006.10.021
33. Rita Jordan. 2003. Social Play and Autistic Spectrum Disorders: A Perspective on Theory, Implications and Educational Approaches. *Autism* 7, 4: 347–360. http://doi.org/10.1177/1362361303007004002
34. Rita Jordan. 2008. THE GULLIFORD LECTURE: Autistic spectrum disorders: a challenge and a model for inclusion in education. *British Journal of Special Education* 35, 1: 11–15.
35. Janet E. Lainhart and Susan E. Folstein. 1994. Affective disorders in people with autism: A review of published cases. *Journal of autism and developmental disorders* 24, 5: 587–601.
36. Mathias Lasgaard, Annette Nielsen, Mette E. Eriksen, and Luc Goossens. 2010. Loneliness and Social Support in Adolescent Boys with Autism Spectrum Disorders. *Journal of Autism and Developmental Disorders* 40, 2: 218–226. http://doi.org/10.1007/s10803-009-0851-z
37. Brenda Laurel. 2004. Narrative construction as play. *interactions* 11, 5: 73–74.
38. Sarah Libby, Stuart Powell, David Messer, and Rita Jordan. 1998. Spontaneous play in children with autism: A reappraisal. *Journal of autism and developmental disorders* 28, 6: 487–497.
39. Leslie S. Liu, Kori M. Inkpen, and Wanda Pratt. 2015. "I'm Not Like My Friends": Understanding How Children with a Chronic Illness Use Technology to Maintain Normalcy. ACM Press, 1527–1539. http://doi.org/10.1145/2675133.2675201
40. Molly Losh and Lisa Capps. 2003. Narrative ability in high-functioning children with autism or Asperger's syndrome. *Journal of autism and developmental disorders* 33, 3: 239–251.
41. Hazel Markus and Paula Nurius. 1986. Possible selves. *American psychologist* 41, 9: 954.
42. Pat Mirenda. 2001. Autism, Augmentative Communication, and Assistive Technology: What Do We Really Know? *Focus on Autism and Other Developmental Disabilities* 16, 3: 141–151.
43. Mojang. 2014. Minecraft. *Minecraft*. Retrieved January 10, 2014 from https://minecraft.net/
44. James Morgan and Yagiz Mungan. 2014. Fine Arts, Culture, and Creativity in Minecraft. In *Understanding Minecraft: Essays on Play, Community, and Possibilities*, Nate Garrelts (ed.). McFarland & Company, Inc., Jefferson, NC, 175–190.
45. Eve Müller, Adriana Schuler, and Gregory B. Yates. 2008. Social challenges and supports from the perspective of individuals with Asperger syndrome and other autism spectrum disabilities. *Autism* 12, 2: 173–190. http://doi.org/10.1177/1362361307086664
46. Bonnie Nardi. 2010. *My Life as a Night Elf Priest An Anthropological Account of World of Warcraft*. University of Michigan Press.
47. Bonnie Nardi and Justin Harris. 2006. Strangers and friends: Collaborative play in World of Warcraft. *Proceedings of the 2006 20th anniversary conference on Computer supported cooperative work*, ACM, 149–158. Retrieved February 12, 2014 from http://dl.acm.org/citation.cfm?id=1180898

48. Elinor Ochs and Olga Solomon. 2010. Autistic Sociality. *Ethos* 38, 1: 69–92. http://doi.org/10.1111/j.1548-1352.2009.01082.x

49. Gael I. Orsmond, Marty Wyngaarden Krauss, and Marsha Mailick Seltzer. 2004. Peer relationships and social and recreational activities among adolescents and adults with autism. *Journal of autism and developmental disorders* 34, 3: 245–256.

50. Tyler Pace, Shaowen Bardzell, and Jeffrey Bardzell. 2010. The rogue in the lovely black dress: intimacy in world of warcraft. *Proceedings of the SIGCHI Conference on Human Factors in Computing Systems*, ACM, 233–242. Retrieved November 11, 2014 from http://dl.acm.org/citation.cfm?id=1753361

51. Celia Pearce and Artemesia. 2009. *Communities of Play: Emergent Cultures in Multiplayer Games and Virtual Worlds*. MIT Press.

52. Amit Pinchevski and John Durham Peters. 2015. Autism and new media: Disability between technology and society. *New Media & Society*: 1461444815594441.

53. Anne Marie Piper, Eileen O'Brien, Meredith Ringel Morris, and Terry Winograd. 2006. SIDES: a cooperative tabletop computer game for social skills development. *Proceedings of the 2006 20th anniversary conference on Computer supported cooperative work*, ACM, 1–10. Retrieved January 23, 2014 from http://dl.acm.org/citation.cfm?id=1180877

54. Amit Pitaru. 2008. E is for everyone: The Case for inclusive game design. *The Ecology of Games: Connecting Youth, Games, and Learning*: 67–86.

55. Michael D. Resnick, Peter S. Bearman, Robert Wm Blum, et al. 1997. Protecting adolescents from harm: findings from the National Longitudinal Study on Adolescent Health. *Jama* 278, 10: 823–832.

56. Michael D. Resnick, L.J. Harris, and Robert Wm Blum. 1993. The impact of caring and connectedness on adolescent health and well-being. *Journal Paediatric Child Health* 29.

57. Catherine M. Ridings and David Gefen. 2004. Virtual Community Attraction: Why People Hang Out Online. *Journal of Computer-Mediated Communication* 10, 1. http://doi.org/0.1111/j.1083-6101.2004.tb00229.x

58. Kathryn E. Ringland, Christine T. Wolf, Lynn Dombrowski, and Gillian R. Hayes. 2015. Making "Safe": Community-Centered Practices in a Virtual World Dedicated to Children with Autism. *Proceedings of the ACM 2015 Conference on Computer Supported Cooperative Work*, ACM.

59. Marsha Mailick Seltzer, Marty Wyngaarden Krauss, Paul T. Shattuck, Gael Orsmond, April Swe, and Catherine Lord. 2003. The symptoms of autism spectrum disorders in adolescence and adulthood. *Journal of autism and developmental disorders* 33, 6: 565–581.

60. Chantal Sicile-Kira. 2004. *Autism Spectrum Disorders: The Complete Guide to Understanding Autism, Asperger's Syndrome, Pervasive Developmental Disorder, and Other ASDs*. The Berkeley Publishing Group, New York, New York.

61. Laurence Steinburg. 1997. *Beyond the Classroom: Why School Reform Has Failed and What Parents Need to Do*. Simon & Schuster, New York.

62. P. S. Strain and I. Schwartz. 2001. ABA and the Development of Meaningful Social Relations for Young Children with Autism. *Focus on Autism and Other Developmental Disabilities* 16, 2: 120–128. http://doi.org/10.1177/108835760101600208

63. Michael Thomét. 2014. Look What Just Happened: Communicating Play in Online Communities. In *Understanding Minecraft: Essays on Play, Community, and Possibilities*, Nate Garrelts (ed.). McFarland & Company, Inc., Jefferson, NC, 121–131.

64. Robert S. Tokunaga. 2010. Following you home from school: A critical review and synthesis of research on cyberbullying victimization. *Computers in Human Behavior* 26, 3: 277–287. http://doi.org/10.1016/j.chb.2009.11.014

65. Patti M. Valkenburg and Jochen Peter. 2009. Social consequences of the internet for adolescents a decade of research. *Current Directions in Psychological Science* 18, 1: 1–5.

66. Emily C. Weinstein, Robert L. Selman, Sara Thomas, Jung-Eun Kim, Allison E. White, and Karthik Dinakar. 2015. How to Cope With Digital Stress The Recommendations Adolescents Offer Their Peers Online. *Journal of Adolescent Research*: 0743558415587326.

67. Susan W. White and Roxann Roberson-Nay. 2009. Anxiety, Social Deficits, and Loneliness in Youth with Autism Spectrum Disorders. *Journal of Autism and Developmental Disorders* 39, 7: 1006–1013. http://doi.org/10.1007/s10803-009-0713-8

68. Dmitri Wiliams, Nicolas Ducheneaut, Li Xiong, Yuanyuan Zhang, Nick Yee, and Eric Nickell. 2006. From Tree House to Barracks: The Social Life of Guilds in World of Warcraft. *Games and Culture* 1, 4: 338 – 361.

69. Keith L. Williams and Renee V. Galliher. 2006. Predicting depression and self-esteem from social connectedness, support, and competence. *Journal of Social and Clinical Psychology* 25, 8: 855–874.

70. Pamela Wolfberg, Kristen Bottema-Beutel, and Mila DeWitt. 2012. Including Children with Autism in Social and Imaginary Play with Typical Peers. *American Journal of Play* 5, 1. Retrieved February 20,

2014 from http://search.ebscohost.com/login.aspx?direct=true&profile=ehost&scope=site&authtype=crawler&jrnl=19380399&AN=83926198&h=XG6m1I3MccHsrbv%2FUCoH1VSYm%2FfZzGkU1f0CeeMjx8ZzeRG2rfYtiJkawjQby9TL3fqt8ErFyEISGFM%2BUQj3lw%3D%3D&crl=c

71. Pamela J. Wolfberg. 2009. *Play & Imagination in Children with Autism*. Teachers College Press, New York City, New York, USA.
72. 2002. *Developing Adolescents: A Reference for Professionals*. American Psychological Association, Washington, D.C.

Anxiety and Autism: Towards Personalized Digital Health

Will Simm[1], Maria Angela Ferrario[2], Adrian Gradinar[3], Marcia Tavares Smith[4], Stephen Forshaw[5], Ian Smith[6], Jon Whittle[7].
[1,2,4,5,7] School of Computing and Communications, [3] Imagination Lancaster,
[6] Division of Health Research.
Lancaster University, UK.
{[1] w.simm, [2] m.a.ferrario, [3] a.gradinar, [6] i.smith, [7] j.n.whittle } @lancaster.ac.uk.
[4] marcia@marciadesigns.co.uk, [5] muveon@gmail.com

ABSTRACT
For many people living with conditions such as autism, anxiety manifests so powerfully it has a big impact on quality of life. By investigating the suitability of truly customizable wearable health devices we build on prior research that found each experience of anxiety in people with autism is unique, so 'one-suits all' solutions are not suitable. In addition, users desire agency and control in all aspects of the system. The participative approach we take is to iteratively co-develop prototypes with end users. Here we describe a case study of the co-development of one prototype, a digital stretch wristband that records interaction for later reflection called Snap. Snap has been designed to sit within a platform that allows the distributed and sustainable design, manufacture and data analysis of customizable digital health technologies. We contribute to HCI with (1) lessons learned from a DIY co-development process that follows the principles of modularity, participation and iteration and (2) the potential impact of technology in self-management of anxiety and the broader design implications of addressing unique anxiety experiences.

Author Keywords
Mental health; Anxiety; Personal Informatics; Autism;

ACM Classification Keywords
H.5.m. Information interfaces and presentation (e.g., HCI): Miscellaneous;

INTRODUCTION
Most of us suffer from anxiety at some point in life: only 1 in 20 people in the UK report never being anxious[1]. To some, anxiety manifests itself so powerfully it has a dramatic impact on quality of life. This is particularly true when anxiety is associated with other conditions such as Autism. Autism is said to affect an individual's ability to communicate and interact socially with others and can result in profound isolation and anxiety with potentially devastating effects [2]. Our research focuses on anxiety in those diagnosed with autism and builds on two fundamental lessons learned from existing autism research in HCI [4, 7, 28, 31]: first, the uniqueness of anxiety experiences and the impracticality of *"one suits all"* solutions; second, end-users' desire for *agency and control* on the system: from aesthetics, to data capture and its use.

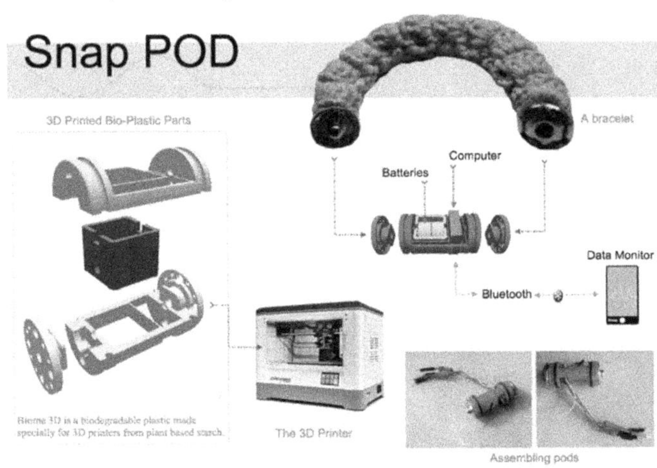

Figure 1 - Customizable Snap Device. Crochet wristband contains conductive cord that changes resistance when stretched, and connects via snap fasteners to a 3D printed pod containing batteries and microcontroller with Bluetooth 4.0.

Our aim is to investigate the challenges and opportunities of building systems that are not only capable of addressing highly unique anxiety management needs, but that can do so at scale. Our approach is to investigate *"by doing"* [19], specifically by combining the modularity of form and function [6, 26] with a participative and iterative co-development process [9, 18, 32]. Our vision is to develop a platform that allows the distributed design, manufacture and data analysis of families of customizable digital health services. This paper reports on the first step towards such a vision starting from the co-development of wearable health devices, using a prototype named Snap as a case study.

[1] http://www.mentalhealth.org.uk/content/assets/PDF/publications/living-with-anxiety-report.pdf

CHI'16, May 07 - 12, 2016, San Jose, CA, USA

ACM 978-1-4503-3362-7/16/05...$15.00
DOI: http://dx.doi.org/10.1145/2858036.2858259

Snap (Figure 1) is a customizable hand-made digital stretch wristband that records interactions for later reflection. It is powered by a *plug and play* 3D-printed (3DP) computing unit, which we refer to as the 'pod'. Snap emerged from a three-month co-development process with and for adults diagnosed with High-Functioning Autism (HFA) and their support. During this phase we engaged in three design workshops with 13 participants (7 people diagnosed with HFA and 6 supporters), followed by a three-week summer study that involved 5 participants and their support wearing a Snap device and reflecting on its value.

Snap co-development is part of a broader six-month participatory design and co-development process that has so far engaged over 300 people including health professionals, the general public, those diagnosed with autism, and supporters. The process follows a values-led, and technology-mediated innovation framework [9, 24, 32] shown in Figure 3. Our design approach is inspired by Phoneblok's **modularity** and **repairability**, Fairphone's approach to **fairness** and community **participation**, Misfit's **adaptability**, and Little Devices' **affordability**.[2] We consider such approaches as promising alternatives to mainstream *one-fits-all* digital health devices (e.g. Fitbit).

Through the co-development of Snap we explore how adults diagnosed with autism experience anxiety, reflect on the role of HCI in anxiety management, and extract lessons learned for anxiety conditions beyond autism. Our contribution to HCI is hence twofold: 1) lessons learned from the DIY co-development of personalized digital health devices following the principles of modularity, participation and iteration 2) the potential role of wearable technology in self-management of anxiety and the broader design implications of addressing unique anxiety experiences and needs.

BACKGROUND

Autism and Anxiety Management

Autism is a condition characterized by difficulties in three main areas, namely social communication, interaction and imagination, commonly referred to as the triad of impairment. Those with autism may have a very literal understanding of language, and think people always mean exactly what they say. They often have difficulty interpreting emotions and expressing their own. Difficulty with social imagination means it is hard to make sense of abstract ideas, and imagine situations outside daily routine[3]. Autism is often described by a 'spectrum'–while all people with autism share these difficulties, their condition will affect them in different ways. Those who are affected most are described as "Low Functioning" and those whose quality of life is impacted less described as "High Functioning".

Adults with HFA are a hard to reach group: their high functioning nature often makes their condition invisible to society, which perceives them as 'simply different' (HFA participant). The fact they are high functioning can make their condition 'invisible' to society, thus allowing them to fall between the gaps of public support. There are no prevalence figures for adults with autism in the UK. As a consequence, it is reasonable to argue that the large majority of adults with HFA lack a formal diagnosis. Not only do they live without an understanding of what make them different, but also in a society that is not aware of their challenges, especially the ones related to day-to-day social interactions. As Bellini puts it *"the anxiety associated with these seemingly simple acts can be devastating [2]"*.

This is a group with hidden needs and whose social interactions are often limited. Yet, interactions outside familiar circles are often sought by most adults with autism and can have a positive impact on their quality of life. However, these very interactions can be a source of great distress [3]: social anxiety has been identified [36,37] as the most common form of autism anxiety, usually affecting half of those with autism .

Prior research [4, 7, 28, 31] shows that the majority of HCI work on anxiety in autism focuses on children, young adolescents and people at the lower end of the autistic spectrum, "*Yet the needs of adults are very different to the needs of children and teenagers, regardless of ASD*" [31].

A similar research 'bias' is found in psychology research where there seems to be a limited number of studies looking at anxiety in adults diagnosed with HFA [14, 15, 34]. In addition, most of these studies are carried out from a statistical perspective to establish the presence of anxiety in association with other mental health conditions. These investigations may be useful to *quantify* the percentage of those diagnosed with autism that suffer from anxiety [3, 35], but few have tried to systematically *characterize* how anxiety is *experienced* in terms of triggers and responses, for example. We argue this is problematic since HCI needs guidance to start addressing the "uniqueness" [4, 31] of anxiety experienced in autism in a holistic way [23, 33].

In summary, anxiety in those diagnosed with autism is *experienced* in a multitude of *subjective* ways. To understand and adapt to its unique manifestations we adopt an iterative, participatory and agile approach to development and a modular approach to system design.

Personal Informatics and health self-management

At the start of our research we considered using and re-purposing a range of mainstream (e.g. Fitbit), emergent (e.g. Angelsensor), leading (e.g. Garmin xt920, Empatica Embrace), and affordable (e.g. Mibands) digital fitness and health tracking devices to explore how they can be used in

[2] phonebloks.com; littledevices.org; misfit.com; fairphone.com

[3] http://www.autism.org.uk/about/what-is/asd.aspx

anxiety self-management. However, after in-the-wild and desk-based evaluations carried out by the research team, we found that none of the above devices could suitably address our research aims for the following reasons: un-reliability of data capture, opacity of data-insight processes [16], black-box designs, patented algorithms, and costs. We argue that these aspects combined can have a 'lock-in' effect on both user and the device, fix them both into rigid functionality and potentially erode user agency and control.

Our main argument is therefore that current PI systems are more focused on the *informatics* aspects than on the *personal* ones. In other words, mainstream PI are simply not personal enough.

To address this shortfall, we expand Li *et al.*'s [23] concept of *iteration* as a potential route towards personalization "*the iterative property of personal informatics suggests that systems should be flexible to support users' changing information needs*". We do so by facilitating active participation with end-users in the system co-development process (see Figure 2). This process is enabled by a modular approach to design, where physical components and system functionalities can be selected, added or removed at any stage of the process.

The biggest challenge is hence to make this process not only relevant to people's needs but also respectful of their individual freedoms [10, 17, 38]. In doing so we find Li's reflections on the dialectic between *system-driven* and *user-driven* approaches particularly helpful in identifying the trade-offs between system automation and user intentions.

Affective vs. Intentive computing

The approach of exploring the role of technology in managing mental health in wearable HCI literature is focussed on tracking users with biosensors, and is typified by Picard et al [27] in the affective computing approach. This approach uses 'always on' biosensors and environment sensors to monitor an individual, and complex algorithms to interpret and present information to the individual in real time and for later reflection. The individual makes a conscious decision to wear a device, once worn the user is not necessarily conscious of what data the device is capturing or when trigger points are reached. Kirkham and Greenhalgh [22] discuss the tensions arising between social inclusion and privacy when developing such sensor driven real-time assistive wearable technologies for those with HFA. Blackwell [5] describes this position as 'prosthetic' – using technology to replace or augment absent ability.

An *intentive* action is defined as requiring the user to consciously and knowingly trigger a system – for example push a button or make a certain gesture. We introduce the concept of intentive computing as the study of the use of such a human-actuated system. Our research differs from the affective computing 'prosthetic' because of the 'intentionality' of actuated interactions. That is not to say the approaches are mutually exclusive – they can be complimentary: for example Fletcher [11] states the importance of synchronizing annotations with data by enabling the user to *"insert data markers to annotate the data as it is being collected"*.

On the role of anxiety support, our argument is that such intentional interactions, not only could provide real-time tactile 'relief', but could also function as cognitive anchors for self-reflection and long-term learning. In this paper we explore the extent to which an intentive action can add value to the coping strategies of those who suffer from anxiety, through designing a modular system in a participatory, iterative and agile manner [9, 32].

DIY and Bespoke Assistive Computing

DIY and bespoke assistive technology (DIY-AT) has a long history for those with physical impairments. There is a high rate of abandonment of "one fits all" technology, estimated at around 35%, and this is used as a justification for individual adaptations to technology[20, 21]. Hurst and Tobias [21] explore how empowering novices to build their own solutions can improve the success and adoption of AT. They propose the use of rapid prototyping to quickly produce and iterate devices, and online sharing communities to expand the reach and discussion of designs. The barriers to uptake of DIY-AT, found through interview with parents of children with mobility impairments, include: lack of skills and time to make and repair devices; the limited practicality, robustness and aesthetics of devices; and concern about the safety and risk of conflict with medical care [20]. The DIY approach may conflict with social acceptability of devices, explored by Shinohara [30], who propose that design for social acceptance will reduce stigma of AT. The lessons learnt from these works on physical impairment are built on here, as we apply a DIY approach to technologies for self management of anxiety.

APPROACH

To engage in research partnerships with any community, and in particular with vulnerable groups, requires sustained motivation, skills, trust and care. The approach we use is a values-led and technology-mediated innovation framework that has been used in several domains involving hard-to-reach vulnerable groups in technology innovation projects [9, 24, 32]. We follow a traditional "plan, act and reflect" action research process [18] across four distinct and overlapping steps, (formative, co-design, co-develop, and sustain) which are shown in Figure 3 and are mapped against milestones and deliverables.

As Figure 2 shows, Snap development was part of a broader six-month participatory design and co-development process that engaged over 300 people including health professionals, the general public and academics from a range of disciplines. The first three months were riskier and more exploratory in nature and involved the **de-construction** of a range of digital health devices down to their core components (*data, materials* and *interactions*).

These in turn were used as the basic ingredients for design fiction [8] activities (e.g. a pop-up *Technology Kitchen* at a national science festival) to broadly envision and reflect on digital-health challenges and possibilities.

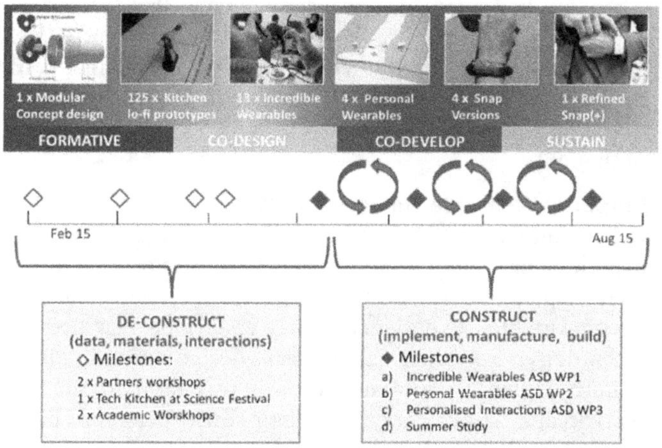

Figure 2 - Research Steps and Milestones

The first phase informed the second phase (**construction**), which is the focus of this paper and from which Snap emerged. During this second phase the majority of the activities were planned and carried out in partnership with a group of adults diagnosed with autism and their support. We held a series of workshops (WP1-WP3) designed to investigate the value of wearable digital health technologies to our user group. Most of these users have been diagnosed with anxiety problems. However, each of our participants described anxiety in different ways, with many not identifying with the language associated with anxiety.

Hence our research is focused on individual experiences of anxiety – how it manifests, its triggers and responses. To facilitate the expression of our participant's experiences, we organized a series of thematically connected 2-hour workshops: **Incredible Wearables (WP1), Personal Wearables (WP2), and Personal Interactions (WP3)**. The timing for each workshop followed a two-week agile development cycle, which was well received by our participants and their support because of its structured approach and the anticipation that was created around the sessions. We found this structured approach to be essential to manage expectations and reduce unknowns for our participants with autism.

Paced by the two-week cycles of the workshops, the research team iteratively distilled design directions into implementable requirements that ultimately converged into 'Snap'. Snap emerged as a digital interaction-recording wristband, which could afford a variety of 'intentive' interactions (e.g. gripping, huddling, and stretching) and that could be fashioned into a variety of styles (e.g. functional, DIY, etc.). Snap was then put to test during a three-week ***Summer Study*** in which 5 participants wore their own Snap in everyday life for three weeks. During the study, feedback was obtained through a group induction, two one-to-one sessions for each participant, and a final group discussion.

Participants

A total of 13 participants were engaged in the workshops comprising 7 diagnosed with autism and 6 of their support (some of whom were also diagnosed with or self identified as suffering from anxiety). One of the challenges of working 'in the wild' outside of a controlled lab environment with people who have autism is the need to create an environment where they are comfortable, with familiar faces, and knowing what to expect well before the event. This is apparently in contrast to working in an agile, responsive manner. However, this challenge was negotiated through meeting in a 'familiar' place – a charity hosted the workshops in their function room, whilst key dates and an activity outline were set well in advance.

INCREDIBLE AND PERSONAL: WP1, WP2 AND WP3

The Incredible Wearables workshop (WP1) was designed to create a relaxed space and inspire participants with the freedom, creativity, and enthusiasm to come up with their very own technology inventions or *incredible wearables*. During the following Personal Wearables workshop (WP2) we narrowed the design scope by inviting participants to construct their previous inventions from a toolkit of parts, or *design tiles,* mimicking real electronics, to be joined together using wooden sticks (Figure 3). Finally the Personal Interactions workshop (WP3) expanded the design focus with an idea generation process, which explored meaningful ways to interact with a range of prototype wearable devices.

Incredible Wearables – WP1

The research aim for WP1 was twofold: first, to gain a broad understanding of the needs, capabilities and aspirations of our participants; second, to start understanding if and how such needs could be addressed by the design and development of personalized digital care technologies. This aim was addressed through the following objectives:

- Create a safe, enjoyable place for shared learning, building trust and mutual understanding in the team.
- Introduce the idea that all can be makers of technology innovation and inventions.
- Stress the importance of creativity and playfulness in learning and innovation.
- Expand the notion of what technology is (e.g. beyond screens and mobile phones).
- Reflect on what technology can and cannot do for us.

Researcher and support participants planned the event together and, most importantly, agreed to **avoid actively prompting ideas around anxiety**. The focus had to be on creativity and the capability of inventing something personal and of real benefit.

The workshop started with a table laid out with a range of objects of different shapes, size, colours and textures. Each participant was asked to select an object, and then people introduced themselves by describing why this object was selected and mattered to them. This gave some initial insight into what was important to each participant – some liked sharp textures and experienced them as calming.

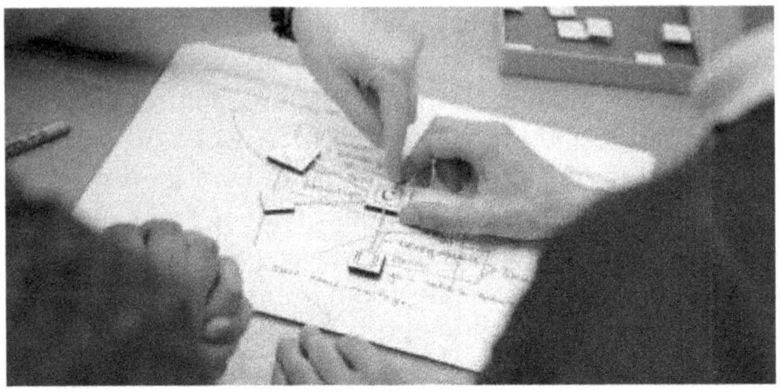

Figure 3 Developing personal wearables with *design tiles*

Participants then broke off into small groups to brainstorm and then prototype wearable technologies that would address their most pressing needs and aspirations. Lo-fi prototypes were built using play-doh, pipe cleaners, and 3DP 'sensor mimics' – small objects designed to mimic a multitude of sensors to which participants could attribute functions of their own choosing.

A total of 13 lo-fi prototypes were constructed, 7 were from those with an autism diagnosis and 6 from supporters. Most interestingly, 7 of these prototypes were designed to directly address stress and anxiety even though the facilitators avoided prompting for anxiety.

Three prototypes dealt with external **auditory triggers**: two by cancelling out noise (*Sound Blocker* and *Acoustic Inhibitor*) and one by providing haptic distractions. *Destresser,* for example, provided relief from high pitch sounds (e.g. children's cries) by stroking a hard yet smooth metallic plaque worn as a bracelet charm. The *Bubble Bracelet* provided stress relief through an actuated **tactile response** triggered by popping plastic bubbles.

Public speaking and demanding **social situations** were cited by the inventor of *Take a Breath* as a source of anxiety. Worn as a brooch, it would emit sounds and smells linked to happy memories inviting to take relaxing breaths. Two prototypes focused on automatically capturing internal **physiological signals** of anxiety: *TempSense* detected rising body temperature as a signal of discomfort; and *AMOK,* worn as a bracelet or an earpiece, monitored change in heart rate, sent messages to family and offered 'digital distractions' when anxious.

The remaining 6 prototypes were not directly related to anxiety. Three of these were related to **engagement**: *Time to Dance*, a pendant that sang bird songs when the wearer sat in one place for too long, was about **physical** engagement; *Contact Glasses*, a pair of glasses that facilitated serendipitous encounters, was about **social** engagement; the *Grounding Ring* was about **mental** engagement: it monitored brain signals and sent warnings when the wearer was perceived as 'zoning out'. The ring had a customizable tactile surface (e.g. sandpaper) that when stroked offered **a sensory snack** that helped re-engaging with reality. *Sonic Whiskers* shoe tag and *Object Detector* bracelet pre-warned the user of objects that could be damaged or cause injury if hit. Finally the *Tele-Personal Assistant* was a pen that helped to write as fast as the speed of thought.

Personal Wearable Devices - WP2

A key finding of WP1 was there is a multitude of ways of experiencing and communicating internal states. Unprompted our group reported anxiety as an uncomfortable experience that could be tackled by technology. For this, rather than designing individually unique devices, a toolkit approach was used to see how participants could assemble their own personal health wearable. The kit contained a DIY plug-together selection of devices and sensors modules or 'tiles' (see Figure 3). Each device had a core 'computing module' (mimicking a microcontroller) to which the sensors, actuators, communications and storage could be attached as required. This process facilitated discussion around how the device they had designed could be implemented.

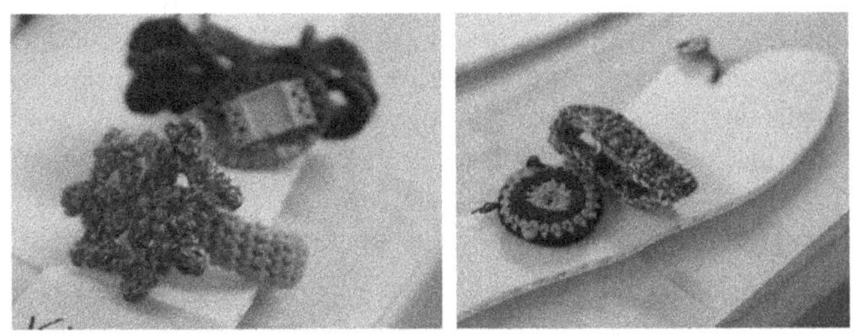

Figure 4 Crochet Prototypes.

Personal Interactions – WP3

WP3 aimed to elicit, capture and map the range of gestures and interactions that participants find useful for dealing with anxiety. To prompt discussion, a range of artefacts inspired by WP2 and WP1 were rapidly prototyped by using crochet and knitting techniques (Figure 4). Participants were invited to select one each, discuss it in pairs and feedback to the group. After that, the participants were invited to list all the possible anxiety interactions that could be afforded by the handmade artefacts. The results of this exercise is shown in Figure 7 and discussed later in "Anxiety Interactions". After that, the first working prototype of Snap was demonstrated to elicit discussions around personal uses of the device.

SNAP DEVICE

The wearable devices designed by our participants are used to inform the design of a toolkit which would enable the construction of a range of personal devices, rather than for individual translation into working devices. The devices can be broadly assigned two functions: alerts based on automatic capture of physiological and environmental data, and tactile interaction (use of bubble wrap, tactile jewellery etc.). As discussed earlier, prior research comprehensively investigates the aspect of automatic capture of physiological and environmental signals in numerous health conditions. We find there is an opportunity to explore tactile intentive interactions where the user is aware of their actions. The first device used as a development case study, is a stretch wristband, called Snap and shown in Figures 1 and 5. The Snap device focuses on intentive interaction and here we investigate its role in anxiety reflection. Embodied in Snap is a 3-pronged philosophy:

Sustainability: The approach is (human) values-driven [13] and has been designed with a three-dimension sustainability framework in mind: material, skills, and human freedom. Its modular design allows the distributed manufacture of each part and easy assemblage by the end-users and health practitioners with little or no engineering experience.

Promiscuity: The computing core (pod) is both independent and promiscuous. Independent because the pod is a complete stand-alone computing unit; promiscuous because is designed to be easily 'plugged in' to different sensors and substrates.

Reflectivity: Snap has been designed to establish a meaningful collaboration between human and machine, where the machine automatically captures data, extract insights and relies on the individual, personal experience to make sense of the data at hand.

Figure 5 - Snap prototypes: first (left) and as used in study with tactile beaded covering (right).

Snap is designed to be customizable physically, electronically and in terms of software functionality. Open source software and widely available 'maker' hardware was used along with DIY techniques such as crochet and 3D printing to build in customizability and DIY manufacture. This was intended to give the devices the widest possible reach: people can make and customise their own, hopefully leading to increased engagement through ownership and personalization.

A minimum-viable prototype of Snap (left of Figure 5) was quickly made with a battery, microcontroller and crochet wristband and taken to WP2 for feedback from participants, who then informed the version used in the study period.

This first prototype has an LED light that increases intensity according to the degree of stretch of the band and communicates this data to a laptop that plots a line on the screen in real time. The second prototype is encased in an enclosure and is described below.

Design and Components

Snap has two main physical components: the pod and the wristband (shown in Figure 1). 'Snap fasteners' of the type found in haberdashery stores are used to provide the mechanical and electrical connection to the wristband.

The pod shown by Figures 1 and 5 is constructed from a 3DP framework, using biodegradable Biome[4] bioplastic made from corn starch. This framework encases the electronic components, and a heat-shrink layer protects the components from the environment while allowing an LED light to show through. The design of the pod uses easily purchased materials and the design files for 3DP can be modified freely.

The wristband is made of conductive rubber cord that has a changing electrical resistance as it is stretched. This is attached to matching snap fasteners by conductive thread. The assembly is wrapped in a personalized outer, and can be encased in any number of outer materials that will allow stretch. We made a selection of wristbands from a variety of materials and styles (crochet in Figure 1 and beaded in Figure 5) inviting participants to choose their favourites to snap onto the pod.

We used a low cost Arduino-compatible RFDuino micro controller, giving access to the popular IDE and variety of open source libraries. Users are free to modify and extend the code and assemble their own devices connected to different sensors. The device can communicate real-time high resolution stretch data live to a Smart phone over Bluetooth (as first prototype) and onto cloud services or social networks, however our users cited trust and privacy concerns with a real-time approach – and indicated they would prefer data to be stored only on the device. This coincided with reduced power and memory demand. However we are aware that others may prefer operation in a similar manner to Clasp [31] and the prototype can be configured in both modes.

The wristband records a timestamp to memory when the device is stretched beyond a threshold value, and then again when the device is relaxed and not stretched for a timeout. This allowed us to record the length of interaction and the frequency of interaction.

Reflection Platform

While the participants were using the wristband during the study, the researchers designed and built a prototype interface to visualize the data collected by the Snap bands. The Snap Visualizer shown by Figure 6 is produced when the data is downloaded from the Snap pod. The Visualizer plots the times of the day over a period of a month when the Snap band has recorded interactions. At the end of the

[4] http://biomebioplastics.com/

study, when the participant data was downloaded the design of this interface was discussed with each participant, and ideas for future features were ideated and discussed. There are a number of emerging design directions that can be taken with this interface, such as automatic pattern extraction and overlay with date from other sources such as GPS log, calendar entries, and physiological wearable.

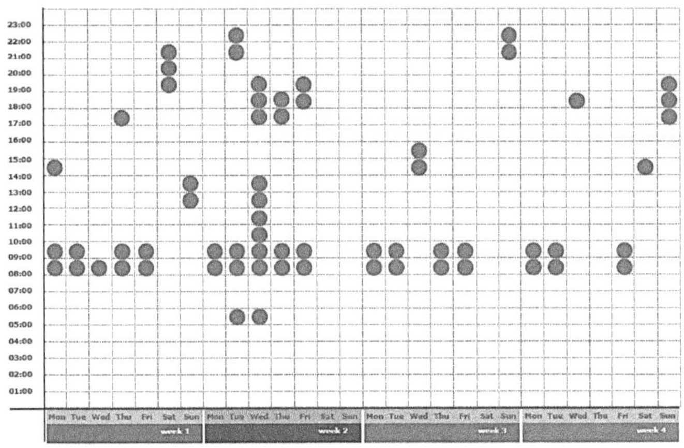

Figure 6 - Snap Visualizer. Interactions by days of the week along the horizontal and hours of the day on the vertical axis.

ANXIETY INTERACTIONS			STEPS
Cover	Play with	Rub	3. Prompted Individual
Feel	Push	Stretch	
Fiddle	Pull	Touch	
Grip	**Tug**		
Bite	Clip -Unclip	**Spin**	2. Unprompted Individual
Click	Flick		
Catch	Roll	Talk to	1. Prompted Group
Hold	Round-Walk	Tap	
Inhale	Scratch	Throw	
Pinch	Spring	Turn	
Poke	Squeeze	Twidle	
Pop	Stamp	Twist	
Press	Stroke	Wave	

Figure 7 - Mapping anxiety interactions: the three-step process elicited 37 anxiety interactions, 11 of which were used with Snap (shown in the inner dark grey square).

ANXIETY INTERACTIONS

During the process we explored a range of anxiety management strategies that could be afforded by wearable interactions. We did so iteratively in three steps: prompted group discussion, unprompted individual feedback, and prompted individual feedback. A total of 37 interactions were identified, and participants used 11 of these with the Snap device. The key findings for each step are summarized below and in Figure 7.

Step 1: Prompted - Group Discussion. During WP3 researchers invited the participants to list all the gestures and interactions that they do or may do to manage anxiety. We did so by using a range of prompts that included rings, belts, pouches, earpieces, brooches and shoe decorations. These prompts had been rapidly prototyped using crochet techniques (Figure 4) to quickly implement ideas that emerged during the WP2. As a result, 34 of the 37 interactions were captured at this stage as shown in Figure 7. The interactions 'spin', 'tug' and 'grip' are shown in bold as they appeared later in Steps 2 and 3.

Step 2: Unprompted - Individual Feedback. The three-week Summer Study included two cycles of individual feedback sessions with each participant. Each session included an unprompted feedback discussion on anxiety interactions followed by a structured discussion about the usage of Snap. The light grey and dark grey areas combined in Figure 7 plot the results of the unprompted part of these discussions, highlighting 13 anxiety management interactions: *"A click I think would be satisfying to me, some kind of, um, sound or click or movement [...] I have a flip cover on my phone, it has a magnetic connection and I just happened to have my phone in my hand and I was flicking it on my phone"*. Figure 7 shows the interaction 'spin' in bold, as it was first mentioned at this stage *"natural for me [] I'm used to it because of spinning my ring [laughs]"*.

Step 3: Prompted – Individual Feedback The dark grey area in Figure 7 shows the 11 interactions participants actually used to interact with Snap. When anxious, excited or both, some of the participants pulled and pushed the band *"Yeah, well in anxiety I just push like that and then it calms things"*, or rubbed their fingers on the bracelets beads: *"My new puppy [] became very upset and ill. I was a bit stressed myself because she was not well so I was rubbing the beads onto my skin it felt nice"*. They also liked to fiddle or play with it just because it felt *"nice and soft"*. 'Gripping' onto the computing pod and 'tugging' the wristband were mentioned at this stage, *"I used my (Snap) bracelet when going into the doctors to pick up my prescription. I was nervous sat in the waiting room to collect my tablets in case someone spoke to me. I tugged a little on my bracelet in frustration of waiting nervously. Which didn't make my nerves go but took my mind off waiting 'cos I was focusing on the bracelet"*.

Design Implications

We draw two main design implications for Snap from the emerging anxiety interaction mapping:

Bite vs. Flick: positive and negative connotations

Different interactions can have different emotional connotations. For example, 'biting' and 'picking' have been described by a participant as harmful habits associated with negative emotions; in contrast 'flicking' or 'fiddling' were associated with a more positive state: *"Um, the harmful habits are when I'm anxious, [] but things like flicking lids I just do that whenever"*, *"to be able to bite it and that's usually what I do when I'm driving and anxious [] and that's a bad habit"*, *"then the positive manifest as fiddling"*.

This reflection matches observations made by health professionals who also argued that only logging times of anxiety, stress and depression (negatives), will over time create a distorted and negative data history of someone's experience of their own life. This observation is echoed by one of the participants *"having something that could focus it [the positive aspect] would [be] beneficial because then there would [be a] positive thing to happen instead of harmful things to happen.*" For this, to design for anxiety and self-reflection could encourage people to be more mindful of positive experiences like happiness, satisfaction, productivity, and flow instead of the negatives. This logging could be done both automatically by the device and inventively by the user. For example, the device could automatically signal lack of interactions as a positive; or the user could actively log times of relaxation and playfulness by interacting with a device in a chosen mode.

INCONSPICUOUS ⟷					CONSPICUOUS	
Secret	Disguised	Functional	DIY/Maker	Fitness	Futuristic	
Hidden under garments, discreet when visible	Looks like ordinary jewelry or garments	Focus on function not on style	Unique, custom made	Matches sportswear, fashionable	Embodies utopian or dystopian visions	Style
When visible tries to blend with body or garments.	Sophisticated, delicate, crafted. Hidden electronics	Industrial, simple and clean. Hidden electronics	Exposed electronics. Hand stitches, boards. DYI, playful	A statement piece. Bright & colorful. Industrial & mass produced. Hidden electronics	Elaborate. Cyberpunk, steampunk, inspired in fiction.	Properties
Skin tones, neutral tones, natural materials	Metallic, jewel-like colors,	Black, grey, neutral tones	Colourful, various colors combined.	Bright, contrasting energy colors	Metallic, natural or geometric forms. Bright/ neon artificial	Colors
Rubber, elastics, adhesives, paint	Metal, wood, textiles, lights	Plastics, rubber, metal, lights	Textiles, plastic, metal, electronics, lights	Rubber, plastics, lights	Combination of materials, metal, natural, glass/ acrylic, plastics	Materials
Small & simple, economical	Pleasing, elaborate shapes and patterns	Straight clean lines, solid shapes, regular, no distractions	Irregular, to suit/follow the use of electronic parts	Clean lines, solid shapes, conveys movement & action	Innovative, elaborate, imaginative	Shapes

Figure 8 - Inconspicuous vs. Conspicuous wearable styles

In summary, the design of bespoke digital health wearables should help to investigate how positive experiences can be appreciated and encouraged as well as how the negatives are triggered and best managed.

Click vs. Stretch, two sides of the same data spectrum:
Snap has been specifically designed to explore intentive (user-actuated) interactions. We chose to use a stretchable wristband as our first 'intentive' prototype for reasons that included participants' feedback in relation to comfort and social acceptability of the device *"I don't think it would draw any attention if you were going like that [fiddling] on a bracelet, whereas if you were like reaching into your pocket and people would be... keep drawing attention to yourself"*. From a researcher perspective, Snap facilitated the exploration of a broad range of anxiety interactions that could be automatically captured, characterized, and analysed: the intensity, length and frequency of a stretch, for example. However, the participants' feedback from the everyday use of the device has highlighted three main challenges: (1) the characterization of the interaction (e.g. a strong pull for me may be a weak pull for another); (2) the ambiguity of the data captured; (3) the risk of false positives (e.g. pulling the band while putting on a jumper). One of the participants explicitly suggested a click button as both inherently satisfying *"I would definitely sit and click that all day"* and as means to reduce data ambiguity and false positives: *"think if it was a clicker that picked up every time you clicked it you have to do it on purpose, you can't do by accident"*.

SOCIAL AFFORDANCES

During our co-development process we asked participants how they felt about wearing Snap in social situations. Not surprisingly, some felt self-conscious about Snap's current *"bulky"* design, *"toy-like"* form, and *"bright colours"*. However, most also agreed that *"as whole the bracelet has a lot of potential"*. Reducing the size of the Snap pod would allow increased adaptability and personalization *"everyone has different likes" "I like black and plain things, some people like bright pink"*. Times of the day were mentioned as important factors "*glow in the dark material could be good wearing at night*". One participant suggested including the Autism logo in future designs, and to make it visible enough to be a conversation starter, but sufficiently discrete to be dismissed as a simple decoration.

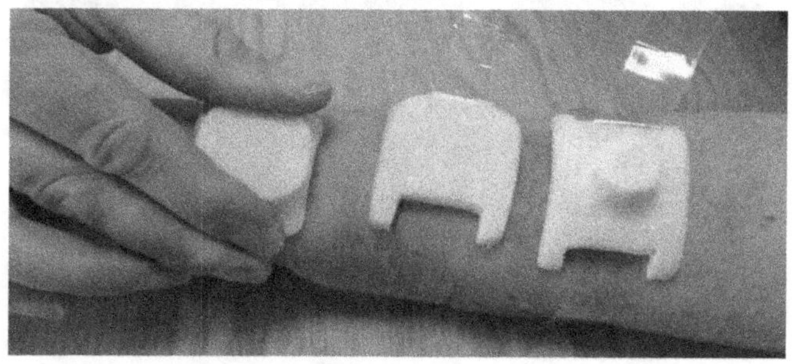

Figure 9 - Concept Designs for Personal Interactions

Design Implications

These observations relate to the concept of "social affordance" that is the *"capability [of wearable devices] of adapting to different social contexts by changing its aesthetic properties and interaction modalities for fitting different social situations"* [29]. The challenge is to translate this concept into practice. We explore three ways:

1. Style taxonomies to guide personalized choices: Snap's modular nature allows personalization in terms of wearable substrate (e.g. where the computing component can be attached to) and styles (e.g. colours, and materials) to adapt to different interaction needs and social situations. Figure 8 shows our first attempt to create a taxonomy of possible styles which we summarized along a spectrum from inconspicuous to conspicuous.

2. Characterization of anxiety in physical designs. Another approach is to map personal anxiety gestures onto the actual form of the system components. For example, we are currently looking into how the 'computing pod' itself could be fashioned in different styles to suit a range of personal interactions. Figure 9 shows how different interchangeable casings could be designed to afford specific interactions. These casings could be affordably and locally manufactured using local 3DP bureau, and combined into functioning devices by health practitioners and users.

3. Putting it all together: the making as part of the therapy. One of the main lessons learned from the co-development process was the importance of the self-reflection activities that took place during the making of the artefacts themselves. During this process the participants, often to the surprise of their support, were able to articulate their experience of anxiety in a very deep, personal and engaged manner. There were several factors at play, including the common factors effect [1] well known in clinical psychology literature, that future studies will need to consider. In practice, the making of the device could be part of the therapy. For example, in one session the health practitioner and client could design their own 'Snap' by combining selected components (e.g. casings, sensors, and actuators) together. Figure 10 shows a 'making kit' prototype as a box of modular and interchangeable components to suit different needs.

Figure 10 - Make Your Own Device from a Kit of Components

DISCUSSION

Experiences of self-management with Snap

Through using the Snap prototype daily, the participants (names changed here) engaged in the summer study revealed much about their experiences and how such a device may be used. 4 of the 5 wore the wristband at some point most days of the duration of the study - only Jamie (male, HFA, early 30's) did not wear it as he does not like things touching his hands.

We learnt something different from each of the participants and their approach to Snap for self management of their condition. Louis (male, HFA, mid 20's) chose to wear Snap only when expecting to experience anxiety or excitement - perhaps Louis can recognise some triggers of his anxiety. Louis chose to wear snap either on the wrist or belt at work, when walking the dog, watching an exciting TV programme, visiting a sensory room (e.g. ball pool) and when tired. Louis liked the soft texture (specifically selected) and would pass it through the hands in use.

Henry (male, HFA, mid 20's) is really motivated to find a pattern to his anxiety. Henry and support are not sure what the triggers are, and think that Snap may help identify them. Henry liked the feel of their chosen wristband and wore it a lot - the band was visibly over stretched (broken) and dirty. Henry claimed the aesthetics weren't a problem for him, although perhaps in this case form follow function and the desire for answers overrides the look.

Susie (female, early 30's, the only non-HFA, but diagnosed with anxiety) usually finds herself *"picking her nails"* when anxious, and would prefer an interaction which can be hidden rather than the Snap requiring both hands. Susie found little satisfaction in stretching the band and would prefer a definite click. Susie described a desire to turn a negative response to anxiety into a positive outlet for that, instead of Susie *"picking her nails"* Snap would be recording interaction for later reflection that Susie would get overall benefit from.

Davina (female, HFA, early 20's) was not part of the initial development workshops, but immediately saw a benefit in Snap. Davina was very enthusiastic, contributing many ideas to improve the aesthetic - as it is, she would not wear it out of the house.

Designing with Adults with Autism

We found our participants wanted to know the time and location of the next meeting, and what to expect well in advance. We kept meetings to familiar places and regular times to minimise anxieties around visiting new places and people. The pacing of the agile development cycles enabled us to set advance milestones, and worked well as participants would know to expect new increments of designs they were contributing to. If plans changed, then significant notice should be given, and detailed explanation of what to expect should be given. During each workshop, accurate timings were given and each participant knew the others already.

In WP1 we asked participants to create their own wearable devices addressing their most pressing health need. Rather than ask directly about experience of anxiety, the creative process allowed participants to describe their experiences not just verbally, but through the physical objects they imagined and produced. In fact, half of the designs were directly addressing anxiety. This was remarkably successful, and support workers gained new insight from this into the experiences of participants.

The participants 'bought-in' to the process and took ownership of the devices they played a role in creating. This process of 'making' became a part of therapy and created a new, shared understanding between participant, support and researchers.

DIY and Bespoke Wearable Devices

WP2 showed participants how they could assemble their 'incredible wearables' using a kit of components. Each participant was able to translate their imaginary object into realistic components, showing how a kit of parts could be used in future DIY health applications. By starting from the imaginary and moving to the realistic, participants were allowed to explore the extremes rather than be restricted by what they know to be possible.

The degree of DIY involved in making DIY health technology - from simple customisation of aesthetics to modifying source code will be highly variable and individual-dependant. It is unlikely our group would modify source code themselves, however the WP2 demonstrates the potential a future DIY health wearable kit holds with suitable facilitation, and would reduce the barriers to making [20].

The participants chose to further personalise Snap by wearing it in a number of ways beyond as a wristband - clipped to the belt loop of jeans, high up on the arm, carried in a bag or pocket. Part of the reason was that the device itself was bulky and unattractive (Davina - *"looks like a bomb"*), nevertheless participants continued to use Snap as they saw benefits in it: Louis: *"I was a bit excited because usually on a Saturday there's some good programmes [] so that's why I wore it to calm me down a bit", "I wore it at work because I found out that somebody was leaving [] and I wore it here, to calm me down a bit"*. The Snap form-factor, although more adaptable than other tactile prototypes [31], still poses challenges for being repurposed. The range of wristbands we created for the study was not wide enough; our users wanted further choice and had their own clear ideas about aesthetics of the device.

A major criticism of wearable activity tracking devices is that typically they show initial promise and promote behaviour change (increased physical activity) in the short term, but are typically worn only for 2 months and then abandoned with the user returning to former behaviour [12, 25]. The approach we have taken is not to encourage behaviour change but to facilitate an understanding and management of anxiety through device interactions and data capture. The process of designing and building these wearable devices has enabled our participants to discuss experiences of anxiety in a way their support indicated they had never before articulated - that in itself is a valuable process. In addition, once the process of learning and understanding is completed, the device itself may become redundant, and components can be passed on, re-used and repurposed for other people's needs. Perhaps as found with DIY-AT, DIY wearable devices will have longer sustained engagement [21] than off the shelf devices.

Deliberate, Intentive Interactions

Characterising when an individual has intended to interact with a device is a challenge - Snap recorded a high number of false positive interactions. Movement and activities like removing clothing would sometimes unintentionally actuate it. Our participants liked the tactile sensory feedback of Snap, but were not interested in recording the resolution of stretch – so the sensitive actuator we used was somewhat unnecessary. This tactile feedback could also be gained with different actuators, requiring more effort to interact (Figure 7) and therefore reducing false positives.

It is noted that participants like to fidget – and this fidgeting may be confused by the system as anxious use. One strategy would be to characterize both interactions for the individual and see if the two uses can be separated in the data. It is recognized that fidgeting has a therapeutic purpose, but clearly it is important for the purposes of reflection to separate usage when anxious from other uses.

Engagement outside of workshops

The participants all indicated they enjoyed the process of developing personal technologies, and want to continue to engage. How much influence this enjoyment had on engagement in the summer study in unknown. However, Davina had no prior engagement to the summer study, had heard of Snap and immediately saw benefit in it so was keen to start using it. In each case, devices are likely to be highly personalised and involve some degree of engagement through customization and use of the reflection platform.

Beyond Autism

Susie's involvement was key in beginning to explore the reach of Snap beyond HFA. Susie has her own experience, quite different from autism and found Snap held promise for her. In future studies we will be recruiting participants who experience anxiety in a wide range of conditions to see how this style of self-management through reflection and DIY assembly of personal technology can have impact.

CONCLUSIONS

We conducted an investigation with adults diagnosed with HFA and their support, to identify the potential role of DIY technology in self-management of anxiety. We explored this through co-developing a technology, from creative DIY prototypes to a 4-week evaluation of Snap. We have specifically looked at individual experiences of anxiety, what kinds of information should be captured and how it might be presented. We found our participants highly engaged in the process, and able to describe their experiences through the prototypes they made.

We propose that as well as helping to identify triggers to the negatives and how best to manage these, devices should help investigate how positive experiences can be appreciated and further encouraged. Focus on the negative may attach negative connotation to the device.

There is a delicate balance to be struck in the social affordance of devices - not only the aesthetic style but how conspicuous it is and how clearly the intended gestures map onto the physical design. This in particular is a challenge to the DIY approach used.

We find that participants both with HFA and without, including one who came late to the process (i.e. was not engaged in early workshops) found benefit in the use of Snap for the management of anxiety.

Indications are that a DIY approach to technology for self management of anxiety may enable design for the whole person, not just one 'component' of diagnosis, thus reducing abandonment and increasing benefits to users. The devices our users made were tailored to their own unique experiences.

ACKNOWLEDGMENTS

We would like to thank our participants, the charity Autism Initiatives and designers from Fluidedge Dublin for supporting this work. This work was funded by Research Councils UK EP/L023644/1.

REFERENCES

1. Ted Asay and Michael J. Lambert. 1999. The empirical case for the common factors in therapy: Quantitative findings. (1999).
2. Scott Bellini. 2004. Social Skill Deficits and Anxiety in High-Functioning Adolescents with Autism Spectrum Disorders. *Focus on Autism and Other Developmental Disorders*, 19/2, p.78-86.
3. Scott Bellini. 2006. The Development of Social Anxiety in Adolescents With Autism Spectrum Disorders. *Focus on Autism and other Developmental Disabilities*, 21/3, p.138-145.
4. Laura Benton, Asimina Vasalou, Rilla Khaled, Hilary Johnson, and Daniel Gooch. 2014. Diversity for design: a framework for involving neurodiverse children in the technology design process. In *Proceedings of the SIGCHI Conference on Human Factors in Computing Systems*, pp. 3747-3756. ACM, 2014.
5. Alan F. Blackwell. 2010. When Systemizers Meet Empathizers: Universalism and the Prosthetic Imagination." *Interdisciplinary Science Reviews* 35, no. 3-4 (2010): 387-403.
6. Eli Blevis. 2007. Sustainable interaction design: invention & disposal, renewal & reuse. In *Proceedings of the SIGCHI Conference on Human Factors in Computing Systems* (CHI '07)
7. Louanne E. Boyd, Kathryn E. Ringland, Oliver L. Haimson, Helen Fernandez, Maria Bistarkey, and Gillian R. Hayes. 2015. Evaluating a Collaborative iPad Game's Impact on Social Relationships for Children with Autism Spectrum Disorder. ACM Trans. Access. Comput. 7, 1, Article 3 (June 2015).
8. Anthony Dunne, and Fiona Raby (2013). *Speculative everything: design, fiction, and social dreaming.* MIT Press, 2013.
9. Maria Angela Ferrario, Will Simm, Peter Newman, Stephen Forshaw, and Jon Whittle. 2014. Software engineering for 'social good': integrating action research, participatory design, and agile development. In *Companion Proceedings of the 36th International Conference on Software Engineering* (ICSE Companion 2014). ACM, New York, NY, USA, 520-523.
10. Maria Angela Ferrario, Zoltán Bajmócy, Will Simm, and Stephen Forshaw. 2015. Towards a Sustainable Framework in Digital-Social Innovation: Integrating Circular Economy, Capability Approach and Action Research. In *Proceedings of the 11th International Conference of the European Society for Ecological Economics (ESEE 15)*. Leeds, UK.
11. Richard Ribon Fletcher, Kelly Dobson, Matthew S. Goodwin, Hoda Eydgahi, Oliver Wilder-Smith, David Fernholz, Yuta Kuboyama, Elliott Bruce Hedman, Ming-Zher Poh and Rosalind W. Picard. "iCalm: Wearable Sensor and Network Architecture for Wirelessly Communicating and Logging Autonomic Activity," in *Information Technology in Biomedicine, IEEE Transactions on* , vol.14, no.2, pp.215-223, March 2010
12. B. J. Fogg. 2002. Persuasive technology: using computers to change what we think and do. *Ubiquity* 2002
13. Batya Friedman. 1996. Value-sensitive design. *interactions*, *3*(6), 16-23.
14. Alinda Gillott, and P. J. Standen. 2007. Levels of anxiety and sources of stress in adults with autism. *Journal of intellectual disabilities* 11, no. 4 (2007): 359-370.
15. Matthew, S. Goodwin, Groden, J., Velicer, Wayne, F., Diller, Amy. 2007. Brief Report: Validating the Stress Survey Schedule for Persons With Autism and Other Developmental Disabilities. *Focus on Autism and other Developmental Disabilities*, 22/3, 183-189.
16. Hamed Haddadi , Richard Mortier, Derek McAuley, and Jon Crowcroft. 2013. Human-data interaction. *University of Cambridge* (2013).
17. Gillian R. Hayes and Gregory D. Abowd. 2006. Tensions in designing capture technologies for an evidence-based care community. In *Proceedings of the SIGCHI Conference on Human Factors in Computing Systems* (CHI '06), Rebecca Grinter, Thomas Rodden, Paul Aoki, Ed Cutrell, Robin Jeffries, and Gary Olson (Eds.). ACM, New York, NY, USA, 937-946.
18. Gillian R. Hayes. 2011. The relationship of action research to human-computer interaction. *ACM Trans. Comput.-Hum. Interact.* 18, 3, Article 15 (August 2011)
19. Gillian R. Hayes. 2014. Knowing by Doing: Action Research as an Approach to HCI. In *Ways of Knowing in HCI*, pp. 49-68. Springer New York, 2014
20. Jonathan Hook, Sanne Verbaan, Abigail Durrant, Patrick Olivier, and Peter Wright. "A study of the challenges related to DIY assistive technology in the

context of children with disabilities." In *Proceedings of the 2014 conference on Designing interactive systems*, pp. 597-606. ACM, 2014.

21. Amy Hurst and Jasmine Tobias. "Empowering individuals with do-it-yourself assistive technology." In *The proceedings of the 13th international ACM SIGACCESS conference on Computers and accessibility*, pp. 11-18. ACM, 2011.
22. Reuben Kirkham, and Chris Greenhalgh. "Social Access vs. Privacy in Wearable Computing: A Case Study of Autism." *Pervasive Computing, IEEE* 14, no. 1 (2015): 26-33.
23. Ian Li, Anind Dey, and Jodi Forlizzi. 2010. A stage-based model of personal informatics systems. In *Proceedings of the SIGCHI Conference on Human Factors in Computing Systems*, pp. 557-566. ACM, 2010.
24. Peter Newman, Maria Angela Ferrario, Will Simm, Stephen Forshaw, Adrian Friday, and Jon Whittle. 2015. The role of design thinking and physical prototyping in social software engineering. In *Proceedings of the 37th International Conference on Software Engineering - Volume 2* (ICSE '15), Vol. 2. IEEE Press, Piscataway, NJ, USA, 487-496.
25. Tekla S Perry. 2015. Giving your body a" check engine" light. *Spectrum, IEEE* 52, no. 6 (2015): 34-84.
26. Phonebloks. 2015. About Phonebloks Retrieved September 22, 2015 from http://phoneblocks.com/about-phonebloks/
27. Rosalind W. Picard.1997. Affective computing. Vol. 252. Cambridge: MIT press, 1997.
28. Cynthia Putnam and Lorna Chong. 2008. Software and technologies designed for people with autism: what do users want?. In Proceedings of the 10th international ACM SIGACCESS conference on Computers and accessibility (Assets '08). ACM, New York, NY, USA, 3-10.
29. Amon Rapp and Federica Cena. 2015. Affordances for self-tracking wearable devices. In*Proceedings of the 2015 ACM International Symposium on Wearable Computers* (ISWC '15). ACM, New York, NY, USA, 141-142.
30. Kristen Shinohara and Jacob O. Wobbrock. "In the shadow of misperception: assistive technology use and social interactions." In *Proceedings of the SIGCHI Conference on Human Factors in Computing Systems*, pp. 705-714. ACM, 2011.
31. Will Simm, Maria Angela Ferrario, Adrian Gradinar, and Jon Whittle. 2014. Prototyping Clasp': implications for designing digital technology for and with adults with autism. In *Proceedings of the 2014 conference on Designing interactive systems* (DIS '14). ACM, New York, NY, USA, 345-354
32. Will Simm, Maria Angela Ferrario, Adrian Friday, Peter Newman, Stephen Forshaw, Mike Hazas, and Alan Dix. 2015. Tiree Energy Pulse: Exploring Renewable Energy Forecasts on the Edge of the Grid. In *Proceedings of the 33rd Annual ACM Conference on Human Factors in Computing Systems* (CHI '15). ACM, New York, NY, USA, 1965-1974.
33. Anja Thieme, Jayne Wallace, Thomas D. Meyer, and Patrick Olivier. 2015. Designing for mental wellbeing: towards a more holistic approach in the treatment and prevention of mental illness. In *Proceedings of the 2015 British HCI Conference* (British HCI '15). ACM, New York, NY, USA, 1-10.
34. David Trembath, Carmela Germano, Graeme Johanson, and Cheryl Dissanayake. 2012. The experience of anxiety in young adults with autism spectrum disorders. *Focus on Autism and Other Developmental Disabilities* 27, no. 4 (2012): 213-224.
35. Francisca, J., Van Steel, A., Bogels, Susan, M., & Perrin Sean. 2011. Anxiety Disorders in Children and Adolescents with Autistic Spectrum Disorders: A Meta-Analysis. *Clinical Child and Family Psychology Review.* 14, 302-317.
36. White, S.W., Donald., O., Ollendick, T., Scahill, L. Anxiety in children and adolescents with autism spectrum disorders. Clinical Psychology Review, (2009), 216-229. 40.
37. White, S.W., Bray, B.C., Ollendick, T. Examining Shared and Unique Aspects of Social Anxiety Disorder and Autism Spectrum Disorder Using Factor Analysis. Journal of Autism and Development Disorders 42, 5 (2012), 874-84.
38. Bajmócy Zoltán, and Judit Gébert. 2014. The outlines of innovation policy in the capability approach. *Technology in Society* 38 (2014): 93-102.

EnhancedTouch: A Smart Bracelet for Enhancing Human-Human Physical Touch

Kenji Suzuki **Taku Hachisu** **Kazuki Iida**
University of Tsukuba
Tennodai, Tsukuba 305-8577, Japan
kenji@ieee.org hachisu@ai.iit.tsukuba.ac.jp kaz@ai.iit.tsukuba.ac.jp

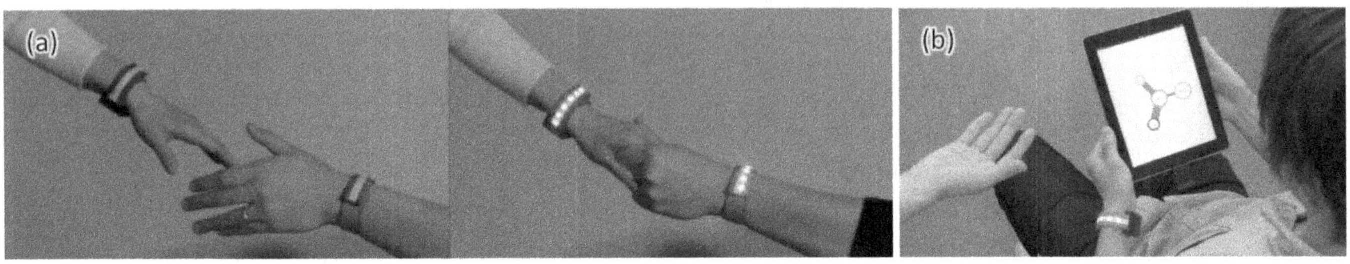

Figure 1. EnhancedTouch: (a) wearable devices measuring, recording and visually augmenting human-human touch events; (b) tablet computer shows touch records with correlation diagram (see also Figure 8 and Figure 10).

ABSTRACT
We present EnhancedTouch, a novel bracelet-type wearable device for facilitating human-human physical touch. In particular, we aim to support children with autism spectrum disorder (ASD), who often exhibit particular communication patterns, such as lack of physical touch. EnhancedTouch is a unique device that can measure human-human touch events and provide visual feedback to augment touch interaction. We employ personal area network (PAN) technology for communication with partner devices via modulated electrical current flowing through the users' hands. Our user study show that the visual feedback provided by the developed bracelet motivates children with ASD to touch one another. Moreover, EnhancedTouch offers a function to record the time and duration of a touch event as well as the identity of the touched person. This allows us to identify and evaluate intervention based on physical touch in a quantitative manner.

Author Keywords
Ambient playware; Autism Spectrum Disorder; EnhancedTouch; Personal Area Network; Touch Interaction.

ACM Classification Keywords
B.4.1 **[Input/Output and Data Communications]:** Data Communications Devices—*receivers, transmitters*; K.4.2 **[Computers and Society]:** Social Issues—*assistive technologies for persons with disabilities*; H.5.2 **[Information Interfaces and Presentation]:** User Interfaces—*Input Devices*

CHI'16, May 07-12, 2016, San Jose, CA, USA
© 2016 ACM. ISBN 978-1-4503-3362-7/16/05...$15.00
DOI: http://dx.doi.org/10.1145/2858036.2858439

INTRODUCTION
Human-human physical touch is a fundamental element of communication, and several benefits and positive effects induced by positive touch and massage have already been reported in the therapeutic domain [4, 9, 29, 36]. Children with autism spectrum disorder (ASD) often experience difficulty in both verbal and non-verbal communication including physical touch, owing to the absence of the desire to communicate and oversensitivity to tactile input [32, 37], which seriously affects their social interaction capabilities [38]. The frequency of touch is considered as an important index to evaluate intervention. Field et al. reported that their intervention method increased the frequency of physical touch, thereby enabling children with ASD to become more social [7, 10]. In these studies, precise measurement of the timing and duration of physical touch is crucial; however, such measurement has thus far been performed only via human review of video footage. This approach is tedious, especially when the number of test participants is large.

We are interested in quantitative measurement of the time and frequency of the touch as well as identification of the touched partner. However, there is no practical equipment for this purpose. Although a number of tactile/force sensors have been reported, it remains difficult to measure physical touch with other persons, e.g., shaking hands or touching bare skin, without any surface sensors.

In this study, we present a novel wearable device, EnhancedTouch, which not only measures but also augments human physical touch among participants in real time. The device is worn on the user's wrist, like a bracelet, and consists of light-emitting diodes (LEDs) that are illuminated by touch detection (Figure 1a). An environment in which several users wear this device motivates the users to touch one another. Furthermore, the device instantaneously provides data on the time and duration of touch, and shows the identity of the peer touched by user by the user on a tablet computer (Figure 1b), thereby allowing us to quickly view the user's social relationship.

Contributions

The contributions of this work are as follows.

1) Implementation of a wearable device that can measure (not just detect), record, and visually augment touch events in real time.

2) Evaluation of the device's response to touch events in laboratory experiments.

3) User study in a class of children with ASD to confirm the children's acceptance of the device and demonstrate that the device offers more efficient measurement and analysis of touch events than video recording.

4) User study in a class to demonstrate the potential of the device as ambient playware that motivates children with ASD to actively touch their peers, by observing their behaviors with/without illumination of the device.

The remainder of this paper is organized as follows. First, we review the existing literature on computer-assisted intervention and personal area network (PAN) technology, which is a key technology of our device. Next, we describe the implementation of EnhancedTouch. Then, we describe a user study in which EnhancedTouch was used by therapists and children with ASD in a classroom. Finally, we conclude the paper by summarizing the results of the user study and discussing the directions for future research.

RELATED WORK

Computer-assisted Intervention and Ambient Playware

Proper interventions for children with ASD will enable them to be independent in their adulthood. For several decades, researchers and therapists have been exploring the potential of computer-assisted intervention in the treatment of ASD [3, 28]. Chen and Bernard-Opitz reported that computer-assisted intervention highly motivates children with ASD [2]. Thus far, various studies have shown that computer-assisted intervention enables children with ASD to significantly improve their social interaction skills, such as learning vocabulary [17, 25] and expressing emotion [35]. In these cases, children generally face a computer (e.g., monitor) and perform the given tasks. Such an approach can be regarded as human-computer interaction, which involves fewer distractions from the tasks.

Interventions based on human-human interaction assisted by computers have been developed in recent years. Sharing a multi-touch screen provides an environment in which children can collaborate with their peers [11, 12, 19]. For example, Gal et al. evaluated the effectiveness of a three-week intervention in which a tabletop interface was presented to children with ASD, and they engaged in collaborative storytelling using widgets on the screen [11]. In other studies, mobile devices [8] and robots [20] have been used for mediated communication and collaborative tasks between children with ASD. Because the child interacts with actual humans, such interventions seem more practical for fostering natural social interaction skills than approaches based on human-computer interaction.

Lund et al. suggested the terms "playware" and "ambient playware" [23]. Playware refers to intelligent hardware and software for creating leisure activities (play) among users, of which computer games are a sub-genre. Ambient playware is playware with ambient intelligence characteristics. Ambient intelligence is provided by a large number of small, intelligent devices built into our surroundings.

Inspired by human-human interaction assisted by computers and ambient playware, we apply these concepts to computer-assisted intervention involving physical touch.

Personal Area Network

Research in the field of human-computer interaction has led to the development of various physical touch detection technologies, including camera/photo sensing [15, 18], resistance sensing [27, 33], acoustic sensing [16, 31], and capacitive sensing [5, 34]. Although several sensing technologies are capable of detecting human-human touch [15, 16, 34], it is difficult to implement wearable devices or identify the person who touches or is touched by the user.

To meet this requirement, we employ personal area network (PAN, or specifically, body area/intra-body networks) technology. Zimmerman proposed the concept of using the human body as a communication channel in order to expand the freedom to design devices attached to the human body [39, 40]. Various applications of this technique have been developed, including communication between consumer electrical appliances [24, 30], tangible interfaces [1, 13, 24], and human-robot interaction [22].

PAN technology can be categorized into two types: electric field type and electrical current type. The former does not require the user to directly attach the device (electrode) on the skin, because the electric field induced around the surface of the human body is used as a communication channel. On the other hand, the latter performs communication via electrical currents in the human body, and the user has to attach the device/electrode on the skin. Considering the measurement of human-human touch, we employ electrical current PAN technology because a channel is established only when two users touch each another, and while the channel exists, information about the touch event and touching parties can be exchanged.

Creating a ground path is the major technical challenge for the electrical current PAN technology. Passing electrical current requires at least two paths, i.e., signal path and ground path. The human body can be regarded as a single conductive wire consisting of a resistor and a capacitor. Thus, the human body can be used as the signal path while the ground path is established by the capacitive coupling between devices in the air (Z_{AirD} in Figure 2a) because the wearable device is driven by a battery and not grounded with wires. Although the stability of communication depends on the intensity of the capacitive coupling, it significantly changes according to the spatial relation between the grounds of each device, such as size, distance, and direction. Doi and Nishimura improved the stability by using the human body as not only a signal path but also a ground path (Figure 2a) [6]. The device has signal and ground electrodes in contact with the skin of the user (Figure 3c), dividing the user's body into signal and ground paths shown in red and blue, respectively (Figure 2a). As a result, a large area of the user's body works as a ground electrode, achieving capacitive coupling with the body of another user (Z_{AirH} in Figure 2a). This improves the communication stability considerably.

Figure 2b shows an equivalent circuit of Figure 2a, where Z_{XS} and Z_{XG} are the impedances of the signal and ground paths in user X's body, Z_{Xs} and Z_{Xg} are the impedances of the signal and ground paths at the contact point between the electrode and the skin, Z_{XW} is the impedance of user X's skin between the electrodes, and Z_{AirD} and Z_{AirH} are the impedances of the capacitive coupling between the devices/human bodies, respectively. Further, SW is a switch that is turned on when users touch each other with their hands on which the devices are worn.

ENHANCEDTOUCH

Design Requirements

We define four design requirements for the device. These requirements majorly derive from the insights of our research partner, Smile Club—a non-profit organization (NPO) that holds classes for children who are not adept at physical activities.

First, the device should be easy to wear. This is necessary for reducing the therapist's load in attaching the devices to children with ASD and for saving time. Furthermore,

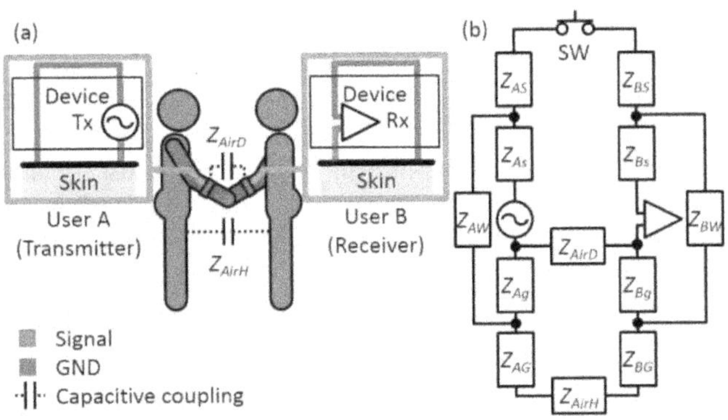

Figure 2. Principle of electrical current PAN technology: (a) human body as signal and ground path [6]; (b) equivalent circuit.

because the children may be oversensitive to wearable artifacts [38], complex mechanics for fixing the device on their wrists would not be acceptable.

Second, the device should be capable of measuring the time and duration of a touch event as well as the identity of the touched person. This is necessary for quantitatively evaluating the effect of the intervention on physical touch. In addition to measuring the start time and duration of touch, identifying the person whom the user touches is important for analyzing the user's social relationship.

Third, it should be possible to use several devices simultaneously. This is necessary for using the device in a class in which several children and therapists participate. Because it is difficult to predetermine the master and slave devices, the devices need to dynamically communicate with each other (ad-hoc network) to share the data on physical touch.

Fourth, the device should measure the touch events in real time. This is necessary for quickly representing the touch event with sensory feedback (in this paper, we employ visual feedback), which is expected to motivate the children to touch their peers.

First Prototype Device Implementation

Hardware

We developed the first prototype device of EnhancedTouch consisting of a 35×35×10 mm PAN module (Figure 3a), a lithium polymer battery, conductive tape and an LED indicator. The device has two copper boards as signal and ground electrodes in contact with the skin, and an analog switch (TS5A23157, Texas Instruments) connecting the signal electrode with the transmitter or receiver (Figure 3b and c). The device is fixed on the wrist with conductive tape.

Using a microcontroller, the transmitter outputs a universal asynchronous receiver transmitter (UART) signal, which is modulated by a carrier wave using on-off keying. We employed a 5 Vpp 10 MHz square wave as the carrier wave because it has been shown that 10 MHz signals can conduct through the human body quite effectively [14]. According to ICNIRP guidelines [21], to avoid side effects such as nervous system interference, whole-body heat stress, and excessive localized tissue heating when using a 10 MHz signal, the maximum contact current should be lower than 20 mA; our transmitter outputs less than 3 mA.

The receiver demodulates the signal transmitted by the partner device. First, the signal passes through a bandpass filter (SFSCE10M7WF03, Murata) whose nominal center frequency and 3-dB bandwidth are 10.7 MHz and ±500 kHz, respectively. Next, the signal is amplified by an intermediate frequency amplifier (NJM2549, New Japan Radio Co.), which outputs the received signal strength indication (RSSI). Then, the RSSI passes through a comparator and the original UART signal is received by the microcontroller.

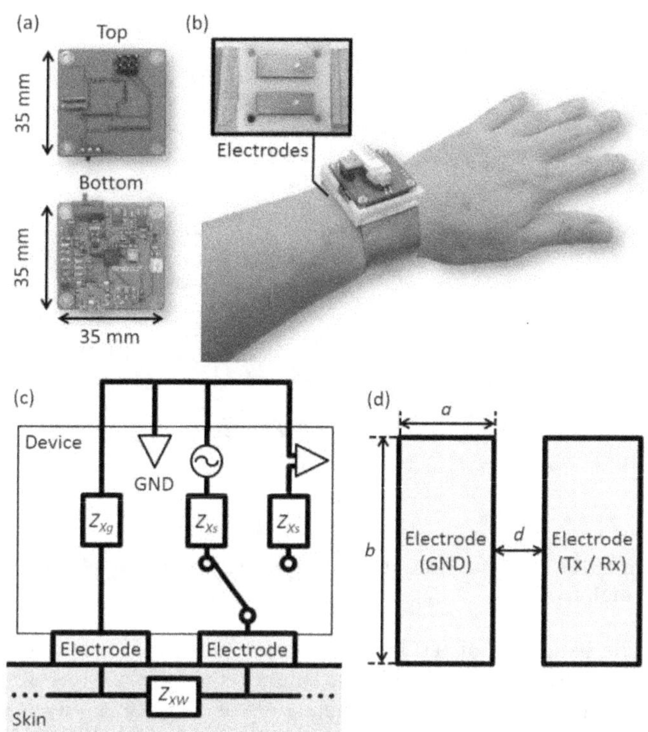

Figure 3. First prototype device: (a) PAN module (35×35×10 mm); (b) device worn on the wrist with conductive tape to expand the ground electrode; (c) module configuration; (d) electrode design.

According to [6], Z_{XW} in Figure 2b and Figure 3c should have a large value for stable communication. To increase Z_{XW}, the electrodes' short side *a* and the long side *b* should be small, while the distance between the electrodes, *d*, should be large (Figure 3d). The values of *a*, *b*, and *d* for the developed device are 8.8, 24, and 6.4 mm, respectively, resulting in an impedance of 50.1 – 6.6j Ω according to the simulation by Muramatsu et al. [26].

We used conductive tape as a wristband to attach the device on the skin. The tape is connected to the ground electrode on the module, which expands the surface area of the ground electrode and strengths the capacitive coupling in Z_{AirD}. A cardboard layer is inserted between the tape and the skin to reduce the capacitive coupling between the tape and the skin, as well as to strengthen the capacitive coupling in Z_{AirD}.

Software

For bi-directional communication through a single path, we use time division to enable transmission and reception in alternating time slots (half-duplex communication).

A 5-byte packet transmitted and received consists of a 2-byte header, 1-byte data (e.g., device ID), and 2-byte cyclic redundancy checks (CRCs). Each device attempts to transmit a synchronous signal with its own ID at intervals selected randomly from ten alternatives (e.g., 1, 2, 3, …, 10 ms at 9.6 kbps) to detect whether touching has occurred and to synchronize with other devices. Using random intervals helps avoid collisions between multiple transmitted signals. When the microcontroller is not transmitting, it waits to receive signals from other devices. If a signal is received successfully by a microcontroller, it replies with an acknowledgement header and its own ID. After this handshake, the device that transmitted the synchronization packet is set as the master, the device that received the packet and acknowledged it is set as the slave, and the communication channel is established. The master device then leads the communication, allowing information to be exchanged. When the contact ends, the communication channel is terminated, and the devices return to their initial state.

Figure 4 shows an example of the communication procedure between two devices. Phase (a) indicates the period prior to synchronization, in which the devices transmit at random intervals. In phase (b), the transmission channel is established, but synchronization initially fails because of a collision between transmissions. In phase (c), synchronization finally succeeds, and the two devices can communicate smoothly.

Thus, each device detects touches according to its state of synchronization with the other device. By this method, the device not only detects touches but also identifies the partner by receiving its ID. In addition, using a timer in the microcontroller allows us to measure the time and duration of a touch event.

As soon as successful synchronization is achieved, the microcontroller turns the LED on. To prevent LED chatter due to bouncing of the initial contact, the microcontroller turns the LED off if disconnection lasts for more than 500 ms.

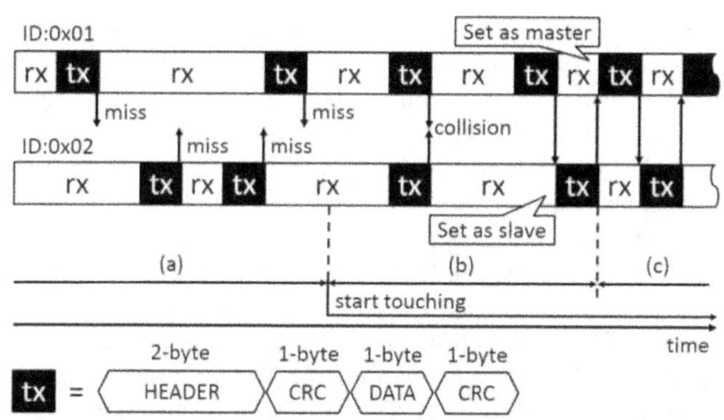

Figure 4. Procedure of communication between two devices: packet contains a header, data (e.g., device ID), CRC; (a) prior to synchronization, the devices transmit at random intervals; (b) the transmission channel is established, but synchronization initially fails because of a collision between transmissions; (c) synchronization finally succeeds, and the two devices can communicate smoothly.

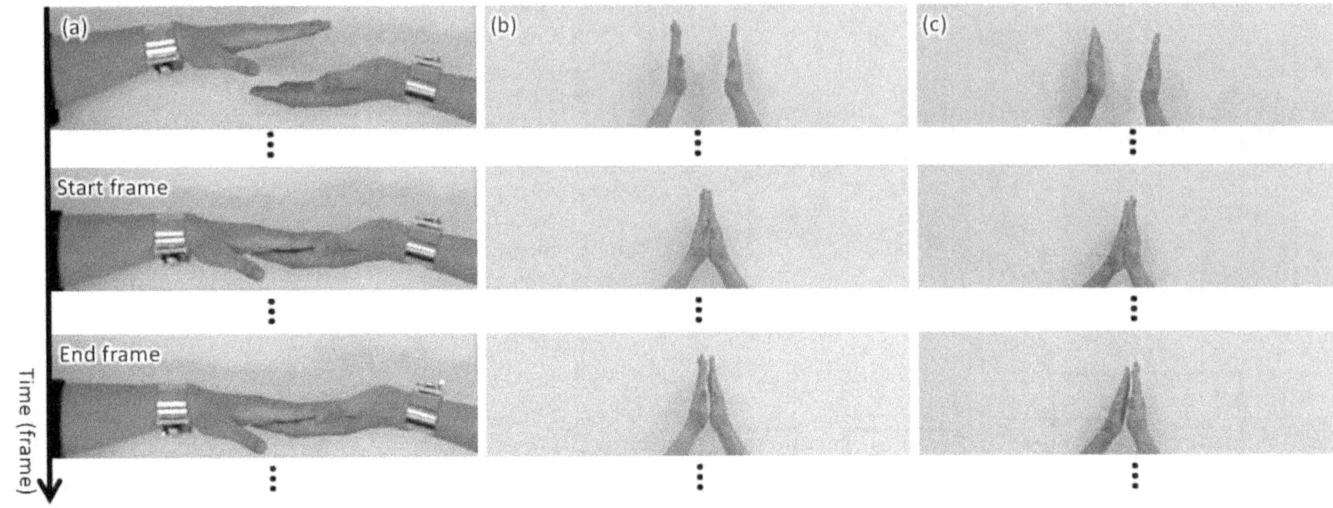

Figure 5. Frames from response time evaluation: (a) measurement of the response time of the device; touch duration of (b) handclap and (c) high five.

Response time evaluation

To validate our prototype device and overall system, we evaluated the response time involved in detecting touch events and compared it with the duration of common physical touch.

The response time of the device (the period between the moment when a touch is initiated and the moment when the LED on the device lights up) generally falls within an expected range determined by the algorithms involved, but it can vary beyond this range when transmissions collide. Therefore, to measure the actual response time, we devised an experiment.

We instructed two participants, each fitted with a device, to touch each other using their fingers. Both devices were configured to light up their LEDs immediately upon touch detection. The experiment was recorded using a high-speed camera at 1200 fps, and the time was calculated from the number of frames between the two relevant actions. Figure 5a shows a single frame captured during the experiment. Note that the participants stood erect and face-to-face. One participant (participant A) held out his arm straight, with the palm of his hand facing up, and the other participant (participant B) held out his arm straight, with the palm of his hand facing down. Participant B touched participant A's fingers fifty times. When each touch occurred, both participant A's hand and participant B's hand were observed to be in synchronized movement, because participant A's hand pushed participant B's hand downward. We defined the start frame as the one in which synchronized movement of the hands began and the end frame as the one in which the LED of both the devices started to light up. Touching was limited to the fingers in order to make the moment of initial contact as distinct as possible.

The baud rate of the UART was set to 9.6, 19.2, and 57.6 kbps. Setting the baud rate higher than 57.6 kbps was possible and allowed the detection of large-area physical touches such as shaking of hands, but could not detect small-area contact such as finger-finger contact reliably because the signals became unstable due to low signal-to-noise ratio resulting from the high baud rate.

Handclaps and high fives were selected as examples of common touching activities for which durations would be measurably short and thus suitable for testing the performance of the device. The handclap experiment involved 10 participants, and the high five experiment involved 10 pairs of participants (one participant paired with ten different partners). Again, we recorded the experiment using a high-speed camera at 1200 fps. To define the duration of physical touch in these activities, we marked the beginning of contact as the frame in which vibration is first observed in the hypothenar muscle in reaction to the force of physical touch, and the end of contact as the first frame in which a gap is observed between the hands. Figure 5b shows a frame from the handclap experiment, and Figure 5c shows a frame from the high five experiment.

The response times of the device are shown in Figure 6. The medians (interquartile range: IQR) of the response times for 9.6, 19.2, and 57.6 kbps were 34.7 (68.1), 13.3 (30.2), and 0.8 (10.6) ms, respectively. We presume that the considerably large variance of the response time is a result of unstable contact between the skin and the electrodes because Z_{XW}, which is important for stability of communication, is strongly dependent on the contact area. Several response times are faster than the sum of the transmitting and receiving time. This could be because contact has occurred earlier than that according to our definition, i.e., the time

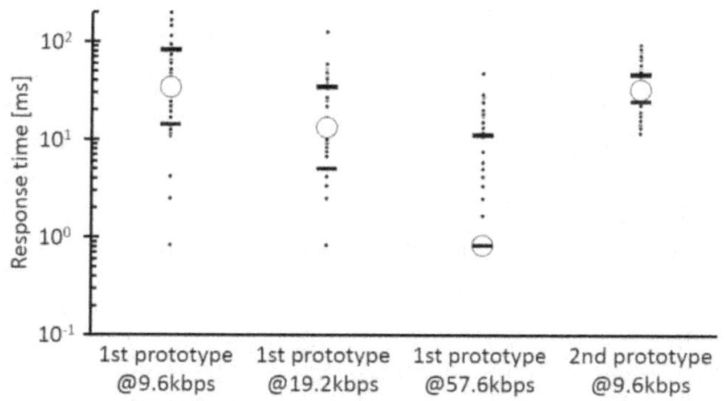

Figure 6. Response times of the first and second prototype devices: the black dots, white circles, and black bars denote raw data, median, and interquartile range (IQR), respectively.

when the hands were observed to be in synchronized movement.

The contact durations of the handclaps and high fives are around 20–80 ms, showing considerable variance. The response time is adequately small compared to slow touch. This result suggests that the device is capable of measuring various kinds of touches that are slower than slow handclaps and high fives.

Second Prototype Device Implementation

Hardware

We developed the second prototype device by modifying the first one. This section describes the major modifications.

Six full-color LEDs and a PAN module are installed on a flexible printed circuit board (Figure 7a), which allows the board along with the embedded LEDs to wrap around the wrist like a watch strap, making the LED output more visible to both the user and others in the vicinity (Figure 1a). All components including a lithium polymer battery are contained in a small case with a cloth strap and Velcro tape (Figure 7b).

A pair of electrodes is located on the inside surface of the case (Figure 7b). Considering the result of response time evaluation, by making a slight arch, the electrodes are designed to fit the wrist comfortably, and using the Velcro tape, the electrodes are firmly attached to the skin.

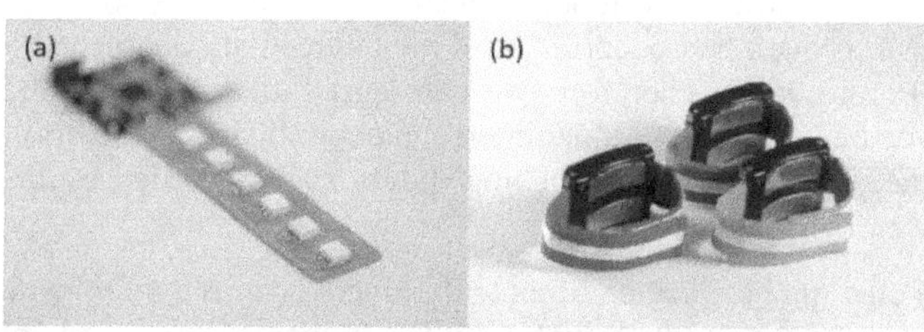

Figure 7. Second prototype device: (a) flexible printed circuit with a PAN module and six full-color LEDs (152×41×5mm); (b) the circuit and a battery are contained in a plastic case with cloth straps and Velcro tape.

Electrically erasable programmable read-only memory (EEPROM) built in the microcontroller is used for recording touch events, i.e., the start time of a touch event, its duration, and the ID of the touched partner. This data can be accessed through an external PC. Each device is capable of recording up to 200 entries.

Software

The procedure of communication is the same as that of the first prototype device. However, the baud rate of the UART is fixed at 9.6 kbps to guarantee stable communication and detect fingertip-fingertip contact. We evaluated the response time of the device using the same protocol as that in the previous evaluation, but touching was limited to fingertip-fingertip touches. The median and IQR of the response time are 32.5 and 22.1 ms, respectively (Figure 6). The results show that the variance is lower than that of the previous device, which indicates that re-designing the electrodes has improved the device. Comparing the duration of the handclaps and high fives, we can conclude that the device is partially capable of measuring common touch activities of very short durations and entirely capable of measuring touches of longer durations.

The device also features color blending, implemented as a form of visual feedback for the duration of a touch event. Each device is assigned a unique color from the set of primary colors (red, green, blue). When users touch each other, their devices activate LEDs showing their respective colors. These colors then begin to blend over the duration of the touch, eventually settling on a shared, intermediate color. This is accomplished by having the master device measuring the touch duration and sharing it with the slave device through the communication channel. When the touch event ends, the duration and color blending state are reset for subsequent touches. To compensate for the insufficient response time of fast touch, the device gradually turns on or fades off the LEDs after connecting or disconnecting with the partner device.

In addition to the positive feedback based on the users' actions, visual feedback is expected to serve the following purpose. Assigning a primary color to one user and implementing color blending engages the user to see the resulting color and provides awareness of the peer; the pair experiencing touch augmentation can be clearly seen by another user, which motivates her/him to touch the peer her/himself. A combination of visual and tactile/audio feedback could be considered, but we implemented only visual feedback for the sake of simplicity.

Our approach for visualizing touch records is based on correlation diagrams, which can combine touch events and their durations over a long period of time, and make degrees of familiarity between users easy to observe. Because records of physical touch between people are a matter of

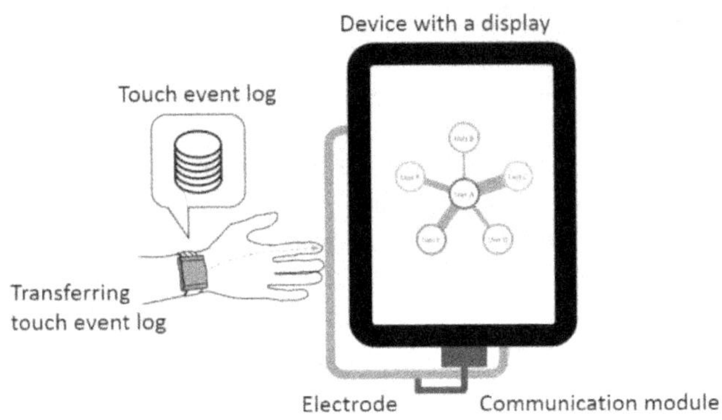

Figure 8. Illustration of correlation diagram visualization

personal privacy, we chose to produce our visualizations on a tablet computer, which allows controlled sharing with devices and people.

Our implementation of correlation diagrams is shown in Figure 8. A tablet computer connects to the device worn by the user holding it, and provides a correlation diagram of the touch log of the device. Communication between the tablet and the worn device is similar to communication between users. An electrode connected to a circuit similar to that used in the bracelet type device, which in turn is connected to the tablet over serial communication is placed on the back of the tablet. When a user holds the tablet, the bracelet device automatically connects to the circuit of the tablet computer through the body, and touch records are downloaded from the EEPROM of the bracelet device to the tablet. Once the records have been received, an application on the tablet immediately visualizes the records. In the correlation diagram, the circle in the center indicates the user holding the tablet computer, and the circles around the center indicate others who made contact with the user (see also Figure 10). The center circle is connected to each of the surrounding circles by lines, and the line thickness indicates the comparative duration of touches between the users. When the user releases the tablet computer, the visualization ends and the tablet computer returns to waiting for a new user.

EXPERIMENT 1: ACCEPTANCE OF THE DEVICE

This section describes the evaluation of our devices used in a class of children with ASD. The objectives of the experiments are to observe the children's acceptance of the device and to study the efficacy of the device in measuring and analyzing the touch events, as compared with video recording by a human coder. The study was conducted with the approval of the institutional review board of the University of Tsukuba.

Method

This experiment was conducted in cooperation with Smile Club. Five boys and one girl with ASD (from 5–8 years; most of the children were not suffering from intellectual disorders or severe autism), along with two male and two female trainers, participated in the class. The class was held in the gymnasium of an elementary school. After the participants finished their warm up, the devices were strapped to their left wrists. The results were recorded using two video cameras, and the recorded videos were later analyzed by a human coder who was not aware of the purpose of our research. The devices were set to record physical touches with an accuracy of the order of 1 s. All LEDs were disabled during this experiment so that they would not influence the children's desire to touch.

The class was divided into two sessions: a physical competition to reverse cards and perform ringtosses, and a bingo game. The bingo game required each child to shake hands with the main female trainer (trainer A) upon finishing his/her bingo card to receive a gift. For effective assessment of the capability of the device, deliberate physical touch from the trainers was needed, as the children were not naturally inclined to initiate touches by themselves.

The total time between wearing the device and completing both sessions was 50 min. The first 20 min comprised the physical competition session, and the last 30 min comprised the bingo game session.

The collected data included observation of the children's behavior (qualitative evaluation), touch events (frequency, duration, and partner) recorded by our devices and video cameras, and times measured by our system and a human video decoder.

Results

Children's Reaction to the Device

The club trainer and the author of this paper helped each child to wear the device. None of the children resisted the device while wearing it or during the subsequent sessions, indicating general acceptance of the device. Moreover, many children showed strong interest in the device, touched its case or switched it on, and stared at it for 5–20 s. Only one child disrupted the function of the device by repeatedly switching it off, thereby erasing its touch data. We did not consider this data for the following analysis.

Touching During the Physical Activity Session

The recorded results of the physical activity session are shown in Table 1a-1 and a-2. Note that it includes only touches involving the left hands of the participants observed by both the device and the video camera. The camera did not always show these touches clearly, though it was obvious that a touch had occurred, and the device data confirmed it (Figure 9a-1). Therefore, we considered this case valid and verified the time of touching (time elapsed since the start of the experiment) and touching duration, as recorded by the wearable device.

Touching between children and trainers occurred often, with most of the events initiated by the trainers. An example of this is seen in Figure 9a-1, depicting trainer D touching the left hand of child A while teaching him a game.

Experiment elapsed time	Touching pair	Touch duration
(a-1) 14'33"	child A - trainer D	1"
(a-2) 15'29"	child A - child F	2"
(b-1) 37'47"	child B – trainer A	3"
(b-2) 42'20"	child A – trainer A	3"

Table 1. Touching events during (a) the physical activity and (b) the bingo game session

As expected, the children had a tendency to not interact with each other. However, child A and F, who are brothers, did touch each other more often than the other children. The recording given in Table 1a-2 at 15'29" was between the brothers, also shown in Figure 9a-2. Physical touches other than touching with the left hand, such as those shown in Figure 9c-1 and c-2, were not considered.

Touching During the Bingo Game Session

The records for the bingo game session are shown in Table 1b-1 and b-2. Participants in the bingo game showed less movements; thus, touches could be clearly recorded by both the wearable device and the video camera. In this session, we confirmed that the time and duration of touches recorded by the wearable device matched those taken from the video footage. Note that Table 1b-1 is the recording at 37'47", as seen in Figure 9b-1, and Table 1b-2 is the recording at 42'20', as seen in Figure 9b-2.

Analyzing Time

Our system allowed us to analyze the touch events in around 3 h. On the other hand, it took around 15 h for the human video decoder to analyze the touch events. The decoder reported that monitoring the touch events was a complex task because it was difficult or impossible to (i) see the initiation and end of touch owing to the low spatial and temporal resolution of the video, (ii) see the touch events beyond the range of the camera, and (iii) track the actively moving children.

Correlation Diagrams

To visualize the results of this experiment, we plotted all the values using correlation diagrams, as shown in Figure 10. Each participant was assigned a unique ID, and the ID for the center circle of the diagram was always that of the owner of the given correlation diagram. The IDs were assigned as

(a-1) 14'33" (a-2) 15'29" (b-1) 37'47" (b-2) 42'20" (c-1) (c-2)

Figure 9. Pictures captured by video camera during Experiment 1 with video footage: (a) the exercise session; (b) the bingo game session; (c) physical touch other than touching with the left hand between two brothers (child A and child F).

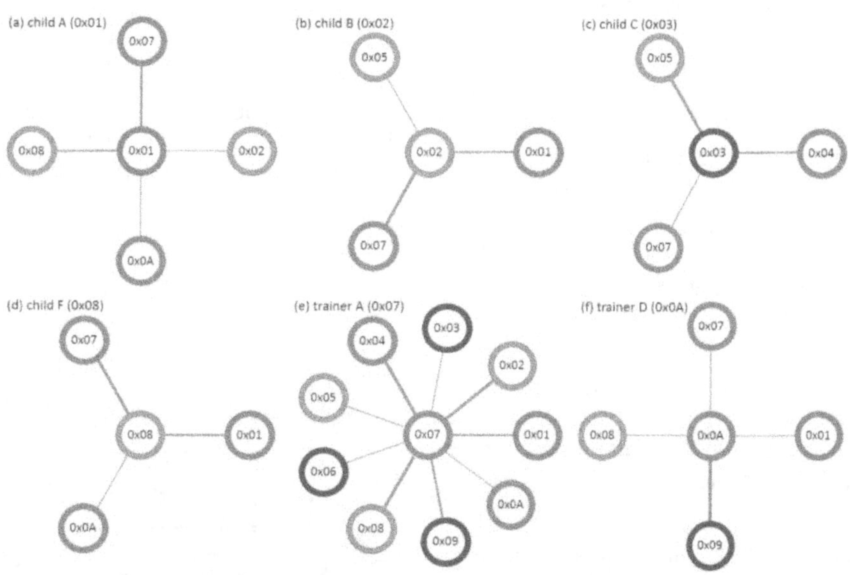

Figure 10. Correlation diagrams for the records of Experiment 1 (excerpt): the circle in the center indicates the user holding the tablet computer, the circles around the center indicate others who made contact with the user, and the thickness of the lines indicate the comparative duration of touches between the users.

follows: a) 0x01 is child A; b) 0x02 is child B; c) 0x03 is child C; d) 0x08 is child F; e) 0x07 is trainer A; and f) 0x0A is trainer D.

Figure 10d shows the correlation diagram for child F. Note that the line connecting to 0x07 (trainer A) is the thickest, indicating that the total touching time with trainer A was the longest among all of the child F's touching partners. As mentioned earlier, 0x01 (child A) was child F's brother and the second most touched person after trainer A. The thinnest line is the line connecting with 0x0A (trainer D), indicating that child F very seldom touched trainer D. Another interesting example is provided in Figure 10e, which shows the correlation diagram for trainer A. Note that trainer A touched all the children in order to shake their hands during the bingo game session. The results indicate that our devices can analyze social relationship by identifying the person whom the user touched.

EXPERIMENT 2: ENHANCED TOUCH

It was shown in the previous experiment that our device can be used to measure physical touch among children with ASD without the children's resistance. These results allow us to proceed to the next experiment to study the potential of our devices as playware that motivates the children to actively touch their peers. The objective of the experiment is to investigate the degree to which physical touch among the children is motivated by the visual feedback provided by our devices via embedded LEDs.

Method

Two sessions were conducted on different days, once again in collaboration with Smile Club. During each session, the children played together and engaged in a light soccer game while wearing the devices. For the first session, the LEDs were deactivated. For the second session, conducted a week after the first, the LEDs were active, providing visual feedback whenever a touch was detected and performing color blending for the duration of the touch. On completion of these two sessions, the recorded data was downloaded to a PC and the total duration and numbers of touches among the children were calculated for each child in each session. The numbers and durations were then compared to determine whether visual feedback had encouraged touching. Only touches among children were considered. All the children wore the devices on their right hands, and none of the children knew anything about the function of the devices beforehand.

During the session, the children were instructed to assemble and wear the device, do a warming up exercise, do a ring ladder exercise, playing a light soccer game, do a cooling down exercise, and remove the device.

Results

Eight boys and two girls with ASD participated in the first session, and four boys and three girls with ASD participated in the second session (four boys and two girls aged 5–8 years participated in both sessions; most of the children were not suffering from intellectual disorders or severe autism).

The total numbers and durations of touches of the six children for each of the sessions are shown in Figure 11. The mean (±95% confidence interval (CI)) number of touches significantly increased by 30.3 (18.6) (paired t-test: $t = -4.19$; $df = 5$; $p < 0.01$) with the visual feedback. The mean (95% CI) touch duration also significantly increased by 45.2 (19.8) s (paired t-test: $t = -5.85$; $df = 5$; $p < 0.01$).

It is also worth noting that the children discovered the visual feedback mechanisms provided by the LEDs entirely on their own through the course of touching one another during the warming up exercise. As the children discovered these mechanisms, they showed a strong positive response. Most of the touches were observed during the intervals between the exercises. We also noted that a child showed interest in the visual feedback while she/he saw a pair experiencing the visual feedback and tried to do the same by her/himself with others as expected. Further, the children gathered around one another, trying to explore the capabilities of the device. Some touches were also observed during the exercise when the children performed well, such as doing well in the ladder exercise or scoring in the soccer game, following which they shook hands or high-fived their peers. They also showed more curiosity and surprise through their facial expressions during the second session than they did in the first session.

DISCUSSION

Effectiveness of EnhancedTouch

Having used video analysis to track touches among the participants, we noted considerable difficulty in covering large spaces, such as the gymnasium used in one of our experiments. Using a fixed camera placed high above and pointed down toward the action, and another handheld camera for recording nearby participants, we found that many of the participants' touches could not be captured. Using additional cameras is an option, but the video analyzer's job may quickly become intractable, as an increasing amount of footage will need to be viewed synchronously. Note that video analysis for Experiment 1

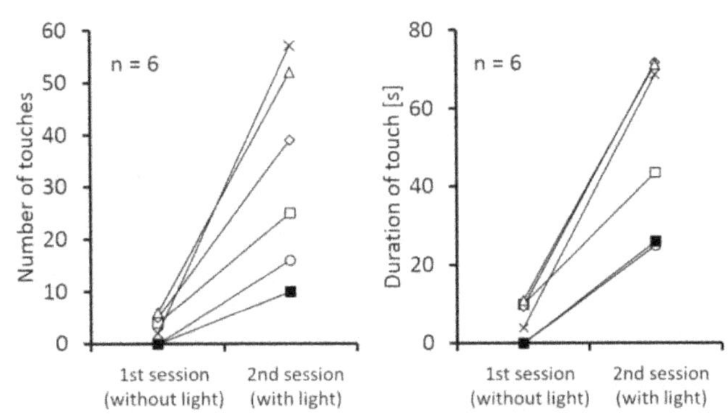

Figure 11. Total number and duration of touches among the children with/without visual feedback (n = 6).

took around 15 h, whereas analysis using the device took only about 3 h. Furthermore, the device can be used regardless of the lighting conditions, depth of field, and so on. Therefore, our device can help to reduce the analytical load involved in studying touch interactions, and it provides a more accurate and versatile platform for measuring physical touch.

Experiment 2 indicates a significant increase in the touch events when visual feedback is provided, as expected. Although it is possible that this increase is mainly due to initial curiosity, we intend to investigate it further in order to confirm our results. Furthermore, although we have employed visual feedback, we plan to consider other representations, such as audio and vibration feedback, to develop more interactive protocols as a means of sustaining children's interest.

Limitations

The current EnhancedTouch prototype and present study have several limitations.

The device cannot stably measure a touch event whose duration is less than 100 ms, as demonstrated in the response time evaluation (Figure 6). We achieved trade-off between the minimum touching area for measuring a touch event and the response time (i.e., baud rate). On the other hand, in the user study, such short-time touches were not observed. Thus, we do not currently consider this limitation as a major issue for our purpose.

The device cannot measure touch events involving body parts other than the hand on which the device is worn or when the electrodes are not in contact with the skin. A possible solution is to employ electric field PAN technology, where the electric field induced around the surface of human body is used as a communication channel and the electrodes do not have to attach to the skin. However, in this case, accurately differentiating the touch and proximity is a challenging task because RSSI depends not only on the contact states but also on the spatial relationship between the devices. The current solution for floating electrodes is to simply watch the device and refasten the belt.

Experiment 2 constituted exploratory work involving small number of participants. In addition, owing to short duration of the session (i.e., two weeks), it may not be possible to generalize the results. We plan to conduct further studies by including long-term sessions and post-sessions without visual feedback in order to determine how long the expected effect remains. One of the most important findings of this work is that our devices was accepted by children with ASD and it was compatible with the class activity.

CONCLUSION

In this paper, we presented EnhancedTouch, a wearable device for recording physical touches among people. The system consists of an easy-to-wear, bracelet-type device that can measure touch events, provide visual feedback for these touch events, and record and share touch data, i.e., the person whom the user touched as well as the time and duration of the touch event. The response time of the device was shown to be sufficient for measuring most everyday touch activities, and with the inclusion of a tablet computer interface, we were able to provide convenient, informative visualizations of the touch data. In tests involving children with ASD, we found that the bracelet device was met with no notable resistance and succeeded in measuring most, if not all, interpersonal touches during experiment sessions. We also found that the visual feedback provided by the devices helped to motivate physical touch among the children, although further study is required to confirm this finding.

We foresee two directions for future research. The first is to establish a technology to identify and represent social interaction. We have been investigating a method to identify various touches by using the developed device. We are also interested in understanding a human being's implicit and explicit behavior for social interaction by observing facial expressions, eye contact, and so on as well as by considering physical touch. For this purpose, we plan to develop a particular environment in which various devices, including EnhancedTouch, measure and augment human-human interaction.

The second is to consider methods for motivating children with ASD to interact more deeply. While our method provides visual feedback of touch events via full-color LEDs, there are numerous other feedback methods, such as tactile and audio feedback. We will investigate the advantages and disadvantages of these sensory feedback methods in representing the states of touch, which will enable us to design more engaging ambient playware.

ACKNOWLEDGMENTS

This research was supported by CREST, JST. The authors would like to thank Ms. Atsuko Ohama of Smile Club for her assistance in the experiments involving children with developmental disorders.

REFERENCES

1. Tetsuaki Baba, Taketoshi Ushiama, and Kiyoshi Tomimatsu. 2008. Freqtric drums: a musical instrument that uses skin contact as an interface. In *Proceedings of the 7th International Conference on New Interfaces for Musical Expression* (NIME '07), 386-387.
2. Shen Hsing A. Chen and Vera Bernard-Opitz. 1993. Comparison of personal and computer-assisted instruction for children with autism. *Mental Retardation* 31, 6: 368–376.
3. Kenneth Mark Colby. 1973. The rationale for computer-based treatment of language difficulties in nonspeaking autistic children. *J Autism and Childhood Schizophrenia* 3, 3: 254-260.
4. Lesley Cullen and Julie Barlow. 2002. 'Kiss, cuddle, squeeze': the experiences and meaning of touch among parents of children with autism attending a touch

therapy programme. *J Child Health Care* 6, 3: 171-181.

5. Paul Dietz and Darren Leigh. 2001. Diamondtouch: a multi-user touch technology. In *Proceedings of the 14th Annual ACM Symposium on User Interface Software and Technology* (UIST '01), 219-226.
6. Kenji Doi and Tokuhisa Nishimura. 2005. High-reliability communication technology using human body as transmission medium. *Matsushita Electric Works, Ltd. Technical Rep* 53, 3: 72-76. (Japanese)
7. Angelica Escalona, Tiffany Field, Jacqueline Nadel, and Brenda Lundy. 2002. Brief report: imitation effects on children with autism. *J Autism and Developmental Disorders* 32, 2: 141-144.
8. Lizbeth Escobedo, David H. Nguyen, LouAnne Boyd, Sen H. Hirano, Alejandro Rangel, Daniel Garcia-Rosas, Monica Tentori, and Gillian R. Hayes. 2012. Mosoco: a mobile assistive tool to support children with autism practicing social skills in real-life situations. In *Proceedings of the SIGCHI Conference on Human Factors in Computing System* (CHI '12), 2589-2598.
9. Tiffany Field. 2002. Infants' need for touch. *Human Development* 45, 2: 100-103.
10. Tiffany Field, Tory Field, Chris Sanders, and Jacqueline Nadel. 2001. Children with autism display more social behavior after repeated imitation sessions. *Autistic Soc* 5, 3: 317-323.
11. Eynat Gal, Nirit Bauminger, Dina Goren-Bar, Fabio Pianesi, Oliviero Stock, Massimo Zancanaro, and Patrice L. (Tamar) Weiss.2009. Enhancing social communication of children with high-functioning autism through a co-located interface. *J Human-Centered Sys* 24, 1: 75–84.
12. Leonardo Giusti, Massimo Zancanaro, Eynat Gal, and Patrice L. (Tamar) Weiss. 2011. Dimensions of collaboration on a tabletop interface for children with autism spectrum disorder. In *Proceedings of the SIGCHI Conference on Human Factors in Computing System* (CHI '11), 3295-3304.
13. Tobias Grosse-Puppendahl, Sebastian Herber, Raphael Wimmer, Frank Englert, Sebastian Beck, Julian von Wilmsdorff, Reiner Wichert, and Arjan Kuijper. 2014. Capacitive near-field communication for ubiquitous interaction and perception. In *Proceedings of the 2014 ACM International Conference on Pervasive and Ubiquitous Computing* (UbiComp '14), 231-242.
14. Keisuke Hachisuka, Yusuke Terauchi, Yoshinori Kishi, Ken Sasaki, Terunao Hirota, Hiroshi Hosaka, Katsuyuki Fujii, Masaharu Takahashi, and Koichi Ito. 2006. Simplified circuit modeling and fabrication of intrabody communication devices. *Sensors and Actuators A: Physical* 130-131: 322-330.
15. Chris Harrison, Hrvoje Benko, and Andrew D. Wilson. 2011. Omnitouch: wearable multitouch interaction everywhere. In *Proceedings of the 24th Annual ACM Symposium on User Interface Software and Technology* (UIST '11) 441-450.
16. Chris Harrison, Desney Tan, and Dan Morris. 2010. Skinput: appropriating the body as an input surface. In *Proceedings of the SIGCHI Conference on Human Factors in Computing System* (CHI '10), 453-462.
17. Mikael Heimann, Keith E. Nelson, Tomas Tjus, and Christopher Gillberg. 1995. Increasing reading and communication skills in children with autism through an interactive multimedia computer program. *J Autism and Developmental Disorders* 25, 5: 459–480.
18. Steve Hodges, Shahram Izadi, Alex Butler, Alban Rrustemi, and Bill Buxton. 2007. Thinsight: versatile multi-touch sensing for thin form-factor display. In *Proceedings of the 20th Annual ACM Symposium on User Interface Software and Technology* (UIST '07), 259-268.
19. Juan Pablo Hourcade, Stacy R. Williams, Ellen A. Miller, Kelsey E. Huebner, and Lucas J. Liang. 2013. Evaluation of tablet apps to encourage social interaction in children with autism spectrum disorders. In *Proceedings of the SIGCHI Conference on Human Factors in Computing System* (CHI '13), 3197-3206.
20. Bibi Huskens, Annemiek Palmen, Marije Van der Werff, Tino Lourens, and Emilia Barakova. 2015. Improving collaborative play between children with autism spectrum disorders and their siblings: the effectiveness of a robot-mediated intervention based on lego therapy. *J Autism and Developmental Disorders* 45, 11: 3746-3755.
21. International Commission on Non-Ionizing Radiation Protection. 1998. Guidelines for limiting exposure to time-varying electric, magnetic, and electromagnetic fields (up to 300 GHz). *Health Physics* 74, 4: 494–522.
22. Ryo Kodama, and Hiroyuki Kajimoto. 2014. EM Package: augmenting robotic intimate space interaction using EM field fluctuation sensing. In *Proceedings of the 33rd Annual ACM Conference Extended Abstracts on Human Factors in Computing Systems* (CHI EA '14), 2061-2066.
23. Henrik Hautop Lund, Thomas Klitbo, and Carsten Jessen. 2005. Playware technology for physically activating play. *Artificial Life and Robotics* 9, 4: 165-174.
24. Nobuyuki Matsushita, Shigeru Tajima, Yuji Ayatsuka, and Jun Rekimoto. 2000. Wearable key: device for personalizing nearby environment. In *Proceedings of the 4th International Symposium on Wearable Computers* (ISWC '00), 119-126.

25. Monique Moore and Sandra Calvert. 2000. Brief report: vocabulary acquisition for children with autism: teacher or computer instruction. *J Autism and Developmental Disorders* 30, 4, 359–362.

26. Dairoku Muramatsu, Takahiko Yamamoto, Kohji Koshiji, and Ken Sasaki. 2012. Study on structural design of transmitter electrodes and surrounding electric field for human body communication based on impedance matching. *J Life Support Engineering* 24, 7: 70-78. (Japanese)

27. Albert Ng, Julian Lepinski, Daniel Wigdor, Steven Sanders, and Paul Dietz. 2012. Designing for low-latency direct-touch input. In *Proceedings of the 25th Annual ACM Symposium on User Interface Software and Technology* (UIST '12), 453-464.

28. Marion V. Panyan. 1984. Computer technology for autistic students. *J Autism and Disorders* 14, 4: 375-382.

29. E. Michelle Pardew and Carol Bunse. 2005. Enhancing interaction through positive touch. *Young Exceptional Children* 8, 2: 21-29.

30. Duck Gun Park, Jin Kyung Kim, Jin Bong Sung, Jung Hwan Hwang, Chang Hee Hyung, and Sung Weon Kang. 2006. Tap: touch-and-play. In *Proceedings of the SIGCHI Conference on Human Factors in Computing System* (CHI '06), 677-680.

31. Esben Warming Pedersen and Kasper Hornbæk. 2014. Expressive touch: studying tapping force on tabletops. In *Proceedings of the SIGCHI Conference on Human Factors in Computing System* (CHI '14), 421-430.

32. Sally J. Rogers, Susan Hepburn, and Elizabeth Wehner. 2003. Parent reports of sensory symptoms in toddlers with autism and those with other developmental disorder. *J Autism and Developmental Disorders* 33, 6: 631-642.

33. Ilya Rosenberg and Ken Perlin. 2009. The unmousepad: an interpolating multi-touch force-sensing input pad. *ACM Transactions on Graphics* 28, 3, 65.

34. Munehiko Sato, Ivan Poupyrev, and Chris Harrison. 2012. Touché: enhancing touch interaction on humans, screens, liquids, and everyday objects. In *Proceedings of the SIGCHI Conference on Human Factors in Computing System* (CHI '12), 483-492.

35. Miriam Silver, and Peter Oakes. 2001. Evaluation of a new computer intervention to teach people with autism or asperger syndrome to recognize and predict emotions in others. *Autism* 5, 3: 299-316.

36. James Keng Soon Teh, Adrian David Cheok, Roshan L. Peiris, Yongsoon Choi, Vuong Thuong, and Sha Lai. 2008. Huggy pajama: a mobile parent and child hugging communication system. In *Proceedings of the 7th international conference on Interaction design and children* (IDC '08), 250-257.

37. Scott D. Tomchek, and Winnie Dunn. 2007. Sensory processing in children with and without autism: a comparative study using the short sensory profile. *American J. Occupational Therapy* 61, 2: 190-200.

38. Lorna Wing. 1996. *The Autistic Spectrum: A Guide for Parents and Professionals.* Constable and Robinson.

39. Thomas Guthrie Zimmerman. 1995. *Personal area networks (PAN): near-field intra-body communication.* Master's thesis. Massachusetts Institute of Technology, Cambridge, MA.

40. Thomas Guthrie Zimmerman. 1996. Personal-area networks: near-field intrabody communication. *IBM Systems J* 35, 3.4: 609-614.

"This is how I want to learn": High Functioning Autistic Teens Co-Designing a Serious Game

Benoît Bossavit
Public University of Navarre
Campus Arrosadia s/n,
31006 Pamplona, Spain
benoit.bossavit@unavarra.es

Sarah Parsons
Southampton Education School
University of Southampton
SO17 1BJ, Southampton, UK
S.J.Parsons@soton.ac.uk

ABSTRACT
This paper presents a project that developed a Serious Game with a Natural User Interface, via a Participatory Design approach with two adolescents with High-Functioning Autism (HFA). The project took place in a highly specialized school for young people with Special Educational Needs (SEN). The teenagers were empowered by assigning them specific roles across several sessions. They could express their voice as user, informant, designer and tester. As a result, teachers and young people developed a digital educational game based on their experience as video gamers to improve academic skills in Geography. This paper contributes by describing the sensitive and flexible approach to the design process which promoted stakeholders' participation.

Author Keywords
Participatory Design; Educational game; Natural User Interface; Autism

ACM Classification Keywords
H.5.2 [Information Interfaces and Presentation]: User Interfaces - User-centered design

INTRODUCTION
Autism Spectrum Disorder (ASD) is diagnosed according to pervasive difficulties in social interaction and communication, coupled with restrictive, repetitive and stereotyped behaviors [1]. ASD affects at least 1 in 68 children in the US [2], with significant social and economic impacts for individuals, families [28], and society [24]. The application of interactive technologies for children with ASD has shown some benefits for supporting learning in the core diagnostic areas of social communication and interaction [37]. Many projects in the field usually prototype activities based on Serious Games (SGs) mechanisms [20] in order to motivate users to improve specific skills. SGs are recognized to be effective mainly due to the engagement and motivation they provide for children [27,39]. SGs developed for children with ASD mainly focus on communication, affective and interaction skills, to the neglect of academic subjects [7]. Although studies present insights of efficacy, there is limited evidence about whether such skills are generalized to real life [38]. This situation could be improved by the integration of these tools at school with greater involvement of, and collaboration with, stakeholders and end-users [31].

CHI'16, May 07-12, 2016, San Jose, CA, USA
© 2016 ACM. ISBN 978-1-4503-3362-7/16/05...$15.00
DOI: http://dx.doi.org/10.1145/2858036.2858322

Participatory Design (PD) seeks to involve representative users in the design and evaluation processes of technological activities [29]. Furthermore, involving children in the design process acknowledges their expertise [13]. The degree of involvement can be organized by role such as user, tester, informant, or design partner [13] and be influenced by the specific needs of those involved [17]. PD can be a very effective process but methods need to be developed and applied sensitively and creatively when seeking to involve children with special educational needs (SEN), such as those with ASD [15]. This is because particular communication needs and preferences of children may make it difficult for children to participate in standard methods such as the use of personas or usability questionnaires [30]. For example, when involving children with autism, researchers have successfully used more visual and structured methods and materials, and provided concrete examples to initiate and prompt ideas rather than relying on abstract concepts for discussion [4,12,26]. Given the need for sensitivity and different methods, research processes should be rigorously reported [14].

This paper presents a project that developed a SG via a PD approach with the 'hardest to reach' teenagers with ASD who had experienced multiple exclusions from previous schools and attended a specialized school for young people with SEN. The contribution of this paper is a description of how teenagers with ASD participated in the co-design of a SG. We also note the novelty of the SG in focusing on academic skills [21,33] using a Natural User Interface (NUI). We focus on the design process that was sustained over a number of weeks, highlighting key elements of the process, using the frameworks [6] and [11]. Below, we summarize the design process, give examples of stakeholders' participation and reflect on how their particular needs were considered.

DESIGN PROCESS

Pre-requisites of the project

NUIs offer natural, intuitive and motion-based ways of communicating [22] that are easily accepted by children [3] and adults [36] with ASD. Additionally, using the body for interaction can improve task engagement [8] and learning [23]. Thus, we wanted to make the body the main element of interaction. The Body Menu (BM) is a technique that uses advantages of proprioception to interact with the software [9]. We used the Kinect [25] since it is affordable, compact and easy to use; all of which are important criteria for planning technology use in schools.

Participants

Key stakeholders were gathered in two groups:

(1) The *designer-team* comprised 4 males with ASD, three of them aged 15 years and one aged 11, the ICT teacher, his teaching assistant and the researcher (first author). However, all the students did not always attend sessions due to timetable clashes. Only two of them (Nathan and Jack (pseudonyms)) participated in most of the sessions.

(2) The *teacher-team* comprised 13 teachers from the same specialized school as the *designer-team*.

Organization

Previous projects involving youth with autism in a PD process organized their sessions based on specific models, such as TEACCH or SCERTS [4,14,26]. Although we did not incorporate these models in their entirety, we drew upon the good practices identified in this research to plan our sessions, for example through using digital prototypes and visual questionnaires within sessions, and clearly communicating the objectives of each session. For each session, the stakeholders flexibly and informally adopted specific roles based on those described in Druin's research [13]: *user, tester, informant* or *design partner*. The overall sequence of the sessions is presented in figure 1. All the sessions were audio-recorded.

Stakeholders' engagement and motivation

Benton and Johnson [6] defined four levels of engagement on tasks and the relationship between adults and children in PD processes; *viz. indirect, feedback, dialogue, and elaboration.* In our study, teachers' engagement was mostly via *feedback,* before and during the PD process. Crucially, teachers provided initial validation for the project by agreeing that the BM could be applied to the subjects taught at the school (e.g. Math, Geography, English) because of the potential to design the surrounding context or task in a flexible way. They also suggested that the NUI could be valuable for supporting children's interaction with each other and motivation to engage with learning materials.

Previous research recommends the use of specific methods to promote participation in PD [4,12,14,26]. Although we provided tools such as visual schedules, and blank paper to sketch ideas or screenshots of the prototype to support further discussion, none of these were used in practice by the teenagers. A visual questionnaire used in the *context setting*, was one of the few tasks which promoted *feedback*; otherwise the tools used by the teenagers were mainly *dialogue*-based.

Foundation (session 1: teacher team)		
Researchers : *facilitators* Teacher team: *informants*	Introduction to the BM with demos [10] Generation of ideas for school use	Digital demo Prompt sheet for feedback

Context setting (session 2: designer team)		
Students: *users, informants* ICT teacher: *motivator* Researcher: *facilitator*	Free play with the Kinect and BM; Narrowing of game ideas for prototype development	Digital demo, visual schedule Visual questionnaire about game preferences

Idea generation (session 3 & 5: designer team)		
Students: *designers* Teacher, researcher: *co-designers*	Generating games ideas for competition and co-operative modes	Demo video Prompt sheets for ideas

Iteration (session 4 & 6: designer team)		
Students: *testers, designers* ICT teacher: *motivator,* Researcher: *facilitator*	Playing with the prototype Feedback on specific features	Digital prototype Screenshots of features

Figure 1: sequence of the PD sessions

Nathan's engagement in the PD process was high and consistently at the *dialogue* level across all sessions. This was unusual but welcome, according to the ICT teacher: *"He is usually shy, stays quiet and sits formally, but today he was very active, thinking on how to improve the interaction - sitting on the table touching his chin, moving all over the room and trying and trying again to discover the limits of the Kinect."*

By contrast, Jack's engagement varied substantially. During the *context setting*, he was mainly distracted by the computer games set in the ICT classroom and almost did not play with the demos. Then, during the first *idea generation* session, Jack's participation was high (*dialogue* level) providing several ideas and taking decisions. However, a 'pivotal moment' appeared during the first *iteration* session when Jack lost the game quickly against Nathan. From then, he was demotivated and withdrew from the project being *indirectly* engaged and mostly distracted by playing PC games. Adults tried to integrate him back to further discussions but he mostly answered the questions by "*I don't mind*" or "*I don't know*".

Ideation

In this project, ideation took place through the roles that each designer-team member adopted within each session. Such roles were informal and flexible but were nevertheless shaped by the planned activities and, therefore, led by the researcher based on session objectives. For example, when the students were asked to play with the Kinect they automatically became *users*; when completing the visual questionnaire about game preferences they were *informants*. Consequently, at many points the process was arguably less reciprocal and so the extent to which the students could be considered *co-designers* is questionable. However, there were also key points in the PD process where the students had more decision-making power i.e. as *designers*, and these points proved to be pivotal in the development of the game.

The first pivotal idea generation occurred between the *context setting* and the *idea generation* session. At the end of the *context setting* session, for homework, students were asked to think about a game which takes advantage of the BM and were reminded that the next session would take place the following week during their ICT class. Subsequently Nathan proposed a game for learning Geography because he struggles in learning that subject. This was later checked and agreed with the other student team members via discussion with the ICT teacher, who then communicated back to the researchers. This plan also aligned with the results of the *foundation* session, where it was suggested that the BM could be applied to any part of the curriculum.

The other key exchanges occurred during the *idea generation* sessions. These sessions were organized as a discussion group around a table. For the first session, Jack was the only student and although he had been given one week to think about the game design, he was not able to give initial ideas. Consequently, we showed a prepared video, inspired by Nathan's Geography idea that illustrated a prototype in which users could select countries by using the BM. This provided a concrete starting point for developing the idea [5,32], and this supported Jack in providing suggestions which were then discussed between the team members.

For both *idea generation* sessions, every new idea was verbally integrated within the scenario by the researcher taking into account the possible causes and consequences it would imply. If the new scenario presented incoherence, the idea was discarded, mostly by the researcher but with consent of all the stakeholders, or modified if the stakeholders considered the initial idea important. If no more ideas were given, the researcher asked questions on game features in order to further develop the concept. All the ideas were represented by hand gestures such as pointing or mimicking or were verbally described. This scenario was frequently repeated to detect incoherence or missing features. This process made the development of ideas for the game transparent for all team members, being clear about what decisions were made and why. We suggest this is one of the reasons why the students' engagement in *idea generation* was so high.

Decision making

Decision-making within PD can be classified in four categories: *values and concept*, *implementation*, *negotiations with the outside world* and *non-decision* [11].

The students proposed initial ideas based on *values and concept* such as suggesting Geography as the topic and deciding on the content of the game. However, the final decisions about the *values* were made by the adults. For instance, after watching the video Jack proposed ideas such as a race of country selections where the first player who answers the teacher's questions wins. This idea was rejected by the teacher as content veto because educational content was provided by the teacher only. Then, Jack proposed a war game by attacking countries via missiles, which was rejected by the researcher as ethical veto. Nonetheless, these adult-led decisions enabled Jack to generate more ideas and propose a questions-based game to 'win' the countries, which formed the starting point of subsequent discussion. Most of the students' decisions were *implementation*-based. For instance, Jack proposed a system of hierarchy within the countries where a weak country could not directly access a stronger one. This was appreciated by Nathan who stated: *"It's a mix of Risk and Civilization, I think it is actually a really good idea ... I think it is a good balance between fun and education"*.

DISCUSSION

PD approaches give 'voice' to stakeholders by providing roles for them in the design process; therefore, it is important to clarify the different roles and contributions made by the participants within such processes. We have used the frameworks of [6,11] to document the specific contributions made by each participant, how this changed over time and who made decisions at different stages of the design. Full details are not possible within the constraints of this paper, but some of the pivotal moments in the design process are highlighted. These moments raise important questions about whether there are boundaries of participation that need to be considered.

Students and the teacher almost exclusively took on *implementation* roles with the researcher mostly taking decisions about *values and concepts*. This reflects that equity on all aspects was not something that could be achieved consistently through the project [32]. However, this confirms that adults also play an important role [6,16]. Not only did adults' interventions impact the design outcomes by having the final decision [35] but this influenced the students' participation in valuable ways by constraining the design space and encouraging them to think again. Nevertheless, the students' ideas were pivotal when making final decisions and even though adults generated some initial ideas such as the first video for inspiration, the main concept was initiated by one of the students based on his self-identified struggle with learning in Geography. This project's PD process shows how each stakeholder contributed their own spheres of expertise to the task: the researcher regarding programming feasibility and the structure of the design sessions; the teacher in relation to pedagogy of the game itself; and the students about gaming features of technologies based on their familiarity with games more widely. This highlights that equity in design partnership is not about all partners sharing all decisions, but about respectfully managing the different expertise that each partner brings [32].

Relatedly, each of the student participants made very different contributions through the design process: one was less engaged in the process, eventually withdrawing, and one was much more dominant, contributing to more decisions. PD is particularly challenging when it involves children with autism because they can be exposed to excessive pressure [14]. Visual schedules [26], visual recap [4] or physical objects [14] have been shown to support the sustained engagement of children. However, the teenagers ignored the visual schedule and recaps via screenshots. Consequently, we used a more informal approach for prompting ideas and gaining feedback, with the support of teachers who knew the students well. This informal approach led to transparency of decision-making within the *ideas generation* sessions. We suggest that this direct tangibility of the 'trace' [34] between participation and design outcomes could be one of the reasons for high engagement of the students during this stage.

Most of the sessions were long (about one hour) which suggests that the engagement was sustained regardless of design stage or tools used. However, we believe that by being flexible about the context of work the engagement of the stakeholders is naturally strengthened because sessions are tailored specifically for their needs, varied moods and interests. This reflection is in line with [16,32] who emphasize the importance of taking a flexible approach. Although a specific period of time was planned for the session, the amount of effective work achieved during that time varied considerably. Pupils needed time to chat, to speak about their interests, and sometimes they were absent from class or school. Due to other timetabling needs, sometimes the amount of time given to the sessions was reduced or simply cancelled shortly before they were due to start. As a result, we suggest that researchers come prepared for this and be willing to respond flexibly. In this case, it was an advantage because it revealed how differently the students responded in individual sessions compared to group sessions. Furthermore, the varying nature of sessions could be considered a strength because the participants took part on their own terms and we aimed to make the process as natural as possible (e.g. using observations and in-class discussion rather than formal questionnaires). Another aspect that requires a flexible approach is the need for children to be able to explore the features of the technology even if it is not the assigned task. For instance, players tended to play with their own projection giving kicks in the air or "dancing". Exploration and testing the technology boundaries remains an important part of young people's experiences with technologies and so we need to accept and allow space for them to do this constructively, not least so that they can be more informed about the technical possibilities in order to be able to think about how aspects of the game can be designed.

It is also important to consider the context for informing and shaping how and where PD processes take place [12]. There are benefits of context-specific design [19] but potential challenges too. In this case, the sessions took place in the school's ICT room. This supported the initial motivation of the students to attend class. For instance, the ICT teacher observed Nathan's desire to attend the sessions and improvements in his behavior after a difficult week. However, the ICT room easily distracted the students because of familiar expectations about activities that took place there e.g. playing *Minecraft*. Indeed, the growing temptation to play PC games rather than focus on the design sessions led to Jack's withdrawal. Therefore, we recommend integrating sessions during teaching lessons but in a room where students cannot be distracted by the other technologies available [12,18].

CONCLUSION

This project shows what is possible when designers work closely with teachers, and students with ASD, in a flexible and open way. We show that previously published techniques were not always successful here and, instead, a much more informal, discussion-based and experiential approach was taken to the design sessions. The context of work was engaging enough to maintain the interest of the teenagers, especially through transparent discussions when ideas were being generated, retained and rejected. This is important because these were teenagers with histories of exclusion and disengagement from school and so it is vital to understand how engagement of these students can be supported more effectively.

This project was conducted in one school with a small number of participants only and so it would be interesting to reproduce the process with several groups of teenagers in different contexts in order to understand how the methodology could be extended and adapted for different groups. Moreover, more formal evaluation of the potential of the game to support learning outcomes in the area of Geography, for students with and without ASD, is needed to provide further validation for the approach and implementation of this project.

ACKNOWLEDGMENTS

We are grateful the New Forest Care of Fawley, UK, and all the children who shared their time in our study. Benoît Bossavit has a grant from the Universidad Pública de Navarra, Spain; this research was conducted while he was on a Visiting Student placement at the University of Southampton, UK.

REFERENCES

1. American Psychiatric Association. (2013). *Diagnostic and statistical manual of mental disorders* (5th ed.). Washington, DC: Author
2. Baio J. (2014) Prevalence of Autism Spectrum Disorder Among Children Aged 8 Years — Autism and Developmental Disabilities Monitoring Network, 11 Sites, United States, 2010 *Surveillance Summaries*. March 28, 2014 / 63(SS02);1-21. http://www.cdc.gov/mmwr/preview/mmwrhtml/ss6302a1.htm?s_cid=ss6302a1_w
3. Bartoli L., Corradi C., Garzotto F., Valoriani M. (2013). Exploring Motion-based Touchless Games for Autistic Children's Learning. *In Proc. of IDC'13, pp.102-111*
4. Benton L., Johnson H., Ashwin E., Brosnan M., Grawemeyer B. (2012). Developing IDEAS: Supporting children with autism within a participatory design team. *In Proc. of CHI'12, pp. 2599-2608*
5. Benton L., Johnson H. (2014). Structured approaches to participatory design for children: can targeting the needs of children with autism provide benefits for a broader child population? *Journal of Instructional Science, 42,* pp. 47-65
6. Benton, L. & Johnson, H. (2015). Widening participation in technology design: a review of the involvement of children with special educational needs and disabilities. *International Journal of Child-Computer Interaction, 3-4,* 23-40
7. Bernardini S., Porayska-Pomsta K., Smith T.J. (2014). ECHOES: An intelligent serious game for fostering social communication in children with autism. *Journal of Information Sciences, 264, pp. 41-60.*
8. Bianchi-Berthouze N., Kim W., Patel D. (2007). Does body movement engage you more in digital game play? And Why? *Affective Computing and Intelligent Interaction, pp. 102-113*. Springer
9. Bossavit B., Marzo A., Ardaiz O. and Pina A. (2014). Hierarchical Menu Selection with a Body-Centered Remote Interface. *Journal of Interacting with Computers, 26(5), pp. 389-402*
10. Bossavit B., Pina, A. (2014). Designing educational tools, based on body interaction, for children with special needs who present different motor skills. *In Proc. of iTAG'14, pp. 63-70.*
11. Bratteteig T., Wagner I. (2012). Disentangling power and decision-making in participatory design. *Participatory Design Conference*
12. Davis M., Dautenhahn K., Powell S., Nehaniv C. (2010). Guidelines for researchers and practitioners designing software and software trials for children with autism. *Journal of Assistive Technologies, 4(1), 38-48*
13. Druin A. (2002). The role of children in the design of new technology. *Behaviour and IT, 21(1), pp. 1-25*
14. Frauenberger C., Good J., Keay-Bright W., Pain H. (2012). Interpreting input from children: a designerly approach. *In Proc. of CHI '12, pp. 2377-2386*
15. Frauenberger C., Good J., Alcorn A., Pain H. (2013). Conversing through and about technologies: Design critique as an opportunity to engage children with autism and broaden research(er) perspectives. *International Journal of Child-Computer Interaction*, 1(2), 38-49
16. Frauenberger C., Good J., Fitzpatrick G., Iversen O.S. (2015) In pursuit of rigour and accountability in participatory design, *International journal of Human.-Computer. Studies. 74,* pp. 93–106
17. Guha M.L., Druin A., Fails J. (2008). Designing With and for Children With Special Needs: an Inclusionary Model. *In Proc. of IDC'08, pp 61–64*
18. Guha M.L., Druin A., Fails J.A. (2013). Cooperative Inquiry revisited: Reflections of the past and guidelines for the future of intergenerational co-design. *Journal of Child-Computer Interaction, 1(1),* pp. 14-23.
19. Harrison, S., Sengers, P., & Tatar, D. (2011). Making epistemological trouble: Third-paradigm HCI as successor science. *Interacting with Computers*, 23(5), 385-392
20. Kapp, K. M. (2012). The gamification of learning and instruction: Game-based methods and strategies for training and education. San Francisco, CA: Pfeifer.
21. Knight V., McKissick B.R., Saunders A. (2013). A review of technology-based interventions to teach academic skills to students with autism spectrum disorder. *Autism and Developmental Disorders, 43(11), pp. 2628-2648*
22. Kynigos C., Smyrnaiou Z., Roussou M. (2010). Exploring rules and underlying concepts while engaged with collaborative full-body games. *In Proc. of IDC'10, pp. 222-225*
23. Latham S.O., Stockman I.J. (2014). Effect of Augmented Sensorimotor Input on Learning Verbal and Nonverbal Tasks Among Children with Autism Spectrum Disorders. *Journal of autism and developmental disorders, 44(6), 1288-1302*
24. Lavelle T. A., Weinstein M. C., Newhouse J. P., Munir K., Kuhlthau K. A., Prosser L. A. (2014). Economic burden of childhood autism spectrum disorders. *Pediatrics*, *133*(3), 520-529
25. Microsoft Kinect. https://dev.windows.com/en-us/kinect. [Accessed on January 2016]

26. Millen L., Cobb S., Patel H. (2011). Participatory design approach with children with autism. *International Journal on Disability and Human Development, 10(4), 289-294*

27. Molins-Ruano P., Sevilla C., Santini S., Haya P.A., Rodríguez P., Sacha G.M. (2014). Designing videogames to improve students' motivation. *Journal of Computers in Human Behavior, 31, pp. 571-579*

28. Montes G., Halterman J. S. (2008). Association of childhood autism spectrum disorders and loss of family income. *Pediatrics*, *121*(4), e821-e826

29. Muller M.J. (2003). chapter Participatory Design: The third Space in HCI. *The Human-Computer Interaction Hand- book, pp. 1051–1068*. Lawrence Erlbaum Associates, London, UK

30. Neale H., Cobb S., Kerr S. (2003). An inclusive design toolbox for development of educational Virtual Environments. Presented at: *Include2003, Royal College of Art*, London, 25-28 March 2003

31. Parsons S., Charman T., Faulkner R., Ragan J., Wallace S., Wittemeyer K. (2013). Commentary – bridging the research and practice gap in autism: The importance of creating research partnerships with schools. *Journal of Autism, 17(3), pp.268-280.*

32. Parsons S., Cobb S. (2014). Reflections on the role of the 'users': challenges in a multi-disciplinary context of learner-centred design for children on the autism spectrum. *International Journal of Research & Method in Education, 37(4)*, 421-441.

33. Pennington, R. C. (2010). Computer-assisted instruction for teaching academic skills to students with autism spectrum disorders: A review of literature. *Focus on Autism and Other Developmental Disabilities*, *25*(4), pp. 239-248

34. Porayska-Pomsta (2015) Processes contra outcomes: On the uncomfortable search for balance between inclusive participation, design and engineering. Presentation at the ESRC seminar series: *Innovative technologies for autism–critical reflections on digital bubbles*. University of Bath, 9th July 2015. http://digitalbubbles.org.uk/wp-content/uploads/2015/09/DigitalBubbleBath-final.compressed.pdf

35. Ruland C.M., Starren J., Vatne T.M. (2008). Participatory design with children in the development of a support system for patient-centred care in pediatric oncology, *Journal of Biomedical Informatics. 41(4),* pp. 624–635

36. Saiano M., Pellegrino L., Casadio M., Summa S., Garbarino E., Rossi V., Dall'Agata D., Sanguineti V. (2015). Natural interfaces and virtual environments for the acquisition of street crossing and path following skills in adults with Autism Spectrum Disorders: a feasibility study. *Journal of NeuroEngineering and Rehabilitation, 12*

37. Wass S.V., Porayska-Pomsta K. (2014) The uses of cognitive training technologies in the treatment of autism spectrum disorders *Autism,* 18(8), 851-871

38. Whyte E.M., Smyth J.M., Scherf K.S. (2014). Designing Serious Game Interventions for Individuals with Autism. *Journal of Autism and Developmental Disorders*

39. Wrzesien M., Raya M.A. (2010) Learning in serious virtual worlds: evaluation of learning effectiveness and appeal to students in the E-Junior project. *Computers & Education 55, pp. 178–187*

Challenging the Car Norm: Opportunities for ICT to Support Sustainable Transportation Practices

Hanna Hasselqvist
KTH Royal Institute of Technology
Stockholm, Sweden
hannaha@kth.se

Mia Hesselgren
KTH Royal Institute of Technology
Stockholm, Sweden
miahes@kth.se

Cristian Bogdan
KTH Royal Institute of Technology
Stockholm, Sweden
cristi@kth.se

ABSTRACT
The use of practices as a unit of analysis has been suggested in order to scale up efforts within sustainable HCI and to shift the focus from changing individual behaviours to supporting transitions at a societal level. In this paper, we take a practice approach to the case of sustainable transportation, and more specifically to car-free transportation. Car use is intertwined in many practices and managing life without a car is difficult, particularly for people in contexts where owning at least one car per family is the norm. We studied three families in Stockholm who replaced their cars with different combinations of light electric vehicles during one year. From the families' experiences, we identified a number of opportunities for designers of interactive technologies to support environmental pioneers in the particular case of car-free living, as well as to support transitions towards sustainable practices in general.

Author Keywords
Sustainable HCI; practice theory; practice-oriented design; transportation.

ACM Classification Keywords
H.5.m. Information interfaces and presentation (e.g., HCI): Miscellaneous.

INTRODUCTION
In the past years sustainable HCI has dealt with numerous interactive technologies aiming to support, inspire or persuade people to adopt pro-environmental behaviours. A central feature in this approach has been eco-feedback: information to users about the impact of their behaviours on the environment. However, sustainable HCI has been criticised for *"turning the problems of environmentalism into questions of personal moral choice"* [8:8], focusing too much on individual consumers [7] and using persuasive technology with a narrow focus on individual behaviours [5]. The same authors see opportunities in supporting environmental movements [8], addressing collective, regional and national levels [7] and shifting the focus from behaviours to practices [5].

CHI'16, May 07-12, 2016, San Jose, CA, USA
ACM 978-1-4503-3362-7/16/05.
http://dx.doi.org/10.1145/2858036.2858468

Figure 1. Examples of the light electric vehicles used in the study: a scooter (top left), a four-wheeled motorcycle (top right), a box bike (bottom left) and a bike (bottom right).

The use of practices as a broader unit of analysis is increasing within HCI in general, although the practice approach is often not explicitly stated [17]. In this paper, we explore how a practice approach can be used to inform sustainable HCI for the specific case of support for sustainable transportation practices, with a focus on car-free transportation.

Cities have for many years been designed with the car as the principal and ideal mode of transportation. However, with local issues of congestion and pollution, and global challenges such as climate change and peak oil, a change is needed in how cars are used. In Sweden, about 60% of all commute trips are made by car [27] (which can be compared to the US where the car is used for almost 90% of the commute trips [9]). Car use is lower in metropolitan municipalities in Sweden (Stockholm, Göteborg and Malmö), with about one third of the commute trips made by car and another third by public transport. Stockholm, with nearly 1 million inhabitants in the city and about 2 million living in the region, has a well functioning public transport infrastructure with buses, commuter trains, trams, boats and a subway system stretching from the city and out to the suburbs and neighbouring cities. Several initiatives have been carried out to reduce car traffic in the region, such as introduction of congestion charges for cars and investments in extended public transport infrastructure.

However, owning a car is in Stockholm still a norm in many contexts, particularly for families with children, and it may indeed be challenging to manage life without a car, despite good public transportation and existing cycling infrastructure. In the project *A Car-free Year*, we have studied the changes in the practices of three families with children, living in Stockholm, when they replaced their car with light electric vehicles for one year. The project supported the families throughout this change by storing their car for the year and providing rental agreements for the light electric vehicles: scooters, four-wheeled motorcycles, box bikes and bikes (see Figure 1 for examples of the vehicles). By following the families during the year we have learned about challenges, as well as positive aspects, of living car-free. We analysed this radical, and very local, change with the aim of identifying ways that design and ICT can support change, also on a societal level.

In this paper we first present a case study of the families' car-free year, including their motivations, challenges and changes in practices. Secondly, we use a practice theory lens to analyse the positive and negative experiences associated with the families' new practices. Finally, we present a number of opportunities for ICT and services to build on these positive experiences or overcome negative experiences in order to support the specific case of sustainable transportation practices, as well as transitions towards other sustainable practices.

RELATED WORK AND THEORETICAL FRAMEWORK

The widespread use of cars has changed how cities are built and citizens have, to a great extent, become dependent on cars to move around between home, work and various leisure activities: *"[the car] forces people to juggle fragments of time so as to deal with the temporal and spatial constraints that it itself generates"* [28:4]. Habits play a central role in the choice of transportation mode and information about alternatives may not be enough for people to change their habits [29]. To break the car habit and decrease the use of cars in city centres, congestion charges have been introduced, and successfully reduced traffic, for example in Stockholm [2] and London [23]. While the overall effect of the congestion charges was positive, such a change negatively affected some citizens and to a great extent influenced their practices [23].

There are many factors influencing our transportation choices and numerous studies of how this process can be supported by ICT, particularly in the form of travel planning information, to encourage more sustainable travelling. It has been suggested that travel planning tools should provide information not only about time and cost of different alternatives, but also about convenience, comfort and privacy [6]. Personal recommendations that nudge people to choose transportation modes or routes with lower carbon emissions have also been proposed [3]. A review of existing travel planning tools found opportunities for improvement by providing: information about non-travel options (e.g. virtual meetings and e-shopping), information about ridesharing options and easy access to online payment and tickets [13]. Eco-feedback has also been explored as a means for influencing travel behaviours, for example in a study of the system UbiGreen [10] where some of the "least green" users thought that the feedback helped them to make more eco-friendly transportation choices. Additional factors the users believed would encourage them to make more green trips were: reliable transportation, financial incentives and more knowledge about alternatives. UbiGo [24] is another travel information system that, during a six-month field study, provided a travel service for multimodal travelling together with rewards for green trips. The UbiGo study found that perceived benefits in terms of convenience and cost were more important for long-term engagement than the rewards for green trips.

While travel information and services tend to focus on individual choices, there are also factors beyond the individual that are important to take into account. Specifically for sustainable transportation, it has been suggested that HCI should, in addition to personal aspects, also consider social values (e.g. environmental concern), societal factors (e.g. financial situations) and structural factors (e.g. infrastructure) [20]. Proposed approaches are designing for: entertainment, education, community support and political activism. Social norms, for example related to being on time and being a good parent, have also been identified as important influences on travel practices [19].

In order to increase the understanding of the complexity of what influences how we do things and to create support for more sustainable practices, practice theory and practice-oriented design have been proposed as ways forward [16, 18, 21, 25]. Such approaches have been investigated for energy related practices such as doing laundry [12], bathing [14] and thermal comfort [15].

Practices are constituted by elements that can be divided into *material*, *meaning* and *competence* [22]. *Material* refers to the technologies and objects involved in a practice, *meaning* refers to shared symbolic meanings and ideas of a practice, and *competence* refers to knowledge and skills used in a practice. Shove et al. suggest that

	Housing & area	Family members	Electric vehicles (monthly fee)	Previous car use	Distance to main activities
Family 1	Detached house in suburb	Mother, father, three children (aged 8-15)	1 four-wheeled motorcycle (€240) 1 scooter (€80) 1 bike (€50)	Daily for work (mother). Regularly for family activities, occasionally for renovations.	Work: 4/20 km Sports activities: 2-12 km Visit family: 6/50 km
Family 2	Apartment in suburb	Mother, three children (aged 11-13)	1 two-wheeled box bike (€70) 1 bike (owned by the family)	Regularly for evening and weekend activities. Visit summer house during holidays.	Work: 7 km Sports activities: 2-50 km Visit family: 470 km Summer house: 480 km
Family 3	Apartment in centre	Mother, father, three children (aged 2-9)	1 three-wheeled box bike (€70) 1 two-wheeled box bike (€70)	Occasionally for evening and weekend activities. Visit summer house during weekends and holidays.	Work: 7/3 km Sports activities: 1-11 km Visit family: 1/170 km Summer house: 70 km

Table 1. The families who participated in the car-free year.

"opportunities for effective intervention may lie in the generation and circulation of elements of which variously sustainable practices are made" [23:472]. This approach has been built upon and adapted for HCI by Mose Entwistle et al. [18], who presented the *Contextual Wheel of Practice* as a framework for understanding practices within HCI research. We will detail how we applied practice theory to our analysis in the next section.

METHODS

In the car-free year study we have combined participatory action research with a practice-oriented design approach. With this intervention "in the wild", we as investigators have participated in the study at the same time as the participants have been investigators; *"as analysts of their own and others' practices"* [4]. Our participants have been encouraged to reflect throughout the study, while the project team helped the families by providing car-free expert advice. This intervention has been the first phase of a practice-oriented design process, aiming to increase the understanding of car-free transportation practices in order to inform design for sustainable transportation.

To recruit families for the car-free year, we advertised a call for participants on the project's Facebook page and in Facebook flows targeting people with an interest in sustainability. The call included three requirements to qualify for the study: the family had to live within the urban region of Stockholm, there had to be at least one child living with the family and they had to currently own a car. The reason for selecting families with cars, rather than families who were already car-free, is that we were interested in understanding the changes required to adapt to car-free living. This approach is different from studying people who already have a certain lifestyle, such as the "simple living families" in [11].

We received 74 applications and, after interviews with 11 families, 3 families were selected for the car-free year. To ensure richness in the collected data we selected families to cover both households in apartments and in detached houses, single parents and two-parent families, families living in the city centre and in the suburbs, and families with young children and with teenagers. There was also a mix of ways in which the car was previously used (see Table 1). The differences between the families were reflected in the challenges they met, and particularly the type of housing and the age of the children came with different challenges. Also the location of work, sports activities, friends, family and summer houses affected the families' car-free experiences.

There were also similarities between the families: all of the adults had university degrees, lived in middle-income areas and were well aware of sustainability issues. They were active families, with particularly the children attending, and needing transportation to, different sports activities (e.g. handball, football, athletics and martial arts). Other activities where the car was used included shopping, visiting friends and family, travelling to the summer house, and going on ski trips and other holiday trips. All three families lived a few minutes walk from the nearest subway station and they already before the study used public transport for some of their activities.

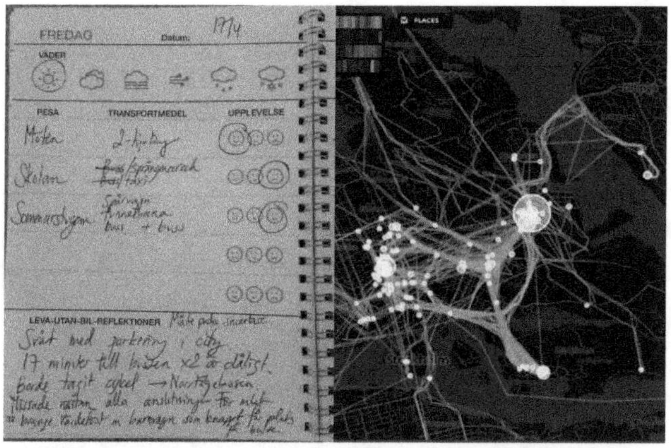

Figure 2. Trigger material used in the interviews: a trip diary (left) and a visualisation of trips colour coded by transportation mode (right).

The families' car-free year started in October 2014. The project provided, for a monthly fee paid by the participants, the families with the light electric vehicles of their choice (see Table 1). Included in the fee were maintenance of the vehicles and expert advice on appropriate equipment and other practical aspects of using the vehicles. During the year the families did not have access to their own car but they were allowed, if needed, a maximum of 24 car trips by taxi or using a borrowed or rented car (at their own cost). We conducted monthly interviews with the parents from September 2014 until May 2015, and final interviews in September 2015. The interviews mainly took place in the families' homes. One of the interviews had specific questions for the children, who joined their parents for a part of the interview. Each interview lasted for 1-1.5 hours, with one main interviewer in charge of the interview and one note-taker making detailed notes. Audio from the interviews was recorded to support the notes. Prior to the interviews the parents had a "log week" when they noted down all their trips, their experiences of the trips and other reflections on car-free living (see Figure 2). In addition, during all weeks the parents used the smartphone app *Moves*[1] that automatically tracked their trips. This data was visualised on a map with the connected app *Move-o-scope*[2] (see Figure 2). The trip visualisations and the notes from the log week were used as probes in the interviews. Other such probes were: a 24-car-trips card where the families registered any car trips they made, photos they posted on the project's public Facebook page and other photos they had taken related to their car-free life. The interviews were complemented with observations of practical arrangements for the vehicles and their charging, of associated equipment and of other physical manifestations of the new practices.

[1] http://www.moves-app.com

[2] http://move-o-scope.halftone.co/

The application forms, notes and photos from interviews and meetings, log material and posts by the families and other visitors on the project's Facebook page have been analysed with a practice theory lens. The first step in the analysis was to gain a broad understanding of the elements of the families' new practices and whether they contributed to positive or negative experiences. We used the four categories proposed in the *Contextual Wheel of Practice* (COWOP) [18] to structure the different types of elements. The COWOP categories correspond to Shove et al.'s [22] division of elements, but the names differ: *meaning* becomes *societal structure* in COWOP, *competence* becomes *the individual*, and *material* is split into *near materiality* and *infrastructure*. This distinction between *near materiality* and *infrastructure* is the main inspiration we have taken from COWOP. In transportation, infrastructure is a dominant topic for example in political proposals and discussions in media. This was also reflected in discussions with the families and within the project team, but the distinction helped to not forget elements of near materiality. Although COWOP describes *near materiality* and *infrastructure* as categories of "physical" elements (the technologies, objects and infrastructures involved in a practice), we decided to include also services in these categories, since we found services to be an important part of life without a car.

As a second step in the analysis, we focused on the role ICT and connected services played in the new emerging practices and on the potential roles for ICT in supporting sustainable transportation practices.

ELEMENTS OF A CAR-FREE LIFE

This section introduces stories and examples that illustrate the most central elements of the families' car-free lives, divided into: motivations for abandoning the car, new practices, planning, the norm of the car, practical challenges, emotional challenges and benefits of not owning a car. As the car-free year project has been presented nationwide in various media, we are protecting the privacy of the families by not revealing which family each story comes from. However, we have provided relevant contextual information about the respective family whenever needed.

Motivations for abandoning the car

The applicants to the car-free year had many different reasons for wanting to get rid of the car, and the motivations were both practical and emotional. Practical motivations included saving money, doing more physical exercise and not having to worry about maintenance of the car, while emotional reasons were mainly related to concern about the environment and the coming generations future lives in cities.

Environmental concern was by far the most common motivation given and applicants often listed other things they did for the environment: buying organic food, reducing their meat consumption, recycling or having energy efficient homes. Many applicants expressed that this is not enough and they wanted to push themselves to do more. While the car is a norm, it also clashes with ideals of having a sustainable lifestyle, which motivated some applicants: *"we are members of the green party and are ashamed to have such an old car but we haven't found any good alternative"* and *"we are environmental geeks who are ashamed of our car"*.

Social responsibility was also given as a reason for wanting to get rid of the car. Some applicants thought it is everyone's responsibility to contribute to a better world, particularly related to life in cities: *"We need to change our behaviour if we are going to continue living in big cities"*. Applicants were also thinking about their children's future. A family with three-year-old twins wanted to participate in the project *"to contribute to a cleaner world we can give to our children"*.

The motivations of the three families selected for the project were very much in line with the environmental and societal concerns described above. Two of the families were also motivated by the opportunity to inspire others to find alternatives to owning cars. These concerns are elements on both an individual and a societal level; they personally cared about doing good for the environment at the same time as they were bothered by the car norm that is dominant in many parts of society. In addition, one family not only had environmental concerns, but also a wish to scale down and live a life with fewer things. One family particularly disliked the hassle of parking and maintaining the car and also gave economic reasons for wanting to not own a car. This motivation concerns the practicalities around the car and can be seen as belonging to elements of *near materiality*.

New practices

During the car-free year, the light electric vehicles became significant elements in the new practices of the three families. However, these vehicles alone could not compensate for the absence of the car. For longer trips, the families travelled by train and they adapted their holiday plans to their new situation. There was an increase in online shopping, which replaced the need of taking the car for buying groceries or larger items needed for the household: *"We have ordered everything online. This works well as long as you don't forget something."* From a practice perspective, the tools and services for online shopping with home delivery can be considered elements of *near materiality* that facilitate car-free living.

For the children, the car-free year led to more responsibility of walking, biking or travelling by public transport by themselves. These practices depended on elements related to the existing infrastructure and well working and reliable public transportation, widely used by different groups of people, in Stockholm. Walking, biking, running and using public transport also

Figure 3. Photo posted on the project's Facebook page by one of the families who bought a second-hand table and took it home with their box bike.

complemented the use of the electric vehicles for the parents. When nothing else worked, such as when going home late at night after a company party or when the toilet broke down and they urgently needed a new one, they made use of taxi services or borrowed cars. The families sometimes also skipped visiting friends or going to activities at places that were difficult to get to by the electric vehicles or by public transport.

For all the families, the car-free year led to significantly more biking: to work, to school and to evening and weekend activities. The families also, to a greater extent than before, biked during the cold and dark winter months. To overcome the barrier of winter biking, and to make it a new practice, the participants had to acquire knowledge about what equipment to use to make it feel safe and more comfortable. Examples of means they used to increase their knowledge were: a Facebook group for box bikes, advice in bike stores and discussions with experts tied to the project. In this way, the combination of individual elements (the new knowledge) and material elements, such as winter tires, good clothes and strong bike lights, enabled the new practice.

For the family with younger children, the electric box bikes worked particularly well as a replacement for the car. They found that the box bike had the car's flexibility; it leaves when one wants it to and takes the rider to the exact destination of their choice. Compared to public transport, the box bike was also much more convenient for "serial activities", such as when picking up the children from school, dropping off one child at a friend's place, then stopping by the grocery store, before finally going home. In addition, the entire family of two adults and three children could fit on the three-wheeled box bike, which the family named "the truck", and the electricity made the load manageable. The storage capacity was also welcome when buying second hand furniture (see Figure 3).

Planning

Irrespective of transport mode or trip purpose, the new practices required considerable amounts of planning. For occasions when a car was needed, such as when transporting furniture to the summer house or for renovating at home, the families tried to coordinate activities and use the car for many different things. While they previously might have taken the car the first time they came to think of something they needed, they now thought twice and waited for several reasons and a possibility for coordinating trips, before actually using a car. Going on holidays without a car required planning in terms of choice of destination, route planning and finding out how to manage the luggage. This planning was not only focused on time aspects, but also on costs. When fuel cost was compared to the cost of train tickets for the entire family, the train was sometimes perceived as an expensive option. However, the fuel cost is only a part of the actual cost of owning and using a car, and even though the family members were aware of this, they tended to forget it when evaluating different transportation options.

The trips within the city, including the daily trips, also required planning. The families had to find suitable routes for the different types of vehicles since, for example, the four-wheeled motorcycle was not comfortable to drive on highways and they wanted to avoid biking with children on city streets without dedicated bike lanes or with too much traffic. They also needed to plan their trips by public transport and to learn about different options. As support for these decisions they used different types of digital travel planning tools. Such tools can be regarded as *near materiality* elements, closely linked to elements of *infrastructure*. These tools also have implications on the *individual's knowledge*, since they helped the families learn about new ways of getting around. However, the planning was not only related to route, time or transportation mode, but also, for example, to ensuring that the children had something to eat between school and after-school activities, to charging the vehicles and taking the charger to work if necessary, and to taking useful equipment for the trip, such as warm and protective clothes and gloves when biking in cold or wet weather.

With the car gone, the families could no longer use it to compensate for poor planning or to manage unexpected events. Previously, the car was not only used when it was the most advantageous option but also for occasions when the original plan failed: when a child missed the bus to an activity, when the family was too late for walking or when the weather was bad. In this sense, the car was associated with flexibility. However, the lack of flexibility also turned out to have positive sides. One family found that their trips became less stressful when they did not have a backup option: *"it saves time and is more efficient to not have that flexibility"*.

The norm of the car

Owning a car and not owning a car can both be provocative. Challenging the car norm can be sensitive in some groups, while other groups have strong norms linked to sustainable lifestyles and find car-free life perfectly normal. Already when the call for participants was posted on Facebook, we received comments that were strongly against the idea of not owning a car as well as comments that did not see any problem in being car-free.

Examples of pro-car posts were: *"Of course we can manage one year without a car. We can also manage one year without a job, without an apartment, without a phone, without tv, without meeting family and friends. The question is why one would make it so hard on purpose."* and *"I don't go anywhere without a car. Could maybe consider going by bike if it wasn't for the wholesome label that comes with the bike. It almost makes me puke."*

Examples of comments in favour of not owning cars were: *"Of course we live without a car. We are modern people, right? Walk to kindergarten, dog daycare and work. Or bike sometimes. If we need a car we rent it."* and *"It has not been a problem at all to be extremely mobile, with family and without a car. Would rather want to try if I really would stand a year with a car and all misery that brings in terms of high costs, increased travel time, traffic jams, hunt for parking space, damage to the environment and worsened health."*

The three families in the project were all aware of that their participation in the car-free year project could be provocative and they were careful not to judge car owners. While they still thought there is a lot of unnecessary car use in cities, they also recognised that there are situations where cars are necessary, such as when you live or work in places with poor public transport or in the countryside. Nevertheless, they sometimes got the impression that relatives, friends and colleagues who own cars felt criticised by their participation in the project: *"They [some car owners] cannot see that society could be better by people living car-free. They think society should adapt to make it easier for cars to get around."* To make their car-free lifestyle less provoking in the contexts where the car was a norm, one family stressed that they were part of a *research* project. Another family said they joined the project for economic reasons: *"I have to say that I need to live car-free because it is too expensive [to have a car]. This argument is easily bought. That it would be for environmental reasons is really provoking."*

Practical challenges

One of the major challenges for the three families in the car-free year was related to taking the children to various activities, particularly sports practices. Another significant challenge for two of the families was to get to their summer houses and, once there, to do grocery shopping, to get to activities, and to visit family and friends nearby. In addition, two of the families had renovation plans already when the project started and had to figure out ways of managing that with minimal use of cars, which was not always easy: *"Renovating is difficult. It is really hard if you are not a builder to plan exactly what and when things are needed [to know what to order online]. It is frustrating and lead times are long."* The renovations also led to a need of transporting old stuff *away*, which was more difficult and more expensive than getting things delivered *to* the home. For the families living in apartment buildings it was easier to deal with bulky waste and recycling, since that was provided in the houses or close to the buildings. However, for the detached housing areas and the summer houses, where owning a car is a norm, it was considerably more challenging to handle recycling, bulky waste and garden waste without a car.

The challenges increased during the winter season: the families needed good clothes for cycling, the bikes needed winter tires and strong bike lights, and the parents were worried about driving the vehicles in snowy or icy weather. Using the vehicles in the city, particularly the box bikes, was sometimes also challenging. Even though there are bike lanes in many places in and around the city, not all of them were broad enough for the box bikes and poor maintenance made some bike lanes difficult to use. These issues often forced the families to ride the box bikes on the roads with the cars, where they felt out of place and vulnerable: *"Sometimes you feel a bit like you are in the face of car drivers. Like you're making a statement. Sometimes you are in the way: not being able to drive that fast and being rather wide. You are somewhat unpredictable because they are simply not used to seeing such a vehicle."*

Emotional challenges

Many of these challenges of how to solve practical matters were expected beforehand, but the challenges also turned out to have more emotional aspects that the families realised along the project. Without the car, one family could no longer help a grandmother with shopping and transportation to family gatherings. Instead, other relatives had to take the grandmother more often, and the family was unhappy about not being able to help as usual. In another family, one of the teenagers considered quitting a sports activity that required one hour of travelling with public transport each way, and the parents felt bad about not being able to help with driving.

One family was concerned that other parents would consider it bad parenting to let the children travel alone by public transport: *"with the lifestyle they have, you just don't do it that way [let the children go by public transport]"*. At the same time, the family did not want to always be the one asking other parents in the sports teams for rides. However, in one team this was less of a problem since the team used an online tool for ridesharing, which was part of the process of signing up for activities: *"They register to matches through their website. You fill in if you're going to attend, if you have car or not and if you have space in the car. So getting a lift with someone is resolved incredibly naturally in this team."* In addition, not having a car made the families more dependent on relatives and friends for the few occasions when they needed a car, and one family pointed out the negative feeling of owing someone after borrowing their car.

These feelings are elements of the *individual's values* of being able to help as well as elements of norms and social values. The participants felt a sense of not fitting in and following the norms, since they always had to ask for help, without being able to offer help.

Benefits of not owning a car

The car-free year not only brought challenges, but also many positive experiences. The family members valued spending time with each other, and the increased use of train, instead of car, for longer trips provided new opportunities for this. On the train all family members could enjoy the trip, since none of the parents had to focus on driving. One family also found that travelling by train, and sitting facing each other, encouraged more conversations compared to travelling by car: *"You rarely sit together the whole family for over two hours and talk. It is not the same when you are going in a car because then the children listen to [music on] their mobile phones."* The box bike parents had similar experiences when biking with their children sitting in the box in front of them.

Another clear benefit for the parents who biked was daily exercise, which they otherwise found difficult to fit into their busy schedules. With the bike they also got to spend more time outdoors and they enjoyed the fresh air and sunlight. These are all aspects of biking that contribute to defining the bike as a healthy means of transportation. In addition, the families could choose more scenic routes with the bike than by car and enjoy the trip through a positive experience of nature.

Biking was also given as an example of how to get to know a city better and to "make it your own". Even though lack of knowledge of the city was a barrier to travelling by bike to new places, biking was at the same time perceived as a good way of extending the knowledge. The parents were particularly keen on that their children should learn to find their way, both for practical reasons but also for them to feel "grown-up" and to feel that the city is "their city".

POSITIVE AND NEGATIVE EXPERIENCES OF THE NEW PRACTICES

Just as a car can be used in many different practices, not owning a car affects numerous practices. The families have changed how they go to work, run errands, go on holidays and spend time with family and friends. Different practices can also have shared elements [22], which we have seen for example in "good planning skills" being part of several practices and in the norm "not having a car is odd/extreme" being present in many different situations.

Social Structure (Norms and shared ideas)	Infrastructure (Infrastructure and services in the city)
(+) Biking is healthy (4) (+) Owning a car in a big city is not "green" (3) (-) A sustainable lifestyle is odd/extreme (-) Not having a car is odd/extreme (1, 2, 3, 4) (-) Asking for help leads to owing someone (3) (-) Young children should not travel alone with public transport	(+) Frequent public transport (+) Easy access to household waste recycling systems (+) Dedicated bike lanes (-) Unreliable or crowded public transport (-) Poorly planned/maintained bike lanes (1) (-) Poor access to recycling systems for bulky waste (2)
The Individual (Skills, values and knowledge)	**Near Materiality (Technologies, stuff and services)**
(+) Good planning skills (+) Caring about the environment (+) Wish to scale-down (+) (-) Knowledge of the city (4) (+) (-) Valuing spending time with the family (4) (-) Lack of knowledge of equipment for winter biking (1)	(+) Appropriate biking equipment (1) (+) Facebook community for box bikes (1) (+) Online system for ridesharing (3) (+) Online services for shopping (2) (+) Home delivery services (2) (+) (-) Light electric vehicles (1, 3, 4) (+) (-) Travel planning tools (1, 4)

Table 2. Elements of car-free practices that the families experienced as positive (+) or negative (-). The numbers next to the elements indicate which of the design opportunities below these elements are parts of.

During the car-free year the families experienced some elements of the new practices as positive while other elements were related to negative experiences, see Table 2 for an overview. The overview is in no way a complete picture of all elements involved in all transportation related practices of the families – that would be practically impossible. Instead, we selected elements that occurred frequently or that we found particularly interesting or inspiring for future design work.

We chose to highlight the positive and negative experiences related to the elements since we believe that this is useful not only to understand the practices of the three families in the study, but also to investigate how other people may be recruited to, or deterred from, sustainable transportation practices. Many of the elements can, in different contexts, be either positive or negative, depending on the quality of the element in the specific context. Good knowledge or well working infrastructure was related to positive experiences, while lack of knowledge or poor infrastructure led to negative experiences. For the analysis we chose to include the most dominant characteristic of the element in the context of the three families' practices in Stockholm. In addition, some elements, such as the light electric vehicles, were associated with both positive and negative experiences, since they on one hand worked very well for the families in many situations but on the other hand added new challenges that the families found frustrating.

It is clear that many elements of transportation practices are not directly in the hands of HCI. Nevertheless, we believe there are opportunities for HCI to support change on a societal level, as well as there are risks of reinforcing unsustainable norms, by the way technologies and services are designed.

OPPORTUNITIES FOR DESIGN AND ICT TO SUPPORT SUSTAINABLE (TRANSPORTATION) PRACTICES

ICT and related services were very present in the *near materiality* of the families' new practices. We also found examples of how ICT supported the families in overcoming negative experiences on societal, infrastructural and individual levels. In addition, we identified opportunities for ICT to further strengthen elements related to positive experiences or to challenge elements that may deter people from adopting sustainable transportation practices. In Table 2 it is indicated which the key elements are for each of the design opportunities in this section.

From our case we have also identified a few more general themes that may inspire designers concerned with sustainability but not necessarily with transportation. Firstly, we believe that design work aiming at supporting transitions towards sustainable practices should be characterised by *designing at the tension between the odd and the norm.* When designing something for "the odd" there is a risk of further distancing it from the norm, which may work against the goal of making the odd more mainstream. Secondly, we want to re-emphasise, and give examples of, what many others already have proposed: *designing with a focus beyond the individual.* Finally, we see opportunities for sustainable HCI in *designing for alternatives to resource optimisation,* to highlight values that are important for sustainable practices. These themes are further discussed below through the example of transportation.

(1) Supporting odd types of vehicles
Many of the challenges the families faced with their new vehicles were related to the city infrastructure not being adapted to light electric vehicles; the families were the odd ones on the roads and in the parking spaces. Just as bicycles were strange vehicles when they were introduced two centuries ago, so are box bikes, electric bikes and other light electric vehicles today.

In transportation, ICT already to some extent supports sustainable choices, for example through travel planning tools that suggest suitable bike routes. However, the information such tools provide may be insufficient or inadequate for electric bikes or box bikes. Even though a box bike is per definition a bike, it has very different properties than a regular bike, mainly due to its size and shape. For example, a bike route that works well for a regular bike may be too narrow for a box bike, and obstacles such as roadwork pose a greater challenge for a larger bike. Consequently, travel information for box bike users could be improved by including if the bike road is "box bike size" and if there is ongoing roadwork.

Another aspect travel planning tools for electric bike users could capture better is the different experience the electricity provides. With an electric bike it is possible to travel faster and at a more constant speed compared to a regular bike, even if the route is hilly, which reduces travel times and the cyclist gets less sweaty. Since convenience has been identified as an important factor for transportation choices [24], such benefits should be highlighted in the design of travel planners. There are examples of dedicated travel planners for electric bikes, which for example take weather conditions into account [26]. However, when designing for the tension between the odd and the norm it becomes important to integrate such solutions with mainstream travel planning, not only to make electric bike users feel less odd but also to challenge current transportation norms and make the benefits of the alternative visible also to people who are currently choosing "normal" modes of transportation.

Specific information for odd travel modes can be provided through online communities, such as the Facebook group for box bikes that one of the families followed. Apart from practical tips, these types of groups can also contribute to a community feeling that encourages use of the specific mode of transportation [1]. From a practice perspective, the Facebook group both addresses elements at the individual level, by increasing knowledge that facilitates the use of the box bikes, and elements at the societal level, by providing a forum that challenges the car norm and suggests alternatives. Such communities could be more easily created and spread by involving actors "beyond the individual". Based on our data we see opportunities in engaging workplaces, schools and sports teams as creators and facilitators of such norm-challenging digital forums, as these are situations where transportation discussions often occurred and the oddities were exposed (and also spread). This knowledge exchange could be combined with services, such as joint bike maintenance or the provision of light electric vehicle leasing contracts by workplaces.

(2) Providing services for transporting stuff *away*
Transportation is not only about moving people between places and activities, but also about moving all sorts of stuff. Without the car, the families changed their shopping practices and in many cases ICT, in the form of online services for shopping, was a part of the new practices. Home delivery services were often free or provided for a small fee, which further enabled online shopping.

While the online shopping providers did not let the families' lack of transportation get in the way of shopping, the families faced greater challenges when things needed to be transported away from the home, particularly for the case of disposing of bulky waste. There are online services for ordering or coordinating such transportations, but they are less accessible and not as integrated into current practices as home delivery services. Renting a car or buying services to have something transported away may also seem expensive, particularly when it is compared to home delivery prices, where the actual delivery cost often is hidden in the cost of the product that is being bought and not explicitly labelled as delivery.

One existing services for coordinating transports is provided by the company Baghitch[3]. It acts as a matchmaker between people who are driving and have space for taking something in the car, and people who need to transport stuff. However, to become more accessible such services need to be better integrated into the situations where transportation is needed and may need to involve other actors than individuals. In the case of disposal of bulky waste, the City of Stockholm, which provides the physical infrastructure for recycling, could complement its recycling service with digital services for coordinating transports, and at the same time challenge the norm that all households in areas with detached houses have access to cars. ICT coordination of transporting stuff away could also be designed for delivery companies or construction workers who already transport stuff as part of their business.

(3) Facilitating helping
One barrier to not owning a car is the norm in Western societies that asking for help leads to owing someone. Lately we have seen an increasing number of ICT enabled services that aim to facilitate the sharing of for example cars or homes between strangers. However, these

[3] www.baghitch.com

typically include predefined rules and clear transactions (the user pays for the service) and no one is left in debt. In our study we found an interesting case in supporting people in being helped with things they could not manage without a car, but by friends, colleagues or other acquaintances.

One example of current technology, facilitating this type of helping between people already acquainted, is the system for signing up for sports activities and coordinating ridesharing, which was used by a sports team of one of the car-free families. By encouraging people to offer help with rides, the system partly hides the oddness of not having a car and makes it easier for car-free families to get a ride to the activities. Another opportunity in the design of ICT solutions is to turn around the roles of the helper and the person being helped. It is questionable whether it is always the person not owning a car who is helped by a car owner, when borrowing a car or getting a ride. A person without a car could, for example, help a car owner to get to work faster in cities with dedicated lanes for car-pooling. Car-free people can also help car owners to lower their carbon footprint (from the embodied emissions of the production and transportation of the car), and perhaps also reduce any associated feelings of guilt for owning a car in a city.

There is, however, a risk that such technologies reinforce the role of the car as the normal mode of transportation. In the case of the ride-sharing tool for sports teams it also means that families without cars cannot contribute to solving the team's transportation needs, and in the long run they might still be considered the odd ones. To better balance the tension between the odd and the norm, the ride-sharing tool could include also options to offer transportation help for example by taking the children by public transport or by box bike. We believe that this tension between the odd and the norm, and the risk of unintentionally reinforcing norms, is important to consider also for other sharing services that aim to support sustainable practices.

(4) Optimising beyond time

The families' choice of not owning a car was often questioned by other families who wondered how they had time for all the hassle. While many trips by public transport or bike are faster, or equally fast, as the same trip by car, there are still many situations where the car clearly is the fastest option to move from one place to another. Time, as in number of minutes, is also very dominant information in travel planning tools [13]. However, when optimising primarily for time, other values that are important elements in sustainable transportation practices are neglected.

If certainty of the travel duration is included as optimisation criterion (higher for bikes than for cars due to unforeseen traffic jams), cars may not be necessarily so attractive. The families also mentioned other, more subtle, criteria: getting physical exercise and being outdoors in the fresh air and sunlight, being with the family without having to focus on driving, sitting face-to-face and talking while travelling, driving a scenic path which can only be approached by bike and getting to know the city better. Finally, our participants suggested that time optimisation and too much flexibility may lead to stress: leaving by car for a long trip "as soon as possible" may be more stressful than taking a train at a certain time.

These are all opportunities for ICT and travel services. Currently in travel planning tools, it is not at all visible that replacing a 20-minutes car trip with a 40-minutes bike trip means "winning" 40 minutes of exercise, sunlight or increased knowledge of the city, instead of "losing" 20 minutes in the car. There might also be possibilities of enhancing positive experiences of sustainable transportation by linking travel planning tools to other services, such as fitness tools or time reporting systems at workplaces.

A resource efficiency perspective on optimisation may leave out values that are important elements also for other types of sustainable practices, for example related to food or consumption. We believe that designers must be aware of this tension between traditional optimisation and sustainability that is present in many practices.

CONCLUSION

In this paper we presented a case study of three families who radically changed their transportation practices by replacing their car with light electric vehicles for one year. We used the case of transportation to exemplify how practice theory can be applied to sustainable HCI and to inform and inspire design of digital services supporting transitions towards sustainable practices. In the study, positive and negative experiences related to elements of sustainable transportation practices were identified. We have shown how design for sustainability can be focused on overcoming negative experiences, spreading elements associated with positive experiences and turning negative experiences into positive ones. We believe that making both positive and negative experiences explicit is useful in order to encourage a focus not only on how to address problems, but also on how to use ICT to build on positive experiences that may be useful for recruiting people to sustainable practices. Furthermore, we suggest sustainable HCI to focus on the *tension between the odd and the norm*. This may include new ways for ICT to approach optimisation as well as provide opportunities to identify actors, beyond the individual, who are crucial for the transformation of the odd into norms.

ACKNOWLEDGEMENTS

This study has been funded by the Swedish Energy Agency. We are also grateful to the families participating in the study, to the project partners involved in the setup and execution of the car-free year, and for the reviewers' valuable comments.

REFERENCES

1. Caroline Bartle, Erel Avineri, and Kiron Chatterjee. 2013. Online information-sharing: A qualitative analysis of community, trust and social influence amongst commuter cyclists in the UK. *Transportation Research Part F: Traffic Psychology and Behaviour* 16: 60–72. http://doi.org/10.1016/j.trf.2012.08.013
2. Maria Börjesson, Jonas Eliasson, Muriel B. Hugosson, and Karin Brundell-Freij. 2012. The Stockholm congestion charges-5 years on. Effects, acceptability and lessons learnt. *Transport Policy* 20: 1–12. http://doi.org/10.1016/j.tranpol.2011.11.001
3. Efthimios Bothos, Dimitris Apostolou, and Gregoris Mentzas. 2013. Choice Architecture for Environmentally Sustainable Urban Mobility. *CHI 2013*, 1503–1508.
4. Barry Brown, Stuart Reeves, and Scott Sherwood. 2011. Into the Wild: Challenges and Opportunities for Field Trial Methods. *CHI 2011*, 1657–1666.
5. Hrönn Brynjarsdottir, Maria Håkansson, James Pierce, Eric Baumer, Carl Disalvo, and Phoebe Sengers. 2012. Sustainably Unpersuaded: How Persuasion Narrows Our Vision of Sustainability. *CHI 2012*, ACM, 947–956.
6. Caspar G. Chorus, Eric J. E. Molin, and Bert Van Wee. 2006. Use and Effects of Advanced Traveller Information Services (ATIS): A Review of the Literature. *Transport Reviews* 26, 2: 127–149. http://doi.org/10.1080/01441640500333677
7. Carl DiSalvo, Phoebe Sengers, and Hrönn Brynjarsdóttir. 2010. Mapping the landscape of sustainable HCI. *CHI 2010*, ACM, 1975–1984. http://doi.org/10.1145/1753326.1753625
8. Paul Dourish. 2010. HCI and environmental sustainability: the politics of design and the design of politics. *DIS 2010*. http://doi.org/10.1145/1858171.1858173
9. Federal Highway Administration. 2010. *2009 National Household Travel Survey*.
10. Jon Froehlich, Tawanna Dillahunt, Predrag Klasnja, et al. 2009. UbiGreen: Investigating a Mobile Tool for Tracking and Supporting Green Transportation Habits. *CHI 2009*: 1043–1052. http://doi.org/10.1145/1518701.1518861
11. Maria Håkansson and Phoebe Sengers. 2013. Beyond Being Green: Simple Living Families and ICT. *CHI 2013*, 2725–2734. http://doi.org/10.1145/2470654.2481378
12. Tuillia Jack. 2013. Nobody was dirty: Intervening in inconspicuous consumption of laundry routines. *Journal of Consumer Culture* 13, 3: 406–421. http://doi.org/10.1177/1469540513485272
13. Anna Kramers. 2014. Designing next generation multimodal traveler information systems to support sustainability-oriented decisions. *Environmental Modelling and Software* 56: 83–93. http://doi.org/10.1016/j.envsoft.2014.01.017
14. Lenneke Kuijer and Annelise De Jong. 2009. A practice oriented approach to user centered sustainable design. *Ecodesign 2009 Conference, Saporo, Japan*: 1–6.
15. Lenneke Kuijer and Annelise De Jong. 2012. Identifying design opportunities for reduced household resource consumption: exploring practices of thermal comfort. *J. of Design Research* 10, 1/2: 67. http://doi.org/10.1504/JDR.2012.046140
16. Lenneke Kuijer. 2014. Implications of Social Practice Theory for Sustainable Design.
17. Kari Kuutti and Lj Bannon. 2014. The turn to practice in HCI: towards a research agenda. *CHI 2014*, 3543–3552. http://doi.org/10.1145/2556288.2557111
18. Johanne Mose Entwistle, Mia Kruse Rasmussen, Nervo Verdezoto, Robert S Brewer, and Mads Schaarup Andersen. 2015. Beyond the Individual: The Contextual Wheel of Practice as a Research Framework for Sustainable HCI. *CHI 2015*.
19. Åsa Nyblom. 2014. Making plans or "just thinking about the trip"? Understanding people's travel planning in practice. *Journal of Transport Geography* 35: 30–39. http://doi.org/10.1016/j.jtrangeo.2014.01.003
20. Sebastian Prost, Johann Schrammel, and Manfred Tscheligi. 2014. "Sometimes it"s the weather's fault': sustainable HCI & political activism. *CHI 2014*, 2005–2010. http://doi.org/10.1145/2559206.2581358
21. Kakee Scott, Conny Bakker, and Jaco Quist. 2012. Designing change by living change. *Design Studies* 33, 3: 279–297. http://doi.org/10.1016/j.destud.2011.08.002
22. Elizabeth Shove, Mika Pantzar, and Matt Watson. 2012. *The Dynamics of Social Practice: Everyday Life and how it Changes*. SAGE Publications.
23. Elizabeth Shove and Gordon Walker. 2010. Governing transitions in the sustainability of everyday life. *Research Policy* 39, 4: 471–476. http://doi.org/10.1016/j.respol.2010.01.019
24. Jana Sochor, Helena Strömberg, and Marianne Karlsson. 2014. Travelers' motives for adopting a new, innovative travel service: Insights from the UBIGO field operational test in Gothenburg, Sweden. *World Congress on Intelligent Transportation Systems*.
25. Yolande Strengers. 2011. Designing eco-feedback systems for everyday life. *CHI 2011*, ACM Press, 2135–2144. http://doi.org/10.1145/1978942.1979252

26. Irina Tal, Aida Olaru, and Gabriel Miro Muntean. 2013. eWARPE - Energy-efficient weather-aware route planner for electric bicycles. *International Conference on Network Protocols, ICNP.* http://doi.org/10.1109/ICNP.2013.6733680
27. Trafikanalys. 2015. Resvanor. *RVU Sverige 2011-2014 Den nationella resvaneundersökningen*. Retrieved August 12, 2015 from http://www.trafa.se/statistik/resvanor/
28. John. Urry. 2004. The “System” of Automobility. *Theory, Culture & Society* 21, 4: 25–39. http://doi.org/10.1177/0263276404046059
29. Bas Verplanken, Henk Aarts, and Ad Van Knippenberg. 1997. Habit, information acquisition, and the process of making travel mode choices. *European Journal of Social Psychology* 27, 5: 539–560. http://doi.org/10.1002/(sici)1099-0992(199709/10)27:5<539::aid-ejsp831>3.0.co;2-a

Learning from Green Designers: Green Design as Discursive Practice

Earl Friedberg and Edward Lank
Cheriton School of Computer Science, University of Waterloo
Waterloo, ON, Canada
earl.friedberg@gmail.com, lank@uwaterloo.ca

ABSTRACT

This paper looks at the activities of environmentally minded technology designers and provides an account of how these designers think, behave and differ. In contrast to traditional designers, green designers appear to: (1) Bias decisions (2) Design from a deep, personal ethos; (3) Accept 'not knowing' as a part of the design process; (4) Rely on alternative ways of knowing, and; (5) Shift roles as needed throughout the design process. While a superficial treatment of these differences might seem to disenfranchise green designers, we show that an analysis of green design as a discursive practice highlights how, through engagement with others, green design can enhance pro-environmental dialog and enact meaningful change.

Author Keywords

Sustainability; designers; product design; mobile.

ACM Classification Keywords

H.5.m. Information interfaces and presentation (e.g., HCI): Miscellaneous.

INTRODUCTION

Even prior to the emergence of designers as technology professionals, researchers have been studying designers' thought processes and how their thought processes differ from non-designers [8, 24, 38]. As designers have become critical components in the creation of technology, an understanding of the discipline of design has become of interest to the field of Human-Computer Interaction (HCI).

Alongside an interest in design and design thinking, the field of HCI has seen work driven by the perspective of sustainability [21, 26, 36]. In particular, DiSalvo et al. [9] have called for HCI to continue to explore the role of design (and designers) in creating sustainable technologies. While research continues to be developed in this area [10, 36], we agree that understanding and contrasting designers' practices regarding sustainability remains an important area of inquiry to many fields, including HCI; technology and interaction designers make deliberate choices about the utility of products and systems, the materials used, the manufacturing process, the length of useful life, and what happens after a system is no longer needed [11].

Many designers work, both privately and within larger organizations, in roles focused on environmental sustainability. These individuals frequently have job titles of sustainable, green, or eco designer. While there is a difference between sustainable design and eco/green design [4, 31] – specifically *sustainable design* is an emerging discipline that advocates for a balanced approach to social, economic, and environmental concerns [42], whereas eco and green design focus on environmental concerns – the intent of sustainable design roles within many corporate environments is to foster more environmentally sustainable products or artifacts. In this paper, we discriminate between these two terms by using *green design* to describe design that seeks to minimize environmental impact. This paper's focus is on green design.

When exploring green design, one often finds green design articulated through a set of practices [28]: optimizing material selection to limit environmental harm, emotionally durable design to encourage longer-term ownership, cradle-to-cradle design to promote secondary product uses and zero-waste artifacts, design for shared ownership models to limit over-production of goods, design for ecological footprint minimization to reduce the total ecological cost of a product, etc. While the goal of green design is to design in such a way that the environmental impact of production, use and disposal of any artifact is reduced, these practices, ideally, would be adopted by any designer as part and parcel of the overall design process. How then does the role of an individual working as a green designer differ from that of any other designer? What aspects of viewpoint or action would characterize a green designer? Given the role of design in a consumer-driven society, is it even possible to be a green designer?

Probing these questions in general is beyond the scope of any one paper: Design as a discipline pervades all aspects of human endeavor. However, within the domain of HCI, the intersection of environmental sustainability and mobile devices has been frequently explored [17, 18, 22, 46], undoubtedly because, at heart, mobile device design and

CHI'16, May 07 - 12, 2016, San Jose, CA, USA

ACM 978-1-4503-3362-7/16/05...$15.00
DOI: http://dx.doi.org/10.1145/2858036.2858124

manufacturing is driven by planned obsolescence [18, 22, 26, 46]. To scope our work, in this paper we focus specifically on mobile designers – that is visual, interaction and industrial designers who design smartphone and tablet experiences. We examine designers in roles designated as green design roles and their contrast with other designers. We perform this analysis specifically within the context of one large, mobile device manufacturer. It is our hope that this case study may provide data that can inform additional exploration in design in HCI and in other research fields.

As with any work contrasting behaviors, it is important to recognize that designers, even those not designated as green designers, do consider aspects of sustainability, including environmental sustainability, in their work practice. While overlap in roles exists between green designers and other designers, this paper explores the articulation of differences between the work practices green designers and their (non-designated) designer-colleagues within the specific organizational context studied. Through semi-structured interviews we contrast the responses of 12 green designers with 10 non-designated-green designers to discover how our green designers employ their problem-solving skills differently than other designers. We identify five attributes within our interview data distinct to our green designers:

- Biased advocacy within design discussion.
- Designing driven by ethos.
- Response to uncertainty and incomplete information.
- Relying on alternative ways of knowing.
- Serving multiple roles simultaneously during design: facilitator, supporter and catalyst.

After describing the data that gives rise to these themes, our case study data are then leveraged to explore how the role-specific nature of green design influences the everyday communicative interactions of green designers. Within the large organizational context of the study, the view of role-specific green design that emerges is one of green design as discursive practice. The goal of green design is not to halt consumption or fully alter the business model of mobile device consumption; instead, through on-going face-to-face dialog, the presentation of alternatives, and the articulation of ideologies, a new reality within design – defined as new social norms and structures – is created. Green design emerges as an application of the design process where the role of green designer within the confines of the design discussion reinforces meaning and creates new values that pervasively influence design.

BACKGROUND

Cross identifies six key aspects to a designer's job: solving ill-defined problems, problem shaping, goal and constraint management, ideation, thinking through drawing, and intuitive reasoning [8]. He defines the designers' ability to solve ill-defined problems as 'design intelligence'.

Early views of design perceived it as a mysterious art. There are still some who view design as ineffable. Marcel Duchamp, for one, writes about how we should not attempt to dissect the creative process [11]. He claims that the creative process cannot be fully subject to rationalized explanations. However, more contemporary views recognize that design can be studied and researched, so that the discipline can better solve ill-defined problems. Newland, Powell and Creed discuss how, within 'design intelligence', designers may employ different styles of thinking [30]. Some styles may be common among all designers, e.g., envisioning, communicating concepts, and collaboration. Other, perhaps undiscovered styles may be less common but may be of benefit in certain domains. Whether one considers a full analysis of design thinking appropriate, we believe that it is still important to gain insights on the roots of current design practices so that designers may respond in ways that are more appropriate to the design context in which they work.

Through much of the 20th century, technology designers played a critical role in western economic growth and created systems that made people's lives easier. An unanticipated consequence of this commercial success was a consumerist culture based on disposability and planned obsolescence [27]. Consumerism narrowly focused designers' work on desirability rather than on creating happier and healthier lives [16, 19, 23, 45]. Consumerism also created the trend towards short-term fashion cycles, rather than providing long-lasting, durable value [18]. More recently, the trajectory of the design profession has been re-oriented towards a more sustainable set of design practices. Victor, a prominent advocate of socially and ecologically responsible design, describes the changing role of the designer as follows: "Our role is changing to that of a facilitator who can bring the needs of the people to the attention of manufacturing, government agencies, and the like. The designer then logically becomes no more (and no less) then a tool in the hands of the people." [44]. As one example of this change, McDonough discusses how designers are moving away from considering their client as one single manufacturer and instead considering the needs of all stakeholders across any aspect of the life cycle [27].

Technology organizations have identified benefits to increased social and environmental responsibility. Brands adopting sustainable design see increased customer loyalty and greater growth opportunities [13, 40]. Businesses that neglect product sustainability can discredit their brands and reduce their market share; consumers are willing to reject products based on negative information about their environmental records and production methods [20].

In addition to significant consumer pressure driving sustainable approaches to design, regulatory directives such as Waste Electrical and Electronic Equipment (WEEE) [33], Restriction on Hazardous Substances (RoHS) [34] and Registration, Evaluation, Authorization and Restriction of Chemical substances (REACH) [35] require organizations to reduce environmentally harmful outputs. As a result, designers and manufacturers have evolved their capabilities and methods towards environmental sustainability [32].

Beyond the commercial context, many individuals are seeking more environmentally sustainable alternatives within their everyday lives. Mobile technology, in particular, has put designers in a direct position to shape people's behaviors. Applications have allowed people to favor public transportation over driving, help people reduce energy use and encourage consumer recycling [26, 43].

An assortment of frameworks, strategies and product lifecycle tools provide insights to designers for thinking about the outcomes of a product design [10, 16, 45]. Alongside work designing these processes and tools, Lindahl [25] explores barriers to the adoption of design tools and processes in general, but with a discussion of implications for eco-design tools. Tingström and Karlsson [41] explore how two specific eco-design tools, Life Cycle Assessment and Environmental Effect Analysis, can be best used together in design. As a final example of work in this area, Baumann et al. [1] surveyed the literature to identify gaps in research on green product development processes.

In summary, over the last 30 years there has been a growing understanding of design thinking [24]. As well, researchers continue to explore ways that sustainable or green concepts can be incorporated into design processes, or design processes can be adapted to foster sustainable practices [10, 16, 21, 23, 28, 31. 46]. The specific goal of our work is to explore how green designers perceive and act differently than other designers within a specific industry, smartphone manufacture, in one organizational context.

METHOD

Participants were enlisted from a large, mobile device manufacturer. Our primary goal in recruiting was to interview a diverse sample of designers whose professional activities varied in terms of output produced. The sample consisted of 22 designers from the disciplines of product design, user experience, industrial design, visual design, interaction design and user research. All participants were responsible for shipping various user experiences. Purposive sampling was employed, as the study required access to a specialized, difficult to reach population of professional designers. The roles in which these designers served all required well-developed awareness of the designer's reflections and procedures used either broadly across the organization or in particular depth with respect to a specific design project.

Of our 22 designers, twelve were green designers, and ten were non-green designers, i.e. traditional designers. As we note in the introduction, any delineation of designers into distinct roles is challenging: designers, by nature, must consider many factors during design. For the purpose of this study, participants labeled as green designers were identified as green designers through the use of the word 'sustainable' or 'sustainability' in their job title and were required to have designed or co-designed a technology product, feature or initiative that aimed to improve environmental welfare. Other/traditional designers were designers serving in a non-green-designated design role within the organization. We anticipate that some ambiguity of role will exist for designers in our study; we will return to this issue in our discussion of results.

For the purposes of data presentation, we identify green designer participants with the label 'G' for green designer (G1, G2, etc.…) and traditional designers with the generic label 'D' for designer. Demographics of green and non-green designers are shown in Table 1. Purposive sampling allowed us to ensure a similar seniority level across both groups. We do note that our green designers are, on average, younger, but with a narrower range of ages than our traditional designers.

Designers	Age	Junior	Intermediate	Senior
Green (G)	35 (5)	2	7	3
Traditional (D)	39 (13)	3	5	2

Table 1: Demographics of our groups of designers including Age (standard deviation), and experience levels. As noted, there were 12 green and 10 non-green designers in our sample.

Data was collected over the course of a 16-month period. Each participant partook in at least 3 semi-structured interviews. Participants were informed of the research intent so that they could prepare to speak in depth about relevant topics while ensuring commonality among interviewees. The interviews were conducted at their place of work, so that supporting materials such as drawings, artwork or digital models could reinforce the interview.

Codes, categories, and themes were developed inductively and working hypotheses were generated. Due to the human cognitive bias towards confirmation, an active search for disconfirming evidence was essential in achieving saturation. During the final round of interviews with participants, our hypotheses were combed with individual participants to validate assertions resulting from the analysis. One concern was evidentiary adequacy – that is adequate time in the field collecting and analyzing data. The data consisted of 55 hours of interview audio, as well as 13 hours of follow-up interactions.

When talking to experts in most fields, the passion often lies with what was created, rather than how it was created. Designers were no different. Often, they had to be redirected to explain their thinking process and procedures. Even the most senior designers had a difficult time focusing their conversation on the activities of design, rather than outcomes. To overcome this challenge, our interview was in the style of project walkthroughs, where designers were asked to walkthrough the conceptualization, development and implementation of particular works of design, focusing particularly on their interactions and the decisions they made. Throughout the walkthrough, designers were probed on specific details around their thought processes.

FINDINGS

Open coding produced 22 thematic elements or concepts in our data. To synthesize these elements into themes, selective coding was guided by our goal of identifying differences between our two participant groups. Five themes were identified on how green designers think, behave and feel they differ from other designers in our sample. Specifically, our green designers appear to: (1) Bias Decisions (2) Articulate a guiding ethos; (3) Embrace uncertainty and "not knowing" as design outcome; (4) Rely on intuition, experience and unusual ways of knowing; and (5) Adopt to multiple roles in design.

Biasing Decisions

As expected when analyzing our data, the biggest contrast between green designers and other designers involved the rationale behind design decisions that the designers advocated for. Although traditional designers were certainly aware of environmental issues, they felt a greater tension between business needs and environmental outcomes. Traditional designers were often in a role of mediation between business needs, user needs and environmental concerns, whereas green designers were not as constrained by conflicting needs. D5 elaborates on this tension. "If there's a higher cost up-front, it is much harder to argue for that particular solution, even if it's better for the environment (…) As much as I'd like it (the environmentally preferred solution) to win out, the needs of our shareholders come first." D2 elaborates: "Often, we're at the mercy of the (corporate executive board), and what our shareholders believe will turn a profit. Most of the time I have to cede to those asks to get my job done. (…) It's about what's best for business."

Contrast this response, with G7, a green designer. "My design decisions revolve around the future of the planet. (…) If I can satisfy both the needs of people and shareholders, then even better." For instance, it was easier for a green designer to prioritize using a more expensive, environmentally preferred material for a product, than it was for a traditional industrial designer. "This (material) was chosen due to its environmental performance. (…) If it was up to a different designer, perhaps the environmental performance wouldn't be a deciding factor. If it was up to the business, it (environmental performance) probably wouldn't be a factor at all. For me, it was the most important thing that guided the material selection phase of the project." (G11)

Prioritizing environmental values appears to make the design process less diverging. "Design is always about tradeoffs. However, when you're not willing to compromise because of the environment, then it makes making decisions easier. … If there's a higher cost (in making an environmentally preferred product), that's managements job to figure out how the business is going to afford to make it. (…) If it's healthier for the environment, it means it's better for our customers. Period." (G7) G4 describes an underlying theme of technological novelty restraint: "For some designers here, it's about the 'tech'. How fast is the processor, how much memory, how many megapixels there are. Just talk to the concept designers here (laughter). For me, it's about creating something that makes lives better. … At the beginning (of my career), I definitely overvalued what the technology could do."

Designing From a Guiding Ethos

All twelve green designers reported practicing a number of pro-environmental behaviors in their personal lives. These included reducing the amount of possessions, being mindful of work-life balance and reducing their carbon footprints at home or while travelling. These pro-environmental behaviors are not significantly different from those who practice simple living [12, 19], where individuals voluntarily move towards a 'simpler' lifestyle.

We labeled these designers commitment to sustainability as 'deep' because their personal commitment to environmentally-minded lifestyles appeared to have a deep influence on their professional activities. A designer describes how environmental commitment in his personal life affects his design decisions at work. "I'm an environmentalist on many different levels. At home, I try to do all the right things (…) At work, I find myself incorporating the simpler, lower-impact lifestyle that I've chosen. (…) Everything that I design at work has been thought of in terms of carbon impacts, not that different than my personal life. It's very important that I stay true to my roots." (G6)

Designers cited a transpersonal orientation as a source for their commitment to a sustainability perspective – that is, they were often motivated by a source that transcended themselves. In four of the twelve green designers interviewed, "doing good" was described as their life's calling. G10 describes this phenomenon: "My calling has always been to improve the lives that this planet contains – whether it be human or other. To me, this is a service that I need to offer. It's something greater than myself (…). And so my (green) design work has been a calling." Other ways of communicating this transpersonal element were "making the world a better place" and "serving those less fortunate." G3 describes the motivation for his work as 'leaving a mark on the world'.

Four of the twelve green designers reported that their commitment to a sustainability perspective was motivated by a spiritual practice. This spiritual practice helped participants confine their excitement towards the novelty of the technology, and give focus on the intent of the application. "It (religion) brings daily routines. Five times a day, I'm forced to reflect on my contributions. (…) In terms of my office work, this helps me put things in perspective." The designer further elaborates on how his spirituality forces him to release personal attachment from the work, and think about his work on a removed level. "I sometimes feel like I'm designing in a completely different world (…)

The level of consciousness I get from my daily spiritual habits helps me think about my work and my users as human beings, rather than simply users. Many other designers don't get that, especially the ones that aren't working in the area of (environmental) sustainability."

Embracing Uncertainty

In the context of discovery, cognitive psychology supports the notion that 'not knowing' may enhance analytical thinking [5]. Design literature has written about uncertainty in the design process [8]. Uncertainty is used to explore opportunities for discussion and critiquing. It is well argued that uncertainty is an important design activity that helps promote ideas around design development.

Nine of the green designers acknowledged 'uncertainty' as a significant part of the design process. A green designer explains what uncertainty means to his design process. "Uncertainty means not knowing what solution is best. Of course, you can reduce the amount of uncertainty. But you have to remember not to be rigid and inflexible. (…) I think many sustainability practitioners understand and respect the feeling for ambiguity." This uncertainty was something that green designers were comfortable expressing during design discussions and to management. In contrast, traditional designers did not have a similar openness to uncertainty. If they were 'uncertain', they felt like they were regarded as less of an expert in their domain. "I wasn't sure if it (a particular design solution) was going to work (…) but I still presented the concept as a path the business should take. (…) I'm under constant pressure to know what's best. If I don't know something, my job is to find out fast." (D3)

Alongside a comfort with 'uncertainty' and 'not knowing', some green designers suggest that there may be negative consequences to 'knowing'. G2 explains how 'knowing' is an external construct that undermines work in the area of sustainability. "I tell most of the designers in this area (those who work on matters of sustainability), that thinking about your design through the perspective of sustainability is very complex. You can't possibly know what the right path is, especially not right away. You have to embrace that the uncertainty you have will become certainty somewhere down the line. (…) You have to remind yourself of this all the time (…) If you think you know the solution right away, guess again. It's probably premature."

An underlying theme was that of trust, both in themselves and in other designers they collaborate with. Seven of the twelve green designers reported a deep confidence in themselves, their peers and/or the design process. "I go by my gut a lot. I have a lot of years of experience in this field. By now, I have a good sense of what works and won't work." (G5). G10 highlights trust in others, even those not directly involved in fostering sustainability. "I treat my peers with a lot of respect. When we're working together, I truly believe that the solution will be answered between us. (…) I may need to facilitate the discussion, to provoke questions or reframe problems, but my entire assumption is that these are the right people to figure this out. (…) You just have to have faith in the design process itself."

Relying on Alternative Ways of Knowing

Green designers described relying on ways of knowing other than analytical deduction. 'Channeling instincts' and 'gut' were some of the words that described how participants accessed sources of knowledge as well as 'unconsciousness', 'intuition', and 'inner-self'. G8 describes this phenomenon. "It's a shift in my state of thinking, where I try to believe that I know the answer. I'm the creator of the design. I have to empower myself to think so. (…) I think the design becomes stronger because of it. "

While using words like intuition and instincts, it was also clear that green designers still relied on data and knowledge. As one example, green designers reported that it was acceptable for their designs to be drawn from personal experiences. G5 articulates this trust in person knowledge and experience as a source of data: "I often get the question from upper management, 'How do you know?'. I'm comfortable saying, 'Listen, based on my 20 years of experience listening and understanding (issues), I think this is a better decision." Traditional designers, on the other hand, felt they needed to articulate more concrete data about where there design came from. "All my decisions are grounded in user data." (D4)

Green designers in this study acknowledged the importance of involving non-designers to make environmentally preferred products. Green designers noted that, like traditional designers, the systems they design are better when they involved collaborating with end users and with other departments and collect expertise from each of these diverse groups. G3 explains how assembling a multi-disciplinary team helped create an improved product. "The approach was unconventional, assembling a team from all disciplines. (…) Project teams are increasingly looking more and more like this. Engineers mixed with Sales. Sales with technical writers…"

Green designers also explored different ways of understanding problems. One green designer, G8, was interested in interviewing people who experience homelessness to learn how to do more with less. G8 describes how he felt this could bring a different perspective to his work: "I tried to bring a homeless man into our studio for a week, to get his perspectives on a couple of projects. He would have had some very unique experiences, that I think, would have offered a fresh look on some the things we were looking at." G8's goal was to expose, for the design team, a viewpoint on minimalism in life that might alter perceptions on needed features and speed of upgrade cycles with respect to design.

Serving Multiple Roles Simultaneously

While the first three themes focused on designers and their engagement with design work, the last theme concerns relationships to peers, managers and stakeholders.

Environmentally minded designers reported adapting to different roles in the design process, as needed. The roles typically fell into three categories: facilitator, supporter and catalyst. The role of facilitator was one shared by all designers. The latter two roles, supporter and catalyst, were roles described only by the green designers we interviewed.

The first role was commonly referred to as 'facilitator'. Both green designers and traditional designers reported attending to the varying opinions of management, while 'listening' and reserving judgment. G1 offers an explanation. "I've told them (stakeholders) that it's not a matter of imposing my own ideas, but rather it's about them coming in, listening, talking and engaging with me, and the work. My job is to listen (…) It's very much about 'outreach', and bringing them in. (…) All my judgments can come later." G9 offers a similar explanation, where she reserves judgment so that she can facilitate building a shared vision among stakeholders. "I create a safe environment so that anybody can offer their ideas. I try to remain neutral, even though I have strong opinions about which paths to take. (…) I was trying to create a space where we can hear each other's opinions openly and honestly. The trick is to actively manage tensions to let natural inquiry occur. (…) Once (stakeholders are) all on the same page, it's much easier to agree on the next step (…). Without that mutual understanding, it would have been harder to agree on a solution."

In G9's comment, and in the comments of other green designers, we note discomfort with the facilitator role, a discomfort not evident in traditional designers. Green designers, by nature of their role, have an agenda during the design process which is sometimes at odds with the role of facilitator. However, G3 explains how this role is important to his work. "I'm trying to create the conditions so that everyone can offer a different view on the problem. (…) I'm aware this is my role at every design review, product management meeting and actually, pretty much, with any conversation." By doing so, G3 reports supporting the emergence of solutions that need to be identified, and the ability to influence design decisions so that they are more environmentally responsible. Similarly, G11 reports how his role is to remove barriers to design problems. He "holds the space" and creates the necessary conditions for people to collaborate. Some of the other phrases designers used to describe this role are: 'tension holders', 'mediators', and 'intermediaries in the design process'.

The second role that green designers took on was that of 'supporter'. In the role of supporter, designers actively took sides on what solutions would be best for their users and for the environment. "Not everyone agreed so I had to leverage the support of my peers to get buy-in at the executive level. I was no longer playing the role of the unbiased facilitator. Now I was playing the role of (green) designer." Here, the designer's responsibility was to advocate for a direction they believed in, in this case a pro-environmental decision. Their goal was to remove any barriers towards that vision, such as timing or development resources.

G3 describes how he removes barriers by directly working through tensions. "I'd like to give the analogy of a masseuse, I believe you call them a massage therapist here. What they do is not that different. They find a point of tension, and push on it as hard as possible, until the tension gets release. What I do is the same thing. I anticipate the pressure points, make sure they get addressed and discuss them thoroughly until everyone is comfortable with ruling out the point. To anticipate this pain points, I usually talk to each of the stakeholders before a big meeting like this occurs." Because green designers are advocating an approach that can be at odds with the most cost effective or expedient approach to design, this process of anticipating resistance, and of acting as a supporter of a specific decision, was particularly important to them in incorporating their vision into any final design artifact.

The third role that green designers adopted was that of 'catalyst' of progress. Other words to describe this role were "driver" and "owner." G5 describes this role: "I believe I was the catalyst. (Pointing to a project) I tried to push the boundaries. It was definitely years upon years of struggles before I was able to see the fruits of my labor." Another (G11) designer describes his role as catalyst. "Designers are responsible for creating great user experiences. Some of us take on much more than that (referring specifically to green design). (…) Lately, I've driven (environmental) projects from start to end. I don't mind this responsibility, but it does take a lot out of you."

Other designers described themselves as 'pushing and shifting boundaries'. G12 contends that his "real job" is to "make people uncomfortable, especially managers." He goes on to note: "We've got many people (in the company) saying (an environmentally beneficial result) is impossible to achieve. 'This was tried before, and it didn't work.' As a designer, you have hold down the fort, and question why it's impossible. From there, you get answers on what is possible."

In our study, all green designers reported taking on the role of 'catalyst' at one time or another, while it was uncommon for traditional designers to take on this role. Green designers reported quite frequently evangelizing to various teams in support of sustainability projects. Rather than directly engaging with these teams, as in the role of 'supporter', this role was much more active and sometimes controversial. This is evidenced by some of the phrases the green designers used like 'pushed', 'drove' and 'exposed '.

Green designers often view their role as more adversarial than traditional designers. One describes the role of 'catalyst' as a balance between pushing on people's boundaries, while not dissuading them for the project at hand. "It's a fine balance between pushing people to edge, asking them to grow, as well as not making them feel like they are being personally attacked." (G8) G4 explains the role of 'catalyst' quite clearly. "I guess you can say I'm a mover and shaker. A lot of people may not like me or my ideas, but what I build wins out every time with users." This participant also suggests that these roles may overlap or also be concurrent. "I wear many hats. I know when to push, but also know when to pull back and just listen."

Finally, we note that, while, in our data, the roles of supporter and catalyst were unique to green designers, the context within which this research occurred had a strong culture of design, but a commercial context (smartphone manufacturing) at odds with environmentalism. In environments where, for example, user-centered design is not embedded in the work culture, designers practicing user-centered design may also need to become supporters and catalysts of a design philosophy.

GREEN DESIGN AS A DISCURSIVE PRACTICE

In exploring themes and building theory in our data, one aspect of our data that continued to unify the results we synthesized to highlight the distinction between green designers and traditional designers involved *communicative interactions* during discussions of actions and behaviors during design, specifically the conceptualization of green design as a *discursive practice*. Here our use of the term discursive practice borrows most heavily on its application with respect to communications research. We use the term discursive practice to represent a set of habituated actions that is informed by role and serves to transform socially structured resources, values, and ideologies through recurring episodes of face-to-face interaction. Note that this interpretation relates to its interpretation in philosophy (a study of the mechanism by which language shapes social norms and structures) [15] and cultural anthropology (an analytical tool used to understand meaningful inter-personal interactions in actual situations).

To crystallize our use of the term discursive practice, consider the question "How are you doing?" Depending on the speaker's role, as friend or as doctor, and on context, on a busy street versus in a medical appointment, how one understands the statement changes. The role (doctor) and context (medical appointment) alters the nature of the interaction, creating expectations for the sharing of information that is distinct from other interactions. Similarly, characterizing a field of design as one that advocates for biased decision making, leverages personal ethos, recognizes uncertainty, and relies on intuition or alternative information could be considered insulting to the role of designers unless the role and context of one participant as green designer are considered. Within role and context, the nature of face-to-face interaction is materially altered. In this section, we explore green design as discursive practice by synthesizing discussion around role, behavior, context and success.

Differing Roles

As we note in our Background, the role of designers has traditionally been to create working systems. In our interviews with traditional designers, we see this goal play out through the need for concrete, actionable solutions during design. Traditional designers lack comfort in acknowledging their uncertainty (despite its importance to design) and justify their designs by grounding the solutions they propose in data they collect, either from prospective users or from other experts within the organization.

One crosscutting observation about our green designers is that the role of a green designer during design is different. The green designer's role is to advocate for one worldview, specifically sustainability. The advocacy role that green designers serve is simultaneously more liberating and more challenging. The liberating aspects of green design play out in two different ways. First, the tolerance for uncertainty allows green designers to question in a way that traditional designers are uncomfortable with. From overall themes of embracing uncertainty to lower level actions of considering what the homeless may reveal to technology design, the comfort of green designers to 'go out on a limb' is distinct.

Second, green designers were able to draw inspiration and data from themselves. Green designers used the terms 'instinct' and 'intuition' as rationales for design decisions, but we believe, instead, what they describe as intuition is, instead, knowledge and experience. All designers in our study (even those characterized as junior) were experienced designers with multiple years and multiple product release cycles completed. Intuition may be another way of describing abductive thinking, something design researchers have identified as crucial to the logic of design [24]. This thinking allows green designers to shift between the articulated goals of the design and more varied forms that satisfy that goal.

Continuing this analysis of experience, we note that the role of traditional designer is to channel data from end users or other experts within the organization, but the role of green designer is to serve *as expert,* a source of data, in the design process such that, within the constraints of a product development and release cycle, designs decisions are made with awareness of ecological considerations during each part of the design process. Green designers articulate considering a much broader range of factors, such as material sciences, lifecycles, and supply chains, among others. The overall goal is both to spur other participants in the design process to consider alternatives which are more environmentally sustainable and to serve as an expert on those practices which might support more environmentally sustainable outcomes.

In interactions around design, because everyone is aware of the green designer's role, the process of advocacy and bias becomes accepted and appropriate. Green designers exist for a reason, to serve a specific role, and, recognizing that role, nuance is applied to each interaction by all participants. Characterizing green design as discursive practice allows us to identify the way that role affects the interpretation of interactions around design.

Differing Constraints on Behavior

In discussions with traditional designers, we did find that environmental sustainability was a concern of traditional designers, but that this concern was balanced against what was viable. Within any corporate environment, the polarization implicit in ecotopianism [37], or radical environmentalism, is impractical and must be balanced against social and economic concerns. This balanced view of sustainability is well-accepted; for example, the United Nations Sustainable Development Knowledge Platform identifies sustainable development as development that balances environmental sustainability, economic sustainability, and social sustainability [42]. Traditional designers, while not articulating aspects of economic and social sustainability, were clearly aware that, in their role where the goal of design was a final, profitable artifact, the laudable goal of environmental sustainability had to be balanced against the needs of the company and its shareholders to make a profit.

Green designers, instead, articulated a need for patience and a need to understand when to advocate and when to step back, listen, and accept others' views. Green designers described waiting months to see if something would work or "years and years" to see their ideas come to life. Green designers also adopt non-traditional roles of supporter and catalyst, and must sometimes step back from these roles, give ground, listen, and mediate between concerns.

While at surface these trade-offs appear different to the designers that we interviewed, we argue that there are similarities in the trade-offs. Each designer is aware of the fact that the role of design is to leverage data, to balance concerns, and to collectively devise a working solution when participating in a large design team. While traditional designers viewed their role as balancing aspects such as user experience, business needs and release cycle concerns during design, green designers articulated their role as advocating for an awareness of issues of environmental impact, while understanding that trade-offs must be made.

The distinction is not in trade-offs in the design process, primarily because design involves compromises between concerns. Instead, the distinction involves one of approach to design interactions. Traditional designers mediate between needed tradeoffs, and their approach to design is informed by this. They collect data, organize data, examine alternatives, and support decisions between those alternatives driven by an objective function that is motivated, primarily, by the desire to create a successful product. Green designers operate almost as *tempered radicals* [29], biasing toward pro-environmental actions, maintaining focusing on pro-environmental goals, and by example and advocacy, promoting professional conversations around eco-design. There is an expectation, based on role in design, that a green designer's interactions will be constrained and motivated by sustainability concern, i.e. the discursive practice of green design enforces on the green designer an expected approach to each new project they tackle.

Differing Context and Values

Design literature extensively writes about the creative process, and the methods used to stimulate creativity [8, 24]. Whether a designer is a traditional designer or a green designer, designers are both providing a professional service and exercising creativity. To foster creativity of *design thinking* in design education, students are introduced to problem-solving exercises, brainstorming techniques and analytical thinking: however these exercises often fail to recognize that the act of design is uniquely personal to the designer, deeply rooted in their individual lives. An understanding of the deep, personal nature of design can enhance the designer's awareness of their process, and contribute to their development. Furthermore, by recognizing the basis on which creative decisions are made, designers may be better able to question their work and challenge expectations.

All of the designers we spoke with cared deeply about the products they designed, but the green designers were unique in the ownership they took of their personal investment in design as a *personal* process, describing comfortably the spiritual aspects they brought to design and the link between their design ethos and their personal life. Traditional designers, in contrast, did not express these same spiritual aspects to design. It remains an open question whether green designers' roles fostered a spiritual connection to the designs they created, or whether people who wanted a spiritual connection to their designs or to their work because of the importance of environmentalism in their lives chose to take on roles as green designers. We suspect the latter. However, regardless of whether green design promoted spirituality and personal investment in design or whether individuals sufficiently invested in environmentalism in their personal lives become green designers, the articulation of personal investment and the spiritual dimension of design was unique to our green designers. When exploring green design as discursive practice, this discussion of personal values was central to our interpretation of behavior-in-context.

Alongside the observation of a personal nature of design and the value-belief structure that informs design is an articulation of the different standards designers hold themselves to. Green designers measure their success by whether they reduced, in any way, the environmental footprint of shipped products. "Good" green design is both a pragmatic and an altruistic endeavor. In contrast, traditional designers articulate their success in the practicalities of the real world, specifically metrics such as how many units shipped, or the differential between the price of the product and the cost of the product. For traditional designers, the reduced altruism inherent in the commercial success that measures any design's outcome may make traditional designers more hesitant to link their ethos to the design work that they do.

The personal context of design that allows green designers to articulate a personal link between their work and themselves relates to an *ethic* [14] within design, i.e. "the intentional work of an individual (in this case a designer) to subject himself or herself to a set of moral recommendations for conduct (in his or her work)." All green designers referred to this ethic outside work as well as within their work – a reduction in possessions in their personal life, their focus on personal ecological impact, or their faith – as a set of moral recommendations that they intentionally applied broadly to themselves.

Differing Measures of Success

As we note above, the goal of designers is to create successful products, and, overall, these goals are aligned with the goals of organizations for which designers work. Our traditional designers talked about the successes of those products in terms of units shipped and market influence, and the user experiences these products fostered. Measuring the success of green design also revolves around success in the product life cycle. Green designers talked about their influence on product design decisions, the value they create for end users and the company, and the influence on the broader market.

At a superficial level, the difference between green designers and traditional designers might appear to be the domain of impact and decision: Green designers valued the influence they had on more environmentally-minded decisions within design. Essentially, given the environmental cost of smartphone manufacturing and two-year upgrade cycles, it might appear that the over-riding success criterion for green design is any slight reduction of environmental harm in the product.

Looking more deeply at green design, the goal of the green designer is often articulated as one of advocacy. However, this, too, shortchanges green design as a design practice. Advocacy implies the raising of issues such that those issues may be acted upon. The purpose or goal of green design is, instead, to transform the values and ideologies at play in design decisions such that design choices are significantly impacted by environmental concerns.

IMPLICATIONS AND DISCUSSION

Impact of Green Design: From Compliance and Efficiency to Strategic Proactivity

If the goal of green design is to materially alter behaviors, values and ideologies, is green design successful? Obviously, this is not a question that can be answered in general given the limited scope and context of our data, but we can pose the question with respect to the socio-cultural context within which this work was performed.

In any case study, the context within which data is collected is an important consideration. In their work on corporate sustainability, Benn et al. [2] posit the existence of six phases or levels of environmental sustainability for a corporation: Rejection, Non-responsiveness, Compliance, Efficiency, Strategic Proactivity, and The sustaining corporation. Clearly, the corporation wherein this study occurred had addressed issues of compliance, but at what phase, then, was the corporation in its integration of environmental sustainability into its design and manufacturing processes? Was green design merely seeking efficiency? Or had the corporate culture begun to transition beyond that point?

All green designers in our study felt that they had influenced design decision making within the corporate environment that they worked, whether through material selection, component design, supply chain design, packaging, or design for disassembly. As well, in discussions with traditional designers, all were aware of environmental concerns, knew that green design was an important component of the business environment, and many had worked with green designers to ensure better decision making at all phases of the product life cycle. There was a pervading notion that environmental impact was a concern for the industry, and that green designers in the organization had done much to advance these concerns.

A more difficult analysis for us, as researchers, is whether the perceptions of impact by our participants corresponded to actual impact, or if, instead, environmentally positive design decisions would have been made regardless of the presence of green designers – perhaps driven by regulatory requirements, cost savings or marketing advantage. In other words, had any changes extended beyond the level of *Efficiency* [2]? Undoubtedly, in some cases, the personal successes that green designers highlighted were design decisions that also made business sense. The design of smartphones to promote materials recovery became a regulatory requirement in some jurisdictions, forcing a change in behavior. The reduction in packaging, while environmentally beneficial, also saved costs.

The risk of green design as discursive practice is that the interjection of contradictory discourse by green designers has limited impact on socio-cultural norms within the work environment, and, instead, serves to entrench pre-existing practices. Specifically, the business can claim to have explored and adopted green alternatives throughout the design process, but simply selected alternatives that were easy to implement rather than making meaningful change. Aligned with this viewpoint, smartphone manufacture remains driven by planned obsolescence [18].

Arguing for the success of green design within the context of our case study, however, was a feeling of agency among our green designers in the design process. Each of our green designers described concrete decisions they had made recently in the design process, decisions that were guided by environmental concerns and over-rode commercial concerns. We probed these issues earlier in the paper when exploring the theme of Biasing Decisions in the Findings section. Because green designers had this agency, their focus on environmental concern allowed some decisions to be made that valued the environment over corporate interests, thus arguing that green design did materially impact the context in which this research was performed, at a minimum indicating an organizational context that had reached the level of *Efficiency* with respect to corporate-adopted environmental sustainability.

Beyond efficiency, examples exist of green designers moving beyond discrete decision making and generating data more relevant to longer product life cycles and greater device longevity. As one example, we note, earlier, the pervading view of green design as important to the smartphone industry by all designers in our study. As other examples, both G8's exploration of minimalist living with respect to projects and product life cycles and G4's move beyond low-level features to high-level needs represent more strategic, long-term, opportunistic thinking. The move beyond discrete decision making to aspects of product life cycle and overall feature sets may be an early instance of *Strategic Proactivity* within the corporate environment of this case study vis a vis environmental sustainability [2].

Relevance to Research and Practice

A significant body of work in HCI focuses on issues of design of artifacts. This includes work on technology design [7], design education [6] and green design [9]. In the area of green design, the exploration of the discursive structures surrounding green design is not new. In his essay on HCI and Environmental Sustainability, Dourish [10] argues that a view of green design as persuasive technology shortchanges issues of scale required for meaningful impact. In a similar vein to Dourish's critiques of scale when green design is framed solely as individual-focused persuasive technology, Sheppard et al. [39] note the challenges associated with motivating local-scale actions when studies describe the problem at a global level. Both Dourish [10] and Sheppard et al. [39] argue for the role of design practice in issues of environmental sustainability. Dourish advocates providing individuals with an awareness of collective effects of their actions to shape environmental movements; Sheppard et al. advocate leveraging techniques within design to allow people to grasp the potential of widespread individual action through scenarios and visualization.

Alongside Dourish's [10] and Sheppard et al.'s [39] identification of the potential of design to foster scaled, impactful behavior, our work provides an alternative view of green design where designers work within existing contexts such as smartphone manufacturers to promote pro-environmental outcomes. Through economies of scale, the actions of green designers as supporters of and catalysts can drive larger-scale environmentalism. Sometimes green design can be about fostering large-scale collective action [10], and sometimes green design can be about fostering small-scale targeted persuasive behavior changes [9. 22]. Sometimes, as in our case study, green design can involve understanding how even the advocacy of or persuasion toward small scale decisions via either the discursive practices we identify or via more traditional design behaviors [39] can foster change that is impactful on a global scale, potentially assisting the movement of corporations through phases in the adoption of environmentally sustainable practices [2].

Beyond these complimentary views of the role of green design, we also believe that a framing of the discursive practice of green design has a role in understanding sustainability in other industries. We acknowledge that, as with any individual case study, our view of green design in the smartphone industry is constrained by the context of one manufacturer. Further work is necessary, both within smartphone design and in other contexts, to continue to develop an understanding of the evolving nature of green design. In informal discussion with free-lance green designers we find echoes of many of the sentiments expressed by our green designers. Specifically, the role of green designer as consultant within a larger design context – be it the automotive industry, urban planning, or resource extraction – is to recognize that, while development may not halt, expert knowledge and the promotion of better alternatives may result in small improvements scaled large. Whether at the level of Compliance, Efficiency, or Strategic Proactivity [2], expertise in green design can foster the transition companies from non-responsiveness to sustaining entities with respect to environmental concerns.

CONCLUSIONS

This paper contrasts the design process of green designers with the design process of traditional designers. We identify five key attributes that arise from our discussion of process with our green designers that appear unique to green designers, specifically a bias in design, the leveraging of ethos; the ability to embrace uncertainty during design; the affinity for intuition or unusual sources of data; and the need to serve multiple roles simultaneously during design activities. Understanding these attributes of green design through the lens of discursive practice leads to an identification of the differing roles, constraints, context, and success for green designers.

ACKNOWLEDGEMENTS

The research described in this paper was approved by the University of Waterloo Research Ethics Committee. Funding was provided by the Natural Science and Engineering Research Council of Canada (NSERC Discovery Grant Program) and by the Networks of Centres of Excellence Project on Graphics, Animation, and New Media (NCE-GRAND). Finally, the authors thank our participants and gratefully acknowledge the constructive comments of the reviewers of this manuscript.

REFERENCES

1. Henrikke Baumann, Frank Boons, and Annica Bragd. 2002. Mapping the green product development field: engineering, policy and business perspectives. *Journal of Cleaner Production* 10, 5: 409–425. http://doi.org/10.1016/S0959-6526(02)00015-X
2. Suzanne Benn, Dexter Dunphy, and Andrew Griffiths. 2014. *Organizational change for corporate sustainability*. Routledge.
3. Hugh Beyer and Karen Holtzblatt. 1997. *Contextual design: defining customer-centered systems*. Elsevier.
4. Eli Blevis. 2007. Sustainable interaction design: invention & disposal, renewal & reuse. *Proceedings of the SIGCHI conference on Human factors in computing systems*, ACM, 503–512. DOI=http://dx.doi.org/10.1145/1240624.1240705
5. Kenneth S. Bowers, Glenn Regehr, Claude Balthazard, and Kevin Parker. 1990. Intuition in the context of discovery. *Cognitive psychology* 22, 1: 72–110. http://doi.org/10.1016/0010-0285(90)90004-N
6. Daniel Boyarski. 1998. Designing design education. *ACM SIGCHI Bulletin* 30, 3: 7–10. DOI=http://dx.doi.org/10.1145/565711.565716
7. Bill Buxton. 2010. *Sketching user experiences: getting the design right and the right design: getting the design right and the right design*. Morgan Kaufmann.
8. Nigel Cross. 2006. *Designerly ways of knowing*. Springer.
9. Carl DiSalvo, Phoebe Sengers, and Hrönn Brynjarsdóttir. 2010. Mapping the landscape of sustainable HCI. *Proceedings of the SIGCHI Conference on Human Factors in Computing Systems*, ACM, 1975–1984. DOI=http://dx.doi.org/10.1145/1753326.1753625
10. Paul Dourish. 2010. HCI and environmental sustainability: the politics of design and the design of politics. *Proceedings of the 8th ACM Conference on Designing Interactive Systems*, ACM, 1–10. DOI=http://dx.doi.org/10.1145/1858171.1858173
11. Marcel Duchamp, Marc Dachy, Richard Hamilton, et al. 1994. *The creative act*. Sub Rosa, Brussels, Belgium.
12. Vernard Eller. 1973. *The simple life: The Christian stance toward possessions*. WB Eerdmans Publishing Company.
13. Daniel Esty and Andrew Winston. 2009. *Green to gold: How smart companies use environmental strategy to innovate, create value, and build competitive advantage*. John Wiley & Sons.
14. Michel Foucault. 1987. The ethic of the care for the self as a practice of freedom: An interview with Michael Foucault on 20th January 1984. *In Foucault Live: Interviews 1961–1984*. (1996). Sylvère Lotinger (ed.). New York: Semiotext(e).
15. Michel Foucault. 1998. The Will to Knowledge: The History of Sexuality vol. I.
16. Batya Friedman, Peter H. Kahn Jr, Alan Borning, and Alina Huldtgren. 2013. Value sensitive design and information systems. In *Early engagement and new technologies: Opening up the laboratory*. Springer, 55–95. DOI=http://dx.doi.org/10.1007/978-94-007-7844-3_4
17. William Bradley Glisson, Tim Storer, Gavin Mayall, Iain Moug, and George Grispos. 2011. Electronic retention: what does your mobile phone reveal about you? *International Journal of Information Security* 10, 6: 337–349. http://doi.org/10.1007/s10207-011-0144-3
18. Gerard Goggin. 2012. *Cell phone culture: Mobile technology in everyday life*. Routledge.
19. Maria Håkansson and Phoebe Sengers. 2013. Beyond being green: simple living families and ICT. *Proceedings of the SIGCHI Conference on Human Factors in Computing Systems*, ACM, 2725–2734. DOI=http://dx.doi.org/10.1145/2470654.2481378
20. Ann Harrison and Jason Scorse. 2004. *Moving up or moving out? Anti-sweatshop activists and labor market outcomes*. National Bureau of Economic Research. Retrieved January 12, 2016 from http://www.nber.org/papers/w10492.
21. Elaine M. Huang, Eli Blevis, Jennifer Mankoff, Lisa P. Nathan, and Bill Tomlinson. 2009. Defining the role of HCI in the challenges of sustainability. *CHI'09 Extended Abstracts on Human Factors in Computing Systems*, ACM, 4827–4830. DOI=http://dx.doi.org/10.1145/1520340.1520751
22. Elaine M. Huang and Khai N. Truong. 2008. Breaking the disposable technology paradigm: opportunities for sustainable interaction design for mobile phones. *Proceedings of the SIGCHI Conference on Human Factors in Computing Systems*, ACM, 323–332. DOI=http://dx.doi.org/10.1145/1357054.1357110
23. Heekyoung Jung, Eli Blevis, and Erik Stolterman. 2010. Conceptualizations of the materiality of digital artifacts and their implications for sustainable interaction design. *University of Indiana* .
24. Bryan Lawson. 2006. *How designers think: the design process demystified*. Routledge.
25. Mattias Lindahl. 2006. Engineering designers' experience of design for environment methods and tools–Requirement definitions from an interview study. *Journal of cleaner production* 14, 5: 487–496. http://doi.org/10.1016/j.jclepro.2005.02.003
26. Jennifer C. Mankoff, Eli Blevis, Alan Borning, et al. 2007. Environmental sustainability and interaction. *CHI'07 extended abstracts on Human factors in*

computing systems, ACM, 2121–2124. DOI=http://dx.doi.org/10.1145/1240866.1240963

27. William McDonough and Michael Braungart. 2010. *Cradle to cradle: Remaking the way we make things*. MacMillan.
28. Jason F. McLennan. 2004. *The philosophy of sustainable design: The future of architecture*. Ecotone publishing.
29. Debra Meyerson. 2001. *Tempered radicals: How people use difference to inspire change at work*. Harvard Business Press.
30. Paul Newland, James A. Powell, and Chris Creed. 1987. Understanding architectural designers' selective information handling. *Design Studies* 8, 1: 2–16. http://doi.org/10.1016/0142-694X(87)90026-3
31. Peter Nicholson. 2005. Green Design vs. Sustainable Design. *Dexigner*. Retrieved January 12, 2016 from http://www.dexigner.com/news/4166.
32. Ram Nidumolu, C. K. Prahalad, and M. R. Rangaswami. 2015. Why sustainability is now the key driver of innovation. *Engineering Management Review, IEEE* 43, 2: 85–91. http://dx.doi.org/10.1109/EMR.2015.7123233
33. *Official Journal of the European Union*. Directive 2002/95/EC of the European Parliament on the restriction of the use of certain hazardous substances in electrical and electronic equipment. 37/19, (2003).
34. *Official Journal of the European Union*. Directive 2011/65/EU of the European Parliament on the restriction of certain hazardous substances in electrical and electronic equipment. 174/88, (2011).
35. *Official Journal of the European Union*. Regulation (EC) No 1907/2006 of the European Parliament concerning the Registration, Evaluation, Authorisation and Restriction of Chemicals (REACH), establishing a European Chemicals Agency. (2006)
36. Yue Pan, David Roedl, John C. Thomas, and Eli Blevis. 2012. Re-conceptualizing fashion in sustainable HCI. *Proceedings of the Designing Interactive Systems Conference*, ACM, 621–630. DOI=http://dx.doi.org/10.1145/2317956.2318049
37. David Pepper. 2007. Tensions and dilemmas of ecotopianism. *Environmental Values* 16, 3: 289–312. http://doi.org/10.3197/096327107X228364
38. Donald A. Schön. 1983. *The reflective practitioner: How professionals think in action*. Basic books.
39. Stephen RJ Sheppard, Alison Shaw, David Flanders, et al. 2011. Future visioning of local climate change: a framework for community engagement and planning with scenarios and visualisation. *Futures* 43, 4: 400–412. http://doi.org/10.1016/j.futures.2011.01.009
40. Stefan Thomke and Barbara Feinberg. 2009. Design thinking and innovation at Apple. *Harvard Busyness School*: 1–12.
41. Johan Tingström and Reine Karlsson. 2006. The relationship between environmental analyses and the dialogue process in product development. *Journal of Cleaner Production* 14, 15: 1409–1419. http://doi.org/10.1016/j.jclepro.2005.11.012
42. UN Resolution A/60/1, adopted by the General Assembly on 15 September 2005. United Nations General Assembly, (2005).
43. US Environmental Protection Agency. My Green Apps. http://www.epa.gov/greenapps/.
44. Papanek Victor. 1982. *Design for the real world: Human ecology and social change*. New York, Pantheon Books.
45. Ron Wakkary, Audrey Desjardins, Sabrina Hauser, and Leah Maestri. 2013. A sustainable design fiction: Green practices. *ACM Transactions on Computer-Human Interaction (TOCHI)* 20, 4: 23. DOI=http://dx.doi.org/10.1145/2494265
46. Galit Zadok and Riikka Puustinen. 2010. The green switch: Designing for sustainability in mobile computing. *The First USENIX Workshop on Sustainable Information Technology*. http://static.usenix.org/legacy/events/sustainit10/tech/full_papers/zadok.pdf.

Understanding and Mitigating the Effects of Device and Cloud Service Design Decisions on the Environmental Footprint of Digital Infrastructure

Chris Preist, Dan Schien
Department of Computer Science,
University of Bristol, Bristol, BS8 1UB, UK
{chris.preist, daniel.schien}@bristol.ac.uk

Eli Blevis
SoIC, Indiana Univ. at Bloomington, Indiana USA
SD, The Hong Kong Polytechnic Univ, HK
eblevis@indiana.edu

ABSTRACT
Interactive devices and the services they support are reliant on the cloud and the digital infrastructure supporting it. The environmental impacts of this infrastructure are substantial—and for particular services the infrastructure can account for up to 85% of the total impact. In this paper, we apply the principles of Sustainable Interaction Design to cloud services use of the digital infrastructure. We perform a critical analysis of current design practice with regard to interactive services, which we identify as the *cornucopian paradigm*. We show how user-centered design principles induce environmental impacts in different ways, and combine with technical and business drivers to drive growth of the infrastructure through a reinforcing feedback cycle. We then create a design rubric, substantially extending that of Blevis [6], to cover impacts of the digital infrastructure. In doing so, we engage in design criticism, identifying examples (both actual and potential) of good and bad practice. We then extend this rubric beyond an eco-efficiency paradigm to consider deeper and more radical perspectives on sustainability, and finish with future directions for exploration.

Author Keywords
Sustainability; Interaction Design; Green Computing; Cloud Computing; Sustainable HCI

ACM Classification Keywords
H.5.m. Information interfaces and presentation (e.g., HCI): Miscellaneous.

INTRODUCTION
The importance of incorporating sustainability principles in the design of digital products and services is becoming increasingly recognised by both academia and industry. Such principles should be applied both when considering how a product is made, but also when considering how a product might be used. Many companies now incorporate reviews of energy efficiency of products, including models of expected user behaviour, and reviews of substances which are potentially hazardous (to people and the environment) in their design process. They also incorporate consideration of the end-of-life of a product—how to encourage recycling of products, and in some cases refurbishment for reuse [27]. In the perspective of Sustainable Interaction Design, Blevis [6] argues that designers of digital products must also be responsible for explaining how resource use is impacted by the artefacts and services they design, as an intrinsic part of the design. As an instrument of fulfilling this responsibility, designers may minimise resource use by moving away from a paradigm of 'invent and dispose' towards one encouraging longevity and sharing of digital devices.

However, one area has received relatively little consideration in the design process—the environmental impact of the infrastructure that grows in support of interactive devices and the cloud services they use. A service on a device does not live in a vacuum. Infrastructural support is required to create the service, to create or source associated content supplied through the service, and to deliver the service over time. Doing this requires use of servers, core and edge network equipment, and potentially content creation equipment such as cameras, sensors etc. We refer to this as the *digital infrastructure*.

People increasingly use digital services for socialising, communicating, organising and entertainment, and such services are often cloud-based. As a result, the infrastructure is a significant contributor to the environmental impact of a device and the services it supports. Furthermore, with the nascent Internet of Things, the impact is likely to increase.

Based on figures for 2007, Malmodin et al. [39] estimate the greenhouse gas impact of the manufacture and running of this digital infrastructure to be 253 Mt CO_2e per annum, of similar order of magnitude to that of computers and other end user devices (278 Mt CO_2e p.a.).[1] Hence a focus on the impact of a device is only considering half the problem.

[1] The infrastructure figure quoted here excludes the share of the fixed telecoms network associated with non-broadband customers.

CHI'16, May 07-12, 2016, San Jose, CA, USA
© 2016 ACM. ISBN 978-1-4503-3362-7/16/05...$15.00
DOI: http://dx.doi.org/10.1145/2858036.2858378

Furthermore, with the growth of streamed media and cloud services, the impact is increasing rapidly. More recent studies of specific digital services [1],[61] show that, especially with the trend towards smaller end-user devices, the infrastructure can account for up to 85% of the environmental impact.

The impact of this infrastructure has begun to draw attention of policymakers, campaigners and researchers. The US EPA [70] identified the growth of energy consumption by data centers as a cause for concern, and Greenpeace [24] has campaigned on the issue. What has drawn less attention in the public eye is the network. This is despite the fact that the network is responsible for over half the impact of the infrastructure [39]. Furthermore, although data centers are used for a number of applications besides the provision of consumer services, the network is primarily used for this. Consumer services, in particular video, make up by far the largest category of data traffic, accounting for 80% of throughput [9].

Design decisions taken when creating an interactive device or service can have a significant impact on the use and development of this digital infrastructure—and hence on the environmental impacts it creates through resource consumption and energy use. Despite this, it has received relatively little consideration in the Sustainable HCI literature, and impacts of infrastructure use do not form part of design considerations used within companies.

In this paper, we apply the principles of Sustainable Interaction Design to cloud services use of the digital infrastructure. We perform a critical analysis of current design practice with regard to interactive services. We show how user-centered design principles induce environmental impacts in different ways, and combine with technical and business drivers to drive growth of the infrastructure through a reinforcing feedback cycle. We then create a design rubric, extending that of Blevis [6] to cover impacts of the digital infrastructure. In doing so, we engage in design criticism, identifying examples (both actual and potential) of good and bad practice. We then extend this rubric beyond an eco-efficiency paradigm to consider deeper and more radical perspectives on sustainability, and finish with future directions for exploration.

RELATED WORK

The work in sustainability related to HCI has mainly focused on front-end interactions between people and digital devices rather than with issues of infrastructure. However, on the level of theory, philosophy, and politics, we as a community have aspired to wider coverage. In this section, we trace the history of notions of sustainability in HCI to support our understanding of digital infrastructure in relation to this.

Origins of the Notion of Sustainable Interaction Design

The notion of Sustainable Interaction Design (SID) originates in Blevis [6]. With respect to infrastructure, Blevis appealed to Kumar et al.'s [36] reformulation of the IPAT equation [8] to show the need to address per-capita energy consumption in our global collective future. In the same year, the *Environmental Sustainability and Interaction* [40] workshop built on notions like VSD [19] to advocate sustainability as a key concern in a values-rich conception of HCI.

Sustainability through Design & Sustainability in Design

This workshop also introduced a distinction between *Sustainability in Design* and *Sustainability through Design*. Sustainability in Design [40]:2122 is characterised as *'how to take account of sustainability as part of the material design of products.'* This is contrasted with Sustainability through Design [40]:2123, which is characterized as *'how to support sustainable lifestyles and decision-making through the design of technology.'* These terms *Sustainability in Design* and *Sustainability through Design* owe to another distinction: that of *Research in Design* and *Research through Design* [16],[75].

Sustainable Interaction Design and Sustainable HCI

In 2010, diSalvo et al. [13] published a survey of the 157 papers on sustainability and HCI to that date, adopting the term *Sustainable HCI. Sustainable Interaction Design* and *Sustainable HCI* have become near-synonyms. Nonetheless, the authors of [13]:1977 make a distinction: *'Sustainable Interaction Design (SID)... describes papers oriented around using sustainability as a 'critical lens'* [25] *...[which]...tend to see a need to fundamentally rethink the methods of HCI in order address sustainability...[and]... see designers as complicit in the unsustainability of current interactive products, aiming to change design to encourage more sustainable effects.'* They contrast this approach with other Sustainable HCI research that *'take known approaches in HCI and apply them to sustainability as a problem domain.'* Our work is clearly situated in this tradition: we will firstly provide a critique of the current design paradigm and highlight its shortcomings, and then propose alternative paradigms illustrated with examples of good and bad practice.

Research in Sustainability in Design

As noted in diSalvo et al. [13], research on sustainability in design has focused primarily on the issue of material use and waste reduction associated with interactive devices. It has studied people's attitudes and practices with regard to mobile technology to guide design in this direction [25],[28]. Remy and Huang [55] categorize research approaches used to encourage device longevity. Some of these are focused on encouraging attachment to the device in different ways, encouraging users to keep them for longer [7],[21],[48],[50],. Others focus on the re-using of old devices by passing them on to others [29],[25], repurposing them in different ways [48],[29],[38] and reusing their subcomponents [30],[74].

In addition to the issue of resource use, some attention has been paid to the energy impacts of design decisions in IT systems. McLachlan and Brewster [41] explore the energy implications of alternative interaction techniques with a laptop computer. Tarzia et al. [67] conduct an in-the-wild study of display power management practices.

More recent work has focused on understanding practices that develop around domestic digital technology, and their resulting impact both in terms of resource and energy usage [4]. This work is notable for adopting a holistic, practice-based perspective on environmental impact, rather than focusing on a single device. It identifies the higher impact associated with 'connoisseurs' who create larger 'constellations' of devices and domestic infrastructure.

Despite the significant impact associated with the digital infrastructure, relatively little research has been conducted by the Sustainable HCI community in this area. It is interesting to note that a sustainability framework developed based on literature study and expert interviews provides thorough coverage of device issues but no mention of broader infrastructure issues [12].

Pan et al. [49] frame key sustainability issues associated with trends in cloud computing of relevance to the HCI community. Bates and Hazas [3] estimate the climate impact of the domestic infrastructure associated with home sensing equipment. Preist and Shabajee [54] quantify the long-term increase in energy use by the internet that results from current trends in user behavior, and propose possible design interventions to mitigate this. Lord et al. [37] identify practices associated with tablet use, estimate the associated infrastructural energy use, and propose design interventions to mitigate this. Bates et al. [5] identify practices which grow ownership and usage of domestic digital technology, including demand on digital infrastructure. Schien et al. [60] model end-to-end energy use of a digital media service, quantify its annual impacts, and estimate reductions in impact enabled by different design interventions. Our work builds on the insights from these, situating them within a wider perspective based on the principles of Sustainable Interaction Design.

Recent Studies and Visions

Our work aligns with many of the recommendations made by Silberman et al. [63]. In particular, we are concerned with both an immediate and a longer timescale understanding of the drivers and impacts of digital infrastructures. In understanding digital infrastructure, we appeal to much work that is outside of HCI, particularly industrial ecology and systems modeling, to contextualize and scope the problem and its components. Like Knowles et al. [34], we also draw inspiration from political science [14] to identify existing discourse within design paradigms, and explore more radical alternatives to this. As alternatives to the current status quo in design thinking with regard to the infrastructure, we firstly consider a reformist, eco-efficiency paradigm and then more radical paradigms. Our inspiration for the latter comes from recent work on collapse informatics [69], computing within limits [51] and sustainability 2.0 [35], which we discuss in more detail later in the paper. Firstly, in the critical tradition of Sustainable Interaction Design, we turn our attention to current design practices and their inadequacies.

THE CURRENT DESIGN PARADIGM AND ITS IMPACT

User-centered design and customer-driven business, together with societal values of individuality, choice and convenience lead to designers working to provide ever faster, richer and more pervasive digital services. They do this through both the design of device ecosystems offering richer functionality and more varied affordances, and through the design of services that exploit such ecosystems. In doing so, designers make the implicit assumption that the digital infrastructure is abundant, relatively cheap to the end-user and will expand to meet future demand. As Lord et al. [37] observe, this means that designers, users and providers assume that 'devices have access to certain intensities and continuities of network service'. Innovation in infrastructure provision tends to support this perspective, with Nielsen's law [45] observing that bandwidth available to a high-end user is increasing by 50% every year.

The majority of innovation in interactive device ecosystems and their associated services focuses on provision to such high-end customers, under the assumption that these are the early adopters of new technologies. Such customers are encouraged to buy increasingly rich device ecosystems, which in turn are reliant on a rich and bandwidth-intensive set of services in the cloud. This strategy also makes the (currently correct) assumption that innovation in the infrastructure, resulting in increased bandwidth and reduced price over time, will allow the majority of users to access such services in the future.

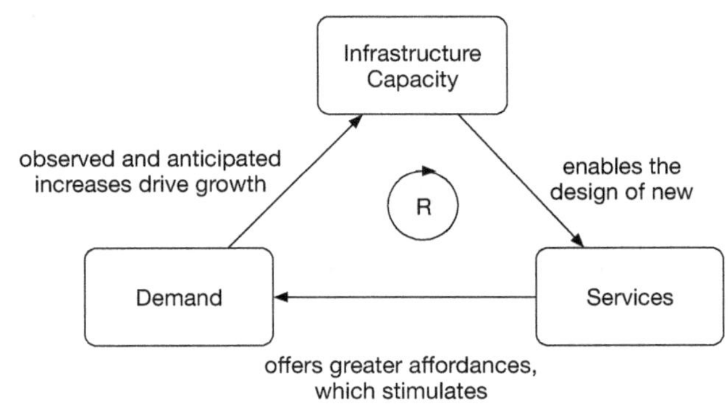

Figure 1: Reinforcing feedback stimulating Infrastructure Growth

Effectively, the provision of digital services to high-end users stimulates latent demand in mainstream users for such services, which means there is a market for infrastructure expansion provided it goes alongside cost reduction in bandwidth provision. The mainstream users then pick up devices and services which were formerly high-end, and they become embedded in everyday practice. Services that most users were happy without become essential to everyday life for the majority of the populace in developed countries. This results in a reinforcing feedback loop encouraging growth of the digital infrastructure.

The (Undesirable) Cornucopian Paradigm

This dominant paradigm, which we refer to as the *cornucopian paradigm*, is reinforced both by faith that Moore's law will continue to hold and deliver efficiency improvements, and by discourse around the cloud which emphasises the 'infinite scalability' [43] of services. The cornucopian paradigm has a number of (often implicit) design principles. We now present the first explicit consolidation of such principles and identify the ways each principle drives increase in infrastructure demand. Elements of these principles are often referred to in academic, design and product advertising literature; we give pointers to examples of this literature to illustrate each of them.

(C1) PERSONAL: Some services are necessarily personal—such as email—but users increasingly expect services traditionally shared by groups of people (family TV, home sound system) to be available on an individual basis: a move from an ideal of a 'happy family' to 'happy individuals' [52]. This means that the infrastructure must deliver more services simultaneously, meaning that more servers and network capacity are required than for shared services.

(C2) VARIETY: Users expect a very large choice of service to be available. Based on this, because of the cheapness of storage, service providers 'make everything available and let the customer decide' [2]. Given the amount of content available, particularly with the rise of user-created content, it means a large amount is never used again. This increases the amount of storage devices required, and hence both use of raw materials to create them and energy to power them.

(C3) INSTANT: Users expect to receive a service straight away, with almost no noticeable access time [44]. To provide this, both servers catering for the individual service and the network infrastructure catering for the combined load of all services must be sufficient to cater comfortably with peak demand, resulting in the need for more servers and network capacity than would otherwise be necessary.

(C4) SHAREABLE: Users want to create content that is available to others, and share it with them [22]. This increases cloud server and storage infrastructure needs, and bandwidth demand to view the content.

(C5) HIGH QUALITY: Users expect increasingly high quality, in the sense of audio, image and video resolution, and services respond by offering increasingly higher resolution video and fidelity of sound [68]. This increases the demand on the network infrastructure, and servers and storage involved in the provision of services. Increasing resolution of user devices means that user-generated content is higher resolution, leading to increased storage requirements both for personal cloud storage services, and also for services that publically share user generated content such as YouTube. The desire for higher quality services also affects content creation equipment, leading to the deployment of new higher resolution cameras (both amateur and professional) and associated infrastructure.

(C6) PERVASIVE: Users increasingly expect each service to be available from any of their devices, transparently [23]. This means that services that historically would be provided locally (such as word processing, diary and music provision) now must be provisioned either partly (through synching of data) or wholly through the infrastructure. This increases server, storage and network provision requirements.

(C7) CONTINUOUS ACCESS: Users expect to access services at any time, anywhere. They want to be able to contact others (increasingly often via video) or view entertainment in any 'down time' [37], wherever they may be. This stimulates the growth of network coverage—particularly mobile networks and Wi-Fi, which are energy intensive components of the infrastructure.

(C8) ETERNAL: Users expect content that they generate to be 'always alive and always available' [58] (unless they choose otherwise) to themselves and others. This increases cloud server and storage infrastructure needs.

(C9) EPHEMERAL: Users create and save content without regard to whether they (or others) will actually use it again. It is easier just to save it just in case than to think about whether it may or may not be used again. Hence a lot of what is saved is ephemeral and never used again. This increases demand on storage infrastructure.

(C10) RICH, CROSS-MODAL AND UBIQUITOUS: Users increasingly look for, and businesses encourage, a collection of services that interact and support each other, providing a richer experience overall [46]. They also increasingly use services in the 'background' of their attention to provide ambient experiences and/or control through the Internet of Things [10]. Hence users use services more often, and use multiple services simultaneously. This increases the demand for services in general, and so amplifies the impact of the other nine factors.

Cloud-based services are at times (particularly in a corporate context) able to reduce energy and resource consumption by consolidation and more efficient use of servers stored in state-of-the-art green data centers [71]. However, in the consumer context, the design principles described above result in growth both of energy consumption by the infrastructure, and in demand on raw materials for infrastructural construction.

In many ways, these principles are desirable to the user. This contrasts with design approaches such as Choreographed Obsolescence [72] and Disposable Technology [28], which arguably encourage waste primarily to improve revenue rather than to benefit the user. A human-centered design process would identify these principles as giving an improved user experience, and offering services to make life easier and more pleasurable. However, as design theorists have observed [20], a human-centered design process is not necessarily humanity-centered. The choices that an individual user may make can result in collective longer-term outcomes that are detrimental to the overall sustainability of the system [57].

Having considered the current design paradigm, and its consequence on the digital infrastructure, we now consider approaches to mitigate its environmental impact.

STRATEGIES FOR 'SOLVING' THE PROBLEM

Broadly, there are two approaches to trying to contain this problem without addressing user interaction.

1. Efficiency improvements in the underlying infrastructure. Network equipment is increasing both in the bandwidth it can provide and also the energy (and, to a lesser extent, resource) efficiency with which it does this. Similarly, servers within data centers provide computational power more efficiently. Such efficiency improvements can be used to partly offset the increasing demand.

2. Smart use of the infrastructure
As well as improving efficiency of the underlying infrastructure, the infrastructure can be used more efficiently through appropriate algorithms and architectures. On a local level, compression algorithms partly compensate the growth of bandwidth from increases in resolution and use time. Video streams can adapt to the resolution of a device to ensure that unnecessarily large images are not sent. Peer-to-peer architectures can reduce the need for data centers by exploiting unused compute resources [32]. Local caching and the use of content delivery networks can reduce the load on the core network [59]. Such interventions are already taking place as increased efficiency of services has the potential to provide better performance and thus improve user experience.

Both of these approaches have value, and are already making significant contributions to the efficiency of the infrastructure. Despite this, the overall infrastructure is growing too fast for the efficiency gains to offset this growth, and there is currently an unsustainable absolute growth in energy consumption. If this is not adequate, then something else will need to change to reflect this future reality: the design paradigm discussed above.

A DESIGN RUBRIC: ALTERNATIVES TO THE CORNUCOPIAN PARADIGM

If we are to move interaction design away from the cornucopian paradigm, it is important to reflect on the consequences of a design of a digital product or service on the wider infrastructure and develop an awareness of the resulting environmental impact of such consequences. We now present a design rubric, in the form of a number of questions for designers to reflect on, which aims to do this. Our rubric, the Rubric of Infrastructural Effects (RoIE) is intended as an extension of Blevis' [6] Rubric of Material Effects (RoME). Following Blevis, we use two core principles to generate a set of questions to encourage reflection on the environmental consequences of design decisions and how to mitigate them. Blevis identified the *invention and disposal* of new types of device as being a driver of increased ownership and therefore material use and waste generation. The corresponding principle behind RoIE is *infrastructural expansion and obsolescence*: to what extent does a device, and the services it enables, encourage deployment of new infrastructure or the replacement of existing infrastructure as no longer adequate. Blevis' second principle, *renewal and reuse*, identifies the use and replacement of existing devices as a source of material and energy impact, and the potential for reuse to reduce this. The RoIE equivalent of this is *infrastructural use and sharing*: the energy consumption in the infrastructure to support services a device enables, and the more efficient use of the infrastructure through sharing to reduce energy and material use. The resultant questions that emerge from these two principles are:

(E1) *Does the design encourage infrastructural expansion or obsolescence?*

(E2) *Does the design encourage increased infrastructural use?*

(E3) *Does the design mitigate or reduce infrastructural use in some way?*

(E4) *Does the design encourage digital waste, or avoidance of it?*

(E5) *Does the design promote the sharing of infrastructure?*

We now discuss each question in more detail, and illustrate them through a number of examples—both potential and actual. Through these illustrations, we engage in design criticism, pointing to existing practice both positive and detrimental, and giving examples of potential new positive practice. We also refer back to principles in the cornucopian (C) paradigm where relevant.

(E1) Does the design encourage infrastructural expansion or obsolescence?

There are broadly three ways in which a new service can strongly encourage or require new infrastructure to be deployed: (a) It can require new functionality of the infrastructure. (b) It can require greater reach of the infrastructure. (c) It can require larger capacity in the infrastructure. We consider each of these in turn.

When a new interactive digital service requires new functionality of the infrastructure, it can require new infrastructural equipment to be deployed. This infrastructure will have environmental impacts, resulting from materials used in its deployment, energy consumption during its use, and impacts of equipment disposal associated with its ongoing maintenance and renewal.

For example, the 'Surfcam' service [64] provides real-time and continuous views of surfing beaches (C5,7). Uptake of this service is resulting in the new deployment of cameras around the world, together with local access network connectivity, primarily or exclusively for the provision of this digital service. As another example, cloud gaming services provide a local high-end gaming experience (C3,5,7,10) with the rendering and game logic taking place in remote data centers. This is resulting in the deployment of additional specialised graphics rendering hardware.

Qualitative changes in existing services may also require new functionality of the infrastructure. This can result in the obsolescence of existing infrastructural equipment, forcing the upgrading of it by organisations providing content to the service. For example, the potential move to 8K video would result in the obsolescence of existing professional filming and editing equipment in media providers, meaning a large turnover of equipment in a short period of time to meet new user expectations of image quality (C5). This would result in resource consumption and electronic waste.

Secondly, new devices and their associated services can require greater infrastructural reach. This is currently happening in the home. Users look to their personal devices for entertainment anywhere in the home (C1,6,7). Furthermore, the Internet of Things becomes more of an everyday reality (C10). IP-enabled devices and services such as networked TVs, smart home technologies and home audio mean that a home WiFi connection is becoming an essential in many households. As a result, WiFi equipment together with signal boosters are being deployed to ensure good coverage throughout the home. This trend has combined with the trend towards lower power devices (laptops, tablets etc.) so that domestic WiFi routers are often the single largest consumer of energy among IT equipment in UK homes [11].

Thirdly, a new service may require a greater capacity infrastructure to support its wide deployment. An example of the first is the move away from broadcast and cable transmission of home TV/film viewing towards streaming on-demand of such services (C1,2,3). This results in a step-change in demand for internet bandwidth, and so will stimulate significant expansion of the core internet [33] as on-demand moves increasingly into the mainstream.

Another example of a step-change in digital service is the 'always on' remote videoconference [31]. If it becomes the norm in remote working to have high-quality video connections with the rest of one's team (C1,3,5,7), it will significantly increase bandwidth demand.

(E2) Does the design encourage increased infrastructural use?

Some services may not result in a step-change in demand on the infrastructure, but nonetheless may encourage increased use and therefore increased impact. This impact consists of the energy to provide the service, and also the longer-term expansion of the infrastructure to handle this usage along with other new services. For example the move from SD to HD video (C5). While not a step-change service change on its own, it does roughly double the infrastructural demand for each video streamed.

Similarly, the deployment of mobile services on smartphones has significantly increased the demand on the mobile network, as it means people are using networked devices more often and more intensively than they used to. This demand for mobile services, particularly those associated with audio and video often connected with the practice of 'filling down time' observed by Lord et al. [37] is driving the move to 4G mobile networks. Such networks, while more energy efficient in terms of the delivery of a given service, use more energy overall.

Another digital product (and it's associated services) that is increasing demand in this way is the Action Cam. Sales of Action Cams are over 5m units per year and increasing [66]. New practices that are developing around their use, e.g. by cycle commuters, extreme sports fans and other communities, are resulting in significant amounts of video content being uploaded to the cloud. A deeper understanding of how these new practices are developing, their associated environmental implications, and what potential there is to 'guide' such practices to be lower impact is a fruitful area for further research.

Services that are used at peak times make stronger contributions both to energy usage and the longer-term drive towards network expansion. The main driver for expansion of network and server infrastructure that support digital services is not the total use over the whole day, but rather the highest (peak) demand requiring servicing at a given time. As peak demand increases, more infrastructure is deployed to ensure continuity of service. Furthermore, the higher peak demand is compared with average demand on a given resource, the less efficiently that resource is used—resulting in waste of energy and material resources. If a service increases demand at such peak times, it is likely to contribute to increased infrastructure deployment over time. For example, the drive for personalised on-demand video (C1,2,3) and other services used at peak times.

(E3) Does the design mitigate or reduce infrastructural use in some way?

Our first two questions in the rubric focus on negative impacts and examples. We now turn to approaches for reducing such impact. Three possible approaches to this are (i) design a service to encourage users to choose less intensive options within it; (ii) design a service to encourage users to use it, rather than other more intensive services; (iii) design a service to reduce or avoid usage of infrastructure at peak times. We consider each in turn.

As noted above, both users and service providers often assume that they want the highest quality possible. For that reason, there is a move towards higher resolution (HD, UHD, 8K) though it may have limited impact on user experience once a certain resolution has been reached. Many video streams will automatically default to the highest resolution available that the end user device will accept. However, some services do not do that. For example, the BBC iPlayer service defaults to standard definition, and the user must explicitly select 'view in HD' if they wish a higher definition image. This is an example of the use of a 'nudge' approach to encourage users by default to use the lower bandwidth option. Audio also can use such an approach. Spotify defaults to 160Kbps as 'normal' with the option of 'high' quality requiring accessing the settings to change. Interestingly, it has different defaults for mobile devices—with 'normal' being 96Kbps. From an impact perspective, this default behaviour will reduce demand on the mobile network—the most energy-intensive part of the network infrastructure.

Secondly, one service can 'compete' with a more intensive service and encourage people away from it. For example, text messaging reduces the number of calls made over the mobile network. Services such as HipChat [26] provide rich (but primarily text-based) environments for collaborative working and so encourage voice or visual connection only when it provides additional value rather than as a default. If these replace regular audio and visual connections, it will reduce infrastructure usage.

Thirdly, if a service is designed to use less resource at peak times and 'time shift' that use to times of reduced demand, then it will reduce the need for infrastructure expansion and use the existing infrastructure more efficiently. An example of a service that already does this is Apple newsstand. It downloads content overnight, at times when the network is less used for media streaming. Other downloads of content that do not need to be used in real time, such as app updates [37], could also be done in this way. Similarly, uploads of content (such as from an Action Cam) could be timed to take place automatically off-peak. Where data or content is used on-demand, such as media streaming, proactive local caching [54] at off-peak times could be used to reduce peak demand. This would be personalised, based on user behaviour—such as downloading at off-peak times the next episodes in a series that a user is regularly watching. Or, in the case of on-demand music streaming, inserting some previously locally cached tracks known to be acceptable to the user (for example, because they have played them more than once before) into a stream, allowing the rate of download at peak times to be reduced. More sophisticated approaches to reducing peak demand while maintaining a good user experience of different services is another rich area for research.

(E4) Does the design encourage 'digital waste', or the avoidance of it?

Digital waste [54] is the accessing of a cloud-based digital service without actually making use of it, or only making partial use of it. It is the digital equivalent of leaving the lights on in an empty room and can take several forms.

Downloading of content that is never used.

For example, podcast subscriptions that download automatically to allow instant access (C3), but a person no longer listens to or is heavily behind on. More intelligent download strategies, based on the number of prior episodes stored locally and the speed at which the user is accessing them, would mitigate this.

Another example of digital waste through non-use of downloaded content is web page bounce. If a user downloads a page, but leaves it straight away because it was not what they were looking for, this is waste. Sometimes this is simply a necessary part of the search process: the user cannot assess the value of the page to them without actually looking at it. However, at other times it may be because either the source-linking page or the search service used to locate the destination page provides inadequate or misleading information. Hence, the design of web pages and search algorithms that reduce the chance of the 'wrong' content being accessed in the search process will reduce digital waste.

Downloading of content that is already available locally.

For example, users download PDF articles that they have downloaded before because it is easier to locate them online than locally. It would be relatively simple for a browser plug-in to perform an automatic local search for an article downloaded from the same url, and then checking with a conditional request to determine if the article has been modified before commencing the download.

Streaming/downloading content that is only partially used.

A common practice, particularly but not exclusively among teenagers, is the streaming of (free) YouTube videos to provide music, without watching the visuals [37]. This anecdotally widespread practice is likely to be responsible for substantial energy waste, both in Google data centres and in the network. Technically, it would not be difficult to remotely detect such behaviour (e.g. when the page visibility API determines the YouTube tab/window is in the background, or when a user queues a long music playlist.) A 'video on/off' option could be provided to override this detection where it makes an error. However, it may be the case that legal (copyright) issues mean this waste cannot currently be resolved in such a way.

Another example is the partial use of video. Some video players force download from the beginning, so even if you are interested in a late section in it you must download the whole thing. Others encourage 'scrubbing'—resulting not in the whole video being downloaded, but sections of it in an attempt to find the relevant bit. A recent design innovation on YouTube—video scrubber preview images—makes it easier to find the relevant spot in a video (or to assess whether it appears interesting overall) without downloading sections, and so helps reduce associated digital waste.

Web pages have increased to approximately 150 times their size in 1995, now averaging over 2MB [15]. Long webpages may only have the top section of them read, and the rest be 'waste' to the user. The size of a page is increased by the use of scripts and embedded video content (C10)—again often providing content not of direct interest to the user. This may be necessary for the business model of the site provider—advertisements aiming to catch people's attention benefit from animation, even if this uses more energy [62] and are an unwelcome distraction for many users. Awareness of the consequence of web page bloat could be encouraged through the use of an enhanced version of a service such as 'noscript' which blocks plug-ins on a page unless the user chooses to activate them. By providing an estimate of the energy or environmental cost of activating each one, and the total 'saved' on the page through deactivation, it could encourage improved design practices around web page bloat.

Uploading content that is never accessed.

Waste can occur through upload as well as download. With cloud storage and backup now commonplace and automated, content (such as photos) users take are often uploaded automatically (C4,8,9). Some of this content is consciously intended as ephemeral—for example, taking a joke photo to text to a friend, or photographing a whiteboard brainstorm to type up. Other content is not intended as ephemeral, but is uploaded without regard for whether it has sufficient interest and quality to be worth using in the future. Waste occurs both in the use of infrastructure to upload, and also in the ongoing use of infrastructure to store the content.

It may not be straightforward to identify ephemeral content prior to upload. However, research into understanding practices associated with image and video use could identify behaviours associated with ephemeral use. These in turn could be automatically detected, and the user given the option of deleting associated content. For example, if a user regularly sends ephemeral images by text, the sending device could offer the option of deleting the image at the moment of sending. If a user takes a number of similar images, planning on keeping the best few, then automated software could detect those with obvious flaws (such as motion blur or poor exposure) and propose which to keep and which to delete prior to upload.

(E5) Does the design promote the sharing of infrastructure?

The desire to have personalised on-demand entertainment (C1,2,3,5,7) is a significant driver in infrastructure expansion. Techniques that encourage sharing (either overtly or covertly) are of value here. Lord et al. [37] propose encouraging people back to broadcast media. Less radical approaches would be to find ways of synching viewing between people who are accessing the same content to allow multicast. One example of this is micro-registration, where several unicast streams in video-on-demand with approximately similar timings are aligned in order to bundle them into a multicast stream and thus to reduce bandwidth use in upstream network links [17]. This is relatively transparent to users, but more intrusive techniques could be used to combine more streams—for example, by delaying the start of some by inserting some other content (such as adverts, if that is part of the business model). How much delay is acceptable, and techniques to make such a delay more acceptable, is an area for research.

A very different approach to sharing infrastructure is provided by Freifunk [18]. It is a non-commercial initiative for free wireless networks. Its members provide free access to their WiFi routers to other members. They operate their routers with a custom firmware that enables additional services. Together the routers form a mesh network over which members can access a variety of services including Internet access. This makes more effective use of (usually underused) WiFi infrastructure through sharing, and will reduce usage of (often overused, and energy intensive) mobile networks for data access.

From Cornucopian Paradigm to Eco-Efficiency Paradigm

These questions provide a rubric, extending that of Blevis [6], to incorporate sustainability considerations related to infrastructural impact within the design process. These move treatment of the infrastructure from a *cornucopian* paradigm to an *eco-efficiency* paradigm: a paradigm in which environmental impacts are considered alongside other factors within design and are reduced where possible. Such a paradigm is already widespread in progressive business practice [73] when applied to a specific product. However, it currently rarely extends further, to the impact of the infrastructure induced by a given product and the services it enables. We believe it would be relatively straightforward, and beneficial, for companies to incorporate infrastructural considerations within Design for Environment guidelines for such products and services.

OTHER PARADIGMS

Many argue that the eco-efficiency paradigm is not adequate to meet the challenges society faces. Hence we now turn to other paradigms from the Sustainable HCI literature and elsewhere, consider how they can apply to the digital infrastructure, and extend our rubric with further questions addressing the issues this raises.

Computing within Limits

The paradigm of computing within limits [51] considers that the Earth's planetary boundaries [56] impose limits within which technical, social and economic development must take place if it is to be sustainable. Information technology must take account of such limits as it is deployed and used in the future.

A global digital infrastructure operating in a world that remains within planetary boundaries would need to (i) take an appropriate (and probably relatively small) share of the total energy generated in such a world; (ii) use an appropriate share of non-renewable resources (such as rare earth metals) in its deployment and maintenance, and use circular economy [47] techniques to wholly reuse these when replacing old equipment with new; (iii) ensure that any new or improved services which require more of the infrastructure (such as higher bandwidth) are only deployed when technological advancement in the infrastructure results in efficiency gains which will at least offset the increased energy use of wide deployment of such services.

If IT is not to become elitist, and to remain something which is available to the majority of the world's population, a further constraint is required: The infrastructure must be capable of providing acceptable levels of service to the global population, within the first 3 constraints. Could current trends with regard to digital service demand be supported in such a world ([54][5])? To determine if this is the case is a key research question. It requires (i) quantifying the infrastructural impacts of existing service demand, and extrapolating these to assume worldwide deployment; (ii) quantifying likely increases in future levels of service demand, including the impact of potential new trends such as Internet of Things and Quantified Self; (iii) understanding and quantifying anticipated technological advancements and the efficiency improvements they bring.

Broadly, the key question is: Are expected efficiency improvements sufficient to allow 'western' levels of service consumption (including its anticipated growth) to take place globally within an appropriate energy and resource budget. It is interesting to note (as has been observed in the context of network use by media services [54]) that such global deployment *may* be feasible within planetary boundaries, based on current technical trajectories. This is very different from many other sectors, such as travel (car, plane) and food (particularly meat) where a qualitatively different breakthrough will be necessary if current western service levels are to be used by all.

However, such 'cornucopia-within-limits' may *not* be possible, and the limits may place restrictions on what service levels can be provided. If so, it is important to understand the environmental costs of different services, and consider what bundles of digital services could be deployed worldwide within environmental limits. Progressive providers could use nudge approaches, 'choice editing' [65] of particularly intensive services and throttling of service levels to encourage or require users to remain within their personal share of the global budget. This leads to questions beyond the eco-efficiency set listed above.

(R1) If this service were to be used by all the world's population, what would the overall environmental impact of the infrastructure be? Can we imagine a future scenario where this would lie within limits imposed by planetary boundaries?

(R2) Is the service able to deal robustly with reduced availability of infrastructure levels?

(R3) Does the business model assume continued growth in infrastructure? If so, what is the risk associated with this?

Collapse Informatics

Collapse informatics [69] can be considered as a more pessimistic version of computing-within-limits: environmental and other pressures risk precipitating a retreat in living standards or even societal collapse. What can Information Technology do to make us more resilient?

From this perspective, in addition to the questions posed above, we must consider what infrastructure might be available in such a scenario, and what services could, or should, run on it. This brings in questions of societal value against the level of infrastructural use of such services. For example, it is likely that the value (to individuals and society) of unlimited text email is worth the relatively low burden in all but the most extreme scenarios. However, the higher infrastructural burden of unlimited video sharing, together with the arguably lesser social value of yet another kitten video, means that such a service may become restricted within many collapse scenarios. This leads to further design rubric questions:

(R4) What is the societal value of the proposed service, and in what scenarios of restricted infrastructure would this justify the resultant usage?

(R5) Can a restricted version of the service be imagined, and what would its value and infrastructural burden be? In what collapse scenarios would this be deployable?

Responsible Design and Sustainable HCI 2.0 [19][35]

In their different ways, these paradigms provide an alternative perspective to the techno-positivist assumption that more and richer digital services are necessarily better for individuals and society. They argue that certain forms of technology use can, at times, increase stress and reduce wellbeing in an individual, reduce a sense of community and quality of life, and distance people from the natural environment and so not engender a sense of caring and responsibility to the world. In such cases, it may be better not to design and deploy such services [53]. As with collapse informatics, this is a form of value judgment on different services, but the criteria of what is valued is different. Rather than prioritizing what can support societal cohesion at times of crisis, these paradigms prioritize what encourages improved wellbeing, slow living and engagement with the natural world. (Though, of course, the two are not necessarily mutually exclusive.)

In this context, it is appropriate to question our increasing need to be connected, which at times can feel almost neurotic. Perhaps a healthier relationship with digital technology and the digital infrastructure will be better both for us and the planet. Lord et al. [37] have proposed using techniques to encourage reflection on our relationship with connectivity, and the use of apps to encourage 'filling time' in more healthy ways without the need for connectivity. We incorporate this within our rubric as follows:

(R6) Does the service encourage a healthy relationship with digital technology, and avoid promoting inappropriate dependency on the digital infrastructure?

More generally, the call for Value Sensitive Design, which was one of the original inspirations for Sustainable Interaction Design, argues that designers must bear some ethical responsibility for the broad impact of the services they create on society. This leads us to our final, and most challenging, question:

(R7) Is the service in tune with your values, as a designer? Can you say with heart that the benefits it brings humanity is worth the environmental costs of the supporting infrastructure?

DISCUSSION

Like Blevis' RoME, we are interested in Material Effects; however, the material effects of infrastructural use are often outside the 'boundary' of awareness of the designer. The underlying issues are the same–does it stimulate additional resource or energy use–but are easier to 'not notice'. This explains why so little literature has considered them up to now. It is only through consideration of systems [54] and practice [37] that such questions begin to emerge.

It is not necessary for designers of new devices, new interaction modalities and new services to be unconsciously trapped between the desires of the user and the promises of unlimited infrastructure. The underlying principles of the reformist rubric–namely that resources and energy should be used efficiently–are widely accepted, but not yet applied in the specific domain of the digital infrastructure. We believe that *all* designers have a responsibility to be aware of, and mitigate where practical, the environmental impacts of their work. Blevis advocates reflection on the principles in his Rubric of Material Effects to integrate consideration of the environmental impact of interaction design, specifically the use of physical resources, in the design process. We advocate use of our reformist rubric in exactly the same way, to encourage reflection of the impact of design decisions on the infrastructure–in terms of increased use and expansion–and the resulting environmental effects.

We believe that this is necessary, but may not be sufficient. The more radical additions to the rubric, which consider questions of *limits to growth* and *societal values* as they apply to the digital infrastructure, have less widespread acceptance. Instead, it is vital that *some* interaction designers who resonate with these principles explore them more deeply, question the mainstream assumptions and develop alternative design paradigms, and that consideration of the infrastructure forms part of such work. Such a 'design counterculture' is a key part of the social dialectic, and through the work of 'tempered radicals' [42] will increasingly influence the mainstream position.

CONCLUSIONS AND FUTURE DIRECTIONS

In this paper, we have argued that the cornucopian paradigm implicitly adopted by interaction designers towards the infrastructure is inappropriate. In the short term, it leads to unnecessary environmental impact. In the long term it increases risk—both for individual companies with business models dependent on this assumption but also for humanity as a whole, which needs to find a way of living within planetary boundaries to ensure its long-term survival. We have substantially extended the design rubric of Blevis to consider impacts associated with the digital infrastructure, and provided numerous examples illustrating this—both of bad and potential good practice. We have initially adopted a reformist, eco-efficiency perspective on the problem, to produce a rubric that can be used to inspire enhancements to existing design-for-environment processes used by progressive companies. However, recognizing the many voices that argue that such an approach does not go far enough, we also extend the rubric to encourage designers to incorporate more radical perspectives in their consideration of the infrastructure.

Expanding Sustainable Interaction Design to consider the digital infrastructure significantly broadens the research space. The few papers published so far, though making valuable contributions, only touch the tip of the iceberg. We have highlighted in our discussions above a number of specific research topics our analysis opens up. More broadly, we see four strands of inquiry necessary:

1. Development of accessible guidelines based on the above rubric for designers to take infrastructure into account in design of interactive devices and services.

2. Further integration of Sustainable Interaction Design with the quantification of environmental impact developed in Industrial Ecology can allow the impact of different facets of the problem to be estimated, and how effective different potential interventions may be. This will aid prioritization of research.

3. Development of a more nuanced understanding of user need with regard to cloud services. Rather than treating want as a need to be satisfied through expanding the cornucopian infrastructure, develop an understanding of the value of different service aspects to users, and which of these aspects are more 'negotiable' (e.g. immediate on-demand video vs. wait a minute). Furthermore, development of a theory of design to make compromises in performance or functionality more comfortable to the user.

4. Scenario analysis of potential future trajectories of infrastructure and associated services, considering the spread of service technologies, user practices and improvements in infrastructure technology and efficiency. Through this, development of an understanding of the overall challenge to remain within planetary boundaries, and identification of viable future trajectories and what is necessary to follow them.

By broadening Sustainable Interaction Design to deeply consider the digital infrastructure in this way, we open opportunities for significant environmental improvements in the short term. Furthermore, the improved understanding of the overall impact of IT in the longer term can be used to shape development to move towards sustainability.

ACKNOWLEDGEMENTS

Thanks to Paul Shabajee, CHI reviewers, and all at 'Table 2' of the ICT4S2015 Sustainable Data Centers workshop.

REFERENCES

[1] Mohammad Ahmadi Achachlouei,, Åsa Moberg, and Elisabeth Hochschorner. 2015. Life Cycle Assessment of a Magazine, Part I: Tablet Edition in Emerging and Mature States. *Journal of Industrial Ecology* (2015).

[2] Chris Anderson, 2006. *The Long Tail.* Hyperion.

[3] Oliver Bates and Mike Hazas. 2013. Exploring the hidden impacts of HomeSys: energy and emissions of home sensing and automation. In *Proceedings of the 2013 ACM conference on Pervasive and ubiquitous computing adjunct publication* (UbiComp '13 Adjunct). ACM, New York, NY, USA, 809-814.

[4] Oliver Bates, Mike Hazas, Adrian Friday, Janine Morley, and Adrian K. Clear. 2014. Towards an holistic view of the energy and environmental impacts of domestic media and IT. In *Proceedings of the SIGCHI Conference on Human Factors in Computing Systems* (CHI '14). ACM, New York, NY, USA, 1173-1182.

[5] Oliver Bates, Carolynne Lord, Bran Knowles, Adrian Friday, Adrian Clear, and Mike Hazas. 2015. Exploring (un) sustainable growth of digital technologies in the home. In Proceedings ICT4S 2015, Atlantic Press, 300-309.

[6] Eli Blevis. 2007. Sustainable interaction design: invention & disposal, renewal & reuse. In *Proceedings of the SIGCHI Conference on Human Factors in Computing Systems* (CHI '07). ACM, New York, NY, USA, 503-512.

[7] Eli Blevis, Kevin Makice, William Odom, David Roedl, Christian Beck, Shunying Blevis, and Arvind Ashok. 2007. Luxury & new luxury, quality & equality. In *Proceedings of the 2007 conference on Designing pleasurable products and interfaces* (DPPI '07). ACM, New York, NY, USA, 296-311.

[8] Marian Chertow. 2000. The IPAT equation and its variants. *Journal of Industrial Ecology 4,*4:13–29.

[9] Cisco Visual Networking Index: Forecast and Methodology, 2014-2019 White Paper. Retrieved 23rd September 2015 from:

http://www.cisco.com/c/en/us/solutions/collateral/service-provider/ip-ngn-ip-next-generation-network/white_paper_c11-481360.html

[10] Andy Daecher and Tom Galizia, 2015. 'Ambient Computing: Putting the Internet of Things to work'. In *Tech Trends 2015: The Fusion of Business and IT.* Deloitte University Press.

[11] Department of Energy and Climate Change. 2013. Household Electricity Survey. Retrieved 24th September 2015 from https://www.gov.uk/government/publications/household-electricity-survey--2

[12] Tawanna Dillahunt, Jennifer Mankoff, and Jodi Forlizzi. 2010. A proposed framework for assessing environmental sustainability in the HCI community. In *Examining Appropriation, Re-use, and Maintenance of Sustainability Workshop at CHI.* 2010.

[13] Carl DiSalvo, Phoebe Sengers, and Hrönn Brynjarsdóttir. 2010. Mapping the landscape of sustainable HCI. In *Proceedings of the SIGCHI Conference on Human Factors in Computing Systems* (CHI '10). ACM, New York, NY, USA, 1975-1984.

[14] John S. Dryzek, 2013. *The politics of the earth: Environmental discourses.* Oxford University Press.

[15] Tammy Everts. Page Bloat Update. Retrieved 24th September 2015 from http://www.soasta.com/blog/page-bloat-average-web-page-2-mb/

[16] Daniel Fallman. 2003. Design-oriented human-computer interaction. In *Proceedings of the SIGCHI Conference on Human Factors in Computing Systems* (CHI '03). ACM, New York, NY, USA, 225-232.

[17] Reza Farrahi Moghaddam, Fereydoun Farrahi Moghaddam and Mohamed Cheriet. A Graph-based Perspective to Total Carbon Footprint Assessment of Non-marginal Technology-driven Projects—Use case of {OTT/IPTV}. In *Computing Research Repository,* September 2014. arXiv:1409.0876

[18] Freifunk. Retrieved 23rd September 2015 from https://freifunk.net/en/

[19] Batya Friedman (Editor). 1997. *Human Values and the Design of Computer Technology.* Stanford CA: CSLI Press.

[20] Tony Fry. 1999. *A New design philosophy: an introduction to defuturing.* UNSW Press.

[21] Silke Gegenbauer and Elaine M. Huang. 2012. Inspiring the design of longer-lived electronics through an understanding of personal attachment. In *Proceedings of the Designing Interactive Systems Conference* (DIS '12). ACM, New York, NY, USA, 635-644.

[22] Google. Google Photos Shared Albums Advert. Accessed 30th December 2015 at https://www.google.com/photos/about/?page=shared-albums

[23] Google. Google Photos from All Devices advert. Accessed 30th December 2015 at https://www.google.com/photos/about/?page=auto-backup

[24] Greenpeace. (2012). How Clean is Your Cloud ? Retrieved 18th September 2015 from http://www.greenpeace.org/international/en/publications/Campaign-reports/Climate-Reports/How-Clean-is-Your-Cloud/

[25] Kristin Hanks, William Odom, David Roedl, and Eli Blevis. 2008. Sustainable millennials: attitudes towards sustainability and the material effects of interactive technologies. In *Proceedings of the SIGCHI Conference on Human Factors in Computing Systems* (CHI '08). ACM, New York, NY, USA, 333-342.

[26] https://www.hipchat.com, retrieved 23rd September 2015.

[27] HP Design for Environment. Retrieved 24th September 2015 from http://www8.hp.com/us/en/hp-information/environment/design-for-environment.html

[28] Elaine M. Huang and Khai N. Truong. 2008. Breaking the disposable technology paradigm: opportunities for sustainable interaction design for mobile phones. In *Proceedings of the SIGCHI Conference on Human Factors in Computing Systems* (CHI '08). ACM, New York, NY, USA, 323-332.

[29] Huang, Elaine M., Koji Yatani, Khai N. Truong, Julie A. Kientz, and Shwetak N. Patel. 2009. Understanding mobile phone situated sustainability: the influence of local constraints and practices on transferability. *IEEE Pervasive Computing* 1 (2009): 46-53.

[30] Jina Huh, Kevin Nam, and Nikhil Sharma. 2010. Finding the lost treasure: understanding reuse of used computing devices. In *Proceedings of the SIGCHI Conference on Human Factors in Computing Systems* (CHI '10). ACM, New York, NY, USA, 1875-1878.

[31] Inc.com. An all-day video conference for remote workers: crazy or brilliant? Retrieved 23rd September 2015 from http://www.inc.com/yakowicz/how-shutterstock-handles-remote-workers.html

[32] Dmytro Karamshuk, Nishanth Sastry, Andrew Secker, and Jigna Chandaria. 2015. ISP-friendly Peer-assisted On-demand Streaming of Long Duration Content in BBC iPlayer. In *Proceedings of INFOCOM 2015,* 289-297.

[33] Kiyo Ishii, Junya Kurumida, Ken-ichi Sato, Tomohiro Kudoh, and Shu Namiki. 2015. Unifying Top-down and Bottom-up Approaches to Evaluate Network Energy Consumption. *Journal of Lightwave Technology, 99*, 2015.

[34] Bran Knowles, Lynne Blair, Mike Hazas, and Stuart Walker. 2013. Exploring sustainability research in computing: where we are and where we go next. In *Proceedings of the 2013 ACM international joint conference on Pervasive and ubiquitous computing* (UbiComp '13). ACM, New York, NY, USA, 305-314.

[35] Bran Knowles, Lynne Blair, Paul Coulton, and Mark Lochrie. 2014. Rethinking plan A for sustainable HCI. In *Proceedings of the SIGCHI Conference on Human Factors in Computing Systems* (CHI '14). ACM, New York, NY, USA, 3593-3596.

[36] Vishesh Kumar, Danny J. Bee, Prasad S. Shirodkar, Serdar Tumkor, Bernhard P. Bettig, and John W. Sutherland. 2005. Towards sustainable 'product and material flow' cycles: identifying barriers to achieving product multi-use and zero waste. In *ASME 2005 International Mechanical Engineering Congress and Exposition*, pp. 433-442. American Society of Mechanical Engineers, 2005.

[37] Carolynne Lord, Mike Hazas, Adrian K. Clear, Oliver Bates, Rosalind Whittam, Janine Morley, and Adrian Friday. 2015. Demand in My Pocket: Mobile Devices and the Data Connectivity Marshalled in Support of Everyday Practice. In *Proceedings of the 33rd Annual ACM Conference on Human Factors in Computing Systems* (CHI '15). ACM, New York, NY, USA, 2729-2738.

[38] Leah Maestri and Ron Wakkary. 2011. Understanding repair as a creative process of everyday design. In *Proceedings of the 8th ACM conference on Creativity and cognition* (C&C '11). ACM, New York, NY, USA, 81-90.

[39] Jens Malmodin, Åsa Moberg, Dag Lundén, Goran Finnveden & N. Lövehagen 2010. Greenhouse Gas Emissions and Operational Electricity Use in the ICT and Entertainment & Media Sectors. *Journal of Industrial Ecology 14*(5).

[40] Jennifer C. Mankoff, Eli Blevis, Alan Borning, Batya Friedman, Susan R. Fussell, Jay Hasbrouck, Allison Woodruff, and Phoebe Sengers. 2007. Environmental sustainability and interaction. In *CHI '07 Extended Abstracts on Human Factors in Computing Systems* (CHI EA '07). ACM, New York, NY, USA, 2121-2124.

[41] Ross McLachlan and Stephen Brewster. 2012. Towards new widgets to reduce PC power consumption. In *CHI '12 Extended Abstracts on Human Factors in Computing Systems* (CHI EA '12). ACM, New York, NY, USA, 2153-2158.

[42] Meyerson, D. (2001). *Tempered radicals.* Boston, MA: Harvard Business School.

[43] Microsoft Azure. Retrieved 24th September 2015 from https://azure.microsoft.com/en-gb/services/cloud-services/

[44] The Minions. Xfinity Internet Commercial. Retrieved 29th December 2015 from https://www.youtube.com/watch?v=Ok39RWPb-XI

[45] Jacob Nielsen. Nielsen's Law of Internet Bandwidth. Retrieved 23rd September 2015 from http://www.nngroup.com/articles/law-of-bandwidth/

[46] Nielsen. Global Digital Landscape report, March 2015. Retrieved 31st December 2015 from: http://tinyurl.com/hbscghx

[47] Duan Ning. 2001. Cleaner Production, Eco-industry and Circular Economy. *Research of Environmental Sciences* 6 (2001).

[48] William Odom, James Pierce, Erik Stolterman, and Eli Blevis. 2009. Understanding why we preserve some things and discard others in the context of interaction design. In *Proceedings of the SIGCHI Conference on Human Factors in Computing Systems* (CHI '09). ACM, New York, NY, USA, 1053-1062.

[49] Yue Pan, Siddharth Maini, and Eli Blevis. Framing the Issues of Cloud Computing & Sustainability: A Design Perspective. 2010. In *Cloud Computing Technology and Science (CloudCom), 2010 IEEE Second International Conference on*, pp. 603-608.

[50] Yue Pan, David Roedl, John C. Thomas, and Eli Blevis. 2012. Re-conceptualizing fashion in sustainable HCI. In *Proceedings of the Designing Interactive Systems Conference* (DIS '12). ACM, New York, NY, USA, 621-630.

[51] Daniel Pargmann and Barath Raghavan. *Limits'15: First Workshop on Computing within Limits.* First Monday 20(8), Aug 2015. DOI: http://dx.doi.org/10.5210/fm.v20i8.6118

[52] Anne Sylvie Pharabod and Francois de Singly. The Impact of Digital Technology on the Family. Orange Digital Society Forum. Retrieved 29th December 2015 at http://digital-society-forum.orange.com/en/les-forums/52-la_famille_connectee_ce_que_le_numerique_fait_a_la_famille

[53] James Pierce. 2012. Undesigning technology: considering the negation of design by design. In *Proceedings of the SIGCHI Conference on Human Factors in Computing Systems* (CHI '12). ACM, New York, NY, USA, 957-966.

[54] Chris Preist and Paul Shabajee. 2010. Energy Use in the Media Cloud: Behaviour Change, or Technofix? In *Cloud Computing Technology and Science (CloudCom), 2010 IEEE Second International Conference on*, pp. 581-586.

[55] Christian Remy and Elaine M. Huang. 2015. Addressing the obsolescence of end-user devices: approaches from the field of sustainable HCI. In *ICT Innovations for Sustainability*, pp. 257-267. Springer International Publishing, 2015.

[56] Johan Rockström, Johan, Will Steffen, Kevin Noone, Åsa Persson, F. Stuart Chapin, Eric F. Lambin, Timothy M. Lenton et al. 2009. A safe operating space for humanity. *Nature 461, no. 7263 (2009):* 472-475.

[57] Inge Røpke and Toke Haunstrup Christensen. Energy impacts of ICT–Insights from an everyday life perspective. *Telematics and Informatics* 29, no. 4 (2012): 348-361.

[58] Scality. Data that lives forever in the cloud. Press release, June 2011. Retrieved 30th December 2015 from: http://tinyurl.com/hsvnfg3

[59] Daniel Schien, Chris Preist, Mike Yearworth, and Paul Shabajee. 2012. Impact of location on the energy footprint of digital media. In *Sustainable Systems and Technology (ISSST), 2012 IEEE International Symposium on*, pp. 1-6.

[60] Daniel Schien, Daniel, Paul Shabajee, Stephen G. Wood, and Chris Preist. 2013. A model for green design of online news media services. In *Proceedings of the 22nd international conference on World Wide Web*, pp. 1111-1122. International World Wide Web Conferences Steering Committee.

[61] Daniel Schien, Paul Shabajee, Mike Yearworth, and Chris Preist. 2013. Modeling and assessing variability in energy consumption during the use stage of online multimedia services. *Journal of Industrial Ecology 17,* no. 6 (2013): 800-813.

[62] R. J. G. Simons, and A. Pras, 2010. The hidden energy cost of web advertising. Retrieved 24th September 2015 from http://eprints.eemcs.utwente.nl/18066/01/Hidden-Energy-Costs.pdf

[63] M. Six Silberman, Lisa Nathan, Bran Knowles, Roy Bendor, Adrian Clear, Maria Håkansson, Tawanna Dillahunt, and Jennifer Mankoff. 2014. Next steps for sustainable HCI. *interactions* 21, 5 (September 2014), 66-69.

[64] Surfline, Accessed 24th September 2015 at http://www.surfline.com/home/index.cfm

[65] Sustainable Development Commission, 2007. *You are what you sell.* Retrieved 23rd September 2015 from http://www.sd-commission.org.uk/publications.php?id=624

[66] Gregg Tarr. Global action cam sales to hit 9M in 2018. Retrieved 24th September 2015 from http://www.twice.com/news/statistics/global-action-cam-sales-hit-9m-2018/46008

[67] Stephen P. Tarzia, Peter A. Dinda, Robert P. Dick, and Gokhan Memik. 2010. Display power management policies in practice. In *Proceedings of the 7th international conference on Autonomic computing* (ICAC '10). ACM, New York, NY, USA, 51-60.

[68] Tidal Music and Video Streaming Service publicity. Accessed 30th December 2015 at: http://tidal.com/

[69] Bill Tomlinson, Eli Blevis, Bonnie Nardi, Donald J. Patterson, M. SIX Silberman, and Yue Pan. 2013. Collapse informatics and practice: Theory, method, and design. *ACM Transactions on Computer Human Interaction 20,* 4, Article 24 (September 2013), 26 pages.

[70] U.S. Environmental Protection Agency. (2007). Report to Congress on Server and Data Center Energy Efficiency Public Law 109-431.

[71] Daniel R. Williams, Peter Thomond, and Ian Mackenzie. 2014. The greenhouse gas abatement potential of enterprise cloud computing. *Environmental Modelling & Software 56 (2014):* 6-12.

[72] Martin Woolley. 2003. Choreographing obsolescence-ecodesign: the pleasure/dissatisfaction cycle. In *Proceedings of the 2003 international conference on Designing pleasurable products and interfaces*, pp. 77-81. ACM.

[73] World Business Council for Sustainable Development. *Eco-Efficiency: Creating More Value with Less Impact.* 2000. Retrieved 31st December 2015 from http://oldwww.wbcsd.org/web/publications/eco_efficiency_creating_more_value.pdf

[74] Xiao Zhang and Ron Wakkary. 2011. Design analysis: understanding e-waste recycling by Generation Y. In *Proceedings of the 2011 Conference on Designing Pleasurable Products and Interfaces* (DPPI '11). ACM, New York, NY, USA, Article 6.

[75] John Zimmerman, Jodi Forlizzi, and Shelley Evenson. 2007. Research through design as a method for interaction design research in HCI. In *Proceedings of the SIGCHI conference on Human factors in computing systems*. ACM, New York, NY, USA, 493-502.

MyPart: Personal, Portable, Accurate Airborne Particle Counting

Rundong Tian Christine Dierk Christopher Myers Eric Paulos
Electrical Engineering and Computer Sciences
University of California, Berkeley
{rutian, cdierk, chrismyers, paulos}@berkeley.edu

ABSTRACT
In 2012, air pollution in both cities and rural areas was estimated to have caused 3.7 million premature deaths, 88% of those in at-risk communities. The primary pollutant was small airborne particulate matter of 10 microns or less in diameter, which led to the development of cardiovascular and respiratory diseases. In response, we developed MyPart, the first personal, portable, and accurate particle sensor under $50 capable of distinguishing and counting differently sized particles. We demonstrate how MyPart offers substantial enhancements over most existing air particle sensors by simultaneously improving accessibility, flexibility, portability, and accuracy. We describe the evolution and implementation of the sensor design, demonstrate its performance across twenty everyday urban environments versus a calibrated instrument, and conduct a preliminary user study to report on the overall user experience of MyPart. We also present a novel smart-phone visualization interface and a series of simple form factor adaptations of our design.

ACM Classification Keywords
H.5.m. Information Interfaces and Presentation (e.g. HCI): Miscellaneous

Author Keywords
Citizen Science; Air Quality; Environmental Sensors; DIY.

INTRODUCTION
Airborne particles affect more people than any other pollutant, and by far the most health-damaging particles are those with a diameter of 10 microns or less (PM10). These particles can penetrate and lodge themselves deep inside the lungs, contributing to the development of cardiovascular and respiratory diseases including lung cancer [1, 2, 21], not to mention these pollutants' role in global climate change. In most countries, government environmental agencies (the EPA in the US) typically report concentrations of PM10 particles in terms of mass per cubic meter of air volume ($\mu g/m^3$), which maps into a more human readable Air Quality Index (AQI) value. However, these air quality measurements reported by the government (1) use expensive calibrated equipment, (2) operate at fixed locations, (3) are sparsely and strategically distributed for regulatory enforcement rather than situated to provide overall neighborhood coverage for human health, and (4) do not afford a personal experience in terms of data reporting, data collection, or device interaction.

Figure 1. The small wrist-worn MyPart sensor and optional accompanying smartphone visualization and data logging app.

While there are "air quality" sensors even less expensive than our MyPart system, many of them either attempt to "measure" a pollutant that is not the primary health concern, such as mixtures of various gasses (carbon monoxide or ozone), or they do not measure small particles accurately at all and simply report "dust".

As we move towards more personal and crowdsourced environmental monitoring systems, there are numerous HCI research questions - the sensor and hardware design, its usability, accuracy, form factor, expressiveness, visual legibility, interpretation, sharing, and acting on data, privacy, society and community engagement, and long term usage models. In this paper, we focus our contribution on the design of a novel, low-cost, accurate, usable air quality sensor that measures the most critical pollutant affecting human health and well being - airborne particles.

CHI'16, May 07-12, 2016, San Jose, CA, USA
ACM 978-1-4503-3362-7/16/05.
http://dx.doi.org/10.1145/2858036.2858571

Through an extensive engineering and HCI iterative design cycle, we have developed a system that for the first time satisfies four primary design equirements when compared to other air quality measurement systems - MyPart is more accessible due to its low cost which makes it available to a much wider demographic; more flexible due to its ease of fabrication and adaptation across a wide range of context specific forms factors (i.e. easily embedded into watches, strollers, carabiners, toys, bicycle attachments, etc); more accurate than any previous air quality system of similar cost; and smaller and more portable than comparable systems. There are air quality sensing systems that may satisfy some of these requirements, but none that satisfy all of these requirements simultaneously - low-cost, accurate, flexible design, and wearable, portable size.

Most often it is the accuracy that suffers. This is an extremely critical component of the overall design since by sacrificing accuracy, the overall reliability and usability of the data from such system is, at best, called into question and, at worst, unusable. In this paper we will demonstrate the novelty of our approach in engineering a solution that is comparable to air quality systems costing thousands of US dollars more than the $50 MyPart.

We address many of these issues in more detail later in the paper. As HCI practitioners, we were motivated to design a low-cost, accurate, portable, and personal particle counter whose design can be readily adapted into a range of form factors, including a small wrist worn device, in order to expand the design space. MyPart is the culmination of that effort (Figure 1). While accurate measurements are critical to our design, we wanted to develop a new mobile phone interface that would provide a compelling real-time visualization that invites curiosity into a deeper exploration of personally collected particle datasets.

In this paper we describe a range of prior work, outline our iterative design process, describe the technical components of our system, report accuracy measurements, explain our mobile interface, describe the results of a preliminary user study, and discuss alternative form factors for our system.

RELATED WORK

In this section, we provide an overview of other technologies that sense air quality and HCI work in air quality monitoring.

Consumer Air Quality Sensing Technologies

There are a number of different techniques for measuring air quality. In this section we detail each and highlight the tradeoffs across various designs.

Thermal Based Gas Sensors

Low-cost air quality sensing devices often consists of some form of gas sensor. These systems typically use a thermal conductivity based detector tuned to respond to carbon monoxide, ozone, nitrogen oxides, or other gases. However, these devices do a poor job of accurately measuring the actual gas concentrations due to sensor response selectivity and gas interaction problems with the sensor. Furthermore, these gas sensors are high-power due to their thermal heating requirements. Most

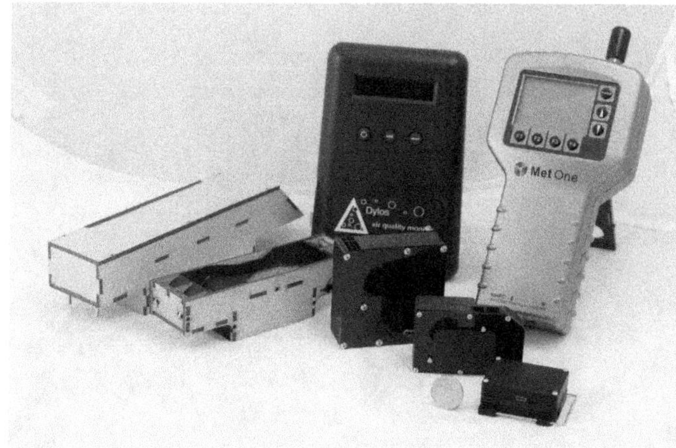

Figure 2. Design iterations, from initial cardboard mock-up to current 3D printed wrist worn prototype. The large commercial Dylos & MetOne are shown for comparison.

importantly, these gas sensors do not measure airborne particles, the primary air pollutant in regards to human health [19].

Low Cost LED and Photodiode Based Sensors

For air quality monitoring of particles at the personal scale, one low-cost solution is LED infrared emitter/detector based sensors such as those produced by Sharp[1], Shinyei[2], and Samyoung[3]. The majority of air quality sensing products, startups, and personal devices also embed this form of sensor. These include the Air.Air![4], Speck [22], and Airbeam[5]. While infrared LED based sensors are inexpensive (typically $10- $30 US) and small (the Sharp sensor is 46.0 x 30.0 17.6 mm), they often give extremely unreliable readings, especially at lower particle concentrations [5]. Many of these systems were engineered to be incorporated into a feedback control circuit for air purifiers, not as general purpose air particle counters [6]. In addition, many of these low cost sensors rely on a heating element to generate flow, which puts strict limitations on the orientation of the sensor, response rate, and battery life when used in a mobile device.

Laser and Photodiode Based Sensors

A second class of consumer-level sensors are those that incorporate a laser, such as the Dylos Indoor Air Quality Monitor[7]($300 US) (Figure 2). While the Dylos performs well against standard commercial instruments [14], it is limited by its large, inflexible size (7 in x 4.5 in x 3 in), cost, user interface, and external computer requirements for data acquisition. More importantly, the Dylos is designed to operate indoors only, meaning it lacks the portability of our everyday mobile

[1] `www.sharpsme.com/optoelectronics/sensors/air-sensors/GP2Y1010AU0F`

[2] `http://www.sca-shinyei.com/particlesensor`

[3] `http://www.samyoungsnc.com/products/3%20Specification%20DSM501.pdf`

[4] `http://www.airair.info`

[5] `http://aircasting.org/`

[6] Samyoung's own product literature lists air conditioners and air cleaners as the primary applications.

[7] `http://www.dylosproducts.com`

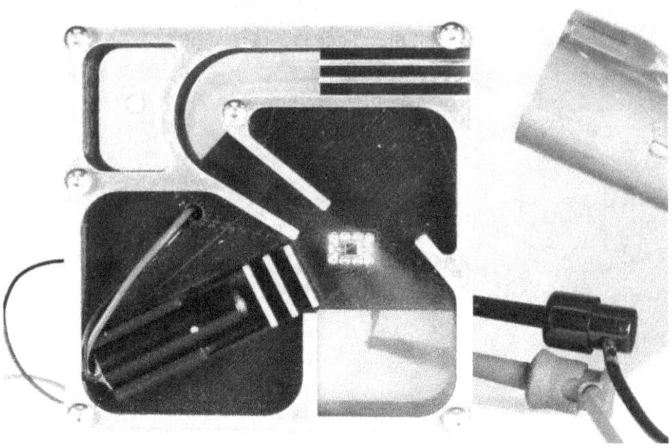

Figure 3. Smoke is injected into an earlier prototype to qualitatively examine the air flow over the photodiode.

Figure 4. MyPart configured as a wrist worn device (40x55x23mm) with LED particle count display illumniated.

devices, severely limiting its ability to truly be on-the-go with people. To emphasize the point, because both the LED/Laser and photodiode systems, by design, respond to light, they perform poorly outdoors since they suffer significantly from ambient light leakage. This restricts the context of their usability to indoors only - the Dylos product literature calls out this limitation directly by warning that it should "not be operated in direct sunlight or other bright light source as this could affect count accuracy".

HCI Research in Air Quality sensing

As environmental monitoring, in particular air quality, becomes more accessible through low-cost components, we have seen its adaption into many HCI and ubiquitous computing projects. It has been truly remarkable to see such a wide range of impressive research into personal air quality sensing across a wide range of contexts - cars [4, 6, 16], municipal vehicles [3, 8], bikes [15], balloons [11], clothing [10], and handheld devices [7, 12, 24] to name a few. Much of this research has made significant contributions towards understanding the design of such sensing tools for interpreting and sharing data, privacy, activism, community engagement, and long term usage models. Because many of these previous studies focused on these important research questions, there was less consideration given to the actual sensor selection, integration, and design. Most incorporated available, off-the-shelf hardware for measuring air quality into their system. As we pointed out earlier, many of these devices contain significant design problems that make them unsuitable for adaption into such HCI applications. In fact, this rich body of prior work has directly inspired us to design and evaluate MyPart. What if a new more accurate, affordable, accessible, low-cost flexible, portable design could be developed and shared with this community? How could such a system encourage a broader landscape of designs, form-factors, applications, and participation all while improving accuracy? MyPart is, in part, a starting point in this research conversation.

SYSTEM DESIGN AND IMPLEMENTATION

The design of the MyPart borrows elements from traditional laser based photodiode systems with several notable improvements: (1) engineered airflow to remove ambient light leakage while maintaining consistent airflow across the photodiode, (2) dense system integration of structural design and circuity to enable wrist worn form factor with ambient visualization, (3) integrated BLE transceiver for low-power networking with mobile devices, and (4) a mobile phone app for visualizing collected data.

In MyPart, a laser and photodiode are arranged orthogonally such that the focal point of the laser is located directly above the photodiode (Figure 5). Air is drawn through the system across the photodiode using a small, low-power, 3 volt, centrifugal fan. Particles in the air stream that intersect the path of the laser scatter light onto the photodiode, and the resulting voltage signal is amplified by an operational amplifier circuit and sampled by a micro-controller. The resulting waveform is analyzed for peaks, which correspond to particle detection. Our final system is able to identify and count particles of 2 different size ranges. The measured values are visualized through a scattered array of eight individually controlled LEDs embedded into the top of the sensor (Figure 4). The MyPart system also has an onboard temperature and humidity sensor to further improve particle readings under high humidity conditions.

As pointed out previously, our innovation is not the use of lasers to count particles. In fact, this technique is used in both high (MET-ONE HHPC-6 at $4,000 USD) and low (Dylos DC1100 at $300 USD) end systems. Rather, MyPart is a result of an iterative design process (Figure 2) and engineering efforts (described below) to lower the cost, reduce the overall size, and provide a flexible design platform for easy integration into other form factors - all while maintaining the overall accuracy of the system. We were particularly motivated to lower the cost in order to increase the accessibility of personal air quality monitoring for at-risk, low-income communities and developing regions where health concerns and air quality are most contentious and misrepresented. The final costs of parts for MyPart is under $50 US.

Mechanical Design: Air Flow and Ambient Light

The design of the airflow channel geometry is constrained by two main factors. First, the flow of air over the photodiode

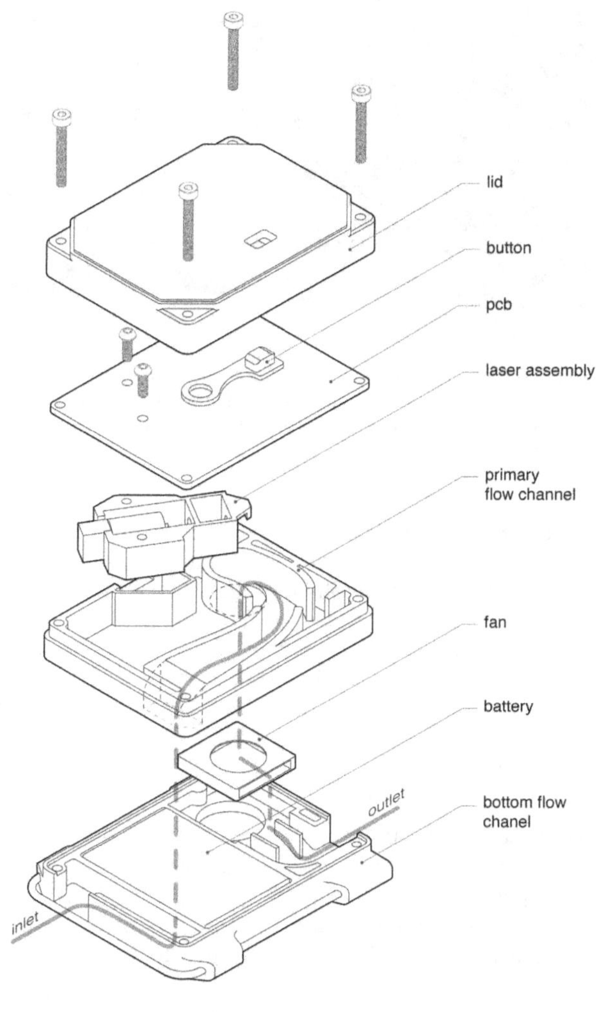

Figure 5. An exploded drawing of the MyPart Design detailing the air-flow and laser placement.

must be constant and free of eddies and turbulence, characteristics which introduce unstable flow velocities and particle recirculation that decrease the responsiveness and accuracy of the sensor. Second, ambient light must be shielded from the photodiode such that changing light conditions do not affect the calibration of the sensor. These two criteria often impose conflicting design constraints. For example, a more complex flow geometry designed to reduce ambient light sensitivity can negatively affect the quality of the air flow, introducing eddies and turbulence. No existing consumer sensor has addressed both of these issues simultaneously. This is a significant limitation for air particle monitors if they are to be portable and functional across a wide range of environments where people go, including outdoors.

To maximize the ambient light rejection of our device, the air channels leading to and from the photodiode were designed with multiple turns that prevent ambient light from directly illuminating the photodiode (Figure 5). In addition, a centrifugal fan and baffles at the outlet were used to further discourage light from directly entering the system (Figure 5). Meanwhile, the air flow channel leading up to the sensor region is a gentle curve designed using cubic splines. At each bend, fillets were used to minimize the formation of turbulence at these transitions. A similar effect for reducing the amount of ambient light entering the system can be achieved by decreasing the cross-sectional size of the inlet and outlet. However, this method reduces the air flow rate and the responsiveness of the sensor since it samples less air per unit of time.

Because of the complex channel geometry, qualitative smoke tests were conducted after each major design revision (Figure 3). High speed videos were used to analyze and confirm the absence of undesirable air flow characteristics.

Counting and Sizing Particles

When light is scattered onto the photodiode by incoming particles, a current is induced in the photodiode which is then converted into a voltage through a high gain transimpedance (current to voltage) amplifier. This analog signal is then high-pass filtered, then low-pass filtered to reduce electrical noise as well as shape the characteristics of the pulse waveform. In particular, choosing a higher cutoff frequency for the high-pass filter decreased the pulse width seen by the analog-to-digital converter (ADC) which prevent successive pulses from overlapping and distorting the measured amplitude for each pulse. The rise time of the resulting pulses in our current configuration is approximately 50 microseconds.

The analog signal is sampled at 88kHz using an external 12-bit ADC driven by a low power system-on-a-chip with a microcontroller and Bluetooth transceiver (Nordic NRF51822). A simple thresholding algorithm is used to detect peaks of various amplitudes, and can be calculated in the time between successive ADC captures. Our algorithm is most similar to a hardware comparator with hysteresis and measures the number of times the thresholds are crossed. Though this algorithm is very simple, it yields good results that will be discussed later. More complex algorithms that consider the pulse width, or the maximum amplitude of the pulses can be designed to further increase sensor accuracy.

Electromechanical Design Evolution

The mechanical design of our sensor has evolved significantly (Figure 2), from initial laser cut prototype to our final 3D printed wrist watch form factor. We began with several laser cut designs for rapid fabrication and iteration speed. However, as the requirements for the flow channel were recognized, the complexity of the required flow channel necessitated the use of 3D printing. Our final mechanical enclosure is optimized to be easily 3D printed, as the overall geometry is partitioned in a way that eliminates overhangs. In addition, the consistent wall thickness and minimal undercuts throughout the entire design make it easily adaptable for injection molding.

The laser is mounted onto the PCB with a piece of 3D printed plastic that also has a series of apertures to prevent stray laser light from illuminating the photodiode (Figure 5). For optimal optical performance, the aperture should be metal to block the stray light entirely, and thin to minimize reflection at the inside diameter of the aperture. We used this method at first, and constructed apertures out of milled pieces of 0.005 inch thick steel. Though effective, this added an additional degree of complexity to the fabrication of our device. Ultimately, we found that comparable performance can be achieved by using successive thin pieces of plastic, which were then integrated into the component for fixturing the laser. More than one aperture is needed for plastic because the thin pieces become slightly transparent.

In earlier designs, we used off-the-shelf photodiodes with integrated transimpedance amplifiers, such as the TSL12 produced by AMS, and the OPT101 produced by Texas Instruments. Using these off the shelf sensors decreases the complexity of the electronics, as the high gain transimpedance amplifiers can be difficult to design and be sensitive to noise. However, the mechanical size of these sensors were not suitable for the small form factor we were pursuing and limited the geometry of the the flow channel, as well as the overall device. A device as small as the current version of the MyPart requires tight integration between the electronics and the mechanical enclosure, and the photodiode is the key interface between these two elements of the design. By using a low profile photodiode soldered directly to the PCB, various mechanical design constraints around the interface between the electronics and enclosure were loosened.

Because of the power limitations of a battery powered device, substantial effort was placed to reduce the power consumption of the device, especially in sleep mode. For example, to minimize digital noise affecting the high gain analog circuitry, two separate voltage regulators are used. Conveniently, the entire analog voltage regulator can then be shut down by the micro-controller when samples are not being taken. Cumulatively, these efforts reduce the power consumption in sleep mode to less than 100 micro-Amps.

Our most current design files, as well as a more detailed explanation of the design, is all available open source. These files can be found online at `http://hybrid-ecologies.org/projects/mypart`.

User Interaction Flow

The device is normally in a sleep mode, in which the micro-controller and other components in the circuits are programmed to be in a low power state. The device is configured to wake up from a button press, but can also be activated at a timed interval, or by any peripheral that can generate a hardware interrupt.

When the device wakes up from sleep mode, onboard LEDs, embedded within the top of the device flash and then fade to intimate to the user that an air sample is being taken (Figure 4). The micro-controller turns on all peripheral devices including the fan. After waiting 500ms for the airflow to stabilize, MyPart begins counting particles by size. As particles are counted, the onboard visualization is updated in real-time. Throughout the fifteen second sampling period, the visualization updates as more particle are counted. After the sampling period, the data is broadcast using Bluetooth, and is also displayed on the LEDs of the physical sensor itself (Figure 4). To conserve energy, the broadcast and LEDs stop after 10 seconds, after

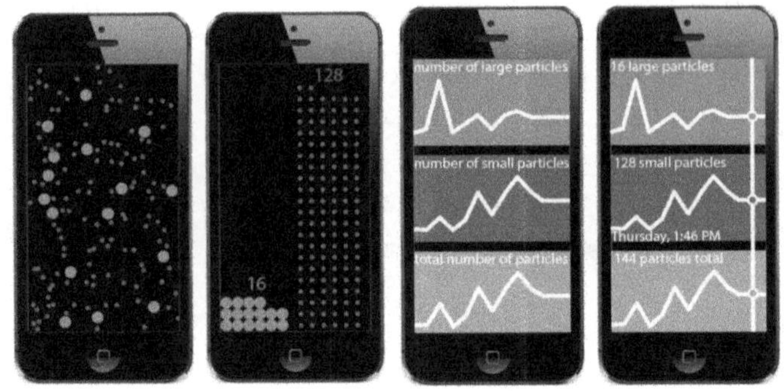

A B C D

Figure 6. The MyPart smartphone application has an ambient animated particles view (A), stacked column view for visual comparisons (B), and a historical view (C) with numerical values revealed from user interaction with the data (D).

which the device returns to the sleep mode. However, the data can easily be logged and visualized on another device such as as mobile smartphone (Figure 6). In this configuration, the sampling period consumes an average of 75 mA. Using a 400 mAh LiPo battery, our sensor can conservatively take 250 readings before needing to be recharged. Our wristwatch form factor (Figure 1) uses this battery which gives very reasonable sensor coverage over a full day without the need for recharging.

Visualizing Air Quality

While MyPart can operate standalone and log data, its usage is more persuasive and compelling when its data is experienced in real-time through a mobile phone interface. Using BLE, live particle count data is transmitted to an iOS application (Figure 6).

Building off a suite of inspirational related work on air quality visualization [9, 13, 18, 23], the MyPart smartphone interface was designed to support scaffolding a user into the data - from a compelling real-time visualization that invites curiosity, to a deeper exploration of the rich particle dataset with time and location patterns. The actual smartphone app design was intended to augment the overall experience of the MyPart system, not be the primary design contribution. Therefore, we focus on describing the design goals and final app design rather than the intermediate prototypes.

There were several initial design goals motivating the visual and interactive design of our smartphone app. First, it was important that users could access the real data from the sensor. We did not want to obscure or abstract the data in such a way that users would have difficulty visualizing the actual sensor data. At the same time, we felt that by offering exclusively numbers and charts, the users would become disengaged with the overall experience we desired. We wanted to deliver an experience with the data that would feel more alive, invite curiosity, and perhaps even feel playful as a means to draw in and retain user interest in the system. We also wanted our design to accommodate quick (1-2 second) engagements through a glanceable interface that would require little to no interaction with the phone. Next, we expected that exploring related contextual information such as time and location along with the MyPart data would be valuable in engaging users and helping them conduct their own sensemaking. Finally, it was important that there was some visual design language elements linking the smartphone app to the physical MyPart sensing hardware device.

We iterated through several prototype designs that each foreground various elements of our design goals. However, the challenge was to arrive at a smartphone app design that struck the proper balance across all of our design goals and was usable for eliciting feedback with users when operating the entire MyPart system. The final design we arrived at is composed of three screens: (1) an animated, ambient display that allows users to easily visualize the air quality, (2) a bar graph view that communicates precise particle counts and corresponding health related information, and (3) an interactive graph view that displays historical readings across time and location.

The initial screen of the application displays particle counts as colorful, animated circles that move and interact in a particle simulation system (Figure 6A). The two sizes of particles are distinguished by their color (blue/purple), size, and movement (fast/slow). Updates to this screen are deliberate, with particles slowly fading in and out such that the user is made aware of changing air quality conditions. This screen is unique in that it is factual, yet playfully aesthetic. In fact, we envision such a display as a compelling element in ambient situations such as a phone lock screen or smartwatch face since its is both easily glanceable and presents an abstract aesthetic visualization [20].

To explore the data more concretely, the user swipes down to access a bar graph view. From the ambient view, the individual particles quickly animate to form two stacked columns, allowing easy interpretation of the quantity of differently sized particles (Figure 6B). The precise count for each particle size is displayed at the top of the stack. When the user clicks on a particular stack of particles, more information is displayed: the size ranges for each particle category, common origins of such particles, and health concerns associated with the current air quality conditions.

A third view is provided when a user swipes up on either screen. This historical view (Figure 6C) displays past readings over time. On this screen, there are three separate graphs displaying three datasets for large particle counts, small particle counts, and total particle counts. This view is interactive - when the user touches any of the graphs, all three graphs are activated and the relevant particle count information is displayed (Figure 6D).

VALIDATION STUDIES

Throughout our design process, we knew that if the resulting particle counts reported by the sensor were inaccurate, we would not have a usable system. To really have impact, provide actionable data, and be convincing, our system would have to maintain a high degree of accuracy with regards to particle counts. This is a step that is often overlooked or at best partially addressed in most HCI air quality crowdsourcing studies. Our aim here was to be able to develop a system that would hopefully be used in further studies by ourselves, other researchers, and the general public and that in those deployments an improved level of accuracy would be provided.

Laboratory Calibration and Comparison Studies

In the analog signal from the amplified photodiode, the amplitude of the pulses correspond to the intensity of light seen by the photodiode. Though there are other factors at play, such as the location at which the particle crosses the laser beam and the optical properties of the particle, the amplitude of the pulses can be used as an approximate metric for the size of the particles detected.

As a first approximation for correlating the response of the analog circuitry to the size of particle detected, we expose our sensor to particles of known size ranges, such as smoke and household dust. The pulses in the raw analog signal are analyzed, and approximate cuttoffs for large and small particles are chosen. Though approximate, the cutoffs determined using this method resulted in very strong correlations against a calibrated instrument costing $4000 US. In future work, our sensor can be tested with particles of precisely known sizes, such as mono-dispersed polystyrene latex beads to further increase accuracy.

Real World Performance Studies

While laboratory and bench top studies are important to characterizing the response of our system, it is important that we study the performance of MyPart in real world everyday context of use. We conducted a validation study across a series of real-world indoor and outdoor locations to test our sensor with naturally occurring particles in various lighting conditions. For our reference monitor, we chose the Met-One HPPC-6 ($4000 US), a laser based optical detector similar in principle to our sensor. The Met-One HHPC-6 is a professional, industrial grade handheld particle counter that offers six particle counting channels (0.3, 0.5, 0.7, 1.0, 2.0, and 5.0 micron) with built-in relative humidity and temperature sensors. It is suitable for use in clean office settings as well as harsh industrial workplaces, construction and environmental sites, and other outdoor applications. The Met-One provides highly calibrated, independent, ground truth measurements of airborne particles to compare the performance accuracy of our MyPart system.

Our sensor was tested against the Met-One across these indoor and outdoor locations. Twenty locations were tested, and two consecutive data points were taken by each sensor at each location. Locations were chosen to adequately represent a broad range of everyday contexts. They included both indoor and outdoor locations such as parking lots, parks, bus stops, downtown urban areas, office workspaces, and indoor cafes to name a few.

We summed the total particle count on the Met-One from its 0.5, 0.7, and 1.0 micron channel measurements as "small particles". Similarly we used the 2.0 micron and 5.0 micron count as "large particles". We used these small and large sizes as comparison against the MyPart sensor's small and large size particle counts. The results of this study are shown in Figure 7 and demonstrate high correlation in signals for both small ($r^2 = 0.96$) and large ($r^2 = 0.91$) particle counts. These results

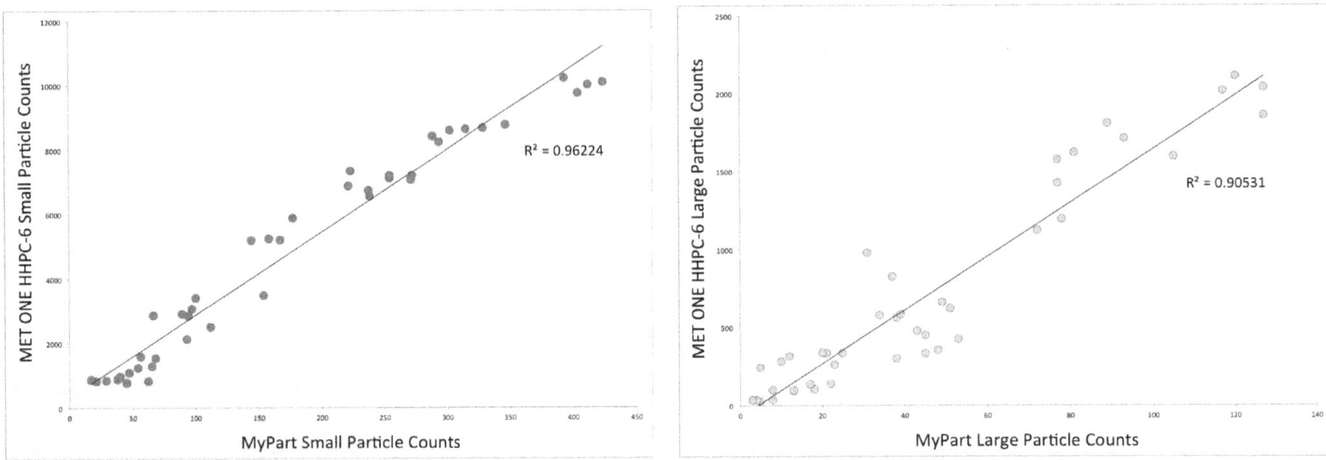

Figure 7. Graphs demonstrating the performance of MyPart ($50 US) in correlation with the calibrated Met-One HHPC6 ($4000 US).

demonstrate the sustained accuracy of the MyPart system in contexts outside of the laboratory setting and in everyday landscapes of typical expected usage.

Calibration to Air Quality Index

The Environmental Protection Agency in the United States reports air quality using an Air Quality Index (AQI) for PM2.5 and PM10. PM2.5 refers to airborne particles smaller than 2.5 micrometers (100 times thinner than a human hair) while PM10 refers to particles smaller than 10 micrometers in diameter, the smaller particles pose the greatest health risk to humans [19]. Environmental statistics for clean air (the AQI) is calculated from mass concentrations per volume using linear interpolation [1].

Since our system, as well as most others, is unable to measure the mass or exact chemical composition of the particles we are measuring, we cannot directly map the particle counts from our system onto an EPA equivalency for "healthy" or "unhealthy" scale. Instead, we report out the particle counts for large and small sized particles approximating the PM2.5 and PM10 particle measurements. This approach is commonly used and provides good correlation with the mass values as measured by the EPA.

PRELIMINARY USER STUDY

In addition to validating the sensor's accuracy, we were interested in evaluating the system with users. In our study, participants were introduced to MyPart and asked to perform a predetermined walking tour of a series of locations with our system. Interviews were conducted before and after the walking tour and focused on perceptions of air quality, feedback on the design and user experience of MyPart, and reactions to MyPart and how it affected air quality awareness.

Study Participants

We recruited 6 participants (3 male, 3 female) through targeted email-lists for a local community center, a homeschooling parents group, and college students. Our study included representation from all of these demographics and across a broad age range (18 to 59 years old). All participants were paid $50 US.

Procedure

The user study consisted of three parts: (1) an initial interview, (2) a "walkabout", and (3) a followup interview. During the initial interview, we asked participants general questions about air quality to gauge their understanding about the topic. Participants were then introduced to MyPart and shown how to operate the device with the accompanying app. A phone was provided to participants to avoid having to load the custom MyPart app onto their personal phones. The participants then took readings at the interview location in order to verify their understanding of the system.

For the walkabout portion of our user study, users took a prespecified walking route through a range of locations around a college campus and the surrounding urban areas. We provided a map marked with the suggested route and eight specific locations, and did not accompany them on the walk. The participants were asked to take a reading at each of the eight locations. The locations were selected to represent broad range of environments and situations, in order to prompt the participants to think about their locations in relation to the air quality. These locations included a bus stop, a grove of trees, a library, a coffee shop, and a construction site. Participants were also told that they were free to take other readings at any time through the walk. The walk was designed to take roughly 40 minutes over a 2.7 km distance. All six participants completed the full study, including the walkabout which lasted from 25 minutes to 38 minutes to complete.

When participants returned from the walk about, we showed them their data and conducted an interview. In this interview, we asked more directly about their experience of using the MyPart system, the visualization, and the legibility of the data. We prompted each participant to discuss how, where, and why (or why not) they would potentially use this system. We also asked them to comment on the the form-factor, comfort, and wearability of the sensor system.

Discussion

We examined our interview data using thematic analysis to reveal patterns across users. These themes become the categories for analysis and are discussed in the subsections that follow.

Lack of General Knowledge About Air Quality
Consistent with previous studies, many of our participants had little understanding of air quality, where it was measured, by whom, and how it was measured and reported. In the initial interview, three participants admitted to not understanding air quality in their area very well and only one participant thought that they understood local air quality and how it affects them.

Engagement and Personal Curiosity
While not required in the study, nearly all of our participants took additional sensor measurements with the system. Five out of our six participants took extra readings for a total of eight additional readings. Participant P4, who did not take additional readings, said that he did not take extra readings because of the weather, but would have taken additional readings given more time. These additional readings came from locations including a building that P1 spent a lot of time in, an indoor space after using a vaporizer (P2), a building vent (P5), a grassy area on campus (P6), and an outdoor exercise class (P5). During the final interview, when participants were asked to discuss additional locations they would use MyPart, all participants listed additional locations that they would like to test including their homes (all participants), their workplaces (P1, P4, P5), higher altitudes (P2, P3, P4), inside of cars (P5), and down by a major highway (P4). Several participants also expressed interest in taking the same readings but at different times, on different days, or during different weather conditions (P4, P6). Overall, we observed that participants easily engaged with MyPart. Many used it to take additional measurements and all had clear ideas of desired future usage, indicating that the MyPart device and visualization were legible and easily understood by participants.

MyPart as part of a larger conversation about air quality
Initially, several participants made assumptions on air quality based on smell (P2, P3, and P6) or other visual cues such as smoke (P3). With our system, participants experienced first hand that these cues do not always accurately reflect air quality. Participants P1 and P6 stated that their perception of air quality had changed in that it is imperceptible and appreciated MyPart as a way to make air quality visible.

Use of the Mobile Phone Data Visualization
Participants noted that the initial ambient display on the mobile application was playful and easy to read (P2 and P4). This view provides a low floor for participants to easily interact with the application and engage with air quality readings, without prior knowledge and experience with the subject. When initiating richer interactions with data, participants preferred the bar graph and chart views (P1, P3, P4, and P5), which allowed the users to associate readings with time, location, weather, and other related factors.

MyPart as a Carryable, rather than a Wearable
Our user study allowed participants to experience MyPart in a unique wristwatch form factor (40x55x23 mm). However, while we found that this form factor was compelling, it was not always desired in all contexts. While participants found the device comfortable and lightweight (P3, P4, and P6), they thought that the device should be much smaller if kept in watch form (P1, P4). This was expected since we have not pushed the system integration to the level that an industrial corporation would for a real product. As such, participants were reacting to the size, which although extremely small, was not close enough to being a usable wristwatch form factor for everyday use. We envision such applications and appropriately sized air quality sensing devices in the near future, however. As such, we were interested in initiating the exploration and understanding of this body location for air quality sensing in our design and studies. Several participants suggested attaching the sensor to a backpack, a briefcase, or another accessory (P1, P2, P3, P4). A few participants wished the sensor could be physically embedded within their mobile device (P1, P5, P6). Overall, participants thought that the device would be most useful if it could be attached to everyday things that the user is already accustomed to carrying (P3, P4, P6). Participant P4 argued that the device should be embedded in a "crucial piece of technology" in order to truly make it ubiquitous. All of these comments strengthen our argument for a small design that can be flexibly adapted into a range of everyday objects and experiences.

Limitations of MyPart
Several participants noted that that the readings are only useful when compared to each other (P3, P4). Participants also expressed interest in knowing exactly what the particles were, rather than just particle sizes (P1, P2). While most of our participants were surprised by one reading or another, two of our six participants thought that using our device consistently would not influence their behavior (P3, P5). One of these participants stated, "day to day I take [the subway], there's not much that I could do to avoid that" (P3). Two other participants thought that they would only change their behavior in very specific situations: cleaning the house if it were messy and contributing to poor air quality, and exercising indoors rather than outdoors if the air quality was particularly poor (P2, P4). Finally, two participants argued that knowing particle counts might stress a person out more so than influence their behavior (P3, P4). For example, if there is consistently a high particle count in the area that a person lives and they do not have the resources to relocate.

Several other broad themes emerged from our user study. When using on body glance-able interfaces, people were more likely to explore locations other than the ones we specified. This was likely due to the lower activation energy required for taking a sample since there is no need to take out a phone to engage with the technology. In all of our users, we observed increasing awareness and concerns for air quality after using the MyPart system. Overall, the user study helped us validate several of the design elements as well as understand the usage limitations.

FLEXIBLE DESIGN EXPLORATION

As we mentioned earlier, one of the central elements of our design was to develop an easily extensible platform that is accurate, but easily adaptable by others into a variety of application specific form factors. To do this, we engineered all of

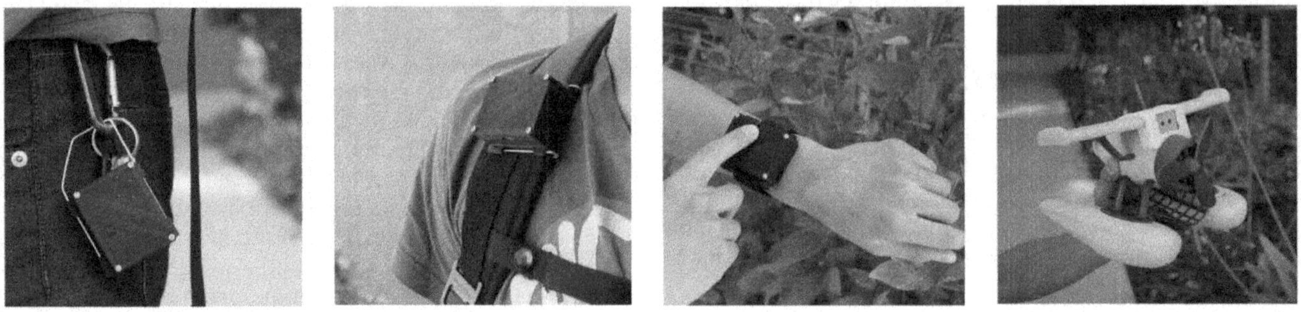

Figure 8. Highlighting the flexibility of the MyPart design form factor by demonstrating the ease of adapting it to function as (from left to right): a carabiner, a backpack strap, a wristwatch, and even embedded into a toy airplane

the electronics to be on a single PCB (Figure 5). This includes the power management, microcontroller, photodiode, analog amplification circuit, led driver, temperature/humidity sensor, and BLE radio. We envision this component being either mass produced, sold as a kit, or published publicly. The top and bottom housing are then simply distributed as open-source 3D model files suitable for printing on any 3D printer. However, we lock the internal geometry, since it contains the tested, calibrated, and accurate design for the airflow and particle measurement, and allow free form designs of the remaining model. Again, because we have pushed the engineering efforts to an extremely small form factor, we have enabled what we believe is a range of interesting potential artifacts into which the MyPart design can be embedded. For example, the core design can be used to embed and achieve accurate air quality measurements into watches, strollers, carabiners, toys, bicycle attachments, etc.

Though the geometry of the flow channel is constrained, there are many other opportunities for modification and customization. For example, the default wire loop design (Figure 4) that is currently used to hold the watch strap can be replaced with any other geometry of 1/16 inch diameter wire, allowing for rapid exploration of other body worn and carried form factors. With minor changes, the mounting for the wire loop can be modified to become general mounting points for fasteners, allowing for its integration within other objects - from domestic Internet of Things devices to urban landscape installations. Because of the small size of our sensor, fewer geometric constraints are imposed on the range of potential form factors. In addition, the battery compartment can be easily enlarged to accommodate higher capacity batteries, opening up even more possibilities for remote data-logging.

Several such alternative form factor designs are showcased in Figure 8. We detail some of these designs below:

Carabiner/Clip On - With changes in the exterior loop, this application enables air quality measurements from book-bags, purses, etc.

Bike and Stroller - MyPart can take on a familiar water bottle like form factor, allowing it to be easily integrated into activities with bikes and strollers.

Children's Toy - We have also prototyped the integration of MyPart into a children's toy airplane [17]. The fuselage allows for easy integration of our sensor in its current form and enables a new culture of participation into sensing by children. In this variation, an e-ink display has been added for facial expressions.

We believe that the ease of appropriation and redesign of MyPart into a wide range of everyday objects and contexts is a powerful element of its overall design. Our hope is that by explicitly calling out this feature and providing a direct mechanism to encourage such redesign of MyPart, broader participation of air quality measurements and context will emerge. Specially, those that are more culturally or context appropriate in order to further usage and meaning.

CONCLUSION

Effective personal air monitoring necessitates the combination of accuracy, low cost, and portability into a single design. Lacking an existing solution, we developed MyPart to address this need as well as provide opportunities to redesign and reimagine alternative form factors. In addition to correlating strongly with calibrated commercial instrumentation, the design of our system remains flexible in terms of both shape and size, enabling a variety of personal designs and context specific applications. A mobile phone app was designed to complement the physical hardware, and a preliminary user study was conducted to evaluate the experience of using the overall system.

ACKNOWLEDGMENTS

We appreciate the valuable input of our anonymous reviewers. We would also like to thank Ethan Chiou for his help conducting user studies and automating field tests. This research was funded by NSF IIS-1211047 and IIS-1451465.

REFERENCES

1. 2013. Technical Assistance Document for the Reporting of Daily Air Quality. (2013). http://www3.epa.gov/airnow/aqi-technical-assistance-document-dec2013.pdf

2. 2014. WHO Ambient (outdoor) air quality and health. (2014). http://www.who.int/mediacentre/factsheets/fs313/en/

3. Paul M. Aoki, R. J. Honicky, Alan Mainwaring, Chris Myers, Eric Paulos, Sushmita Subramanian, and Allison Woodruff. A vehicle for research: using street sweepers to explore the landscape of environmental community action. In *Proceedings of the SIGCHI Conference on Human Factors in Computing Systems* (2009). ACM, 375–384. http://dl.acm.org/citation.cfm?id=1518762

4. E. Bales, N. Nikzad, N. Quick, C. Ziftci, K. Patrick, and W. Griswold. Citisense: Mobile air quality sensing for individuals and communities Design and deployment of the Citisense mobile air-quality system. In *2012 6th International Conference on Pervasive Computing Technologies for Healthcare (PervasiveHealth)* (2012-05). 155–158. DOI:http://dx.doi.org/10.4108/icst.pervasivehealth.2012.248724

5. Matthias Budde, Mathias Busse, and Michael Beigl. Investigating the use of commodity dust sensors for the embedded measurement of particulate matter. In *Networked Sensing Systems (INSS), 2012 Ninth International Conference on* (2012).

6. Jeffrey A. Burke, D. Estrin, Mark Hansen, Andrew Parker, Nithya Ramanathan, Sasank Reddy, and Mani B. Srivastava. 2006. Participatory sensing. *Center for Embedded Network Sensing* (2006). http://escholarship.org/uc/item/19h777qd

7. Carl DiSalvo, Illah Nourbakhsh, David Holstius, Ayça Akin, and Marti Louw. The Neighborhood Networks project: a case study of critical engagement and creative expression through participatory design. In *Proceedings of the Tenth Anniversary Conference on Participatory Design 2008* (2008). Indiana University, 41–50. http://dl.acm.org/citation.cfm?id=1795241

8. David Hasenfratz, Olga Saukh, Christoph Walser, Christoph Hueglin, Martin Fierz, Tabita Arn, Jan Beutel, and Lothar Thiele. 2015. Deriving high-resolution urban air pollution maps using mobile sensor nodes. *Pervasive and Mobile Computing* 16, Part B (2015), 268 – 285. DOI:http://dx.doi.org/10.1016/j.pmcj.2014.11.008 Selected Papers from the Twelfth Annual {IEEE} International Conference on Pervasive Computing and Communications (PerCom 2014).

9. Sunyoung Kim and Eric Paulos. inAir: Measuring and Visualizing Indoor Air Quality. In *Proceedings of the 11th International Conference on Ubiquitous Computing* (2009) *(UbiComp '09)*. ACM, 81–84. DOI: http://dx.doi.org/10.1145/1620545.1620557

10. Sunyoung Kim, Eric Paulos, and Mark D. Gross. WearAir: expressive t-shirts for air quality sensing. In *Proceedings of the fourth international conference on Tangible, embedded, and embodied interaction* (2010). ACM, 295–296. http://dl.acm.org/citation.cfm?id=1709949

11. Stacey Kuznetsov, George Noel Davis, Eric Paulos, Mark D. Gross, and Jian Chiu Cheung. Red balloon, green balloon, sensors in the sky. In *Proceedings of the 13th international conference on Ubiquitous computing* (2011). ACM, 237–246. http://dl.acm.org/citation.cfm?id=2030145

12. N.D. Lane, E. Miluzzo, Hong Lu, D. Peebles, T. Choudhury, and A.T. Campbell. 2010. A survey of mobile phone sensing. *Communications Magazine, IEEE* 48, 9 (Sept 2010), 140–150. DOI: http://dx.doi.org/10.1109/MCOM.2010.5560598

13. Nima Nikzad, Nakul Verma, Celal Ziftci, Elizabeth Bales, Nichole Quick, Piero Zappi, Kevin Patrick, Sanjoy Dasgupta, Ingolf Krueger, Tajana Šimunić Rosing, and others. CitiSense: improving geospatial environmental assessment of air quality using a wireless personal exposure monitoring system. In *Proceedings of the conference on Wireless Health* (2012). ACM, 11. http://dl.acm.org/citation.cfm?id=2448107

14. Amanda L. Northcross, Rufus J. Edwards, Michael A. Johnson, Zhong-Min Wang, Kunning Zhu, Tracy Allen, and Kirk R. Smith. 2013. A low-cost particle counter as a realtime fine-particle mass monitor. *Environ. Sci.: Processes Impacts* 15 (2013), 433–439. Issue 2. DOI: http://dx.doi.org/10.1039/C2EM30568B

15. Christine Outram, Carlo Ratti, and Assaf Biderman. The Copenhagen Wheel: An innovative electric bicycle system that harnesses the power of real-time information and crowd sourcing. In *EVER Monaco International Exhibition & Conference on Ecologic Vehicles & Renewable Energies* (2010).

16. Eric Paulos, R. Honicky, and Ben Hooker. 2008. Citizen science: Enabling participatory urbanism. *Urban Informatics: Community Integration and Implementation* (2008), 414–436.

17. Eric Paulos, Chris Myers, Rundong Tian, and Paxton Paulos. Sensory Triptych: Here, Near, out There. In *Proceedings of the 27th Annual ACM Symposium on User Interface Software and Technology* (2014) *(UIST '14)*. ACM, 491–496. DOI: http://dx.doi.org/10.1145/2642918.2647410

18. Sameera Poduri, Anoop Nimkar, and Gaurav S. Sukhatme. 2010. Visibility monitoring using mobile phones. *Annual Report: Center for Embedded Networked Sensing* (2010), 125–127. http://robotics.usc.edu/~mobilesensing/visibility/MobileAirQualitySensing.pdf

19. C. Arden Pope, Majid Ezzati, and Douglas W. Dockery. 2009. Fine-Particulate Air Pollution and Life Expectancy in the United States. *New England Journal of Medicine* 360, 4 (2009), 376–386. DOI: http://dx.doi.org/10.1056/NEJMsa0805646

20. Tobias Skog, Sara Ljungblad, and Lars Erik Holmquist. Between aesthetics and utility: designing ambient information visualizations. In *Information Visualization, 2003. INFOVIS 2003. IEEE Symposium on* (2003). IEEE, 233–240. http://ieeexplore.ieee.org/xpls/abs_all.jsp?arnumber=1249031

21. J. Sundell. 2004. On the history of indoor air quality and health. *Indoor Air* 14 (2004), 51–58. DOI: http://dx.doi.org/10.1111/j.1600-0668.2004.00273.x

22. M. D. Taylor and I. R. Nourbakhsh. 2015. A low-cost particle counter and signal processing method for indoor air pollution. *Air Pollution XXIII* 198 (2015), 337–348.

23. Sean White and Steven Feiner. SiteLens: Situated Visualization Techniques for Urban Site Visits. In *Proceedings of the SIGCHI Conference on Human Factors in Computing Systems* (2009) *(CHI '09)*. ACM, 1117–1120. DOI: http://dx.doi.org/10.1145/1518701.1518871

24. Yu Zheng, Furui Liu, and Hsun-Ping Hsieh. U-Air: When urban air quality inference meets big data. In *Proceedings of the 19th ACM SIGKDD international conference on Knowledge discovery and data mining* (2013). ACM, 1436–1444. http://dl.acm.org/citation.cfm?id=2488188

Evaluating the Influence of Targets and Hand Postures on Touch-based Behavioural Biometrics

Daniel Buschek, Alexander De Luca, Florian Alt
University of Munich (LMU), Germany
{daniel.buschek, alexander.de.luca, florian.alt}@ifi.lmu.de

ABSTRACT

Users' individual differences in their mobile touch behaviour can help to continuously verify identity and protect personal data. However, little is known about the influence of GUI elements and hand postures on such touch biometrics. Thus, we present a metric to measure the amount of user-revealing information that can be extracted from touch targeting interactions and apply it in eight targeting tasks with over 150,000 touches from 24 users in two sessions. We compare touch-to-target offset patterns for four target types and two hand postures. Our analyses reveal that small, compactly shaped targets near screen edges yield the most descriptive touch targeting patterns. Moreover, our results show that thumb touches are more individual than index finger ones. We conclude that touch-based user identification systems should analyse GUI layouts and infer hand postures. We also describe a framework to estimate the usefulness of GUIs for touch biometrics.

Author Keywords

Touch Targeting; Behavioural Biometrics; Mobile Device

ACM Classification Keywords

H.5.2. Information Interfaces and Presentation (e.g. HCI): Input devices and strategies (e.g. mouse, touchscreen)

INTRODUCTION

Observing touch behaviour can yield important information about the user. This attractive data has been widely used in recent HCI research to personalise interfaces and to recognise individuals. Related work observed touches to tailor keyboards to the individual typist [3, 16, 20, 24, 45], to personalise fonts [14], to add an implicit layer to authentication (e.g. for unlock patterns [1, 18]), or to create new authentication methods based on touch biometrics [38]. Targeting personalisation, privacy and security, these applications demonstrate the usefulness and importance of extracting and recognising user-specific information in mobile touch behaviour.

Related work has mostly targeted specific applications of touch biometrics, for example pattern unlock screens [18]. Recently, features for touch biometrics have also been studied across a greater range of tasks [44]. Improving our knowledge of *what to observe* (i.e. touch features) is important. On the other hand, to develop robust touch-based behavioural biometrics, we also need to investigate *what influences* the degree to which users will exhibit individual touch behaviour. We also lack a formal metric for such individuality.

CHI'16, May 07–12, 2016, San Jose, CA, USA.

ACM 978-1-4503-3362-7/16/05...$15.00
DOI: http://dx.doi.org/10.1145/2858036.2858165

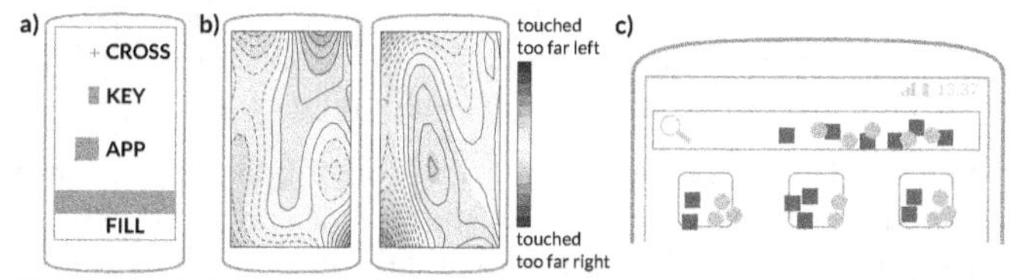

Figure 1. To inform applications of behavioural touch biometrics, we evaluate how characteristically and consistently users touch at *(a)* four target types with thumb and index finger. We measure user-revealing information via *(b)* touch-to-target offset patterns, and describe a method to evaluate GUIs accordingly: *(c)* In this illustrative example, touches of two users (■/●) are less individually distributed at the search bar than at the app-icons. Such insights help applications relying on user-specific behaviour to focus on the most individual and thus prolific interactions.

Hence, to facilitate research and applications that use touch biometrics, we contribute: 1) an approach for *measuring* user-revealing information in targeting behaviour; 2) insights into *influences* of interface targets and hand postures on this individuality; and 3) an *evaluation framework* to estimate the expected amount of user-revealing information in touch interactions with given interfaces. Our insights inform applications of touch biometrics – focus on characteristic interactions and ignore those revealed as less individual (Figure 1).

APPLICATION CONTEXT

To illustrate the kind of application we aim to facilitate with our analytical contributions in this paper, consider that a user accidentally leaves behind a phone in a bar after unlocking it. A stranger, or a nosey friend, picks it up to read emails, view pictures and so on, thus compromising privacy and security.

This threat can be addressed with continuous implicit authentication [44]. If the observed touch behaviour deviates from the legitimate user's characteristic behaviour, the phone raises alarm, locks itself, or blocks access to sensitive data and apps.

For such a system, it is vital to know which touch interactions *consistently* yield *characteristic* information about the user – and which ones are generally not very individual. For example, we will see that large buttons lead to little individual information compared to smaller ones. Hence, the system described above could mitigate the risk of false user rejections and false attacker acceptances by taking into account that touches at large buttons should not be used to determine whether the legitimate user is interacting.

RELATED WORK

We relate our work to 1) research that shows why and how touch targeting behaviour varies between users; and to 2) systems which use such implicit individual touch information.

Variations in Touch Behaviour

Related research found sources for variations in touch behaviour and models to describe it, such as Fitts' Law [21] and its refined version for touch input [9]. Furthermore, research showed that finger angles affect touch contact areas on tabletops [22, 40]; touch-to-target distances and directions depend on the finger's pitch, roll and yaw, as well as head position [27]; fingers occlude the target [5], and users rely on different visual features of the finger tip to align it with the target [26].

Other related work examined how touch behaviour is influenced by target size [34], location [35], and hand postures [43], but without deriving individual user models. Targeting errors (i.e. offsets) were compensated with polynomial functions derived from touches of many users [25]. This was improved with flexible models trained on user-specific touch data for thumb input aiming at cross-hair targets [15, 41, 42]. In this paper, we also employ offset models, but for representing and recognising users touching at four different target shapes and with two hand postures.

In summary, we can expect individual touch behaviour due to variations in targeting, perception and anatomy. Without special hardware or expensive computations [37], features like finger angles or head locations remain hard to assess in practice. Hence, to develop an applicable measuring approach and evaluation framework, we consider such influences based on how they reflect in users' targeting error patterns. These can be captured with offset models on any off-the-shelf mobile touchscreen device.

Utilising Individual Touch Behaviour

Many systems utilise individual touch behaviour: on-screen keyboards adapt to the typist's touch behaviour to decrease error rates [2, 3, 45]; users can be identified by typing rhythm [32], and strokes on gesture keyboards [10]; pattern unlock can be enhanced with an implicit authentication layer using touch sequences [1, 7, 18]; other work proposed touch biometrics to replace passwords or patterns entirely [38].

Further work distinguished users on rear-projected tabletops based on typing touches [31] and fingerprints [28]. Identification with offset models has been tested for pairs of users with thumb input and cross-hairs [15]. In general, a wide range of touch features is used to infer or verify user identity: acceleration, pressure, size or timing [1, 7, 47], as well as gestures for zooming and scrolling [23, 46]. Xu et al. [44] have recently evaluated touch features for implicit authentication in four such tasks, including on-screen writing with the finger.

In conclusion, individual touch behaviour has been successfully utilised to improve usability and security of mobile interactions. However, behavioural observations were either interface-agnostic (e.g. scrolling [23, 46]) or tailored to specific interfaces (e.g. keyboard [2, 3, 45], unlock screens [1, 7, 18, 47]). These interfaces were mostly assumed to yield characteristic behaviour without further comparisons. We lack

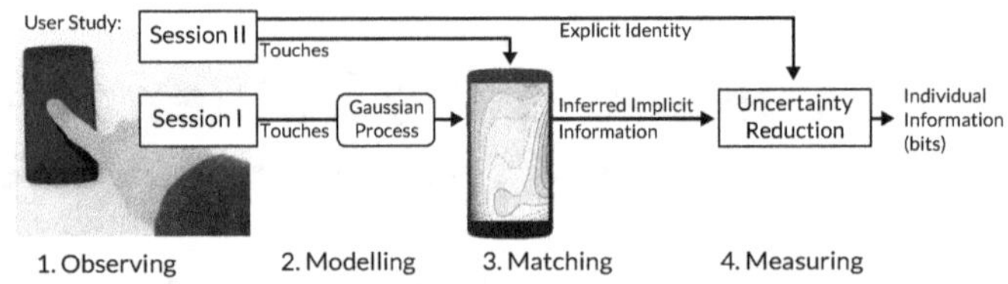

Figure 2. Measuring characteristic and consistent information ("individuality") in touch targeting behaviour: (1) Based on observed behaviour, we derive (2) targeting models to represent individual users. (3) These models recognise how well behavioural patterns in new data match each user. Hence, we gain implicit information about which user is likely touching. (4) This can reduce uncertainty about the identity of the truly interacting user, and this reduction quantifies individual information.

an understanding of the interface's influence on user-specific touch information. To inform applications of touch biometrics, possibly across different apps and interfaces, we evaluate how interface targets and hand postures influence individuality of touch behaviour. Our insights allow applications of touch biometrics to optimise user observation schemes by focusing on the most individual interactions.

Recent work [8] has simulated touches to evaluate keyboards (e.g. error rates). We present a framework to simulate touch behaviour, not restricted to keyboards, to predict expected individuality of user behaviour with given interfaces. This helps applications of touch biometrics to gain useful expectations and to favour – during runtime or UI design – those interfaces that provoke highly individual touch behaviour.

MEASURING TOUCH INDIVIDUALITY

We present an information-theoretic measure for individuality of touch targeting behaviour, computing an "index of individuality" I. We define individuality as behavioural information (i.e. patterns), which is *characteristic* (varies between users) and *consistent* (stays similar for a user over time).

Rationale: Intuitively, our metric considers behaviour individual if it allows an observer to recognise individual users. Note that we do not aim to create a running identification application, but a concept to analyse collected touch targeting data. This only *hypothetically* includes recognising users to measure how characteristically and consistently they touch. More precisely, we compute an "index of individuality" I (in bits) by measuring reduction in uncertainty about a user's identity, achieved by analysing this user's touch data.

Overview: The remainder of this section develops our measurement process. Figure 2 shows this, from left to right:

1. *Observing* touch targeting behaviour in a study with two sessions per user yields touch data for different tasks.
2. *Gaussian Process regression* applied to data from the first session captures users' targeting error patterns. Figure 2 shows an example contour plot of a user's horizontal errors.
3. *Matching patterns* with touch data from the second session results in probabilities indicating how likely each user is responsible for the analysed touches.
4. *Individuality* of user behaviour is quantified by the extent to which the uncertainty of user identity can be reduced with this extracted implicit user information.

Hence, the metric considers users' individual *characteristics* (user-specific modelling in step two) and *consistency* (recognition of users' patterns across two sessions in step three). We next describe modelling, matching, and measuring in detail.

Representing Users

To represent and recognise users' individual targeting behaviour, we adopt touch-to-target offset models, originally proposed to correct sensed touches to improve accuracy [42].

Model: We use Gaussian Processes (GPs) [36] following Weir et al. [42], a method shown to capture user-specific touch behaviour. We refer to these sources for details on the model.

Training: We measure offset vectors between target centres and touch locations by asking users to touch targets on the screen. Assuming centres is no limitation: If users aim for a different point, offsets will simply be shifted with no change to the pattern. The model is trained on this data to predict offsets for touches (see [36, 42] for details on training GPs).

Prediction: Trained models predict a bivariate Gaussian of likely offsets, $\mathcal{N}(\mu, \mathbf{\Sigma})$. To improve touch accuracy, we can add the mean prediction μ to the sensed location $\mathbf{t}$ to correct it. The full predictive distribution of likely target locations is $\mathcal{N}(\mathbf{t} + \mu, \mathbf{\Sigma})$. We use these predictions to recognise users.

Recognising Users

To recognise users, we match observed offsets with offsets predicted by users' models to derive the likelihood of each user being responsible for the analysed touches: We evaluate the true target location under the GP's predicted distribution (Figure 3). This likelihood is high if the prediction matches the observed behaviour. We thus interpret it as $p(u|\mathbf{t})$, the likelihood of user u given touch $\mathbf{t}$. For touches $\mathbf{t}_i$, we update our belief that the k-th of N users is touching at time T:

$$\textbf{User Recognition Model:} \quad p(u_k) = \frac{\prod_{i=1}^{T} p(u_k|\mathbf{t}_i)}{\sum_{j=1}^{N} \prod_{i=1}^{T} p(u_j|\mathbf{t}_i)} \tag{1}$$

The prediction for the currently touching user is then given by the user with the highest probability $p(u_k)$ at T touches. The next step employs this user recognition model to quantify individual information in touch interactions.

Quantifying Individual Information

To develop our approach for calculating the amount of individual information in touch targeting behaviour, we consider the problem of hypothetically encoding a user's identity. Abstractions like this are commonly considered to measure information, for example by Fitts' Law [21], which relates distance and target size to signal and noise in information theory to compute an "index of difficulty" in bits.

Following a similar view, we define an "index of individuality" I: the extent to which costs of *explicitly* encoding identity can be reduced with *implicit* information. In other words, we compare uncertainty of guessing user identity to the uncertainty after analysing users' touch behaviour. We next describe explicit and implicit identity within this approach.

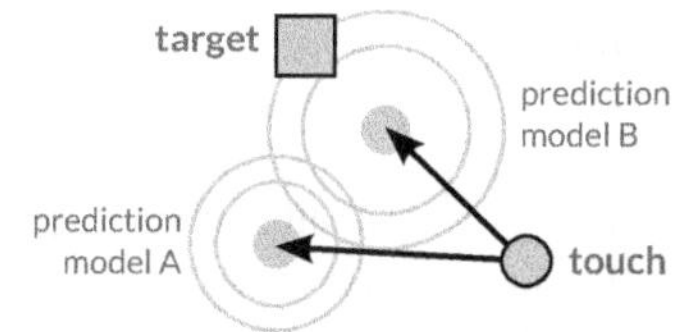

Figure 3. Recognising users with offset models. We predict a distribution of intended locations with each user's model to evaluate the true target location. In this example, the target is more likely under the predictive distribution from model B. Hence, we predict that user B is touching.

Explicitly Encoding User Identity

In a theoretic view, explicitly encoding identity requires $\log_2 N$ bits per user for N different users, since we need to represent numbers 0 to N-1 (hypothetical user IDs). This is the maximum entropy [30] of a uniform distribution over N states (i.e. users):

$$\textbf{Explicit Costs:} \quad H_{max} = -\sum_{i=1}^{N} \tfrac{1}{N} \log_2 \tfrac{1}{N} = \log_2 N \tag{2}$$

Entropy can be seen as *a priori* uncertainty [4]: Highest uncertainty (H_{max}) occurs when all users are equally likely (e.g. guessing). In other words, we need H_{max} bits (of explicit information) to resolve this uncertainty about the user's identity. We consider this the cost of explicitly encoding identity.

Implicitly Inferring User Identity

We consider a model (e.g. Eq. 1) that predicts the probability $p(u_i)$ that analysed touch data comes from user u_i. The entropy of the model's predicted distribution over users is [30]:

$$\textbf{Implicit Gains:} \quad H = -\sum_{i=1}^{N} p(u_i) \log_2 p(u_i) \tag{3}$$

Relying on such predictions, users are no longer equally likely (compare Eq. 2 and 3). Illustratively, if we "rule out" half of the users with the predictions, we save one bit to explicitly encode IDs of the remaining users ($\log_2 N$ - $\log_2 \frac{N}{2}$ = 1). We consider this the gains of implicit information.

Individuality as Reduction in Uncertainty

In summary, analysing behaviour reduces uncertainty about the user's identity. It is this difference in uncertainty that we have gained as user-specific information. Hence, we measure the index of individuality I via this reduction in uncertainty:

$$\textbf{Uncertainty Reduction:} \quad I = H_{max} - H \tag{4}$$

If we interpret this equation as information gain (e.g. as in decision trees), it compares uncertainty before and after analysing user behaviour with the model. In information theory, it is also an equation for *redundancy* (see [30]).

To illustrate this interpretation, consider the extremes: $I = H_{max}$ if analysing behaviour removed all uncertainty ($H = 0$). If we are already certain about the user's identity based on behaviour, the explicit identity seems redundant. However, if analysing behaviour cannot reduce uncertainty ($H = H_{max}$), we gained no implicit information and $I = 0$. Then, explicit identity is not redundant. Between these extremes lies a continuum where uncertainty is only partly reduced by analysing the user's behaviour with the model.

Considering Correctness of Inferred Identity

While low entropy H indicates certainty, it does not imply correctness. For example, a model might predict user A with high certainty, while ground truth is user B. Even if the model is entirely certain, if it is wrong, we cannot say that the explicit (true) identity is redundant information. Hence, we cannot reduce the costs of explicit identification, when a decision based on the model's predicted probabilities would be wrong. Thus, we consider $I = 0$ in these cases:

$$\textbf{Index of Individuality:} \quad I = \begin{cases} H_{max} - H & \text{if} \max p(u_i) = u_t \\ 0 & \text{otherwise} \end{cases} \tag{5}$$

Here, u_t denotes the ground truth user. In this paper, we use this equation to quantify individual information in user behaviour. To estimate user probabilities $p(u_i)$ needed for H, we use our user recognition model defined in Equation 1.

Remarks on the Metric

In summary, we measure individuality as reduction of uncertainty about user identity, achieved by observing touch behaviour. Equation 5 can be related to common classification accuracy (ratio of correct user identifications). For discrete predictions (i.e. $p(u_i) = 1$ for exactly one user, and 0 for all others), accuracy is equivalent to the average value of I, except for its scaling factor H_{max} and unit (bits).

In our probabilistic perspective, I is more informative than classification accuracy, since it measures reduction of uncertainty with correct predictions, instead of just counting them. Moreover, we consider bits more appropriate than accuracy for the amount of individual information in user behaviour. Our metric also respects the sample size of the analysed dataset (N in H_{max} term), whereas accuracy values always fall between 0 and 100% regardless of N.

We defined individuality as *characteristic* and *consistent* information in behaviour. We will see that our metric is sensitive to both: 1) It is sensitive to *consistency*, as shown by higher values when analysing behaviour within one session compared to analyses over a week. 2) It is sensitive to *characteristic* behaviour – obtained values reflect that behaviour characteristic among many users is to be considered more individual than if it was only characteristic among two users.

TARGETING STUDY

Touch targeting data was collected in a user study (see [11] for other analyses on this data, not related to individuality).

Study Design

The study followed a repeated measures design with independent variables *hand posture* (right thumb with device in right hand; right index finger with device in left hand), *target location* (400 locations), and *target type*: CROSS, KEY (4×7mm), APP (9×9mm), and FILL (height 9mm), shown in Figure 1a). The dependent variable was *touch location*. There were two sessions per participant with a gap of a week.

Hence, the dataset contains 24 *subjects* × 2 *sessions* × 2 *hand postures* × 4 *target types* × 400 *target locations* = 153,600 touches.

Apparatus

Data was collected with a custom Android app on a smartphone (Nexus 5). Per task, it displayed 400 targets, one at a time, with locations chosen from a grid in randomised order. Targets were always fully visible – their centres were placed at least half their width/height away from screen borders.

Participants

The study was completed by 24 participants (10 female, 3 left-handed, mean age 26), all students. Almost all participants stated in a questionnaire prior to the study that they used either hand to operate touchscreens, all including their right hand. Hence, using the right hand in the study was not an unusual task for the left-handed people. Hand sizes were measured from the index finger to the bottom of the palm (mean: 179mm; range: 159mm to 194mm) [11]. Participants were compensated with a €15 gift card for an online shop.

Procedure

Each participant was invited to two study sessions in the lab, with at least 6 days in between. A session consisted of a series of 8 targeting tasks (2 hand postures × 4 target types) and lasted for one hour, including a short questionnaire at the end.

Participants sat on a couch and held the phone in portrait orientation. They were asked to neither emphasise accuracy nor speed, but to tap "naturally". A 8×8 latin-square was used for task order to minimise learning effects. Tasks alternated between thumb and index finger to reduce fatigue. Participants were encouraged to take breaks between tasks.

RESULTS

To evaluate individuality of touch targeting behaviour, we present four analyses on the described dataset: 1) we evaluate our method of representing user behaviour, 2) we measure individuality with the described approach, 3) we evaluate user differences in targeting features in more detail, and 4) we take a closer look at the role of the screen location of targets.

Evaluating the User Representation

This first analysis confirms that offset models *trained per individual* improve accuracy for all our tasks (related work studied different tasks/models [11, 42]). This shows that the models capture user-specific targeting behaviour and are thus suitable user representations for measuring individuality.

Touch Accuracy

Figure 4 compares touch-to-target-centre distances (i.e. offsets) per target type. GP models reduced offsets for all tasks, evaluated with ten-fold cross-validation per user and task. Hyperparameters (γ=2, a=0.1, α=0.9, σ^2=0.001) were chosen by cross-validation on one arbitrary session [42].

Greenhouse-Geisser corrected ANOVA found significant main effects of hand posture ($F_{1,23} = 9.34, p < 0.01, \eta^2_G = 0.02$), target type ($F_{1.10,25.21} = 104.38, p < 0.001, \eta^2_G = 0.44$) and model ($F_{1,23} = 201.72, p < 0.001, \eta^2_G = 0.36$). The interaction effect of target type × model was significant ($F_{1.01,23.22} = 163.15, p < 0.001, \eta^2_G = 0.55$). Bonferroni corrected paired t-tests showed significantly smaller RMSEs with the model than without (index/KEY, index/APP: $p < 0.05$; others: $p < 0.01$). Models thus significantly improved touch accuracy.

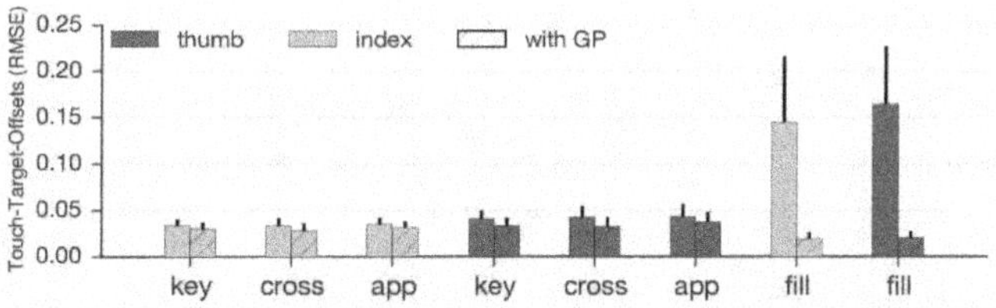

Figure 4. Touch offsets by target type and hand posture. Thumb input resulted in larger distances (i.e. touch RMSEs) to the target centres than using the index finger. The predictions of the GP offset models shifted touch locations towards the target centres, resulting in smaller RMSEs.

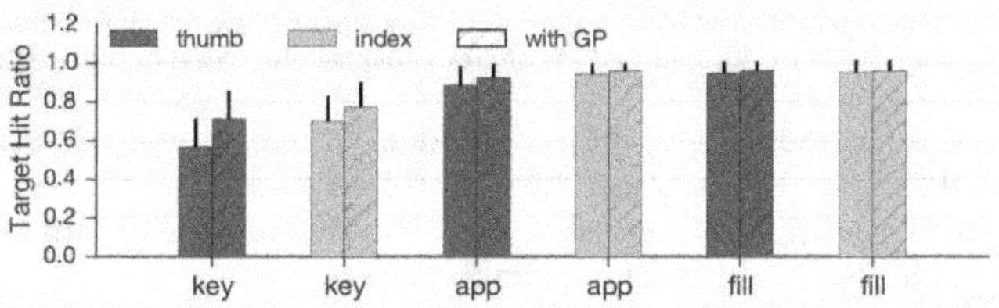

Figure 5. Target hit ratios. Larger targets were easier to hit. Index finger input was more successful than the thumb. Offset models improved hit ratios for all target types.

Area Targets: Hit Ratios

To evaluate accuracy for area targets, we examined the ratio of hits (touch in target bounding box). Figure 5 shows that larger targets were hit more consistently, and that thumbs missed targets more often than index fingers.

Greenhouse-Geisser corrected ANOVA revealed significant main effects of posture ($F_{1,23} = 19.62, p < 0.001, \eta^2_G = 0.06$), target type ($F_{1.17,27.00} = 183.72, p < 0.001, \eta^2_G = 0.61$) and model ($F_{1,23} = 52.56, p < 0.001, \eta^2_G = 0.06$). All interaction effects were significant: posture × target type ($F_{1.75,40.33} = 17.49, p < 0.001, \eta^2_G = 0.04$), posture × model ($F_{1,23} = 21.36, p < 0.001, \eta^2_G = 0.01$), target type × model ($F_{1.08,24.86} = 25.19, p < 0.001, \eta^2_G = 0.05$) and posture × target type × model ($F_{1.32,30.36} = 9.34, p < 0.01, \eta^2_G = 0.01$). Bonferroni corrected paired t-tests revealed significantly higher hit ratios with the model than without for index/KEY, thumb/KEY and thumb/APP (all $p < 0.05$). The model also improved hit ratios for the other tasks (not significant).

Applying Models Across Tasks

Improvements by models trained and tested on different tasks were not as large as with task-specific data. Models trained on FILL only reduced RMSEs for the other posture with FILL. Models trained on index finger tasks reduced RMSEs in all tasks, but thumb models only improved other thumb tasks (and FILL with index). We conclude that offset models are more robust across target types than postures.

Conclusions

The results show that GP offset models fit individual behaviour in all tasks, demonstrated by significant improvement in targeting accuracy and hit ratios. Hence, the models can represent individual users. Furthermore, our analyses revealed that thumb input was less accurate than index finger input, and that models trained with thumb data only reduced offsets for thumb tasks, but regardless of the target type. As an exception, models trained on FILL targets did not reduce offsets for other targets.

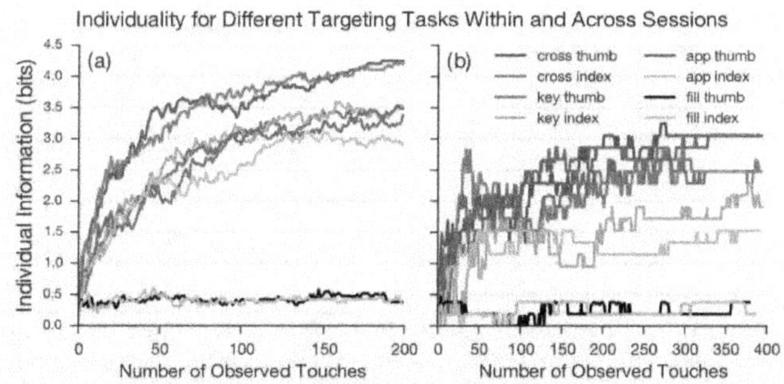

Figure 6. Individuality of targeting behaviour measured with our approach. Results show: 1) more individual information was extracted *(a)* within one session than *(b)* across sessions; 2) thumb touches were more individual than index finger touches; 3) smaller targets tended to result in more individual behaviour than larger ones. Numbers in Table 1.

Individuality of Targeting Behaviour

We now apply the developed approach (Figure 2) to measure targeting individuality according to Equation 5.

This section reveals a ranking of targets and hand postures by individual information in resulting touch targeting behaviour. We also compare measuring individuality based on data of all users to the most basic case of comparing only two users at a time. Finally, we apply our user representation and recognition method (Equation 1) to user identification, reporting achieved accuracy and practical implications.

In general, we plot individuality over time: We update measured values after each touch, using all touches so far to infer user identity implicitly (see Equation 1). This matches practical applications of touch biometrics, which can also consider all available information to identify users (e.g. a continuous implicit authentication system).

Ranking of Targets and Hand Postures

Here, we measure the amount of individual information that can be extracted within sessions (*how characteristic?*) and across sessions (*how characteristic and consistent?*).

Within sessions: We trained offset models for all users on half of their data from the first/second session. With the resulting trained system (Equation 1), we measured the individual information in the other half of each user's data from the same session, then averaged over all users per task (Figure 6a): FILL did not reveal much individual information (<0.5 bits), but other targets reached ≈ 3 to 4 bits after 100-200 touches. Thumb input with CROSS and KEY reached the highest amount of individual information (>4 bits).

Across sessions: We trained offset models on each user's first session data, using the resulting system to measure individual information in each user's second session data, again repeated for all combinations of users per task, then taking the average. Figure 6b) shows that about 1 to 1.5 bits less individual information was measured than in the within-session case, since behaviour varied over time. Thumb input resulted in 1.5 to 3 bits for all target types (but FILL). Interestingly, APP targets were more consistent than KEY targets here, as indicated by higher individuality across sessions. Table 1 summarises these results, also including numbers from the following comparison to measuring individuality on pairs of users.

Rank	Target	Hand Posture	Individual Information (bits)			
			group (24 users)		pairs of users	
			within	*across*	*within*	*across*
1	cross	thumb	3.45	2.48	0.95	0.91
2	key	thumb	3.45	2.15	0.95	0.92
3	app	thumb	2.70	2.45	0.91	0.86
4	cross	index	2.64	2.18	0.91	0.84
5	key	index	2.80	1.45	0.92	0.86
6	app	index	2.44	1.27	0.90	0.79
7	fill	index	0.41	0.26	0.50	0.42
8	fill	thumb	0.42	0.23	0.54	0.44

Table 1. Tasks ranked by individual information, based on the average value within and across session evaluations when measuring on the whole group of users. Smaller targets and thumb input led to more individual behaviour. APP was more consistent than KEY for thumbs (higher values across sessions in the group case).

Comparison to Pairs of Users

If a user A tends to touch too far left, and B too far right, then these very simple patterns are individual. Such simple patterns will not be unique to a single user any more, if we observe many more users. Hence, behaviour is inherently more individual, if it is individual in a larger group of users. This analysis demonstrates that this is reflected by our metric.

We repeated the analysis both within and across sessions for all *pairs of users* to measure the most basic user recognition task (binary: "A vs B"). The ranking of targets and hand postures overall matched the previous results (see Table 1). However, absolute values were different: Our metric showed the desired sensitivity to *characteristic* patters – behaviour unique among many users was correctly considered more individual than behaviour unique among only two users.

User Identification

Beyond their role as a measuring instrument, the methods for representing/recognising users with offset models (steps 2 and 3 in Figure 2) could also be applied to identify users as part of a continuous implicit authentication system. Hence, we evaluated user identification accuracy as well.

Accuracy is the number of correct user predictions, divided by the total number of predictions. For each group size $2 \leq N \leq 20$, we drew 100 random groups and computed average identification accuracy, splitting data for training and testing as in the previous analyses. Figure 7 shows the results. They match our expectations based on the preceding analyses and our metric: Users were more accurately identified based on behaviour observed with smaller targets and thumb input.

In general, accuracy was lower for larger groups. Consistent behaviour (i.e. within session) resulted in up to about 90% accuracy after 150 touches. Varying behaviour across sessions resulted in up to about 70% after 300 touches. We also computed F1-scores in the same way, which resulted in the same rankings of the tasks, with values for all but FILL tasks ranging from 0.70 to 0.89 within sessions for groups of size 20, and from 0.37 to 0.74 across sessions.

Conclusions

Table 1 shows the ranking of targets and hand postures by individuality: thumb input is more individual than index finger, and CROSS and KEY overall yield more individual information than APP. Little to none user-revealing information can be extracted from touches aimed at FILL targets.

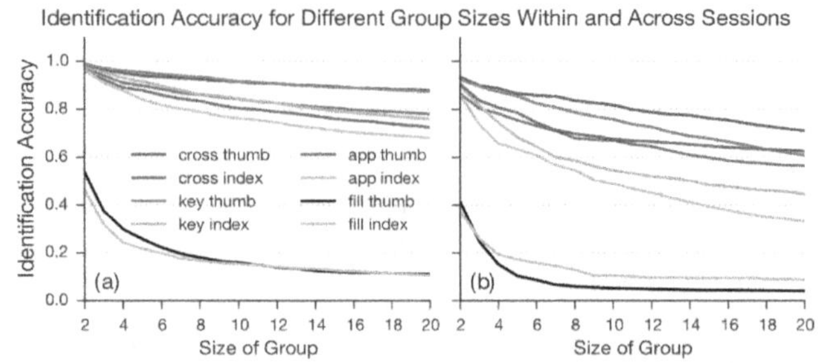

Figure 7. Identification accuracy for different group sizes *(a)* within sessions after 150 touches, and *(b)* across sessions after 300 touches. Predicting the current user from a group of known users was easier for smaller groups. The ranking of tasks matches expectations based on our metric.

As a second insight, more individual information is extracted within a single session than across sessions. Hence, our results reveal higher consistency of individual touch targeting behaviour within one session than over time.

We also compared individual information measured for all 24 users to measuring pairs of users at a time. While, for example, identification accuracy is always in the range 0-100% regardless of N, our metric captures that behaviour information characteristic among many users is more individual than information which is only characteristic among two users.

Predicting the user from a group of 4-6 reached about 75-90% accuracy with thumb across weeks. While this may seem too low for practical systems, note that we are only looking at a single feature here. Further considering that recent work utilised offsets with only a few touches to help identify typists [13], we conclude that offsets present an interesting additional touch feature for continuous implicit authentication. Ideally, they should be combined with other touch features [23, 44, 47] or methods (e.g. gait recognition [19]), since combining biometrics improves the system's accuracy [17].

Features of Individuality

The preceding section has shown that the amount of individuality in touch targeting behaviour is influenced by hand posture and target type. Now, we examine this targeting behaviour in further detail by analysing the variations in touch offset lengths and angles between users for each task.

Behavioural Differences in Offset Lengths

For each target type and pairing of two users we computed the difference in offset lengths for each observed target location. Averaging over all locations yielded a difference score for this pair of users. We limit this analysis to descriptive statistics, since ANOVA is not applicable to user differences, where each user necessarily contributes to more than one pair.

Figure 8 shows that thumbs resulted in greater offset length variations between users than index fingers. We explain this with users' different hand and finger sizes: offset lengths are likely to be influenced by the reachable area of the thumb when holding the device in the same hand [6]. In contrast, the index finger of a free hand can reach any point on the screen more easily. The largest differences were observed for the FILL targets, since they provide a larger touch area in which users can operate. Hence, to complete the picture, we need to assess a length-invariant feature as well.

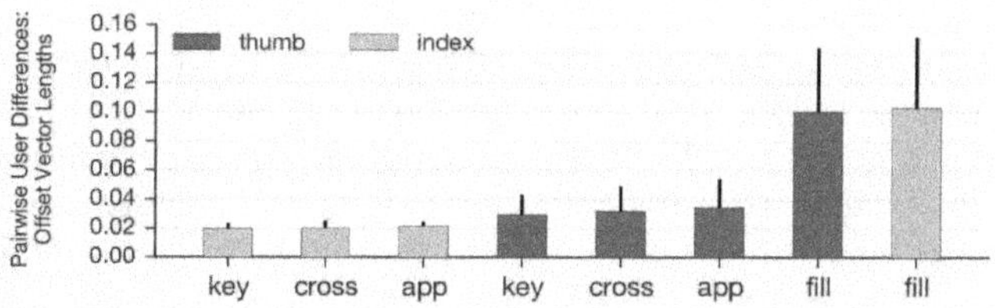

Figure 8. Pairwise user differences in offset vector lengths. Thumbs led to larger differences between users than index fingers. The biggest targets (FILL) showed the largest differences.

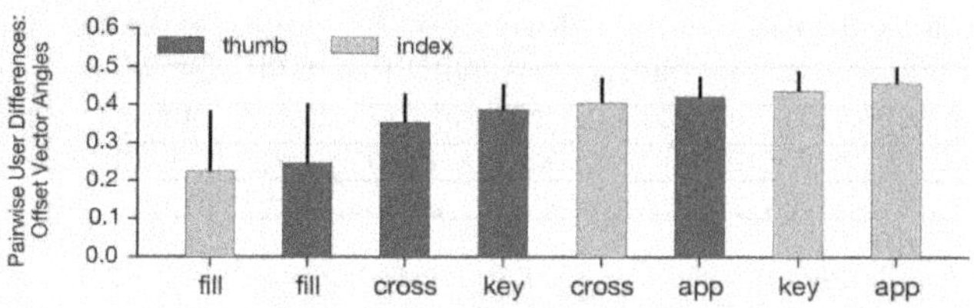

Figure 9. Pairwise user differences in offset vector angles. For all but FILL targets, the thumb led to smaller offset angle differences between users than the index finger.

Behavioural Differences in Offset Angles

We examined angles between offset vectors $\mathbf{o_1}, \mathbf{o_2}$ from two users at the same target location, using a shifted and inverted cosine similarity (to measure distance, not similarity):

$$d(\mathbf{o_1}, \mathbf{o_2}) = \frac{1}{2} - \frac{\mathbf{o_1} \cdot \mathbf{o_2}}{2\|\mathbf{o_1}\|\|\mathbf{o_2}\|} \quad (6)$$

For each target type and pair of users we computed this distance at each target location. Averaging over all locations yielded the user difference scores.

Figure 9 shows that angles varied less between users for thumbs than index fingers, likely due to anatomical constraints: a thumb's angle relative to the device is more restricted than a free hand's index finger.

In contrast to offset lengths, FILL resulted in the smallest angular user differences. The shape of these targets offered little space to vary the angle relative to the centre. In addition, users mostly touched on the right half of these targets due to the use of the right hand in the study. For the other target types, differences grew with increasing area (CROSS < KEY < APP). Hence, we conclude that users individually made different use of touch areas with respect to targeting angles.

Conclusions

These results show that thumb input leads to similar offset angles, but individual offset lengths. In contrast, index finger input leads to similar lengths, but individual angles. Target size and shape, as well as hand postures, influence the main features of individuality in touch targeting errors.

Relevant Screen Locations

We also analysed which parts of the screen are most important to describe users' individual touch targeting error patterns, using the Relevance Vector Machine (RVM) algorithm [39]. Related work used this method for touch offset prediction and for training set analysis [41]. RVMs solve regression problems like GPs, but their predictions are based on a small subset of all training examples, the *relevance vectors* (RVs). In contrast, GPs use the full training set for predictions.

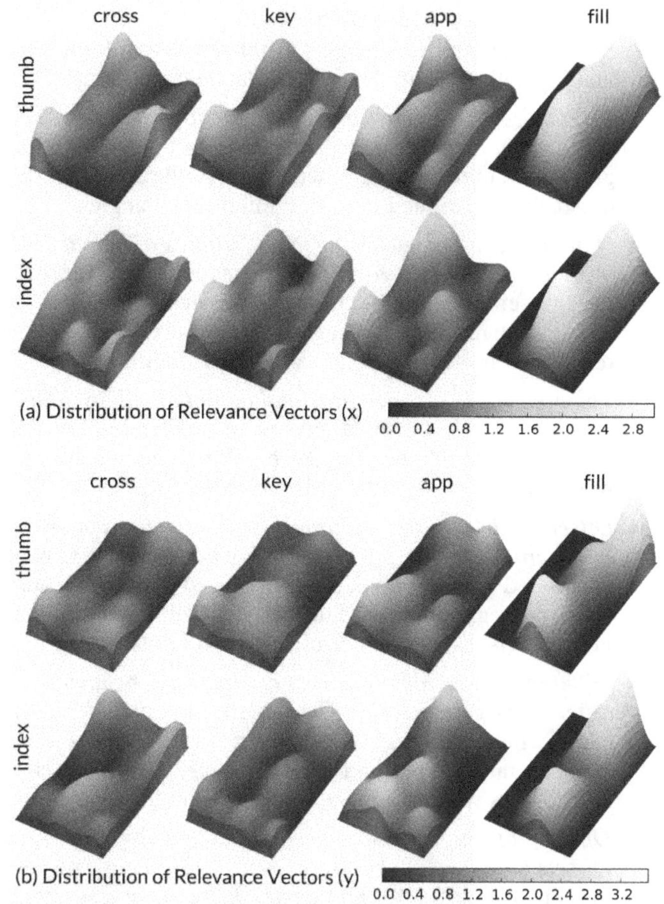

Figure 10. Kernel density estimates (i.e. smoothed histograms) of the distribution of relevance vectors (RVs) on the screen across all users, found with a Relevance Vector Machine. High values indicate the most important touches for predicting user-specific offsets in *(a)* horizontal and *(b)* vertical dimension. These plots show in which regions touches can be expected to yield more descriptive information.

The RVs found by the algorithm can be interpreted as the most important touches for modelling user behaviour. Thus, screen regions with many relevant touches across users are more descriptive. Figure 10 shows the distribution of RVs per task for both screen dimensions (x, y).

Overall, most of the touches that the RVM found to be relevant for describing users' targeting patterns were located near screen borders and corners ("peaks" in Figure 10 mostly near edges and corners). Hence, interface elements (and thus touches) at these locations are expected to yield more characteristic information. In contrast, fewer RVs were located in the centre of the screen.

These results are in line with the findings in related work on cross-hair targets [41]. Moreover, we found that the RVM used less training touches to describe index finger patterns compared to thumbs. This suggests that index finger input leads to less complex offset patterns.

INSIGHTS INTO TOUCH TARGETING

We summarise our key insights to inform research on touch modelling and implicit identification/authentication:

- *Target size and shape influence the main features of individuality in touch targeting errors:* Offset lengths and angles varied more between users for larger targets, but broad target shapes resulted in more similar offset angles.
- *Hand posture influences the main features of individuality in touch targeting errors:* Offset lengths varied more between users for thumbs than index fingers, as thumb size restricts the reachable area. However, these restrictions also resulted in less offset angle variations for thumbs.
- *Thumb input is less accurate and more individual than index finger input:* Offset lengths were smaller and hit ratios were higher with index fingers, but thumb input resulted in more characteristic and consistent offset patterns.
- *Offset modelling for accuracy improvement is more robust across target types than across hand postures:* Models trained with thumb data only reduced offsets for thumb tasks, but regardless of the target type. Training on the large FILL targets did not reduce offsets for other targets.
- *Different screen locations best characterise behaviour for different targeting tasks*: The most informative screen areas for modelling individual touch offset patterns varied between target types and hand postures, but screen edges and corners were in general more relevant than the centre.
- *Offset patterns are user-specific, but not for all targets*: Offsets are known to be user-specific [42], but we revealed that this is not true for all targets. Patterns are less characteristic and consistent if only one dimension matters (FILL).
- *Individual touch characteristics stay more consistent for small targets*: User-specific behaviour can be recognised a week after training, but with lower accuracy, especially for targets which allow for multiple targeting strategies (e.g. aiming at the centre or right half of broad targets).

IMPLICATIONS FOR APPLICATIONS

In summary, our results show that GUIs could optimise their expected gain in individual information per touch as follows:

- *Use interface elements at the screen borders*: Touches at these locations are more descriptive of users' patterns.
- *Avoid unnecessarily large targets*: Users touch less consistently if they can choose from a large area to hit the target.
- *Avoid very elongated target shapes:* Such targets lead to less diverse offset angles, reducing pattern individuality.
- *Use thumb-friendly layouts:* User characteristics are more evident with thumb input than with the index finger.

We could try to improve implicit identification by designing interfaces with the above statements in mind, but usability considerations should obviously come first. Hence, these implications are mainly meant to help choose between *usable* designs, with optimisation for biometrics as a secondary goal. Moreover, instead of changing GUIs, developers can use our implications to optimise which touches to "watch out for". Coming back to our initial example, an implicit continuous authentication system could mitigate the risk of false decisions by weighting touches higher, which are aimed at small compact targets near screen borders. With approaches to infer hand postures [11, 29, 45], systems can put more weight on thumb than index finger touches to infer user identity (e.g. via weighted samples in SVMs, or a prior in Bayesian methods).

INTERFACE EVALUATION

To facilitate application and verification of our implications, we now present an interface evaluation method. It takes a GUI layout as its input and outputs a (rough) estimate of the amount of individual information that could be derived from touch targeting interactions with that GUI. Developers and researchers can use this method to computationally compare different GUIs with respect to their expected usefulness for touch-based user identification and authentication.

Rationale: Intuitively, we use the collected data to train touch models for different interactions (target types, hand postures). We then simulate touches based on these models. Finally, we measure individuality of the simulated interactions. These values can then be compared between interfaces. In summary, our method comprises of the following three steps:

1. *Creating a model:* For a given interface, we train an interaction model on the study data from the *second* sessions.
2. *Simulating touches*: We next sample from this model's distribution to simulate touch interactions for this interface.
3. *Interface evaluation*: Simulated touches are fed into our measurement system, trained on the *first* sessions' data.

In summary, we use our study observations to enable evaluation of target combinations/layouts not directly observed before. The approach considers *consistency*, since touches are generated by a model trained on users' second sessions, and fed to a system trained on their first sessions. It also considers user *characteristics*, since it evaluates interfaces with our measuring system based on individual targeting patterns.

Applications and limitations: Predicted individuality is not meant to be interpreted absolutely, since simulated behaviour is less complex than real interactions. Nonetheless, we can *compare* predictions (e.g. higher individuality predicted for interface A than B). With this knowledge, developers and researchers can 1) alter interfaces iteratively or 2) weight observations accordingly, both to yield more user-revealing touch information. Figure 11 summarises our evaluation framework. The corresponding detailed formal description follows.

Touch Interaction Model

We consider an interface E with a set of GUI elements $e \in E$, and a set of users $u \in U$. Our touch interaction model for E is then defined by the following factorisation of the joint distribution of users u, elements e and touches t:

$$\textbf{Touch Interaction Model:} \quad p(t,e,u) = p(t|e,u)p(e)p(u) \tag{7}$$

The individual parts are explained in detail below.

Expected touch locations per GUI element: $p(t|e,u)$ describes the distribution of touches for interface element e targeted by user u as a bivariate Gaussian:

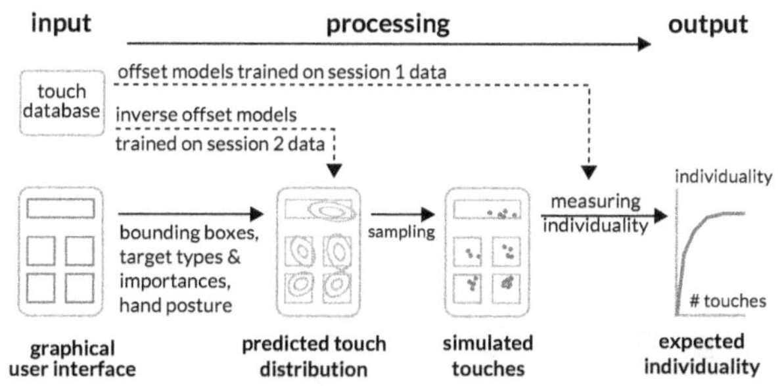

Figure 11. Graphical user interface evaluation framework. An interface is given as a set of elements (blue). Each element e is described by its bounding box, type (e.g. APP), and importance $p(e)$. We train inverse offset models from collected touches to predict a distribution of likely touch locations $p(t|e, u)$ for each target e and user u. Over all users and targets, this results in a touch distribution for the whole interface (orange): $p(t|e, u)p(e)p(u)$. We sample touches (red) from this distribution by drawing a user from $p(u)$, an element from $p(e)$, and then a touch location from $p(t|e, u)$. Finally, we feed these simulated touches t into our measurement system to predict individuality (green). Values can be compared between different interfaces, for example to evaluate which one has higher potential for behavioural touch biometrics.

$$p(t|e, u) \sim \mathcal{N}(\mu_{\mathbf{e,u}}, \mathbf{\Sigma_{e,u}} + \varepsilon\mathbf{\Sigma_n}) \quad (8)$$

Here, $\mu_{\mathbf{e,u}}$ denotes the mean prediction of an *inverse* offset model for user u given location and type of element e. $\mathbf{\Sigma_{e,u}}$ is the covariance matrix of this predictive distribution. *Inverse* means that the model (here we again use the GP model) is trained to predict touch locations given a target location [12].

We add noise with zero mean and covariance $\varepsilon\mathbf{\Sigma_n}$, set proportional to the element's width/height with scaling ε, a hyperparameter of the model. This reflects that users may touch different parts of (larger) elements, as revealed by varying behaviour in our study, and also allows us to estimate behaviour for elements with sizes not exactly observed during training.

Relative importances of interface elements: $p(e)$ models the elements' relative importances. For example, when evaluating a keyboard we can use the relative frequency of the characters in a given language. A uniform distribution means that each element is equally important to the user.

Relative user frequencies: $p(u)$ models how often users interact. We assume uniformity – each user is equally likely.

Possible extensions: Our model assumes fixed hand postures, since participants were told which postures to use. However, it can easily be adapted to freely chosen postures h, for example as $p(t, e, u, h) = p(t|e, u, h)p(e)p(u)p(h)$, where $p(h)$ is the observed relative posture frequency. We can also include terms like $p(h|u)$ (different users favour different postures), or $p(h|e)$ (different elements provoke different postures).

Simulating Touch Interaction

To simulate interactions for the given interface, we sample touches from the joint distribution $p(t, e, u)$ as defined by our model: 1) we draw a user u from $p(u)$; 2) we draw an element e from $p(e)$; and 3) we draw a touch location t from $p(t|e, u)$.

Example Application

Three example applications show that the model's predictions match the study insights. Figure 12 presents a list, a homescreen, and a keyboard. The figure further shows each GUI's touch interaction model (Equation 7, density shown via contours for thumb input) and predicted (pairwise) individual information. The method predicts the highest individuality for the keyboard, followed by the homescreen and finally the list. We discuss these results in the light of our previous insights:

Keyboard: Keys are smaller than app-icons and list entries; thus, users touch more consistently. Predicted high touch density (Figure 12c) also lies in the most descriptive screen regions (Figure 10), yielding more informative touches.

Homescreen: In contrast, the homescreen uses larger targets, including the elongated searchbar at the top. Such targets lead to less consistent behaviour. Moreover, the homescreen features targets in the less descriptive centre region of the screen.

List: Finally, the list yielded little individual information. It only features FILL targets, which the study revealed to lead to very inconsistent behaviour.

Hand postures: Our method predicted higher accuracy for thumbs than index fingers, matching our study findings.

In summary, we demonstrated that our method can rank interface layouts according to expected individuality in targeting behaviour. Predictions match expectations from our previous analyses. The model can thus utilise given touch data to estimate targeting behaviour for interface layouts. This complements our insights with an applicable evaluation tool.

SUMMARY AND DISCUSSION

Individuality of targeting behaviour: We analysed and ranked eight targeting tasks by individuality (Table 1). Using data from two sessions, our measuring approach considered both user characteristics and consistency. Small targets result in more individual touch behaviour. Targets and hand postures influence whether targeting error length or angle is the main feature of individuality in targeting behaviour. Moreover, thumb input is less accurate but more individual than index finger input. The most descriptive touch locations are near the screen corners and edges.

Measuring individuality: We presented an approach to measure the amount of individual information in touch targeting behaviour. Our analyses showed that the metric has desirable properties: 1) Comparison of evaluations within and across sessions (Figure 6) showed that the metric is sensitive to consistency. 2) It is easier to extract characteristic behaviour for two users than for 24 – the metric also proved to be sensitive to this complexity of individuality. We thus conclude that our measuring approach renders the amount of individual information in mobile touch targeting behaviour assessable.

Interface evaluation: We applied our findings in a probabilistic touch interaction framework for interface evaluation and discussed three example cases. The predicted ranking matched our expectations based on the manual analyses of the collected data. The framework can thus help to comparatively assess which interface leads to more individual information.

Implications for Touch Biometric Systems

Observe offsets: Our results show that touch offsets are useful to distinguish users and could thus complement previous feature sets (e.g. [44]).

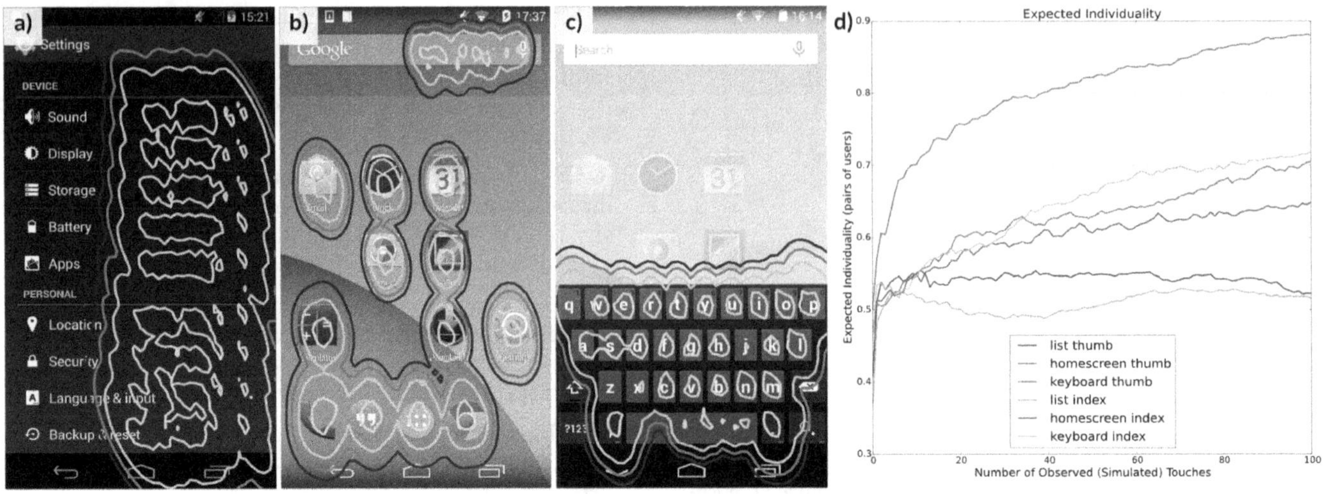

Figure 12. User interface evaluation framework for three examples: *(a)* list, *(b)* homescreen, and *(c)* keyboard. Our model uses target bounding boxes, types (e.g. APP, FILL), and importances (e.g. letter frequencies for the keyboard) to predict touch densities, as shown with contour plots (shown for thumb input only, yellow is high). We sample touches from these distributions to simulate user interaction and *(d)* measure expected individuality. In this example, we conclude that the keyboard allows us to observe more individual behaviour than homescreen and list.

Consider context: Hand postures and targets render some touches more "telling" than others. In particular, to distinguish users, we recommend to rely on thumb touches targeting small, compactly-shaped targets near screen edges.

Integrate with other systems: Influences of targets and hand postures imply that applications relying on touch biometrics can benefit from close integration with other systems. GUI targets are known to the OS and (touch-based) recognition systems could provide the current hand posture [11, 29, 45].

Use multi-model methods: Our results show that touch-based biometric systems could potentially improve accuracy with target-specific and posture-specific models instead of one-fits-all models. A promising approach is a hierarchy of models that increase in specificity, as successfully used in keyboard individualisation [45].

Opportunities for Future Applications

Holistic biometrics across GUIs: While most current systems focus on one GUI or app (e.g. keyboard [13], Android pattern [18]), our results help biometric systems to utilise touch observations across multiple GUIs, by weighting relative importances (e.g. keyboard touches are more important than list touches to infer user identity).

Applications with prior knowledge: Our insights inform default parameters for biometric systems, for example to treat touches on small targets and in screen corners as more reliable. This could be realised, for instance, via weighted samples in an SVM or via priors in a Bayesian approach.

LIMITATIONS

Influence of user representation: Measuring individual information I requires a model to recognise characteristic behaviour. Absolute values of I thus depend on the chosen model, as in other information measures of behaviour [33]. To handle model-dependency, we chose the well-researched offset model and evaluated its suitability as a user representation in all our tasks. In general, our approach can also be used with other models for other biometrics (e.g. based on gait).

Analyses: Future work could study further element properties (e.g. their visuals), landscape device orientation, and other touch interactions (e.g. scrolling), possibly in every-day use. While a controlled targeting study like ours is more abstract than real GUIs, this control is needed to examine the factors' influences. Nevertheless, our tasks used common GUI element shapes/sizes and natural hand postures, and single taps are the most fundamental and common touch interaction.

Interface evaluation: We do not claim to predict exact absolute individual information with our interface evaluation framework, which would require analyses on more interfaces and testing to fine-tune the parameters. This is beyond the scope of this paper. However, here we have shown that the ranking of three typical mobile interfaces, as predicted by our method, matches expectations based on manual data analyses. While limited by available data (e.g. with respect to target types), our concept is flexible to work with any dataset of touches and targets. It can thus easily be adapted, for example to respect hand postures chosen by users.

CONCLUSION AND FUTURE WORK

We have evaluated individuality of mobile touch targeting behaviour, measuring how characteristically and consistently users target GUI elements with over 150,000 touches in eight tasks. We presented a metric, data analyses, and an interface evaluation framework. As a key insight, applications of touch biometrics (e.g. implicit continuous authentication) should consider hand postures and properties of GUI elements.

With this knowledge, biometric systems can 1) favour interfaces which yield characteristic and consistent touch information, and 2) optimise user observation schemes to appropriately focus on the most individual and thus prolific interactions. We regard these contributions as a fundamental step towards robust, holistic applications of mobile touch biometrics for interface personalisation and usable privacy and security.

In future work, we plan to build a continuous posture recogniser and user authentication system, with this paper's results as prior knowledge of individuality of touch interactions.

REFERENCES

1. Julio Angulo and Erik Wästlund. 2012. Exploring Touch-Screen Biometrics for User Identification on Smart Phones. *Privacy and Identity Management for Life* 375 (2012), 130–143.
2. Shiri Azenkot and Shumin Zhai. 2012. Touch Behavior with Different Postures on Soft Smartphone Keyboards. In *Proceedings of the 14th International Conference on Human-computer Interaction with Mobile Devices and Services (MobileHCI '12)*. ACM, New York, NY, USA, 251–260.
3. Tyler Baldwin and Joyce Chai. 2012. Towards Online Adaptation and Personalization of Key-target Resizing for Mobile Devices. In *Proceedings of the 2012 ACM International Conference on Intelligent User Interfaces (IUI '12)*. ACM, New York, NY, USA, 11–20.
4. David Barber. 2012. *Bayesian Reasoning and Machine Learning*. Cambridge University Press.
5. Patrick Baudisch and Gerry Chu. 2009. Back-of-device Interaction Allows Creating Very Small Touch Devices. In *Proceedings of the SIGCHI Conference on Human Factors in Computing Systems (CHI '09)*. ACM, New York, NY, USA, 1923–1932.
6. Joanna Bergstrom-Lehtovirta and Antti Oulasvirta. 2014. Modeling the Functional Area of the Thumb on Mobile Touchscreen Surfaces. In *Proceedings of the SIGCHI Conference on Human Factors in Computing Systems (CHI '14)*. ACM, New York, NY, USA, 1991–2000.
7. Michael Beton, Vincent Marie, and Christophe Rosenberger. 2013. Biometric secret path for mobile user authentication: A preliminary study. In *Computer and Information Technology (WCCIT), 2013 World Congress on*. 1–6.
8. Xiaojun Bi, Shiri Azenkot, Kurt Partridge, and Shumin Zhai. 2013a. Octopus: Evaluating Touchscreen Keyboard Correction and Recognition Algorithms via. In *Proceedings of the SIGCHI Conference on Human Factors in Computing Systems (CHI '13)*. ACM, New York, NY, USA, 543–552.
9. Xiaojun Bi, Yang Li, and Shumin Zhai. 2013b. FFitts Law: Modeling Finger Touch with Fitts' Law. In *Proceedings of the SIGCHI Conference on Human Factors in Computing Systems (CHI '13)*. ACM, New York, NY, USA, 1363–1372.
10. Ulrich Burgbacher and Klaus Hinrichs. 2014. An Implicit Author Verification System for Text Messages Based on Gesture Typing Biometrics. In *Proceedings of the SIGCHI Conference on Human Factors in Computing Systems (CHI '14)*. ACM, New York, NY, USA, 2951–2954.
11. Daniel Buschek and Florian Alt. 2015. TouchML: A Machine Learning Toolkit for Modelling Spatial Touch Targeting Behaviour. In *Proceedings of the 20th International Conference on Intelligent User Interfaces (IUI '15)*. ACM, New York, NY, USA, 110–114.
12. Daniel Buschek, Alexander Auch, and Florian Alt. 2015a. A Toolkit for Analysis and Prediction of Touch Targeting Behaviour on Mobile Websites. In *Proceedings of the 7th ACM SIGCHI Symposium on Engineering Interactive Computing Systems (EICS '15)*. ACM, New York, NY, USA, 54–63.
13. Daniel Buschek, Alexander De Luca, and Florian Alt. 2015b. Improving Accuracy, Applicability and Usability of Keystroke Biometrics on Mobile Touchscreen Devices. In *Proceedings of the 33rd Annual ACM Conference on Human Factors in Computing Systems (CHI '15)*. ACM, New York, NY, USA, 1393–1402.
14. Daniel Buschek, Alexander De Luca, and Florian Alt. 2015c. There is more to Typing than Speed: Expressive Mobile Touch Keyboards via Dynamic Font Personalisation. In *Proceedings of the 17th International Conference on Human-Computer Interaction with Mobile Devices and Services (MobileHCI '15)*. ACM, New York, NY, USA, 125–130.
15. Daniel Buschek, Simon Rogers, and Roderick Murray-Smith. 2013. User-specific Touch Models in a Cross-device Context. In *Proceedings of the 15th International Conference on Human-computer Interaction with Mobile Devices and Services (MobileHCI '13)*. ACM, New York, NY, USA, 382–391.
16. Daniel Buschek, Oliver Schoenleben, and Antti Oulasvirta. 2014. Improving Accuracy in Back-of-Device Multitouch Typing: A Clustering-based Approach to Keyboard Updating. In *Proceedings of the 19th International Conference on Intelligent User Interfaces (IUI '14)*. ACM, New York, NY, USA, 57–66.
17. Heather Crawford, Karen Renaud, and Tim Storer. 2013. A framework for continuous, transparent mobile device authentication. *Computers & Security* 39, Part B (2013), 127 – 136.
18. Alexander De Luca, Alina Hang, Frederik Brudy, Christian Lindner, and Heinrich Hussmann. 2012. Touch Me Once and I Know It's You!: Implicit Authentication Based on Touch Screen Patterns. In *Proceedings of the SIGCHI Conference on Human Factors in Computing Systems (CHI '12)*. ACM, New York, NY, USA, 987–996.
19. Mohammad Omar Derawi, Claudia Nickel, Patrick Bours, and Christoph Busch. 2010. Unobtrusive User-Authentication on Mobile Phones Using Biometric Gait Recognition. In *Proceedings of the 2010 Sixth International Conference on Intelligent Information Hiding and Multimedia Signal Processing (IIH-MSP '10)*. IEEE Computer Society, Washington, DC, USA, 306–311.
20. Leah Findlater and Jacob Wobbrock. 2012. Personalized Input: Improving Ten-finger Touchscreen Typing Through Automatic Adaptation. In *Proceedings of the SIGCHI Conference on Human Factors in Computing Systems (CHI '12)*. ACM, New York, NY, USA, 815–824.

21. Paul M. Fitts. 1954. The information capacity of the human motor system in controlling the amplitude of movement. *Journal of Experimental Psychology* 47, 6 (1954), 381–391.

22. Clifton Forlines, Daniel Wigdor, Chia Shen, and Ravin Balakrishnan. 2007. Direct-touch vs. Mouse Input for Tabletop Displays. In *Proceedings of the SIGCHI Conference on Human Factors in Computing Systems (CHI '07)*. ACM, New York, NY, USA, 647–656.

23. M. Frank, R. Biedert, E. Ma, I. Martinovic, and D. Song. 2013. Touchalytics: On the Applicability of Touchscreen Input as a Behavioral Biometric for Continuous Authentication. *Information Forensics and Security, IEEE Transactions on* 8, 1 (Jan 2013), 136–148.

24. Asela Gunawardana, Tim Paek, and Christopher Meek. 2010. Usability Guided Key-target Resizing for Soft Keyboards. In *Proceedings of the 15th International Conference on Intelligent User Interfaces (IUI '10)*. ACM, New York, NY, USA, 111–118.

25. Niels Henze, Enrico Rukzio, and Susanne Boll. 2011. 100,000,000 Taps: Analysis and Improvement of Touch Performance in the Large. In *Proceedings of the 13th International Conference on Human Computer Interaction with Mobile Devices and Services (MobileHCI '11)*. ACM, New York, NY, USA, 133–142.

26. Christian Holz and Patrick Baudisch. 2010. The Generalized Perceived Input Point Model and How to Double Touch Accuracy by Extracting Fingerprints. In *Proceedings of the SIGCHI Conference on Human Factors in Computing Systems (CHI '10)*. ACM, New York, NY, USA, 581–590.

27. Christian Holz and Patrick Baudisch. 2011. Understanding Touch. In *Proceedings of the SIGCHI Conference on Human Factors in Computing Systems (CHI '11)*. ACM, New York, NY, USA, 2501–2510.

28. Christian Holz and Patrick Baudisch. 2013. Fiberio: A Touchscreen That Senses Fingerprints. In *Proceedings of the 26th Annual ACM Symposium on User Interface Software and Technology (UIST '13)*. ACM, New York, NY, USA, 41–50.

29. Markus Löchtefeld, Phillip Schardt, Antonio Krüger, and Sebastian Boring. 2015. Detecting Users Handedness for Ergonomic Adaptation of Mobile User Interfaces. In *Proceedings of the 14th International Conference on Mobile and Ubiquitous Multimedia (MUM '15)*. ACM, New York, NY, USA, 245–249.

30. David J.C. MacKay. 2003. *Information Theory, Inference, and Learning Algorithms*. Cambridge University Press.

31. Philipp Mock, Jörg Edelmann, Andreas Schilling, and Wolfgang Rosenstiel. 2014. User Identification Using Raw Sensor Data from Typing on Interactive Displays. In *Proceedings of the 19th International Conference on Intelligent User Interfaces (IUI '14)*. ACM, New York, NY, USA, 67–72.

32. Mohammad Nauman, Tamleek Ali, and Azhar Rauf. 2013. Using Trusted Computing for Privacy Preserving Keystroke-based Authentication in Smartphones. *Telecommunication Systems* 52, 4 (April 2013), 2149–2161.

33. Antti Oulasvirta, Teemu Roos, Arttu Modig, and Laura Leppänen. 2013. Information Capacity of Full-body Movements. In *Proceedings of the SIGCHI Conference on Human Factors in Computing Systems (CHI '13)*. ACM, New York, NY, USA, 1289–1298.

34. Pekka Parhi, Amy K. Karlson, and Benjamin B. Bederson. 2006. Target Size Study for One-handed Thumb Use on Small Touchscreen Devices. In *Proceedings of the 8th Conference on Human-computer Interaction with Mobile Devices and Services (MobileHCI '06)*. ACM, New York, NY, USA, 203–210.

35. Keith B. Perry and Juan Pablo Hourcade. 2008. Evaluating One Handed Thumb Tapping on Mobile Touchscreen Devices. In *Proceedings of Graphics Interface 2008 (GI '08)*. Canadian Information Processing Society, Toronto, Ont., Canada, Canada, 57–64.

36. Carl Edward Rasmussen and Christopher K. I. Williams. 2006. *Gaussian processes for machine learning*. The MIT Press.

37. Simon Rogers, John Williamson, Craig Stewart, and Roderick Murray-Smith. 2011. AnglePose: Robust, Precise Capacitive Touch Tracking via 3D Orientation Estimation. In *Proceedings of the SIGCHI Conference on Human Factors in Computing Systems (CHI '11)*. ACM, New York, NY, USA, 2575–2584.

38. Napa Sae-Bae, Kowsar Ahmed, Katherine Isbister, and Nasir Memon. 2012. Biometric-rich Gestures: A Novel Approach to Authentication on Multi-touch Devices. In *Proceedings of the SIGCHI Conference on Human Factors in Computing Systems (CHI '12)*. ACM, New York, NY, USA, 977–986.

39. Michael E. Tipping. 2001. Sparse Bayesian Learning and the Relevance Vector Machine. *Journal of Machine Learning Research* 1 (Sept. 2001), 211–244.

40. Feng Wang and Xiangshi Ren. 2009. Empirical Evaluation for Finger Input Properties in Multi-touch Interaction. In *Proceedings of the SIGCHI Conference on Human Factors in Computing Systems (CHI '09)*. ACM, New York, NY, USA, 1063–1072.

41. Daryl Weir, Daniel Buschek, and Simon Rogers. 2013. Sparse Selection of Training Data for Touch Correction Systems. In *Proceedings of the 15th International Conference on Human-computer Interaction with Mobile Devices and Services (MobileHCI '13)*. ACM, New York, NY, USA, 404–407.

42. Daryl Weir, Simon Rogers, Roderick Murray-Smith, and Markus Löchtefeld. 2012. A User-specific Machine Learning Approach for Improving Touch Accuracy on Mobile Devices. In *Proceedings of the 25th Annual ACM Symposium on User Interface Software and Technology (UIST '12)*. ACM, New York, NY, USA, 465–476.

43. Jacob O. Wobbrock, Brad A. Myers, and Htet Htet Aung. 2008. The Performance of Hand Postures in Front- and Back-of-device Interaction for Mobile Computing. *International Journal of Human-Computer Studies* 66, 12 (2008), 857–875.

44. Hui Xu, Yangfan Zhou, and Michael R. Lyu. 2014. Towards Continuous and Passive Authentication via Touch Biometrics: An Experimental Study on Smartphones. In *Symposium On Usable Privacy and Security (SOUPS 2014)*. USENIX Association, Menlo Park, CA, 187–198.

45. Ying Yin, Tom Yu Ouyang, Kurt Partridge, and Shumin Zhai. 2013. Making Touchscreen Keyboards Adaptive to Keys, Hand Postures, and Individuals: A Hierarchical Spatial Backoff Model Approach. In *Proceedings of the SIGCHI Conference on Human Factors in Computing Systems (CHI '13)*. ACM, New York, NY, USA, 2775–2784.

46. Xi Zhao, Tao Feng, and Weidong Shi. 2013. Continuous mobile authentication using a novel Graphic Touch Gesture Feature. In *2013 IEEE Sixth International Conference on Biometrics: Theory, Applications and Systems (BTAS)*. 1–6.

47. Nan Zheng, Kun Bai, Hai Huang, and Haining Wang. 2014. You Are How You Touch: User Verification on Smartphones via Tapping Behaviors. In *2014 IEEE 22nd International Conference on Network Protocols (ICNP)*. 221–232.

Enhancing Mobile Content Privacy with Proxemics Aware Notifications and Protection

Huiyuan Zhou[1], Khalid Tearo[1], Aniruddha Waje[1], Elham Alghamdi[1], Thamara Alves[2], Vinicius Ferreira[2], Kirstie Hawkey[1], Derek Reilly[1]

[1]GEM Lab, Dalhousie University
{hzhou,tearo,waje,elham,hawkey,reilly}@cs.dal.ca

[2]Federal University of São Carlos
{thamara.alves, vinicius.ferreira}@ dc.ufscar.br

ABSTRACT
Given the widespread adoption of mobile devices and the private personal and work information they carry, casual or deliberate shoulder surfing is an increasing concern with these devices. We iteratively designed a tablet interface that detects when people nearby are looking at the screen, providing awareness through glyph notifications, and response through visual protections, and evaluated its use in two experiments. The results indicate that mobile content privacy management systems such as ours could help alleviate the cognitive and social burden of managing mobile device privacy in dynamic settings. We identify physical privacy behaviours and preferences that can inform the design of privacy notification and management protocols on mobile devices. We argue that such systems require *subtlety* so as not to advertise the users' intention for privacy, *flexibility* in addressing dynamic privacy needs and *trustworthiness* to promote adoption.

Author Keywords
Mobile content privacy management; shoulder surfing; proxemics interaction; mobile interface; tablet.

ACM Classification Keywords
H.5.m. Information interfaces and presentation (e.g., HCI): Miscellaneous.

INTRODUCTION
Given the explosive growth of the mobile device market and the popularity of large screen smartphones, tablets, and subnotebooks, shoulder surfing has moved off the laptop and onto mobile devices. In the US people spend more time on average using mobile devices than desktop computers [12]. Mobile devices often carry sensitive or personal data, and their mobility means that such data can be accessed in environments that carry a real or indeterminate threat to privacy. Thompson [45] surveyed 800 professionals and found that for organizations, sensitive data such as internal financials (42%), private HR information (33%) and trade secrets (32%) were the most commonly accessed data outside the office. Surveys indicate growing concern about the privacy of personal information such as passwords, emails and text messages on smartphones [33]. At the same time, 72% of office commuters in the UK admit to looking over their neighbours' shoulders on the bus or train [41]. Similar behaviours occur in queues, at cafes, and in dynamic, semi-public workplaces such as hospital wards.

ACM 978-1-4503-3362-7/16/05$15.00
DOI: http://dx.doi.org/10.1145/2858036.2858232

From a traditional social and interpersonal perspective, privacy, defined by Altman as *"selective control of access to the self"*, concerns controlling the desired level of one's accessibility to others, or interaction with others [1]. Contemporaneous social research identified interpersonal privacy behaviours such as verbal and nonverbal communication, the maintenance of personal space, territory and cultural norms [1]. For example, people may block, turn, or move in response to nearby intruders [36].

From an information control perspective, privacy issues evolve with changes in technology [28], and privacy research defends against new opportunities technology has brought for intrusion [29]. We define *mobile content privacy management* as controlling the accessibility of visual information to others on mobile devices. Mobile content privacy is also a social concern, but the focus shifts from self-other interaction to self-device-other interaction.

As with interpersonal privacy, mobile content privacy could be managed by *physical* means. Taking advantage of spatial elements of the built environment is one basic way to do this [34]. For example, in a library mobile content privacy could be managed by moving from a busy foyer to a quiet alcove. However, mobile devices are also physically manipulated relative to the user (e.g., moved, tilted) to preserve privacy. Luff and Heath argue that *"micro-mobility"*—the way artefacts and objects can be subtly placed, mobilized and interwoven into interactions—is critical for collaboration [31]. There is currently little understanding of the role that a device's micro-mobility can play in mobile content privacy.

Mobile content privacy can also be managed through the device itself *digitally*. Possible approaches can be classified and understood using Brunk's privacy framework, in which privacy management is seen as an ongoing process of awareness, prevention, detection, response and recovery [10]. For example, hardware privacy filters that limit screen visibility to a small range from perpendicular [39], and indirect password entry schemes such as Convex Hull Click scheme [47] and gaze-based input methods [27] provide *prevention*, however the user must maintain *awareness* of when it should be used (not when sharing content, for example). When the privacy characteristics of a setting are fluid, or when an individual accesses information across a range of settings, solutions that focus on *awareness, detection* and *response* may be useful. Portnoff et al. showed notifications (e.g., on-screen icons, LED lights) could raise users' awareness of privacy-related events such as unexpected webcam recording [38]. Tarasewich et al. designed privacy blinders that could cover specific types of data (e.g., banking numbers) with opaque squares [44] in response to a perceived or real threat to privacy.

Recent work explores detection of shoulder surfing to trigger just-in-time notifications or protection mechanisms with marker-based motion trackers [8], and front camera-based eye detection and counting [30]. Apple and Samsung have patented gaze-tracking technologies. Given the transient need for screen privacy and increasing processing power, battery life, and lens quality, practical systems will become available. However, it is not clear how people respond to and use such systems. We wondered how shoulder-surfing detection could integrate with physical privacy management behaviour (e.g. tilting the device, turning away), and how mobile privacy management might differ in individual vs. collaborative tasks [11].

We began by designing potential notification and protection mechanisms, and evaluated them in a Wizard of Oz study. Results favoured an iconic rather than literal representation for notification, and demonstrated that the most suitable protection technique varies with both context and content attributes [48]. We then implemented a working mobile shoulder-surfing detector prototype which used motion tracking sensors to locate and orient an onlooker relative to the tablet, and designed content and related scenarios to elicit privacy behaviors and gather feedback in an experimental simulation, which is the focus of this paper. Results indicate that digital techniques for mobile content privacy management are most effective when physical management is constrained by cognitive capacity and/or social norms. Our techniques also improved awareness, confidence in privacy, and the ability to balance privacy with task efficiency, particularly during solo tasks. Mobile content privacy is an underexplored area. We contribute to this area and to proxemic interaction research by classifying physical privacy practices, exploring how physical and digital mechanisms can be integrated, and informing design through a synthesis of participant feedback and behaviour.

RELATED WORK

Physical Privacy Management Practice

In organizational settings, people strategically manage physical space to achieve privacy. Dourish et al. reported how people positioned their computer screens to avoid the gaze of visitors, and used seats and desks as barriers to separate public and private areas of the office [15]. Murphy et al.'s ethnographic study in a hospital setting showed that staff used physical proximity (e.g., stay close to logged in computers), secured space (e.g., choose a private office, close the door), and protected verbal communication (e.g., lower voice, cover mouth when speaking) as privacy practices [32]. To the best of our knowledge, there is no prior research considering how individuals physically manage visibility of content on mobile devices.

Privacy Notifications and Protections

Goucher argued that shoulder surfing mostly happens when task focus and cognitive load reduces awareness of changes in the environment [18]. Notification cues such as visual glyphs, sounds or vibrations can help raise awareness, but they must be carefully designed to manage tradeoffs between obtrusiveness, noticeability, and information conveyed [5,6,9]. Glyph design considers dimensions such as color, shape, motion and blinking [46]. Auditory notifications are more intrusive and public while tactile notifications are more subtle and private [21].

Overlay techniques have been explored as a means of protecting digital content [8,30,44]. Fined-grained coverage requires searching for and recognizing sensitive information (e.g., currency formatting) which adds implementation complexity but reduces interference. Decreasing visible areas is potentially useful for hiding information not needed at the moment. Other approaches alter attributes of graphical or media content: for example, blurring, scrambling [26], or removing details [7] of images or video. More research is needed to assess when and how well these methods will work for mobile visual content privacy.

Proxemics as a Mediator for Privacy

In the field of nonverbal communication, Hall defined four interpersonal zones by distance: intimate (less than 1.5 feet), personal (1.5-4 feet), social (4-12 feet) and public (12-25 feet) [20]. Hall emphasized that the interaction possibilities (e.g., via sight or touch) rather than the distance *per se* is important. Greenberg et al. operationalized this into five dimensions (distance, orientation, movement, identity, location) and envisioned a number of applications that employ what they dub proxemic interaction [4]. For example, the distance between people and screens in always-on video connections could be used to alter video and audio fidelity to preserve privacy [19]. Brudy et al. used proxemics data to provide visual cues of potential privacy intrusion and to protect large public displays by, for example, blacking out windows [8]. However, large displays are fundamentally different from mobile devices in terms of visibility, the expectation of public vs personal access, and the types of physical privacy actions possible (e.g. stand in front of the screen vs. tilt the screen away from onlookers). Lian et al. combined shoulder surfing detection and environmental brightness to dynamically adjust smartphone screen brightness [30]. Results showed that with view distance greater than 0.3m and view angle greater than 40°, changing brightness could protect screen details. Multi-view applications display distinct views to different viewers [14] which could be used to maintain privacy. These use glasses or specialized (e.g., TN) display hardware, which might not be a realistic requirement. Explicit human body movement such as leaning postures can be interpreted and used to control information size [22]; this could also potentially be adapted for privacy purposes but requires correct inference of user intentions or explicit user control, which can be ineffective if a privacy breach is unexpected or when mobile.

Challenges of Privacy Evaluation in the Lab

Designing a study that poses plausible privacy threats and elicits realistic responses in the lab is difficult. Using actual personal data may preclude those who hold strong concerns about the privacy of that data [35], while participants are unlikely to value fake data or feel the consequences of their behaviors. The lab context may also import a sense of trust, impacting behaviour [42]. Nonetheless, researchers have developed strategies to evaluate privacy and security in the lab. Role playing can help participants engage in study tasks [16,17]. Tan et al. assigned adversarial roles of user and onlooker to participant pairs, to evaluate a spy-resistant keyboard [43]. Iachello and Hong suggest using realistic tasks, motivating participants to protect their data, and evaluating in target settings [24]. Using unrelated primary tasks is also useful for examining the secondary nature of privacy and security goals [35].

DESIGN EXPLORATION

In this section we summarize preliminary design work and results from a first evaluation, in order to motivate the design of the study presented in this paper. More details are provided in [48,49]. Through brainstorming sessions and design sketches we created four privacy notification designs and four protection techniques for evaluation (see Figure 1).

We used an eye glyph in three designs, varying in granularity of notification from on/off (A1), three discrete intensities (A2), and a continuous range (A3). The fourth design (A4) was a literal "radar" representation that maps the relative spatial relationship between the user (the black dot in the middle) and the onlooker (a red dot showing location and a triangle representing field of view). Protection techniques removed certain visual attributes of the content to limit the ability of onlookers to see the information. Grayscale (B1) alters content color. Dim (B2) covers the whole page with a semi-opaque layer. Mask (B3) reduces the visible area to a small circle-shaped viewport that can be moved around by touch and drag. Selective Hiding (B4) anonymizes data, replaces sensitive pictures with placeholders, etc.

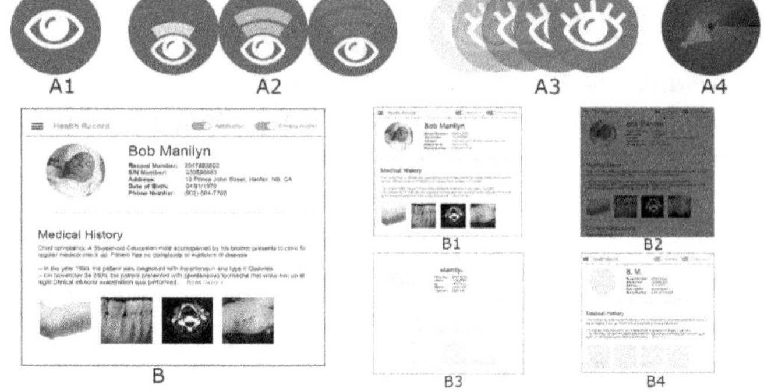

Figure 1. Notification and protection design. A1) simple (on-off). A2) 3 coarse levels. A3) fine-grained levels. A4) radar map. B) Normal electronic health record. B1) Grayscale. B2) Dim. B3) Mask. B4) Selective Hiding.

We conducted an evaluation with 12 participants in a busy university library atrium. Using a Wizard of Oz approach participants were able to use what seemed to be a privacy-aware tablet. Different notification designs (order randomized) appeared 3-5 times while the user was engaged in a primary task using a tablet. Participants ranked the notifications in terms of understanding, awareness, distraction and overall preference. Next, different protection techniques (order balanced) were triggered while participants were engaged in 4 primary tasks (information retrieval from Facebook chat, online banking, a photo album, and a health record) on a high-fidelity prototype. Participants ranked the protection techniques in terms of protection, interference and usefulness. Participants explained their rankings in a post hoc interview.

Overall, participants preferred notifications that could be immediately understood, and that would capture attention when necessary and not distract from the primary task with subtle changes or movement. We combined attributes of A1 (simple, not too distracting) and A3 (highly noticeable when opaque) into a new on/off notification (see Figure 2, B). There was no clear preference for protection method, but participants preferred Mask in the personal banking task to have precise control over what is visible, and Dim was thought to provide practical protection in all cases. Participants were split as to whether notification and protection should be used together (6 participants), or in isolation (6 participants), but found both useful.

STUDY DESIGN

We designed a study to examine physical privacy management behaviours (individually and collaboratively), and the role and impact of the digital privacy management system (e.g., notifications, protections).

Apparatus and Setting

We implemented a prototype for the purposes of the study that monitors potential shoulder surfing events around a tablet computer. It calculates the relative distance and orientation between the device and a designated onlooker to monitor potential privacy breaches in real time. When the onlooker is approaching the personal zone (<5 feet) of the user, and is oriented toward the tablet (within a 60° field of view, at which shapes and icons become recognizable [25]), a shoulder surfing event is triggered.

To track the position and orientation of the tablet and onlookers, we used a 6 degree-of-freedom electromagnetic motion tracker (Polhemus G4) with an update rate of 120HZ per sensor within a range of 6 feet from the source [37]. One sensor was attached to a thin wooden plank 12 inches from the top of the tablet to mitigate magnetic field distortion. A second sensor was attached to the back of the onlooker's head with a headband. Hubs were attached to the collar or belt of the user and the onlooker. Sensor data is transmitted wirelessly to a central server that logs the data and forwards it to a custom application that calculates the distance and relative orientation between the sensors and determines whether the proximity conditions are met. The prototype does not consider occlusion by the person using the device in this calculation. Once a shoulder surfing event is detected, a Node.js server communicates the event to a client (on the tablet) using the WebSocket protocol.

On the tablet (Windows Surface Pro 2), two applications were developed in HTML5 with variants supporting each experimental condition. Depending on the condition, a notification may pop up and/or a protection may be applied to the contents on the tablet. Aside from automatic protection, a manual protection mode allowed tablet users to decide when and for how long to use a protection by clicking a button. System behaviors could be overridden via toggle buttons for enabling/disabling notification and protection. While this setup is not realistic for field deployment, precisely tracking position and orientation allows us to detect, probe and explore user behaviors.

The study was conducted in the middle of an open lab, where other researchers might be quietly working. A single Polhemus G4 source was hung from the ceiling with a plastic rope and secured with a sandbag on the floor. It was positioned slightly behind and 2ft above a couch (See Figure 2, A) to cover a sensing area about 10 ft in diameter.

Recruitment

We recruited 26 participants (14 female, 12 male) in pairs from the Dalhousie University community via a campus-wide mailing list and website. Participants were required to use tablets on a monthly basis, have normal or corrected-to-normal eyesight, and sign up with a partner, as piloting suggested that familiar pairs would engage more fully in our competitive and collaborative tasks. Each participant was compensated $20. Participants averaged 28 years in age (range 18-46), with 10 undergrad students, 9 graduate students, and 7 faculty and staff. 12 participants were from Computer Science, and the rest were from across the campus (humanities, social science, engineering, medicine, biology). 9 pairs were friends, 3 pairs were family (husband and wife), and 1 pair were colleagues.

19 of 26 participants used tablets on a daily basis. On average participants used tablets 10 hours a week, 64% for personal use, 24% for study and 12% for work use. The main locations to use tablets are home, workspace (office, school, lab) and public places (buses, airplanes, coffee shops etc.). Participants had the highest concern about accessing financial data in public (M= 5.7 out of 7, SD=2.2), followed by health information (5.4), email (5.0), photo (4.9), chat (4.7). When asked if they would participate if the study used their real bank accounts, 12 participants said no, 11 said hard to say, only 3 said yes.

Activities

Participants completed three activities: a game, a personal banking scenario, and a collaborative finance scenario. For all activities, the participant(s) using the tablet sat on the sofa, while an onlooker occasionally passed by (in the banking and finance scenarios) or did so repeatedly (in the game scenario). We used the same on/off notification (see Figure 2, B) but varied protections (see Table 1) to best support each activity.

	Game		Individual		Collaborative
Tablet User	P1	P2	P1	P2	P1+P2
Onlooker	P2	P1	Confederat		Confederate
Protection	Dim		Mask		Dim

Table 1: Lab study configuration across 3 activities.

Figure 2. The game activity setup. A) One participant (the user) hid tablet information while performing a primary task. The other participant (the onlooker) tried to see the information. B) Screenshots of the game interface with a notification and Dim protection.

Activity 1: Hide-and-Seek Game

Two participants played a game described as a "competition". In each round, one participant played a memory match game (see Figure 2, B) while hiding the screen from the other participant (onlooker). The matching game required the player to tap on two cards at a time to reveal pictures of national flags. Matched pairs would disappear. The player was told to use any technique to hide the information while remaining on the couch. The onlooker was encouraged to use any technique to look with the constraint of observing only at specified intervals and staying outside a green-dashed circle with a radius of 4 feet to simulate the personal zone around the couch. A 'Ding' sound signaled the onlooker to observe for 10 seconds and in the following 10 seconds they recognized and circled the flags seen on a recording sheet. The process was repeated until the player finished the game. After two rounds, the player and the onlooker switched roles and played for another two rounds. The player would lose points for either playing slowly or when their opponent correctly identified information (flags), and the winner of the game got a $1 compensation bonus. The matching game was chosen to simulate a primary task taking up most attentional resources. We used *Dim* in conditions where a protection mechanism was used, as our design evaluation suggested it would provide reasonable protection without interfering too much with the time-sensitive primary task.

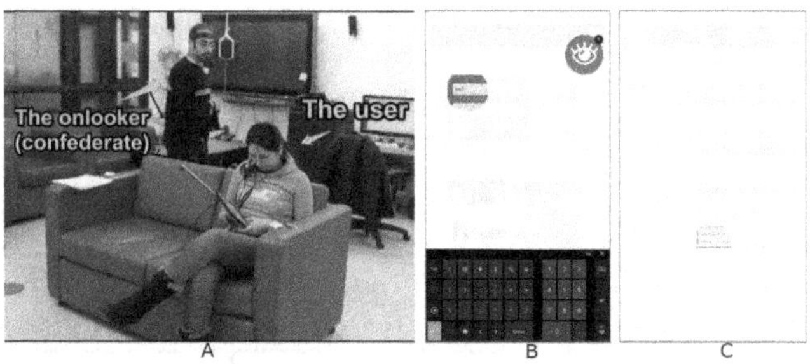

Figure 3. The individual banking activity setup. A) One participant performing banking tasks and a research confederate looking over her shoulder. B) Online banking login interface with a notification and Mask protection. C) The user searching for bank account information with Mask.

Activity 2: Individual Online Banking

Participants were asked to role play a person ("Casey" or "Jessie") who works at Dalhousie University, and "*occasionally does online banking on tablet at a non-enclosed office where colleagues may pass by*". This activity was done individually. Participants were given an authentic looking bank card with password and asked to perform two information retrieval tasks using an online banking site: to log in to the account and retrieve the last two digits of the amount paid on a particular account on a particular day or for a particular item. A research confederate who was not introduced to the participants until the end of the study acted as the onlooker (he was made conspicuous by the headband he wore). He walked around the couch area pretending to do lab work (e.g. measuring, making coffee), and discreetly looked over participants' shoulders to trigger privacy intrusion. We used *Mask* as a protection mechanism for this activity, as it was most preferred for a similar scenario in the design evaluation.

Activity 3: Roommates Splitting bills (Collaborative)

Using the same roles as Activity 2, participants acted as roommates sharing a bill in a coffee shop (See Figure 4). In each task, participants were shown a webpage with "Casey and Jessie's" apartment information, shared bills (e.g. electricity, internet, furniture), and an embedded calculator. They were asked to first calculate their balance. Then the person who owed their roommate money logged into their bank account and paid using email transfer. Participants were asked to calculate and fill in the transfer information together, and to discuss realistic security questions. The same confederate acted as the onlooker. Each pair completed 3 similar tasks with different bill values and different payers. We used *Dim* as a protection technique in this activity in order not to interfere with collaboration.

Figure 4. The collaborative activity setup. A) Two participants performing shared tasks and a research confederate looking over their shoulders. B) Bill calculation interface with Dim protection.

Conditions and Study Procedure

Four experiment conditions were defined, based on the use of notification and protection: no notification and no protection as a baseline of physical privacy management, only notification, only protection (protection was triggered automatically), and having both (protection was turned on manually as automatic notification and protection were considered redundant by participants in the previous study). Due to time limitations, each participant experienced the 4 conditions distributed across game (2 tasks) and individual (2 tasks) activities, but only 3 in the collaborative activity (3 tasks). The assignment was random and condition order was counterbalanced across participants.

Participants filled in a demographic questionnaire prior to the study. Two researchers greeted participants, obtained informed consent and introduced them to the tablet and the study setting. Each participant pair then performed the game, individual, and collaborative activities in turn. Participants completed a short questionnaire and interview after each activity. The questionnaire asked participants to rate the system used in each task in terms of awareness, confidence in protection, balance of efficiency and privacy, and overall satisfaction on a 7 point Likert scale. In individual and collaborative tasks, they also rated task realism, role play realism, and ranked their preferences over the 4 interface conditions and over Dim and Mask. The follow-up interview asked participants to explain their choices, reflect on privacy strategies used and differences from real-world experience. At the end of the study, they participated in a final semi-structured interview. The interview collected feedback on various design aspects (e.g., notification versus protection, automatic versus manual protection, individual versus collaborative scenarios), potential usage scenarios of the system, concerns, and suggestions for improvement. All the questionnaires and interviews were done independently in separate rooms except the interview after the collaborative activity, for which both participants reflected on their experience together. We videotaped the study, captured the tablet screen and took handwritten notes.

Data Analysis

Video and screen capture were synchronized in Adobe Premiere and placed side by side for coding. Two researchers watched all the videos independently, assigned a unique code to each privacy management behavior, and compared the code list to agree on a single code list. This list was then compared with participants' reported privacy strategies and any code not mentioned by participants was removed from the list. This step was taken because non-verbal behaviors are often ambiguous, especially in relation to privacy intentions [3]. We settled on 5 verbal codes and 13 non-verbal codes. One researcher rewatched the videos and coded them with the complete code list and made video annotations in Vcode. It was possible that some non-privacy driven behaviors (e.g., natural body leaning) were counted. The interviews were fully transcribed. One researcher reviewed all the video annotations and interview transcriptions to capture interesting details on more than 1,000 individual notes and organized them into 6 themes.

RESULTS

We found that adding digital privacy notification and protection mechanisms improved participants' self-reported awareness, confidence in privacy, ability to balance work and privacy and overall satisfaction, but this didn't significantly alter observed physical privacy behaviours. We provide a classification of physical privacy behaviours used by our participants and identify activity-based differences. We then summarize interview responses regarding system support for awareness, detection and response. For brevity, we name the no notification no protection condition as *NN*, notification only as *YN*, protection only as *NY*, and having both as *YY*.

Digital Privacy Management System Perceptions

In solo (game and individual) tasks, participants ranked having both notification and protection as their favorite (mean rank YY = 3.6 out of 4) for "*maximum protection*", followed by only protection (NY=3), only notification (YN=2.3) and no protection (NN=1). The ranking was similar in collaborative tasks (YY=3.6, NY=2.9, YN=2.4 NN=1.2). All conditions with digital support (YY, NY, YN) were ranked higher than NN (p<.001).). Protection only was preferred over notification because it provided a response rather than requiring a physical privacy action.

We examined the impact of the digital privacy system on participants' attitudes (measured by questionnaire) across the 3 activities. We found significant improvement in digital privacy management (YN, NY, YY) compared to physical management (NN) in terms of perceived awareness, easiness to hide information, balance between work and privacy, and overall satisfaction in both individual and collaborative tasks but not in the game tasks. For example, there was a difference in awareness that somebody was nearby in both individual ($\chi^2(3)$ =21.074, p<.001) and collaborative ($\chi^2(3)$ =40.360, p<.001) activities but not in the game ($\chi^2(3)$ =2.771, p=.428). Post hoc analysis showed all conditions with the digital system (YN-p<.001, NY-p=.024, YY-p<.001) were better than physical management (NN) in raising awareness. The differences for the game could be because participants were vigilant and relied heavily on physical cues (e.g. footsteps) and measures (e.g., turning the body around) to play the game, regardless of what digital interface they were using. P13 said: "*I was into the game, you know, observing her [opponent] going around me...I depend more on my own vision than on that icon [notification].*"

Impact on Behaviours

We observed both verbal and non-verbal privacy management behaviors. Verbal behaviors (overall 54 occurrences, 90% in collaborative tasks) included explicitly asking the onlooker to leave, lowering one's voice in discussion, speaking a different language, being vague when talking about sensitive information (e.g., security questions), and reminding their partner to be careful. Non-verbal behaviors (overall 542 occurrences, 76% of these in game tasks) included scanning the vicinity, leaning over the tablet, bringing the tablet closer, tilting the tablet, changing location, and turning their body angle to face towards or away from the onlooker. To block the view of the tablet they used parts of their body (e.g., arms, hands, long hair), objects (e.g., clothes, bank card), or the environment (e.g., lie on the couch or use the back of the couch as a barrier). They also glared at the onlooker or temporarily stopped working. In the collaborative task, participants sat close together or blocked the screen while their partner worked.

On average, participants demonstrated 16 physical privacy behaviors in game (SD=8), 3 in individual (SD=3) and 2 in collaborative tasks (SD=1.9). We didn't observe an impact of interfaces on privacy behaviors in game (YY=14.6, NY=15.9, YN=16.6, NN=16.2), individual (YY=2.2, NY=2.7, YN=3.6, NN=1.8) or collaborative (YY=3, NY=1.6, YN=2.9, NN=1.8) tasks. For the financial scenarios, the reason might be we only observed a small number of privacy behaviors (individual 71 and collaborative 58). For example, in 44% of individual tasks, we observed 0-1 occurrences of explicit privacy behavior.

We didn't observe differences in task completion time (on average 1-4 minutes) or error rate across conditions.

Although we didn't observe a clear change in behaviours given digital support, participants identified several issues with physical privacy management. 8 participants said it is difficult to stay aware of the surroundings when concentrating on a task. Other issues include the need for precautionary behaviors like looking behind one's back (5 participants), less convenience to work with hands covering the tablet (3), advertising through their actions that they are engaging in a private activity (3), and concerns about appearing awkward or signaling that they don't trust those nearby (5). Digital support can alleviate these issues so that there is no need to "*look around behind you*" (P25), "*find a better spot*" (P8), "*move our hands*" (P5) or "*be obvious[ly] trying to protect things*" (P2).

Physical Privacy Behaviours across Activities

As discussed, the game scenario was designed to elicit rapid and frequent privacy management behavior. We recorded the most frequent and most obvious privacy management behaviors during the game. We focused on 9 types of non-verbal behaviors (verbal behaviours were rare in the game) to categorize and used Hierarchical Clustering Analysis (R-type) with Between-groups Linkage as the cluster method and Pearson correlation as the distance measure.

Hierarchical clustering joins pairs of behaviors that are most similar based on distance calculations, and repeats the process until all behaviors are joined hierarchically. We chose the cluster threshold of 15 to yield clusters that best correspond with privacy processes: cluster 2 as awareness, cluster 1, 3, 4 as response, and cluster 5 as prevention. The dendrogram (see Figure 5) illustrates that behaviors seem to cluster by nature of body movement: moving body position and angle (we name it **macro protection**) and looking around (**awareness**) are large-scale behaviors; body leaning, using objects or body parts (**micro blocking**) require less movement and manage the immediate surroundings of the device; moving the tablet position and angle (**device maneuver**) merely manipulates the device itself; using barriers to block vision (**environment utilization**) doesn't require movement once a spot is chosen and is more preventative in nature.

Using the 5 behavior categories, we compared physical privacy management patterns across the 3 scenarios regardless of condition (see Figure 6). In the more realistic financial tasks, macro protection behavior, which was heavily used in the game and very effective, almost disappeared. Instead, participants mainly relied on less conspicuous behaviors such as manipulating the device or micro body movement for privacy management. This illustrates that very obvious privacy behaviors, while effective, are not appropriate in many circumstances. The collaborative task had the least number of privacy protection behaviors but more looking around. While participants may have felt the information in the collaborative task was not as sensitive as in the individual task, we note that collaboration means extra capacity (i.e., eyes, ears) to monitor the environment.

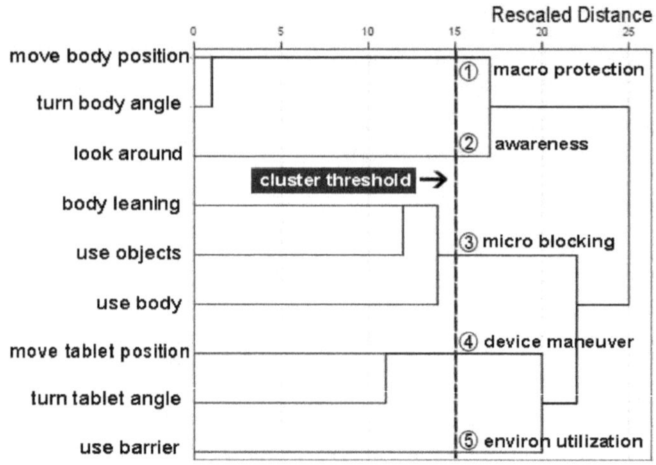

Figure 5. Dendrogram showing clusters of physical privacy management behaviors in the game tasks.

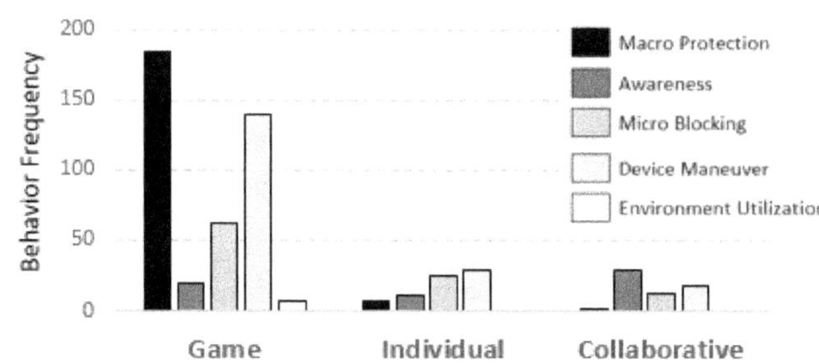

Figure 6. Total non-verbal physical privacy behaviors observed by activity.

Participants' self-reported behaviors corroborated our observations. For example, 7 participants in the individual banking tasks reported "*use[ing] my body in not obvious way*", "*hold[ing] the tablet a little bit closer*", or "*tilt[ing] it a little bit*". In addition, some privacy strategies were too subtle to be observed. 8 participants reported slowing down and being more careful about their interactions when a threat was around. 11 tried to finish tasks as fast as possible to reduce exposure. 6 participants reported listening for and responding to audible cues in the game such as footsteps or the "ding", which signaled that the opponent could eavesdrop. We asked participants to compare privacy strategies used in daily life. The primary difference was that several prevention strategies (e.g., avoid private activities in public, move to the back or a corner of a room) were common that weren't possible in our study.

Small Group Privacy Management

Two thirds of participants felt that privacy issues in the collaborative scenario were different from the individual one. Three stated the tablet was held between collaborators and was more easily seen. Two felt overall awareness was enhanced by an extra person, and four mentioned that the system needs to accommodate potentially conflicting needs of collaborators. Three stated that the importance of task efficiency increases thus techniques that slow tasks down would be less tolerable. Participants were asked to consider what it would be like to use Mask in a collaborative task, and Dim for an individual task. Preference was reversed: 18 preferred Mask to Dim for individual tasks whereas 22 preferred Dim to Mask for collaborative tasks. One participant said *"for collaboration, dimming is the way to go just because we both need to be able to look at the screen"*—P23. 8 participants thought notification became more noticeable by the extra person and thus more useful whereas protection was described as *"problematic"* and *"challenging"*. 8 thought protection didn't suit teamwork and 4 claimed it should be as unobtrusive as possible.

Role of Notification and Protection

Privacy notifications were seen as somewhat useful or better by 20 participants, with 4 undecided and 2 who did not find them useful. 12 participants felt they would help promote awareness in unfamiliar or dynamic surroundings. Other benefits include helping address human perceptual limitations (e.g., *"you don't have an eye on the back of your head"*, P26), saving attention for primary tasks, reducing the need for precautions, and indicating whether a protection action was successful (*"If you didn't protect yourself well, the notification will come again"*. P14). Notification is not useful if there are many false alarms or misses (10 participants). 4 participants worried that frequent notification in busy environments would be overly disruptive or cause confusion about when to take action. Other cited concerns include distraction (5), being too obvious to the onlooker (5), occluding display content (4), or going unnoticed (2).

Almost all participants agreed that protections were useful. Dim was seen as adding subtle protection and made 15 participants feel content was safer but not completely protected. 8 participants had already adopted it as a privacy strategy in daily life (e.g., when using Facebook, Tumblr, IM). Participants expected it to be useful when working with a whole document containing medium-sensitive information, and it could protect detailed text information from a distance. Mask was trusted by 19 of users to be *"totally safe"* and *"effective"*, suitable for highly-sensitive data within close proximity given familiarity with the information layout and the ability to work in a small region.

Preferences for combinations of notification and protection were mixed: 12 preferred both notification and protection, 8 preferred only (automatic) protection, 2 preferred only notification and 4 emphasized that it depended on information sensitivity, location and potential viewers.

Automatic and Manual Protection

We asked participants about their preferences for protection techniques automatically triggered by the system and protection manually turned on by the user. 9 preferred automatic protection, 13 preferred manual protection, and 4 thought both had their merits and demerits. The benefits of automatic protection are that it promotes task focus (5), users might forget to turn on manual protections (4), it is fast (2) and it is *"almost two [notification and protection] in one [automatic protection]"* (1). For *manual protection*, 54% participants chose to turn on the protection throughout the task, 20% turned it on when they realized someone was around or they were accessing sensitive data. 26% participants turned it off in the middle or didn't use it to avoid interference with the current task. Stated benefits of manual protection were feeling more in control (5), avoiding an unpredictably changing screen (5), and not being dependent on the system's reliability (4). For example, P17 noted: "*...In this way I will not be worried about the system catching that guy [onlooker] or not... It is not dependent on the technology implementation.*" Others simply used it as a prevention turned on throughout the task without worrying about people walking by or looking.

DISCUSSION

In this section, we discuss factors to be considered in designing usable visual privacy management systems.

Holistic Privacy Management

Dourish et al. proposed *"holistic security management"* to illustrate how online data security is protected not only online but also in the physical world by space arrangement and demarcation [15]. Similarly, we found participants didn't perceive visual privacy management of digital information solely through a digital system. The existing physical mechanisms and the physical world were considered to be integral parts of *"holistic privacy management"*. Users' physical movements and changing screen appearances are parts of privacy management that can be used together to reduce the possibility of privacy breach. Hawkey and Inkpen found users wanted to conceal privacy-related feedback from collaborators [23]. Our results showed users also tend to manage physical behaviours and are concerned about the appearance of notification and protection mechanisms when faced with casual shoulder surfing threats. A holistic design should consider ways of reducing the user's physical obviousness as well as the digital system's ability to attract attention or to advertise the intent for privacy. For example, a privacy notification could resemble a regular system notification or notify through vibration. Secondly, our prototype was expected to consider the user's and the onlooker's physical circumstances. For example, the system might kick in when there is loud noise or when an onlooker is detected beyond the user's visual field, but not when an onlooker is at an obtuse angle or their vision is occluded. Finally, no matter how users choose combinations of physical and digital measures, the underlying awareness and response privacy processes are both integral parts of a whole. Different choices reflect personal preference over trust in technology versus self-control, or responsibility distribution between physical and digital privacy mechanisms. For example, a user could be aware of a privacy breach while delegating the response to the digital system or be reminded by the digital system and respond physically on one's own. System designs should allow for such choices.

Social and Cultural Implications

A mobile content privacy management system is meant to be used in social situations. Such a system should be socially acceptable for the user, her collaborators, and bystanders. Most participants thought the obvious physical protection used in the game would be "*difficult*", or "*awkward*" in real life, making them look "*creepy*" or like "*a freak*". Some participants suggested more subtle notification glyphs (e.g., an animal, star) and less prominent protection. 5 participants wanted to switch the eye to a customizable icon "*only known to the user*" (P15). Traditional notification design values universality and visibility, but obfuscation may be more appropriate for privacy. The need for privacy is a delicate matter among friends or colleagues. For example, P2 commented: "*I think I'd be embarrassed that I want privacy... Feeling like I have something to hide, or that I don't trust people around me.*" Appearing not to trust nearby strangers was also a concern. Systems could reflect these concerns by offering flexibility in establishing the parameters for detection, and the nature of notification and protection.

Altman et al. claimed that privacy management involved cultural-specific regulatory mechanisms [2]. Half (13) of our participants were from North America and the other half were from Asia and the Middle East. Brudy et al. argued designs that enhance mutual awareness between the user and the onlooker could exploit social protocol to regulate both parties' behavior [8]. This strategy was only mentioned by 3 participants from North America. They described the obvious eyeball design "*a good thing*" to make onlookers back off or "*teach people to not look at other people's screens.*" Only 1 North American participant expressed concern for the impropriety of the eyeball design. On the contrary, no participants from Asia or the Middle East perceived mutual awareness as a strategy but 9 of them repeatedly used "*impolite*", "*unfriendly*" or "*not respectful*" to judge the social appropriateness of a design and suggested resorting to more secretive designs. 1 Middle Eastern and 1 Asian participant also seemed to be hesitant to take actions upon a privacy breach because hiding or questioning "*in my culture, it is not really respectful. But in Western culture, it's quite normal*" (P11). While we have interesting observations that suggest potential cultural implications for further research, we don't claim to have validated any cross-cultural differences. Further research is required to explore the impact of culture in more detail.

Issues of Trust

The trustworthiness of a visual privacy management system became a recurrent theme in participant feedback. 12 participants expressed concerns about reliability and accuracy about the system, 6 due to false alarms and 6 missed detection. This could be due to the limited tracking range of our sensor (1.5m around the source) or magnetic field distortion from metal in the environment. False alarms caused participants to be confused, hyper-vigilant, or to ignore the system. P24 said: "*...a couple of tries at me not really understanding what was happening before ...[it] was not helpful to me anymore. The problem is when it comes to privacy that trust factor is so big.*" Missed detections had a similar impact. As P25 noted: "*...at times it didn't pop up, like it didn't know I was there [as an onlooker]. So just improve accuracy. That's always something, I guess, everything.*" Trust can easily be lost due to system inaccuracy, but might be reinforced by a clear understanding of the technology's capabilities and limitations both during design and in use. 3 participants expressed that they thought the notification only considered distance and not the field of view of the onlooker. This may have created the impression of missed detections. As P22 stated: "*I don't know how else it would notify you. I wouldn't have known that technology existed.*"

On the other hand, trust in the protection techniques (Dim in particular) seemed to grow with experience. For example, 5 participants reported not having confidence in the Dim technique at first but changing their opinion after playing the onlooker in the game, and another expressed having learned through the collaborative task how well the dimming helps to hide numbers. Similarly, Iachello et al. found that positive direct experiences are the most important influencers of a user's trust in a system [24].

Design Aspects of Protection Techniques

In our study we encountered three kinds of privacy: information, context and intention privacy, and protection techniques vary in their capability of preserving them. Both Dim and Mask are good for protecting detailed on-screen data – thus **information privacy**. Mask is also useful when protecting the activity and meaning of the information – **context privacy**. As P8 commented: "*when you're doing banking, that one spot, that piece of information is meaningless unless you know the context it is in.*" However, the high contrast and magnified focus of Mask was thought to attract unwanted attention thus revealing the fact that people are trying to hide something – **intention privacy**. Dim, on the other hand, is subtler and less noticeable for onlookers and so could better preserve intention privacy.

Automatic protection was seen as implicitly encompassing detection, awareness and response, and so could stand alone. For example, P2 commented: "*The whole screen dimmed, so I find that's enough of an indicator that someone is around.*" Standalone manual protection mechanisms offer response and prevention at the expense of detection and awareness support. This is an attractive option especially where the system is unable to provide reliable detection. Issues notwithstanding, most of our participants expected manual protection to be combined with notification to facilitate awareness.

Design Guidelines

We summarize design principles for just-in-time mobile content privacy management systems as follows:

- **Subtlety**: for many, a notification should be clear to them but obscure to onlookers. Protections should avoid striking contrast with the primary interface.
- **Complementarity**: system decisions based on an understanding of the environment and both user and onlooker capabilities and limitations to fill in the gaps would help create seamless privacy management.
- **Flexibility**: the system should allow for flexible configuration of design aspects to accommodate subjectivity and context-dependency of privacy issues.
- **Socio-cultural awareness**: the visual presentation of the system should be sensitive to social norms.
- **Trustworthiness**: accuracy, design within technical limitations, managing expectations, and customization can all help build user's trust towards the system.
- **Unobtrusiveness**: notification should not trigger continually in busy environments; protection should reduce interference particularly in work-related tasks.

Limitations

While the privacy behaviors observed in our study were analogous to those in the real world, we must note they are by no means precise reflections of real-life behaviors. Real privacy behaviors may be less frequent, less obvious, and contain more prevention behaviors – the study setting restricted participants to complete the task regardless of their actual concern and did not offer many environmental features to use in a preventive manner. However, the lab method allowed us to systematically study behaviors that would have been too context-dependent and ephemeral to capture or too subtle to observe in situ, and explore new possibilities to support collaborative work. It also enabled us to ask participants for comparisons and probe the reasons for their choices.

A lab study can also lead to a lack of realism for not having retained the integrity of environmental causal factors [13]. The demographic data indicates that our recruitment didn't exclude participants with high concern for privacy. This would have been difficult if we were to use real data for a social privacy transaction. The individual and collaborative activities were rated 6.38 and 5.92 out of 7 in terms of realism. Task designs were also reported as "*natural*". By choosing competitive games and highly sensitive task material (e.g., bank data), applying a role playing paradigm and not introducing the confederate, we mitigated the problem of insufficient motivation due to fake data to the extent that only 2 participants felt that they were not as protective as they would be in real life. Nonetheless, we must acknowledge that participants were primed to behave protectively, and the task location did not match expected usage locations. With longer tasks, the impact of protections on performance could be larger.

The Polhemus tracking didn't work ideally due to tracking ranges and environmental distortion (metal in the ceiling / floor, objects not able to move) which caused some inaccuracy in detection. Participants may have undervalued the usefulness of notification as a result, because the sole purpose of notification is to provide accurate just-in-time awareness. For similar reasons the inaccuracy might have biased some participants to prefer manual control over automatic control. We argue the flaw didn't fundamentally affect participants' attitudes, as shown by the distribution of ratings.

Future Work

There are a number of possible directions for future designs of mobile content privacy management systems. For awareness indicators, parameters such as size, frequency, duration, sensitivity, and modalities such as vibration, sound, or combinations could be further explored. Protection techniques suitable for specific contexts such as information (e.g., text, image), tasks (e.g., typing, reading), environmental features (e.g., brightness, noise) could also be considered. For a feasible deployment, on-board cameras need to address problems of limited field of view and might capture subtle events like shoulder surfing with the corner of eyes by integrating eye tracking technology. Google's Project Tango prototype has the ability of motion tracking, object detection and environment construction [40] and could be a platform for shoulder surfing detection. The impact of culture and contextual factors such as number, transientness, and identity of people nearby, nature of tasks, and features of the space are also worth more exploration.

CONCLUSION

Human physical mechanisms alone are not sufficient for visual privacy management on mobile devices due to cognitive limitations and social concerns. We created a range of software-based privacy notifications and protection techniques triggered by proxemic interactions between the device and the onlooker to support privacy management without breaking workflow. We demonstrated that people manage visual privacy in inconspicuous ways to avoid attention as well as be socially agreeable. Digital privacy systems serve as extension of physical measures that is useful for improving awareness and facilitating information protection. Our research paves the way for designing a digital system that is trustworthy, socio-culturally aware and deeply integrated with physical behaviours to offer holistic mobile content privacy management.

REFERENCES

1. Altman, I. (1975). The Environment and Social Behavior: Privacy, Personal Space, Territory, and Crowding. Monterey, Calif.: Brooks/Cole.
2. Altman, I. (1977). Privacy regulation: culturally universal or culturally specific?*Journal of Social Issues*, *33*(3), 66-84.
3. Altman, I., & Chemers, M. M. (1984). *Culture and environment* (No. 2). CUP Archive.
4. Ballendat, T., Marquardt, N., & Greenberg, S. (2010, November). Proxemic interaction: designing for a proximity and orientation-aware environment. In ACM *International Conference on Interactive Tabletops and Surfaces* (pp. 121-130). ACM.
5. Bartram, L., Ware, C., & Calvert, T. (2003). Moticons:: detection, distraction and task. *International Journal of Human-Computer Studies*, *58*(5), 515-545.
6. Bellotti, V., & Sellen, A. (1993, January). Design for privacy in ubiquitous computing environments. In *Proceedings of the Third European Conference on Computer-Supported Cooperative Work 13–17 September 1993, Milan, Italy ECSCW'93* (pp. 77-92). Springer Netherlands.
7. Boyle, M., Neustaedter, C., & Greenberg, S. (2009). Privacy factors in video-based media spaces. In *Media Space 20+ Years of Mediated Life*, 97-122.
8. Brudy, F., Ledo, D., & Greenberg, S. (2014, April). Is anyone looking?: mediating shoulder surfing on public displays (the video). In *CHI'14 Extended Abstracts on Human Factors in Computing Systems* (pp. 159-160).
9. Brunk, B. (2002). Understanding the privacy space. *First Monday*, 7(10).
10. Brunk, B. (2005). A user-centric privacy space framework. *Security and Usability, LF Cranor and S. Garfinkel, Eds.* O'Reilly, 401-420
11. Chen, Y., & Xu, H. (2013, February). Privacy management in dynamic groups: Understanding information privacy in medical practices. In *Proceedings of the 2013 conference on Computer supported cooperative work* (pp. 541-552). ACM.
12. Comscore. (2014). The U.S. mobile app report. Retrieved from: http://www.comscore.com/Insights/Presentations-and-Whitepapers/2014/The-US-Mobile-App-Report
13. Dhami, M. K., Hertwig, R., & Hoffrage, U. (2004). The role of representative design in an ecological approach to cognition. *Psychological bulletin*, 130(6), 959.
14. Dostal, J., Kristensson, P. O., & Quigley, A. (2013, June). Multi-view proxemics: distance and position sensitive interaction. In *Proceedings of the 2nd ACM International Symposium on Pervasive Displays* (pp. 1-6). ACM.
15. Dourish, P., Grinter, R. E., De La Flor, J. D., & Joseph, M. (2004). Security in the wild: user strategies for managing security as an everyday, practical problem. *Personal and Ubiquitous Computing*, 8(6), 391-401.
16. Downs, J. S., Holbrook, M., & Cranor, L. F. (2007, October). Behavioral response to phishing risk. In Proceedings of the anti-phishing working groups 2nd annual eCrime researchers summit (pp. 37-44). ACM.
17. Egelman, S., Oates, A., & Krishnamurthi, S. (2011, May). Oops, I did it again: mitigating repeated access control errors on facebook. In *Proceedings of the SIGCHI conference on Human Factors in Computing Systems* (pp. 2295-2304). ACM.
18. Goucher, W. (2011). Look behind you: the dangers of shoulder surfing. *Computer Fraud & Security*, 2011(11), 17-20.
19. Greenberg, S., Marquardt, N., Ballendat, T., Diaz-Marino, R., & Wang, M. (2011). Proxemic interactions: the new ubicomp?. *interactions*, 18(1), 42-50.
20. Hall, E. T., & Hall, E. T. (1969). The hidden dimension (Vol. 1990). New York: Anchor Books.
21. Hansson, R., Ljungstrand, P., & Redström, J. (2001, January). Subtle and public notification cues for mobile devices. In *Ubicomp 2001: Ubiquitous Computing* (pp. 240-246). Springer Berlin Heidelberg.
22. Harrison, C., & Dey, A. K. (2008, April). Lean and zoom: proximity-aware user interface and content magnification. In *Proceedings of the SIGCHI Conference on Human Factors in Computing Systems* (pp. 507-510). ACM.
23. Hawkey, K., & Inkpen, K. M. (2007, May). PrivateBits: managing visual privacy in web browsers. In *Proceedings of Graphics Interface* 2007 (pp. 215-223). ACM.
24. Iachello, G., & Hong, J. (2007). End-user privacy in human-computer interaction. *Foundations and Trends in Human-Computer Interaction*, 1(1), 1-137.
25. Ishiguro, Y., & Rekimoto, J. (2011, March). Peripheral vision annotation: noninterference information presentation method for mobile augmented reality. In *Proceedings of the 2nd Augmented Human International Conference* (p. 8). ACM.
26. José Ramón Padilla-López, Alexandros Andre Chaaraoui, Francisco Flórez-Revuelt. (2015).Visual privacy protection methods: A survey. In *Expert Systems with Applications*, 42(9), 4177-4195
27. Kumar, M., Garfinkel, T., Boneh, D., & Winograd, T. (2007, July). Reducing shoulder-surfing by using gaze-based password entry. In *Proceedings of the 3rd symposium on Usable privacy and security* (pp. 13-19). ACM.

28. Langheinrich, M. (2001, January). Privacy by design—principles of privacy-aware ubiquitous systems. In *Ubicomp 2001: Ubiquitous Computing* (pp. 273-291). Springer Berlin Heidelberg.
29. Lee L. (2014).Digital media technology and individual privacy. *Communication technology and social change: Theory and implications, Lin, C. A., & Atkin, D. J. (Eds.).* Routledge, 257-279.
30. Lian, S., Hu, W., Song, X., & Liu, Z. (2013). Smart privacy-preserving screen based on multiple sensor fusion. *Consumer Electronics, IEEE Transactions on*, 59(1), 136-143.
31. Luff, P., & Heath, C. (1998, November). Mobility in collaboration. In *Proceedings of the 1998 ACM conference on Computer supported cooperative work* (pp. 305-314). ACM.
32. Murphy, A., Reddy, M, & Xu, H. (2014). Privacy practices in collaborative environments: a study of emergency department staff. In *Proceedings of the 17th ACM conference on Computer supported cooperative work & social computing*.(pp.269-282).
33. Muslukhov, I., Boshmaf, Y., Kuo, C., Lester, J., & Beznosov, K. (2013, August). Know your enemy: the risk of unauthorized access in smartphones by insiders. In *Proceedings of the 15th international conference on Human-computer interaction with mobile devices and services* (pp. 271-280). ACM.
34. Palen, L., & Dourish, P. (2003, April). Unpacking privacy for a networked world. In *Proceedings of the SIGCHI conference on Human factors in computing systems* (pp. 129-136). ACM.
35. Patrick A. (2007). Commentary on Research on New Security Indicators -essay. http://www.andrewpatrick.ca/essays/commentary-on-research-on-new-security-indicators.
36. Patterson, M. L., Mullens, S., & Romano, J. (1971). Compensatory reactions to spatial intrusion. *Sociometry*, 114-121.
37. Polhemus, Inc.(2013). *G4 user manual*. Retrieved on March 15, 2013 from http://polhemus.com/_assets/img/G4_User_Manual_URM10PH238-D.pdf.
38. Portnoff, S.R., Lee, N.L., Egelman, S., Mishra, P., Leung, D., & Wagner, D. (2015, April) Somebody's watching me?: Assessing the effectiveness of Webcam indicator lights. In *Proceedings of the SIGCHI conference on Human factors in computing systems* (pp. 1649-1658). ACM.
39. Probst, G. (2000). Analysis of the Effects of Privacy Filter Use on Horizontal Deviations in Posture of VDT Operators (Doctoral dissertation, Virginia Polytechnic Institute and State University).
40. Project Tango Depth Perception. (n.d.) In Google Developers. Retrieved on July 23, 2015 from https://developers.google.com/project-tango/overview/depth-perception
41. Regus. (2014). Business people globally describe their ideal work environment. Retrieved from: press.regus.com/united-kingdom/download/60669/gbs11theidealworkplaceenvironmentreport_final.pdf.
42. Sotirakopoulos, A., Hawkey, K., & Beznosov, K. (2011, July). On the challenges in usable security lab studies: lessons learned from replicating a study on SSL warnings. In *Proceedings of the Seventh Symposium on Usable Privacy and Security* (p. 3). ACM.
43. Tan, D. S., Keyani, P., & Czerwinski, M. (2005, November). Spy-resistant keyboard: more secure password entry on public touch screen displays. In *Proceedings of the 17th Australia conference on Computer-Human Interaction: Citizens Online: Considerations for Today and the Future* (pp. 1-10). (CHISIG) of Australia.
44. Tarasewich, P., Gong, J., & Conlan, R. (2006, April). Protecting private data in public. In *CHI'06 Extended Abstracts on Human Factors in Computing Systems*, 1409-1414.
45. Thompson. H.(March, 2011). *Visual data breach risk assessment study*. For People Security and 3M. Retrieved from: http://solutions.3m.com/3MContentRetrievalAPI/BlobServlet?locale=en_US&lmd=1291398659000&assetId=1273672752407&assetType=MMM_Image&blobAttribute=ImageFile
46. Ware, C. (2012). *Information visualization: perception for design*. Elsevier.
47. Wiedenbeck, S., Waters, J., Sobrado, L., & Birget, J. C. (2006, May). Design and evaluation of a shoulder-surfing resistant graphical password scheme. In*Proceedings of the working conference on Advanced visual interfaces* (pp. 177-184). ACM.
48. Zhou, H., Ferreira, V., Alves, T., Hawkey, K., & Reilly, D. (2015, April). Somebody Is Peeking!: A Proximity and Privacy Aware Tablet Interface. In*Proceedings of the 33rd Annual ACM Conference Extended Abstracts on Human Factors in Computing Systems* (pp. 1971-1976). ACM.
49. Zhou, H., Ferreira, V., Alves, T. S., MacKay, B., Hawkey, K., & Reilly, D. (2015). Exploring Privacy Notification and Control Mechanisms for Proximity-Aware Tablets. *International Journal of Mobile Human Computer Interaction (IJMHCI)*, *7*(3), 1-19.

CalendarCast: Setup-Free, Privacy-Preserving, Localized Sharing of Appointment Data

Florian Echtler
Mobile Media Group
Bauhaus-Universität Weimar, Germany
florian.echtler@uni-weimar.de

ABSTRACT

We introduce CalendarCast, a novel method to support the common task of finding a suitable time and date for a shared meeting among co-located participants using their personal mobile devices. In this paper, we describe the Bluetooth-based wireless protocol and interaction concept on which CalendarCast is based, present a prototypical implementation with Android smartphones and dedicated beacons, and report on results of a user study demonstrating improved task performance compared to unaugmented calendars.

The motivating scenario for CalendarCast occurs quite often in a variety of contexts, for example at the end of a prior meeting or during ad-hoc conversations in the hallway. Despite a large variety of digital calendar tools, this situation still usually involves a lengthy manual comparison of free and busy time slots. CalendarCast utilizes Bluetooth Low Energy (BTLE) advertisement broadcasts to share the required free/busy information with a limited, localized audience, on demand only, and without revealing detailed personal information. No prior knowledge about the other participants, such as email addresses or account names, is required.

ACM Classification Keywords

H.5.2. User Interfaces: Mobile Interfaces; H.5.3. Group and Organization Interfaces: Synchronous Interaction; H.4.1. Office Automation: Time Management

Author Keywords

Bluetooth; Low Energy; BTLE; calendar; appointment; broadcast; anonymous; sharing

INTRODUCTION

As personal mobile devices have become ubiquitous, it is now also commonplace to use them for fixing appointments, especially in a work context. Consequently, we often see several people standing together, staring at their respective smartphones or tablets, while trying to find a common date and time for a meeting. This scenario repeatedly occurs at the end of a prior meeting, or during ad-hoc conversations in the hallway, and usually involves a back-and-forth with multiple proposals from one participant which are then rejected by one of the others until a common free time slot is found. Although cloud services, shared calendars and similar tools promise to ease this tedious task, they require a willingness to share calendar information with third parties, a commitment to using the same service from all participants, and particularly prior knowledge of the other persons. As soon as even one person does not use the same tool as the others or has just joined the group, the promised support breaks down and again needs to be replaced by manual comparison of calendars.

CHI'16, May 07 - 12, 2016, San Jose, CA, USA

ACM 978-1-4503-3362-7/16/05...$15.00
DOI: http://dx.doi.org/10.1145/2858036.2858100

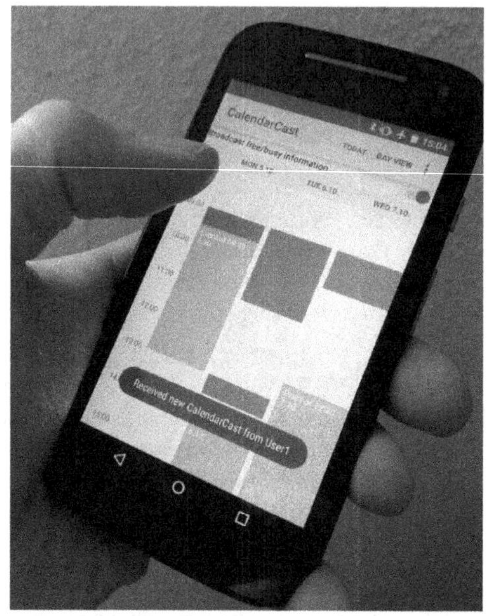

Figure 1. CalendarCast user interface. Own calendar entries are shown colored, while received broadcasts are shown as anonymous grey events in the background. Reception of a new broadcast is indicated by a popup message.

To address these issues, we introduce CalendarCast, a privacy-preserving, localized, and time-limited method of sharing free/busy information with co-located participants without requiring disclosure of personal information. CalendarCast uses Bluetooth Low Energy (BTLE) advertisement broadcasts with a very low range of 5-10 meters which can be sent and received by most modern smartphones and tablets. While these broadcasts are primarily designed to simply ad-

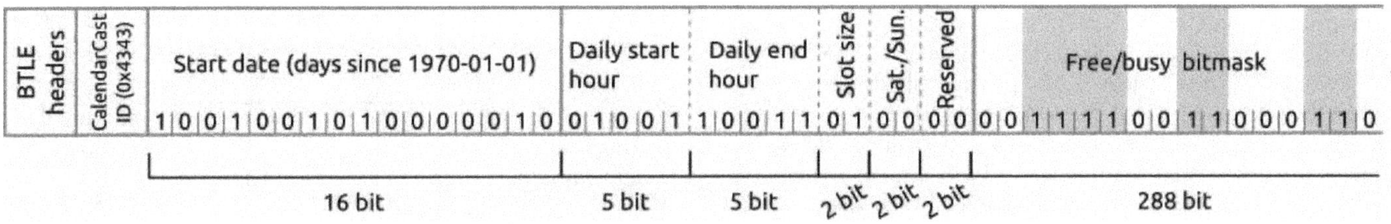

Figure 2. Bit-level description of CalendarCast message format (all numbers represented in network byte order, i.e. big endian format as suggested by [14]). This message is split and encapsulated in two BTLE broadcast frames.

vertise the presence and availability of a device, they offer limited space for additional user-specified data.

We re-purpose this reserved space to embed a bit pattern representing free and busy timeslots of the device's owner within a certain timeframe. Multiple devices can simultaneously broadcast and receive this information, thereby creating an ad-hoc shared calendar which is visible on all participating devices. Additionally, dedicated broadcasting devices can be used to distribute information about the availability of shared resources, such as a meeting room.

RELATED WORK

The topic of spontaneous interaction between co-located participants using their mobile devices has been explored by numerous researchers. Sarigol et al. present AdSocial [15], a mobile instant messaging application built around an ad-hoc wireless network. Shuttleworth et al. [17] propose using a similar network to facilitate an automated discovery process for appointments. However, both approaches require a shared local WiFi network which may have security implications or access restrictions and is therefore not always available.

Google Nearby [10] attempts to remove this restriction by providing a framework to determine nearby devices using a variety of techniques, such as WiFi, Bluetooth and inaudible sound. Nevertheless, this framework still requires a permanent Internet connection to a Google server to actually retrieve the list of peer devices. Similar functionality without the cloud connection requirement is offered by NFC+ [5] and Android Beam [9]; however, due to the use of NFC for the initial connection, both approaches are limited to two participating devices.

Do and Gatica-Perez use Bluetooth as a measure of proximity to discover the social context a person is in [8], while Davies et al. interact with public devices without a setup procedure by changing the device name broadcast by Bluetooth devices [7]. This technique has since been superseded by Bluetooth Low Energy. More recently, Aditya et al. present Encore [1] which employs BTLE broadcasts to create a personal log of encounters with people while at the same time creating event-specific secure encryption keys only available to those involved in the encounter.

Regarding the topic of calendar management, Schaub et al. show PriCal [16], a semi-public calendar display which preserves privacy by changing the detail level of the displayed information based on presence of other persons. Beard et al. present an early version of calendar overlays [3] to show the aggregate availability of multiple persons.

PhoneEar by Nittala et al. [12] uses inaudible sound embedded in regular audio streams to broadcast small data snippets to nearby devices. Tan et al. use "silence signatures" [18] to determine which mobile devices are in the same meeting without disclosing private information through audio recordings.

Despite this large body of existing work, we consider CalendarCast the first approach to combine setup-free interaction, preservation of privacy, and peer-to-peer techniques for sharing small information snippets such as calendar data.

CALENDARCAST

As described above, the main usage scenario for CalendarCast is finding a common free timeslot for an appointment among co-located participants, possibly including free/busy information for shared resources such as meeting rooms. We assume that users will quickly agree up front on a broad time range (e.g., "sometime next week", "in early November") within which the desired appointment should take place. Once this initial agreement has been made, each participant will then select individual constraints such as exact start day, duration of the time window and earliest/latest acceptable time of day.

Once these selections have been made, the devices will start broadcasting free/busy information for the chosen time window while at the same time listening for CalendarCast transmissions from peer devices. As soon as a broadcast from a peer is received, the contained information is integrated into the local calendar display as anonymous, untitled appointments which recede behind the users' own calendar entries (see also Figure 1). As more and more peer messages are received and integrated, the calendar fills up to display a union of all participants' free/busy information, thereby immediately highlighting which time slots are free for everyone. The final agreement on a specific time slot can then be confirmed verbally.

Low-Level Data Format

CalendarCast is based on Bluetooth Low Energy (BTLE) advertisement messages. These messages are periodically broadcast by BTLE devices with adjustable transmit power and interval, usually in the range of several 100 ms. The messages are unencrypted and can be received by all BTLE devices within range (usually 5-10 m) without prior pairing, in particular even by those which are simultaneously broadcasting themselves. One message can contain up to 31 bytes of payload [4] in the most basic "passive advertising" mode; when "active advertising" is used, a second message with 31 additional bytes will be broadcast upon request. These requests are performed automatically by listening devices, resulting in a total of 62 bytes which can be broadcast to nearby devices without setup or user intervention.

Of course, it would be possible to extend the amount of data using an additional protocol layer on top of the broadcasts which could employ, for example, sequence numbers to combine several successive messages. A generic implementation of this approach was presented by Corbellini et al. [6]. However, this solution would proportionally increase the duration until a full message has been received by peer devices and would also increase sensitivity to packet loss on the shared wireless channel, further increasing the time required to deliver all data. For these reasons, we decided to base CalendarCast on the small amount of data available in unmodified broadcasts. Nevertheless, even the comparatively tiny broadcast messages are already sufficient for our purpose of sharing free/busy information.

Of the 62 available bytes, between 10 and 13 bytes (depending on the BTLE implementation) are reserved for protocol-related header fields such as device capabilities and transmit power, while up to 7 additional bytes can be claimed for the "human-readable" device name which is always included in the broadcast. While this device name is often pre-set to a generic model identificator (such as "Galaxy" or "iPhone") and rarely changed by the user, this does not hinder the function of CalendarCast, as our focus is on creating an aggregate and *anonymized* calendar.

Due to these constraints, at most 42 bytes can be assumed to be available for CalendarCast data across all device types. Of these, 2 bytes are required for the CalendarCast identifier (0x4343, 'CC') and another 4 bytes for a CalendarCast-specific header describing the format of the bit pattern in the remaining 36 bytes or 288 bits of the message. This bit pattern represents a sequence of time slots, beginning at a start date specified in the header, and simply tells all receiving peers if the corresponding time slot is free (0) or busy (1).

An example message is illustrated in Figure 2. Here, the starting date is October 5th, 2015, i.e. 16713 days after January 1st, 1970. The daily time range is 9:00 - 19:00, and the slot size is 30 minutes (0 = 15min, 1 = 30min, 2 = 1h, 3 = 2h). This means that in this case, every day contains a total of 20 available slots. As weekends are excluded (bits for Sat./Sun. are set to zero), the 288 slot bits in the message can then cover a total of 14.4 days or just under three work weeks, which should usually be sufficient to find a common free timeslot. The end date is always implicitly specified by the number of slots available in the bitmap and the slot size.

User Interface

The user interface of CalendarCast mostly consists of a "classic" calender view with an additional button on top to start the broadcast. Upon tapping this button, the user is presented with a modal dialog in which the rough time window for the desired appointment can be adjusted (start date, daily start and end times, size of time slots).

	Sparse A/B	Dense A/B	Room
Time range	Oct. 5 - Oct. 16, 9am - 7pm		
Time slot duration	30 minutes (20/day)		
Total time slots	200 (weekends excluded)		
Busy time slots	40	80	80
Common free slots	133	67	n/a
# of individual events	22	24	28
Distance to first match	24	44	n/a

Table 1. Characteristics of all four test calendar pairs. Sparse/dense calendar pair A was tested with CalendarCast, sparse/dense pair B without.

Once this dialog has been completed, the calendar view is shown again and the broadcast of free/busy information starts in the background. At the same time, the device also starts listening for broadcasts with the custom CalendarCast identifier. As soon as a compatible broadcast is received from a previously unknown device, the contained free/busy information is added to the calendar view as "background events", i.e. untitled events in muted colors which recede behind the user's own events in the foreground. These events serve as a visual aid to quickly locate timeslots that are available to all participants in a kind of "focus & context" view, with the user's own events being in *focus* and the background events from other users providing the *context*. Ad-hoc modification of calendar entries is of course still possible, and will quickly propagate to other users' displays.

EVALUATION

We evaluated a prototypical implementation of CalendarCast on Android smartphones. We used Motorola *moto e* (2nd generation) devices running Android 5.0, as this hard- and software combination is known to support simultaneous sending and receiving of BTLE broadcasts [13]. Our hypotheses were that CalendarCast will enable participants to find a suitable time and date for a planned appointment faster than using manual comparision of calendars, and that this effect will be more pronounced for more complex search tasks, e.g. on calendars with more events which have less overlap of free time slots. We intentionally excluded usability-related questions from our study and focused on task completion times, as any calendar interface would include numerous confounding variables (e.g. number of days in view) that would be difficult to control for. Consequently, we did also not yet compare CalendarCast to existing calendar tools.

Our test setup consisted of two *moto e* smartphones preloaded with test calendars in a custom app, a BTLE dongle[1] for broadcasting availability data of a hypothetical meeting room, and a paper calendar representing the meeting room's door calendar (showing the same data as broadcast by the dongle). Participants were tested in pairs of two, and given the task of finding two common appointments within a given time window (first two weeks of October 2015) based on the

[1]based on Nordic nRF51822 BTLE SOC

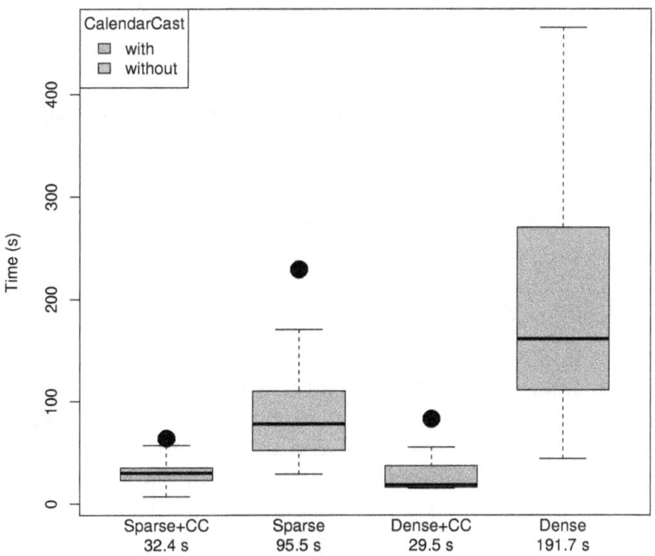

Figure 3. Task performance (boxes show 2nd and 3rd quartile, with median highlighted). Mean value is indicated below each condition.

available calendar data, including the meeting room. As additional constraints, both appointments had to span two hours and occur on the same weekday and time (i.e., a recurring appointment) to simulate a non-trivial search task in a realistic setting. Time was taken from the simultaneous start of the app on both devices to the confirmed agreement on a time slot.

We tested four conditions in a within-subject design using balanced Latin square order [11]: sparsely populated calendars and densely populated calendars, both with and without CalendarCast support. The time window was already pre-set in the app to match the test calendars. The calendar data was different for each scenario, but contained the same amount of overlap, i.e. the same number of possible time slots. Distance from the start of the week to the first suitable event was identical for the two pairs of sparse and dense calendars, respectively, to ensure comparable search times. Details of the different data sets are described in table 1.

Our test was completed by 20 participants recruited from students and researchers of our university (N = 10 teams in total, average age 24.3 years, 7 female, 13 male). Test subjects did not receive any compensation for their participation, and consented to the anonymized and aggregated use of their recorded data. On average, subjects reported to use smartphones "several times daily" and digital calendars at least "several times weekly".

Although the total number of samples is small, the results clearly support our two initial hypotheses as illustrated in Figure 3. Without CalendarCast, the average task completion time was 95.5 seconds for the sparse calendar and 191.7 seconds for the dense calender. The ratio between these two results (1:2.01) also roughly corresponds to the ratio between the distances to the first match (24:44 = 1:1.83, see also table 1). When using CalendarCast, however, task time dropped to 32.4 seconds for the sparse and 29.5 seconds for the dense calendar, a reduction by a factor of 2.9 and 6.5, respectively.

A tentative statistical analysis using the Shapiro-Wilk test shows that the data is likely not normally distributed ($p < 0.05$ for two conditions), and a subsequent Wilcoxon Signed-Rank test confirmed that both in the sparse ($p = 0.0078$) and dense ($p = 0.0039$) conditions, a statistically significant difference between the variants with and without CalendarCast exists. Interestingly, when testing for difference between the two CalendarCast-based conditions, the result suggests ($p = 0.3131$) that *no* difference exists. This implies that using CalendarCast reduces the task time to a constant value, regardless of how much overlap between the calendars exists.

DISCUSSION & OUTLOOK

We have presented CalendarCast, a privacy-preserving, localized, and time-limited method to share calendar data with one's immediate surroundings without requiring prior setup. Our evaluation confirms that CalendarCast improves task completion time when trying to find a common free time slot for an appointment among co-located participants, particularly for more complex search tasks with multiple constraints.

Although our prototype was developed and tested on Android, similar techniques could also be applied on iOS-based devices. However, it is worth noting that iOS as of v9.0 offers only limited control over the low-level message contents. Currently, it is only possible to include UUIDs into the broadcast data [2], i.e. fixed-size values of either 16 bit or 128 bit length. Consequently, while it is still possible to create CalendarCast messages using custom UUID values, the effective payload size will be lower on these devices.

While the app developed for the evaluation employed an internal database to provide the calendar data for the different test scenarios, a future deployment "in the wild" would use standardized mobile OS interfaces to access the users' own calendar entries and build CalendarCast messages from them.

We consider several possible extensions to CalendarCast which we will investigate in future experiments. The first extension involves the semi-automated broadcast of appointment proposals (either auto-selected or initiated by one user) to the other participants, who then only have to confirm the proposed time slot after specifying the acceptable time frame.

Another possible extension would be to re-purpose the bitmask used by CalendarCast to represent a set of interests instead; in a venue such as a large conference, attendants could periodically broadcast the specific topics they are interested in and be notified of persons nearby who share a noticeable number of topics. An even more generic approach would be to allow sharing of arbitrary data items by using compact representations, e.g. a PGP global key ID for contact information or a shortened URL for media data.

ACKNOWLEDGMENTS

We thank Raphael Wimmer, Stefanie Wetzel, and Sven Bertel for their valuable comments, and Felix Schmidt for his help in conducting the study. This work is in part supported by BMBF through grant T_209_M_SB.

REFERENCES

1. Paarijaat Aditya, Viktor Erdélyi, Matthew Lentz, Elaine Shi, Bobby Bhattacharjee, and Peter Druschel. 2014. EnCore: Private, Context-based Communication for Mobile Social Apps. In *Proceedings of the 12th Annual International Conference on Mobile Systems, Applications, and Services (MobiSys '14)*. ACM, New York, NY, USA, 135–148. DOI: http://dx.doi.org/10.1145/2594368.2594374
2. Apple, Inc. 2015. Peripheral Role Tasks - Advertising Your Services. (2015). https://developer.apple.com/library/prerelease/ios/documentation/NetworkingInternetWeb/Conceptual/CoreBluetooth_concepts/PerformingCommonPeripheralRoleTasks/PerformingCommonPeripheralRoleTasks.html#//apple_ref/doc/uid/TP40013257-CH4-SW5 Retrieved September 25, 2015.
3. David Beard, Murugappan Palaniappan, Alan Humm, David Banks, Anil Nair, and Yen-Ping Shan. 1990. A Visual Calendar for Scheduling Group Meetings. In *Proceedings of the 1990 ACM Conference on Computer-supported Cooperative Work (CSCW '90)*. ACM, New York, NY, USA, 279–290. DOI: http://dx.doi.org/10.1145/99332.99361
4. Bluetooth SIG. 2014. Core Specification 4.2. (2014). Retrieved September 25, 2015.
5. Kuang-Ming Chen, Yu-Cheng Liou, and Mike Chen. 2011. NFC+: NFC-assisted Media Sharing for Mobile Devices. In *Proceedings of the 13th International Conference on Ubiquitous Computing (UbiComp '11)*. ACM, New York, NY, USA, 575–576. DOI: http://dx.doi.org/10.1145/2030112.2030220
6. Giorgio Corbellini, Stefan Schmid, and Stefan Mangold. 2015. Two-Way Communication Protocol Using Bluetooth Low Energy Advertisement Frames. In *Proceedings of the 1st International Workshop on Experiences with the Design and Implementation of Smart Objects (SmartObjects '15)*. ACM, New York, NY, USA, 19–24. DOI: http://dx.doi.org/10.1145/2797044.2797049
7. Nigel Davies, Adrian Friday, Peter Newman, Sarah Rutlidge, and Oliver Storz. 2009. Using Bluetooth Device Names to Support Interaction in Smart Environments. In *Proceedings of the 7th International Conference on Mobile Systems, Applications, and Services (MobiSys '09)*. ACM, New York, NY, USA, 151–164. DOI: http://dx.doi.org/10.1145/1555816.1555832
8. Trinh Minh Do and Daniel Gatica-Perez. 2013. Human Interaction Discovery in Smartphone Proximity Networks. *Personal Ubiquitous Comput.* 17, 3 (March 2013), 413–431. DOI: http://dx.doi.org/10.1007/s00779-011-0489-7
9. Google, Inc. 2015a. Android Beam. (2015). Retrieved September 25, 2015.
10. Google, Inc. 2015b. Nearby. (2015). Retrieved September 25, 2015.
11. I. Scott MacKenzie. 2013. *Human-Computer Interaction: An Empirical Research Perspective* (1 edition ed.). Morgan Kaufmann, Amsterdam.
12. Aditya Shekhar Nittala, Xing-Dong Yang, Scott Bateman, Ehud Sharlin, and Saul Greenberg. 2015. PhoneEar: Interactions for Mobile Devices That Hear High-frequency Sound-encoded Data. In *Proceedings of the 7th ACM SIGCHI Symposium on Engineering Interactive Computing Systems (EICS '15)*. ACM, New York, NY, USA, 174–179. DOI: http://dx.doi.org/10.1145/2774225.2775082
13. Radius Networks. 2015. Android Beacon Library. (2015). Retrieved September 25, 2015.
14. John Reynolds and John Postel. 1994. RFC1700 - Assigned Numbers. (1994). Retrieved September 25, 2015.
15. Emre Sarigöl, Oriana Riva, Patrick Stuedi, and Gustavo Alonso. 2009. Enabling Social Networking in Ad Hoc Networks of Mobile Phones. *Proc. VLDB Endow.* 2, 2 (Aug. 2009), 1634–1637. DOI: http://dx.doi.org/10.14778/1687553.1687611
16. Florian Schaub, Bastian Könings, Peter Lang, Björn Wiedersheim, Christian Winkler, and Michael Weber. 2014. PriCal: Context-adaptive Privacy in Ambient Calendar Displays. In *Proceedings of the 2014 ACM International Joint Conference on Pervasive and Ubiquitous Computing (UbiComp '14)*. ACM, New York, NY, USA, 499–510. DOI: http://dx.doi.org/10.1145/2632048.2632087
17. Saxon Shuttleworth, Rebecca Chan, Julka Trajic, and Henricus Gerardus Spaay. 2003. System and method for synchronous peer-to-peer appointment scheduling facilitation. (July 2003). CIB: G06Q10/10; (IPC1-7): G06F17/60.
18. Wai-Tian Tan, Mary Baker, Bowon Lee, and Ramin Samadani. 2013. The Sound of Silence. In *Proceedings of the 11th ACM Conference on Embedded Networked Sensor Systems (SenSys '13)*. ACM, New York, NY, USA, 19:1–19:14. DOI: http://dx.doi.org/10.1145/2517351.2517362

SkullConduct: Biometric User Identification on Eyewear Computers Using Bone Conduction Through the Skull

Stefan Schneegass
Human-Computer Interaction Group
University of Stuttgart
stefan.schneegass@vis.uni-stuttgart.de

Youssef Oualil
Spoken Language Systems Group
Saarland University
youssef.oualil@lsv.uni-saarland.de

Andreas Bulling
Perceptual User Interfaces Group
Max Planck Institute for Informatics
bulling@mpi-inf.mpg.de

ABSTRACT
Secure user identification is important for the increasing number of eyewear computers but limited input capabilities pose significant usability challenges for established knowledge-based schemes, such as passwords or PINs. We present *SkullConduct*, a biometric system that uses bone conduction of sound through the user's skull as well as a microphone readily integrated into many of these devices, such as Google Glass. At the core of SkullConduct is a method to analyze the characteristic frequency response created by the user's skull using a combination of Mel Frequency Cepstral Coefficient (MFCC) features as well as a computationally light-weight 1NN classifier. We report on a controlled experiment with 10 participants that shows that this frequency response is person-specific and stable – even when taking off and putting on the device multiple times – and thus serves as a robust biometric. We show that our method can identify users with 97.0% accuracy and authenticate them with an equal error rate of 6.9%, thereby bringing biometric user identification to eyewear computers equipped with bone conduction technology.

Author Keywords
User Authentication; User Identification; Bone Conduction; Eyewear Computer; Google Glass

ACM Classification Keywords
H.5.m. Information Interfaces and Presentation(e.g. HCI): Miscellaneous; K.6.5 Computing Milieux: Security and Protection: Authentication

INTRODUCTION
Secure user authentication is important for personal devices, such as mobile phones, given that these devices store an increasing amount of personal information. To address limitations of established knowledge-based authentication schemes, such as passwords and PINs, recent works exploit the sensors readily integrated into these devices. For example, previous works proposed the analysis of keystroke dynamics [12], gait patterns [13], ambient sound [10], micro-movements while interacting [2], the shape of the user's ear [8], bioimpedance [5], or the way a user places or answers a phone call [4].

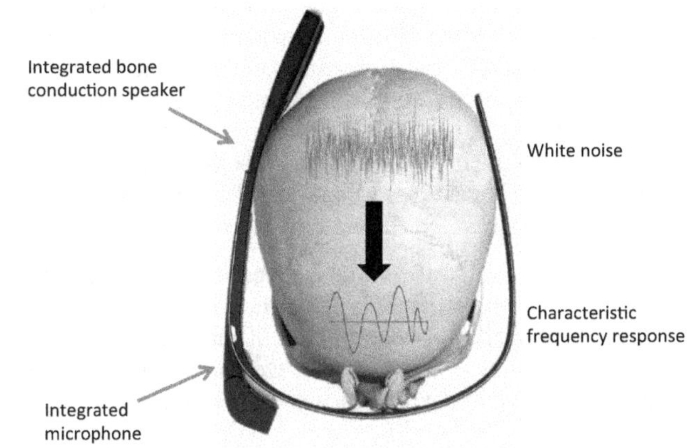

Figure 1. SkullConduct uses the bone conduction speaker and microphone readily integrated into the eyewear computer and analyses the characteristic frequency response of an audio signal sent through the user's skull.

In contrast, secure user authentication on another type of personal device, namely eyewear computers, remains largely unexplored. Simkin et al. described an approach to use Google Glass in combination with challenge-response protocols for authentication with an external system, such as an ATM or an entrance door [21]. The lack of methods to authenticate with eyewear computers themselves is partly because these devices only recently became widely available but also because their limited input capabilities and unique affordances pose usability challenges for traditional authentication schemes. Google glass for example uses the combination of strokes and taps on the touch-sensitive side of the device for authentication. Another notable exception is the recent work by Rogers et al. who explored the analysis of users' blinking patterns and head movements for user identification on Google Glass [19].

We present *SkullConduct*, a biometric system that uses bone conduction of sound through the user's skull for secure user identification and authentication on eyewear computers. Bone conduction has been used before as a transmission concept in different consumer devices, such as hands-free head-

CHI'16, May 07 - 12, 2016, San Jose, CA, USA

ACM 978-1-4503-3362-7/16/05...$15.00
DOI: http://dx.doi.org/10.1145/2858036.2858152

sets and headphones, bone anchored hearing aids, as well as special-purpose communication systems, such as for diving or high-noise environments. Bone conduction has only recently become available on eyewear computers, such as Google Glass, as a privacy-preserving means of relaying information to the user. SkullConduct uses the microphone readily available on many of these devices to analyse the frequency response of the sound after it travelled through the user's skull (see Figure 1). As shown in this work, individual differences in skull anatomy result in highly person-specific frequency responses that can be used as a biometric.

The contributions of this work are two-fold. First, we present SkullConduct, a biometric system that uses bone conduction for secure user identification and authentication on eyewear computers. The system combines Mel Frequency Cepstral Coefficient (MFCC) based features with a light-weight 1NN classifier that can directly run on Google Glass. In contrast to established uses of bone conduction, our system uses a microphone close to the user's head – in our case readily integrated into Glass – to measure and analyze the frequency response after the sound traveled through the user's skull.

Second, we report on a controlled experiment with 10 participants that shows that this frequency response serves as a robust biometric, even when taking off and putting on the device multiple times. We show that we can identify users with 97.0% accuracy and authenticate them with an equal error rate of 6.9%.

THE SKULLCONDUCT SYSTEM

There are, in general, two different pathways audio can take to get from a source to the user. The most widely used pathway, as for example in the case of headphones or speakers, is via air conduction in which the audio travels through the air and the auditory channel to the user's inner ear. The second pathway is via bone conduction, i.e. directly through the skull to the inner ear. Especially for eyewear computers that already are located close or even at the head of the user, using bone conduction yields the advantage that the audio is not well audible to bystanders and thus more private.

So far, systems typically used speech to identify different users (see [18] for an example). In contrast, SkullConduct exploits the characteristic changes in an audio signal while it travels through a user's skull (see Figure 1). When audio is played back with a bone conduction speaker (i.e., the audio travels through the head) it is modified by the user's head. If recorded with a microphone, the changes in the audio signal reflect the specific characteristics of the user's head. Since the structure of the human head includes different parts such as the skull, tissues, cartilage, and fluids and the composition of these parts and their location differ between users, the modification of the sound wave differs between users as well. First, the speed of sound transmission differs for each of the parts of the human head [15] and, second, the different signal frequencies are damped differently [22]. In this work we opted for Gaussian white noise as the input signal since it covers the whole frequency range and therefore all frequency bands that might get affected by individual skull characteristics.

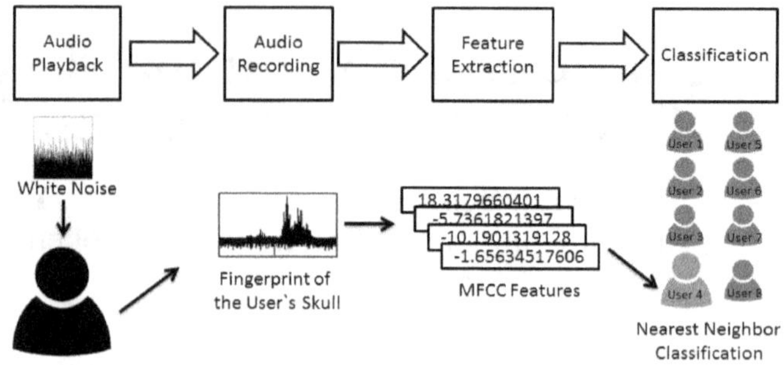

Figure 2. The recognition pipeline we used to authenticate users: (1) white noise is played back using the bone conduction speaker, (2) the user's skull influences the signal in a characteristic way, (3) MFCC features are extracted, and (4) a 1NN algorithm is used for classification.

We implemented SkullConduct on Google Glass as one of the most common used smart eyewear devices. We developed an application that plays back an audio file using the integrated bone conduction speaker and records concurrently with the integrated microphone. The recording is saved on the Glass as a byte file with 44100 samples per second, a single channel (i.e., mono), and a precision of two bytes per sample. To authenticate users, the system is capable of extracting features from the recording and comparing it to a training set using a 1NN classifier.

Recognition Pipeline

Our recognition pipeline to identify and authenticate users combines Mel Frequency Cepstral Coefficients (MFCCs) [6] as acoustic features with a computationally light-weight 1-nearest-neighbour classifier (see Figure 2). MFCCs are commonly used in speech classification and speaker identification but were shown to also perform well for non-speech event classification (see [17] for an example). In a first step, the signal as a whole is transformed using a Fourier transform. Afterwards, the power spectrum is mapped to the Mel scale using a Mel Filter Bank (MFB). Then, the Discrete Cosine Transform (DCT) is calculated after taking the logarithm. Finally, the MFCCs are given by the 2-13 DCT coefficients. In this work, we extend the 12 MFCCs features with their first derivatives (deltas) resulting in 24 features. All features are then used as input to a 1-nearest-neighbor classifier to identify or authenticate users. As a distance measure we used the sum of the Euclidean distances of each feature of a sample.

Application Scenarios

We envision two main application scenarios in which our system will be useful.

Personalization of Eyewear Computers

Eyewear computers are used in an increasing number of applications, such as for training in laboratories [9], medical documentation [1], educational purposes [11], or even during surgeries [14]. In all of these domains, multiple users may use a single device on a regular basis. As soon as a user puts on the device, SkullConduct can immediately identify the user and configure user-specific settings, such as preferred applications or system preferences.

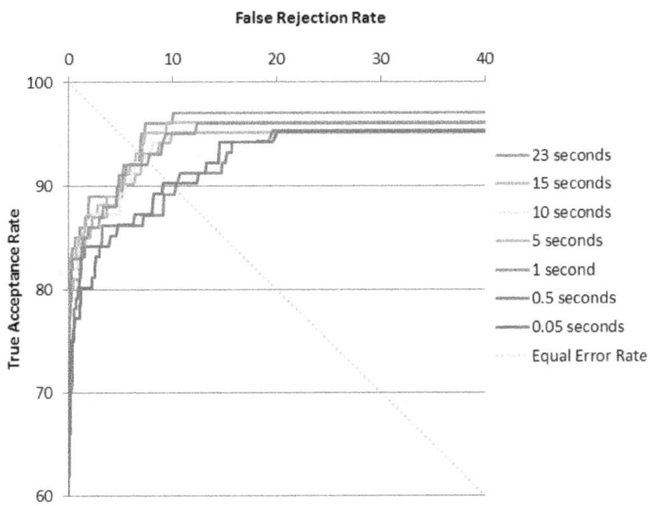

Figure 3. Receiver operating characteristic (ROC) curves summarizing the performance in terms of true acceptance rate vs. false acceptance rate for different recording lengths.

Protecting Private Content

Most eyewear computers are personal devices that contain sensible information about the owner, such as social media logins or bank account details. Current systems, such as Google Glass, are not protected and attackers can simply put on the device and access sensitive information. User authentication could automatically be triggered after the device has been put on by a new user. In addition, as soon as specific applications are started, such as the banking application, SkullConduct could re-authenticate the user to ensure he is allowed to access the application data.

EVALUATION

We evaluated SkullConduct with respect to the two main operating modes of biometric systems, namely user identification and authentication [16]. We designed a user study to record characteristic frequency responses for multiple people wearing Google Glass in a controlled laboratory setting.

Data Collection

We recorded data of 10 participants (9 male, 1 female) aged between 21 and 36 years ($M = 28$, $SD = 4.35$). The recording took place in a quiet room without any other source of noise and the participants sat down on a chair in the middle of the room. In this initial evaluation of the approach, we opted to have no confounding audio sources that may influence our results, such as sounds of other electronic devices or people. As mentioned before, we used a randomly generated Gaussian white noise audio signal with a length of 23 seconds. We recorded each participant 10 times with the same audio signal. After five recording trials, we asked participants to take off the device and put it back on to include different placements of the device on the participant's head.

Analysis

After recording the samples of all users, we analyzed the recorded data using 10-fold cross validation. In each fold, similar to Holz et al. [8], we excluded all recordings of one

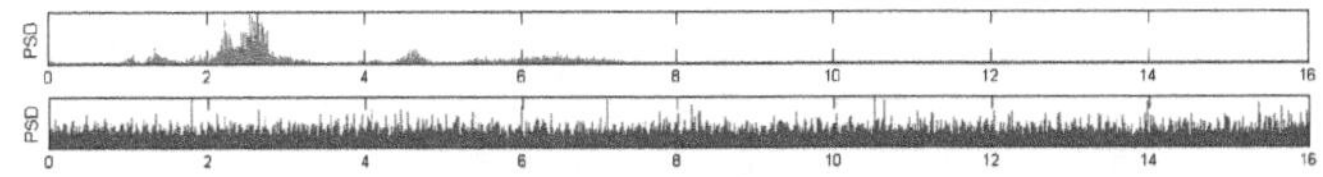

Figure 4. The user-specific modification (top) of the white noise input signal (bottom) takes place in the range of 1 kHz to 8 kHz with most modifications occurring between 2 kHz and 4 kHz.

participant (i.e., the attacker). Within each fold, we did an additional two-fold cross validation. To this end, we grouped the recordings of the nine remaining participants into two folds. The first five recordings went into the first fold and the second five recordings, recorded after taking off Google Glass and putting it back on, went into the second fold. In total, we trained our system with 45 recordings (i.e., fold 1) of the nine known participants and used 55 recordings (i.e., fold 2, 45 recordings from known and 10 from unknown participants) for testing. We deliberately chose to split the data of each user since the placement of the Google Glass might influence the results [7, 22].

User Identification

The first evaluation task for our SkullConduct system is to identify a known user. This might be necessary when an eyewear computer is shared within a group of users (i.e., a family or at work) but not require authentication since, for example, this information is only used for personalization of the device and not to protect content. In our case, the system achieves a 97.0% accuracy (cf., Figure 3 – True Acceptance Rate (TAR)). Thus, the lowest Euclidean distance between the new sample is with a recorded sample of the same user. In only 3% of the cases, a user is mistaken with another one.

User Authentication

The second evaluation task for our system is to authenticate a known user while rejecting unknown ones. The main measure of goodness for authentication system is the Equal Error Rate (EER) which is the point for which the false acceptance rate (FAR) and the false rejection rate (FRR) are equal [16]. We calculate both rates for our system for specific thresholds that decide whether a user will be authenticated or rejected (i.e., the euclidean distance between a training data and the authentication data needs to be lower than the threshold). Next, we calculated the EER out of the FAR and FRR (cf., [16]). The FAR is the percentage of samples that are mistakenly granted access even though they are from an unknown user. in contrast, the FRR is the percentage of samples that are mistakenly refused to access even though they are from known users. In our case, both rates were the same at 6.9%. The receiver operating characteristic (ROC) curve in Figure 3 shows the SkullConduct precision for different thresholds. For a high true authentication precision (97.0%), the FAR was 10.2%.

Influence of Different Frequency Bands

As related work suggested [22], different frequencies are influenced in characteristic ways by the head and skull. To investigate this phenomena, we calculated the Power Spectral Density (PSD), which describes how the power of the signal traversing the skull is distributed over the frequency range (see Figure 4). As can be seen from the figure, the head and skull for each participant influenced the PSD of the original signal in a specific way (see Figure 5). This influence varies

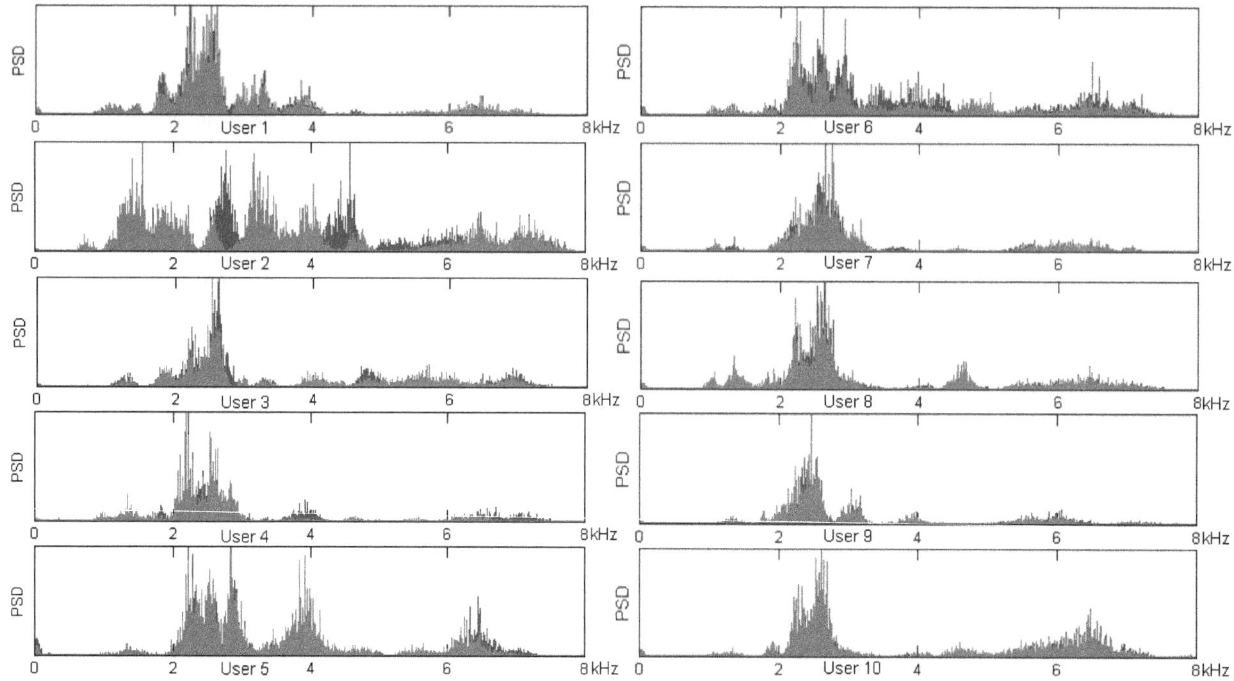

Figure 5. The power spectral density visualized for two recordings of each of the ten participants before and after removing and putting the device back on (trial 1 shown in red and trial 2 in blue) in the range of 0 kHz to 8 kHz. The changes in the power spectral density are almost similar for the different placements but differ between participants.

among participants but is constant for the same user even over several trails (i.e., only slightly affected by misplacement of the eyewear computer). Furthermore, the user-specific differences are skewed towards the lower frequency ranges and the main influence of the user's skull is for frequencies between 2 kHz and 4 kHz.

Influence of Audio Length

Current authentication systems on mobile devices require about 1.5 seconds to authenticate a user [20]. We used audio recordings of 23 seconds length which would take significantly longer for a user to authenticate. Therefore, we evaluated the performance of our system using audio with shorter lengths. Specifically, we cut each recording after 15, 10, 5, 1, 0.5, or 0.05 seconds and calculated a ROC curve for each length of audio samples using the same procedure as described before. As shown in Figure 3, the EER significantly drops when using audio samples shorter than 1 second.

DISCUSSION AND LIMITATIONS

The evaluation of our system yielded promising results. We showed that bone-conduction audio is well suited as a biometric security system for eyewear computers. However, we tested our approach only in a controlled setting without any background noise. Thus, we used a best-case scenario for our user study to explore the general feasibility of our approach. It will be interesting to see if and how much additional noise, such as other people talking in the room or appliances, reduces performance. One potential solution to this problem are algorithms that preserve the specific characteristics of each skull but remove the environmental influences [3]. Furthermore, there might be additional influences such as hair growth or gained weight that might impact the accuracy of our approach and need to be evaluated in the future. Although we show that a white noise signal of 1 second is sufficient to achieve high authentication accuracy, white noise signals may be unpleasant for the user. In the future, we envision that white noise could be replaced by more pleasant audio sounds such as common start-up jingles or even short music clips. Any alternative sound, however, needs to cover a sufficient number of frequency bands to discriminate well between different users.

CONCLUSION

We presented SkullConduct, a biometric system that exploits the characteristic frequency response of the human skull for user identification and authentication on eyewear computers equipped with bone conduction technology, such as Google Glass. While other biometric systems require the user to enter information explicitly (e.g., place the finger on a fingerprint reader), our system does not require any explicit user input. We implemented our system on Google Glass and evaluated its performance in a controlled user study with 10 participants. We demonstrated that our approach works well and can identify users with 97.0% accuracy as well as an EER of 6.9%.

ACKNOWLEDGMENTS

This work has in part been funded by the Cluster of Excellence on Multimodal Computing and Interaction (MMCI) at Saarland University, DLR Technology Marketing, the Helmholtz Validation Fund, the Deutsche Forschungsgemeinschaft (DFG) under grant SFB 1102, the European Union through the FP7 project Metalogue under grant agreement 611073, and the EU 7th Framework Programme under grant agreement no. 323849.

REFERENCES

1. Urs-Vito Albrecht, Ute von Jan, Joachim Kuebler, Christoph Zoeller, Martin Lacher, Oliver J Muensterer, Max Ettinger, Michael Klintschar, and Lars Hagemeier. 2014. Google Glass for documentation of medical findings: evaluation in forensic medicine. *Journal of medical Internet research* 16, 2 (2014).
2. Cheng Bo, Lan Zhang, Xiang-Yang Li, Qiuyuan Huang, and Yu Wang. 2013. SilentSense: Silent User Identification Via Touch and Movement Behavioral Biometrics. *Proceedings of the 19th annual international conference on Mobile computing & networking - MobiCom '13* (2013), 187. DOI: http://dx.doi.org/10.1145/2500423.2504572
3. Pedro Cano, Eloi Batlle, E Batle, T Kalker, and J Haitsma. 2002. A review of algorithms for audio fingerprinting. In *Multimedia Signal Processing, 2002 IEEE Workshop on*. 169–173. DOI: http://dx.doi.org/10.1109/MMSP.2002.1203274
4. M. Conti, I. Zachia-Zlatea, and Bruno Crispo. 2011. Mind how you answer me!: transparently authenticating the user of a smartphone when answering or placing a call. *Proceedings of the 6th ACM Symposium on Information, Computer and Communications Security* (2011), 249–259. DOI: http://dx.doi.org/10.1145/1966913.1966945
5. Cory Cornelius, Ronald Peterson, Joseph Skinner, Ryan Halter, and David Kotz. 2014. A Wearable System That Knows Who Wears It. In *Proceedings of the 12th Annual International Conference on Mobile Systems, Applications, and Services (MobiSys '14)*. ACM, New York, NY, USA, 55–67. DOI: http://dx.doi.org/10.1145/2594368.2594369
6. Steven B. Davis and Paul Mermelstein. 1980. Comparison of parametric representations for monosyllabic word recognition in continuously spoken sentences. *IEEE Transactions on Acoustics, Speech, and Signal Processing* 28, 4 (1980). DOI: http://dx.doi.org/10.1109/TASSP.1980.1163420
7. Paula Henry and Tomasz R Letowski. 2007. Bone Conduction : Anatomy , Physiology , and Communication. May (2007).
8. Christian Holz, Senaka Buthpitiya, and Marius Knaust. 2015. Bodyprint: Biometric User Identification on Mobile Devices Using the Capacitive Touchscreen to Scan Body Parts. In *Proceedings of the 33rd Annual ACM Conference on Human Factors in Computing Systems (CHI '15)*. ACM, New York, NY, USA, 3011–3014. DOI: http://dx.doi.org/10.1145/2702123.2702518
9. Grace Hu, Lily Chen, Johanna Okerlund, and Orit Shaer. 2015. Exploring the Use of Google Glass in Wet Laboratories. In *Proceedings of the 33rd Annual ACM Conference Extended Abstracts on Human Factors in Computing Systems*. ACM, 2103–2108.
10. Nikolaos Karapanos, Claudio Marforio, Claudio Soriente, and Srdjan Čapkun. 2015. Sound-Proof: Usable Two-Factor Authentication Based on Ambient Sound. *arXiv:1503.03790 [cs]* (2015). http://arxiv.org/abs/1503.03790
11. Paul Lukowicz, Andreas Poxrucker, Jens Weppner, B. Bischke, Jochen Kuhn, and Michael Hirth. 2015. Glass-physics: Using Google Glass to Support High School Physics Experiments. In *Proceedings of the 2015 ACM International Symposium on Wearable Computers*. 151–154. DOI: http://dx.doi.org/10.1145/2802083.2808407
12. Emanuele Maiorana, Patrizio Campisi, Noelia González-Carballo, and Alessandro Neri. 2011. Keystroke dynamics authentication for mobile phones. *Proceedings of the 2011 ACM Symposium on Applied Computing SAC 11* (2011), 21–26. DOI: http://dx.doi.org/10.1145/1982185.1982190
13. Jani Mantyjarvi, Mikko Lindholm, Elena Vildjiounaite, Satu-Marja Makela, and Heikki Ailisto. 2005. Identifying users of portable devices from gait pattern with accelerometers. In *Acoustics, Speech, and Signal Processing, 2005. Proceedings. (ICASSP '05). IEEE International Conference on*, Vol. 2. ii/973–ii/976 Vol. 2. DOI: http://dx.doi.org/10.1109/ICASSP.2005.1415569
14. Oliver J Muensterer, Martin Lacher, Christoph Zoeller, Matthew Bronstein, and Joachim Kübler. 2014. Google Glass in pediatric surgery: An exploratory study. *International Journal of Surgery* 12, 4 (2014), 281–289.
15. William D. Jr. O'Brien and Y Liu. 2005. Evaluation of acoustic propagation paths into the human head. 2005 (2005), 1–24. http://oai.dtic.mil/oai/oai?verb=getRecord&metadataPrefix=html&identifier=ADA437351
16. P. Jonathon Phillips, Alvin Martin, C. L. Wilson, and Mark Przybocki. 2000. Introduction to evaluating biometric systems. *Computer* 33, 2 (2000), 56–63. DOI: http://dx.doi.org/10.1109/2.820040
17. Axel Plinge, Rene Grzeszick, and Gernot A. Fink. 2014. A Bag-of-Features approach to acoustic event detection. In *2014 IEEE International Conference on Acoustics, Speech and Signal Processing (ICASSP)*. 3704–3708. DOI: http://dx.doi.org/10.1109/ICASSP.2014.6854293
18. Sandra Pruzansky. 1963. Pattern Matching Procedure for Automatic Talker Recognition. *The Journal of the Acoustical Society of America* 35, 3 (1963), 214–215.
19. Cynthia E Rogers, Alexander W Witt, Alexander D Solomon, and Krishna K Venkatasubramanian. 2015. An Approach for User Identification for Head-mounted Displays. In *Proceedings of the 2015 ACM International Symposium on Wearable Computers (ISWC '15)*. ACM, New York, NY, USA, 143–146. DOI: http://dx.doi.org/10.1145/2802083.2808391

20. Stefan Schneegass, Frank Steimle, Andreas Bulling, Florian Alt, and Albrecht Schmidt. 2014. SmudgeSafe: Geometric Image Transformations for Smudge-resistant User Authentication. In *Proceedings of the 2014 ACM International Joint Conference on Pervasive and Ubiquitous Computing (UbiComp '14)*. ACM, New York, NY, USA, 775–786. DOI: http://dx.doi.org/10.1145/2632048.2636090

21. Mark Simkin, Dominique Schrder, Andreas Bulling, and Mario Fritz. 2014. Ubic: Bridging the Gap between Digital Cryptography and the Physical World. In *Proc. of the 19th European Symposium on Research in Computer Security (ESORICS 2014)* (2014-09-01), Vol. 8712. Springer International Publishing, 56–75. http://dx.doi.org/10.1007/978-3-319-11203-9_4https://perceptual.mpi-inf.mpg.de/files/2014/09/Simkin14_ubic1.pdf

22. Stefan Stenfelt and Richard L Goode. 2005. Transmission properties of bone conducted sound: measurements in cadaver heads. *The Journal of the Acoustical Society of America* 118, 4 (2005), 2373–2391. DOI: http://dx.doi.org/10.1121/1.2005847

Use Your Words: Designing One-time Pairing Codes to Improve User Experience

Sarah Wiseman
Goldsmiths,
University Of London
London, United Kingdom
s.wiseman@gold.ac.uk

Gustavo Soto Mino,
Anna L. Cox,
Sandy J.J. Gould
University College London
London, United Kingdom
{*gustavo.mino.*14|*anna.cox*|*sandy.gould*}
@ucl.ac.uk

Joanne Moore,
Chris Needham
BBC
London, United Kingdom
{*joanne.moore*|*chris.needham*}
@bbc.co.uk

ABSTRACT
The Internet of Things is connecting an ever-increasing number of devices. These devices often require access to personal information, but their meagre user interfaces usually do not permit traditional modes of authentication. On such devices, one-time pairing codes are often used instead. This pairing process can involve transcribing randomly generated alphanumeric codes, which can be frustrating, slow and error-prone. In this paper, we present an improved pairing method that uses sets of English words instead of random strings. The word method, although longer in terms of character length, allows users to pair devices more quickly, whilst still maintaining the complexity necessary for secure interactions.

ACM Classification Keywords
H.5.m. Information Interfaces and Presentation (e.g. HCI): Miscellaneous

Author Keywords
Pairing; passcodes; passwords; data entry; authentication; Internet Of Things; typing; transcription; text entry

INTRODUCTION
Thanks to innovations in technology and the Internet of Things (IoT), it is becoming more common for previously "dumb" devices to become smart. Everyday interactions with lights [8], heating [18] or even washing machines [4] can be conducted with sophisticated remote controls that are accessed via smartphones. However, linking these devices to the associated web accounts can be difficult if they do not come pre-paired. Providing your email address, for example, to a smart TV using only a standard remote control can be tedious.

The alternative to this is to allow a 'pairing' process. In this scenario, the device displays a unique code, which a user must then enter into a web-based account on a laptop, smart phone, tablet or any device capable of browsing the web. The IoT device is then linked with the account, and all future interaction can take place online, using a device that is better designed for complex user interaction.

CHI'16, May 7–12, 2014, San Jose, USA.

ACM 978-1-4503-3362-7/16/05...$15.00
DOI: http://dx.doi.org/10.1145/2858036.2858377

The idea of generating a code in order to create a pairing of two devices is not new [11] and has been used commonly to allow people to, for example, remotely access secure systems when working from home [9]. The current standard in these situations is to generate a numeric or alphanumeric string for the user to transcribe. However, these strings can be awkward to type on touchscreen devices [10] and difficult to memorise [5], forcing multiple glances between the input screen and the device displaying the code.

When trying to improve the design of systems that require data transcription, researchers have focused on redesigning the process [6, 26] or the data entry interface [7, 27]. Rarely is there an opportunity to design the data string itself. In the context of a pairing action, codes are not semantically meaningful and it is therefore possible to design pairing codes that are optimized for their use in practice. In this way, we can explore the design not only of the underlying technology, but the data they use as well.

We present an investigation of alternatives to standard alphanumeric string codes. We show that by using a set of short words, the pairing process can be made faster and less taxing for users. This method not only improves the experience for the user, it also offers a sufficient number of permutations to generate multiple, non-clashing codes. This allows many users to pair at the same time and reduces the chances of security breaches due to malicious attacks.

RELATED LITERATURE
Pairing processes are used to connect devices so that they can share information. It is possible to complete this process through technology alone, for instance using an infrared channel [2]. However, this requires that both devices be in close proximity to one another, and that both have the specialized technology necessary for physical communication. An alternative to this method is to ask the user to verify and authenticate the device. There are a number of possible processes that can be utilized, from asking users to compare two values on two different devices, to selecting the correct value from a

possible list, to copying a value from one device into another [25]. Research has shown that, although Selection is preferred by users, the Copying method is the most secure [25]. Indeed, many systems use this method to display a text-based code to a user in order to verify a pairing. An example of this process is seen on banking websites, which display numeric codes which must be given to a phone operator to verify the caller's identity. Although text-based codes are common, alternative pairing solutions have been suggested that make use of pictorial comparisons [20] or comparing sounds [21]. However, text-based numeric or alphanumeric passcodes have been found to be safer [15, 17] and users show strong preference for word-based comparisons [16]. In addition, sound- or picture-based systems require that the display device has the ability to display images and create sounds; something many IoT devices with simple displays cannot do.

The design of the text-based passcode can be compared to the generation of passwords. A password, unlike a passcode however, is used multiple times and must be memorized by the user. When a user generates a password, they are often required to create a complex string containing special characters to ensure a high level of security. Research shows that this can result in users forgetting their passwords or using workarounds [1, 14].

It is not just recall that can cause issues with complex string passwords, but the process of entry can itself be problematic. Research into the manual processes associated with entering complex passwords also suggests that the use of alphanumeric passwords can be problematic for smartphone users [10]. This stems largely from the need to switch between multiple different keyboard levels in order to navigate to the various characters required. However, passcodes often contain multiple character types, as this ensures a high level of complexity and thus better security.

SCENARIO

This work was completed in response to a request from a large broadcasting company's requirement for pairing codes to enable users to pair smart devices (such as radios and TVs) with their personal accounts [19]. This would allow users to save songs or programmes from their devices to their account for later use. The issue faced in this scenario is that the entry of account details is difficult on a TV remote, and is near impossible on a radio. Additionally, the output of a radio is particularly limited, often using only a 16 character LCD display to scroll song information. The solution to this problem is to issue temporary pairing codes that can be displayed on the smart device and then entered on a separate device better designed for input, such as a laptop or smartphone. Once logged-in to the personal account on a browser-capable device, the generated code can be entered, joining that account to the smart device so that all future interactions can be linked to the account.

The important factor here is that the codes need to be easily read and entered by users, and additionally that the number of possible codes needs to be large enough to ensure that during moments of high levels of pairing, there are enough possible codes to issue to users. For instance, a suggestion to pair on a TV programme which would result in large numbers of people pairing their devices at the same time. Additionally, there are security constraints to prevent brute force attacks from linking a malicious device to the user's account.

The requirements in this particular scenario called for a code set in the magnitude of 500 million. Commonly, text-based pass codes use either numeric or alphanumeric randomly generated strings. The aim of our investigation was to improve the readability, memorability and typability of the codes. Familiar text is faster to type than randomised strings (see point 5 in [22] for a summary), suggesting that word-based codes may perform better than randomly generated numeric or alphanumeric codes. We conducted an experiment to test this hypothesis.

METHOD

Participants

The experiment was conducted with 20 participants (13 female) with a mean age 27 (*SD*=5). The participants were recruited from a university subject pool and social media; they were reimbursed £8 for the 35 minute session.

Design

The experiment used a within-subjects design, with each participant taking part in each of the six conditions. These conditions were presented in two different orders to the participants, counterbalanced for device.

The 2x3 design used two factors: device and code type. Two devices were used in the experiment: a laptop and a touchscreen smart phone. The three levels of code type were numeric, alphanumeric and words. The dependent variables include time per trial, number of uncorrected errors, eye glances to the display device and NASA TLX scores which allow the participants to self-assess their workload during the task [12].

Materials

Table 1 shows the complexity of the three types of codes used in this experiment: numeric, alphanumeric and word-based. Note that each offers more than 500 million possible codes.

The numeric codes were generated as a random string of nine digits from 0-9, displayed in three blocks of three digits. The alphanumeric codes were similarly randomly generated, using the characters a-z, A-Z and 0-9, removing characters that could be easily visually confused (i, o, l, I, O ,L). From this set, a string of five characters was created and chunked into two blocks of two then three characters as splitting groups of alphanumeric characters can make them more memorable, which aids in the transcription process [23]. A word code was generated by randomly sampling three words from a set of English words and displaying them with spaces between each word. For the word codes to be feasible, the number of possible combinations of words would need to exceed 500 million in order to be comparable to the complexity of the numeric and alphanumeric codes. There are around 1100 three-letter English words, although many of these are likely to be obscure. When computing the word code complexity, a conservative estimate of 800 possible words was used, thus resulting in

Code Name	*Size*	*Example*	*Complexity*
Numeric	9 digits	180 487 101	10^9
Alphanumeric	5 characters	s4 5vB	56^5
Words	3 words	pot bee rid	800^3

Table 1. Different code generation schemes with set size. Numeric codes include digits 0-9. Alphanumeric codes include digits and all upper and lower case letters (excluding i,o,l,I,O,L). Word codes include three 3-letter English words.

$800^3 = 512,000,000$ possible combinations of three three-letter words. This estimate was based upon an upper limit of 1135 three-letter words found in the Unix "words" file and a lower limit of 754 three-letter words reported in [24], which took words from a spell-checking dictionary and thus excluded highly obscure words. For the purposes of the experiment, the word codes were generated from a list of 242 common English three-letter words taken from the easily accessible Google Books database.

The experiment was set up as two websites: one display and one input. The display website ran on a 22 inch computer monitor, whilst the input website ran on either a laptop (a MacBook Pro) or the participant's smartphone depending on the condition. A Tobii X120 eye-tracking device was set up to record the glances at the display screen.

The display screen showed the codes in 32px Helvetica font. The input screen displayed a text entry box and an enter button in the centre of the screen. In the laptop condition, the participant copied the code into this box using the physical keyboard. In the phone condition, the user used the installed keyboard on their smart phone to enter the code.

Procedure

Participants completed the experiment sat in front of the display monitor. Prior to two test trials, the eye tracker was calibrated for each participant. Each participant was able to freely move their head throughout the experiment. The 20 participants were counterbalanced: half entered codes on the laptop and then their smartphone whereas the the other half used the smart phone first and then the laptop.

The display screen began by showing a fixation cross for 3 seconds in the centre of the screen. After this, the first code was displayed in the centre of the screen. Once the user had entered the code on the separate input device, the fixation cross on the display screen would appear for 3 seconds before displaying the next code to be entered.

In each of the six conditions (two devices and three code types) the user copied 20 codes, for a total of 120 codes. The duration of code entry was measured from the point at which the code was shown on the display screen to the point the user pressed the 'enter' key on the input screen. After each condition, the participants were given a NASA TLX survey to fill in to self-assess the workload. This was completed six times in total.

After all trials had been completed, the participants were asked about their preference for the different codes; they were asked which code they found easiest to input on the laptop, then the smartphone. Finally, the participants were asked which code they would find easiest and safest to use in a device pairing situation.

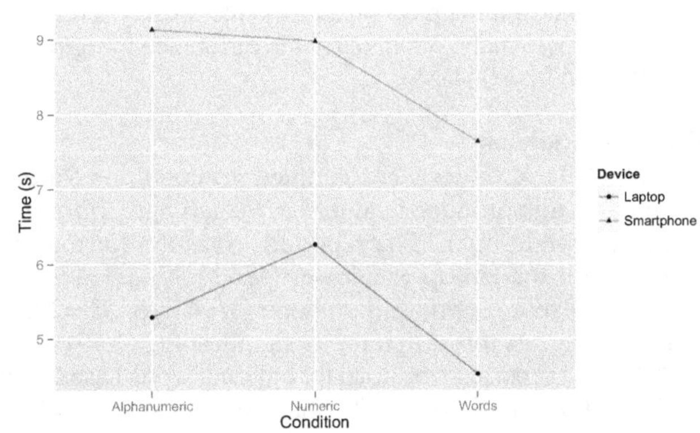

Figure 1. Mean time across all participants to enter one code

RESULTS

Speed of Transcription

Figure 1 shows the mean time taken to enter one code in each condition. Participants entered codes faster on the laptop (*M*=5.36-s, *SD*=1.97-s) than on the smartphone (*M*=8.58-s, *SD*=2.72-s). A two-way repeated ANOVA analysis of this result suggests that this difference was significant ($F(1,19)=65.04$ $p<.001$). Despite being longer in terms of character length, in both device conditions, the word codes were faster to enter (*M*=6.09-s, *SD*=2.24-s) than both the alphanumeric (*M*=7.62-s, *SD*=3.06-s) and numeric (*M*=7.21-s, *SD*=3.07-s) conditions. Analysis suggests that this speed difference is significant ($F(2,38)=6.72$ $p=.003$). A post-hoc pairwise comparison suggests that words are significantly faster to type than both numeric ($p=.010$) and alphanumeric codes ($p<.001$). The interaction between device and condition was non-significant, indicating that the advantage of word codes is not device-specific.

Error Rate

Error rate was calculated as the percentage of trials that resulted in the code being entered incorrectly. The mean error rate for codes entered in the laptop condition (*M*=3%, *SD*=4.6%) and smartphone condition (*M*=4.3%, *SD*=6.1%) was not significantly different. Similarly, the differences between error rates for numeric codes (*M*=3%, *SD*=4.9%), alphanumeric codes (*M*=4.3%, *SD*=5.9%) and word codes (*M*=3.8%, *SD*=5.5%) were also non-significant.

Eye gaze data

The eye tracking data was not recorded for six participants due to an equipment limitation. Additionally, the eye tracking data for the smartphone condition was unusable because of excessive head movement in this condition. In the laptop condition however, the data showed that the mean number of gazes to screen in the numeric condition was 1.8 (*SD*=0.73), in the alphanumeric condition it was 1.76 (*SD*=0.74) whereas in the word condition the mean glances to the display screen was 1.3 (SD=0.53). Analysis suggests this difference is significant ($F(2,26)=3.53$ $p=.044$).

Workload analysis

The NASA TLX values were summed per condition for each participant (this produced values between 0 and 20 for each of the six conditions). The reported workload for entering the codes on the laptop was lower (M=37.37, SD=21) than the reported score for the smartphone (M=45.98, SD=22.45). Analysis suggests this difference is significant ($F(1,19)=19.86$ $p<.001$). The reported workload for entering word-based codes was lower (M=31.15, SD=17.22) than both numeric (M=44.95, SD=22.72) and alphanumeric (M=48.78, SD=22.33) codes. A repeated measures ANOVA test suggests this difference is significant ($F(2,38)=36.65$ $p<.001$). A post-hoc pairwise comparison suggests that word codes resulted in a significantly lower reported workload than both numeric ($p<.001$) and alphanumeric ($p<.001$) codes. The difference between workload for numeric and alphanumeric codes was non-significant, as was the interaction between device and condition.

Code Style Preference

When asked which code the participants preferred when using the laptop, 85% chose the word-based codes and 15% chose numeric codes. In the smartphone condition, 80% of participants preferred word-based codes, 15% preferred numeric codes and 5% preferred alphanumeric codes. In a device pairing scenario where security was emphasized as an important factor, 75% of users said they would prefer the word-based codes and 25% said they would prefer the numeric codes.

DISCUSSION

The alphanumeric condition required users to type five characters, whereas the numeric and word conditions required the users to type nine characters. Despite this difference in length, the words condition resulted in the fastest code entry time on both devices with no reduction in accuracy.

It is known that typing familiar words is faster than typing random strings [22]. The results of this experiment replicate this finding, as the randomly generated strings in the numeric and alphanumeric conditions were transcribed slower than the more familiar words. This cognitive facilitation of familiarity during the transcription process may explain the increase in speed for word-based codes. The eye gaze data suggests that the word-based codes were easier to store in short term memory, with participants making fewer glances back to the display screen in the word condition compared to the other two conditions.

The device used had a significant effect upon the speed of code entry also, with codes being entered significantly faster on the laptop than on the users' smartphones. This replicates research that has found typing on physical keyboards faster than touchscreens or flat keyboards, particularly on smaller mobile phone screens [13, 3].

Ultimately, in a pairing situation, the key measure is that the method used should be no more error-prone than an alternative. This suggests that any of the three conditions tested here would be usable. However, the indications of user preference and perceived workload alongside the improved speed suggest that the word-based codes are better than number or alphanumeric codes, whilst maintaining a similar level of complexity.

Further to this analysis, the words condition also has a "safer" fail mode than the other two code options. For example when entering an alphanumeric code, if the user was to slip whilst typing and enter 'rT 5v6' instead of 'rT 5v5', this incorrect code is still valid in the system, meaning there is a chance it could represent a code another user has been given and thus incorrectly pairing their device with the other user's account. In the word-based code condition, a user accidentally entering 'win cat trt' instead of 'win cat try' has entered a string of characters that does not constitute a word and therefore represents an invalid code. The user can then be immediately alerted to the error. Although it is still possible that a typing slip when using the words system could produce a valid code, the likelihood of this happening is greatly reduced compared to other systems. This means the word-based codes are less likely to result in accidental pairings of devices and accounts: the syntactical rules inherent in word creation mean that word-based codes have some level of built-in error checking.

Gallagher and Byrne, in [10], highlight the problems of entering mixed character passcodes on touchscreen devices such as a smartphone, where each switch between keyboard levels adds time to the text entry process. In the current study, participants were required to navigate multiple keyboard levels in the alphanumeric condition when using the smartphone (switching keyboard between lower case letters, upper case letters and numbers). Despite the alphanumeric codes being 45% the length of the numeric codes, the time difference between these two conditions was not significant. This finding appears to support the previous research that suggests switching keyboard levels increases time for data input.

CONCLUSION

The results of this study strongly support the use of word-based codes in a device pairing context. Not only are word-based codes faster to transcribe, they also require fewer glances to the display screen to memorise, result in a lower perceived workload and are preferred by users. These improvements in the pairing process are not associated with an increase in error rate, nor do they result in codes that are less secure: the search space of possible codes is still in the same order of magnitude as numeric codes of the same length, and is greater than the needs of an example scenario set by a company using a pairing system. This research suggests that when pairing devices with poor input interfaces, and low fidelity output displays, word-based codes are a preferable alternative to the current standard of randomly generated numeric and alphanumeric codes.

ACKNOWLEDGMENTS

This work was supported by the UK Engineering and Physical Sciences Research Council grant EP/L504889/1. We thank the anonymous reviewers of this manuscript for their insight.

REFERENCES

1. Anne Adams and Martina Angela Sasse. 1999. Users are not the enemy. *Commun. ACM* 42, 12 (1999), 40–46. DOI: http://dx.doi.org/10.1145/322796.322806
2. Dirk Balfanz, Diana K Smetters, Paul Stewart, and H Chi Wong. 2002. Talking to Strangers: Authentication in Ad-Hoc Wireless Networks. In *NDSS*.
3. Julia Barret and Helmut Krueger. 1994. Performance effects of reduced proprioceptive feedback on touch typists and casual users in a typing task. *Behaviour & Information Technology* 13, 6 (1994). DOI: http://dx.doi.org/10.1080/01449299408914618
4. Berg Cloud Limited. 2014. Cloud Wash. (2014). http://bergcloud.com/case-studies/cloudwash/
5. Roy Brener. 1940. An experimental investigation of memory span. *Journal of Experimental Psychology* 26, 5 (1940), 467–482. DOI: http://dx.doi.org/10.1037/h0061096
6. Duncan P. Brumby, Anna L. Cox, Jonathan Back, and Sandy J. J. Gould. 2013. Recovering from an interruption: Investigating speed-accuracy trade-offs in task resumption behavior. *Journal of Experimental Psychology: Applied* 19, 2 (2013), 95–107. DOI: http://dx.doi.org/10.1037/a0032696
7. Abigail Cauchi, Andy Gimblett, Harold Thimbleby, Paul Curzon, and Paolo Masci. 2012. Safer "5-key" number entry user interfaces using Differential Formal Analysis. In *Proceedings of the 2012 BCS Conference on Human-Computer Interaction*. 29–38.
8. Easy Bulb. 2015. Easy Bulb. (2015). http://easybulb.com/
9. EMC Corporation. 2015. RSA. (2015). http://www.emc.com/domains/rsa/index.htm
10. Melissa A Gallagher and Michael D Byrne. 2015. Modeling Password Entry on a Mobile Device Modeling. In *Proceedings of the International Conference on Cognitive Modeling*. 45–50.
11. Richard H Guski, Raymond C Larson, Syephen M Matyas Jr, Donald B Johnson, and Don Coppersmith. 1997. Authentication system using one-time passwords. (1997). https://www.google.com/patents/US5592553
12. Sandra G. Hart and Lowell E. Staveland. 1988. Development of NASA-TLX (Task Load Index): Results of empirical and theoretical research. *Advances in psychology* 52 (1988), 139–183. DOI: http://dx.doi.org/10.1016/S0166-4115(08)62386-9
13. Eve Hoggan, Stephen A Brewster, and Jody Johnston. 2008. Investigating the Effectiveness of Tactile Feedback for Mobile Touchscreens. In *Proceedings of the SIGCHI conference on Human factors in computing systems*. 1573–1582. DOI: http://dx.doi.org/10.1145/1357054.1357300
14. Phillip Inglesant and M. Angela Sasse. 2010. The true cost of unusable password policies: password use in the wild. In *Proceedings of the SIGCHI Conference on Human Factors in Computing Systems*. 383–392. DOI: http://dx.doi.org/10.1145/1753326.1753384
15. Ronald Kainda, Ivan Flechais, and A.W. Roscoe. 2009. Usability and Security of Out-Of-Band Channels in Secure Device Pairing Protocols. In *Symposium on Usable Privacy and Security*. DOI: http://dx.doi.org/10.1145/1572532.1572547
16. Ronald Kainda, Ivan Flechais, and A. W. Roscoe. 2010. Secure and Usable Out-Of-Band Channels for Ad Hoc Mobile Device Interactions. *Information Security Theory and Practices. Security and Privacy of Pervasive Systems and Smart Devices* 6033 (2010), 308–315. DOI: http://dx.doi.org/10.1007/978-3-642-12368-9
17. Alfred Kobsa, Gene Tsudik, and Yang Wang. 2009. Serial Hook-ups : A Comparative Usability Study of Secure Device Pairing Methods. In *Proceedings of the 5th Symposium on Usable Privacy and Security*. DOI: http://dx.doi.org/10.1145/1572532.1572546
18. Nest Labs. 2015. Nest. (2015). https://nest.com/
19. Sean O'Haplin, Chris Needham, and Michael Barroco. 2014. *The Cross Platform Authentication Protocol*. Technical Report September. EBU Operating Eurovision And Euroradio, Geneva. 1–39 pages.
20. Adrian Perrig and Dawn Song. 1999. Hash Visualization : a New Technique to improve Real-World Security. *International Workshop on Cryptographic Techniques and E-Commerce* (1999), 1–8.
21. Ramnath Prasad and Nitesh Saxena. 2008. Efficient device pairing using "human-comparable" synchronized audiovisual patterns. In *Applied Cryptography and Network Security*. 328–345. DOI: http://dx.doi.org/10.1007/978-3-540-68914-0{_}20
22. Timothy A. Salthouse. 1986. Perceptual, cognitive, and motoric aspects of transcription typing. *Psychological bulletin* 99, 3 (1986), 303–319. DOI: http://dx.doi.org/10.1037/0033-2909.99.3.303
23. Jan Maarten Schraagen and Kees van Dongen. 2005. Designing a licence plate for memorability. *Ergonomics* 48, 7 (2005), 796–806. DOI: http://dx.doi.org/10.1080/00140130500123720
24. Reginald Smith. 2012. Distinct word length frequencies: distributions and symbol entropies. *Glottometrics* 23 (2012), 7–22.
25. Ersin Uzun, Kristiina Karvonen, and N. Asokan. 2007. Usability Analysis of Secure Pairing Methods. *Financial Cryptography and Data Security* (2007), 307–324. DOI: http://dx.doi.org/10.1007/978-3-540-77366-5_29
26. Sarah Wiseman, Anna L. Cox, Duncan P. Brumby, Sandy J. J. Gould, and Sarah O'Carroll. 2013a. Using Checksums to Detect Number Entry Error. In *Proceedings of the SIGCHI Conference on Human Factors in Computing*. 2403–2406. DOI: http://dx.doi.org/10.1145/2470654.2481332
27. Sarah Wiseman, Orla Hennessy, Anna L. Cox, and Duncan P. Brumby. 2013b. Tailoring Number Entry Interfaces To The Task of Programming Medical Infusion Pumps. In *International Annual Meeting of the Human Factors and Ergonomics Society*. 683–687. DOI: http://dx.doi.org/10.1177/1541931213571148

Reconstituting the Utopian Vision of Making: HCI After Technosolutionism

Silvia Lindtner
University of Michigan
Ann Arbor, USA
lindtner@umich.edu

Shaowen Bardzell
Indiana University
Bloomington, USA
selu@indiana.edu

Jeffrey Bardzell
Indiana University
Bloomington, USA
jbardzel@indiana.edu

ABSTRACT
HCI research has both endorsed "making" for its innovation and democratization capacity and critiqued its underlying technosolutionism, *i.e.*, the idea that technology provides solutions to complex social problems. This paper offers a reflexive-interventionist approach that simultaneously takes seriously the critiques of making's claims as technosolutionist while also embracing its utopian project as worth reconstituting in broader sociopolitical terms. It applies anthropological theory of the global and feminist-utopianism to the analysis of findings from research on making cultures in Taiwan and China. More specifically, the paper provides ethnographic snippets of utopian glimmers in order to speculatively imagine and explore alternative futures of making worth pursuing, and in so doing reconstitute the utopian vision of making.

Author Keywords
Making; maker movement; DIY; innovation; neoliberalism; capitalism; utopianism; policy; HCI; China; Taiwan.

ACM Classification Keywords
H.5.m. Information interfaces and presentation (e.g., HCI): Miscellaneous.

INTRODUCTION
In recent years, a collection of emerging technologies and practices has co-evolved into what is now often referred to as "making," or "the maker movement." Hailed in the media as *the* contemporary site of technological innovation and as a revamp of economies and broken educational systems, making is promoted as having diverse potential benefits for society. What was largely understood as a hobbyist movement, associated with the early hackerspaces in the 1990s in Europe and the founding of Arduino in 2006 [20], has over the last 10 years transformed into an aspiring interdisciplinary arena of social computing [2,10,48].

ACM 978-1-4503-3362-7/16/05...$15.00 DOI:
http://dx.doi.org/10.1145/2858036.2858506

Making is often articulated in utopian terms; it is envisioned to democratize technology production. Through the transformation of the self, empowered by the tools of production, making will have broad social, economic, and political impacts, so the story as portrayed by advocates of the maker movement often goes, *e.g.*, [3]. This largely utopian vision of making has already had impact as the growing number of investments in maker-related activities, projects, events, and spaces evidence [19, 48]. The rapid transformation of making from the fringes to the mainstream has been in part enabled by the financial and/or political support of large corporations including Intel, Qualcomm, Microsoft, Ford; by educational institutions ranging from local libraries to American ivy league universities; and by city and national governmental entities including but not limited to the US White House, the US National Science Foundation, the Chinese national and local city governments, Singapore, the Taipei city government and "creative industry policy" bureau, the European Union, and many more.

The HCI research community has shared this enthusiasm and expressed diverse interests in making. These include an interest in making as a new domain of computing [32,42, 48,60,77], which HCI can investigate to theorize interaction, to pursue new design methodologies, and to which HCI can contribute tools and infrastructure [7,14,16,21,35, 40,41,43,44,54,68,76]. HCI researchers have also explored the potentials of making to contribute towards a sustainable IT agenda [61]. One of the central interests that these diverse projects share is making's contribution to the democratization of technology use and design. For instance, making is envisioned to move IT innovation out of university and corporate labs into everyday society [29,71]. Making is also seen as enabling marginalized groups to participate in computing innovation, including children [26,34], women [28,64] and people in the Global South [18].

At the same time, HCI research has also expressed skepticism towards some of these projects, suggesting that they are unrealistic or even naïve [1,2,10,25,28,37,39,47,60,61, 62,69,74]. This research suggests that there is a technosolutionism underlying making and much of the research on the topic. Technosolutionism is the view that technology can unilaterally solve difficult social problems. Technosolutionism is visible in promotions of making that portray it as furthering sustainability, social justice for women, economic development for the Global South, and empowerment for all. HCI research has also problematized this view as it largely rests on the deployment of Western conceptions of democracy and empowerment to characterize what is in fact a global phenomenon [17,37,39,40,46, 47,47,69].

Taken together, the utopian vision of making has been unmasked as resting on a kind of technosolutionism and ideological colonialism, in a literature of critical studies in and beyond HCI that is hard to dismiss. Yet, the body of critical HCI scholarship on making has not replaced the techno-utopian vision with an equally aspirational vision. Thus, HCI researchers are in a dilemma. We can pursue making as an avenue to increase participation and democracy in technology use and design, if we take what has been criticized as a naïve technosolutionist stance. Or we can take a critical stance and thereby risk abdicating our agency in contributing towards making's sociopolitical potentials.

This paper seeks to deconstruct this dilemma and to explore a way of pursuing making research that robustly pursues a democratizing agenda, while remaining technically, critically, and empirically sophisticated. We argue that a methodological blind spot has made it hard for HCI to pursue technical and sociopolitical agendas simultaneously: common methodological stances tend to prioritize either the possibilities of technical innovations or careful sociopolitical critique—but not both equally and at the same time. This is not to suggest a rigid binary between the utopian project of make and its critics. Rather, we acknowledge that both share a commitment to critical intervention and change, although each construes change and intervention differently. For instance, the utopian project of making is also a form of critique; it challenges perceived conceptions of computing and design (and who gets to do them), as is visible, for instance, in Leah Buechley's work [14,15,16]; and making's project to democratize production is positioned to disrupt passive consumer culture, *e.g.,* [71]. Similarly, critical scholarship is also committed to a form of intervention. We propose to reconstitute the utopian vision of making to harmonize the interventionist and utopian impulses of the technical and critical agendas.

Reconstituting the Utopian Vision of Making

We ask: how can we blend the contributions of technologists who are opening up making to new uses and users with the contributions of more critical voices to pursue the democratization of making as an equally sociotechnical research practice? What is needed is both a technical and a sociopolitical perspective, because (obviously) democratization itself is a sociopolitical issue, implicated in problems of hegemony and structural disenfranchisement. Technological innovations, such as new tools and kits, may well have democratizing potential, but realizing that potential is not merely a technical problem; it is also a sociopolitical one.

To summarize, this paper offers an attempt to pursue making's democratizing potentials, by constructing and deploying a perspective that is equally fluent in, and equally prioritizes, technical and sociopolitical perspectives. We say "attempt" because this project is bigger than any of us, let alone a single paper. Rather than seeing our contingent perspective as a reason to shy away from our sociopolitical agency as researchers, we see it instead as a place to start. Throughout, we strive to maintain a critical sensibility to prevent devolving into cheerleading and fad-ism.

To do so, we adopt the reflexive-interventionist approach of feminist utopianism [12] and speculative sociology [45] as developed by Shaowen Bardzell [6,8]. Specifically, we propose a double move to outline how HCI can begin such a reflexive-interventionist approach. The first move constitutes a *critique of the present* to reveal both problem spots and opportunities for intervention as well as practices, spaces or moments where alternatives to dominating modes are revealed. We deploy the concept of "global assemblages" in order to analyze making on both levels (technological and sociopolitical), without normalizing making in Western terms. The second move is rooted in our critique of the present; in it, we employ an *anticipatory design* approach to move forward. Anticipatory design is an approach from feminist philosophy and speculative sociology [6,8,12,45] that is reconstructive, working with fragments as raw materials out of which to speculatively imagine and explore alternative futures worth pursuing (which is what makes this activity "utopian"). Anticipatory design provides models and tactics to pursue ambitious social goals of making in a pragmatic and participative way.

In what follows, we provide a detailed explanation of the analytical commitments of each of these two moves. To articulate each, we draw from our extensive fieldwork on making in China and Taiwan. This includes many years of ethnographic research with diverse making cultures including but not limited to hobbyist makers, makerspaces, hardware entrepreneurs, policy makers, artists, designers, crafters, manufacturers, and more. Details of our methods and long-term work are documented here: [6,7,9,46,47,48,61, 74,79]. A central commitment in our ethnographic engagements in China and Taiwan has been the close collaboration with our interlocutors, including co-authorship and the hosting of workshops aimed at bringing together hands-on making with critical intervention. Throughout, we continuously reflect on our own positionality in relation to our fieldsites, as described in [9,10,47,49]. For purposes of clarity, we first tackle *critique of the present: making as global assemblages* and then turn to move 2 *anticipatory design: utopian glimmers of making,* with each section teasing out stories and aspects of making from our fieldwork as potential raw materials for a critique of the present and an anticipatory design practice. The written format forces a kind of sequencing, which does not mean to suggest that the two moves necessarily have to occur in the order presented here. On the contrary, the two moves work hand-in-hand, unfold alongside one another in and through our empirical and analytical work. The double move is aimed at articulating a sensibility (rather than a firm recipe) for future research on making in HCI and cultures of production more broadly.

The discussion brings the two moves together in order to reconstitute the utopian vision of making. Throughout this paper, we build on prior research on non-Western making [17,18,37,39,40,41,46,47,48,69,70,79] to continue decenter a predominantly Western narrative of making (and technology design writ large) by opening up alternatives and other possible futures.

MOVE 1: CRITIQUE OF THE PRESENT

Any critique of the present requires substantive empirical work informing us of the present. Reading and doing such empirical research critically implies taking seriously that making means different things across regions and is practiced in relation to situated technological and cultural processes, while acknowledging that at the same time making can not be divorced from global processes of capital flows, investments, geopolitical tensions, and so on. Prior research has emphasized that much of the techno-utopian idealism and visions of democratization are articulated from a largely Western perspective [17,69,70]. Reframing democratization of technology as a sociopolitical problem thus benefits from a decentering of this Western-centric perspective. We also need a theoretical perspective to account for making in its sociopolitical and technomaterial complexities. We draw from a body of work in global anthropology. Specifically, we use the concept of "global assemblages" [58], which refers to a conceptual approach to understanding and accounting for emerging "material, collective, and discursive relationships" that are articulated as global forms [58]. Examples of such forms, as collected in [58], include organ selling, bond trading, and DNA self-testing; to which list we would add making, as we explain in what follows below. These forms of life are global in the sense that they move across cultural situations (*e.g.,* stem cell research as a global practice), and yet they are also locally enacted and performed (*e.g.*, stem cell research in the US is legally and politically constrained in ways that such research is not elsewhere).

Key to this approach is the concept of "assemblage," which according to [58] "is the product of multiple determinations that are not reducible to a single logic. The temporality of the assemblage is emergent.... As a composite concept, the term '*global* assemblage' suggests inherent tensions: global implies broadly encompassing, seamless, and mobile; assemblage implies heterogeneous, contingent, unstable, partial, and situated" (12, emphasis in original). In summary, global assemblages are emergent and heterogeneously composed forms of life situated both in local and global practices, materials, and discourses. Such an understanding counters the abstract and structural notion of a global universal, replacing the latter with concrete little histories of situated forms of life as they participate in, are shaped by, and also do not relate to "the global."

Making, we argue, is such a global assemblage. In other words, we do not see a single maker movement as a global universal with local instances. Rather, we examine in this paper specific "ensembles of heterogeneous elements – the assemblages" [58] through which making and its significance is articulated and practiced. This becomes evident in the following two ways.

First, maker groups are spread across the globe, view themselves as part of a global movement, and articulate values and practices using global networks, from wikis to globally disseminated maker franchises such as FabLab. Part of this phenomenon is the dissemination of ideas (*e.g.*, "everyone can be a maker" and "making is a whole new paradigm of IT innovation"), which when widely disseminated, become global ideas that are interpreted and put into action in diverse ways in particular sites and situations.

Second, making is linked to global capital, though its flows are socially, institutionally, and technologically concentrated in contingent ways. For instance, making as start-up culture has in part proliferated because of new channels such as crowdfunding, which remains predominantly accessible to a fairly elite network of technologists [2, 19]. Making also can't be divorced from broader "techno-capitalist" processes such as the utilization of (free) user participation and open innovation as business model, *e.g.*, companies that remained open source long enough to build up a robust product and user base and then switched to a proprietary model, *e.g.,* MakerBot and 3DRobotics [20,25,47]. Making is simultaneously a symptom and a transformation of global processes of capitalism: while making feeds off of existing structures of power, it is also aimed at and specifically motivated by democratizing technology production.

The "maker movement" is often presented as a global universal, applying equally to Silicon Valley, Taipei, Changsha, and Windhoek. Ong and Collier's [58] approach to "global assemblages" provides a means to problematize such a view by investigating the "petit recits" of particular locales as these ideas come into contact with praxis. This approach reveals that global practices such as making do not fit under a single definition but are better understood as sharing family resemblances. In perceiving the resemblances, we can construct an account of the global form. But in perceiving the variations, which resist or fail to fit the unifying narrative, we can find alternative practices and potentials. In other words, viewing making as global assemblages gives us the methodological and epistemological tools to account for heterogeneous aspects of making without losing sight of the fact that they are all "making." The global assemblages approach provides tools to expand prior research with a reflexive program for the study of global processes of technology, *e.g.*, [23,24,36,47,61,72,79], avoiding the binary between universals like globalization or innovation on the one hand and place-based struggles on the other. Instead, global assemblages replace the global universal with "petit recits" of situated forms of life through which the global is produced. We now continue by unpacking how the making practices we observed in China and Taiwan unfolded as global assemblages.

Making in China as Global Assemblages

Making as global assemblage in China figures in the following key ways: 1) aspirations to position making, and with it China, as a key site in global networks of technology innovation and on par with Western innovation hubs like Silicon Valley; and 2) a wave of entrepreneurs, who turn their maker visions into commercial products by engaging with manufacturing in the South of China. We now articulate how these two aspects of making as global assemblages come to the fore in China.

In 2012, China witnessed its first international maker event; the Maker Carnival. Since around 2010, a steadily growing number of open source hardware enthusiasts had come together across a variety of Chinese cities. They had opened up maker and hackerspaces, organized local workshops and events, and written about their open source hardware projects online. The 2012 Maker Carnival was intended not only to bring together makers from various places in China, but also to help legitimize and generate visibility for their efforts in international maker circles. The organizers, a group of makers in China, considered the event a success: while the Maker Carnival did not generate profit (on the contrary, its organizers contributed personal funds to make it happen), the event triggered significant international visibility. Mitch Altman, a key figure in the American hackerspace scene, gave one of the keynote lectures, and 28 foreign makers received stipends to attend the event. The Maker Carnival was the first of many maker-related events to follow, culminating in two featured Maker Faires in Shenzhen in 2014 and 2015, drawing significant investment from the Chinese government and from international corporations such as Intel, Qualcom, Microsoft, and Arduino.

Over the years, through maker events and the efforts of a continuously growing number of hackerspaces [46,48,50], China's makers have carefully crafted a particular kind of image of making in China in relation to what many imagine to be a *global* maker movement. For instance, two of China's most prominent open source hardware companies, Seeed Studio and DFRobot, sell the majority of their products and services to individual makers, start-ups, educational entities and hackerspaces in North America and Europe. Similarly, prominent hardware incubator programs like HAXLR8R and Highway1, while leveraging the manufacturing ecosystem of the city of Shenzhen [47,49], are backed by European Venture Capitalists, and operate through a powerful network of start-ups, media relations, venture capitalists, and big corporates, many of which have ties into Silicon Valley. Alongside foreign venture capitalists, Western tech media have joined in to promote Shenzhen as the new "Silicon Valley for Hardware," *e.g.,* [4,13, 78]. In this imaginary of a global future, regions like Shenzhen are portrayed as being modernized by the intercessions of ideas or practices of (predominantly Western) venture capitalists, entrepreneurs, and designers, who move the region from "copycat culture to innovation" [78]. But this story of China's transformation from "backwards" copy to "international" innovation culture is problematic, which Shenzhen's roots in alternative (not-Western centric) global assemblages make immediately visible. Let us briefly elaborate.

As a special economic zone, Shenzhen was a key region during the West's outsourcing boom [47] (see [56,57] for a detailed account of Shenzhen's urbanization). Since the 1980s, many electronics manufacturing companies had set up shop in Shenzhen, the most well-known being the Taiwanese companies Foxconn and HTC [33,52]. From the Apple iPhone to the Tablet sold at Wal-Mart, Shenzhen had become a key site in global end-consumer electronics production. However, over the last 20 years, the region has not only produced computers and mobile devices commissioned by corporations such as Apple, Nokia and HP, but has also begun develop its own lines of products, shipped to markets that had remained largely untapped by international tech firms: populations in Africa, India, Asia, South America unable to access and/or afford the international brands. This manufacturing practice is often described as *shanzhai* (山寨) in Chinese, referring to a network of some thousand factories in the South of China, whose open sharing practices have enabled them to become competitive in global markets [47]. The global assemblages of *shanzhai* production extend beyond the more familiar China-US-Europe triangle, and include other regions typically not associated with global tech innovation and original design.

In their theory of global assemblages, Ong and Collier suggest staying close to the practices that "rearticulate and reassemble material, technical and discursive elements in the process of remaking particular contexts" [58]. Following this approach, we account here for the ways in which aspirations of China's makers play out in both their material engagements with and their discursive construction of Shenzhen and *shanzhai*. China's makers position China's history and culture of manufacturing, especially as lived and practiced through *shanzhai*, key to the ideals of the maker movement; only if the global maker movement (and with it the West) took seriously Chinese manufacturing as equal partner in IT design and innovation, will the maker movement be able to accomplish its ideal to truly democratize technology production [46].

Making Assemblages in Taiwan

The maker scene in Taiwan reflects its present political situation. Taiwan evolved to a multiparty democratic government in the 1980s and 90s. Taiwan's young democracy is situated in a complex history. The island itself was originally peopled by aboriginals, but beginning in the 17th century saw immigrants from nearby China come to the island as well as a succession of foreign rulers: the Dutch, Spanish, Chinese, and Japanese all occupied Taiwan from the 17th century through the 1940s. In 1949, the government of the Republic of China (ROC), having lost the Chinese Civil War to the communists, relocated to Taiwan. Today, citizens of Taiwan are politically divided between those seeking eventual reunion with China and those who wish to declare independence from China, though all view Taiwan/ROC as a sovereign nation. For its part, China considers Taiwan a renegade province and has made credible threats to invade it, if Taiwan does not submit to PRC rule.

In short, Taiwan has an ongoing project of self-identity—ROC vs. Taiwan, Chinese vs. Taiwanese, nation vs. province. But this project has urgency; people of Taiwan feel threatened that their way of life could disappear. This includes the threats of the destruction of their liberal democracy by a Chinese invasion, Taiwan's fading influence as it is politically and economically isolated from the rest of the world, internal divisions between a Chinese- vs. Taiwanese-identifying electorate, and the threat of distinctively Taiwanese ways of life, rituals, and craft traditions dying out in the age of global entertainment media. Taiwan's maker movement views the democratizing of making as a resource for pursuing the very existence of this society; that is, the democratization of computing in Taiwan is a proxy for a larger conversation about Taiwan itself.

Making is enmeshed in Taiwan's creative and cultural industry policy. This policy seeks to build on the economic significance of professionals operating in the overlapping creative (*e.g.*, design, computing, advertising, media, *etc.*) and cultural (*e.g.*, tourism, heritage, parks and recreation, museum, *etc.*) industries. In Taiwan, as in many other places pursuing such policies, the goals are not merely economic but they are also part of the project of forging a national identity. The policy seeks to construct a vision of Taiwanese culture that can drive the economy and also identify Taiwanese styles and products globally. It does so first by identifying distinctively Taiwanese creative industries (*e.g.*, traditional Taiwanese crafters) and also industries where Taiwan is particularly strong (*e.g.*, computer science and engineering); then this policy seeks to experimentally fuse these industries, in an attempt to cross-pollinate their respective strengths. For example, the government has hired design firms to engage with crafters in hopes of transitioning crafts to exportable products [9]. More recently, it is supporting the maker movement as it combines fabrication, design, art, entrepreneurship, and hacking. In March 2015, the former Air Force Command Headquarters in Taipei City was transformed into a world-class "TAF [Taiwan Air Force] Innovation Base," a co-working space for making-enabled entrepreneurship with substantial technical and economic support. However, the movement itself offers distinctly different visions for making's role in Taiwan's society, which we articulate through examples.

Taiwanese "puppet opera" (布袋戲) was originally a popular form of street theater. This 200-year-old tradition can be seen everywhere in Taiwan, in streets and festivals, government-sponsored cultural events, and in popular media. A typical performance includes elaborately decorated traditional stage, stylized performance techniques, and handcrafted wooden puppets. Puppeteers undergo extensive apprenticeships in both performance and fabrication. Chen Bo-Jian (陳伯健) is a master in this tradition, and he is also well known in the Taipei maker scene. He has collaborated with FabLab Taipei, OpenLab Taipei and other maker groups to use 3D printing, laser cutting, and other emerging technologies to transform and update the painstaking fabrication of puppet opera stages and puppets, combining traditional techniques and materials with new ones.

Chen also uses this work to make a strong political statement. In public presentations and interviews, Chen argues that "culture and creativity industry must exist to be in service of Taiwanese tradition, not the other way around." Chen is not arguing against an entrepreneurial vision of making in favor of a hobbyist vision in which makers should be free to do what they like. He is more specifically rejecting the notion, pursued by the government through its creative and cultural industries policy, that Taiwanese arts, crafts, styles, and rituals should be pursued for their market potential. He argues instead that Taiwanese ways of life themselves are the highest goods, and that economic development is a tool to support them. His political enemy is not an external threat, such as that of the Chinese military, but an internal threat: the subjection of Taiwanese ways of life to global capitalism by well-intentioned bureaucrats. Chen's political position is common among many (but not all) of the maker spaces in Taipei. They view the rise of making as an opportunity to perpetuate distinctively Taiwanese forms of life into the future, and for such a project to be successful, making has to become a widespread cultural practice. This view provides a substantive basis for specific educational reform proposals, in which educational institutions are tasked with disseminating the Taiwanese cultural practice of making, as it disseminates Taiwan's history, language and literature, and everyday skills such as arithmetic, writing, and civic participation.

Yet an alternative position is also prevalent in the Taipei maker scene. This view emphasizes making as key to innovation and entrepreneurship. For example, Taiwan's government has sponsored making-related innovation competitions, hackathons, and co-working spaces with the goal of cultivating the next generation of IT professionals. The government also supports major local, regional, and Asia-Pacific conferences such as COSCUP (Conference for Open Source Coders, Users and Promoters) and the FabLab Asia Network Conference 2015, which featured participation from over 80 labs located in 20 Asia-Pacific nations.

In this spirit, Taipei maker communities MakerPro and FutureWard focus on the economic potentials of making. Both MakerPro and FutureWard are supported in part by government funding, work closely with city and national government agencies, and are well positioned to execute the agenda of the creative and cultural industries policy. MakerPro focuses on maker-to-entrepreneur pathways, providing workshops, consulting, and networking opportunities. FutureWard operates on a membership dues model, but its

1,000m^2 facility is physically located on the campus of Ta-Tung University in central Taipei, and students use its facilities as part of their coursework. Interestingly, FutureWard also hosted a week-long hands-on workshop for a couple dozen employees of the Labor Department within the Taipei City Government in 2015, the purpose of which was to educate government employees about making.

The two ideologies of making outlined here—the culture and the economic framings—are often articulated by makers as though they are in opposition. For example, OpenLab Taipei aligns itself with artistic maker practices and argues against making as a form of entrepreneurship; informants at places like MakerPro and FutureWard stress the need to realize making's economic potential. These conflicting visions of making are reflected in a hotly contested debate between two translations for "maker": 自造者 vs. 創客. Both terms translate as "maker" but they have very different connotations. The first aligns itself with notions of the self-made, while the latter has strong connotations of entrepreneurship. Puppet master Chen uses the former, while the latter is common at MakerPro and FutureWard. Makers in different spaces use these different formulations both to articulate their individual identities and also affiliation with a normative stance about what making in Taiwan should be.

These two formulations of making are strongly and frequently asserted. But we noticed in our ethnographic work that clear ideological lines are blurrier in practice. For example, the same individuals who sharply criticize government policies—to the point of joining in major public demonstrations against them—nonetheless collaborate in spaces that are government subsidized; they collaborate with government officials; they participate as judges in government-sponsored competitions; they show up to and work in spaces with an entrepreneurial focus. It is also a credit to these government officials that they financially and professionally support makers who are publicly criticizing them. In short, there appears to be a sense of a shared enterprise, but exactly what it is, and how it should be prioritized and perpetuated, is being actively and openly debated in a democratic way.

In their theory of global assemblages, Ong and Collier [58] stress the inability to reduce assemblages to a single logic, and we see that at work in the Taipei maker scene. Taiwan's take on creative and cultural industries helps explain this in part. All of the diverse maker sites are instances of the global "maker movement" in their (flexible) deployment of maker technologies, tools, ethos, recruitment methods, self-presentation tactics, sanctioned maker identities, and so on. Additionally, they all make credible arguments that they are operating broadly within objectives, principles, and values of the culture and creative industries policy, because they promote distinctively Taiwanese practices, styles, materials, and traditions (common practices at OpenLab and FabLab) and/or they contribute to Taiwan's engineering and IT culture (common practices at MakerPro and FutureWard). Many makers vocally disagree with the specific ways that the policy (in their view) subordinates cultural ends to economic ones, rather than the other way around. Others criticize the artistic crowd of failing to make a real impact (often understood in market terms). The government appears to be willing to let both sides hold this debate and support them in diverse ways.

MOVE 2: ANTICIPATORY DESIGN

We now turn to our second move, *anticipatory design*, in which fragmentary images—in our case, images of making from our empirical work—are used in a way analogous to how an archaeologist reconstructs past cultures from fragments of pots and houses left behind: to creatively and speculatively imagine the wholes that these fragments were part of. The difference is that whereas the archaeologist is attempting to construct a holistic understanding of an actual culture in the past, in this anticipatory design practice the holistic understanding is of a world not yet existing, but potentially worth pursuing. The anticipatory design practice is a method to study forms of life to discover and build on the glimmers of the utopian in them, however partial or imperfect they may be. These glimmers are then brought forward to form actionable aspirations and alternatives. Importantly, anticipatory design is not about assessing if a utopian project meets or fails to meet the standards of utopianism. Instead, feminist utopian sociologist Ruth Levitas writes of anticipatory design that it proposes "provisional hypotheses about how society might be" which are not intended as forecasts, but rather as invitations to "both writer and reader to imagine themselves, as well as the world, otherwise," initially considered with "a suspension of disbelief" [45].

Applied to HCI's relationship to making, anticipatory design can support intervention within making to bring about participation and democracy in technology use and design. In this paper, we apply anticipatory design to our analysis of making as global assemblages, precisely to uncover concrete and specific moments where technology appears to have been deployed, however provisionally or temporarily, in a utopian way. In collecting these moments, our goal is to contribute towards realizing the democratic potential of making, in which the empirical present is articulated as a vision of how it can be otherwise. We align our approach with work by Introna and Nissenbaum [38], pushing technology towards more democratic outcomes. In the following pages, we use this approach to draw out utopian glimmers from our ethnographic research in China and Taiwan.

Utopian Glimmers in China

What started out with a single hackerspace in Shanghai in 2010 morphed into a complex sociopolitical project of "mass making" that spans industries and regions today: China currently is estimated to have more than 1,000 maker spaces, and a new national policy entitled "mass makerspace" (众创空间) that enrolls making into a much larger social, economic, and educational program aimed at transforming China from a manufacturing to a global knowledge economy. Within only 5 years, making in China has become part of a national policy and attracts foreign investment. Intel has invested millions of USD in the South of China to support China's "mass makerspace" initiative, and hundreds of makers-turned entrepreneurs from across the globe have traveled to China to realize their commercial Internet of Things product visions by partnering with local factories [47].

Much like elsewhere though, these activities started out much earlier, in part driven by the efforts of a few idealists [46,50], an eclectic collective of artists, social entrepreneurs, open source hardware geeks, and bloggers, active since 2007 and operating within tech companies, coworking spaces, makerspaces, and non-for profit organizations in China. Their underlying rationale was that by adopting the principles and values of the free culture movement, China's society as a whole could be opened up so to enable individuals to explore alternative life- and workstyles, different from what the government or their parents' generation had set out for them [46,50].

A sense of euphoria was central to these early projects; many believed that the values associated with the free culture movement such as open source, peer production, and collaboration would lead to both individual and collective freedom, civic engagement, and economic transformation. It was a utopian project that coincided with the rise of Chinese social media such as Sina Weibo, celebrated as enablers of digital democracy and the birth of a new liberated citizen – the netizen (网民) [51, 80]. China was on the upswing; with a rapidly swelling economy, it seemed almost immune to the 2008 economic crash. It was an enticing moment documented by China's tech enthusiasts, international journalists and scholars alike [53].

Fast forward to 2015; the Chinese economy is witnessing a major slow-down with ripple effects in the global economy and stock market. Earlier visions of open sharing are now packaged under the banner of "mass innovation" or "mass making," promoted by the government as the crux to get the economy back on track by turning citizens into entrepreneurs, innovators, and makers. On first glance, the counterculture from 2007 appears co-opted by capitalism with Chinese characteristics. Since President Xi Jinping took over office in 2012, arrests and central control over media outlets and digital media have reportedly increased [59, 78], while start-up culture and venture capital investment are encouraged in ways comparable to the West [11, 30, 55].

And yet, to portray China's maker scene as a story of coopted counterculture would render invisible earlier and continuous efforts by China's makers to situate their work, neither outright against nor for the system [50]. A story of co-option would run the risk to critique these efforts, utopian they might be, as elitist or technologically deterministic. Our goal here, then, is to intervene and amplify the glimpses and moments of alternatives we observed in China's maker culture, rather than shut them down. Here we deploy the utopian anticipatory design move to seek the materials of a preferable future in fragmentary form in the present.

Open Source & Partnership

In 2007, Ricky Ye (叶琛) returned to Shanghai from graduate school in England, where he had begun working on an open source robotics project with a group of fellow enthusiasts distributed across Europe and China. Upon his return to China, Ye continued the work and began showcasing some of the early DIY robotics hacks in the Shanghai coworking space XinDanWei (新单位), which was at that time an important meeting spot for advocates of the free culture movement in China. Today, Ricky Ye is the CEO of one of China's most well-known open source hardware businesses: DFRobot. In some ways, DFRobot might be reminiscent of a typical Silicon Valley start-up success story. And yet, the ways DFRobot began and continues its operations offer an open source business model that differs from the more widespread Silicon Valley approach of creationist capitalism [11]; DFRobot's business model is structured around enabling hobbyist roboticists, newcomers to making as well as aspiring hardware start-ups to either expand their prototyping skills and/or move into professional product development. The business is rooted in a model of partnership: DFRobot offers expertise in design for manufacturing, prototyping, and engineering, while hobbyist makers offer a continuous stream of ideas. Start-ups and hobbyists can build on the company's open source hardware platforms, working with its designers and engineers to improve and expand both hardware and ideas. If one side decides to move into production, the revenue is shared.

This model of partnership, which might be better characterized as peer-entrepreneurship than peer production, is fundamentally different from the much more widespread tendency to exploit participants in technology production as contributors of free labor [11, 73]. This includes business models of prominent social media sites like Facebook, mining online behavior to sell it back its users in the form of advertisement, but also newer companies like MakerBot, which has productively leveraged its online community of enthusiastic contributors in order to gain reputation, free contributions and eventually economic value. In a 2014 keynote at the first featured Maker Faire in Shenzhen, Chris Anderson, former editor of *Wired* Magazine and now CEO of 3DRobotics articulated this business model as follows: "This is really the main asset of the maker movement… it creates a community of enthusiastic people who share for free. Our company has hundreds of developers around the world, who we don't have to pay or to hire, because we have created a place where they can feel part of something… how do we reward them? We teach them. How do we pay them? With a coffee mug! If they commit code, we give them a t-shirt. They love that, because it's an official recognition of their contribution." Open source, here, is rendered as a business model that rests on low-paid or even free labor. It recalls what Gina Neff [55] has termed "venture labor" where people began to "think of their jobs as an investment or as having a future pay-off other than regular wages." Similarly, here, Anderson bets on the fact that "hundreds of developers around the world" are offering their know-how and expertise in exchange for "feeling part of something."

DFRobot offers an alternative. It is not a big step or a revolutionary program. It is a pragmatic business model, aimed at making revenue and not at overthrowing existing structures of state control or the global processes of capitalism. It also remains a fairly exclusive project; reserved to those who can afford to traverse in international start-up land or engage in hobbyist production. It is not a revolutionary tool for the masses of workers on the factory floor. And yet, its underlying business tactic is exactly what makes it an alternative worth exploring; in contrast to companies like MakerBot, DFRobot demonstrates that open source hardware can be part of a successful business model. It is a hint of utopia practiced within (not against) a capitalist mode. DFRobot's business model firmly incorporates the ideals of many open source hardware enthusiasts – peer production and open sharing of knowledge, code and other resources – extending them into business: the sharing of profit and revenue or peer-entrepreneurship. We do not mean to imply, here, that DFRobot stands for some kind of authentic Chinese utopianism that would be intrinsically better than projects in the US or elsewhere. Rather, DFRobot's story allows us to show how a utopian alternative materialized as an economic model in a place typically associated with tight state control and authoritarianism. The DFRobot case, in other words, makes visible what Suchman has called "the multiplicity of places in which different but also potentially related future-making practices occur" [Suchman in: 25].

With this account from China, we aim to offer two particular take-aways: First, the opportunity of peer-entrepreneurship. We have outlined earlier in this paper that China's makers (like those working at DFRobot) reframe Chinese manufacturing in the global imaginary as a partner in both design and production. The tagline of China's first featured Maker Faire in 2014, for instance, was "Innovate with China," used to demonstrate that Chinese manufacturing can mean something else than copycat or low quality production. The business model of DFRobot is organized around this ambition to position manufacturing as partner in innovation. A possible stance that follows for HCI is to envision ways to engage in such partnerships during research and design. HCI has a long tradition of partnering with industry; however, this involves mostly large international corporations such as Microsoft, IBM, Intel, Nokia, and so on. What would a partnership look like with a small open source hardware business like DFRobot? Possible outcomes could include the developing of open hardware platforms for education and design research, and the ideation of alternative economic models that might also be taken up by larger corporations and educational institutions. Thinking about research impact in terms of business and market has been explored peripherally in HCI, but becomes pressing as HCI visions and approaches from participatory design to ubiquitous computing are commodified [5].

Second, DFRobot shows that innovative forms of entrepreneurship within a capitalist framework do not have to be antithetical to critical intervention. This observation extends a body of work in HCI that has challenged the sharp distinction between critical design and affirmative design [6]. Looking for moments of critical intervention in entrepreneurship can be productive for HCI to expand its critical scholarship beyond the confined circles of people who can afford attend conferences like ACM CHI.

Utopian Glimmers in the Taipei Maker Scene

In its many makerspaces, with free or inexpensive access to cutting edge tools and skilled communities to support their use, Taiwan replicates one of the major democratizing tactics of the global maker movement. What makes it specifically Taiwanese? Taiwan in general, and in its maker scene, is engaged in a kind of dialectic. On the one hand is the threat to its existence as an autonomous nation-state—hardly a utopian source—which has the silver lining of creating solidarity among Taiwan's people in spite of their other divisions: a solidarity that is committed to its democratic way of life, to presenting a coherent picture of itself to the rest of the world, and to perpetuating all of the above in future generations. On the other hand is its internal heterogeneity and divisions, the bitter debates concerning its relationship with China, whether people are "Taiwanese" or "Chinese from Taiwan," whether the history of China or the island of Taiwan should be taught in schools, and so forth.

The meaning of making is among other things a proxy conversation for this dialectic. Makers are thrown together as a community by the global maker movement, including its organizational, technical, and ideological apparatuses. Taipei's makers are eager to convince others of the potentials of making, but they are also divided about what those potentials are. Is making a life skill through which one enacts and perpetuates cultural citizenship? Is it a professional skill through which one contributes to the national economy? Can making contribute to the commodification of Taiwan as a style or brand in the global marketplace or encourage tourism? Common to all of these questions is a focus on collective, rather than individual, interest. We saw no evidence of making pitched as a way for an individual to "get ahead" or to expressing oneself creatively. The collective tended not to be framed in terms of fellow makers, either, but of all Taiwan, present and future. Again, we believe that collective interest may have something to do with the sense of threat shared by Taiwan's citizens, and perhaps more broadly by collectivist tendencies in Asian culture. Regardless, *making is pursued in Taiwan as a technology of the national self*, as a collection of national self-making techniques organized by a social vision.

But it is also important to stress the democratic nature of this process. There is no authority in charge of making in Taiwan, no one institution that has the power to decide how it unfolds. The makers see themselves as ambassadors of the global maker movement, but as we have seen they offer different interpretations of its significances and potentials for Taiwan. Both national and city governments also have an interest in making, because of its potentials for creative and cultural industries, which they are eager to promote. Policymakers have framed this policy in more market-driven terms than many of makers like. Yet the government has supported strands of making that would seem to yield little hope of impact on strictly market terms. Taipei seems to be testing, through trial and variation, many forms and ideologies of making to see which ones stick.

One of our informants, an entrepreneur born in Hong Kong who earned graduate design degrees at an Ivy League university before returning to Asia, told us that he decided to open up his making consultancy and design business in Taipei, rather than Hong Kong, Shanghai, or Shenzhen for two reasons: he felt that Taiwanese engineers were inexpensive relative to their ability, and that Taiwan was the only free Chinese society in the world. This combination was promising, he said, because it meant that high quality startups would be less expensive in Taipei than elsewhere, and because the freedoms of a democratic society meant that their creativity would be unfettered. For this entrepreneur, Taiwan's freedom is not merely a political ideal; it serves in an epistemic capacity, as a condition of possibility for heightened creative practice.

Taiwan's maker scene is functioning today as a workshop for discovering ways that a democratized technology can contribute to a social vision of a lasting, self-sufficient, and sovereign society, yet divided, even extremely divided, on what that vision should entail and how to bring it into being. A key mechanism of this project—in whichever of its many forms it is construed—is that the democratization of technology via making is seen as a national need. We never heard in Taiwan, as we have in the U.S., the relatively passive approach to recruiting participation in making, "our doors are open and everyone is welcome." Instead, there are diverse tactics of taking making to the public: by placing it in a university and requiring students to use it; putting maker tools and kits on 500 trucks and driving them out to rural communities in Taiwan [75]; inviting the public to free workshops on entrepreneurship; updating and reinvigorating everyday Taiwanese cultural practices, such as puppet opera, via making; bringing in policy makers to makerspaces and teaching them to make; and by the government publicly embracing and supporting conflicting forms and ideologies of making, even when those very makers take to the streets to attack those same policies.

The utopian glimmer is our amplification of the point that the Hong Kong-based entrepreneur raised: the idea that democracy can serve in an epistemic capacity to intensify creative potential at scale. Specifically, we see the union of the cultural value of *collectivism* merging productively with the democratic value of policy supportive of and also informed by *robust debate*. The debate allows for the proliferation of alternative visions and models of making and maker practices, as we saw in the debate between making as cultural work vs. making as entrepreneurial work. The collectivism orients making towards a common good, rather than an individual good; in other words, the development of distinctively Taiwanese practices of making is oriented towards a national future—be it economic, pedagogical, or cultural. Meanwhile, government agencies do not sit on the sidelines but actively participate, both materially and symbolically supporting divergent maker groups and ideologies, even as they make their own priorities known (e.g., to stimulate economic growth and to promote Taiwan's creative and cultural life). We thus understand democracy serving in an epistemic capacity to support collective creativity at scale in the context of Taiwanese making as follows: it entails a model that robustly allows for heterogeneous experiments in peer-based innovation, which both influences and is influenced by government agencies, and which contributes towards an evolving conception of the public good.

DISCUSSION

This paper began with the articulation of one of making's central commitments – the democratization of technology production. Making gives new appeal to HCI's own long-held values and commitments to user participation; making challenges whether there is (or needs to be) a gap between designers and engineers on the one hand, and between designers and end users on the other. Making also raises questions about computing itself. It challenges the long-standard view that end users manipulate software but not hardware. Making and HCI, in other words, are not separate phenomena but instead mutually implicated. And yet, while HCI has pursued making as an avenue to increase participation, HCI research has also critiqued that there is an underlying technosolutionism to making, *i.e.* technology is seen as solution for social, economic and political problems. One feature of the technosolutionist vision is that it tends to treat making as an undifferentiated global form. Such a reduction abstracts out the local work in diverse sites. Following anthropologists of the global, we have argued that it is in the specific instances of global forms where possibilities of making are developed and realized.

Throughout the paper, we have articulated preferable futures, rooted in a critique of the present, to offer a way out of the dilemma of HCI as it both contributes to and critiques making's utopian vision. We now return to the question we posed up front: Could we blend the contributions of technologists who are opening up making to new uses and users with the contributions of critical voices to pursue the democratization of making as an equally sociotechnical research practice? What we have hopefully demonstrated throughout this paper is that the answer to this question is yes, but it demands a reflexive-interventionist move, which we characterize as "democratizing from within."

HCI: Democratizing from within

As scientists, we HCI researchers often view ourselves as outside observers of computational domains of interest. Such a view is disadvantageous not only because it does not acknowledge our own participation in such domains—via the development of tools, the framing of research issues, and the marshaling of resources—but it is also self-disempowering. HCI researchers share in many ways making's utopian vision to democratize technology. This, we believe, creates an opportunity and obligation to pursue the democratization of maker assemblages and do so through approaches we outlined in this paper – a critique of the present and anticipatory design. In many obvious ways, we already do this. When HCI technologists develop a new tool to support making, we introduce at least the potentiality for the democratic uptake of that tool. When HCI social scientists help us understand a collaborative behavior, such that we can better support it, we introduce at least the potentiality for democratic empowerment. But there are more subtle ways that we do (or at least could). In naming and framing making as an object of inquiry, we ourselves end up resourcing, judging, championing, inhibiting (and so forth) making. When we understand the projects and materials that appear in *MAKE Magazine* or at Maker Faires as exemplars of making, this is not an innocent description. When we justify making research because it stimulates economies or functions as a crowdsourced laboratory of the Internet of Things, this is not an innocent description. In each case we are contributing to the discursive formulation—and to the assemblaging—of making. This is a form of agency, of power/knowledge [27], that we have.

If we view ourselves as implicated in global assemblages of making, what power does that grant us as actors to contribute towards the democratization of computing? We argue that it might inhere in our field's ability to engage technologies and situated actions at the same time, *i.e.*, to perceive how technologies do and do not democratize. Put another way, a given technology or social formation can be directed towards more versus less democratic outcomes. We need a stance, then, that acknowledges and augments our agency to push towards more rather than less democratic outcomes.

Making inevitably poses opportunities and challenges for the democratization of computing. If technologies are expensive, difficult to use, or if their functionalities or aesthetics speak to some ways of life more than others, they can inhibit widespread use. It was Leah Buechley's insight that Arduino seemed to resonate with men more than women, and she sought to redesign it in a way that would resonate more with women [14]. But this is not just a technological issue. If individuals cannot see themselves in an existing collective, they will not join it. If laws make certain forms of making difficult or impossible, they also affect who makes, and what they make [61]. Clearly the mantra "everyone can be a maker" is optimistic—certain kinds of makers and making are encouraged or discouraged based on the spaces, ecologies, networks, and discourses in which making is construed as a reflexive practice.

In this last point there is a role for HCI researchers: to leverage our empirical accounts of maker practices in a utopian analysis to identify those specific and situated democratizing forms and bring them back into the global conversation. In this paper, we showed how making in China can thrive using labor partnerships instead of exploitative labor relations, and can, despite its business-focus, also pursue and achieve critical outcomes. As we showed in Taiwan, making can be democratically debated and diversely pursued without becoming so individualistic that it loses its political capacity to democratize technology as part of a more ambitious social project. Taken together, these two maker scenes demonstrate that the democratizing potential of making can occur not only by empowering individuals (*i.e.*, as often articulated in the West), but also by empowering collectives—maker groups, entire cities, even nations—to pursue their collective goals in and through making.

What is needed, then, in research on making is a reflexive-interventionist stance, if HCI is to pursue the democratization of technology in a sociotechnical way. In its reflexivity, it seeks to account for, and be accountable to, our positions as actors in the computing arenas we research and design for. In its interventionism, it seeks to give substance and new resources to the pursuit of democratization beyond technosolutionism. In our practice, we have sought to decenter our own HCI theoretical predispositions as Western academics by engaging in making praxis in Shenzhen and Taipei. We have sought to acknowledge and celebrate the technological achievements that have created so much potential to empower people to design hardware. But we have sought also to understand the sociopolitical, legal, national, urban, and ideological contexts in which these technologies are deployed, to reveal in them glimmers of democratization that are not part of the global currency. Out of those glimmers, we seek to fashion new practices, models, technologies that could be used to augment and amplify their democratizing potentials.

ACKNOWLEDGMENTS

We thank all of our participants, as well as Morgan Ames, Seyram Avle, Marissa Cohen, Jean Hardy, Cindy Lin, Stefanie Wuschitz for comments on drafts. We also thank long-term research collaborators and commentators Paul Dourish, Ingrid Fischer-Schreiber, Anna Greenspan, Ted Hung, Lyn Jeffery, David Li, Pei-Ying Lin, C.H. (Mach) Ma, Eric Pan, Ricky Ye, 陳伯健, 何偉光, 歐敏銓, 楊育修, and 鄭鴻旗. This work was supported in part by the National Science Foundation under awards 1513596, 1321065, and 1513604, the Lieberthal-Rogel Center for Chinese Studies, the Intel Science and Technology Center for Social Computing, and Participatory Information Technology (PIT) at Aarhus University.

REFERENCES

1. Morgan G. Ames, Daniela K. Rosner and Ingrid Erickson. 2015. Worship, Faith, and Evangelism: Religion as an Ideological Lens for Engineering Worlds. In Proceedings of the 18th ACM Conference on Computer Supported Cooperative Work & Social Computing, CSCW'15, pp. 69-81.
2. Morgan Ames, Jeffrey Bardzell, Shaowen Bardzell, Silvia Lindtner, David Mellis, and Daniela Rosner. 2014. Making Cultures: Empowerment, Participation, and Democracy - or Not? *In Proc. Panel at CHI'14*, ACM Press (2014), pp. 1087-1092.
3. Chris Anderson. 2012. Makers. The New Industrial Revolution. Crown Publishing Group, New York.
4. Zachary Bako. 2015. How a Nation of Tech Copycats transformed into a Hub for Innovation. Wired Magazine. http://www.wired.com/2015/12/tech-innovation-in-china/, last accessed Jan 3, 2016.
5. Liam Bannon and Pelle Ehn. 2012. Design Matters in Participatory Design. In: J. Simonsen and T. Robertson (eds) Routledge Handbook of Participatory Design, pp. 37-63.
6. Jeffrey Bardzell and Shaowen Bardzell. 2013. What is "critical" about critical design? In Proc. of CHI'2013. ACM: New York.
7. Jeffrey Bardzell, Shaowen Bardzell, and Austin Toombs. 2014. "Now that's definitely a proper hack": Self-made tools in hackerspaces. In Proc. of CHI'2014. ACM: New York
8. Shaowen Bardzell. 2015. Utopian Design. In Reconceptualizing Critical Utopia panel at Aarhus 2015, the Decennial Conference on Critical Alternatives. Aarhus, Denmark.
9. Shaowen Bardzell. 2014. Utopias of Participation: Design, Criticality, and Emancipation. Keynote address at the 2014 Participatory Design Conference. In Windhoek, Namibia.
10. Shaowen Bardzell, Daniela Rosner, and Jeffrey Bardzell. 2012. Crafting quality in design: Integrity, creativity, and public sensibility. In Proc. of the Designing Interactive Systems Conference, DIS 2012. ACM: New York, pp. 11-20.
11. Tom Boellstorff. 2008. The coming of age in Second Life: an anthropologist explores the virtually human. Princeton University Press.
12. Seyla Benhabib. 1992. Situating the Self: Gender, Community, and Postmodernism in Contemporary Ethics. Routledge: New York.
13. Gareth Branwyn. 2015. An Insider's Guide to Shenzhen Manufacturing. Makezine. http://makezine.com/2015/06/15/making-in-shenzhen/ last accessed September 2015.
14. Leah Buechley and Benjamin Mako Hill. 2010. LilyPad in the wild: How hardware's long tail is supporting new engineering and design communities. In Proceedings of the Designing Interactive Systems Conference, DIS 2010. ACM: New York, pp. 199-207.
15. Leah Buechley, Qiu, K., and de Boer, Sonja. Sew electric: a collection of DIY projects that combine fabric, electronics, and programming. HLT Press, Cambridge, MA, USA 2013.
16. Leah Buechley and H. Perner-Wilson. 2013. Crafting Technology: Reimagining the Processes, Materials, and Cultures of Electronics. Journal ACM Transactions on Computer-Human Interaction (ToCHI), Vol 19, Issue 3, Article No. 21.
17. Anita Chan. 2014. Networking Peripheries. Technological Futures and the Myth of Digital Universalism. Cambridge, MA: MIT Press.
18. Ruy Cervantes and Bonnie Nardi. 2010. Innovating from the Global South: practices to connect local and global networks of innovation. In Proc. of ICIC'10, pp.259-262.
19. Susan Currie Sivek. 2011. "We Need a Showing of All Hands" Technological Utopianism in MAKE Magazine. Journal of Communication Inquiry 35, 3, pp. 187-209.
20. David Cuartelles. 2014. How Deep is your Love? On Open-Source Hardware. In: Making Futures. Marginal Notes on Innovation, Design and Democracy (eds Pelle Ehn, Elisabet M. Nilsson, Richard Topgaard), Cambridge, Massachusetts: MIT Press.
21. Laura Devendorf and Kimiko Ryokai. 2014. Being the machine: exploring new modes of making. In Proc. of the Designing Interactive Systems Conference, DIS'14, pp. 33-36.
22. Laura Devendorf and Daniela K. Rosner. 2015. Reimagining Digital Fabrication as Performance Art. In: Extended Abstracts of the ACM conference on Human Factors in Computing Systems (CHI'15), pp. 555-566.
23. Paul Dourish. 2006. Implications for Design. In Proceedings of the ACM SIGCHI Conference on Human Factors in Computing Systems (CHI'06), pp. 541-550.
24. Paul Dourish and Scott D. Mainwaring. 2012. Ubicomp's Colonial Impulse. In Proceedings. of UbiComp'12, Springer, pp. 133-142.
25. Pelle Ehn, Elisabet M. Nilsson, Richard Topgaard (eds). 2014. Making Futures. Marginal Notes on Innovation, Design and Democracy. Cambridge, Massachusetts: MIT Press.
26. Daniel Fiton, Janet C. Read, John Dempsey. 2015. Exploring children's designs for maker technologies. In Proc. of IDC'15, pp. 379-382.

27. Michel Foucault. (1977). *Discipline and Punish: The Birth of the Prison.* Alan Sheridan, trans. New York: Vintage Books.
28. Sarah Fox, Rachel Rose Ulgado, Daniela Rosner. 2015. Hacking Culture, not Devices: Access and Recognition in Feminist Hackerspaces. In Proc. of CSCW'15, pp. 56-68.
29. Neil Gershenfeld. 2005. Fab. The coming revolution on your desktop – from personal computers to personal fabrication. Basic Books.
30. Mel Gregg. 2011. Work's Intimacy. Cambridge: Polity.
31. Donna Haraway. 2008. When Species Meet. Minneapolis, MN: University of Minnesota Press.
32. Hartman, B., Doorley, S., Klemmer, S. Hacking, Mashing, Gluing: Understanding Opportunistic Design. IEEE Journal of Pervasive Computing, 2008, Vol. 7, No. 3, pp. 46-54.
33. Josephine Ho. 2010. *Shanzhai*: Economic/Cultural Production through the Cracks of Globalization. Crossroads: Cultural Studies Conference.
34. Jonathan Hook, Sanne Verbaan, Abigail Durrant, Patrick Olivier, Peter Wright. 2014. A study of the challenges related to DIY assistive technology in the context of children with disabilities. In Proc. of DIS'14, pp. 597-606.
35. Scott Hudson. 2014. Printing teddy bears: a technique for 3D printing of soft interactive objects. In Proceedings of the ACM SIGCHI Conference on Human Factors in Computing Systems CHI'14, pp.459-458.
36. Lilly Irani, Janet Vertesi, Paul Dourish, Kavita Philip, and Rebecca Grinter. 2010. Postcolonial Computing: A Lens on Design and Development. In Proceedings of the ACM Conf. Human Factors in Computing Systems CHI 2010 (Atlanta, GA), pp.1311-1320.
37. Lilly Irani. 2015. Hackathons and the Making of Entrepreneurial Citizenship. Science, Technology & Human Values (Sage), Vol. 40, No. 5, pp.799-824.
38. Lucas Introna and Helen Nissenbaum. 1999. Sustaining the Public Good Vision of the Internet: The Politics of Search Engines. Center for the Arts and Cultural Policy Studies, Working Paper #9, 1999, Princeton University.
39. Steve J. Jackson, Alex Pompe, and Gabriel Krieshok. 2012. Repair worlds: maintenance, repair, and ICT for development in rural Namibia. In Proc. of the ACM 2012 conference on Computer Supported Cooperative Work, pp.107-116.
40. Denisa Kera. 2010. ''Bionetworking over DNA and Online Forms of Biological Citizenship: STS and Design Perspectives.'' Genomics, Society and Policy 6 (1): 47-60.
41. Denisa Kera and Connor Graham. 2010. Collective Sensor Networks and Future Communities: Designing interaction across multiple scales. In Proc. of OZCHI'10, pp. 396-399.
42. Beth Kolko, Alexis Hope, Brook Sattler, Kate MacCorkle, Behzod Sirjani Hackademia: Building Functional Rather than Accredited Engineers. In Proc. of the Participatory Design Conference (ACM), PDC'12, pp.129-138.
43. Stacey Kuznetsov, Nathan Wilson, Scott Hudson, Carrie Doonan, Swarna Mohan, and Eric Paulos. 2015. DIYBio Things: Open Source Biology Tools as Platforms for Hybrid Knowledge Production and Scientific Participation. In Proc. of ACM SIGCHI Conference on Human Factors in Computing Systems, pp. 4065-4068.
44. Stacey Kuznetsov, Alex Taylor, Nick Villar, Time Regan, and Eric Paulos. 2012. At the Seams: DIYBio and Opportunities for HCI. In Proc. of Designing Interactive Systems (ACM), DIS'12, pp. 258-267.
45. Ruth Levitas. 2013. *Utopia as Method: The Imaginary Reconstitution of Society.* Palgrave Macmillan.
46. Silvia Lindtner. 2015. Hacking with Chinese Characteristics: The Promises of the Maker Movement against China's Manufacturing Culture. Science, Technology & Human Values (Sage), Vol. 40, No. 5, pp.854-879.
47. Silvia Lindtner, Anna Greenspan, David Li. 2015. Designed in Shenzhen: Shanzhai Manufacturing and Maker Entrepreneurs. In Proc. of 5th Decennial Aarhus Conference on Critical Alternatives, Denmark, Aug 17-21, 2015, pp. 85-96.
48. Silvia Lindtner, Garnet Hertz, Paul Dourish. 2014. Emerging Sites of HCI Innovation: Hackerspaces, Hardware Start-ups, Incubators. In Proc. of the ACM SIGCHI Conference on Human Factors in Computing Systems (Toronto, Canada), pp.439-448.
49. Silvia Lindtner and David Li. 2012. Created in China: The Makings of China's Hackerspace Community. ACM Interactions , XIX. 6 November + December.
50. Silvia Lindtner. 2014. Hackerspaces and Internet of Things in China: How Makers are reinventing Industrial Production, Innovation & the Self. Journal of China Information, Special Issue on "Political Contestation in Chinese Digital Spaces" (ed. Guobin Yang), Vol. 28, No. 2, pp. 145-167.
51. Fengshu Liu. 2011. Urban Youth in China: Modernity, the Internet and the Self. New York: Routledge.
52. Boy Lüthje, Stefanie Hürtgen, Peter Pawlicki, and Martina Stroll. 2013. From Silicon Valley to Shenzhen. Global Production and work in the IT industry. Rowman & Littlefield Publishers.
53. Rebecca MacKinnon. 2012. Consent of the Networked: The Worldwide Struggle for Internet Freedom. New York: Basic Books.

54. David Mellis and Leah Buechley. 2014. Do-It-Yourself Cellphones: An Investigation into the Possibilities and Limits of High-Tech DIY. In Proceedings of the ACM SIGCHI conference on Human factors in computing systems, pp. 1723-1732.

55. Gina Neff. 2012. Venture Labor. Work and the Burden of Risk in Innovation Industries. Cambridge, Massachusetts: MIT Press.

56. Mary Ann O'Donnell. 2001. Becoming Hong Kong, Razing Baoan, Preserving Xin'an: An Ethnographic Account of Urbanization in the Special Economic Zone. Cultural Studies 15(3/4), 419-443.

57. Mary Ann O'Donnell. 2006. Attracting the World's Attention: The Cultural Supplement in Shenzhen Municipality. Positions 14:1.

58. Aihwa Ong and Stephen J. Collier (eds.). 2004. Global Assemblages: Technology, Politics, and Ethics as Anthropological Problems. Wiley-Blackwell.

59. William Overhault. 2015. The politics of China's anti-corruption campaign. EastAsiaForum. http://www.eastasiaforum.org/2015/09/15/the-politics-of-chinas-anti-corruption-campaign/ last accessed September 20, 2015.

60. Matt Ratto and Megan Boler (eds). 2014. DIY Citizenship. Critical Making and Social Media. Cambridge, Massachusetts: MIT Press.

61. David Roedl, Shaowen Bardzell, Jeffrey Bardzell. 2015. Sustainable Making? Balancing Optimism and Criticism in HCI Discourse, ACM TOCHI Journal, VOl. 22, Issue 3, Article No. 15.

62. Daniela K. Rosner and Morgan G. Ames. 2014. Designing for Repair? Infrastructures and Materialities of Breakdown. In Proc. of CSCW, pp. 319-331.

63. Ananya Roy and Aiwah Ong. 2011. Worlding Cities. Asian Experiments and the Art of Being Global. Blackwell Publishing.

64. Gabriela T. Richard, Yasmin B. Kafai, Barrie Adleberg, Orkan Telhan. 2015. StitchFest: Diversifying a College Hackathon to broaden participation and perceptions in computing. In Proc. of SIGCE'15, pp.114-119.

65. Lucy Suchman. 2008. Striking Likeness to Difference. Paper presented at 4S/EASST (annual meeting of Society for Social Studies of Science), Rotterdam.

66. Sunflower student movement: http://tinyurl.com/p58tjor

67. Tom Phillips. 2015. Families of China's 'disappeared' say country is a place of fear and panic. The Guardian. http://www.theguardian.com/world/2015/aug/31/families-of-chinas-disappeared-say-country-is-a-place-of-fear-and-panic, last accessed September 20, 2015.

68. Jie Qi and Leah Buechley. 2014. Sketching in Circuits: Designing and building electronics on paper. In Proceedings of the SIGCHI conference on Human factors in computing systems (CHI'14), pp 1713-1722.

69. Yuling Sun, Silvia Lindtner, Xianghua Ding, Tun Lu, Ning Gu. 2015. Reliving the Past & Making a Harmonious Society Today: A Study of Elderly Electronic Hackers in China. In Proc. of the 18th ACM Conference on Computer Supported Cooperative Work & Social Computing, pp. 44-55.

70. Yuri Takhtezev. 2012. Coding Places. Software Practice in a South American City. Cambridge, MA: MIT Press.

71. Joshua G. Tanenbaum. Amanda M. Williams, Audrey Desjardins, Karen Tanenbaum. 2013. Democratizing technology: pleasure, utility and expressiveness in DIY and maker practice. In Proc. of ACM CHI'13, pp. 2603-2612.

72. Alex Taylor. 2011. Out there. In Proceedings of the ACM SIGCHI Conference on Human Factors in Computing Systems (CHI'11), pp. 685-694.

73. Tiziana Terranova. 2000. Free Labor: Producing Culture for the Digital Economy. Social Text 63, Vol. 18, No. 2, Duke University Press.

74. Austin L. Toombs, Shaowen Bardzell, Jeffrey Bardzell. 2015. The Proper Care and Feeding of Hackerspaces: Care Ethics and Cultures of Making. In Proc. of ACM CHI'15, pp. 629-638.

75. vMaker action plan: http://tinyurl.com/o6s38vt

76. Ron Wakkary, Markus Lorenz Schilling, Matthew A. Dalton, Sabrina Hauser, Audrey Desjardins, Xiao Zhang, Henry W.J. Lin. 2015. Tutorial Authorship and Hybrid Designers: The Joy (and Frustration) of DIY Tutorials. In Proc. of ACM CHI'15.

77. Tricia Wang and Josef 'Jofish' Kaye. 2011. Inventive Leisure Practice: understanding hacking communities as sites of sharing and innovation. In Proc. of ACM CHI Extended Abstracts, pp. 263-272.

78. Tom Whitwell. 2014. Inside Shenzhen: China's Silicon Valley. The Guardian. http://www.theguardian.com/cities/2014/jun/13/inside-shenzen-china-silicon-valley-tech-nirvana-pearl-river last accessed September 20, 2015.

79. Amanda Williams, Silvia Lindtner, Ken Anderson, and Paul Dourish. 2014. Multisited Design: An Analytical Lens for Transnational HCI. Journal of Human–Computer Interaction, Vol. 29, Issue 1, pp. 78-108.

80. Guobin Yang. 2011. The Power of the Internet in China: Citizen Activism Online. New York: Columbia University Press.

Values in Repair

[1]Lara Houston, [1]Steven J. Jackson, [2]Daniela K. Rosner, [1]Syed Ishtiaque Ahmed, [3]Meg Young, [1]Laewoo Kang

[1]Information Science
Cornell University
Ithaca, USA
{lh573, sjj54, sa738}
@cornell.edu

[2] Human-Centered Design
and Engineering
University of Washington
Seattle, USA
dkrosner@uw.edu

[3]Information School
University of Washington
Seattle, USA
megyoung@uw.edu

ABSTRACT

This paper examines the question of "values in repair" – the distinct forms of meaning and care that may be built into human-technology interactions through individual and collective acts of repair. Our work draws on research in HCI and the social sciences and findings from ethnographic studies in four sites — two amateur "fixers' collectives" in Brooklyn and Seattle, USA and two mobile phone repair communities in Uganda and Bangladesh — to advance two arguments. First, studies of repair account for new sites and processes of value that differ from those appearing at HCI's better-studied moments of design and use. Second, repair may embed modes of human interaction with technology and with each other in ways that surface values as contingent and ongoing *accomplishments*, suggesting ongoing processes of valuation that can never be fully fixed or commoditized. These insights help HCI account for human relationships to technology built into the world through repair.

Author Keywords

Repair; maintenance; design; values; ethnography.

ACM Classification Keywords

H. 1. 2. Human Factors

INTRODUCTION

A growing body of scholarship in HCI and the social sciences has called attention to the problem of "values in design": the myriad ways in which social and ethical concerns may be built into and out of artifacts, systems, and infrastructures through the process of design. Parallel work in science and technology studies has emphasized the embedding of values in larger forms of infrastructure and its consequences for deep social concerns around the distribution of power, knowledge, and authority in technically mediated social orders [5,36]. HCI scholars have brought these concerns back to the work of design itself, advocating for design approaches that make explicit and systematic attention to values a core feature and contribution of HCI analysis and design. [2,6,15,17].

CHI'16, May 07 - 12, 2016, San Jose, CA, USA

ACM 978-1-4503-3362-7/16/05…$15.00
DOI: http://dx.doi.org/10.1145/2858036.2858470

Our research extends this work by tackling the related but distinct problem of "values in repair": the forms and processes of value grounded in the ongoing work of fixing and maintaining the objects and systems around us. From this standpoint, questions of value in and around objects don't stop at moments of design and adoption, but extend to the long and rich history of relations through which worlds of human-computer interaction are sustained and held together. We keep our technologies going through acts of repair, from on-the-fly improvisations to faithful restorations. Just as values may be embedded in and through design, alternate processes of valuation may be set in motion through repair. This points us to different sites and agents of technological work: from HCI's usual suspects of designers and users, to a broader and often overlooked cast of actors and activities *also* central to human-computer interaction (at least where those interactions are sustained through time). It also reopens the question of value itself, and redirects HCI attention to the ongoing process by which value (and *valuation*) are achieved, sustained, and evolved through time in real-world computing environments.

Our paper builds on HCI traditions of value-centered analysis and a small but growing body of HCI and social science work dedicated to problems of maintenance and repair. Reporting on larger programs of ethnographic fieldwork with "fixer" movements in Brooklyn and Seattle and mobile phone repair workers in Uganda and Bangladesh, we make two central contributions. The first concerns the forms of value to be found in work and interaction surrounding the practice of technology repair in both amateur and livelihood communities. We show how systems of value originating in industrialized production meet local ecologies of care and expertise, where different moral relations and imperatives may unfold. We also explore values that draw people to repair, ranging from the economic and personal to the social and environmental: people choose to fix (or not) the objects around them for a wide variety of reasons, many of which have little to do with the instrumental "means-ends" logics central to standard HCI discussions around technology use and design.

Our second contribution concerns the *nature* (rather than the *content*) of the values so discovered. In particular, we show how repair can help us reorient how we think about values, from static achievement or fixed set of affordances (a position we'll describe as the "commodity fiction" of value) towards a more fluid and emergent model that treats value as an active and ongoing *process*. We understand *valuation* as the processes through which something is rendered important, or treated as worthy or useful, and *values* as moments where these broader processes become stabilized. From this perspective, acts of repair may extend but also *enliven* the landscape of things, building forms of meaning and attachment that help *thicken* human relationships to technology. Generic manufactured objects may be deepened or ennobled through repair, adding affective and social valences. Within an industrial and consumption-centered economy, new forms of durability can be achieved, and things meant to be discarded can be turned into things to be cared for and saved. At the same time, repair can change its human participants, transforming "mere users" into something slightly more, better versed and engaged with the object worlds around them. In short, repair may support ongoing forms of valuation that continue to unfold through the lifetime of our objects, reshaping values and meanings "originally" made durable through design.

This paper begins by reviewing parallel but largely separate bodies of work on repair and values in HCI. We track how early theoretical work treats each of these themes, and how more recent scholarship has reoriented and extended these claims. We then turn to vignettes from our four empirical sites in order to make two distinct contributions: first, to show how HCI discussions of value can be usefully extended beyond moments of design into moments of breakdown and repair; and second, to show how values in repair (and indeed other HCI contexts) are better conceived as *processes* rather than *things:* in effect, *verbs* rather than *nouns*. We conclude by discussing implications of our findings for wider HCI research and practice, and how attending to values (and *valuation*) in repair may open up new theoretical and empirical terrains for the field.

HCI AND REPAIR

While HCI scholarship has accorded vastly more attention to practices of technology design and adoption, questions of maintenance and repair are not wholly foreign to the field. Pragmatist and ethnomethodological traditions of HCI scholarship have long called attention to the importance of breakdown and repair as crucial but understudied moments in the life of technological objects, systems, and social interaction more generally. Breakdowns of (social) order and expectation hold a special place in American pragmatist traditions of social science, accounting most famously for the separation of thought and consciousness from more rote patterns of habit and routine that structure human interactions with the world [8,28]. The same instinct animates mid-century work in the American social sciences, from the Chicago School sociology of Hughes and Strauss [22,39] to Bateson's cybernetics [3], to traditions of ethnomethodology and conversation analysis [2,20,35] which are pragmatism's most obvious jumping off point into HCI. In contrast to their structural and/or functionalist social science competitors, these pragmatist traditions feature breakdown and repair as variously: a) ever-present realities of the social orders we engage; b) engines for learning, change, and adjustment across situation, difference, and context; and c) methods for surfacing the tacit and hidden features of social life in its smoothly functioning form.

The few extended empirical studies of repair in the HCI canon follow directly from this pragmatist tradition. A leading example is Julian Orr's book-length ethnography of Xerox repair technicians, [31] which calls into sharp relief the contingent nature of repair work, and the forms of collaboration required to diagnose and resolve the myriad forms of breakdown that routinely challenge and undermine effective human-computer interaction. As Suchman [40] famously demonstrated, these breakdowns also posed deep challenges to models of thought and action then dominant in Artificial Intelligence, necessitating a sea change from "planning" to "situated action" as the dominant mode and challenge of HCI work. Building on the same pragmatist foundation, influential work by Star and Ruhleder has noted the tendency of functioning infrastructure to disappear, reappearing only at moments of breakdown [37]. Subsequent work in infrastructure studies and HCI has articulated the significance of tensions and breakdowns as generative, even formative, moments in the emergence of new infrastructural systems and practices [32].

More recent work has extended these insights, moving beyond the organizationally bound worlds of the Xerox repair technicians studied by Orr and Suchman. Rosner et al. [34] and Jackson [24] have shown how technology breakdown and repair may expose facets of human-computer interaction that exceed or frustrate design or engineering-centered expectations, and reveal dimensions of human-technology relations obscured under the field's traditional emphasis on design. Ethnographic projects in Namibia [26], Uganda [21], Kenya [43] and Bangladesh [25] have explored the nature and operation of mobile phone repair worlds in the global South, outlining forms of collaboration, innovation, value, and exchange through which technical infrastructures are sustained and extended. This growing body of scholarship takes sites of amateur and informal repair work seriously as skilled spaces of knowledge production and transmission. A separate body of work in collapse informatics has sought to reorient HCI design efforts from a future predicated on growth towards one marked by the breakdown, disruption, and contraction of existing social, technical and environmental systems

[41]. These themes connect in turn to a growing body of analytic and design-based work in sustainable HCI that has considered the field's relationship to problems of environmental change and sustainability (see inter alia [4,9,10]).

Our work is heavily indebted to these prior bodies of HCI work. Our arguments draw on the recognition that breakdown is everyday rather than exceptional, and that the recuperative processes of repair are central to the maintenance of social and material orders across time. Insights from the HCI repair canon around the contingent and situated nature of repair work and the impossibility of its full encompassing within predictable plans of action contributes to our re-specification of "values" as processes of valuation. Finally, our case also points to the deep material embedding of repair, and its reliance on sometimes tacit or skill-based knowledges that may be difficult to convey through the abstractions of formal and linguistic description. As a consequence, stories loom large in the empirical accounts that follow; like Orr's technicians *talking about machines* is a crucial part of the sensemaking that surrounds and supports repair work [31].

VALUES AND DESIGN

Since the early 1990s, discussions of value within the HCI community have called attention to the "social, moral, and political consequences" of design practices [14,18]. Mirroring growing recognition of the social responsibilities of technologists more generally – marked for example by the founding of Computer Professionals for Social Responsibility in 1983 – the new "values" scholarship sought to call attention to design as an inherently value laden endeavor, and offer specific strategies by which the often tacit nature of values in design work could be more carefully and systematically accounted for.

In the early 1990s, Friedman, Nissenbaum and others opened calls for value-based approaches that were oriented to producing technological systems that were "good" to use in a moral as well as a functional sense [18]. Working on problems ranging from bias in computer architectures and search engines to the challenges of designing for user autonomy [18,19] and developing in counterpoint with related work in computer ethics, social informatics, CSCW, and participatory design, value sensitive research sought to integrate ethical concerns and socio-technical analyses directly into the process of design itself [16]. An influential variant of this work was developed across a series of articles in the 1990s and early 2000s by Friedman, Borning and others under the heading of "Value Sensitive Design" (VSD).

VSD was intended as a methodological framework to ensure structured and systematic attention to values within processes of design [15–17]. VSD is defined as a tripartite methodology enfolding conceptual enquiry (such as scoping values and identifying primary and secondary stakeholders), empirical enquiry (including ascertaining real-world preferences and attitudes among actors), and technical enquiry (the development and/or critical analysis of the technology itself) [17]. Iterations between these forms of enquiry present opportunities for embodying values in the design of individual systems or artifacts. At its core VSD seeks to account for and protect human values: "what a person or group of people consider important in life" [17, p.70]. While twelve "universal" values are explicitly named within early VSD work (including *privacy*, *autonomy*, and *freedom from bias),* Friedman et al. emphasize that these may take on different forms in particular times and places, and that other values may also be located and operationalized in and through VSD methodologies.

In the early 2000s, Flanagan, Howe and Nissenbaum advanced a parallel values in design framework, arguing once again for the moral role and responsibility of design and urging designers to engage their work as a "form of political or moral activism" [11, p.323]. Flanagan et al. discerned three forms of activity used to methodically embody values in design - *discovery*, *translation* and *verification* – which once again relied on the integration of technical, philosophical and empirical modes of enquiry [11]. Values could be embodied in systems or artifacts in three ways: through direct visual representations within the design itself; through its "material" affordances (the practices that a system or artifact enables or hinders) and within a wider situation where values "emerge indirectly as a property of the system's interaction with the contextual setting in which it operates" [11, p.345].

These values-based approaches have proved highly generative, being taken up in HCI research ranging from the security of wireless implantable medical devices [7] and the values of computational modelers [12], to homeless young people's experiences with information technology [42] and the development of co-design spaces [44]. The impact of this early values work is also reflected in initiatives such as the Values In Design (VID) Council, created in 2010 by Helen Nissenbaum, bringing together social scientists and designers under the Future of Internet Architectures project. A series of values in design workshops convened by Nissenbaum and Bowker have continued to renew and reset the agenda for values work in the field.

Generative critiques have reoriented this core methodological literature, questioning the specification and scoping of values themselves: for example, as universal or particular. Le Dantec et al. [6] locate VSD's twelve "universal" values as commitments arguably specific to computing cultures in Northern liberal democracies. They observe that this heuristic "privileges a discursive definition of values over values that may be discovered or encountered through investigation" [p.1141]. Instead, they argue VSD should encourage open-ended and exploratory empirical engagement with sites for design, in order to uncover local values that are appropriate to this specific context, taking care to distinguish between the values of designers and stakeholders [6]. Alsheikh et al. address similar concerns in their work on technology use in long distance relationships, highlighting how the privacy of the family (rather than the individual) is central within an Arab cultural context [1]. Knobel and Bowker [29] have explored forms of "cultural valence" which may imbalance global representations in and through technology, observing how a Google search for "Cameroon" produced exactly zero page one results emanating from the country itself. Reflecting on next steps for VSD, Borning and Muller [4] respond by arguing for a pluralist position, where no claims are made for the universality or specificity of values, instead leaving them open for empirical researchers to take up.

A second point of debate concerns the ontological status of values within wider interactional environments. JafariNaimi et al. [27] have argued that the definition of values as universal properties "emphasizes the identification of values rather than their service in design situations" [p.93]. This leads to an "*identify/apply logic,*" in which scholars aim to find and define relevant values so that they may be applied more comprehensively to design practice. But JafariNaimi et al. argue that values are always surfaced *in action*: "practicing designers... make sense of values not at remove, as in scholarship, but in the often-confused design situations in which value has value" [p.93]. Similar insights can be drawn from science and technology studies: for example, Lepawsky and Mather's tracing of the movement of e-waste from Canada to Bangladesh, which discovers not waste but *re-use*, as discarded artifacts are disassembled and remade into other things [30]. This causes the authors to turn from noun to verb in their ontological re-framing, asking "what we might learn if we followed *actions*; if we studied not waste and value, but wast*ing* and valu*ing*' [p.247].

In sum, value-centered approaches have made real and generative contributions to HCI theory and practice, not least by adding an explicitly ethical layer to HCI's traditional design orientation. More recent work has extended this early values work in two directions: first, away from ideas of "universal" human values and towards more specific questions of values in situ; and second, towards the recognition of value as a culturally organized process that is produced and reproduced through action. Our work shares this orientation, and approaches questions of value as an (inter)active and ongoing accomplishment, rather than a fixed stock of ethical "things" in the world – a position we describe after Foucault [13] as the "commodity fiction" of value. When played out at the global scale, this in turn lines up with other emerging HCI research programs – for example, around "postcolonial computing" [23] which attempts to situate these questions of difference within wider political discourses of technology design and manufacture between the global North and South. It also aligns well with investigations that take seriously the proposition that questions of value and valuation in and through technology are never fully fixed and answered through design, but may persist across the myriad processes by which technologies unfold and are sustained within the contexts and lifeworlds around them. This leads us to the ethical question(s) of repair, and the empirical studies that follow.

METHODS

This paper is part of a collaborative project undertaken by the authors to generate comparative insights about the values and processes of valuation surfaced in repair, an important contribution given the single-case nature of prior work in this area. We bring together four different repair sites: firstly, two amateur fixers' groups located in the USA: the Fixers' Collective in Brooklyn, New York and the Northeast Seattle Fixers' Collective in Seattle, Washington, and secondly, two mobile phone "repair worlds" [26] in Kampala, Uganda and Dhaka, Bangladesh.

All four sites were the subject of deep and sustained ethnographic engagement by one or more of the authors, including participant observation, the "hands on" learning of embodied repair skills, interviewing, photography and video recording (as a supplementary material). Interviews, field notes and video recordings were transcribed and coded based on grounded theory analysis [38]. Regular fieldwork visits to the Brooklyn-based Fixers' Collective began in November 2012 while engagement with the Northeast Seattle Fixers' Collective began in March of 2015; both are still ongoing. The Ugandan study draws on six months' ethnographic fieldwork spanning a three-year period from October 2010 to September 2012, while the Bangladeshi study was undertaken over a four-month period in 2013. All participants have been assigned pseudonyms.

While these projects began in partial independence and range in form and type, all of the sites demonstrated the continual negotiation of values in repair and involved analyses significantly shaped by shared theoretical foundations (notably pragmatist and ethnomethdological traditions of HCI work). The case vignettes that follow are representative of key themes surfaced within these larger bodies of ethnographic work. Our first case pairing speaks to the situated action of repair in Northern, amateur, activist repair sites, while the second Southern case pairing deals with wider social valuations of repair.

AMATEUR REPAIR IN NEW YORK AND SEATTLE

Our first two cases emerge from the small but rapidly growing amateur repair movement developing in parallel in Europe and North America. In 2009, organizers in Berkeley, Amsterdam and New York separately launched public events to help local residents fix (and learn to fix) their broken consumer appliances. The vignettes that follow demonstrate the values of collaboration and learning that frequently characterize and support ongoing participation in this space. They also however reveal the presence of other systems of valuation – including socially coded relations of expertise and sometimes gender – that may also mark and inflect these spaces. Our fieldwork highlights how these processes serve to legitimate certain aesthetics and practices of repair while limiting or undermining others, in ways that both expand and limit the reach and impact of repair practice in such settings.

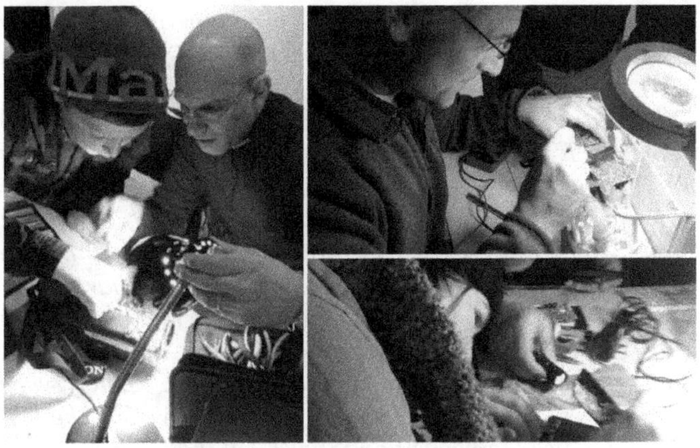

Figure 1: Repairs underway at the Fixers' Collective NYC, March 2015

Fixers' Collective, Brooklyn

Our first case involves the Fixers' Collective, an amateur repair organization that has since 2009, met the third Thursday of every month at the Proteus Gowanus gallery in Brooklyn, New York. With roots in an earlier installation called "Mend" (2008), and drawing inspiration and resources from groups like iFixit and the Repair Café movement in Europe and beyond, the group's goal is to provide a public and collaborative space where repair skills can be practiced, shared, and supported. On any given night, the group attracts an eclectic cast of participants and objects. These include regulars with specific repair skills to offer (designated within the group as "master fixers"). It also includes occasional or one-off participants ranging in age from 8 to 80, all of whom are invited to bring items in need of repair. Objects repaired by the group run the full gamut from household items (lamps, toasters, clothing, etc.) to consumer electronics. Over the course of our fieldwork organizers and participants emphasized the group's role in the transmission of repair skill and knowledge, and note a distinction between their activities and a simple drop-off repair operation: in the Fixers' Collective, *participants are expected to actually fix;* to join with other participants and the master fixers in learning and performing repair operations themselves. The vignettes that follow illustrate both the importance and the complexity surrounding this hands-on and collaborative ideal.

One February evening in 2014, Rita a female participant in her mid-20s arrives at the Fixers' Collective with a non-functioning MacBook Pro. She explains that the laptop is hers, that water was accidentally spilled on the keyboard some weeks ago, and since then it won't turn on when the power button is pressed. Following her explanation a master fixer called Tom looks over the laptop. He tells her they should start by finding the model number, and looks for a repair manual or other information online. He points her to the model number engraved on the bottom of the backplate. As she reads him the number, he searches online, finding a hit on the iFixit website – a group the Fixers' Collective regularly depends on for online resources, spare parts, and specialized tools. Having located the appropriate resource, Tom and Rita now work together to disassemble the laptop, following the instructions laid out on the iFixit site. Upon removing the front plate, Tom plugs the power cable back into the charging slot. The indicator light turns green. "Oh, it's going on now. It didn't go on before!" Rita exclaims. She presses the power button, but the laptop still won't boot up. Tom suggests removing the RAM memory, in case the units have been damaged by water. They work their way through a separate set of instructions on the iFixit site describing RAM removal, with Rita holding the front plate as Tom first locates and them removes the RAM cards.

As they are working, Mike (another master fixer with more experience in laptops) wanders by to join the conversation. "Do you know what this indicator means?" he asks. "It means that the processor is inactive," Tom replies. After another 20 minutes of discussion and a variety of trials, the MacBook suddenly makes a beeping noise and starts booting. Everyone around reacts with surprise and pleasure. Mike points to the other fixer and exclaims "You reset the P-RAM!" Tom smiles and responds, "Right! Yeah, yeah. That's probably what I did. Because it automatically turns on everything." "So what was the problem?" Rita asks. "We're not sure," Tom explains. "It could be a bad RAM slot. I put one chip in the slot, and got a blinking sleep light. Then I put the same chip in the other slot and reset the P-RAM, so…". As this explanation is concluding, the laptop finishes its boot sequence, and the screen changes to a picture of Rita standing in front of a bridge. She exclaims in pleasure, and smiles are exchanged all around.

The scene above embodies the principles of collaboration and learning that are central to the Fixers' Collective and related organizations in the wider "fixer" movement. This is in some ways an ideal case: the participant shows up with a problem, and members of the group work with the participant and with each other to assemble relevant resources and expertise (including those located in online sources). Rita walks away with a functioning laptop, a better understanding of how it works, and possibly with a story and memory now attached to the device itself. Educated guesses are made, fixes are attempted, and at some point in the process of trial and error produces a positive result. Along the way, small bits of understanding and belonging are also produced, through the shared puzzle of the broken laptop. The small victory of the water-damaged laptop becomes a point of hope and connection among participants and fixers alike, and buoys the group through other not-always-so-successful attempts. For of course, not all interactions end so happily. In many instances, devices are found to be unfixable, and master fixers advise participants on the best way of disposing of broken items (which may include recycling or salvaging parts for other purposes). In others, participants stand idly by, as expertise and other forms of difference reassert themselves, and the task of diagnosing and responding to broken objects returns to those with longer experience or specific training in this space. This tension between expertise, collaboration and learning figures more centrally in the second vignette shared below.

Northeast Seattle Fixers' Collective

The Seattle Fixers' Collective developed in 2011, after a former engineer read about the Brooklyn-based Fixers' Collective and decided to start one locally, prompted by the breakdown of his two-week-old salad spinner which could not be fixed due to embedded, inaccessible screws. Two years later, the Northeast Seattle Tool Library — a community-run organization that lends tools much like libraries lend books — began its own Collective as a way to meet their sustainability mission and increase membership. Today the group meets monthly for 3 hours in the workshop space of the Northeast Seattle Tool Library, which is run out of a standalone building in a church lot. Inside, shelves of tools lead to a check-out at the front; a large, long work table fills the space in the back. Most days, fixers help attendees from the neighborhood and members of the tool library repair broken household items, including shovels, lawn mowers, and food processors. When few or no attendees come to a session, the fixers tend to stay the full three hours anyway, often tinkering with items from the tool library inventory in need of repair. However, the dynamic of control between fixers and attendees reveals some important concerns for authorship and visibility, impacted by who shows up to help fix. Most fixers are white men in retirement from engineering jobs. The following vignette illustrates the limits and contours of collaborative repair.

In May 2015, a woman named Kay enters building with a broken lamp and a shattered pot lid. Kay is an effervescent woman in her early sixties with silver-blonde hair. She is a longtime volunteer at the Tool Library, and has been to the Fixers' Collective many times. Soldering her broken lamp back together had been straightforward, she says, so she is excited to start a more complicated repair—a cooking pot lid. Alex, a tall, talkative fixer in his fifties, approaches her to help. Kay dropped the glass lid at home, leaving her with only its metal rim and a handle that had been screwed into the glass. She has an aluminum turkey-basting pan she hopes to use as raw material to create a new top for the lid. Once he learns of Kay's plans, Alex becomes doubtful. "You want to fix this?" he exclaims holding up the lid in disgust. He goes on, however, to help her cut out a piece of aluminum to fit the metal rim, using rubber wedges and a mallet to pound it into its crevices without tearing the aluminum's surface.

There is an open question of how to get the aluminum to stay attached to the lid. Alex adamantly advises her to use bathtub caulk, saying "she wouldn't eat off of it" so there is nothing to worry about. Another fixer, Bo, is much more concerned, warning Kay that she needs to make sure it would be fire rated silicone, if she used it at all, and that he doesn't think it is a good idea. "Don't put it in the oven. This one never goes in the oven," Bo directs. When Kay steps outside Alex begins making veiled criticisms of the project. "It will be a piece of art, knowing Kay. A piece of recycling." Then, he says something a bit more judgmental: "It's up to Kay if she wants to show her friends or not." I stand with Alex, considering ways to attach the lid handle to the top. Kay's aluminum pan had a hard wire undergirding; I think that Kay wants to cut and use it as an exoskeleton to attach the handle securely. Alex disagrees, saying that Kay wants that part to "be waste." Later, when Alex leaves, Kay stands talking with me. Kay says she had wanted to use the heavy-gauge wire, but that "Alex was not going for it."

Here, the fixer evaluates Kay's repair in unflattering terms. He suggests that the repair is something that she should be ashamed of, and should possibly not show to her friends. Kay's fix restores function to the pot—she looks specifically for food-safe materials so she can use the pot lid as she did before. However, the appeal to restoring function to an object stands in contrast to an appreciation for tidy and professional-grade workmanship. Alex's criticism stems from a sense that the work is inelegant or embarrassing in form. Alex tries to take the repair in a different direction than the one that Kay had intended. Counter to the many electronic devices that that come into the Collective, the workmanship of repair for this pot lid is necessarily fully exposed, open to visual critique and technical interrogation. For other fixers and participants, a repair and its analysis carries traces of its repairer, and his or her competencies. This dynamic reflects other cases of repair that we observed, where male fixers exercised authorship over repairs, asserting forms of technical mastery historically equated to the assumed pleasures men attain through technical work. Participation in this community of amateur invites confronting cultures of masculinity — and associated questions of visibility — developing in and around repair.

Bounding participation

The values of collaboration and learning are central to the two Fixers' Collectives and they underpin two significant organizational ideals. The development of collective bodies of knowledge and skills around repair prevents the wasting of objects that might still have a useful life; extending the use of resources, and deferring replacement purchases for the benefit of the environment. Secondly, learning through participation in repair increases the sense of agency that members of the public have over the objects in their lives. Fixers' Collectives attempt to normalize careful, technical and materially engaged ways of knowing and living with everyday consumer objects. Appeals to collaboration and learning are used by repair organizations to distinguish their free events from traditional paid-for, drop-off repair services. Participation-value replaces exchange-value.

Within the two vignettes we see how values, rather than stable properties of organizations, become negotiated in action, as processes of valuation unfold in repair. In the first vignette Rita, the owner of the MacBook Pro, and the two master fixers Tom and Mike work together in an open exchange within the unfolding process of diagnosing and repairing the machine: a situation where everybody learns something. Skills and knowledges of repair are assembled and shared between fixers and participants, in ways driven by shared motivations and affective connection. In these interactions, social meanings are also being negotiated and passed on, about what it means to shape repair practices, the boundaries of participation and performances of mastery.

Collaboration and learning play out quite differently in the second vignette, as tensions emerge between the valuations of master fixer Alex and participant Kay in the repair of a broken pot lid. Valuing is a central dimension of repair, as practitioners first make sense of whether artifacts are "worth" repairing in a particular social and material context, and secondly, as they work to preserve value by restoring or transforming artifacts before they fall into the category of waste. Although Kay believes in the pot lid repair, fixer Alex maligns it as an example of "art" or "recycling" - leading to disagreements about how to take the repair forward, in the choice of materials and how to combine them. Authority is a central question: this exchange makes visible dynamics of control that shape the collaborative learning relationship between participants and master fixers. Processes of valuing are crucial to the ways that public participants and master fixers negotiate the social and material asymmetries of knowledge and skills inherent in the organization of these activist events. The gendered framing of repair here is particularly striking, as Alex performs an identity of mastery that reflects historical linkages between masculinities and repair [33].

LIVELIHOOD REPAIR IN KAMPALA AND DHAKA

Our second set of repair endeavors locate repair as part of livelihood communities in Kampala and Bangladesh. In these sites of mobile phone repair we find corporate systems of value and socioeconomic status confront the concerns and competencies of local fixing ecologies. Our fieldwork surfaced difficulties of valuation in the shifting material configuration of electronic devices, revealing moments where skilled technical work sits in tension with financial and social reward.

Mobile Repair in Kampala, Uganda

Within the mobile phone repair world of downtown Kampala, livelihood businesses predominate: technicians run their own informal and independent micro-enterprises, sometimes employing an assistant or apprentice. However, corporate actors are also represented, as four larger repair workshops maintain relationships of "authorization:" two with mobile manufacturers and two with mobile network providers. The following case explores tensions in the valuing of particular repair practices between these regimes of repair.

Sitting upstairs in an airy repair workshop one afternoon in September 2012, a technician describes how mobile repair is becoming more difficult. Peter works in a mobile dealership authorized to sell and repair two leading mobile brands: one European and the other East Asian. He juxtaposes two motherboards from the same European manufacturer and points out how the newer model has an on-board microphone, where the microphone pierces the motherboard with the component on one side and an output on the other. Peter explains that it can no longer be replaced using a soldering heat gun (called a "blower" for the way that it blows a stream of hot air), but needs an infra-red soldering station which he doesn't have access to. I remember seeing an independent technician replace this type of mic using a different technique called looping, and I show Peter the picture below. This skillful work involves soldering thin copper wires from the contacts on the motherboard to the contacts on the mic.

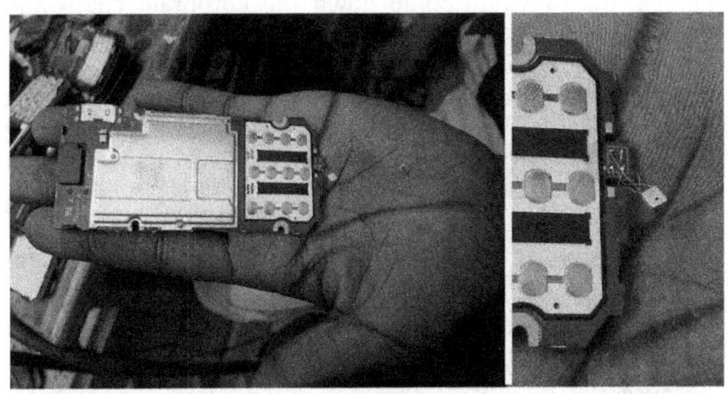

Figure 2: The discarded microphone is visible on Jason's palm. He has connected a replacement microphone using four copper wires, rather than mounting it on the motherboard, as can be seen in the magnified image, September, 2012.

Peter is unimpressed, describing looping as "just tampering" saying that "it creates noise in the circuit, it's unprofessional and doesn't last". He explains that if the phone was dropped, the loop would break and the customer would be back when the repair had failed... his company would never allow it. I ask Peter if looping has a place for those who want to extend the life of their phone, even for a short time. He replies no, "it's about your own standards," explaining that he wants to do quality work that makes him feel good and sleep well at night. But other standards are also at work here: this workshop was only authorized to a

Level Two standard by the mobile manufacturer, meaning that Peter is unable to undertake any repairs of onboard components. This microphone repair was simply unable to be performed in the "authorized" way, in this workshop.

This vignette demonstrates the changing material forms between older and newer mobile handsets, even those made by the same manufacturer, raising vital questions for designers around repairability. Replacing a damaged microphone was once one of the easiest repairs for technicians in training; now it increasingly requires the specialist skill of looping. This vignette demonstrates how repairability does not simply index material affordances, but takes shape in relation to organizational contexts for repair, configurations of knowledge, embodied skills, and access to tools within "repair worlds" [26,34]. Crucially, this case illuminates the central role that values and processes of valuation have in negotiating the limits of repair practice.

Looping, for example is contested practice across authorized and independent sites. It has different material properties than the like-for-like replacement of a part: as a skilled technique it makes the phone function again, but it is more fallible than the original design and less safe in the case of a power surge. Peter devalues looping as "just tampering", framing it as an intervention that would not be legible or acceptable to his company's standards. This case reveals how relationships of authorization are one way in which corporate values in repair impact local repair worlds, as systems of value come down the corporate chain and meet the local ecology in Kampala.

In response to accusations of "just tampering," independent technicians argue that authorized workers "don't even repair". In Peter's case, authorized values in repair restrict his work to the replacement of non-integrated parts, rendering whole generations of handsets unfixable after the simple failure of a mic, or other on-board component (at least using any authorized technique). For independent technicians, authorized standards are a rejection of the idea that repair itself is a form of valuing in action, simply because the quality of the restoration work cannot meet original design specifications. Independent technicians value successful repairs above all else - firstly because customers only pay for working devices. Yet much more is happening here than simple functionalism: repairing "by any means" is understood by independent technicians as creative, improvisational and masterful work, which makes the most of materials, and is deeply connected to professional pride and identities of mastery in downtown Kampala.

Mobile Repair in Dhaka, Bangladesh

As with the Kampalan case, the mobile phone repair world in Dhaka consists of a range of workshops, including high-end brand "authorized" workshops and informal, independent livelihood businesses. The educational background of repair workers ranges widely: some are engineers from low-ranking universities, others had graduated in unrelated disciplines, and a subset had very little or no educational background. Repair waste collectors, locally called "Bhangari," (from the Bangla word "bhanga," meaning broken) worked closely with repairers, visiting workshops to buy discarded electronic objects cheaply and selling them on at a higher price to Chinese recyclers. Our study surfaces uncertainties about the social status of repair workers in Bangladesh, taking the role of repair technicians and the economic valuation of waste materials performed by Bhangari waste collectors as counterpoints.

I meet Rimon a 35-year-old mobile phone repairer, in May 2013 at his workshop in a busy shopping mall in Dhaka. He explains that he comes from a very modest family and did not continue his education after the 9th grade, instead starting his career as an ornaments maker. He fell in love with a woman in his community, but her higher family status did not allow Rimon to propose to her, so he decided to change his profession to work with the latest electronic technologies, which at that time meant the repair of mobile phones. As a first step, he started working with one of his friends in an electrical workshop, and then he got an apprenticeship in a mobile repair shop and learned the basic techniques. At that point, he considered himself good enough to propose, but, it was too late; the woman he loved had already married somebody else. Rimon continued building his career in mobile phone repair, and he is now a renowned repairer with his own shop.

Like Rimon, we found that many of our participants switched jobs into mobile phone repair in order to upgrade their social status, yet many were still frustrated with the lower social status of repair compared to engineering. None of our participants wanted their children to be repairers: most of them wanted their children to be engineers or doctors. Wasim, a senior repairer in Gulistan Underground Market was sharing his frustration about this when he explained: *"A lot of boys from good families cannot complete their education, and could easily come into the repair profession. The problem is nobody calls a repairer an "engineer". I have seen many engineers who know nothing, but just managed a certificate. They get better social status, while repairers are considered as 'service men'. This is unfortunate; some of our repairers could teach many things, even in the universities."*

Yet even within the Dhaka repair world, the appreciation of academic education determines a repairer's place of work. Software repairers are more highly paid and valued than hardware technicians, because being able to read and write in English is a prerequisite for this work, whereas it is assumed that even an illiterate person can work with hardware. University graduates get jobs at the authorized service centers of multinational brands. As in our Kampalan repair site, we observed distinctions between the valuing of authorized and independent repair work. In Dhaka, independent repairers described authorized work as replacing rather than fixing components, which most of the independent repairers did not consider to be "actual repairing". They explained that technicians in the authorized workshops would often come to take help from the independent repairers, a practice that remained secret through financial contacts.

On the other hand, the Bhangari community is concerned about the value of the materials within the electronic waste that they buy. At the Bhangari shops, the collected objects are classified based on the residual components left on their motherboards. Lutfur, a senior Bhangari, does not differentiate between motherboards of different companies. Instead, he checks how many integrated chips the motherboards have. The condition of the motherboards also does not matter much to him. He looks at his weighing scale and tells me, "*The only thing that matters is the weight.*"

These tensions in social status and value judgments present a broader socio-economic framework within which the livelihood repair communities of Bangladesh operate. The status of mobile phone repairers may be higher than the ornament makers, however, this is a reflection of the social appreciation of their expertise with electronic devices and not particularly of repair; something which becomes evident when they are compared with engineers. The knowledge, skills, and hard work of the repairers cannot lift them up to the level of the engineers. This distinction between professions, described by the repairers themselves, highlights the different values assigned to the work of building the new and repairing the old. Invisibility plays a dual role in repair, in that "good repairs" erase or minimize the evidence of breakdown (both in terms of aesthetics and functionality), while repair practitioners themselves inhabit backstage roles that come with low pay and low status, such as mobile phone repair in Dhaka.

When repair fails, value begins to fall away from an object: most notably use-value, but also other forms of affective attachment that exist between people and their possessions. The Bhangari waste collectors work to revive value from discarded motherboards by stripping and selling them in bulk. Here, value is framed solely in terms of the price by weight that the Chinese buyers will pay. At the same time, we see forms of valuation assigned to people, tied into the social status of repair. Forms of work are better and less regarded, with categories of work, such as waste collecting excluded even from the "technological" status that attracted Rimon to the profession.

DISCUSSION

The cases above make visible the specific embedding of repair across a variety of economic, social and material settings not usually considered together. This comparative framing enables us to point out both shared and divergent processes of valuation in repair. In all four of our sites, technicians, customers, master fixers and participants work towards the careful rejuvenation of objects and the restoration or preservation of their usefulness; from low-tech pot lids and the ubiquitous MacBook Pro to the many mobile handsets that are part of expanding infrastructures in Uganda and Bangladesh. At the same time these acts are enlivened by very different motivations and imperatives that move this discussion beyond the organizational settings highlighted in much of the HCI repair canon.

In our two amateur sites in the USA, working products are not the only ends: repair is made valuable as a collaborative activity centered around participation and shared learning, oriented towards producing different affective and practical relations to objects, illuminated most clearly in the New York case. New values are introduced through practices of repair: repairing *together* becomes a way to address the various concerns of master fixers and participants, including a sense of alienation from the workings of devices, wasteful consumption patterns and environmental damage. At the same time, the situated process of collaborative repair reveals competing understandings of what is worth repairing and how, particularly in the Seattle case, which points towards repair as a gendered framing.

In Kampala and Dhaka, we surface different regimes of value active within repair communities themselves and the wider social settings in which they operate. In Kampala, design impacts repair worlds not only through the material affordances of devices (values "embedded" in design), but in the way authorized values in repair limit particular forms of practice. In contrast, independent technicians see repair as a form of valuing in and of itself, where the limits of repair are defined by technicians' own skill and mastery. These findings are echoed in Dhaka, where we also see vast imbalances in credit and compensation allocated to repair versus those allocated to the production of new technologies through engineering. When technologies break down into "waste" materials, we see further retrenchment of value, as Bhangari waste collectors are denied even the "technological" status that repair work enjoys.

Using insights drawn from these four case vignettes, the first core contribution of this paper has been to highlight the centrality of *values* in repair, and to argue for repair as an important site through which values are achieved and maintained. Despite their many and important gains, we suggest that design-centered approaches to questions of value and technology may suffer precisely from a narrow or over-weighted orientation to design itself – and that this orientation reflects in turn a larger imbalance in the field that actively obscures and disadvantages the forms of work described here.

Our exploration of "values in repair" renders visible the social and collective organization of value, whether in amateur activist sites, or across livelihood repair communities. By examining the collective negotiation of values across four very different repair worlds, we have moved beyond the dominant relation in HCI values scholarship between a technological artifact and its single user. This suggests a different agenda for HCI work, firstly in continuing to take repair work seriously, but in addition, further exploring the way questions around value surface in how communities care for their technologies collectively. Our research pushes the values in design literature to move outward in scope to encompass new sites and actors that are not envisaged in current modes of evaluation, which focus narrowly on how well values have been "embodied" or "embedded" in design during the privileged moments of user adoption. Our work points to multiple and ongoing moments of adoption as items are recycled, resold gifted, shared and repaired together.

In addition, our case studies have shown that questions of value are central to how (and whether) objects are sustained over time, particularly in amateur and livelihood repair settings, which are relatively new areas to the HCI community [25,26,33,34]. Within different repair worlds, valuation may include the pleasure of an avocation, the building of community, a contribution to activist agendas, the pursuit of professional pride, in addition to economic reward. Values are clearly not settled at the point of design, but are repeatedly negotiated as objects wear, age, and malfunction, and are cared for (or not) by the removal of these traces and the resetting of broken parts. Our cases demonstrate the multifaceted nature of the values at stake in sustaining objects across time, opening up new avenues for exploration that move beyond calculations of the economic worth or sentimental value of an object to an individual, or the functionalist life cycle analyses of particular products.

By extension, this work questions the ontological status of values themselves, and how we understand their implications for social and political life: the second core contribution of this paper. Generative critiques of VSD and values in design methodologies such as Le Dantec et al. [6] have sought to question the framing of values as universal properties, arguing instead for the empirical exploration of particular design contexts in order to locate values relevant to users (rather than drawing primarily on analyst categories). Likewise JafariNaimi's more recent analysis [27] argues against a two-step "identify/apply" logic within values literature, proposing that values cannot be understood as prior properties outside of action.

Repair literatures offer analytic resources to advance these critical agendas: pragmatist and ethnomethodological influences have oriented the HCI repair canon towards breakdown and repair as everyday processes, in a world where shared understanding is contingent on ongoing collaborative interaction, including between humans and technologies [31,40]. Drawing on JafariNaimi et al. [27], work by Lepawsky and Mather on e-waste [30], and our own case studies, we argue that values are better conceptualized as processes of *valuation*. In this, we turn away from a "commodity fiction" of values [13] (a position where values are a fixed stock of things in the world, divorced from action). This change in focus emphasizes the contingent, ongoing processes through which things are rendered valuable in a wider social and material context.

We suggest that focusing on processes of valuation may be a generative theoretical and methodological shift for values in design scholarship, providing ways to address open questions in the literature about how, and whose, values are materialized within design practice [6,27]. Thinking in terms of processes rather than properties, it becomes clear that *what* values are materialized and *how* they are made visible are deeply intertwined issues. Our comparative work suggests the need to empirically engage with valuation as a situated and collective process unfolding within a particular context that includes sites and processes of design. Our cases also point towards conflicts between different regimes of value and valuation that often remain unresolved and require accounting for.

Accounting for repair practices as sites of valuation, we can begin to see broader programs of HCI design as ethical provocations and starting points rather than final words. Rather than determining final outcomes, design practices may be best conceived as social mechanisms by which a host of economic, social and material arrangements are born and set in motion, rather than definitively concluded. Our intention is not to suggest that values never stabilize, but rather that they continue to do so across the entire trajectory of the object(s) in question – a course that includes the forms of maintenance and repair by which objects are continually sustained and kept live. Approaching such processes as sites of valuation invites recognition of these stabilities as temporary outcomes of social and material change. Rather than universal properties of human subjects, valuations forge new relations. For HCI scholars seeking to expand our design practice and understand such interventions, this highlights the power of valuations to not only represent social and material orders but to help build them differently, enlivening new landscapes of technological development along the way.

ACKNOWLEDGEMENTS

Research for this paper was supported by funding from NSF Grant IIS-1422621, and the Intel Science and Technology Center for Social Computing.

REFERENCES

1. Tamara Alsheikh, Jennifer A. Rode, and Siân E. Lindley. 2011. (Whose) value-sensitive design: a study of long-distance relationships in an Arabic cultural context. *Proceedings of the ACM 2011 conference on Computer supported cooperative work*, ACM, 75–84.
2. Morgan G. Ames, Janet Go, Joseph 'Jofish' Kaye, and Mirjana Spasojevic. 2011. Understanding technology choices and values through social class. *Proceedings of the ACM 2011 conference on Computer supported cooperative work*, ACM, 55–64.

3. Eli Blevis. 2007. Sustainable interaction design: invention & disposal, renewal & reuse. *Proceedings of the SIGCHI conference on Human factors in computing systems*, ACM, 503–512.
4. Alan Borning and Michael Muller. 2012. Next steps for value sensitive design. *Proceedings of the SIGCHI Conference on Human Factors in Computing Systems*, ACM, 1125–1134.
5. Geoffrey Bowker and Susan Leigh Star. 1999. *Sorting things out: Classification and its consequences*. MIT Press. Massachusetts, USA.
6. Christopher A. Le Dantec, Erika Shehan Poole, and Susan P. Wyche. 2009. Values as lived experience: evolving value sensitive design in support of value discovery. *Proceedings of the SIGCHI conference on human factors in computing systems*, ACM, 1141–1150.
7. Tamara Denning, Alan Borning, Batya Friedman, Brian T. Gill, Tadayoshi Kohno, and William H. Maisel. 2010. Patients, pacemakers, and implantable defibrillators: Human values and security for wireless implantable medical devices. *Proceedings of the SIGCHI Conference on Human Factors in Computing Systems*, ACM, 917–926.
8. John Dewey. 1922. *Human nature and conduct*. Dover Edition. 2012 Print. Dover Publications. Mineola, USA.
9. Carl DiSalvo, Phoebe Sengers, and Hrönn Brynjarsdóttir. 2010. Mapping the landscape of sustainable HCI. *Proceedings of the SIGCHI Conference on Human Factors in Computing Systems*, ACM, 1975–1984.
10. Paul Dourish. 2010. HCI and environmental sustainability: the politics of design and the design of politics. *Proceedings of the 8th ACM Conference on Designing Interactive Systems*, ACM, 1–10.
11. Mary Flanagan, Daniel C. Howe, and Helen Nissenbaum. 2008. Embodying values in technology: Theory and practice. *Information technology and moral philosophy*. Jeroen Van Den Hoven and John Weckert (eds.) Cambridge University press, UK. 322–353.
12. Kenneth R. Fleischmann, William Wallace, and Justin M. Grimes. 2010. The values of computational modelers and professional codes of ethics: Results from a field study. *System Sciences (HICSS), 2010 43rd Hawaii International Conference on*, IEEE, 1–10.
13. Michel Foucault. 1980. *Power/knowledge: Selected interviews and other writings, 1972-1977*. Pantheon Books, New York.
14. Batya Friedman. 1990. Societal Issues and School Practices: An Ethnographic Investigation of the Social Context of School Computer Use. *Annual Meeting of the American Educational Research Association. Boston. April 16-20.* Retrieved 8 January 2015 from http://files.eric.ed.gov/fulltext/ED321740.pdf
15. Batya Friedman. 1996. Value-sensitive design. *Interactions* 3, 6: 16–23.
16. Batya Friedman and Peter H. Kahn Jr. 2003. Human values, ethics, and design. *The Human-Computer Interaction Handbook*. Andrew Sears and Julie A. Jacko (eds.) L. Erlbaum Associates Publishers. Mahwah, USA. 1177–1201.
17. Batya Friedman, Peter H. Kahn, and Alan Borning. 2008. Value sensitive design and information systems. *The Handbook of Information and Computer Ethics* Kenneth E. Himma and Herman T. Tavani (eds.) Wiley, Hoboken, USA. 69–101.
18. Batya Friedman and Helen Nissenbaum. 1996. Bias in computer systems. *ACM Transactions on Information Systems (TOIS)* 14, 3: 330–347.
19. Batya Friedman and Helen Nissenbaum. 1997. Software agents and user autonomy. *Proceedings of the first international conference on Autonomous agents*, ACM, 466–469.
20. Harold Garfinkel. 1967. Studies in ethnomethodology. 1991 Print. Polity, Cambridge, UK.
21. Lara Houston. 2014. Inventive Infrastructure: An Exploration of Mobile Phone Repair Practices in Downtown Kampala, Uganda. PhD Dissertation. Lancaster University, Lancaster, UK.
22. Everett Cherrington Hughes. 1971. *The sociological eye: Selected papers*. 1984 Print. Transaction publishers. Herndon, USA.
23. Lilly Irani, Janet Vertesi, Paul Dourish, Kavita Philip, and Rebecca E. Grinter. 2010. Postcolonial computing: a lens on design and development. *Proceedings of the SIGCHI Conference on Human Factors in Computing Systems*, ACM, 1311–1320.
24. Steven J. Jackson. 2014. Rethinking Repair. In *Media Technologies: Essays on Communication, Materiality, and Society* Tarleton Gillespie, Pablo J. Boczkowski, Kirsten A. Foot (eds.) MIT Press, Cambridge, USA. 221-240.
25. Steven J. Jackson, Syed Ishtiaque Ahmed, and Md Rashidujjaman Rifat. 2014. Learning, innovation, and sustainability among mobile phone repairers in Dhaka, Bangladesh. *Proceedings of the 2014 conference on Designing interactive systems*, ACM, 905–914.
26. Steven J. Jackson, Alex Pompe, and Gabriel Krieshok. 2012. Repair worlds: maintenance, repair, and ICT for development in rural Namibia. *Proceedings of the ACM 2012 conference on Computer Supported Cooperative Work*, ACM, 107–116.
27. Nassim JafariNaimi, Lisa Nathan, and Ian Hargraves. 2015. Values as Hypotheses: The Service that Values Provide. *Design Issues* 31, 4.
28. William James. 1910. *The Meaning of Truth. A Sequel to Pragmatism*. Longmans, Green, and Company, New York, USA.
29. Cory Knobel and Geoffrey C. Bowker. 2011. Values in design. *Communications of the ACM* 54, 7: 26–28.
30. Josh Lepawsky and Charles Mather. 2011. From beginnings and endings to boundaries and edges: rethinking circulation and exchange through electronic waste. *Area* 43, 3: 242–249.

31. Julian Orr. 1996. *Talking About Machines: An ethnography of a modern job*. Cornell University Press, Ithaca, USA.

32. David Ribes and Thomas A. Finholt. 2009. The long now of technology infrastructure: articulating tensions in development. *Journal of the Association for Information Systems* 10, 5: 5.

33. Daniela K. Rosner. 2014. Making citizens, reassembling devices: on gender and the development of contemporary public sites of repair in Northern California. *Public Culture* 26, 1 72: 51–77.

34. Daniela K. Rosner and Morgan Ames. 2014. Designing for repair?: infrastructures and materialities of breakdown. *Proceedings of the 17th ACM conference on Computer supported cooperative work & social computing*, ACM, 319–331.

35. Harvey Sacks. 1992. *Lectures on conversation.* Gail Jefferson (ed.) 1995 Print. Blackwell, Malden, USA.

36. Susan Leigh Star and Geoffrey C. Bowker. 2007. Enacting silence: Residual categories as a challenge for ethics, information systems, and communication. *Ethics and Information Technology* 9, 4: 273–280.

37. Susan Leigh Star and Karen Ruhleder. 1996. Steps toward an ecology of infrastructure: Design and access for large information spaces. *Information systems research* 7, 1: 111–134.

38. Anselm Strauss and Juliet M. Corbin. 1997. *Grounded theory in practice*. Sage. Thousand Oaks, USA.

39. Anselm Leonard Strauss. 2008. *Continual permutations of action*. AldineTransaction. New Brunswick, USA.

40. Lucy A. Suchman. 1987. *Plans and situated actions: the problem of human-machine communication*. Cambridge University Press. Cambridge, UK.

41. Bill Tomlinson, M. Silberman, Donald Patterson, Yue Pan, and Eli Blevis. 2012. Collapse informatics: augmenting the sustainability & ICT4D discourse in HCI. *Proceedings of the SIGCHI Conference on Human Factors in Computing Systems*, ACM, 655–664.

42. Jill Palzkill Woelfer, Amy Iverson, David G. Hendry, Batya Friedman, and Brian T. Gill. 2011. Improving the safety of homeless young people with mobile phones: Values, form and function. *Proceedings of the SIGCHI Conference on Human Factors in Computing Systems*, ACM, 1707–1716.

43. Susan Wyche. 2015. Exploring mobile phone and social media use in a Nairobi slum: a case for alternative approaches to design in ICTD. *Proceedings of the Seventh International Conference on Information and Communication Technologies and Development*, ACM, 1–8.

44. Daisy Yoo, Alina Huldtgren, Jill Palzkill Woelfer, David G. Hendry, and Batya Friedman. 2013. A value sensitive action-reflection model: evolving a co-design space with stakeholder and designer prompts. *Proceedings of the SIGCHI conference on human factors in computing systems*, ACM, 419–428.

Making Community: The Wider Role of Makerspaces in Public Life

Nick Taylor
DJCAD
University of Dundee
Dundee, UK
n.x.taylor@dundee.ac.uk

Ursula Hurley
School of Arts and Media
University of Salford
Salford, UK
u.k.hurley@salford.ac.uk

Philip Connolly
Disability Rights UK
London, UK
philip.connolly@
disabilityrightsuk.org

ABSTRACT
Makerspaces—public workshops where makers can share tools and knowledge—are a growing resource for amateurs and professionals alike. While the role of makerspaces in innovation and peer learning is widely discussed, we attempt to look at the wider roles that makerspaces play in public life. Through site visits and interviews at makerspaces and similar facilities across the UK, we have identified additional roles that these spaces play: as social spaces, in supporting wellbeing, by serving the needs of the communities they are located in and by reaching out to excluded groups. Based on these findings, we suggest implications and future directions for both makerspace organisers and community researchers.

Author Keywords
Makerspace; FabLab; making; DIY; community; Men's Shed; wellbeing; inclusion.

ACM Classification Keywords
H.5.m. Information interfaces and presentation (e.g., HCI): Miscellaneous;

INTRODUCTION
Makerspaces—also referred to variously as hackerspaces and Fab Labs—are one of the most visible manifestations of an emergent maker culture. They provide communal facilities in an openly accessible space, giving access to resources including digital fabrication and open electronics, which have been collectively hailed as enabling a revolution in personal manufacturing. As digital fabrication increasingly enters the public consciousness, makerspaces are dramatically lowering barriers to entry, enabling anyone to create their own solutions to problems or even bring products to market. Initially emerging from universities, makerspaces are now found everywhere from industrial estates to high streets, schools, museums and libraries.

CHI'16, May 07 - 12, 2016, San Jose, CA, USA

ACM 978-1-4503-3362-7/16/05...$15.00
DOI: http://dx.doi.org/10.1145/2858036.2858073

Figure 1. Typical makerspace facilities. Image © Rory Hyde.

As with most innovations, access to the benefits of makerspace facilities is unevenly spread. Although makerspaces are open to all, many of those making use of these facilities are early adopters with technical or creative backgrounds and a large proportion are affluent males [4]. Many makerspaces have grown out of existing software clubs run by programmers and reflect the demographics of these groups. Our research considers the potential benefits of makerspaces to the broader public and the challenges that might be faced in making this a reality. Initially, our focus had been on the disabled community and how disabled people might make use of makerspaces for their own benefit. While there has been much research focusing on the use of DIY assistive technologies by disabled people [e.g. 8, 13, 14], we sought to understand broader benefits, including wellbeing and entrepreneurship.

However, in surveying existing makerspace usage and outreach activities, we discovered that the potential sources of value to disabled people are in fact sources of value for the wider communities surrounding the facilities. We found evidence that makerspaces have much to offer the communities in which they are located. This is a finding that would not surprise makerspace organisers themselves—for almost all the spaces we surveyed, community engagement was either a core activity or an aspiration. However, for those working in other community organisations or researching the intersection of technology and community, these findings reveal new resources that cam be harnessed in supporting communities.

In this paper, we report on findings from site visits to makerspaces throughout the UK and interviews with makerspace organisers. For the purposes of our research, we subscribe to the definition of a makerspace as "an open workshop with different tools and equipment, where people can go independently to make something" [31]. These varied between incredibly small spaces that primarily catered to a community of enthusiasts to large spaces providing commercial services. Activity ranged from digital fabrication and traditional crafts to hardware and software hacking. Based on an analysis of the interviews, we describe the different ways in which makerspaces support community beyond those which are most widely known. Building on these experiences, we offer suggestions for makerspaces, communities and researchers on how the value of makerspaces might reach a still wider audience.

BACKGROUND

Maker culture describes a worldwide movement of individuals using a mix of digital fabrication, open hardware, software hacking and traditional crafts to innovate for themselves, underpinned by an ethos of openness and skill sharing rather than commercial benefit [17]. There is a belief that individuals with the right skills can produce solutions that are better and cheaper than mass produced products—or at the very least, they can learn something and have fun while trying to do so.

Much of the focus on making and DIY in HCI has been around individual creativity and craft communities [e.g. 27], but it has also come to be recognised as a potentially democratising revolution for design and manufacturing [33]. Chris Anderson's *Makers* [2] describes a range of examples in which access to rapid prototyping technologies has allowed inventors to rapidly iterate over designs and ship products themselves. This is possible because digital fabrication defies economies of scale, negating the need for mass production to make a product viable. Lindtner et al. [21] pay particular attention to the growth of maker culture in emerging economies, where local innovators can begin to develop their own products rather than simply manufacturing products designed elsewhere. Other examples include hacking and repairing the infrastructure of their environment [1] and empowering technology owners to repair their own devices [28].

Other research has begun to consider the application of digital fabrication and maker culture to wider challenges in society, often aiming to broaden participation in making [e.g. 7, 14, 15, 26]. In particular, a large body of research has explored DIY assistive technologies (DIY-AT). Digital fabrication allows rapid and cheap customisation of existing assistive technologies or even the creation of entirely new solutions [8, 13, 14, 15], aligning with an emerging agenda of designing for user empowerment [18, 25]. For example, E-Nable [9] is a network of makerspaces that are capable of producing 3D printed prosthetic limbs that can be customised according to individual needs—both in terms of functionality and aesthetics.

Alongside the rise of maker cultures has been the appearance of shared spaces where people can come together to share skills, ideas and equipment. The idea of a Fab Lab emerged from MIT's Centre for Bits and Atoms before being replicated in other cities and countries [11]. Fab Labs form part of a global network and sign up to a particular set of shared values—the Fab Charter—that defines them as community spaces, with business as a secondary activity that must not interfere with the primary function. Other spaces, more commonly just referred to as makerspaces, might not be part of this network, although they typically have many of the same facilities and share much of the Fab Lab network's ethos. However, these spaces play a wide range of roles, including co-working space, clubhouse, community centre, school innovation space, museum education centre and shop [19].

Although the dominant focus within HCI has been on "individual makers and their skills" [35], past work has noted that the community within these spaces is often one the most valuable resources they have [21]. Toombs et al. [35] document the implicit and explicit effort required to maintain this community within a makerspace, such as donating equipment, teaching other users, welcoming new members or taking on quasi-official roles within the space. Other research has explored feminist hackerspaces [10], paying particular attention to boundaries defining who does and does not fit within the space's community. Even in these cases, the focus has typically been on the community *within* the makerspace amongst those who could already be considered enthusiasts.

Other fields of study, particularly education and library studies, have been quick to capitalise on the benefits of makerspaces for those outside maker communities [20, 29]. Although the makerspaces in library environments might at first seem at odds, they share a common goal of making resources available to everybody at little or no cost. Usage patterns for libraries have shifted significantly in recent years, offering a broader range of services and sometimes being integrated with delivery of other public services. Makerspace values strongly echo libraries' core mission of providing equal access to knowledge resources [30], so access to digital fabrication has been seen as a natural progression beyond existing ICT provision [5].

The existence of makerspaces in libraries also places them in a space that has traditionally served as a hub of community activity and information. This can be a significant aspect of a makerspace's identity: they are "both a community space and a space for communities" [36], and consequently respond to local factors. Kohtala and Bosqué [16] in particular emphasise the importance of people and locality in the Fab Lab network, describing how Norway's first Fab Lab responded to the unique characteristics of the community in which it was established, transforming into something quite different to MIT's original Fab Lab. Making is often—arguably always—a political act, as makers aim to intervene to create a world different to the one we live in [24]. Making in communities thus often contains a streak of activism. Barcelona's Ateneu de Fabricació Digital (an *ateneu* is a traditional Catalonian civic space) were intended to allow citizens to take an active role in shaping the city [32]. These spaces recognised that they exist in specific social, political and economic contexts that shape their use. In the case of Barcelona, the facilities opened against a backdrop of economic strife and political dissatisfaction that greatly influenced them [32].

This civic and community facet of makerspaces, recognised by existing work but remaining underexplored, is the focus of our attention in this paper. We focus outwards to consider not just communities of makers who frequent makerspaces, but to the wider environment in which these facilities are sited. We demonstrate a wide range of roles that makerspaces can play in civic life, acting as a hub for both making and other activities, and imparting value in a much broader variety of ways than just the economic potential and hobbyist communities on which past research has focused. In doing this, we begin to see intersections with other topics of HCI research, such as community technology and wellbeing.

STUDY

This paper draws on data collected through a series of site visits and interviews intended to scope out existing activity in UK makerspaces to identify opportunities and challenges in engaging a wider audience. Below, we describe the process of surveying makerspace provision across the UK and analysis to derive common themes of activity. We also provide examples of makerspaces demonstrating typical configurations and community roles.

Data Collection and Analysis

Three members of the research team independently visited a total of 15 makerspaces and similar facilities (the varying self-descriptive terminology reflects differences in origins, provision and philosophy, but all the spaces acted as a publicly accessible workshop supporting something recognisable—but not necessarily identified—as maker culture). Each site visit included a tour of the facilities and a semi-structured interview conducted with makerspace organisers. Question prompts used by the researchers sought information about the history, motivations and ambitions of the facility, its user base, typical activities, promotion and outreach, and specific examples relating to excluded communities. Interviews typically lasted between 30 and 60 minutes and were followed by a tour of the facilities. Most interviews were conducted with a single representative of the makerspace, but in smaller and less formal spaces, a number of members were present and contributed to the discussion. One Skype interview was also conducted with an arts organisation who worked with profoundly disabled people and had made use of makerspaces, but who did not have their own facilities. Based on an analysis of the collected data, the team derived themes of activity presented in the subsequent sections.

Example Makerspaces

Using a broad definition of makerspaces, our site visits ranged from large commercial spaces to small spaces run by volunteers that identified themselves variously as makerspaces, Fab Labs and hackerspaces, but also facilities that do not identify with maker culture at all. Below, we describe a number of spaces that exemplify different scales, business models and activities observed, and that we will draw heavily on in the following sections.

MAKLab Glasgow

MAKLab in Glasgow is the largest and longest-established makerspace in Scotland and one of the most successful in the UK. Their main space is a highly visible shopfront near the city centre that houses digital fabrication equipment, electronics facilities, a fabric/textiles workshop and an events space. They have a number of other spaces, including a 'dirty' workshop for woodworking equipment and a growing network of smaller, specialist facilities across Scotland, including in museums and libraries. They operate as both a provider of commercial digital fabrication services and a charity aiming to broaden access to these facilities. By comparison to many spaces, they are able to employ a relatively high number of staff, which allows them to invest time in a range of outreach activities.

Dundee Makerspace

Unlike their more commercial counterparts, Dundee Makerspace is one of a number of grassroots facilities started by a small number of enthusiasts with little or no financial support. As is typical of smaller spaces, they do not have formal leadership but rather operate as a collective—although in reality a small number of members play a larger organisational role. They have less capacity for outreach, and while they do run some public events the provision of the space itself for members is their core activity. The space is located in an office building within walking distance of the city centre, which is part of a cluster of buildings housing many of the city's digital and creative sector companies. They rely on membership dues and a small amount of external funding.

FabLab Northern Ireland

The two associated makerspaces located in Belfast and Derry/Londonderry were the first makerspaces in Northern Ireland, but are also notable for the unique political role that they play. Northern Ireland suffered many years of conflict between the 1960s and 1990s, with lingering divisions and sporadic incidents of violence up to the present day. The two Northern Irish facilities were intended to play a part in the peace process by bringing people together around shared creative activities regardless of their backgrounds. The facilities themselves are located at "interface areas" where nationalist and unionist areas of the city meet and are combined with other community arts facilities, including music studios, practice rooms and other bookable spaces.

Westhill Men's Shed

Westhill Men's Shed (Figure 2) is part of an international movement that originated in Australia in response to concerns about mental health in older men. Like makerspaces, Men's Sheds provide a communal workspace where members can come together to work on their own projects—although the workshops provide traditional wood and metalwork tools rather than digital fabrication equipment. The shed also provides communal areas outside the workshop and like many makerspaces they have expanded their provision into other areas, such as cookery lessons. Attendees are mostly older men who may be feeling isolated following a major life event such as retirement, bereavement or a stroke. The shed provides social contact and a sense of purpose without foregrounding the mental health issues that men may be unwilling to confront explicitly.

FINDINGS

The roles that makerspaces played in their communities fell into four broad themes: acting as social spaces; supporting wellbeing; serving the needs of the communities they are located in; and reaching out to excluded groups. While not exhaustive, these roles presented themselves in almost all of the spaces, manifested in a variety of ways.

A Social Space

Makerspaces are rarely just where fabrication could be carried out. Rather, they are hubs of community, where people come together to work together, learn from each other, or simply socialise. Some of the spaces we visited, such as the Men's Shed, had dedicated communal areas, while others emphasised the value of socialising with others over the machinery itself. Many of the spaces included kitchen facilities and most included at least facilities to make hot drinks—facilities were seen as being just as integral to the space's mission as any digital fabrication equipment.

The smallest of the spaces that we visited, located in a single small office at the top of a tenement building, was most adamant about this point. Identifying themselves as a hackerspace, they were primarily engaged in computer hardware and software. With none of the large pieces of equipment seen in a typical makerspace, the provision of shared equipment was not their main priority, but being in the space had additional value:

> *"Most of our members could afford to reproduce the facilities without any issue* [...] *It's mostly the access to other people that drives them in. You don't really want to be sat in your house all weekend by yourself soldering.*

Figure 2. Westhill Men's Shed offers workshop facilities similar to a makerspace, but also prioritises its social spaces. Image © Scottish Men's Sheds Association.

> *But if you come here other people might come through and you speak to them and you feel like you're socialising."*

This had the effect of turning otherwise solitary activities such as coding into communal activities that could be shared with others. However, this was echoed even by spaces with larger pieces of equipment. In these spaces, the equipment—particularly 3D printers with widespread appeal—were seen as a 'hook' that drew in visitors, who would subsequently stay for the community:

> *"Quite a few people who come to the makerspace are interested in microfabrication* [sic] *and the kind of fabrication boom that's come from 3D printing in recent years. I think the allure of that is something that's got a lot of people on-board, but we all kind of stay for the community aspect and to try help it grow."*

Membership-driven spaces typically had at least one open evening per week. Although these were theoretically designed as times when any member of the public could stop by to learn about the space, they had a secondary purpose as designated meeting times for the community. Particularly in the smaller spaces with limited numbers of members, it was at these designated times that the majority of users visited the space and usage outside these times was often very light. Although many regular members had ongoing projects in various stages of completion or planning, these were frequently long-term, tinkering projects (most notably a perpetual motion machine). Instead, we saw members spending much of their time socialising, helping others or just observing members who were actively working on projects, maintaining or tinkering with pieces of shared equipment, or other activities that contributed to the greater good of the space.

In this sense, the smaller spaces had much in common with the Men's Shed. In both cases, the facilities being provided and even the making being carried out were secondary to the social value that was being gained by sharing the facilities and being connected with fellow makers. At the time of our visit to the Men's Shed, very few of the attendees were engaged in making at all. Rather, most of the attendees were located in the social area, mostly chatting with other members or playing games.

> *"The big catch is the workshop* [...] *but actually its not about that, it's about health and wellbeing and sociability out there* [in the social space]. *"*

By comparison, the Men's Shed organiser described another space he had visited that had not succeeded in gaining a critical mass. He saw their key problem as a lack of communal facilities:

> *"Guy comes in, has a cup of tea, might talk to someone while he makes his cup of tea, does his project and goes home* [...] *you're telling them its not available to socialise, there's no possibility for that."*

Many of the spaces were also self-organising, grassroots initiatives, typically started by friends or an existing group, such as a software club. They had little in the way of organisational structures, and what structures they had often existed only for legal purposes so that they could be registered as a social enterprise (a business with a social mission that reinvests profits in itself). In one case, the contact person for a space reacted sharply to an email request to speak with the space's organisers, as the idea of a hierarchy conflicted with strongly-held values:

> *"There are directors because there have to be directors. There's nobody organising anything. It's very different from the way* [other] *makerspaces are probably structured as* [...] *companies and arts organisations. We just want to have the space."*

This space represented one extreme on a spectrum: in reality, most of the grassroots spaces had a small group of founders and core members who took it upon themselves to keep the space open by applying for funding, maintaining equipment and acting as a public face for new members.

However, the social qualities of makerspaces were less apparent in the larger, more commercial spaces. Although there were normally tables where people could work and sometimes kitchen facilities, there were no apparent regular events or core members outside the staff. Owing to their larger size and organisational needs, there were also more defined hierarchies and they were often created by partnerships between local councils, arts organisations or knowledge institutions rather than emerging in a grassroots fashion. These spaces did have other roles in the community, as we will discuss in subsequent sections.

Serving Local Needs

While the makerspaces were broadly similar in their equipment and ethos, we were struck by the subtler diversity in their activities and goals. Makerspaces very much served the communities in which they were located, responding to local needs and issues and tailoring their provision accordingly, much as the Fab Lab model was customised as it moved from a North American university to the Norwegian countryside [16]. One of the makerspace organisers spoke explicitly about the effort that they put into this:

> *"We've had to work hard to make this relevant* [...] *there's a utility to what we do, it's useful in some way rather than just proving the concept."*

One way in which makerspaces responded to the local community was in catering to industry and employment needs. Most literally, many of the spaces had helped local industry to create custom parts—in one case a police forensics team wanted to build a DIY alternative to an expensive piece of equipment. More broadly, it was common for spaces to have a training programme, some of which were accredited and recognised (e.g. OCN Level 1 in Digital Fabrication). Even where formal training was not provided, they still saw the skills being developed—both by young people and those retraining—as being useful for a future career in industry:

> *"It's a good way to* [...] *start thinking about a creative career or an engineering career* [...] *you can use the FabLab as a platform to find jobs and get experience."*

This makerspace was able to identify several examples of users who had gained apprenticeships either directly or indirectly through their experience, and was now offering its own apprenticeships. A number of spaces also took on young, unemployed people in work experience roles. This trend was particularly visible in spaces located in industrial cities and towns or where unemployment rates are high. In one case, the entire makerspace was funded by the nuclear industry, which was a major employer in the local area. Although this was partly a goodwill activity, it also served to develop skills and an enthusiasm towards science and technology in local young people that would be useful to a future career in the energy sector.

However, the economic contribution was not entirely industry-focused. In one example, a makerspace in a small town had enabled a local café to create unique decor that was a defining feature of the business. For the café owner, this had a double impact, enabling her to keep costs down when starting her business, but also making her venue unique—visitors would frequently comment on the decor and such comments also featured heavily in TripAdvisor reviews:

> *"Every room in the bistro has got at least one item that was created by the FabLab. They played a very big part in the making of the decor and the atmosphere* [...] *people love it* [...] *they say it's more of a big city style."*

For the Men's Shed, taking on jobs from the local community was a core part of their business model, alongside upcycling tools and equipment. Small jobs received were posted on a jobs board, where members could choose to take them on. Typical jobs included building benches and mailboxes for clients ranging from private individuals to schools and local government. By taking on these tasks, they were not only able to provide value to the local community, but also perpetuate the space, effectively reinvesting the funds into the community:

> *"Last year the guys did thirty-two community projects which they charged for* [...] *they're completely self-sufficient after a year and a half."*

However, they were careful to do this without undermining local businesses:

> *"The projects that they do are pretty much projects that people don't want, that charities and schools can't afford* [...] *and they know that their fathers and grandfathers are benefiting from* [doing the work]*."*

The Men's Shed emphasised that jobs should come without stress and deadlines, which would interfere with the space's core mental health goals.

Meeting local needs did not only take the form of service provision benefits. One of the most striking examples of makerspaces responding to local issues was in the Northern Irish FabLabs. The Belfast FabLab was located in the north of the city, which—in addition to being an interface area between nationalist and unionist neighbourhoods—was one of the most socially and economically deprived areas of the city. Part of their mission was to bring together people from both sides of the Northern Ireland conflict around shared, constructive tasks and activities that helped to develop skills and economic prosperity:

> *"We're moving into* [...] *having a focus on social enterprise and social innovation, partly because we believe that those two elements are ways of normalising post-conflict society* [...] *if people feel that they have a future and they play a part in that future then you're offering hope and you're more likely to take the tension out of divided communities."*

Their sister site in Derry/Londonderry likewise engaged in civically engaged making as part of David Best's *Temple* (Figure 3), a crowdfunded installation built in 2015 [6]. Over a week, the 22-meter wooden temple was visited by 60,000 visitors, who were encouraged to attach a memory to the structure, leaving it behind and symbolically letting go. At the end of a week, the entire temple was burned in front of an audience of 15,000 people. The city's FabLab contributed a series of ornate panels made by young people, who completed the work as part of a training course. Other community groups helped to build lanterns that were used during the burning of the installation. In this example, we see the entire city being engaged in a collaborative act of making that cumulated in the creation of a substantial artwork with ambitions to have an impact on societal issues

Figure 3. Inside David Best's *Temple*, Derry/Londonderry. Panels were covered with personal messages before the structure was burned. Image © Kenneth Allen

affecting the city. Although the FabLab itself played a tangential role, it was nonetheless able to harness enthusiasm around making to deliver training to young people—thereby contributing to efforts around both reconciliation with the past and development for the future.

Wellbeing and Empowerment

For most of the makerspaces, wellbeing was not an explicit goal, but nevertheless manifested itself in a number of ways. The idea of craft and other creative endeavours as an activity for wellbeing is not a new one or one that is exclusive to makerspaces [37]—as part of our study, we interviewed one disabled arts organisation who have spent the past 20 years working on long-term arts projects with profoundly disabled people. For them, there was little doubt that both the act of making was highly beneficial:

> *"You get lost in a process* [...] *what happens as a result of making means a lot."*

Due to the overall focus of our project on disability in makerspaces, many of the wellbeing activities identified in interviews related to this. As documented by existing research, assistive technologies were an obvious use case, and one of the spaces had recently printed its first prosthetic limb. However, for many users of makerspaces, the wellbeing aspect of the facilities is not about solving particular problems, but about the simple joy of making something. A common sentiment expressed was that *what* was made didn't matter, but rather *how*—the act of making itself was more important. In most cases, disabled users were not building anything that related to their disability. Rather, the benefit was in being in a space that empowered them to be creative:

> *"It would be more about bringing them into a creative space and doing things* [...] *the technology takes away some of the barriers."*

"I was surprised by it [...] *what that does for people, how they feel liberated."*

For others, makerspaces presented an opportunity to develop skills and to engage with the world in a productive way. Inspiring examples from our interviews included a teenager who had not left his home for six months prior to visiting the makerspace, but who was able to engage with other people his own age and publically reach out to the makerspace on social media to thank them for the experience. At another space, one of the volunteers was in rehabilitation from an unspecified condition: his volunteer position allowed him to build confidence and skills—not just in terms of utilising machinery, but also in engaging with members of the public.

"It's a way for him to engage with the public again, where he didn't have the confidence before, and so he's learning how to use the machinery, but at the same time he's building skills that he could use to get a job once he's fully rehabilitated."

Many of the examples fitting this theme included similar individuals who had difficulty interacting with others for varying reasons—reports of makerspace users with autism arose in a large proportion of the interviews, for example. This highlights the importance of providing the form of social space described previously.

While most makerspaces do not actively aim to achieve wellbeing outcomes, the Men's Shed made it central to their existence—even if it wasn't foregrounded. The Men's Shed that we visited formed part of a worldwide movement that originated in Australia in response to mental health issues amongst men and their unwillingness to seek help. This was particularly acute amongst retired men, whose identity and social circles may have been closely tied to their jobs. Men's Sheds directly address loneliness in this population, but also provide a space with less perceived stigma attached than traditional wellbeing provisions, in which men may eventually feel able to address other issues affecting them. This movement has been replicated in many other countries, including Scotland, where a single pilot shed started by a council worker has subsequently grown into a nationwide network.

Wellbeing benefits were readily apparent during the site visit. For example, several stroke victims who lived alone were visiting the social space to practice speaking. Another attendee, a World War II veteran in his 90s, repeatedly remarked how the space had given him a new lease of life following his retirement and the subsequent death of his wife. He had learned new woodworking skills and now made wooden chairs and benches, some of which had been commissioned for public spaces in the local area (as described in the previous section). In addition to 'making' in the sense of wood and metal, the Shed also ran cooking lessons targeted at helping widowers to become more independent and improve their health. The fact that this took place in a safe environment alongside activities perceived as being more 'masculine' allowed them to reach those who—as with mental health—might not be willing to access other provisions.

The wellbeing outcomes were remarkable: a social return on investment analysis showed a tenfold return in terms of reductions in loneliness and reliance on public health services and other forms of support. Members were happier and more active, in some cases leading to physical health benefits and reduced reliance on medication—the organiser cited research findings that loneliness alone has the same health impact as 15 cigarettes a day [12]. It also provides a place where consumption of alcohol is not possible in an area and population with high levels of alcoholism. Health research in Australia has confirmed these outcomes in some of the original Men's Sheds [3]. At both the Men's Shed and the other examples provided, making is a hook that brings people together and places those with different wellbeing needs on a similar footing around a shared activity.

Widening Access

Almost all of the makerspaces were engaged in some form of outreach, most commonly by running workshops with members of the public who might not normally engage with making. These sometimes included bringing external groups into the makerspace, but often involved taking equipment out of the makerspace, either to public events or to particular groups of users such as schools. The importance placed on reaching a wider audience was evident even in the way spaces described their objectives:

"Make digital technologies and software as available to as wide a range of the public as possible at as low cost as possible."

"Enabling everyone to create anything."

Even in the smallest of spaces, there was an expressed desire to be more inclusive. Organisers cared greatly about openness and accessibility, and were often frustrated with their inability to meet these needs. For example, the smallest space was located in a cramped office with no elevator, but their funds were insufficient to allow them to move elsewhere:

"We've tried [to move] *twice, but we struggle to maintain a positive balance* [...] *it's unfair to block off a resource like this."*

For some makerspaces, being able to secure a premium location on the high street, typically with the backing of local authorities, was seen as a core method of reaching a wider audience:

"We get everybody [...] *they walk past and they stick their head in the door and they say 'what's this all about?'"*

Figure 4. Workshops with members of the public engage a wider audience who might not otherwise access makerspaces. Image © Mitch Altman.

But for all types and size of space, dedicated public events (e.g. Figure 4) both inside and outside their own facilities were the most common form of outreach. Broadly speaking, these events were intended to introduce attendees to the possibilities of digital fabrication, usually through a small, structured task that resulted in a tangible outcome. These were generally intended to act as an inspiration and starting point for people who want to do more, especially for school children:

> *"We do after school clubs for kids* [...] *people who've completed that* [...] *they go away and sit on their own or in groups and come up with their own ideas."*

Although this might be seen as a natural avenue for recruitment, organisers reported mixed successes in converting attendees at outreach events into regular users of the facilities. For larger spaces with varied income streams, this is not a problem, but for membership driven spaces, growing their subscribers was necessary to achieve their ambitions. Rather, these spaces reported that recruitment was often by word of mouth, which presents greater challenges in reaching outside typical demographics.

In responding to the demands of their community, some of the spaces were broadening their provision beyond the most commonly found digital fabrication and electronics equipment. For example, one of the makerspaces has recently added a textiles workshop with professional sewing equipment and, at the time of writing, are advertising an introductory course to domestic sewing machines. This had brought in a different audience, but has encouraged learning and collaboration between different communities of interest:

> *"It's bringing in a different type of user, at the same time they're then feeding back into* [other activities...] *you're getting a different sort of overlap, just broadening again the range of users, that maybe they wouldn't normally have come to this sort of space before."*

Like 3D printing, these activities might be considered as 'hooks' that draw in people with varying interests who might subsequently branch out to explore other materials and processes, or take advantage of the social benefits of makerspace usage described previously.

However, despite the best intentions of the makerspaces, it was availability of resources, particularly staff, that was the primary factor in determining the level of outreach activities they were capable of conducting. In this area, there was a marked difference between small grassroots makerspaces and larger commercial facilities—larger spaces had more staff, but they were also able to reinvest income from commercial work to support the charitable and outreach aspects of the space's ambitions.

> *"We don't have any employees. There's nobody to do it. There's nobody trained to work with any sort of people."*

> *"Whatever activities we have here, more commercial enterprises* [...] *all that money then goes back into funding outreach programmes."*

At the same time, the fact that most makerspace users are there to engage with things they are passionate about can be a boon when this intersects with outreach. For example, one of the full-time staff members we interviewed had a background in caring for people with mental health problems. This background manifested itself in the organisations the space chose to work with, the types of activity that they organised, and in her acute awareness of accessibility issues. Conversely, even in those spaces that had resources to conduct outreach activities, staff and volunteers were cautiously enthusiastic, but aware of their own lack of skills in dealing with people who might need extra consideration, particularly when resources did not extend to additional training or facilities:

> *"We are not trained for work with disabled people. I'm more worried about that. But I'd see it like a challenge* [...] *I'd like to do it just to see how."*

Finally, some factors influencing outreach are more culturally ingrained. For example, for some new users, the ability to create anything was intimidating and some makerspaces discussed using designers as facilitators for inspiration. But there were more varied reasons for exclusion, even amongst those who might otherwise want to use the facilities. For various segments of society, there might be a feeling that they simply don't 'fit in'. In one example, a child was unable to return to the makerspace due to his parents' feelings of exclusion:

> *"One of the young gentlemen who was involved from the school* [said his parents] *don't speak English. They felt very much like they couldn't come in, that it wasn't for them, no matter how much we talked to him."*

Although public events and the increasing public awareness of digital fabrication—particularly through its presence in schools—might help to ease this, most makerspaces are in their infancy and clearly some way from meeting their ambitions of being truly accessible to everybody. This last point in particular speaks of deeper inclusion issues that makerspaces share with other public resources, where exclusion is not just about access to technology or facilities, but a more fundamental exclusion from large parts of society.

DISCUSSION

Through a survey of 15 makerspaces, we have identified a number of broad themes describing ways in which these resources support public life. These impacts are much broader than just those that are commonly reported on, having implications for wellbeing, social life, local communities and potentially reaching a wide audience. In identifying these wider impacts, we begin see overlaps with other areas of HCI research, such as the role of technology in community and in supporting wellbeing. Below, we reframe the wider civic role of makerspaces in terms familiar to HCI and describe a number of remaining areas of potential that HCI researchers may be well-equipped to support makerspaces in exploiting.

Makerspaces as Third Places

Throughout our survey, we saw many spaces that matched the image of a makerspace held in popular imagination: stylishly utilitarian rooms filled with exciting equipment and brimming with ideas. But we also saw spaces being shared with museums, galleries and games companies, and utilised for events that ranged from Robot Wars to hairdressing lessons. It is clear, then, that makerspaces are not just homes for 3D printers and laser cutters. Rather, they are public resources dedicated to creativity, learning and openness. This comes at a time when many communities do not have a community spaces and where civic life is often seen as being in decline.

A number of scholars have already argued that makerspaces are effectives effectively *third places* [22, 34]. The notion of third places—social spaces separate from the home and workplace that play a critical role in public life [23]—has been a popular one in HCI, but some of the critical features of Ray Oldenburg's term have tended to be disregarded. His third places were homes away from home that acted as social levellers, places where one can find both regulars and friends old and new, places that never became overly serious. Almost all of these properties are embodied by makerspaces. Perhaps the only aspect where they do not align is in being accessible to all, where the ideals held by makerspaces are not always achieved, despite best intentions. Regardless, viewing makerspaces in this way gives us a starting point for understanding the role that they might play in communities, and learning from other research around third places might provide indications of further possible sources of value to communities.

Playing an Active Role

As we have shown, makerspaces play various roles in public life and have been very successful in that role. Despite this, we were struck by how few of the spaces had an explicit agenda beyond making digital fabrication equipment available to as many people as possible. Indeed, some of the spaces actively rejected any notion of a further agenda. However, where there was an agenda—such as wellbeing in the Men's Shed or reconciliation in Northern Ireland—the makerspaces had been able to make a remarkable difference in their communities. The success of these ventures causes us to reflect on whether makerspaces should be encouraged to take a more active stance on creating positive change, despite the inherent tension that this introduces.

One way in which this tension might be resolved is through a more concerted effort to connect makerspaces with those who *do* have agendas. On the whole, even those makers who did not want to push an agenda for their space remained enthusiastic about tackling problems brought through the door by visitors. Providing a challenge, especially in an area that makers aren't familiar with but are keen to engage with, can be highly motivating. This might mean connecting makers with local communities, national campaigns or even international networks. One area where we can see this happening is in the E-Nable community of makerspaces who offer to work with disabled people to produce prosthetic limbs. Issues remain, particularly the risk that makerspaces might be put under pressure to deliver, where they see themselves as hobbyists—"no deadlines, no stress", as one organiser put it. However, opening these channels of communication presents opportunities for both makerspaces and communities.

Making the Case for Makerspaces

Over the course of our research, we have been struck by the difficulty that makerspace organisers had in identifying and highlighting concrete examples of positive outcomes for makerspace users. This included not only the intangible social benefits that we have focused our attention on here, but also the more widely discussed economic benefits. One organiser spoke openly about their inability to track outcomes and the difficulties that this created—even pondering how they could be sure that the effort put into maintaining the space was worthwhile. To a certain extent, this is a reflection of the freedom that members had to access equipment independently and also the lack of central coordination in the smaller spaces. Organisers were enthusiastic makers, not administrators, whose primary focus was on making the resource available.

However, being able to communicate these outcomes is important in securing the future of this resource, especially against a backdrop of funding cuts. For example, being able to calculate a social return on investment and identify intangible benefits to the local area allowed the Men's Shed to gain support from local authorities and propagate quickly. Although there have been some efforts to document the extent of makerspaces [e.g. 31], the sheer variety of scale and activity makes it difficult to grasp their social and economic impacts. If makerspaces are to be sustainable and to play a role in communities akin to libraries—which appears to be a reasonable goal for at least a subset of the facilities—then it will be necessary to communicate their benefits more effectively.

CONCLUSION

In this paper, we have discussed a variety of roles that makerspaces play in civic life, which extend far beyond those roles they are most commonly associated with. These roles speak of huge potential for makerspaces to benefit communities and individuals. While not all of the roles we have observed are present in all makerspaces—this is to be expected given how responsive many of the spaces are to the particular needs of their communities—the desire to be more than just a workshop is widespread.

It is clear that makerspaces should be seen not as a gimmick or just the preserve of technologists, but taken seriously as a resource for communities. However, barriers remain that must be addressed if this potential is to be reached. In particular, future work might focus on the barriers that prevent individuals who might otherwise be interested in utilising the spaces from doing so. While the motivations of makerspace users have been documented previously, non-use is a more complex issue that deserves further attention.

ACKNOWLEDGMENTS

This research was funded by the AHRC *In the Making* project (AH/M006026/1). We would like to thank all of the participants who made time to speak to us.

REFERENCES

1. Syed Ishtiaque Ahmed, Nusrat Jahan Mim and Steven J. Jackson. 2015. Residual mobilities: infrastructural displacement and post-colonial computing in Bangladesh. In *Proceedings of the 33rd Annual ACM Conference on Human Factors in Computing Systems* (CHI '15), 437–446. http://dx.doi.org/10.1145/2702123.2702573
2. Chris Anderson. 2012. *Makers: The New Industrial Revolution*. Random House.
3. Megan L. Ballinger, Lyn A. Talbot and Glenda K. Verrinder. 2009. More than a place to do woodwork: a case study of a community-based Men's Shed. *Journal of Men's Health* 6, 1 (March 2009), 20–27. http://doi.org/10.1016/j.jomh.2008.09.006
4. Jonathan Bean and Daniela Rosner. 2014. Making: movement or brand? *Interactions* 21, 1 (January 2014), 26–27. http://doi.org/10.1145/254166
5. Nicole Belbin and Pat Newcombe. Fab Labs at the Library. 2012. *Government Technology* 25, 10 (October 2012), 30–33.
6. David Best. 2015. Temple. Retrieved July 13, 2015 from http://templederry-londonderry.com
7. Leah Buechley and Benjamin Mako Hill. 2010. LilyPad in the wild: how hardware's long tail is supporting new engineering and design communities. In *Proceedings of the 8th ACM Conference on Designing Interactive Systems* (DIS '10), 199–207. http://doi.org/10.1145/1858171.1858206
8. Erin Buehler, Amy Hurst, and Megan Hofmann. 2014. Coming to grips: 3D printing for accessibility. In *Proceedings of the 16th International ACM SIGACCESS Conference on Computers & Accessibility* (ASSETS '14), 291–292. http://doi.org/10.1145/2661334.2661345
9. E-Nable. Retrieved September 23, 2015 from http://enablingthefuture.org
10. Sarah Fox, Rachel Rose Ulgado and Daniela Rosner. 2015. Hacking culture, not devices: access and recognition in feminist hackerspaces. In *Proceedings of the 18th ACM Conference on Computer Supported Cooperative Work & Social Computing* (CSCW '15), 56–68. http://doi.org/10.1145/2675133.2675223
11. Neil Gershenfeld. 2005. *Fab: The Coming Revolution on Your Desktop*. Basic Books.
12. Julianne Holt-Lunstad, Timothy B. Smith, J. Bradley Layton. 2010. Social relationships and mortality risk: a meta-analytic review. *PLoS Medicine* 7, 7 (July 2010), e1000316. http://doi.org/10.1371/journal.pmed.1000316
13. Jonathan Hook, Sanne Verbaan, Abigail Durrant, Patrick Olivier, and Peter Wright. 2014. A study of the challenges related to DIY assistive technology in the context of children with disabilities. In *Proceedings of the 2014 Conference on Designing Interactive Systems* (DIS '14), 597–606. http://doi.org/10.1145/2598510.2598530
14. Amy Hurst and Jasmine Tobias. 2011. Empowering individuals with Do-It-Yourself assistive technology. In *Proceedings of the 3rd International ACM SIGACCESS Conference on Computers and Accessibility* (ASSETS '11), 11–18. http://doi.org/10.1145/2049536.2049541
15. Amy Hurst and Shaun Kane. 2013. Making "making" accessible. In *Proceedings of the 12th International Conference on Interaction Design and Children* (IDC '13), 635–638. http://doi.org/10.1145/2485760.2485883
16. Cindy Kohtala and Camille Bosqué. 2014. The story of MIT-Fablab Norway: community embedding of peer production. *Journal of Peer Production*, 5 (October 2014).
17. Stacey Kuznetsov and Eric Paulos. 2010. Rise of the expert amateur: DIY projects, communities, and

cultures. In *Proceedings of the 6th Nordic Conference on Human–Computer Interaction* (NordiCHI '10), 295–304. http://doi.org/10.1145/1868914.1868950

18. Richard E. Ladner. 2015. Design for user empowerment. *Interactions* 22, 2 (March 2015), 24–29. http://doi.org/10.1145/2723869
19. Micah Lande and Shawn Jordan. 2014. Making it together, locally. In *Frontiers in Education Conference* (FIE '14), 1–7. http://doi.org/10.1109/FIE.2014.7044394
20. Breanne K. Litts. 2015. Resources, facilitation, and partnerships: three design considerations for youth makerspaces. In *Proceedings of the 14th International Conference on Interaction Design and Children* (IDC '15), 347–350. http://doi.org/10.1145/2771839.2771913
21. Silvia Lindtner, Garnet D. Hertz, and Paul Dourish. 2014. Emerging sites of HCI innovation: hackerspaces, hardware startups & incubators. In *Proceedings of the SIGCHI Conference on Human Factors in Computing Systems* (CHI '14), 439–448. http://doi.org/10.1145/2556288.2557132
22. Jarkko Moilanen. 2012. Emerging hackerspaces – peer-production generation. In: *Open Source Systems: Long-Term Sustainability*, 94–111. http://doi.org/10.1007/978-3-642-33442-9_7
23. Ray Oldenburg. 1989. *The Great Good Place: Cafes, Coffee Shops, Community Centers, General Stores, Bars, Hangouts, and How They Get You through the Day*. Paragon.
24. Matt Ratto and Megan Boler. 2014. *DIY Citizenship: Critical Making and Social Media*. MIT Press.
25. Yvonne Rogers and Gary Marsden. 2013. Does he take sugar?: moving beyond the rhetoric of compassion. *Interactions* 20, 4 (July 2013), 48–57. http://doi.org/10.1145/2486227.2486238
26. Yvonne Rogers, Jeni Paay, Margot Brereton, Kate Vaisutis, Gary Marsden and Frank Vetere. 2014. Never too old: engaging retired people inventing the future with MaKey MaKey. In *Proceedings of the SIGCHI Conference on Human Factors in Computing Systems* (CHI '14), 3913–3922. http://doi.org/10.1145/2556288.2557184
27. Daniela Rosner and Jonathan Bean. 2009. Learning from IKEA hacking: I'm not one to decoupage a tabletop and call it a day. In *Proceedings of the SIGCHI Conference on Human Factors in Computing Systems* (CHI '09), 419–422. http://doi.org/10.1145/1518701.1518768
28. Daniela K. Rosner and Morgan G. Ames. 2014. Designing for repair?: infrastructures and materialities of breakdown. In *Proceedings of the 17th ACM Conference on Computer Supported Cooperative Work & Social Computing* (CSCW '14), 319–331. http://dx.doi.org/10.1145/2531602.2531692
29. Kimberly M. Sheridan, Erica Rosenfeld Halverson, Breanne K. Litts, Lisa Brahms, Lynette Jacobs-Priebe and Trevor Owens. 2014. Learning in the making: a comparative case study of three makerspaces. *Harvard Educational Review* 84, 4 (Winter 2014), 505–531. http://doi.org/10.17763/haer.84.4.brr34733723j648u
30. Diane Slatter and Zaana Howard. 2013. A place to make, hack, and learn: makerspaces in Australian public libraries. *The Australian Library Journal* 64, 4, 272–284. http://doi.org/10.1080/00049670.2013.853335
31. Andrew Sleigh, Hannah Stewart and Kathleen Stokes. Open dataset of UK makerspaces: a user's guide. 2015. Retrieved September 8, 2015 from http://www.nesta.org.uk/publications/open-dataset-uk-makerspaces-users-guide
32. Adrian Smith. 2015. Tooling up: civic visions, FabLabs, and grassroots activism. Retrieved July 27, 2015 from http://gu.com/p/478pv/sbl
33. Joshua G. Tanenbaum, Amanda M. Williams, Audrey Desjardins and Karen Tanenbaum. 2013. Democratizing technology: pleasure, utility and expressiveness in DIY and maker practice. In *Proceedings of the SIGCHI Conference on Human Factors in Computing Systems* (CHI '13), 2603–2612. http://doi.org/10.1145/2470654.2481360
34. Austin L. Toombs, Shaowen Bardzell and Jeffrey Bardzell. 2014. Becoming makers: hackerspace member habits, values, and identities. *Journal of Peer Production*, 5 (October 2014).
35. Austin L. Toombs, Shaowen Bardzell and Jeffrey Bardzell. 2015. The proper care and feeding of hackerspaces: care ethics and cultures of making. In *Proceedings of the 33rd Annual ACM Conference on Human Factors in Computing Systems* (CHI '15), 629–638. http://doi.org/10.1145/2702123.2702522
36. Ding Wang, Nick Dunn and Paul Coulton. 2015. Grassroots maker spaces: a recipe for innovation? In *11th European Academy of Design Conference* (EAD '15).
37. Karen Yair. 2011. Craft and wellbeing. Retrieved September 10, 2015 from http://www.craftscouncil.org.uk/content/files/craft_and_wellbeing.pdf

Continuing the Dialogue: Bringing Research Accounts Back into the Field

Sarah Fox and Daniela K. Rosner
Human Centered Design and Engineering
University of Washington
sefox, dkrosner@uw.edu

ABSTRACT
This paper examines the work to bring HCI research back to the people and sites under study. We draw on our ongoing collaboration with members of feminist hackerspaces in Northern California where we conducted fieldwork over eighteen months in 2014 and 2015. Together we created and distributed a zine — a self-published magazine produced with a photocopier — that knit together content of a published paper with local histories of feminist print production. By tracing the efforts involved in this collaboration and its effects on our research project, our research community, and ourselves, we extend HCI's efforts to foster continued dialogue with our sites of study. We end by outlining strategies for bolstering this mission both within and beyond HCI.

Author Keywords
Alternative distribution; zine; feminism; design research.

ACM Classification Keywords
K.4.0 Computers in Society: general.

INTRODUCTION
Over the years, the HCI community has developed multiple and varied approaches to maintaining connections within and beyond its sites of investigation. From postcards to pots of clay, a tradition of probes has called on designers and researchers to develop conversational artifacts left open to interpretation [9,21]. In neighborhoods and among grassroots organizations, community-based projects organize initiatives that cultivate dialogue among multiple actors, priorities and interests [3,4,7]. At workshops and conferences, organizers invite industry colleagues and interlocutors to serve on panels and attend gatherings [22].

Yet, this work to extend conversations from the "field," or those people and sites so studied, exists primarily as a form of inquiry or professional development, and less as a mode of *knowledge transmission*, as sociologist Kat Jungnickel [13,14] would describe. Despite an ongoing interest in broadening research audiences, "innovative findings are often transformed back into conventional presentational formats" [14, p.138]. Beyond sending papers to our interlocutors and delivering presentations, we rarely communicate research insights to those we study — or the broader audiences we engage when we develop HCI papers, but who never encounter the work in its finished form. As HCI's research programs involve increasingly indeterminate and collaborative methods, we need to ask what new kinds of translations our scholarship might require.

This paper is about the work to communicate HCI research and continue conversations from the field. We examine our extra-academic collaborative activities to refigure traditional models of participation for researcher and subject. After publishing an academic paper on our study of feminist hackerspace in 2015 [8], a chance encounter led us to collaborate with members of these sites on a zine — a self-published magazine typically made with a photocopier — that knit together content from our published paper with local histories of feminist print production. Since 2012, community-organizers have developed feminist hackerspaces as workspaces oriented toward alternative legacies of technology development. We use this case to illustrate the opportunities and limitations of alternative modes of research distribution. In creating our zine, we not only acknowledged the active role our interlocutors played in our research process, but also broadened the impact of our work and sharpened our analytic focus. In doing so, we advance two central arguments. First, connecting modes of knowledge transmission with our methods of knowledge production may help researchers communicate in the field, reflecting the range of concerns that reach beyond textual authorship. Second, ongoing communication helps, in turn, extend the scope of our studies, enabling collaborations that cut across the seams of our research worlds.

BACKGROUND
Before discussing our efforts to reimagine our work for new audiences, we wish to revisit a growing body of research within and beyond HCI that seeks to treat interlocutors as collaborators. From the adoption of action-research methods to co-design [3,11,18], this research has sought to upend the researcher/subject dynamic as traditionally constituted. Rather than passive participants, community mem-

CHI'16, May 07 - 12, 2016, San Jose, CA, USA

ACM 978-1-4503-3362-7/16/05$15.00
DOI: http://dx.doi.org/10.1145/2858036.2858054

bers contribute to and shape research outcomes. Projects range from the development of neighborhood sensor networks [4], a collaborative system for a social movement [3], and a digital photo-album to facilitate cultural sharing among residents of a women's center [1]. In addition to the design of some artifact or system that may benefit the community in question and a peer-reviewed publication accounting for the work, several of these projects have organized a means of sharing the knowledge gained from this collaborative process beyond academic or industrial circles. For instance, Clarke et al. regularly facilitate exhibitions of workshop participants' photos in community settings [1] and Taylor and colleagues describe a process of 'insight journalism' [19], claiming it provides both design inspiration and a means for locals to represent themselves through a written newsletter.

Just outside HCI, similar concerns have emerged predominantly in the fields of sociology and science and technology studies. These include Lury and Wakeford's [16] inventive methods, Junknickel and Hjorth's [14] methodological entanglements, and Rabinow and Marcus' [17] studio-based inquiry. Margery Wolf's [23] early experiments involved comparing her presentation of the same story, a Taiwanese woman's departure from her village, in three different authorial accounts: a fictional tale, field notes, and anthropological argument. In her analysis, she suggests retaining firm boundaries between fiction and ethnographic research. Otherwise, she affirms, "[w]e will have blurred the ethnical assumptions of our craft" [23, p.59].

In other work this skeptical relation to authorial encoding extended to new media. Wakeford's [20] analysis of PowerPoint recommends "keeping open the relationship between the researcher and the PowerPoint" by, for example, "leaving traces of our own relationship to the participants within the slides." Drawing on the anthropological notion of "thick description," she frames PowerPoint as "thick" events locally informed and contextually dependent; for the corporate ethnographer, they require significant descriptive work to comprehend [20, p.100]. Highly influential on our work is the related series of experiments discussed by Junknickel and Hjorth [14] that draw on Wakeford to illustrate the promise of entangling methods and knowledge transmissions. Most recently, Junknickel's *Bikes and Bloomers* project prompts people to reconstruct and wear bloomers designed for Victorian women bicyclists. The project asked "what making *and* wearing your research bring to an understanding of mobility, gendered citizenship and the changing nature of public space" [13]. Our work expands these experimental modes of collaborative making and performance to wrestle with the "mess of method" [15] not in our empirical studies as much as the curation, summation and dissemination of research insights. Rather than approach the development of a single account, we show how knowledge transmissions might originate from multiple perspectives, take several forms, and appeal to different audiences.

METHODS

Our project draws on ethnographic methods that foreground engagement and interpretation over analytic distance and transcription of empirical phenomena. We conducted fieldwork and 13 ethnographic interviews in four hackerspaces that engaged in processes of redefining the role of marginalized groups, primarily women, in technology production and hacking. The second author additionally interviewed ten organizers of related technology development endeavors such as Survival Research Labs and the Flaming Lotus Girls in Northern California. Lastly, the first author visited and conducted participant observation within two zine festivals: one in Seattle, Washington and one in New York, New York. We subsequently transcribed interviews and reviewed our empirical materials during weekly meetings to discuss and draw out relevant themes.

CASE OF THE ZINE

Our efforts to collaboratively produce a zine came on the heels of an eighteen-month multi-sited ethnographic study. In the first several months of the research, we primarily occupied the role of a participant-observer. Over time our work became more collaborative as we organized workshops with members of two hackerspaces around questions of feminist technology design. Before publishing a paper about our fieldwork to that point, we sent a copy of the paper to the groups with whom we worked, hoping for any comments or reactions to our writing. Instead, we received an email asking for the rewording of one sentence (conveying a member's background more accurately). We ultimately published the paper with this change, but found ourselves underwhelmed by the modest response. Their reaction seemed markedly out of character for members of a group who had devoted hours to speaking candidly with us about their frustrations around the treatment of gender in sites of male-dominated technology development. Beyond these conversations, they let us sit alongside them at workshops in their spaces and answered questions about their finances and how they interpreted their own positions of power and privilege. We suspected that they had more to say about the work we had been doing, but perhaps we weren't talking in a way that prompted discussion.

Developing the Zine

The idea for the zine came out of this dissatisfaction with existing models of knowledge transmission — and a chance encounter. While attending a Seattle's Short Run festival — a temporary zine fest for artists to showcase and sell their own work — the first author ran into Amy Burek, a feminist hackerspace member. Burek was a scientist who had previously been a PhD student herself and, thus, found the academic style of writing and the format of the conference paper more-or-less familiar. Through this zine fest we also met Emily Alden Foster, an independent illustrator and animator who had recently completed a zine of personal histories and comics around the theme of women in the workplace. She also ran a subscription service that delivered a collection of zines called the Womanzine Delivery Service made by women on a quarterly basis. Over email and video chat, we continued to discuss combining our research findings with Burek's own experience as a member and the illustrator's watercolor images into a single piece named for the academic paper. After the initial meetings, Burek and Foster worked together for just over a month, combining text and image, before they asked us for final comments and edits. We compensated both artists for their work through a fund that had also covered the observational research.

The zine differed from our published paper. The artists added evocative comic imagery illustrating key ideas. They removed sections of our paper discussing theory and related literature to focus, instead, on our descriptions of the spaces: how they were run, what activities happen within them, and what motivated members to create them. Pushing beyond our published academic paper, our collaborators reframed a buried discussion of race and economic privilege, moving it from the middle of a section in our published paper to a page titled "The problems with 'hacking' and 'making'." With new language and sharp imagery, they described how "the terms 'hacker' and 'maker' may not properly represent people of color and the economically disadvantaged groups." Together these edits had the unanticipated outcome of sharpening our analytic focus on questions of marginality.

The artists then attributed the zine to multiple sources, noting that the work was "inspired by and sourced from research" published in our original paper [8]. Otherwise our names did not appear on the zine. But should they have? Should the zine have articulated who paid the artists and who curated the content? Whose zine was this anyway? Through attribution, the zine drew attention to multiple authorial voices and details of their relation.

In electing to put together a zine, we were situating the work in the prior practice of Burek and others who were a part of the spaces we studied. For instance, a cofounder of the San Francisco site had made zines since childhood and the hackerspace regularly hosted workshops for its members to come together to craft zines as a group. Several members also spoke of the commonalities between feminist hackerspaces and the Riot Grrrl movement of the 1990s, which sought to challenge the masculine culture of punk rock through the exchange of craft-based knowledge and the formation of spaces to practice and record music [10]. Zines were an important means of communicating sometimes highly personal stories of abuse and injustice and to document their own histories of the movement.

Debuting the Zine

We debuted the zine at a feminist zine festival hosted by Barnard College in New York. In the winter of 2015, the first author traveled from the Pacific Northwest with about 150 handmade zines and 50 copies of the academic paper to distribute to the hundreds of students, community organizers, professors, activists, and curious locals who gathered at the event. Also exhibiting were some 40 other zine makers "who [identified] on the feminist spectrum" [24].

Figure 1: Zine illustrations, © Emily Alden Foster & Amy Burek

Over the course of the day, the zine received several consistent reactions. Visitors regularly inquired about the types of activities that the feminist hackerspaces facilitated and a few people asked what constituted 'hacking'. Several conversations concerned concepts of invisible work mentioned in the zine. When visitors seemed particularly interested, the first author offered them a copy of the conference paper.

Yet, even with this consistent interest, we saw a striking difference among visitors emerge. *"So are you a hacker?"* one man asked. *"Do you code?"* The visitor only ceased asking questions when the first author explained she had done some front-end web development. At an adjacent table, a woman presented a zine openly grappling with histories of American slavery. Her zine used images she had digitally manipulated to contest the continued regulation of black women's bodies. At about midday, another visitor stopped at her table after circling a few times. As he thumbed through a zine, he paused to ask where she had gotten the photos. When she said she'd downloaded them from the Internet, he probed again, asking about the digital textures they featured and eventually suggested they be altered in Photoshop.

We share this vignette to show how an alternative means of research transmission opened our project to new observations. Notable here is a focus on technical ability over other forms of work, which found its way into a space meant to hold up voices and knowledges often unacknowledged. The visitors' comments recall Ron Eglash's discussion of masculine geek identity, which can play a gatekeeping role [6] that, in Christina Dunbar-Hester's words, "restricts nonwhites or women from embracing a geek identity" [5, p.67]. At the festival, this sort of questioning was not limited to zine makers whose zine titles included the word 'hack'. Like our prior encounters within feminist hackerspaces, our interlocutors surfaced an imposing regulation of what does and does not belong and a concentration on the technical. However, we were only able to surface these connections because of our own involvement in this alternative form of publication. In this sense, the zine helped expand our questions and sites of inquiry.

Extending the Dialogue

Over the coming months, the conversations and ideas that developed at the zine fest continued through the circulation of our zine. After the Barnard festival, the zine found a home in several sites just beyond it. The Barnard zine library and the Philadelphia Public Library took copies to add to their collections. We soon hosted a .pdf version of the zine on our project website, along with an offer to mail a printed copy to interested parties at no cost. A few months after this release, the popular feminist writer Ann Friedman recommended the zine in her newsletter. With this endorsement, we immediately noticed a marked increase in traffic to our project website. Several mentions of the piece on Twitter and Facebook and dozens of requests for paper copies soon followed. In a surprising turn of events, the zine even reappeared in our own research circles. Mentions of the work popped up in Twitter chats about civic media and in a blogpost about limitations of discussions of in/visibility by a digital humanist. Over time the zine helped us gather and broaden a conversation on issues of feminism and design.

DISCUSSION

This paper has so far examined the processes of knowledge production and sharing that emerged from our zine case study. The zine makers rewrote our original paper in ways that blurred authorship and claims, trusting, perhaps, that a reader might decide whose authority to accept. In the process, we learned how definitions of hacking (what one member called "shit-testing") circulate well beyond the walls of San Francisco and Portland hackerspaces to meet local patterns of zine distribution. But what do these hackerspace members, zine makers, and festivals have to do with HCI's sites of study? How do the inner workings of our extended dialogue speak to other areas of technological production such as sustainable computing or ICTD? How do they shed light on HCI knowledge transmissions more broadly?

As HCI's empirical focus continues to grow beyond conventional sites of technology production, our understanding of participation among those represented will continue to change, complicating our expectations for knowledge transmission in the field. Intertwining our objects of study with the people and ideas represented changes the accounts we produce. The moments of production, debut and distribution outlined above show the importance of reflecting back on our techniques of representation — and imagine what translations (while always partial) might effectively extend them.

Alongside highlighting this possibility for knowledge transmission, our project reveals something for the research study itself. The zine development not only helped the research team bring our accounts back to the field and reinterpreted it for new audiences; it also extended the scope of our project. For example, our experience observing the zine fest prompted us to ask what makes something a *feminist* design, where the design might entail a feminist hackerspace, zine, technology, and so on. Conversely, it prompted us to ask how a design activity may refigure feminist ideals. Following up on these questions in ongoing fieldwork, our publication — as a product of our methods and transmissions — created a "thick" [20] device for thinking with our communication media.

However, the zine's role in our project was by no means a given. The zine would not have been appropriate in every setting and it was certainly not the only form for this site either. Perhaps a hackathon with a critical bent would have opened our conversations to broader audiences. Or a Twitter chat would have more thoroughly catalogued our conversations beyond local sites. Each mechanism offers a different set of partial openings into HCI's sites of study. To help HCI researchers produce their own extensions, we submit three questions for those reporting back to the field:

(1) *What transmissions emerge in the site?* Within a given field site particular communication media (zines, tweets, tumblr feeds, podcasts) come to convey insights and shape enrollment. These media provide a means of examining alternate platforms for distribution (here, short-run publications).

(2) *What kinds of authorship do people gather around?* Exploring moments of acknowledgement and visibility already reverberating in a site suggests alternative modes of recognition (here, often collective and collaborative).

(3) *What rhetorical devices do people use to make their arguments?* The ways arguments circulate — and the form they take — offer lessons for overturning the "form fetish" [2,23] of paper presentations, wherein an established textual presentation prefigures evidentiary claims (here, comic illustrations and manifestos).

Together these questions help us imagine new knowledge representations that might inhabit HCI research. Their commonsense form invites us to ask why so little experimentation has occurred already. Perhaps one answer lies in the feminist case study we began with. Feminist anthropologists like Marilyn Strathern and Margaret Wolf have long questioned representations of the "other" by recognizing the remnants of colonialism in their wake (see [23]). As a community engaged in the examination of technology development, HCI has a similar responsibility to surface and make sense of the power relations within [12]. Beyond telling a convincing or evocative story, our transmissions require incorporating new kinds of participation for those being represented and, in doing so, reaching beyond our paths for research dissemination already underway.

ACKNOWLEDGEMENTS

We greatly appreciate our collaboration with Amy Burek and Emily Alden Foster. We also thank Elizabeth Churchill, Andrés Monroy-Hernández, Laura Devendorf, and Tad Hirsch for invaluable feedback on this paper. The research was supported by funding provided under NSF #1453329.

REFERENCES

1. Rachel Clarke, Peter Wright, Madeline Balaam, and John McCarthy. 2013. Digital Portraits: Photo-sharing After Domestic Violence. *Proceedings of the SIGCHI Conference on Human Factors in Computing Systems*, ACM, 2517–2526. http://doi.org/10.1145/2470654.2481348
2. James Clifford and George E. Marcus. 1986. *Writing Culture: The Poetics and Politics of Ethnography : a School of American Research Advanced Seminar*. University of California Press.
3. Jill P. Dimond, Michaelanne Dye, Daphne Larose, and Amy S. Bruckman. 2013. Hollaback!: The Role of Storytelling Online in a Social Movement Organization. *Proceedings of the 2013 Conference on Computer Supported Cooperative Work*, ACM, 477–490. http://doi.org/10.1145/2441776.2441831
4. Carl DiSalvo, Illah Nourbakhsh, David Holstius, Ayça Akin, and Marti Louw. 2008. The Neighborhood Networks Project: A Case Study of Critical Engagement and Creative Expression Through Participatory Design. *Proceedings of the Tenth Anniversary Conference on Participatory Design 2008*, Indiana University, 41–50. Retrieved August 28, 2015 from http://dl.acm.org/citation.cfm?id=1795234.1795241
5. Christina Dunbar-Hester. 2014. *Low Power to the People: Pirates, Protest, and Politics in FM Radio Activism*. The MIT Press, Cambridge, Massachusetts.
6. Ron Eglash. 2002. Race, Sex, and Nerds: From Black Geeks to Asian American Hipsters. *Social Text* 20, 2: 49–64.
7. Sarah Fox and Christopher Le Dantec. 2014. Community Historians: Scaffolding Community Engagement Through Culture and Heritage. *Proceedings of the 2014 Conference on Designing Interactive Systems*, ACM, 785–794. http://doi.org/10.1145/2598510.2598563
8. Sarah Fox, Rachel Rose Ulgado, and Daniela Rosner. 2015. Hacking Culture, Not Devices: Access and Recognition in Feminist Hackerspaces. *Proceedings of the ACM 2015 conference on Computer Supported Cooperative Work*.
9. Bill Gaver, Tony Dunne, and Elena Pacenti. 1999. Design: Cultural Probes. *interactions* 6, 1: 21–29. http://doi.org/10.1145/291224.291235
10. Kathleen Hanna and Johanna Fateman. 2014. *The Riot Grrrl Collection*. The Feminist Press at CUNY, New York.
11. Gillian R. Hayes. 2011. The Relationship of Action Research to Human-computer Interaction. *ACM Trans. Comput.-Hum. Interact.* 18, 3: 15:1–15:20. http://doi.org/10.1145/1993060.1993065
12. Lilly Irani, Janet Vertesi, Paul Dourish, Kavita Philip, and Rebecca E. Grinter. 2010. Postcolonial Computing: A Lens on Design and Development. *Proceedings of the SIGCHI Conference on Human Factors in Computing Systems*, ACM, 1311–1320. http://doi.org/10.1145/1753326.1753522
13. Kat Jungnickel. In Press. Making things up: Design perspectives from a study of Victorian women's convertible cycle. *interactions*.
14. Katrina Jungnickel and Larissa Hjorth. 2014. Methodological entanglements in the field: methods, transitions and transmissions. *Visual Studies* 29, 2: 136–145. http://doi.org/10.1080/1472586X.2014.887263
15. John Law. 2004. *After Method: Mess in Social Science Research*. Routledge, London ; New York.
16. Celia Lury and Nina Wakeford (eds.). 2013. *Inventive Methods: The Happening of the Social*. Routledge, Place of publication not identified.
17. Paul Rabinow, George E. Marcus, James D. Faubion, and Tobias Rees. 2008. *Designs for an Anthropology of the Contemporary*. Duke University Press.
18. Elizabeth B.-N. Sanders and Pieter Jan Stappers. 2008. Co-creation and the new landscapes of design. *CoDesign* 4, 1: 5–18. http://doi.org/10.1080/15710880701875068
19. Nick Taylor, David M. Frohlich, Paul Egglestone, et al. 2014. Utilising Insight Journalism for Community Technology Design. *Proceedings of the 32Nd Annual ACM Conference on Human Factors in Computing Systems*, ACM, 2995–3004. http://doi.org/10.1145/2556288.2557054
20. Nina Wakeford. 2006. Power Point and the Crafting of Social Data. *Ethnographic Praxis in Industry Conference Proceedings* 2006, 1: 94–108. http://doi.org/10.1111/j.1559-8918.2006.tb00039.x
21. Jayne Wallace, John McCarthy, Peter C. Wright, and Patrick Olivier. 2013. Making Design Probes Work. *Proceedings of the SIGCHI Conference on Human Factors in Computing Systems*, ACM, 3441–3450. http://doi.org/10.1145/2470654.2466473
22. Amanda Williams, Johanna Brewer, Alicia Gibb, Wilhelm Eric, and Hugh Forrest. 2012. Indy R&D: doing HCI research off the beaten path. *CHI'12 Extended Abstracts on Human Factors in Computing Systems*, ACM, 1131–1134.
23. Margery Wolf. 1992. *A Thrice-Told Tale: Feminism, Postmodernism, and Ethnographic Responsibility*. Stanford University Press, Stanford, Calif.
24. NYC Feminist Zine Fest: A Showcase. *Barnard College*. Retrieved from http://barnard.edu/events/nyc-feminist-zine-fest

Author Index

www.ingramcontent.com/pod-product-compliance
Lightning Source LLC
LaVergne TN
LVHW080107011026
849160LV00013B/1048